BIOGRAPHICAL DICTIONARY
OF FRENCH
POLITICAL LEADERS
SINCE 1870

BIOGRAPHICAL
DICTIONARY
OF FRENCH
POLITICAL LEADERS
SINCE 1870

Edited by

David S. Bell

Douglas Johnson

Peter Morris

ASSOCIATION FOR THE STUDY OF MODERN AND
CONTEMPORARY FRANCE

SIMON & SCHUSTER

New York   London   Toronto   Sydney   Tokyo   Singapore

First published in the UK in 1990 by
Harvester Wheatsheaf
66 Wood Lane End, Hemel Hempstead
Hertfordshire HP2 4RG
A division of
Simon & Schuster International Group

and in the USA by
Academic Reference Division
Simon & Schuster
15 Columbus Circle
New York, NY10023

Printed and bound in Great Britain at
The University Press, Cambridge

Library of Congress Cataloging-in-Publication Data

Biographical dictionary of French political leaders since 1870/
    edited by David S. Bell, Douglas Johnson, Peter Morris.
        p.   cm.
    "Association for the Study of Modern and contemporary France."
    First published 1990 by Harvester Wheatsheaf, Hemel Hempstead,
England.
        ISBN 0-13-084690-2
        1. Politicians—France—Biography—Dictionaries. 2. France—
Politics and government—1870–1940—Dictionaries. 3. France—
Politics and government—20th century–Dictionaries. I. Bell,
David Scott. II. Johnson, Douglas W. J. III. Morris, Peter.
IV. Association for the Study of Modern and Contemporary France
(Great Britain)
DC342.B56   1990
944.08′092′2–dc20
[B]
                                90-9662
                                CIP

---

1 2 3 4 5   94 93 92 91 90

CONTENTS

EDITORS' PREFACE

The preparation of this biographical guide to French politics owes much to the support of the members of the Association for the Study of Modern and Contemporary France. Very early on the editors circulated a preliminary list of potential entries to the ASMCF membership in order to ascertain the names not only of those political figures who should be included in (or excluded from) the guide but of those colleagues who might be willing to contribute individual biographies. The response was immediate and generous. It would be quite impossible for us to thank individually the scores of people in the ASMCF who have helped to bring the project to completion. To them, and to all the others who wrote entries or suggested names, the editors express their gratitude; without such support the book could not have appeared.

The guide aims to be of use to the many people in many countries who are interested in the past and present of the politics of France and who may not always have a reading command of French. The editors have sought where possible to provide an English equivalent of French terms. To cover the many cases where translation would be difficult or inappropriate, a glossary of terms has been provided. It may be that some discrepancies exist over the spelling of some proper names; French nineteenth-century usage was sometimes inconsistent and English usage may differ from the French. In the latter case we have used the English rather than the French form (Lyons rather than Lyon).

Though this guide is very much a collective enterprise, the editors naturally accept responsibility for such errors and omissions as it contains.

DSB
DJ
PM

LIST OF ENTRIES

The initials of the author of each entry are given in brackets: see Notes on Contributors.

LIST OF ACRONYMS

AD	Alliance Démocratique
AF	Action Française
ARD	Alliance Républicaine Démocratique
ARLP	Alliance Républicaine pour les Libértés et le Progrès
ARS	Action Républicaine et Sociale
BBC	British Broadcasting Corporation
BDS	Bloc Démocratique Sénégalais
CAPES	Certificat d'Aptitude au Professorat de l'Enseignement Secondaire
CC	Central Committee (of Communist Party)
CD	Centre Démocrate
CDS	Centre des Démocrates Sociaux
CEDEP	Centre d'Etudes et de Promotion
CERES	Centre d'Etudes, de Recherches et d'Education Socialistes
CERM	Centre d'Etudes et de Recherches Marxistes (formerly Institut Maurice Thorez)
CES	Collège d'Enseignement Secondaire
CELIB	Comité d'Etudes et de Liaisons Bretons
CFDT	Conféderation Française Démocratique du Travail
CFLN	Comité Français de Libération Nationale
CFTC	Confédération Française des Travailleurs Chrétiens
CGC	Confédération Générale des Cadres
CGE	Compagnie Générale d'Electricité
CGPF	Confédération Générale du Patronat Français
CGT	Confédération Générale du Travail
CGTU	Confédération Générale du Travail Unitaire
CIR	Convention des Institutions Républicaines
CNAM	Caisses Nationales d'Assurance Maladie
CNE	Conseil National Economique
CNFF	Conseil National des Femmes Françaises
CNIP	Centre National des Indépendants et Paysans
CNPF	Conseil National du Patronat Français
CNR	Conseil National de la Résistance
CNRS	Centre National de la Recherche Scientifique
CNT-FAI	Confederación Nacional de Trabajo-Federación Anarquista Ibérica (Spanish anarchists unions)
CODER	Commission pour le Développement Economique Régional
CPSU	Communist Party of the Soviet Union
CRS	Compagnies Républicaines de Sécurité
DATAR	Délégation à l'Aménagement du Territoire et à l'Action Régionale
ECCI	Executive Committee of the Communist International
ECSC	European Coal and Steel Community
EDC	European Defence Community
EEC	European Economic Community
EMS	European Monetary System
ENA	Ecole Nationale d'Administration
ENS	Ecole Normale Supérieure

LIST OF ACRONYMS

EURATOM	European Atomic Energy Community
FEN	Fédération de l'Education Nationale
FFI	Forces Françaises de l'Intérieur
FGDS	Fédération de la Gauche Démocrate et Socialiste
FGE	Fédération Générale de l'Education
FLN	Front de Libération Nationale (Algeria)
FN	Front National
FNC	Fédération Nationale Catholique
FNRI	Fédération Nationale des Républicains Indépendants
FNSEA	Fédération Nationale des Syndicats d'Exploitants Agricoles
FNSP	Fondation Nationale des Sciences Politiques
FO	Force Ouvrière
FRF	Fédération Républicaine de France
FTP	Francs-tireurs et Partisans
FTSF	Fédération des Travailleurs Socialistes de France
GAM	Groupes d'Action Municipale
GAJ	Groupe Action Jeunesse
GRECE	Groupement de Recherche et d'Etudes pour la Civilisation Européene
IAEA	International Atomic Energy Authority
IEP	Institut d'Etudes Politiques
IFOP	Institut Français d'Opinion Publique
IGAME	Inspecteurs Généraux de l'Administration en Mission Extraordinaire
ILO	International Labour Organization
INSEE	Institut National de Statistiques et d'Études Économiques
ISB	International Socialist Bureau
IUT	Institut Universitaire de Technologie
JAC	Jeunesse Agricole Chrétienne
JC	Jeunesses Communistes
JCR	Jeunesse Communiste Révolutionnaire
JEC	Jeunesse Etudiante Chrétienne
JOC	Jeunesse Ouvrière Chrétienne
JP	Jeunesses Patriotes
LCR	Ligue Communiste Révolutionnaire
LO	Lutte Ouvrière
MJR	Mouvement Jeune Révolution
MLF	Mouvement de Libération des Femmes
MLN	Mouvement de Libération Nationale
MPPT	Mouvement pour un Parti des Travailleurs
MRG	Mouvement des Radicaux de Gauche
MRP	Mouvement Républicain Populaire
MSDF	Mouvement Social Démocrate de France
MSF	Mouvement Solidariste Français
MSR	Mouvement Social Révolutionnaire
MUR	Mouvements Unis de la Résistance
NATO	North Atlantic Treaty Organization
NKVD	Narodnyi Kommissariat Vneshnei Torgovli (People's Commissariat of Internal Affairs − Soviet secret police)
OAS	Organisation de l'Armée Secrète
OCM	Organisation Civile et Militaire
OECD	Organization for Economic Co-operation and Development
OEEC	Organization for European Economic Cooperation
ORTF	Organisation de la Radio-diffusion−Télévision Française
OSARN	Organisation Sécrète d'Action Révolutionnaire Nationale
OURS	Office Universitaire de Recherche Socialiste

PCF	Parti Communiste Français
PDCI	Parti Démocratique de la Côte d'Ivoire
PDM	Progrès et Démocratie Moderne
PDP	Parti Démocrate Populaire
PO/POF	Parti Ouvrier Français (sometimes Parti Ouvrier)
POSR	Parti Ouvrier Socialiste Révolutionnaire
POUM	Partido Obrero de Unificación Marxista (Spanish)
PPF	Parti Populaire Français
PR	Parti Républicain
PRL	Parti Républicain de la Liberté
PRNS	Parti Républicain National et Social
PRP	Parti Républicain Populaire
PS	Parti Socialiste
PSA	Parti Socialiste Autonome
PSF	Parti Social Français
PSdeF	Parti Socialiste de France
PSOP	Parti Socialiste Ouvrier et Paysan
PSR	Parti Socialiste Révolutionnaire
PSU	Parti Socialiste Unifié
PTT	Postes Télégraphes Téléphones
PUF	Presses Universitaires de France
PUP	Parti d'Unité Prolétarienne
RDA	Rassemblement Démocratique Africain
RFSP	Revue Française de Science Politique
RGR	Rassemblement des Gauches Républicaines
RI	Républicains Indépendants
RNP	Rassemblement National Populaire
RPF	Rassemblement du Peuple Français
RPR	Rassemblement pour la République
RTF	Radio-Télévision de France
SAC	Service d'Action Civique
SDI	Strategic Defense Initiative
SFIO	Section Française de l'Internationale Ouvrière
SNCF	Société Nationale des Chemins de Fer
SOFRES	Société Française d'Enquêtes par Sondages
SOL	Service d'Ordre Legionnaire
SPD	Sozialdemokratische Partei Deutschlands (German)
TPPS	Toujours prêt pour servir
UA	Union Anarchiste
UCRG	Union des Clubs Pour le Renouveau de la Gauche
UDCA	Union de Défense des Commerçants et Artisans
UDF	Union pour la Démocratie Française
UDR	Union des Démocrates pour la République
UDT	Union Démocratique du Travail
UDSR	Union Démocratique et Socialiste de la Résistance
UFF	Union et Fraternité Française
UFF	Union des Femmes Françaises
UFSF	Union Française pour le Suffrage Féminin
UGDS	Union de la Gauche Socialiste et Démocrate
UNESCO	United Nations Educational, Scientific and Cultural Organization
UNC	Union Nationale des Combattants
UNEDIC	Union Nationale pour l'Emploi dans l'Industrie et le Commerce
UNO	United Nations Organization
UNR	Union pour la Nouvelle République
UR	Union Républicaine

NOTES ON CONTRIBUTORS

APT Adamthwaite (APA) (BA, Phil.) is the author of numerous books and articles on French history including *France and the Coming of the Second World War* (Cass, 1977) and he has also published *The Lost Peace* (E. Arnold, 1981).

Martin S. Alexander (MSA) is a former Franco-British Council fellow and since 1982 has been a lecturer in modern French and British history at the University of Southampton. A contributor to *Makers of Modern Strategy* (ed. P. Paret) (Princeton University Press, 1986), he is co-editor (with Helen Graham) of *The French and Spanish Popular Fronts: Comparative perspectives* (Cambridge University Press, 1989) and is the author of *The Republic in Danger: Maurice Gamelin, the defence of France and the politics of rearmament, 1933–39* (Cambridge University Press, forthcoming).

Robert Anderson (RDA) is Reader in History at Edinburgh University, where he has taught since 1969. His publications include *Education in France 1848–1870* and *France 1870–1914: Politics and society* (Routledge & Kegan Paul, 1977). His current research interests centre on the history of universities.

Margaret Atack (MA) is Head of the School of Humanities at Sunderland Polytechnic and is author of articles as well as a recent book on literature and the Resistance.

Nicholas Atkin (NA) is lecturer in history at Reading University and is currently preparing a book on the Church in France since 1905. His Ph.D thesis is on 'Catholics and schools in Vichy France 1940–44'.

Daniel C. Bach (DCB) (D.Phil., Oxon.) is *Chargé de recherche* of the Centre National de la Recherche Scientifique, Centre d'Etude d'Afrique Noire, Bordeaux I University.

David S. Bell (DSB) is lecturer in politics at Leeds University.

Laurence A. Bell (LAB) is lecturer in the department of international studies at Surrey University.

David G. Berry (DGB) (BA, Oxon.; MA, Sussex; D.Phil.) is lecturer in French at the Department of European Studies, Loughborough University. His doctoral research was on the French anarchist movement between the wars.

Serge Berstein (SB) is professor at the Paris Institut d'Etudes Politiques. Among his many books are a two-volume *Histoire du Parti Radical* (Presses de la Fondation Nationale des Sciences Politiques, 1980–2) and a biography of Edouard Herriot (Presses de la Fondation Nationale des Sciences Politiques, 1985).

John Bramley (John B) has taught French language, history and politics at Wolverhampton Polytechnic and Newcastle-upon-Tyne Polytechnic and is now senior lecturer at Oxford Polytechnic.

Jeff Bridgford (JB) is lecturer in French at Heriot-Watt University, Edinburgh. Prior to this he was engaged in postgraduate work at the Universities of Nice, Manchester and Strasbourg before talking up a post at the Ecole Supérieure du Commerce in Le Havre and afterwards at Newcastle-upon-Tyne Polytechnic. He has written articles on political parties and interest groups in French politics and aspects of French industrial relations.

Patrick Bury (JPTB), who died in 1987, was one of the most distinguished scholars working in the field of modern French history and was for many years a fellow of Corpus Christi College, Cambridge. Among his books are biographies of Gambetta and Thiers and *A History of France 1914–1940* (Methuen, 1979).

Eric Cahm (EC) is a former Professor of French Studies at Portsmouth Polytechnic, joint editor of *Modern and Contemporary France* and a specialist on Péguy. He is now *Professeur d'Histoire* at the University of Tours.

Philip G. Cerny (PGC) is senior lecturer in politics at the University of York and has been a visiting professor at New York University and Dartmouth College (USA). He is the author of *Une Politique de grandeur* (Flammarion, 1986) and co-editor of *Socialism, the State and Public Policy in France* (Pinter, 1985).

Tony Chafer (TC) is senior lecturer in French and African studies at Portsmouth Polytechnic. He has written extensively on the anti-nuclear and Green movements in France and on French policy in Africa. He is an editor of the review *Modern and Contemporary France.*

Rosemary Chapman (RC) is lecturer in French and German at Nottingham University. Her main research interests are proletarian literature in France and Germany between the wars and, more generally, the relationship between the writer and politics in twentieth-century France.

A. Cole (AC) wrote his thesis on the French Socialist Party before its accession to power in 1981. He has written on other areas of contemporary French politics and taught at Oxford, Caen and Aston Universities before being appointed to his present position of lecturer in politics at Keele University.

Robert Cornevin (RC) (*Docteur ès Lettres*) is Secretaire Perpetuel de l'Academie des Sciences d'Outre Mer and President of l'Association des Ecrivains de Langue Française.

Martyn Cornick (MC) (MA, Ph.D., Warwick) is lecturer in French in the department of

European studies at Loughborough University. His Ph.D was on 'History and politics in the *Nouvelle Revue Française* under Jean Paulhan, 1925–1940'. He is currently working on a study of the French secret services with Peter Morris, and is preparing a study of Jean Paulhan.

Byron Criddle (BC) is senior lecturer in politics at the University of Aberdeen. He co-authored *The French Socialist Party: the emergence of a party of government* (Oxford University Press, 1988) and has written extensively of aspects of French and British politics.

M. Cross (MCr) graduated from the University of Ulster in West European studies. After postgraduate studies at Reading University, she taught in Paris and the University of Newcastle-upon-Tyne where she completed her Ph.D. thesis on Flora Tristan. Her present post of lecturer is in the modern languages department, Newcastle-upon-Tyne Polytechnic.

Brian Darling (BD) is principal lecturer in sociology at Polytechnic of North East London, and is currently doing research on the Ecole Nationale des Cadres d'Uriage. He has been Secretary of the ASMCF since 1979 and is Chevalier de l'Ordre National du Mérite. He is a regular broadcaster on issues of Anglo-French concern.

Keith Dixon (KD) (MA, *Docteur ès Lettres*) is *Maître de conférence* in the English department of the University of St Etienne. He has been active in French politics – in the French Communist Party from the early 1970s until his expulsion in 1988 – and has written on French politics in *Marxism Today*, *Radical Scotland* and the *Swedish Socialist Review*.

François Duchêne (FLD) worked with Jean Monnet as head of his private office from 1958–63 in the action committee for a United States of Europe. He ran the Institute of Strategic Studies from 1969–74 and the Sussex European Research Centre from 1974–82. He has published studies of the poet Auden, and of industrial and agricultural policies in Western Europe. He is currently researching Jean Monnet.

Claire Duchen (CD) is lecturer in French at University of Bath and author of *Feminism in France from May '68 to Mitterrand* (Routledge & Kegan Paul, 1986), *French Connections: Voices from the women's movement in France* (Hutchinson, 1987). She is currently working on a book about women in France from the Liberation to May 1968.

Roger Eatwell (RE) is lecturer in politics at the University of Bath. His publications on France include articles on Poujadism, and the 1986 and 1988 legislature and presidential elections. His latest publication is R. Eatwell and N. O'Sullivan (eds) *The Nature of the Right* (Pinter, 1989).

Dr Howard Evans (HE) worked in the executive secretariat of an international organization based in Paris before moving to Leeds University where he is senior lecturer in French. He has written on local and regional government in France, French Third World policies, François Mauriac and Emmanuel Mounier, and on social and political aspects of the evolution of the contemporary French language. He is also the co-author, with Professor Philip Thody, of *Faux Amis and Key Words – A Dictionary-Guide to French Language, Culture and Society through Look-alikes and Confusables* (Athlone Press, 1985).

Christopher Flood (CF) (D.Phil., Oxon.) is lecturer in French Studies at the University of Surrey. He has written a number of articles on the politics of French intellectuals and a book on the diplomat–playwright Paul Claudel (forthcoming 1989). His current research is on the ideologies and discourse of the French right.

Hilary Footitt (HF) is Head of Languages at the Polytechnic of Central London and has written – with John Simmonds – 'The resistance experience: Teaching and resources' in *Vichy France and the Resistance*, R. Kedward (ed.) (Charles Hurst, 1977). She is the author (with John Simmonds) of *The Politics of Liberation: France 1943–45* (Leicester University Press, 1988). She is currently working on Women and the Resistance.

John Frears (JF) is reader in politics at Loughborough University and the author of various books and articles on French government and politics including *Political Parties and Elections in the Fifth Republic* (C. Hurst, 1976) and *France in the Giscard Presidency* (Unwin, 1981).

John Gaffney (JG) is lecturer in French at Aston University, author of *The French Left in the Fifth Republic* (Macmillan, 1989), editor of *France and Modernization* (Gower, 1987) and of *The French Presidential Elections of 1988* (Gower, 1989).

Ralph Gibson (RG) teaches history and French studies at the University of Lancaster. He has published various articles on French Catholic history, and *Social History of French Catholicism 1789–1914* (Routledge, 1989).

B.D. Graham (BDG) is professor of politics at the University of Sussex. He is working on the internal politics of the SFIO in the 1930s and 1940s.

Richard Griffiths (RMG) was formerly professor of French at University College, Cardiff. He has specialized in French right-wing and Catholic politics. Among his books are: *The Reactionary Revolution* (Constable, 1966), *Marshal Pétain* (Constable, 1970) and *Fellow Travellers of the Right* (Constable, 1980).

Paul Hainsworth (PH) is lecturer in politics at the University of Ulster. He is co-author of *Decentralisation and Change in Contemporary France* (Gower, 1986), as well as numerous articles/ chapters on French politics in *Partliamentary Affairs, West European Politics, Contemporary French Culture, The World Today*, etc.

Bernard Hamilton (BH) is founder of the Oxford Human Rights Institute and the Oxford Minority Rights Group. He has taught at colleges in Oxford, London and Washington DC.

David Hanley (DH) is Professor of French at University College, Cardiff and he is the author of *Keeping Left: Ceres and the French Socialist Party* (Manchester University Press, 1986).

Tony Harding (TH) is dean of the faculty of business, languages, and hotel management at Oxford Polytechnic and lectures in French politics.

Dr Geoffrey Hare (GH) is a lecturer in French Studies at the University of Newcastle-upon-Tyne, having previously lectured at Leeds Polytechnic, Aberdeen University, Bradford University and the British Institute in Paris. His main interests (apart from travel) are language teaching methodology and materials and contemporary French society and politics, especially the media and political communication. He has also published advanced French language learning materials and articles on French radio and television.

Alec G. Hargreaves (AGH) is lecturer in French at Loughborough University. His principal publications are in the fields of French colonial literature and post-war immigration.

Trevor A. le V. Harris (TAleVH) (BA, B.Sc. (Econ.), Ph.D.) is a lecturer in French in the Department of Modern Languages, Salford University. His main research interests are literature and the history of ideas during the period 1870–1914. His most recent work has been a major study of Guy de Maupassant, to be published by Macmillan in 1990.

Geoffrey T. Harris (GTH) (Ph.D) has been senior lecturer in the department of modern languages in the University of Salford since 1976. He is currently working on Malraux's politics and on Claude Simon.

Martin Harrison (MH) has been professor of politics at the University of Keele since 1966. His books on France include *French Politics* (D.C. Heath, 1969), and (with Philip Williams) *De Gaulle's Republic* (Longman, 1960) and *Politics and Society in de Gaulle's Republic* (Longman, 1971). He is an occasional resident in the 7th *arrondissement* of Paris.

Diana Holmes (DiH) is senior lecturer in French and member of the women's studies team at Wolverhampton Polytechnic. Her main research interests are women writers in France and the representation of gender in the novel, and she is currently preparing a book on Colette for the Macmillan Women Writers series.

Peter Holmes (PH) (MA, Ph.D.) is lecturer in economics in the School of European Studies at the University of Sussex and was a visiting assistant professor at the University of British Columbia, Vancouver in 1979–80. He is the author with Saul Estrin of *French Planning in Theory and Practice* (Unwin, 1983).

J. Horne (John H) has written on the French and British labour movements during the First World War and on French labour history. He has completed a book on the first of these subjects and is currently writing a social history of France in 1914–18.

Jolyon Howorth (JH) is professor of French civilisation at the University of Bath. His two main areas of research are the social and political history of the early Third Republic, and contemporary French defence and security policy. He has published several books and many articles on both these subjects.

Marie-Monique Huss (M-MH) teaches French and economic history at the Polytechnic of Central London. She has written on population, *mentalités* and popular culture.

NOTES ON CONTRIBUTORS

Julian T. Jackson (JTJ) is lecturer at the University College of Swansea and author of *Politics of Depression in France 1932–36* (Cambridge University Press, 1985) and of *The Popular Front in France* (Cambridge University Press, 1988).

Paul Jankowski (PFJ) (D.Phil., Oxon.) is the author of *Communism and Collaboration* (Yale University Press, 1989) and a study of Simon Sabiani. He currently teaches history at the University of Stanford, California.

Brian Jenkins (BJ) is senior lecturer in French studies at Portsmouth Polytechnic, and joint editor of the Review *Modern and Contemporary France*. He is joint author (with G. Minnerup) of *Citizens and Comrades: Socialism in a world of nation states* (Pluto Press, 1984) and has published articles on contemporary French politics and French history. He is currently preparing a book on class and nation in France since 1789.

Douglas Johnson (DJ) is professor of French history at University College, London and is Hon. President of the ASMCF and is the author of numerous books and articles on contemporary France and French history.

J.F.V. Keiger (JFVK) is senior lecturer in French history and politics in the department of modern languages at Salford University. In 1983 he published *France and the Origins of the First World War* and has just finished editing the nineteen volumes of documents on *Europe 1848–1914* in *British Documents on Foreign Affairs* (general eds K. Bourne and D.C. Watt) published in 1989 by University Publications of America. He is currently preparing a biography of Raymond Poincaré.

A.P. Kerr (APK) is a member of the French studies department of Reading University. Her research interests are the history and political thought of the nineteenth century, particularly the period of the consitutional monarchies.

Andrew Knapp (AFK) (D.Phil., Oxon.) wrote his thesis on the French communist municipality of Le Havre, and has since written a number of articles on French communism, elections, and local government, working most recently on the Paris municipality under Chirac. He was a Research Fellow at Nuffield College, Oxford and taught at the Ecole Supérieure du Commerce, Le Havre, and Paris University before taking up his present editorial post with Oxford University Press.

Eleonore Kofman (EK) is senior lecturer in geography at Middlesex Polytechnic and has also lectured at the University of Caen. She has written on regionalism and nationalism in France.

Myron Kofman (MK) wrote his master's thesis on Proudhon's and Bakunin's stances on nationalism. His doctoral thesis was on French ex-Communists and the problem of commitment. He teaches modern European history on the humanities degree course at Bolton Institute of Higher Education.

Raymond Kuhn (RK) is lecturer in the department of political studies at Queen Mary and Westfield College, University of London. He has written numerous articles on the media in France.

Maurice Larkin (ML) is Richard Pares professor of history in the University of Edinburgh. His books include *Church and State after the Dreyfus Affair: The separation issue in France* (Macmillan, 1974), *Man and Society in Nineteenth Century Realism: Determinism and literature* (Macmillan, 1977) and *France since the Popular Front: Government and people 1936–1986* (Oxford University Press, 1988).

Howard Lewis (HDL) took his degree and MA at the University of Wales and later obtained his doctorate in French at the University of Leeds. He has published articles and talks on the French political scene and more recently has concentrated on the education system. He is the author of *The French Education System* (Croom Helm, 1985). He lectures at Derbyshire College of Higher Education.

David A.L. Levy (DALL), (D.Phil., Oxon.) has researched and written on the French popular front, taught French politics and history at Salford University and is currently a reporter for BBC television.

David Looseley (DL) is lecturer in French studies at the University of Bradford, where he teaches courses on French society and culture. He is the author of a book on the dramatist Armand Salacrou, published in 1985, and is currently engaged in a research project on cultural politics in France, funded by the Leverhulme Trust.

Jill Lovecy (JL) is lecturer in European politics at the University of Manchester Institute of Science and Technology. She is the author (with G.K. Roberts) of *West European Politics Today* (Manchester University Press, 1984) and of articles on regional policy and regionalism in France, as well as on the *'cohabitation'* experiment.

Howard Machin (HM) is lecturer in French government and politics at the London School of Economics and Science.

Mairi Maclean (MMac) has lectured in French studies at the University of Aston. She has taught French language and economic affairs at the University (since 1985). Her articles and book chapters on nationalization, privatization and business policy in France have appeared in G. Yannopoulos (ed.), *Privatisation Worldwide* (Macmillan, 1989), and elsewhere; she has also published on other aspects of French society and literature.

J.F. McMillan (JFM) (Ph.D.) teaches history at the University of York and is the author of two books, *Housewife or Harlot: The place of women in French society 1870–1940* (Harvester, Brighton, 1981) and *Dreyfus to De Gaulle: Politics and society in France 1898–1969* (Edward Arnold, 1985) as well as a large number of articles and reviews.

J.S. McClelland (JSM) is lecturer in politics at the University of Nottingham. His most recent work is a study of *The Crowd and the Mob in History: From Plato to Canetti* (Unwin Hyman, 1988).

Margaret A. Majumdar (MAM) teaches French language and politics at the Polytechnic of Central London and is engaged in research on the work of Louis Althusser, and on the French colonial presence in Bengal.

Sonia Mazey (Sonia M) (D.Phil., Oxon.) is a senior lecturer in politics at Brunel University. She is currently working on public policy-making and decentralization in France and has published articles on these subjects. She is also editor of, and a contributor to, *Mitterrand's France* (Croom Helm, 1987).

Susan Milner (SM) (Ph.D.) is lecturer in French at Aston University. Her doctoral research examined the relationship between the French labour movement and foreign labour movements before 1914. She is currently researching comparative aspects of the European labour movements.

Annette F. Morgan (AFM) is lecturer in politics and recent history at Brunel University. By 'politics', understand 'politics of the European Community' – from a Candide vantage-point and spiritedness dating back to the first wails of the Council of Europe – and 'politics of the French Fifth Republic – from both the botanist's and the rose's point of view'. 'Recent history' covers the macrocosm as well as the microcosm of Charles Peguy's *Cahiers de la Quinzaine* – a human tragicomedy.

Peter Morris (PM) is lecturer in politics at the University of Nottingham. His Ph.D. was on the French Radical Party in the period before 1914. He has written on aspects of contemporary French and British politics and history.

M. Palmer (MP) is professor in communication studies at the University of Paris having previously lectured at the Universities of Aston and Rennes. He has written extensively on the history of the French press.

Dorothy Parkin (DP) has taught French language and French studies at Coventry Polytechnic and is now senior lecturer in politics. As well as French politics, other interests include the European Community and academic translation.

Kevin Passmore (KP) is currently writing a thesis on 'The right and the extreme right in the department of the Rhone, 1928–39' at the University of Warwick.

Dr Alan Butt Philip (ABP) is a senior lecturer in politics at the Centre for European Industrial Studies, Bath University. His research interests include regional, banking and small firms policies in France. He is the co-author (with Professor B.T. Bayliss) of *Capital Markets and Industrial Investment in Germany and France: Lessons for the UK* (Gower, 1980).

Keith A. Reader (KAR) is senior lecturer in French at Kingston Polytechnic. He has taught in France at the University of Caen, at the Ecole Normale Supérieure and the British Institute in Paris. He is the author of *Intellectuals and the Left in France since 1968* (Macmillan, 1987). He is one of the editors of *Paragraph* and has written extensively on French cinema and intellectual life.

Jean-Paul Révauger (JPR) is *maître assistant* in English at the University of Grenoble III. His interests include contemporary history and the socialist and labour movements in Britain and France. He is the author of a doctoral thesis on 'The far left in Britain in the 1970s' and a *Thèse d'etat* on 'Worker's control and self-management in Britain 1900–1983'.

Siân Reynolds (SR) is senior lecturer in French (politics and history) at the University of Edinburgh. She has translated various books including Fernand Braudel's *The Mediterranean* (Collins, 1972–3), has edited a collection of essays, *Women, State and Revolution* (Wheatsheaf, 1986) and published a number of articles on recent French history.

Martin Rhodes (MR) is lecturer in politics in the Department of Government, University of Manchester. He is the author of *Steel and the State in France 1946–1986: The politics of industrial change* (Oxford University Press, forthcoming).

Adrian C. Ritchie (ACR) (MA Manchester – Docteur de l'Université-Strasbourg) is lecturer in French studies at University College of North Wales (Bangor). He has published on late nineteenth-century literature and on modern French political institutions. His special interest is the political consciousness of nineteenth century French writers.

Ella Ritchie (ER) (Ph.D., London) is lecturer in politics at Newcastle University where she has taught since 1974. Her research interests are contemporary conservatism in France and European Community politics.

Colin Roberts (CR) is senior lecturer in French at Coventry Polytechnic. He has written on aspects of modern French literature and on decentralization and education in modern France.

Adrian Rossiter (AR) is a senior lecturer in European politics at the Civil Service College in London, has published on the Popular Front and his thesis covered politico-corporatist developments in France between the wars.

Bernard Sasso (BS) is a research student at the University of Wales at Swansea where he is currently working on a thesis on Lord Lyons, the British Ambassador in Paris between 1867 and 1887.

Peter Savigear (PWMS) was senior lecturer in the department of politics at the University of Leicester and has published in the fields of Corsican politics and international relations.

James Shields (JS) is currently researching into the French right and extreme right. He has published on a range of topics relating to contemporary French politics and to French literature and philosophy in the post-revolutionary period. He is a lecturer at the University of Warwick.

J.C. Simmonds (JCS) (Ph.D.) is senior lecturer in European history at Anglia Higher Education College (Cambridge), researches on the French Communist Party and has recently published (with H. Footitt) *The Politics of Liberation: France 1943–45* (Leicester University Press, 1988).

Malcolm Slater (MS) (MA, B.Sc. (Econ.), LLB) is lecturer in French studies at the University of Bradford. His main research interests are French foreign policy and European Community politics. His recent publications include *Contemporary French Politics* (Macmillan, 1984).

Anne Stevens (AS) is lecturer in politics at the University of Sussex and has written extensively on aspects of French government and administration.

Judith F. Stone (JFS) is assistant professor of history at Western Michigan University, Kalamazoo, Michigan. She is author of *The Search for Social Peace. Reform legislation in France, 1890–1914* (SUNY Press, 1985) and is currently working on a study of Camille Pelletan and his place within the political culture of French radicalism.

Francis de Tarr (FdeT) is European representative of the Hoover Institution, Stanford University, was former counsellor for political affairs in the American embassy in Paris and is author of *The French Radical Party from Herriot to Mendès-France* (Oxford University Press, 1961; Greenwood Press, 1980).

Pippa Temple (PT) has researched into the politics of inter-war France and has lectured at the Anglia Higher Education College.

Philip Thody (PTh) is professor of French literature at the University of Leeds. He has published books on Anouilh, Barthes, Camus, Genet, Huxley, Laclos, Proust and Sartre. He has recently published *French Caesarism from Napoleon 1st to Charles de Gaulle* (Macmillan, 1989).

Robert Tombs (RT) is fellow and director of studies in history at St John's College, Cambridge, and a university lecturer in modern history. He is the author of *The War Against Paris 1871* (Cambridge University Press, 1981) and co-author of *Thiers 1797–1877: A political life* (Allen & Unwin, 1986) and is currently working on *France 1815–1914* and on nineteenth-century French nationalism.

Robert Turner (Robert T) is senior lecturer in French studies at Newcastle Polytechnic and is currently researching into French attitudes towards European integration.

Michalina Vaughan (MV), obtained a *Doctorat d'Etat* in France. She taught Sociology at the London School of Economics before becoming professor of sociology at Lancaster University (1972–87). She has written extensively on French society, education and politics.

Richard Vinen (RV) is part-time research fellow at Trinity College Cambridge and half-time lecturer at Queen Mary College London. His thesis is entitled 'The politics of French business 1936–1945'.

David Robin Watson (DRW) studied at the University of Oxford and at the Fondation Nationale des Sciences Politiques in Paris and has taught European history at Dundee since 1961. He has published a biography of Georges Clemenceau (1974) and many articles on French history. At present he is researching French policy towards Russia and the USSR between 1914 and 1928.

M.K. Weed (MKW) (BA California, *Doctorat d'Etat*, Pol., Paris) works in marketing and business communications in Paris, and has taught international trade at the University of Paris (Sorbonne) and international relations at the American College in Paris; she is the author of *L'Image publique d'un homme secret: Michel Jobert et la diplomatie française* (Lanore, 1988).

Anne Whitmarsh (AW) is senior lecturer in French at Coventry Polytechnic where she teaches French language and contemporary politics. Her main interest is Simone de Beauvoir and she is the author of *Simone de Beauvoir and the Limits of Commitment* (Cambridge University Press, 1981).

Stephen Wilson (SW) (BA, MA, Ph.D., Cantab.) is reader in European history at the University of East Anglia. His publications include *Ideology and Experience: Anti-semitism in France at the time of the Dreyfus Affair* (Fairleigh Dickinson University Presses, 1982) and *Feuding, Conflict and Banditry in Nineteenth-Century Corsica* (Cambridge University Press, 1988).

G. Wigglesworth (GW) completed a doctorate on politics and the French Army, 1904–14, and continues to research in this area. She has lectured in British and American Universities and also practises law.

BIOGRAPHICAL DICTIONARY
OF FRENCH
POLITICAL LEADERS
SINCE 1870

A

'ALAIN' (pseud.), Emile-Auguste Chartier (1868–1951)

The son of a vertinary surgeon, Alain was born into a poor family of peasant stock deep in the provinces at Mortagne. After excelling at his studies, in 1886 he entered the philosophy class of Jules Lagneau at the Lycée Vanves (secondary school) in Paris; this decisive encounter marked Alain for the rest of his career. Lagneau taught him Cartesian and Kantian philosophy and of the primacy of the spirit; here Alain acquired a reverence for the concepts of liberty and free thought which were to underpin his philosophical and political thinking. In 1889 he won a place at the prestigious Ecole Normale Supérieure in Paris (among his fellow-students was Léon Blum, future leader of the Popular Front). Despite discipline problems, in 1892 Alain received the highest teaching qualification in France, the *agrégation*, and began his own career as philosophy teacher. After periods in Pontivy, Lorient and Rouen (1892–1902), Alain reached Paris in 1903. In 1909 he obtained his most influential appointment at the Lycée Henri-IV; he taught there (and at the Collège Sévigné) until his retirement in 1933.

Alain is best remembered for his famous series of 'Propos', which began to appear daily in the *Dépêche de Rouen* newspaper in February 1906. He had already contributed material to this publication from 1903, the culmination of a period during which Alain committed himself fully to the Radicals' cause after the Dreyfus affair. The 'Propos' represent the essence of Alain's philosophy and style; in *Histoire de mes pensées* (1936) he wrote that he had felt destined 'to raise journalistic writing to the heights of metaphysics'. Despite his antimilitarism and his unwavering commitment to the cause of peace, Alain joined up as a volunteer in 1914 at the age of 46. This experience gave rise to *Mars, ou la guerre jugée* (*Mars, or the War Judged*, published in 1921) and reinforced his subsequent pacifism – he co-founded the Comité de Vigilance des Intellectuels Antifascistes (Committee of Antifascist Intellectuals) in 1934. After creating his own publication, *Libres propos* in 1921, Alain was then invited to join the regular contributors of the renowned *Nouvelle Revue Française* in 1927, where his 'Propos' appeared until 1936. Alain's last significant 'political' act was to sign Louis Lecoin's *Paix immédiate!* (*Immediate Peace!*), a tract published after the declaration of war in September 1939; for this he was interrogated by the military authorities. The rest of Alain's life was relatively uneventful, and he died at Le Vésinet, near Paris, on 2 June 1951, aged 83.

Politically, Alain is most often remembered as the influential survivor of a 'golden age' of radicalism dating from the 1900s. Indeed Alain saw himself as the last remaining 'combiste', Combes (q.v.) being one of the most effective Radical politicians (see *Le Citoyen contre les pouvoirs – The Citizen Against Authority*, 1926). In 1925 Gallimard collected and published a number of texts by Alain dating from before 1914; these were his *Eléments d'une doctrine radicale* (*Elements of a Radical Doctrine*). Albert Thibaudet has recounted how a number of Radical ministers, on receiving complimentary copies of Alain's 'doctrine', replied: 'If there really were a Radical doctrine, wouldn't we be the first to know it?' Alain's radicalism, reduced to its basic principle, extolled the virtues of the individual citizen (i.e. 'le citoyen') who, whilst living in complete and respectful obedience for the Republic, its ideas and ideals, should exercise the rights of the individual 'against authority' (*contre les pouvoirs*). Alain's political thinking was based on his own idealistic brand of philosophy. For Alain intolerance and fanaticism were the enemies of true democracy and, he believed, party divisions and loyalties in the French system reflected this only too clearly.

It is in his role as teacher of numerous intellectuals that Alain is also remembered. If it is difficult to agree with André Maurois' claim that Alain was a 'modern-day Montaigne', Raymond Aron is justified in stressing that the cult which grew up around his personality exercised an undeniably powerful influence over his pupils and disciples.

Bibliography

Selected works by Alain:
Eléments d'une doctrine radicale (Paris: Gallimard, 1925).

Le Citoyen contre les pouvoirs (Paris: Gallimard, 1926).
Histoire de mes pensées (Paris: Gallimard, 1936).

The definitive study is Alain Sernin, *Alain: un sage dans la cité* (Paris: Laffont, 1985).

MC

ALLAIN-TARGÉ, François Henri René (1832–1902)

Allain-Targé is of interest as a follower of Gambetta, as a Radical spokesman on economic and financial affairs, and as a Republican notable.

He was one of a band of Republicans, among whom Gambetta was a leading spirit, who came together in the 1860s and rose to prominence in Gambetta's wake after the fall of the Second Empire. Like many of them Allain-Targé had had some legal training, having enrolled at the Bar in Angers in 1852. Also like many he was a provincial who gravitated to Paris (1864), turned to journalism, writing for various opposition papers, and aspired to enter Parliament. His views were, however, too radical for the largely rural electors of his home department of Maine-et-Loire; he was unsuccessful there in 1869 and in two elections in 1871 despite having briefly served as prefect in 1870. This appointment he owed to Gambetta, by then a forceful member of the emergency Republican government of national defence against the Prussians. Gambetta subsequently nominated Allain-Targé a commissioner to the improvised armies in the West and finally prefect of the Gironde, which included Bordeaux the provincial capital, in the last stage of the war.

After the Franco-Prussian War Paris was the natural centre of his political activity. Allain-Targé first served on its municipal council and then from 1876 as a deputy for its 19th district (*arrondissement*) which he represented until his retirement from parliamentary life in 1889. Throughout he continued his journalistic activities, in particular writing for Gambetta's newly-founded paper *La République Française*. It was Gambetta who gave him his first ministerial post in his short-lived ministry (November 1881–January 1882) while Brisson (q.v.), another pre-war friend, made him minister of the interior in 1885.

Although loyal to Gambetta, Allain-Targé was a man of independent mind and for most of his career spoke and wrote as a political Radical; he favoured constitutional revision and reforms such as the election of the judiciary. His speeches and articles on economic and social affairs (see Sanford Elwitt's *The Making of the Third Republic*) are important testimony to some of the objectives and limitations of Republican policies. He was well known for his hostility to the big railway companies and unsuccessful advocacy of state purchase of their lines.

By his family connections Allain-Targé counts as a 'notable'. His father was briefly a deputy, his father-in-law was a minister under the July Monarchy and his daughters both married future deputies. He died at the Château de Targé, which in 1982 was still inhabited by descendants.

Bibliography

Elwitt, S. (1975), *The Making of the Third Republic*, Baton Rouge: Louisiana State University Press.
Kayser, J. (1962), *Les Grandes batailles de radicalisme*, Paris: M. Rivière.

JPTB

ALLEMANE, Jean (1843–1935)

A leading figure in the early days of socialism in France, giving his name to the 'Allemanist' party of the 1890s, Jean Allemane was born in a village in Haute-Garonne in 1843, the son of a peasant turned wine-seller. The family moved to Paris in 1849 and thereafter Allemane became strongly identified with the Parisian working class, working as a compositor. He took an energetic part in the Paris Commune of 1871, as organizer in the Latin Quarter, and fought on the barricades to the end. Sentenced to hard labour in New Caledonia, he returned under amnesty in 1880, to take up his old trade. Throughout the 1880s, Allemane was a leading figure among Parisian printers (as a founder member of the printers' union, the Fédération du Livre) and in the newly-founded Socialist party, the Fédération des Travailleurs Socialistes de France (FTSF). In 1882, he remained with the 'possibilist' Paul Brousse when the followers of Jules Guesde left the party. But Allemane, who was influential in the thriving Paris branch of the FTSF (largely made up of skilled workers), became a focus for grassroots dissatisfaction with Brousse's leadership, deemed over-electoralist. In 1890, the FTSF split at the Châtellerault congress. The bulk of the membership left, taking a new name, the Parti Ouvrier, Socialiste Révolutionnaire (POSR), but it was always known popularly as the Allemanist party, because of Allemane's celebrity. In fact, he was never its formal leader, and at times dissented strongly from the party line. He did however own, edit and print its newspaper, *Le Parti*

Ouvrier, and was active throughout the POSR'S existence, until it finally merged with the other Socialist groups in the early 1900s to form the unified Section Française de l'Internationale Ouvrière (SFIO) of 1905. By then Allemane was in his sixties, and his two terms in parliament (1901–2 and 1906–10) were unremarkable. He continued for a while to run his small printing-house, acquired in 1890 to print Socialist literature, and lived to a great age, dying in 1935.

Allemane was virtually unique among French Socialist leaders of his time in being a worker and living in a working-class milieu. It is no accident that he is associated with the most *ouvriériste* of the Socialist parties, deeply conscious of its class identity, distrustful of parliamentary socialism, and rejecting both the broad municipal alliances of Brousse and the inspirational politics of Guesde, though most Allemanists revered Marx. The Allemanists retained a vision of the revolution as made from below, and many of them, including Allemane, later sympathized with revolutionary syndicalism. Some aspects of their party organization – notably strict control over those elected to Parliament or municipal councils, and a compulsory levy on their salaries for party funds – caused problems during the party's short life, but were later adopted by the Communist Party. Allemane himself was a popular orator in the heroic mould, a propagandist rather than a theorist of socialism, a fierce anticlerical who remained marked by his experience of the Commune. Like others of his generation who had known the Empire, he was divided between revolutionary opposition to the Republic and rallying to its defence, for instance during the Boulanger and Dreyfus affairs. His importance as a printer has been neglected by historians: his trade union career and his role as printer for Socialist, feminist and other groups at the turn of the century should be considered alongside his always ambiguous relationship with the party which, against his wishes, bore his name.

Bibliography

Reynolds, S. (1984), 'Allemane avant l'allemanisme, jeunesse d'un militant 1943–1890', in *Mouvement Social,* no. 126, January–March, pp. 3–28.

Reynolds, S. (1985), 'Allemane, the Allemanists and le *Parti Ouvrier,* problems of a socialist newspaper 1888–1900', in *European History Quarterly,* vol. 15, no. 1, pp. 43–70.

Wincock, M. (1971), 'La scission de Châtellerault et la naissance du parti allemaniste 1890–91', in *Mouvement Social,* no. 71, April–June, pp. 33–62.

See also D. Stafford, *From Anarchism to Reformism: The political activities of Paul Brousse* (London: Weidenfeld & Nicolson, 1971).

SR

ANDRÉ, General Louis Joseph Nicolas (1838–1913)

Born in 1838, General André served as Minister of War during the years 1900–4 successively under Waldeck-Rousseau (q.v.) and Emile Combes (q.v.) before his enforced resignation in November 1904. Although his period of office showed that his real ambitions were political rather than military in nature, he had no previous experience of French political life. His background was that of a career army officer. André was educated in Dijon and Paris before entering the prestigious Ecole Polytechnique where he was a brilliant student and underwent a further period of military training in Metz. Despite active participation in the war of 1870–1 against Prussia his rise up the military hierarchy was far from spectacular and he did not attain the rank of general until 1893. He was head of the Ecole Polytechnique from 1893 to 1896 and was put in charge of his own division in 1899 prior to his appointment as minister of war.

During his time at the War Office he did much to improve the material well-being of the army as well as setting in motion a realistic programme of development for the artillery in the light of his own professional experiences. Apart from supporting technological improvements in weaponry, André actively encouraged sports societies as a form of pre-military training and brushed up the army's image by prohibiting the sale of alcoholic drinks in army barracks. Army pay and pensions were also increased during his tenure of office.

None the less, it is for his role in the notorious 'affaire des fiches' that André is primarily remembered. His term of office witnessed the introduction of a new scheme of promotion in the army, designed to republicanize the army by making military promotions heavily dependent on the political and religious convictions of the individual rather than on age and military merit. His objective was to ensure that the military would stand firmly behind the Republic by making it virtually impossible for potentially subversive royalist, reactionary and Catholic elements to rise to positions of responsibility and power within the army. André set about his purpose by implementing a numerical grading system in the files ('fiches') kept on each member of the army which was itself dependent on secret information supplied by the lodges of the Freemasons, under the aegis of the Grand Orient. The delation system, in essence a form of spying, raised the controversial issue of the extent to which political considerations could, or indeed should, be allowed to influence military promotions and in the end this brought about André's political downfall.

On 28 October 1904 a nationalist deputy, Guyot de Villeneuve, exposed the practice of delation for what it was; though the breach of parliamentary privilege by another nationalist deputy, Syveton, a week later, in violently assaulting André, enabled the government to hang on to power in the short term, André had to go. He continued to abide by his political philosophy in retirement and made several unsuccessful attempts at a political come-back.

Bibliography

There is an interesting file on André at the Préfecture de Police archives in Paris, BA series 932. See also D.B. Ralston, *The Army of the Republic: The place of the military in the political evolution of France, 1871–1914* (Cambridge, Mass: Yale University Press, 1967).

GW

ANDRIEU, René Gabriel (1920–   )

René Andrieu is known chiefly for his editorials in *L'Humanité*, of which he was principal editorialist and editor (*rédacteur-en-chef*) from 1958 to 1987. As a polemicist and stylist Andrieu attained a certain notoriety and it is his aggressive campaigning style rather than an unconditional support for Soviet Russia, the Communist Party, or literary work that merits attention. On this last point Andrieu, who is given to quoting Stendhal, has some literary reputation although his judgement in his book *(Stendhal ou le bal masqué*, Stock, 1983) suffers from a constricting Marxist framework.

Andrieu is the son of Alphonse Andrieu, a small farmer in the department of the Lot; his father became a left-wing city councillor and then an anti-war activist. Despite this background Andrieu went to a Church school and seems to have been politicized by the Popular Front and by the works of André Malraux on Spain. He progressed up the academic ladder, evincing a passion for literary studies, and by 1942 got to the point of completing a Masters

(*Licence ès lettres*) whilst teaching at Figeac. On gaining this degree, Andrieu went into the PCF's National Front Resistance in the Toulouse region after the suppression of the unoccupied zone in November 1942. Refusing to become a conscripted (STO) worker, Andrieu went into clandestinity at the end of 1943 in the Maquis in the Lot and ended as an officer in the FTP (Croix de Guerre and Resistance Medal).

After the liberation Andrieu became a full-time party employee and in 1946 a full-time journalist (diplomatic editor) for the Communist evening paper *Le Soir*. As a foreign correspondent he was in Belgrade in December 1947 and in Bucharest from 1948–52: he was one of the editors of the Cominform weekly bulletin. All this implies a high degree of orthodoxy. Whatever dark nights of the soul Andrieu underwent they never interfered with his progression in the hierarchy. Andrieu's broadcasts to France on the Eastern European radio service argues a similar reliability; after the 20th CPSU Congress in 1956, however, he was promoted. Perhaps scenting changes in the air, Andrieu became an assistant editor of *L'Humanité* at the beginning of 1956, and chief editor in 1958 when the paper required modernizing (whatever the change in political line). Andrieu was astute enough to grasp that need, as well as not to get too far in front. Andrieu may have supported the Khrushchevite reformism of Laurent Casanova (q.v.) and Servin at this time, but if so it did not prevent his steady, if unspectacular, progression on to the Central Committee in 1961, as substitute, and a full membership in 1964 (until 1987).

Andrieu's talents, as a writer and on television (a political as well as a literary figure), have been those of a loyal Communist ploughman willing to drive a furrow through the minefields. Hence there have been many exhausting polemics: but *Lettre ouverte à ceux qui se réclament du socialisme* (1978), one of the many ephemeral, if stylish, attacks on the Socialists during the dog days of left unity, and other works (*Choses dites*, for example) will be recognized as insubstantial in the long term.

Bibliography

Andrieu's autobiographical testimony appears in numerous places, for example *Du Bonheur et rien d'autre* (Paris: Stock, 1976) but is of interest mainly to specialists and is unrevealing on key questions such as the Resistance in 1944–5.

DSB

ARAGON, Louis-Marie (1897–1982)

During his long life Aragon was a prolific poet, novelist and essayist. Since he also maintained his active role within the French Communist Party (PCF), he is regarded as a prime example of the politically committed writer, unusual for his long involvement with the party and for his eminence within it.

Aragon's literary career began after he was demobilized in 1919 when, with fellow-poet André Breton, he joined the surrealist Dada movement. In the 1920s both were key figures in the anti-establishment surrealist movement which sought to liberate artistic creation by drawing on images from the unconscious and from dreams. However, from 1930 Aragon saw the PCF, which he joined in 1927, as the new focus of his revolutionary activities. Abandoning surrealism, he adopted the new Socialist realist style favoured by the party, producing a series of novels entitled *Le Monde réel* (The Real World), which offer a critical portrait of decadent bourgeois society. In the early 1930s Aragon visited the Soviet Union several times with Elsa Triolet – the Russian-born writer whom he had met in 1928 and later married. From 1933 Aragon worked to rally intellectuals to join a broad left front against war and fascism. As a journalist he worked for the party daily *L'Humanité*, was co-founder in 1933 with Paul Nizan of *Commune* which served as platform for the anti-Fascist movement, and in 1937 he and Jean-Richard Bloch became co-editors of *Ce Soir*, a new Communist evening paper.

After fighting in the campaign of 1939–40, Aragon organized a Resistance network of writers and intellectuals, emerging as one of the outstanding poets of the period. Now recognized as the PCF's cultural figurehead, he resumed his editorship of *Ce Soir* in 1947 and became editor of the Communist monthly literary journal *Les Lettres Françaises* in 1953. In 1954 he was elected a full member of the party's Central Committee. He remained loyal to the party through de-Stalinization and the Hungary crisis in 1956, although some self-questioning and loss of optimism are expressed in works such as *Le Roman inachevé* (The Unfinished Novel, 1956). In May 1968 Aragon supported the students' cause by offering them a platform in *Les Lettres Françaises*. After Elsa's death in 1970, Aragon devoted himself to his literary work and to his friendships with young people.

Bibliography

L. Becker, *Louis Aragon* (New York: Twayne, 1971)

offers a brief introduction to Aragon's life and works up to the death of Elsa. D. Caute, *Communism and the French Intellectuals* (London: André Deutsch, 1964) explores the political commitment of French intellectuals such as Aragon, Gide, Malraux and Sartre between 1914 and 1960. In French the best general studies of Aragon are R. Garaudy, *L'Itinéraire d'Aragon* (Paris: Gallimard, 1961), P. Daix, *Aragon, une vie à changer* (Paris: Seuil, 1975) and J. Verdès-Leroux, *Au Service du Parti* (Paris: Fayard, 1987).

RC

ARON, Raymond Claude Ferdinand (1905–83)

Raymond Aron was born, as was Sartre (q.v.), in 1905. Aron died in 1983 (three years after Sartre). Aron's parents were Jews (unlike Sartre's). In Germany, between 1930 and 1933, Aron studied German philosophy, while witnessing the Nazi takeover. Politically a vegetable between 1933 and 1940, he sympathized with the Popular Front, but expected its economic programme to end disastrously. (It did.) In those years he pioneered Weberian sociology in France; he handled Husserl's phenomenology and gave it to Sartre.

In 1940 he escaped to London, where he edited the journal *France Libre* until 1944. From 1945 to 1947 he was a prudent journalist on *Combat* (with Camus as its editor) and *Les Temps Modernes* (with Sartre as editor). In 1947, the year tripartism was liquidated, Aron moved to *Le Figaro*, where he remained until 1977. He defended Nato, European unity and German rearmament against the threat of Soviet Communist expansion. He was no Gaullist, even though he joined the RPF in support of constitutional reform. In 1955 came the 'scandalous' book, *The Opium of the Intellectuals* (London: Secker & Warburg, 1957). It attacked the three 'word-myths' of the French left: 'the left' itself, 'revolution' and 'proletariat'. In 1955 he was appointed professor at the Sorbonne; his lectures on industrial society broached the question on convergence between the Western and Soviet systems. Henceforth, Aron with his two ideological power bases (Sorbonne and *Le Figaro*) was to frequent the corridors of power. But he aspired to be the Tocqueville of the twentieth century, even more than to be the Kissinger of France. A supporter of decolonization from Vietnam to Algeria, of the Gaullist state but not its sordid birthmark, and of decentralizing the French university system, he was the purest of liberal mandarins.

Inevitably, in 1968, the students in revolt saw him as a dinosaur. Aron returned the compliment with an unstarry-eyed analysis of the revolt as adolescent 'psychodrama'.

Aron risked all his intellectual capital by ridiculing 'the Revolution' of May *in* May 1968: subsequently, as the passing years 'confirmed' his analysis, the dividends multiplied. Admittedly Aron could not spearhead the disintegration of the 'marxisant' culture of the French intelligentsia. Only a literary 'immortal' – Solzhenitsyn – could cripple the reign of Sartre, but Aron was the major French beneficiary. On the left the resentful could ask, as Benny Levy did, 'Is it better to be Sartre wrong than Aron right?'. The repentant 'discovered' him as God's window on the age. The symbolic matrix of this transformation arrived in June 1979 at a press conference of the campaign on behalf of the Vietnamese refugees known as the 'boat people'. The campaign was founded by Claudie and Jacques Broyelle, repentant Maoists, now friends of Aron. Sartre entered, assisted by André Glucksmann (who had persuaded him to join). Aron uttered their youthful recognition call 'Bonjour, mon petit camarade'. Blind, Sartre could not see the other's rueful smile, probably did not hear the old words, and simply shook the forgiving hand.

The repercussions of 1968 also brought political influence. De Gaulle had an icy disdain for Aron; Aron sensed a certain anti-Semitism, which reminded him he was a Jew. After de Gaulle resigned in 1969, Aron could dabble in presidential politics and his support was valued by both Pompidou (q.v.), and Giscard (q.v.). His shift from *Le Figaro* to *L'Express* in 1977 caused ripples to spread as far as the Elysée palace. Aron was less pro-Giscard than anti-Mitterrand, since he mistook Mitterrand's presidential candidacy for a Communist-impregnated new Popular Front.

Aron's error defines his historic significance. A conservative might have intuited Mitterrand's genius in exploiting the deep ebb tide of Marxism in France. Aron, personification of analytic intellect, was a liberal who hated revolutionism. He was the lucid 'other' whom Sartre feared but refused to be. By acknowledging itself to be a myth and bowing to Aron, the left caused the oracle to run dry.

Bibliography

Among Aron's many works in translation are *The Opium of the Intellectuals* (London: Secker & Warburg, 1957); *Eighteen lectures on industrial society* (London: Weidenfeld & Nicolson, 1967); *France Steadfast and Changing: The fourth to the fifth republic* (Oxford: Oxford University Press, 1960); *The Elusive Revolution: Anatomy of a student revolt* (London: Pall Mall Press, 1969). His *Mémoires* were published by Juilliard (Paris) in 1983. There is a two-volume biography by Robert Colquhoun, *Raymond Aron* (London: Sage, 1986).

MK

ARRIGHI, Pascal Laurent (1921–   )

Born in Vico (Corsica), Pascal Arrighi has led a distinguished and often controversial career on a number of levels. From 1986 to 1988 he represented the National Front as deputy for the Bouches-du-Rhône stronghold, after leading the movement's breakthrough in the Corsican Regional Assembly elections of 1984. Between 1975 and 1982 Arrighi helped to establish and presided over Corsica's university, at Corte. Much of Arrighi's success is based on his native Corsica. Educated at the Collège Fesch (Ajaccio) Arrighi proceeded to the Facultés de Droit et des Lettres in Paris and, in 1947, to the influential Ecole Nationale d'Administration (ENA). After ENA, Arrighi commenced a chequered career as an academic, politician and top-level political, legal and economic adviser. Elected as a 'Radical-Socialist' deputy for Corsica in 1956, he was re-elected as a Gaullist (UNR) two years later, only to fall out with de Gaulle over Algerian decolonization. At the same time, Arrighi enjoyed political office as a general councillor, mayor of Vico and representative at the European Parliament. In 1972, following academic and law appointments, Arrighi became a member of the prestigious Conseil d'Etat, France's highest judicial authority. In the military field, too, Arrighi was widely decorated for bravery, distinguishing himself in the Resistance and exhibiting a strong preference for a French imperial role.

Thus Arrighi's career has been rich and varied. One particular theme stands out: his attachment to the extreme right of the political spectrum. In 1958 Arrighi played a significant part in the historic (13 May) revolt which brought de Gaulle back to power because of the Algerian problem. Arrighi vacated his parliamentary seat to play a major role in the revolt in Corsica against the Fourth Republic's Algerian policy. Pro-de Gaulle in 1958, Arrighi identified with the French Algeria (*Algérie française*) lobby. With the latter's failure and disillusionment with de Gaulle, Arrighi lost his seat in 1962 and entered into political hibernation.

After decolonization and the consolidation of the Gaullist Fifth Republic, Arrighi primarily concentrated upon academic and legal matters. However, the rise of the National Front provided Arrighi with a second wind, enabling the movement to draw upon his influence in the Corsica–Provence–Côte d'Azur areas. As an elder statesman within the National Front and a vice-president of the Corsican Assembly, Arrighi enjoys considerable prestige and deference and represents a certain continuity within the extreme right political family.

In the 1988 presidential election, the National Front emerged as Marseilles' leading political force and, on that basis, Arrighi aspired to be mayor after the 1989 municipal elections. Arrighi's many credentials (politician, lawyer, educationalist, Resistance fighter, *Algérie française*, etc.) make him a key figure on the far right of French politics. However, Arrighi fell out with Le Pen in September 1988 as the latter aspired to a dominant role in Marseilles and planned to stand for mayor. Arrighi quit the National Front with éclat but has kept his own counsel.

Bibliography

There is nothing significant in English on Arrighi but he is the author of several works in French: *Hiérarchie et tutelle administrative: mémoire* (Paris: Ecole Libre des Sciences Politiques, 1942); *Essai sur le caractère administratif des marchés de fournitures* (Paris: R. Foulon, 1945), *Le Statut des partis politiques* (Paris: Librairie Générale de Droit et de Jurisprudence, 1948); *La Corse atout décisif* (Paris: Plon, 1958); and *L'Organisation des régions en France et en Italie: étude comparée* (Paris: CNRS, 1983).

PH

d'ASTIER DE LA VIGERIE, Emmanuel 'Bernard', Baron (1900–69)

Emmanuel d'Astier de la Vigerie's aristocratic background and glamorous debut stand out in contrast to his later involvement in left-wing politics. He even contributed anti-Semitic and anti-Popular Front articles in a weekly, *1935*. A journalist for *Time* and *Life* in the 1930s, he married an American actress and drew an income from the management of newsreel companies. He became an officer in the navy, whose traditional class snobbery and pro-Pétain feelings he rejected in 1940, when he founded the Resistance network Dernière Colonne, which published an underground paper, *Libération*, from July 1941. The

group, subsequently named after the paper, attracted left-wingers and trade unionists, especially after the d'Astier–Jouhaux (q.v., leader of the *CGT*) agreements in August 1941, and was particularly successful in the south-east of France.

From the start d'Astier was hostile to the Vichy regime, and castigated the right-wing Resistance leader Henri Frénay (from the Combat Resistance network) for holding negotiations with Pucheu, Pétain's police chief, in January 1942. Similarly, he scuppered the American-inspired tentative conciliation talks with General La Laurencie. In April 1942 he pressed de Gaulle to speak out clearly on the issue of political democracy, and allow political parties to play a part as such in the Resistance. From December 1942 it appeared that Communists were overrepresented on the leading bodies of *Libération*, to the detriment of Socialists, who strongly objected to this, and who branded d'Astier, with some justification, as a fellow traveller.

In December 1943 he became *Commissaire à l'intérieur* of the Comité Français de Libération Nationale in Algiers, then minister for home affairs in the French provisional government in September 1944. He met Churchill in January and February 1944 in a dramatic and personal move to obtain British weapons for the Resistance groups in the Alps and Auvergne. Although Churchill tried to restrain the French authorities and the Resistance from tracking down and sentencing collaborators, he acceded to d'Astier's demands – which was somewhat resented by the orthodox Gaullists.

D'Astier seemed to condone the rising influence of some Communist individuals in *Libération*, but he came under fire from Communist leaders in July 1944 for enhancing the authority of de Gaulle – whom he called 'le symbole' – over independent Resistance groups.

After the war, d'Astier maintained this ambiguous relationship with Gaullism and communism, which he never managed to blend. Elected to the Constituent Assembly on a Resistance ticket in 1945, he kept his parliamentary seat until 1958, and mostly sided with the Communist Party. Under his editorship, *Libération* developed into a fully-fledged daily (with a circulation of 150,000 copies in its heyday in 1948), attracting journalists and readers from the rival *Franc-Tireur*. Then it declined, and was eventually wound up by its virtual owner, the PCF, in 1964. In 1950, together with Pierre Cot, d'Astier was party to the creation of the *Union Progressiste*, a left-wing Resistance-inspired group which lacked coherence and dwindled away in the 1950s.

Although he was sentimentally attached to the

Soviet Union – he was awarded the Lenin Prize in 1957 – d'Astier disagreed with the PCF, to the point of supporting de Gaulle after the 1962 referendum. *L'Evénement*, a magazine he founded in 1966, in support of his 'left-wing Gaullism', did not survive him.

Bibliography

d'Astier de la Vigerie, Emmanuel (1961), *Les Grands*, Paris: Gallimard.
d'Astier de la Vigerie, Emmanuel (1965), *De la chute à la Libération de Paris*, Paris: Gallimard.
E. d'Astier de la Vigerie is also mentioned in Henri Noguères, *Histoire de la résistance en France* (Paris: Robert Laffont, 1981) five volumes; and also Jean Lacouture, *De Gaulle* (Paris: Seuil, 1984, 1985) three volumes.

JPR

ATTALI, Jacques José (1944–   )

Of African settler origin (a *pied noir*) and the son of a businessman in Algiers, Jacques Attali had a spectacularly successful career in higher education before turning to politics as a close collaborator with François Mitterrand. He graduated first from the prestigious Ecole Polytechnique in 1963, entered the civil service (Mines), and graduated from 'Sciences Po' and ENA. He went on to teach courses in the Polytechnique and ENA as well as becoming a member of the Conseil d'Etat. His brother, Bernard, is the head of Air France.

Although he had met Mitterrand when on secondment to the Prefecture of the Nièvre, it was as a result of his association with Jean-Pierre Chevènement (q.v.), who was then recruiting for Socialist Party working groups, that he became acquainted with the Socialist Party which he joined in 1973. He became Mitterrand's principal economic adviser in 1974 and (as 'Simon Ther') helped in the election campaign of that year. It was in this capacity that he went on a secret visit to the Bundesbank to obtain help to sustain the franc if Mitterrand won. He continued to help Mitterrand as an economic expert (preparing, for example, the famous debate with Raymond Barre in 1977) but also contributed to many other Socialist working groups. He was unsuccessful in his attempt to be adopted for a winnable Socialist constituency but in 1981 became a key figure in the Elysée as head of Mitterrand's private staff. In this position he had privileged access to the president and controlled much of the advice given. He was

not, however, the principal influence even on economics and was overruled on a number of key issues.

Attali has achieved some renown as a writer, but most of it outside the mainstream of the economics profession. His *Anti-Economique* (1974) was a critique of orthodoxy. His *Nouvelle economie française* (1978) contains a vision of where capitalism is heading and what to do about it. One fear expressed is that of a change in social relations brought about by information technology. Social status will depend on your ability or otherwise to get access to the network of computers that will control society. Top dogs would be those who could still afford to write letters by hand! The analysis of the service sector plays a big part in Attali's writing. His *Bruits* (1977), an essay on the 'political economy of music', has more appeal for cultural theorists than economists. Attali's claim to fame is thus basically as a propagator of stimulating ideas; his reputation is more literary than economic.

Bibliography

Attali, J. and M. Guillaume (1972), *Anti-economique*, Paris: PUF.
Attali, J. (1978), *La Nouvelle economie française*, Paris: PUF.
Attali, J. (1977), *Bruits*, Paris: PUF, translated (1985) as *Noises: the Political Economy of Music*, Manchester: Manchester University Press.
See also *Le Point*, 24 July 1989 for a profile.

PH

d'AUDIFRET-PASQUIER, Edmond Armand Gaston, duc (1823–1905)

Nephew and adopted son of the Chancelier Pasquier from whom he inherited the dukedom created in 1844, d'Auddiffret-Pasquier entered the Conseil d'Etat where his career was cut short by the advent of Napoleon III. He retired then to his estates in the department of L'Orne where twice he tried but unsuccessfully to be elected to the Assembly (Corps Legislatif) against official candidates. All his life he remained a fierce opponent and bitter enemy of Bonapartism. Following the débâcle of the Franco-Prussian War he was elected (from 1871 to 1875) to the National Assembly where he perfectly expressed the feeling of the mainly royalist dominated assembly when he declared that he belonged 'to that provincial aristocracy, honourable and full of respect for God and King'.

D'Audifret-Pasquier was soon acknowledged along with the duc de Broglie as one of the leaders of the centre-right. In the Assembly he constantly voted with the conservative majority on the acceptance of the peace treaty with Germany, against the return of the government to Paris after the Commune and for the abrogation of the law of exile for members of former royal families. After the fall of Thiers in May 1873 he tried to have the duc d'Aumale chosen as the new head of state but Marshal MacMahon, the duc de Broglie's nominee, was preferred. He also vainly attempted to bring a reconciliation between the royalist factions but that failed when the royalist pretender, the comte de Chambord refused to accept the *Tricolore* as the national flag.

In 1875 d'Audifret-Pasquier voted for the constitutional laws (*lois constitutionnelles*) but against the establishment of the Republic as proposed in Wallon's amendment. However, he gradually made so many friends within the moderate left that he was elected, by a large majority, President of the Assembly in place of Buffet. From 1875 to 1905 he was a senator: he was elected the first of the life senators and from 1876 to 1879 he presided over the Senate. During the constitutional crisis following the 16 May 1877 he refused to give the duc de Broglie a vote of confidence in the Senate. Fearing that president MacMahon might be tempted to resolve the conflict with the Republican National Assembly by a *coup d'état*, he advised the president against any unconstitutional move and urged him to appoint a Republican as the new head of the government. In 1879 he was elected at the Academie française where he succeeded the formidable Bishop of Orléans Mgr Dupanloup (q.v.).

In contrast to Thiers who identified his own political success with the Republic, d'Audifret-Pasquier remained a sturdy champion of the monarchical ideas; as one commentator put it, 'He refused to repudiate his past, he merely adjourned his hopes'. However, this uncompromising liberal Orleanist (allied to the *haute-bourgeoisie*) was also by temperament and conviction more at ease with the centre-left than the fanatical right and as such paved the way to a moderate Republic where social order and property would be safe.

Bibliography

Audifret-Pasquier, duc d' (1938), *La Maison de France et l'assemblée nationale – souvenirs*, Paris: Plon.

Chapman, G. (1962), *The Third Republic of France – The First Phase 1872–1894*, London: Macmillan.

de Rémusat, C. (1967), *Mémoires de ma vie* (C.H. Pouthas), Paris: Plon.

BS

AURIOL, Jules Vincent (1884–1966)

Born in Revel (Haute-Garonne), the son of a baker, Vincent Auriol was elected Socialist deputy for Muret in 1914. He allied himself with Léon Blum (q.v.) in the great schism that occurred within the French Socialist Party (SFIO) in 1920 and soon became prominent as the SFIO's financial expert. He was president of the finance committee of the Chamber of Deputies between 1924–6 during the period of left-wing government known as the *Cartel des Gauches* and was a natural choice as finance minister in Blum's Popular Front government of 1936. He served as justice minister in the Chautemps (q.v.) government of 1937 and also participated in Blum's brief second administration in 1938. He was among those at Vichy who voted against granting full powers (*pleins pouvoirs*) to Pétain in 1940 after the fall of France and was for a period interned by the Vichy authorities, using this time to work on plans for constitutional reform. In October 1943 he flew to join de Gaulle and in the following year served as president in the foreign affairs committee of the Algiers Assembly.

His most notable achievements, however, were to lie in the post-war period. After de Gaulle's resignation as head of the provisional government in January 1946, he replaced Félix Gouin (q.v.) as president of the Constitutional Assembly when the latter took over from de Gaulle. He presided over both Constituent Assemblies and, a year later, was elected president of the new Republic by the Senate and National Assembly by 452 votes to 242 in the first round. His part in the elaboration of both draft constitutions had been vital, since he was the arbiter between the Socialist, Communist and Christian Democrats coalition known as 'tripartism'. He distanced himself from the SFIO's opposition to the preservation of presidential authority (which he favoured) and also conducted the delicate negotiations for a prime minister when neither the Communist Thorez (q.v.) nor the Christian Democrat Bidault (q.v.) were acceptable. It was Auriol who successfully proposed his fellow Socialist Blum. After his election as president, Auriol was to admit privately that he had in effect begun to act as president a month earlier during the difficult process of government formation.

As president, Auriol had to imprint a new style on an office which the extreme left had wished to abolish completely. Though wielding much less power than would a Fifth Republic president, he adopted a firmer stance on many matters than had most of his pre-war predecessors. Events conspired to give Auriol the opportunity to flex his muscles, and to demonstrate the importance of that continuity which his office alone could represent, as ephemeral centrist (third-force) governments came and went. Though he deplored Ramadier's (q.v.) dangerous willingness to accept opposition questions (*interpellations*), his own support of his prime minister in 1947 enabled the latter to remove the obstructionist Communist ministers. During the ensuing years of 'third-force' cabinets, Auriol's overall management was a precious factor in safeguarding a Republic threatened from the Communist left and the Gaullist right. In an Assembly where up to six parties jostled for supremacy, he realized that a responsible president could vitally affect events by his non-partisan appraisal of a situation. Convinced that the gravity of the situation early in 1952 demanded a man of the right who was at the same time a moderate, Auriol chose Antoine Pinay and thus gave a whole new complexion to French politics.

By virtue of his presidential office, Auriol was also president of the French Union, and so had the power to influence policies in an area which, though particularly vital at this juncture, interested the general public less than the bread-and-butter issues of domestic politics. In Indo-China, the Auriol–Bao Dai agreements of 1949 maintained a façade of Vietnamese independence while retaining a French colonial presence. Elsewhere, and particularly in North Africa, nationalism grew apace helped by the lack of a firm voice from Paris, and it was Auriol who represented a measure of permanence during these years as Tunisia and Morocco moved towards independence.

An active president but one who, in the eyes of some, broke the unwritten law that presidents should be non-controversial, Auriol could be outspoken: his own dislike of the idea of German rearmament, for example, was a secret to no one and he was hostile to the proposal for a European Defence Community. Towards the end of his mandate (May–June 1953) he upbraided the Communists and Gaullist RPF for making parliamentary government unworkable by their destructive blocking tactics during the five-week crisis after the fall of the Mayer (q.v.) cabinet.

A dramatic example of the faults of the stalemate system over which he was forced to preside came a few months later when it took thirteen ballots to break the deadlock in the election of his own successor.

Four years later Auriol played a small but significant role in the events leading to the establishment of a new Republic. In May 1958 he exchanged letters with de Gaulle and it was after he and Mollet (q.v.) visited Colombey-les-Deux-Eglises that the Socialist parliamentary group agreed, by a very small majority, to support the investiture of de Gaulle as prime minister. Auriol himself resigned from the Socialist Party in December 1958. As a former president of the Republic, he was a life member of the newly-created Constitutional Council but resigned from it in 1960. He did this out of opposition to what he saw as the increasingly authoritarian nature of presidential power, something that was incompatible with his view of Republican democracy. He opposed the 1962 constitutional amendment on the direct election to the presidency and his last political act was to support the Mitterrand (q.v.) presidential candidacy in 1965.

Auriol's overall achievement was to have maintained and indeed strengthened the prestige of (and respect for) the presidency when it had been the intention of many of the founders of the Fourth Republic to make it an even weaker office than it had been in the Third. From being, in Clemenceau's memorable phrase, as superfluous to political constitutions as the prostate gland is to man, during these seven years the presidency had evolved for itself a role, a function and an honourable place within the political institutions of France. As for Auriol, he had been in some measure the most influential French politician of his day. Only Adolphe Thiers among his predecessors in the Third Republic could have made a similar claim.

Bibliography

Auriol, V. (1970), *Journal du septennat, 1947–1954*, Paris: A. Colin.

Cuvillier, J.-P. (1978), *Vincent Auriol et les finances publiques du Front Populaire*, Paris: Publications de l'Université de Toulouse.

Dansette, A. (1966), *Histoire des Présidents de la République*, Paris: Fayard.

Guilleminault, G. (1970), *La France de V. Auriol (1947–53)*, Paris: Denoël.

ACR

B

BADINTER, Robert (1928–)

Appointed president of the Constitutional Council in 1986, Badinter had previously been a campaigning lawyer and, from 1981, a reforming minister of justice.

Born in Paris, he attended leading Paris *lycées* and the Faculty of Law; he also has an MA from Columbia University. A lawyer at the Paris Court of Appeals from 1951, he also taught in Paris, Dijon, Besançon and Amiens before becoming professor of law at the Sorbonne (Paris I) from 1974–1981. Highly respected for both his intellect and his ideals, he is widely seen as the representative of a certain liberal humanitarian tradition in French public life.

Before 1981, he was best known for his opposition to capital punishment, and defended several notable cases. His book *L'Exécution* (Paris: Grasset, 1973) is an impassioned description of the guillotining of his client Roger Bontems; he concludes that 'The crime had, physically, changed hands'. His plea in a celebrated 1977 case influenced the highest appeal court to quash death sentences thereafter, despite a rash of them in the lower courts in 1980–1.

He chaired the Socialist Party's commission on a new 'charter of liberties', the report of which appeared in the book he edited, *Liberté, libertés* (Paris: Gallimard, 1976), and was a leading opponent of harsh measures against terrorism and violent crime in 1978–80. He also defended a wide range of notable clients in leading non-capital cases, including businessmen, politicians of all colours, and the terrorist suspect Klaus Croissant. His law firm was considered to be one of the best in Paris.

His tenure as minister of justice from 1981–6 was described by *Le Monde* as 'an historic accomplishment'. Perhaps his most important achievement was the abolition of the death penalty in 1981; the two guillotines still in service were consigned to the Musée National des Arts et Traditions Populaires.

In the same period, France first recognized the principle that individuals could take appeals to the European Court in Strasbourg (Article 25 of the European Convention on Human Rights). The government also abrogated several 'exceptional' legal procedures, for example abolishing the State Security Court (a legacy from the Algerian War) and the anti-riot laws which followed the events of May 1968). The 1980 'Security and Liberty Act' was revised in 1983 in a compromise with the more hardline minister of the interior, Gaston Defferre (q.v.).

Other initiatives failed, such as increasing the independence of judges and dealing with overcrowded prisons, while a U-turn took place on the extradition of terrorist suspects. But measures were also taken to institute community service sentencing and to support the victims of crime. Badinter presided over a major modernization of court facilities with videos, word processing, etc.

His liberalism is sometimes seen as having fuelled the extreme right-wing backlash of 1984–6. However, his work is widely respected across party lines. This has helped to mute cricitism of his obviously political appointment to head the Constitutional Council just prior to the 1986 elections. He managed to steer the Council, evenly divided between left and right, through a number of shoals made more treacherous by the 'cohabitation' of a Socialist president and a right-wing government – including parliamentary reapportionment, privatization, laws on the press and broadcasting, antiterrorist measures, etc.

His main adviser called the decision to uphold the privatization law a 'flashing amber light' to proceed while respecting basic rights. Badinter has described the Council's role as one of preventing political 'passions' from encroaching on 'fundamental liberties'; nevertheless, its 'essential function', he says – one which is 'not found in any text but which is the most effective' – is 'the function of dissuasion'. The campaigning lawyer and reforming minister is now the discreet arbiter of constitutional propriety.

PGC

BALLADUR, Edouard (1929–   )

Edouard Balladur has played a major role both as an adviser to Georges Pompidou and Jacques Chirac and, from March 1986 to May 1988, as finance minister in the second Chirac government. Like many members of the Fifth Republic elite, he has occupied senior posts in business and in the civil service as well as in politics.

Balladur was born in Smyrna, but his family, after several generations of mercantile and banking activity in Turkey, returned to France shortly afterwards. He was educated at the Lycée Thiers in Marseilles, the law faculty at Aix-en-Provence, the Paris Institute d'Etudes Politiques, and the Ecole Nationale d'Administration, whence he graduated (late, owing to illness) in 1957. He then spent six years at the Conseil d'Etat, occasionally working on secondment for Radio-Télévision de France. The head of RTF recommended him to Prime Minister Pompidou, who appointed him to his *cabinet* as adviser on social and industrial relations in December 1963, keeping him through his short 'crossing of the desert' in 1968–9 and then at the Elysée. Balladur was part of Pompidou's May 1968 crisis team at Matignon, participating in the Grenelle negotiations with the unions and working with Chirac, who had left Pompidou's *cabinet* to become junior employment minister in 1967. He proved a discreet and effective staff manager for Pompidou as president (limiting the damage of a running feud between his colleagues Michel Jobert against Marie-France Garaud and Pierre Juillet) and becoming Elysée secretary-general in 1972.

After a brief return to the Conseil d'Etat on Pompidou's death in 1974, he moved to industry, where he held several directorships and managed two subsidiaries of the Compagnie Générale d'Electricité. He thus acquired direct experience – rare for a future finance minister – of the sharp end of the private sector, cutting the workforce at the Compagnie Européenne d'Accumulateurs by 40 per cent. After 1980 Chirac increasingly turned to him for unofficial political and economic advice. Part of this was given publicly, in an article in *Le Monde* (16 September 1983) where he argued for 'cohabitation' between a right-wing majority and President Mitterrand after the March 1986 parliamentary elections.

Elected in third place on the Rassemblement pour la République (RPR) Paris list in March 1986, Balladur, as minister of the economy and finance, had overall responsibility for ensuring that the new government's free-market programme worked well enough to win Chirac the presidency in 1988. Balladur is not a free-market ideologue, and some of his policies – liberalizing the stock market, phasing out price controls, limiting public spending – show continuity with the Socialists. But other measures, such as extensive privatizations, abolition of the wealth tax, priority to top earners in income tax cuts and to lower business taxation rather than investment incentives and grants, showed a clear break with the past.

The results achieved by April 1988 were insufficient to win Chirac's gamble for him. To a middling performance on inflation and investment, slow growth, and poor unemployment and foreign trade figures, was added the sudden fall in share values of newly privatized firms after the stock market crash of October 1987. Chirac was thus unable to campaign on the basis of a resoundingly successful economic record.

Balladur's main contribution to the campaign was an article in *Le Monde* (18 March 1988) advocating early steps towards a merger between the RPR and the main rival grouping of the respectable right, the Union pour la Démocratie Française (UDF). Re-elected for a Paris seat at the first ballot in the June 1988 parliamentary elections that followed Mitterrand's second presidential victory, Balladur became a leading champion of the transformation of the RPR–UDF alliance into a moderate conservative grouping fielding a single presidential candidate. In this he differed from rivals on the left and the right of the RPR who sought a return to the party's Gaullist roots.

Bibliography

Profiles have appeared in the *Financial Times* (15 September 1986), *Le Monde* (21 March and 11 September 1986) and *L'Evènement du jeudi* (11–17 September 1986), as well as an extensive profile/interview in *L'Expansion* (12–25 September 1986). Balladur himself has written *L'Arbre de Mai* (Paris: Librairie M. Jullian, 1979), a book on May 1968 which he describes as half-fact, half-fiction, *Je crois en l'homme plus qu'en l'etat* (Paris: Flammarion, 1987) and *Passion et longueur du temps* (Paris: Fayard, 1989), his own account of cohabitation.

AFK

BARANGÉ, Charles (1897–1985)

It is unlikely that Charles Barangé would have found a place in the history books were it not for the 1951 Law that bears his name (or more precisely the Marie/Barangé laws). Elected to Parliament in 1945 as a member of the newly-formed Christian Democrat Mouvement Républicain Populaire, MRP, he became chairman of the influential finance committee of the National Assembly. Re-elected in 1951, he did not wish to continue in 1956 and played no further part in national public life.

The general election of June 1951 resulted in the election of an increased number of right-wing candidates, favourable to the granting of state aid to private (mainly Catholic) schools. In the autumn of the same year the education minister, André Marie, introduced a bill authorizing the award of education grants to needy parents of children in private – as well as state – secondary schools. A private member's bill was then introduced by Barangé and a Gaullist deputy, Barrachin, instituting a per capita grant to be paid from Treasury funds for each child attending primary school, state or private; the money was to be paid in the case of state schools to the local authorities and in the case of the private schools to the schools' parents' associations. Although the grants were not in themselves munificent, these bills were only passed after bitter controversy in Parliament and in the nation at large, reaching a degree of virulence that was to be echoed, often with the same arguments and slogans, in the debate on the Socialist Savary bill of 1984.

The significance of this episode may be seen to be two-fold. First, it showed the permanency in France, since the nineteenth century, of the 'school war', that is, the left/right rift on the question of state aid to private, to a very large extent confessional schools. Secondly, by widening the rift between the Socialist SFIO, whose long-standing belief in a single state secular education system, *l'école unique*, was unshakeable, and the Christian Democrat MRP, which supported educational pluralism and aid to church schools, it rendered virtually impossible a coalition between these two parties (with the Radicals), against the combined opposition of the Communists on the left and the Gaullist Rassemblement du Peuple Français (RPF) on the right. However, it can be argued that this split was perhaps inevitable in view of the existence within the MRP, alongside more progressive elements, of an increasingly dominant right-wing faction, and of its largely conservative electoral clientele.

Bibliography

Most histories of the Fourth Republic devote a couple of pages to this episode: see, for example, J. Fauvet, *La Quatrième République* (Paris: Fayard, 1959), pp. 185–6. For a detailed account of the parliamentary debates, see *L'Année politique – 1951*, Editions du Grand Siècle (Paris: PUF, 1952), pp. 217–24.

HE

BARBÉ, Henri (1902–66)

Born in 1902, Henri Barbé's political career began young, at the age of 15 when he joined the Jeunesses Socialistes. His early political trajectory is representative of the generation of working-class activists who were propelled into politics by the twin radicalizing influences of the First World War and the Russian Revolution and whose first political experience was acquired in the waves of highly politicized strikes which spread out from the Parisian engineering industry between 1918 and 1921. As with others of his generation, Barbé's trade union activity was accompanied by an enthusiasm for the Bolshevik cause, and a desire to make a break with the traditions of native French socialism through joining forces with the Third International. As such he was one of those who welcomed the split in the SFIO at the Tours Congress of December 1920 which gave birth to the PCF.

Once the PCF was created Barbé immediately took on an influential position in his local branch at Saint-Denis in what was to become a bastion in the 'red belt' of Communist suburbs around Paris. Saint-Denis was to become Jacques Doriot's fiefdom but Barbé also played an active role there from 1924 until 1940. Within the new PCF Barbé's career seemed to progress in tandem with both those of Doriot and of Pierre Célor. All three were roughly the same age and their youth aided their rapid advancement in the PCF to a point where by the early 1930s they were all very close to the pinnacle of power within the party. By 1934 all three had been disgraced and excluded from the PCF, and had begun a move rightwards which would take them first towards fascism, and then later into collaboration politics.

Within the PCF Barbé's rise was evident in 1925 when he made his first visit to Moscow (where he was received by Trotsky and Stalin) and became a member of the Central Committee and a full-time official. Until then his political activity had been conducted among the Jeunesses Communistes (JC) but thereafter the JC leadership took on an increasingly important role within the national party. Barbé joined the PCF Political Bureau in 1927 and then, after the party's poor showing in the 1928 elections, he went to a Comintern youth congress in Moscow where he was singled out as one of those JC leaders who were to be given the task of reviving the fortunes of the party. In 1928 Barbé became one of the most important men in the PCF when he, along with Thorez, Frachon and Célor joned the four-man Party Secretariat – an instrument of collective leadership entrusted with implementing the disastrous new tactic of 'class against class' – a policy which succeeded only in precipitating the PCF decline it was designed to stem.

Barbé's rapid rise came to an abrupt halt in 1931 with the uncovering of the so-called Barbé-Célor 'group', by the very same Comintern official (Manouilski) who had been responsible for the rapid promotion of these supposed conspirators (see entry under Célor). A Central Committee meeting in August 1931 expelled Barbé from the Political Bureau but he remained active in Communist politics until 1934 when he joined with Doriot in opposing the party's initially lukewarm attitude towards anti-Fascist unity. Barbé was expelled from the PCF along with Doriot in September 1934, and he went on to join with Doriot in founding the Parti Populaire Français in 1936, where Barbé as general secretary approved of the move towards fascism. He broke with Doriot in 1939 and then entered into collaborationist politics under the aegis of Marcel Déat's Rassemblement National Populaire (RNP) in 1941. He was an enthusiastic collaborationist and played an important role in trying to unite the various rival groups. He was imprisoned at the liberation for his collaborationist activities. After his release in 1949 he became active as an anti-Communist writer for journals such as Est-Ouest and Le Figaro and was baptized a Catholic. He died in May 1966.

Bibliography

Jean Maitron, *Dictionnaire Biographique du mouvement ouvrier* (Paris: Editions Ouvrières 1973) gives a good account of Barbé's life as does the entry in P. Robrieux, *Histoire interieure du parti communiste,* vol. 4 (Fayard, 1984).

Jean-Paul Brunet, 'Une crise du parti communiste français: l'affaire Barbé-Célor', *Revue d'Histoire Moderne et Contemporaine,* vol. xvi, 1969, pp. 439–61, gives a full account both of Barbé's rise within the PCF and of the circumstances surrounding the uncovering of the supposed Barbé-Célor 'group'.

DALL

BARBUSSE, Henri (1873–1935)

Henri Barbusse – novelist, journalist, pacifist and Communist fellow-traveller – will perhaps be best remembered as the author of one of France's greatest war novels: *Le Feu: Journal d'un escouade* (1916). Awarded the coveted Prix Goncourt in 1917, the novel had taken France by storm on its release, for its sketches of daily life in the trenches, behind the lines and on attack – based on Barbusse's own trench diaries and written during convalescence – were described with an uncompromising realism which aimed to convey the brutal reality of combat to the often complacently optimistic civilians far from the front. But he is also remembered as a committed internationalist who founded associations for veterans from both sides of the divide, and for his role in opening up dialogue between French and Soviet intellectuals in the 1920s and 1930s.

Barbusse began his career as a journalist, working for the *Petit Parisien* and the *Echo de Paris*, and as a poet. His early verses, notably *Pleureuses* (1895), bore the traces of a late-Romantic sensitivity, the influence of Catulle Mendès whose daughter Barbusse married. Here, the profound social message with which all of his later work is imbued, is entirely lacking. But in his novel *L'Enfer* – his second, published in 1908 – the almost obsessive quest for truth and the desire for social justice which characterize his subsequent writings can already be felt.

Barbusse was 41 when war broke out. Despite his declared pacifism – his chronic ill-health alone would have excused him from active service – he enlisted voluntarily. *Le Feu*, which emerged from his experiences 'under fire' (the title of the English translation) in the front trenches of Artois and Picardy, was written in the hope that war might transform humanity for the better. One final sentence, hesitantly voiced, contains the novel's essential message: *'If the present war has advanced progress by one step, its miseries and slaughter will count for little.'* It also explains the direction his career now took.

On his return from the front, Barbusse founded several associations for ex-soldiers from all countries, including France's former enemies. His novel *Clarté,* published in 1919, calls upon men to found a 'Universal Republic' and to stamp out slavery in every form. As a literary work it is disappointing; but it led to the formation of the *Clarté* group and the founding of an international review of the same name which Barbusse edited for many years.

The precise nature of Barbusse's relationship to the French Communist Party is the subject of some controversy. For a while Barbusse was increasingly fascinated by the ideas of Lenin and the Third International. Though critical of Zola who had, in his opinion, ignored the call to political commitment, he nevertheless proved curiously reluctant to become a fully-fledged party member. His *Lettre aux intellectuels* (1921) in defence of communism seems to clarify his position; in it he announced his sympathy, but reserved the right to an independent stance which he felt could be more useful. However, in 1923, when the Communist Party and the association for ex-soldiers fell foul of the authorities, and the Communist leaders were imprisoned, it seems that Barbusse joined in protest. Despite the ambivalent nature of this relationship, it is certainly the case that Barbusse was one of a comparatively small number of intellectuals to be taken seriously by the Communist Party. In 1927, Barbusse journeyed to the Soviet Union where he helped to set up the International Union of Revolutionary Writers, and in 1933 and 1934 he organized several international conferences against fascism and war.

Although Barbusse will be remembered primarily as the author of *Le Feu*, he was above all a committed pacifist and internationalist, concerned even in the 1920s with East–West relations. In his own terms, 'to be both nationalist and internationalist would be dishonest'. Born in Asnières, he died, in 1935, in Moscow.

Bibliography

Barbusse's best works are *L'Enfer* (Paris: Flammarion, 1908) and, clearly, *Le Feu* (Paris: Flammarion, 1916; translated as *Under Fire*, London: Everyman, 1969). See also: Brett, V. (1963), *Barbusse, sa marche vers la clarté, son mouvement 'Clarté'*, Prague: Orbis.
Caute, D. (1967), *Communism and the French Intellectuals 1914–1966*, London: André Deutsch.
Duclos, J. and J. Fréville (1946), *Henri Barbusse*, Paris: Editions Sociales.
Field, F. (1975), *Three French Writers in the Great War: Barbusse, Drieu la Rochelle, Bernanos*, Cambridge: Cambridge University Press.

MMac

BARDÈCHE, Maurice (1907–   )

Having graduated from the Ecole Normale Supérieure in Paris to which he was admitted in 1928 Maurice Bardèche began a career as a literary academic. In 1934 he married Suzanne the sister of the Fascist author Robert Brasillach (q.v.) with whom he wrote *Histoire du cinéma* (1935) and *Histoire de la guerre d'Espagne* (1939). Professor at the Sorbonne from October 1940 to October 1941 Bardèche was appointed to the chair of nineteenth-century French literature at the University of Lille in 1942. His university career came to an end in 1945 when he was dismissed from this post, no doubt because of his close association and friendship with Brasillach and also on account of his own political views.

Brasillach's execution in 1945 for collaboration and anti-Semitic propaganda during the occupation goaded Bardèche into taking an overt political stance and from 1947 to 1952 he became one of France's most reviled intellectuals. In his *Lettre à François Mauriac* (1947) and *Nüremberg ou la terre promise* (1948), two books which caused a scandal and increased his notoriety and his isolation, he defended collaboration by state employees, questioned the military effectiveness of the Resistance, attacked the liberation purges, criticized the Nüremberg trials and denounced the Allies' blanket bombing of Germany. The second book was banned and Bardèche charged with writing an 'apologia for murder'. After a series of trials and retrials lasting three years he was sentenced to one year's imprisonment. He was pardoned but until 1952 remained under police surveillance and was forbidden to leave France.

In close contact with Oswald Mosley and other leading European Fascists he co-founded the *Mouvement Social Européen* and throughout the 1950s and early 1960s continued to publish political essays. In parallel with his political writing he pursued his career as a literary scholar, founded a publishing house, Les Sept Couleurs, and launched the monthly *Défense de l'Occident*. In 1986 he published a study of Céline.

A contemporary at the Ecole Normale Supérieure of Brasillach, Thierry Maulnier and Jacques Soustelle (q.v.) who would all sooner or later become identified with extreme right-wing politics, Bardèche has become a figure of considerable importance in postwar European Fascist thinking. Although he belonged to no political party during the occupation and adopted no overt political stance, in many ways he continues the intellectual Fascist tradition of Brasillach and Drieu la Rochelle (q.v.). He does however underline, particularly in *Qu'est-ce que le fascisme?* (1961) and perhaps with the benefit of hindsight, the idealistic dimension of fascism, presenting it as a utopia quickly compromised in government. His appearance on the French TV programme *Apostophes* in April 1987 demonstrated none the less that his defence of fascism and his minimization of Nazi war crimes can still shock public opinion.

Bardèche's extreme political views have not prevented him becoming one of France's most eminent literary scholars even when, as in the case of his *Stendhal romancier* (1947) (Paris: Plon, 1977), his studies are politically loaded.

Bibliography

Algazy, J. (1984), *La Tentation néo-fasciste en France 1944–45*, Paris: Fayard.
Bardèche, M. (1957), *Suzanne et le taudis*, Paris: Plon.
Bardèche, M. (1961), *Qu'est-ce que le fascisme?*, Paris: Les Sept Couleurs.
Brasillach, R. (1941), *Notre avant-guerre*, Paris: Plon.

GTH

BARRE, Raymond Octave Joseph (1924–)

An academic, a deputy, a former European commissioner, a minister and prime minister; independent centre-right candidate in the 1988 presidential elections, Raymond Barre was born into a Catholic bourgeois family in the French Pacific island of La Réunion. He was educated first in La Réunion and then in Paris where he graduated in law and economics.

His academic career as an economist took him to the Universities of Caen and Paris, where he became professor of economics. Between 1959 and 1962 he worked as a ministerial adviser in the private staff (*cabinet*) of Jean-Marcel Jeanneney (q.v.), the minister of industry in the new Gaullist administration. In 1967 Barre was appointed by de Gaulle as one of the two French representatives on the European Commission where he was given the portfolio of economic affairs.

He returned to France in 1972, after five highly successful years in the Commission, resumed his university career and took up a seat on the board of the Bank of France. In January 1976 he was appointed minister of overseas trade in the Giscard administration, before becoming prime minister in August 1976. He became a deputy for a seat in Lyons in 1978 under the UDF label and was re-elected in

1981 and 1986. He stood unsuccessfully in the 1988 presidential elections, failing to obtain enough votes to reach the second ballot.

Barre has been a distinguished and prolific author. He has produced several economic texts, including *Economie politique* (PUF, vol. 1 1961, vol. 2 1965), and a number of works outlining his political ideas, *Une Politique pour l'avenir* (Plon, 1981), *Réflexions pour demain* (Pluriel, Hachette, 1984), *Au tournant du siècle* (Plon, 1987), *Questions de confiance* (Flammarion, 1988). He is also editor of the political journal *Faits et Arguments*.

Many biographers and commentators claim that the traumatic childhood experience of his father's involvement in a case of business fraud and the parental separation which followed, when his father left La Réunion, had a significant effect on Barre's personal development. It is alleged that this episode induced in Barre both a strong ambition to succeed and the adherence to a traditional set of values.

Barre's first, and in his eyes primary, career as a university academic and economist has brought him considerable acclaim. He has been an influential teacher and scholar in the fields of economics and European affairs since the mid-1950s, holding posts at the Universities of Caen and Paris, the Political Science Institute in Paris and the National School of Administration. Throughout his political career his love of lecturing students and, his critics add, of hectoring the general public, has never left him, earning him the epithets of 'le Professeur Barre', and 'Barre la Science'. His commitment to his academic career was illustrated during the 1988 election campaign when he continued to give his weekly classes in Paris.

Like many other leading politicians, Raymond Barre's entry into the world of politics was through a ministerial *cabinet*. As the head of Jeanneney's team of personal advisers, Barre found himself at the heart of industrial policy-making at a time when France's economy was rapidly changing and expanding. He gained first-hand experience of planning, management, international economic relations and dealing with the unions. Barre left Jeanneney's *cabinet* in 1962 but remained part of a circle of university academics, sympathetic to the Gaullists, who were frequently consulted by the government, either formally or informally, on matters of policy. It was from this circle that Barre was unexpectedly chosen by de Gaulle to serve on the European Commission. During his time in the Commission Barre's international reputation as an economist widened among politicians and policy-makers. He was also acknowledged among European leaders as an administrator capable of handling complex financial and economic matters. The period spent in Brussels converted Barre into an ardent and committed European and paved the way for future ministerial office. Whilst working in Brussels Barre kept in close touch with domestic policy-making and was, for example, instrumental in advising de Gaulle against the devaluation of the franc in 1968.

When Barre's five-year term as a commissioner ended in 1972, he continued to keep in close touch with government circles, acting as an adviser on higher education and economic matters during the Pompidou administration.

He entered the government in January 1976 as minister for overseas trade; after only a few months ministerial experience, President Giscard d'Estaing appointed Barre prime minister to replace the Gaullist Jacques Chirac. Barre's appointment was unexpected and many thought that he had insufficient political experience for such a key office. However, Giscard was facing both a delicate situation within his own right-wing majority and an economic crisis. Hence Barre's relative political obscurity and lack of political ties, coupled with his economic and financial expertise, made him seem the ideal choice as premier. Giscard hailed him as the 'best economist in France' and initially gave him the portfolios of both finance and prime minister in order to sort out France's increasing economic problems. Barre's close relationship with the president and his dominance over other ministers meant that he had a relatively free hand in determining economic policy between 1976 and 1981, and it is in this sphere of policy that he made his most significant contribution as prime minister.

The economic policy of Barre's premiership, labelled as *Barrisme*, involved a package of economic measures designed to aid France's economic recovery and restore the trade balance. The two Barre Plans of 1976 and 1977, and other economic measures, introduced an austerity programme which gave priority to cutting the budget deficit, reducing public expenditure, and setting tight monetary controls. Barre also introduced a set of neo-liberal policies which privatized minor parts of French industry and attempted to liberalize labour and capital markets. The policy of rigour had the effect of lowering living standards and allowing unemployment to rise. Barre's economic programme was extremely unpopular, not only with all the unions (including the moderate Force Ouvrière), but also with the wider electorate which had been used to a prolonged period of economic growth and rising living standards. The unpopularity of *Barrisme* was undoubtedly

one of the factors contributing to the defeat of Giscard in the 1981 presidential elections.

Barre consolidated his own political position in 1978 by winning one of the constituencies in Lyons as a candidate for the newly-formed Union pour la Démocratie Française (UDF), an alliance of non-Gaullist centre and right-wing parties. His bonhomie and empathy for provincial France made him an appealing candidate and he readily adopted the Rhône Valley as his political home. Barre's standing as a national figure improved considerably when his period in government ended following the right's electoral defeat in 1981. With the experience of rampant inflation and rising unemployment during the first two years of the socialist government, Barre's policies were seen in retrospect as 'safe and sensible' and his premiership was viewed in a more favourable light by the public. Against this background Barre began a long campaign to promote his candidature for the presidency and built up a network of support groups around the country. By 1987 Barre was predicted to be the right-wing candidate most likely to defeat Mitterrand in the 1988 presidential elections. In the event, Barre lost the first ballot to the better organized and more assertive Gaullist candidate, Jacques Chirac (Barre 16.9 per cent, Chirac 19.1 per cent). A poorly organized campaign, a lack of a clearly defined political support base and an inability to present a coherent set of alternative policies, were all contributory factors in Barre's defeat. Most importantly, however, Barre appeared avuncular, serious and lacklustre compared to the more dynamic Chirac. Nevertheless, he emerged from the election relatively unscathed and his popularity remained high in the immediate post-election period.

Barre has described himself as having 'the head of a Gaullist and the heart of a Christian Democrat'. In addition he is committed to many of the broad principles of economic liberalism. His Gaullism is based upon support for the person and policies of General de Gaulle and a strong commitment to the institutions of the Fifth Republic. As a young man, Barre was inspired by de Gaulle's policies of economic modernization and a strong independent France. His support for constitutional Gaullism is perhaps best illustrated by the campaign he waged between 1985 and 1988 against '*cohabitation*', or power sharing, between a left-wing president and a right-wing government. Barre argued that '*cohabitation*' was against the spirit of the Fifth Republic Constitution and would cause instability and weak government. His high principled stance went unheeded when, in June 1986, the narrowly elected conservative majority agreed to form a government under the presidency of François Mitterrand.

His Christian Democratic principles are reflected in his Catholicism, his ardent Europeanism and his commitment to *solidarité*, a French version of one-nation conservatism. Barre believes in the importance of the state as a 'guarantor of the social equilibrium of the nation', and as responsible for the provision of welfare. These centrist positions are interwoven with a number of conservative and neo-liberal doctrines. Barre's neo-liberalism embraces a commitment to the deregulation of businesses and the labour market in order to enhance competition. However, it does not encompass what Barre sees as 'blind, unthinking privatization' advocated by the majority of the neo-Gaullist RPR and the Republican Party. Essentially, Barre believes that the state should play some role in industrial policy-making, that privatizations should be limited, and that the state has a responsibility for the provision of welfare to its citizens. In summary, Barre's political views are eclectic, pragmatic and non-ideological. They represent a blend of traditional values, modern conservatism, neo-liberalism and Christian Democratic principles.

Although Barre advocates the creation of a party similar to the West German Free Democrat Party, he has a Gaullist dislike of party politics. Since his election as a deputy in 1978 he has been attached to the UDF, although his relations with this federation of parties has remained ambivalent. Whilst he has much in common with the Centre Democrate (the centrist grouping of the UDF), he is at odds with the younger generation of economic liberals in the Republican Party (the conservative wing of the UDF). The federation did however give him their backing in the 1988 presidential election.

Barre has been a very significant figure in French politics during the last fifteen years. His advocacy of neo-liberal ideas in the 1970s helped to set a new political and economic agenda in France. His failure to achieve presidential office, which he has so coveted, should not overshadow his importance as a central figure in French right-wing politics. Barre's failure to win office is emblematic of the failure of the right to construct a presidential coalition in the 1980s. The fragmentation of right-wing politics has made it difficult to secure consensus on a single presidential candidate of the right. Furthermore, although Barre has considerable popular appeal, he has been unable to extend his party support beyond a narrow, and by no means secure, base in the UDF. His political shortcoming has been a reluctance to recognize that a strong party base is an essential prerequisite for political success – in Fifth Republic politics. Barre has remained in many senses an independent, identifying himself in the post-1988 election period as a man of the centre.

Bibliography

For a discussion of Barre's political views see R. Barre *Une Politique pour l'avenir* (Plon, 1981) and *Questions de confiance* (Flammarion, 1988). Henri Amouroux's biography, *Monsieur Barre* (Robert Laffont, 1986), gives a detailed and sympathetic account of Barre's life.

ER

BARRÈS, Maurice (1862–1923)

Novelist, journalist and politician, Barrès was born at Charmes-sur-Moselle in 1862, and educated at the *lycée* of Nancy. In 1883 he moved to Paris, and soon was writing regularly for a number of prominent journals. In 1888 he published the first novel in his trilogy *Le Culte du moi*, in which he emerged as a fashionable exponent of the cult of individualism.

Meanwhile, he was showing a strong political interest, as a fervent Boulangist. Having founded, in Nancy, a political journal *Le Courrier de l'Est*, he stood successfully for Nancy as a Boulangist in the 1889 elections, on the platform of 'Nationalisme, protectionisme et socialisme'. His complex political attitudes at this stage combined an authoritarian republicanism, a strong nationalism, and an anticapitalist desire for social reform. After the loss of his seat in 1893, these ideas were further elaborated during his short-lived political editorship of *La Cocarde* from 1894 to 1895.

From 1893 to 1906 Barrès was to try repeatedly but unsuccessfully to return to the Chamber. These years saw, however, the development of his philosophy of 'la terre et les morts' in his influential novel *Les Déracinés* (1897); the vivid depiction of the Boulangist and Panama episodes, in his political novels *L'Appel au soldat* (1900) and *Leurs figures* (1902); and the start, from 1904 onwards, of his campaign for the restitution of the lost provinces of Alsace-Lorraine, both in the press and in his novels *Au service de l'Allemagne* (1905) and *Colette Baudoche* (1908). He involved himself heavily (1898–9) in the battles of the Dreyfus affair as an anti-Dreyfusard, his attitudes being strongly laced with anti-Semitism.

In 1906 he became a member of the French Academy. He also, finally, became deputy for the 1st *arrondissement* of Paris, which he was to remain until his death. Strangely, though he was a brilliant speaker, and commanded much respect, he was an isolated figure in the Chamber, and not part of any parliamentary grouping. His main themes, apart from the ever-present Alsace-Lorraine question, were (despite his agnosticism) the defence of the Church against anticlerical policies, and the preservation of France's churches from the decay caused by official unconcern. Throughout the 1914–18 War he wrote a daily article in *L'Echo de Paris*, and paid numerous visits to the front. He played a crucial part in the 'treason' campaign against Caillaux and Malvy in 1917, which was to bring Clemenceau to power. For the last years of the war, and the first years of the peace, he was obsessed with France's need for a Rhine frontier. He deplored the Versailles Treaty on this score, and thereafter openly encouraged Rhineland separatism. In home affairs, he started a campaign for the proper funding of scientific research, and for loans for students. He died suddenly of a heart attack in 1923.

Barrès was not a particularly successful practical politician, but he was a highly influential political thinker, who with Maurras had a considerable impact on the pre-war young generation, whose later actions and attitudes were to be strongly marked by his example.

Bibliography

Ouston, P. (1974), *The Imagination of Maurice Barrès*, Toronto: University of Toronto Press.

Soucy, R. (1972), *French Fascism: The case of Maurice Barrès*, Berkeley, Cal.: University of California Press.

Domenach, Jean-Marie (1958), *Barrès par lui-même*, Paris: Seuil.

Maurras, Hélène and Nicole (eds) (1970), *La République ou le roi* (Barrès–Maurras correspondence, 1888–1923), Paris: Plon.

RMG

BARTHOU, Jean Louis (1862–1934)

In his very early student days Barthou had already achieved prominence in the political sphere. He joined the Union de la Jeunesse Républicaine when his legal career first took him to Paris and he became its president in 1889 after he returned to the capital as a newly elected deputy. He was then just 27 years old. He represented the Basses Pyrénées first as a deputy for Orloron and then as a senator, continuously from 1889 until his death.

Ministerial office was not long in coming, for Barthou was an excellent debater, and his interventions in the Chamber attracted considerable notice. In 1893 he was appointed minister of public works (a key patronage post), and found himself in conflict with the leading Socialist Jaurès (q.v.). This conflict was finally satisfied, with honour, after a duel between the two protagonists.

Despite this duelling, Barthou was always a man of moderation, and nowhere was this more in evidence than during the Dreyfus affair. His views ensured his election to the presidency of the 'progressive wing' of the Moderate Republicans, but kept him temporarily out of office. However, in 1906 he returned to the Ministry of Public Works and remained in cabinet office until his appointment as prime minister in 1913. His premiership was marked by a verbal battle with Caillaux (q.v.) who unsuccessfully opposed the extension of military service, but who brought him down when Barthou tried to raise a new loan to cover the budget deficit.

In December 1914 Barthou learnt of the death of his son in battle. It was a tragedy that was to colour profoundly his outlook on the world: provoking firstly a complete withdrawal from public life which was to last until 1917, and then by an adherence to a rigid attitude against the German nation. This rigidity was of some import, for he briefly held the post of minister of foreign affairs in 1917, reported on the Treaty of Versailles to parliament in 1919, and represented France in the immediate post-war conferences as minister of war and president of the war reparations committee.

In 1922 he abandoned foreign affairs on his appointment as minister of justice (*Garde des Sceaux*). It was a post that he was to occupy for the greater part of a decade, and which he used to effect judicial reforms close to his heart. With the onset of increasing ministerial instability, Barthou returned to his former area of expertise, at one stage being considered for the premiership, but taking on the Ministry of Foreign Affairs in Doumergue's 'government of national union', after the night of the 6 February 1934.

Once again his fears of Germany came to the fore. He sought to re-establish the traditional French diplomatic entente with Russia despite the nature of the Bolshevik regime. He gave additional impetus to the system of eastern alliances that France had begun to build up in the mid-1920s, by attempting to shore up faltering relations with Yugoslavia and Poland. It was for this purpose that King Alexander of Yugoslavia was invited to France in October 1934, there to be received in Marseilles by Barthou. Both were to fall to the bullets of the Croatian assassin, Gueorguiev.

PT

BARZACH, Michèle (1943–)

Michèle Barzach, minister of health and the family in Jacques Chirac's government from 1986–8, was one of that government's most popular ministers. She was born in Casablanca, the daughter of a Polish emigré (who arrived in France by way of Moscow) and was brought up in Morocco. Ambitious from an early age, she was outstanding at school and determined to become a doctor despite the family's lack of means. This was accomplished through hard work and the award of a grant after her exam success.

At the start of her medical studies she married a Protestant industrialist and made contact with a wider Parisian world. As a doctor she specialized in gynaecology and Jungian psychoanalysis. She remarried the newspaper columnist J.-P. Remard in 1970 and in 1973 started practising as a doctor (in the 15th *arrondissement* of Paris), and was highly successful. A certain political skill was already evident in the mid-1970s.

Apparently untouched by the ferment of May 1968 and not initially interested in politics, she became associated with Jacques Chirac's aide, Jacques Toubon and subsequently 13th *adjoint* at the City Hall of the 15th *arrondisement*. In 1984 she became a 'shadow' for social affairs in the RPR team and in 1986 was made minister of health.

As a politician Barzach is associated with a number of issues. Along with Noir (q.v.) and others she made clear that 'her soul had a price' and that she would not participate in a government with Le Pen (q.v.) or any other National Front member. Although a practising Catholic she helped the family planning and abortion campaigns in Aubervilliers. As minister of health she launched the French government's anti-AIDs campaign. That she was made minister of health, the first doctor at that ministry since the Fourth Republic, was a tribute to the medical lobby in the RPR; one of her first acts was to restore the private beds to public hospitals. She also defended the monopoly held by pharmacies, and unrestricted free entry to medial schools (no *numerus clausus*), increased the family allowance for the third child, and partially restructured the hospital service. Barzach's lack of vigour in the campaigns against alcohol and tobacco have been criticized, although a lower tar cigarette was negotiated and the anti-Aids campaign

(which included the issue of free syringes) has been widely praised, even though its efficacy is not yet clear. The anti-abortion issue was also adeptly handled.

Barzach is famous for elegance and charm and knows how to use the media. But she is very much a lone figure, probably better equipped for discreet actions than the construction of a *grand dessein* for health. After the defeat of the right in 1988 she became an associate of the RPR 'renovators' (Noir and Séguin) but also became the party's national secretary on cultural affairs, and in 1989 an adjoint to the mayor of Paris, a Paris councillor and a European MP.

Bibliography

See M. Barzach, *Le Paravent des Egoïsmes* (Paris: Odile Jacob, 1989).

DSB

BAUDIS, Dominique Pierre Jean Albert (1947–)

Dominique Baudis emerged as a rising political star during the 1980s, successfully combining the deft manipulation of parochial loyalties and party political machines in south-west France with American-style media hype and technocratic managerial skills. A former television news presenter, he belonged to no party and vowed never to join any. Yet in just three years, beginning in 1983, he captured virtually every major elected office in the Toulouse region, and won seats in the National Assembly and the European parliament. Though still in his 30s he was widely tipped as a future government minister.

His youthful looks mirrored the changing face of Toulouse, the principal city in the Haute-Garonne department, in the Midi-Pyrénées region, which had long been an economic backwater. The area experienced comparatively little industrialization during the nineteenth century, but became a centre for high-tech developments such as aeronautics and computing after the Second World War. It has been described as a French California in the making, and there is more than a whiff of things American in Baudis's media-oriented campaign style. But his carefully distanced relations with party political machines are uniquely French. From de Gaulle to Raymond Barre, the Fifth Republic has a long tradition of statesmen who have made their reputation by boasting their independence from any narrow party allegiance. While there is sometimes an element of pretence in such claims – Baudis, for example, could not have been elected to the European Parliament in 1984 had he not been nominated as a candidate by the CDS – one of the component parties in the centrist UDF – their appeal is none the less potent.

Throughout most of the twentieth century, Toulouse was a stronghold of the left. The mould began to crack when Baudis's father Pierre won a seat there as a centrist *député* in 1958; he was elected mayor of the city in 1971. Dominique, who was educated at Le Caousou, a Jesuit school in Toulouse, and the Institut d'Etudes Politiques in Paris, played a leading role during his early twenties in the youth section of Jean Lecanuet's Centre Démocrate, predecessor of the CDS. After being called up for military service in 1971, he had no further involvement in party politics. He began a career as a television journalist in 1974, and was a news presenter on national television from 1978 until 1982, when he stood down as a result of disagreements over editorial policy following the Socialists' election victories the previous year. By chance, Pierre Baudis was now nearing political retirement, and he immediately began grooming his son to take over as mayor of Toulouse in the municipal elections due to be held in 1983.

Dominique's main asset was the reputation for trustworthiness and impartiality associated with his career in broadcasting. With the support of the local UDF machine, together with that of the neo-Gaullist Rassemblement pour la République (RPR), Baudis's list of candidates in the municipal elections won a comfortable victory over their Socialist-led rivals. As mayor of Toulouse, the younger Baudis quickly proved himself to be both dynamic and efficient in his management of France's fourth largest city. This provided the springboard for further election victories, bringing him seats in the European Parliament in 1984, on the Departmental Council of Haute-Garonne in 1985, and in both the National Assembly and the Regional Assembly of Midi-Pyrénées in March 1986. To conform with a recent law limiting the number of elected offices which any one individual may hold, Baudis decided, after securing the presidency of the Regional Assembly, to resign his newly-won seat in Parliament, and brought his father out of retirement to serve as his official substitute there. When a parliamentary by-election was held in Haute-Garonne in September 1986, the RPR and UDF fielded a combined list under Baudis's leadership. The local Socialists were in organizational disarray, and even the presence of national party secretary Lionel Jospin at the head of

their list failed to prevent Baudis from increasing his support. He again relinquished his seat to his father, but finally entered the National Assembly after winning a further parliamentary victory in the 1988 general election.

Re-elected Mayor of Toulouse with an increased majority in March 1989, Baudis attempted to grab the national spotlight in the run-up to the European elections held in June of that year by joining a group of young centre-right politicians in an unsuccessful challenge to the leadership of the UDF and RPR. Despite the setback which he suffered at the hands of the old guard, Baudis still had time on his side and had clearly established himself as a force to be reckoned with in the long-term renewal of centre-right politics in France.

Bibliography

Baudis has been profiled in *The Economist* (20 April 1985). See also *Le Monde* (21 October 1985) and *L'Express* (29 March 1985).

AGH

BAUMEL, Jacques (1918–   )

The son of a general practitioner, Jacques Baumel was born in Marseilles on 6 March 1918 into a Protestant family, and himself studied medicine at the University of Marseilles.

He is a good representative of those politicians whom Jean Charlot calls 'the Gaullists of the war, of the first age'. Having joined the Resistance, he was in charge of political agitation in the southern zone, and became a member, then the secretary-general of the Mouvement Unis de la Résistance (MUR) in 1943, quite naturally following on to become a member of the executive committee of the National Liberation Movement in 1944 and of the Provisional Consultative Assembly in 1944 and 1945. He was decorated by de Gaulle who made him a Companion of the Resistance.

Having first joined and then been made assistant secretary of the small Resistance party, the UDSR, he was elected to the first Constituent Assembly by the voters of the Moselle constituency, and to the second Constituent Assembly by those of the Creuse. Answering de Gaulle's call in Strasbourg on 7 April 1947, however, he was one of the founding members of the French People's Rally (RPF), was duly appointed to its executive committee and in 1950 became its delegate for the Paris region.

Apart from his career both as a party leader and a parliamentarian, Jacques Baumel has had varied experience in national and international organizations. However, his main claim to fame is his role as party leader. He was in turn deputy secretary-general (1958) of the UNR and secretary-general (1962–7) of the UNR–UDT, at a time when the party was under considerable pressure for reform, a change of personnel and growing independence from de Gaulle. Baumel, who was probably authoritarian, and whose rather rigid interpretation of party rules generated some degree of resentment within party ranks, was a victim of these changes: he had to surrender his post of secretary-general at the Lille Party Conference of November 1967.

That demotion did not prevent him from successfully continuing his parliamentary career throughout the Fifth Republic, first as senator for the Seine department from 1959 to 1967, then as deputy for the Hauts-de-Seine department continuously from 1967 to the present day. He was in the ranks of Chirac's Rally for the Republic (RPR) from its foundation. The Hauts-de-Seine department in 1976 became virtually his home base, where he was a local elected representative, first as *conseiller général* (departmental delegate) for the Garches canton in 1967, then deputy chairman and finally chairman of the General Council (1970–82), and mayor of the town of Rueil-Malmaison since 1971. He has also served as member of the governing board of the Paris regional district for the past twenty odd years, and is vice-president of the governing board of the Green Spaces Agency of the Ile-de-France region.

Jacques Baumel has had limited ministerial experience, serving as junior minister to the Prime Minister in the Chaban-Delmas Cabinet (1969–1972). Not much younger than François Mitterrand, and a member of the Opposition, he is unlikely to get another chance to play a prominent role in French politics.

Bibliography

Jacques Baumel gets fleeting mentions in Philip Williams's books *Crisis and Compromise* (London: Longman, 1964) and *Politics and Society in de Gaulle's Republic* (London: Longman, 1971) (the latter co-authored by Martin Harrison), and in Jean Charlot's *The Gaullist Phenomenon* (London: Unwin, 1970).

AM

BEAUVOIR, Simone Bernard de (1908–86)

Born into an impoverished bourgeois family, Simone de Beauvoir was educated privately and then – unusually for a girl at that time – studied philosophy at the Sorbonne. There she was brilliantly successful, coming second to Jean-Paul Sartre in the competitive *agrégation* – teaching – examination in 1929, the youngest of her year at 21. From then on her name would be associated with his, not only because of their unconventional relationship but also because of their public image as free thinkers, leaders of the existentialist movement, writers and supporters of the radical left. Members of a numerous, interactive group of writers, thinkers and artists of every kind, they came to epitomize the French left-wing intellectual after the liberation.

Although she considered herself a supporter of the revolutionary left, she was uninterested in politics until the Second World War convinced her that political commitment, or *engagement*, was essential. She left organized activity to Sartre, disliking it intensely herself, but she was always willing to lend her name to political protests, to sign petitions and manifestos, or make statements. Occasionally in later years, during the Algerian War for instance, she would join in demonstrations against brutality, torture or censorship. Considering herself first and foremost a writer, she preferred above all to exemplify her *engagement* through publications, as in the left-wing review they founded in 1945, *Les Temps Modernes*, whose critical and demystifying role was intended to lead to radical social change. In her view, though, this could also be done through her fictional and autobiographical works; it was sufficient that she was aware of the contemporary world and able to reveal it to her readers, thereby changing their perceptions.

The Second Sex, published in 1949, achieved immediate notoriety but its significance only became clear when the feminist movement gathered momentum in the early 1970s. Her highly original analysis of the feminine condition made the work very influential and it became a classic of feminist literature, although many of her views are disputed by modern feminists. In the 1970s, when she had become increasingly disillusioned with the various revolutionary regimes she had supported over the years, she found a new concern which was to occupy her – independently of Sartre for the first time – until her death. Approached in 1970 by the MLF – Women's Liberation Movement (Mouvement de Libération des Femmes) – she joined in the campaign for reform of the abortion law, becoming president of the pressure group *Choisir* and then of the League for Women's Rights; she started a journal, *Questions Féministes*, and a feminist column in *Les Temps Modernes*; and she appeared at conferences, at demonstrations, in television programmes. Finally, with the election of François Mitterrand as president in 1981, she set aside her decision to work only outside political parties. Invited by Yvette Roudy, the minister for women's rights, she agreed to be spokesperson for the Commission on Women and Culture, and she also collaborated with the government in a television series called 'The Second Sex'.

In spite of her somewhat ambivalent relationship with the various women's groups, it is as a militant feminist that she is popularly remembered today.

Bibliography

A. Whitmarsh in *Simone de Beauvoir and the Limits of Commitment* (Cambridge: Cambridge University Press, 1981) analyses de Beauvoir's political theory and practice, and M. Evans' *Simone de Beauvoir: A Feminist Mandarin* (London: Tavistock, 1985) is a critique of de Beauvoir's contribution to feminism. Of de Beauvoir's own works the most significant politically are *The Second Sex* (London: Jonathan Cape, 1953) which was first published in 1949, and her novel *The Mandarins* (London: Collins, 1957), first published in 1954, a fictionalized account of the French intellectuals of the left after the liberation.

AW

BELIN, René Joseph Jean-Baptiste (1898–1977)

René Belin was a hardworking, effective and dedicated trade unionist who acquired considerable prominence in the 1930s. His career prospects were permanently broken by the decision he made after the fall of France to work with the new regime of Marshal Pétain (q.v.). But his role as Vichy's minister of industrial production and labour did not, in his eyes, reflect an abandonment of his trade union beliefs and he is an interesting example of the diversity of motives among those who made what came to be the wrong choice in 1940.

Belin's devotion to trade unionism arose out of his childhood experiences. The son of a teacher who died young and penniless, he knew great poverty as a child and was at one stage obliged, because of his mother's illness, to live in an orphanage. At the age of 11 he was sent out to work. After service in the First World War, he entered the French postal service in Lyons and was soon promoted. He was an energetic member of the post workers' trade union, becoming regional secretary in 1925. Dismissed for his role in a 1930 strike, he was reintegrated in 1932, by which time he had acquired national status in the union and had come to the attention of the leader of the CGT, France's largest union confederation, Léon Jouhaux (q.v.). He entered the confederal bureau of the CGT in 1933 and used its library resources to acquire the theoretical knowledge of which he had been deprived as a child. He became an effective speaker and journalist and was seen as heir apparent to Jouhaux. As an organization man, he disliked the way in which the Communists sought to take over all the positions of union responsibility after the CGT merged with the Communist-led CGTU in 1936. He founded the review *Syndicats* as a focus for those who, like him, saw communism as a threat to the crucial value of trade union independence. In the climate of the late 1930s hostility to Communist infiltration merged into hostility to the war policy which the Communists were seen to advocate. A strong pacifist, Belin was by 1939 on the road that would bring him to Vichy. His relations with Jouhaux were by now very bad, he opposed the war and welcomed the armistice.

On the recommendation of Laval (q.v.) and Marquet (q.v.) he was appointed minister of industrial production and labour. He saw his remit as being to modernize and protect trade unionism rather than to destroy it (in his memoirs he gleefully describes how many future union leaders sought to work with him and how in 1940 Jouhaux's CGT was ready to abandon the statutes which referred to strike action and to the disappearance of the employer class). Though he acceded to the dissolution by Vichy of trade union confederation, he claims to have protected the existence of ordinary unions and federations and to have initiated what would after 1945 become work place committees (*comités d'entreprise*). He left government on the return of Laval in April 1942 and spent the rest of the occupation running a pension fund for gas and electricity employees.

At the liberation, he went into hiding and then spent some time in Switzerland. At the beginning of 1949 all legal charges against him were dropped on the grounds of his resistance to German demands and he returned to France. Though he failed to make the trade union comeback for which he hoped, he re-emerged as a prolific writer and lecturer and was a long serving mayor of the commune to which he retired. He made a notable intervention at the symposium on Vichy organized by the Fondation

Nationale des Sciences Politiques in 1972, still attempting to justify what seemed to most people in the post-war world to have been a betrayal of the trade unionism that he always espoused. Belin was mayor of Lorrez-le-Bocage in the Seine-et-Marne from 1959 to 1965.

Bibliography

Belin, R. (1978), *Du Sécretariat de la CGT au gouvernment de Vichy*, Paris: Editions Albatros.

Maitron, J. (ed.) (1967), *Dictionnaire biographique du mouvement ouvrier français*, Paris: Editions Ouvrières.

PM

BENDA, Julien (1867–1956)

Julien Benda was born into a family of Jewish background in 1867. His education at the Lycée Condorcet had a profound effect on him; the teaching he received there inculcated rationalist and Republican principles and ideals which remained fundamental in his subsequent work. Initially he specialized in mathematics and had intended to prepare for the entrance examinations for the Ecole Polytechnique, but he later changed discipline and studied history at the Sorbonne.

His writing career began in earnest during the 1890s and, at the height of the Dreyfus affair (1898), he started to contribute material to the pro-Dreyfus *Revue Blanche*. He was a *dreyfusard* 'through reason', he insisted, and his firm commitment to the 'eternal values' of truth, justice and reason engendered by the debates surrounding the 'affair' underpinned his thinking for the rest of his career. During the 1900s Benda submitted material to Charles Péguy's *Cahiers de la Quinzaine* and by 1912 he had published a novel – *L'Ordination* – which was denied the prestigious Goncourt literary prize due to the anti-Semitic prejudice of certain jury members. The same year his attack on Bergsonist philosophy (*Le Bergsonisme ou Une philosophie de la mobilité*) appeared. This formed the basis of his subsequent work on literature in which he argued for the restoration of a rigorous classicism (*Belphégor*, 1919 and *La France byzantine*, 1945).

Benda's most famous and best remembered work is *La Trahison des clercs (The Treason of the Intellectuals)* which was published in 1927 by Grasset. The 'clercs' (i.e. intellectuals, artists and writers) had betrayed their calling, Benda believed, through their promotion of temporal, political or national interests to a place superior to those 'eternal values' which they were duty-bound to protect before all else. Yet it should be stressed that Benda was not advocating a return to the 'ivory tower'; in successive defences of his position he asserted that the 'clerc' was fully justified in entering the public arena when he did so in the name of reason or justice, as in the Dreyfus affair.

As the 1930s progressed it became increasingly clear that such conviction to justice would inevitably involve some form of political commitment. Thus, in common with many other intellectuals active in the 1930s, he saw the rise of fascism in Europe as the greatest threat to the eternal values he defended so passionately. This led him into support for the anti-Fascist cause, and by 1938 he was recognized as a leading 'fellow-traveller'. By this time he was convinced that the only truly 'patriotic' political group in France was the French Communist Party. Seeing the French Communists as the natural heirs of Jacobinism, Benda believed that they alone had the political will to combat the Fascist menace, especially in view of the chronic ineffectiveness of successive Third Republic governments.

His Jewish background made Benda a potential target for anti-Semitic polemic and, indeed, Charles Maurras and his acolytes on the extreme right attacked him relentlessly throughout the inter-war period. During the German occupation Benda was forced into hiding and lived out the war in and around Carcassonne. After the liberation he returned to the intellectual scene, but broke with some of his former supporters at the *Nouvelle Revue Française* over the issue of intellectual collaboration. Benda was against clemency being shown to those intellectuals who had collaborated with the Nazis, for he was sure that their attacks on the Republic before the war had not only betrayed their calling, but their country too.

Apart from *The Treason of the Intellectuals*, much of Benda's work is forgotten today. Yet, like Alain, he exerted considerable influence in intellectual circles, and in his life and thought he can be seen as a typical product of the educational culture of the radical Third Republic. Ever since the Dreyfus affair intellectuals have played a major role in political culture in France. It is in this way that Benda's work represents a major contribution to continuing debates on the role and responsibilities of intellectuals. Today his influence can be felt in the work of those contemporary writers who, disillusioned by the reality and practice of communism, have taken a more distanced position regarding political commitment.

Bibliography

For works by J. Benda see: *La Trahison des clercs* (Paris: Grasset, 1927, published as *The Great Betrayal*, trans Richard Aldington, London: G. Routledge and Son, 1928) and *La Jeunesse d'un clerc, Un Régulier dans le siècle* and *Exercice d'un enterré vif* (preface by Etiemble) (Paris: Gallimard, 1968) which is a revealing three-volume autobiography.

R.J. Niess, *Julien Benda* (Ann Arbor: Michigan University Press, 1956) remains the best study in English. See also David Caute, *Communism and the French Intellectuals* (London: André Deutsch, 1964) and D.C. Schalk, *The Spectrum of Political Engagement (studies on Nizan, Benda, Brasillach, Sartre)* (Princeton, NJ: Princeton University Press, 1979).

MC

de BENOIST, Alain (*a.k.a.* Fabrice LAROCHE and Robert de HERTE) (1943–)

De Benoist was born into the middle class. Like many contemporaries he became politically active at university in the 1960s, but he was attracted to the right rather than the left. By the late 1970s he had emerged as the leading intellectual of the *nouvelle droite*. This has sought to develop a strategy of 'Gramsciism of the right'. Right-wing political ideas would gradually attain hegemony not only through their intellectual force, but also through the cultural sphere, and more surreptitiously by a careful infiltration of individuals in key institutions.

De Benoist has worked for various organizations since leaving university, and written prolifically. Publicly, he is best known for his contributions to *Le Figaro Magazine* in the period after 1977, when the paper (under the influence of Hersant and Pauwels) tried to develop a more intellectual right-wing position. He has been closely associated with GRECE (Groupement de Recherche et d'Etudes pour la Civilisation Européenne), formed in the late 1960s to disseminate right-wing ideas. He has been a regular contributor to its journal *Eléments*, writing mainly about European culture, and psychological and scientific developments which underpin inegalitarian ideas. Since 1969 he has also been editor of the journal *Nouvelle Ecole*, which has links with other European right-wing, racist and Fascist organizations.

Three themes are central to de Benoist's thought. First, there is a rejection of the Judaeo-Christian tradition. This is seen as having brought monotheism, thus paving the way for totalitarianism. It has also stressed egalitarianism, when the laws of nature show that man is not created equal. In this sense, Marxism is seen as a form of secular Christianity. Secondly, there is a strong attack on the social and political systems of both the USA and USSR. In differing ways, each involves a totalitarian narrowing of viewpoints. Each fails to achieve what de Benoist sees as the Indo-European values necessary for a good society. American society is founded on an alienating pursuit of money; the Soviet Union is ultimately based on coercion. The third theme in de Benoist's writing is a quest for identity – a need to define a European community, especially in cultural terms.

Many critics have argued that there is little that is new about these ideas; some even perceive them as a form of neo-fascism. However, previously the French right had often been characterized as 'the most stupid' in the world. It had frequently sought to hide under names such as 'démocrates', 'libéraux', or 'républicains'. De Benoist has been proud to stress his membership of Mensa, and describes himself as right wing. He has failed to create a group of like-minded intellectual theorists, but the *nouvelle droite* has almost certainly played a part in the development of French opinion in the 1980s, most notably by contributing to the attack on immigration and Marxism.

Bibliography

Benoist, A. de (1977), *Vu de droite*, Paris: Copernic (winner of Prix de l'Essai de l'Académie française).

Benoist, A. de (1979), *Les Idées à l'endroit*, Paris: Libres Hallier.

RE

BENOIST, Charles Augustin (1861–1936)

Benoist combined a political career with those of journalist, academic and diplomat. Born at Courseulles-sur-Mer (Calvados) in relatively humble circumstances, he went to Paris in 1883 as the protégé of Henri Baudrillart, former editor of *Le Constitutionnel*. He worked as secretary to Baudrillart and then to Hervé-Mangon, minister of agriculture in Brisson's 1885 government, while studying at the Ecole des Hautes Etudes. Baudrillart introduced him to Yung's *Revue Bleue*, for which he wrote a series of satirical portraits of politicians, republished in book form as *Croquis parlementaires* in 1891. The pieces attracted the attention of Adrien Hébrard of the daily paper *Le Temps*, who sent Benoist to Italy, Germany, Holland and Algeria to write articles for the paper. He then received a similar commission from the *Revue des Deux Mondes*, which took him to Austro-Hungary, Belgium and Switzerland. In the course of these journeys he met Bismarck and Cardinal Lavigerie (q.v.) and had several audiences with Pope Leo XIII.

He first stood for the Chamber of Deputies in the sixth *arrondissement* of Paris in 1898. He was elected there in 1902 and continued to represent the constituency until 1919. In the Chamber, he joined the Union Républicaine group, which included J. Méline (q.v.) and A. Ribot (q.v.), and he eventually became its leader. He was active in debates and committee work on a wide range of issues, from labour legislation, strikes by state employees and the remuneration of deputies to foreign affairs. He campaigned with particular vigour for independent education (he was a Catholic), for the three-year conscription law and for proportional representation. In his work for electoral reform, he was associated with Jaurès (q.v.) and with Joseph Reinach (q.v.).

During the war, in 1915, he was twice sent to Rome on important diplomatic missions. After the death of Francis Charmes in January 1916, Benoist took over the influential political column of the *Revue des Deux Mondes*. He was chairman of the Chamber of Deputies committee, which examined the territorial clauses of the Versailles Treaty in 1919, and he expressed serious misgivings about the viability of the new nations which they created and about France's failure to obtain a secure natural eastern frontier. He did not stand for re-election that year, having been offered the post of ambassador to The Hague by Clemenceau. Since the Kaiser had taken refuge in Holland, this was a position of some importance. Benoist stayed there five years and hoped to be transferred to the Vatican. The advent to power in 1924 of the *Cartel des Gauches* removed this prospect. He was recalled and returned to his writing and scholarship.

In 1895 he had been given the chair of European constitutional history at the Ecole des Sciences Politiques, and in 1908 he was elected to the Académie des Sciences Morales et Politiques. Among his many books on politics, political theory and social questions, special mention may be made of *Les Ouvrières de l'aiguille à Paris* (1895) and *Le Machiavélisme* (1907–36) in three volumes.

Les Lois de la politique française (1927) announced his despair of ever satisfactorily reforming the republican regime, and the following year he joined the royalist Action Française, a conversion which caused some stir. He never belonged to the movement's leadership, though he wrote on current affairs for the right-wing fellow-travelling *Revue Universelle* and he was later appointed as tutor to the Pretender to the French throne, the Comte de Paris. He died in August 1936 at Courseulles.

Bibliography

Benoist, C. (1932), *Souvenirs*, 3 vols, Paris: Plon.
Reclus, M. (1939), *Notice sur la vie et les travaux de M. Charles Benoist*, Paris: Institut de France, Académie des Sciences Morales et Politiques.

SW

BÉRÉGOVOY, Pierre Eugène (1925–)

Pierre Bérégovoy was one of the leaders, under François Mitterrand (q.v.), of the new Socialist Party (Parti Socialiste) in the 1970s. After the left-wing victory in the 1981 presidential and parliamentary elections, he became a key figure in Mitterrand's personal team and in the governments of Pierre Mauroy (q.v.), Laurent Fabius (q.v.) and, after 1988, Michel Rocard (q.v.).

Bérégovoy left school at 16 to become a manual worker in the textile industry and then on the railways. He was a member of the French Resistance, and after the war joined the Socialist Party (SFIO). He obtained a job with Gaz de France in 1950, and rose by autodidactic efforts to a managerial position. Based in Paris from 1957, his opposition to the Algerian war, and then the return of de Gaulle in 1958, led him to break with the SFIO and become a prominent member of a party to its left which in 1960 became the main component of the Parti Socialiste Unifié (PSU).

In the 1960s he was influenced by the forward-looking ideas of Pierre Mendès France (q.v.), and in 1967 founded Socialisme Moderne, one of many clubs and discussion groups for the renewal of the non-Communist Left. With the demise of the SFIO in 1969, Bérégovoy was able to find a political home in the new Parti Socialiste as it emerged during the period 1969–71; he became a member of the leadership first under Alain Savary (q.v.) and then under François Mitterrand after 1971.

Bérégovoy had already in the 1960s shown sympathy with Mitterrand's strategy of a strong, broad-based Socialist party cooperating with the Communists, and he became one of Mitterrand's closest collaborators in the continuation of this strategy in the 1970s, first as adviser on social questions, then in charge of relations with the Communist Party (PCF). In the latter position, he played the central role in the effort, which finally proved unsuccessful, to update for the 1978 elections the Joint Programme for Government, signed in 1972 by Socialists, Communists and left radicals.

Bérégovoy failed to win a parliamentary seat in the elections of 1973 and 1978 (he lacks charisma), but he was returned in the Socialist landslide of 1981; he was elected mayor of Nevers two years later. Mitterrand made him secretary-general of the president's office, the first in the Fifth Republic not to have been a senior civil servant.

His value to Mitterrand as a solid and trustworthy colleague, with the right mix of Socialist commitment and pragmatic administrative talent, was shown by his appointment to two key government posts – minister of social affairs and national solidarity (1982–4), where he put the social security system back on a sound footing, and, from 1984 to 1986, minister of finance, in which post he applied the Socialist government's policy of economic austerity and modernized the financial markets.

His closeness to Mitterrand meant that he became his campaign director in the 1988 presidential election and was spoken of as a possible prime minister. In the event, he returned to the Ministry of Finance in the government headed by Michel Rocard.

Bibliography

There is nothing on Bérégovoy in English and no biography of him in French. References to his role can be found in books about the political clubs in the 1960s, the growth of the PS in the 1970s, and the left-wing governments of the 1980s.

MS

BERGERON, André Louis (1922–)

André Bergeron became general secretary of the trade union confederation Confédération Générale du Travail – Force Ouvrière, more generally known as Force Ouvrière (FO), in 1963 when he took over from Robert Bothereau. Apprenticed as a printer in Belfort, he joined the recently reunified Confédération Générale du Travail (CGT) in 1936. During the war he was sent to work in Germany and Austria for two and a half years. On his return he became the secretary of the printer's union in Belfort and after the split in the CGT and the founding of FO, he became a full-time official of the latter in 1948, a member of its executive commission in 1950 and its Confederal Bureau in 1956.

Bergeron has presided over a confederation which has slowly increased its support to the point where in the 1980s FO has regularly obtained between 11 and 14 per cent of the votes at the elections for works committees and has become particularly strong in the civil service and among white collar workers in general.

During his period of office the FO has reinforced its identity as a trade union confederation wedded to the ideas of reformism and political autonomy. It has not been an advocate of the overthrow of capitalism nor of the introduction of a Socialist economic and political system. Bergeron has always considered that the interest of his members could best be defended by participating in collective bargaining, which in turn would lead to the gradual improvement of wages and working conditions, and also by playing a major role in the administration of a number of semi-public organizations, such as Union Nationale pour l'Emploi dans l'Industrie et le Commerce (UNEDIC) and the Caisses Nationales d'Assurance Maladie (CNAM), responsible for unemployment benefit and health insurance respectively.

FO has always emphasized its autonomy *vis-à-vis* political parties and the state. In spite of the fact that Bergeron himself has been a member of the Socialist Party, the confederation has shunned close institutional links with political parties and has in fact campaigned vigorously against the French Communist Party to which it has always been violently opposed. This autonomy has not however prevented Bergeron from enjoying the occasional visit to the Hôtel Matignon and the Elysée Palace for discussions with various prime ministers and presidents.

FO's reformism has had significant consequences for its dealings with the other trade union confederations. It has tended to spurn the advances of the self-styled revolutionary confederations, the Confédération Générale du Travail (CGT) and the Confédération Française Démocratique du Travail (CFDT), which in turn have criticized it, particularly during the 1970s, for being a 'class collaborator'. It has often joined forces with FEN, the teachers' union, the CGC, the white-collar union, and interestingly the CFTC, the rump Catholic trade union confederation – an intriguing choice since Bergeron and other FO members would describe themselves as being resolutely secular.

André Bergeron announced that he was going to

stand down at the 1989 FO national conference and did so. He will be sorely missed within the confederation and his successor Marc Blondel (q.v.) will find it difficult to replace his influence.

Bibliography

There is no biography of André Bergeron in English. The book by Jean-Louis Validire, *André Bergeron – une force ouvrière* (Paris: Plon, 1984) provides some interesting biographical elements but is primarily a brief history of Force Ouvrière itself. Apparently a biography is being prepared to coincide with his retirement. André Bergeron has himself written *FO* (Paris: Epi, 1971), *Lettre ouverte à un syndiqué* (Paris: Albin Michel, 1975), *Ma Route et mes combats* (Paris: Ramsay, 1976) and *Quinze cents jours (1980–1984)* (Paris: Flammarion, 1984).

JB

BERGERY, Gaston Frank (a.k.a. Gaston François) (1892–1974)

Initially, Gaston Bergery seemed to be heading for an academic career, when, following his graduation in 1912, he combined the profession of law with research for a doctorate. This work was interrupted by the onset of the First World War, in which he enlisted as a private soldier, working his way through the ranks, and receiving both citations and the Military Cross for distinguished service. Promoted to the officer corps in 1918, he was attached to the Versailles Peace Conference Secretariat and it was there that his extensive knowledge of international politics was gained.

During the early 1920s Bergery, as well as being a member of the war reparations committee, was sent on missions to both Great Britain and the United States. He was principal private secretary (*chef de cabinet*) to Edouard Herriot (q.v.) in the first (1924) government of the *Cartel des Gauches*. Thus it soon became clear that a political career beckoned and in 1928 he stood as a Radical candidate in Mantes (Seine-et-Oise), winning a seat at the first attempt. Inevitably he was appointed to the prestigious Assembly foreign affairs committee where, in particular, he applied his knowledge of the German reparations problem. He also played a large part in the famous 'coup d'Angers' of 1928 when the Radical Party withdrew its participation in the Poincaré government.

At the same time he took up a career in journalism, which he was to use increasingly, as a forum for his stringent views on constitutionalism. It was these views that were to halt his political advancement, and eventually leave him isolated from his Radical colleagues. He became the most outspoken critic of the way in which a democratically elected majority could be undermined by parliamentary manipulation of procedure. Frequently he spoke out in the Assembly against the way in which, within a short space of time, a left-wing majority could be transformed into a right-wing government, denying the will of the electorate.

In 1934 his criticism of the vulnerability of the parliamentary regime appeared vindicated with the riots of the night of 6 February. He resigned his seat in protest at these events, forcing a by-election expressly on this issue – a contest which he lost. But in the general election of 1936 he stood with his colleague, Izard, at the head of the Parti Frontiste, and was re-elected on a platform of constitutional and economic reform. The party made little impact on the Assembly, for its membership never exceeded three deputies, and it generally aligned itself with the Radical Party on the votes. Nevertheless, Bergery was an outstanding speaker and his condemnation of the political manoeuvering in the period 1936–40 made uncomfortable listening for many senior politicians.

In 1940 he was called upon by the Vichy regime to utilize his expertise in foreign affairs in their service and, in 1941, he became the French ambassador in Moscow until diplomatic relations between the two were severed. Subsequently he was posted to Ankara, and remained there until the liberation. He returned to France to stand trial. He was acquitted and returned to his old profession of the law. For a while afterwards he contributed a diplomatic column to *Paris-Presse l'Intransigeant*.

Bibliography

Gaston Bergery wrote a number of books, among them a study of the economics of the Popular Front, *L'Economie frontiste* (Paris: La Flèche, 1939). There is no full biography, but some detail can be found in P. Larmour, *The French Radical Party in the 1930s* (Stanford, Cal.: Stanford University Press, 1964); S. Berstein, *Histoire du Parti Radical* (Paris: Presses de la FNSP, 1982) and P. Burrin, *La Dérive fasciste* (Paris: Seuil, 1986).

PT

BEUVE-MÉRY, Hubert (1902–89)

Beuve-Méry was the founder of *Le Monde:* the first issue appeared on 18 December 1944 and he edited it until his retirement on 29 December 1969. Born in Paris, the son of a jeweller, Beuve-Méry's religious upbringing enabled him to climb the educational ladder, first at the Collège du Sacré-Coeur d'Yssingeaux, then with the help of the Dominican R.P. Janvier to undertake a thesis on Francisco de Vitoria, and by 1928 he was the head of the legal and economic section of the French Institute in Prague.

He had also been involved with the periodical *Les Nouvelles Religieuses* and while in Czechoslovakia became a regular correspondent to a number of newspapers principally *Le Temps.* However, he became disenchanted with the standard of contemporary French journalism and when his anti-Munich articles were suppressed he resigned. The experience of the 1930s was to set his commitment to objective journalism free from the government control characteristic of *Le Monde.*

After service in the Second World War he was demobilized and went to Portugal in the foreign service before moving to Lyons where he joined Mounier's *Esprit* group. In December 1940 he became director of studies in Vichy's Ecole des Cadres d'Uriage. In December 1942 (just before the Ecole was dissolved) he was an active participant in the *Maquis* and ended as an FFI officer.

At the liberation he edited the weekly *Temps Présent* but his principal work was the foundation of the *Le Monde* – discreetly supported by de Gaulle who wanted France to have a journal of record. His politics brought him into contact with many milieux: he was a neutralist at the onset of the cold war and maintained a certain hostility to the USA. These attitudes were at the origin of the board conflict in *Le Monde* in 1951 which was eventually resolved in his favour. He also took an anti-colonial line when that was unpopular (and cost circulation) and his house was bombed by the OAS because of his approval of Algerian independence.

Mendès France's government which ended the Indo-China war was the only one which Beuve-Méry supported and his relationship with de Gaulle was tense. He supported de Gaulle at the liberation (but not de Gaulle's Atlanticism) and supported de Gaulle's return to power in 1958 (but not his foreign policy). Under his habitual pseudonym 'Sirius' he was critical of de Gaulle's domestic politics during the 1960s but he was also dismissive of the students in 1968.

Beuve-Méry was a difficult man to work with but his service to journalism in France is unquestionable. He continued to advise *Le Monde* even when retired (for example during the severe financial crisis of 1984 in which he supported the directors) and was active on a number of boards and committees, as well as being a teacher at Paris University (1970–3).

Bibliography

Jeanneney, J.-N. and J. Juillard (1979), *Le Monde de Beuve-Méry*, Paris: Seuil.
H. Beuve-Méry, *Réflexions Politiques: 1932–52* (Paris: Seuil, 1951) contains articles on Eastern Europe in the 1930s and European politics in the immediate post-war period. See also *Onze Ans de Règne 1958–69* (Paris: Flammarion, 1974) which contains many of the editorials on Algeria as well as on de Gaulle's domestic policies.

BD

BICHELONNE, Jean (1904–45)

Bichelonne was an academic prodigy at the Ecole Polytechnique (where he achieved the highest marks on record) and at the Ecole des Mines. He was a member of the cabinet of the minister of works from October 1937 until March 1938 and head of the cabinet of the minister of armaments from September 1938 until June 1940. But he first achieved real prominence in the Secretariat (which eventually became the Ministry) of Industrial Production set up by the Vichy government. He was head of technical services in June 1940; he was secretary-general for commerce and industry from July 1940 until April 1942 and minister of industrial production from November 1942 until his death.

Bichelonne's formidable intellect and capacity for hard work gave him a complete mastery of the technical aspects of his job. However, some colleagues, notably René Belin (q.v.), suggested that his lack of political realism undermined his effectiveness. This lack of realism was most clearly reflected in Bichelonne's interest in schemes for Franco-German economic collaboration even when it was obvious that Allied victory would soon render such schemes irrelevant. In 1943, when more prudent colleagues such as Couve de Murville were seeking to distance themselves from the losing side, Bichelonne met with the German minister of armaments – Albert Speer. The two men agreed that French labour would serve the German war economy more effectively in France than in Germany. Bichelonne was still drawing up carefully documented fantasies about a 'New European Economic Order' after Allied troops had entered Paris.

Some believed that Bichelonne's 'technocratic' view of the world conflicted with the traditionalist elements in the Vichy government and it was alleged that he was associated with a 'synarchic' group which was trying to undermine the Marshal's policies. But Bichelonne himself believed that his plans for modernization could be carried out within the traditional social structure of France. This belief was reflected in his attempts to protect small business at his meetings with Speer. Bichelonne's dedication to Franco-German collaboration led him to follow the Vichy government into exile/captivity in Germany after the Allied invasion of France. His death, while undergoing an operation at a German army hospital in 1945, led to rumours, apparently without substance, that he had been murdered.

Bibliography

Ehrmann, H. (1957), *Organized Business in France*, Princeton, NJ: Princeton, University Press.

RCV

BIDAULT, Georges Augustin (1899–1983)

The civilian, short in stature, seen walking alongside de Gaulle down the Champs Elysées in the legendary photograph taken after the liberation of Paris in August 1944, was virtually unknown at the time to the French public at large; yet Georges Bidault was to play a major and controversial role in French politics in the succeeding twenty years. As a student in the 1920s he had been an active leader of one of the Catholic Action movements that were to contribute to the growing political and social awareness of important sections of French catholicism. A history teacher by training (he came first in the prestigious national competitive *agrégation d'histoire*), he contributed to Francisque Gay's Christian Democrat newspaper *L'Aube*, applauding the Vatican's condemnation of Charles Maurras' extreme right-wing Action Française and in 1938 writing a famous series of articles condemning the Munich Agreement.

During the war he was a co-founder of the Combat Resistance movement, and, after the arrest and execution of de Gaulle's appointee, Jean Moulin (q.v.) in 1943, was – unbeknown to de Gaulle – elected president of the National Resistance Council, the body established at de Gaulle's instigation to coordinate Resistance activities in occupied France and comprising representatives of the various resistance movements, of the unions and of the political parties hostile to Vichy. At the liberation he was a co-founder of the Christian Democrat Mouvement Républicain Populaire (MRP) and, during the Fourth Republic, was between 1946 and 1955 president of the Council (prime minister) on two occasions and foreign minister on several others. In spite of the latent hostility between Bidault and de Gaulle (dating back to the war years), Bidault supported the latter's return to power in May 1958, but as de Gaulle's Algerian policy developed so did the virulence of Bidault's opposition to any form of self-determination in Algeria; he founded a new 'National Resistance Council', expressed unequivocal support for *l'Algérie française* and for the Organisation de l'Armée Secrète, OAS, the pro-settler terrorist organization which, in Algeria before independence and also in metropolitan France, opposed de Gaulle's solution to the Algerian problem. Threatened with arrest and prosecution, Bidault went into exile in 1962 and did not return to France until 1968. In his later years he did not enjoy good health and his condition was reportedly aggravated by a 'drink problem'.

The latter part of Bidault's career, his commitment to *l'Algérie française*, should not perhaps detract from the importance of his earlier public career. Under his presidency, in March 1944, the National Resistance Council drew up the Resistance Charter, crystallizing the spirit of the Resistance in its hostility both to the Vichy regime and to the Third Republic and in its determination to achieve radical economic and social change in liberated France. It was reputedly Bidault who coined the expression: 'The Revolution by legal means' to characterize this spirit. The Charter called for 'economic democracy', a planned economy, nationalization of energy, banks and insurance, extended trade-union rights, a generalized system of social security, a more democratic education system and wider political rights for the inhabitants of the French colonies. In short, a blueprint for post-war France. It is not Bidault's fault that so few of these aims were achieved.

In foreign affairs he believed first and foremost in national independence, and some of his pronouncements in the late 1940s are distinctly Gaullist in spirit. Although he was closely associated with the setting up of the Council of Europe, Western European Union, the signature of the North Atlantic and European Coal and Steel Community Treaties, and the European Defence Community negotiations, he feared the re-emergence of a strong Germany, was more 'Atlanticist' than 'European' and did not share the federalist enthusiasm for Europe of Robert Schuman and some other members of the MRP. In colonial affairs he was an inflexible supporter of the French Empire (*l'Union française*), the association of the French colonies under the French umbrella, established (without consultation of those primarily concerned) by the Constitution of the Fourth Republic and which, in spite of the generous intentions expressed in its preamble, effectively closed the door to any form either of assimilation or of self-government or self-determination. Indeed, it has been argued that in his opposition to decolonialization Bidault suffered from a sort of 'Munich complex'.

Bibliography

Bidault has attempted to defend his pro-*Algérie française*, anti-Gaullist stance in two works: *Algérie: l'Oiseau aux ailes coupées* (Paris: Table Ronde, 1958) and the (autobiographical) *D'Une Résistance à l'autre* (Paris: Presses du siècle, 1965). The latter has been translated into English as *Resistance* (London: Weidenfeld & Nicolson, 1967; New York: Praeger, 1967). Otto Barthélemy, *Georges Bidault l'indomptable* (Annonay: Imprimerie du Vivarais, 1975) is hagiographic and written from an extreme right/Catholic integrist standpoint. A more balanced assessment may be found in the four substantial articles published in *Le Monde* of 28 January 1983, on the occasion of Bidault's death. See also: R. Rémond, *Les Droites en France* (Paris: Aubier, 1982) and a 1969 English translation of an earlier version, *The Right Wing in France, from 1815 to de Gaulle* (Philadelphia, University of Pennsylvania Press); for Bidault and Christian Democracy: W. Bosworth, *Catholicism and Crisis in Modern France* (Princeton, NJ: Princeton University Press, 1962); R.E.M. Irving, *Christian Democracy in France* (London: George Allen & Unwin, 1973); E.-F. Callot, *Le M.R.P., Origine, structure, doctrine, programme et action politique* (Paris: M. Rivière, 1978). For Bidault and the Algerian War, see A. Horne, *A Savage War of Peace* (London, Macmillan, 1977) and, in French, B. Droz, and E. Lever, *Histoire de la guerre d'Algérie (1954–1962)* (Paris, Seuil, 1982).

HE

BILLÈRES, René (1910–)

René Billères was leader of the Radical Party from 1965 to 1969 and as such was a leading force in the efforts to revive the non-Communist left by means of the FGDS in the early years of the Fifth Republic. A teacher (*professeur*) by profession, Billères was born in 1910 in the Hautes-Pyrénées, one of the southwestern strongholds of the Radical Party. The son of a legal functionary (*greffier*), he was educated at *lycées* in Tarbes and Paris (Lycée Lakanal) and after study at the Ecole Normale Supérieure he taught at *lycées* in Mont-de-Marsan and his native Tarbes. He was elected to the National Assembly for the Hautes-Pyrénées in 1946 and served continuously until his retirement in 1973. He made the traditional progression to the Senate in 1974 and finally retired from elected office in 1983. His career in the Fourth Republic was not uncharacteristic of a Radical politician. He presided over the education committee of the Assembly from 1948 to 1954, and was minister of education in three consecutive governments – that of Mollet, Bourgès-Maunoury and Gaillard – in the late 1950s (1956–8). Not that he was from an anticlerical background: he was in fact a devout Catholic as well as being – in the words of his one-time Radical colleague, Charles Hernu, 'a sincere *laïc* Radical'. In the debate on the *loi Barangé* restoring state aid to *écoles libres* in 1951, he spoke of a dialogue between Voltaire and Pascal which was sometimes carried on 'within each of us'. He also saw the debate as archaic, reviving old oppositions and hostilities, dead passions and buried quarrels.

As a minister in the 1956–7 Mollet government he defended it against the attacks of his leader Mendès France, whose brief membership of the government had ended over opposition to the one-sidedly tough policy applied in Algeria. At the same time Billères and his fellow Radical Bourgès-Maunoury, the defence minister, sought modifications to the policy.

In 1958 the Radicals split almost evenly over the investiture of de Gaulle as prime minister, with Billères voting for. He did not, however, follow other Radicals such as Edgar Faure, into support for the de Gaulle presidency, but rather devoted his energies to the realignment of the non-Communist left, first through membership of Defferre's abortive *Comité Horizon 80* and then in the executive of the Mitterrand-led FGDS.

His short leadership of the Radicals ended with his replacement by the more meteoric Servan-Schreiber in 1969. A pragmatic 'radical de gestion' by nature, his role as a relatively minor foot-soldier in the politics of his day owed much to the larger talents and stronger characters of those in his party with whom he had to coexist.

BC

BILLOUX, François (a.k.a. Laudrer) (1903–76)

François Billoux made more political mistakes than any other French Communist Party leader and escaped from their consequences just as regularly through the device of self-criticism. Born of a sharecropping family, he became a textile worker in 1919 and a Socialist in 1920. Secretary of the Young Socialists in Roanne he led them to vote for the Third International and to join the Communist Party in 1920. In the same year he became a paid organizer of the Young Communists (*Jeunesse Communiste* – JC) and in 1926 was promoted to general secretary of the JC, member of the Central Committee and of the Political Bureau. From 1929 to 1931 he attended the Marx–Lenin school in Moscow.

As one of the younger generation of leaders in the PCF he was implicated in the Barbé-Célor group – whose members were 'unmasked' in 1931 – but made a public self-criticism admitting his complicity. He recovered sufficiently by 1934 to be appointed regional secretary for the PCF in Marseilles and in 1936 he won a parliamentary seat after a violent election contest against the right. Arrested with other members of the PCF in 1939 and deported to North Africa, he (along with other Communist leaders) wrote a letter to Pétain (q.v.), offering to testify in the Riom trials against Blum (q.v.), Daladier (q.v.) and Reynaud (q.v.). He was released with other prisoners when the Allies landed in November 1942, became a member of the Consultative Assembly of the Comité Français de la Libération National and commissaire d'état in the provisional government (April 1944). In September he was named minister of health and was subsequently minister for the economy and minister for reconstruction under Gouin (q.v.). He remained in this post under Bidault (q.v.) and was finally minister of defence from January to May 1947. This was a post which the PCF had long been denied and which they had always coveted, because it seemed to legitimize them as a trusted pariotic party. Unfortunately for Billoux, the resumption of the Indo-China war, the problems of wages and the economy persuaded the PCF to vote against Ramadier (q.v.) and the latter took the opportunity to get rid of them from government.

Billoux accepted the subsequent hard line policy shift with apparent enthusiasm. In January 1952 he visited the ailing party leader Thorez (q.v.) at Soukhouin in the USSR and returned to France with a note from Thorez calling for a 'class against class' policy and the mobilization of the workers against American imperialism. He turned this into an intemperate article in *Cahiers du Communisme* which called for mass action in the streets against US General Ridgeway, the new Nato commander, whom the PCF accused of bacteriological warfare in Korea. This resulted in serious rioting, but in June the Central Committee corrected 'a misinterpretation' of the original note and Billoux made a discreet self-criticism in the August number of *Cahiers du Communisme*. After Thorez' return in 1953, Billoux resumed his post as faithful lieutenant, fought 'opportunism' and 'sectarianism', challenged the socialist, Defferre, (q.v.) in Marseilles and resisted de-Stalinization.

In 1957 he became the editor of *France Nouvelle*, the PCF political monthly and lost influence along with the decline of the journal. He lost his position on the Secretariat, made an intemperate attack on the students in 1968, and when the PCF began to liberalize its image in the early 1970s he retired to be a respected, but unheeded member of the 'old guard'. He was removed from the Central Committee by Marchais in 1972 because of his opposition to liberalization, but his book, *Quand nous etions ministres*, published in the same year, seemed to argue in favour of much that Marchais was doing.

He was typical of the surviving early leadership; men who were naturally attracted by a 'hard line', who sometimes took such a line too far, who were often disciplined and who always accepted the 'decisions of the party'. He was the sort of man who made the PCF a powerful but inflexible force in French politics.

Bibliography

Billoux, F. (1972), *Quand nous etions ministres*, Paris: Editions Sociales.
Robrieux, P. (1984), *Histoire intérieure du Parti Communiste français*, Paris: Fayard.

JCS

BLANC, Louis Jean Joseph (1811–82)

Louis Blanc exerted a significant influence on both nineteenth-century Socialist theory and on the practice of Radical Republican politics. The eldest son of a southern bourgeois family in straitened circumstances, Blanc was given a royalist and Catholic education. He arrived in Paris in 1830 at the very moment of the July Revolution. Within two years Blanc had plunged into political journalism and Jacobin republicanism. By 1834 he had joined an opposition journal, becoming its very young editor-in-chief the following year. He continued to move steadily to the left, calling for an ever more thorough republicanism and linking the cause of popular sovereignty with the growing concern about the working class.

In 1838 he established his own monthly journal *La Revue du progrès* in which he developed his particular version of Jacobin-socialism. A series of articles appearing in 1839, later published as a book in 1840, *L'Organisation du travail*, was the most important and most widely read statement of his analysis and solution of the 'social question'. At the heart of Blanc's programme stood the democratic state which would promote the reorganization of work through social workshops. Easy credit supplied by the state would enable these producers' associations to flourish. Eventually, the workers' cooperatives, *ateliers sociaux*, would replace capitalist competition and the citizens' right to work would easily be met in this new social arrangement. The agent of change in Blanc's scheme was the state, legitimated by universal male suffrage. *L'Organisation du travail* was the most widely read socialist tract of the 1840s. The right to work and the social workshop became popular slogans among the more organized and more militant Paris workers.

In 1843 Blanc joined other radicals on the editorial board of a new journal *La Réforme* which appealed to the growing opposition to the July monarchy. This position, as well as his Socialist and historical writings, made Blanc a well-known figure. During the February days of the 1848 Revolution, Paris workers insisted that Blanc be included in the provisional government in order that they be represented. Blanc's position in the provisional government was always marginal and the moderate majority succeeded in removing him from day-to-day decisions by appointing him to the Commission of Labour. Whilst he was kept outside the centre of power, the Luxembourg Commission which Blanc headed did contribute to later working-class and socialist developments. It did provide workers with an opportunity to organize and express their views, strengthening their class consciousness.

Although isolated in the provisional government, Blanc supported the early efforts to introduce social reform, such as the declaration of the right to work and the ten-hour day. He was equally concerned with the protection of the fragile Republic. Throughout the three months of the provisional government's existence Blanc attempted to balance his calls for more radical actions with efforts to avoid a second revolution. He was not an organizer of the mass demonstrations during the spring of 1848. Nor did he have any connection with the desperate worker uprising of June. Despite his repudiating violence, the conservative Constituent Assembly elected in April identified Blanc as a leader and symbol of working-class revolution. In August 1848 a parliamentary Commission of Enquiry accused him of revolutionary activity, revoked his parliamentary immunity, and was about to demand his arrest. Blanc fled to England. He left few followers behind: his working-class support had declined drastically because of his insistence on moderation at the very time when moderates suspected him of plotting revolution.

Blanc never recovered the importance and popularity which he had had in the 1840s. He feuded with the Radicals and he rejected the growing emphasis on independent working-class action which dominated French socialism during the 1850s and 1860s. Blanc did, however, remain an intransigent opponent of the Second Empire, refusing the amnesties of 1859 and 1869.

He returned to France the day after the declaration of the Third Republic, 5 September, 1870. His views had changed little. Following his election to the National Assembly, he publicly denounced the Commune and supported Thiers (q.v.), thus gaining the enmity of a new generation of revolutionaries. None the less, he took his place on the far-left of the Assembly as one of the grand old men of radical socialism. In the last years of his life he influenced the small group of young radicals led by Clemenceau (q.v.). From Blanc they learned that the 'social question' and reform policies had an important place in the Republican programme. Louis Blanc was a Socialist who rejected revolution and stressed instead the important role of the democratic state as an instrument for social and economic change. He always remained committed to his slogan 'The Republic: the means; social regeneration: the objective.'

Bibliography

Loubère, L. (1961), *Louis Blanc. His Life and his Contribution to the Rise of French Jacobin-Socialism*, Evanson, Ill: Northwestern University Press. This is the most recent biography of Blanc in English which analyses both his political activity and his theoretical contributions.

JFS

BLANQUI, Louis Auguste (1805–81)

Revolutionary Republican activist, political prisoner, ardent patriot, journalist and quasi-mythical symbol of the nineteenth-century French 'left'. Blanqui, a brilliant young law student, was first imprisoned for revolutionary activities against the Bourbon restoration in 1828. He was subsequently associated with almost every insurrectionary uprising from July 1830 to the Paris Commune of 1871. Blanqui is remembered more for his inextinguishable *spirit* of Republican revolt than for any specific political 'programme'. When he died at the age of 75, he had spent over thirty-four years in jail, four years under house arrest and six years in exile: over forty-three years in all. His austere and ascetic personality attracted a devoted following, mainly from *déclassé* Parisian intellectuals and adventurers who were trained in the insurrectionary methods of Carbonarist secret societies. The streets of Paris were his political arena, the ministries, arsenals and other nerve-centres of power his political targets. Convinced that the seizure of power by a dedicated elite was the key to transformation of French society, he avoided the elaboration of anything approaching a political programme. During the Paris Commune, he remained incarcerated by the (bourgeois) Republican government and so highly was he valued by the communards as a figurehead to give inspiration (rather than a sense of direction) to the movement, that offers were made to the *Versaillais* to exchange him against the dozens of hostages held in Paris. It is a measure of the fear which his very name evoked among the conservative bourgeoisie that these offers were rejected.

The campaign for amnesty of the communards was intimately associated with the campaign to liberate the man now best known as *L'Enfermé*. Blanqui was elected a deputy for Bordeaux while still in prison in 1879 as part of this campaign. But the advent of 'formal' republicanism merely showed up his lack of a political programme. When he emerged from prison only a year before he died, he hailed Clemenceau as the leader of the left. For Blanqui, the fundamental 'social problem' sprung not from capitalism or the economic system, but from 'ignorance' and the hegemonic role of the Church. In the struggle for what he called 'socialism', he considered the obstacle presented by capitalism as a 'mere hedge' which could be swept away in twenty-four hours. On the other hand, the real obstacle posed by ignorance would, in his view, take fifty years to clear away. The fundamental solution was therefore a secular state, the generalization of atheism and of free,

compulsory and secular education. Beyond that, Blanqui's 'political' programme is hard to decipher. His fervent patriotism and Germanophobia, his anti-Semitism, his penchant for ironing out class struggle through some form of labour–capital association and his ardent belief in *putschism* square awkwardly with Marxism, internationalism and democracy. His major disciples, such as Ernest Granger, were by no means straying from the Blanquist straight and narrow when they opted for Boulangism in 1889.

French historiography, dominated as it has been by Marxists, has tended to portray Blanqui as the 'French origin of scientific socialism' (Garaudy q.v.). Lenin was clearly influenced by his example, which was indeed awe-inspiring for those with insurrectionary aspirations. But by the early Third Republic, Blanqui's ideology and example were, in effect, of increasingly little relevance. The fact that he died before anybody had understood this has resulted in the construction, around his memory, of a mythology which the colloquium marking the centenary of his death, in 1981, did nothing to dispel. The 'true' history of Blanqui and of Blanquism remains to be written.

Bibliography

Bernstein, S. (1970), *Auguste Blanqui*, Paris: Maspéro.

Dommanget, M. (1957), *Les Idées politiques et sociales d'Auguste Blanqui*, Paris: M. Rivière.

Hutton, P.H. (1981), *The Cult of the Revolutionary Tradition*, Berkeley, University of California Press.

Vigier, P. (ed.) (1986), *Blanqui et les Blanquistes*, Paris: SEDES, Cal.: (Acts of centenary colloquium).

JH

BLOCH-LAINÉ, François (1912–   )

Bloch-Lainé's career and approach can be taken as typifying a certain relationship between politics and administration – including the public sector of commerce and industry – that is often regarded as especially characteristic of the Fifth Republic, at least in its first two decades. Born and brought up largely in Paris, his membership of the Catholic boy scout movement, then in its early days, had, he claims, a greater influence on him than his formal education. He thus came into contact with the Catholic social movements, and his thesis for his doctorate of law in 1934 was on workers' education movements in Europe. He joined the civil service in 1936 as a member of the prestigious *corps* of finance inspectors, a *corps* of which his great uncle and his father were members and into which his eldest son followed him.

He was active in the Resistance, acting in Paris as a banker on behalf of de Gaulle's provisional government-in-exile. In 1947 he was appointed head of the Treasury division of the ministry of finance and in 1952 he became director-general of the Caisse de Dépôts et Consignations, which as the government's central banking and investment institution for all the French savings banks plays a key role in national credit and investment policies. From 1967 to 1974 (when he was rather suddenly removed from the post by President Giscard) he was chairman (*président*) of the big nationalized French bank, the Crédit Lyonnais. Alongside these posts he has held many appointments, as non-executive director in public and private companies. For many years he taught at the Paris Institut d'Etudes Politiques. He was one of the 'three wise men' appointed by the government to settle the 1963 miners' strike. In 1968 he chaired a committee of enquiry into civil service training. In 1981 the incoming Socialist government asked him to head a committee which produced a multi-volume report on 'the state of France'.

Bloch-Lainé holds a view of the role of the civil servant as combining both loyalty and independence that forbids any overt political allegiance; he twice refused de Gaulle's offer of a ministerial post. He was, however, associated in the 1960s with the *Club Jean Moulin*, a left-wing political (but not partisan) discussion group and was one of the organizers of the group that published *Pour nationaliser l'etat* (1968). He was actively involved in the post-war strategy of reconstruction, modernization, planning and public intervention. He supports notions of economic 'concentration' and of democratic planning. His much discussed book *Pour une réforme de l'entreprise* (1963) advocates the remodelling of company structures with increased participation and more internal democracy.

The political-administrative system in France allows considerable scope and prominence to certain senior officials. Bloch-Lainé exemplifies an independence and autonomy of action, and a view of relations between state and society in a mixed economy that has been very influential, especially within the administration.

Bibliography

Bloch-Lainé, F. (1976), *Profession: Fonctionnaire*, Paris: Seuil (a volume of autobiographical reminiscences in the form of an extended interview).

For his ideas see also:

Alphandéry, C. *et al.* (1968), *Pour nationaliser l'Etat*, Paris: Seuil.

Bloch-Lainé, F. (1963), *Pour une réforme de l'entreprise*, Paris: Seuil.

AS

BLONDEL, Marc (1938–)

Marc Blondel was born in Courbevoie, a working-class suburb of Paris, in 1938 but spent his childhood in the mining district of Henin-Liétard (in the Nord). Although his family were miners he himself passed his secondary school examination (*baccalauréat*) and started to study law. However, he quickly abandoned his law studies and took on a number of temporary jobs before becoming a supply teacher.

In 1966 he joined the Force Ouvrière unions and his activism was remarked on at his first congress in April 1966 when he made a stirring and militant speech. For a period he condemned as old-fashioned the refusal of Force Ouvrière to associate with the newly-created CFDT and the Communist CGT in joint negotiations. However, he subsequently became more favourable to his union's autonomy which he saw as strengthening its bargaining position and by 1986 was opposed to any *rapprochement* with the CFDT.

Marc Blondel has always been located on the left of the French political spectrum. He was an opponent (in student union politics) of the Algerian War and was briefly a member of the anticolonial Parti Socialiste Autonome. Expelled from the SFIO at the time of Algeria, he rejoined the new Parti Socialiste in 1970 and remains a member. Marc Blondel is a close associate of former Prime Minister Mauroy (q.v.) and is a Freemason with an anticlerical zeal which recalls former Republics. He is also a friend of Trotsky's one-time secretary Fred Zeller although in 1989 he denied having Trotskyist support in the elections for secretary-general of Force Ouvrière.

Marc Blondel is a fiery orator and a tough negotiator, and at the same time a typical product of the Nord Socialist tradition. He has the back-slapping, familiar approach common to Socialist politicians in the old industrial area from which he comes, is a raconteur and somewhat flamboyant – being well-built and given to wearing coloured braces.

In 1974 he was narrowly elected general secretary of the white-collar union of the Force Ouvrière and in 1980 was elected to the unions' confederal bureau where he ran, with success, the economic department.

Although often spoken of as the 'dauphin' to André Bergeron (q.v.), Blondel won the fight for the leadership of the Force Ouvrière by the narrowest of margins on 4 February 1989 at the unions' national confederation. In a bitter and divisive fight he defeated Pitous, his more moderate rival, to become secretary-general and had to start immediately on recruiting the quarrelling parties in the unions.

Bibliography

See C. Lévy, *Les Trois Guerres de succession* (Paris: Alain Moreau, 1987) and *Le Monde* (7 February 1989).

DSB

BLUM, Léon (1872–1950)

Léon Blum was born in Paris to solidly Republican, middle-class Jewish parents. He was a brilliant pupil and in 1890 won a scholarship to the prestigious Ecole Normale Supérieure. He left after a year, took a law degree at the Sorbonne and in 1895 entered the Conseil d'Etat, the supreme administrative court of France. While still a student he became actively involved in the intellectual ferment of the time and was literary critic for the *Revue Blanche*, an important literary and intellectual publication. He became a supporter of the Socialist leader, Jean Jaurès, first in the Parti Socialiste Français and, after 1905, in the Section Française de l'Internationale Ouvrière (SFIO).

As a writer Blum displays both rigorous logic and purity and clarity of style. These were to become the hallmarks of his later political speeches. As a critic he identified most with the novelist, Stendhal, whose characters agonize over whether or not to act and are tempted to give in to nostalgia and regret. It is possible that Blum recognized in their dilemma his own inner conflict between a desire to act and a reluctance to commit himself and he made a study of the novels in *Stendhal et le Beylisme* (1914). His interest in ideas led him away from literature into a growing preoccupation with politics. The shift is seen most clearly in the *Nouvelles conversations de Goethe avec Eckermann* (1901). By donning the mantle of Goethe he stakes his claim to speak with the voice of universal reason. Mankind, he writes, forms part of the infinite immensity of the universe but harmony between man and the world has been broken. Prophets are needed to remind men that they have lost their way. At one point he makes Goethe sketch a Faust Part III. Faust discovers that progress cannot be guaranteed by science alone because the more wealth science creates the greater the social inequalities that ensue. The solution lies in Socialism. Faust, who represents the French Socialist leader Jean Jaurès, believes in man's innate sense of justice which modern civilization has corrupted and he wants to convert man to justice through education and persuasion. He fails, whereas Mephisto, who stands for the Marxist Jules Guesde, seems to succeed by bringing about violent revolution. In the long run, however, Blum believes that it is Faust's slow and deliberate strategy which will prove the more effective way of creating a just society.

In *Nouvelles conversations de Goethe avec Eckermann* Blum attributes to the Jews an active as well as passive role in the future Socialist revolution. As a result of their centuries-old suffering the Jews are predestined to accept suffering and to bend with the tide of history. If revolution is to be bloodless, he argues, it will be thanks to the Jews' critical insight into the social order, to their readiness to discard traditional values when they no longer reflect reality and to their capacity to rebuild society. The Hebrew bible preaches a religion of justice and the Jewish messianic spirit is in accord with the revolutionary and republican traditions of France. Although many of his collaborators were Jewish he was completely assimilated and eschewed all forms of separatism in national life. In 1918 he was converted to Zionism and in 1938 he proclaimed his solidarity with German Jews suffering Nazi persecution.

The Dreyfus affair had a crucial impact on Blum's political development. It brought him face to face with anti-Semitism and injustice in French society. He had first been won over to socialism by Lucien Herr (q.v.), the librarian at the Ecole Normale Supérieure. It was Herr who introduced Blum to Jaurès in 1897. For Blum, Jaurès was a prophet bringing a new gospel of universal morality and humanism of which the ultimate expression is socialism. Like Jaurès, Blum was attracted to the defence of Dreyfus because it offered an opportunity to uphold justice, the rights of man and universal conscience. Socialism became, for Blum, a continuation of the *dreyfusard* struggle becaue it was rooted in the conviction that it is possible to achieve justice with the right political and social policies. Blum wrote in support of Zola and helped at his trial. In the 1930s, however, he was to reflect that the *dreyfusards* had failed to turn the revisionist coalition into a permanent army in the service of human rights because society had not been transformed at the socio-economic level.

Jaurès' assassination on the eve of the war was a serious personal and political blow to Blum who always maintained that, had Jaurès lived, he would have supported the war effort on the grounds that the establishment of socialism in France was conditional upon the survival of the Republic. With the formation of the cabinet of the Union Sacrée in 1914, Blum was appointed *chef de cabinet* to the Socialist, Marcel Sembat, who became minister of public works. His new post, which he occupied till December 1916, brought him into contact with industrialists. He was involved in the increasingly bitter internal party quarrel over support for the Union Sacrée. His responsibilities also gave him invaluable insight into the machinery of government and he set out his ideas on how it could be improved in *Lettres sur la réforme gouvernementale* (1918). His recommendations, which have nothing particularly socialist about them, reflect his admiration for British parliamentary democracy in which stable governments are led by prime ministers who have time to concentrate on overall strategy because they are not burdened by responsibility for a particular ministry. Blum also analysed weaknesses in the French political system: the lack of party discipline and the often obstructive role played in the legislative process by the parliamentary commissions.

Blum was elected to the Chamber of Deputies in 1919 to represent a Paris constituency. He lost to the Communists in 1928 but was found a safe seat in Narbonne. The 1920 Party Congress in Tours saw the split between the minority SFIO and the majority who rallied to the Third International. Blum was the leader of a small group which refused to abandon the old party and intervened forcefully at the congress to attack Bolshevik authoritarianism and inflexibility. He defended the decentralized nature of the SFIO and justified support of the Union Sacrée, rejecting the Leninist thesis that the overthrow of capitalism should override national defence. He described the Bolshevik's stress on violent revolution as doomed to failure in an advanced industrial society like France and asserted that revolutionary consciousness needed to be raised over a long period of time. Blum rejected the Marxist thesis that a society's code of morality is determined by its economic infrastructure. Such a view was incompatible with his belief in unchanging universal values.

After Tours Blum and the other Socialist leaders rebuilt the party by winning back support from the Communists. A party newspaper, *Le Populaire*, was founded, of which Blum became director until his death. As leader of the parliamentary Socialist group he was effective in leading opposition to the *Bloc National* and in supporting the *Cartel des Gauches*. His theoretical writings in the 1920s moulded party doctrine and strategy. While upholding the party's commitment to equality and collective property he was careful to remove overly Marxist connotations from its commitment to internationalism and class struggle. Internationalism was defined in vague terms as the interdependence of nations while class struggle was softened to 'class action'. He interpreted working class in the widest sense to embrace all those who struggle for a new society. Violent overthrow of the bourgeois state was rejected in favour of social revolution, namely the slow transformation of social and economic structures by an educated and politically conscious work-force.

The key doctrinal issue which confronted Blum in the inter-war years was whether or not the party should participate in government. There were swings to the left in the 1924 and 1932 elections and on both occasions approaches were made to the Socialists to enter Radical-led governments. Each time participation was turned down on the grounds that it would be incompatible with the party's stated intention of changing society. The only circumstances when it would be justified were if the nation was threatened as in 1914. Blum was also concerned for the party not to lose its revolutionary credentials and thereby play into the hands of the Communists. Between 1924 and 1928 he elaborated an original doctrine on participation. This was the famous distinction between the conquest of power and the exercise of power. The conquest of power would occur when the party was in a position to reorganize society on Socialist lines. However, if the Socialists became the largest party and were asked, in time of national crisis, to exercise power by forming a government it would be legitimate to do so provided they were able to introduce legislation that hastened the advent of a truly Socialist society. In exercising power Socialists should always be careful to act within the framework of the constitution. Here we find another expression of Blum's belief in revolution through evolution.

By 1933 the policy of non-participation had led to the neo-Socialists splitting with the party, accusing Blum of being more concerned with ideological purity than with assuming the responsibility of government. The threat of fascism which first became apparent during the violent anti-government demonstrations on 6 February 1934 represented the sort of national emergency which would legitimize

Socialist participation in government. Blum became a forceful champion of the Popular Front coalition which brought together Radicals, Communists and Socialists. He was surprised by the size of the Socialist vote in 1936 and when he accepted the premiership he expressed his doubts about succeeding and revealed his concern to avoid misunderstanding with the working class about the limits of what it was possible to achieve. He feared the wave of strikes which followed his electoral victory was the result of the working class mistaking the exercise of power by the left for the conquest of power. Under the terms of the Matignon agreements collective contracts governing wages and conditions were signed between representatives of the trade unions and the employers' organizations. Social and economic legislation was rushed through parliament: paid holidays, a central marketing organization for grain, a public works programme, nationalization of the armaments industry and a forty-hour week. The paramilitary right-wing leagues were banned and national rearmament was embarked upon, although Blum has since been criticized by some, notably by de Gaulle, for not giving enough attention to detail in matters of defence.

The outbreak of the Spanish Civil War in July 1936 presented Blum with an agonising political dilemma: whether or not to intervene to help the Republican government in Madrid. He adopted a policy of non-intervention much to the dismay of the Communist Party and of many Socialists. The policy clashed with his instincts but it made sense on rational grounds. A military intervention would have created a rift with London, thereby weakening Anglo-French solidarity in the face of Hitler and Mussolini. It would also have deepened the division between right and left in France. On the other hand, non-intervention was responsible for putting Communists at loggerheads with the government and ran counter to the Popular Front's stated aim of defending democracy against fascism.

In February 1937, under pressure from the Radicals, Blum announced a 'pause' in the programme of social legislation and public expenditure in order to restore confidence to financiers. This provoked Communist hostility and, in a renewed climate of unrest, serious disturbances broke out on 16 March in the Paris suburb of Clichy which left a number of Communist supporters dead or wounded. Blum resigned in June 1937 after his request for exchange control powers to stop the outflow of capital had been rejected by the Senate. The economic failure of Blum's government has been ascribed to the forty-hour week, to the refusal to devalue the franc on

taking office and to the inherent contradiction of enacting Socialist legislation within a capitalist system. Although Blum continued to serve in the second Popular Front government as deputy prime minister little remained of the original programme. In January 1938 Blum made another attempt to form a government of national unity but failed. In March 1938 he tried again but had to fall back on a government of Socialists and Radicals. It fell after only three weeks when the Senate refused Blum yet again the financial powers he needed.

He opposed the ending of the Third Republic after the fall of France in 1940. The Vichy authorities had him arrested on the 16 September 1940 and charged with responsibility for France's defeat on the grounds that he had presided over industrial unrest and failed to rearm the nation. Blum, however, defended his record as prime minister so brilliantly that, under pressure from the German authorities, the trial was suspended. His wartime writings were smuggled out of Vichy prisons where he had been kept between September 1940 and April 1943. *A l'Echelle humaine* (1945), which is a testament of faith in socialism, inspired the reorganization of the party in the post-war period. In it Blum argues for a fair redistribution of wealth and blames the bourgeoisie for France's defeat through failing to convert society into a genuine social democracy. The institutions of the Republican state, he maintains, could be instrumental in building a Socialist society provided they were controled by Socialist and progressive forces.

After his return from Buchenwald concentration camp in 1945 he continued to write in *Le Populaire*. By now he had become an elder statesman and remained active in politics even though he did not stand for election to the Chamber again. He ensured that the Socialists rejected rigid Marxism and that they declined the Communist offer to form a united party. He also opposed the Gaullist attempt to give France a presidential constitution. In 1946 he negotiated, on behalf of the French government, financial agreements with Washington. His last brief spell as prime minister was at the end of 1946 and early 1947. It was a time of economic crisis with rapid price rises. The National Assembly had failed to produce a majority and, although the new constitution had been voted, neither the president nor the Council of the Republic had been elected. Blum, who was not a member of the cabinet, took office for one month and introduced measures to control the economy by ordering price reductions. By an unhappy coincidence it was during that month that the Indo-China War began. Blum's last political initiative, which proved abortive, was to call for the creation of a third force which would bring together the Socialist Party and the Catholic Mouvement Républicain de Gauche to form a French labour party.

Léon Blum's name is linked above all with the first Popular Front government and with its failures. In his defence it must be said that he had to tackle a series of problems for which no amount of experience could equip him: how to manage a policy of economic reflation, how to confront fascism in Europe and, in particular, what policy to adopt towards the Spanish Civil War. Although not a charismatic leader he commanded the respect and even devotion of his followers within the party although to his opponents on the right he remained a figure who evoked deep suspicion and even hate. The Socialism he espoused, however, far from being narrowly Marxist and revolutionary was in fact moderate and reformist. A man of eminently bourgeois tastes and life-style he was also a sensitive intellectual who was part of a European cultural elite. He had no first-hand experience of working-class life and his socialism grew out of moral and intellectual convictions while his political actions were deduced from general principles. According to his critics, his determination to ensure that party action accorded with Socialist theory made him doctrinaire and ineffectual; in the eyes of his supporters it made him an honest and principled politician.

Blum believed that socialism was compatible with liberal democracy and indeed that democratic structures were a precondition for the creation of a Socialist society. In line with the constitutional views of the left he wanted to retain only the directly elected Chamber and abolish the Senate. However, with the right's assault on the institutions of the Third Republic in the 1930s he became a stout defender of the constitutional status quo. While arguing that in theory no Socialist should allow himself to be hemmed in by legality, in practice he was always careful to act within the law as his doctrine of the exercise of power illustrates. Blum was a lawyer by training and after he resigned from the Conseil d'Etat he continued to work as a barrister for a number of years. His legal background made him an able legislator and stood him in good stead during his trial in 1942. He believed that the task of socialism, as defined by Jaurès, was to complete the work of the Enlightenment. He was above all a humanist whose socialism was rooted in a faith in the innate goodness of man. Because socialism was the art of making society just and harmonious it was committed to ending the bourgeoisie's exploitation of the working class.

Bibliography

The fullest biography is Jean Lacouture's *Léon Blum* (Paris: Seuil, 1977). On Blum's political philosophy the following are recommended: Joel Colton, *Léon Blum. A Humanist in Politics* (New York: Alfred A. Knopf, 1966) and James Joll, 'Léon Blum: The intellectual in politics' in *Intellectuals in Politics. Three Biographical Essays* (London: Weidenfeld and Nicolson, 1960), pp. 3–56.

CR

BONNET, Georges (1889–1973)

Georges Bonnet was a Radical-Socialist deputy, minister and prime minister, remembered principally as a leading exponent of the policy of appeasing Hitler while foreign minister 1938–9. Born at Bassillac (Dordogne), the son of a prominent lawyer, he studied law and in 1913 entered the civil service as *auditeur* at the Conseil d'Etat. In 1911 he made a politically advantageous marriage by marrying Odette Pelletan, granddaughter of Eugène Pelletan, a founding father of the Republic. During the First World War he served with distinction, winning the Croix de Guerre. Thereafter he continued as a successful career bureaucrat until elected to parliament in 1924. Immediately recognized as *ministrable* he held a wide variety of cabinet posts, establishing a reputation in particular for expertise in financial and economic affairs. As under-secretary of state in the cabinet of his patron Painlevé, he set up the Economic Council (1925) and as minister of finance under Daladier he created the National Lottery in 1933. At the Ministry of Commerce and Industry he prepared the International Exhibition of 1937. To remove an adversary of its financial policy the Blum government sent him as ambassador to Washington in 1936 but he was recalled to the Ministry of Finance in 1937 by Chautemps to try to restore 'confidence' among the financial community during the protracted financial crisis. He failed: another devaluation of the franc was necessary at the end of June 1937). Unable to form a viable government himself in January 1938, he served again as minister of state responsible for the coordination of financial and economic policy.

The most significant phase of Bonnet's career was his time as foreign minister in the third Daladier government (April 1938 to September 1939). Ambitious, able and intelligent, but considered excessively devious even by the standards of the Third

Republic, Bonnet was widely and rightly distrusted. His five volumes of self-congratulatory memoirs reveal little of the real thrust of his policies. Though genuinely interested in a long-term accommodation between France and Germany, he was motivated primarily by fear of communism both at home and abroad. Convinced that war could only benefit Bolshevism, he favoured the maintenance of peace at virtually any price. In public his policy was to stress France's obligations to her allies and to blame others – especially the British – for difficulties in meeting them. Behind the scenes, he was known to be ready to renege on French commitments in Eastern Europe and to favour disengagement from the area. He was a strong advocate of concessions to Germany on the part of Czechoslovakia at Munich in 1938 and hampered attempts to achieve cooperation between France, Britain and the Soviet Union in the spring of 1939. In the Polish crisis which led to the outbreak of the Second World War, he supported further accommodation of Hitler regarding Danzig and the Polish Corridor and hoped that a second Munich might be organized through the offices of Mussolini. Daladier removed him from the Foreign Office to the Ministry of Justice in his re-shuffle of September 1939. Reynaud dropped him altogether in May 1940.

A supporter of Laval after the French collapse in 1940, Bonnet voted for full powers to Pétain on 10 July 1940. His activities under Vichy are obscure but probably more extensive than his memoirs make out. Characteristically more of a wait-and-see *attentiste* than an all-out collaborator or resister, he escaped to Switzerland in April 1944. He was allowed to return to France only in 1950 but remained ineligible for elective office until 1953 on account of the Fourth Republic's ban on persons deemed a 'national disgrace' because of their record between 1940 and 1944. Having reactivated his electoral machine in the Dordogne, he returned to the Chamber in 1956 and was re-elected in 1958. He retained his seat until June 1968, though without ever regaining ministerial office.

Bibliography

Adamthwaite, A. (1977), *France and the Coming of the Second World War 1936–1939,* London: Cass.

Bonnet, G. (1946–8), *Défense de la paix*, 2 vols, Geneva: Les Editions du Cheval Ailé.

Duroselle, J.-B. (1979), *La Décadence (1932–1939),* Paris: Imprimerie Nationale.

JFM

BOUCHARDEAU, Huguette (1935–)

Huguette Bouchardeau has combined a career in general leftist politics as a leading figure in the PSU (Parti Socialiste Unifié) with active involvement in the women's movement, where she has been a link spanning the generations. Born at Saint-Etienne, she pursued an academic career, from 1961 to 1970 at the Lycée Honoré d'Urfé, then at the University of Lyons II, whilst working as an activist in the family planning movement, the Mouvement pour la Liberté de l'Avortement et de la Contraception (MLAC), the Centre Lyonnais d'Etudes Feministes, the trade union SGEN-CFDT and the PSU, where she assumed responsibility for women's affairs. In 1979, she became general secretary of the PSU and was a candidate in the presidential election of 1981, receiving 1.1 per cent of the vote. In 1983, she entered the Socialist government as environment minister. In the general election of 1986, having left the PSU, she was guaranteed a safe seat in the Doubs by the Socialists.

Her book, *Pas d'histoire les femmes*, deals with the period from the First World War to 1968. It talks about ordinary 'forgotten' women, as well as the 'stars' of the movement prior to its resurgence in the 1970s, not just because history is also made by the masses but, more significantly, taking the feminist position that their private struggles were also political.

Her involvement in the MLAC is also primarily a political act. When the movement restarted after the war in the 1950s, publishing information about contraception was still illegal in France. For many of the women activists, their involvement was going beyond the confines of social work to make a real contribution to the struggle for women's freedom. The right to contraception and then in the 1970s the right to abortion were important issues on which mass mobilization of women could take place. They are also issues which provide the basis for the continuity of the women's movement. Moreover, Huguette Bouchardeau was able to take on board the radical newness of the renascent women's movement of the 1970s with its recognition of the difficulties arising from sexist ideology and from interpersonal relationships with men.

On the general political stage, Huguette Bouchardeau is aware of the sexual division of labour whereby women are saddled with the 'caring', 'social', 'family' areas of responsibility, and has both assumed this responsibility – on the grounds that since these are areas neglected by men, women have to take them on – while at the same time managing to go beyond the particularly feminine to become leader of the PSU and presidential candidate.

Bouchardeau rejects the idea that women should have nothing to do with power. For her, women need to use the weapons of the current political struggle to compete for power. None the less she also believes that the nature of that power will be different as a result of the women's movement with its questioning of patriarchal power, based on authoritarianism, bureaucracy, centralism and hierarchy, and its aspirations towards antihierarchical relations, local and individual autonomy, and self-management (*autogestion* – a principal theme of the PSU).

Her strong links with the ecology and antinuclear movement probably influenced her appointment to the environment ministry. Her time there was characteristic of her political realism: she recognized at the outset that there was no possibility of moving the Socialists in a non-nuclear direction. It was marked by the outbreak of the Seveso dioxin barrels affair, the establishment of a 'Mutuelle de l'Air' to combat atmospheric pollution, the beginnings of a European agreement to reduce pollution from cars and cooperation with Mediterranean countries to reduce coastal pollution.

Bibliography

On the women's movement:

Bouchardeau, H. (1977), *Pas d'histoire des femmes* Paris: Syros.

Bouchardeau, H. (1978), *Hélène Brion, la voie féministe*, Paris: Syros.

Bouchardeau, H. *et al.* (1981), *Pour une politique des femmes, par les femmes, pour les femmes: les propositions du PSU*, Paris: Syros.

An account of her time at the Environment Ministry:

Bouchardeau, H. (1986) *Le ministère du possible*, Paris: Alain Moreau.

MAM

BOUISSON, Fernand Emile Honoré (1874–1959)

Born in 1874 in Algeria to a Marseilles industrial family, Fernand Bouisson settled in Aubagne in the department of the Bouches-du-Rhône at an early age and went on to make a career, first in local, and then in national, politics. He was elected to the Conseil Municipal of Aubagne in 1904, became a *conseiller général* in 1907, mayor of Aubagne in 1908, and president of the general council des Bouches-du-Rhône in 1912. It was in 1909 that Bouisson was first elected as a deputy, a post he retained until the end of the Third Republic. His career as a national politician peaked during his period as president of the Chamber of Deputies from 1927 to 1936. For a few days in June 1935 he moved on to the centre stage when after the fall of Flandin he became leader of a short-lived and highly heterogeneous 'National' government whose members included Marshal Pétain, Joseph Caillaux, Edouard Herriot, Georges Mandel and Pierre Laval. The Bouisson government was defeated as soon as it was presented to the Chamber, to be replaced by a government led by Laval. Later, at the National Assembly's special session at Vichy on 10 July 1940 Bouisson was again allied with Laval and was among the most forceful advocates of handing the country over to Marshal Pétain. In spite of this early enthusiasm for Vichy, Bouisson then withdrew from politics, resigning as mayor of La Ciotat in 1941 (a post to which he had been elected in 1935) and retiring to the Côte d'Azur where he died at his villa at Cap d'Antibes in 1959.

Bouisson's career can be seen as typical of that of many of the political notables of the Third Republic. Progressing from a local base, first Aubagne and then La Ciotat, Bouisson always nurtured these local roots as he went on to achieve national office. Although elected as a Socialist, Bouisson's watchwords were clientelism, patronage and moderation and the national roles which he sought were those which used his powers of negotiation, reconciliation and arbitration and required only a minimal degree of ideological commitment.

Much of Bouisson's appeal rested on his own personal prestige. Initially this was boosted by his size, his renown as an international class rugby player and his role as a local employer. Later, his position as president of the Chamber of Deputies was put to good use, helping him to develop an aura of gravitas, one which was compounded by the practice of always referring to him as 'le president Bouisson'. He was helped by the support of the Marseilles-based daily paper *Le Petit Provençal* (for which he was a regular leader-writer) as well as that of key local Socialist power brokers. Above all Bouisson presented himself as a man attached to his adopted home, Provence, and as the only local politician with a sufficiently grand national role to ensure that the needs of his electors received due attention. He took a special interest in shipping and shipbuilding, sitting on every parliamentary commission which dealt with these subjects, always doing his best to defend the interests of the Marseilles shipping lobby and to ensure that the shipyards of La Ciotat and Marseilles were supplied with work.

Bouisson's personalized politics were typical of the day. But they were also accompanied by that other feature of the Third Republic, a very weak sense of attachment to party. His relations with the Socialist Party were always tense and as a powerful local figure in Aubagne and La Ciotat he was resistant to the demands both of local and national party discipline. He first entered the Chamber as an 'independent Socialist' in 1909 having fought a campaign against the official SFIO candidate and in the face of denunciations from Jaurès. He joined the SFIO thereafter but was never really happy as a party member. In the 1930s as politics became more polarized Bouisson was increasingly ill at ease in the SFIO. His resignation from the SFIO in 1934 made the break formal and opened the way for his later attempt at forming a 'National' government. In the 1936 parliamentary elections he fought the seat of La Ciotat on an independent ticket, but with the backing of powerful local Socialists who preferred him to the officially endorsed Popular Front candidate, who was a Communist. Bouisson won the election but shortly thereafter lost his post as President of the Chamber to Edouard Herriot. Deprived of the patronage of his old office Bouisson's final electoral victory proved to be a rather hollow success.

Bibliography

(There is nothing in English specifically on Bouisson although he is referred to briefly in D.W. Brogan, *The Development of Modern France (1870–1939)* (London: Hamish Hamilton, 1940), pp. 679–80, in W. Shirer, *The Collapse of the Third Republic* (London: Heinemann, 1970), pp. 914–15 and in A. Werth, *The Destiny of France* (London: Hamish Hamilton, 1937), pp. 145–50. In French the best single source is L. Jeansoulin, 'Fernand Bouisson (1874–1959)', in *Marseille*, 121, 1980, pp. 85–92. Two contemporary portraits are P. Carrere, *Profils*, (Paris: Le Contemporain, 1935), pp. 122–5 (flattering) and G. Suarez, *Nos seigneurs et maîtres* (Paris: Les Editions de France, 1937), pp. 37–40 (vitriolic). Jules Jeanneney gives a contemptuous account of Bouisson's role in July 1940 in his *Journal Politique* (Paris: A. Colin, 1972), pp. 98, 104, 333, 337, 443 and 444, while Marceau Pivert singled him out for attack in his intervention at the SFIO Congress of June 1936, SFIO, *Congrès 1936, compte rendu stenographique des débats* (Paris: SFIO, 1936), pp. 30–6.

DALL

BOULANGER, Georges Ernest Jean-Marie (1837–91)

General Boulanger and the movement of which he was the figurehead came closer than any other to destroying the Third Republic. In the political and economic doldrums of the late 1880s, his banner of political radicalism and anti-German nationalism united left- and right-wing enemies of the Opportunist Republic in a populist movement prefiguring fascism while also recalling the popular Bonapartism of the late 1840s. The unstable and contradictory nature of the movement, aggravated by Boulanger's personal failings, made it a short-lived threat, though it left permanent traces on the political life of the Third Republic.

Boulanger was the son of a provincial solicitor. After the military school of Saint-Cyr, he served in North Africa, Italy and Indo-China in the 1850s and 1860s, and in 1870–1 commanded a regiment during the German siege of Paris and against the Commune, winning a reputation for bravery, ambition and self-publicity. He was frequently wounded, though never seriously enough to harm his career: perhaps this helped to convince him that dash and recklessness paid off. His last wound was particularly lucky: a bullet in the arm during the fighting in Paris against the Commune allowed him to be absent from the worst atrocities of the 'Semaine Sanglante', and thus his later political career as darling of the left was safeguarded. His summary shooting of communard prisoners, carried out at least in part to curry favour with his superiors at the beginning of the Civil War, never came to light. Similar luck and unscrupulousness in the pursuit of advancement marked Boulanger's career thereafter. During the MacMahon period he ingratiated himself with the Duc d'Aumale, his superior officer and a prince of the house of Orléans, then, when the wind shifted towards the left, he tacked accordingly, showing himself to be not only a Republican soldier – a rare enough phenomenon – but even a Radical. Advancement was rapid: general of brigade in 1880; director of infantry in 1882; general of division in 1884, and commander of the occupation troops in Tunisia. This was his first 'political' command, and showed signs of things to come: when one of his men was involved in a brawl with an Italian, he publicly ordered his troops to take the law into their own hands in defending the honour of the uniform. This led to a row with the civilian Resident, Paul Cambon (q.v.), and Boulanger's recall to Paris. Once again rashness paid, for he was supported by Clemenceau and the Radicals. After the 1885 elections, which had seen a severe fall in support for the Opportunists and a consequent rise in importance of the Radicals, Boulanger was appointed minister of war in the Radical-backed Freycinet government of January 1886, and in the Goblet (q.v.) government that succeeded it in December.

His tenure of the ministry was perhaps the most eventful in French history. He achieved some important reforms, principally the speedy introduction of the new Lebel rifle and the long-delayed adoption of universal three-year military service, with the abolition of exemptions and loopholes (especially for priests) which the left had demanded for years. He also made many improvements in the standard of living of the soldiers. On the other hand, his ministry was marked by blatant publicity-seeking at home and abroad, some of it cynical and even highly dangerous. He delighted the left by expelling his former patron Aumale from the army, encouraging troops to share their rations with strikers, and allowing soldiers to grow beards (a mark not only of fashion but also of Republicanism – Clemenceau remarked that Boulanger's decision to grow a beard himself in 1886 was the most important decision he ever made). On the patriotic front he had sentry boxes painted blue, white and red (an enduring reform), tried to conduct personal diplomacy with the tsar, patronized a fête at the Opera featuring 'a great military ball given in camp on the evening of victory', and, as if to turn fantasy into reality, escalated a minor frontier incident with Germany in May 1887 – the Schnaebelé affair – to the brink of war, with both sides contemplating mobilization. Cooler heads prevailed in Paris and Berlin, but the public was convinced that Boulanger's toughness had forced Bismarck to back down. These antics were making him a popular hero, aided by his looks (he had, said one contemporary, the virile air that pleased crowds and women) and the city-dweller's passion for military display. The Longchamps army review on 14 July 1886 was his apotheosis, and was celebrated in a music-hall song of infectious verve and vulgarity, 'En revenant de la revue', which extolled 'Le brav' général Boulanger' and became the marching song of his growing band of admirers – 'the Marseillaise of bakers' boys and petty businessmen, of seamstresses and counter-jumpers' as Anatole France remarked superciliously but not inaccurately. Dozens of other songs, toys, playing cards, soap, pictures and books dedicated to Boulanger showed how attractive the patriotic image was to the urban masses. Jingoistic nationalists such as Paul Déroulède's Ligue des Patriotes believed that at last they had found the man who would sweep aside pusillanimous politicians and lead the nation to 'revenge' for 1870.

The politicians took fright, René Goblet's government fell, and Rouvier (q.v.), the successor, would accept neither Clemenceau nor Boulanger into the cabinet. In spite of the rage of the leading left-wing Parisian newspapers, especially *L'Intransigeant* and *La Lanterne*, and big popular demonstrations, Boulanger was despatched to a command in Clermont-Ferrand. He and his supporters maintained an agitation which earned him thirty days' close arrest for insubordination and then, when in early 1888 his supporters put him forward as a candidate in seven by-elections, he was removed from his command and placed in retirement. This added fuel to the flames, and he was elected as deputy for both Dordogne and the Nord. By now, most Radical and Socialist Party leaders were as alarmed as the Opportunists, and began to organize to resist him. In June 1988, Boulanger demanded in the Chamber revision of the constitution and in July a dissolution of Parliament. Angry scenes led to his resigning and fighting a duel on 13 July 1888 with the prime minister, Floquet. The aged Floquet severely wounded Boulanger in the neck. This did not prevent his immediate re-election by three departments.

Boulanger and his 'catch-all' campaign for revision of the constitution were now supported both by monarchists of various hues, notably Baron Mackau, Comte Dillon, Comte Albert de Mun, de Cassagnac and the Duchesse d'Uzès (q.v.), the source of most of his funds, and by much of the extreme-left, who provided many of his most active organizers and advisers, principally the journalist Rochefort, the nationalist Déroulède, the left-wing Radical politicians Naquet and Laguerre, and the Blanquist socialists Granger and Roche. Both sides were hoping that with Boulanger as a figurehead an irresistible mass movement would sweep away the constraints of the moderate Republican system, entrenched behind its seven-year presidency and undemocratic Senate, and by calling a constituent assembly create an opportunity for either a popular monarchical restoration or an ultra-democratic republic. Boulanger secretly encouraged the hopes of both sides.

In January 1889 a seat fell vacant in Paris, and Boulanger stood against a Republican, Jacques, who was supported by the government and the combined Republican groups. The power of Boulanger's appeal was shown by his crushing victory by 245,236 votes to 162,875: half of the Republican electorate had rallied to him, most markedly in the extreme-left working-class districts; so had practically all the right.

In the 15th *arrondissement*, for example, where he polled most strongly – 51 per cent of the registered voters – he gained the support both of the lower-middle class and the Javel factory workers. Many – including the government – now feared a *coup d'état*, but Boulanger and his advisers, sure that they were winning electorally but far from sure of support among the generals, played safe.

The Tirard government, with the tough and unscrupulous Constans as minister of the interior, immediately altered the rules to prevent an electoral landslide by Boulanger: in February 1889 single-member constituencies were rapidly reintroduced, with a ban on any individual's standing simultaneously in several places. Heavy pressure was put on government employees to vote against the Boulangists. The Ligue des Patriotes was dissolved, and steps were taken to prosecute three leading Boulangists, Laguerre, Laisant and Naquet. To the government's delight, Boulanger himself fled to Brussels – appropriately on 1 April – to avoid prosecution for high treason. This showed a lack of sense as well as of courage: a political trial would have been more dangerous for the government than for Boulanger himself, while his flight was a humiliation and his absence from the scene a disadvantage. On 14 August, the Senate, sitting as a high court, sentenced *in absentia* Boulanger and two of his leading supporters, Rochefort (q.v.) and Dillon, to transportation for plotting against the state. The Boulangists continued to win elections – most notably another victory in Paris when in the left-wing stronghold of Montmartre Boulanger beat the Socialist Joffrin in the general elections of September 1889. But even spectacular isolated successes could not beat the system of single-member constituencies and individual candidatures: Boulanger's followers won only forty-two seats. Moreover, the limits of the movement's support were becoming clear. Outside a few urban areas, most notably Paris, where a disaffected and adventurous left-wing fringe was willing to combine with an anti-Republican right, and the few historic rural strongholds of royalism, a solid, safe Republic could command majority support. Local elections in 1889 and 1890 gave the Boulangists disappointing results. Revelations in the press, and in a widely read book by an erstwhile supporter (Gabriel Terrail), Mermeix's *Les Coulisses du Boulangisme* (Paris: L. Cerf, 1890), made public the duplicitous relations of the general with the royalist leadership. Many supporters grew disillusioned. The waning of his political fortunes coincided with personal anguish: his mistress, Marguerite de Bonnemains, died of consumption in July 1891. Ten weeks later, on 30 September, Boulanger shot himself on her grave in a Brussels suburb. This romantic, indeed melodramatic, end inspired a characteristically acerbic epitaph from his enemy and sometime ally, Clemenceau: 'Here lies General Boulanger who died as he lived: like a second-lieutenant.'

Boulanger, the handsome blond-bearded Republican general on the black horse, a lightweight without principles or scruples, was for a time the most popular man in France, and one of the most charismatic figures in modern French history. That there was widespread discontent with the Opportunist Republic in the late 1880s is understandable: at a time of serious economic slump the left was disillusioned with centrist governments, and the right frustrated by its exclusion from power. The 1885 elections, which showed an advance by both the radical left and the right at the expense of the Opportunists, provided both a temptation and an opportunity to intensify the attacks on the moderates, entrenched behind constitutional barriers. That it was a soldier who catalysed the opposition demonstrates the appeal of militarism and jingoism to a significant part of the urban population, working class and middle class, in the generation after 1870. The Paris elections of 1889 might be seen as the dying echo of the revolutionary and patriotic tradition of the Paris *sans-culottes*. After the death of Boulanger, radical nationalism remained on the French political scene; but throughout the Third Republic, it was never able to attract the breadth of working-class support that Boulanger, momentarily, had enjoyed, and which thereafter was drawn towards socialism – though a socialism which, despite its internationalist ideology, always contained a broad streak of Jacobin-style patriotism.

Bibliography

The standard work in English is Frederic Seager, *The Boulanger Affair: Political crossroads of France 1886–1889* (Ithaca, NY: Cornell University Press, 1969) while a recent examination of the movement in the national context is Michael Burns, *Rural Society and French Politics: Boulangism and the Dreyfus Affair, 1886–1900* (Princeton, NJ: Princeton University Press, 1984). An important analysis of the revolutionary element in Boulangism is Zeev Sternhell, *La Droite révolutionnaire, 1885–1914* (Paris: Seuil, 1978) and an examination of the links with royalism is Philippe Levillain, *Boulanger, fossoyeur de la monarchie* (Paris: Flammarion, 1982). The most lively narrative history is Adrien Dansette, *Le Boulangisme* (Paris: Fayard, 1946).

RT

BOULIN, Robert (1920–79)

Born on 20 July 1920 at Villandraut (Gironde) in a middle-class family (his father was inspector of the state tobacco manufacture), Robert Boulin was educated in the provincial *lycées* of Talence and Bordeaux and in the arts and law schools of the University of Bordeaux.

His *cursus honorum* is the archetypal example of a successful twentieth-century French political career abruptly interrupted in tragic circumstances. As a young man of 20, he went to London to fight in the Resistance and became a member of the French committee of national liberation. In 1946, he joined the Bar in his home town of Libourne, and soon became active in politics. His talents quickly appreciated by his neighbour Chaban-Delmas (q.v.), he was a member of the National Council of the Gaullist RPF from 1947 to 1953 then of its offshoot the Social Republican Party.

Having been elected in 1958 deputy of the newly-formed Union pour la Nouvelle République in the Libourne constituency of the Gironde (a seat he was going to hold or pass on to his 'substitute' throughout the 1960s and 1970s), he was also elected mayor of Libourne in 1959, and re-elected after each successive local election in 1965, 1971 and 1977. His obvious popularity as a notable in d'Artagnan country stood the test of national politics, and he started a brilliant ministerial career in the none too enviable post of under-secretary for the repatriated in the Debré Cabinet from August 1961 to April 1962, then in the first Pompidou Cabinet from April to September 1962. He was also a member of the Central Committee of the UNR.

From then on until his death, he was to hold portfolios (junior minister for the budget, then for economy and finance, minister in charge of the civil service, minister of agriculture, minister for health and social security, minister in charge of relations with parliament, and finally labour minister) in every Fifth Republican Cabinet except for three years in the political 'wilderness' (1973–76), obviously paying the price for his unfailing loyalty to Chaban-Delmas (q.v.), whose campaign manager he was for the 1974 presidential election. In December 1974 he resigned from the UDR as a protest against Jacques Chirac's election as secretary-general of the party.

A very competent technician, he was also an outstanding negotiator thanks to his easy personal manner, his skill at dealing with concrete matters, and his flair for compromise. As a minister for health and social security from June 1969 to July 1972, he carried through important pieces of legislation on the completion of social security provisions for the self-employed and the improvement of pension rights (the Boulin Bill of 20 December 1971), as well as on hospital reform. He also successfully negotiated new forms of contract between the illness insurance offices and the medical profession, without jeopardizing the fundamental principle of liberal medical practice.

It was as minister for labour and participation [*sic*] in the third Barre Cabinet (April 1978 to his death) that he achieved his last major pieces of legislation: a reform of the National Agency for Employment and of unemployment benefits, and a reform of the industrial conciliation boards ('Conseils de Prud'hommes') in January 1979.

Widely tipped as a future prime minister and probably successor to Raymond Barre, he appears to have mismanaged his private affairs as lamentably as he had brilliantly handled the affairs of the State. Probably the victim of misplaced trust in a former Resistance fighter whose wife was a friend of Madame Boulin, and who is said to have made substantial contributions to Boulin's own electoral campaigns, he was named in a real estate scandal involving the purchase of land and building permits at a suspiciously low price in the expensive and select commune of Ramatuelle (near Saint-Tropez). It has also been rumoured that political enemies (including some in the Cabinet) were out to destroy him. He was found drowned in a pond near Rambouillet on 30 October 1970. Predictably, Jacques Chirac failed to attend the funeral at which Raymond Barre was present, while President Giscard d'Estaing sent the secretary-general of the Elysée to represent him. This particular scandal, the circumstances of which were never made clear (Robert Boulin's family rejected the verdict of suicide) undoubtedly damaged the president's own reputation and that of his cabinet. The young Socialist deputy Laurent Fabius (q.v.), casting himself as a new Revolutionary prosecutor (Fouquier-Tinville), thus indicted the president in the National Assembly on 11 November 1979: 'What we are telling you is that your society is decaying and you are responsible!'

Bibliography

No biography of Boulin has yet been published, but numerous articles appeared in the French and international press at the time of his death and in the first few days of November 1979.

AM

BOURGEOIS, Léon Victor Auguste (1851–1925)

Born in Paris in the year of Louis-Napoléon Bonaparte's *coup d'état*, Léon Bourgeois became one of the most prominent figures of the Third Republic as a leader and theoretician of the Parti Radical. The son of a watchmaker, he started his career in the French Civil Service, first as secretary-general of the Marne *préfecture*, then as a sub-prefect in that department, eventually becoming prefect of police at the age of 36. He then switched to politics, using the Marne department as his base, and his career progressed at an astonishing pace, from *député* to under-secretary of state in the ministry of the interior in the same year, 1888.

One of the striking features of Léon Bourgeois' fate is the contrast between the eminent place he occupied in French politics during his lifetime and the relative obscurity of his posthumous reputation as compared with such figures as Briand, Caillaux, Clemenceau, Jaurès or Poincaré, all broadly his contemporaries. Not only was he twelve times a minister and once a prime minister, but he was also repeatedly approached and nominated to be prime minister, characteristically declining to meet the challenge of being defeated by a hostile Chamber of Deputies. A minister of the interior in 1890, then of public instruction until December 1892, he became minister of justice in 1893, which was an uncomfortable portfolio to hold at the tail end of the Panama scandal (though Bourgeois' own reputation remained unsullied). He had by then become leader of the Radicals, of whom there were about 120 in the Chamber of Deputies. In a speech at Châlons-sur-Marne in his own constituency, he thus summarized his own doctrine of government: 'Government of all, by all and for all, . . . that is . . . exclusively republican, essentially democratic, absolutely opposed to any form of violence and to any violation of the law, resolutely opposed to any lowering of human dignity, and to any enslavement of human beings.' This meant a moderate form of government, based on the rule of law, with an implied concern for social welfare and protection against all forms of tyranny (including that of the Church and the army), in order to preserve and enhance the development of the individual.

Having declined to become President of the Council when the newly-elected president of the Republic, Félix Faure, asked him in January 1895, he failed soon afterwards to be elected President (speaker) of the Chamber of Deputies by forty votes. But on 1 November of that year, Bourgeois even-

tually became head of an all-Radical cabinet, in which he was easily the outstanding figure. This minority government, already moderate by vocation, would have to content itself with a programme of extreme moderation. Bourgeois nevertheless managed to antagonize the Catholic right with a bill on associations (the first step in a ten-year span of Republican policies that would lead to the separation of Church and state legislation of 1905). Committed to a long overdue tax reform, Bourgeois also earned for himself the tenacious hostility of the Senate as well as the opposition of fifty-five *conseils généraux* (departmental assemblies) when he tried to introduce some form of income tax, a reform that would be passed by the Chamber of Deputies only in 1907, and by the Senate in 1914! The Senate dealt its death blow when it refused to vote the money for the continuation of the French army's expedition in Madagascar (23 April 1896). Although technically Bourgeois' cabinet was not overthrown, he resigned six days later, and would never again agree to become prime minister.

Bourgeois became successively minister of public instruction (in the era of primary school teachers as the foot-soldiers of the Republic), minister for foreign affairs and French delegate to the Hague Peace Conference of 1899, and again at the time of the Algeciras Conference in 1906, and minister of labour in the pre-war years when at last the Republic showed some concern for welfare legislation. In between ministerial posts, having become a senator, he was also chairman of the Senate's foreign affairs committee, and after the war he assisted Clemenceau at the Peace Conference, when he wisely though unsuccessfully tried to endow the League of Nations with a military support force. His personal commitment and competence were publicly recognized when he was awarded the Nobel Peace Prize in 1920. His career was crowned by his holding the presidency (speaker) of the Senate from 1920 to 1923.

Bourgeois also exercised considerable influence as leader and theoretician of the Radical Party. He developed the doctrine known as solidarism, which owed much to the values of the French Revolution, and was located somewhere between liberalism and socialism. According to this doctrine, the individual is born with a debt towards society, the repayment of which is a legal obligation; thus those born with social privileges must in justice compensate for them by endorsing a programme of social welfare and progressive income tax, free education, a minimum wage, insurance, etc., in order to help the disadvantaged. The doctrine, however, far from advocating the abolition of private property, aimed to generalize access to property, and in that sense it was socially conservative, promoting reforms not for the sake of redistribution, but of clearing a 'social debt'. Bourgeois' defiant question to the French right in a speech at Nantes in 1893: 'You say you rally to the Republic. So be it. But do you accept the Revolution?' hardly went beyond Sieyès' claims for the Third Estate, and that with a time lag of over a century . . .'

A man of great charm and personal integrity, Bourgeois was anticlerical because clericalism was perceived by French Radicals as the root of tyranny; he was a revisionist in 1898 when the Brisson cabinet had to decide whether to call a retrial for Dreyfus (this being seen as a snub to the French army); he was a constant advocate of the supremacy of civilian over military power, and he was a supporter of international arbitration. Yet this front-rank politician of his time is largely forgotten nowadays. A good orator and a consummate parliamentarian, he seems to have been reluctant to play other roles than that of 'second fiddle' to the maestros of the day, with few achievements to his name in terms of implemented policies, in spite of his wide-ranging interests and considerable influence. For all his limitations, he is one of the most honourable and characteristic representatives of his contemporaries' moods and attitudes, and would serve well as an 'ideal type' figure of the first half of the Third Republic.

Bibliography

It is revealing that Léon Bourgeois has not attracted the attention of any modern biographer, though numerous books contain references to him. In the French literature, the most notable contributions are to be found in Jean-Denis Bredin, *Joseph Caillaux* (Paris: Hachette, 1980), and *L'Affaire* (Paris: Juilliard, 1983); Jacques Chastenet, *Histoire de la troisième république* (Paris: Hachette, 1952 and 1954); François Goguel, *La Politique des partis sous la troisième république* (Paris: Seuil, 1946); Jacques Kayser, *Les grandes batailles du radicalisme* (Paris: Marcel Rivière, 1962); Albert Thibaudet, *Les Idées politiques de la France*, (Paris: Stock, 1932). In English, one can usefully consult the translation of Emile Bourgeois, *Modern France 1815–1913*, (Cambridge: Cambridge University Press, 1919); D.W. Brogan, *The Development of Modern France* (London: Hamish Hamilton, 1940); Guy Chapman, *The Third Republic of France* (London: Macmillan, 1962); J. Hampden Jackson, *Clémenceau and the Third Republic* (London: Hodder and Stoughton, 1946); and Theodore Zeldin, *France 1848–1945* (Oxford: Oxford University Press, 1977).

AM

BOURGÈS-MAUNOURY, Maurice Jean-Marie (1914–)

Educated at the Ecole Polytéchnique, an artillery officer (1935–40), a Resistance fighter, a *Campagnon de la Liberation*, and a grandson of Marshal Maunoury, Bourgès-Maunoury as a young man seemed headed for an outstanding career. He was regional commissioner (prefect) for Bordeaux in 1945. He hesitated over joining the Socialist Party and then entered the Assembly as a Radical deputy for the Haute-Garonne in 1948. (He represented the constituency until defeated in 1958.) As a young Radical he made a rapid reputation by attacking ministries but he was a poor orator (although a good organizer) and stood in opposition to the strong Mendésiste tide in the Radical Party.

Bourgès-Maunoury made an impression as a hardliner particularly on colonial matters which came increasingly to dominate the Fourth Republic. He was minister of the interior for Edgar Faure, minister of industry for Mendès France (q.v.) and minister of defence for Guy Mollet (q.v.). When Faure's government was formed he promised Jacques Soustelle (q.v.), the Gaullist leader, who was a long-time friend, that he would appoint him governor-general of Algeria which he did. On the Algerian problem Bourgès-Maunoury supported the view that the revolt should be squashed and for this purpose supported the invasion of Suez by Anglo-French forces in 1956. However, when he was informed of an army conspiracy in Algeria he hoped that 'the affair would not make it impossible to go skiing'. Mollet referred to him as the twerp ('ce con là').

On the fall of the Mollet government there were twenty-two days of comings and goings before he was able to form a government supported by Socialists, Radicals, the MRP and Gaullists. His government lasted from 12 June 1957 to 30 September 1957 and mainly took up where Mollet left off. Félix Gaillard (q.v.) was able to push through a finance bill much like the one which sank Mollet's ministry. The government was able to construct the 'Morice line', a barrage around the Algerian frontier to prevent the movement of insurgents across the border, and pursued the policy of 'pacification' – i.e. military victory over the FLN. The government was defeated when it tried to pass the outline law prepared by the

Mollet government to create eight or ten administrative assemblies in the Algerian departments. The law did not make clear whether they would be dominated by settlers or not but in any case the government was defeated before its intentions were tested.

On the fall of the Bourgès-Maunoury government the Republic was plunged even deeper into crisis and it was thirty-three days before a new ministry was formed by Félix Gaillard (q.v.).

In the Fifth Republic Bourgès-Maunoury virtually retired from politics. He was one of the 121 signatories of the 'Vincennes Committee' of colonial Algerian die-hards on 20 June 1960. The declaration stated that 'Algeria is a part of French sovereign territory' but it was rapidly overtaken by events. He then devoted his time to business and was the director of a number of companies including the financial conglomerate Rivaud. He emerged briefly from obscurity in September 1970 to announce his resignation from the Radical Party and his support for Chaban-Delmas against the then Radical leader Servan-Schreiber (q.v.) in the Bordeaux by-election.

DSB

BOUSSEL, Pierre (1920–)

Pierre Boussel, also known as Pierre Lambert, is one of the Grand Old Men of Trotskyism. He was born in Montreuil (on 9 June 1920) on the outskirts of Paris and adopts a rather courteous manner from behind round spectacles and a dapper moustache. He was a Post Office worker in 1935 and joined the Trotskyist group within the SFIO (the *Gauche révolutionnaire* led by Pivert – q.v.) in the same year. In 1938 he was excluded from the SFIO and joined the Parti Socialiste Ouvrier et Paysan (PSOP).

It was as a Resistance fighter that Boussel took the name Lambert. Boussel's political activity after the war was as a social security official in the CGT unions. He was involved in the strikes in Nantes in 1953 and then in the postal strikes of the same year and sheltered Algerian FLN during the Algerian War (this resulted in several months in prison). He had represented the Trotskyists at the Belgrade union conference in 1953 (which resulted in his exclusion from the CGT) and then worked to build up the network of contacts which eventually became the Mouvement pour un Parti des Travailleurs (MPPT). In 1962 he joined the Force Ouvrière union and at the same time worked for the reconstruction of the IVth (Trotskyist) International. For thirty-three

years he was a clerk in the family allowance office in Paris, finally retiring in 1980.

In 1981 Boussel's group called for a vote for François Mitterrand but in 1987 he was nominated MPPT presidential candidate and in 1988 managed to get the 500 local elected officials to sign the nomination. This platform rejected the 'treason' of the 1986–8 'cohabitation' of a left-wing president and right-wing government and called for an immediate 10 per cent increase in wages. The Parti Communiste Internationaliste (which ran the MPPT) polled 0.9 per cent in the 1984 European elections and 0.6 per cent in the Assembly elections of 1986.

Boussel's achievement in getting the 500 elected councillors needed to sign the nomination papers seems to have exhausted the MPPT, whose meetings were badly attended – for example only 120 in Paris on 20 May. The campaign centred on the unity of the workers, Mitterrand's non-respect for the promises of 1981, the Communists' 'amnesia' about the cost to people of hospitalization and the 'boycott' by the media of the MPPT's campaign. Boussel had no friendly words for Juquin (q.v.) – supported by Krivine's Lutte Ouvrier, or Arlette Laguillier (q.v.), the Trotskyist's other 1988 candidate. Boussel was against giving the vote to immigrants 'because it is reactionary' (that is, it integrated them into the system). His 0.38 per cent vote in 1988 (116, 474 votes) enabled Boussel to *re-establish* leadership over a disintegrating party (many ex-Trotskyists joined the Socialist Party) and was the equivalent of the vote for Alain Krivine (q.v.) in 1974.

Bibliography

There is a profile of Boussel in *Le Monde* (20th April 1988).

DSB

BOUTHILLIER, Yves Marie (1901–77)

Yves Bouthillier was born in 1901 at Saint-Martin-de-Ré, and made his career as a civil servant in the *inspection des finances*. He held major administrative posts for financial affairs in local and central government during the inter-war period, and was brought into the government itself as minister of finance in March 1940 by Paul Reynaud (q.v.). After the fall of France, and the establishment of the Vichy State under Philippe Pétain the following July, he was again nominated to the post of minister of finances, where he remained until 1942. It is for this period of his life that he is noted, and even though some historians have questioned the gloss he has placed on events, particularly in relation to collaboration with the Germans, his memoirs of this chapter in France's history are still an important reference for students of the Vichy government. With other prominent Vichy figures, he was arrested by the Germans and deported in 1944; he was also an actor in the trials of the collaborators after the liberation, and was given a three-year sentence. After the war he became public prosecutor with the revenue court (Cour des Comptes), returning to Saint-Martin-de-Ré as mayor from 1959 to 1972.

His elevation to the rank of minister is widely interpreted as consonant with the hostility to politicians characteristic of Vichy. He was one of the 'techniciens' or experts, who considered themselves to be efficient administrators rather than politicians, although the importance of his post meant that he inevitably played a political role. He was a major figure in negotiations with the German authorities over the interpretations of the armistice and the economic relations between the two countries, particularly the exchange rate and the cost of the occupation army. The Germans also sought a substantial stake in France's nationalized companies, and much of his effort went into trying to save France's economy from being taken over by Germany. He advocated a spirit of collaboration as being the most effective means to this end. The very strong inflationary pressures on the French economy were also a constant preoccupation. Hostile to economic liberalism, he was sympathetic to the authoritarian controls Vichy used over the economy, again in the name of efficient administration.

The thesis of a 'good' Vichy represented by Pétain and opposed to the 'bad' Vichy of Pierre Laval has been rather discredited in recent years, but it is certainly true that Yves Bouthillier was Pétain's man, and known not to be sympathetic towards Laval. He was one of a group of ministers who plotted against Laval and succeeded in engineering his removal on 13 December 1940. When Laval returned to power in April 1942, Bouthillier lost his ministerial position, although he later returned to Vichy as an adviser, and played an important part in drawing up a secret 'act of succession', the aim of which was to prevent Laval from succeeding to Pétain.

Bibliography

See Yves Bouthillier, *Le Drame de Vichy*, vol. I, *Face à l'ennemi, face à l'allié* (Paris: Plon, 1950); vol. II, *Finances sous la contrainte* (Paris: Plon, 1951). For Bou-

thillier's role at the Ministry of Finance and in the plot to remove Laval, Alan S. Milward's *The New Order and the French Economy* (Oxford: Clarendon Press, 1970), and Robert Aron, in collaboration with Georgette Elgey, *The Vichy Regime*, trans Humphrey Hare (London: Putnam & Co. Ltd, 1958), are useful.

MA

BOUTMY, Emile Gaston (1835–1906)

Emile Boutmy was the founder of political science as an organized academic field in France. He was from a well-connected, Protestant, bourgeois background, but the premature death of his father left him with family responsibilities which prevented him from entering higher education when he completed his secondary schooling at the prestigious Lycée Henri IV. Through the patronage of his godfather, Emile de Girardin, he became a journalist for the liberal, opposition press under the Second Empire. Among his close contacts during that period, the philosopher, Hippolyte Taine, and the former Orleanist prime minister, François Guizot, were probably the most notable. It was largely through Taine that Boutmy was offered the chair in history of civilizations at a new, privately-funded architectural college, the Ecole Spéciale d'Architecture, in 1865. Both Taine and Guizot were also among the backers who enabled Boutmy to found the Ecole Libre des Sciences Politiques (forerunner of the Institut d'Etudes Politiques and the Ecole Nationale d'Administration) in 1871. Boutmy directed the school until his death in 1906, selected its teaching staff, and helped to foster its climate of conservative, political and economic liberalism.

Part of the impulsion to found Sciences Po (as it came to be nicknamed) was the shock of France's recent defeat in the war with Prussia and the quasi-revolutionary upheaval of the Commune. Boutmy aimed to provide France with a new elite, drawn from the traditional ruling classes, but justifying its pre-eminence through competence in the skills needed to lead society in an era of democratization. The school was thus intended to fulfil a social mission, combining national and class interests, while closing a gap in the higher education system, where there had been no specialist institution bringing together the political, administrative and economic sciences. Boutmy believed the teaching of the school should provide an understanding of the contemporary world through courses sharing a positivistic methodology centred on comparative, historical analysis. Boutmy himself was a disciple of Taine, and his own major works, such as his *Essai d'une psychologie politique du peuple anglais au XIXe siècle* (1901), though less rigidly systematic than Taine's, show a similarly deterministic conception of collective psychology, the factors which condition it, and the institutional forms which it produces.

In practice, although the more general courses shared the approach originally envisaged by Boutmy, the development was towards greater diversity. To survive, the school had to extend its clientele to lower strata of the bourgeoisie, and to offer an increasing number of courses with a more vocational slant. It functioned primarily as a private *grande école* (higher level university) preparing candidates for the entrance examinations giving access to the administrative grades of the civil service. For this purpose, Boutmy hired senior practitioners from the relevant ministries to hand on their specialities. By the mid-1880s it had achieved a near-monopoly of successful candidates taking the entry exam for the elite Civil Service jobs in the Conseil d'Etat, the Cour des Comptes, the Inspection des Finances and the Ministère des Affaires Etrangères. Therefore, while it is true that Sciences Po under Boutmy's directorship included a substantial number of politicians among its teachers, sponsors or graduates – most of them conservative Republicans, such as Léon Say, Alexandre Ribot, Paul Deschanel or Raymond Poincaré – its real importance was as a training ground for state administrators.

Bibliography

In English, see Thomas R. Osborne, *A 'Grande Ecole' for the 'Grands Corps'. The Recruitment and Training of the French Administrative Elite in the Nineteenth Century* (New York: Columbia University Press, 1983), and the same author's 'Social science at the Sciences Po: Training the bureaucratic elite in the Third Republic', *Historical Reflections*, vol. 8 (1981), pp. 58–62. In French, Pierre Favre, 'Les Sciences d'État entre déterminisme et libéralisme. Emile Boutmy (1835–1906) et la création de l'Ecole libre des Sciences politiques', *Revue Française de Sociologie*, vol. 22 (1981), pp. 429–65, is particularly valuable, as is Dominique Damamme, 'Genèse sociale d'une institution scolaire: l'Ecole libre des sciences politiques', *Actes de la Recherche en Sciences Sociales*, vol. 70 (1987), pp. 31–46; and for the official history of the school, Pierre Rain and Jacques Chapsal, *L'Ecole libre des sciences politiques, 1871–1945, suivi de l'école et la guerre, la transformation de son statut* (Paris: Fondation Nationale des Sciences Politiques, 1963).

CF

'BRACKE' (Desrousseaux, Alexandre-Marie) (1861–1955)

Alexandre Desrousseaux was born in Lille on 29 September 1861, the son of the popular singer Alexandre Desrousseaux. Later Alexandre junior was to adopt the name of his mother, Marie Bracke, in public life. His academic ability won him a scholarship to the Lycée Louis-le-Grand secondary school in Paris. In 1884 he graduated first of his year in grammar from the arts section of the prestigious Ecole Normale Supérieure. Whilst working as a tutor in Paris, 1884–5, he studied Greek language and history at the Sorbonne and the Ecole des Hautes Études, and then worked in the archaeology section at the French School in Rome until 1887. After returning to France, he lectured in the arts faculty at Douai and then Lille. In 1891 he moved to the Ecole des Hautes Études in Paris to continue lecturing in Greek language and was promoted to deputy head in 1896 and head of studies in 1915. He continued to lecture there until well into his old age and acquired a considerable reputation as a Greek expert. Bracke was also a Germanist and translated several works of socialist theory from German; he also translated some works from English.

Bracke made his political choice early in life after, it would appear, reading Marx's *Capital* in 1886. Once he moved to Paris he quickly made contact with Jules Guesde (q.v.) and became actively involved in socialist politics in 1898. In December 1899 he acted as secretary at the first General Congress of Socialist organizations in Paris where he was nominated on to the general committee. Between 1900 and 1905 he was a member of the Parti Ouvrier Français's National Council and attended all the POF and Parti Socialiste de France's National Congresses. A deputy secretary of the POF, he became secretary of the PSdeF in 1902. In December 1905, he represented his native Nord department at the second General Socialist Congress (Wagram). During this period he was known as the right-hand man of Guesde. Bracke was involved in preparations for unification of the Socialist movement in 1904–5. He sat on the permanent administrative commission of the unified party 1905–8 and 1914–39. After the Congress of Tours (1920) Bracke remained with the minority but fought against opportunism within the SFIO; for instance, he opposed ministerial participation from 1924 and he campaigned for women's emancipation.

An ardent internationalist (he fought to ensure that the title SFIO was included in the name of the unified Socialist Party), Bracke represented France at many congresses of the Socialist International and at congresses of the German SPD. He was Guesde's deputy on the Bureau of the Socialist International and, after the war, a member of the secretariat of the reconstituted Socialist International based in Hamburg. However, Bracke did not see nation and internationalism as incompatible, and he supported ministerial participation during the First World War.

Bracke's parliamentary career began in 1912, when he was elected deputy in Paris, a seat which he retained until 1924, when he refused to stand on a joint platform with non-Socialists. For Bracke, the Socialist Party could not be other than a class party. He returned to Parliament between 1928 and 1936 and accepted the vice-presidency of the Chamber during the last months of his parliamentary career.

Bracke remained active in the party and as a municipal councillor until the Second World War. He and his wife were arrested by the Gestapo in 1944; he was released after the university intervened, but his wife was not released until the liberation. He remained in close touch with his Socialist colleagues until his death at the age of 94 in December 1955.

Bibliography

Biographical details on Bracke appear in Claude Willard, *Les Guesdistes* (Paris: Editions Sociales 1965), p. 607, Compère-Morel (Adéodat Constant Adolphe), *Grand dictionnaire socialiste du mouvement politique et économique national et international* (Paris: Publications Sociales, 1924), p. 83, and Jean Maitron, *Dictionnaire biographique du mouvement ouvrier* (third part: 1871–1914) (Paris: Editions Ouvrières, 1973–7, vol. XI (1973), pp. 37–40. A dossier on Bracke exists in the Archives de l'Assemblée Nationale.

SM

BRASILLACH, Robert (1909–45)

The son of an officer in the colonial army, Robert Brasillach was born in Perpignan into an established Roussillon family on 31 March 1909. Six years later his father was killed in action in Morocco and, his mother having remarried, the family moved to Sens. A brilliant student, in 1925 Brasillach won a place at the Paris secondary school, Lycée Lois-le-Grand, where his teacher, the nationalist André Bellessort noticed his undoubted talents. He successfully took the entrance examinations for the Ecole Normale Supérieure and took his place there in 1928, in the same 'promotion' as Thierry Maulnier, Paul Guth and Maurice Bardèche, all of whom were to distinguish themselves as right-wing writers (Bardèche, in fact, became Brasillach's brother-in-law and co-author). Not only was Brasillach encouraged by Henri Massis (another of Maurras' influential lieutenants) to contribute material to *La Revue Universelle*, but in 1931, aged only 22, he was also appointed literary critic on the famous nationalist daily newspaper *L'Action Française*; this marked the beginning of a highly active career as a journalist and literary critic.

Already sympathetic to nationalist ideas, the shock of the 6 February anti-parliamentary riots in 1934 reinforced Brasillach's commitment to right-wing thinking and, by 1937, he had taken over as editor-in-chief of *Je Suis Partout*, a notorious and extreme weekly newspaper, in which he was able to give free rein to his pronounced anti-Semitic and pro-Nazi opinions. Believing that France was decadent and that European civilization was on the brink of a crisis, Brasillach turned with increasing conviction towards fascism. A visit to a spectacular Nuremburg rally in September 1937 reinforced his emotional admiration for the achievements of the Nazis; the episode is remembered in a novel published in 1939, *Les Sept couleurs*. With the outbreak of war in 1939, he was mobilized as a lieutenant, was captured and made a prisoner of war in 1940, and then released in April 1941 after the intervention of Admiral Darlan, minister of information in the Vichy government. Upon his release he enthusiastically resumed his activities as a journalist in much of the press, including *Je Suis Partout*, now totally pro-Hitler and unashamedly in favour of collaboration. In August 1943 he resigned, refusing, he said later, to 'further conceal from his readers the critical situation confronting the Axis powers'. After the liberation of Paris, Brasillach was arrested and, during the purge of the collaborators, appeared in one of the most controversial trials of the period. Found guilty of 'intelligence with the enemy', Brasillach was executed by firing squad in the morning of 6 February 1945, aged 35, despite a petition to de Gaulle on his behalf, signed by numerous intellectuals and writers, including François Mauriac, Albert Camus and Paul Valéry.

Politically Brasillach was an admirer of the many established or growing Fascist movements in Europe (especially Mussolini in Italy, Salazar in Portugal, Franco in Spain and Degrelle's 'Rex' in Belgium). He was persuaded by the promise of what he called (in his intellectual autobiography, *Notre avant-guerre*, 1941) a 'new human type'. 'Fascist man' had appeared and had to be nurtured as a natural stage in the evolution of human society. In Brasillach's view democracy had irrevocably corrupted France; he believed that Fascism had to be encouraged there, particularly for the hope it held out to the young people of the country.

Brasillach's case remains controversial. For some his execution represents a just punishment meted out to those who willingly served the Nazi cause through collaboration. For others, however, Brasillach is a martyr who, like the poet André Chénier, ultimately had the interests of the French nation at heart.

Bibliography

Written in collaboration with Maurice Bardèche *Histoire du cinéma* (Paris: Plon, 1935), has been revised and republished many times since and is regarded by some as a classic. *Léon Degrelle et l'avenir de 'Rex'* (Paris: Plon, 1937) gives a sympathetic view of Belgian fascism. *Les Sept couleurs* (Paris: Plon, 1939) is perhaps Brasillach's most interesting novel. *Histoire de la guerre d'Espagne* (in collaboration with Maurice Bardèche) (Paris: Plon, 1939) is a pro-Franco history. *Notre avant-guerre* (Paris: Plon, 1941, 1968 and 1981): an autobiography; the best introduction. *Poèmes de Fresnes* (Paris: Les Sept Couleurs, 1949) are poems written while in captivity and awaiting execution.

There exists a 12-volume edition of the *Oeuvres complètes de Robert Brasillach*, edited and annotated by Maurice Bardèche (Paris: Club de l'Honnête Homme, 1963–6).

Studies on Brasillach:

Sérant, P. (1959), *Le Romantisme fasciste*, Paris: Fasquelle.

Tucker, W.R. (1975), *The Fascist Ego: A political biography of Robert Brasillach*, Berkeley, Cal.: University of California Press.

Vandromme, P. (1956), *Robert Brasillach, l'homme et l'oeuvre*, Paris: Plon.

MC

BRIAND, Aristide (1862–1932)

Aristide Briand was one of the most remarkable politicians of the Third Republic. Eleven times prime minister, a member of the twenty-five governments and in office for a total of sixteen and a half years, he was living proof that an unstable governmental system was compatible with continuity of political personnel. Without the technical or intellectual virtuosity of many of his rivals, he was a superb parliamentary speaker, a consummate political operator and a man of great personal charm. By the end of his life, he inspired great affection among sections of the French political nation. Yet both his career and his legacy attracted much controversy. For the first part of his career he was viewed as an unprincipled opportunist who had betrayed his Socialist origins in the pursuit of office. The charge against his later years was, ironically, exactly the reverse. His enemies accuse him of having allowed himself to become enveloped in a fog of misty, pacifist idealism that left France unprepared to resist the rise of Hitler.

Briand was born in 1862 in Nantes, the son of a café owner, who subsequently moved to St Nazaire. He was educated at the Nantes *lycée*, studied law in Paris and set up in practice in St Nazaire. He wrote for local newspapers, became a municipal councillor, stood unsuccessfully for Parliament in 1889, and came to hold radical, indeed revolutionary views. As a friend of Ferdinand Pelloutier – one of the legendary figures in the history of French syndicalism – he preached the doctrine of the general strike in St Nazaire and subsequently, after a morals charge forced him to leave town, in Paris where he combined revolutionary politics with legal advocacy, defending in court the then antimilitarist Gustave Hervé (q.v.). It is measure of his ideological slipperiness that though by the late 1890s he was close to the Jaurès (q.v.) wing of French socialism, he continued to advocate bullets as well as ballots virtually up to his election as deputy for the working-class constituency of St Etienne (Loire) in 1902. Two years later, he collaborated on the new Socialist daily, *L'Humanité*.

French socialism has always been haunted by the emasculating effects of parliamentarism and in the years before 1914 Briand came to symbolize the corruption that the so-called 'Republic of Pals' could wreak on an ambitious newcomer. Quickly adapting to the techniques and conventions of the Chamber of Deputies, he seized his chance with the bill on the separation of Church and state. He became *rapporteur* of the bill and showed skill and tenacity in preventing the more extreme anticlericals on the left from turning separatism into an anti-Catholic crusade. His evident taste and talent for parliamentary life led to his progressive estrangement from the bulk of his erstwhile colleagues, who, like Jaurès, were prepared to sacrifice short-term government opportunities in the name of Socialist unity. The SFIO was formally created in April 1905. The consensus politics of the *bloc des gauches* was dead and Briand soon demonstrated that he did not intend to see his career prospects buried with it. In 1905 Jaurès was able to dissuade him from entering the businessman's government of Rouvier (q.v.). But Briand told a friend that this was the last time he would obey and a year later accepted the Education Ministry in the Sarrien government. The sometime revolutionary had entered the inner sanctum of French high politics.

Briand was in office for the whole of the 1906 legislature. As minister of education and religion and then of justice under Clemenceau (q.v.) between October 1906 and July 1909 he was thus closely involved in the strikes and disturbances that punctuated the period (schoolteacher syndicalism was a particular problem). At this stage his relations with Clemenceau were good and it was on the latter's advice that Fallières (q.v.) appointed him prime minister in July 1909. In office he soon showed his indifference not only to his Socialist past but also to broader themes of traditional leftist discourse. His speeches denouncing the 'stagnant pools' of single-member constituencies and calling for a consensual, non-sectarian Republic offended Radical susceptibilities and his actions in the 1910 railway strike outraged the Socialists. He conscripted the striking railwaymen in the name of the national interest and provoked a parliamentary sensation when he declared that he would be prepared to break with law in order to defend order. By the time Briand left office in February 1911, he was the sworn enemy not only of the Socialists but of the left wing Radicals who were soon to find a champion in Caillaux (q.v.), a politician whose ambition matched Briand's but who was much less good at concealing it.

In the run up to 1914, Briand was firmly identified with the nationalist, albeit parliamentary, Right, whose other leaders were Barthou (q.v.), Millerand (q.v.) and Poincaré (q.v.) – the latter made him minister of justice and deputy prime minister in his 1912 government. After Poincaré's election to the presidency in 1913 Briand again became prime minister of a government that was defeated, (significantly, in the 'Republican' Senate) over the issue of proportional representation just a week after it had introduced a bill to extend the length of military service to three years. In this last great conflict between the peace-loving left and militarist right in pre-war France, Briand was the leader of the centre right *Fédération des Gauches* against the revived Socialist Radical *entente* of Jaurès and Caillaux.

Thus by 1914 Briand seemed to have turned full circle; the apostle of the general strike was a leader of the war party, agreeing to attend the funeral of the veteran anti parliamentary nationalist Déroulède. He held office as prime minister from October 1915 to March 1917 and thus presided over the grim slaughter of trench warfare in the Somme and Verdun and over the unsuccessful Salonika expedition. By the time he left office, his government had lost all authority. Yet paradoxically the war saw the start of Briand's slow march back to the French Left. While in office, he sought, via intermediaries, to make contact with the German diplomat Lancken over the possibilities of a compromise peace. The negotiations came to nothing and Clemenceau, who came to power in November 1917 on a 'prosecute-the-war' policy, used the threat of their exposure to keep a by now implacable enemy quiet. Briand took no part, and received no acclamation, in the celebration of victory and was excluded from any participation in the Versailles peace negotiations. Yet to be Clemenceau's enemy was not without its advantages to a politician of Briand's subtlety. In 1920 he was able to use his pre-war reputation for religious moderation and Clemenceau's reputation for militant atheism to convince members of the Catholic right that Clemenceau should not be elected president of the Republic. And at the same time, the fiercely anti-Clemenceau Socialists could not but see virtue in their enemy's enemy, particularly given Briand's wartime attempts to stop the carnage through negotiation.

Briand was still sufficiently identified with the right to switch constituencies in 1919 (he moved to his native Loire Inferieure) and to become prime minister in 1921 of a government supported by the conservatives of the *Bloc National*. Yet the shape of his future evolution was clear. In March 1922 he resigned after the unusually assertive President Millerand accused him of being too willing to accept English arguments about the need to negotiate with Germany on economic problems. (His crime was made worse by the fact that he was photographed taking a golf lesson from Lloyd George in Cannes.) His identification with the goal of international reconciliation grew steadily and struck a responsive chord with the democratic left's aspirations for a peace that would last because it was just. By 1925 he was back in office as prime minister – but this time supported by Radicals and Socialists.

He now embarked on the last, and most celebrated, part of his career. Four times prime minister between 1925 and 1929, his real power base lay in the Ministry of Foreign Affairs which he held continuously for seven years – save for twenty-four hours – until January 1932. He became a passionate advocate of peace through reconciliation and sought to end the causes not only of Franco-German enmity but of international conflict in general. He found an ally in the German Chancellor Stresemann and was an architect of the Lucarno Pacts that brought Germany back into the concert of Europe in return for guarantees of her western frontier. Briand was the real inspiration of the Briand-Kellogg Pact of August 1928 that outlawed war as an instrument of national policy and constantly proclaimed that international affairs should be regulated through the 'spirit of Geneva', and the League of Nations. He also in 1929 and 1930 put forward proposals for a form of European union that would harmonize not simply economic interests but political values. Briand was no technician of diplomacy and he was greatly assisted in the formulation of his ideas by career diplomats like Philippe Berthelot and Alexis Léger (q.v.). But there can be no doubt that his were the skills and the charisma that gave the ideas their emotional, and political, force. He was not a utopian – but he became an idealist.

By 1931 it became clear that not only was Briand ageing fast but that the peaceful Europe he had hoped to build was starting to crumble under the twin effects of depression and chauvinism. Stresemann was dead and the proposal for an Austro-German customs union suggested that Briand's optimism about central Europe was the naïvety of near senility. An ambitious ex-protégé, Pierre Laval (q.v.) kept him on as foreign minister but tried to kick him upstairs to the presidency of the Republic. His defeat, at the hands of Paul Doumer (q.v.) was a severe blow to his prestige and his morale. He visited Berlin with Laval (the first official visit by a French leader since 1878) but looked – and was – increasingly feeble. In January 1932 Laval brutally dumped him. He retired to his country home at Cocherel (Eure) but two months later, back in Paris, was dead. He was spared the collapse of his dreams that occurred in the mid-1930s – and also the sight of some of his closest disciples using his pacifistic idealism to justify their collaborationism under the occupation. Only a political system as fluid as the Third Republic could have produced a figure like Briand; half a century after his death he remains, for all his ubiquity, an elusive figure.

Bibliography

Craig, G. and F. Gilbert (eds), (1953), *The Diplomats 1919–1939*, 2 vols, Princeton, NJ: Princeton University Press.
Larkin, M. (1974), *Church and State after the Dreyfus Affair*, London: Macmillan.
Suares, G. (1938), *Briand,* 6 vols, Paris: Plon.

PM

BRISSON, Eugène Henri (1835–1912)

Henri Brisson was a prominent figure in the politics of the first half of the Third Republic. A committed Republican, his career and attitudes are typical of the school of Radical politicians who sought to reshape French national values without transforming France's socio-economic structure. Brisson was born in Bourgès (Cher) in 1835, the son of a lawyer. He studied law in Paris where he became active in Republican politics and journalism, alongside such future luminaries of the Third Republic as Gambetta (q.v.) and Allain-Targé. In 1871 he was elected to the National Assembly for the Seine and remained a parliamentarian (sitting in the Chamber of Deputies) until his death. Originally a leading figure in the opportunist party led by Gambetta, he quickly showed that he stood closer to the intransigent Radicals on the great symbolic issue of anticlericalism (throughout his life he would be a hammer of the religious orders – congregations). He was also a Freemason. With the republicanizing of the Republic, he became president of the Chamber of Deputies in 1881 and this was a position he would hold for a total of fifteen years (1881–5, 1894–8, 1904–5, 1906–12). By contrast, he was prime minister on only two, relatively brief, occasions, once in 1885 when he took over from the deeply unpopular Ferry (q.v.) and consolidated the decisions to annex Tonkin; and again in 1898 for a brief, and unsuccessful, period during the high noon of the Dreyfus affair.

Brisson's ambitions seem to have focused on the presidency of the Republic, for which he stood no fewer than four times (1885, 1887, 1894, 1895). On each occasion he was wholly unsuccessful. He seems to have been a rather stiff and remote figure, though his combination of personal austerity and political reliability made him the ideal figure to chair the commission of inquiry into the Panama scandal of 1892. In the 1890s, the generation of Republicans to which he belonged, alongside Clemenceau (q.v.) and Floquet (q.v.), went into partial eclipse with the emergence of new figures (Poincaré, Barthou) (q.v.) and a growing concentration on social issues. The Dreyfus affair, however, revived the traditional Republican themes and gave Brisson something of an Indian summer. He pursued his old enemy, the congregations, by writing a book about them and was a firm supporter of all the anticlerical reforms of Waldeck-Rousseau (q.v.) and Combes (q.v.). He was also a strong champion of the Radical's favourite general, Sarrail. His last year was spent back in the Chamber presidency and it was characteristic of his reputation that he should have been accused by the right of making the Masonic sign of distress during the noisy debate that followed the 1906 decision to increase the pay of the parliamentarians.

Bibliography

Chapman, G. (1962), *The Third Republic*, London: Macmillan.

PM

de BROGLIE, Jacques Victor Albert, duc (1821–1901)

The duc de Broglie was the foremost of the dukes who achieved political prominence in the first decade of the Third Republic. He came of an ancient, talented and cultivated family which had served the monarchy in many capacities. His father had been a minister and he himself was a diplomat under the July Monarchy. Orleanist in his sympathies, he had resigned his post after the 1848 Revolution and during the Second Empire devoted himself to historical studies and the furtherance of a well-known liberal Catholic paper.

One of many monarchists elected to the National Assembly in February 1871, he was immediately appointed ambassador in London, but, dismayed by the leftward turn of Thiers' direction of affairs, he returned to France in May 1872 and tried to rally the divided and dispirited right-wing groups in the Assembly. Largely responsible for engineering Thiers' overthrow and replacing him by the conservative soldier MacMahon in May 1873, he then headed a ministry which espoused a policy of 'moral order'. In effect he had become the leader of the right in their last serious attempts to block the advance of radical, anticlerical republicanism (which they saw as a menace to Church and state alike) and to keep a way open for a restoration of monarchy. He succeeded in having MacMahon's term of office prolonged to seven years (a long time in politics), but resigned in May 1874 when part of the right failed to support his proposals for a strongly conservative Second Chamber. In 1877, when MacMahon's dismissal of the moderate Republican Jules Simon opened the *Seize Mai* crisis, de Broglie was called upon to form a new cabinet that would restore the fortunes of the right. For this it was essential to secure parliamentary majority. De Broglie therefore dissolved the Chamber of Deputies elected only the year before, but, despite the utmost official pressures exerted in the ensuing elections, the right were defeated and he was soon forced to resign. Active as a senator until he lost his seat in 1885, he subsequently resumed his studies and made important contributions to eighteenth-century diplomatic history.

A shrewd and able man of somewhat sceptical temperament, de Broglie had an almost impossible task. The right were too divided by mutual jealousies and suspicions to be welded into a reliable whole. Their leaders, like de Broglie himself, were often remote from the ordinary voters, many of whom failed to see the need for fresh electoral turmoil, and their organization and propaganda were inferior to those of the Republicans. In 1877 de Broglie loyally responded to MacMahon's call in a situation not of his choice. He had little hope of victory and the consequences of his defeat were far-reaching.

Bibliography

De Broglie's posthumously published memoirs (*Mémoires du duc de Broglie*, 2 vols (Paris: Calmann-Lévy, 1938) are of considerable interest. He has no modern biographer but is well if briefly described in books such as Guy Chapman's *The Third Republic of France* (London: Macmillan, 1962) and R. Rémond's *The Right Wing in France from 1815 to de Gaulle* (Philadelphia: University of Philadelphia Press, 1966). Daniel Halévy's classic study is still of interest *La Fin des notables II. Volume Two: La République des ducs* (Paris: Grasset, 1937).

JPTB

BROSSOLETTE, Pierre (1903–44)

A left-wing journalist before the Second World War, Brossolette was a supporter of the Popular Front, a contributor to the Socialist daily *Le Populaire* and a member of the Socialist Party (SFIO). He was strongly anti-Munich and anti-Nazi, so it was natural that he should join the Resistance in late 1940 through his contacts with Jean Cassou and the Musée de l'Homme group. With his wife he opened a bookshop in the rue de la Pompe in Paris, which became a centre of Resistance activity and he became involved in the foundation of groups such as Libération Nord and L'Organisation Civile et Militaire. He also wrote for clandestine journals including *Résistance*, which he edited, and *Libération Nord*. By December 1941 he was in contact with Colonel Rémy, de Gaulle's main representative in the north and in April 1942 he arrived in London to represent the views of the northern Resistance. He assumed an important position in the Free French movement as one of the earliest Socialists to wholeheartedly support de Gaulle and as a close collaborator of his chief of secret services, 'Passy' (Dewavrin). In March 1943 Brossolette and Passy returned to France with the 'Arquebuse-Brumaire' mission. The aim of this was to unify the northern Resistance in the same way that Jean Moulin was attempting to unite the southern groups. Given Passy's leadership of the Gaullist secret service and Brossolette's loyalties, the northern mission set out to form a military command for the movements of the north and ensure that Gaullist elements dominated, whereas in the south, Moulin was prepared to countenance political leadership of the left.

During April it became clear that Brossolette and Passy were opposed to Moulin's plan for national Resistance unity, including political parties, and a race developed to unify the northern groups before the National Resistance Council (CNR) could be founded. Brossolette returned to London at the end of April 1943, but was back in France by September ('Marie-Claire' mission) to sort out the chaos which had suddenly developed among the northern groups. Although he initially supported the Central Committee of the Resistance – a rival to the CNR which excluded political groups – Brossolette could not deny Moulin's Gaullist credentials and he eventually accepted the CNR as the unified leadership of the domestic Resistance. By January 1944 Brossolette was ready to return to England, but several attempts were aborted and the last, a sea crossing, led to his arrest. Imprisoned in Rennes, he was moved to Paris once the Germans realized what an important resister they had captured. Rather than succumb to torture, he threw himself from the fifth floor of the Gestapo building in the Avenue Foch on 22 March 1944.

Brossolette frequently battled with Moulin, with the Provisional Government's *délégués généraux* – especially Seurelles – and with Moulin's successor in the CNR, Bidault, because he had lost faith in political parties and wanted a military command for the Resistance. He was determined that the Free French in London and the provisional government in Algiers should control the domestic movement and having been Passy's deputy, he always represented the Gaullist viewpoint. Brosselette's importance was as an indefatigable organizer, as a man who helped to build the early movements and who worked to bring the northern Resistance under the aegis of de Gaulle. This was a vital part of the process which legitimized the Free French leader and built his power base in France.

Bibliography

Brossolette, G. (1976), *Il s'appelait Pierre Brossolette*, Paris: Albin Michel.

Noguères, H. (1970 & 1972), *Histoire de la résistance en France*, vols 2 & 3, Paris: Robert Laffont.

Passy, Colonel (1957), *Missions sécrètes en France*, Paris: Plon.

Passy, Colonel (1968), *Souvenirs,* vol. 2, Paris: Editions Raoul Solar.

JCS

BROUSSE, Paul Louis Marie (1844–1912)

Doctor, journalist and Socialist leader, Brousse was born into a bourgeois family in Montpellier. His first involvement in politics came in 1871 when, as a medical student in his home town, he appeared on the administrative committee of Jules Guesde's (q.v.) paper *Les Droits de l'Homme* and was thereby associated with that publication's defence of the Paris Commune. Incensed by the repression of the Paris movement, he became involved with the First International at precisely the moment (1872) when the government was set to ban it and Marx and Engels were set to destroy it. The heat of the disputes between Marxists and Bakuninists saw Brousse, who sided openly with the latter, take refuge in Barcelona, where he came increasingly under anarchist influences. Moving to Switzerland in 1873, he played a visible part in the anarchist Fédération Jurassienne, became a close associate of Kropotkin and gradually moved to a more extreme position, even expounding the doctrine of propaganda by the deed. He was eventually expelled from Switzerland as a result of articles he had written in favour of political assassination.

However, despite this apparent ideological extremism, Brousse was already reflecting on the lessons of the Paris Commune and, as early as 1878, was beginning to elaborate the theory of 'municipal socialism' with which he was to be identified for most of the rest of his career. His early anarchism, once tempered by the quest for practical achievement, thus led logically to a decentralizing reformism based on local politics.

Returning to France after the amnesty in 1880, he passed his final medical exams in Montpellier and set up practice as a doctor in one of the poorest districts of Paris. At the same time, he participated in the nascent Socialist movement and took an early lead, within the Parti Ouvrier, against the statist Marxism then associated with Jules Guesde. It was his polemic with Guesde between 1882 and 1884, during which Brousse coined the expression 'possibilism' (settling for reforms which were immediately realizable) that he rose to national prominence. After the expulsion of the Guesdists from the infant Socialist Party in 1882, Brousse became, along with Jean Allemane (q.v.), de facto leader of the Fédération des Travailleurs Socialistes de France (FTSF). He developed his theory of progressive reformist socialism, concentrating particularly on the potential of municipal socialism: conquest of the municipality offered not only possibilities of practical reform and an education in local self-management, but also a series of decentralized power-bases from which to whittle down the omnipotence of the state. In 1887 he was elected to the Paris Municipal Council, of which he became vice-president in 1888. An ardent advocate of social reforms at local level, Brousse also found himself siding with the radicals in defence of the Republic against Boulangism.

His rapid shift towards Republican alliances with the Radical Party, added to his bourgeois background and lifestyle, sparked a revolt against him by his former comrade Jean Allemane who, in 1890, left the FTSF to set up his own, more 'revolutionary' and *ouvriériste* party. This effectively left Brousse high and dry at a time when the advent of Jean Jaurès (q.v.) as a Socialist leader of real stature would, in any case, have caused his personal star to decline. He was elected as a deputy for Paris in 1906, but lost his seat again in 1910. Both as a municipal councillor and as a deputy, he worked hard on problems of public assistance and health and specialized in legislation concerning psychiatric patients. An ardent Anglophile, he organized, as president of the Paris Municipal Assesmbly in 1905, the Anglo-French 'municipal entente'. Brousse remained with the Jaurès wing of the Socialist Party until his sudden death in 1912.

Bibliography

Maitron, J. (1967), *Dictionnaire biographique du mouvement ouvrier français,* vol. 4, Paris: Editions Ouvrières. See also vol. 11, 1973.

Jolly, J. (1962), *Dictionnaire des parlementaires français,* vol. II, Paris: PUF.

Stafford, D. (1971), *From Anarchism to Reformism: A study of the political activities of Paul Brousse,* London: Weidenfeld & Nicolson.

Humbert, S. (1912), *Les Possibilistes,* Paris: M. Rivière.

JH

BRUNSCHVICG, Cécile (née Kahn) (1877–1946)

Cécile Brunschvicg is best known as a feminist of the inter-war period, but she was also a junior minister in Léon Blum's government of 1936–7. Born in 1877, Cécile Kahn was the daughter of an industrialist. Her father being opposed to girls' education, she took her *brevet supérieur* secretly. In 1899, she married the philosopher Léon Brunschvicg and their four children were born between 1901 and 1919. In the late 1900s, she joined the women's suffrage association Union Française pour le Suffrage Féminin (UFSF), quickly became its secretary-general, and began her lifelong work as an activist for women's rights and practical reform. During the First World War she organized, among other things, lodgings for refugees and the introduction of women factory inspectors. Between the wars, she became a leading figure among suffragists of the moderate Republican tendency, presiding over both the UFSF and the weekly paper *La Française* published by the Conseil National des Femmes Françaises. She had joined the Radical Party in 1924, hoping to promote the idea of women's rights on this somewhat unpromising ground. When, in 1936 Léon Blum asked the Radicals to nominate a woman for one of the three junior ministries he proposed to create, Cécile Brunschvicg was an obvious choice. As under-secretary of state for education, she was concerned with various measures of educational welfare, only some of which came to fruition in the short life of the Popular Front government. She remained active in women's causes until 1940 when she and her husband had to flee from Paris, taking refuge under assumed names in the south, where Léon Brunschvicg died in January 1944. Cécile Brunschvicg survived to see French women vote for the first time in 1945, but died soon after in October 1946.

Cécile Brunschvicg was an indefatigable activist, one of the generation of women who undertook public service during the First World War. As the wife of a Sorbonne professor, she was both comfortably provided for and a member of intellectual Parisian society between the wars, thus acquiring a certain reputation as the 'grande dame' of a feminist movement whose leaders in this period often came, like herself, from the Parisian bourgeoisie. Her politics were not very left-wing (somewhat to the right within the Radical Party) so it is ironic that she should have become a minister under the Popular Front. But she undertook her mission with the zeal and practical reforming spirit she had always shown, taking responsibility for school canteens and clinics, special schools for the handicapped and for the children of deep-sea fishermen.

She was in constant demand both before and after her term of office to give lectures, write articles and organize campaigns on every aspect of women's rights. She firmly believed, as did her husband, that only with the vote would women achieve full civil rights in France, though she shared the fears of republicans that it might benefit clerical parties. Many of her most determined efforts went into practical piecemeal reforms such as the revision of the Civil Code and the admission of women to professions and the civil service. Outside France, she was a well-known figure in the international women's movement, and tributes from many quarters were paid at a memorial ceremony held at the Sorbonne in 1946.

Bibliography

The 1946 tributes, which contain some biographical details, are collected in a small book, *En mémoire de Madame C.L. Brunschvicg,* published privately (Paris, n.d. but 1946). In English, there is some information in S. Hause and A. Kenney, *Women's Suffrage and Social Politics in the French Third Republic* (Princeton, NJ: Princeton University Press, 1984).

SR

BUCARD, Marcel (1895–1946)

Although outside the mainstream of French politics, Marcel Bucard is a perfect representative of an avowedly Fascist tendency in the French extreme right. The Franciste movement, over which he presided from 1933 to 1945, never hid its admiration for Mussolini and Hitler. It preached the construction of a Fascist Europe in the 1930s, and was collaborationist during the occupation. In 1944–5 the few remaining Francistes were integrated into special squads parachuted behind Allied lines by the Germans.

Bucard was born into a prosperous family of horse dealers of St Clair-sur-Epte (Seine-et-Oise). Originally destined for a career in the Church, his life was transformed by the First World War. Much decorated and three times wounded, he rose from the ranks to finish the war as a captain. Like so many others on the far right Bucard devoted the rest of his life to the propagation of the 'spirit of the trenches'. His special ingredient was a cult of violence: 'I love my revolver,' he wrote, 'I shall use it against the vultures and the scum, who, in their lairs and in their

unspeakable newspapers, try to question my honour as a citizen, soldier and father of a family' (*Le Franciste,* 20 January 1935, quoted by A. Jacomet).

After the war Bucard collaborated with André Tardieu (q.v.) the Fédération Nationale Catholique of General Castelnau, and briefly with Georges Valois in the Faisceaux groups. In 1927 he became secretary to François Coty, with whom he helped to organize the Croix de Feu. Bucard launched his own movement, the Francistes, in the summer of 1933. It was explicitly modelled on Mussolini's *squadristi.* He attracted only 8,000 followers. Hostile to rival leagues, they played no part in the 'fascist' riots of 6 February 1934 but their violence, together with the leading role played by Bucard in Mussolini's 'Fascist international', led to their dissolution by the Popular Front government in June 1936. Most adherents deserted to Jacques Doriot's PPF, only a handful supporting abortive attempts to reform the party.

There was no trace of defeatism in Bucard's attitude when war broke out in 1939. Indeed, he re-enlisted. But collaboration was a logical step for the Francistes. In September 1940 Bucard set about the reconstitution of the party. It was to furnish volunteers for the French contingent of the Waffen-SS, and played a part in the enforcement of anti-Semitic measures and in the fight against the Resistance. Its political weight was, however, limited, even within the tiny collaborationist world. Bucard himself suffered increasingly from the effects of wounds received in the First World War, while his lieutenants struggled for control over the party. There was little left of the Francistes when in August 1944 Bucard led them into exile in Germany.

Convicted of 'intelligence with the enemy', Bucard was executed in 1946.

Bibliography

Bucard, M. (1930), *Paroles d'un combattant,* Paris: Les Etincelles.

Bucard, M. (1938), *L'Emprise juive,* Paris: Editions du Coq de France.

Deniel, A. (1979), *Bucard et le francisme,* Paris: Editions Jean Picollec.

Gordon, B. M. (1980), *Collaborationism in France during the Second World War,* Ithaca and London: Cornell University Press, especially chapter seven.

Jacomet, A. (1975), 'Les chefs du francisme: Marcel Bucard et Paul Guiraud', *Revue d'histoire de la deuxième guerre mondiale,* no. 25, January, pp. 45–66.

KP

BUFFET, Louis-Joseph (1818–98)

Louis Buffet was a prominent, if hardly eminent, figure in the French politics of the late 1860s and 1870s; he was one of those conservatives who helped to shape the institutional structure of the Third Republic but found themselves almost immediately outsiders in the new political order. Born in 1818 in the Vosges, Buffet was a lawyer and entered Parliament in 1848 as a progressive conservative (Orleanist), formally accepting the Republic but strongly opposing radicalism. Briefly minister of commerce and agriculture in governments in 1849 and 1851, he opposed the *coup d'état* by Louis Napoleon Bonaparte and retreated in internal exile to his native Mirecourt. He was elected as an independent to the Corps Legislatif in 1864. As a classic liberal, he strongly advocated a balanced budget and in 1869 played a large part in the establishment of the so-called 'Liberal Empire', becoming minister of finance in the government of Emile Ollivier (it was characteristic that he should resign his post over the decision to ratify the new constitution by plebiscite).

He took no part in the Franco-Prussian War but was elected to the National Assembly, again for the Vosges, in 1871. Sitting with the centre-right, he refused the offer of the Finance Ministry in January 1871 and thereafter became a firm opponent of Thiers (q.v.). Voting for all the conservative causes, such as the abrogation of the exile laws affecting members of France's royal families, he was elected president of the National Assembly in April 1873 and was active in the manoeuvres that led to the fall of Thiers and his replacement by MacMahon (q.v.).

Fear of the risks of political uncertainty led him, like many conservatives to vote for the constitutional laws establishing the Third Republic in 1875. In March of that year he had become a highly conservative head of government, and minister of the interior, and he was instrumental in the decision to use the single-member electoral system (*Scrutin d'arrondissement*) rather than the list system favoured by Gambetta (q.v.). An aggressive debater, he failed to be elected a life senator by the National Assembly, largely because of Orleanist–Legitimist hostility; he also failed to win a seat in the Senate and Chamber elections of 1876, despite standing in the latter in four constituencies. He sat with the Senate conservatives, supported (though he was not part of) the de Broglie (q.v.) ministry that followed the so-called coup of 16 May 1877 and spent the rest of his political career resisting the social and political measures that led to the republicanizing of the Republic.

Bibliography

Halévey, D. (1937), *La République des ducs*, Paris: Grasset.

Vapereau, G. (1893), *Dictionnaire des contemporains*, Paris: Hachette.

PM

BUISSON, Ferdinand-Edouard (1841–1932)

As much as any other figure, Buisson articulated, and indeed, personified the values that the Third Republic sought to promote. Throughout his long, and incredibly active life he was a zealous propagandist for the moral code of republicanism – the belief in progress, the cult of patriotism, the search for international harmony and, perhaps above all, the commitment to a secular morality enshrined in *laïcité*. The fact that Buisson was born a Protestant is one, though not the only, factor explaining his intellectual and political development. Buisson's father died young and he had to earn his living as a tutor while preparing for the examination (*agrégation*) in philosophy. On graduating, he refused to take the oath of loyalty to the emperor that was necessary to teach; he went instead to a chair of philosophy in Protestant Neuchâtel in Switzerland where he wrote books attacking the dogmatic religious instruction that was given in schools and participate in international peace conferences attended by, among others, Garibaldi and Victor Hugo (q.v.). With the collapse of the Second Empire he returned to France and was appointed inspector of primary education, a post from which he had to resign following an attack on his supposedly irreligious writings from Bishop Dupanloup (q.v.). He visited Vienna and Philadelphia to study their education systems.

His hour struck in 1879 when Ferry (q.v.) appointed him first inspector-general, and then director of primary education. He thus played a key role in what was perhaps the Third Republic's proudest achievements, the establishment of a system of free, compulsory, secular primary schools which taught factual knowledge and civic humanism. In 1896 he became professor of education at the University of the Sorbonne, having completed a vast thesis on the sixteenth-century Protestant liberal (and enemy of Calvin) Sebastien Castellion. By this time Buisson's protestantism had evolved into a profound commitment to the moral value of *laïcisme* – though he never became a vulgar anti-Christian. The Dreyfus affair galvanized his political energies.

Its polarization of left and right meant that the former vice-president (alongside Déroulède) (q.v.) of the Ligue des Patriotes was one of the founders of the Ligue des Droits de l'Homme. In 1902 he entered the Chamber of Deputies, for a Paris constituency, as a Radical Socialist and supported all the anti-clerical measures of the government of Emile Combes (q.v.). In 1907 he published *La Politique radicale*, a justification of the social and economic progressivism of the Radical Party. He was in some senses the conscience of the party and this, together with his high-minded support for good causes like women's suffrage and proportional representation, probably helps to explain why he never became a minister. Government radicalism had a keen sense of the incompatibility of reformist priority and political advantage. In 1913 he became president of the Ligue des Droits de l'Homme and extended its interest, in a manner reminiscent of the future Amnesty International, to persecuted groups like the Poles, the Austrian Italians, the Jews and the Armenians. After the war, which showed the fundamental patriotism of his brand of progressive republicanism, he became a strong supporter of the League of Nations and in 1926 was awarded the Nobel Peace Prize. He was defeated in 1924 and failed to be nominated by his party (to whom he seemed by now an excessively venerable eminence) for a Senate seat. Nothing could alter the convictions he held as to the universal message of republicanism; and it was probably merciful that he died before the final collapse of the optimism about mankind and progress that had informed his entire career.

Bibliography

Buisson was a prolific Bourgeois writer. Among his works are *Le Christianisme libéral* (Paris: J. Cherbulie, 1986) and *La Politique radicale* (Paris: Giard and Brière, 1908); see also F. Buisson, *Un Moraliste Laïque,* introduction C. Bouglé (Paris: Félix Alcan, 1933) and C. Nicolet, *L'Idée républicaine en France* (Paris: Gallimard, 1982).

PM

C

CACHIN, Gilles Marcel 1869–1958

A Socialist activist of long standing, Marcel Cachin symbolizes the Communist Party's roots in the pre-1914 Socialist movement. He was born to a poor, Catholic family in the Côtes-du-Nord and, after a brilliant school career, studied classics and philosophy at the University of Bordeaux. At Bordeaux, he joined the Parti Ouvrier Français, the sectarian and energetic Marxist grouping led by Jules Guesde (q.v.). He also participated in 1895 and 1890 in a much decried coalition in Bordeaux City Council in which the Guesdists joined forces with nationalist and royalist councillors in order to oppose the Radicals and weaken whatever hold 'bourgeois republicanism' might have on the working-class vote.

He became a full-time worker for the newly-formed SFIO with responsibility for propaganda and moved to Paris, where he wrote regularly for *L'Humanité* and was elected city councillor in 1912 and deputy in 1914 (in 1910 his parliamentary election had been invalidated). In 1914 he was one of the leading lights of the majority wing of the SFIO which supported the war effort and even went to Italy in 1915 to try to persuade his fellow Socialist Mussolini to help bring Italy in on the Allied side. Two years later he visited Kerensky in Petrograd to persuade him to keep Russia fighting, an action which earned him harsh criticism from Lenin's supporters. In October 1917, however, he supported the Bolshevik coup which he hoped would spread to Germany, thus ensuring a French victory in the war. His support led to his being refused a passport to the Socialist International Conference in Stockholm in 1918.

Cachin kept his seat in the 1919 general election and also became editor of the Socialist daily, *L'Humanité*, a post he held nominally until 1957. He and L.-O. Frossard were the two French delegates sent to Moscow in 1920 to investigate the Revolution and hold exploratory talks with the Communist leadership about joining the Third International. He was quickly won over by Lenin and became an enthusiastic supporter of the Bolsheviks, accepting the nine conditions of membership of the Comintern that were laid down in 1920 and the additional twelve that were revealed a little later. He played a large part in the process whereby a majority within the French Socialist Party moved over to the Communist Party in December 1920. A leader of the new party, Cachin witnessed – and accepted – the first Russian-inspired purge of its leadership in December 1922, when his friend Frossard was demoted.

Thereafter his personal career exactly mirrored the fortunes of the PCF. Charged in 1923 with inciting French troops to mutiny and make common cause with the German working class in protest against the occupation of the Ruhr, Cachin defended himself poorly in a parliamentary debate and a scuffle ensued. Although he was eventually cleared of the charge, he was arrested again in 1927 for anti-militarist propaganda and, though still a deputy, served six months in prison. A fervent advocate of the Popular Front strategy he became the first Communist to enter the Senate from which he was expelled in 1939, along with the other Communist parliamentarians during the campaign that followed the signing of the Nazi–Soviet pact. He did not play any significant role in the Resistance and even signed an appeal condemning attacks on German soldiers. Nevertheless, at the liberation he resumed his place as a major Communist dignitary, remaining a member of the Political Bureau until his death. He continued to express absolute confidence in the leadership of Thorez (q.v.) and he never voiced the slightest criticism of the French party's line or of the merits of the Soviet Union.

He was always an effective speaker and his distinctive moustache contributed to his popularity as an attractive ornament of the French Communist Party; but he lacked an independent mind and his role in party decision-taking was in the last analysis a subordinate one.

Bibliography

Fauvet, J. (1977), *Histoire du PCF*, Paris: Fayard.
Robrieux, P. (1980), *Histoire intérieure du PCF*, Paris: Fayard.

JPR

CAILLAUX, Joseph Pierre Marie Auguste (1863–1944)

Joseph Caillaux was virtually coterminous with the Third Republic, not only in the flesh (1863–1944), but also in spirit: we see him as one symbol of progressive bourgeois France, self-confident yet frustrated, universalist in its dreams and yet provincial in its roots, combining secularism with a rigid code of chivalry.

In 1888 Caillaux became an inspector of finances; in 1896 he entered politics. Such a career was inscribed in the logic of his family's historic associations. The Caillaux fortune (an ample but not excessive capital of 1 million francs) was founded by Caillaux's great grandfather, who speculated in property nationalized during the great revolution. The family, already bourgeois, ascended to the revolutionary *haute bourgeoisie*. Eugène, father of Joseph, was a functionary of the Second Empire, before serving in the Orleanist cabinets of MacMahon (q.v.) (1874–6 and 1877). Caillaux *fils* only had to be his father's son to envisage a career beginning in the civil service and transferring into politics. That his 'choice' of a moderate left orientation caused no friction with his moderate right father underlined the continuities. But eventually Caillaux would become a 'conviction politician': how did the man of principle emerge from the family careerist?

In 1896 he entered parliament as a 'staunch' Republican, but initially he had explored entry under the wing of the duc de Rochefoucault-Doudeauville, a less than staunch Republican. The small and very provincial town of Mamers in the Sarthe was to be his constituency – almost a political fief for his entire career.

A year later he was invited by Waldeck-Rousseau (q.v.) to enter the Cabinet as minister of finance. Finance was to be the focus of his ministerial career, as well as of his moderate radicalism. Except for the brief but crucial sojourn as prime minister in 1911–12, the finance portfolio would be the only one he would hold. Between 1898 and 1914 he made the quest for income tax the hallmark of his tenure of office. Almost by accident his period as prime minister coincided with the Agadir crisis of 1911: he brought to its solution his abilities as a financial negotiator. 'Overnight' he began to become a symbol – for the left, proof of the powers of reason in international affairs, for the nationalists, of the disloyalty of international finance. After 1914, he held office but briefly, the final occasion, virtually an anachronism, being only three days in 1935.

Why did he fade out after 1914? The 'aficionado' of the Third Republic's affairs will look for a woman. After a number of 'elegant liaisons' (mistresses, not sauces) Caillaux married: the first marriage (1906) was forced upon him by his then mistress Berthe Gueydan, who 'snookered' him by divorcing her husband. Caillaux's unhappiness was exacerbated by Berthe's ignorance of thrift. He divorced her, and in 1911 married his current mistress, Henriette Rainouard. In March 1914, the second Madame Caillaux shot and unfortunately killed Gaston Calmette, editor of *Le Figaro*. Possibly she also killed Caillaux's political prospects. She was acquitted days before war began, but a taint was to hang over Caillaux. Calmette's campaign was directed aganst Caillaux the tax reformer, but still more the man of Agadir. *Le Figaro*'s publication of erotic letters marks the methods of the nationalist press: French lovers wrote such letters, but French ladies were then allowed to pretend not to receive them – Henriette Caillaux saved her honour as a woman and that honour saved her from prison.

During the war, Caillaux, most cautiously, supported a negotiated peace. His arrest followed the 1917 crisis, when the ultra-Jacobin Clemenceau squashed all peace initiatives. Some of Caillaux's contacts had received German money and were shot for treason. Clemenceau sought to convict Caillaux through his associates. Fortunately for Caillaux, the Senate trial came after the war, and Paris 1920 was not Moscow 1937 or Berlin 1944. The entire left, remembering Dreyfus, rallied round Caillaux. Caillaux was acquitted but forbidden political activity for five years. Caillaux used his pen 'instead'. He denounced the Poincaré policy aimed at massive gold reparations and the political disintegration of Germany. Like Keynes he attacked the economic folly of vast reparations and their destabilizing, revolutionary political consequences. By now, a semi-martyred symbol for the left, the careerist had found his vocation. After the 1924 amnesty his faithful Sarthe electors sent him to the Senate where he would remain for the rest of his career. His recruitment, in 1925, as the *Cartel des Gauches*' minister of finance mingled defiance and faith. The left defied Poincaré and demonstrated faith that Caillaux would lift the debt mountain weighing on France and Europe. If Briand was the political face of the reconciliation symbolised by Locarno, Caillaux was the economic face. Caillaux went to Washington: he failed. The legacy of war could not be banished by 'wizardry'. The budget had to be balanced somehow; Caillaux resorted to increasing indirect taxation, thus destroying the promises on which the cartel had come to power. After its final collapse,

Caillaux was a muted presence, part ghost, part relic. Raised to the Senate in 1929, his last major political act was to deny Blum full financial powers in 1937. The symbol had been severely tarnished, but Caillaux had remained faithful to his deflationist ideal of budgetary rectitude.

In retirement after 1940, Caillaux shunned both Vichy and the Germans: we note the distance between his liberal internationalism and the varieties of Fascist collaboration. He expected the liberation and restoration of the Third Republic. Death in November 1944 left his beliefs intact.

Our *aficionado* of the Third Republic should instantly recognize Caillaux's photograph. The face, superbly moustached, fronts a bald Gallic cockerel: it unites a certain idea of a raffish Third Republic politician with the legendary Frenchman of the music-hall – just the man whose second wife shot the editor of *Le Figaro*. Those shots marked the beginning of the end: Caillaux would lose a pre-eminence, held particularly from 1911 to 1914, and decline to little more than a symbol. We ask: had not the high tide of the radical bourgeoisie come and peaked by 1914? If so, Caillaux was a victim of what he symbolized. We might suspect that Henriette Caillaux's revolver merely anticipated the verdict of history: the shots which really sent Caillaux downhill were those fired at Sarajevo.

Caillaux, on the contrary, after 1914 repeated and embroidered a counter-factual scenario: had he been in office in July 1914, war would not have happened. Just as in the Agadir crisis, he would have tamed German arrogance without humiliating German pride.

Our interpretation of Caillaux's role in French politics will therefore take three steps. First, we present his vision of the Third Republic and its role in world affairs; secondly we analyse his argument that he could have harnessed both the forces of and threats to liberalism to ensure uninterrupted progress. We have already acknowledged that Caillaux's vision was a fantasy, heavily tinged with personal vanity. Our final step relates Caillaux's fantasy to the unresolved tensions between universalism and provincialism in the political and social constituency of French radicalism. Ultimately, therefore, Caillaux, the most perspicacious of the Radicals, exemplifies their failure to grasp the European crisis unleashed in 1914.

Caillaux's arguments were based on the May 1914 elections: these consolidated the parliamentary preponderance of the left. *Retrospectively*, he envisaged a Caillaux–Jaurès partnership dominating French politics, ushering in an era of social reform, based on European concord. In Caillaux's bourgeois-humanitarian dream, a united Western Europe, cleansed of Prussian militarism and French chauvinism, would extend its civilizing gifts to its African and Asian colonies. Caillaux, we note, was no friend of despotism ruled by the Camarilla of a weak-minded tsar. Caillaux saw Russia as the key to war in 1914: the plot which drowned hope in blood was forged between Isvolsky (Russian ambassador to France) and President Poincaré. The social forces behind the plotters were a handful of 'feudals' – French oligarchs unwilling to let Caillaux's proposed income tax touch their wealth, joined with the servitors of the tsar. The two champions of peace, Caillaux and Jaurès, were marked for destruction. *Le Figaro*'s campaign removed Caillaux; when Poincaré, unsupervised by Caillaux, had ripened his plot, Jaurès was killed.

Caillaux's scenario reads like a primitive French version of the Fischer thesis of German responsibility for the First World War: an overlapping elite of land and money manipulates nationalism as a counter to the progress of political and social democracy – war is their gamble. But Caillaux's obsessive affirmation of conspiracy with himself as victim no. 1 indicates the mental horizons of French parliamentary radicalism. The vagueness of the institutional features in the conspiracy alleged by Caillaux is a counterpart to the homogeneity of the Third Republic when compared to Willhelmine Germany. Given the Republican culture of France, the absence of a *junker* class or Wotanesque industrialists, Caillaux saw war as the outcome of a personal duel between himself and Poincaré. Caillaux's devotion to parliamentary combinations was a corollary of the weakness of organized political parties. We noted that Mamers was effectively his 'fief' – within the Radical Party he behaved like a 'feudatory' rather than an official. Before 1914 he had intrigued with Clemenceau or Poincaré quite willingly if that would arrange a ministerial majority. The psychological accompaniment to Caillaux's conspiratorial world-view was vanity: as Caillaux aged, it degenerated from arrogance to light-headed fury.

We are tempted to read vanity into Caillaux's manoeuvres against the Popular Front. Resentment against Blum, who had opposed his demands for full fiscal powers in 1925 may have prompted his role in 1937. But the vanity expresses the practitioner of parliamentary combinations. What sense could the politics of streets and factories make to a man who saw himself as a statesman of the *ancien régime*? One might as well expect Necker to have been Mirabeau or Danton. His belief that class conflicts could be smoothed out by parliamentary combinations and tax reforms gels with belief that he could have secured peace in 1914. The Jaurès whom Caillaux admired was a gentlemanly dreamer of utopias: an 'idealist' necessarily subordinate to the 'realist' Caillaux in the parliamentary game. (The utopias were just nowhere lands.)

Socially, Caillaux's break with the Popular Front represented the clash of two 'Frances', Caillaux's provincial France of peasants and artisans, and the France of the factories. Caillaux's radicalism posited a real France, eternal and progressive, precisely and only because he did not take the other seriously. Characteristically, Caillaux was not 'anti-Communist' after 1917 – the Bolsheviks, he thought, were basically children: they would grow up and return to common sense. Common sense excluded all violations of good budgetary management such as Keynesian expansionism. Caillaux never grasped that Jaurès – or Blum – had to deal with people who took any such nonsense seriously. Communism, the Popular Front, like pre-1914 syndicalism, were so many *Frondes* against the real France of peasants, artisans and small businesses.

We pictured Caillaux as a self-confident, clever politician: he glimpsed the tidal waves of 'history' lapping around France as Poincaré or Clemenceau could not. Until 1914, he was in his element, but once his word began to crumble he could see no other solution than to restore the world he had lost. His Europeanism looked back, not forward: rightly, if harshly, 'history' remembers Caillaux the husband of Henriette, and forgets the precursor of Europeanism.

Bibliography

There is no full biography in English. Caillaux wrote a three-volume autobiography, *Mes Mémoires* (Paris: 1942–7). His disciple, Emile Roche, wrote *Avec Joseph Caillaux: mémoires, souvenirs et documents* (Paris: Publications de la Sorbonne, 1980). The most complete scholarly treatment is J.C. Allain, *Joseph Caillaux*, 2 vols (Paris: Imprimerie Nationale, 1981). See also S. Berstein, *Histoire du parti radical*, 2 vols (Paris: FNSP, 1980–2); R. Binion, *Defeated Leaders* (Westport, Conn.: Greenwood Press, 1975).

MK

CAMBON, Jules Martin (1845–1935)

Born in Paris on 5 April 1845 Jules was the younger brother of Paul Cambon, and like him became a respected administrator and one of the best known diplomats of the Third Republic. Jules' career followed an identical path to Paul's. He graduated in law, was called to the Paris Bar in 1866 and following the Franco-Prussian War (1870–1), in which he served as a captain, he moved into the civil service. He was appointed prefect in Constantine (Algeria) in 1878, then secretary-general of the prefecture of Paris, followed by prefect of the departments of the Nord (1882) and Rhône (1887) finally returning to Algeria as governor-general in January 1891. Like his brother he was made ambassador, first to the United States (October 1897) and then to Spain in 1902. His last ambassadorial appointment was to Germany in 1907 where he remained until the outbreak of the war. In 1915, he became secretary-general of the Foreign Ministry. In 1919 he was made one of the five-men French delegation at the Versailles peace conferences where he served as chairman of the commissions for Greek, Czech and Polish affairs. After signing the Peace Treaty in 1919 he was made chairman of the ambassadors' conference but retired in 1922. It was an active retirement devoted principally to writing, his talents having been recognized in this area by his election in 1918 to the French Academy. He died at Vevey (Switzerland) on 19 September 1935.

Though perhaps more intelligent than Paul, Jules always lived in the shadow of his brother. But his modest, retiring manner belies major achievements. After a conspicuously successful term in Algeria where he replaced direct rule by greater decentralization, his period in the United States gained him an international reputation for having mediated in the Hispano-American War and for having brought about the Peace Treaty of 1898. It was only natural that his next appointment should be to Madrid, where he improved Franco-Spanish relations and played an important role in the international Algeciras conference to settle in particular Franco-German differences over Morocco. But it is as ambassador to Berlin that he played his greatest and perhaps least known role in attempting to bring about Franco-German détente. Though this policy was persistently opposed by nationalist permanent officials in the French foreign ministry and overseas it had many successes in settling Franco-German diplomatic incidents and bringing about colonial settlements between the two countries, such as the 1909 Moroccan and 1914 Ottoman Empire Agreements. His policy towards Germany, based on firmness yet conciliation, may have been designed in the long run to bring off the diplomatic coup of convert ing an enemy into a friend that had crowned his brother's life's work. The fact that Germany declared war on France on 3 August 1914 ensured that Jules Cambon's reputation continued to be overshadowed by his brother's.

Bibliography

In English see Geneviève Tabouis, *The Life of Jules Cambon* (London: Jonathan Cape, 1938). For a description of his policy towards Germany, see J.F.V. Keiger, 'Jules Cambon and Franco-German détente, 1907–14', *The Historical Journal*, vol. 26, no. 3 (1983), pp. 641–59.

JFVK

CAMUS, Albert (1913–60)

Albert Camus's career as a leading creative writer and political commentator flowered during the middle decades of the twentieth century. His international reputation as a moral figurehead of the non-Communist left was reflected in the award of the Nobel Prize for literature in 1957. Before his death in a road accident in 1960, his political reputation went through three main phases. The first and least problematic of these arose from Camus's involvement in the French Resistance movement during the Second World War. The aura of moral heroism associated with the struggle against fascism carried over in the eyes of his admirers to the cold war period, when Camus became a fierce opponent of Soviet Communism. It was during this period that, in 1952, he quarrelled publicly with Jean-Paul Sartre, a fellow-writer and former Resistance activist who was by then sympathetic to the French Communist Party. Sartre was among those who argued that Camus was becoming politically ineffectual as a result of abstract moralizing and narrow literary concerns. At the time of his death, Camus's political reputation had entered its third and most damaging phase, dominated by his equivocal stance on the Algerian war of independence (1954–62).

Algeria's indigenous Muslim inhabitants had been brought under French rule during the nineteenth century. Camus was born in 1913 into a poor working-class family among the white settler (*pied noir*) community there. He joined the Algerian Communist Party in 1935, and left it two years later in circumstances which have never been fully explained. After beginning a career in journalism, he emerged from the obscurity of colonial North Africa

when he moved to France during the Second World War. In 1943, he began to work for the clandestine Resistance newspaper *Combat*. By the time France was liberated the following year, he had taken over as editor of *Combat*, and his journalistic commentaries continued to command widespread attention during the immediate post-war period.

During the 1930s he had broken ranks with most of the *pied noir* community by advocating reforms which would have benefited Algeria's Muslims, but he always opposed the idea of independence from France. When Muslim nationalists bent on independence launched a guerilla war in 1954, Camus refused to support it and eventually retreated into silence on the issue. His critics regarded this as proof at the very least of his political impotence and at worst of his complicity with the politically reactionary *pieds noirs*.

Bibliography

Informative biographical studies include Herbert Lottman, *Albert Camus* (London: Weidenfeld & Nicolson, 1979) and Patrick McCarthy, *Camus: A critical study of his life and work* (London: Hamish Hamilton, 1982); Germaine Brée, *Camus and Sartre* (London: Calder and Boyars, 1974) offers a politically sympathetic assessment of Camus; while Conor Cruise O'Brien, *Camus* (London: Fontana, 1970) highlights the more problematic aspects of his Algerian roots. There is a useful editorial introduction in Jonathan H. King (ed.), *Albert Camus, Selected Political Writings* (London: Methuen, 1981).

AGH

CANDACE, Gratien (1873–1953)

Gratien Candace was born on 18 December 1873 in Bailliff (Guadeloupe) to a family of planters. He was a brilliant student at the secondary school – Ecole Primaire Supérieure – of Basse-Terre. At 18 he was a teacher in a town on his native island and as a school inspector he went to Toulouse to continue his studies at the teacher training college – Ecole Normale d'Instituteurs. (He also took courses in the agricultural college.) As a graduate in science he was part of a delegation sent to North Africa to organize agriculture. Another delegation to the British Antilles enabled him to compare the British and French practice in the Caribbean.

He was a member of the Socialist Party and from 1906 to 1909 assistant head in René Viviani's private office at the Ministry of Labour. From 1910 to 1911 he taught at the Ecole Professionelle in Creil (Oise). Candace submitted articles to the influential Radical daily *Dépêche de Toulouse* and was editor of *La Justice*. On 10 February 1912 he was elected deputy for Guadeloupe and represented the constituency until 1942.

Despite his age he enlisted in 1914 but was recalled to parliament where he founded, with Henri Bérenger, 'Le foyer Colonial du combattant' and 'le Comité d'aide et assistance Coloniale'. After the war with Henri Bérenger and Alcide Delmont he founded the French Colonial Institute (L'Institut Colonial Français) and headed, in the Colonial Union, the section for French colonies in the West Indies and the Pacific. In 1930 he published *Marine marchande française, son importance dans le vie nationale*, for which he received the *grand prix* from L'Academie de Marine. He also founded the journal *Colonies et Marine* in collaboration with Henri Bérenger.

In June 1932 Edouard Herriot made him his secretary of state for the colonies, a portfolio he kept in the Paul-Boncour government: during this seven months in government he was able to start the French banana boat fleet.

In 1936 Candace was one of the stars of the tricentennial celebrations of the annexation of the Antilles by France and a small book was dedicated to him. Elected deputy speaker of the Assembly in 1938, he voted full powers to Marshal Pétain and in 1940 became a member of the National Council of the French State.

He retired from active politics when the Vichy government was in power and died in Lormaye (Eure-et-Loir) on 12 April 1953. In the obituary sketch of him in the Académie des Science d'Outre Mer, Henry Lemery noted that throughout his life Gratien Candace was an intransigent patriot seeing France is a 'protector of the weak', the 'emancipator of peoples' and the 'most humane of motherlands'. These patriotic views, it need hardly be underlined, were then the main credo of Antilles' elites.

Bibliography

See J. Binoche on Gratien Candace in *Hommes et Destins*, vol. II, pp. 171–3 (Paris: Académie des Sciences d'Outre-mer, 1975).

RC

CAPITANT, René (1901–70)

A law professor and politician, Capitant was a member of Léon Blum's private staff in the 1936 Popular Front government, helped to found the 'Combat' resistance movement in North Africa in 1941, before being appointed education minister in de Gaulle's provisional government in Algiers (1943). In 1955 he founded (with Louis Vallon) the small and uncomfortably-placed left-wing Gaullist party, L'Union Démocratique du Travail, UDT (Democratic Labour Union), of which he was to be a leading figure until it merged with the main Gaullist party, L'Union pour la Nouvelle République, UNR (Union for the New Republic) in 1962. For some years he was chairman of the influential legislation committee of the National Assembly. During the events of May 1968, he resigned his seat in the National Assembly in order not to have to support a vote of confidence in Prime Minister Pompidou, and three days later, on de Gaulle's insistence, he was appointed minister of justice in Pompidou's Cabinet reshuffle. In April 1969, he resigned as a result of de Gaulle's referendum defeat and resignation.

His political beliefs, expressed in the columns of the UDT paper, *Notre République*, are marked by unfailing loyalty to de Gaulle and his ideas and to Gaullist institutions; he was a staunch supporter not only of colonial emancipation and Gaullist foreign policy but also of direct democracy, democratic planning and worker/capital association or 'participation'. In the 1960s he showed increasingly overt hostility towards de Gaulle's first two prime ministers: he criticized Michel Debré for placing obstacles in the way of Algerian independence and Georges Pompidou for what was, in Capitant's eyes, a betrayal of true Gaullism: conservative economic and social policies, subservience to the Employers' Federation and reluctance to introduce real reforms in respect of worker participation. Although it is perhaps with the latter idea that the name of René Capitant (and that of his fellow left-wing Gaullist, Louis Vallon) is most readily associated, it has been suggested that de Gaulle's genuine if rather vague views on this subject owed less to Capitan and to Vallon than to his deep-seated mistrust of the capitalist class and to ideas on the social role of the industrialist and of the Army officer that had been prevalent in France in the early twentieth century.

Although the impact of de Gaulle on left-wing electors cannot be denied (it has been estimated that 3 million left-wing electors voted for de Gaulle in the 1965 Presidential election), 'left-wing Gaullism' – or Gaullist 'social democracy' – must be seen as failure in the inability of its supporters (the UDT was only one of several similar organizations) to form a politically significant group or to influence substantially the policies of the main Gaullist party. It has been said of René Capitant that he was 'more Gaullist than de Gaulle', and the latter is reputed to have said to him: 'Capitant, you are too honest!' These two comments sum up perhaps one of the more independent and engaging political figures of the Gaullist era.

Bibliography

A selection of Capitant's *Nouvelle République* articles has been published, with a substantial introduction by Louis Vallon, in *Ecrits politiques (1960–1970)* (Paris: Flammarion, 1971). He is one of the Gaullists studied in Pierre Viansson-Ponté's *Les Gaullistes, rituel et annuaire* (Paris: Seuil, 1963), and the Institut Charles de Gaulle has devoted a special number of its journal, *Espoir*, to Capitant, no. 36 (Paris: Plon, 1981). See also: J. Touchard, *Le Gaullisme (1940–69)* (Paris: Seuil, 1978), and J. Charlot (*Le Phénomène gaulliste* (Paris: A. Colin, 1970), translated into English as *The Gaullist Phenomenon* (London: George Allen & Unwin, 1971).

HE

CARNOT, Marie François Sadi (1837–94)

Grandson of the hero of the French Revolution Lazare Carnot and son of a Republican minister of 1848, Sadi Carnot was born into a family of illustrious politicians and scientists. A talented public works engineer, he was appointed prefect and extraordinary commissar of the Republic by Gambetta in January 1871 with the specific brief of organizing the defence of western France against Prussian invasion. Within a few weeks, he resigned from that post and ran for election to the National Assembly the following month, and was one of the 107 deputies who voted against the Treaty of Frankfurt which imposed the loss of Alsace-Lorraine on France. This marked the beginning of an uninterrupted parliamentary career, when he was successfully returned to the Chamber of Deputies in the elections of 1876, 1877, 1881 and 1885 as deputy for the Côte d'Or department. Notwithstanding his competence, which earned him several ministerial posts in public works and finance, his notoriety might not have rippled much beyond the Palais Bourbon and his own constituency (where he was also president of the *conseil*

général), had he not been elected, almost by accident, President of the Republic in December 1887.

A reserved, shy and rather unbending man, apparently better suited to committee work than to the glitter of parades and society gatherings, Sadi Carnot seemed an odd choice as a candidate for the presidency. Indeed, this ultra moderate Republican was elected, without any regard to his own merits, as a result of manoeuvring by Clemenceau (q.v.) who thus successfully blocked the election of his arch enemy Jules Ferry. The election had been called after the enforced resignation of Jules Grévy, whose son-in-law had traded in official decorations. Having thus acceded to the presidency in somewhat inauspicious circumstances, Sadi Carnot had to face some of the stormiest and most violent events of the Third Republic.

Within a few weeks of his settling in, there unfolded the first serious challenge to the Republic through the meteoric rise of General Boulanger (q.v.), culminating in an aborted march on the Elysée on 27 January 1889. The Republic was saved by default, and its resilience was further tested throughout Carnot's term of office which was punctuated by ten ministerial crises, a financial scandal of cataclysmic proportions, labour unrest and anarchist outrages which culminated in his own assassination in Lyons on 24 June 1894. The most politically damaging of these episodes was undoubtedly the Panama scandal, a sorry story of bribes to prominent parliamentarians who vaunted the merits of the doomed enterprise in order to encourage private investment, causing considerable funds to be literally sunk in the apparently bottomless marshes of Panama. A violent press campaign disparaged parliamentary ways and gave considerable muscle to *La Libre Parole*, the newspaper of the extreme right-wing and anti-Semitic publicist Drumont (q.v.), who contributed massively to raising the level of intolerance of Third Republican politics.

Carnot did not, however, merely weather these troublesome episodes. He presided over, and indeed took an active part in varied achievements of the Republic. Anxious to enhance the prestige of the presidency, he not only travelled extensively through France, including the hapless visit to Lyons which cost him his life, but he inaugurated with some panache the 1889 exhibiton. This celebrated the centenary of the French Revolution and was dedicated to French industry, with the Eiffel Tower the most prominent of a number of architectural and engineering showpieces, lit up at night by electricity. Very keen to put an end to France's diplomatic isolation, he personally encouraged the *rapprochement* with Russia, a negotiation made somewhat delicate by Alexander III's distaste for a republic, but which nevertheless led in 1892 to a military agreement between the two governments as a first step towards a defensive alliance. Finally, Carnot presided over the Republic's political coming of age, not just by surviving the commotions of the various scandals, but by witnessing the about-face of the Catholic Church, the signal for 'rallying' the Republic being spectacularly given by Pope Leo XIII in an encyclical published in French.

Little was expected of Sadi Carnot when he was elected, and indeed the years of his presidency had a momentum of turbulence which he could do little to control, and to which he himself fell victim; but he turned a sinecure into an influential office, and endowed the Republic with much needed poise to overcome the turmoils to which it was then subjected.

Bibliography

Clio has not been very generous towards Sadi Carnot, who barely gets passing references in most books dealing with the Third Republic, either in French or in English. A fairly detailed but perfunctory account of Carnot's career appears in Dominique Frémy, *Quid des présidents* (Paris: Robert Laffront, 1981).

AM

CASANOVA, Danièle (Danielle) (1909–43)

A Corsican, born Vincentella Périni, Casanova adopted the name Danièle (also commonly spelt Danielle). A dentist by profession, and married to the Communist, Laurent Casanova, she was a lifelong and devoted activist of the Communist Party, elected to the central committee of the youth organization (Jeunesse Communiste) in 1932. Despite some initial resentment within that group, she, Claudine Chomat, Marie-Claude Vaillant-Couturier and Jeannette Vermeersch formed a women's youth organization, Union des Jeunes Filles de France, in 1935 whose committees were active in giving support to the 1936 French strikers and the Republicans in the Spanish Civil War. After the dissolution of the Communist Party in 1939, Casanova shared the direction of the party's clandestine women's organization which became the Union des Femmes Françaises, setting up local committees and using the material difficulties which women faced as a means

of stimulating general discontent. After the summer of 1941, in her position as a Jeunesse Communiste leader, she helped to organize armed groups of partisan fighters. In February 1942 she was arrested in a major Gestapo round-up along with many other Communists. She was imprisoned in La Santé and the Fort of Romainville before being deported to Auschwitz in January 1943, part of a group of some 230 women, of whom only forty-nine were to return. In May 1943 Danièle Casanova died in Auschwitz of typhus.

Danièle Casanova is widely revered as an undoubted heroine of the French Resistance, posthumously awarded the Legion of Honour. A Paris street was named after her, and the Mauroy government issued a stamp dedicated to her in 1983. For the French Communist Party in particular she is the archetypal Communist martyr, and was regularly compared, in post-war Communist publications, with Joan of Arc. A series of *hommages* to the memory of Danièle Casanova have been held by the Party, and there is a painting (1950) by the artist Boris Taslitzky of 'The Death of Danièle Casanova'.

In paying such marked attention to Danièle Casanova, the Communist Party was underlining its case that it had been involved in some form of continuous Resistance activity since the outbreak of war. The party's adulation of Casanova should however be seen in the context of its official histories of the Resistance, e.g. *Le P.C.F. dans la Résistance* (Paris: Editions Sociales, 1967), where the place accorded to women resisters has been surprisingly slight.

Bibliography

A biography by S. Téry, *Danielle* (New York: International Publishers, 1953), has been translated by Helen Simon Travis. M.L. Rossiter, *Women in the Resistance* (New York: Praeger, 1986) has a brief mention of Danièle Casanova. See also, R. Rousseau, *Les Femmes rouges* (Paris: Albin Michel, 1983), and H. Bidouze *et al.* (eds), *Les Femmes dans la Résistance* (Paris: du Rocher, 1977).

HF

CASANOVA, Laurent (1906–72)

Laurent Casanova ('*Le Cardinal*') was one of those *éminences rouges* without whom the PCF could not have functioned as the exceptional party it once was.

Born to a revolutionary Socialist family in Algeria,

he joined the PCF in 1928. In 1934, after military service, he was entrusted with the clandestine anti-military section. Thereby he came in close personal contact with Thorez (q.v.). When, in 1936, the Comintern's Popular Front strategy liquidated such activities, Casanova became Thorez' direct subordinate.

The Comintern sent him on special mission to Moscow in 1939. On his return he was mobilized; captured by the Germans, he escaped in 1942. He resumed contact with the Resistance in Paris through Claudine Chomat, later the second Madame Casanova.

After the liberation he became a deputy (Seine et Marne), minister (for ex-servicemen), member of the party's Central Committee and, in 1947, the Political Bureau. His task, mapped at the Strasbourg Conference of June 1947, was to direct the party's ideological struggle by reorganizing its relationship with the house intelligentsia. The specific problem was to demonstrate total loyalty to Marxism–Stalinism while retaining the Resistance's idealization of France. At first Casanova encouraged the *cercles de critiques* which provided intellectuals with a semi-autonomous forum. But as the Zhdanov offensive unfolded, the intellectuals were sent back to the (party) cells. Their Frenchness was not repudiated, but Casanova emphasized their place in the ideological war between proletarian science and bourgeois ideology. In 1948–9 he organized support for Lyssenkoism, supervised the silencing of the idealists who later created *Arguments*, and yet preserved some autonomy for the PCF's ideological apparatus. In 1950 he replaced Tillon (q.v.) in charge of the Peace movement. 'Casa' well earned his soubriquet 'Le Cardinal'.

In 1956, after Kruschev's secret speech, 'Casa' decided the moment had come: the dialectic in its course demanded de-Stalinization and his special relationship with 'Maurice' made him the proper messenger. Encouraged by Kruschev, Casanova and Servin demanded the public repudiation of Stalin's 'crimes' and an analysis of the new phase of capitalism, in which revolution came from social, not economic contradictions. After 1958 Casanova identified Gaullism as a national adaptation to neo-capitalism, not regression to fascism – and argued the need to join the Algerian struggle.

Opposed by Jeanette Vermeersch, 'Casa' envisaged a campaign for the 'king's ear' (Thorez), not a political battle. In 1960 he received the Lenin prize. Thorez replied by breaking Casanova's hold over the Communist Youth in 1960, and in 1961 removing Casanova and Servin from the leadership.

The fall-out among Casanova's student following was a major aspect of the PCF's contemporary ideological collapse. Casanova remained bitter but loyal.

'Casa' exemplified 'L'Homme communiste'. His two marriages articulated the ideal of Communist coupling. Before 1960 the Casanovas, joined in friendship with 'Maurice and Jeanette' and 'Louis and Elsa' (Aragon) embodied French communism as an infinite progression of committed couples. He died a servant of 'Le Parti'.

Bibliography

There is no biography but his former disciples have penned portraits: see Pierre Daix, *J'ai cru au matin* (Paris: Robert Laffont, 1976) and *Les Hérétiques du P.C.F.* (Paris: Robert Laffont, 1980), Philippe Robrieux, *Thorez, vie secrete et vie publique* (Paris: Fayard, 1975) and *Histoire intérieure du parti communiste*, vol. II (Paris: Fayard, 1981). Casanova's epistles to the intellectuals were gathered in *Le parti communiste, les intellectuels et la nation* (Paris: Editions Sociales, 1949).

MK

CASIMIR-PÉRIER, Jean-Paul-Pierre (1847–1907)

Casimir-Périer was a member of one of the great political and industrial dynasties of the nineteenth century, the equivalent in some ways of the English Whigs. His grandfather was a senior minister in the July Monarchy, his father demonstrated his commitment to constitutional liberalism by his resolute opposition to the political system of Napoleon III.

Casimir-Périer's first experience of public life was as political secretary (*chef de cabinet*) to his father in the Thiers (q.v.) government and he entered the Chamber of Deputies in 1876 as representative of his native department of the Aube. His high-principled constitutionalism led him to oppose the actions of the de Broglie government after the 16 May 1877; his equally high-principled sense of honour led him in 1883 to resign his parliamentary seat in protest against the measures that deprived the Orleanist princes of their military ranks. He was immediately re-elected and in 1885, after a short period as under-secretary for war, became vice-president of the Chamber of Deputies.

The 1893 elections saw the arrival of a strong Socialist group in the Chamber but the majority was conservative and Casimir-Périer became first president of the Chamber and then, for a six-month period, prime minister. His government saw the creation of the Ministry of Colonies but made most impact for the introduction of a series of measures (known as the 'wicked laws' – *loi scélérates*) designed to cope with a series of anarchist outrages. It was these measures that would be responsible for promoting – but also destroying – his career. What to the right seemed evidence of firmness, was to the left evidence of the repressiveness of the class interests which he, more than anyone else, symbolized. On the defeat of his government, he was immediately re-elected president of the Chamber and was then well placed to succeed to the presidency of the Republic after the assassination of Carnot (q.v.). On 27 June 1894 he was elected president, obtaining 451 votes against 195 for the Radical Brisson (q.v.) and 97 for the Centrist Depuy (q.v.). The unimpressive margin of his victory marked an ominous beginning to a seven-year term (*septennat*) that would last only six months. He was quite unable to win the respect of his political opponents and became the victim of a violent press campaign from the left, who denounced both his background and his behaviour. Prominent socialists like Millerand (q.v.) and Jaurès (q.v.) led the attack. When another journalist–politician, Gérault-Richard, was prosecuted for defaming the president, Jaurès defended him in court and launched an enormous attack on Casimir-Périer and on the class which he represented. Sentenced to a year's imprisonment, Gérault-Richard was promptly elected to Parliament in a sensational Paris by-election. Beneath a somewhat bulldog appearance, Casimir-Périer was in fact extremely sensitive and by January 1895 he had had enough: he quit not simply the presidency but political life altogether. In his post-election address, he had stressed the constitutional rights which the presidency possessed. He was later to reveal that as president his ministers had refused to keep him informed on matters of public policy (including such central issues as the Dreyfus affair) and that his foreign minister would not even show him diplomatic telegrams.

The political career of Casimir-Périer was short and his achievements were few. Yet he is a not insignificant figure in the development of the political culture of the Third Republic. His tenure of the presidency consolidated its reputation as a weak institution and the controversy that raged round him indicated the growing importance of class rhetoric in shaping the discourse of the French left. Jaurès' speech attacking the Casimir-Périer dynasty became an immensely popular pamphlet and Casimir-Périer himself was the last member of the great nineteenth-century dynasties to test the waters of democratic politics.

PM

CASSIN, René Samuel (1887–1976)

René Cassin's long life was one of devotion to humanity, a devotion which found two particular forms in response to the inhumanity of the two world wars that he witnessed. Cassin was educated in Nice, Aix and Paris. Soon after completing his legal training, he was called to active service in the First World War, for which he was decorated. The ceaseless suffering experienced by his many injured compatriots moved Cassin to found a national organization for war *invalides*. Cassin continued to develop his deep interest in justice and education between the wars. He was professor of law at the Universities of Lille and Paris, and at the Hague Academy of International Law. From 1924–38, Cassin was a French delegate to the League of Nations.

In the Second World War, Cassin was appointed to de Gaulle's staff; and, from 1941–3, served as national commissioner for justice and public education. From 1943–5, he worked on the UN War Crimes Commission. Between 1946 and 1972, Cassin was a member of the UN Commission on Human Rights. He was the first *rapporteur* of the Universal Declaration of Human Rights, and became a presiding judge at the European Court of Human Rights.

Cassin's response to the holocaust of the Second World War was in keeping with his major interests and with his Judaism. He had the vision to see the contribution to the prevention of crimes against humanity that could be made by law and by education. Cassin saw that the way to raise and maintain people's awareness of human rights was through instituting conventions, based upon the rule of law, against which the basis of a state's activities could be tested. He also saw that educating people about human rights would play a vital role in preventing infringements of those rights. Speaking in 1960, Cassin expressed a belief that he was to repeat eleven years later in London in the light of the French response to the troubles of 1968. He said that, 'Legal force of itself is only a secondary safety valve: it is the education of young people and even of adults that constitutes the primary and real guarantee for minority groups faced with racial hatred which leads so easily to violence and murder' (*L'Alliance Israélite Universelle* (Paris: PUF, 1961), p. 123).

In 1968, Cassin was awarded the UN Human

Rights Prize and the Nobel Peace Prize. He used the latter award to found the International Institute of Human Rights, in Strasbourg, which continues to provide opportunities for young people from all over the world to learn about human rights. In 1973, Cassin was awarded the Goethe Prize. He also received honorary doctorates from Oxford, Mainz, Jerusalem, London and Brandeis universities. At home, his contribution was recognized by the award of the Grand Croix Légion d'Honneur.

Cassin was a citizen of France, a Jew, a jurist and an educator; but he will be remembered by the world as a humanitarian.

BH

de CASTELNAU, Noël Marie Joseph Edouard de Curières, General (1851–1944)

General de Castelnau played a large part in the conservative politics of inter-war France. As leader of the National Catholic Federation a mass lay movement of Catholics, he became for a period the leading spokesman of nationalist traditionalism. His origins and his attitudes made him a perfect target for those on the left who viewed generals, in or out of politics, as booted and bigoted reactionaries. It is significant that his greatest influence occurred in the middle 1920s, a period when the old themes of right–left conflict enjoyed their last period of supremacy before being superseded by the harsher confrontations of the 1930s.

De Castelnau came from the landed and deeply Catholic nobility. Educated at a Jesuit college and at the military academy of Saint Cyr, he pursued a conventionally successful career in the service of the Republic whose principles he despised but which left him and his equivalents free to run the army. During the First World War (in which three of his sons were killed) he held a series of senior but not crucial posts and began to develop contacts with right-wing figures in Parliament and the press. (His intermediary was his personal secretary, who was a Jesuit chaplain and also his nephew.) In the conservative landslide of 1919 he was elected to the Chamber of Deputies for his native Aveyron where he was also president of the departmental council. As a back-bencher, he soon showed that he possessed better political skills and greater energy than many of his conservative colleagues and became president of the Chamber army commission. The experience of the 1919 Chamber demonstrated that the traditionalist, Catholic right had far less influence over

the course of Republican politics than its numbers warranted. But it was the victory of the Radicals and socialists in the 1924 elections (in which de Castelnau lost his seat) that provided the catalyst for his subsequent fame. He was convinced that behind the Socialist–Radical left lurked the hidden hand of Freemasonry with its diabolical commitment to atheism at home and pacifist internationalism abroad. He detested both the anticlerical measures which the Herriot (q.v.) government proposed – abolition of diplomatic relations with the Vatican, reactivation of the anticongregation laws suspended in 1914 and, above all, the application of the 1904–5 laws to Alsace Lorraine – and the foreign policy of Franco-German reconciliation that came to be associated with Briand (q.v.) and the Locarno Treaty. It was to defend the civil rights of Catholics against secularism that in February 1925 de Castelnau founded the Fédération Nationale Catholique (FNC). The FNC soon became enormously successful, with well over a million members, and Castelnau had a powerful press ally in the nationalist daily, the Echo de Paris, for which he wrote regularly. Acting as a pressure group of the moral majority, the FNC sought influence rather than direct political power (in this it differed from the Leagues of the 1930s) and was highly successful. The anticlerical legislation of the Herriot government was for the most part abandoned and in 1928 277 deputies accepted the FNC policy statement on freedom of association and education.

De Castelnau continued to write and organize with unflagging energy in the 1930s, but the FNC now occupied a less central position in conservative policies. The emergence of the leagues created an alternative – and more modern – focus for activism, the right was now radical as well as traditionalist. Simultaneously, a more progressive trend emerged among French Catholics and de Castelnau found himself in fierce conflict with Catholic democrats like Bidault (q.v.). His militarism and hatred of the 'spirit of Geneva' (which led him to support Mussolini's invasion of Abyssinia) provoked Mounier (q.v.) to write the savage attack 'Général, trois fils, n'est ce pas assez?' Though naturally opposed to the Popular Front he seems to have been less neurotically antagonistic than others. He spent his last years in his Hérault property, far away from Vichy, but still active in the FNC. He died in March 1944.

The Fédération National Catholique unquestionably helped to rouse French Catholics from their political torpor. But it also contributed to the continuing antagonism between parliamentary republicanism and catholicism. To this extent, de Castelnau contributed to the spirit of penitential antidemocratic conservatism that found expression at Vichy and to the national catholicism of some of the defenders of French Algeria. He himself seems to have been an engaging figure, popular even with his opponents; but it was from among the ranks of his supporters that would come such apostles of collaboratism and anti-Semitism as Philippe Henriot (q.v.) and Xavier Vallat (q.v.).

Bibliography

Nobecourt, J. (1967), *Une Histoire politique de l'armeé*, Paris: Seuil.
Rémond, R. (1960), *Les Catholiques, le communisme et les crises 1929–39*, Paris: A. Colin.
Viance, G.D. (1930), *La Fédération national catholique*, Paris: Flammarion.

PM

CÉLOR, Pierre Louis Joseph Jean (1902–57)

Célor's name usually appears as a footnote in histories of the French Communist Party (PCF) because of the celebrated Barbé–Célor 'group' which was accused of having dominated the PCF between 1929–31. Célor's career is, however, also illustrative of three broader phenomena within the early history of the PCF. The first is the importance assumed by the first generation of activists to reach political maturity after the creation of the PCF, many of whom went on, like Célor himself, to become influential within the young Communist movement, (Jeunesses Communistes – JC) and indeed to lead the PCF itself during the 1920s and early 1930s. The second factor concerns the role of the Comintern in promoting and then purging this early PCF leadership. Finally, while not typical, Célor's progress from a career in the early history of the PCF to a later period of fascism, and then collaboration during the Second World War was mirrored by that of other prominent political activists of his generation, among them, Jacques Doriot (q.v.) and Henri Barbé (q.v.).

Born in Tulle in 1902, Célor moved to Morocco where he joined the Communist Party and the Jeunesses Communistes in 1923 while he was undergoing his military service. He was involved in the PCF's antimilitarist and anticolonial campaigns in Morocco in 1924–5 and these led to his expulsion from the territory, together with the loss of his job in May 1925, at the age of 23. Thereafter he returned to Paris where he became a full-time PCF official responsible for anti-imperialist propaganda. He swiftly became one of the key figures in charge of the JC and as such he was among those Young Communist members who in 1927 were singled out by the Comintern to apply the new ultra revolutionary 'class against class' line within the PCF. From 1928 he was a member of the PCF's Political Bureau where he was heavily involved in illegal antimilitarist campaigns. Célor was a member of the French delegation to the 6th Congress of the Comintern held in Moscow in the summer of 1928 and he remained in the USSR until November of that year. He was elected to the PCF Central Committee in April 1929 and between 1929 and 1930 along with Thorez, Frachon and Barbé he made up the collective leadership of the party. This period was the most revolutionary and the least successful in the party's history and by 1930 the Comintern was beginning to worry about the PCF's failures. In 1931 the Comintern representative Manouilski, who had himself encouraged the JC faction to take over the PCF leadership, discovered the existence of the so-called 'Barbé–Célor group' which was blamed for the party's problems. Barbé and Célor were called to Moscow where they were interrogated in the autumn of 1931 about the existence of a police spy within the 'group'. Barbé's evidence turned the focus on Célor whose interrogation continued in Moscow until the autumn of 1932. In December of that year the PCF Central Committee decided to relieve him of all his official functions in the party and Célor was expelled from the PCF on his return to France in October 1932. The allegations against him have never been substantiated and are now regarded as fabricated.

Célor ceased political activity until 1941 when he joined Marcel Déat's Rassemblement National Populaire (RNP) and went on to sit on the party's Central Commitee. In September 1942 he left the RNP to join his former Communist comrade Jacques Doriot in the PPF, where he became a full-time official and member of the Political Bureau. In August 1944 he fled first to Germany with other PPF leaders and then to Italy. After the liberation Célor's involvement in collaborationist politics led to him being sentenced to seven years' forced labour. He was released in 1949 after serving two years of this sentence. He was an active Catholic and anti-Communist until his death in 1957.

Bibliography

The best account of the Barbé–Célor affair is by Jean-Paul Brunet, 'Une Crise du parti communiste français: l'affaire Barbé–Célor', *Revue d'Histoire Moderne et Contemporaine*, vol. xvi, 1969, pp. 439–61.

J.-P. Brunet also touches on Célor's career at several points in his biography, *Jacques Doriot: du communisme au fascisme* (Paris: Balland, 1986). See also B. Lazitch, *Biographical Dictionary of the Comintern* (Stanford, Cal.: Heover Press, 1973) and P. Robrieux, *Histoire intérieure du parti communiste*, vols 1 and 4 (Paris: Fayard, 1981).

DALL

'CHABAN-DELMAS', Jacques Pierre Michel Delmas (1915–)

Jacques Chaban-Delmas is, together with François Mitterrand, the most enduring figure in the post-war history of French politics. First elected to the National Assembly in 1946 and mayor of Bordeaux since 1947, over a period of forty years he has cultivated the reputation of a reformer who is at once dynamic and pragmatic. Though a committed Gaullist, he has always prided himself on his ability to establish good relations with other political formations and he lacks the passionate, almost mystic, intransigence of a Michel Debré (q.v.). At the highest level his career has been unsuccessful. In the whole of his political life he held ministerial office for only five years and his bid for the presidency in 1974 ended in humiliating failure. Yet his three periods of president of the National Assembly, his role in Gaullist politics and his position as regional boss of the Gironde (he is known as the 'Duke of Aquitaine') mean that he has never been absent from the centre stage of politics.

Jacques Delmas was born in Paris in 1915 the son of a self-employed automobile designer and inventor and stepson (after his parents' divorce) of a furniture dealer. Educated at the Lycée Lakanal, he was an unmemorable student, though he managed to obtain a law degree and the diploma of the Ecole Libre des Sciences Politiques (which he describes in his memoirs as 'that citadel of intellectual snobbishness'). Often unwell in childhood he took up sport with enormous enthusiasm while a student and became a highly accomplished player of rugby and then tennis. (This sporting image would be an important part of his political persona.) After graduation, he became a journalist, working on the Radical Socialist economic daily *L'Information* and then joined an infantry regiment for his military service. He passed out top of his class at the military academy of Saint-Cyr. When war came, he fought in the brief Italian campaign. From 1941–3 he worked in the Ministry of Industrial Production while preparing the entry

exam for the prestigious *Inspection des Finances*, an exam which he passed on his second attempt. But at the same time he embarked on the Resistance activity that would be the foundation of his subsequent political career. He played an extremely important role in the Resistance, working closely with future political friends like Félix Gaillard (q.v.), Maurice Bourgès-Maunoury and Lorrain Cruse (of the Bordeaux wine family), and eventually becoming the national military delegate of de Gaulle's provisional government. As such, he was closely involved in the liberation of Paris.

He ended the war, aged 29, as a brigadier-general, with a double barrelled surname (Chaban was his Resistance pseudonym) and all the star qualities needed to play a leading part in the fluid situation created by the collapse of the legitimacy of the political elites of both Vichy and the Third Republic. After a brief period as secretary-general of the Ministry of Information (he resigned over what he saw as the unjust treatment of the owners of the occupation newspaper industry) he quit the *Inspection des Finances* and turned to politics. His choice of party and region were significant. In the absence of political Gaullism, he turned, as did Debré, to the Radical Party and he decided to try his luck in Bordeaux. Both the Radicals and Bordeaux were badly in need of the political rehabilitation which Chaban-Delmas' youth, glamour and record could offer; he for his part found in the Radicals what de Gaulle called a 'sense of the state' and also a reformist, but undoctrinaire tradition. In quick succession he became both deputy and mayor and used the latter post to build up the power base that is necessary in a political system where organized party loyalties are weak. For a while he faced a considerable challenge from the pre-war boss of Bordeaux, Adrien Marquet (q.v.) who had been disbarred from political life in 1945 because of his role under Vichy but who maintained a strong local position. After Marquet's death in 1955 his position was unassailable and he became, together with Defferre (q.v.) at Marseilles, France's best known big-city boss.

In his memoirs, Chaban-Delmas says that he revered de Gaulle as a national symbol and loved him as a father. Thus his decision in 1947 to join the Rassemblement du Peuple Français was inevitable and he played an important part in its history. Yet it was typical of his essential moderation and flexibility (his enemies would call it opportunism) that he did not leave the Radical Party until he was excluded, and that he was willing to serve in Fourth Republic governments. Attracted to the modernizing reformism of Mendès France (q.v.) he served in his government as minister of public works, transport and tourism and led a fraction of the Gaullists into the 1956 electoral pact with Socialists and Radicals known as the 'Front Républicain'. After these elections, he served under Mollet (q.v.) as minister of state and in 1957 became defence minister in the government of his war-time friend Félix Gaillard (q.v.).

As defence minister he was of course responsible for army discipline. But he was also a Gaullist baron and he took on to his staff Léon Delbecque, who became his ears and eyes in the events leading up to the collapse of the Fourth Republic and who played a crucial role in getting the army leaders in Algeria to declare for de Gaulle. If this somewhat unusual concept of ministerial responsibility showed clearly where Chaban's real loyalties lay, his decision in 1959 to run for the presidency of the National Assembly against de Gaulle's preferred candidate, the veteran parliamentarian Paul Reynaud (q.v.), demonstrated his dynamic independence. His victory not only showed that a new political generation was ready to take over from the existing leadership of the right, it also guaranteed that de Gaulle would have a loyal ally in a crucial place during his battle to tame the power of the parliamentary monster. Chaban held the presidency for eleven years, never challenging de Gaulle's conception of the National Assembly but managing at the same time to cultivate his image as a progressive. He built up a brains trust of advisers, who included members of the administrative elite like Bloch-Lainé (q.v.) and also reformist trade unionists and representatives of that civil society which de Gaulle, for all his concern with a third way between capitalism and communism, seemed to disdain.

It was this 'social' dimension that would be so valuable to Chaban-Delmas in 1969. The explosion of 1968 demonstrated that the right needed a social conscience and Chaban unquestionably had one. He was the ideal counterpart – energetic, conciliatory, sympathetic – to the solid, but uncharismatic competence of Pompidou (q.v.). It is a measure of his reputation at this time that Poher (q.v.) – the centrist candidate in the 1969 presidential election – indicated that he too wanted him as prime minister. As it was, he became Pompidou's prime minister and immediately declared his programme to be the creation in France of a 'new society' (he had first used the term, with its Kennedy resonances, on 30 May 1968). The 'new society' was essentially an attempt in the aftermath of 1968 to reduce the rigidities and inequalities in French social relations by progressive social measures, a systematic attempt to improve the status and function of trade unionism in collective bargaining and the liberalization of government, notably in the area of public sector broadcasting. Chaban-Delmas paid highly publicized visits to the slums (*bidonvilles*) around Paris that were the underside of the much-trumpeted Gaullist prosperity; he also appointed to his staff two members of the social democratic opposition, Simon Nora, a *Mendésist*, and Jacques Delors (q.v.). They argued that the Gaullist dream of a classless society via *participation* was impossible but that French society could be unblocked.

In his speech on Chaban-Delmas' ministerial declaration, François Mitterrand declared that he did not doubt its sincerity but did doubt that his political majority would ever let the reforms happen. This was an accurate enough prediction of what happened. A number of deals (*contrats de progès*) were signed by government and trade unions in an attempt to de-dramatize industrial relations – even the Communist-led CGT accepted the SNCF package – and there were significant moves to liberalize broadcasting. Yet by the time Chaban-Delmas left office in July 1972, his programme had lost much of its credibility and his own image was in decline. There are a number of reasons for this. The growing trend to left unity meant that the (highly politicized) unions were unlikely to moderate the intransigence of their rhetoric and became cooperative 'social partners'. More seriously, Chaban's social and political liberalism was suspect to a highly-conservative Gaullist majority in parliament which saw firmness rather than reform as the proper response to 1968. Relations between the prime minister and the Gaullist group became extremely bad (the latter detested the broadcasting reform in particular). This might not have mattered – in the Fifth Republic parliamentarians exist to support rather than to challenge government – had Chaban-Delmas been able to keep the support of the president of the Republic. But he was not. Pompidou's worldly scepticism about impetuous reformism rapidly hardened into suspicious conservatism and an impatience with the superficiality of a 'new society' (and a premiership) that could neither conciliate opponents nor satisfy supporters. Urged on by his advisers Juillet (q.v.) and Garaud (q.v.), Pompidou came to see Chaban-Delmas as an irresponsible activist who threatened his own authority (on several occasions he was not informed about prime ministerial initiatives) and risked alienating conservative support. Suddenly Chaban-Delmas was vulnerable. His reformism began to look frayed when it was revealed that he had (quite legally) paid virtually no taxes thanks to an exemption scheme and he was made to pay the price for the politically unsuccessful referendum on British entry into the EEC (April 1972) by being deprived of responsibility for broadcasting. He attempted to shore up his position by calling for a parliamentary vote of confidence on 23 May 1972 and this he was massively accorded. But he had committed the cardinal sin of not informing Pompidou first and for this act of lèse-président he would be quickly punished. Six weeks after winning his vote of confidence he was sacked. There could hardly have been a more brutal assertion of where real power lay in the Fifth Republic.

After his dismissal, Chaban-Delmas fought back and appeared to consolidate his position as leader of the Gaullist movement and potential successor to a rapidly declining Pompidou. He created a team of advisers and made what was at that time the statutory statesman's visit to China. His presidential aspirations were obvious; when Pompidou died, he immediately announced his candidature. Justifying his haste and determination in terms of the sportsman's dynamism, he managed to get the support of the Gaullist movement. Yet it soon became clear that the election was not going to be the sprint for which he had hoped. If he was able to crush his potential rivals Edgar Faure (q.v.) and the prime minister Messmer (q.v.) the manner in which he did so greatly annoyed the latter who pointedly refused to campaign for him. The entry on to the scene of Giscard d'Estaing (q.v.) presented him with a formidable opponent who never tired of boasting that he had been able to keep Pompidou's confidence until the end. Doubts emerged about Chaban-Delmas' suitability for the presidency. He was three times married, the tax story would not go away, he had announced his candidature before Pompidou was even buried and he was unconvincing on television. Above all, the unremitting hostility of Pompidou's friends led the most influential among them, Jacques Chirac (q.v.), to mobilize a group of forty-three Gaullist deputies against him and to use his position as interior minister to leak government intelligence reports saying that whereas Giscard could defeat Mitterrand, Chaban-Delmas could not. Chaban-Delmas' appeals to Gaullist inter-classism coming at a time when the class-based nature of electoral sociology was clearer than ever, seemed as archaic as the Gaullist old guard whose prisoner he now appeared to be. The prophet of the 'new society' had ended up as the representative of all that was unpopular in the Gaullist-dominated State – L'Etat UDR. Once the polls put Giscard ahead, Chaban-Delmas' campaign rapidly ran into the ground and he ended up with a humiliating 14.76 per cent of the vote, compared with Giscard's 32.76 per cent.

Chaban-Delmas' presidential hopes were permanently dashed by the 1974 result. He withdrew to his political base of Bordeaux and was unable to prevent his political assassin, Chirac, from taking over the Gaullist party. Yet his innate flexibility – and a party system which resists the absolutes of discipline – soon enabled him to recover much political ground. In 1978 the right unexpectedly won the parliamentary elections and Giscard was able to use Chaban-Delmas as an ally in his struggle against the violently antagonistic Chirac. Chaban-Delmas became Giscard's candidate for the presidency of the National Assembly against the incumbent, Edgar Faure (q.v.), another floating heavyweight of French politics who was supported by Chirac. Chaban-Delmas won the election, thanks to the defection of a number of anti-Chiraquian Gaullists and was able, as twenty years earlier, to defend the president of the Republic against the turbulence of a section of the parliamentary right. The victory of his old friend Mitterrand naturally led to his departure from office. But with the coming of the politics of 'cohabitation' in 1986 he once again hoped that the hour had struck for his brand of flexible reformism and that he would become prime minister. Chirac's control of the Gaullist party and determination to use the premiership as a launching pad for his presidential campaign meant, however, that Chaban-Delmas had to be content once again with the presidency of the National Assembly. It was in a way appropriate that a figure who symbolizes, despite his Gaullism, a continuing Radical sensibility in French politics, should end up as one of the great *notables* of the Fifth Republic.

Bibliography

Bunel, J. and Meunier, P. (1972), *Chaban-Delmas*, Paris: Stock.

Chaban-Delmas, J. (1975), *L'Ardeur*, Paris: Stock.

Guillebaud, J.-C. and P. Veillet (1969), *Chaban-Delmas ou l'art d'être heureux en politique*, Paris: Grasset.

PM

CHALANDON, Albin Paul Henri (1920–   )

A minister during the de Gaulle and Pompidou presidencies (1968–72) Chalandon was minister of justice in the Chirac government of 1986–8. He was Deputy for Asnières between 1967 and 1976 and was re-elected for the Nord department in the Gaullist

RPR list in 1986. Born into a wealthy industrialist family he was educated in Lyons and Paris at the secondary school, the Lycée Condorcet and the Faculté des Lettres, and after graduating entered the *Inspection des finances*. He spent two years seconded to the personal ministerial staff (*cabinets*) of Blum, Ramadier and then Mayer (January–May 1953) before taking up a career in banking and industry. Chalandon's industrial experience and expertise made him a key member of many state bodies, most notably in the areas of economic planning and energy policy, and eventually gained him the post of president of Elf Acquitaine (1977–83). He has had a long-standing link with the Gaullist Party, holding party office in 1958–9 and 1974–5 (deputy general-secretary).

Chalandon's political career in many ways reflects the changing facets of Gaullism. His first encounter with the movement came with the Resistance and the early days of the Fourth Republic when he was active in the Gaullist *Rassemblement du Peuple Français* participating in a working group set up by General de Gaulle (1947–9) to study the 'general problems of the country'. After ten years' working both in the private and public sectors as an industrialist and banker he re-emerged on the political scene, along with the Gaullists in 1958, and was influential in the UNR as treasurer and secretary-general. He came to the political forefront as minister of industry (1968) in the Pompidou premiership and then held the Ministry of Equipment between 1968–72. Chalandon regained political prominence under the Chirac premiership with the acquisition of the highly prestigious Ministry of Justice. It is however difficult to categorize Chalandon. He keeps his own counsel; a part of the generation of Gaullist 'barons' who remained separate from them; a close supporter of Pompidou, but never in the heart of the Pompidolian clan; and admirer of Chirac but with reservations. He was perhaps the greatest 'neo-liberal' of the pre-1985 Gaullist era, favouring privatization and competition in an era when *dirigisme* and *étatisme* were largely taken for granted by the right. As minister of justice he has become a controversial figure over his radical and intransigent solutions to the problems of security and terrorism. He has also advocated hardline policies on the nationality issue and for solving youth delinquency and has argued for the privatization of prisons.

As a minister, Chalandon has always been able, assertive and assiduous. Never afraid to fight ministerial battles, he was also uninhibited about shaking up the civil service. He took many of these strengths with him to the public sector and as chief executive of the oil conglomerate Elf Acquitaine had many public rows over policy with the tutelage – supervising – ministers, André Giraud and Laurent Fabius, which more than once precipitated presidential intervention. A discrete man of eclectic taste, Chalandon has also produced significant academic works: *Les joueurs de flûte* (Paris: Plon, 1977) and economic treatises with others (*Le système monétaire internationale*, Paris: France Empire, 1977; and *Quitte ou double*, Paris: Grasset, 1987).

ER

CHALLE, General Maurice (1906–)

Maurice Challe had a successful professional career as a general of the French air force and as a senior military commander. He became the commander-in-chief of the French forces in Algeria, taking up the post on 19 December 1958, until his appointment as the commander of the central European forces in April 1960. He soon retired, troubled by the direction events were taking in Algeria. He was involved in the attempted *putsch* in Algiers (April 1961), directed against the policies of President de Gaulle for the future of Algeria. For his part in this plot, General Challe was condemned to fifteen years' imprisonment.

Maurice Challe had a distinguished record during the Second World War and received the DSO for passing the Luftwaffe's order of battle at the time of the D-Day landings to the Allies. At a later date he was the representative of Guy Mollet to the British government, participating in the preparations for the Suez campaign in 1956. His personal qualities have been somewhat lost in the many accounts of events in Algeria, but he was a respected officer, with a noted sense of humour and warmth. His loyalty was above all to his forces.

In Algeria, Maurice Challe's name became associated with the achievement of military victory by the French in the years 1958 to 1960. The 'Challe plan', although prepared by his predecessor General Salan, was developed and executed under his authority. The mobile units, the 'commandos de chasse', carried the war into the hills and strongholds of the National Liberation Front and army of the Algerian nationalists, especially into their securest areas in the Kabylie. The powerful air support, appreciated by an air force officer like Challe, enabled the 'crack' units of paratroops and Foreign Legion to winkle out resistance. The operations included the widening and extension of the protective barriers between Algerian territory and that of Tunisia and Morocco (the Morice Line). Challe also encouraged the use of double agents and of locally-recruited Muslim troops.

General Challe was resolute in affirming order in Algeria. His handling of the 'week of the barricades', a serious civil disturbance in January 1960 which disrupted the city of Algiers and obliged his retreat outside the centre, was marked by condemnation of violence and insistence on the need for responsible military action, even against white colonists. This loyalty to his troops drew him into a political stand against the government of de Gaulle. The army had fought and sustained serious losses in defending the idea of French Algeria, and Challe determined to support this army. He was invited to lead the attempted military 'coup' of April 1961.

He flew to Algiers on 20 April, but his appeal to senior serving officers to rebel went largely unheeded. His refusal to contemplate major civil disorder or acts of violence and bravura, left him isolated. The plot failed, with Challe standing before the crowd in Algiers inaudible because of the failure of the microphones. He gave himself up, unlike some others involved, and anticipated the death penalty. His long prison sentence was ended by an amnesty in December 1968.

Bibliography

Challe, M. (1968), *Notre révolte*, Paris: Presses de la Cité.

Droz, B. and E. Lever (1982), *Histoire de la guerre d'Algérie*, Paris: Seuil. A full, authoritative account.

Horne, A. (1977), *A Savage War of Peace*, New York: Viking. The best account in English, not accurately up to date with the latest work.

Montagnon, P. (1984), *La Guerre d'Algérie*, Paris: Pygmalion. This is a sharp account by a former officer, a participant in the events.

PS

CHAMBORD, Henri, Comte de (1820–83)

As 'Henri V', Chambord was the Legitimist Pretender to the throne of France for forty-seven years, from 1836 to 1883. Described as 'l'enfant du miracle', he was born in September 1820 seven months after the assassination of his father, the Duc de Berri, elder son of the Comte d'Artois, who in 1824 was to succeed to the throne as Charles X. Created Duc de Bordeaux at birth, one year later he was given the Chateau de Chambord by the government. At Charles X's accession, he became heir to the throne.

Artois had, both at the Revolution and during the Restoration, been prominent in the reactionary party, and his grandson was educated in hatred of the French Revolution, and in ignorance of modern political issues. At the 1830 Revolution, Charles abdicated in favour of Chambord, but the proclamation of Louis-Philippe led to the exile of both grandfather and grandson. On Charles's death in 1836 Chambord became the Pretender. He was the last male descendant of the elder Bourbon line (he himself having no children).

The 1848 Revolution, which drove the Orleanists from the throne, seemed for a time to present a possibility for Restoration; but despite legitimist strength in the Assembly, the monarchist cause was already bedevilled by the problem which it was to face throughout Chambord's life: the inability of Legitimists and Orleanists to work together. Chambord himself could never forgive Louis-Philippe's utilization of the coup of 1830; the Orleanists were alienated, in their turn, by Chambord's rigid and reactionary views.

For the first years of the Second Empire Chambord played a very small political role, though he continued to hold his Pretender's court at the Castle of Frohsdorf, in Austria. With Napoleon III's Italian venture of 1859, however, Chambord re-entered politics as the champion of the Church. The Royalist campaign culminated, in 1865/6, with a series of manifestos in which Chambord appealed to all groups in the country, including the workers ('La Royauté a toujours été la patronne des classes ouvrières'). Most of his policies, while having a gloss of social concern, were corporatist, paternalist, and authoritarian.

The fall of the Empire, in 1870, led to further opportunities. There was a majority of the right in the National Assembly, and a real possibility of a Restoration. Again the split with the Orleanists played its part, however, as did Chambord's own assertions of principle. When, in 1873, Thiers (q.v.) was succeeded by MacMahon (q.v.), the time again seemed ripe; emissaries were sent to him in Austria, but his insistence on a return to the white flag of the Bourbons, in place of the *tricolore* (almost certainly a more general attempt to assert the manner in which he intended to reign) finally finished all possibility of his return. He died at Frohsdorf in 1883.

Chambord was a limited man, out of touch with France, and with his times. His intransigence, however, possibly saved France from the disaster of a new Restoration based on a temporary and misleading parliamentary majority, which would have been followed by further instability; as it was, the Third Republic, which had started so inauspiciously, was to last till 1940. He also destroyed the monarchist cause, which never fully recovered from his policies, even under the Orleanist pretenders who succeeded him.

Bibliography

Brown, M. (1967), *The Comte de Chambord*, Durham, NC: Duke University Press.
de Luz, P. (1931), *Henri V*, Paris: F. Nathan.
Valois, G. (Grassent a.k.a.) (1908), *La Révolution sociale ou le roi*, Paris: Nouvelle Librairie Nationale.
Zeldin, T. (1973), *France 1848–1945*, vol. I, Oxford: Oxford University Press.

RMG

CHAUTEMPS, Camille Gabriel (1885–1963)

Camille Chautemps was the third man in the trinity of leaders who dominated the Radical Party in the last twenty years of the Third Republic. Lacking the star quality – and self-importance – of Daladier (q.v.) and Herriot (q.v.), his formidable skills as a political conciliator and fixer made him a ubiquitous figure in the parliamentary politics of the day. He was a minister in fourteen governments. As post-war (1919) mayor of Tours, he worked closely with the American forces stationed there and subsequently established good relations with many US leaders, including notably Roosevelt. Yet his career is associated much more with scandal and failure than with any legislative or personal achievement. Whereas Herriot and Daladier were able to make political comebacks after the Second World War, Chautemps saw himself condemned, in absentia, to imprisonment and national degradation for his alleged role in the collapse of 1940. He spent the last years of his life as an exile without honour, living mainly in Washington and remains a largely forgotten – and discredited – figure.

Born in Paris in 1885, Chautemps came from an intensely political family and one that identified strongly with the new Republic. His father was president of the Paris municipal council, a deputy and then senator; and his brother (who was killed in the First World War) was a deputy for the Savoie, where the family had its origins. Chautemps himself took the classic road to Radical political advancement – law, the prefectoral administration, freemasonry, ministerial cabinets and the patronage of a political grandee, the Radical parliamentarian, René Besnard. He entered the Chamber of Deputies in 1919 and immediately acquired a reputation for technical competence and personal skills. It is a measure of his standing that after the virtue of the Socialist–Radical coalition in 1924, Herriot made him, despite his relative youth and inexperience, minister of the interior. He held several ministries – justice, education, as well as the interior – in this period of great governmental instability. Defeated in the 1928 elections, he almost immediately returned to parliament and was, very briefly, prime minister in 1931. Two years later, in November 1933, he again became prime minister at a time when the comfortable certainties of traditional radicalism had to face the full blast of economic depression and international tension. His premiership crashed into the Stavisky affair, which was the response of political discontent to the worsening situation. Not only was the Radical Party the target of those who saw in Stavisky the corruption of the political system, Chautemps was directly linked with the scandal by the fact that his brother-in-law, Pressard, was the head of the Paris prosecutor's office, which had so signally failed to pursue the crook. Chautemps always denied any wrongdoing and was unusually, and successfully, aggressive in defending himself. He left office without losing a vote of confidence but was back in office in the Sarraut government of January 1936. His speedy return showed the extent of his popularity within (and beyond) his own party and it was characteristic of his flexibility that, although no left-winger, he went along with the Popular Front.

He was minister of state in the Popular Front (1936) government and then succeeded Blum (q.v.) as prime minister. His administration saw the departure of the Communists from the government majority. More seriously, for his reputation, Chautemps once again chose to resign without being defeated, this time at the height of the tremendous crisis provoked by the Anschluss. His departure suggested political weakness if not actual bankruptcy. Once again, his skills as a political conciliator and tactician ensured that he was almost immediately back in government and he represented the voice of Radical so-called good sense in the governments of Daladier and Reynaud (q.v.). Yet it was this good sense that would ultimately destroy him. In the supreme crisis of 1940, his was the voice that suggested that the terms of an armistice with Hitler should be sought. He always claimed subsequently that he did so to prove that the terms would be unacceptable and that

France must continue to fight; but few then, or subsequently, have accepted this explanation. In November 1940 Pétain (q.v.) sent him to Washington as official representative of the Vichy government. He soon broke with Vichy and, developed, as we have seen, good relations with Roosevelt who much preferred clever politicians to intransigent generals. This closeness was hardly likely to appeal to either Gaullists or Communists and after a short visit to Algeria in 1944 he returned to Washington. His judicial condemnation in 1947 was an almost exemplary punishment for the sins of the Third Republic. Though he was allowed to return to France in 1954, he spent most of the rest of his life in America where he died, aged 78, in 1963. No official French statement acknowledged his death.

Bibliography

Berstein, S. (1980 and 1982), *Histoire du parti radical*, 2 vols, Paris: FNSP, 1982.
Le Monde obituary (3 July 1963).

PM

CHEVÈNEMENT, Jean-Pierre (1939–)

This son of primary school teachers has been a key figure on the left for twenty years. Winning a scholarship to the Institut d'Etudes Politiques, he then entered the Ecole Nationale d'Administration after service in Algeria. Until 1972 he worked in the foreign trade divisions of the finance ministry and also lectured. He became a political full-timer with his election as deputy for his home town Belfort in 1973 and has since added to this post the mayoralty of that city (1983) and also briefly in 1981 the presidency of the regional council of Franche-Comté. His governmental career saw him as minister of state from 1981 to 1983 with responsibility for research and technology, to which he briefly added industry before resigning in spring 1983. From July 1984 to March 1986 he was education minister. He is married with two sons.

His major claim to fame lies however in his contribution to the revival of the PS. Since 1966 he has led the party's left wing CERES (Centre d'Etudes, de Recherches et d'Education Socialistes), since 1986 known as *Socialisme et République*. This highly organized faction had a clear programme of alliance with the PCF. It sought a disciplined and principled party, which would be transformative and not just 'social-democratic'. It dreamed of introducing a decentralized and highly participatory socialism (*autogestion*) aided by an increased growth to be secured by extension of *dirigisme* and by expanding the public sector into profitable areas. In foreign policy CERES approved Gaullian notions of independence based on French nuclear capacity; it was hostile to US leadership of the Western camp and opposed European integration, fearing Germany. Elements of these radical views influenced PS programmes before 1981 thanks to CERES' organizational sophistication, its skill at sectarian polemic and the presence of Chevènement on the party secretariat from 1971 to 1975 and from 1979 to 1981, usually with responsibility for drafting programmes.

Strongly associated with the phase of economic expansion in 1981–2, Chevènement left government in March 1983 in protest at the deflationary turnaround. But his return to education signalled a change of emphasis; now he took a pragmatic '3 R's' line, seeing schooling as a vocational preparation and also increasingly in meritocratic terms (*élitisme républicain*). The replacement of *autogestion* by Republican themes shows his awareness that the French public is now less receptive to radical messages. But republican ideology does enable him to keep some of his old themes (patriotism, social solidarity) while introducing more notions of competition in tune with the times. Today Chevènement is positively enthusiastic about joint European collaboration, even in defence. CERES is now kept in the background as Chevènement works more through a group, La République Moderne, which is really a coalition of backers for a presidential bid whereby he hopes to extend his support, American style, beyond the mere PS. This skilful, tough and very obstinate man may never win his party's or the French people's nomination; but he will keep alive in difficult times the message of a characteristic segment of the modern left, which seeks not to manage capitalism but to transform it. In May 1988 he became minister of defence in Rocard's government but soon clashed with the prime minister over plans to reduce defence expenditure and increase the budget for education. After some discussion he remained at his ministry.

Bibliography

In English, see D. Hanley, *Keeping Left? Ceres and the French Socialist Party* (Manchester: Manchester University Press, 1986) and also 'CERES – an open conspiracy?' in E. Shaw (ed.), *The Left in France*, (Nottingham: Spokesman, 1983). A useful biography in French is C. Makarian and D. Reyt, *Un Inconnu nommé Chevènement* (Paris: Table Ronde, 1986), and there is much autobiography in J.-P. Chevènement, *Etre socialist aujourd'hui* (Paris: Cana, 1980). For the vintage period of the 1970s see his *Les Socialistes, les communistes et les autres* (Paris: Aubier-Montaigne, 1977).

DH

CHIAPPE, Jean (1878–1940)

Born in Ajaccio, Corsica in 1878, Jean Chiappe qualified in law and occupied several administrative posts in the Ministry of the Interior before his appointment in 1927 as Paris prefect of police. Relieved of these functions in 1934, he turned to politics, winning a seat in 1935 on the Paris Municipal Council which immediately elected him its president. At the legislative elections of 1936 he won a parliamentary seat as deputy for the Seine, and became one of the main spokesmen in the Chamber of Deputies for the right-wing leagues which had been banned by the incoming Popular Front government of Léon Blum. After the fall of France in 1940, he accepted Marshal Pétain's offer of the post of high commissioner for Syria and the Lebanon. He was on his way to take up this position in November 1940 when his plane was shot down by unidentified aircraft over the Mediterranean. His body was never recovered.

Jean Chiappe's name is remembered chiefly in association with the right-wing Paris riots of 6 February 1934, which were the pretext for the French left's first moves towards the construction of the 'Popular Front against fascism'. As Paris prefect of police, Jean Chiappe's tough handling of Communist demonstrations had won him the confidence of conservative opinion in the capital as the guardian of 'law and order'. In January 1934 the left's suspicions of him were further aggravated by his apparently lenient attitude towards the right-wing demonstrations which accompanied the development of the 'Stavisky affair'. When the government of Camille Chautemps fell on 27 January under the weight of this politico-financial scandal, the Socialists allegedly made the removal of Chiappe a condition of their parliamentary support for the new government Edouard Daladier was trying to form.

As part of an administrative reshuffle, Daladier offered Chiappe the governorship of Morocco, a post which the latter declined. Though there was evidence that Chiappe, along with other sections of the police and the judiciary, was himself compromised in the Stavisky affair, the right put a very different interpretation on his removal. Daladier was accused of capitulating to Socialist and Communist pressure and of clearing the Paris streets for a left-wing 'coup'. Chiappe thus became the focus for right-wing protest which culminated in the demonstration called for the evening of 6 February to coincide with the investiture of Daladier's government in the Chamber of Deputies. When the police guarding the bridge between the Place de la Concorde and the Chamber of Deputies opened fire on the crowd, killing seventeen, 6 February 1934 became a symbolic date in the calendar of the French right. Jean Chiappe's subsequent political career was launched on the notoriety of this incident, and his later campaign on behalf of the right-wing leagues tends to bear out the left's doubts about his political neutrality as a public official in 1934.

Bibliography

The 'Chiappe affair' figures in all political histories of France in the inter-war period and the following are particularly recommended:

Berstein, S. (1975), *Le six février*, Paris: Gallimard-Julliard.

Chavardès, M. (1966), *Le 6 février 1934. La République en danger*, Paris: Calmann-Lévy.

Le Clère, M. (1967), *Le 6 février*, Paris: Hachette.

Rémond, R. (1959), 'Explications du six février' in *Politique: Revue Internationale des Doctrines et des Institutions*, II (Nouvelle Série 7–8) July–December, pp. 218–30.

In English, see:

Beloff, M. (1955), 'The sixth of February' in *The Decline of the Third Republic*, edited by James Joll, (St Antony's Papers no. 5, London).

Jenkins, B. (1979), *The Paris Riots of February 6th 1934: The crisis of the Third French Republic*, doctoral thesis (University of London).

BJ

CHIRAC, Jacques René (1932–)

Jacques Chirac became, in March 1986, the first prime minister under the Fifth Republic to 'cohabit' with a president of the opposite political tendency. This second premiership was a prelude to his own second unsuccessful presidential candidacy. It was preceded by a triple political career as a government minister and parliamentarian under Presidents de Gaulle, Pompidou and Giscard d'Estaing: as leader of the Gaullist party in the post-Pompidou period: and as the first twentieth-century mayor of Paris. Elected deputy for Ussel, in the department of Corréze, in 1967 and at every general election since then, he was successively junior minister for employment (1967–8) and finance (1968–71), before becoming minister for relations with parliament (1971–2), minister of agriculture (1972–4), minister of the interior (1974) and Giscard's first Premier (1974–6). The leading member of the Gaullist movement after 1974, he refounded it as the Rassemblement pour la République (RPR) and became its president in 1976. He was elected mayor of Paris in March 1977 and he was handsomely returned to office in both 1983 and 1989.

Chirac was born in Paris, the grandson of a Corrèze schoolteacher and the son of a banker who joined the Potez aircraft firm in 1936. He attended the prestigious Lycée Louis-le-Grand and the Paris Institut d'Etudes Politiques, gaining entry to the Ecole Nationale d'Administration in 1954. He was then conscripted, and volunteered for active military service in Algeria after six distinguished months at the Saumur officers' training school. He returned to ENA in 1957, graduated in 1959, and spent a further ten months in Algeria as a civil servant before joining the Cour des Comptes. He then moved to the government secretariat in April 1962 and to Prime Minister Pompidou's *cabinet* the following November.

This appointment was of twofold importance. First, Chirac established an almost filial relationship with Pompidou. Second, this helped him to launch what was almost the prototype of an early Fifth Republic Gaullist political career – from the centre of government down to the localities rather than by the more traditional opposite route. Chirac has family roots in Corrèze, a backward and traditionally left-voting *département* that was an obvious electoral target for the Gaullists. Joining the region's Commission pour le Développement Economique Régional at its creation in 1964, he then used his position in Pompidou's office to channel unprecedented amounts of government money into Corrèze. He became councillor for the village of Sainte-Féréole in 1965, deputy for Ussel in March 1967, a member of the Corrèze Departmental Council in September 1967 and its president in March 1970.

These elected offices were then the basis of a ministerial career that brought him to the premiership twelve years after joining Pompidou. His period at employment was an apprenticeship, but one that led him to take part in the May 1968 Grenelle negotiations. At finance he was responsible, from 1969, for the budget under finance minister Valéry Giscard d'Estaing, and attempted to keep a tight rein on spending departments. He was then a disastrous minister for relations with parliament, making no effort to compensate for his ignorance of an institution where he had hitherto spent little time. In addition, he was caught between Prime Minister Chaban-Delmas' ambitions for a 'new society' and the conservatism of many Gaullist deputies, of Pompidou's advisers Pierre Juillet and Marie-France Garaud, and of the president himself. As minister of agriculture in Messmer's government he succeeded in his main task of buying back the farmers' vote in time for the 1973 elections and improved the position of many tenants and dairy and livestock farmers: but his aggressive tactics at European negotiations brought few results, and he failed to achieve his declared ambition of halting the decline of French peasant agriculture. On his arrival at the Interior Ministry he cut down on the extensive telephone tappings effected by his predecessor Raymond Marcellin (q.v.), and planned a large-scale liberalizing reform. This appointment was probably intended by Juillet, Garaud and even Pompidou as a staging-post towards the premiership a few months later and the presidency in 1976: but such a perspective was radically altered by Pompidou's early death in April 1974.

Two candidates for the succession emerged on the right: Chaban-Delmas, former premier and a leading Gaullist 'baron', and Giscard, finance minister and leader of the Républicains Indépendants. Chirac, by getting a carefully-coded message of support for Giscard signed by forty-three Gaullist deputies and by leaking confidential Interior Ministry polls damaging to Chaban-Delmas, helped materially to ensure that Giscard, not Chaban-Delmas, went through to the second ballot against the left-wing candidate François Mitterrand. There are three possible explanations for this behaviour. First, he, and above all Juillet and Garaud, mistrusted Chaban-Delmas and his 'new society' and thought Giscard more suitable for their (conservative) purposes. Second, he was convinced that only Giscard could beat Mitterrand. Third, his own political prospects, severely damaged by the death of his patron Pompidou, would be no brighter under Chaban-Delmas (who would not be beholden to Chirac if he won the presidency), but would improve under Giscard. This proved to be the case: after a narrow victory against Mitterrand, Giscard made Chirac prime minister in May 1974.

Relations between the two men were rapidly strained by a profound divergence of political aims. Giscard expected his prime minister to 'deliver' the Gaullist party and consent to its dilution into a 'presidential majority' under his own leadership. Chirac saw his premiership as a means of preserving the Gaullist movement's strength and independence (after the loss of the presidency) and of establishing his own leadership of it. Thus when Chirac won election as the Gaullists' secretary-general in December 1974, Giscard, through his lieutenant Michel Poniatowski, moved to organize the non-Gaullist right: this type of manoeuvre continued through the Chirac premiership. Conflicting objectives were compounded by policy differences. All the reforms of the 'advanced liberal society' – the vote at 18, easier divorce, contraception and abortion, a mayor for Paris, tighter environmental controls on building, a capital gains tax – were Giscard's initiatives, not Chirac's, and were seldom to the taste of the Gaullists. Chirac was more identified with anticrisis measures – such as restrictions on firing personnel and generous unemployment benefit for redundant workers, as well as a local tax reform – that were contested by Gaullists a few years after the event. The reflation package of 1975 – brought in against opposition from Finance Minister Jean-Pierre Fourcade – was the only policy in nearly ten continuous years of office to bear Chirac's name. In addition to policy differences, there was also a clash of temperaments between the president and the prime minister. Giscard was twice high-handed enough to reshuffle the cabinet without either consulting or informing the prime minister, with whom the choice of ministers constitutionally lay. Chirac ended by resigning noisily – the only prime minister under the Fifth Republic to have done this – in August 1976.

He thus started a second career as a party leader, ensuring the survival of the Gaullist movement as an independent force, contributing even more to Giscard's downfall in 1981 than he had to his election in 1974, and emerging as 'leader of the opposition' under the Mitterrand presidency. Chirac was returned as deputy for Ussel at a by-election in November 1976 (Fifth Republic ministers have to resign their parliamentary seats). After the (re-)foundation of the RPR the following month, with himself as its president, Chirac kept the Gaullists in an uneasy halfway position, not really in the right-wing majority (in 1979 they went as far as to vote against the budget), but not really in the opposition either (they never voted a motion of censure against the government). This was difficult not only because some Gaullists (notably Alain Peyrefitte) remained in government but also because preserving the Gaullists' hegemony on the right and the right's position in government became increasingly incompatible aims.

Election campaigns became increasingly competitive between the RPR and the Union pour la Démocratie Française (UDF), Giscard's federation of the non-Gaullist right. In March 1977 Chirac won a vicious battle for the Paris City Hall against the president's candidate Michel d'Ornano. At the parliamentary elections a year later, the RPR retained the biggest parliamentary group, with 153 seats to the UDF's 138, but the overall right-wing majority benefited Giscard more than Chirac. Chirac ran a stridently nationalist, anti-Giscardian campaign for the European elections of 1979, but won only 16.3 per cent of the vote against the UDF's 27.6 per cent. By 1981 it was clear that Chirac had more to lose if Giscard won a second term in the Elysée than if the left took the presidency. At the first ballot of the presidential election, he took 18 per cent of the vote to Giscard's 27.8 and Mitterrand's 26.1. He then failed to offer his support to Giscard for the second ballot, and 800,000 Chirac voters switched to Mitterrand at the run-off with discreet encouragement at the highest levels of the RPR.

Yet at the June parliamentary elections that followed Mitterrand's presidential victory, the RPR survived the Socialist landslide better than the non-Gaullist right, taking 88 of the opposition's 158 seats. With the UDF in disarray, Chirac's position on the opposition was (temporarily) unrivalled. His claim that 'the Socialist experiment would not last two years' presumably looked forward to early elections from which he would emerge president. Four obstacles presented themselves. First, Chirac's own popularity suffered from the public's (not unfounded) perception of him as divisive and ambitious. Second, Raymond Barre emerged as an alternative presidential candidate, particularly after the Socialists had adopted similar economic policies to those he had applied as prime minister from 1976 to 1981. Third, when the tide of opinion began to move sharply rightwards in 1983, it benefited the far-right National Front more than the RPR and the UDF. Fourth, in order to reduce the impact of a right-wing victory at the 1986 parliamentary elections and to facilitate his own continuation in office, Mitterrand changed the electoral system to a form of PR based on lists in departments. In response, Chirac eschewed any electoral deals with the National Front (but leaned towards many of its policies); he admitted publicly the possibility (which Barre refused) of 'cohabiting' with Mitterrand in government after March 1986; and he negotiated a common platform and common lists in most departments (though not for most seats) with the UDF, excluding as many Barre supporters as possible. At the elections, the 'respectable' right won a narrow majority and RPR a leading position within that majority (292 and 155 seats respectively). Mitterrand then called on Chirac to form a government, giving him the chance to acquire the presidential stature he had hitherto lacked.

The party tool with which Chirac reached his second premiership was different from the Gaullist movement Pompidou had bequeathed in 1974, in three respects. Firstly, its organization was much re-inforced. By 1984 the RPR claimed 700,000 members, as many as the Communists, traditionally France's biggest party in terms of activists (though the figure of 300,000 would probably be more accurate in both cases). Secondly, the RPR corrected the Gaullists' traditionally weak local implantation. Chirac himself provided the paradigm of this change (just as he had represented a prototype of the Gaullists' development in the 1960s) by winning and running the Paris City Hall. This has represented an enormous asset for him. Paris has a strong tax base allowing low rates. It offered opportunities for municipal improvements, for patronage (some thirty leading city officials took posts in ministries or *cabinets* – private offices – in March 1986) and for attracting national and international media attention. And as the city's first twentieth-century mayor (the executive was previously a government-appointed prefect), Chirac started out with a particularly high degree of legitimacy. On the whole he has used these advantages astutely. Paris has become somewhat greener, cleaner and livelier since 1977, and a highly effective public relations department ensures both that improvements are credited to the mayor and that the failure to deal with more intractable problems such as traffic are not held against him. In March 1983 he was triumphantly re-elected, his lists winning majorities in all twenty *arrondissements*: this was partly a personal vote of confidence, since some 60 per cent of Parisians consistently considered Chirac a good or very good mayor. March 1983 also, though, saw a wider reinforcement of the RPR's municipal positions: the number of RPR mayors in towns of over 30,000 inhabitants rose from twenty-three to forty-four, the biggest gains being in the Paris suburbs.

As well as reinforcing its organization and putting down local roots, the RPR changed many of its policies. Many elements that made the Gaullist movement a curiosity for a European right-wing party – the prickly nationalism, the penchant for state intervention, the (always unfulfilled) belief in workers' 'participation' – were toned down, especially after 1981. Questions of organization, style

and temperament became as important as policies in differentiating the RPR from the UDF. This made it easier to negotiate the 1986 joint RPR–UDF platform, which promised a panoply of free-market economic measures and tighter policing and anti-immigration policies. In the longer term the RPR–UDF convergence could lead to the merger that Chirac's close adviser Edouard Balladur called for in March 1988.

The gamble of Chirac's second premiership was that he could, by applying the 1986 platform, produce sufficient economic and social improvements to emerge as the right's leading presidential contender for 1988, and thus a strong challenger to the incumbent. Economic conditions at the time, with a falling dollar and lower oil prices, looked favourable. But by early 1988 his economic record was clearly insufficient to propel him into the Elysée: rising unemployment for most of the two years, disappointing foreign trade figures, and slow growth scarcely constituted a resounding vindication of government policy, while the crash of 1987 had knocked value off the shares of recently-privatized firms. Other elements of the programme, such as the ill-fated Devaquet higher education bill, the new nationality bill, and television privatizations, were handled ineptly and lost the government support. They were balanced, in part, by the real and popular achievement of falling crime figures. But in the last week of the presidential campaign, Chirac still felt sufficiently short of a useful record to get interior minister Charles Pasqua to organize a series of spectacular releases of French citizens held in New Zealand, New Caledonia and Lebanon. His political weakness in spring 1988 was due not only to his patchy performance in government but also to the greater political skill of President Mitterrand, who managed simultaneously to maximize the impact of Chirac's rivals on the right, to present the RPR as a dangerous, power-hungry faction, and to cultivate his own concerned but consensual image as national patriarch.

Chirac won just over 6 million votes, just under 20 per cent of votes cast, at the first ballot of the 1988 presidential election. This allowed him through to the second ballot, but he was too far behind Mitterrand and too close to the other right-wing candidates, Barre and Le Pen, for him to be a convincing challenger: at the run-off he trailed Mitterrand by 46 per cent to 54, and resigned as premier days later. The RPR was, with the National Front, the main victim of the parliamentary elections that followed, losing 26 of its 155 seats.

With two presidential defeats behind him, and leading a party that was both a prey to factional strife and increasingly unable to reach beyond its classically conservative constituency of farmers, small traders, the old and the well-off, Chirac faced an uncertain future in the summer of 1988. But his continuing assets in the shape of a relatively strong party organization and the bastion of the Paris City Hall, as well as his own steel in the pursuit of political ambition, remained sufficiently important to ensure a place at the centre of French politics.

Bibliography

Three books cover his relations with Giscard: Françoise Giroud, *La Comédie du pouvoir* (Paris: Fayard, 1977); Ann Noury and Michel Louvois, *Le Combat singulier* (Paris: Denoël, 1980); Catherine Nay, *La Double méprise* (Paris: Grasset, 1980).

Articles on the RPR are grouped in *Pouvoirs*, no. 28, 1984.

Articles in English on recent elections include: David B. Goldey and Andrew F. Knapp, 'Time for a change: The French elections of 1981', in *Electoral Studies*, vol. I, no. 1 (pp. 3–42) and 2 (pp. 169–94), 1982; David B. Goldey and R.W. Johnson, 'The French general election of 16 March 1986', in *Electoral Studies*, vol. V, no. 3, 1986, pp. 229–252; and David B. Goldey and R.W. Johnson, 'The French elections of 1988' *Electoral Studies*, vol. VII, no. 3, 1988, pp. 195–223.

There is nothing of length in English on Chirac, though the *Financial Times* (20 November 1986) contains a profile.

There are five biographies of Chirac in French: Catherine Clessis, Bernard Prévost, and Patrick Wajsman, *Jacques Chirac ou la république des 'cadets'* (Paris: Editions de la Cité, 1972) – Chirac compared with other leading young right-wing politicians of his generation; Henri Deligny, *Chirac ou la fringale du pouvoir* (Paris: Alain Moreau, 1977) – hostile, with extensive coverage of early 'scandals'; Thierry Desjardins, *Un Inconnu nommé Chirac* (Paris: La Table Ronde, 1983) – journalistic, very pro-Chirac; Franz-Olivier Giesbert, *Jacques Chirac* (Paris: Seuil, 1987) – the most authoritative biography; Maurice Szafran, *Chirac, ou les passions du pouvoir* (Paris: Grasset, 1986) – also journalistic, but more critical than Desjardins.

AFK

de CISSEY, Ernest Louis Octave Courtot (1810–82)

General de Cissey played an important part in the crushing of the Paris Commune in 1871, and in the reorganization of the army as minister of war from 1871 to 1873 under Thiers, and 1874 to 1877 under MacMahon. He was also prime minister in 1874–5. He was a politically nondescript soldier, typical of the majority who put their own careers and the interests of the army before questions of ideology.

Born in Paris of a noble family, he was educated at the military schools of La Flèche and Saint-Cyr, and had a successful career as a staff officer under the July Monarchy and Second Empire. He commanded a division with some success against the Germans in 1870, and was taken prisoner after the capitulation of Metz. In April 1871 Thiers appointed him commander of the 2nd Corps of the army of Versailles, and he immediately became his protégé and informant within the high command. De Cissey was primarily responsible for the final stages of the siege of Paris during May 1871 and his Corps captured and occupied the left-bank districts of the city during the *semaine sanglante* (21–8 May 1871). He took merciless reprisals against what he considered to be a revolt of professional revolutionaries, criminals and foreigners, and hundreds of executions were carried out at his headquarters at the Luxembourg Palace. His order to shoot the deputy Millière on the steps of the Pantheon became notorious.

Thiers appointed him minister of war on 1 June 1871, and he was elected a deputy for the Seine (i.e. Paris and suburbs) in the by-election of 2 July, on the united conservative list, receiving 109,780 votes (of 290,823 cast). As minister he was Thiers' obedient instrument in the post-war reorganization of the army, giving priority to rapid reconstruction, with improvements in training, planning and equipment, but without fundamental reform. For political and military reasons, Thiers and de Cissey stubbornly and successfully opposed the demand – widespread in the army and the country – to shorten the period of military service from seven years to three, with reliance on recalled reservists in time of war rather than a long-service standing army. In political matters de Cissey also faithfully followed a Thierist 'conservative-Republican' line, forbidding public manifestations of political loyalty by officers, and punishing both Radicals and Bonapartists who persisted. For this reason he was regarded with favour by moderate Republicans. He left office when Thiers resigned in May 1873, but thereafter moved towards the right-centre, supporting MacMahon and de Broglie.

When the de Broglie government fell in May 1874, MacMahon called on de Cissey to form a cabinet. No doubt his reliable but non-ideological conservatism and ministerial experience were the reasons. During the life of the government, France finally received a Republican constitution (in February 1875), though neither de Cissey nor MacMahon had much control over the political process by which this was done. In so far as any minister did, it was duc Decazes, the Orleanist foreign minister, who helped to bring together a majority of Republicans and Orleanists. After the vote of the constitution, the government resigned, but de Cissey immediately returned to the War Ministry in the Buffet and Dufaure governments. During his tenure, in 1875, occurred the alarming but short-lived 'war scare' with Germany. He was elected a life senator in December 1875. There was criticism of his administration, his opposition to reform and his weakness in debate, and he left the ministry in 1876. In March 1878 he was appointed to command the 11th Army Corps at Nantes, but in 1880 was the victim of a scandal in which he was accused of having as mistress a known German spy and of giving her military secrets and public money. This was the end of his career, although he was unanimously exonerated by a parliamentary committee of enquiry. The Radicals continued to imply that there had been shady dealings under his administration, but the real reasons for their enmity were perhaps his conservative military policy, his support for MacMahon, and his ruthless butchery of the communards.

Bibliography

For his activities against the Commune, see Robert Tombs, *The War Against Paris 1871* (Cambridge: Cambridge University Press, 1981), and as minister of war, Allan Mitchell, *Victors and Vanquished: The German Influence on Army and Church in France after 1870* (Chapel Hill and London: University of North Carolina Press, 1984). There are a few details concerning his political activities in Jacques Silvestre de Sacy, *Le Maréchal de Mac-Mahon* (Paris: Inter-Nationales, 1960), and a general outline in A. Robert, E. Bourloton and G. Cougny, *Dictionnaire des parlementaires français*, 5 vols (Paris: Bourloton, 1889–91).

RT

CLEMENCEAU, Georges Eugène Benjamin (1841–1929)

Georges Clemenceau was born in a remote village of the Vendée to a family whose earlier Protestant traditions had evolved into support for the Revolution, the Republic and anticlericalism. Like his father, he took a medical degree, but the family were landed gentry who did not need to practise medicine in a serious way. His political career began in 1862 with a student demonstration against the Second Empire that earned him a short spell in prison. On graduation in 1865 he emigrated to the United States, returning to France in 1869 with an American wife from whom he was divorced in 1891.

With the proclamation of the Third Republic on 4 September 1870, his father's political contacts brought him the post of mayor of the Paris suburb of Montmartre. He played his part in organizing the National Guard to defend Paris against its Prussian besiegers and, albeit with misgivings, in supporting the government of national defence against the extreme left. He was elected to the National Assembly on 8 February 1871, and opposed the cession of Alsace and Lorraine in the peace settlement. His position as mayor placed him at the centre of the incident that produced the revolt of the National Guard leading to the Paris Commune. He resigned his seat as deputy in protest at the Assembly's refusal to make concessions to Paris, and tried to mediate between the Commune and the government. To this end, along with other Radicals, he formed the Ligue d'Union Républicaine pour les Droits de Paris (League of Republican Union for the Rights of Paris). Seeking to mobilize support for mediation, he left Paris in disguise. His mission failed, but it probably saved his life which would have been at risk from both the communards and from governmental troops when the city was recaptured.

After the suppression of the Commune he was elected to the new Paris municipal council and became its president. The general election of 1876 brought him back to Parliament as deputy for Montmartre, as a Radical-Socialist on the extreme left of the Republican Party. He helped Gambetta defeat the threat to the Republic in 1877, but as early as 1879 sought to make himself leader of a Radical opposition to the ruling Opportunist Republicans who formed the new governmental establishment. With this in mind, he set up a daily newspaper *La Justice* and campaigned tirelessly against the government. After Gambetta's death in 1882 political life became virtually a duel between the dominant Opportunist figure of prime minister Ferry and Clemenceau. He attacked Ferry over constitutional reform, the social question and colonial expansion. The Langson incident, a supposed French defeat on the borders of Indo-China allowed him to bring down Ferry's government in 1885, and had a powerful influence on the general election of that year, producing a new Chamber divided into three roughly equal parts, the right, the Opportunists or moderate Republicans, and the Radicals. But although Clemenceau had thus gained a powerful blocking position, he remained excluded from office.

His reputation as an unreliable and purely negative figure was reinforced when his protégé, General Boulanger, embarked in 1888 on a political campaign that for a time seriously threatened the survival of the parliamentary republic. Clemenceau by this time opposed Boulanger, but several of his associates became Boulangists, and the Boulangist threat convinced many of the dangers of Clemenceau's past tactics. The Panama scandal was to complete his political eclipse. The central figure in this affair of parliamentary corruption was Herz (q.v.) who had been a financial backer of *La Justice* thus tainting Clemenceau, although Clemenceau himself was not touched by the bribery charges. He had abandoned his Paris seat in 1885 for a southern constituency in the Var department, and after a vicious election campaign was defeated there in 1893.

This was the nadir of Clemenceau's career. He had lost his wife, his money and his newspaper, and his political position seemed irretrievably compromised. He set out to make a new career as a journalist and writer. He wrote vaguely philosophical pieces, a weak novel and even feebler play. The Dreyfus affair first revealed his real talent as a writer and then restored his political fortunes. From the end of 1897 he campaigned with passionate conviction on Dreyfus's behalf, arguing that his acquittal would defend the honour of France and her army, not the contrary as the anti-Dreyfusards believed. The Dreyfus affair produced a political realignment that favoured his return to the political stage. It ended the *ralliement* in which a *rapprochement* between catholicism and moderate republicans had been attempted. This amounted to a conjunction of the centres against extremes – intransigent Catholics on the right, Socialists and Radicals on the left. As such it was anathema to Clemenceau, who had expressed his belief in a clear cut left/right polarization in a famous phrase 'The Revolution is a bloc'. When the great majority of French Catholics opposed the Dreyfusard campaign, this issue was given dramatic human embodiment. Thus the victory of the Dreyfusards set the scene for the subsequent attack on the Church and the emergence of the Radical Party as the leading political force. Although Clemenceau was never a leader of the Radical Party, his pro-Dreyfus journalism made him a leading Radical politician in a wider sense. After gaining a secure political base when elected senator for the Var in 1902, he played a moderating role over the next four years, distancing himself from the extreme anticlericalism of the Combes cabinet.

In March 1906, at the age of 64, he held office for the first time, as minister of the interior in the Sarrien cabinet. Taking over as prime minister, while remaining minister of the interior, in October 1906, he remained in office until July 1909, one of the longest uninterrupted periods of any political leader during the Third Republic.

This period saw Clemenceau's reputation shift from that of dangerous radical to the opposite – the strikebreaker and scourge of the CGT (Confédération Générale du Travail, the trade union confederation), *le premier flic* (chief policeman). But his ministry was not without its achievements, including the settlement of Church and state relations, the nationalization of the Western Railway Company, and the passing of a law instituting income tax, by the Chamber of Deputies, although it remained vetoed by the Senate. That Clemenceau was able to ride out at least three dangerous periods of labour unrest, the coal-miners' strike, the Draveil strike, and the wine-growers' strike, was in itself an achievement. By the end of his ministry, fears of a revolutionary syndicalist wave could be seen to have been enormously exaggerated. There was achievement too in foreign affairs, notably the Franco-German agreement on Morocco in 1909. Contrary to the view that he was bound to antagonize Germany, he could be said to have followed firm but conciliatory policies.

Clemenceau's first ministry ended on 20 July 1909, in a surprise defeat over a minor issue, typical of Third Republic parliamentary habits. After a lecture tour to South America (the lectures being subsequently published as *Sur la Democratie*), he made his return to the forefront of French political life in January 1912 by overthrowing the Caillaux ministry over the compromise settlement with Germany that followed the Agadir crisis. He now emphasized the need for France to stand up to German bullying. In 1913 he founded another newspaper *L'Homme Libre*, which he continued to edit until November 1917. It was renamed *L'Homme Enchaîné* after being suspended by the wartime censor. He campaigned in 1913 for the law extending conscription to three years.

Though he is now best known as France's wartime leader, Clemenceau was only prime minister for the last twelve wartime months. Until November 1917 he was a formidable critic, in newspaper editorials, and influential parliamentary committees, where his leading role was demonstrated when he became president in 1915 of the Senate committees for the army and for foreign affairs. He only rarely spoke in full Senate sessions.

His criticism was based on the failure to prosecute the war successfully, not from the opposite viewpoint – on hope for a compromise peace. The conflict between the two views came to a head in the summer of 1917, after the failure of the April offensive and the widespread mutinies among French troops, which were kept secret from the general public, but were well known to inner political circles. Clemenceau's return to office began with his attack on the minister of the interior, Malvy, for not acting vigorously against German spies, traitors and in a wider sense against left-wing pacifist agitation. Malvy's resignation brought down the Ribot government in September 1917. The president, Poincaré, then sent for the independent Socialist Painlevé, but his government was very weak, and clearly not destined to last. It coincided with the most disastrous period of the war for the Allies, with the Italian defeat at Caporetto, the Bolshevik revolution in Russia, the exhaustion of British and French armies on the western front, and the long delay before United States help arrived.

Painlevé was defeated in the Chamber of Deputies, and Clemenceau became prime minister again on 16 November 1917. In his inaugural speech he promised 'No more pacifist campaigns: no more German intrigues, neither treason, nor semi-treason: the war, nothing but the war.' His cabinet consisted of second-rank Radical Party politicians, 'obedient underlings', and of technicians from outside parliament.

He retained Pétain as commander of the French armies. His strategy was to avoid further offensives on the western front, while awaiting the arrival of the Americans. The Germans sought to achieve a decisive victory before the American arrival, with the great offensive of March 1918, which almost achieved the decisive tactical advantage of breaking through to the Channel and separating the British and French armies. At this point Clemenceau played a decisive role by overruling Pétain's defeatism and imposing the aggressive Foch as supreme Allied commander with power to give orders to both British and French.

After another desperate German offensive in July, the tide turned and by October the Germans asked for an armistice. Clemenceau's political position had at first seemed weak, and observers thought that his government was bound to fall on several occasions during its first six months. But victory brought him

immense prestige, and the nickname Père-La-Victoire (Father Victory). His position was now unassailable. No other leading political figure shared this prestige, and Clemenceau had a free hand to speak for France in the peace negotiations. The foreign minister, Pichon, a protégé of Clemenceau from the 1880s, was totally eclipsed, and although Clemenceau faced opposition from Poincaré and Foch, he was able to outmanoeuvre them both.

In spite of the huge assembly of statesmen and officials from the Allied powers in Paris for the peace settlement, the crucial decisions were taken in intimate informal meetings of the council of four, Wilson for the United States, Lloyd George for Britain, Clemenceau for France, and Orlando for Italy. In fact only the first three really counted. In this forum, Clemenceau, playing a weak hand – for France's military, economic and above all financial, strength was now far below that of her Anglo-Saxon allies – did remarkably well. The essential issue was the treatment of Germany. Neither Lloyd George, and still less Wilson, were willing to provide France with what Clemenceau and the overwhelming majority of French opinion regarded as essential for future security. Finally a compromise was achieved.

Clemenceau abandoned his proposal to separate the Rhineland from Germany, in return for a fifteen-year military occupation, which could be prolonged if the Germans had not fulfilled all their obligations under the Treaty, and a mutual treaty of guarantee between Britain, France and the United States. Unfortunately this promise was not honoured, as the Treaty was not ratified by the American Senate, and France was left feeling cheated and vulnerable. Clemenceau presided over the ceremony in the Palace of Versailles on 28 June 1919, when the Treaty was signed by German plenipotentiaries.

The elections of November 1919 saw the triumph of the centre-right electoral coalition of the Bloc National. Clemenceau was clearly the national hero, and expected to be elected president in January 1920. But the president was elected, not by the populace, but by the members of Parliament: Briand's behind the scenes manoeuvrings ensured that Clemenceau could not have been elected by an overwhelming majority, but only after a contest in which right-wing votes would have compensated for opposition from the left. In these circumstances he withdrew his candidature.

Although now nearly 80, he still had another nine years to live, years filled with travel (to India and to the United States) and with writing on a wide range of subjects – studies of Demosthenes, and of his friend Monet, a philosophy of life entitled *In the evening of my thought* . . . . He had time to complete a first draft of a reply to Foch's attack on his policies in 1917–19, published posthumously as *Grandeurs and Miseries of Victory*, before succumbing to a sudden and fatal illness on 24 November 1929.

A superficial verdict on Clemenceau's career would be that it exemplifies the dictum that 'un Jacobin ministre n'est pas un ministre Jacobin', that we see in him an example of the political challenger from the left who becomes a reactionary authoritarian when in power. This view is not totally wrong. For instance he abandoned his opposition to the 1875 constitution and spent the productive part of his political career in the Senate whose abolition he had advocated: his arguments against colonial conquests were abandoned and he extended the French empire in 1919: his criticisms of *laissez-faire* capitalism, and his support for the claims of organized labour were, to say the least, toned down after 1906. Nevertheless a strong case can be made for the continuity of his basic political stance. There are two central points. The first is that in domestic politics Clemenceau certainly did not move from extreme left to extreme right, but at the most from left of centre to right of centre. Although he changed his views about the details of constitutional arrangements, his basic belief was the defence of representative democracy against opponents from left and right. He detested the Second Empire, and held that it was legitimate to overthrow it by violence, as it had itself been established by a *coup d'état*. But once democracy was restored he refused to support revolutionary attempts to overturn the verdict of the polls however much he hated the policies of those elected, as in 1871. His insistence in 1906–9 on the need to maintain the authority of the State against strikers and theorists of revolutionary syndicalism followed logically from his earlier position. Throughout he was neither revolutionary nor reactionary, but a believer in liberal parliamentary democracy. The second element of continuity is provided by his patriotism, which it would be unjust to call nationalism. In this context it must be realized that Clemenceau stayed constant while the political landscape revolved around him. During the first part of his life the polarities of the revolutionary and Restoration period still held good; that is, the left was nationalistic, the more revolutionary the more fervent, while the right rejected such emotions. By 1900 the situation was reversed and polarity went from a nationalistic right to an internationalist, pacifistic or, in wartime, defeatist, left. Here also, Clemenceau can be seen as holding a central position,

avoiding both extremes, a defender of Dreyfus but also a patriot who believed in the need for a strong French army. His rejection of Bonapartism included distaste for the military glories of the first Napoleon, as well as for the disasters of the third. He did not seek to engineer a war of revenge against Germany, but only to resist further German encroachments on France's status as an independent great power.

The view that Clemenceau ended as a reactionary and a dictator cannot be sustained. It is based on misconceptions arising from contemporary polemics. His two governments, and especially his wartime government, provided strong leadership, but were based on parliamentary support. France survived the war with the principle of civilian rule and the details of her constitutional system intact, while Germany succumbed to military rule. A second misconception is that he prevented a compromise peace with Germany in 1917, and then imposed a harsh and retributory settlement on her in 1919. Germany never offered an acceptable compromise, and there was no alternative to victory over her. In the negotiations of 1919, contrary to the view so widely promulgated by J. M. Keynes, Clemenceau did not press the extreme demands of the real French reactionaries, who argued for the dismemberment of Germany. Instead he insisted on the importance of maintaining unity between France and her Anglo-Saxon allies, and thus accepted a moderate treaty, which, if it had been maintained, could have provided for French security. It was because Clemenceau came from the left, and was still in 1917–20 not on the right, but at the centre of the political spectrum, that he could inspire the great majority of French people with determination to survive the terrible ordeal of the war.

Clemenceau's career is at the centre of the paradox of the Third Republic – a regime which was adopted as an unloved compromise, intended to be only a temporary expedient, but which proved to be the longest-lasting regime France has known since 1789. It is paradoxical also in that it provided the governmental framework in which the country recovered from the defeat and despair of 1870 to the victory of 1918, and then that the same system failed in such a dramatic fashion in the next twenty years. Clemenceau is central here because of his part in establishing in the formative years 1879–89 a way of operating the political system that made weak government and stalemate endemic. Then his periods in office showed that, at least in exceptional circumstances, it was possible to use that system to provide strong, effective and yet democratic government. That very success, in turn, ensured that there would be no change, either in the constitution or in the wider political culture, so that the Third Republic continued down its road to deadlock and disaster in 1940.

Bibliography

There are many biographies, but very few are serious works of scholarship.

In English: G. Brunn, *Clemenceau* (Harnden, Conn.: Anchor Books, 1943); D.R. Watson, *Georges Clemenceau, a Political Biography* (London: Eyre Methuen, 1974); J.B. Duroselle, *Clemenceau* (Paris: Fayard, 1988).

In French: *Clemenceau et La Justice, Actes du Colloque de décembre 1979* (Paris: Publication de la Sorbonne, 1983). Preface by A. Wormser; Serie France XIX–XXI, no. 15.

The following works by collaborators are useful for the primary source material they contain:

Martet, J. (1930), *Clemenceau, the events of his life as told by himself*, London, Longmans.

Mordacq, H. (1930–1), *Le Ministère Clemenceau, journal d'un Témoin*, 4 vols, Paris: Plon.

Wormser, G. (1961), *La République de Clemenceau*, Paris: PUF.

Wormser, G. (1979), *Clemenceau vu de prés*, Paris: Hachette.

DRW

CLÉMENTEL, Etienne (1864–1936)

In many ways Clémentel was a typical politician of the Third Republic: he came from an agricultural background, entered politics after studying law, and maintained a strong base in local government (in the Riom–Puy de Dôme area) while active in central government. Soon regarded as being of ministerial potential ('ministrable'), he had a solid rather than brilliant career, and was a member of many cabinets and even more committees, often as rapporteur or chairman: he was one of the reliable figures who gave continuity to the Third Republic in spite of its apparent lack of stability. He was elected deputy in 1900 as a left-wing Radical but, like many politicians of his generation, served in a number of centre left coalitions. When he lost his seat in 1920, he was elected to the Senate where he remained until 1935.

Clémentel was nevertheless distinctive in some respects: although he shared a legal training with many Third Republic politicians, his own aspirations (as opposed to his family's ambitions for him) were

artistic. A friend of Rodin and Monet, he sculpted, painted and was co-author of an opera, *Vercingétorix*. As a politician, however, his main area of action was not culture or education but the economy. In this field he was far from being a mere executive: during the First World War, in particular, he was very much at the centre of the economic war effort (together with such figures as A. Thomas) and his analysis of France's economic shortcomings as well as the style of action he advocated make him something of a precursor of economic planning 'à la française' who came too early or whose plans were perhaps, as R. Kuisel suggests, too ambitious.

Throughout his career one can trace a common theme: the importance of collaboration and concerted action as a means of improving France's economic performance. Thus, before the war he was an early advocate of farming cooperatives and, in colonial matters, of concertation with local populations. In the liberal and individualistic climate of the prewar era, however, his ideas had little influence. It was only the wartime spirit of national unity, the 'Union sacrée', which enabled him to force certain sections of the economy to work together under his direction at the Trade Ministry, where he remained through five different governments, and which was expanded to take in army supplies, industry, transport, posts and telecommunications, labour and agriculture, thus making him in effect a sort of minister of the national economy. He was particularly successful in using Allied pressure to bring importers and users of key raw materials to an acceptance of concentration. He was very much aware that France's industrial under-achievement was to a large extent a problem of attitude: his eloquent appeals to 'men of good will' to work together for a common purpose and to accept the role of the state as leader and arbiter of the economy prefigure de Gaulle's famous description of the Plan as an 'ardent obligation' for all French people. With the return of peace, however, the desire to reject the constraints and controls imposed by the war, and the fear of corporatism and dirigism, led to Clémentel's plan for reconstruction being abandoned in favour of Loucheur's pragmatic liberalism.

Some of Clémentel's ideas nevertheless survived: his National Association for Economic Expansion was to develop into today's French employers' federation (Conseil National du Patronat Français); he introduced an arbitration procedure to resolve conflicts between workers and management, and he reorganized chambers of commerce on a regional basis: this was in fact a much watered down version of an earlier grand design for economic planning regions, an approach which would have to wait until the 1950s to be seriously considered again.

Bibliography

Clémentel gives his own account of his wartime economic policies in *La France et la politique économique interalliée* (Paris & Newhaven: Carnegie Foundation, 1931). For a recent critical analysis see R. Kuisel, *Capitalism and the State in Modern France* (Cambridge: Cambridge University Press, 1981).

M-MH

COCHIN, Denys Pierre Augustin (1851–1922)

Denys Cochin is chiefly remembered as the first prominent Catholic politician to have been included in a post-1879 French government. Minister of state between 1915 and 1917, he first entered parliament in 1893 as the liberal monarchist deputy for the 8th *arrondissement* in Paris, a seat he retained until 1919. A staunch defender of Church rights, in 1903 he attempted to create a Catholic party, the Comité Catholique, and in 1905 worked to modify the Law of Separation. It was for his skills as a negotiator that he was later included in Briand's cabinet of 1915, where he was in charge of blockades. In 1917, however, he resigned his post, believing that the government no longer embodied the ideals of the Union Sacrée. By then an old man, he chose not to stand in the 1919 elections and died shortly afterwards in 1922.

Throughout his career Cochin retained an ambivalent attitude towards the Third Republic. Although he was a monarchist, he was prepared to accept the Republic as long as it was governed by moderates. Yet in the early 1900s it was the Radicals who were in charge. The creation of the Comité Catholique was, therefore, an attempt to head off the anticlerical challenge. Here, however, Cochin betrayed a political naïveté and the Comité Catholique came to naught. The French right was too divided to rally to the cause of religious defence, whereas the papacy was against the establishment of a Catholic party. Only later did Cochin reconcile himself to the Republic. In 1915 he recognized the need for national unity and was happy to accept a government post, even though this meant sitting alongside anticlericals and Socialists.

Cochin was always more successful as a conciliator and negotiator than as a political leader. His diplomatic skills were clearly demonstrated in 1905 when he acted as an unofficial intermediary between Paris and Rome. Although he questioned the Separation of Church and state, he realized that it was futile to oppose the law in its entirety. Accordingly, he was one of the twenty-three Catholic intellectuals who signed an open letter urging the Church hierarchy to accept the Separation. In this, the 'green Cardinals', so-called because they wore the green robes of the Académie française, argued that the Church must adopt some form of organization recognized by the state; otherwise catholicism would become a minority religion. Although some clerics disputed this, such counsels of caution were important in ensuring that the Church did not adopt a posture of outright defiance.

In many ways Cochin's career illustrates the dilemmas confronting the French right before 1914. Having lost power in 1879, members of the right were uncertain how to proceed. One option was to seize control illegally through a *coup d'état*, yet Cochin refused to support General Boulanger. A further possibility was to exploit a popular issue such as religious defence which might win a parliamentary majority. Cochin tried this, but with little success. The remaining option was for members of the right to organize themselves into a united party with a clear legislative programme, yet the Comité Catholique fell far short of this ideal. Nevertheless, Cochin's career did offer some hope to the right. His inclusion in government in 1915 showed that it was possible for a Catholic to become a minister and helped pave the way for the Bloc National in 1919.

Bibliography

Dansette, A. (1961), *A Religious History of Modern France,* 2 vols, Freiburg: Herder, 1961 (provides an overview of the whole period).

Larkin, M. (1974), *Church and State after the Dreyfus Affair. The Separation Issue in France,* London: Macmillan, 1974 (useful for Cochin's role during the separation).

Martin, B.M. (1978), *Count Albert de Mun. Paladin of the Third Republic,* Chapel Hill: University of North Carolina Press, 1978 (good on the Comité Catholique).

Shapiro, D. (1962), *The Right in France, 1890–1919. Three Studies.* St Antony's Papers, no. 13, London: Chatto & Windus, 1962 (little on Cochin himself, but good on the problems of the French right before 1914).

NA

COHN-BENDIT, Daniel (1945–)

Born in southern France but of German nationality, Cohn-Bendit more than any other single figure came to epitomize the 'spirit of 1968' in Paris, its anarchistic provocativeness and ludic indefinability. A sociology student at the University of Nanterre (where in September 1968 he received an outstanding degree in his enforced absence), Cohn-Bendit came to the fore as an animator of the 'Movement of 22 March', named after the date of a meeting at Nanterre called to protest against the arrest of six members of the National Vietnam Committee. The movement saw parliamentary politics and peaceful demonstrations as at best outmoded, at worst counter-productive; occupation of the university and its eventual conversion into a 'red base' or 'anti-university' to debate problems of capitalism and imperialism was what was called for instead. However utopian this may now sound, the fact remains that the May events started from the universities, and that it was there that their most durable effects were (perhaps still are) felt; the forcible exclusion of politics from the university campus became, as a result of the actions of Cohn-Bendit and his associates, a thing of the past.

It is not surprising that Cohn-Bendit was detested with equal fervour by the Communist Party, for whom he was a spoilt bourgeois playing at revolution, and the right and far right. The latter's stercoraceous mouthpiece, *Minute*, dubbed him a 'German Jew' (an obvious allusion to Marx); 'we are all German Jews' immediately became a rallying-cry among demonstrators . . . The 'respectable' right, for its part, expelled him on 20 May 1968, and not until ten years later did Giscard restore his right of residence. (There is a persistent, but unconfirmed, rumour that he was smuggled across the German border after one clandestine return visit in the back of Lacan's Jaguar.) To see Cohn-Bendit as merely a prankster, however, would be to underestimate the seriousness and intensity of his political commitment. In *Le gauchisme – remède à la maladie sénile du communisme* (Obsolete Communism – the Left-Wing Alternative, 1968), written for publishers untroubled by 'the fact that their cash will be used for the next round of Molotov cocktails' (p. 11), the role of the vanguard party is insistently called into question, and the Communists and the trade union movement alike are branded as incorrigible enemies of the spontaneous revolutionary process. 'The barricades were no longer simply a means of self-defence, they became a symbol of individual liberty' (p. 63); classes and the wider social formation make much the same

kind of periodic appearance in this rhapsodic view of existential deliverance as they must have seemed to do while the events were going on.

Yet the failure of all the Stalinist leopard's attempts to change its spots, and the broadening of the sense and scope of political activity that was one important factor in the Socialist victories of 1981, show, like 'Danny the Red's' meteoric rise to fame, how surely as well as erratically he had put his finger on the major social changes that were going on. His own subsequent career has remained (in so far as this can be said) true to his 1968 origins; he lived (mostly in Frankfurt) for four years with the former Maoist, now feminist, Barbara Koster, and is currently in a commune. He is now active in the (ecologist) Green Party, declaring himself a supporter of what might appear to be the very 'democracy' he so despised in 1968 – except that the Greens' prominence in it is for him an index of how far it has changed: 'Today, even the idea of revolution has deserted our contemporaries' imagination. We have had to bow to democratic formalism.

'But what is this democracy we talk about? For me, it is the kind that strives to improve day-to-day relations between men, women, men and women, men and children, women and children, that tries to shed light on our day-to-day lives.

'That is the idea for which I am active in the Green Party.' (*Nous l'avons tant aimée, la Révolution – Oh, how we loved the Revolution*, 1986).

Bibliography

Obsolete Communism: The left-wing alternative (Harmondsworth: Penguin Books, 1969). An inevitably euphoric account of the 'events' backed up by analysis of 'the Gaullist phenomenon' and of the omnipresent bureaucracy of communism.

Nous l'avons tant aimée, la Révolution (Paris: Barrault, 1986). Based on four television programmes (made with government subsidy . . .) Cohn-Bendit made in 1986 to interview, and trace the divergent evolution of, prominent 1968 activists (French and others). The glossy 'coffee-table' format at once makes it possible to savour many of the great photogenic moments of 1968 anew and leaves Cohn-Bendit wide open to the classic *gauchiste* charge of 'recuperation'.

KAR

COMBES, Emile Justin Louis (1835–1921)

'Le petit père Combes' is synonymous with the militant anticlericalism of the Third Republic. He had witnessed the dangers of Church influence under the Second Empire and again during the mid-1870s, and he was determined to prevent it re-emerging. At the same time, an unhappy start on an ill-chosen ecclesiastical career had added a personal bitterness to this resolution, giving his anticlericalism a markedly obsessive character. His subsequent fortunes exemplified all that was most typical of small-town radicalism. While practising as a country doctor, he acquired his Masonic grades and rose through successive layers of local government to a seat in the Senate in 1885 – which he was to occupy for the rest of his life, while keeping his feet firmly rooted in the modest little municipality of Pons in the Charente-Inférieure. He was briefly minister for education, fine arts and religions in Léon Bourgeois's (q.v.) cabinet of 1895–6, when he conducted a vigorous enquiry into the clientele of Catholic private education, foreshadowing his celebrated onslaught on Catholic schools and the religious orders during his subsequent premiership (7 June 1902 to 18 January 1905).

The aftermath of the Dreyfus crisis created a parliament in 1902 that was favourably disposed to tough measures against the Church, but Combes surpassed what many expected of him, disquieting Waldeck-Rousseau (q.v.) who had been partly responsible for his becoming premier. He brought about the expulsion of all but five of the unauthorized religious orders, and was directly and indirectly responsible for the closure of a third of France's Catholic schools by 1911. He greatly extended his predecessor's attempts to make advancement in the civil service, the army and other forms of public employment dependent on sympathy towards current Republican policy, and instructed prefects 'while you owe justice to everyone . . . you keep your favours for those who have unmistakably proved their fidelity to Republican institutions'. The revelation that the Masonic secretariat was systematically supplying the war office with information on the policies and religious inclinations of candidates for promotion discredited the government and led indirectly to Combes' resignation.

It was ironic that Combes' anticlerical campaign should eventually escape his control and result in the disestablishment of the Church under his successor in December 1905. Combes had always feared that disestablishment would strengthen the Church, through the freedom Rome would gain in the nomination of bishops; but his attempts to intimidate the Vatican into accepting his stringent interpretation of the concordat created a situation that he could no longer master. He was to make a brief come-back to ministerial office, when Aristide Briand gave him a token seat in his cabinet of national union in 1915–16.

Bibliography

The years of his ministry are discussed in his somewhat tendentious memoirs, *Mon Ministère: mémoires, 1902–1905* (Paris: Plon, 1956), and in Maurice Larkin, *Church and State after the Dreyfus Affair* (London: Macmillan, 1974).

ML

CONSTANS, Jean Antoine Ernest (1833–1913)

Ernest Constans played a large part in the agitated politics of the late 1880s and early 1890s. He was minister of the interior in two successive crises – Boulangism and the Panama affair – and showed in his handling of them the sort of unscrupulous toughness that would make him a model for some of his successors. Born to a family without means in Béziers (Hérault) he studied law but soon turned to business and spent some time in Spain. The manner in which he carried out his business activities attracted much criticism and gave rise to the image of shady ruthlessness that would carry over into his political career. By the end of the Second Empire he was teaching law at the Faculty of Toulouse, where he became a municipal councillor. Under Thiers (q.v.) he was very active in promoting the secularization of local primary schools, an action which led to the right-wing government that succeeded Thiers forcing him out of his municipal office and attempting to deprive him of his university job.

Elected to the Chamber of Deputies in 1876, he opposed the 16 May 1877 *coup* and voted solidly with the Opportunist group. He first became minister of the interior in the 1880 government of Freycinet (q.v.). His aggressiveness in dealing with the Congregational orders led to the breakup of the government but he kept his post in the succeeding ministry of Ferry (q.v.). He undertook an administrative organization of Algeria and presided over the successful elections of 1881. Between 1881 and 1887 he was out of office, though in Parliament; he led an official mission to China shortly after the 1885 elections and was briefly governor-general of Indo-China in 1887 (his time there was not very successful and he was, characteristically, accused of illegally profiting from licensed gambling houses). He returned to the Interior Ministry under Tirard (q.v.) in 1889 at the height of the scare provoked by Boulanger's (q.v.) revisionist campaign. Managing to convince Boulanger that he was about to be arrested he provoked the latter's flight to Brussels, an action from which Boulanger's reputation never recovered. Constans' also rushed through the bill reintroducing single-member constituencies (*scroutin d'arrondissement*) and forbidding multiple candidatures. Once the election campaign began he leaned heavily on the prefects to make sure that Boulangist candidates did not win. It was this hard-nosed use of state power that gave him his enduring reputation (the incorruptible Waldeck-Rousseau (q.v.) greatly admired his political skill).

His role in the Panama affair showed his capacity for intrigue. He had resigned as interior minister in March 1890 after a quarrel with Tirard but was back in office in 1892 when the Panama affair started to unravel. Like so many of the politicians of the time, he had known Cornelius Herz (q.v.) but he also knew the names of the deputies who had accepted bribes from the Panama company and he was rumoured (though he denied it) to be behind the press exploitation of the scandal. Like many other such affairs, the Panama scandal was never fully explained. It marked the end of Constans' ministerial, though not his public, career. In 1898 he embarked on a ten-year stint as ambassador to Constantinople which brought him very close to Abdul-Hamid and which ended, at his own request, with the arrival to power of the Young Turks.

Bibliography

Chapman, G. (1962), *The Third Republic of France*, London: Macmillan.

Sorlin, P. (1962), *Waldeck Rousseau*, Paris: A. Colin.

PM

COSTE-FLORET, Paul (1911–79)

An eminent constitutional lawyer, and politician in the Mouvement Républicain Populaire (MRP) – the French equivalent of a Christian Democrat party – Paul Coste-Floret was one of the main inspirers of the Constitution of the Fourth Republic, approved by referendum in October 1946, and also a member of the committee which drew up the Fifth Republic Constitution, approved by referendum in September 1958.

In the inter-war years, Coste-Floret was active in the Association Catholique de la Jeunesse Française, as was his twin brother, Alfred, whose own career as a constitutional lawyer and Christian Democrat politican was remarkably similar. Paul Coste-Floret became law lecturer at Montpellier in the 1930s and developed his specialism of constitutional law. He was a member of the Resistance, and deputy from 1945 to 1967 for the MRP and then the Centre démocrate.

Coste-Floret's role in the shaping of the Fourth Republic Constitution was central. He was *rapporteur* of the National Assembly's constitutional committee when this body was drawing up, in summer 1946, a second draft constitution, the first having been rejected in a referendum. He urged the Constitutional Assembly to adopt a solution mid-way between a presidential regime, which for him led to 'personalized power' and an all-powerful parliament (*régime d'assemblée*), which led to revolution. He wanted a parliamentary regime, with a prime minister, modelled on the British system. The re-emergence of the political habits of the Third Republic made this hope unrealistic as the National Assembly came more and more to challenge rather than support incumbent governments.

Coste-Floret as an MRP politician occupied several ministerial posts in Fourth Republic governments, not least as colonial minister and minister responsible for Indo-China, where, with some reluctance, he applied a tough antiliberal, anti-independence policy.

Disappointed with the way the Fourth Republic Constitution worked out, and opposed to devices such as the grouping of electoral lists (*apparentement*) which magnified support for pro-system parties in the 1951 election, he came round to the view of de Gaulle and Debré that a parliamentary regime would not work unless it was 'rationalized' by preventing the Assembly from imposing its will and unless the president of the Republic had the power to step in and mediate when necessary. Coste-Floret served as one of the three MRP members of the consultative constitutional committee for the Fifth Republic Constitution in summer 1958.

Coste-Floret's reaction to the first phase of de Gaulle's presidency was that of many French centrists – he was not happy when de Gaulle distorted the Constitution, by increasing presidential powers, though he approved of his policy over Algeria.

Moreover, he joined with most constitutional lawyers in attacking de Gaulle's 'unconstitutional' method of changing the Constitution (i.e. by referendum) in October 1962. Although active in moves to reconstitute a new centre political group from the defunct MRP in 1966, Coste-Floret turned more and more to university teaching.

MS

COT, Pierre (1895–1977)

Perhaps the most brilliant of all the politicians who came to prominence in the inter-war period, Pierre Cot failed to achieve the positions of responsibility for which he seemed destined. He was twice minister of aviation in the 1930s and showed imagination and energy in his efforts to improve France's civil and military air force. After the Second World War he was a highly visible and articulate political personality; but he never again held ministerial office. Hostile to the main thrust of French foreign policy in a Europe divided by superpowers' rivalries, his admiration for the Soviet Union led him to become one of France's most prominent fellow travellers and he thus virtually excluded himself from power.

Cot came from the Savoie and was born to a family with a long tradition of involvement in local politics. He studied law in Grenoble, fought – and was wounded – in the First World War, came to Paris where he performed outstandingly in the law teaching examination (*agrégation*) and was briefly a law professor at Rennes. His ability attracted the attention of Poincaré (q.v.) who brought him into his private office; but it was as a Radical that he entered the Chamber of Deputies in 1928 for a Savoy constituency. (He also succeeded his father and grandfather as mayor of Coise.) A superb speaker, he quickly became a leader of the Radical left (the 'Young Turk' movement) and in 1933, still under 40, he succeeded Painlevé (q.v.) at the Air Ministry. He immediately set about the amalgamation of France's many – and weak – civil air lines into a national company, Air France, using as pretext the scandal that surrounded the collapse of Aéropostale. His interest, however, were much more than technical. He was a strong supporter of the League of Nations, an equally strong advocate of the Popular Front dynamic that followed the collapse of parliamentary authority on the 6 February 1934, and above all, a champion of the cause of Republican Spain against Franco and his Fascist allies. As minister of air in the Popular Front governments of June

1936 to January 1938, he strove to overcome the official policy of non-intervention and ensured that war material, including planes, did reach the Republicans. His head of private office and close collaborator was the future head of the Resistance, Jean Moulin (q.v.). His very obvious leftism made him a target for intense right-wing animosity, and he enraged his opponents even further by his success in nationalizing France's aircraft industry, though he managed to win the cooperation of its former owners, like Marcel Dassault (q.v.).

Cot was in the United States when France fell. Deprived of his citizenship by the Vichy government, he vigorously defended the record of the pre-war governments of the left and went to Algiers. De Gaulle sent him on a study mission to the USSR (which he had already visited in 1933) and he came back greatly impressed with the Soviet achievement. Before the war he had advocated Franco-Soviet cooperation in military procurement; now he became a champion of close ties at all levels. The nature of his post-war political evolution was emerging. Back in Parliament in 1945, he played a major role in the debates on the first draft of the constitution supporting, as the Communists did, an Assembly-led regime. With the onset of the cold war, he was active in the opposition to the westward thrust of French foreign policy. He rejected the Atlantic Alliance in favour of 'active neutralism', helped run the Communist Mouvement de la Paix, and founded the fellow travelling Union Progressiste and was awarded the Stalin Peace Prize in 1954. Elected with Communist support in the Rhône in 1951 and 1956, he was thereafter out of Parliament except for the short legislature of 1967–8 when he was a deputy for Paris and made an effective attack on the Pompidou government in the parliamentary censure motion of May 1968. He was always much in demand as an international lawyer and university professor and his links with his native Savoie remained strong (he was mayor of Coise from 1928 until 1971 when his son – the Socialist politician Jean-Pierre Cot – took over). He always retained the radicalism of his youth; and it was this that ensured that he would end his career as a talented outsider.

Bibliography

Pierre Cot figures in books on the Popular Front but has written his own account of those years in:
Cot, P. (1939), *L'Armée de l'air*, Paris: Grasset.
Cot, P. (1944), *Le Procès de la République*, 2 vols, New York: La Maison Française, which are

translated as *Triumph of Treason*, Chicago and New York: Ziff-Davis, 1944.

PM

'COTY', François Spaturno (1874–1934)

Born in Ajaccio, Corsica in 1874, François Coty began his career in provincial journalism whilst at the same time developing his talent as a connoisseur of perfume. After his arrival in Paris in 1904, he rapidly established a flourishing perfume business, and by the outbreak of the First World War the Maison Coty had a worldwide reputation. His immense wealth encouraged him in the 1920s to indulge his two other passions, the press and politics. He gained control of *Le Figaro* in 1922 but, dissatisfied with its limited popular appeal, turned his attention in 1927 to the production of a cheap mass circulation newspaper of a kind France had not yet seen. Despite the efforts of the 'big five' Paris dailies and the Hachette group to block him in the courts, Coty launched *L'Ami du Peuple* with some initial success in 1928, and followed it with an evening version of the paper one year later. His acquisition of several weekly periodicals had made him a genuine 'press baron' by the early 1930s, and in 1933 he made his most spectacular political move, founding the extreme right-wing league Solidarité Française (French Solidarity) and turning *L'Ami du Peuple* into its mouthpiece. He was elected senator for Corsica in 1933, but crippled financially by a damaging divorce settlement which lost him *Le Figaro* and forced him to sell *L'Ami du Peuple*, he died in the summer of 1934.

Coty's ambitions as a newspaper proprietor have some interesting contemporary echoes, but he is best remembered for his associations with a succession of right-wing extra-parliamentary organizations during the 1920s and early 1930s. The rise of fascism in Europe, which was seen by the Communist International and Marxists at large mainly in terms of armed bands financed by big business, made the French left particularly sensitive to any evidence of links between the paramilitary right-wing leagues and the interests of 'capital'. Coty, along with the electrical industry magnate Ernest Mercier (q.v.) and the wealthy champagne producer Pierre Taittinger (leader of Jeunesses Patriotes), was thus at the heart of the left's fears that France might tread the same path as Italy and Germany.

Coty's political connections in the 1920s were the subject of rumour and speculation, and it is hard to discern the truth behind the allegations of the left

and the internecine polemics of rival right-wing factions. It seems likely that Coty used his wealth to try and gain influence with both Action Française and Georges Valois' short-lived Faisceau (1924), but there is no doubt about his involvement in the foundation of Solidarité Française in 1933 and his use of *L'Ami du Peuple* to launch this new league. However, the movement was never much more than an anti-Communist street-fighting organization modelled on foreign fascism. Though it gained a brief notoriety for its pro-Nazi stance in 1933 and its involvement in the Paris riots of February 1934, its influence was marginal even in the narrow enclaves of the extreme-right, where it was overshadowed by Action Française, Jeunesses Patriotes and Croix de Feu. Despite the sinister image he had acquired for the left, Coty never achieved the political returns he expected from his energetic financial patronage.

Bibliography

The most useful source on Coty's press career is R. Manévy, *Histoire de la presse 1914–39* (Paris: Corréa, 1945). An interesting, if possibly biased view of Coty's early involvement with the right-wing leagues is given by the founder of the Faisceau, Georges Valois, in *L'Homme contre l'argent: souvenirs de dix ans 1918–28* (Paris: Librairie Valois, 1928).

BJ

COTY, René (1882–1962)

The son of a primary-school teacher, René Coty was trained as a lawyer and worked his political apprenticeship as a municipal councillor in the town of his birth, Le Havre. He was elected to Parliament in 1923, where he sat with the left Republican group until 1935, briefly holding a junior ministerial post in 1930. A senator from 1935 until 1940, he was among those who voted full powers to Pétain, though refusing to accept nomination by Vichy as mayor of Le Havre.

His major political achievements belong to the post-war era when he led the Independent group in the National Assembly (1946) and briefly tasted ministerial office in 1947–8 as minister of reconstruction and town planning. Elected to the Council of the Republic, he eventually became vice-president of the upper house. René Coty's career as the second president of the Fourth Republic began and ended in controversial circumstances. It required seven days of discussion, and thirteen ballots, before Coty, a complete outsider who only entered the fight on the eleventh ballot, broke the deadlock and secured an overall majority.

Though his mandate coincided with a difficult stage in the decolonization process, it was his pragmatism and, as a specialist in constitutional matters, his determination that the presidential office should be and be seen to be a meaningful institution which historians particularly remember. His concern for unity was always apparent; he liked to play down partisan quarrels, aware that the circumstances of his own election had made many cynical about parliamentary institutions. He particularly tried to keep the Communist Party within the Republic, being more conciliatory in this respect than his predecessor, Vincent Auriol (q.v.). Declaring that the president should not make public pronouncements on matters which the Assembly alone was competent to decide, he was in many ways a traditionalist and a man of the Third Republic. He sought to retain the presidential right to address messages to Parliament, a right which he exercised spectacularly in 1958 during the political crisis that led to de Gaulle's return to power. He was not averse to taking initiatives: his unease about Mendès France led him to facilitate Guy Mollet's accession to the premiership in 1956, and he was open in his support for the maintenance of French Algeria.

In May 1958, his threat to resign – and thereby perhaps let in a Popular Front government – unless the Assembly voted the investiture of 'le plus illustre des Français' helped de Gaulle become the last prime minister of the Fourth Republic. Coty remained president for seven months after de Gaulle's assumption of power, retiring as soon as the Fifth Republic was installed. As an indirect homage to Coty, de Gaulle was to make ex-presidents life members of the Constitutional Council, and in 1962 he praised Coty posthumously for having recognized in his successor that 'profound legitimacy' alone could ensure the survival of the Republic.

Bibliography

Fauvet, J. (1971), *La IVe République*, Paris: Livre de Poche.

Melnik, C. and Leites, N. (1958), *The House Without Windows: France selects a president,* Evanston, White Plains: Row, Peterson and Co., (on Coty's election).

Williams, P. (1958), *Crisis and Compromise: Politics in the Fourth Republic*, London: Longman.

ACR

COUVE DE MURVILLE, Jacques Maurice (1907–)

Maurice Couve de Murville was close to the centre of French foreign policy for a period of nearly thirty years. Intensely orthodox in manner and appearance, and notably ill at ease in the rough and tumble of French electoral politics, he seemed to epitomize the mandarin style of the French administrative elite to which he belonged. Yet his orthodoxy was less obvious than it might appear. Always identified with Gaullism, he first acquired prominence as one of the most senior officials in Vichy; and his icily correct diplomatic skills were placed for a decade at the service of a foreign policy that was highly individualistic and often destabilizing.

Couve de Murville came from a Protestant family, married the daughter of a Protestant banker and entered public service through the royal road of the Lycée Carnot, the law and literature faculties of the University of Paris and the Ecole Libre des Sciences Politiques. He joined the prestigious Inspection des Finances in 1932, spent a period as financial attaché at the Brussels embassy and in 1937 moved to a senior post in the Treasury. His career took off under Vichy. In September 1940, Yves Bouthillier (q.v.), who was Pétain's minister of finance, made him head of Vichy's foreign financial desk and, as such, president of the finance sub-committee of the Armistice Commission. He was continuously engaged in negotiations with the German occupation authorities right up to spring 1943 when he made his way, via Spain, to Algiers. After a brief period with the General Giraud (q.v.) he placed his talents and his loyalty at the service of the infinitely more capable de Gaulle and became financial commissioner of the French committee for national liberation. His next years were spent in a series of increasingly senior positions in the diplomatic service, working in Italy, in the negotiations over the Saar and in the 1947 conference of the 'big four'. In 1950 he became ambassador to Egypt and subsequently to the United States (1954) and West Germany (1956).

He became minister of foreign affairs in June 1958. The choice of a senior diplomat indicated clearly that de Gaulle wanted a capable technician to implement a policy which he himself would determine; the fact that Couve held the post for ten years is testimony to the confidence with which he was regarded. Couve had long believed in the inevitability of Algerian independence and the good relations that he had been able to establish in Bonn with Adenauer made him a useful agent in de Gaulle's quest for a special relationship with West Germany.

He was also the implacable defender of other more controversial aspects of de Gaulle's foreign policy – the vetoes on British entry to the EEC, the partial withdrawal from Nato, the encouragement to Quebec separatism and above all, the great 1965 crisis over the future direction of the European Community. De Gaulle's absolute hostility to the supra-national aspirations of the commission led Couve to boycott community institutions for a six-month period, an action which provoked much resentment among France's partners. The crisis was finally resolved by the so-called Luxembourg compromise (1966) which enshrined the primacy of states' – as opposed to the commission's – rights in determining EEC affairs.

It seems clear that by 1967 de Gaulle was seeking to groom Couve for the premiership in succession to Pompidou (q.v.). But in the general election of that year Couve showed his political limitations by failing to dislodge the notably un-Gaullist conservative Frédéric-Dupont (q.v.) from his Paris constituency: his awkward style led to him being portrayed as 'English without the umbrella, which he had probably swallowed'. (He is a great lover of Victorian fiction.) In the government reshuffle that accompanied the crisis of 1968 he briefly took over the finance portfolio on 30 May and then, after the Gaullist landslide in the June parliamentary elections, finally became prime minister. His period in office was not particularly happy. Pompidou, seen by most as the real victor of 1968, was angered by the manner of his replacement and then enraged by what he saw as Couve's passive disloyalty in the face of the smear campaign launched against Madame Pompidou. Couve's status was inevitably under threat from the reputation – and the availability – of his predecessor at a time when de Gaulle himself had been visibly weakened. Fully aware of his declining authority, de Gaulle sought to recreate his legitimacy by a referendum on regional and Senate reform, a referendum about which Couve was unenthusiastic but which, as usual, he loyally defended. A coalition of discontents led to the defeat of the referendum proposal in April 1969. De Gaulle immediately resigned, leaving Couve to carry on as prime minister under the interim presidency of Poher (q.v.).

With the election of Pompidou, Couve left office. The symbol of a defeated Gaullism, he was again unsuccessful in his bid to enter Parliament in October 1969 (he was beaten by Michel Rocard (q.v.)) but finally managed to win a seat in the National Assembly in the elections of 1973. He presided over the Assembly's foreign affairs committee between 1973 and 1978, and was for ten years a member of the regional council of the Ile-de-France. An elder stateman of Gaullism – describing himself with characteristic irony as a *baron à titre posthume* – he remains a marginal but respected figure, the most prominent survivor of the heroic age of Gaullist foreign policy.

Bibliography

Couve de Murville, M. (1971), *Une Politique etrangère*, Paris: Plon.

Kolodziez, E. (1974), *French International Policy under de Gaulle and Pompidou: The politics of grandeur*, Ithaca, NY: Cornell University Press.

Willis, F.R. (1968), *France, Germany and the New Europe 1945–67*, Stanford, Cal.: Stanford University Press.

PM

CRÉPEAU, Michel Edouard Jean (1930–   )

Crépeau has two important qualifications for a French Radical politician: he is a lawyer by training and has a strong local power-base in south-west France (he has been an energetic mayor of La Rochelle since 1971). With the Radicals split between the Parti Radical (allied to the right and, since 1978, a constituent part of the Union pour la Démocratie française, UDF) and the Mouvement des Radicaux de gauche, MRG (allied to the Socialists and a signatory of the 1972 common left-wing programme), since the early 1970s Crépeau has been a leading figure in the latter (he replaced Fabre as its president in 1978) and was its candidate in the 1981 Presidential election (polling 2.21 per cent of the votes cast in the first round). He held ministerial appointments in the Socialist governments between 1981 and 1986, but, after the left's electoral defeat of March 1986, was ousted from effective leadership of his party by the advocates of greater independence from the Socialist Party and of closer links between the MRG and the Parti Radical.

For Crépeau, radicalism belongs to the left and is a necessary component of the left. While paying lip-service to the ideal of a reunited Radical Party, he advocates a 'special relationship' with the Socialists. However, he rejects what he sees as the dogmatic elements of the French left, the 'collectivist' aspects of socialism and the Jacobin conception of the State. He favours pragmatism and gradual change, decentralization and the existence of effective counter-balancing powers within the state and society (against, for example, the dangers of presidentialism).

In this – as in his denunciation of 'technocracy' and the multinationals, his frequent appeals to the Revolutionary ideals, to secular humanism and to the ideas of the Radical philosopher of the inter-war years, Alain – he may be seen as an up-dated representative of traditional French radicalism, that of the provincial *notables*, whose party dominated so much of Third and Fourth Republic politics.

The mere survival of organized radicalism in France, let alone in the form of two separate, often pussy-footing, Radical parties, each with only very limited electoral support, is perhaps one of the paradoxes of Fifth Republic politics. The fact that the separation of left and right passes between the two Radical parties highlights the age-old dilemma of the French Radical Party, with, as the saying goes, 'its heart on the left and its wallet on the right'. Unless 'centrism' is once again destined to play a major role in French politics, it is not easy to see a Radical Party in France as being more than a relic of the past.

Bibliography

Crépeau's political ideas are set out in his *L'Avenir en face* (Paris: Seuil, 1980). For a detailed study of the French Radical Party up to the early 1970s, see: J.T. Nordmann, *Histoire des radicaux (1820–1973)* (Paris: Table Ronde, 1974).

HE

CRESSON, Edith (1934–)

Born in 1934, the daughter of a civil servant, Edith Campion – who married Jacques Cresson, currently managing director of the automobile company Peugeot, in December 1959 – was given the new title of minister of industrial restructuring and external trade in the cabinet of Prime Minister Laurent Fabius on 19 July 1984. One of only two women ministers to serve during the first Socialist term of office (1981–6), she had previously participated in all three Mauroy cabinets: as minister of agriculture from May 1981 to March 1983, and thereafter as minister of foreign trade and tourism until July 1984. With the return (albeit partial) of the Socialists to power in June 1988, Cresson was appointed minister for European affairs; it was in this capacity that in August 1988 she launched a virulent attack on Margaret Thatcher 'for not having understood that the European Community is more than a glorified grocer's shop'. She holds a degree in business from the prestigious Parisian business school Hautes Etudes Commerciales, and has also been awarded a doctorate in demography for a thesis on the life of women in a rural canton. Outside the political arena, her professional life has been primarily engaged in economic investment and in marketing.

Cresson's political career began in 1965, when she joined the Convention des Institutions Républicaines and participated in the election campaign which took François Mitterrand through to the second round against General de Gaulle. Cresson remained in the leadership of the CIR until 1971; she therefore found herself 'at the centre of things' when, that year, the CIR was supplanted by the newly-formed Parti Socialiste. For five years – from 1974 to 1979 – she served as national secretary of the party, in which she was further responsible for youth organization. She was elected as a member of the European Parliament in 1979, and two years later, on 21 June 1981, she ran successfully for deputy from Vienne, western France, as the Socialist candidate – although, in the event, she resigned her seat shortly afterwards to take up office as the first woman minister of agriculture. Her third spell of ministerial office, as minister of industrial restructuring and foreign trade (1984–6), was no doubt the most problematic. This was a time of general disenchantment with State ownership, which had set in almost as soon as the left's vast nationalization programme of 1982 was complete. There was a movement towards a reduction in state control ('moins d'Etat'), a new focus on the firm, an emphasis on company profitability, and an awareness that the government's room to manoeuvre was ultimately conditioned by market forces. This clearly posed problems of an ideological nature for the then minister of industrial restructuring. In the general mood of economic pragmatism, Cresson made political history in France when, at the introduction of the Carrefour National des Créateurs d'Enterprise in April 1985, she articulated the logical consequence of this new company-oriented stance adopted by the Socialists: 'Denationalize the public sector? Why not? I don't have any religious theory about it, neither one way nor the other'.

Bibliography

See Danièle Loschak, *La Convention des institutions républicaines: F. Mitterrand et le socialisme*, (Paris: Presses Universitaires de France, 1971). Edith Cresson is herself the author of a book: *Avec le soleil* (Paris: J.C. Lattès, 1976).

MMac

D

DALADIER, Edouard (1884–1970)

Edouard Daladier epitomized the Third Republic middle classes who used the public education system as a means of advancement. His importance lies in the fact that he played a central role in three crucial moments of inter-war French history. He was a prime minister at the time of the 6 February 1934 crisis. As president of the Radical Party he was the author of its acceptance – and subsequent – rejection of the Popular Front. And in 1939 he was head of the government that declared war on Germany on the 3 September 1939, having held the defence portfolio since 1936.

Born in Carpentras (Vaucluse) the son of a baker, he was taught at the Lycée in Lyons by Edouard Herriot (q.v.) and subsequently passed the prestigious *agrégation* degree in history and geography. Politics attracted him very early and in 1911 he succeeded in being elected mayor of Carpentras at the head of a 'youth' list. He joined up in 1914, spent the entire war at the front and ended with the rank of lieutenant. In 1919 he was elected to Parliament in his native Vaucluse and held his seat throughout the inter-war period. His highly successful political career began under the patronage of Edouard Herriot whose minister of colonies he became in 1924; he held the portfolios of war and education and arts in the various governments of the Cartel des Gauches. In 1926, however, he broke with Herriot over the latter's decision to enter the national union government of Poincaré (q.v.) and emerged as the leader of the left wing of the Radical party whose president he was between 1927 and 1931.

The left's victory in the 1932 Chamber elections reopened his ministerial career. As minister of public works in succeeding Radical governments, he became one of the figures without whom it was difficult to form a government of the left. By a natural progression he became prime minister himself in January 1933 and held office until October. He suffered from the congenital difficulty which faced all Radical governments of being torn between a parliamentary majority that included the Socialists and an economic policy, supported by business, that saw deflation as the means to resolve the economic crisis. It was moreover very irritating for this staunch supporter of the union of the left to see the Socialists continually rebuff his efforts. Already in 1929 they had refused to participate in a government which he was attempting to form and in 1933 the national committee of the SFIO overrode the decision of its parliamentary group to enter his ministry.

On 30 January 1934, as the Stavisky crisis reached its peak, he was recalled to the premiership thanks to his reputation for dynamism and integrity which made him the leading figure on the political left. Having once again failed to win the support of the Socialists (he approached individual members of the SFIO but did not negotiate directly with the party), he formed a government of Radicals and Centrists. One of his first actions was to remove the Paris prefect of police, Jean Chiappe, whose negligence he blamed for the delay in dealing with the Stavisky dossier; Chiappe disdainfully refused his compensatory offer of the residency-general in Morocco. Chiappe's dismissal led to the resignations of the centre-right ministers. The right accused Daladier of having sacrificed his prefect of police to get the votes of Socialists and the dismissal became the pretext of the 6 February demonstrations which brought together the ex-servicemen of the politically moderate Union Nationale des Combattants (National Union of Combattants) and the various nationalist and quasi-Fascist leagues. Daladier stood firm, resisted the pressures of those on the right who sought to force his resignation and planned a series of measures to defend the regime. But it became clear that the army, the police and the judiciary were unwilling to support his proposals and were engaging in a series of delaying measures to prevent their application. By the morning of 7 February he was faced with the resignation of several of his ministers and with pressure for his resignation from the president of the Republic, the presidents of both Senate and Chamber and even from Edouard Herriot, the president of the Radical Party. Driven from power, branded by the right and the Communists as an executioner his political career seemed broken.

He was brought back to political life by the

creation of the Popular Front. From spring 1935 onwards, he made himself the champion of those Radicals who favoured the union of the left in the face of Herriot's reluctance. He attended the early meetings of the Popular Front and on the 14 July 1935 participated in the huge Paris procession alongside Thorez (q.v.) and Blum (q.v.). It seemed inevitable that after the elections he would become the leader of a Popular Front government. The election results, however, decided otherwise. As leader of the largest parliamentary group in the new left-wing Chamber majority, the Socialist Blum became prime minister. Daladier, however, was clearly the number two in the new government and became deputy prime minister and minister of defence. His position was made all the stronger by the fact that in January 1936 he had once again become president of the Radical Party, replacing Herriot who had little desire to lead a political formation that had become part of the Popular Front. Even though the Radicals had lost many seats, their 106 deputies made them an essential part of a left parliamentary majority that simply could not exist without them. Thus Daladier, at the head of a phalanx of Radical ministers, became the arbiter of the government's fate. There is no doubt that in the early days he loyally supported the Popular Front experiment, approving the social legislation that was voted in the summer without any protest from the Radicals.

It was in September 1936 that Daladier became aware of the deep anxiety which the Blum government's policy was causing to those sections of the middle class which formed the electoral base of the Radical Party. They were deeply unhappy at the government's unwillingness to sanction what looked to them like revolutionary strikes and factory occupations; they disliked a social policy that increased employers' costs; and they were angry at the damage done to savings by the October devaluation. Daladier thus had to employ a double strategy. On the one hand, he wanted to defeat those on the right wing of his party who were using grassroots discontent to get the Radicals to withdraw from their Popular Front engagements. Obviously he could not accept the rejection of a policy which he had initiated nor take the risk of a challenge to his position at the head of the party. But at the same time he constantly warned his prime minister about the need to take account of the aspirations and interests of the middle classes. It became increasingly difficult for him to maintain this balanced position, since the anti-Popular Front Radicals were making more and more progress and he had increasingly to distance himself from government policy to preserve his in-fluence within the party. In June 1937 he made a speech in Biarritz which was widely seen as posing his candidature for the succession. A few days later, Blum's government was defeated in the Senate by a vote in which a number of Radicals joined the opposition.

Daladier had to wait until April 1938 to become prime minister, remaining minister of defence in the Popular Front governments of Chautemps (q.v.) (June 1937–March 1938) and Blum (March–April 1938). The fact that his own government, which included moderates but no Socialists, received a virtually unanimous vote of confidence showed the ambiguity of its position – it encapsulated the two possible majorities within the 1936 Chamber, one based on the Popular Front, the other on centre-right concentration. Very soon, however, his own preferences became clear. In a speech on 21 August 1938 he announced his intention of 'getting France back to work' by amending legislation on the 40-hour week. Since this was something that neither Communists nor Socialists could accept, Daladier by his action broke the Popular Front. The process of disintegration took place in two stages. In signing the 1938 Munich agreements that preserved peace but sacrificed France's ally Czechoslovakia, Daladier unquestionably spoke for the pacifist segments of the majority of French people; but those who still believed in the Popular Front accused him of having betrayed its anti-Fascist ideals. The violent campaign which the Communists unleashed against him led the Radicals in November 1938 to quit the National Committee of the Popular Front, thereby signing its death warrant. On 1 November 1938 he appointed the conservative Paul Reynaud (q.v.) as finance minister. Reynaud immediately produced a series of decree laws, one of which undermined the forty-hour week and thus marked a rejection of the social programme of the Popular Front. The parties and unions of the left retaliated by organizing a general strike on 30 November, which became a decisive trial of strength between Daladier and his former allies in the Popular Front. The measures he took were successful both in defeating the strike and in reducing the left to silence.

At the end of 1938 Daladier stood at the height of his power. He had vanquished the Marxist left and made himself the unchallenged leader of a National Union organized around his person. He was able to exercise a virtual moral dictatorship over not only a docile Parliament but also a public opinion that saw in him the 'strong man' for which it yearned. His overwhelming purpose was to prepare France for the war which he saw as inevitable. At the start of 1939, he firmly rejected Italy's colonial demands and joined with Britain in offering guarantees to states threatened by Hitler and Mussolini. The same determination led him to declare war on Germany on 3 September 1939. But the phoney war would see the capital of confidence which he had acquired drain away. His confidence in the judgements of his military commanders led him to accept a defensive military strategy that went against his foreign policy decisions. France did not come to the aid of Poland, for whose defence she had declared war in the first place, and stood by passively as it was crushed, waiting for the German forces to destroy themselves on the fortifications of the Maginot Line. In the absence of a mobilization of national energy for the war effort, political conflict continued after hostilities had been declared. Daladier arrested the pacifists who were calling for negotiations with Hitler and, with the support of a part of public opinion, launched an attack on the Communists. When Soviet troops entered Poland on 17 September, he decided on the dissolution of the Communist Party and in October ordered the prosecution of the Communist deputies who had urged France to reply to Hitler's not yet formulated offers of peace. But as time went on, he began to be criticized in Parliament for refusing to choose between a peace policy (which some people favoured) and a war policy (for which the strategy of his high command did not provide). His parliamentary majority fell away and on 20 March 1940 he resigned as prime minister. He held on to the defence portfolio in the Reynaud government that succeeded his and attempted to intrigue his way back into the premiership. After the fall of France he was imprisoned by the Vichy authorities in September 1940 and was brought before the Riom Court in 1942 as one of those responsible for the defeat. Alongside Léon Blum (q.v.) he presented a courageous defence of the Third Republic and turned himself into the prosecutor of his judges. Deported into Germany in 1943 he was liberated by the Americans at the end of the war. In the face of violent attacks from the Communist Party, he picked up the threads of his political career and was again elected deputy for the Vaucluse. But he never acquired the prominence he had formerly held. It was perhaps unsurprising that this symbol of the parliamentary Republic should oppose de Gaulle's return to power; and his political career ended with his defeat in the parliamentary elections of November 1958.

Bibliography

Berstein, S. (1975) *Le 6 Fevrier 1934*, Paris: Gallimard-Juillard.

Berstein, S. (1980–2), *Histoire du parti radical,* (2 vols), Paris: Presses de la Fondation Nationale des Sciences Politiques.

Rémond, R. and Bourdin, J. (eds) (1977), *Edouard Daladier, chef de gouvernement*, Paris: Presses de la Fondation Nationale des Sciences Politiques.

SB

DARLAN, François (1881–1942)

Admiral and politician, born at Nérac in Gascony in 1881. His father (mayor of Nérac) was minister of justice in Méline's cabinet, 1896–8. Though of strong Republican stock, Darlan entered the Navy. In the First World War he fought mainly on land, in the Salonica, Verdun and Champagne battles.

In the inter-war period he became very much a 'political' sailor, serving extensively as *chef de cabinet* to Georges Leygues, in his several terms as navy minister. He was largely responsible for the expansion in naval construction, at a time when money for equipment of the services was scarce. By the outbreak of war the French navy was stronger than it had ever been before, and Darlan was a full admiral, in command of all French naval forces. His emotional commitment to 'his' fleet was to be a major factor in his subsequent political attitudes.

In 1940 at Bordeaux, he was navy minister in the short-lived last government of the Third Republic, under the premiership of Marshal Pétain, where he was solidly in the camp of those seeking an armistice. In the Vichy government he continued as navy minister. His ingrained Anglophobia was exacerbated by the British attack on the French fleet at Mers-el-Kébir. His conviction that Germany had won the war, and that France must have its proper place in the new Europe, made him a strong advocate of collaboration. He was involved, by late 1940, in plans to 'reconquer' by force of arms those parts of Africa which had followed de Gaulle.

After the dismissal of Laval on 13 December 1940, Darlan first became part of the triumvirate that succeeded him, and then, in February 1941, head of government (deputy premier). He formed a government of 'technocrats', whose *dirigiste* approach was very much the precursor of post-war 'planning'. In foreign affairs, he introduced military concessions into collaboration for the first time, with the so-called Paris protocols, only the first of which (German use of Syrian airfields and military supplies) came into force. The loss of Syria to Allied troops made him declare the other protocols dependent on much larger concessions by the Germans; and stalemate ensued. By April 1942 Laval had returned to power, Darlan becoming commander-in-chief of the armed forces.

When the Allies landed in North Africa in November 1942, Darlan happened to be on the spot, visiting his seriously sick son. The Vichy forces strongly resisted the Allied landings, and it soon became clear that only orders from the senior officer on the spot could resolve the situation. Darlan negotiated a cease-fire, and then brought the armed forces over to the Allies. To the horror of British and American public opinion, to the disarray of the Giraudists and the dismay of the Gaullists, the Americans gave him full military and administrative control over French North Africa. This complicated and potentially dangerous situation was solved by his assassination on Christmas Eve 1942; it is still a matter of doubt as to who gave the orders to his assassin.

Bibliography

Coutan-Bégarie, H. (1989), *Darlan*, Paris: Fayard.

Michel, H. (1966), *Vichy année 40*, Paris: Robert Laffont.

Mikes, G. (1943), *Darlan: A Study*, London: Constable.

Paillat, C. (1967), *L'Echiquier d'Alger* (vol. 2), Paris: Robert Laffont.

Paxton, R. (1972), *Vichy France*, London: Barrie and Jenkins.

Tompkins, P. (1966), *Le Meurtre de l'amiral Darlan*, Paris: Albin Michel.

RMG

DARNAND, Aimé Joseph Auguste (1897–1945)

Ambitious, not over-endowed intellectually, blue-eyed, square-jawed and of Catholic working-class stock, Darnand was physically and biographically the epitome of the Fascist leader and became one of the principal hardline collaborators during the occupation. A highly decorated hero of the First World War he became involved in extreme right-wing politics after the Armistice and by 1928 was the local leader in Nice of the Camelots du Roi, the league affiliated to Action Française. Subsequently he left the latter and in 1936 joined Jacques Doriot's Parti Populaire Français, arguably the only Fascist party to have existed in France. He was also associated with the *Cagoule*, the conspiratorial anti-republican Comité Secret d'Action Révolutionnaire founded by Eugène Deloncle, and was imprisoned for five months on this account in 1938.

After a brief, but again outstanding career as an officer in the Second World War he was taken prisoner, escaped and returned to Nice where in July 1940, by now a fervent admirer of Italian fascism, he founded the local branch of the Légion Française des Anciens Combattants (the French Legion of Ex-Servicemen). In 1941 he created the elitist Service d'Ordre Légionnaire (SOL), an anti-Gaullist, anti-Semitic, anti-democratic political police force which was officially recognized by Marshal Pétain in January 1942. Although its strong-arm tactics were not always appreciated by the Vichy government they met with the approval of the hardline collaborators in the occupied zone. With its efficient administrative and political machine Darnand's SOL was the precursor of the Milice, Vichy's dreaded paramilitary political police. The Milice, which from early 1944 would become notorious for its brutal repression of Resistance members, was formed in January 1943 with Darnand virtually in sole command. In August of the same year he reached the point of no return in his Fascist stance when he joined the Waffen SS, pledging loyalty to Hitler. When Darnand was appointed secretary for the maintenance of order in December 1943 Franco-German anti-Resistance collaboration gathered considerable momentum. In February 1944 he became minister of the interior in the Vichy government and in August of that year fled to Sigmaringen with other members of the government. After the Allies' victory he fled to Italy where he was arrested. Sentenced to death by the High Court in Paris he was executed on 10 October 1945.

Ultra-nationalistic, violently anti-German and an unconditional admirer of Marshal Pétain, Darnand was led to support German militarism by his hatred for liberal democracy and for communism. Such a paradoxical itinerary was not altogether uncommon among French Fascist sympathizers.

Bibliography

There is nothing in English or in French exclusively devoted to Darnand. His activities are however described in varying detail in:

de Bayac, J.D. (1969), *Histoire de la milice 1918–1945*, Paris: Fayard.

Lottman, H.R. (1985), *Pétain, Hero or Traitor*, London: Viking.

Ory, P. (1976), *Les Collaborateurs 1940–1945*, Paris: Seuil.

Paxton, R.O. (1972), *Vichy France: Old guard and new order 1940–1944*, New York: Alfred A. Knopf.

GTH

DASSAULT, Marcel Ferdinand (né Bloch) (1892–1986)

Born in Paris, the son of a bankrupt doctor, and educated at the newly-created state aviation school, Marcel Bloch began to build aeroplanes towards the end of the First World War. The coming of peace led him to turn his attention to property development but he returned to aeroplane construction in the early 1930s and by the time of the Popular Front was, with Henry Potez, an established aircraft constructor. He was a great admirer of Léon Blum (q.v.) and did not allow the nationalization of the air industries to interfere with his career; he continued to design fighter and civil aircraft (including the one that brought Daladier – q.v. – back from Munich) and acted as a research consultant to the government. A Jewish industrialist who refused to work for the Germans, he was arrested and deported to Buchenwald where he narrowly escaped execution, thanks largely to the protection of Communist inmates. After the war he changed his name to Dassault and built up the empire for which he became famous. With the exploitation of the jet engine in the Mirage and Mystère and with the mass production of the Languedoc 161 (4-engine transport) Dassault became synonynous with the French aircraft industry. His companies built over 6,000 planes in post-war France and by the end of the Fourth Republic most of French military production (in which there had been a six-fold increase) came from Dassault.

His dependence on state purchase meant that he needed to have politically influential people on his staff. Among those he recruited were Generals R.M. Gallois and Dugit-Gros, Admiral Ruyssen, Albin Chalandon (q.v.) and the father of Jacques Chirac. A highly effective lobbyist in the Fourth Republic (he also advised Prime Minister Laniel – q.v. – on housing programmes), he nevertheless played an important, if occult, role in de Gaulle's return to power by providing credit to Jacques Soustelle (q.v.). Before the war, Dassault had been a Radical Socialist but in 1947 he supported de Gaulle's Rassemblement pour la France and in 1951 he was elected to the National Assembly for the Alpes-Maritimes. Defeated in 1956 he was elected the following year a senator for the Oise (possibly at the instigation of Resistance leaders who wanted a counterweight to Robert Hersant – q.v.) and in 1958 became Gaullist deputy for Beauvais (Oise) a constituency he represented until his death shortly after the 1986 election.

Invariably elected on the first round, his financial largesse became legendary and he could be seen at election time signing cheques for the construction of swimming pools, sports grounds and community centres in the constituency. In 1978 the Socialists unsuccessfully tried to have him disqualified for electoral fraud but he always maintained that he helped communities not individuals. He owned the successful weekly journal *Jours de France* and in the 1970s became involved in film productions. In 1963, the *Le Monde* journalist Pierre Viansson-Ponté painted a highly unflattering portrait of Dassault referring to his arrogance and disdain, but by the 1980s he had become virtually above criticism. After 1981 he co-operated with the Socialist government's nationalization policy and was publicly thanked by Prime Minister Mauroy (q.v.). He always prided himself on being a good employer (he had given his workers paid holidays before the 1936 legislation and towards the end of his life took to buying full-page advertisements in newspapers in which he would enunciate simple truths about the economy and society that recalled his pre-war Radical-socialism). The antithesis of a contemporary industrial tycoon, he became something of a folk hero as well as a symbol of France's aeronautical prowess.

Bibliography

Assouline, P. (1983), *Monsieur Dassault*, Paris, Balland; see also *Le Monde* (20–1 April 1986) for an obituary.

PM

DAUDET, Léon (1867–1942)

Léon Daudet was, with Charles Maurras (q.v.), one of the two most prominent figures in the Action Française movement. Born in Paris in 1867, son of the famous writer Alphonse Daudet, at first he shared his parents' republicanism, being a youthful opponent of Boulangism. He also inherited from his father a fervent anti-Semitism, Drumont (q.v.) being a frequent visitor to the family home. Léon was one of the first members of the Ligue Antisémite, and became a writer for Drumont's daily *La Libre Parole*.

The Dreyfus affair confirmed these prejudices, and was to be a lasting theme in his writings. It was in the early years of the new century, however, that he underwent a strong conversion to catholicism, and also became a member of Action Française, adding royalism and nationalism to his anti-capitalistic anti-Semitism. He speedily became one of the movement's leading polemicists, and in 1908 founded the daily newspaper *L'Action Française*, of which he became editor.

Daudet has been described as 'the Sancho Panza to Maurras' Don Quixote'; certainly there was a great difference of style. Alongside the logical, restrained reasonings of Maurras' articles Daudet's daily editorials created a wild splash of colour. He was a specialist in invective, and spattered with mud everyone he attacked. This violence flourished in an incredible world of make-believe, in which conspiracy theories abounded.

In the years just before the First World War, Daudet conducted a campaign against suspected German spies within France. For the first few years of the war he suspended attacks on the Republic, in the interests of national unity, but by 1917 his attacks on the *embochés* betraying France homed in on Malvy (q.v.), the minister of the interior, and on Caillaux (q.v.). Though most of these attacks were unjustified, there were enough murky secrets surrounding the journal *Le Bonnet Rouge* for credence to be given to them. Clemenceau's rise to power was brought about by his climbing on the bandwagon which Daudet had created.

In the 1919–24 parliament (during Action Française's brief parliamentary experiment), Daudet was one of their very few members to be returned. Though isolated, he exerted some influence on international issues. His policies were uncompromisingly anti-German.

From 1923 onwards, his life was dominated by the drama surrounding the death of his son Philippe. Suicide or murder? Daudet claimed that there had been a plot involving the police. Condemned to five months' imprisonment for libel, he was spirited away from prison by Action Française members thanks to a spectacular hoax, and spent the years 1925–7 in exile in Belgium. Politically, in the inter-war period he was to suffer two grievous blows: the papal condemnation of Action Française in 1926, and the disavowal of the movement by the Pretender in 1937. Typically, Daudet remained more integrist than the pope, and more royalist than the king; it was they who were out of step.

Unlike Maurras he was profoundly depressed by the fall of France. Already a seriously ill man, he agreed that the *L'Action Française* should continue to appear in the Vichy zone, and sent articles to it; but he retired to his property at Saint-Rémy, taking no prominent part in the politics of Vichy. There he died in July 1942.

Bibliography

Dresse, P. (1947), *Léon Daudet vivant*, Paris: Robert Laffont.

Germain, A. (1959), *Les Croisés modernes*, Paris: Nouvelles Editions Latines.

Weber, E. (1962), *Action Française*, Stanford, Cal.: Stanford University Press.

RMG

DÉAT, Marcel (1894–1955)

Born the son of a junior civil servant at Guérigny (Nièvre) in 1894, Marcel Déat went on to study at the Lycée Henri IV in Paris, and was about to enter the Ecole Normale Supérieure when the First World War broke out. Having served with distinction as an infantryman, he resumed his studies in 1919 and qualified in philosophy. It was while teaching in the *lycée* in Reims that he became involved in the local Socialist Party. He won a seat on the city council in 1925, and a year later became Socialist deputy for the Marne after a parliamentary by-election victory. He lost this seat at the 1928 elections, but returned to the Chamber as deputy for a Paris constituency in 1932.

By this time, however, his ideas had begun to diverge sharply from mainstream socialism, and he left the party in the famous split of 1933. He served as minister for the air force in the centrist Sarraut government of January–May 1936, and his ambivalent attitude towards the Popular Front cost him his parliamentary seat when the left swept to power at the 1936 elections. By then his major preoccupation was the threat of war, and as a journalist he worked to regroup the pacifist elements on the left in favour of a *modus vivendi* with Nazi Germany. His article 'Die For Danzig?' ('Mourir pour Dantzig?') in May 1939 is famous in the annals of appeasement.

Returned to the Chamber of Deputies in a 1939 by-election at Angoulême (Charente), he voted full powers to Pétain in June 1940 but remained hostile to the Vichy regime which he saw as profoundly reactionary. Persuaded that nazism was a variant of socialism, he sought to convince the German authorities of the need for a genuine Fascist regime in France and attempted unsuccessfully to turn his Rassemblement National Populaire into the focus for a Fascist movement. He fled to Germany after the Allied landings, was received by Hitler in August 1944, and tried to form a government in exile. He escaped the death penalty in France by reaching Italy in 1945, where he lived in exile under the protection of Catholic priests until his death of tuberculosis in 1955. In these last years this life-long anticlerical was converted to catholicism, and a special papal dispensation allowed him to sanctify his marriage to the woman who had been his civil-law wife for twenty-three years.

The career of Marcel Déat, like that of the erstwhile Communist Jacques Doriot, is often cited as a prime example of how certain dissident sections of the French left were drawn towards fascism in the 1930s. In Déat's case the origins of this evolution are complex. His socialism was never entirely orthodox, owing more to the intellectual legacy of Saint-Simon and Durkheim than to the historic debates of the French labour movement. From these antecedents he derived his preoccupation with rational economic organization, his ideal of a harmonious and unanimous social order, and a quest for class reconciliation that was reinforced by his memories of the fraternity of the trenches. All of this tended to distance him from the Marxist discourse of the party rank-and-file, but when he first emerged as an economic theorist in the late twenties there was little to distinguish his ideas from the other reformists in the Socialist parliamentary group. Like them he emphasized the practicalities of economic organization, the constructive involvement of trade unions in the planning process, and the abandonment of revolutionary 'workerist' rhetoric in favour of wider social alliances.

What marked Déat out even at this early stage was his ambition as a propagandist and organizer to forge a new ideological synthesis for the party, and a tendency to intellectual abstraction which often led him to underestimate strictly political obstacles. This was already evident in his 1930 book, *Perspectives Socialistes* (Paris: Librairie Valois). However, it was above all the growing threat of fascism, brought to a head in the early thirties by Hitler's success in Germany and by the heightened activity of the French right-wing leagues, which drove Déat to his first act of heresy.

The reformist wing of the Socialist Party, which was particularly well-represented among the party's deputies, had long favoured a closer alliance with the Radical Party and even, on occasions, Socialist participation in Radical governments. After the left's election victory in 1932, these demands became more intense, and the arguments were reinforced by

evidence that the German left's disunity had paved the way for nazism. When in 1933 a large number of Socialist deputies broke discipline by voting for a deflationary Radical budget against party instructions, a split became inevitable. At the party's National Council in November 1933, those who would not toe the line were either expelled or forced into voluntary exile. In all twenty-seven deputies, five senators and a number of Socialist departmental federations left the SFIO.

Marcel Déat was among those who left, but he cannot be equated with the main bloc of reformists who departed behind Pierre Renaudel. At the height of the internal crisis, during the party Congress in Paris in July 1933, Déat and his colleagues Adrien Marquet and Barthélemy Montagnon had made speeches which filled the Socialist leader Léon Blum with 'horror' and which were soon to be identified as 'neo-socialism'. The gist of their arguments was that socialism, if it was to combat fascism, must appeal to ideals of order and national unity rather than liberty and justice, and construct a strong state based on a corporate economy and a new sense of national mission. In Déat's case this reflected his belief that in this age of crisis and confusion the French craved security and discipline. If this was not to lead to fascism, socialism itself must adapt its principles. Like the Belgian Socialist Henri de Man, he felt that socialist materialism had neglected the emotional dimension of political mobilization, the transcendent idealism which could unite the nation across the barriers of class.

The 'neo-socialists' were however only a minority within the new party formed by the exiles, the Parti Socialiste de France. Déat's ideas had little appeal for traditional reformists like Renaudel, whose moderate left republicanism was identical to that of earlier defectors from the SFIO who sat in the Chamber with other independent Socialist groups like the Parti Socialiste Français and the Parti Républicain Socialiste. Déat's efforts to win a mass base in the CGT trade-union confederation and the ex-servicemen's associations met with no greater success. The new party rapidly lost members, and in November 1935 it merged with the other independent Socialist formations under the umbrella *Union Socialiste et Républicaine.*

With his efforts at breaking the ideological mould frustrated, and the new left-wing alliance of the Popular Front gaining ground, Déat entered a rather ambiguous and, some would say, opportunist phase of his career. As secretary of the Union Socialiste Républicaine, he persuaded his party to join the Popular Front in November 1935. On the other hand he remained highly critical of the Popular Front's programme, and with the approval of his parliamentary group joined the centrist government of Albert Sarraut as air minister in January 1936. He thus entered the May 1936 elections with a rather ambivalent image, and he did nothing to enhance his reputation on the left when, outdistanced by a Communist on the first ballot, he maintained his candidacy at the second in the hope of attracting tactical anti-Communist votes. His defeat meant that for the next three years journalism was to become his main political activity.

After the victory of the Popular Front, Déat became increasingly hostile not only to the Communists but to the whole experience of the left in power. Like so many political dissidents in the mid-thirties he subscribed to vague planning (*planiste*) and corporatist economic theories as an alternative to liberalism and Socialist 'interventionism', and argued for the widening of the Front Populaire into a Front National. His major preoccupation from 1935 onwards, however, was the worsening international situation and the danger of war. His deep pessimism about the weakness of a 'decadent' France faced with the ruthless dynamism of the Fascist regimes, which had inspired his neo-Socialist 'solution', now led him to see the preservation of peace as the only chance of national survival. He opposed intervention in the Spanish Civil War, became increasingly suspicious of the Franco-Soviet pact, and began to call into question France's obligations to her East European allies. He was in fact eager to avoid any commitment that might drag France into a full-scale European war, and came to place his main hopes in the British alliance and in preventing Italy from joining the German camp.

Such attitudes were of course widespread from 1936 to 1938, when the issue of war caused bitter divisions within every major political formation except the Communist Party. Déat worked tirelessly to rally support for the pacifist cause from across the political spectrum, but he came no nearer to his old ambition of building a cohesive movement. Indeed, by the time he wrote his notorious article recommending that France abandon her obligations to Poland in May 1939, many former appeasers in all camps were reconciled to the inevitability of war, and Déat's action drew widespread condemnation.

Déat continued to press for conciliation right through the period of the phoney war, and France's rapid military collapse in May–June 1940 fulfilled his pessimistic predictions. However, he saw defeat and occupation as an opportunity for the regeneration of France within a new European order. His initial hopes were placed in Vichy, where he was entrusted by Laval with plans for establishing a new single party that would be the mass movement of the 'Révolution Nationale', but he was soon disillusioned as the Vichy regime staffed itself with elements from the traditionalist and clerical right and denied him the prospect of any significant role. He moved to Paris where he continued his efforts to lay the foundations of the (*parti unique*) one-party state and where he endeavoured to win the support of the German authorities for the Vichy reshuffle that would offer him a place in government. However, his ambitions were frustrated by the partisan rivalries in the collaborationist community in the occupied zone, and by the fact that the Germans had little interest in the establishment of a genuine Fascist movement in France. Déat's Rassemblement National Populaire never achieved the following he hoped for, but in his efforts to win German approval he fashioned it increasingly along Fascist lines and, in mid-1942 turned it into a party modelled directly on the Nazi movement. In 1940 he had invoked the values of 'discipline', 'heroism', 'asceticism', 'sacrifice' and 'service of the state'. By August 1942 he was talking of 'blood, soil, and race'.

It was under the shadow of German defeat that Déat finally won a post at Vichy as minister of labour in Laval's government of March 1944, and six months later he fled France in a German baggage train. For some, his final identification with the Nazi cause was the natural conclusion of an ideological odyssey that began with his authoritarian 'neo-socialism' of 1933. Others have seen it more in terms of his profound pessimism about France's national survival, which led him to follow the tide of events in the vain hope that circumstances would eventually favour the reconstruction of which he dreamed.

Bibliography

The most accessible studies are Donald N. Baker, 'Two paths to socialism: Marcel Déat and Marceau Pivert, in *Journal of Contemporary History*, vol. II, no. 1, pp. 107–28, January 1976 and Eugen Weber, 'Nationalism, socialism and national-socialism in France', in *French Historical Studies*, vol. II, no. 3, spring 1962, pp. 273–307. In French, the most recent study, with a comprehensive bibliography, is Philippe Burrin, *La Dérive fasciste: Doriot, Déat, Bergery 1933–45* (Paris: Seuil, 1986). See also M. Déat, *Mémoirs Politiques* (Paris: Denoël, 1989).

BJ

DEBRÉ, Michel Jean-Pierre (1912–   )

Michel Debré was the first prime minister of France under the constitution (the Fifth Republic) inroduced in 1958. His term of office (1959–62) saw the establishment of the new regime on a firm basis and the end of the Algerian War. He has, however, spanned both the political and the administrative arenas in France, and although he is perhaps best known as a Gaullist politician, the most lasting achievements of his career may have been in the legal and administrative fields. He was born in Paris. Both his parents were doctors, his father being the great paediatrician Robert Debré. After studies in the law faculty of Paris and the Ecole Libre des Sciences Politiques and military service in the cavalry, he entered the Conseil d'Etat in 1935. The intellectual atmosphere of the Conseil d'Etat helped to foster his sense of the necessity of achieving a perception of the general interest and his conception of the unitary state. In 1938 he joined the private office of Paul Reynaud (q.v.). He rejoined the army in 1939. On escape from captivity he soon began to attempt to organize a measure of resistance and in 1941 decided that de Gaulle (q.v.) offered the only hope of rebuilding France; although he did not meet de Gaulle until after the liberation this was the start of a lifelong attachment to the Gaullist cause. By March 1943 he was obliged to become completely clandestine, and under the pseudonym Jacquier returned to Paris. There he became a member of the Comité Général d'Etudes – the study commission set up by the National Resistance Council to prepare plans for post-war France. In collaboration with Emmanuel Monick he published, pseudonomously, two studies advocating administrative and constitutional reforms. From July of 1943 onwards he took responsibility, in consultation with a small Resistance group, for choosing and alerting those who as *commissaires de la République* (Republican commissioners) took control of each part of France on liberation. His work was largely instrumental in ensuring that relatively orderly and legitimate French civilian government was re-established everywhere. He himself became regional commissioner for the Angers region.

In the spring of 1945 he was recalled to Paris to join de Gaulle's personal office with the special task of undertaking the reform of the civil service. Debré had been associated with abortive pre-war efforts at reform, and was well acquainted with the long history of reform proposals. Building upon that knowledge and bringing to it both an acute perception of the limits of the possible and a clear view of a need for a renewed, strengthened, unified, active and forward-looking top civil service he drew up, and saw through to its official promulgation in October 1945, the legislation creating the Ecole Nationale d'Administration (ENA) as a recruiting and training establishment for senior civil servants. He briefly acted as director of the school and watched over its earliest stages. A potential student of the period recalled him as resembling in his enthusiasm 'a man with a newly established business, delighted to have found a client'. Important among his personal contributions was the opening of the ENA on equal terms to both men and women.

From 1948 to 1958 Debré represented the Indre-et-Loire in the Senate. He remained closely associated with de Gaulle throughout the rise and decline of de Gaulle's political movement the Rassemblement du Peuple Français and was active in the Gaullist parliamentary group. He supported the Gaullist insistence upon the standing and independence of France and advocated constitutional reform along Gaullist lines. He inveighed against the weakness of the Fourth Republic, for instance, in his 1957 book *Ces Princes qui nous gouvernent* (*Our Ruling Princes*). From the outbreak of the Algerian revolt he was strongly committed to the retention of Algeria as part of metropolitan France. He founded a polemical periodical, the *Courrier de la Colère*, to support both this cause and that of the return of de Gaulle and was deeply implicated in the manouevring which preceded de Gaulle's appointment as prime minister in 1958. De Gaulle appointed him minister of justice in his first government.

As minister of justice his first major task was to see to the drafting of a new constitution. He brought together a small group of mostly young experts with official and legal backgrounds to assist him and, in the brief space of just over a month, this group, working in consultation with de Gaulle's personal advisers and with a consultative group with a wider membership of leading politicians, produced the constitution. In the constitution of the Fifth Republic many of Debré's own attitudes are reflected: his ardent Jacobin republicanism which pre-dated even his Gaullism, his own elevated view of the role of the state combined with his attachment to de Gaulle's principles which required a strong central presence and a strengthened executive, and his commitment to parliamentary institutions which should be stable and constructive, as he held the British Parliament to be. Given the extent of his personal contribution to the creation of both institutions, Debré may with some justice be regarded as the 'father' of both the ENA and the Fifth Republic's constitution.

After his election as the first president under the new regime, de Gaulle appointed Debré as prime minister. It therefore fell to him to commence the definition of the role of prime minister within the new balance of institutions. The political circumstances of the time were dominated by concerns, especially the war in Algeria, in which de Gaulle played a leading role. Debré did not challenge that role. He was none the less an active and energetic prime minister. He was closely interested in the activities of all the ministers, would intervene where there was conflict, and was prepared to take decisions which might run counter to their advice. The departure from office in 1961 of the minister of justice, Edmond Michelet (q.v.), a devoted Gaullist, has been interpreted as Debré's reaction to a minister who was not, ultimately, prepared zealously to follow the prime-ministerial line. Debré's strongly cenralist and reformist cast of mind encouraged him to use the balance of the institutions that he had been so instrumental in creating to permit the resolution of a number of long-standing problems (including some like the attack upon alcoholism through the limitation of rights to the domestic distilling of spirits, which were also personal concerns shared with his eminent medical father). He was able, for example, to tackle the thorny problem of state subsidies to church schools, regulating the matter through a law which bears his name, the *loi Debré* of 1959.

As prime minister, Debré took a close personal interest in economic affairs. De Gaulle, in 1958, laid down the main lines of an economic policy, but it was Debré's legislative programme, aimed at stabilizing the economy, containing inflation and strengthening the franc, that effected the necessary measures. He was prepared to be seen to intervene very directly, writing, for example, to the employers' organization to remind them that wage rises were exceeding what the government thought desirable. He was clear that the state had a guiding role to play within the economy and he saw the area as one for prime-ministerial, not presidential, action.

An agreement signed at Evian on 18 March 1962 brought the Algerian War to an end and opened the way to Algerian independence. The issue had been a particularly difficult one for Debré. His total loyalty to de Gaulle was never called into question. On the other hand, he had been a strong advocate of a French Algeria and came into conflict with the president on the issue. Contemporary commentators noted that he was being pulled in two directions. The end of the Algerian War meant for him, however, the end of an exceptional period. Government in which the balance of the institutions as he

had envisaged them could be ensured, should now be possible. He had been careful to see that Parliament did not overstep the bounds that had been set for it. These bounds should, he thought, enable the processes of government to be conducted along lines that would enable a full role to be played both by prime minister and parliament. He had clashed privately with the president on previous occasions over the interpretation of the constitution. His approach was not accepted and his resignation in early April 1962 was presented as the result of a recognition by both president and prime minister that an era had ended.

Debré remained politically active. Defeated in the Indre-et-Loire in the general election of 1962, he was returned in 1963 as the member for the Indian Ocean island of Réunion, which he represented, except during his periods as a minister, until 1988. He was one of the founders of the Gaullist Party (then called the Union pour la Nouvelle République – UNR) in 1958, and one of the original members of its directorate. He served as minister of finance for two spells between 1966 and 1968, as foreign minister between 1968 and 1969, and as minister of defence throughout the Chaban-Delmas and Messmer (q.v.) governments under President Pompidou (q.v.) from 1969 to 1973. All these posts were well suited to his energetic, interventionist style of ministerial activity, and to his loyalty to the Gaullist priorities especially in the field of defence and foreign affairs.

Throughout the 1970s, however, he saw the Gaullist party moving, in his view, steadily away from some of these priorities. He perceived an increasing tendency to support policies which favoured greater European integration, and a more Atlanticist stance. His concept of the role of the state, whilst strongly opposed to collectivism or socialism, is not easily accommodated to a more liberal outlook that would lessen the state's role and withdraw it from major areas of economic and social life. He stood as a candidate in the presidential election of 1981, but gained only a derisory 1.65 per cent of the votes cast in the first ballot.

Debré's career has consistently demonstrated courage, energy and an ability to translate reformist zeal into real administrative achievement. During his early life he developed both a staunch republicanism and an idea of France which found their fulfilment in a loyalty to de Gaulle that overrode the difficulties and conflicts he certainly experienced. His family background, as well as his attachment to the idea of a strong and independent nation, may help to explain his ardent advocacy of policies designed to halt the falling birthrate. His early administrative and legal experience certainly developed his lofty view of the nature and role of the state, and of the officials who serve it. He writes and speaks robustly, but seems scarcely at home and indeed oddly outmoded in a more polarized political world where he incarnates too many paradoxes – reformist yet orthodox, Jacobin yet favouring participation, interventionist yet anti-Socialist, insistent upon a strong state yet profoundly parliamentary, a politician whose major achievements have been administrative and legal.

Bibliography

Debré has published the first three volumes of his memoirs as Michel Debré, *Trois Républiques pour une France: mèmoires* (Paris: Albin Michel, 1984–).

Of his other books the most representative are probably: Michel Debré, *Ces Princes qui nous gouvernent* (Paris: Plon, 1957) and Michel Debré, *Une Certaine idée de la France* (Paris: Fayard, 1972).

On his assessment of the Fifth Republic's constitution see his chapter in W.G. Andrews and S. Hoffmann (eds), *The Fifth Republic at Twenty* (Albany, NY: State University of New York Press, 1980).

On the foundation of the ENA see his introduction to Marie-Christine Kessler, *L'Ecole Nationale d'Administration: la politique de la haute fonction publique* (Paris: Presses de la Fondation Nationale des Sciences Politiques, 1978).

AS

DECAZES, Louis Charles Elie Amanieu, duc de Glücksberg, then marquis, then duc de (1819–86)

Decazes was one of those dukes whose role in the founding years of the Third Republic was analysed by Daniel Halévy. The family from which he came was not one of France's great historical dynasties – his grandfather had been a public prosecutor in the Gironde – but it had acquired great wealth (through its ownership of mines) and great status (through Elie Decazes' career under Louis XVIII and Louis Philippe). Louis Decazes entered the diplomatic service in the July monarchy. Like many Orleanists he abandoned all his public functions in February 1848 and had the aristocratic liberal's distaste or plebiscitary Bonapartism. The overthrow of the Second Empire brought him into politics as a Gironde representative to the National Assembly. He saw the

political situation as ripe for the brand of parliamentary liberalism he supported and he became an extremely active advocate of the cause of the Orleanists, hoping that the Orleanist prince, the duc d'Aumale, would become lieutenant-general of the kingdom. Having supported the removal of Thiers (q.v.) in 1873, he briefly became ambassador to London and then entered government as foreign minister. He stayed in this post for four years, playing a skilful role in the defusing of Bismarck's war scare in 1875 and moving towards acceptance of Italy's rights over the former papal states.

The sceptical moderation that made him such an archtypical Orleanist led him to support the 1875 constitutional laws with less heart searching than his fellow duke, de Broglie (q.v.). It also meant that he was an acceptable member of the Republican government that Jules Simon (q.v.) formed after the elections of 1876, elections in which he was returned for a Paris constituency. This centrism would, however – as for others – lead to his political demise. The resentment of legitimists and Bonapartists at his preference for constitutionalism over dynasticism caused him to fail to be elected a life senator. And though he did not exhibit the aggressive activism of most of his political allies in the crisis that followed the 16 May 1877, he was inevitably linked by his origins and wealth with the anti-Republican cause. The collapse of the political authority of Marshal MacMahon (q.v.) led to his departure from office.

Bibliography

Chapman, G. (1962), *The Third Republic*, London: Macmillan.

Elwitt, S. (1975), *The Third Republic*, Baton Rouge: Louisiana State University Press.

Halévy, D. (1937), *La Républicque des ducs*, Paris: Grasset.

PM

DEFFERRE, Gaston Paul Charles (1910–86)

Born in Marsillargues (Hérault) in 1910, Gaston Defferre came from a Cevenol Protestant family. His father practised law in Nîmes and, after a period spent with his family in Dakar in West Africa, Gaston Defferre completed his secondary education in Nîmes. From there he went to the law faculty of Aix-en-Provençe, reading law as a first degree but economics as a postgraduate. When he was 21 he enrolled at the bar in Marseilles where his sister, who was married to a prominent industrialist André Cordesse, already lived. For the rest of his life Defferre's political fortunes at both local and national level would be inextricably linked with the city of Marseilles. He first joined the Socialist Party (SFIO) in 1933 but his career as a full-time politician really began with his Resistance work.

As early as August 1940, Defferre was busy creating a clandestine SFIO network which included André Boyer, Henry Frenay and Daniel Mayer (q.v.). Defferre defended Resistance workers in the tribunals established by the Vichy regime after November 1942 while at the same time, under the name 'Danvers', participating in the Froment Resistance network and helping to set up the Socialist militia under Paul Trompette. The political base of his Resistance activity is shown by the fact that, after flying to London to make contact with de Gaulle and the Free French, he declined to go to Algeria in 1943 and returned to France to re-establish the Socialist Party. Nevertheless, at the liberation, he was nominated by de Gaulle's regional commissioner, Raymond Aubrac, to be president of the committee established to rebuild the shattered city of Marseilles. Defferre's Resistance group took over the offices of *Le Petit Provençal* and he himself wrote the first editorial for the new *Provençal*. The *Provençal* group would in time become the most powerful newspaper group in the Midi and, in 1973, it acquired ownership of its principal right-wing opponent, *Le Méridional*. Defferre carefully developed a vast sprawling empire of holding-companies and interlocking directorships and ended his life a very rich man.

Defferre's power rested on the Socialist Party in Marseilles. In the late 1940s he battled with the Communists (who ran the municipality from 1946 to 1947); with a section of the regional Socialist Party who wanted an alliance with the PCF; and with Gaullists who won control of the municipality in November 1947, an event that led to the famous Communist-inspired disturbances which the riot police (CRS) could not control. The Socialist Party, in coalition with the centrists, won back the City Hall in 1953 and Defferre was made mayor, a position he held continuously until his death thirty-three years later.

This anti-Communist alliance with the centrist parties survived the Algerian War, the Gaullist onslaught on local government in the elections of 1965 and the national agreement which the Socialist Party signed with the Communist Party in 1972. But the growing left-right polarization of French politics in the Fifth Republic made centre leftism more and more difficult to sustain. In 1976 Defferre broke up

the coalition, although in 1977 Marseilles still stood out against the local government trend to joint Communist-Socialist lists; he survived with the support of left Radicals, various community leaders and prominent local figures. In 1983, he was forced to accept a formal alliance with the PCF as the price of his sixth, and last, victory – a victory that was very narrow indeed (and which owed a good deal to creative redistricting).

Much of the change in the city took place as a result of the general post-war growth but Defferre's achievements, as mayor, were substantial. In 1953, Marseilles was a poorly administered, run-down, under-industrialized and politically unstable city, with a long history of bad management and a large burden of debt. Despite these difficulties, Defferre immediately embarked on an ambitious modernization programme. The 1953 City Council undertook numerous projects but two were especially notable: the city was given a new water supply and school building was undertaken in earnest. Before 1953 the city depended precariously on unfiltered water from works engineered in the nineteenth century; Defferre's Council invested in a massive new water system, something which also allowed the city to expand (the population rose from 650,000 to 920,000 by 1965). The school building programme, highly visible ('one new classroom per day' as the slogan put it) continued well into the 1960s and included the primary as well as the more prestigious secondary schools. The second City Council (1959–65) continued these works but also tackled housing deficiencies (public housing was particularly necessary for a rapidly expanding city) as well as a major road building programme; the third Defferre Council continued these works ((1965–71) and the fourth (1971–7) saw the start of the metro, of which Defferre was particularly proud, and the introduction of a well-funded cultural policy. As in most big cities, the helter-skelter expansion of concrete tower blocks has subsequently been highly criticized.

Defferre always stated that his main concern as a politician was with Marseilles; yet his work at national level was also significant. At the very highest level, that of the presidency, he was of course unsuccessful and his two bids for the Elysée both ended in humiliation. This was due in large part to the tension between the national leadership of the Socialist Party (and especially its long-time secretary Guy Mollet – q.v.) and Defferre's Bouches-du-Rhône federation. Defferre's opposition to the visionless trimming of Mollet's SFIO led him to being labelled right-wing despite the fact that, although leader of a city that depended on colonial trade, he consistently argued for a liberal colonial policy and against the war in Algeria. In 1965, after a brilliant publicity campaign (*Monsieur X*) organized in *L'Express* by J.-J. Servan-Schreiber (q.v.), Defferre sought to weld Socialists, Radicals and Catholic centrists into a national electoral coalition akin to that existing in Marseilles. But internal tensions and rivalries brought about the demise of this 'Great Federation' even before the election campaign began and Defferre withdrew from the race. In 1969, at a time when the national political credibility of the non-Communist left was at its lowest, Defferre stood as Socialist Party candidate in tandem with Pierre Mendès France. The result was a disaster for Defferre who polled only 5.1 per cent of the vote.

Defferre represented Marseilles in the French Parliament from 1945 to 1986 mainly as a deputy (but from 1959–62 in the Senate). He was president of the Socialist group from 1977–81, a junior minister for information (1946–7), the merchant navy minister (1950–1), minister for overseas France (1956–7), minister of the interior (1981–4) and the planning minister (1984–6). Two things probably stand out in a distinguished parliamentary and ministerial career. One was the outline law for overseas France which paved the way for the decolonization of the French Empire. The other was the series of decentralization laws which transferred powers from the central state to the regions and departments and which was one of the major reforms of the Socialist legislature (1981–6). Defferre's work at the Planning Ministry was essentially devoted to problems of the technological revolution and at the same time thought was given to Marseilles' position in the 'third industrial revolution' of computing and hi-tech.

Defferre used the Bouches-du-Rhône federation's bloc vote (it was for a long time the largest in the party) for power-broking, for example, in the coup that made François Mitterrand first secretary in 1971. Latterly there were signs that Defferre's grip on the Federation was slackening: in 1986 Michel Pezet's group made substantial inroads into the traditional areas of Defferre's support within the party. But it should be noted that over the years Defferre had beaten off many challenges and in 1979 had demoted Emile Loo (long considered the 'dauphin') ostensibly for not supporting his motion at the 1979 Metz Congress of the PS. Had Defferre lived, there is no telling what would have happened: Pezet was not the person who stepped into Defferre's shoes at City Hall (that was Robert Vigouroux, first adjoint) and the Federation was deeply split. Despite his avuncular appearance, Defferre was no push-over and ran the City party in autocratic style.

Bibliography

See J.F. Bizot *et al., Au parti des socialistes* (Paris: Grasset, 1975) and Defferre's 1965 presidential programme *Un Nouvel horizon* (Paris: Gallimard, 1965), and his *Si Demain . . . La Gauche* (Paris: Robert Laffont, 1977); on Marseilles there is the partisan work by D. Bleitrach et al, *Classe ouvrière et social-démocratie: Lille et Marseille* (Paris: Editions Sociales, 1981); Gilbert Rochu, *Marseille: les années Defferre* (Paris: A. Moreau, 1983).

DSB

DELCASSÉ, Théophile Pierre (1852–1923)

The longest serving foreign minister in the history of the Third Republic, Théophile Delcassé was born in Ariège, close to the Spanish border, in 1852. The son of a court official, he attended university at Toulouse and became a teacher of literature in Paris at the secondary school (*lycée*) St Louis. His political career began under the patronage of Gambetta (q.v.) for whose daily newspaper, *La République Française* he became a correspondent in the early 1880s, working on the foreign news desk. After standing unsuccessfully for the Chamber of Deputies in his native Ariège in 1885 he was elected for the Foix constituency four years later as an Opportunist – moderate Republican. His maiden speech was on the Foreign Ministry budget and it was his deep interest in foreign and colonial questions that brought him prominence at a time when most French politicians concentrated on domestic matters.

Although the loss of Alsace-Lorraine had been the catalyst for his involvement in politics, he lacked the visceral anti-Germanism of most French nationalists and was for a long time bitterly critical of what he saw as Britain's usurpation of France's legitimate aspirations, particularly in Egypt. He was also prepared to court unpopularity by advocating a policy of vigorous colonial expansion and was very close to the influential colonial group (Parti Colonial) headed by Etienne (q.v.). In 1894 he was appointed to the newly-created Ministry of Colonies and was very active in attempts to develop France's position in Africa, notably the organization of Colonel Marchand's famous expedition to the Upper Nile. He became foreign minister in 1898 in the Brisson (q.v.) government at a time of the crisis caused by the Dreyfus affair. It was the very intensity of domestic political controversy – together with the strong support of President Loubet (q.v.) – that enabled

Delcassé to shape the contours of French foreign policy for the next seven years. Given that his name is inextricably linked with the creation of the *entente cordiale* with Great Britain, it is ironic that his first great problem was the Fashoda affair, described by one historian as the worst crisis in Anglo-French relations since Waterloo. He had to accept the British demand for Marchand's unconditional withdrawal from Egypt. French Anglophobia was intense and became even more so during the Boer War. Yet the more intelligent among the French imperialists were now beginning to speculate on the possibility of a deal whereby France would concede Egypt to Britain in return for British recognition of her preponderance in Morocco. Urged on by Paul Cambon, French ambassador to London, Delcassé became converted to the idea of an Egypt-Morocco swap and the British too became favourable once the Boer War had shown that isolation was not always splendid. The *entente cordiale*, signed in April 1904, was essentially a bargain over Morocco and contained few entangling ties. But when a year later, Germany tried to sabotage French claims to Morocco, Britain stood solidly behind her new ally. The 1905 crisis, however, brought an end to Delcassé's tenure of the foreign ministry – his prime minister, Rouvier (q.v.), who feared a German attack, secretly promised the Germans to get rid of him. Delcassé stayed active in politics and contributed in 1909 to the overthrow of the first government of Clemenceau – another nationalist, but one of his bitterest political enemies. He was navy minister between March 1911 and January 1913 and also served for several months as ambassador to Russia.

It was a tribute to his reputation that on the outbreak of war in 1914, he returned to the Foreign Ministry in Viviani's (q.v.) government. His second period of office was, however, less successful and together with Viviani he resigned in October 1915 after Bulgaria entered the war. He died in 1923.

Bibliography

Andrews, C.M. (1968), *Théophile Delcassé and the Making of the Entente Cordiale*, London: Macmillan.

PM

DELESCLUZE, Louis-Charles (1809–71)

An eternal insurrectionary, Charles Delescluze mirrored the revolutionary tradition of nineteenth-century France, drawing its inspiration from the Great Revolution and always seeking the establishment of the popular Republic of Jacobin legend. A member of the Société des Amis du Peuple and the Droits de L'Homme secret societies, Delescluze was not involved in the 1830 revolution, but was wounded later in a demonstration demanding a Republic. Arrested in April 1834 at the offices of the *Tribune*, he fled to Belgium in 1836, pursued by the police on a charge of plotting against the government. He edited the *Journal de Charleroi*, returned to Valenciennes in 1840 as the editor of *L'Impartial du Nord*, was arrested briefly in 1844 and became a friend of Ledru Rollin. In 1848 he declared the Republic in Valenciennes and was named *commissaire du Nord* by the minister of the interior, Ledru Rollin.

After a turbulent and unpopular administration he left for Paris and established the weekly *La République Démocratique et Sociale* in November 1848 to propagate his radical ideas. But the support of the nation and Paris had turned to Louis Napoléon. Delescluze was arrested in March 1849 for attacking Cavaignac, re-arrested a month later and fled to clandestinity, followed by exile in London. After returning secretly in 1853, he was arrested in 1854 as a member of the Marianne secret society, imprisoned and transported to Cayenne until the amnesty of 1859. On his return, Delescluze published *Le Panthéon de l'industrie et des arts* (1860), launched *Le Réveil* in 1868 and returned to prison for two brief spells as a result of opening a subscription for a statue to Alphonse Baudin, the deputy killed in the protests which followed Louis Napoléon's *coup d'état* in 1851. He maintained his anti-Bonapartism and had to flee the country again in 1870 after *Le Réveil* was closed for antiwar sentiment. Delescluze returned after the collapse of the Empire and was immediately involved in the attempted *coup d'état* of 31 October 1870. Elected as a radical mayor for the 19th *arrondissement* in November 1870, he resigned in protest at General Trochu's actions and was imprisoned when *Le Réveil* was closed again. Elected as deputy for the Seine in February 1871, his bitter opposition to Thiers led him inevitably to support the Commune. He was elected to its committee for the 11th *arrondissement*.

During the Commune he was *commissaire des rélations exterieures*, sat on its Executive Commission, was *commissaire de guerre* and finally *délégué général de guerre* in its final days. It was he who exhorted the Parisians to a last ditch effort against the Versaillais once they had broken into the city. But on 25 May, with the Commune almost on its last barricade, he hoped to end the carnage through a parley arranged by the Prussians. Prevented from attending by national guardsmen, and conscious that he could not bear another revolutionary failure, he sought death on the barricades and found it in the Rue Voltaire near the Place du Château d'Eau.

Delescluze made an important contribution to the nineteenth-century French revolutionary movement. Like other revolutionary figures – such as Blanqui – he spent a lifetime of activism and adversity, writing, propagandizing, plotting and fighting for the establishment of the popular Republic. In his journalism he seemed to bring the ideas of Jacobin radicalism and socialism together, but his disputes with Socialists before and during the Commune demonstrate that he was not an orthodox Socialist. During the Commune he expressed his policy as 'integral emancipation of the workers', but his attachment to the republicanism of 1793 and his radical spirit led back in his last days to Jacobinism. Delescluze was a legendary figure in the French revolutionary movement.

Bibliography

Delescluze, C. (1869), *De Paris à Cayenne, journal d'un transporté*, Paris: Le Chevalier.

Dessal, M. (1936), *Les Origines, l'enfance et la jeunesse de Charles Delescluze*, Rennes: Imprimerie Réunis.

Dessal, M. (1952), *1809–1871: un révolutionaire jacobin: Charles Delescluze*, Paris: M. Rivière.

JCS

DELONCLE, Eugène (1890–1942)

Born in Brest in 1890, Eugène Deloncle studied at the Ecole Polytechnique and established a considerable reputation as a marine engineer before involving himself in politics in 1934. His sympathies for the royalist Action Française (AF) led him to join the street-fighting Camelots du Roi, and he soon became an Action Française section leader in Paris. However, in the wake of the riots of 6 February 1934 he and others became impatient with what they saw as the inactivity of the Action Française leadership, and at the end of 1935 Deloncle was among the ninety-seven who were expelled from the organization. This split furnished Deloncle with the team of violent former *camelots* who were to be the nucleus of the right-wing terrorist group La Cagoule (literally the hooded men) formed in July 1936. After the Armistice he formed the Mouvement Social Révolutionnaire and vied with Doriot and Déat for leadership of French pro-Nazi collab-

oration. However, he remained suspect to the German authorities, and he was shot dead when resisting arrest by the Gestapo in Paris in 1942.

Deloncle's name is primarily associated with the Organisation Sécrète d'Action Révolutionnaire Nationale, more commonly known as La Cagoule, which carried out a series of terrorist attacks between July 1936 and November 1937. The group's most notorious crime was the assassination of two leading Italian anti-Fascists, Carlo and Nello Rosselli, allegedly on the request of Mussolini's secret service and in exchange for arms. In the highly charged political atmosphere of the Popular Front period, the Cagoule was inconclusively linked with a number of other incidents and it was seen by the left as the agent of a far-reaching right-wing conspiracy to overthrow the Republic. Arms caches were found and there was evidence that the organization had links with clandestine insurrectionary groups within the French army. In a crude imitation of the Reichstag fire, the Cagoule blew up the headquarters of the French employers' association on 11 September 1937 in the hope that the Communists would be blamed and that a military 'coup' would ensue. The Socialist minister of the interior, Marx Dormoy, uncovered this plot in November 1937 and took measures to break the organization, an act that was later to cost him his life under the occupation.

Deloncle's penchant for terrorist violence found fresh outlets under the occupation. Members of his new organization, the Mouvement Social Révolutionnaire are believed to have been responsible, in complicity with the German SS, for the blowing-up of seven synagogues in Paris on 2 October 1941. His ambitions to become the privileged interlocutor of Franco-Nazi collaboration led him to try and outmanoeuvre both Marcel Déat (q.v.) and Jacques Doriot (q.v.) and to seek control of the Légion des Volontaires Français (French volunteers to fight for the Nazi cause). The rivalry and mistrust he thereby aroused in the collaborationist camp no doubt cost him his life.

Bibliography

Though Deloncle and the Cagoule are discussed in most standard historical studies of the period, there is nothing specifically on him and his movement in English. In French, see F. Fontenay, *La Cagoule contre la France* (Paris: Editions Sociales Internationales, 1938); C. Bernadac, *Dagore, les carnets secrets de la Cagoule* (Paris: France-Empire, 1977); P. Bourdrel, *La Cagoule* (Paris: Albin Michel, 1970).

BJ

DELORS, Jacques Lucien Jean (1925–)

A pure product of social-catholicism, Jacques Delors was minister of finance from 1981 to 1984 and, as such, was the architect of the French Socialists' conversion to orthodox economics. Paris born, he entered the Banque de France as a trainee in 1944. He did not achieve recognition as an expert in social affairs and economics until he was asked by P. Massé to contribute to the preparation of the Fifth Plan in 1962. His appointment was due both to his capacity for hard work and to his political connections with the Catholic CFTC union, whose research team he led from 1957. Influenced by Emmanuel Mounier's ideas, he associated briefly with the Mouvement Républicain Populaire and then with Socialist splinter groups, although he strongly disapproved of the radical posturing of the Parti Socialiste Unifié. He also belonged to Vie Nouvelle, a Catholic group involved in community and political action, and led its offspring, the Citoyen 60 club.

In the 1960s, as a high ranking civil servant, he advocated a less authoritarian and more consensus-based system of industrial relations. His ideas appeared very attractive to a ruling elite who were traumatized by the events of May 1968. When Chaban-Delmas became prime minister in 1969, he chose Delors to be his counsellor on social affairs in an effort to strengthen the credibility of his project for a 'new society'. This earned Delors much publicity, although his version of productivity deals (contrats de progrès) did not yield the hoped-for results of social peace. His emphasis on the development of adult education was in the long run a more rewarding enterprise. After leaving government, he was from 1972 to 1979 professor at the University of Paris-Dauphine and he also created the Echanges et Projets club, an exclusive group of enlightened captains of industry.

In 1974 he joined the increasingly powerful Socialist Party. He became a European MP in 1979 and saw his role as economic adviser steadily expand, the more so since he supported François Mitterrand against Michel Rocard, whose economic views were actually closer to his own. By the time Mitterrand won the presidency in 1981, Delors was one of the few Socialist leaders with a reputation for professionalism and with an international standing in financial circles. He was thus extremely influential as minister of finance, even though he displayed little enthusiasm for the anticapitalist rhetoric of the Socialist Party. He tolerated a brief period of reflation, unrealistically based on an elusive world recovery, before using the threat of resignation to impose his views on the government as early as December 1981. Supported by Mauroy, he kept France within the European Monetary System and in spring 1982 implemented a first austerity plan, curtailing consumption to reduce the trade deficit. Wages remained frozen for six months but prices did not, so as to boost company profits. As a result, themes like the 'entrepreneurial spirit' and the 'morality of profit-making' came to gain wide acceptance among Socialist officials. A second, and more stringent austerity package was adopted in March 1983, in the wake of a new devaluation of the franc. Collective bargaining was severely curtailed, especially in the public sector, by the uncoupling of wage from the price index with a consequent period of cuts in real wages.

By the time Delors left the government in July 1984, the Socialist Party's popularity was at its lowest. However, considerable reduction in inflation and a slight increase in unemployment meant that Delors' actions were deemed quite satisfactory by the financial community. The Paris Stock Exchange index rose by 60 per cent in 1983 and he himself was often described as a 'left-wing' Raymond Barre. In 1985, he became president of the European Commission but he is still talked of as a possible candidate for high office within France itself.

Bibliography

Bihr, A. (1986), *La Farce tranquille*, Paris: Spartacus.

Hamon, H. and Rotman, P. (1982), *La Deuxième gauche*, Paris: Ramsay.

Milesi, G. (1985), *Jacques Delors*, Paris: Belford.

JPR

DEPREUX, Edouard Gustave (1898–1981)

As a Socialist politician, Edouard Depreux played a prominent part in the public life of both the Fourth and the Fifth Republics.

He was born at Viesly, in the Nord department, but his family moved to Sceaux, on the southern outskirts of Paris, in 1913. Having completed his education after a period of war service, he qualified as an advocate and began practising in the Court of Appeal in Paris in 1923. He belonged to the Sceaux branch of the French Socialist Party (SFIO) and worked closely with Jean Longuet, one of the national leaders of that party. Depreux took the first steps of his political career in the late 1930s; in 1935 he won a place on the Sceaux Municipal Council, in

1937 he accepted the post of principal private secretary to Vincent Auriol during his period as minister of justice in the Chautemps government (June 1937–January 1938) and at the end of 1938 he was elected to the General Council of the Seine department.

He saw military service again in 1939–40 but after demobilization he made contact with Vincent Auriol, Léon Blum and others of his party who were opposed to the Vichy regime. In December 1941 he refused to accept appointment as a member and as president of the newly-created administrative committee for the Seine department and was subsequently interned in a camp in Compiègne. Fortunately he was released and played a full part in the Resistance movement as a member of the liberation organization and as part of the underground Socialist network.

After the liberation of France he was a member of the Consultative Assembly, of the two Constituent Assemblies and of the National Assembly, representing the Seine department. He was minister of interior in the Bidault, Blum and the Ramadier governments spanning the period from June 1946 to November 1947, and took charge of the education portfolio in the Robert Schuman administration between February and July 1948. He still maintained his interest in local affairs and served as mayor of Sceaux from 1944 to 1959.

Although Depreux had always been a loyal and disciplined member of his party, he disagreed strongly with the Algerian policy of the Mollet government of 1956–7 and became one of the leaders of a dissident minority within the SFIO. In the political crisis of 1958 his group favoured a change in the leadership and policy of the party. In September 1958, when the National Congress of the SFIO voted to support the policies recommended by the existing leadership, Depreux and his colleagues broke away to form the Autonomous Socialist Party (PSA), which in 1960 merged with two other groups to constitute the Unified Socialist Party (PSU). He served as national secretary of the new party until 1967, when he was succeeded by Michel Rocard.

Bibliography

Depreux, E. (1972), *Souvenirs d'un militant: cinquante ans de lutte: de la social-démocratie au socialisme: (1918–1968)*, Paris: Fayard.

See also *Le Monde* obituary notice (18–19 October 1981) and a memoir by Daniel Mayer (21 October 1981).

BDG

DÉROULÈDE, Paul (1846–1914)

Paul Déroulède was a prominent volunteer at the time of the Franco-Prussian War, shortly after which he published a volume of stridently patriotic verse: *Les Chants du soldat* (1872). Founder of the Ligue des Patriotes, in 1882, and a supporter of Boulanger, Déroulède continued to espouse the Boulangist cause long after *le brav' général* had been driven into political oblivion. Déroulède was elected as deputy for Angoulême in 1889 and for a second time in 1898. In what is now seen as a farcical episode, he attempted a *coup d'état* early in 1899. He was arrested and stood trial, being sentenced to ten years' exile. Pardoned in 1905, he stood for election in 1906, but was defeated. Undeterred, he continued on his hardline nationalist course and in 1910 again stood for election but was once more defeated.

Following the capitulation of 1870 and the Treaty of Frankfurt in 1871, Déroulède had emerged as a leading nationalist figure and exponent of *revanchard* sentiment. His political career advanced rapidly, building on a solid and broad base of popular support. Indeed, the Ligue des Patriotes, in its early years, operated from what was, in many ways, an orthodox parliamentarian base, boasting Gambetta, Hugo and Waldeck-Rousseau among its members.

A number of factors, however, combined to drive the Ligue away from a parliamentarian approach towards a blatantly authoritarian one. First, Gambetta's death, in 1882, removed the man whom Déroulède had always seen as best equipped to drag France from the ruins of defeat and, as he saw it, degeneration. Second, Déroulède quarrelled increasingly with Ferry (q.v.), most notably over the question of military education, Ferry preferring to diminish its importance. Third, Déroulède viewed with growing dissatisfaction France's involvement in a number of colonial ventures which he saw as sapping the vital energies of the nation, energies better spent, in his opinion, in working towards revenge against Germany. Déroulède took the presidency of the Ligue des Patriotes in 1885 and immediately had the movement adopt a tougher style, often indulging in open opposition to the parliamentary regime.

At the time of the Boulanger crisis Déroulède turned to Boulanger as the strong man capable of providing the authoritarian impetus needed to prepare France for revenge. Boulanger's spectacular failure to exploit a favourable situation in 1889, finds an extended if less dramatic parallel in Déroulède's increasing political impotence during the last years of the century. Although he favoured an appeal to the masses and advocated direct, authoritarian rule, he was never able to imagine a strategy to implement his ideas. His political career has to be seen as that of a man who veered away, successfully at first, from parliamentary republicanism, only to find himself straying close to proto-Fascist arguments. He never really espoused the latter, however, and remained locked in a sterile antagonism between opposition to what he saw as the ineffective institutions of representative government and an inability to launch any serious, coherent alternative.

Bibliography

Le Nationalisme français 1871–1914, a collection of contemporary documents chosen and presented by Raoul Girardet (Paris: A. Colin, 1966) remains a useful introduction to the broader issues. Z. Sternhell, 'Paul Déroulède and the origins of French nationalism', in *Journal of Contemporary History*, vol. 6, no. 4, 1971, pp. 46–70, provides an interesting account, in English, of Déroulède's main activities. By the same author, *Maurice Barrès et le nationalisme français* (Paris: Presses de la Fondation Nationale des Sciences Politiques, 1972) and *La Droite révolutionnaire 1885–1914* (Paris: Seuil 1978) contain important pages on Déroulède and the Ligue des Patriotes.

TAleVH

DESCAMPS, Eugène Paul (1922–)

In 1961 Eugène Descamps succeeded the little-known Georges Levard as general secretary of the Confédération Française des Travailleurs Chrétiens (CFTC) – a reformist trade union confederation originally established in 1919 and inspired by the consensual teachings of the Roman Catholic Church, which themselves were based on the papal encyclical on social affairs, *De Rerum Novarum* (1891).

He left school at the age of thirteen and tried his hand at a number of different jobs. At the same time he joined the Jeunesse Ouvrière Chrétienne (JOC), a young Catholic workers' organization, which was to provide the focus of his activities for many years. During the war he avoided being sent to work in Germany and became involved in the Resistance movement. At the end of the war he was sent to the Alsace-Lorraine region to build up the JOC, but after starting to work in the engineering industry, he joined the CFTC and started to become active in trade union affairs, with the result that by 1954 he had become the general secretary of its Metalworkers

Union and by 1957 he was a member of its executive body, the Bureau Confédéral.

Descamps will be remembered for his part in the 'deconfessionalization' of the confederation. At an extraordinary conference held in November 1964 it was finally decided that the reference to Christianity in the statutes of the CFTC should be modified and that the name of the confederation should be changed to the Confédération Française Démocratique du Travail. A minority of members wanted to retain their close link with Christian humanism and so they left to set up their own trade union confederation which was to keep the original title, the CFTC. In spite of this split, membership of the CFDT was to return to its 1964 level within three years.

Descamps was instrumental in convincing many of the other members of the CFDT of the necessity of unity of action with other trade union confederations. This was sealed in January 1966 by an agreement on industrial demands with the largest trade union confederation, the Communist Confédération Générale du Travail (CGT). Although this unity broke down during the strike wave in May–June 1968, it was to resurface at the beginning of the 1970s.

He will also be remembered for the decision taken at the 1970 Conference which was to launch the CFDT into a new phase of development as a self-styled revolutionary trade union confederation. At this conference, the 35th, held in Issy-les-Moulineaux, the CFDT was to base its analysis of capitalism on the class struggle and was to opt for *socialisme autogestionnaire*, a somewhat hazy concept based on three pillars: workers', control, the socialization of the means of production and exchange and decentralized planning. *Autogestion* was to inspire the confederation's activities for the next decade.

In 1971 Descamps was obliged to stand down for reasons of ill health and he handed a relatively thriving trade union organization with a growing membership over to his successor Edmond Maire (q.v.). Afterwards he developed a new career as a lecturer in industrial relations at various universities in Paris.

Bibliography

There is no biography of Eugène Descamps in English. He has written an autobiographical work, *Militer* (Paris: Fayard, 1971) and is the subject of a major, if rambling, profile in H. Hamon and P. Rotman *La Deuxième gauche* (Paris: Ramsay, 1982).

JB

DESCHANEL, Paul Eugène Louis (1855–1922)

Paul Deschanel was born in Brussels 1856, the son of a professor of classics who was expelled from France in the aftermath of Louis Napoleon's *coup* of 1851. Throughout his career, the legitimacy of his political origins was to serve Deschanel as guarantor of a republicanism that might otherwise have seemed somewhat lukewarm. Having studied literature and law in Paris, he decided on a political career very early on. In 1877 he became sub-prefect of Dreux in the Eure-et-Loir and began a connection with the department that would survive until his death.

He was first elected to the Chamber of Deputies in 1885; thereafter he was constantly re-elected and on five occasions did not even have to face an opponent. This massively strong electoral base – in 1919 he obtained 43,000 of the 52,000 votes cast – enabled him to pursue the career of gentleman politician. He engaged in literary and historical scholarship, cultivated a reputation as a parliamentary orator, and specialized in foreign and colonial affairs and in the defence of small property holders. He was a great admirer of English political style and indeed of style *tout court*; his slightly overdressed elegance became legendary. Refusing all offers of ministerial office, he preferred to base his reputation on his writings, his speeches and his profile. Thus his election to the Academie française in 1899 complemented his first election as president of the Chamber of Deputies in 1898. The Dreyfusard coalition that gained political power in 1899 had little use for the political or personal manner of a figure whose republicanism was too obviously conservative and he did not regain the presidency of the Chamber until 1912. Thereafter his ambitions were fixed on exchanging one presidency for another. He was able to exercise his oratorical talents during the First World War as Chamber president and acquired prominence without responsibility. The circumstances of the 1920 presidential election also worked to his advantage. The Chamber elected in 1919 was far more overtly conservative than any of its immediate predecessors and Clemenceau (q.v.) – the natural choice to succeed Poincaré – was deeply suspect to the hard right because of his intransigent anticlericalism. At the same time he was equally unpopular with the system politicians of the centre and centre-left who had fallen victims to his aggressive patriotism both before and after he became prime minister. Deschanel played on the right's dislike of Clemenceau's absolute refusal to re-establish diplomatic relations with the Vatican and on the left's fear of an authoritarianism that posed a threat to Republi-

can conventions about the role of the presidency. In a secret ballot held before the formal election, the parliamentarians gave 408 votes to Deschanel and only 389 to Clemenceau who had not formally proclaimed his candidature and who, on hearing the result immediately withdrew. On 17 January 1920 Deschanel was elected President of the Republic with 734 votes, the highest total ever.

Nine months later, mental illness compelled him to resign. The pathetic tragicomedy of his presidency – whose point of absurdity was reached when he fell off a train and was found wandering along the track in his nightshirt – seemed a dreadful conclusion to an ultimately sterile career. Critical of the leniency of the Versailles peace settlement for maintaining the territorial unity of Germany, he even found his prime minister, Millerand (q.v.), too soft. He seems to have had an activist conception of the presidency, arguing for its right to communicate with the Chambers without ministerial countersignature. After his resignation, he spent a period in a mental hospital before returning to the Senate, to which he was narrowly elected by the department in which he had so often triumphed. He died in 1922. It is a measure of the paucity of his record that all that is remembered of him in politics is the manner of his departure from it.

Bibliography

Sonolet, L. (1926), *La Vie et l'oeuvre de Paul Deschanel*, Paris: Hachette.
Dansette, A. (1960), *Les Presidents de la république*, Paris: Le Livre Contemporain.

PM

DIENESCH, Marie-Madeleine (1914–   )

Marie-Madeleine Dienesch has enjoyed a lifelong career as a pro-Gaullist politician, concerned primarily with social issues, who nevertheless has always retained her independence from political parties.

Born in Cairo, Marie-Madeleine Dienesch had a classical education crowned by the teaching qualification – *agrégation de lettres*. During the war she taught in Brittany and at the liberation sat in both Constituent Assemblies and was elected as an MRP Deputy for Côtes-du-Nord from 1946–58. She was vice-president of the National Assembly from 1958–9 and part of the Christian democrat (MRP) executive committee in 1958. During the Fifth Republic, she presided over the group of deputies who were attached, but not part of (*apparentés*) the Gaullist party (UDR and later RPR). In Georges Pompidou's Fourth cabinet, she was secretary of state for national education (May–July 1968); under the premiership of Couve de Murville she was secretary of state for social affairs (July 1968–9); under Chaban-Delmas she held on to this portfolio (July 1969–72); under Pierre Messmer she was secretary of state attached to the Ministry of Health and Social Security (1973–4).

Dienesch's varied political career also took her to Luxembourg as ambassador (1975–8); to a departmental council in Brittany (1976–82) and to Brittany's Regional Council. She was re-elected deputy for her former constituency in 1978–81. This list of her political activities is by no means exhaustive.

She has always been a Gaullist, but not part of the parliamentary Gaullist parties. She believed that a party could not be both a party of government and a party of *rassemblement* (rally), which she considered to be the corner-stone of de Gaulle's thinking.

CD

'DORGÈRES', Henri Auguste d'Halluin (Henri d'Halluin) (1897–1985)

In spite of the apparently aristocratic name, Henri d'Halluin was the son of a butcher. He changed his name to Dorgères after becoming a journalist. During the 1920s he turned *Le progrès agricole de l'ouest* into a major weekly paper in the north-west, organizing around it a series of Comités de Défense Paysanne. These were to provide a major focus of the extensive agricultural protest which characterized the inter-war period. In the late 1920s the immediate cause of growing rural violence was the decision to adopt compulsory social insurance for farm labourers. During the 1930s France's small scale, backward, agricultural sector was further hit by a serious decline in real prices for its produce.

In 1934 Dorgères formed a Front Paysan with other rural leaders. By 1936 this had broken down. The problem was partly one of personality, but there were also serious differences of policy when discussions moved beyond tax strikes, or protest meetings. Dorgères had emerged as a forceful demagogue, who was attracted by Mussolini's fascism. The Jeunesses Paysannes side of his movement wore green shirts, and adopted aspects of paramilitary organization. His slogan, 'Believe, Obey, Serve', clearly echoed Mussolini. However, it would be wrong to see the movement as Fascist. It never developed a full Fascist ideology, stressing more a celebration of rural life

and defence of the small man in his fight against the encroachments of the state. Moreover, although Dorgères revered Marshal Pétain (whom he called 'Maréchal paysan'), and was named a member of the Vichy Conseil National and the Peasant Corporation, he strongly opposed collaboration. He was placed on trial after the liberation, but was given a suspended sentence in a view of evidence that he had finally turned to the Resistance.

After the war, Dorgères resumed his journalistic and political activities. During the 1950s France underwent rapid economic change, in particular a movement away from the land. Dorgères picked up a particularly potent issue in his defence of the *bouilleurs du cru* (home distillers) against Mendès France's anti-alcohol measures. Once again, tens of thousands flocked to the banners of the Comités de Défense, and in the 1956 elections Dorgères was elected a deputy for Ille-et-Villaine. In the following year he formed an alliance with Pierre Poujade, who had leapt to prominence as leader of a shopkeepers' pressure group and party, and Paul Antier, the Peasant Party leader. However, these right-wing groups were riven by internal dissent, and their supporters were beginning to desert in droves well before de Gaulle's return to the political scene in 1958.

Dorgères initially supported de Gaulle as the saviour in France's hour of need, but in 1965 he supported Tixier-Vignacourt in the presidential elections. By this time he had slipped back into obscurity. Rural protest continued, but it had taken on a younger leadership, and less extreme right-wing complexion.

Bibliography

Dorgères, H. (1975), *Au temps des fourches*, Paris: France-Empire.

Fauvet, J. and Mendras, H. (1958), *Les Paysans et la politique*, Paris: Librairie A. Colin.

Ory, P. (1975), 'Le Dorgèrisme: institution et discours d'une colère paysanne', in *Revue d'Histoire Moderne et Contemporaine*, vol. 22, no. 2, pp. 168–90.

RE

DORIOT, Jacques Maurice (1898–1945)

Doriot is remembered for his astonishing political journey from the leading circles of the Communist party, through the Fascist Parti Populaire Français (PPF), to an enthusiastic collaboration with the Germans during the occupation.

Born in the small town of Bresles (Oise), Doriot was the only child of an artisan-blacksmith. Having finished his studies at the age of 15, he arrived in the Parisian suburb of Saint-Denis in 1915, where he found employment in a number of engineering concerns. In 1916 he joined the Young Socialists, and was mobilized in the following year.

On his release from the army in 1920 Doriot returned to Saint-Denis, where he rejoined the Young Socialists. Having followed the Communist majority at the time of the Tours Congress, Doriot's rise in the hierarchy of the Young Communists (Jeunnesses Communistes – JC), due in part to his reputation as a 'true Bolshevik', was extremely rapid. In July 1921 he visited Moscow. In the spring of 1922 he was given a seat on the Presidium of the Executive of the International.

Doriot returned to France in the winter of 1922–3. In his absence he had received a prison sentence for antimilitary propaganda. Consequently it was as a clandestine militant that he played a leading part in the JC campaign against the occupation of the Ruhr. In May 1923 he was named secretary-general of the JC. He was finally captured by the police in December 1923. His numerous antimilitarist articles earned him a three-year prison sentence.

Thanks to his election as deputy of the fourth constituency of the Seine, Doriot served only four and a half months in the Santé. (From 1928 until 1938 he held the fourth constituency of Saint-Denis.) In the Chamber of Deputies the vehemence of his interventions, particularly his expressions of support for Moroccan rebels in the Rif War, brought his name to the attention of a wider public. His willingness to pass from verbal to physical violence was frequently displayed on the streets.

From 1927 Doriot began to be afflicted by doubts. He personally witnessed the disastrous consequences of the Comintern's Chinese policy. Two more periods in prison (July to October 1927 and April to October 1928) gave him time to reflect on the consequences of the hardening of the Comintern's line represented by the application of the sectarian 'class against class' tactic in France from the summer of 1927. But seeing, at this time, no future for himself outside the party, Doriot endorsed the new line in a humiliating speech of self-criticism at the 6th Party Congress of March 1929. He was content to devote his energies to building a power base in Saint-Denis, of which he was elected mayor in February 1931.

Only after the 'Fascist' riots on the Place de la Concorde of 6 February 1934 did Doriot make public his disagreements with the party leadership.

Backed by a majority of Saint-Denis militants, he called for immediate talks with the Socialist Party (SFIO) with a view to the formation of a united front against fascism. On 27 June 1934 Doriot was expelled from the Communist Party, at the very moment when it was in the process of reversing its own policy by urging negotiations with SFIO leaders. Henceforth he nourished an inextinguishable hatred for communism, and in particular of its leader, Maurice Thorez (q.v.).

The Communist Party ensured that Doriot played no part in the movement for unity of action that culminated in the formation of the Popular Front in July 1935. In the autumn of that year Doriot's hostility to communism was expanded to include the left as a whole. With the support of diverse figures of the extreme right, Doriot formed the PPF (27 and 28 July 1936). Fear of communism stemming from the Popular Front electoral victory of April/May 1936 and the mass strikes of June provided favourable conditions for recruitment. At its peak in late 1937 the PPF may have had 100,000 members. Many adherents were former Communists, though historians may have exaggerated the extent of such support. The PPF has been described as the sole truly Fascist party of the period. In reality there was little in its programme or activities to distinguish it from any other movement of the far right, at least before 1940.

Doriot followed an uncertain political line. His call, in the spring of 1937, for a Front de la Liberté, grouping all the non-Marxist parties, foundered on the opposition of the centre right and of La Rocque's Parti Social Français. In late 1938 he adopted a populist tactic, denouncing both the general strike of 30 November 1938 and the decree laws that had provoked it. This change of tack did not prevent the decline of the party, now that the threat of the Popular Front had receded. Doriot's revocation as mayor of Saint-Denis, on grounds of financial irregularities, on 25 May 1937, followed by the recapture of his deputy's seat by the Communists, had also demoralized supporters. In January 1939, in protest against Doriot's pro-Munich views and his willingness to accept subsidies from the Italian government, a number of Politburo members resigned from the party. Doriot assumed an ultra-nationalist attitude in the months that followed, and was himself mobilized in September 1939. He fought courageously, receiving a citation to add to those of the previous war.

After the 1940 armistice Doriot had no hesitation in preaching collaboration with the Germans. He believed the moment had come for the PPF to take power. In order to advance his cause he posed first as a faithful supporter of Pétain in his quarrel with

Laval, and then from the summer of 1941 attempted to convince the Germans that the PPF was the only reliable collaborationist force in France. This helps to explain the leading role played by him in the creation of the Légion des Volontaires Français, which was to fight with the Germans on the eastern front. Doriot himself was among the first contingent of volunteers, though he remained in Russia for only three months (4 September 1941 to early December). His prestige in collaborationist circles was increased by this gesture. Yet his hopes of power were disappointed. He was distracted by quarrels with rival collaborators, Marcel Déat in particular. In any case the Germans had resolved to back Laval and Pétain. This was clearly demonstrated when they refused to withdraw support from Laval at the time of the American invasion of North Africa.

Seeing no political future in France, Doriot departed once more for the Russian front in March 1943, this time remaining until the end of February of the following year. The PPF, meanwhile, put itself at the service of the Germans, playing a key role in anti-Resistance activities.

On the eve of the liberation of Paris Doriot fled to Germany. His ambition to become the 'French Führer' still unrealized, he formed the Comité de la Libération Française in December 1944 as a means of out-flanking the delegation that had suceeded Laval. On 22 February 1945, on his way to secure the adhesion of Marcel Déat and Joseph Darnand, the only collaborationist leaders who had not yet rallied to him, Doriot was killed when two aircraft, probably Allied, machine-gunned his car.

Bibliography

Allardyce, G. (1966), 'The political transition of Jacques Doriot', in *Journal of Contemporary History*, vol. 1, no. 1, pp. 56–74.

Brunet, J.-P. (1986), *Jacques Doriot. Du communisme au fascisme*, Paris: Balland.

Burrin, P. (1986), *La Dérive fasciste: Doriot, Déat, Bergery, 1933–1945*, Paris: Seuil.

Doriot, J. (1936), *La France ne sera pas un pays d'esclaves*, Paris: Les Œuvres Françaises.

Wolf, D. (1969), *Doriot. Du communisme à la collaboration*, Paris: Fayard.

KP

DOUMER, Paul (1857–1932)

The oldest president of the Republic on taking of-fice, and one of four to die in office, Paul Doumer was born in Aurillac (Dordogne), the son of a railwayman. His background was in education but he quickly turned to politics. He was first elected to the Chamber of Deputies in 1888, in a by-election in the Aisne, after the leading candidate, Boulanger (q.v.), withdrew. From 1890–6 he represented a Yonne constituency and then, after six years out of Parliament, returned first as deputy for the Aisne, and then, from 1912 to 1931 as senator for Corsica.

Doumer's first ministerial experience was as minister of finance in Léon Bourgeois' (q.v.) government of 1895–6 and to him goes the distinction of having presented the first bill advocating a tax on income. Then he left parliamentary politics to become governor-general of Indo-China. A discreet yet active and enterprising governor, he promoted the Yunnan railway project and established a series of levies on salt, opium and rice alcohol to finance the region's development. He returned to domestic politics at a delicate time in the affairs of the ruling Radical-dominated coalition (the *bloc des gauches*), and aligned himself in 1904 with those who opposed Combes' (q.v.) non-aggression pact with the Socialists. Having become president of the influential budget committee, in 1905 he was elected president by the Chamber of Deputies, using the votes of conservatives to defeat the candidate of the left, Henri Brisson (q.v.). Combes resigned as prime minister a week later and Doumer was subsequently excluded from the Radical Party for his dissidence, a dissidence that culminated in January 1906 in his unsuccessful bid for the presidency of the Republic against the candidate of the left, Armand Fallières (q.v.).

After the war, Doumer served in the 1921–2 government of Aristide Briand (q.v.) and his financial expertise earned him the presidency of the Senate finance committee. He was again in a Briand government in 1925–6, sharing financial responsibilities with the industrialist-turned-politician, Louis Loucheur (q.v.). His career then followed the classic pattern of a future president of the Third Republic. In 1927 he became president of the Senate and four years later was elected head of state – in preference to the more high profile Briand – by parliamentarians who distrusted an interventionist presidency. Like Doumergue (q.v.) before him and Lebrun (q.v.) his successor, he was a conservative who was also a Freemason and like them he was elected against left wingers who were not. He was assassinated by a Russian anarchist within a year of taking office, on the eve of the second ballot of the 1932 Legislative elections.

An industrious, rather aloof man, Doumer was

not likely to inspire affection. After the genial and energetic Doumergue, who had rescued the presidency from the Millerand (q.v.) débâcle by his firm but tactful interventions and parliamentary skills, Doumer was by temperament and style ill-suited to maintain that impetus; he had been imposed by a right wing for whom Briand's conciliatory politics were already showing their inadequacy in the face of dangerous international developments.

Bibliography

Doumer, P. (1906), *Livre de mes fils*, Paris: Vuibert-Nony.

de Villiers, A. (1932), *Paul Doumer parle*, Paris: Tallandier.

ACR

DOUMERGUE, Gaston (1863–1937)

Born into a Protestant landed family from the Gard, Doumergue chose the law as a profession and served as magistrate in Indo-China and Algeria. On the death of his father, he returned to France and was persuaded in 1893 to stand for election as deputy for Nîmes (Gard) and won easily with 10,001 of the 10,564 votes cast. He stood as a Radical Socialist and throughout his career would be identified with the moderate wing of French radicalism. He was also a Freemason.

His experience of the colonies made him an effective spokesman on the subject, initially gaining a reputation by opposing Delcassé (q.v.) and subsequently being appointed minister of colonies in the Combes government of 1902–5. He then held ministerial office in the governments of Sarrien (q.v.), Clemenceau (q.v.) and Briand (q.v.) before becoming prime minister himself in December 1913. He kept the foreign affairs portfolio in his own government and in that of Viviani (q.v.) which followed. With the onset of war, Doumergue returned to the Ministry of Colonies and stayed there until 1917, supervising colonial recruitment, preserving the security of France's colonial possessions and pursuing the conquest of the German colonies of Togoland and the Cameroons.

The fall of Briand's *cabinet* in 1917 led to a long period of absence from ministerial office for Doumergue; yet his influence remained considerable. In 1910 he had exchanged the Chamber of Deputies for the Senate and he became its president in 1923. Thus he was well placed to replace Millerand (q.v.) when

the latter was forced to resign in 1924. The early years of his presidency were marked by a series of crises, affecting both the economy and governments, which led to a disastrous fall in the value of the franc. In order to halt this process, Doumergue took a key role in appointing Poincaré (q.v.) to the premiership and he firmly supported the orthodox, right-wing policies, which paved the way for renewed financial stability. The fact that Poincaré's resignation in 1929, on the grounds of ill health, led to a measure of renewed ministerial instability, did not detract from Doumergue's considerable reputation as an effective political operator and conciliator. His regard for constitutional government and his ability to work with men of differing political persuasion was widely recognized in the country and led to his affectionate nickname of *Gastounet*.

It was this popularity that prompted his recall to office in 1934. The Stavisky (q.v.) scandal and the riots of 6 February 1934 had made constitutional government in France look very vulnerable. In desperation, President Lebrun (q.v.) turned to Doumergue who came out of retirement and formed a cabinet which excluded only Communists, Socialists and the extreme right from its membership. Acting on a massive vote of confidence, he used the decree-laws mechanism to introduce unpopular financial measures, a tactic that would become increasingly common during the last years of the Republic. Despite initial success, it was inevitable that political faction fighting should occur within his very heterogeneous cabinet; and to many on the democratic left, he seemed increasingly to advocate an authoritarian executive-led style of government that was an anathema to traditional republicanism. In November 1934 the Radicals resigned from his government, his premiership came to an end and he left the political scene for good. He left behind the reputation of a skilful politician who had few positive achievements to his name.

Bibliography

Berstein, S. (1982), *Histoire du parti radical*, vol. II, Paris: Presses de la Fondation Nationale des Sciences Politiques.

Derfler, L. (1983), *President and Parliament*, Boca Rota: University Press of Florida.

Larmour, P. (1964), *The French Radical Party in the 1930s*, Stanford, Cal.: Stanford University Press.

PT

DREYFUS, Captain Alfred (1859–1935)

Contrary to 'Hamlet without the Prince', one of the most significant books written about 'the affair' is aptly entitled 'L'Affaire sans Dreyfus'. The man whose personal tragedy attracted superlatives like a magnet and who gave French politics a metaphysical dimension, was temperamentally a prime candidate for historical oblivion. Born in Mulhouse from Jewish parents who left Alsace in 1871 and settled in Paris in order to remain French, Alfred Dreyfus graduated from the Polytechnique and the Ecole de Guerre with such a good record that out of 300 Jewish officers then serving in the French Army, he was the only one to be appointed to the General Staff in 1893.

Accused in October 1894 of having passed on to the Germans military secrets in the form of a handwritten document known as the *bordereau*, Dreyus was tried in camera by a military tribunal who convicted him on flimsy evidence wrongly interpreted by a set of incompetent graphologists. He was sentenced in December 1894 to be reduced to the ranks and deported to Devil's Island off French Guyana. Dreyfus never ceased to protest his innocence while, as a loyal and patriotic officer, he accepted that the harsh sentence in itself was just retribution for such a heinous crime.

While Dreyfus endured the torment of solitary confinement in the most inhospitable environment, nobody in France wasted any compassion on the 'traitor' or questioned the validity of the judgment, except for his wife, his brother Mathieu, and within a few months the Zionist Bernard Lazare, whom Mathieu Dreyfus managed to convince that the verdict was reached on the strength of wrong evidence. While various officers of the French intelligence service stored up unreliable testimonies and carried their sense of duty to the extreme of fabricating further incriminating evidence, politicians, journalists and other public figures slowly, gradually came to the conclusion that there had been a miscarriage of justice and that there should be a re-trial.

From 1897 onwards, when the new head of espionage, Colonel Picquart, an Alsatian Protestant, discovered the similarity between the handwriting of the *bordereau* and that of an officer of dubious morals and uncertain financial means, Commandant Esterhazy, he managed to alert another Alsatian Protestant, the much respected vice-president of the Senate Scheurer-Kestner, who supported the campaign for the revision of the trial. From then on, and in spite of the cautious, cool-headed approach both of Picquart and Scheurer-Kestner, passion quickly overtook reason, and war was declared between those who deemed that the Republic's most sacred duty was towards redress of an injustice, and those who considered that any criticism of the army was an attempt against the integrity of the nation.

By then Dreyfus's personal fate hardly seemed relevant. The issue was distorted from the outset by the violently anti-Semitic campaign of Drumont in his newspaper *La Libre Parole*, The anti-Dreyfusards included mainly but not exclusively nationalist 'leagues' and a large contingent of Catholics who saw in the Dreyfusards the seeds of French degeneration. The Dreyfusards included genuine idealists and gave 'intellectuals' the stamp of moral commitment in politics, but some Dreyfusards were also more concerned to score points against 'reactionary elements' of the Church and the army than to maintain high standards of justice, as their blatantly unfair treatment of Catholic officers was to demonstrate a few years later. But in 1898 and 1899, gross disregard for evidence and justice tainted most official decisions pertaining to the affair.

Esterhazy was court-martialled and acquitted on 10 January 1898. On 13 January, Clemenceau published in his newspaper *L'Aurore* what is probably the most famous open letter of all times, the letter 'J'accuse' by Emile Zola to the President of the Republic Félix Faure, an indictment on the major figures of the Ministry of War and the General Staff who had connived to condemn Dreyfus. In February Zola stood trial, as he had wished, and was convicted of libel. Even though the electoral campaign in the spring of 1898 was fought on the issue of the price of bread rather than on that of military justice, the affair rebounded in August with the revelation of Colonel Henry's forgery and his subsequent suicide. The government yielded to the inevitable and in December the Supreme Court of Appeal ordered a retrial. Brought back from Devil's Island in poor health and with broken spirits, Dreyfus attended the retrial in Rennes in August and September 1899 with astonishing passivity, and received the astonishing verdict of 'guilty with mitigating circumstances'. Too exhausted to fight back, he accepted a pardon from the President of the Republic, and in 1906 the Court of Appeal quashed the Rennes verdict. Dreyfus was reinstated in the Army and awarded the Legion of Honour. He retired the following year, took up service again during the First World War, and then led a quiet private life until his death in 1935.

Bibliography

The Dreyfus affair seems to be an inexhaustible

source of inspiration, and the long list of books that go on being published and republished seem to fall into two categories: the chronicles of an unjustice perpetrated and the mystery of the traitor's identity not altogether solved; the analysis of the moral, ideological and political implications and repercussions of the affair on twentieth-century France (all, of course, supported by a massive corpus of primary sources). For a fairly comprehensive bibliography, one should consult the most recent addition to classics of the first category, Jean-Denis Bredin, *L'Affaire* (Paris: Julliard, 1983). The more lucid and/or interesting accounts include Alfred Dreyfus, *Cinq années de ma vie*, with an introduction by Pierre Vidal-Naquet (Paris: Maspéro, 1962); Alfred Dreyfus, *Five Years of My Life* (London: Geo. Newnes, 1901); Mathieu Dreyfus, *L'affaire telle que je l'ai connue* (Paris: Grasset, 1978); Joseph Reinach, *Histoire de l'affaire Dreyfus*, 7 vols, (Paris: Fasquelle, 1929). Relevant to the first category, but in a class of their own because of their value as political credos are the following: Maurice Barrès, *Scènes et doctrines du nationalisme* (Paris: Plon, 1902); Daniel Halévy, *Apologie pour notre passé* (Paris: Cahiers de la Quinzaine, 1910); Jean Jaurès, *Les Preuves* (Paris: Le Signe, 1981); Charles Péguy, *Notre jeunesse* (Paris: Gallimard, 1913); Emile Zola, *L'Affaire Dreyfus. La Vérité en marche* (Paris: Garnier-Flammarion, 1969). The second category is less directly relevant to Dreyfus, but essential to an understanding of French politics, and includes among others, Marcel Thomas, *L'Affaire sans Dreyfus* (Paris: Fayard, 1961); Madeleine Rebérioux, *La République radicale, 1898–1914* (Paris: Seuil, 1975); Douglas Johnson, *France and the Dreyfus Affair* (London: Blandford Press, 1966); Roderick Kedward, *The Dreyfus Affair* (London: Longman, 1965)).

AM

DRIEU LA ROCHELLE, Pierre Eugène (1893–1945)

A First World War veteran, Drieu flirted with the surrealist movement in the 1920s but found it difficult to commit himself then, as later, to any artistic or political movement for any length of time. Progressively more dismayed with the blinkered nationalism of French politicians and by what he considered his country's decadence, by the early 1930s he was convinced that France's only hope of revival lay in a United States of Europe which would abandon liberal capitalism and parliamentary democracy. After the politically polarizing riots of 6 February 1934 he openly declared himself a Fascist and that same year published *Socialisme fasciste*, a book which condemned the bankruptcy of 'bourgeois' political thinking and recommended the Fascist alternative. In 1935 he attended the Nuremberg rallies and in June 1936 joined Jacques Doriot's newly-founded Parti Populaire Français, arguably the only Fascist party ever to exist in France. He wrote regularly for the party's daily newspaper *L'Emancipation Nationale* until he resigned in January 1939, disillusioned with Doriot and increasingly disappointed by what he now saw as Hitler's German rather than European brand of fascism. However, after France's defeat in 1940 he despised the Vichy regime as yet another manifestation of the sterile conservative right and advocated unconditional collaboration with the Nazi occupier. Occasionally using his influence to secure the release of close friends from the Gestapo's clutches, Drieu devoted much of his time during the occupation to his own writing and to editing the prestigious *Nouvelle Revue Française*. He committed suicide on 16 February 1945 the day after a warrant was issued for his arrest.

Typical of the young intellectuals of his generation, Drieu was disenchanted by what he viewed as society's failure to take advantage of the opportunity for radical change afforded by the First World War. He had found the war exhilarating, saw it as a breeding ground for leaders and a chance for national rejuvenation. Politically available in the 1920s and early 1930s, he was attracted by the idea of authoritarian leadership and extreme political solutions. Although he viewed communism as the only viable alternative to fascism in Europe he believed the party had been compromised by its participation in the French democratic process and by its adherence to dialectical materialism which automatically precluded it from the spiritual and moral rejuvenation required to rouse Frenchmen from their lethargy. The violent riots of 6 February 1934 revived his faith in his fellow countrymen and demonstrated that an extremist right- and left-wing potential existed which could be channelled into a single antiparliamentarian force. By 1940 however he had lost faith both in fascism and in what had turned out to be German imperialism, and his unconditional backing of collaboration with Germans during the occupation became more a gesture of despair than of political commitment.

Drieu was one of the most important figures among the French Fascist intellectuals of the interwar years. His biography is that of the failure of fascism in France. His fascinating yet, in the final analysis, disappointing itinerary is perhaps best described in his semi-autobiographical novel, *Gilles* (Paris: Gallimard), first published in 1939.

Bibliography

Introductory material on Drieu may be found in:
Field, F. (1975), *Three French Writers and the Great War: Henri Barbusse, Drieu la Rochelle and Georges Bernanos*, Cambridge: Cambridge University Press.
Leal, R.B. (1982), *Drieu la Rochelle*, New York: Twayne.
More complete and complex studies include:
Andreu, P. and F.J. Grover (1979), *Drieu la Rochelle*, Paris: Hachette.
Grover, F.J. (1958), *Drieu la Rochelle and the Testimony of Fiction*, Berkeley and Los Angeles: California University Press.
Soucy, R. (1979), *Fascist Intellectual: Drieu la Rochelle*, Berkeley and Los Angeles: University of California Press.

GTH

DRUMONT, Edouard Adolphe (1844–1917)

A journalist and leading anti-Semite, Drumont was born in Paris in 1844. After his father's death, he followed him as a minor employee at the Hôtel de Ville. Soon, however, he took up journalism, writing regularly for *La Liberté*, and contributing to other papers. He also had a modest success as an author.

Until he was 42 there was no hint of his coming political fame. *La France juive*, published in 1886, came as a bombshell. Drumont's early struggles, and his humble background, had instilled in him a hatred of the capitalist society, and a belief that behind the façade of that society there lurked an obscure and malevolent force. The product of this belief was a vast, turgid diatribe, in two volumes, about Jewish power in contemporary society. *La France juive* had an enormous success. It channelled the currents of anti-Semitism already existent in French society, and was the starting-point for the strong anti-Semitic movement which was to dominate French politics for the next twenty years. By its vast sales, it made Drumont both wealthy and famous. It was to be followed by other books, of which the most important is *Le Testament d'un antisémite* (1891).

In 1889 Drumont founded the Ligue Nationale Antisémitique de France, which, however, folded in 1890. In 1892, more successfully, he founded the anti-Semitic newspaper *La Libre Parole*, which soon had a very large circulation, and played a leading part during the Panama scandal, stressing the nefarious role of Jewish financiers. In 1894, by its leaks in relation to the interrogation of Captain Dreyfus, it precipitated his trial and condemnation; and during the height of the Dreyfus affair, 1897–9, it was the leading voice in the anti-Semitic chorus which dominated the debate.

In the 1898 elections Drumont was returned for Algiers, as a member of the anti-Semitic parliamentary group, In the Chamber, however, he proved to be surprisingly ineffectual; a hopeless public speaker, he intervened little. In 1902 he lost his seat.

Already his fortunes were in decline. Whereas in the early 1890s he had had a considerable following, and was seen as France's leading anti-Semite, by the end of the century he was being challenged not only by Guérin's successful Ligue Antisémitique Française (founded 1897), but also by a wide variety of other anti-Semitic movements and papers. The founding of the daily *L'Action Française* in 1908, by his *Libre Parole* collaborator Léon Daudet, was a further nail in the coffin. Drumont gradually relapsed into obscurity, and by his death in 1917 had lost most of his money, and was living in a *pension de famille*, from which he was miserably buried in a pauper's grave.

Drumont's cry, before his death, 'Comprenez-vous que Dieu me fasse cela, à moi Drumont, après tout ce que j'ai fait pour lui!', sums up his illusion that in pursuing his anti-Semitic policies he was performing a Christian mission to remove injustice from society. By such illusions he was a forerunner of some of the most dangerous trends in the twentieth century.

Bibliography

Bernanos, G. (1931), *La Grande Peur des bien-pensants*, Paris: Grasset.
Beau de Loménie, E. (1968), *Edouard Drumont ou l'anticapitalisme national*, Paris: J.-J. Pauvert.
Wilson, S. (1982), *Ideology and Experience: Antisemitism in France at the time of the Dreyfus affair*, E. Brunswick, NJ: Associated University Presses.

RMG

DUBEDOUT, Hubert (1922–86)

Born on 9 December 1922 in Paris, son of an industrialist, Hubert Dubedout was late in entering political life. After studying engineering in the Naval

School in Paris, economics at Toulouse University and taking an MSc. at the Carnegie Institute of Technology, Dubedout embarked on a career as a high-ranking officer in the French navy, which lasted from the end of the war until the late 1950s. Unhappy with his role during the Indo-China war, he finally quit the navy in 1958 and settled in Grenoble where he took up a senior administrative post in the Centre for Atomic Studies. It was not however until 1964 that Dubedout made his first, characteristic impact on local politics, when he led a largely apolitical campaign to improve the erratic water supply in the town's high-rise flats. At this time he founded the Grenoble-based Municipal Action Group – Groupes d'Action Municipale (GAM), which was to develop into a national movement in the late 1960s and early 1970s, and was initially intended as a ginger group pressing for improvements in council amenities.

Dubedout created a major political upset in the local elections of 1965 when he defeated the right-wing council in Grenoble at the head of a coalition including orthodox Socialists from the Socialist Party (SFIO), the breakaway left-oriented United Socialist Party (PSU) and the GAM. From this time on his name was to be associated with Grenoble. He was mayor of Grenoble from 1965 until 1983, and under the impulse of the left coalition on the council it was transformed from a conservative, provincial town into a dynamic, modern centre of social, cultural and industrial experimentation. Throughout the late 1960s and 1970s Grenoble was seen as a laboratory for new ideas in town planning, industrial implantation and public transport, as well as in the development of local democracy. Dubedout piloted new methods of council management, a new aesthetic of council house construction, and developed an attractive public image for his town, drawing high-tech companies, among others, from France and abroad to set up their plants in the Grenoble region. By the late 1970s Grenoble had become a major role of the microelectronics industry.

The municipal socialism which Hubert Dubedout came to embody was very much a technocratic, modernizing movement which put efficient and humane council management before politics. Indeed Dubedout was long considered to be apolitical, and even after joining the 'new' Socialist party in 1973, and standing successfully as Socialist parliamentary candidate for Grenoble in the same year, he remained aloof from the internal struggles within the Socialist Party and the left in general. After winning the parliamentary seat which his mentor Mendès France had lost in 1968 he remained deputy until

1983 when he resigned after a surprise defeat in the town council elections at the hands of Alain Carignon, the up-and-coming young neo-Gaullist (RPR) politician. Dubedout's reputation and influence, however, were built around his innovative action as mayor of Grenoble and his original contribution to council management.

After 1983 he withdrew from local politics and worked in Paris at the head of a state agency concerned with coal imports. He died of heart failure during a mountaineering expedition on Mont Blanc on 25 July 1986.

Bibliography

For a full acount of Dubedout's contribution to local politics in Grenoble, see Pierre Frappat, *Grenoble, le mythe blessé* (Paris: Alain Moreau, 1979) and J. Ardagh, *The New France* (Harmondsworth: Penguin, 1986).

KD

DUCHET, Roger Benoît (1906–81)

From classic viticultural peasant proprietor stock, Roger Duchet was always fascinated by politics, by its power brokerage and by its personalities. In 1930, at the age of 24 he founded a small journal, *La Vie Rurale*, which expressed the demands of the small farmer and the rural community, particularly the vinegrowing areas. Using this as a platform he became mayor of Beaune in 1934 and unsuccessful Radical candidate in the Popular Front election of 1936. Mobilized in 1940, captured and liberated, he resumed his post as mayor of Beaune in 1940 and survived the war to continue in office until 1965: a typical French political 'fief'. From 1946 to 1964 he was departmental councillor for Beaune and senator for the *Côte d'Or* from 1946 to 1969.

His great achievement was, almost single-handedly, to establish the Centre National des Indépendants on 6 January 1949 in Paris. He brought together many pre-war centre right remnants which had been devastated by the post-war elections and some newer formations. He toured the country speaking in innumerable small towns, where he set up support committees, which with the addition of some conservative personalities, formed the CNI. He later negotiated the addition of Antier's Peasant Party to form the Centre National des Indépendants et Paysans. The rules of the 1951 elections required lists of candidates in one constituency to belong to an organization that presented lists in thirty constituencies nation-wide. This caused a flood of local 'notables' and renowned independents to join the CNIP (including an alliance with Laniel's Parti Républicain de la Liberté) and led to a 'victory' with ninety-seven deputies under the CNIP banner in the Chamber. It meant that the traditional right, tainted by collaboration with the Germans and support for Vichy, was saved from extinction. Indeed, with the help of dissident Gaullists, its parliamentary leader, Antoine Pinay (q.v.) became prime minister in 1952.

Duchet served as a minister – mostly for the PTT (post and telephones) or for construction – in the governments of René Pleven (1951), E. Faure (1952 and 1955), Antoine Pinay (1952) and René Mayer (1953). In the period 1954 to 1962 his pro-French Algeria (Algerie française) led to his increasing isolation within the party he and Pinay had founded. He always protested that his ideas were 'moderate', but he became increasingly associated with the extreme right. He condemned de Gaulle's betrayal of French Algeria in 1962 and claimed to be a lifelong opponent of Gaullism; but he compromised with the Gaullist party, the UDR, in the 1965 municipal elections and supported de Gaulle for the presidency that year. During the Fifth Republic he held on to his positions of mayor and senator but this was essentially because of his very strong local power base and his constant support of the viticulturalists who controlled politics in Beaune.

Duchet was an outstanding example of the Third or Fourth Republic centre-right politician with a strong local base founded on a single interest. He was always available for ministerial posts, was a declared 'moderate', an alliance builder, a political wheeler-dealer and a gourmet. The alliance which he built with the Alliance Démocratique showed the extent of the CNIP's fortunes and of his influence. Men like Duchet found the Fifth Republic a very harsh environment. By 1958 the Poujadists had already invaded and disrupted the movement and by 1962 he was condemned to the oblivion of Algerié française and ejected from his own party. Duchet's achievement was to build the CNIP, from which a minority split away in 1962 to form the Républicains Indépendants. This would later become the Parti Républicain: the central bulwark of the Giscardian Union Pour la Démocratie Française.

Bibliography

CNIP newspaper – *La France Indépendante*, especially 12 September 1953 for Duchet's history of the CNIP.

See also:

Anderson, M. (1974), *Conservative Politics in France*, London: Allen and Unwin.
Centre National des Indépendants (*c*.1952) *Le Centre National des Indépendants*, Paris.
Duchet, R. (1958), *Pour le salut publique*, Paris: Plon.
Duchet, R. (1975), *La République epinglée*, Paris: Editions Alain Moreau.

JCS

DUCLERC, Charles Theodore Eugène (1812–92)

Duclerc was one of the veterans of mid-nineteenth-century republicanism who played a part in the early years of the Third Republic. He came from the Hautes Pyrenées, worked in Paris as a proof-reader and journalist and became an expert in financial and economic questions. A dedicated Republican, he served briefly as minister of finance in 1848 before resigning in protest at the dictatorial powers given to Cavaignac after the June Days. His political career then seemed to come to an end and he spent virtually the whole of the Second Empire as a businessman in Spain. But when news of the Revolution of September 1870 reached him in Bayonne, he returned to Paris and was immediately appointed president of the supervisory commission of government expenditure. He was elected to the National Assembly for the Basses Pyrenées, became president of the parliamentary group of the Gauche Republicaine and voted the straight Republican ticket on all the great issues of the legislature. Elected life senator in 1875, he was a strong opponent of the duc de Broglie (q.v.) though he was, apparently, well regarded by Marshal MacMahon (q.v.). He became prime minister in August 1882 at a time when more prominent figures (Gambetta (q.v.), Ferry (q.v.), de Freycinet (q.v.)) had all been defeated, the latter over French non-participation in the British naval expedition against the Egyptian leader Arabi-Bey. Duclerc appeared to share this unwillingness, which marked the end of the Anglo-French condominiums in Egypt and would lead to much French bad feeling towards Britain in the following twenty years. It was a sign of Duclerc's moderation – or his age – that he was unwilling to contemplate the expulsion from France of the Orleanist princes, a move that became a litmus test of left republicanism. His refusal led to his resignation in January 1883 and probably explains why the Radicals refused to accept his nomination as prime minister in 1887, at a time when President Grévy (q.v.) was desperately trying to hold on to power.

Bibliography

Dictionnaire de la biographie française, vol. XI (Paris: Letouzey and Ane, 1967).

PM

DUCLOS, Jacques (1896–1975)

The biography of Jacques Duclos is filled with obscurities: he was probably Stalin's 'French Connection' and, as such, hatchet man in the PCF and elsewhere.

Duclos was born in the Pyrénées in 1896. By profession a confectioner, he acquired the physiognomy of a small rubber shark. His path to the PCF was typical in his generation – Verdun, and then a German prison camp. In 1926 he became a deputy and a member of the PCF's Central Committee. 1928 saw the first of many visits to Moscow, and henceforth Duclos worked for the Comintern. A natural negotiator, his first major success was in Spain in 1936: he helped persuade Largo Caballero (the Socialist leader) to accept a Popular Front government without socialism.

When Thorez (q.v.) was mobilized in 1939, Duclos took over; 1939–44 would be the first of two long periods when Duclos ran the PCF. A well-behaved understudy, he never tried to unseat Thorez. Between September 1939 and June 1940 he operated from Brussels, then the Comintern's West European headquarters. He returned to Paris on 10 June 1940. All these circumstances imply that the several overtures he made to the Germans were ordered direct by Moscow. The 'Thorez–Duclos' anti-Vichy manifesto of 10 July was Duclos' work; presumably the Comintern provided Thorez' signature. After September, he formed a 'troika' with Benoît Frachon (q.v.) and Charles Tillon (q.v.). If Tillon was its fire eater, Duclos remained the prudent member. In August 1944 he prevented Tillon's partisans, under Rol-Tanguy, from attempting a single-handed battle for Paris.

After the liberation, Duclos mounted a vast campaign for Thorez' return, thereby deflecting the PCF from armed confrontation with the state. After Thorez returned, Duclos settled into parliamentary life: the speeches, the insults and the back-slapping were second nature to him.

In September 1947 Thorez made Duclos stand in when the French party was summoned by the Cominform. Duclos swallowed many insults that time, but continued to represent the PCF with the Cominform in 1948 and 1949.

Thorez' stroke in October 1950 brought Duclos again into the 'regency'. This time he supervised two simultaneous operations, the 'Marty–Tillon affair' and the anti-Ridgway demonstration of 28 May 1952. The PCF expected a return to outlawry. On the evening of this most violent 'demo', Duclos left his safe place. The police stopped his car. In an excess of zeal, they arrested not only Duclos, thus breaching his parliamentary immunity, but also two dead pigeons. The car also contained all the minutes of the latest Political Bureau meetings, but these did not excite the police. Duclos was lucky: but was he downright careless, excessively 'parliamentarist' or only obeying orders? When this question can be answered, we will know much more about the post-war functioning of the PCF.

Duclos was released from illegal arrest in July. In April 1953 Thorez returned. Duclos supported Thorez' struggle against de-Stalinization. He was none the less demoted in 1956 and, when Thorez died, Waldeck Rochet, not Duclos, became leader. But even when Duclos was understudy he was probably not the 'dauphin'. It is widely held that Auguste Lecoeur was 'dauphin' in 1950–53, but Lecoeur was ejected in 1954. Some monarchy! Duclos twice 'regent' could not, apparently, be 'king'. (The PCF was certainly not 'Un parti comme les autres'.) Duclos was, however, considered fit to represent the PCF in the 1969 presidential elections, in which he pulled a very creditable 21.5 per cent of the vote. He died in 1975.

Bibliography

There is no biography; Duclos' *Mémoires* reveal his love of long speeches. Substantial English language interpretations can be found in Irwin Wall, *French Communism in the Era of Stalin: The quest for unity and integration 1945–1962* (Westport, Conn.: Greenwood Press, 1983) and Ronald Tiersky, *French Communism 1920–1972* (New York: Columbia University Press, 1974). French readers can consult Roger Courtois, *Le PCF dans la guerre. De Gaulle, la résistance, Staline* (Paris: Editions Ramsay, 1980) for the first 'regency', as well as volumes 1 and 2 of Philippe Robrieux, *Histoire intérieure du parti communiste* (Paris: Fayard, 1980–1).

MK

DUFAURE, Jules Armand Stanislas (1798–1881)

Dufaure, son of a former naval officer, was born in western France (Charente-Maritime), a region which he always sought to represent in parliament. A contemporary of Thiers, his long public career resembled that of the first president of the Third Republic at many points. Both were provincials, both were trained as lawyers, both were prodigious workers, both first became deputies and ministers during the July Monarchy, both stood for the restoration of order in 1848 and both in different ways opposed the Second Empire. There were however striking differences. Whereas Thiers abandoned the law, Dufaure first made his name at the Bar, won a reputation as a powerful advocate and enhanced it under the Second Empire; whereas Thiers was a deist, Dufaure was a Catholic; whereas Thiers was brilliant and versatile, Dufaure was a man of narrower outlook and lacked charm. His manner was brusque and, assiduous in parliamentary attendance, he was by 1848 celebrated as a formidable and aggressive debater, earning at one stage the nickname 'the boar'. Regarded as a man of integrity in February 1871 he was one of the more prominent elderly men who had served the Second Republic and it was not surprising that he was elected to the National Assembly by five departments. Thiers immediately appointed him minister of justice and, a few months later, vice-president of the Council of Ministers, in effect his second-in-command. In 1875 he was again minister of justice in another cabinet, in 1876 he was premier for nine months and in December 1877, after the 'seize mai' crisis, he formed his second ministry which lasted until February 1879. He then retired from politics, refusing to stand for the presidency of the Republic against Jules Grévy. He was eighty, the oldest French premier of the nineteenth century.

Dufaure had made himself indispensable to conservative Republicans like Thiers because of his debating skill, his experience and his moderation – he was a man of the centre left who distrusted the more radical policies of the left. He became prime minister because he was acceptable to the conservative Marshal MacMahon rather than for qualities of leadership or any wish to initiate new policies. He was thus a useful man to carry the country through the year of the exhibition of 1878 when a political truce was desirable. Responsible for punitive legislation against the communards and for sponsoring proposals that in part became the basis for the Constitution of 1875, he was probably happiest when working to a specific

brief and transacting day-to-day business as minister of justice, a post which he again held when premier.

An able but somewhat isolated figure, Dufaure has no modern biographer. His ability to combine the callings of barrister and politician indicates that he became a man of some means. His two sons both became deputies.

JPTB

DUFOIX, Georgina (1943–)

Georgina Dufoix was a member of the Socialist government throughout the left's period in office, from 1981 to 1986. Little known outside the party before 1981, she was first appointed secretary of state for family affairs, then in 1983 her area of responsibility was extended to cover immigrants, and in 1984 she was given full ministerial rank and the title minister of social affairs and national solidarity. From December 1984 until the elections of March 1986 she was also spokewoman for the government and responsible for the presentation of its policies to the public.

Her appointment in 1981 was part of the left's attempt to modify the male monopoly of government, and her career profile to that date followed a pattern fairly typical for women politicians. Born Georgina Nègre in 1943 in Nîmes, she graduated in economics before marrying an engineer, Antoine Dufoix in 1963, and for the next several years moved around the country as his career demanded. During this period she also inherited the ownership of her father's small firm, which she managed from 1967 to 1969, and had four children. She began to work for the Socialist party on a voluntary basis in 1967 and was part of the Mitterrand faction at the 1971 Congress at Epinay that saw the growth of the present party. In 1977 she was elected a town councillor in Nîmes, and became a member of the party's directing committee in 1979.

As a minister she undoubtedly represented the caring face of socialism, though in a climate of recession and governmental austerity her scope for reform was limited. In charge of 'family affairs', she attempted to encourage population growth by providing the financial incentives and the practical conditions that would allow women to have children without being disadvantaged in all other spheres. On immigration, she operated a dual policy of formalizing the legal status of immigrants already in France and supporting antiracist measures, whilst at the same time tightening up controls on further immigration. As minister in charge of social security she was judged by *Le Monde* (20 March 1986) to have done a competent management job, leaving the budget healthy despite the structural problems of an ageing and progressively more unemployed population. Her policies were thus clearly in line with the general tenor of the government's cautious reforming mood, and she was an appropriate spokeswoman, albeit fighting a losing battle, in the run-up to the election.

Since her departure from government after the Socialists' electoral defeat in 1986 Georgina Dufoix has continued her political career as a town councillor in Nîmes, and pursued her interest in the development of alternative medicine by becoming president of the Association des Réseaux de Santé, the national organization that links the various branches of *médécine douce* in France. In the Rocard government of 1988 she was minister for social affairs and women's rights.

Bibliography

'Mme Georgina Dufoix, la fraîcheu et la ténacité, *Le Monde* (4 June 1981); 'Mme. G.D., la rigueur malgré tout', *Le Monde* (20 March 1986); Agence France Presse bulletin (7 December 1984) and others which are collected in dossier on Georgina Dufoix in the Bibliothèque Marguerite Durand, Paris.

DiH

DUMONT, René Fernand (1904–)

René Dumont was born on 13 March 1904 at Cambrai. Son of a lecturer in agriculture, he graduated from the Institut National Agronomique and then worked in south-east Asia for the Services agricoles d'Indochine from 1929 to 1933, an experience which was to determine the future course of his career. He has lectured at the Institut National Agronomique, the Institut d'Etudes Politiques and at the Institut du Développement Economique et Social and has travelled widely as a consultant for the United Nations Food and Agriculture Organization.

He has become known as the 'agronomist of famine' and is perhaps best known in the English-speaking world for his works on famine and environmental degradation in the Third World. These include *L'Afrique noire est mal partie* (1962), which has been translated into English as *False Start in Africa* (London: André Deutsch, 1969), and which now reads as a tragically prophetic work as it warned, long before most people were aware of what was happening, of the economic and environmental problems that the models of development being chosen in Africa were already storing up for the future. Other works include *L'Utopie ou la mort* (1973), *Agronomie de la faim* (Paris: Robert Laffont, 1974), *Paysans écrasés, terres massacrées* (Paris: Robert Laffont, 1978), *L'Afrique étranglée* (Paris: Seuil, 1982) and *Pour l'Afrique, j'accuse* (Paris: Plon, 1986). In France he is perhaps better known however as a leading figure in the Green movement. In the 1974 presidential elections he stood as the Green candidate and although he gained only 337,000 votes (1.3 per cent of the total votes cast), his well-publicized campaign from a barge moored on the River Seine in Paris firmly installed the Green movement on the political map of France. At the March 1986 parliamentary elections he re-entered the political arena to head the Green list in Paris but, partly because the Green vote was split by another largely Green list, only gained 1.4 per cent of the votes cast. He has played an important part in the promotion of the ecology movement in France.

Bibliography

Dumont, R. (1962), *L'Afrique noire est mal partie*, Paris: Seuil.

Dumont, R. (1974), *A vous de choisir: la campagne de R. Dumont*, Paris: J.-J. Pauvert.

Dumont, R. (1974), *L'Utopie ou la mort*, Paris: Seuil.

Dumont, R. (1989), *Un Monde intolérable*, Paris: Seuil.

TC

DUPANLOUP, Félix-Antoine-Philibert (1802–78)

Félix Dupanloup was born in a Savoyard village, the illegitimate son of a poor peasant woman; it was often rumoured (though without hard evidence) that he had an aristocratic father. Taken to Paris as a child, he trained for the priesthood at Saint-Sulpice and was ordained in 1825. Rapidly accepted into Parisian high society, he made his name as a catechist, a society confessor, and as headmaster (1837–45) of the minor seminary of Saint Nicolas du Chardonnet (where he taught the historian and theorist E. Renan). His activity as a polemicist in the campaign for the Church's right to open its own secondary schools culminated in his crucial role in the compromise solution which became the Falloux law of 1850. In 1850 he was made bishop of Orleans. He remained a leading spokesman in Church affairs, most notably with his 1865 pamphlet arguing that the condemnations of liberal principles by the Syllabus of Errors (1864) referred only to an ideal world, and Catholics could and should accept modern institutions in practice. At the first Vatican Council he was a leading agitator against the definition of papal infallibility. Elected to the National Assembly in 1871, he campaigned untiringly for a constitutional monarchy based on the 'fusion' of the Bourbon and Orleanist lines. When this project failed, he devoted himself to combating the rising tide of republicanism, supporting in particular the attempt by the de Broglie (q.v.) ministry to manage the elections of October 1877. He was also influential in the passing of laws favourable to the Church, in particular the law of 1875 allowing the establishment of Catholic universities. He was made a life senator in 1875.

Dupanloup is sometimes seen as a liberal Catholic, but with not much justification. He was friendly with liberals like Montalembert and Falloux, and bitterly hostile to the reactionary journalist Veuillot, but he was less concerned to defend liberal principles for their own sake than he was to ensure that the Church did not adopt such a reactionary stance that it would alienate thinking men. The freedom of education campaign of the 1840s sometimes led him to articulate liberal principles, but by the 1870s his fear of de-Christianization and social revolution caused him to look increasingly to the state to defend the interests of the Church. He opposed any attempt to re-establish a divine-right monarchy wielding a secular arm in favour of catholicism, but he was also solidly opposed to the idea of a secular state. He was violently anti-Republican, seeing the Republic as atheistic and leading to social revolution. His greatest claims to fame are probably his gifts as an educator (Renan regarded him as an inspiring headmaster), and his efforts as a diocesan administrator. Appointed to a largely de-Christianized diocese, he drove his clergy to great efforts and achieved at least a temporary increase in religious practice. A natural authoritarian, he made many enemies in the clergy, but he did establish himself as the leading spokesman in France of those who, while in no way democratic, thought the Church would have to come to terms with the post-Revolutionary world.

Bibliography

The best short treatment is R. Aubert's article 'Dupanloup' in the *Dictionnaire d'histoire et de Géographie ecclésiastiques*, vol. XIV (Paris: Letouzey et Ané,

1960), vol. 1070–122; C. Marcilhacy, *Le diocèse d'Orléans sous l'épiscopat de Mgr Dupanloup* (Paris: Plon, 1962) is the most up-to-date and reputable study, though more about the diocese than about Dupanloup himself; F. Lagrange, *Vie de Mgr Dupanloup, évêque d'Orléans* (Paris: Poussielgue, 1883–4), 3 vols, is the most comprehensive biography, but desperately hagiographic; M.R. O'Connell, 'Ultramontanism and Dupanloup: The compromise of 1865', *Church History*, vol. 53 (London) 1984, pp. 200–17 is the only recent contribution in English; E. Renan, *Recollections of my Youth* (London: Chapman and Hall, 1883) for Renan's impressions of Dupanloup as an 'incomparable' educator.

RG

DUPUY, Charles Alexandre (1851–1923)

Charles Dupuy was a moderate Republican who became prime minister five times in the 1890s. One of the so-called Teachers' Republic (*Republique des professeurs*), he was born at Le Puy (Haute-Loire) and, *agrégé* in philosophy, was a teacher and school inspector before entering politics. Deputy for the Haute-Loire in 1885, after only brief ministerial experience he was appointed premier in 1893 mainly because he was untainted by the Panama scandal. He evinced a limited sympathy for the *ralliement*, antipathy towards the workers' movement and enthusiasm for the Russian alliance. In office only between April and November 1893, he presided in the Chamber of Deputies on 9 December 1893, the day when the Chamber was shaken by the bomb thrown by the anarchist Vaillant, and achieved fame for his declaration 'Messieurs, la séance continue'. Premier again in 1894 he resigned after the assassination of President Carnot and stood unsuccessfully for the presidency against Casimir-Périer. Piqued at his failure, he avenged himself when reappointed prime minister by keeping the new president in the dark with regard to policy decisions. His ministry was notable also for its enactment of the fierce *lois scélérates* against the anarchists and its decision in October 1894 to proceed with the prosecution of Dreyfus. On the sidelines between January 1895 and November 1898, he returned as premier when the Dreyfus affair was moving towards its climax, though his own position remained that the case was a matter for the courts alone. The sudden death in 1899 of another President of the Republic (this time Félix Faure's, following ill-advised sexual indulgence) required his resignation but he was reappointed by Faure's successor Loubet. He lasted only until June 1899 when mounting right-wing agitation, culminating in an attack on President Loubet at Auteil races, undermined confidence in the ability of his government to defend Republican institutions. In 1900 he moved to the Senate but went into political eclipse as the so-called Opportunist Republic made way for the Republic of the Radicals.

Bibliography

Chastenet, J. (1977), *Histoire de la troisième république*, Paris: Hachette.

Mayeur, J.-M. and Rébérioux, M. (1984), *The Third Republic from its Origins to the Great War 1871–1914*, Cambridge: Cambridge University Press.

JFM

E

EBOUÉ, Félix Adolphe Sylvestre (1884–1944)

Félix Eboué was born in French Guyana in 1884, the son of black parents who had acquired French citizenship. His intellectual abilities were quickly recognized at school and after passing his elementary exams he was awarded a scholarship to study in France. From 1901 to 1905 he received his secondary education at the Lycée Montaigne in Bordeaux; and having obtained his *baccalauréat* then studied at the Ecole Coloniale in Paris (1905–8). During this period he became friendly with the novelist and poet René Maran. Having received his diploma, he was posted to Oubangui Chari (now known as the Central African Republic). Alongside his work as an administrator responsible for economic development went a great interest in ethnographic research into the languages, social structures and institutions of Africa, areas in which he published several articles and monographs. Eboué became close to the Senegalese deputy Blaise Digne and was a member of the French Socialist Party (SFIO). He was appointed secretary-general and interim governor of Martinique between 1922 and 1934 and he held a posting in the French Sudan (now known as Mali) from 1934–6; in 1936 the formation of the Popular Front government led to his being appointed governor of Guadeloupe, a position he held until 1938.

Eboué was governor of Chad when the French government signed the humiliating armistice with the Germans in June 1940. Against the orders of his superior Boisson (governor-general) Eboué officially proclaimed the adherence of Chad to de Gaulle's Free French movement on 26 August. His decision created a momentum which would draw the Cameroon and subsequently all the territories of French Africa to the Gaullist cause. De Gaulle appointed him in 1940 governor-general of French Equatorial Africa, a position he held until his premature death, of pneumonia, in 1944. Shortly before his death he took a leading part in the Brazzaville Conference at which the future of the French Empire was discussed. In 1949 his ashes were transferred with full honours to the Pantheon.

Bibliography

de la Roche, J. (1957), *Le gouverneur général Félix Eboué, 1884–1944*, Paris: Hachette.
Weinstein, B. (1972), *Félix Eboué*, Oxford: Oxford University Press.

DCB

ELLEINSTEIN, Jean (1927–   )

'Jean Ellen' had a brief Warholesque glory in the 1970s when the Communist Party's 22nd Congress led to a rethink and, to a degree, a movement within French communism but in fact his close association with the party goes further back than that. Elleinstein was born in Paris to a family of Polish origins. He was the son of a small businessman; not a naturally Communist background. He joined the Communist Party in 1944 and became a full-time party employee in 1947 and, until 1952, was employed in the party department for propaganda. He spent a few weeks in prison for distributing anti-Indo-China War leaflets to soldiers at the Clignancourt barracks and, in 1952, went underground because the police sought him in connection with the 'pigeon plot' (in which Jacques Duclos was fatuously accused of sending pigeon messages to Moscow). Although he was promoted to the national bureau of the Young Communists and became director of the Young Communist journal *Avant-Garde*, at the same time he started to study seriously and in 1954 became a teacher of history.

Elleinstein remained a party employee but seems to have been seriously troubled by the Khrushchev report. In 1958 he passed the teaching diploma and became a secondary school teacher and in 1960 passed the teaching exam, the *agrégation*. Elleinstein made his way slowly up the party hierarchy until, in 1970, he became assistant director of the party's research bureau, Centre d'Etude et de Recherches Marxistes, and a history lecturer at the University of Poitiers.

It was with Elleinstein's books *Le PC* (Editions Grasset, 1976) and the *History of the Stalin*

Phenomenon that he sprang to public attention – pushed up, it must be said, by the party. In *Le PC* Elleinstein carried 22nd Congress 'openness' into an examination of the party itself and a defence of Euro-communism as the democratic road to a socialism through an alliance of all 'non-monopolist' social classes – at the time this was orthodox party policy. Elleinstein's dismissal of Stalin – also orthodox – is more complicated.

Neither *L'Histoire de l'URSS* (4 vols, Editions Sociales, 1972–5) nor *The History of the Stalin Phenomenon* contribute new facts or new interpretation; put into the academic acid bath they leave no residue. Nor do they tackle the question Togliatti (the Italian Communist leader) posed in 1956: how could Stalin have ruled in a *Socialist* system? Elleinstein's book stuffed the facts into a blender and wonderfully reconstituted them: Stalinism had nothing to do with the Soviet system – *qua* system – and was limited to peculiar historical circumstances. Although this was the furthest the party had gone at the time in admitting what had actually happened (and there were still numerous gaps) there was no coherent explanation of why Stalin's terror should have occurred and the French party ('profoundly democratic' according to the book) is absolved. Though Elleinstein's book tried to confine Stalinism to a corner of Russian history – an 'epiphenomenon' – and constantly underlined the superiority of socialism, it was nevertheless too critical for some in the party.

At the time of the 22nd Congress Marchais said 'give me 200,000 like Elleinstein and I'll take them' but the party line subsequently changed. While 'Euro-communism' was *à la mode* Elleinstein was much in demand in the media and he even wrote for *Le Figaro Magazine*. In 1978, after the election defeat of the left, Elleinstein wrote two articles highly critical of the party for *Le Monde* and by the beginning of 1979 was out of favour. In January 1980 he was excluded. In signing a contract to write regularly for *Le Figaro Magazine* he was signing his own arrest warrant as far as the party was concerned.

Elleinstein is an intellectual to whom politics has happened – transatively. He does not seem to have realized where his own *démarche* was leading him and he probably did not realize that there was an incompatibility between thought and engagement. Since his ejection Elleinstein has published further and has worked in Laurent Fabius' Socialist club Espaces 89 but he has virtually disappeared from the political scene though within the Communist Party his name is a hissing and a by-word.

Bibliography

Faced with a problem the first instinct of the French intellectual is to fight it, the second to write a book about it. Elleinstein's work therefore comprises a substantial *oeuvre*. See, in particular:

Elleinstein, J. (1976), *The Stalin Phenomenon*, London: Lawrence and Wishart.

Elleinstein, J. (1976), *Le PC*, Paris: Grasset.

Elleinstein, J. (1981), *Ils vous trompent, camarades!*, Paris: Belfond.

DSB

ETIENNE, Eugène Napoléon (1844–1921)

Born in Oran (Algeria) the son of a professional soldier, Etienne was educated at the Lycée Napoleon in Algiers and at the Lycée Imperial in Marseilles. He stayed in Marseilles and went to work for a grain importing company run by Maurice Rouvier (q.v.) who introduced him to Republican politics and would later be his patron. Through Rouvier, Etienne met his great political hero Gambetta (q.v.) with whom he subsequently collaborated. In 1875 Rouvier's support secured him a job in the emerging state railway company. Six years later he was elected Republican deputy for Oran, a constituency which contained many of those deported in 1848 and 1852 and which he turned into an impregnable fief. Utterly loyal to Gambetta, he joined his parliamentary group, the Union Républicaine and soon showed, in the violent debates occasioned by the Treaty of Bardo that made Tunisia French protectorate, where his political interests and ambitions lay. He supported Ferry's Indo-China policy in the teeth of great parliamentary opposition and became dedicated to the expansion of French colonial interests. Though he held the junior ministry of colonies for only four years – first under Rouvier in 1887–8 and then under Tirard (q.v.) and Freycinet (q.v.) (1889–92) – he became the most influential advocate of the imperial cause. In Parliament he presided over the inter-party Groupe Colonial; outside he ran the Ligue Coloniale Française, presided over the Comité de Maroc, and controlled the newspaper *La Dépêche Coloniale*. Though closely linked to business interests (and inevitably criticized on that score) he always placed strategic and emotional considerations of grandeur at the centre of his desire for a greater France. Like many colonial activists before (and after) he was deeply suspicious of British imperial ambitions and he would be a strong supporter of the

Boers. Yet he was one of the first to advocate the 'swap' between Egypt and Morocco that would be at the origin of the *entente cordiale* which Delcassé (q.v.) negotiated with Great Britain in 1904. Etienne subsequently hoped that a similar deal could be negotiated with Germany and visited the Kaiser in 1907.

What gave Etienne his influence were his wider political beliefs and his key parliamentary position. Loyal to the Republican lessons of Gambetta, he separated from the more right-wing members of the progressist group at the time of the Dreyfus affair and the group he presided over became the indispensable right flank of the left-wing governments of Waldeck Rousseau (q.v.) and, above all, Combes (q.v.). It was in this position that he was able to advance colonial interests both out of power (when he was invariably vice-president of the Chamber of Deputies) as well as in office. He was minister of the interior – again under Rouvier – in 1905 and then became, on several occasions, minister of war. It was at the War Ministry that he played a major role in the introduction of the three years law in 1913, a measure that he saw as inevitable given Germany's armament programme. He died in 1921, shortly after being elected to the Senate. A Commune in the Oran department was named after him.

Bibliography

Andrew, C.M. (1968), *Théophile Delcassé and the Entente Cordiale*, London: Macmillan.

Villot, R. (1951), *Eugène Etienne*, Oran: L. Fouque.

PM

F

FABIUS, Laurent (1946–)

One of the leading figures in the Socialist Party (PS), Fabius is none the less an enigmatic character. He was appointed prime minister in July 1984; then aged only 37, he was France's youngest head of government since Decazes (1815–20) under Louis XVIII. With his vision of a more liberal and technology-minded French socialism moving the country into the third Industrial Revolution, he seemed assured of a bright political future.

However, since the defeat of the PS in the parliamentary elections of 1986, his career has been somewhat overtaken by events and eclipsed by rivals. His objective of representing 'modernizing' elements within the PS – concerned with new industrial activities, the diffusion of new technology and education – is counteracted by an elusive personal image and the lack of a strong, autonomous political base, both of which have been attributed to a prior overdependence on the patronage of his mentor, President François Mitterrand. Since June 1988 he has been president of the National Assembly (a more politicized and powerful office than that of speaker of the House of Commons; somewhat more analogous to the speaker of the US House of Representatives).

He comes from a comfortable Parisian background; his father is an antique dealer whose family had converted from Judaism to catholicism. His fast-track educational career took him from highly competitive Paris *lycées* through the Ecole Normale Supérieure, an *agrégation* in modern literature and a diploma from the Paris Institute of Political Studies, to the Ecole Nationale d'Administration – after which, in 1973, he became a junior official (*auditeur*) at the Council of State, France's highest administrative tribunal. At the Council of State, Fabius was noticed by Georges Dayan, a personal friend of Mitterrand, and thus began an extraordinarily rapid political ascent, taking him to the premiership in ten years. He only joined the PS in 1974; a year later he became an economic adviser to Mitterrand, then first secretary of the party; and in 1976 he was appointed director of Mitterrand's advisory staff (*cabinet*).

During the late 1970s, when younger leaders were challenging Mitterrand within the PS, Fabius and others (including Lionel Jospin), representing an even younger generation in the party, organized Mitterrand's power base in a party notorious for its internal competition of formalized personal-cum-ideological factions (*courants*). At the 1979 Metz Congress, faced by a coalition of Michel Rocard and Pierre Mauroy, they negotiated a new alliance with Jean-Pierre Chevènement's (q.v.) more hard-left CERES faction, thus maintaining control of the party organization. The party's philosophical position paper, the 1980 *Projet socialiste*, was thus heavily influenced by CERES; in the 1981 presidential election, however, Mitterrand, with Fabius as his campaign manager, was able to stand on his own more centrist programme.

Meanwhile, Fabius, as is the rule for French politicians, was cultivating a provincial base, at Grand-Quevilly in Normandy. In the 1977 local elections, the then mayor and deputy for Seine-Maritime abruptly replaced his chief assistant (and ostensible successor) with Fabius, said to have been 'recommended' by Mitterrand. Though at first suspect to local activists, Fabius quickly took control of the organization and, by assiduously nursing the constituency, succeeded to the parliamentary seat in the elections of March 1978. Although his attempt to shake up the Regional Council in Haute-Normandie in 1981–2 was cut short by the defeat of the PS there in the 1982 cantonal elections, he has, as deputy and as minister, done well for the region, as is expected in the French system.

Prior to May 1981, Fabius, who had in 1978 become the PS parliamentary spokesman on budgetary matters, had been devoting more and more of his time to party and constituency affairs. However, the newly-elected President Mitterrand appointed him minister for the budget. Thus he was in charge of drawing up and defending the reflationary budget of 1982 which attempted to please all sections of the PS – and their coalition partners, the Communist Party (PCF) – by funding a variety of costly social and economic reforms. These reforms required a budget deficit which, while small by international standards, rose sharply. This increased economic growth temporarily at the cost of a surge of imports, a slower decline of inflation from the high levels of 1979–81 and continued weakness of the franc. Although he was not the main architect of the government's economic strategy, Fabius had much influence on how it was put into practice. The main proposal to which he nailed his colours was a wealth tax – eventually enacted, however, only in an emasculated and ineffective form.

During 1982, however, as opinion in the government (especially that of Jacques Delors) moved first towards a 'pause' in the reform process and then to a full-scale austerity programme, Fabius became a strong proponent of economic rigour. In the major reshuffle of March 1983, in which the leading economic nationalists in the government, Chevènement and ex-Gaullist Michel Jobert, lost their posts, Fabius was promoted to the former's 'superministry' of Research and Industry, to which Telecommunications was added. Thus he took over responsibility for a strategy to take France into the third Industrial Revolution. However, his term at industry is often seen as less concerned with long-term strategy than with completing a U-turn in the government's policy of industrial regeneration.

His predecessors in the post had focused on large-scale restructuring of industry, especially on making the public sector (including the major industries nationalized in 1982) more modern and efficient. This policy was to start with (in Prime Minister Mauroy's phrase) a 'reconquest of the internal market', often seen to imply protectionism; it was hotly disputed in the world crisis of 1982, and split the PS too. A second element was the notion that virtually any industry could be made competitive by restructuring and technological modernization; this was widely seen to imply an open-ended financial commitment while the franc was under pressure on the exchange markets and France was borrowing heavily on the Euro-markets to finance its deficits.

In this context, Fabius was more a trouble-shooter than a strategist. The nationalized sector was a major drain on the French budget not so much because too much money had been spent on effective modernization, but because in the recession years of 1981–2 most of France's major industries had suffered large losses prior to nationalization. Despite the increased allocation of budgetary resources to the public sector, a 'lame-duck' problem had set in, and the policies of 1981–2 were blamed. And despite the importance of a policy of industrial modernization to the fragile unity of the various PS factions in the late 1970s and early 1980s – and to the coalition with the

Communist Party – Fabius, Mitterrand and Delors increasingly stressed the need to re-emphasize profitability and competitiveness over technological prowess in all fields.

The key to Fabius's period at industry was the assertion that nationalized industries must operate like other firms in world markets. Financial losses would have to be cleared up before modernization and expansion could take place. Retrenchment – and increased unemployment – took the place of expansion. Planning for the automobile industry – a world force in the 1970s but hit by shrinking export markets and import penetration in the 1980s – went by the board in favour of rescue measures, leading to plant closures and redundancies. A major U-turn took place in the coal industry, which had been expanded in 1981–2 in the face of very unfavourable international conditions. The same pattern held true for the declining shipbuilding industry and, perhaps most importantly, in the long-troubled steel industry, where according to the EEC's common steel policies, subsidies were due to run out in 1986.

The problem was also political. By mid-1984, unemployment – held steady at just over 2 million from 1981–3 through a variety of social measures and negotiated 'planning agreements' – had risen to over 2.3 million. The working-class electorate, the PS's share of which had expanded in the 1970s, was increasingly split and alienated. Opposition grew most within unions affiliated to the Communist-oriented Confédération Générale du Travail (General Confederation of Labour), which were the most strongly organized not only among the traditional blue-collar workers in coal, steel and shipbuilding, but also among the most threatened group in the automobile industry – immigrant workers.

In February 1984 strikes and protests spread to lorry drivers and middle-class professionals too, and at the same time the old issue of state control over private (mainly religious) education divided the PS as well as the voters. Electoral disaster loomed, as evidenced by the Socialists' poor showing (and the Communists' even more abysmal performance) in the June 1984 European elections. With the government split on social and educational policy, massive demonstrations brought matters to a head in July; massive demonstrations provoked Mauroy's resignation – and Mitterrand replaced him with Fabius. Delors became president of the European Commission; Chevènement returned to the (non-economic) education portfolio; and, most importantly, the Communists were excluded altogether. The new government began with two clear briefs. The first was to streamline and further prioritize the austerity programme in order to produce positive economic results in time for the March 1986 parliamentary elections. The second was to bury divisive social issues and to establish a clear line of authority within party and government reaching up to the president – something which Mauroy's open style of running the government had often undermined.

In fact, Fabius was remarkably successful within a fairly short time. Trade and budget deficits, already more manageable since 1983, continued to come under control. The franc remained steady on the foreign exchanges, and France began to repay her foreign borrowings. Inflation fell dramatically, to a lower level than in Britain for example. Major French firms continued to return to financial health, including the nationalized industries – which were becoming accustomed to operating with greater managerial autonomy. The fashion for 'deregulation' of economic activities was taken up in France, most notably in the financial markets under the direction of Finance Minister Pierre Bérégovoy. Unemployment steadied at around 2.4 million. And economic growth, which after a spurt in 1982 had fallen while other European economies were recovering, rose again.

In the political arena, Fabius succeeded in stamping his (or Mitterrand's) authority on the government, and public opinion in mid-1985 was impressed by its relative tranquillity and smooth operation. His public image was very positive, with his youth and intellectual talents, his regular attempts to explain economic policy on television, and his social-liberal discourse on poverty, human rights, South Africa, etc. – despite doubts among some in his own party as to his Socialist credentials. But it was in the political arena rather than the economic that Fabius's position was eroded towards the end of his term.

Four events stand out from mid-1985. First, he attempted to extend his authority to the PS, staking a claim to control the 1986 campaign, but came quickly into conflict with Jospin, the first secretary, and in July had to accept a compromise among the *courants*. Also in July, the Greenpeace ship *Rainbow Warrior*, which was to shadow the French military during nuclear tests in the Pacific, was sunk by French agents in Auckland harbour (New Zealand). Fabius was asked by Mitterrand to pursue the matter rigorously, but the president was less than pleased with the prime minister's persistence in investigating a cover-up when it led to the resignation of Defence Minister Charles Hernu (q.v.), a senior party figure close to the president.

A third 'banana skin' was Fabius's poor perfor-

mance in a major televised debate against neo-Gaullist leader Jacques Chirac. Abandoning his cool and polish for an aggressive approach, he was out-debated by the usually more aggressive Chirac, whose challenge to the PS was enhanced. And finally, he clashed with the president in December 1985 over the latter's decision to receive the Polish prime minister, General Jaruzelski, on a visit to France. Two of these events, both concerning foreign policy – an issue-area jealously guarded by successive presidents – cooled relations between Fabius and his mentor. The other two damaged his image as an effective election campaigner, while Mitterrand's increasing role in the campaign put Fabius in the shade. Although the PS was defeated in March 1986, it did better than expected – at 31 per cent, 10 per cent up on the 1984 European results – but the economic results of 1984–6 were not sufficient to counteract the disappointments of 1982–4.

Fabius's star waned somewhat after 1986. He lacks a strong, autonomous political base of his own. Within the PS, he has been at loggerheads with Jospin, being able in 1987 to obtain only a post on the national secretariat dealing with the training of party workers and problems of education. The intellectual 'club' associated with his ideas (and partly run by his wife), Espaces 89, has made little impact. He failed in a campaign to become first secretary of the PS during the 1988 elections, and his election as president of the National Assembly has been seen as something of a consolation prize. And his image is still unclear, although in opinion polls he remains a popular figure on the left after Mitterrand and Prime Minister Michel Rocard.

There are three intertwined elements of the image problem: that Fabius is an opportunist, a 'traitor to his class', whose background and gut beliefs without Mitterrand's early patronage might as easily have made him a Giscardian; that in office he lacked strategy and vision, being essentially a pragmatist, tacking to the winds; and that even if he is somehow of the left, he is still not really a Socialist. In December 1986 he undertook a *tour de France* intended to show, in *Le Monde*'s words, 'a Laurent Fabius who is close to the people, smiling, simple, even warm, and firmly anchored in his Socialist beliefs – in sum, to break down whatever remains of his image as a "Giscard of the left".'

Nevertheless, he has perhaps reinforced his non-Socialist image in articles and interviews in the press – for example, emphasizing that the label 'liberal' should not be (as it tends to be in France) reserved to the right, 'because no one has a monopoly of liberty', and claiming that the real dividing line is between progressives and conservatives; or referring to socialism as just an inspiring utopia ('utopie mobilisatrice'), while arguing for a catalogue of precise, limited reforms in contrast to the broad programmes of the left; or stating that previous models of society – Marxism–Leninism, Maoism, Americanism – have all failed and that it is necessary to invent a new model, 'la société de la nouvelle chance' (a 'society of new opportunity'), emphasizing science, technology and education. The rhetoric is that of an American progressive, not a European Socialist.

But his strongest handicap was the loss of Mitterrand's patronage. Perhaps this was inevitable, given that he would be forced sooner or later to develop a distinct image and political line. But Mitterrand's reclaiming of control over the campaign in 1986, his adroit playing of the new 'cohabitation' game with the right for two years, and his dramatic re-election and espousal of *ouverture* in 1988, have left little room for Fabius. Now that Mitterrand has allied with his old foes from Metz – with Rocard as prime minister and Mauroy as first secretary of the PS – Fabius must bide his time. Fabius's position in the party was appreciably weakened by the poor showing of the Socialist list, which he led, in the European elections of 1989. The PS took only 23.61 per cent of the vote (twenty-two seats) which put the party at its lowest standing since 1984 when economic stringency made the Socialists highly unpopular. The young, gifted, eloquent rising star of 1984, the apostle of modernization and technology, now seemingly sidetracked, must re-establish himself in the political game.

PGC

FABRE, Robert Charles Victor (1915–)

Robert Fabre was one of the signatories, with François Mitterrand and Georges Marchais, of the 1972 Joint Programme for Government (Programme Commun de Gouvernement) on which the left intended to base its policies once elected to power. Between 1980 and 1986 he served as the French equivalent of ombudsman (*médiateur*), and in 1986 joined the nine-member Constitutional Council.

Fabre was brought up in the department of Aveyron, and followed in his father's footsteps as a qualified pharmacist. He continued a traditional French political career pattern of *cumul des mandats* (plurality of elected office) by becoming successively – but holding the offices concurrently until the early 1980s – mayor of his native town, member of the

council of the Aveyron department, and Radical Party deputy representing a constituency in the same department.

Fabre was a leading figure in the attempt (1965–68) to coordinate the Radical Party, the SFIO (Section Française de l'Internationale Ouvrière – the Socialist party of the time) and political clubs led by Mitterrand, into a Fédération de la Gauche Démocrate et Socialiste. He was also a member, responsible for regional development, of Mitterrand's short-lived 'shadow cabinet' (*cabinet fantôme*) established in March 1966 – the only time such a phenomenon has appeared in French political history.

When the Radical Party split in 1972 over the question of its political strategy, Fabre was leader of a left-wing Mouvement de la Gauche Radicale-Socialiste, and it was in this capacity that he signed the Programme Commun de Gouvernement with two much larger parties – the Communists and the new Socialist Party – and a new dimension was added to the 'Union de la Gauche'. Fabre's group changed its name the following year to Mouvement des Radicaux de Gauche (MRG) and under this name began a long period of close association with the Socialist Party.

However, when the three signatories met in September 1977 to try to update the Joint Programme, in anticipation of the 1978 elections and in the light of changes brought about by the first oil crisis, Fabre was led to torpedo the attempt (and the programme) because of what he regarded as exorbitant demands by the Communists. The idea of the Union de la Gauche as electoral cooperation was just resuscitated in time for the second round of the March 1978 election.

Already criticized for being the first opposition leader to agree to meet Giscard soon after he was elected president (1974), Fabre was in 1978 regarded by the MRG as 'having put himself outside the party' when he accepted from Giscard a special mission to examine ways of reducing unemployment; the Socialist Party also ended his status as a deputy attached to their group in Parliament.

In 1980, Fabre was appointed as the third *médiateur*. He resigned from the post in March 1986 on being appointed to the Constitutional Council, the supreme arbitral body on constitutional matters, which played an increasingly important part in French politics from the mid-1970s onwards, especially in the changed circumstances of 'cohabitation', brought about by the March 1986 elections.

Bibliography

Nordman, S. (1974), *Histoire des radicaux*, Paris: La Table Ronde.

Fabre, R. (1978), *Toute la vérité est bonne à dire*, Paris: Fayard.

Loncle, F. (1979), *Autopsie d'une rupture*, Paris: Simoën.

MS

FAJON, Etienne Louis-Henri (1906–)

Etienne Fajon was born into a family of vine growers on 11 September 1906 in Jonquières-la-Jolie (Hérault). He went to the Ecole Normale to become an elementary school teacher before joining the Communist-run union the Confédération Générale du Travail Unitaire in 1926 and becoming a party member in 1927. Like other Communists during the 'class against class' phase of sectarianism he was involved in numerous confrontations and demonstrations, including the 1 August 1929 'strike against war' and he was arrested on a charge of subversion. Although the case was abandoned he was unable to continue as a teacher and in 1932 was again charged with subversion just as he was promoted to the Central Committee and moved from the Languedoc to Paris. In 1935 he was given responsibility for training party cadres and for the various party schools – a key post.

In 1936 he was elected deputy for the Courbevoie constituency in the Paris 'Red belt'. Although mobilized to an artillary unit in 1939, he was able to return to the Assembly to put the Comintern's anti-war line in the debate on the dissolution of the party. In April 1940, along with other Communist deputies he was arrested and deported to Algeria but was freed in 1943 and became health minister in the provisional government. In 1945 he entered the Political Bureau and was elected a member of the Constituent Assemblies; in 1946 he was elected deputy for the Seine.

Fajon was a pro-Russian hardliner. In September 1947, along with Duclos, he went to the founding meeting of the Cominform at Szklarska-Poreba, followed this with attacks on Blum ('who gives in to every sacrifice demanded by reactionaries', *L'Humanité*, 14 October 1948) and defences of the Soviet Union (see *Cahiers du Communisme*, September, 1948); he controlled the Belgian party on behalf of the Cominform. On 3 November 1956 after the invasion of Hungary Fajon evoked 'capitulation to

social-democratic ideology' and repeated Russian charges of 'counter-revolution' and 'fascism' in Hungary. Although only officially promoted to the secretariat in 1954, from 1945 to 1956 he was a member of the party's inner core and during Thorez' frequent illnesses made declarations on behalf of the party. Fajon was made assistant editor of *L'Humanité* in 1928, was editor-in-chief from 1958 to 1974 (after which he took charge of political education in the party) and was a member of the Political Bureau from 1947–79.

It was Fajon who in 1970 handed over the PCF transcripts of discussions between the French and Czechoslovakian parties and which were used by the Russians against Dubček, yet perhaps because of Fajon's reputation as a Russophile he was chosen by the PCF to criticize the 'mistakes and insufficiencies in the working of Socialist democracy' in Poland and which had led to the fall of Gomulka in 1970. Although said to be a supporter of Marchais, he was not at the forefront during the mid-1970s. In 1975, however, Fajon's book *L'Union est un Combat* signalled the end of the honeymoon with the Socialists and the beginning of the polemic on the left and as a Central Committee member he was one of those responsible for bringing Fiszbin's Paris Federation to heel in 1979. (This operation typified Fajon's behind-the-scenes work for the PCF). In the 1980s Fajon was one of the last of the 'historical' figures of the party and played a role, though a diminishing one, when the party became more outspokenly pro-Russian. On 10 April 1985 he was awarded the 'order of friendship' at the Russian embassy in Paris for having been 'persecuted several times because of his courageous positions for the Communist cause in France and for friendship with the USSR' (See *Actualités Soviétiques*, no. 517, April 1985).

Bibliography

The book under Fajon's name *L'Union est un combat* (Paris: Editions Sociales, 1975) is remembered chiefly because it contains Marchais' speech to the Central Committee in 1972 after the signing of the common programme with the Socialists. Fajon's autobiography with a 'bourgeois' publisher, *Ma vie s'appelle Liberté* (Paris: Robert Laffont, 1976) is boring and unrevealing.

DSB

FALLIÈRES, Armand Clément
(1841–1931)

Of all the presidents of the Third Republic, Fallières perhaps comes closest to symbolizing the sociological characteristics and political values identified with republicanism. In a culture which distrusted power and lauded the good sense of the provincial notable, Fallières was the ideal head of state. He was born in the Lot-et-Garonne, the son of a clerk of the court and grandson of a blacksmith. Educated in Toulouse and Paris, he became a lawyer and a Republican. His political career began after 1870 as mayor of the town of Nerac in his home department and he acquired the politically useful badge of being dismissed for his advanced views after the fall of Thiers. In 1876 he became deputy for the Lot-et-Garonne and within four years held his first government post as junior minister at the Interior Ministry. He had a busy but unremarkable ministerial career, holding office a total of eight times between 1880 and 1890. He was briefly prime minister in 1883 and at different times held the politically sensitive Ministries of Justice, Education and the Interior. In office he proved to be the classic exponent of the bourgeois middle way.

His strong commitment to republicanism led him to vote against the de Broglie government in 1877 and as a prime minister he introduced a bill banning members of former reigning dynasties from residing in France. Yet he also voted against a complete amnesty for communards and as interior minister was very tough in dealing with labour unrest. His attitude to the religious problem was sensitive and moderate. In 1892 he entered the Senate and after a seven-year period in which he neither held office nor contributed much to political debate, became president of the Upper House. Occurring as it did in the heat of the Dreyfus affair, his election was seen as evidence of the Senate's republicanism. Thereafter he presided over the legislative consequences of the left-wing governing coalition known as the *bloc des gauches*. The tensions and conflicts that this period gave rise to, particularly during the Combes ministry (1902–5) meant that the 1906 presidential election became the focus of the conflict between the Dreyfusard coalition and its opponents, who by now included a number of dissident Radicals and Socialists. The candidate of the Republicans, Fallières easily defeated, by 449 votes to 371, the younger and more dynamic Paul Doumer, who though a Radical and president of the Chamber of Deputies, was supported by the Nationalist Right group. As president, Fallières travelled widely and was praised by Edward VII for the subtlety of his political judgement. Yet he never attempted to challenge his ministers and was perfectly content with the role of constitutional president. He showed a talent for political talent spotting – Clemenceau (q.v.), Briand (q.v.), Caillaux (q.v.) and Poincaré (q.v.) – all held prime ministerial office for the first time in his presidency. The choice of Poincaré as his successor showed a desire among the parliamentarians for a more activist presidency and it was somehow appropriate that on leaving the Elysée, Fallières should simply return to his native Lot-et-Garonne to cultivate his vineyards. To say that as president he restored French unity after the traumas of the Dreyfus affair would be to exaggerate the importance of both man and office. Yet his genial and reassuring manner and his image of avuncular good sense made him a popular head of state and a fitting figure to preside over the legend of the *belle époque*.

Bibliography

Chastenet, J. (1949), *La France de Monsieur Fallières*, Paris: Fayard.
Watson, D. (1974), *Georges Clemenceau*, London: Eyre Methuen.

PM

FAURE, Edgar Jean (1908–88)

Many commentators and politicians of all political persuasions regard Edgar Faure as one of the most clever politicians of twentieth-century France. Trained as a lawyer, he worked from 1929 in the Court of Paris (*avocat à la cour de Paris*). In 1942, he joined de Gaulle in Algiers, where he worked as assistant secretary (legislative issues) for the liberation committee, and later, for the provisional government. In 1945, he was assistant prosecutor representing France at the War Crimes Tribunal in Nuremberg. From 1946 until 1958, he was a Radical-Socialist deputy for the Jura (he hesitated, in 1946, between the Radicals and several other parties of the centre and centre-right). During his post-war political career, as well as holding national office, he has held office as mayor (Port-Lesney 1947–70, 1983–8, Pontarlier 1971–7) and as a local and regional councillor.

Faure claimed in the late 1940s that it was the destiny of the Radicals to be associated with government. This was to prove especially true in his particular case in both the Fourth and Fifth Republics. The many and unstable governments of the Fourth

Republic created a relatively large group of politicians who lined up in varying combinations to form a new government as each successively fell prey to the shifting party alliances in the National Assembly, where no single party held an overall majority. Faure was one of the ablest (and youngest) of this group. After the failure of *tripartisme* (the conflictual Communist, Socialist and Christian Democrat alliance) in early 1947, the centre of gravity of Fourth Republican government moved rightwards, making a centrist political figure like Faure a sure occupant of national office throughout the 1950s. He was, in turn, secretary of state for finance and minister for the budget in 1949, 1950 and 1951, minister of justice (1951), president of the foreign affairs committee (1952–3), finance minister (1953 and 1954), minister of foreign affairs (1955), and again finance minister in Pflimlin's brief ministry in May 1958. He was twice prime minister (*président du conseil*). In 1952, aged 43, he was the youngest prime minister since 1893, in the short-lived government (20 January–29 February 1952) which was defeated when Faure tried to raise taxes. When he became prime minister again (23 February 1955–24 January 1956, a long period by Fourth Republican standards), he demonstrated great political skill, particularly over the Tunisian and Moroccan issues. Defeated on a confidence vote, Faure dissolved the Assembly, the first time this had happened for nearly eighty years.

Faure was one of the few major Fourth Republic figures to return to national office in the Fifth, but he did so stealthily. Between 1959 and 1966, he was a senator (Jura). He refused the education portfolio in 1962, in part because he did not wish to be seen as an opportunist. He wrote, studied (*agrégation*, 1962), and taught (Faculty of Law, Dijon). In 1963, at de Gaulle's request, he went on a diplomatic mission to China, a mission which was instrumental in securing the People's Republic's admission to the United Nations.

The second major phase of Faure's career began in 1966, when he became minister of agriculture (1966–8) in Pompidou's government. In 1967, he again entered the National Assembly (Doubs) as a supporter (*apparenté*) of the Gaullist party (UDR). In July 1968 Faure came to national prominence once again as minister of education. After the May–June uprising and the UDR landslide victory of June, de Gaulle gave him *carte blanche* (for an account see *Ce que je crois*, 1971) to reform radically the education system (minister of education, July 1968–June 1969). The main features of the reforms were the introduction of a core curriculum, a greater emphasis upon mathematics and science within the education sys-

tem, and the devolution of decision-making power to the universities. He was to continue his work in the field of education as president of UNESCO's International Commission for Educational Development (1971). In the Messmer government, he was minister of state for social affairs (1972), and between 1973 and 1978, president of the National Assembly. But it was the education portfolio and the 'Faure reforms' of 1968–9 that assured his lasting place in the history of the Fifth Republic, although – without 'protection' after de Gaulle's resignation in April 1969 – his reform programme was to be curtailed subsequently.

As a political personality, Faure was generally greatly admired. In spite of his right-of-centre position on the political spectrum, he provoked little hostility from the left; his main enemies (especially over the education reforms) being on the right. He was considered a very sound finance minister, a conciliatory prime minister, and a reformist agriculture and education minister. Significantly, perhaps, he held these various posts at particularly difficult times and at moments of major social and political transition. In both 1969 and 1974, he was considered a possible contender for the presidency of the Republic. In international diplomatic circles, he was respected by the Americans, the Soviets and the Chinese. Intellectually too, he was a relatively important figure. He was the author of many works, and his memoirs are a major documentary source for the study of post-war French politics. (He is also the author of several crime thrillers, pseud. Edgar Sanday.) He was elected to the Academie française and was president of the commission organizing the bicentennial of the Revolution when he died.

Edgar Faure, whose political life spanned half a century, is significant, not only because of his effect upon twentieth-century France, but for what he represents and illustrates in French political life. One of the essential qualities he demonstrated was that divisions and convergences within French politics are more complex than the traditional left–right divide might lead us to assume, a divide that Faure himself always denied had any correspondence in French society. He always regarded the political divisions in French life as 'illogical', arguing that the real socio-political divide was between producers and non-producers, and that class antagonisms could be overcome by a planned, regulated, moderately expansionist capitalism in which all (producers) benefited (see *Prévoir le présent*, 1966). It is worth noting that such an approach to economic and political life probably owes much to Faure's origins in a family network of industrious lawyers, doctors, soldiers and peasants of modest means who epitomized the optimism of the Third Republic in its heyday.

At the level of political philosophy, Faure can be characterized as a realist and a pragmatist who, at the high point of his career in the mid-1950s, carried little ideological baggage. He has been likened to a Talleyrand, with all that that connotes of political genius, durability, and opportunism. He always held dear, however, the belief in parliamentarianism (he regarded his presidency of the National Assembly as of great significance and a great honour) and in republican values, and from the early 1960s onwards, propounded a philosophy which eventually added an 'ism' to his name. From 1972, he put forward the idea of a 'New Social Contract' which might 'transcend' Marxism (he was never anti-Socialist, like so many non-Socialist politicians of the Fourth and Fifth Republics) and reconcile the dominant competing political ideologies in contemporary French thought. He argued for the development of a political consensus across party lines on major issues such as education, unemployment and defence. In the bipolarized Fifth Republic, however, few on the left were attracted to his initiatives, and his audience remained that of the centre-right and right, and his most notable political ally was Jacques Chirac. Through the 1970s, much of his conciliatory politics was directed at reducing the growing antagonism between the supporters of Chirac and Giscard d'Estaing.

Three concluding remarks on Faure's political style and beliefs are worth noting. First, though he was of the centre-right, his general outlook, especially on colonialism, was much closer to that of Mendès France than the personal rivalry between the two seemed to suggest. Less dogmatic than Mendès, Faure was prepared to 'play the political game' in order to further his policies and remain in the forefront of politics. With hindsight, there is little to distinguish 'Mendésisme' from Faurism as political philosophies or as policies. It was only the exceptional circumstances of the mid-1950s which, in Faure's words, stopped the two best prime ministers from working together. Second, although it was, in part, Faure's greater adaptability which allowed him to work within the Fifth Republican system, more importantly, what distinguished him from Mendès France was his attitude to de Gaulle. Like so many (though not all, cf. Mendès and Mitterrand), Faure fell under the spell of de Gaulle's mystique in the Resistance period. He believed thereafter that de Gaulle was necessary for France, and even though in North Africa and at home Faure's Fourth Republic was undermined by de Gaulle's supporters, Faure believed, much earlier than 1958, that de Gaulle should be 'called'. This is, in part, the key to an understanding of Edgar Faure: in spite of his epitomizing the best of the Radical Republican tradition, he was, in fact, both practically and sentimentally, a left-wing Gaullist: national independence, a 'strategic' commitment to the nuclear strike force, an activist non-alignment in super-power and in Third World affairs, a commitment to Europeanism while maintaining a scepticism concerning Britain's and West Germany's connections with the US, a belief in a form of social relations which transcends class through 'participation', a belief in national solidarity, a 'romantic' view of republicanism, and a personal allegiance to de Gaulle himself, are the hallmarks of 'Faurism'. It is one of the paradoxes of French politics that the underlying philosophy of the archetypal Fourth Republican, so close to that of Mendès France, is also very close to that of the founder of the Fifth Republic, whom Mendès France opposed so resolutely. Third, it is arguable that Faure's social reformism (concerning, for example, the distribution of wealth, planned economic expansion, and upward social mobility) would have been forced into starker choices if his political career had been at a time of economic recession rather than during the '30 glorious years' of France's and Europe's economic expansion.

Bibliography

Faure, E. (1966), *Prévoir le présent*, Paris: Gallimard.

Faure, E. (1968), *L'Education nationale et la participation*, Paris: Plon.

Faure, E. (1970), *L'Ame du combat. Pour un nouveau contrat social*, Paris: Fayard.

Faure, E. (1971), *Ce que je crois*, Paris: Grasset.

Faure, E. (1972), *Apprendre à être*, Paris: Fayard.

Faure, E. (1973), *Pour un nouveau contrat social*, Paris: Seuil.

Faure, E. (with P. Sollers) (1977), *Au delà du dialogue*, Paris: Balland.

Faure, E. (1982), *Mémoires: avoir toujours raison, c'est un grand tort*, vol. I, Paris: Plon.

Faure, E. (1984), *Mémoires: si tel doit être mon destin ce soir*, vol. II, Paris: Plon.

See also: R. Barral, *Les thèses constitutionnelles du Président Edgar Faure* (Thèse de droit, Montpellier, 1973); D. Colard, *Edgar Faure ou l'intelligence de la politique: 1945–1975* (Paris: Dullis, 1975); Institut de France/Académie Française, *Discours prononcés pour la réception de Monsieur Edgar Faure* (Paris: Institut de France, 1979).

JG

FAURE, François Félix (1841–99)

Born in Paris on 30 January 1841 the future President of the Republic, Félix Faure trained as a tanner and moved to Le Havre where he set up in business becoming a sucessful industrialist and shipowner. He was elected to the Le Havre chamber of commerce, of which he became president, and following the Franco-Prussian War (1870–1) began his political career with local politics. After his election as deputy-mayor for Le Havre he was eventually elected to the Chamber of Deputies for the Seine-Inférieure (now Seine-Maritime) department in 1881, defeating the royalist incumbent. His republicanism and shipping interests gained him a place as junior minister, first for commerce and colonies in Léon Gambetta's 1881 government, and subsequently for marine and colonies in various governments until in 1894 he became minister for marine and colonies. In 1895 he was elected seventh president of the Third Republic and died in office on 16 January 1899.

Félix Faure is perhaps better remembered for the manner of his passing than for his political achievements, following his sudden death at the Elysée Palace in the arms of his mistress (Madame Steinhell, née Marguerite Japy). A moderate Republican, elected on the 'progressist' ticket, he sat on the parliamentary benches as a member of the Union républicaine and proved his commitment to the Republic in the stance he took in the Chamber against General Boulanger and his movement in the late 1880s. His political contribution was greatest in colonial affairs which he worked hard to promote whether as minister or as a member of various parliamentary bodies, some of which, such as the superior council for colonies, he helped set up. But he never really stood out as a leader. Even his election to the Elysée following the resignation of Casimir-Périer was unexpected, when he beat the main left-wing contender Henri Brisson (q.v.).

Never having held a major office of state was probably an advantage at a time when it was believed that the presidential role should remain ceremonial. Here Faure was a success using to effect his distinguished appearance and cordial manner to emblazon the symbolic function of president on state occasions, like the exchange of visits between himself and Tsar Nicholas II of Russia (1896–7) or by his numerous popular presidential visits to the provinces. But during the Dreyfus affair in the latter days of his presidency, he refused to use his position to reopen the case of the army captain falsely accused of treason. In refusing to exercise the presidential role

in anything other than the ceremonial, Faure contributed to the function of President of the Republic being devoted to nothing more, according to one observer's sardonic comment, than 'opening flower-shows'.

Bibliography

There is nothing in English on Faure, but A. Dansette, *Histoire des présidents de la République* (Paris: Amiot-Dumont, 1953) and J. Chastenet, *Histoire de la IIIe République*, vol. III (Paris: Hachette, 1955) may usefully be consulted together with C. Braibant, *Félix Faure à l'Elysée: souvenirs de Louis Le Gall* (Paris: Hachette, 1963).

JFVK

FAURE, Maurice Henri (1922–)

Faure has been one of the great constants of post-war French politics. The son of a schoolmaster, Faure briefly followed the same profession after 1945 until being launched into national politics as a member of a ministerial cabinet in 1947, and moving quickly to the National Assembly.

Faure's career in national and international politics spans forty years. He began life as and stayed a Radical long after the party ceased to be a major political force, shifting his allegiance to the Mouvement des Radicaux de Gauche (MRG) after the party split in 1972. Faure's political life has been conspicuously multi-dimensional and yet it typifies the accepted career path of so many French provincial politicians. He has remained a representative of the Midi in Paris rather than a representative of Paris in the Midi.

Maurice Faure has maintained a presence in local, national and European politics for most of his political life, and has succeeded in accumulating more elected positions ('mandates') than most of his contemporaries and rivals.

At local level, he was first elected to the Departmental Council of the Lot department in 1951, remaining a member into the 1980s and retaining the presidency from 1970. His was initially mayor at Prayssac, but in 1965 he captured the town hall of Cahors, the administrative centre of his constituency and department, and this position he convincingly retained at the 1983 elections. As the regional dimension became defined, so Maurice Faure followed his interests at this level too. He was president of the local nominated Assembly (CODER) for the Midi-Pyrénées between 1964 and 1970, and vice-president of the Regional Council from 1974 to 1986.

In national politics, he was elected and then re-elected for the Lot department at every general election from 1951 to 1981 (two years later he resigned to become a senator). He served as a junior minister under Guy Mollet, then Bourgès-Maunoury, and Félix Gaillard, before serving for three days as minister of the interior and briefly as minister of European institutions in the short-lived Pflimlin government of 1958. Maurice Faure's ministerial career came to an end with the proclamation of the Fifth Republic and he remained in opposition until called upon in 1981 by his former ministerial colleague François Mitterrand to represent the MRG component of the left coalition as minister of justice and *garde des sceaux* in the new Mauroy government. Faure did not enjoy the portfolio he was offered and resigned his post after one month, to the regret of his party and his friends. In 1988, however, he resurfaced as minister of public works and housing in Rocard's governments.

As a young minister, Maurice Faure had signed the EEC Treaty in 1957 on behalf of France. Twenty-seven years later he was to serve as President Mitterrand's personal representative on the Dooge committee which recommended major institutional changes to the European Community, some of which emerged in the Single European Act of 1986. Meanwhile Maurice Faure had served as a nominated member of the European Parliament (1959–67; 1973–9) and as a directly-elected MEP from 1979 to 1981.

Maurice Faure also had prominent posts in the Radical Party. He was secretary-general from 1953 to 1955, and succeeded Gaillard as president, serving from 1961 to 1965 and 1969 to 1971. He was the leading opponent of J. J. Servan-Schreiber's critical stance towards the reformed Socialist Party in the early 1970s, and after his defeat by Servan-Schreiber for the presidency of the Radical Party at its 1971 Congress, Faure led the majority of Radical deputies and senators back to the Socialist group as *apparentés*. This was the first stage in the formation of the Mouvement des Radicaux de Gauche in 1972 and its eventual endorsement of the common programme.

ABP

FAURE, Paul (1878–1960)

Paul Faure was secretary-general of the Socialist Party (SFIO) from the split at the Tours Congress in 1920 until 1940 and a Socialist deputy for Saône-et-Loire from 1924–32 and 1938–40. Remembered now for his pacifist desire to appease the Fascist dictators, he encapsulated the grave dilemmas of ordinary French people in the 1930s: the fear of war and the expectation of defeat. Less than four years after serving in Léon Blum's Popular Front government as a high-ranking minister of state, he was, in the summer of 1940, embracing the Vichy regime of Pétain and Laval.

A native of Périgord, whose accent he strikingly bore, and of bourgeois origins – the journalist son of a provincial lawyer – Faure joined the Guesdist Parti Ouvrier Français in 1901 and on the unification of French socialism in 1905 with the creation of the SFIO became secretary of the Dordogne federation. Despite Guesde's support for the war in 1914, Faure was a prominent leader of the pacifist anti-war minority in the SFIO, co-founding Le Populaire du Centre to articulate the pacifist case. In 1920 he adopted a mid-way position between the left of the party who favoured adhesion to the Leninist Third International and those who opposed, and with the latter (led by Blum) was expelled from the Tours Congress to become secretary-general of the re-formed rump SFIO. As part of a duumvirate comprising himself and Blum, he dominated the party until the Second World War, becoming (for Georges Lefranc) 'the heart of the SFIO' to Blum's 'head'. The two men enjoyed a rather uneasy relationship. Though an indifferent orator, Faure was very much the SFIO's 'chief engineer' (as Jean Lacouture says in his biography of Léon Blum), with an intimate knowledge of the rank and file and a natural provincial down to earth touch; whereas Blum's reputation was more for Parisian intellectual aloofness and certain prima donna-ish qualities.

Faure's whole political position was informed by pacifism. As Lacouture has put it, 'pacifism was the sum, the dead-end of his thought' and it was this that made him incapable of distinguishing between resistance to nazism and the 1914 conflict. And (says Lacouture) 'beyond pacifist blindness, we must also talk of cowardice'. Fear was the basis of his policy: fear of war, fear of defeat and fear of Communist revolution. A staunch anti-Communist, Faure saw Soviet intervention in Spain and the PCF's attack on non-intervention as evidence of a Soviet desire to provoke a Franco-German war. His views were a meld of pacifism and defeatism, believing that France would suffer certain defeat at the hands of a more powerful adversary in the event of a general war. Thus he rejected any action over German reoccupation of the Rhineland, strongly backed non-intervention in Spain, and, in relation to Mussolini's colonial ambitions, argued that 'the skin of a vineyard worker of Mâcon is worth more than the port of Djibouti'. More frightened of Stalin than Hitler, he was prepared to make lavish concessions to Germany to keep France out of a disastrous war which would lead either to a Communist or Fascist victory. He saw the cession of the Sudetenland to Germany as the righting of a wrong imposed at Versailles – an application indeed of the supposed Versailles principle of self-determination.

Leader of the Munichites in the SFIO after 1938, he split the party at the Montrouge Congress in that year over Blum's advocacy of an anti-Fascist front of the major powers and founded Le Pays Socialiste to argue the case for appeasement – for peace at all costs. With the fall of France in 1940 he unsuccessfully sought a government post, but served only as an adviser to Laval and acted as an emissary between Vichy and the German authorities after Laval's dismissal in December 1940. At the Riom Trials in 1941 he testified against his erstwhile colleague Blum, distancing himself from the nationalizations of the Popular Front government, in which he claimed he had no hand. At the liberation he was expelled from the SFIO for his Vichyite involvement and founded the short-lived Parti Socialiste Démocratique. He survived into the Fifth Republic to publish an attack on the disqualification from parliamentary service of those deputies (among whom were a majority of SFIO deputies) who voted powers to Pétain in June 1940.

Bibliography

See Paul Faure, *De Munich à la cinquième République* (Paris: Editions de l'Elan, 1958) and Paul Faure, *Histoire d'un faux et de ses conséquences* (Paris: La République Libre, 1958).

BC

FAURE, Sébastien (1858–1942)

Born in Saint-Etienne of a wealthy and religious family, Faure was educated by Jesuits and was intended for the priesthood. His noviciate in Clermont-Ferrand ended when his father died in 1875, and Sébastien returned home to look after his family, working for an insurance company. In 1885 he married Blanche Faure (no relation) and the couple settled in Bordeaux. Faure's loss of faith and his nascent interest in Socialist politics led to divorce

only three years later. He then moved to Paris, and became increasingly involved with the anarchist movement. Many years later, he became reconciled with his ex-wife and the couple lived together first in Paris and then, from April 1940, in Royan.

Faure was perhaps the last outstanding representative of the romantic anarchism of the nineteenth century, and his life is inseparable from the history of the revolutionary movement over half a century. His political involvement began in Bordeaux in 1885, when he was a candidate for Jules Guesde's Parti Ouvrier in the general election. By 1888, when he was a delegate to the Third Congress of the Fédération Nationale des Syndicats, Faure had become a committed anarchist, influenced by the works of Kropotkin and Elisée Reclus (q.v.).

Faure became renowned as a propagandist for the anarchist movement, gaining a reputation especially as a lucid and convincing orator, although many of his talks were also published in pamphlet form. The collections taken at such meetings were his only income, but they were so successful that he was still able to donate considerable sums to the movement.

1894 saw the 'trial of the thirty', the last act in the notorious era of 'propaganda by the deed', a period which had culminated in the actions of Ravachol (q.v.), for example, and in the assassination of President Sadi Carnot (q.v.) by the Italian anarchist Caserio. In the *Procès des Trente*, well-known anarchist propagandists, Faure among them, were accused of conspiring together with 'illegalists' (those who used anarchist theories to justify common crimes). All the defendants apart from three thieves were eventually acquitted.

In 1895, Faure helped found the weekly Le Libertaire, which was to remain the main anarchist–Communist paper until 1939, and it was through this paper that he first supported Dreyfus early in 1898. The following year, with financial help from a group of Jews, Faure started the daily Le Journal du Peuple, which campaigned on behalf of Dreyfus through till December.

Faure's belief in education as a determinant of social behaviour led him in 1904 to set up La Ruche, a school near Rambouillet which was run on anarchist lines and which catered especially for poor children. La Ruche remains an important experiment in the development of a libertarian approach to education.

During the First World War, Faure adopted a resolutely pacifist approach, launching *Towards Peace: An Appeal to Socialists, Syndicalists, Revolutionaries and Anarchists* in 1915, and helping to found the very successful weekly *Ce qu'il faut dire* in 1916.

In the late 1920s Faure intervened in the bitter debate about organization and discipline within the Union Anarchiste (UA). He opposed those who believed that anarchism's failure to counter the growth of communism was due to the movement's lack of theoretical and organizational coherence. Instead, he proposed an 'anarchist synthesis', whereby the three main tendencies which make up the movement (communist, syndicalist, individualist) should work together within one organization. He left the Union Anarchiste to found the short-lived Association des Fédéralistes Anarchistes, before being reconciled with the UA in the early 1930s, and thereafter working with all tendencies in the movement. During the Spanish Civil War he supported the CNT–FAI, criticizing those anarchist pacifists who did not distinguish between inter-state war and revolutionary war; but his were also the first articles criticizing the CNT's participation in government to appear in the pages of *Le Libertaire*.

Bibliography

Books written by Faure include: *Mon communisme* (Paris: Editions de la Fraternelle, 1921); editor, *Encyclopédie anarchiste* (Paris: Oeuvre Internationale des Editions Anarchistes, 1934–5), 4 vols; *La Synthèse anarchiste* (Paris: 1927; reprinted in *Mouvement Social*, April–June, 1973).

See also Jean Maitron, *Le Mouvement anarchiste en France*, 2 vols (Paris: Maspéro, 1975).

DGB

FAUVET, Jacques Jules Pierre Constant (1914–)

Jacques Fauvet is best known for being editor-in-chief (*directeur*) of *Le Monde* between 1969 and 1982. He joined the newly-created newspaper at the end of the Second World War and in 1948 became head of its politics desk. From there he rose up the editorial hierarchy, acceding to the top post at the same time as France was entering the post-de Gaulle era. He thus succeeded Hubert Beuve-Méry who had founded the paper in 1944 and had been its editor-in-chief for the whole of the intervening 25-year period. Fauvet is also a highly respected political commentator and writer. He is the author (or co-author) of various books on French politics, including: *Les Partis dans la France actuelle* (1947), *Les Forces politiques de la France* (1951), *La France déchirée* (1957), *La Quatrième République* (1959), *La Fronde des Génér-*

aux (1961) and *Histoire du parti communiste français* (2 vols: 1964 and 1965).

Under Fauvet's editorship *Le Monde* remained the favoured newspaper of the political, administrative and economic elites of the Fifth Republic: the top people's newspaper. Its circulation rose from just over 200,000 at the start of the Fifth Republic to around 500,000 by the mid-1970s. Though containing no editorial page and striving to provide as complete journalistic coverage of national and international current affairs as possible, the newspaper's political sympathies during the 1970s clearly lay with the nascent Union of the Left and in particular Mitterrand's Socialist Party. Under Fauvet *Le Monde* adopted a very critical attitude towards the Giscard d'Estaing presidency (1974–81), implicitly advocating and then welcoming the victory of Mitterrand and the Socialists in the 1981 presidential and parliamentary elections.

The final months of Fauvet's editorship were unhappy ones for *Le Monde*. Circulation began to decline and the paper lost readers, especially younger ones, to the refashioned post-1981 *Libération*. At the same time the modernization of the paper's production process and the computerization of its documentation service had imposed severe strains on the paper's finances. It was, therefore, in an atmosphere of uncertainty about the paper's future that Fauvet was succeeded to the post of editor-in-chief by another long-standing *Le Monde* journalist, André Laurens, in the summer of 1982.

Bibliography

There is nothing in English on Fauvet. On *Le Monde* under his stewardship see J. Thibau, *Le Monde, histoire d'un journal . . .* (Paris: Simoën, 1978).

RK

FERRY, Jules François Camille (1832–93)

Of solid bourgeois background and of independent means, later increased by marrying into the industrial plutocracy, Ferry qualified as a lawyer, like his father before him. Prevented by his Republican convictions from embarking on an administrative career under Napoleon III, he practised at the Bar, albeit somewhat desultorily. He was also active as a journalist, eventually joining the staff of the opposition paper, *Le Temps*. In his writings, he uncovered electoral irregularities and specialized in denouncing the financial mismanagement of the prefect of the Seine,

Baron Haussmann, in the implementation of a modern town planning policy in Paris. These attacks were published under the apt title *Les Comptes fantastiques d'Haussmann* (Paris: A. Le Chevalier, 1868).

Under the Second Empire, Ferry was repeatedly prosecuted for breaches of the restrictive legislation which curtailed opposition activities. In 1869 he was elected deputy on an anticlerical platform. His political career took off with the collapse of imperial rule in the aftermath of defeat. On 4 September 1870, he was, with Jules Favre, among those who proclaimed the Republic. As a member of the government of national defence, he was entrusted with Haussmann's prefectoral duties and became mayor of Paris in November 1870. In that capacity he was in charge of maintaining law and order while the city was beseiged and starved of supplies. He was blamed for the food shortages and nicknamed *Ferry Famine*. His lifelong unpopularity with the Paris population – which was held to have precluded his election to the presidency of the Republic in the 1880s – dated from then. It was increased by his tough stance during the Commune. He became so unacceptable to public opinion that he was sent as ambassador to Greece for a cooling-off period in 1872. He always lacked the popular touch and was anything but a charismatic figure. His supercilious manner, reminiscent of some English Victorian politicians, was equally ill-suited to cajoling parliamentarians and to courting the electorate. The persistent antagonism between Ferry and Gambetta, which exacerbated the divisions among parliamentarians until the latter's death in 1882, was rooted as much in temperemental differences as in political disagreements.

From 1876, Ferry was president of the Gauche Républicaine (somewhat misnamed, since it was a centre group) which was in sharp competition with Gambetta's Gauche Démocratique. He had a long and distinguished record as a parliamentarian, first as a deputy for the Vosges from 1869 to 1889. Later, after he lost his seat in a particularly bitter electoral campaign, he became a senator in 1891 (his brother stood down to aid his career). He remained in the Senate until his death in 1893. Though he frequently held ministerial posts, he did not achieve the political eminence or the national recognition to which he aspired. He was only prime minister twice for relatively brief periods in 1880–1 and 1883–5. The presidency of the Republic eluded him, although he would have been acceptable to the Vatican, despite his secularist policies, if he had consented to go through the formality of a church wedding. In the presidential election of 1887, he only gained twenty votes and stood down, making room for the outsider Sadi Carnot (q.v.).

Despite the passions he generated, Ferry was a Republican 'opportunist' rather than an ideologist. His political stance was intrinsically moderate. He voted against putting on trial the ministers involved in the crisis of 16 May 1877, against breaking diplomatic relations with the Vatican, against making divorce legal and against compulsory military service for seminarists. Thus he could not be described as either vindictive in dealing with political opponents or even as systematically anticlerical. It was only in educational matters that he was a relentless adversary of the clergy and particularly of the congregations. However, this is the aspect of his political activity which has had the most lasting consequences. Indeed, it was as minister of education that he made his main contribution to the history of the Third Republic; though his involvement with colonial policy was also significant, it was less creative.

Ferry held the education portfolio for a total period of fifty months between 1879 and 1885, in five out of eight cabinets (including his own). His two bills of 1879 were designed to restore the monopoly of degree-granting to the university and to undermine clerical control over teaching. The famous Article 7 prohibiting members of religious orders from being headmasters, was aimed at the Jesuits. It was a forerunner of Combes' (q.v.) legislation and proved so highly contentious that it caused the fall of the Waddington cabinet. However, during the 1880s Ferry secured the closure of some 300 Catholic schools. More positively, he shepherded through Parliament an array of legislation which transformed the provision of state education. Primary schooling became compulsory and free, secondary schools for girls were instituted by the law of 1880, teacher training was reorganized both at department and at *grandes écoles* level. These were not separate piecemeal reforms, but the gradual implementation of a long-term plan for planned social change through educational provision.

The influence of positivism on Ferry's educational policy is clear. In his youth, he had been a keen student of Comtean philosophy. As a politician, he remained convinced that progress was evolutionary and therefore necessarily slow, but also inevitable. Zeldin describes such a stance as midway between fatalism and utopianism. Ferry's fatalism (or his realism) consisted in accepting that social persistence was unavoidable. He recognized that, despite having become a Republic, France would remain to a large extent and for a long time a static society. The introduction of the universal suffrage was politically progressive, but would lead to the endorsement of conservative policies. Traditionalism, vested interests and an involvement with local rather than national issues – all these features of a predominantly rural electorate had to be taken into account. They could only be altered by engineering a change in the values and attitudes of voters. Ferry's optimism about the possibility of raising ethical standards and propagating enlightenment through popular schooling was derived from Comte. It may have been utopian, it was undoubtedly positivistic.

Ferry's educational reforms of the early 1880s linked the dissemination of knowledge with the inculcation of an altruistic civic morality. This was to replace the catechism, while secular teachers, trained and employed by the state, would become the substitutes of the Catholic clergy. At the political level, it was expedient for the Radical Republicans to undermine and ultimately to destroy clerical control over the rural masses. The provision of education for girls was particularly important in this respect. On the other hand, from a philosophical perspective, it was a central tenet of positivism that the religion of humanity should be disseminated and that superstitious beliefs should give way to scientifically-based knowledge. The array of Ferry's reforms served both sets of objectives. They furthered the electoral interests of anticlerical republicans by secularizing the elementary schools Napoleon had left to the Catholic Church (as well as the instruction of women). They were also intended to further social integration by devising curricula which emphasized the common legacy of French history and the duties of citizenship. The rationale for *éducation civique* was not only to promote republicanism, but also to stimulate patriotism in the aftermath of a humiliating defeat. The primary school teachers became known as the 'black hussars of the Republic', since they were an elite corps engaged in a secularist offensive. Despite the abundant literature recording confrontations between *instituteurs* and *curés* it would be an oversimplification to describe primary teachers merely as enemies of the clergy. Their main commitment was to a task of popular regeneration preparatory to the *revanche*, i.e. to the recovery of the lost provinces (Alsace-Lorraine) and the restoration of national pride. It was no coincidence that military training should have been reintroduced in the secondary schools (*lycées*) by the law of 1881 and that the need for physical education in primary schools should have been asserted by that of March 1882. In this context primary teachers were to be lay missionaries, spreading enlightenment, including a new civic morality, and strengthening patriotism.

The objectives of these educational reforms were not egalitarian. Although social promotion could be achieved through gaining formal qualifications (thus peasants' children become teachers – *instituteurs* – and their grandchildren academics), this mobility was an unintended – if welcome – consequence. The principal aim of Ferry's policies was not to promote equality of opportunity, but rather to enhance freedom (by liberating minds from superstition and prejudice) and, above all, to stimulate fraternity through civic education. It is only in the case of exceptionally gifted individuals that differences of class and inequalities of wealth were to be reduced by education. To Ferry, capitalism was a natural form of economic organization. At most, he thought that the immoral consequences of *laissez-faire* could be offset by the solidarity that the schools would generate. Nor was the emphasis on education for women intended to reduce gender-related differences in society. By freeing females from clerical domination, it was the family – where the wife and mother played a central part – which Ferry wanted to regenerate. The influence of Comtean philosophy is manifest both in the concern for moral change and in the reliance on schooling to bring it about.

The government's duty to ensure sound secular education was part and parcel of the State's main task, which was to promote social hygiene. This entailed compensating for the detrimental effects of capitalism – hence the need to teach altruism and solidarity. But above all, it meant that the beneficial effects of the capitalist system as a generator of wealth had to be maximized. To this end, a large market had to be secured in order to provide for a sustained economic growth. Although Ferry had started as a free-trader, he gave up this belief early on in his career. In 1881, he introduced protectionist tariffs, so as to shelter French producers from the impact of foreign competition. Though he held protection to be necessary, it was not sufficient to turn a predominantly agrarian economy into a modern industrial one. Colonialism was a means of providing outlets for manufactured goods. It was mainly – though not exclusively – on economic grounds that Ferry justified imperialist policies.

French expansion overseas originated from the unconnected initiatives of explorers, soldiers and civil servants rather than from any systematic governmental policy. Ferry supported their moves and took advantage of whatever opportunities arose. Yet he did not seem to be guided by coherent principles. He acted as an empiricist, without being guided by a colonial vision. This is in sharp contradiction to his educational policy, with its theoretical foundation.

At the time of the appropriation of Madagascar, he made a speech in the Chamber of Deputies in July 1885. This was an outline of the main grounds on which he wished France to acquire a colonial empire. First, he used strategic arguments, such as securing bases for the navy. He also referred to increased national prestige on the international scene. Secondly, he stressed the advantage to an industrial economy of expanding the market open to French products. Thus the value of Tonkin was that it provided access to 400 million civilized potential customers. Thirdly, he mentioned the duty of civilized peoples towards 'barbarous' nations. France's civilizing mission was exemplified by Brazza's role in the Congo.

Over time, Ferry laid more stress on the economic aspect of colonialism policy as 'a corrective to protectionism, a safety valve to the steam engine of the protective system' (Preface to L. Sentupéry, *Le Tonkin et la Mère Patrie*, Paris: Victor Havard, 1890). The neo-mercantilist doctrine advanced in defence of his own policies in North Africa and in the Far East appear to have been a rationalization devised after the event. Be that as it may, Ferry's colonialist stance was extremely unpopular. Nationalists accused him of diverting resources from the defence of French security on the Rhine and from the patriotic duty of recovering the 'lost provinces'. They held Germany to be the arch-enemy, whereas colonial politics led to competition with England and, in the case of Tunisia, with Italy. The nationalist vision of France as a European power with a strong army capable of avenging the defeat of 1870, was incompatible with Ferry's advocacy of a colonial empire whose world-wide economic and cultural interests would be protected by its navy and by troops posted overseas.

Paradoxically, Ferry's supporters in the educational debates were his opponents over colonial policies. As anticlericals, they resented the part played by Catholic missionaries and nuns in the new overseas dependencies. Ferry's own secularism was focused on popular education in metropolitan France. He was prepared to treat the Church as an ally in the colonies, since its influence there could be progressive, given the low level of native cultures. Again there is a Comtean cast to this argument, since it rests on the concept of ages (or stages) of evolution. Therefore the inconsistency in the treatment of religious orders was merely apparent. However, it was politically damaging. Furthermore, public opinion was resentful of the public expenditure involved in colonial expeditions and fearful that French lives would be lost. Ferry's overseas policies added to his

unpopularity and earned him yet more disparaging nicknames, e.g. '*le Tunisien*' and '*le Tonkinois*'.

At the Berlin Conference of 1885, Ferry pressed for the recognition of French zones of influence, especially in Tonkin and in the Congo. He had been instrumental in the establishment of a protectorate in Tunisia by the Treaty of Barolo in 1881 and in Annam by the Treaty of Hué in 1883. In the former case, he had sent French troops, with the tacit assent of the main European powers, except Italy. In the latter, Rivière's expedition had been started in 1881 and he was merely consolidating an existing situation. When the peace with China had already been concluded, though not yet announced, in March 1885, a local withdrawal of French troops which became known as the 'Langson incident', was construed by the opposition and the press as a major defeat. This was when Ferry's unpopularity was at its highest. It was beginning to abate towards the end of his life and after the death of his main adversary, Gambetta.

Although he is mainly remembered for his educational reforms and his overseas policies, Ferry was involved with legislation on a number of domestic issues. In addition to his concern for tariff protection, he was responsible for the creation of the savings bank (Casse d'Epargne). In accordance with his early anti-Bonapartist political tenets, he extended the freedom of the press and of association. These relatively minor achievements confirm Ferry's commitment to the values of liberty and of popular capitalism.

Bibliography

Legrand, L. (1961), *L'Influence du positivisme dans l'oeuvre scolaire de Jules Ferry*, Paris: Bibliothèque des Sciences Politiques et Sociales, 1961.

Brunschwig, G. (1966), *French Colonialism. Myth and Realities*, London: Pall Mall, 1966.

MV

FISZBIN, Henri (1930–)

Henri Fiszbin was born in Paris to a Polish, Jewish, immigrant family and was a metal worker for eight years before becoming a full-time Communist Party employee. A militant Communist involved in the demonstrations at the beginning of the cold war, Fiszbin joined the Communist youth movement in 1945, joined the party in 1946 and became a full-time worker in the party at the end of 1956. Fiszbin seems to have been a devoted activist, hard-working, and of an impeccable worker background; as such he was steadily moved up the apparatus, going on to the Central Committee from 1967 to 1979 and being made first secretary of the Paris Federation from 1973 to 1979. In the 1977 city election in Paris, Fiszbin was elected councillor (a position he held until 1983) and was leader of the Paris Communist group. As first secretary of the Federation Fiszbin mounted the 'operation open heart' designed to show the city Communist Party to visitors, the Federation having made a lot of the running after the 22nd Party Congress which inaugurated a more open style of party activity.

If things had stopped there, Fiszbin would almost certainly have remained a minor politician in the Communist Party but in the autumn of 1977 there was a U-turn as the party rejected the alliance of the left with the Socialists and the adventures of the 22nd Congress. Thus began the long 'affair' of the Paris Federation written up in Fiszbin's *Les Bouches s'ouvrent* (Paris: Grasset, 1980). What seems to have happened was that the Federation was particularly prone to anti-Russian sentiments, distrust of the leadership and many members voted against Marchais' report on the 1978 elections. Fiszbin either could not or would not bring the Federation under control and Paul Laurent (an old friend) was sent to apply a little martial law up-country.

Fiszbin's confused book does not make clear what took place but does give an insight into the mentality of the Communist *apparat*: Fiszbin at first went along with the party 'explanation' that he retired from the Federation 'because of illness' and, out of loyalty, voted his own condemnation for 'laxism, opportunism, lack of firmness and lack of class spirit'. The errors of which Fiszbin was accused were a pretext to restructure the refractory Federation and it was handed to his cousin Henri Malberg who took over as first secretary. After the publication of this book, and his consequent disgrace, Fiszbin went further and in October 1980 he and some supporters publicly objected to the way in which Marchais was made the Communist presidential candidate (an odd objection from somebody who had been in the party since 1946).

Marchais' bad result of the 1981 elections led to another wave of discontent inside the Communist Party: Fiszbin, capitalizing on this, founded a weekly paper *Rencontres communistes hebdo* in May 1981. This journal, which claimed to be within the Communist movement but which published the opinions of divergent or dissident activists, was pronounced 'factionalist' and Fiszbin was excluded from the party.

Fiszbin was soon joined by other ex-Communists and the journal claimed a circulation of 3,500 in 1984. In the Paris city elections of 1983 Fiszbin polled a creditable 9 per cent and in 1986 he was elected as a 'rencontres communiste' candidate on the Socialist list in Alpes-Maritimes (his associate Roger Fajnzylberg was elected to the regional council of Ile-de-France). Fiszbin's second book *Appel à l'auto-subversion* (Paris: Luffont, 1984) claims to speak to the Communist movement outside of the party and, at a time when the party itself was hostile to alliance with the Socialists, his position although marginal was important. Although he lost his seat in 1988 he remains an important bridge between the Socialists and disillusioned ex-Communists.

Bibliography

On the affair of the Paris Federation see R.W. Johnson, *The Long March of the French Left* (London: Macmillan, 1981).

DSB

FITERMAN, Charles (Chilek) (1933–   )

Born on 28 December 1933 in Saint-Etienne, Charles Fiterman is the son of an East European Jewish family which emigrated to France in the early inter-war period. Fiterman has been a leading member of the French Communist Party since the early 1970s: he entered the Central Committee in 1972 and the Political Bureau in 1976, when he also took charge of the party's influential Economics Commission.

He began his working life as an electrician in the Schneider factory in Saint-Etienne, and was active throughout the 1950s as the leader of the local Communist youth organization and from 1958 until 1962 as a full-time official of the CGT. In 1963 he moved to the Paris region and obtained a key post within the internal Communist Party hierarchy as director of the party's cadre school. In 1966 he became personal secretary to the reforming Communist leader, Waldeck Rochet. When Rochet retired from political life because of serious illness in 1970, Fiterman stayed on as secretary to the new leader, Georges Marchais, and from this time on his political career has been very much associated with that of the party's general secretary. He has often been described as Marchais's dauphin, although there is also some ill-concealed rivalry in their relationship.

Fiterman became a public figure when he was

elected as departmental councillor in 1973 in the Val-de-Marne, and he was later to win a seat as deputy for Choisy-le-Roi which he held briefly between 1978 and 1981. He is, however, much better known as a spokesman for the Communist Party leadership. Thus he played an important role as head of the Communist Party delegation in the renegotiation of the common programme of the left in 1977 and in the subsequent break-up of left unity. He was also associated with the pro-Soviet turnabout in Communist Party policy during the 1978–81 period.

His reputation as a hardliner was however attenuated after the victory of the left in the general and presidential elections in 1981, when he became one of the four Communist ministers in the first Mauroy government, occupying the post of minister of transport. During this period in office he proved to be a disciplined and persuasive defender of the policies of the coalition government, winning public popularity and even some grudging respect from his Socialist colleagues, despite his somewhat austere image in the media and some virulent campaigns against him (including a politicized road haulage strike in February 1984).

When the Communists refused to participate in the new Fabius government in the summer of 1984, Fiterman returned to his full-time party post, and was careful to distance himself from the growing opposition within the Communist Party. In what had become an internal crisis within the French Communist Party Fiterman none the less proceeded cautiously and avoided alienating any of the contradictory currents which were beginning to manifest themselves openly as the party confirmed its spectacular political decline. Credited with a more reforming vision than Georges Marchais, and certainly less tempestuous and unpredictable, Fiterman could be the compromise leader which the warring factions may agree on. Whatever his political future, he will remain the pure product of the Communist Party's internal career structure which demands low-profile diplomacy and above all unswerving discipline in toeing the party line(s).

Bibliography

Fiterman's role in the renegotiation of the common programme is discussed in R.W. Johnson, *The Long March of the French Left* (London: Macmillan, 1981). See also, in French, the fourth volume of P. Robrieux, *Histoire intérieure du parti communiste* (Paris: Fayard, 1984).

KD

FLANDIN, Pierre-Etienne (1889–1958)

Flandin descended from an affluent family associated with the liberal professions. He gained a doctorate in law and a diploma of the Ecole Libre des Sciences Politiques before qualifying as a lawyer. Somewhat less predictably, he trained as a pilot before World War One. Describing himself as *républicain de gauche*, he was elected deputy for the Yonne department at the minimum legal age of 25. He was re-elected throughout the inter-war period. His career in national politics, which began as secretary to Millerand, was furthered by his aeronautical expertise. He served on the relevant technical committee during the negotiations prior to the Treaty of Versailles. In 1920–1, he became under-secretary of state for aerial navigation and president of the Aero-Club de France. He held ministerial posts in a number of characteristically short-lived moderate cabinets. Minister of trade under François-Marsal in 1924 and twice under Tardieu in 1929–30, he held the finance portfolio under Laval in 1931–2 and that of public works under Doumergue in 1934. President of the Alliance Démocratique (ARD) from 1932 onwards, he was briefly prime minister between November 1934 and May 1935. The turning point in his political life was his resignation as minister of foreign affairs from the Sarraut cabinet in June 1936. This was motivated by his objections to the French mobilization during the Rhineland crisis. From then on, he was a consistent advocate of appeasement. He campaigned against war over Czechoslovakia and congratulated Hitler for saving the peace at Munich. As a result, the Alliance Démocratique split in September 1938.

Flandin opposed the declaration of war in 1939. He appeared at Vichy in due course, though he was not among the early arrivals. He advocated the election of Pétain (q.v.) to the presidency of the Third Republic rather than a change of political regime. In December 1940 he was appointed minister of state in charge of foreign affairs and vice-president of the Council of Ministers. The fact that he was replacing Laval at the helm was welcomed by the Allies as a sign that relations with Vichy could be normalized. In the labyrinth of Vichy politics, it is difficult to assess Flandin's actual contribution or even to define his intentions. He certainly maintained friendly contacts with Otto von Abetz, though Hitler held his appointment to have been a slight. Thus it remains unclear whether his resignation in February 1941 was due – as he later maintained – to his own refusal to cooperate more closely with the German authorities or to the fact that he was operating in a vacuum, systematically ignored by the Nazi establishment in occupied France. He withdrew to Algeria in October 1942 and was arrested as a collaborationist in December 1943 by the Free French. Although both Churchill and Roosevelt had intervened on his behalf, he remained in custody until January 1946. The High Court of Justice condemned him only to the symbolic loss of civic rights (*indignité nationale*). He failed to be elected to the Senate in 1952, but remained a departmental councillor in the Yonne and continued to be prominent in conservative politics.

Bibliography

Flandin, P.E. (1947), *Politique française 1919–40*, Paris: Editions Nouvelles.

MV

FLOQUET, Charles Thomas (1828–96)

Charles Floquet was a left-wing Republican, whose career under the Third Republic was most notable for his role in the Boulanger episode (1886–9). Floquet was a typical figure of the old-fashioned left, interested almost exclusively in political and religious rather than social questions.

Born to a Republican family in southern France, Floquet participated as a student in the 1848 revolution. As a lawyer and journalist, he was a leading member of the Republican opposition to Napoleon III, acting in several political trials, and serving as a candidate in parliamentary elections. When the Second Empire was overthrown, he was appointed as assistant to the mayor of Paris, and in 1871 was elected as deputy for the city. He resigned this post on the outbreak of the Commune, which put him in a difficult position: attempting to mediate between the two sides, he was briefly imprisoned by both.

After a period on the Paris municipal council, Floquet returned to the Chamber in 1876, and was a prominent member of the 'extreme left' in the early years of the Republic. He campaigned especially for an amnesty for the communards, and for thoroughgoing anticlerical policies; like many men of this type, he was an active Freemason. Known for his oratory and his combative views, Floquet was successful as a parliamentarian, acting as president of the Chamber in 1885–8 and 1889–93, but held office only once, as prime minister in 1888–9. General Boulanger (q.v.) had been elected as a deputy, and his anti-parliamentary campaign was at its height. Violent verbal duels between Floquet and Boulanger

led to a real duel, in which Floquet wounded the General. Floquet was still in office at the climax of the Boulangist movement in January 1889, when Boulanger's supporters urged him to exploit electoral victory in Paris and carry out a coup. Floquet's firmness helped to defeat this danger, and his government's last act was to abolish the list system of voting which Boulanger had exploited. Floquet's defence of democracy during this episode had kept him in office, but there had been little support, except from the extreme left, for his wider ambitions, which included a revision of the constitution to allow direct election of the Senate. He lost his Chamber seat in 1893 but returned to Parliament as a senator in 1894.

Bibliography

There is no biography of Floquet, but his role in the Boulanger affair may be studied in works like A. Dansette, *Le Boulangisme* (Paris: Librairie Académique Perrin, 1938) or F.H. Seager, *The Boulanger Affair, Political Crossroad of France 1886–1889* (Ithaca, New York: Cornell University Press, 1968).

RDA

FOCCART, Jacques Guillaume Louis Marie (né Koch) (1913–)

Jacques Foccart was born on 31 August 1913 at Ambrières-le-Grand (Mayenne) into a family of the *grande bourgeoisie*. From an early age he had had contacts with French overseas territories as his father had created a banana export business and married a Creole in Guadeloupe. His youth was therefore split between Mayenne and Guadeloupe. At the beginning of the war he was a sergeant in the French army and subsequently joined the Resistance under de Gaulle's banner. By the end of the war he had risen to the rank of lieutenant-colonel and he first met de Gaulle in June 1944 after the liberation of Laval. This was the beginning of a long association that was only to come to an end with the death of de Gaulle in 1970.

After the war Foccart embarked on a business career in import–export, but was also closely associated with de Gaulle when he founded the RPF (Rassemblement du Peuple Français) in 1947. He was an active member of the party, both in France and abroad, and sat on its National Council from the outset, becoming deputy general-secretary and subsequently general-secretary in 1954. In 1953 he organized de Gaulle's visit to eighteen African countries, thus enabling the latter to make the contacts which were to prove so important in the future. During de Gaulle's period out of the public eye, there are unconfirmed reports that Foccart was a member of France's counter-espionage services. What is certain however is that he made regular visits to France's colonies during this time, building on the many contacts he had made during the Resistance. On de Gaulle's return to power in 1958 he was thus perfectly placed to become his African specialist (conseiller technique chargé des affaires Africaines). In 1960 he became secretary-general of the Communauté Française and in 1961 secretary-general to the president with responsibility for African and Madagascan affairs. He was to retain this post until Pompidou's death in April 1974. He also remained a leading member of the Gaullist party throughout this period.

Africa was his primary interest and field of activity. He was regularly associated, by both political friends and foes, with France's secret 'networks', with her 'alternative' police, with the underground government agents (barbouzes) and with actual or attempted coups in Africa. He gained the confidence, however, of many of the leaders of newly independent francophone African states and was an important intermediary between them and the French president. He was removed from his post by Alain Poher during the interim period between Pompidou's death and the election of Valéry Giscard d'Estaing to the presidency in 1974 and was not recalled by the latter. His role in French political life was apparently at an end. He continued to retain an interest in francophone Africa, however, and travelled there frequently, either for his own business interests or as a representative for various French companies, such as Thomson CSF.

After the victory of the right at the March 1986 elections he made an unexpected return to French politics when he was appointed by Prime Minister Chirac as his personal adviser on African affairs. President Mitterrand having retained his own adviser on African affairs, Chirac clearly felt that Foccart's accumulated knowledge and experience of Africa would be invaluable during the 1986–8 period of 'cohabitation' which was just beginning.

Bibliography

Although there are allusions to Foccart in many works there is no study of his real influence.

TC

FOCH, Ferdinand, Marshal (1851–1929)

Foch's forebears were weavers and wool merchants, though his father opted for the civil service. Foch's immediate ancestors, as well as being devout Catholics, had been imbued with the Napoleonic tradition, and the two main influences in Foch's life were therefore present from an early age – religious devotion and military fervour. Foch volunteered for military service on the outbreak of war in 1870, and though he did not see action, the effect on a young aspiring soldier of the ignominious defeat of Napoleon III and of the loss of Alsace-Lorraine to Germany was significant.

Foch became an artillery officer in the army of the newly-founded Third Republic, but this regime suffered from a fundamental dilemma: it needed its army for its policy of ultimate revenge on Germany (*revanchisme*), yet remained highly suspicious of its anti-Republican tendencies. Foch played a major role in shaping the strategy and tactics of the new French army. He became a major proponent of an assertive military policy emphasizing the spirit of the offensive pushed home at all costs. Foch was determined to inculcate this spirit into the French officer corps, which he did as chief instructor at the Ecole Supérieure de Guerre (Staff College) from 1895 to 1900. On the other hand, Third Republic politicians deeply distrusted those elements in the army whose loyalty appeared to be not to the Republic but to other institutions or values – the Catholic Church, anti-egalitarianism, unrestrained nationalism. Foch's career suffered from the government's desire to bring the army to heel in the wake of the Dreyfus affair, though later a degree of reconciliation allowed him to become director of the Staff College, where he continued to indoctrinate officers with the offensive spirit.

This doctrine proved extremely costly in the first few weeks of the First World War – Foch lost his only son and his son-in-law on 22 August 1914. The advent of trench warfare and three unsuccessful offensives in Artois in 1915 led Foch to revise his views, and he had strong reservations about the 1916 Somme offensive.

If the synthesis of Republic and army appeared to be complete by Foch's appointment as Allied Generalissimo in April 1918 and the final victory in November 1918 to which it greatly contributed, nevertheless two developments in the last years of Foch's life significantly reduced his influence on national affairs, despite his elevation to the rank of Marshal of France in August 1918. One was Clemenceau's rejection of Foch's post-war demand for full separation of the German-speaking Rhineland: when the Treaty of Versailles imposed the lesser condition of permanent demilitarization but temporary occupation, Foch boycotted the signing ceremony in disgust. The second was the emergence of a new image, at odds with Foch's pre-1916 approach, of the French army as cautious and defensive, personified in the public mind by Pétain, the saviour of Verdun and the pacifier of the 1917 mutinies. Foch died in 1929, but already the doctrine of static defence had won the day, leading ultimately to the defeat of 1940, and the taking of power by Pétain.

Bibliography

Foch as military commander is well covered in the book of that name by General Sir James Marshall-Cornwall (London: Batsford, 1972). A good recent biography in French is J. Autin: *Foch* (Paris: Perrin, 1987).

MS

FONTAINE, André Lucien Georges (1921–)

André Fontaine has been a leading journalist at *Le Monde* virtually since the newspaper's creation at the end of the Second World War. He joined the paper in 1947 and became head of the foreign desk in 1951. In 1969 he became editor (*Rédacteur en chef*) under the new head of the paper, Jacques Fauvet (q.v.). He occupied this position until 1985 when he was appointed to the top post of editor-in-chief (*directeur*). He is also the author of various books, principally on foreign affairs: *L'Alliance atlantique à l'heure du dégel* (1960), *Histoire de la guerre froide* (1966), *La Guerre civile froide* (1969), *Le Dernier quart du siècle* (1976), *La France au bois dormant* (1978), *Un Seul lit pour deux rêves* (1981) and *Sortir de l'hexagonie* (1984).

Fontaine undoubtedly made a major contribution to the national and international prestige of *Le Monde* with his well informed articles on foreign and defence matters. However, his most important task came in 1985 at a time when the newspaper was going through a period of major crisis. While the victory of Mitterrand and the Socialists in the 1981 elections had been welcomed by *Le Monde*, it had led to the paper becoming less critical of government policy than had been the case during the 1970s. Circulation declined with *Le Monde* losing readers, particularly in the younger age bracket, to the revamped

Libération newspaper of Serge July. At the same time the changeover to new printing technology had imposed huge costs on the paper. Between 1982 and 1985 *Le Monde* lurched from financial to managerial crisis, culminating in the resignation of Fauvet's successor, André Laurens, as editor-in-chief in December 1984.

Under Fontaine's stewardship the decline in circulation experienced in the first half of the decade was halted and then reversed. Improvements in print quality and the introduction of new features and supplements are only two aspects of the revamped *Le Monde*, which despite its recent problems remains the most prestigious newspaper in France. Fontaine has also presided over the expansion of *Le Monde*'s activities into other media fields, notably private local radio which became legalized in France at the end of 1981. In 1987 the newspaper was part of the failed bid led by Hachette to take control of the newly privatized television channel, TF1.

RK

FOUCHET, Christian (1911–74)

Born into a military family, Fouchet took a degree in law before studying at the Ecole Libre des Sciences Politiques, with the intention of pursuing a career in diplomacy. He was one of the very earliest to join General de Gaulle in London (19 June 1940). Thereafter he served as a war correspondent with the Free French before undertaking several diplomatic missions from 1944 to 1947. He then joined the newly-created Gaullist movement (Rassemblement du Peuple Français – RPF) and was appointed to its executive committee. In 1948 he became RPF organizer for the Parisian region, and was elected as a Gaullist deputy for Paris in 1951. With de Gaulle's authorization, he entered the Mendès France government (1954) as minister of Moroccan and Tunisian affairs. Failing to be re-elected in 1956, Fouchet returned to diplomacy and was ambassador to Denmark from 1958 to 1962. He also presided over the EEC's abortive effort to establish a closer political union (the so-called Fouchet Plan, 1961–2). After the signing of the Evian Agreements, he was appointed high-commissioner of the Republic in Algeria, with the task of organizing the referendum on self-determination and of establishing Algeria's provisional government. He held office as minister successively of information (September 1962), education (December 1962) and of the interior (April 1967), and was thus responsible for law and order during May 1968. He was then opposed to any concessions, in marked contrast with Pompidou's more flexible approach. Although re-elected in the Gaullists' landslide victory of June 1968, he was dropped from the government. Out of office for the rest of his life, he became increasingly critical of the materialistic/conservative tendencies in Gaullism after de Gaulle. He finally resigned from the party in January 1971 whilst still remaining within the governmental majority.

Fouchet's career is fairly typical of the Gaullist 'baron', deriving his prominence from his services to Gaullism from the 1940s onward. Although he had a relatively hardline image, his own brand of Gaullism was not entirely conservative, in matters such as decolonization, for example. His personal loyalty to de Gaulle lasted to the end of his leader's life and beyond. Regarding himself as the defender of pure Gaullism, he became estranged from the Gaullist party in its post-Gaullian development. His contribution to the RPF's rise was outstanding, and it was an achievement in which he took great pride. The longest-serving education minister since Jules Ferry (four years and four months), he also achieved substantial reforms in this domain, the most significant being the creation of the *carte scolaire* (the forward planning of educational resources), of comprehensive secondary education via the *collège d'enseignement secondaire*, the reform of the *baccalauréat*, the reorganization of university education, and, above all, the creation of the university institutes of technology (IUT).

Bibliography

Fouchet's activity as minister of education may be studied as part of the overall development of post-war French education in the following:

Fraser, W.R. (1971), *Reforms and Restraints in Modern French Education*, London: Routledge & Kegan Paul.

Halls, W.D. (1976), *Education, Culture and Politics in Modern France*, Oxford: Pergamon.

Lewis, H.D. (1985), *The French Education System*, London: Croom Helm.

While the Fouchet Plan can be seen in the context of French foreign policy since the Second World War in general studies such as G. de Carmoy, *The Foreign Policies of France*, (Chicago: Chicago University Press, 1970) (translated from the French), more specific studies include A. Silj, *Europe's Political Puzzle, a Study of the Fouchet Negotiations and the 1963 Veto* (Harvard: Harvard University Press, 1967); R. Bloes, *Le 'Plan Fouchet'*

et le problème de l'Europe politique (Bruges: College of Europe, 1970), (very detailed and with a substantial bibliography). On Fouchet himself, *Le Monde* of 13 August 1974, containing his obituary and an appreciation by P. Viansson-Ponté, may usefully be consulted. The best and most revealing source is undoubtedly Fouchet's own memoirs, in two volumes, *Mémoires d'hier et du lendemain* (Paris: Plon, 1971–3).

APK

FOURCADE, Marie-Madeleine (1909–89)

Born in Marseilles in 1909, Marie-Madeleine Bridou (Fourcade after her second marriage) was educated at the Couvent des Oiseaux in Paris, and the Ecole Normale de Musique. In 1929 she married an army officer, the future General Méric, and subsequently went with him to Morocco where he was working for the secret service. In the late 1930s she got a job as assistant to Commandant Georges Loustaunau-Lacau, an officer of pronounced anti-Communist views whose right-wing attitudes were expressed in the monthly magazine, *L'Ordre National*, which Fourcade directed for him. After the armistice in 1940 Loustaunau-Lacau set up an underground intelligence service, 'Alliance', directly linked to the British agencies, which Marie-Madeleine Fourcade ran whilst he maintained his cover of directing veterans' organizations. When Loustaunau-Lacau was arrested in July 1941 Fourcade took over command of the whole network, organizing highly successful intelligence groups throughout France. After a number of arrests of 'Alliance' members, Fourcade decentralized the movement and changed the pseudonyms of her agents, giving them names of animals – she was 'Hedgehog' – hence the title of her memoirs, 'Noah's Ark'.

In Resistance terms, Fourcade's achievements were remarkable. She had commanded one of the most important intelligence networks in France which, among other contributions, had provided a detailed map of German defences around the Cotentin peninsula in Normandy. Her bravery was recognized by a number of awards, including the Legion of Honour, and she became the most famous woman intelligence agent in France.

In the post-war years she used her considerable energy to further the political cause of General de Gaulle. With her second husband, Hubert Fourcade, she organized a massive petition and letter campaign during the Algerian crisis, to persuade President

Coty to recall de Gaulle to power. She was one of the founder members of the Gaullist group, Convention Républicaine, which formed part of the nucleus for the first Gaullist party of the Fifth Republic, the Union pour la Nouvelle République (UNR).

Later, in 1979, she stood on the Gaullist list for the first direct elections to the European Parliament. The list, called *La Défense des Intérêts de la France en Europe*, allowed candidates to replace each other in alphabetical order as representatives, and Fourcade sat in the European Parliament between 1981 and 1982.

Bibliography

Fourcade's memoirs are *Noah's Ark* (London: Allen and Unwin, 1973; New York, 1974) abridged and translated by Kenneth Morgan from the French, *L'Arche de Noé*, 2 vols (Paris: Fayard, 1968). There is some information on her in M.L. Rossiter, *Women in the Resistance* (New York: Praeger, 1986).

HF

FRANCHET d'ESPEREY, Louis Félix Marie François, Marshal (1856–1942)

A professional soldier, Franchet d'Esperey was a corps commander at the outbreak of war in August 1914. He participated in the move by the French Fifth Army, together with the small British Expeditionary Force, to exploit a gap left in their line by the advancing Germans. The manoeuvre – the Battle of the Marne – caused the withdrawal of the German right flank, and the final failure of the Schlieffen Plan for quick victory over France. In September 1914 Franchet d'Esperey took over command of the Fifth Army on Lanrezac's dismissal, and later commanded army groups; British troops gave him the affectionate nickname of 'Desperate Frankie'. In 1917 he was an energetic proponent of the notion that the French army mutinies were not spontaneous disaffection caused by the obtuse policies of the high command, but a Bolshevik plot responsible for the failure of the Nivelle offensive.

In June 1918, Franchet d'Esperey was sent to command the Salonika Army, where Clemenceau, the French prime minister, without consulting Lloyd George, ordered him to go on the offensive. His attack on the Salonika front in September 1918 was so successful that it put Bulgaria out of the war, occupied Belgrade, and threatened Austria-Hungary with invasion. The process was started which led to the 11 November armistice on the western front and though Franchet d'Esperey's idea of marching on Constantinople at the head of the victorious French army was strenuously resisted by Lloyd George, he had the consolation of being made Marshal of France.

Having been horrified by the election of a parliamentary *Cartel des Gauches* in 1924, but being as yet uncertain of what to do about it, his disenchantment with the Third Republic regime led him by the 1930s to be interested in secret rightist anti-Republican groups. On the romantic fringes of the extreme right were the Corvignolles, with cells inside the army and led by an aide of Pétain from 1935 to 1938. Franchet d'Esperey, deeply involved as a fund-raiser, was one of the main links between this organization and the more overtly terrorist Comité Secret d'Action Révolutionnaire, which ran the Mouvement Social d'Action Révolutionnaire, whose members were called 'hooded ones' (*cagoulards*) and whose aim was to set up a regime like Mussolini's.

As a Marshal of France, Franchet d'Esperey was a life member of the Supreme War Council (Conseil Supérieur de Guerre) from the 1920s, but took a less and less active part in the public affairs of a regime which had adopted defensive military policies. In late 1937, however, he was a party to a decision against the scrapping of two cavalry regiments on the grounds that horses could still be vital for reconnaissance purposes in war. 1940 saw him still present in the military corridors of power, though confined to a wheelchair. He died in 1942.

Bibliography

Franchet d'Esperey was co-author of volume 8 of *Histoire de la nation française* (Paris: Plon, 1927), entitled *Histoire militaire et navale*, in which his views on military matters are apparent. A general biography is P. Azan, *Franchet d'Esperey* (Paris: Flammarion, 1949).

MS

FRACHON, Benoît (1893–1975)

One of the major trade union figures of the twentieth century, Benoît Frachon was the leader of the Confédération Générale du Travail (CGT) from the end of the Second World War until 1967 when he was succeeded by Georges Séguy (q.v.).

After leaving school at the age of 13, he became an

apprentice in the engineering industry and three years later he joined a trade union. After some years of trade union activity he became general secretary in 1924 for the Loire area of the increasingly pro-Communist Confédération Générale du Travail Unitaire (CGTU) which had split from the more reformist CGT in 1921. From 1933 onwards he was the *de facto* general secretary of the CGTU. When in 1936 these two confederations merged into one organization, the reconstituted CGT, he became one of the joint general secretaries, the other being Léon Jouhaux (q.v.). He was a key figure in the trade union movement at the time of the strike wave which coincided with the election of the Popular Front government under Léon Blum (q.v.) in 1936 and the subsequent negotiations which were to lead to a number of laws introducing the forty-hour week, paid holidays, workplace representatives and improved collective bargaining procedures.

He joined the French Communist Party (PCF) as soon as it was founded in 1920 and became a member of the Central Committee in 1926 and a member of the Political Bureau and Secretariat two years later. He officially resigned from these posts in 1936 because holding political office was incompatible with holding office in the reconstituted CGT, but he continued to enjoy an intimate relationship with the leadership of the PCF.

Frachon will be remembered for his activities in the French Resistance at the time of the German occupation. Along with other Communists he was expelled from the CGT in 1939 but when the Vichy regime introduced a set of corporatist labour laws banning trade union activities, he found himself at the head of a clandestine trade union movement which sprang up in opposition. His position was reinforced when Léon Jouhaux, the other major trade union leader of the time, was sent to an internment camp. He was the driving force behind the decision taken in 1943 to sign the *Accords de Perreux* which aimed to re-establish a united trade union confederation. Moreover, along with Jacques Duclos (q.v.), he was instrumental in ensuring the survival of the clandestine French Communist Party whose general secretary, Maurice Thorez (q.v.), spent the war in Moscow.

By the end of the war Frachon and his supporters were in a dominant position within the CGT which was becoming ever more identified with the French Communist Party, with the result that Jouhaux and a number of non-Communists resigned from the CGT and set up a rival trade union confederation, Force Ouvrière (FO). The CGT was thrust on to the defensive and was to spend the 1950s in isolation. It

was not until the 1960s that its membership stabilized and it started to emerge from its isolation.

In poor health, Frachon stood down as general secretary of the CGT at the 26th Conference in 1967. However this was not the end of his trade union days. When the strike wave broke in May 1968 he participated in the subsequent negotiations with the government and the employers' organization, the Conseil National du Patronat Français, which led to wage increases and the reinforcement of trade union rights. Afterwards he played a significant role in ensuring that the CGT was not disavowed by the strikers.

Bibliography

There is no biography of Benoît Frachon in English. He has written an autobiographical work in two volumes, *Au rhythme des jours* (Paris: Editions Sociales, 1967) and is the subject of a profile in the 28th volume of Jean Maitron (ed.) *Dictionnaire bibliographique du mouvement ouvrier français* (Paris: Les Editions Ouvrières, 1986).

JB

FRANÇOIS-MARSAL, Frédéric (1874–1958)

François-Marsal was born in Lorraine, went to the Lycée Louis-le-Grand and in 1894 graduated from the military academy of Saint-Cyr (premier in the infantry class). From 1900 to 1904 he was in Indo-China on the personal staff of the governor, Paul Doumer but in 1905 he went into banking, first in Lyons and then in Paris. In 1914 he was mobilized, from 1915 to 1917 he served on Joffre's staff, in 1917 he served on de Castelnau's staff and later that year he joined Clemenceau's office to deal with financial matters. He was awarded the Croix de Guerre and Légion d'Honneur.

Although he returned to banking at the end of the First World War and wrote for the *Echo de Paris* (as 'Custos'), he was in the French delegation to the Versailles Conference working on economic issues. When Millerand became prime minister, François-Marsal was made minister of finance, an innovation because he was not then in Parliament. He remained at that post from 20 January 1920 to 16 January 1921, carrying out a policy of deflation. As a member of Georges Leygues' government (24 September 1920 to 15 January 1921) he was one of the signatories to the pact restoring the Republic's relations with the Vatican and he supported military aid to Poland with material aid (when the Assembly was in recess).

François-Marsal was elected to the Senate for the Cantal department in 1921 (this was a disputed election which required validation by the Senate) and represented it until 1930. On 29 March 1924 he was back at the Finance Ministry in the Poincaré cabinet. From 9 to 14 June 1924 he was prime minister. After the victory of the SFIO and Radicals in the 'Cartel des Gauches' President Millerand cast round for a prime minister who was not from the majority. François-Marsal's minority government fell on 10 June when Herriot's motion of censure was voted by 327 votes to 217. The government's sole act had been to read a statement from Millerand stating his conception of the president's role. Millerand resigned but François-Marsal remained head of the executive until a new president was elected.

After Herriot's victory François-Marsal went on to the offensive against the economic policy of the 'Cartel des Gauches' in speeches in the Senate and in his journalism but his position as a technocrat with no political base made him irrelevant. In 1929 he tried to gain election to the Senate from Paris but after an unpleasant campaign which featured unproven allegations against his business dealings he lost and quit politics.

Bibliography

François-Marsal's oeuvre is vast but most of it is ephemeral, polemical and concerned with now forgotten financial details. F. François-Marsal, *Les Finances* (Paris: Dubois et Bauer, 1921) is representative.

DSB

FRANÇOIS-PONCET, Jean (1928–)

Jean François-Poncet is one of Raymond Barre's closest advisers and supporters in the Union pour la Démocratie Française (UDF). Son of André François-Poncet, one of France's most distinguished diplomats of the 1930s and the early years of the Fourth Republic, he studied both in Paris and at Harvard and graduated top of his year from the prestigious Ecole Nationale d'Administration (ENA). In the last years of the Fourth Republic, as a member of the private office (cabinet) of the junior foreign minister, the Radical Maurice Faure, he was closely involved in the negotiations leading to the setting up of the EEC and EURATOM. In the early years of the Fifth Republic, his lack of sympathy with Gaullism (and in particular with de Gaulle's European policy) was to prove an obstacle to his promotion in the Ministry of Foreign Affairs and, after a series of relatively minor diplomatic postings and a presidential veto of his appointment as ambassador in Madrid, he spent several years working in the private sector (successfully restoring an industrial 'lame duck' to health and prosperity). Under Giscard d'Estaing, he returned to the public service as secretary general of the presidential staff. In 1978 Giscard d'Estaing appointed him minister of foreign affairs, a post he held until Giscard's electoral defeat and the resignation of the Barre government in 1981. In appointing this career diplomat and close personal adviser as foreign minister, Giscard not only followed an established Fifth Republic tradition and marked his determination to maintain a close involvement in all of France's foreign policy decisions but also showed his desire to extend his presidential base towards the political centre. Twice in the 1980s François-Poncet's accession to high office has seemed to hang on the result of a presidential election: after being one of Giscard d'Estaing's possible prime ministers if the latter had been re-elected in 1981, he was favourite to become prime minister, had Barre been successful in the 1988 presidential election.

Jean François-Poncet, the archetypal urbane and wealthy Parisian *grand bourgeois*, has established a powerful regional political base in the traditionally Radical stronghold of the Lot-et-Garonne department in south-west France, which he has represented in the Senate since 1983 (sitting as a member of the centrist 'democratic left' group), and of whose General Council he has been president since 1978. In the latter capacity and as president of the Association for the Development of Aquitaine (ADA), he has been particularly concerned with the economic challenges facing south-west France as a result of Spain's entry into the EEC (about which he had expressed serious reservations). He had been strongly tipped to succeed the latter-day 'Duke of Aquitaine', Jacques Chaban-Delmas, as president of the Aquitaine Regional Council, but in the event, with the implementation of the recent legislation limiting the number of elective posts which can be held simultaneously, he preferred the presidency of the departmental General Council to that of the Regional Council and hence did not stand for election on Chaban's resignation in July 1988. This is further evidence (if further evidence were needed) of where power really lies after the Socialists' decentralization legislation.

Jean François-Poncet is also a Professor at the Institut d'Etudes Politiques in Paris (and as such is an academic colleague of Raymond Barre). Since 1984, he has contributed regular editorials on foreign affairs to *Le Figaro*, displaying caution in respect of recent Soviet disarmament proposals and, on the European Community, enthusiasm for the Single European Act and '1992', 'with Great Britain if possible, without her if necessary'.

Although often seen as a loyal, highly intellegent, hard-working and authoritarian technocrat (he ruffled not a few feathers in the conservative Foreign Affairs Ministry between 1978 and 1981), a tough negotiator rather than an effective orator, he is not without political ambition. However, the centre-ground of French politics is currently fully occupied and Jean François-Poncet, more at home in political 'reflection groups' than in structured political parties, does not possess the support of a strong party machine. His political future may well depend on that of his friend and colleague at Sciences Po, Raymond Barre.

Bibliography

Jean François-Poncet is the subject of a chapter in Alain Duhamel, *Les Prétendants* (Paris: Gallimard, 1983, revised edition 1985) and of a section in Jean-Louis Rémilleux, *Les Barristes* (Paris: Albin Michel, 1987). For his role in the implementation of Giscard d'Estaing's foreign policy between 1978 and 1981, see D.L. Hanley, A.P. Kerr and N.H. Waites, *Contemporary France. Politics and Society since 1945* (London: Routledge & Kegan Paul, 2nd Edition 1984) and J.R. Frears, *France in the Giscard Presidency* (London: George Allen & Unwin, 1981). For Jean François-Poncet's conception of France's foreign policy, see his article, 'Diplomatie française: quel cadre conceptuel?' in *Politique Internationale*, vol. 6, autumn–winter 1979–80, pp. 9–20 and in *Le Monde* (12 December 1978).

HE

FRÉDÉRIC-DUPONT, Edouard Frédéric Dupont (1902–)

Edouard Frédéric-Dupont reigned for over half a century over his fief on the left bank of Paris with a combination of unwavering conservatism and unflagging attention to constituents' interests. A general's son, born in the 7th *arrondissement* in 1902, he studied at the Ecole Libre des Sciences Politiques and became a lawyer at the Court of Appeal in 1926. He entered politics as a conservative councillor for his home *arrondissement* in 1933. Wearing his councillor's sash, he featured prominently in the anti-parliamentary riot of 6 February 1934. But in 1936 he himself entered parliament – as an opponent of the Popular Front. In 1940 he voted full powers to Marshal Pétain, remaining a councillor under German occupation until 1943. One of the rare conservatives to survive the war politically, he was elected to the Constituent Assemblies in 1945–6 and throughout the Fourth Republic. A founder-member of the right-wing Parti Républicain de la Liberté (PRL), he rallied to de Gaulle on the formation of the RPF in 1947, deserting him for the more orthodox conservatism of the Action Républicaine et Sociale (ARS) in 1952. Meanwhile, he tirelessly nursed his constituency. His most celebrated achievement was the abolition of the *cordon*, by which late-returning residents roused *concièrges* to admit them. Ever after he revelled in his title of 'deputy for the *concièrges*' and they reputedly became his most loyal supporters. His devotion to local interests once took the form of asking a parliamentary question when a constituent was refused a post as lavatory attendant. So it was that for decades he was an arbiter of the fortunes of the right on the left bank.

Ferociously anti-Communist, he was a diehard advocate of fighting on in Indo-China. As the situation deteriorated he was brought into the Laniel cabinet in 1954 as minister for Indo-China. The gamble failed; the government fell twelve days later – but ever after Frédéric-Dupont bore the treasured title *ancien ministre*. He fought the Geneva Settlement, then became an ardent defender of *Algérie Française*. In May 1958 he called for de Gaulle's return, surviving the transition to the Fifth Republic as a Gaullist independent. As de Gaulle steered towards 'abandoning' Algeria Frédéric-Dupont again broke with him. However, in 1962 his opposition to the peace settlement stretched constituents' loyalty too far; he met his only electoral defeat. Yet in 1967 he had returned, trouncing de Gaulle's foreign minister, Couve de Murville, and becoming an associate member of the Gaullist group. Still a Paris and regional councillor, in 1983 he became mayor of his native *arrondissement*. Sensing that the Gaullists would drop him for a younger man in 1986 he deftly switched allegiance to the far-right National Front, gaining easy re-election. Now *doyen d'âge* of the Assembly, though nominally in opposition, he gave skilfully calculated voting support to the Chirac government. He reaped his reward in 1988 when a change in the electoral system spelled the doom of the National Front's parliamentary representation, emerging effortlessly with the Gaullist label yet again to retain his seat. To the last he was constant both to his record of having 'no enemies to the right' and to the opportunism which made him the arch political survivor.

Bibliography

There is no full-length study but *Le Monde* published a profile on 27–8 April 1986 and he features in a constituency study by M. Harrison, 'Paris 5: Safe seat', in *Political Studies*, vol. 7, no. 2, June 1959, pp. 147–56.

MH

FREY, Roger (1913–   )

Born in New Caledonia, Frey went to the select Stanislas College in Paris (where he played rugby alongside his future Gaullist colleague, Alexandre Sanguinetti – q.v.) and then returned to Noumea to run the family firm. After distinguished though obscure, wartime service with the Free French, he was sent on undercover missions by de Gaulle in 1945–6 and began an association with Gaullism that lasted throughout his career. He played an important administrative role in the Rassemblement Pour la France (the Gaullist movement of the Fourth Republic), became a member of the Assembly of the French Union in 1952 and was secretary of the Gaullist parliamentary group in the dog days of the mid-1950s.

With the political drama of 1958, Frey's career took off. He was involved in the clandestine side of Gaullist activity in the May events (joining Soustelle (q.v.) in Algiers via Spain and broadcasting coded messages that were meaningless but alarming) and then became a member of the official consultative constitutional committee. He played a key role in the establishment and development of the Union Pour la Nouvelle République which would become the corner stone of Gaullist electoral success in the 1960s.

His ministerial career began in 1959 when Debré (q.v.) appointed him minister of information but it was as minister of the interior for 1961 to 1967 that he acquired both fame and notoriety. The first period of his office was marked by the political violence surrounding the end of French Algeria and Frey showed vigour and determination in rooting out subversion, from both right and left. At the time of the army insurrection in Algiers (22–4 April 1961), he arrested a number of army and civilian conspirators on the mainland and prevented a paratroop insurrection. Although the government's policy was opposed most bitterly by the anti-independence Organisation de l'Armée Secrète (OAS), Frey attracted much criticism from the left for his handling of the protest. Two incidents in particular stood out. In October 1961 the banning of pro-independence demonstrations in Paris led to the death of scores of Algerians (many bodies were fished out of the Seine) and four months later, in February 1962, eight people were crushed to death in the Charonne metro station when police over-reacted to another prohibited demonstration. Frey refused an enquiry and at one point even blamed the deaths on OAS agents disguised as police. Such events – and the circumstances of the disappearance and death of the Moroccan opposition leader Ben Barka in 1966 – contributed to the very negative image that Frey came to have among liberals, an image compounded by his taste for secrecy and over-smart suits. But it was an extraordinarily difficult time to be responsible for order and Frey did manage to achieve the long overdue reform of the administration of the Paris region.

Frey had been elected a Paris deputy in 1962. In 1967 he became minister of state, charged with relations with Parliament, a position he held until 1969 when Chaban-Delmas (q.v.) gave him responsibility for regional reform. He left government in 1972. Less than two years later, the soon-to-die Pompidou (q.v.) made him president of the Constitutional Council. The appointment of such a prominent (and executive-minded) Gaullist alarmed those who believed that the Constitutional Council should not be the watchdog of executive privilege. Yet under his presidency – and helped by the 1974 reform which opened up access to the Council to parliamentarians – the Council showed increasing independence and concern for civil rights. Measures attempting to strengthen identity controls and weaken the rights of illegal immigrants were quashed, as were some articles of the right's controversial security and liberty law of 1981. Despite some criticism from the left, Frey handled the reforms of the 1981 Socialist government with tact. By the time he retired, in 1983, the suspicion and hostility which his first career as minister had provoked had to some extent disappeared in assessments of his second career as guardian of the constitution.

Bibliography

A secretive man, Frey has written no memoirs. Contrasting accounts of his time at the Interior Ministry can be found in C. Melnik *1000 Jours à Matignon* (Paris: Grasset, 1988) and M. Papon, *Les Chevaux du pouvoir* (Paris: Plon, 1988).

DSB/PM

DE FREYCINET, Charles-Louis de Saulces de (1828–1923)

Born at Foix (Ariège) and a civil engineer by training, de Freycinet was to become one of the most experienced and shrewd of Third Republic politicians. He was a member of nine ministries, and four times president of the Council in a career which began under Gambetta at the War Ministry in the government of national defence (1870–1). A specialist in military matters and in public works who served in the civil service *ponts et chaussées* division, he contributed a daily article on military affairs to Gambetta's *République française*, and he was to find time, at the latter's instigation, to write *La Guerre en Province pendant le Siège de Paris* (1871) justifying the tactics of the War Ministry. A senator in 1876, his political career began in earnest in the aftermath of MacMahon's defeat in 1877. A protégé of Jules Grévy and a man of flexible convictions, Freycinet was not over-obsessed with ideology, and soon became an indispensable member of most of the ministerial combinations which filled the next few years. The anchor-man of many a ministry, and a man whom Grévy preferred to Gambetta or Ferry, he first drew attention to himself when, as minister of public works, he inspired and organized a vast plan for ports, canals and railway building (the Freycinet plan).

A Protestant like Waddington whom he replaced in December 1879, Freycinet was to be a safe, even a timid prime minister; lacking in firmness and conviction over the Ferry religious reforms of March 1880, he fell through trying to please both sides. He steered clear of Gambetta's 'great ministry' (*grand ministère*), securing thereby his future career as a man of 'consensus' and a conciliator. He filled the Foreign Ministry post in his own second ministry (1882), but his timid policy in Egypt gave the upper hand there to the British. The first civilian to hold office as minister of war, Freycinet served in three successive cabinets between 1888 and 1893, but it was a measure of his careful approach that his work

on the reorganization of the army, and his pressure for short but universal military service mooted in 1872, only bore fruit in 1889. Always a safe choice if an unadventurous one, he gained much support against Ferry in the presidential election of 1887, before Sadi Carnot (q.v.) was elected on a second ballot.

His career continued in the quieter waters of the Senate until 1920 and he played an influential role in the First World War. Ever the discreet parliamentarian, and a guarded memorialist, his *Souvenirs 1878–1893* (1912) are a useful account of government under the Third Republic, and demonstrate by their lack of polemics those qualities of middle-of-the-road and unexciting moderation which had ensured for Freycinet a long period in political life.

Bibliography

There is little in English on Freycinet, but a good conspectus is to be found in T. Zeldin, *France 1848–1945*; especially the volume entitled *Politics and Anger* (Oxford: Oxford University Press, 1979) and also Hector Depasse, *de Freycinet* (Paris: A. Quantin, 1983).

ACR

FROSSARD, Louis-Oscar (often wrongly referred to as Ludovic-Oscar) (1889–1946)

Frossard, born 5 March 1889 in Foussemagne (Territoire de Belfort), the son of a small farmer with patriotic Republican beliefs, was from his early days drawn almost instinctively (as he later said) into a militant internationalist socialism. As a student at the Ecole Normale Supérieur he was reprimanded for singing the 'Internationale'. During his national service, in 1911, he was stripped of his sub-lieutenant grade for antimilitarist propaganda. He became a primary school teacher in the Territoire de Belfort and continued his Socialist activities as a leading member of the Belfort Federation, campaigning publicly against militarism. In 1913 he married the Socialist activist Rose Pétrequin. In the same year he was brought before a university disciplinary board and dismissed for his part in a demonstration against a military procession.

Deprived of a career, Frossard's life became even more closely bound up with his politics. He founded the local Federation's paper, *Le Socialiste Belfortain*, which became *Germinal*. He stood for Parliament in Belfort in April 1914 but was not elected. Called up in August 1914, Frossard initially supported the war effort and ministerial participation, despite his internationalist standpoint, but as the party split over the issue Frossard's position changed and he became associated with the group around Jean Longuet and was elected on to the SFIO general secretariat at the 1918 Congress. A candidate on the unsuccessful list headed by Longuet (q.v.) at the 1919 legislative elections, Frossard was nevertheless in a key position within the party. At first opposed to the reconstruction of a Third International, Frossard was delegated together with Marcel Cachin to visit Moscow to negotiate conditions of entry. After this visit Frossard argued for membership of the Third International.

His own increasingly flexible approach to socialism did not stand him in good stead for future work within the new Communist Party. He remained on the general secretariat for only two years. Frequently called to order by the leaders of the Third International, Frossard refused to give over his place in the leadership of the party to the left. When the International demanded the expulsion from the French party of non-revolutionary elements, Frossard resigned from the secretariat in January 1923 and left the party later that year. In 1924 he joined the Parti Social-Communiste, a group of ex-Communists, and tried unsuccessfully to get himself elected to Parliament on a *Cartel des Gauches* list headed by Pierre Laval. He moved back towards the SFIO, collaborating with Longuet to launch *La Nouvelle Revue Socialiste* in December 1925. In 1928 he was elected as Socialist deputy for Martinique and soon carved out a name for himself in Parliament as an eloquent speaker. In the 1932 elections, he abandoned his seat for the possibility of one nearer to home and was elected deputy for Lure (Haute-Saône). In the same year he became mayor of Ronchamp.

After his election to Parliament Frossard drifted increasingly to the right of the party. In June 1935 he acted independently of the party in accepting the labour portfolio under Fernand Bouisson and then Laval. In 1936 he was re-elected as an 'independent socialist' against a Socialist Party candidate. He became minister of state and minister of public works in 1938 but resigned in protest against attempts to weaken the forty-hour week law. Between March and July 1940 he was minister of information and then of public works. In July 1940 he voted in favour of the transfer of powers to Marshal Pétain, who later invited him into his government. Frossard continued to serve as mayor for Ronchamp until his death in Paris on 11 February 1946.

Bibliography

Profiles of Frossard are to be found in Jean Maitron, *Dictionnaire biographique du mouvement ouvrier français* (third part: 1871–1914) (Paris: Editions Ouvrières 1973–77), vol. XII (1974), p. 230; Jean Maitron and Claude Pennetier, *Dictionnaire biographique du mouvement ouvrier français* (fourth part: 1914–39) (Paris: Editions Ouvrières, 1982–), vol. XXVIII (1986) pp. 308–10. A dossier on Frossard exists in the Archives de l'Assemblée Nationale.

SM

G

GAILLARD, Félix Achille d'Aimé (1919–70)

Félix Gaillard was one of the brightest political lights to emerge in the Fourth Republic. At 38 he was the youngest prime minister France had ever known, but his political career was cut short, first by the demise of the Fourth Republic and then by his death at the age of 50 – his promise unfulfilled.

The son of a Parisian company director, Gaillard's brilliance was clear as a student. He was a doctor of law at 20 and passed out top in the examination for the Inspection des Finances. After a distinguished career in the Resistance, he was recruited as Jean Monnet's assistant at the Commissariat Général du Plan. But he soon turned to politics and was elected to represent the Charente department as a Radical in November 1946, being re-elected at each election until his death, and serving also as mayor of Barbezieux.

Gaillard quickly distinguished himself in the National Assembly as one of the Radicals' young turks on the right of the party alongside Daladier (q.v.) and Bourgès-Maunoury, making a substantial contribution to debates on economic matters. He built up a reputation within the National Assembly's finance committee, and did not spare ministers from his own party in making his criticisms. Gaillard's progress was swift, for within three years of his election as a deputy he became a junior minister.

Taking with him a reputation for wit and brilliance, Gaillard saw experience as secretary of state attached to the prime minister's office (1953–4) and as minister of finance (1957). Although this progress did Gaillard no harm, in the Fourth Republic it was the premiership that was the politically risky post to hold.

Gaillard was himself surprised to be asked to form a government in October 1957 in succession to Bourgès-Maunoury, after a search for an administration with a make-up acceptable to the National Assembly which had lasted five weeks.

The Gaillard government set out with a certain style and was backed by most groups, from conservative to Socialist, in the National Assembly. It secured the passage of an Algerian reform bill, denied to its predecessor, and also won approval for its budget. It resorted to votes of confidence in the National Assembly in order to push through controversial measures. Gaillard also convened round-table conferences of party leaders in order to secure parliamentary approval for agreed government policies. This technique was not always successful, because of the indiscipline of the deputies rather than failure of the leaders to agree. Gaillard's problems were no different from those of other premiers' whom he succeeded – the round-table device merely highlighted the weakness of the premier's position. After the Gaillard government lost a vote of confidence on the issue of Anglo-US 'good offices' in the French air force's bombardment of Sakiet in Morocco, *Le Monde* described the premier in the Fourth Republic as 'an ephemeral monarch among the barons who enthrone or dethrone him, he can preserve his equilibrium in his high position only by giving way to the most demanding, and otherwise trying to neutralize them by playing one against the other. Nine-tenths of his time is taken up by this task, as futile as it is exhausting. In it he ruins his health, and loses his integrity' (30 April 1958).

Gaillard's prominence in French political life largely ended with the collapse of the Fourth Republic, although he served as president of the Radical Party from 1958 to 1961. Permanently confined to opposition, he did not enjoy the loss of office. He was keen to support moves which united the centre and non-Communist left (such as Defferre's (q.v.) short-lived 'grande fédération') but refused absolutely to be dependent on Communist votes – a point of principle which almost cost him his seat at Cognac in 1968 and which was to divide the Radicals finally four years later. Gaillard died in a yachting accident in July 1970.

Bibliography

See *The Times*, 13 July 1970 (obituary) and P.M. Williams, *Crisis and Compromise* (London: Longman, 1964).

ABP

GALLIFFET, Gaston Alexandre Auguste, marquis de (1830–1909)

General de Galliffet is chiefly remembered for two episodes: his massacre of communards in Paris in 1871, and his participation as minister of war in the Republican Defence government of Waldeck-Rousseau at the height of the Dreyfus crisis in 1899. In between, he had built a reputation as a competent soldier and a loyal – if perhaps self-interested – Republican.

Born of an ancient southern military and *parlémentaire* family, he volunteered for the army as a private soldier (the usual route of stupid or lazy young gentlemen) and quickly obtained a commission. He served in the Crimea and in the vicious counter-guerrilla campaign in Mexico. He also had a checkered career during the Second Empire as courtier and 'swell', and narrowly avoided being cashiered. His bad reputation was repaired by his very public gallantry leading suicidal cavalry charges at the battle of Sedan in September 1870. After the end of the war he was given command of a cavalry brigade in the army of Versailles, which played a minor role in the civil war against the Paris Commune. While escorting captured insurgents from Paris to Versailles, Galliffet indulged in cruelty as exhibitionistic as his bravery at Sedan, picking out prisoners and having them shot on the spot. He was not the only or even the worst culprit, but his doings were widely reported in the press.

Whether by ambition, or through a change of heart not uncommon among those who had experienced the defeat of 1870, Galliffet in the 1870s began to work hard at his profession: promoted general of division in 1875, he commanded the 17th Division at Dijon and then in 1879 the 12th Army Corps at Limoges. In 1880 he was made military governor of Paris. He was a reforming chairman of the cavalry committee and a member of the military inner circle, the Conseil Supérieur de la Guerre. At the same time he was well known as a socialite and acid wit. His remarkable advancement under a Republican government, in spite of his 1871 notoriety, was due to his close association with Gambetta (said to spring from admiration of his struggle against the Germans in 1870–1) and Republican loyalism. Reliable Republican generals were a rare and valuable species, and during the MacMahon period (1873–9) and the Boulanger crisis (1888–9) Galliffet made clear his resolve to oppose a possible coup. He retired in 1895.

His military prestige and known republicanism led to his appointment as minister of war in June 1899,

to the understandable anger of the Socialists – some of them former communards – who greeted him with shouts of 'Murderer!'. Galliffet's intention as minister was to stamp on political dissidence in the high command, while protecting the army from the consequences of its gross mishandling of the Dreyfus case. In an attempt to calm the affair by compromise, he favoured a pardon for Dreyfus rather than exoneration, and followed this with a famous Order of the Day on 21 September 1899 announcing that 'The incident is closed'. This proved over-optimistic, and his attempt at compromise merely prolonged the affair, finally harming the cause of moderation and the army itself. He became the butt of criticisms from both sides: 'If I lay hands on a guilty general, I am accused of massacring the army. If I do nothing I am accused of treason.' He resigned in May 1900, to be replaced by the more politically radical General André, whose clumsy discrimination against Catholic officers caused political and military turmoil.

Galliffet was one member of the small group of senior Republican officers who helped to ensure the army's obedience to the regime in the 1870s and 1880s, but who were too conservative and too devoted to the corporate interests of the army to be able to survive the Dreyfus affair.

Bibliography

For his military role, especially as minister, see Douglas Porch, *The March to the Marne: The French army 1871–1914* (Cambridge: Cambridge University Press, 1981). There are several French biographies, most useful, Louis Thomas, *Le général de Galliffet* (Paris: Dordon Aîné, 1910).

RT

GAMBETTA, Léon Michel (1838–82)

Gambetta was the youngest and one of the most astute, eloquent and dynamic of the founders of the Third Republic. Son of an Italian grocer modestly established in the southern town of Cahors, he was sometimes denounced by political enemies as an alien, but he acquired French nationality in 1859 and his mother was French, as was his upbringing. As the result of an accident in 1849 his right eye was injured and eventually removed in 1867 – hence the nickname given him of 'Cyclops' or 'Le Borgne' (the one-eyed). Short and slim as a young man, he was stout and florid by the age of 40. His career went through four phases. The first culminated in his role as a deputy in the legislative body of the Second Empire, the second followed the fall of the Empire and coincided with the later phase of the Franco-Prussian war of 1870–1, the third spanned the period from July 1871 to December 1877 during which he helped to establish the Third Republic, and the fourth covered the last five years in which he sought to control the Republic's destinies.

The first phase was one of preparation crowned by his first political successes. Like many ambitious young southerners with Republican sympathies Gambetta made his way to Paris (1857), studied law, declaimed in cafes, cultivated Republican politicians, attended parliamentary debates and aspired to a parliamentary career. His eloquent denunciation of the imperial regime in a lawsuit in 1868 (the Baudin trial) made his name and ensured his adoption in two constituencies as a Republican candidate in the general elections of 1869. Successful in both Marseilles and Paris, he chose to sit for Marseilles, where he had defeated Thiers himself, but the fact that he had also been elected in the Parisian working-class district of Belleville was still more important for his future. In Belleville he stood against and defeated a moderate Republican; he had waged a violent campaign and accepted a programme of sweeping reforms which, known as 'the Belleville programme', for years supplied a basis for Radical election manifestos. No less important, his success at Belleville qualified him for membership of a provisional government only fifteen months later. His election campaign at Belleville marked him out again as an irreconcilable foe of the Empire and, many thought as a dangerous demagogue, but through it he achieved his aim of being 'a *force*' in his own right, independent of the Republicans of an older generation. His successes were due to exceptional eloquence (men compared him to Mirabeau), drive and astuteness. Moreover, once in parliament he made speeches there which impressed by their moderation and good sense: he had no wish, he said, to obtain a Republic by the use of physical force but through the peaceful exercise of universal suffrage, and when war broke out, unlike some Republicans, he voted the necessary credits. He showed a statesmanlike awareness of the need to reassure the French people that a Republic need not entail violence; he also showed that a Radical could still be a patriot.

This he demonstrated pre-eminently during the second and most dramatic phase of his career. When Napoleon III was taken prisoner at Sedan the Empire was doomed. A few weeks later Gambetta was exercising virtually dictatorial powers, directing the provincial resistance against the Prussian invaders. His eloquence, powerful voice and popularity had enabled him to play such an influential part in the Parisian revolution of 4 September. He had done much to ensure that the transfer of power from Empire to Republic should be orderly (the revolution was bloodless) and that the new provisional Republican government of national defence should consist mainly of men elected in Paris in 1869, including himself. Outwitting a rival, he had secured appointment to the key post of minister of the interior and promptly replaced the Empire's prefects by Republicans. When Paris was besieged and cut off from the provinces, the government sent him to reinforce its elderly delegation at Tours. His escape from Paris by balloon remains one of the most sensational episodes in a period full of drama. Soon after his arrival he took over the Ministry of War, but his task of galvanizing the provinces, raising new armies and relieving Paris – the paramount military and political objective – was formidable. After the defeat of the army of the Loire in December and the failure of Parisian attempts at a successful sortie were followed by the onset of a bitter winter and further defeats, it became increasingly hopeless. Yet such was Gambetta's determination that even when Paris had fallen at the end of January 1871 he urged continuing the war 'until complete exhaustion'. But the government in Paris had agreed to an armistice to be followed by free elections and when Gambetta issued a degree making Bonapartists ineligible, they overruled him and he resigned. France was war-weary, morale had plummeted and the election results returning a monarchist majority were tantamount to an overwhelming vote for peace.

Thus all Gambetta's efforts were unavailing and his role became a subject of bitter controversy. On the one hand, critics like Thiers regarded him and his colleagues as 'raging madmen' who 'prolonged the defence beyond all reason'; on the other, admirers hailed him as a second Danton (a great leader in the first French Revolution) who improvised new armies. Clemenceau's dry verdict was nearer the mark: 'he had conducted the war . . . more badly than well – but he certainly did conduct it, and as well as he could'. By so doing he had helped to restore the nation's self-respect and, as a German general remarked, its honour. This second phase of his career is a remarkable example both of what could be achieved by a civilian amateur with vision and also of such an amateur's limitations.

Despite his failures, Gambetta's prestige was such that he was elected to the new National Assembly by ten departments. He shrewdly chose to represent one in Alsace, which was about to be ceded to Germany in accordance with the peace treaty. Having formally protested against the cession, thereby championing the unity and indivisibility of France, he and his fellow representatives of Alsace and Lorraine resigned their seats. Worn out after his wartime exertions, Gambetta withdrew to recuperate in Spain.

His re-entry into France and the beginning of the third phase of his career were marked by a notable speech at Bordeaux in June 1871 and his re-election to the Assembly by three constituencies in July. The return of a monarchist majority in February had held out the possibility of a restoration of monarchy, but Thiers, the new head of state, had not committed himself and had declared 'The future is to the wisest'. Gambetta was determined that the Republicans should be the wisest. His main concern at first was to consolidate the *de facto* Republican regime, to win converts to it, to republicanize its personnel and to combat the efforts of the monarchists (or the right as they were often termed) to steer the country in their direction. These aims he pursued not as a minister – he held no government office during these years – but as a powerful leader of the Republican Radicals, endowed with great personal charm, an eloquence that moved crowds, and exceptional skill in political manoeuvring and election management. Furthermore, he had an important new weapon at his command, a newspaper. The *République Française*, founded in 1871, voiced his views and those of many of his closest supporters. These he bade regard themselves not as journalists but future ministers and in due course several of them did hold office.

A key issue was the framing of a constitution. Faced by a monarchist majority, Gambetta at first denied that the Assembly had constituent powers and unsuccessfully campaigned for its dissolution. When it was clear that it would not vote its own demise and that the intransigence of the Pretender and the divisions of the monarchists ruled out any immediate restoration, he shifted his ground and urged it to give France a definitive Republican government. This was narrowly achieved in 1875. Gambetta had helped to ensure that the new parliament should consist of two Chambers, the upper house being elected, not nominated. When the Republic's first Chamber of Deputies was elected (1876) he became president of its important budget committee. He was still deputy for Radical Belleville, his chosen constituency of 1871, but he had in effect become an Opportunist preaching a policy of 'results', still

capable of verbal violence when it suited him, as when he denounced clericalism as 'the enemy', but moderate in fact. The return of the right to government in May 1877 meant that there was one further battle to be fought before the Republican regime appeared secure. It gave Gambetta an unrivalled chance to use his electioneering skills, his eloquence and his continuing influence in the army. He contributed enormously to the Republican's victory in the October polls and emerged as their most dynamic leader.

Had France imitated English practice, Gambetta might well have formed a cabinet at the end of 1877 or the beginning of 1879 but he was not called upon to do so until November 1881. In the meantime he exercised exceptional power ('occult power' some called it), helping to make and unmake ministries and influencing foreign policy and all kinds of appointments from his posts first as president of the budget committee and then as president of the Chamber. This last phase of his career was the 'era of difficulties'. It had been one of Gambetta's ambitions, never achieved, to weld the Republicans into a single homogeneous party. But after their temporary unity in the 16 May battle of 1877 they relapsed into rival groups. When at last he was asked to be prime minister he could not form the 'ministry of all the talents' expected of him and became the victim partly of the jealousies aroused by his 'occult power' and increasing authoritarianism and partly of hostility to some of his policies. His ministry lasted less than three months and eleven months later he died of peritonitis. He was only 44.

Like Thiers, Gambetta is a remarkable example of a man who exercised great influence although he was in government for relatively short periods. He was a dominating and controversial personality whose untiring wartime efforts and post-war concern for France's 'regeneration' under a Republican regime led him to be regarded both as a great patriot and a great Republican. His main preoccupations were political and he was criticized for paying insufficient attention to social problems. When he died, a fellow Republican, Jules Ferry, said that although Gambetta was not very adept at governing, it had been a great relief to know that he was there 'in reserve'; in other words he was the Republic's strong man, a potential saviour in time of crisis. Most French towns named a street or square after him; in Paris his heart was eventually interred in the Pantheon and until the Second World War an imposing monument commemorating him stood on the Place du Carrousel.

Bibliography

Some of Gambetta's most important speeches are to be found in P. Barral's *Les Fondateurs de la troisième République* (Paris: A. Colin, 1968); D. Halévy and E. Pillias edited his lively letters: *Lettres de Gambetta 1868–1882* (Paris: Grasset, 1938). The three main phases of his career are examined in three books by J.P.T. Bury: *Gambetta and the National Defence* (London: Longman Green and Co., 1936; American reprint, 1971), *Gambetta and the Making of the Third Republic* (London: Longman, 1973) and *Gambetta's Final Years* (London: Longman, 1982).

JPTB

GARAUD, Marie-Françoise 'Marie-France' (1934–)

Marie-France Garaud is best known as the *eminence grise* of the Pompidou (q.v.) presidency (1969–74) and has been called the most powerful woman in France in the Fifth Republic.

Garaud studied and practised law in Poitiers, the town where she was born. Her political career began in 1962, when she entered the cabinet of Jean Foyer, minister of justice, as special assistant for parliamentary affairs. In 1967, she became legal adviser to the prime minister, Georges Pompidou, and when he moved from Matignon to the Elysée in 1969, Garaud moved with him as technical adviser in the president's cabinet. With Pierre Juillet, she was credited with being the most influential member of the president's team.

After Pompidou's death in 1974, Marie-France Garaud was reputedly responsible (more than Chirac – q.v.) for the rallying of forty-three Gaullist deputies to the camp of Valéry Giscard d'Estaing (q.v.) in the presidential elections, marking a distance from the Gaullist party. Seeking a new look for Gaullism, she was a founder-member of the Rassemblement pour la République (RPR) in 1976 and a year later supported Jacques Chirac (q.v.), leader of the RPR, in his bid for a further power base as mayor of Paris.

Garaud left her post as Chirac's adviser after the European elections in 1979 to return to the Cour des Comptes, where she still holds the position of adviser on referenda. She is also president of the Institut International de Géopolitique (International Institute of Geopolitics), an international political think-tank which she founded in December 1982.

Universally acknowledged for her influence and power as the figure in the background on whom those in the limelight depend, Garaud has been less successful as a political figure in her own right. She stood as an independent Gaullist candidate in the 1981 presidential elections (receiving 1.33 per cent of the vote) and headed an unsuccessful list in Paris in the 1986 legislative elections.

In many ways Garaud is a classic right-wing political thinker, profoundly anti-Communist, in favour of the death penalty and strong on issues of law and order. Her thinking on political institutions is close to de Gaulle's: hostile to notions of left and right, she has always refused to identify her position in terms of traditional French party divisions. She was opposed to the *cohabitation* experiment of 1986–8 and is a strong believer in presidential power.

CD

GARAUDY, Roger (1913–)

The notoriety of Roger Garaudy rests on events culminating at the 19th Congress of the PCF (1970), after which he was expelled. Garaudy's part stemmed from his past as an ideological godfather of the Thorezian era of the PCF. He was born in Marseilles in 1913, the son of poor parents. He had been a member of a Christian youth circle and he almost became a Christian intellectual before entering the PCF in 1933. In 1937 he was introduced to Thorez as a 'strange intellectual coming from Christianity'. Garaudy did not remain merely an intellectual, he served in the French army in 1939/40; later the Vichy regime sent him to an Algerian camp, whence he emerged weighing 6 stone 7 pounds. After 1945, as a PCF deputy in the Tarn, he was actively involved with the miners' strike of 1947–8 but his leading role was still that of intellectual, and eventually Political Bureau member, responsible for the ideological strategy of the PCF, in the light of which we gauge the significance of his expulsion date.

Garaudy's 'tasks' were to demonstrate both the scientific completeness of Marxism–Leninism–Stalinism and its compatibility with French culture. Indeed, the post-Resistance PCF found France from Jeanne d'Arc to Anatole France impregnated with the roots of communism. Only the existentialists were the rotten apples. The cold war re-shaped this ideological perspective, but did not radically transform it. Dialectical materialism remained pure science (with Stalin its supreme being) and the Communists were still best of Frenchmen. But after 1947 Garaudy had to expose most non-Communist Frenchmen as traitors to France. The events of 1956 would eventually jolt Garaudy out of that orbit. With permission, if not encouragement from Thorez. Garaudy offered a dialogue of many voices: it came to fruition in 1960, when he shared the same platform as Sartre and Gabriel Marcel. When a CPSU representative came West to reaffirm that communism meant militant atheism, Garaudy, with Thorez' discreet support, publicly dissented.

Only after Thorez died would Garaudy lose his party bearings. A series of publications developed the theme of Marx as the best Christian since Jesus. 1968 was the turning point. As prophet of 'alienation' in a cybernetic society, Garaudy wanted the PCF to align itself with the student revolt (he, like others, envisaged a 'new historic bloc' of workers, technicians and students). An enthusiastic proselyte for the Czech experiment, he immediately condemned the Soviet invasion. His response exceeded the PCF's own mild reproach to the Russians, and he was censured for indiscipline. Garaudy's past welled up in a Protestant moment: 'I cannot be silent'. At the 19th Congress he was visibly alone, and his speech testifying to 'the whole truth' was heard in silence. Shortly after this, he was expelled.

Subsequently, Garaudy stood by his 'man-god' Marxism and popularized it in several works. Garaudy's liege-loyalty to Thorez lay at the heart of his historic significance. A comment on *Maurice* is its key: the 1937 policy of the hand outstretched to Catholics (*La Main tendue*) was no manoeuvre, Garaudy declared in 1975. One need not believe in providence to see that the 1937 meeting was no accident, but an element of Thorez' strategy to let the Popular Front flower as Communist culture. Historians can argue whether this non-insurrectionary patriotic visage was mask or face; Garaudy desperately sought convergence between mask and face. As long as Thorez, cultic demi-god of the PCF lived, Garaudy suffered such contradictions with joy. Afterwards, Garaudy's religious drives needed other outlets; most recently he converted to Islam.

Bibliography

Several of Garaudy's works have been translated; politically the most significant is *The Whole Truth* (London: Fontana, 1971); there is no English language biography. His pre-1965 position is discussed in George Lichtheim, *Marxism in Modern France* (New York: Columbia University Press, 1966). his subsequent development is discussed in Michael Kelly, *Modern French Marxism* (Oxford: Blackwell, 1982). The events of the 19th Party Congress are mentioned by Ronald Tiersky, *French Communism 1920–1972* (New York: Columbia University Press, 1974), and in Max Adereth, *French Communist Party: A critical history, 1920–1984* (Manchester: Manchester University Press, 1984). See also: Roger Garaudy, *Karl Marx and His Doctrines* (New York: International Publishers, 1965) and Roger Garaudy, *From Anathema to Dialogue: A Marxist challenge to the Christian churches* (New York: Herder and Herder, 1966).

MK

de GAULLE, Charles André Marie Joseph (1890–1970)

De Gaulle was born in the Rue Princesse in Lille, the third child of Henri de Gaulle who was a teacher in a Jesuit college in Paris and was the descendant of a family of the lesser nobility which had become devoted to study and writing; his mother, née Jeanne Maillot, was from a Lille bourgeois family. They were both dedicated Catholics and patriots, with royalist convinctions. Educated at the College of the Immaculate Conception and (after the expulsion of the Jesuits from France in 1905) at Antoing in Belgium, he then spent a year at the Collège Stanislas in Paris. In 1909 he entered Saint-Cyr and began his military career. When the 1914 war broke out he was an infantry lieutenant. Wounded three times, decorated and then made a prisoner of war in 1916, he used his enforced leisure to begin his study of military history and of Germany. His first book, an analysis of German military leadership during the war, *La Discorde chez l'ennemi* was published in 1924.

In this book, and throughout the inter-war period, de Gaulle showed considerable and unusual qualities. He was studious, thoughtful, well-read. He proved himself to be an eloquent lecturer and an accomplished writer. Believing in the imminence of a future war he urged the French army to equip itself with professional armoured and motorized units and he did not hesitate to criticize official French military policy in ways which proved, eventually, to have been justified. But he was not liked by his superiors. He was accused of arrogance and awkwardness. Many found it unacceptable that a junior officer, with little experience, should pontificate about leadership and strategy, and the fact that he often enveloped his thought in a curious philosophical guise did not help to make his views acceptable. He was assisted in his early career by the friendship of Marshal Pétain (q.v.), but in 1938 they disagreed over de Gaulle publishing under his own name a history of the French army which was based upon a staff study which Pétain had initiated. Before the 1939 war broke out it was only with difficulty that he had been promoted to the rank of full colonel to which he was entitled by seniority. He had, in 1920, married Yvonne Vendrou, the daughter of a biscuit manufacturer in Calais. They had three children, the last of whom, Anne, born in 1928, suffered from Downs Syndrome.

But in the course of the 1930s de Gaulle made a number of important political contacts. In 1934 he explained his ideas on the organization of the army to Paul Reynaud (q.v.), a somewhat isolated but highly respected deputy. This was the start of a long collaboration. Reynaud unsuccessfully proposed in the Chamber of Deputies that a specialized corps of armoured divisions should be created, made up of soldiers who would serve on contract. In 1936 de Gaulle was able to explain his ideas to Léon Blum (q.v.), the prime minister, who was reputedly impressed by them but felt unable to take any action. In spite of his activity, when war came in 1939 and de Gaulle was appointed tank commander of the Fifth Army, and later commander of the Fourth Armoured Division, few of the officers who served with him were acquainted with his views on modern warfare.

On 10 May 1939 the Germans launched their offensive against Holland and Belgium and de Gaulle, with his tanks, found himself at the centre of battles around Laon and Abbeville. In Gaullist mythology these events have become unique victories of French arms within the general melancholy of defeat, whilst opponents of de Gaulle have insisted upon his failure to cooperate with other units and his overall lack of success. The truth lies, inevitably, somewhere between these two interpretations, but there can be no doubt that de Gaulle showed himself to be an effective commander in the practice of war and was far from being a mere theorist of strategy.

As it happened, de Gaulle should not have been in action at all. On 23 March Paul Reynaud had succeeded Daladier (q.v.) as prime minister and had sought to make de Gaulle secretary to the new war cabinet, but Daladier, who had held on to the Ministry of Defence, refused to accept this nomination. On 6 June (5 days after he had been promoted to the rank of general) he was summoned to Paris and appointed under-secretary for defence. In spite of his somewhat lowly rank, his friendship with the prime minister and his own energy and ambition gave him considerable importance in a disastrous situation (the day that he had arrived in Paris the Germans had

broken through the French front on the Somme). He rapidly became aware of the power of the defeatists who surrounded Reynaud and he urged the prime minister, unsuccessfully, to replace the commander-in-chief, Weygand (q.v.), by General Huntziger. On 16 June de Gaulle was in London (for the second time) and played a prominent role in promoting the idea of a Franco-British union (which originated with Jean Monnet (q.v.), René Pleven (q.v.) and a number of British officials). Returning to Bordeaux that evening (where the government had taken refuge) he learned that Reynaud had resigned and therefore that he was no longer a minister. A little later when it was announced that Pétain had become prime minister he determined to leave for London the next day since he was convinced that Pétain would seek an armistice. It is possible that for some days he had envisaged the possibility of establishing himself in London, probably with other French political leaders.

However, he arrived in London alone and no outstanding personality ever joined him there. It was the beginning of an extraordinary story: he was a junior general without an army and without money, with few friends and an uncertain reputation, with a political experience of only a few days as a junior minister. Yet it was de Gaulle who was to stride down the Champs Elysées in August 1944 when Paris was liberated and who was to lead the provisional government. At any moment it would have been possible for any one of a dozen politicians or any one of his military superiors to have nudged him aside and to have replaced him as the leader of *La France Libre*. But none did so. De Gaulle was undoubtedly assisted by two factors. In June 1940 the British prime minister, Churchill, was anxious to demonstrate to the world (and especially to the USA) that Britain was determined to continue the struggle against Germany, and he was glad to welcome a Frenchman who was similarly determined. Therefore, he allowed him to make his famous broadcast on 18 June in which he called upon all free Frenchmen to join him in London. But at the same time, Churchill recognized that the situation in France was uncertain. Preoccupied by the problems of what would happen to the French fleet and to the French colonies, he did not wish to recognize in de Gaulle a government-in-exile. Therefore he came to an agreement (7 August) with de Gaulle as an individual, thereby giving considerable importance to a single man.

De Gaulle was successful in rallying certain colonies to the cause of Free France (Chad, Cameroon, Oubangui-Chari and later Gabon), but an expedition that he led to win over Senegal in September 1940 failed. From these bases in equatorial Africa he ordered a column to be formed, under the command of Colonel Leclerc, which would advance northwards into the desert against the Italians in Libya. During 1942 Free French forces cooperated with their allies in meeting a German threat in Syria and the Lebanon but de Gaulle did not gain the political advantages which he had hoped for in these regions. From London he also established intelligence networks which kept him in touch with what was happening in France, especially with the growing resistance movements.

This period was marked by increasing disagreements with Churchill who, once, for a period of eleven months, would not allow him to leave England. To some extent these quarrels were caused by de Gaulle's desire to demonstrate that he was not a puppet controlled by the British. There was also the influence of Roosevelt who despised the French and distrusted de Gaulle. There were a number of anti-de Gaulle plots, some of them inspired by the British. The climax came when, without informing de Gaulle, Anglo-American forces invaded French North Africa in November 1942, and having attempted to come to an agreement with the Vichyite Admiral Darlan (q.v.) who was in Algiers at the time (he was assassinated on 24 December) appointed General Giraud (q.v.) as the civil and military commander-in-chief of the area. It appeared that de Gaulle was eliminated. However, by obstinacy and skill, de Gaulle succeeded in establishing representatives of his London organization in North Africa. Strengthened by the setting up of the National Council of the Resistance in Paris, which declared its allegiance to him, de Gaulle left London for Algiers on 30 May 1943. In spite of continued hostility from Roosevelt who wished Giraud to be in charge, by the end of July de Gaulle was the effective leader in Algiers. From there he received Resistance leaders and made plans for the setting up of the provisional government in France.

With the invasion of Europe in June 1944 de Gaulle achieved his aim of avoiding the establishment of an Anglo-American military government after the expulsion of the Germans. When, on 14 June he made a brief visit to the beachheads and to Bayeux and other towns in Normandy, the populations demonstrated that he was the leader they wanted. His commissioners began to establish themselves in different parts of France. A French unit, the 2nd Armoured Division under Leclerc (now a general) landed in Normandy in early August and at de Gaulle's insistence it led the Allied advance on Paris.

By 24 August it was in the capital and de Gaulle arrived there the next day. Three particular actions symbolize de Gaulle's carefully considered policies. First he drove to the Ministry of War and to his old office there; in this way he suggested continuity, the idea that after Reynaud's resignation he had carried on the government of the Republic in June 1940, so that the France that had surrendered was the illegal and temporary government of Pétain. Secondly he visited the Préfecture of Police in order to show that the apparatus of the French state still existed and would not be taken over by the Communists. Thirdly, in spite of the dangers present from German units, he organized a triumphal march from the Arc de Triomphe to Notre Dame on 26 August. This meant that he, and his government, were directly acclaimed by the people.

For de Gaulle the most urgent necessities were then to complete the liberation of France and to revive the French economy, devastated by occupation and war. Nevertheless he considered that certain other considerations were vital: that of recovering for France her role in world affairs, notably by negotiating a treaty with Stalin, by securing the right to be one of the occupying forces in Germany, and by re-establishing French rule in Indo-China; that of controlling the revenge of the resistance movements and of preventing a massacre of those who had collaborated with the Germans; that of introducing new structures into French society by a programme of nationalization (the Renault motor-works, aviation production, mines, gas, electricity and certain banks) and by creating the social security system. But de Gaulle had always been convinced that it was through institutions that France could be properly governed. After some hesitation, and after some difficulty, he organized a referendum (21 October 1945) which overwhelmingly decided that an assembly should be elected which would devise a new constitution. That Assembly was elected on the same day, by the system of proportional representation and with women voting for the first time. It produced a left-wing majority (Communists, Socialists and Christian Democrats) which unanimously elected de Gaulle as head of the government (13 November 1945).

But within a short time it became apparent that the Assembly did not wish to allow de Gaulle the authority which he had exercised hitherto. He was excluded from the process of constitution-making, which was all the more important as it became evident that what was envisaged was a return to a Third Republic type of government with the Assembly holding supreme power. His policies on many matters, including the military budget were rejected. On 20 January 1946 he suddenly resigned, claiming that he could not accept the return of the exclusive rule of political parties. But he did not intend to remain inactive. On 16 June 1946, returning to Bayeux two years after his dramatic arrival there, he proposed a constitution that would place power in the hands of a president rather than an assembly. But by a referendum held in October 1946 this advice was rejected, and the Fourth Republic came into being. De Gaulle's answer was to create a new political party, or rally as he preferred to call it, the Rassemblement du Peuple Français. This he announced in April 1947.

The period which follows is a curious one in de Gaulle's life, and there is reason to believe that he might well have come to regret his activities. He was totally opposed to the Fourth Republic and refused to be a candidate for any office. Yet his party campaigned in elections, with the idea of winning enough votes to be able to control the Assembly and to change the constitution. Thus, the RPF suffered from the ambiguity of being both outside and inside the system. De Gaulle was thought by many to have Fascist tendencies, and there is good evidence that certain of the leaders of the Fourth Republic feared a Gaullist *coup d'état* more than they feared a Communist revolution. The two main objectives of Gaullist policy were to attack a regime where political parties flourished and which, it was claimed, rendered France impotent; and to denounce the Communists and the dangers of the cold war. De Gaulle was therefore attacking the vast majority of the Assembly in one way or another.

In the municipal elections of October 1947 the RPF had been very successful, winning some 40 per cent of the votes. Therefore when the legislative elections of 1951 were due, the centre parties devised an electoral law which, by modifying the system of proportional representation and allowing certain lists which were in alliance to win the totality of votes in a department, was deliberately designed to keep out the Communists and the Gaullists. The Communists suffered the most by this manoeuvre, winning 101 seats when they would have had 180 by proportional representation, but the Gaullists, who had hoped for some 200 deputies to be elected, had 117 and would only have had some 27 more had proportional representation been properly applied. From this time onwards the RPF could do little other than demonstrate that there was no workable majority in the Chamber. In March 1952 some twenty-seven of the group voted in favour of Antoine Pinay (q.v.) as prime minister. The

Rassemblement was disintegrating. It had entered the system which it should have destroyed, and de Gaulle distanced himself from it.

De Gaulle became increasingly pessimistic. A European army was proposed in 1952 which he saw as a grave weakening of France's independence; the French were being defeated in Indo-China and by 1954 there was armed rebellion in Algeria. Since the death of Stalin an American–Soviet hegemony had been established in the world which could, he thought, only be broken if France became a nuclear power. De Gaulle became an isolated figure. His reputation was revived by the publication of his first volume of Memoirs in 1954 (*L'Appel*) but he seemed to be a figure of the past without any future. In his family life de Gaulle had been much saddened by the death of his daughter Anne in 1948. In the 1950s he was twice operated upon for cataract.

It was the humiliation of France in the Suez campaign of 1956 and the deterioration of the war in Algeria that changed the situation. There had always been a small number of faithful Gaullists who continued to work for the General's return to power. By 1958 these were increased as a number of individuals came to believe that it was only de Gaulle who could get France out of the Algerian impasse. It was widely rumoured that plots were in existence, both in Algeria and in France, both civil and military, which could create a crisis of the first magnitude and which could even threaten civil war. De Gaulle undoubtedly knew about these conspiracies but did not take part in them. At the age of 67 he knew that this was his last chance and he was extremely prudent, concealing his ideas about the future of Algeria and only making one thing clear in private conversations: he would not work within the constitution of the Fourth Republic and he would insist upon special powers if he accepted any governmental responsibility.

But the chances of success appeared to be slim. There were three sources of power. The first was in the Assembly, but there was no clear majority. The government of Félix Gaillard (q.v.) had been overthrown on 15 April, and it was not until 13 May that a Social Catholic, Pierre Pflimlin (q.v.), was able to present a government to the Assembly. The second was in the army which, afraid of being betrayed by the politicians in Paris, developed a sharper political awareness in Algiers. The third lay in the European settlers in Algeria, and their supporters within France. Whatever their differences, this lobby was united and powerful in its determination that Algeria should remain French. De Gaulle did not figure in any of these sources of power. Although he had certain supporters in the Assembly he had no party there. He was distrusted both by the army and by the settlers. The mechanism whereby he could return to office or be brought there, was difficult to envisage.

The key incidents were the revolt in Algiers on 13 May 1958, and the establishment there of a committee of public safety which included officers and settler representatives (as well as at least one Gaullist agent); the invasion of Corsica on 24 May, when committees of public safety again took control; the threat of a parachute operation against Paris on the night of 27/28 May.

De Gaulle's tactics were superbly calculated. He made no comment on events except to note the degradation of the state. He did not commit himself to any individual or party. He was always reassuring, he would not establish a dictatorship and he would preserve the liberties and the principles of the Republic. But he would not succeed Pflimlin as head of the government as previous prime ministers had succeeded each other.

On 26 May, having (supposedly) learned of the operation against Paris, with all the dangers that that involved of civil war, he suggested that he should meet secretly with Pflimlin. Their nocturnal negotiation did not lead to any agreement, but at midday on the 27 May de Gaulle announced that he had started the regular process necessary for the establishment of a Republican government capable of ensuring the unity and the independence of the country. In these circumstances, the communiqué went on to announce, the land, naval and air forces present in Algeria should abstain from taking any action. It was this last reference which was essential. Pflimlin might well have said that de Gaulle could in no way be starting the regular process of forming a government since there was no agreement that he should do so and since he himself was still prime minister with a majority in the National Assembly. But the threat of an invasion prevailed. The prime minister resigned and although there were last minute attempts to prevent de Gaulle coming to power on his own terms (and he made a number of concessions at the last minute) the idea that without de Gaulle the nervous and uncertain politicians of the Fourth Republic would find themselves in confrontation with armed parachutists was a powerful deterrent to his opponents. It was this atmosphere of threat and blackmail which was, for someone such as Mendès France (q.v.), the original sin of the Fifth Republic, although it would seem to be true that de Gaulle never envisaged the hypothesis of being brought to power as the direct result of a military intervention.

Invited to form a government of 29 May, de Gaulle appeared before the National Assembly on 1 June and was afterwards given full powers for six months, including the power to draw up a new constitution and to present it to the nation for its approval by referendum. Votes were gained with relative ease.

From this time onwards the life-story of de Gaulle is the story of the Fifth Republic. Of course no one was to know that he was to be president from 1959 until 1969. Apart from the consideration of his age many politicians believed that once the Algerian question was settled then he could be got rid of. But this was to underestimate de Gaulle's preoccupation with the constitution. When he went to Algiers immediately after the voting in the Chambers was finished, he told the massed crowds that they had opened the way to a new France and he charged his minister for justice Michel Debré (q.v.) with the task of rapidly drawing up a new constitution. This was approved by referendum on 28 September 1958, but the most important item of the institutions of the Fifth Republic was absent from this, namely the election of the president by universal suffrage. This was introduced in 1962, after an attempted assassination of de Gaulle, and first used in the elections of 1965. It is not clear whether de Gaulle had always intended to introduce this measure and thought it prudent to wait, or whether he found that the spread of television made it possible for him to be a campaigning candidate without having to stump the country, which would have been a daunting prospect for someone of his age. At all events a powerful president elected by universal suffrage is the keystone of the Republic.

The list of de Gaulle's activities and achievements during the eleven years of his presidency is a long one. He ended the war in Algeria and accepted the existence of an independent Algerian Republic, and this was approved by a referendum in April 1962. Having at first supported the idea of a Franco-African community he abandoned this and accepted that all France's African colonies should be independent. On coming to power, he accepted the Treaty of Rome and French membership of the European Economic Community, but he always insisted that the role of the Community should be carefully limited and that there should be little interference with France's sovereignty. On two occasions he rejected British applications to become a member. He attempted to reform the North Atlantic Treaty Organization and having failed to do this, arranged for the French withdrawal from the organization. This insistence upon French independence was obviously linked with the French possession of nuclear weapons (the first explosion of a French nuclear device had taken place in February 1960).

Such actions, often viewed as hostile, by the British and Americans, were balanced by a careful cultivation of friendship with the West German Republic, with Soviet Russia and China. If matters of defence and foreign policy were de Gaulle's chief preoccupations he was interested in promoting trade as part of the booming economy over which he presided, and which was associated with the early prosperous years of the Common Market.

From 1962 onwards criticisms of de Gaulle became more outspoken and there is evidence that his popularity was on the wane. The Algerian danger was over; he became increasingly associated with a political party, the Union Pour une Nouvelle République (or 'Gaullists' as they called themselves); there were complaints about the unequal distribution of wealth in a growing economy. In the 1965 presidential elections (by universal suffrage) in the first ballot he gained only 43.7 per cent of the votes cast. Well over half the population voted for his opponents, who included Mitterrand (q.v.) and Lecanuet (q.v.). On the second ballot de Gaulle won comfortably against Mitterrand (with 54.5 per cent of the vote) but the lesson was clear. By 1967 de Gaulle's position began to deteriorate further as fears grew about increasing unemployment. In the parliamentary elections of March 1967 the Gaullists barely won a majority.

De Gaulle was increasingly criticized. It was said that his solitary exercise of power was too great. There was increasing speculation about what would happen when he ceased to be president. Some of his excursions into foreign affairs were highly controversial; his condemnation of Israel for aggression at the time of the Six-Day War in June 1967 and his reference to the Jews as 'an elite people, self-confident and dominating' in November 1967; his 'vive le Québec libre' speech in Montreal in July 1967.

But, unexpectedly it was the student revolts in Paris, joined by widespread strikes during May 1968, which shook the General's power. He appeared to be nonplussed and unable to cope with events. It was confidently expected, when he left French territory for West Germany on 29 May, that he was going to resign or even exile himself. The fact that he made a dramatic return and a vigorous speech, dissolved the Assembly and won a great victory in the elections, showed that he had lost none of his tactical skills. But he never recovered his position. When in April 1969 he insisted upon a complicated referendum being held on the subject of decentralization and of trans-

forming the Senate into a consultative rather than a legislative chamber, there were many who expected him to be defeated. These included de Gaulle himself. His resignation took effect from midday 27 April 1969.

In his retirement he worked at his new memoirs, publishing the first volume in 1970. He visited Ireland and Spain and planned to go to China and meet Mao Tse Tung. He received no members of the government and never intervened in public affairs. He died suddenly on 7 November 1970, within thirteen days of his 80th birthday.

Bibliography

The major biography of de Gaulle is by Jean Lacouture in three volumes, *De Gaulle* (Paris: Seuil, 1984, 1985, 1986). An English edition is being prepared. In English see Bernard Ledwidge, *De Gaulle* (London: Weidenfeld & Nicolson, 1982).

DJ

GAY, Francisque (1885–1963)

A journalist and publisher, Gay played a vital role in the development of Christian Democrat ideas in France and, more generally, in the growth of political and social awareness among the Catholic elite and activists which was to have a profound influence on catholicism in France between 1920 and 1960. A friend of Marc Sangnier (q.v.), he was a member of the latter's Sillon (the 'furrow'), the Christian Democrat movement which at the beginning of the century – and prior to its condemnation by the Vatican in 1910 – attempted, after the traumas of the Dreyfus affair and the separation of Church and state, to reconcile French Catholics with democracy and the Republic and to provide a structure for French Catholics opposed to Charles Maurras' extreme right-wing Action Française and to the reactionary spirit prevailing in the Catholic Church in France at the time; the Sillon also aimed at bridging the gulf that had grown up in France between the working classes and the Church.

In the inter-war years, as managing director of the Catholic publishing house of Bloud & Gay, he helped to promote the dissemination of these ideas, while helping to found the first Christian Democrat party in France, the Parti Démocrate Populaire, PDP, a party which was to enjoy only limited electoral success. His major role during this period was, however, in the field of journalism with the founding of the weekly *La Vie Catholique* (1924–38) and, more importantly, of the daily *L'Aube* (1932–51). Although not the official organ of the Christian Democrat parties, *L'Aube* provided broad support for their policies. Like Mounier's *Esprit* it came under the Vatican's suspicion in the 1930s. A minority of Catholic opinion, it opposed Franco's 'Christian' crusade in Spain, and in 1938 published a series of articles by Georges Bidault (q.v.) condemning the Munich Agreement. *L'Aube* was one of the first newspapers to be banned after the armistice of June 1940 and, during the war Gay himself narrowly escaped arrest by the Gestapo for his Resistance activities.

His prestige at the liberation may be gauged from the fact that he was deputy prime minister and then minister of state in the 1944–6 provisional governments. He was also instrumental in drafting the decree of 26 August 1944, organizing the French press after the confiscation of those newspapers that had continued to appear officially during the occupation. Gay's insistence on the need for pluralism, democratic control, journalistic freedom and for limits to be placed on purely commercial considerations are still, in spite of the changed circumstances, real issues in France.

With Georges Bidault and Maurice Schumann among others (and Marc Sangnier as a sort of 'father-figure'), in 1944 Francisque Gay founded the Mouvement Républicain Populaire, MRP, the Christian Democrat party which was to enjoy considerable but short-lived electoral success after the liberation. However, in 1947 he broke with the leadership of the party over – among other things – the MRP's support for French repression in Madagascar and its Indo-China policy. In 1948 he gave up control of *L'Aube*, whose plumeting sales brought about its folding in 1951.

The importance of Gay's *L'Aube*, together with Mounier's *Esprit*, the Dominicans' *Sept* and *La Vie Intellectuelle*, in the development of 'left-wing' catholicism in France in the 1930s should not be minimized. These, and the activists of the Catholic youth movements and of the Catholic Trade Union Confederation, the Confédération Française des Travailleurs Chrétiens, CFTC, were to contribute to the opening-out of important sections of the French Church to the modern world, and with the support of the Council Vatican II, to its subsequent transformation. They also permitted, admittedly given the particular circumstances of the time with a discredited right, the emergence at the time of the liberation of the MRP as a political force with an electorate comparable in size to that of the Socialists and the Communists; indeed, its leadership was

entirely composed of active members of one of the three groups mentioned above (the Catholic press, the youth movements or the CFTC). However, its ambiguities and contradictions were immediately obvious: a supposedly 'non-confessional' party run by committed Catholics, a centre-left party with a right-wing Catholic clientele, its ambivalent attitude towards both the Socialist Party and de Gaulle. It was these factors – which were to a large extent to lead to the MRP's early decline and ultimate demise – as much as Gay's own natural independence that were to cause his break with the party and his withdrawal from active political life.

Bibliography

Gay's view of Christian democracy is contained in two pre-war works: *Pour en finir avec la légende 'rouges-chrétiens'* (Paris: Editions de l'Aube, 1937), and *Pour un rassemblement des forces démocratiques d'inspiration chrétienne* (Paris: Editions de l'Aube, 1938). He explained his reasons for his break with the MRP leadership in the late 1940s in *La Démocratie chrétienne à l'épreuve du pouvoir* (Paris: Bloud & Gay, 1952). Maurice Carité, *Francisque Gay, le militant* (Paris: Editions Ouvrières, 1966), is a sympathetic study. Gay's role in *La Vie Catholique* has been studied by his daughter, Elisabeth Terrenoire, in *Un Combat d'avant-garde – Francisque Gay et La Vie Catholique* (Paris: Bloud & Gay, 1976); for his role in *L'Aube*, see: Françoise Mayeur, *L'Aube, étude d'un journal d'opinion* (Paris: A. Colin, 1966). A perceptive analysis of the contradictions of the MRP is to be found in Jacques Fauvet, *Les Forces politiques en France* (Paris: Editions 'Le Monde', 2nd edition, 1951), pp. 165–95. More general works on Christian democracy in France include, in English, W. Bosworth, *Catholicism and Crisis in Modern France* (Princeton, NJ: Princeton University Press, 1962), R.E.M. Irving, *Christian Democracy in France* (London: George Allen & Unwin, 1973), and, in French, E.-F. Callot, *Le MRP, origine, structure, doctrine, programme et action politique* (Paris: M. Rivière, 1978).

HE

GAYSSOT, Jean-Claude François (1946–)

Jean-Claude Gayssot rose without trace through the apparat of the Communist Party to outrank showier figures in a very short space of time. In 1979 he was nominated to the Central Committee, in 1982 he was promoted to the Political Bureau, and in 1985 he became the party's organization secretary. In 1986 he was being talked of as the party's third ranking figure (behind Marchais and Lajoinie) and the organization secretariat, because of its patronage, is an excellent position from which to prepare for eventual leadership. In 1986 he became deputy for the Seine-Saint-Denis in the most powerful Communist Federation.

Yet Gayssot is an organization man. He is not a good speaker, nor is he an engaging personality and has never shown any disposition to depart from the party line of the moment. Nothing in Gayssot's background marked him out for high office: for example his tenure at the head of the Lorraine Federations took place whilst Meurthe-et-Moselle was shattered by dissidence.

Gayssot comes from a poor peasant family in the Languedoc (Hérault) and worked for a diploma in Beziers. At 18 he joined the SNCF and at the same time he also joined the CGT, to emerge two years later as secretary of the local railway union, soon becoming CGT secretary for the Lozère. At 28 he became a full-time CGT official in the Gard department and a member of the PCF Federal bureau. Gayssot moved up to Bosigny near Paris with the CGT and was then recruited by Plissonier (q.v.) to work in the PCF's economic department (he became a local councillor at this time). There is nothing to suggest that Gayssot's views are other than orthodox and he has often moved to hammer the party's dissidents. However, his very rapid promotion and responsibilities at a young age leave open the question of how he got so far and so quickly and who was the moving force behind this career. In 1987 he led the commission which developed the new party programme, accepted at the Congress of December 1987 (the 27th).

Bibliography

Gayssot, J.-C. (1989), *Le Parti communiste français*, Paris: Messidor.

DSB

'GÉRAULT-RICHARD' (pseud.), Alfred Léon Richard (1860–1911)

Gérault-Richard, born in Bonnétable (Sarthe) on 11 October 1860, came to socialism from a working-class background. An upholsterer by trade, he went to Paris to work at the Gare de Lyon before discovering his talent as a journalist, starting at the age of 22 with *Le Réveil*. He went on to work for *La Marseillaise* and *La Bataille* (in the latter case under the pseudonym of Jean Valjean). In 1887 his leading position at *La Bataille* placed him at the forefront of the paper's attacks on the Boulangist movement. In 1889 he published the *Courrier quotidien de l'Exposition*. After the disappearance at *La Bataille*, he joined the editorial staff of *La Marseillaise* and *Germinal* and then *La Petite République*. He also launched the weekly *Le Chambard* in 1893. It was through *La Petite République* that Gérault-Richard wielded the most influence, becoming editor-in-chief in 1897. On the fringes of the organized socialist movement, Gérault-Richard gained a name for himself as an independent Socialist before standing unsuccessfully in the 1893 election. He was an ardent supporter of Alexandre Millerand in the debate on ministerialism.

Gérault-Richard used his articles to expose and denounce right-wing politicians and often had to defend his positions in court. Just after his unsuccessful bid for parliament, he launched an all-out attack in his short-lived paper *Le Chambard* against the government and the President of the Republic, Casimir Périer. For this he was sentenced to a year in prison and a 3,000 franc fine (at a trial in October 1884 where Gérault-Richard was defended by Jean Jaurès). Whilst in prison he was elected to Parliament in a by-election in Paris and was then freed. He was not particularly active in Parliament and lost his seat in 1898.

Having joined the confederation of independent Socialists, Gérault-Richard was involved in moves towards closer ties with the organized Socialist movement, but his role was limited, although he participated in various Socialist congresses. His own socialism was a natural corollary of republicanism and he recognized little in the programme of the newly unified Socialist Party. In particular, he wished to distance himself from Gustave Hervé's group of anti-patriots and other groups which he saw as anarchist. In pursuing his own political route independently of the party he incurred the wrath of the Socialists. Gérault-Richard was elected deputy for one of the Guadeloupe constituencies after his friend Hégésippe Légitimus, who was ill, more or less 'gave' him the seat. When he gave it back, he managed to secure a seat in the other constituency in Guadeloupe. The Socialist Party denounced these practices and called Gérault-Richard a 'renegade'. Undeterred, Gérault-Richard defended himself and was re-elected in 1910. He died soon afterwards, on 7 December 1911.

As well as his work for *Le Chambard* and *La Petite République*, Gérault-Richard founded a monthly publication *Ohé* in 1901 and *Messidor*, which appeared between 1907 and 1908 and gave way to

Paris-Journal (1908–11). His declaration to the court in 1884 is reproduced in Jean Jaurès, *Le Procès du Chambard* (1895).

Bibliography

Biographical details on Gérault-Richard may be found in Compère-Morel, Adéodat Constant Adolphe, *Grand dictionnaire socialiste du mouvement politique et économique national et international* (Paris: Publications Sociales, 1924), p. 328, and Jean Maitron, *Dictionnaire biographique du mouvement ouvrier français* (3rd part: 1871–1914) (Paris: Editions Ouvrières 1973–7), vol. XII (1974), pp. 271–2. There are also documents in the Archives Nationales (F7/12 562 and F17/12 387–8) and in the Archives de l'Assemblée Nationale.

SM

GIGNOUX, Claude-Joseph (1890–1966)

Gignoux was trained as a lawyer. After serving in the First World War he became Secretary of the Economic Commission of the Versailles Peace Conference and then an academic. He also worked as a journalist, editing the *Journée Industrielle* from 1925 to 1928 and from 1932 to 1936. He was a deputy for a constituency in the Loire between 1928 and 1932 and under-secretary at the Ministry of Finance in 1931. He achieved his greatest prominence when he became leader of the French employers' federation Confédération Générale du Patronat Français (CGPF) in October 1936. Gignoux's appointment followed the 'Matignon' accords which business and trade union leaders had signed under the aegis of the Popular Front government. It was suggested that these accords had been concluded in the interests of big business and that Gignoux's appointment represented a reassertion of small business power. In reality, big business itself resented the Matignon accords and supported Gignoux's appointment.

Gignoux's greatest asset as leader of the French employers was the fact that he himself was a lawyer and not an industrialist. This allowed him to pull together the rival factions within large-scale industry. It also allowed him to present himself, with little justification, as a leader of small business. He also promoted corporatism as a means of cementing the new unity in the business movement. However, Gignoux's power in the CGPF was short-lived. He was only useful to industrialists as long as they needed to unite against the Popular Front settlement.

The defeat of the general strike of November 1938 marked the end of that settlement and thus of Gignoux's usefulness. He himself recognized that businessmen showed less interest in organization after November 1938. In 1940 Gignoux entered the army passing the acting presidency of the CGPF to Baron Petiet.

By the time that Gignoux emerged from a German prisoner of war camp in 1941 the CGPF had been dissolved. After this Gignoux did not appear to play a prominent part in political life. He devoted much of his energy to his duties as mayor of a small town in the Loire. However, behind the scenes he exercised considerable influence at Vichy. He headed the economic commission of Pétain's Conseil National and he frequently visited Vichy. Pierre Nicolle reported that he was 'among the Marshal's most trusted advisers' and that he had turned down the Ministry of Industrial Production on at least one occasion. In the 1950s Gignoux became editor of the venerable conservative journal *Revue des Deux Mondes* and in 1959 was appointed to the Committee of experts that reported on France's financial situation.

Bibliography

Gignoux, C.J. (1920), *L'Après-guerre et la politique commerciale*, Paris: A. Colin.

Kolboom, I. (1986), *La Revanche des patrons*, Paris: Flammarion.

Nicolle, P. (1947), *Cinquante mois d'armistice*, 2 vols, Paris: André Bonne.

RCV

GIRAUD, General Henri (1878–1949)

An officer who achieved exceptionally rapid advancement, Henri Giraud was an infantryman whose reputation as a daring and bold soldier was made in the First World War. Wounded several times during the conflict, he spent four months in late 1914 evading capture behind German lines in Belgium after the battle of Guise. Eventually incarcerated, he broke out from his prisoner of war camp in Holland and was assisted back to France by Nurse Edith Cavell's escape network. Later in the war, and after 1918, Giraud's career progressed swiftly through command and staff appointments. In 1936 he became military governor of Metz and commander of the sixth military region (one of the twenty districts into which France was divided for peacetime administration of the army and which acted as skeletons for the mobilized corps in wartime). Successfully directing this key sector which bordered the fast-rearming Germany and contained a large section of the Maginot Line, Giraud made a considerable impression.

Still in only his late fifties, he was reckoned among the French army's brightest stars. In 1936 the British military attaché noted him as 'one of the foremost French commanders and . . . certainly one of the youngest . . . tall for a Frenchman, alert and possessed of tremendous drive and energy'. Around this time the 'Giraud legend' was born, though it rested on little except a sense that Giraud's generalship would be dashing, aggressive and innovative. The myth owed more to his appearance than his achievements. Of slim build, over six feet tall, and a top-class fencer, Giraud had the conventional military good looks which especially endeared him to visiting British officers and politicians. By 1939 he was thought the 'outstanding claimant' to be next-but-one French supreme commander and chief of national defence staff, after General Gaston Billotte, the likely successor when Maurice Gamelin retired in September 1940. Giraud's rise to the head of the French command seemed to be purely a matter of time.

During the Phoney War he was assigned command of the 7th Army, in the French strategic reserve. This force was disposed, at first, behind the centre of the Franco-British front between Lâon and Châlons-sur-Marne, ready to fall in swift counterattack on a German breakthrough. But in November 1939 the army was redeployed in Gamelin's Dyle Plan for the forward support of Belgium. The modification moved Giraud's formations, which included much of the best French motorized infantry and mechanized armour, to the extreme left flank of Allied dispositions, on the Channel. Their task was made more hazardous still, in April 1940, when Gamelin added to his plan the speculative Breda Variant. This required Giraud's powerfully-armed mobile divisions to dash north when the German western blitzkrieg began. Hugging the Belgian coast, they were to race to join the Dutch at Breda and Tilburg, extending the Franco-British lines northwards and incorporating the Netherlands army – as well as the Belgians – into Allied defensive strength. The mission, accomplished from 10–13 May with panache and verve, was too successful. Cut off in the Low Countries, Giraud found himself far removed from the decisive Sedan and Meuse battlefields as the German panzers destroyed the French centre and divided the Allied armies. As the debacle of May 1940 unfolded, Giraud was ordered to counterattack southwards against the panzer advance. The

manoeuvre, involving a change of front behind the retreating Belgian army on roads choked with refugees, was too ambitious even for the best divisions the French possessed. In the confusion, in a repetition of his 1914 misadventure, Giraud himself was captured on the 19 May. It is ironical that the day he was taken prisoner was also the day on which Gamelin, whom Giraud had been tipped to replace, was dismissed. The coincidence seemed to symbolize the inability of the French army of 1940 to regenerate itself from the ranks of its own command.

In 1942 Giraud's career continued to repeat itself. For just as he had escaped in the earlier war, so now Giraud made a daring breakout from his fortress prison at Königstein on the Elbe. The Giraud legend was embellished by his passage in disguise across Germany and occupied France. The romantic escapade was completed in cloak and dagger style through a night-time rendezvous off the Spanish coast with a US submarine, organized by the American general, Mark Clark. This took Giraud to Algeria where a pro-Allied French authority was being constituted in the aftermath of the 'Torch' landings which ended Vichy control in North Africa. Paraded proudly by the Americans on the stage of the Casablanca Conference between Roosevelt and Churchill at the start of 1943, Giraud was the US protégé against the British-backed de Gaulle, to lead Free France. In the cauldron of intrigue, infighting and ambition of North Africa, Giraud, however, showed himself to be as inept a politician as he had been unlucky as a soldier. Gradually, if reluctantly, Roosevelt was obliged to recognize that Giraud did not possess the political skills equal to the immense task wished upon him. Belatedly, the Americans accepted de Gaulle's direction of the fighting French forces and of the French committee of national liberation in Algiers in 1943, precursor of the 1944 provisional government.

Giraud's inadequacies both in high wartime command and under the challenge of political leadership offer a near-classical example of the 'Peter principle'. When tested by the demands of battle and the pressures of politics, Giraud revealed that he was simply a competent corps commander, with an engaging personality, promoted far beyond his abilities. The historical interest of Giraud resides not in asking why he failed in these highest callings but in seeking to understand how he ever came to be called at all. The career of this man of straw does more than exemplify the central importance of defective top-level military performance in producing the catastrophe of 1940. It also brings into doubt the quality of wartime advice about Europe offered to Roosevelt by the US state department and chiefs of staff. Last, but very far from least, the Giraud case poses extremely uncomfortable questions about the judgement of Roosevelt himself.

Bibliography

Alexander, D.W. (1974), 'Repercussions of the Breda Variant', in *French Historical Studies*, vol. VIII, pp. 459–88.
Giraud, H. (1946), *Mes evasions*, Paris: René Julliard.
Kersaudy, F. (1981), *Churchill and de Gaulle*, London: Collins.
Lerecouvreux, M. (1951), *L'Armée Giraud en Hollande*, Paris: Nouvelles Editions Latines.

MSA

GIRAULT, Suzanne (a.k.a. Depollier, Girand, Connier, Olympia, Sauvage) (1882–1973)

This 'brutal, coarse, ferociously ambitious, backstairs Catherine the Great' (in Humbert-Droz' words) merits inclusion here only because, along with Albert Treint (q.v.), she was one of Zinoviev's instruments for the Bolshevization of the French Communist Party in the early 1920s. Both Girault and Treint espoused the Comintern's sectarian 'united front from below', attacked the Socialist parties (which severely weakened the Communist parties) and were vigorous in the witch hunt of 'Trotskyists'. In an act of propitiation to Stalin (who had eliminated Zinoviev from the Russian leadership) they were expelled from the French party as 'Trotskyite faction leaders' in January 1928 before the 9th ECCI Plenum in February. Since Girault and Treint had led the first anti-Trotskyite crusade (in which they had implicated both Thorez – q.v. – and Souvarine – q.v.) this accusation was no mere grace note on the keyboard of abuse.

Girault was born in La Chaux-de-Fonds, Switzerland, and went to Russia as a governess. At some point, possibly as early as 1917, she joined the Communists and in 1919 was a member of the French Communist group in Kiev. During July–August 1920 she served as guide and interpreter for the French syndicalist Alfred Rossmer at the 2nd Comintern Congress in Moscow. Rossmer is thought to have recommended her promotion and she was also supposed to have had connections with the secret police.

In late 1923 Girault returned to France and was coopted on to the French party's Political Bureau; this position was ratified at the Lyons Congress of January 1924 (as a result of Zinoviev's support) and she thereafter ran the party with Treint. In September 1924 she became head of the party's Paris region and continued to act as the Comintern's liaison with France. The aggressiveness of the party's line at this time led to her being in court on several occasions and in 1924 she was condemned to six months in prison and a 500-franc fine for inciting military disobedience (during the Rif War). This was also the period in which Treint and Girault carried through the centralization of the party in exemplary fashion: Girault, with the slate pencil voice and a command of Bolshevik invective, was no mere adjunct to this process.

However when the leadership struggle in Moscow turned against their patron their power slipped away. In February 1926 the ECCI (6th enlarged plenum) condemned the 'ultra-left error' which it blamed on them (in so far as France was concerned) and this judgement was confirmed at the French party's Lille Congress in June 1926: both were dropped from the Political Bureau.

Girault, unlike Treint, did not join another party and did not accept expulsion as definitive and, despite having run the journal *L'Unité Léniniste*, was readmitted in 1930. But she was involved only in a series of secondary administrative tasks in the 1930s and in the Communist National Front Resistance during the war. She was elected to the Senate on the PCF ticket in 1948 and again in 1952. Girault retired in 1958 but was in a delegation of veterans at the PCF Congress in 1967. This provincial Torquemada having run one inquisition was, after the 1920s, no longer in the top ranks of power. Her long-time companion was François Sauvage; she is sometimes known as 'Suzanne Sauvage' among other names.

Bibliography

No reliable account of Girault's contribution to early French communism exists but there is a brief portrait in Jean Maitron (ed.), *Dictionnaire bibliographique du mouvement ouvrier français* (Paris: Editions Ouvrières, 1973).

DSB

'GIROUD, Françoise' (France Gourdji) (1916–   )

Françoise Giroud was already an influential political

figure as editor of the weekly *L'Express*, when she made history as the first minister for women's affairs. She began her career in the cinema as a script-girl. During the war she worked for *Paris-Soir* and was imprisoned for Resistance activities. From 1945 she was the editor of the new magazine *Elle*, which she saw as an instrument of women's liberation, with a new vision of women's place in the world. She left in 1953 to found *L'Express* with Jean-Jacques Servan-Schreiber (q.v.). In 1974, after Valéry Giscard d'Estaing became president, she was appointed secretary of state for women's affairs in Chirac's government. In 1976 she became secretary of state for culture in Barre's government. She left the government in 1977, after her role in the abortive attempt to have the Giscardian D'Ornano elected as mayor of Paris, and returned to journalism.

L'Express was founded to give voice to the ideas of Mendès France and bring him to power. It put forward the policy of rebuilding France through investment in productive industry, democratic planning and a belief in parliamentary democracy, backing this up with economic information. Françoise Giroud saw the situation of women also in terms of the need for modernization, the continued division of labour between the sexes being essentially outdated, but entrenched by habit and therefore requiring positive action to eradicate it.

In spite of her support for Mitterrand in 1974, Giscard d'Estaing invited her to become a minister. He was looking for allies from the centre-left to help him in his project to reform French society. In this strategy, women and young people were seen as key elements: 53 per cent of voters were women, yet, as Françoise Giroud was to find out, 41 per cent of women claimed to have no political opinions (as compared to 10 per cent of men). This was clearly a large segment of political territory to be fought over. Giscard d'Estaing did not have a policy to improve women's situation as the poor legislative record of his presidency bears out. Françoise Giroud accepted the post, in spite of the initial obstacles put up by Chirac and the Gaullists and her own reservations about the extent to which she would have any power to act effectively. Her 'ministry' had no budget of its own and could only persuade other ministries to cooperate to carry out her proposals. After leaving the government, she published *La Comédie du Pouvoir* in which she expressed more general reservations about the unreal nature of ministerial power and the degree to which governments can or should influence the course of events.

Even though some of the major reforms affecting women, such as the abortion law, were not her responsibility but Simone Veil's her achievements as a minister are none the less real. After one year collecting information on women's problems and demands, she drew up a five-year programme of one hundred measures, eighty of which were adopted by the cabinet. The aim of these measures was to improve women's situation by making it easier for them to extend their role from the private to the social and to gain greater autonomy and independence in running their own lives.

Bibliography

Giroud, F. (1977) *La Comédie du pouvoir*, Paris: Fayard.
    See also: *Secrétariat d'état à la condition féminine – cent mesures pour les femmes; presentées par Françoise Giroud* (Paris: La Documentation Française, 1975).

MM

GISCARD D'ESTAING, Valéry (1926–)

Valéry Giscard d'Estaing was elected president of the Republic in 1974 with great hopes of a brilliant and reforming period of office and was defeated by François Mitterrand in 1981. His presidency, which occurred at the end of the period of rapid economic growth which most of Europe had enjoyed until the OPEC oil crisis of 1973, is regarded as a disappointing one in which little of consequence was achieved.

Giscard d'Estaing comes from a wealthy and cultivated Catholic family of conservative tradition. He was born at Koblenz, Germany, on 2 February 1926 when his father, Edmond, an *inspecteur des finances*, was in charge of finance services for the French occupation of the Rhineland. His mother, May Bardoux, descendant, apparently, of a daughter of King Louis XV, belonged to a family long active in conservative political and literary circles. Indeed, in 1956 Giscard was to inherit the parliamentary seat in the Auvergne occupied by his grandfather, Jacques Bardoux. Giscard has two sisters, Sylvie and Isabelle, and a brother, Olivier.

He was educated mainly at the Lycée Janson-le-Sailly and Lycée Louis-le-Grand in Paris. He was too young to have played an active role in the Resistance and the Second World War, though he did participate in the advance into Germany in 1945, receiving the Croix de Guerre and the Bronze Star medal.

One of the most important elements in Giscard's make-up is his technocratic education after the war at the two most famous *grandes écoles* which train the elite of the public service: Polytechnique, where he passed out second of his year, and the newly-created ENA (third).

In 1952 he married Anne-Aymone de Brantes, connected to the wealthy steel family Schneider. They have four children: Henri, Louis-Joachim, Valérie-Anne and Jacinthe.

As one of the top graduates of ENA Giscard became, like his father, an *inspecteur des finances*, and joined the Banque de France. In 1950 he became a Ministry of Finance official and in 1953 a member of the cabinet of Edgar Faure, minister of finance. Edgar Faure took Giscard with him to Matignon as *directeur-adjoint* when he became prime minister in 1955. To join a ministerial *cabinet* has become the classic move from administration to politics that so many graduates of ENA have made since. In 1956 his grandfather retired and Giscard stood on the CNIP (independents and peasants) list in Puy-de-Dôme under his grandfather's label, Independent Republican (Républicain Indépendent). As a parliamentarian, tall and of distinguished appearance and intellect, he immediately impressed obsevers as destined for high office. His first speech, in 1957, called for France to support the creation of the European Community. In the 1958 crisis he backed General de Gaulle and held his seat at the first election of the Fifth Republic. He also added the local constituency roles of mayor of Chamalières (a suburb of Clermont-Ferrand) and local councillor. He was given junior ministerial office in the Finance Ministry in 1959 under Pinay, symbol of prudent conservatism, and in 1962, aged 35, he became minister of finance and economic affairs. He was the first ENA graduate to succeed to such high office.

During 1962–74 Giscard was the brilliant rising star of liberalism in France – a sort of French Kennedy or Pierre Trudeau. As minister of finance, 1962–6, he is best remembered for the *plan de stabilisation* to combat inflation, but above all for his informal pullover-clad television appearances explaining complex economic matters to the nation. He supported de Gaulle over Algerian independence and in the 1962 referendum on direct elections to the presidency. This enabled him and a few of his associates, calling themselves Independent Republicans to hold their seats in the 1962 election when practically all conservatives opposed to direct elections – not to mention opposition parties like MRP, Radicals, Socialists and Communists – fell victim to the pro de Gaulle landslide. The Independent Republicans formed a parliamentary group on their own with Giscard as leader and supported the Gaullist government as coalition partner. Their support,

however, was not unconditional and they acted as a ginger group inside the coalition in favour of Europe and a more liberal, less authoritarian style of government.

In 1966 Giscard left the government and became a much more prominent critic of de Gaulle and de Gaulle's 'solitary exercise of power'. He described his attitude as 'yes . . . but' ('oui . . . mais') – in support of the government but not unconditionally. He criticized de Gaulle's European policy and his famous outburst in Canada *'vive le Québec libre'*. He cultivated the art of attracting maximum attention for his utterances (rather as Chirac did when Giscard was president) – none more so than for his announcement in 1969 that he was not supporting de Gaulle on the referendum on regional and Senate reform. The defeat of this referendum was followed immediately by de Gaulle's resignation – so Giscard to this day is regarded as something of a parricide by Gaullists. The period out of government was also used by Giscard to build the Independent Republicans into a national party (albeit rather too much based on prominent notables rather than a mass membership), and the Perspectives et Réalités clubs as think-tanks for liberal ideas.

In 1969 he supported Georges Pompidou for the presidency and was rewarded by a return to the Finance Ministry, though with something of the aura of a deputy prime minister. In 1974 Pompidou died and Giscard announced that he was a candidate for the succession. Although the Gaullist party adopted Jacques Chaban-Delmas as its candidate it soon became clear that Giscard was the one with the best chance of defeating François Mitterrand, the candidate supported by the united left – Socialists and Communists. Indeed, it was for this reason that Jacques Chirac, a leading Pompidou Gaullist, the man who seven years later contributed to Giscard's defeat, threw his support behind Giscard. Giscard also gained the support of centrists like Jean Lecanuet (q.v.), presidential candidate against de Gaulle in 1965, who had remained in opposition up to 1974. With 32 per cent Giscard ran well ahead of the other candidates of the right and centre at the first ballot and won an exciting second ballot run off against Mitterrand by 13.1 million (50.7 per cent) to 12.7 million (49.3 per cent). The election in 1974 remains as the one which attracted record public interest – huge meetings for the two principal candidates and a turn out of almost 90 per cent.

The new president took office in 1974 amid great hopes of a new reforming era. His election campaign had emphasized change and a more liberal, less authoritarian state. His victory was the defeat of the

Gaullist party and the 'UDR state' in which Gaullists had for so long been dominant in government, parliament, and the public services. He was young (48), brilliant, and with the training and intellect to master the immense and complex organization of the modern state. He seemed to be introducing a more relaxed and less pompous style to the presidency: no uniform for the official photograph displayed in every town hall in France, a new arrangement for the Marseillaise, a stroll on foot to his inauguration, occasions when he drove his own car, the invitation to the local dustmen to come in to breakfast at the Elysée, the famous occasions when he would invite himself and Mme Giscard d'Estaing to dinner with 'an ordinary family'. He also had a parliamentary majority prepared to see presidential supremacy continue; and a French president, with the support of such a parliamentary majority, has more unfettered power, is less subject to checks and balances and constraints, than any other Western political leader. Despite all this, however, the presidency was a disappointment. One looks in vain for the memorable achievements in foreign affairs, for the great economic and social developments that were associated with his two predecessors, General de Gaulle and Georges Pompidou.

It was Giscard's misfortune to be president after the oil crisis of 1973 and through the second oil crisis of 1979, a period in which the price of energy increased fourteenfold. The mid and late 1970s therefore were a period of economic recession and inflation in most Western countries. The golden era for France of perpetual and rapid economic growth, in which governments can always do great things, was over. This was the period of the *Plan Barre* – austerity and unemployment in an attempt to reduce deficits. The main thrust of industrial policy, however, was continued: an interventionist policy of 'national champions' in which state resources are used to ensure that France has an internationally viable firm in each major industrial sector, such as aviation, automobiles, electronics or nuclear power. The greatest success of the period was probably the tremendous nuclear energy programme in which France, aided by a planning system which makes it very easy for the State to ride roughshod over objectors, made rapid strides towards a reduced dependence on imported oil.

Liberal social reforms were surprisingly limited. France was the last country in Western Europe to retain the death penalty – indeed the gruesome method of the guillotine. Giscard failed to abolish it, and was rather sparing in the use of his presidential right of mercy. Abortion was legalized – a reform

which Giscard and his health minister, Simone Veil, had to see through without the full support of the parliamentary majority parties. The franchise was extended to 18-year-olds, and a Ministry for Women was introduced.

Giscard's statements over the years had led to hopes that, as president, he would be more liberal and less nationalist than his predecessors – less hostile to the USA, less divisive of Western unity and Nato, more supportive of Israel, less mercenary in dealing with former African colonies, overall more favourable to a community approach in Europe. These hopes were not realized. In Europe the Giscard period is remembered for three things. The most important was the establishment of the European Council, the regular meetings of EEC heads of government. This, however, belongs much more to the de Gaulle idea of *l'Europe des patries* – dealings between nation states – than a move towards a more integrated community. Another important European initiative backed by Giscard was the European Monetary System (EMS). The third development was the Franco-German entente. Helped by a good personal relationship (in English) between two liberal technocrats, Giscard and Helmut Schmidt, France and Germany became the joint leaders of the EEC with very close regular consultations and exchanges at administrative and cultural levels.

In East/West relations, France finished up, at the end of the Giscard presidency, roughly where it had been under de Gaulle and Pompidou, that is to say doing everything possible to frustrate American policy. France refused to help the USA during the Iran hostages crisis of 1979/80, and refused to support the boycott of the Moscow Olympics of 1980 to protest at the Soviet invasion of Afghanistan. Indeed Giscard actually had a meeting in Warsaw with President Brezhnev, while the Western response was being worked out.

In the Middle East, France continued with its policy of selling military hardware to all and sundry. A French nuclear reactor in Iraq was subsequently bombed by the Israelis, who were convinced it was being used to produce atomic bombs. In Africa the replacement of colonialism by dependence, started under de Gaulle, continued. France continued to feel free to intervene militarily to prop up or remove dictators, and to exploit local mineral resources. Giscard sent the French paratroops into Zaïre in 1979 to rescue some Europeans (mainly Belgian) held hostage by rebel troups in Kolwezi – an excellent example of the power of a French president to do exactly what he liked with no need to explain to Parliament or the public. In the field of defence,

France remained outside Nato, although there was some movement towards a commitment to join in the defence of Europe. France retained and developed its own strategic nuclear force.

Giscard's first prime minister was Jacques Chirac, a Gaullist protégé of Pompidou, who was minister of the interior at the time of Pompidou's death and who had supported Giscard against the official Gaullist candidate in the 1974 election. In retrospect it seems odd that a president with liberal reforming aims should have appointed such an ambitious authoritarian to such a job. At all events, he lived to regret it. Chirac made himself leader of the Gaullist party, left the government when he was ready to do so in 1976, relaunched the Gaullist party as his own creature, the RPR, and defeated Giscard's candidate in a bruising campaign for the Paris City Hall in 1977. Chirac became the president's bitterest rival and played a major part in his defeat in 1981. Under the prime minister, the government, unlike previous Fifth Republic governments, was predominantly Giscardian with Independent Republicans like Michel Poniatowski, or centrists like Jean Lecanuet in key roles. After the resignation of Chirac in 1976 Giscard appointed another future rival, Raymond Barre, 'the best economist in France', as prime minister and finance minister, to be a 'doctor for the economy'. In the period 1976–81 the Gaullists, though still part of the majority and never voting for a motion of censure, were increasingly critical of the government, rather as Giscard and his friends had been under de Gaulle from 1966–9. The principal feature of government during the whole Giscard presidency was the way decision-making power, over almost the whole range of policy, from foreign affairs to social and environmental issues, was concentrated in the hands of the president.

The most significant electoral success for the president was in 1978, when the left, because of the divisions between Socialists and Communists, failed to win the expected parliamentary election victory. It was for this election that the non-Gaullist, or Giscardian, elements of the majority combined to form the UDF. Giscard's main contribution to this election was his clear statement foreshadowing *cohabitation*, that he would not resign if the left won and that it would be permitted to carry out its electoral programme. In this he made a real contribution to the concept of peaceful alternation of power – finally to occur in 1981.

The presidency ended badly. There were a number of political scandals of a characteristically French kind – that is to say the cover-up. A Giscardian deputy, de Broglie, was murdered, a minister in the government, Boulin, committed suicide, both events carrying the faint odour of the abuse of power. Finally there was the scandal of the 'Bokassa diamonds' – a gift allegedly given to Giscard by the extremely unsavoury dictator of the Central African Empire – kept in power, indeed crowned, by France, and removed from power by France in 1979. The damaging point about the diamonds affair was not suspicion of corruption, but that the president, by this time, thought his dignity too offended to make a proper explanation to the public. One of the strange aspects of the Giscard presidency is why a term of office, which began in such a relaxed and approachable style, should have ended in such excessive touchiness about presidential dignity and protocol.

The election of 1981 was won by François Mitterrand, Chirac having stood as a candidate against Giscard in the first ballot. His criticisms of the president and withholding of support in the second ballot ensured Giscard's defeat. The president handed over power to his successor in an exemplary democratic fashion – the first transfer of power to the opposition in the Fifth Republic. Giscard's other democratic memorial was the constitutional amendment allowing sixty members of the Chamber of Deputies or Senate to challenge legislation in the Constitutional Council.

Giscard is the first person to have actively played the role of ex-president. Should one retire, like de Gaulle? Should one renew political activity? If so, to what extent should one be inhibited by the dignity of one's former office? After a period of hesitation, Giscard chose first the method of occasional presidential-type press conferences and declarations, and subsequently re-election. He returned to the National Assembly as a deputy in 1984 and was re-elected in 1986. He was elected to the Auvergne Regional Council in 1986 and became its president. He was not appointed as a minister in the Chirac *cohabitation* government of 1986, though he had always expressed himself favourable to *cohabitation*. In the opposition to President Mitterrand, Giscard's leadership role has been eclipsed – first by Chirac, leader of the new majority, and also by Raymond Barre, principal critic of the government from within the majority. Nevertheless, he attempted a comeback after the 1988 presidential elections which saw the defeat of his rivals Chirac and Barre, and became president of a weakened UDF. For the 1989 European elections Giscard led a joint UDF–RPR list which polled 28.86 per cent of the vote (26 seats).

In conclusion, the story of Giscard is the sad story of a man with brilliant gifts and generous ideas who never became a great political leader.

Bibliography

Giscard d'Estaing, V. (1977), *Towards a New Democracy*, London: Collins.
Giscard d'Estaing, V. (1984), *Deux français sur trois*, Paris: Flammarion.
Giscard d'Estaing, V. (1988), *Le Pouvoir et la vie*, Paris: Compagnie 12.
Frears, J. (1981), *France in the Giscard Presidency*, London: Unwin.

JF

GOBLET, René-Marie (1828–1905)

A lawyer by training, practising in Amiens (Pas-de-Calais), René Goblet later became a journalist of note and one of the leading Radical politicians of his day. Founder of *Le Progrès de la Somme* daily, Goblet was elected deputy for his department in 1871 allying himself with the Republican left – *gauche Républicaine*. Though not re-elected in 1876, he regained his seat in 1877 having, as mayor of Amiens, been an eloquent opponent of MacMahon's constitutional clash with the Republicans. He was a member of the committee of eighteen in the critical last months of that year when the Republican majority had to decide a strategy to deal with MacMahon's refusal to admit defeat. An active and influential parliamentarian, Goblet was *rapporteur* of the amnesty bill of 1878. Under-secretary at the Ministery of Justice in Waddington's cabinet (1879), he was in favour of a purge of law officers thought to be hostile to the new regime. He was also minister of the interior under de Freycinet (q.v.) in 1882, where he was closely involved in legislation for the election of mayors by their municipal councils. Minister of public instruction under Brisson (1885) and holding office under de Freycinet again in January 1886, Goblet gave his name to the law of October 1886, enforcing at last the secularization of the teaching staff in state schools.

Two months later, he was president of the Council, controversially retaining General Boulanger as minister of war, a fact which did not go unnoticed by Bismarck. In addition, Goblet was personally to adopt an aggressive posture in the crisis in Franco-German relations (the 'Schnaebelé affair') of April 1887, proposing that an ultimatum be sent to Berlin.

Perhaps providentially, Goblet's cabinet fell over another matter and Boulanger with it. Foreign minister under Floquet in 1888, Goblet again held office at a time when Franco-German relations were strained. Since 1882 he had given much thought to constitutional reform, and, during a brief interlude away from the forefront of politics, published *La Révision de la Constitution* (1893). He had, in 1889, taken up his legal practice again this time in Paris, having failed to be re-elected by his Amiens constituents. A senator for the Seine, he became a director with Lockroy and Millerand (q.v.) of *La Petite République* daily in the years up to 1893. In that same year, he was again deputy for Paris, being one of the few to return after defeat in 1889; for, with Léon Bourgeois (q.v.) and Poincaré (q.v.) and younger men, a new political generation was taking over. Goblet himself had already started to distance himself from the *concentration républicaine*, turning towards socialists like Millerand, who was to replace him as editor of the *Petite République*. Among the last issues to engage this fiery Radical were the *lois scélérates* – measures against the anarchists and legislation which he opposed vigorously in 1894.

Goblet had only briefly reached the political heights, as a second-choice in 1886 when Grévy had vetoed Freycinet's nominee, Clemenceau. His cabinet, almost identical to the one it succeeded, was referred to, disparagingly, as 'a Freycinet ministry without Freycinet'. Yet he held ministerial office six times between 1879 and 1893, and his notable gifts as a debater had made him over a number of years a useful, even an indispensable, member of many cabinets.

Bibliography

Kayser, J. (1961), *Les Grandes batailles du radicalisme*, Paris: M. Rivière.

ACR

GOUIN, Jean Félix (1884–1977)

Félix Gouin was prime minister (président du Conseil) for five months during the transition period between the resignation of de Gaulle as head of the provisional government and the approval of the Constitution of the new Fourth Republic in October 1946. He was one of the generation of French Socialists which came after the founders of the SFIO in 1905 (Section Française de l'Internationale Ouvrière – French section of the Workers'

International) and before the generation of the early Fifth Republic.

Between the wars, he was a member of the Chamber of Deputies, but first and foremost a lawyer in Marseilles and Aix-en-Provence. In July 1940 he was one of only eighty deputies (later regarded as heroes) who voted against giving Pétain full power to recast the French state. He was an early member of the Socialist Resistance, and one of a group of nine people who reconstituted a clandestine SFIO in Nîmes in March 1941. Having been one of the defence lawyers at the trial of Léon Blum in 1942, Gouin was sent by Blum to London (he was imprisoned for three months in Spain on the way) as representative of the SFIO, but de Gaulle at first refused to recognize organized parties. Gouin himself wavered between support for and opposition to de Gaulle.

In 1944–5 his qualities of conciliation and flexibility served him well as president of the Consultative Assembly, then of the Constituent Assembly, and meant that the Communists did not oppose his appointment as prime minister when de Gaulle resigned in January, 1946. His own ambition at the time was to be French ambassador to a South American country. In his investiture speech, Gouin spoke of the dire economic situation – galloping inflation, huge budget deficit, capital investment at a standstill and industrial production at a third of its 1938 level. His government's austerity programme, involving a wage and partial price freeze, provoked widespread unpopularity for the Socialists.

During Gouin's period of office, the first formal institutions of French economic planning, inspired by Jean Monnet, were established. Moreover, major nationalizations were effected – coal, gas and electricity, banks and credit institutions, and the thirty-two biggest insurance companies. New elections in June 1946, made necessary because the first draft Constitution had been rejected by the people, saw a significant decline in Socialist support, and Bidault replaced Gouin as prime minister on 23 June, though the latter remained deputy prime minister in continuation of the spirit of coalition politics.

An unsuccessful attempt was made in autumn 1946 to implicate Gouin in a scandal involving fraudulent dealing in wine, and the affair surfaced again in March 1950. In fact, Gouin was ill-served by members of his personal staff who owed their position largely to political services rendered. Gouin remained as a deputy until November 1958, after which he retired from active politics. He was opposed to de Gaulle's return in June 1958, drawing a telling analogy between the fear of Socialist parliamentarians at this prospect, and that of their predecessors in the chaos of summer 1940.

Bibliography

Information on Félix Gouin is best obtained from Léon Blum's memoirs, and books on the French Resistance and the Fourth Republic. See, for example, G. Elgey, *La République des illusions* (Paris: Fayard, 1969).

MS

'GRANDVAL' (né Hirsch), Gilbert (1904–81)

Grandval was educated at the Lycée Condorcet and was the commercial director of a chemical company. An enthusiastic flier before the war, he was mobilized as a pilot in 1939. He was one of the first Resisters and he recruited and organized escape routes before he rose to the head of the FFI in the east of France, comprising eight regions. (He was then known as *Planète*.) Grandval went underground after June 1943. It was Grandval who welcomed de Gaulle on his entry to liberated Nancy, the first time the two had met. He was made governor of the Saar (then under French control) by de Gaulle and he remained in the Saar for ten years (1945–55) as high commissioner and then as ambassador. He became associated with the French occupation but helped start the European Coal and Steel Community.

Although a 'liberal' Gaullist, he was made resident general of Morocco from June to September 1955 by Edgar Faure. Arriving in Rabat after the assassination by counter-terrorists of a businessman, he cleared the embassy of reactionary colonialists and tried to form a representative government. He presciently warned of disaster if nothing were done but faced the opposition of the settler community (which he antagonized) and the administration. Resignation was inevitable and Faure replaced him with a more amenable figure after only fifty days.

In 1962 Grandval was minister of labour in Pompidou's government during the period of the miners' strike. From 1958–62 he was the under-secretary for the merchant navy which enabled him, when he left government in July 1966, to head a shipping line, Messageries Maritimes.

Grandval was important as a major figure in the small left-wing Gaullist party the Union Démocratique du Travail (UDT) which put up candidates supported by the main Gaullist party. As minister of labour Grandval was responsible for extending 'participation' with de Gaulle's backing against the objections of the business organizations and the Communist unions. The Grandval reform of 1965 strengthened factory and office committees, made them compulsory, and increased workers' rights to be informed of the state of a firm's affairs. The bill faced 128 amendments but was forced through on a package vote. Grandval also supported the UDT's demand that social security be extended to the self-employed. This, too, was implemented. However, these moderate reforms and the institution of a fourth week of paid holiday made him unpopular with conservative colleagues and he quit government at the beginning of 1966. In 1971 he tried to federate the left-wing Gaullists into a Union Travailliste, of which he became president. The Union made no impact. Grandval was awarded the Croix de Guerre 1939–45.

Bibliography

See the obituary in *L'Espoir* (Paris) no. 38, March 1982, pp. 56–7.

DSB

GRAVE, Jean (1854–1939)

Grave's father, finding success neither as a joiner nor as a farmer, left his native Puy-de-Dôme to find work in Paris in 1857, and he was joined there by his wife the following year. Jean Grave lived with his grandparents before joining his parents in the 5th *arrondissement* in 1860. He gained his *certificat d'études*, and from 1866 served his apprenticeship first as a mechanic, then as a cobbler. He worked together with his father for a while, and although there was a clash of temperaments, their common attachment to the Republican ideal effected something of a *rapprochement* during the siege of Paris and the Commune of 1870–1, when Grave's father was a national guard. Grave's mother died in 1874 and his father in 1876, and he was therefore released from military service as the eldest child. He returned to working as a cobbler, and became involved in the revolutionary movement. In the late 1880s Grave married Clotilde Benoît, a bookbinding worker, but both she and their son were to die in childbirth. In 1909 he married Mabel Holland Thomas, an Englishwoman of aristocratic origin to whom he had been introduced by Kropotkin; she was to die in 1929.

Grave, an autodidact, was not an original theorist and had no oratorical skills. He was extremely shy, and devoted himself to journalism and to writing. He produced five books on anarchist doctrine, numerous pamphlets and ensured the appearance of various anarchist newspapers and reviews from the early 1880s until 1936. Somewhat dogmatic, he was known as the 'high-priest of anarchy', and for thirty years or more was one of the leading figures in the anarchist movement.

Briefly a member of the Parti des Travailleurs de France, which included both Socialists and anarchists, Grave devoted himself exclusively to anarchism from 1880 onwards. In 1883 he went to Geneva to take charge of *Le Révolté* (fortnightly then weekly; founded in 1879 by Kropotkin and others). Two years later he returned to Paris with the paper, which changed its name twice: in 1887, to avoid having to pay a fine, it became *La Révolte*, and in 1895 *Les Temps Nouveaux*. Grave initiated a fortnightly, then weekly, *Supplément Littéraire* to *La Révolte*; despite his personal reservations about syndicalism, *Les Temps Nouveaux* contained contributions from union leaders; he gained the cooperation of writers and artists like Mirbeau, Luce, Pissaro and Signac; and hundreds of pamphlets were published (with print runs of many thousands).

Grave's own political development reflected that of the movement as a whole. In the 1880s he was very sceptical about strikes whose aims were less than violent rebellion, and his book *La Société mourante et l'anarchie* (see below) gained him a two-year prison sentence for *incitation à la révolte*. By the late 1890s his belief in imminent revolution had diminished, and he was more concerned with changing people's ideas; 'propaganda by the deed' no longer meant only violence, but living one's own life according to one's ideals. His opposition to individualism and his rigorous moral standards led him to condemn both 'illegalism' and the industrial sabotage practised by some syndicalists.

The First World War, which he had spent in England, was a watershed in Grave's life. A signatory of the *Manifeste des Seize*, pointing out the need for workers to have their own political organization, he agreed with Kropotkin that the reactionary nature of German militarism necessitated support by anarchists for the war effort. This position was adopted by only a small minority of anarchists internationally, and most of the group around *Les Temps Nouveaux* abandoned Grave to launch a new antimilitarist and internationalist review. In 1920, when the bulletin form of *Les Temps Nouveaux* (1916–19) was to be replaced by a new series of the paper, personal differences led to a further split in the group. From then on Grave was very much isolated, but still managed to produce *Publications de la Révolte et des Temps Nouveaux* from 1920 to 1936.

Bibliography

Books by Grave: *La Société mourante et l'anarchie*, preface by Octave Mirbeau (Paris: Tresse et Stock, 1893); *La Société future* (Paris: P.-V. Stock, 1895); *L'Individu et la société* (Paris: P.-V. Stock, 1897); *L'Anarchie, son but, ses moyens* (Paris: P.-V. Stock, 1899); *Réformes, révolution* (Paris: P.-V. Stock, 1910).

A complete bibliography can be found in the new edition of Grave's autobiography, *Quarante ans de propagande anarchiste*, edited and introduced by M. Delfau, with a preface by Jean Maitron (Paris: Flammarion, 1973; first published in 1930 under the title *Mouvement libertaire sous la troisième république*).

See also: Jean Maitron, *Le Mouvement anarchiste en France* (Paris: Maspéro, 1975), 2 vols; and Jean Maitron (ed.), *Dictionnaire biographique du mouvement ouvrier français* (Paris: Les Editions Ouvrières), vol. 12.

DGB

GREMETZ, Maxime (1928–)

Maxime Gremetz was born in Canchy in the department of the Somme and at 18 was an activist in the Young Communists at Abbeville where he was secretary of the Guy-Môquet 'Communist circle'. Already noted by the leadership, he was at the 7th Festival of Youth in Vienna in 1959. In 1960 he was a metal worker at the Ferodo works in Amiens where he was also an enthusiastic CGT (union) organizer and, it is said, so 'difficult' that he was soon without a job. At this point he entered the party apparatus and became a startling example of upward failure.

In 1965 Gremetz became organization secretary of the PCF's Somme Federation and in 1966 became its first secretary. Gremetz failed to win a seat in the local elections in Amiens in 1965 although he was elected a departmental councillor (*conseiller général*) for Amiens in 1970. But the local election in 1965 does provide one clue to Gremetz' steady promotion: the Amiens ticket was one of the few left-unity lists at a time when the party was looking for a breakthrough in its alliance overtures to the Socialists. This alliance was the first in a series of disastrous central instructions carried out by Gremetz with ex-

emplary discipline: in 1978 Gremetz was rewarded for his loyalty with René Lamps' Assembly seat; he was defeated in 1981 but in 1986 scraped back into the Assembly though with only 14.54 per cent of the vote. (He lost the seat in 1988.)

In 1972 Gremetz was made a substitute member of the Central Committee and in 1976 he was made a Political Bureau substitute member with responsibility for relations with Christian groups. This appointment was a curious one. Gremetz was neither a philosopher nor did he have contacts with religious milieux – the promotion was probably a reward for his loyalty to Marchais. Gremetz was also responsible for the local elections of 1977 and for the negotiations over them with the Socialists and it is commonly agreed that the Communists did well out of the 1977 local negotiations. In 1978 Gremetz took over as director of the PCF intellectual weekly *France Nouvelle*, a position for which he also seems to have had few qualifications, since he had no acquaintance with or understanding of journalists or intellectuals. Gremetz 'survived' this post but took away from it the nickname of 'Minime' and an enhanced reputation as an authoritarian hardliner.

In September 1978 the next promotion was even more astonishing: he took over the party's foreign relations department (although under the *tutelle* of Gaston Plissonnier – q.v.) from Jean Kanapa (on his death) whose understanding and political abilities, as well as innovative approach, were widely appreciated. At the party's 23rd Congress in 1979 when Marchais' closest supporters were promoted, Gremetz was moved into the secretariat: a grey man, in a grey suit, with grey ideas but just what the leadership wanted at a trying time and with the PCF line about to take a U-turn. Gremetz carried out the party's new foreign policy – a return to Moscow – with no qualms but without flair. Maxime Gremetz's book *Et pourtant elle tourne!* (Paris: Messidor, 1987) was a pedestrian exposition of the Communist Party's foreign policies including a severe criticism of French foreign policy, the arms race, 'neo-colonialism', but combined with a traditional defence of the Eastern bloc 'Socialist' societies. He was elected to the European Assembly in 1989, the sixth on the PCF list (seven were elected).

Bibliography

Gremetz is an authentic *apparatchik* and there is nothing on him in French or English and he rarely figures in histories of Communist politics. He is an *eminence très grise* and not much of a public figure.

DSB

GRÉVY, François Judith Paul ('Jules') (1807–91)

Grévy held executive office for two months in 1848 – as *commissaire général de la République* in his home department, the Jura: this was his sole active experience of government before he became President of the Republic in 1879, at the age of 72. Yet, whether presiding over the Republic (January 1879–December 1887), a parliamentary Chamber (the National Assembly, 1871–3, the Chamber of Deputies, 1876–9) or a parliamentary group ('*la gauche fermée*, 1869–70), 'monsieur le président' was allegedly tailor-made for the role; from the early 1870s, some argue, he prepared himself for the post of President of the Republic. This is perhaps surprising: the reputation acquired during his first political career (as deputy for the Jura, 1848–51 and again from 1868 to 1879) was largely based on his opposition to the creation of the post of president and, in particular to the election of the president by universal (male) suffrage. Furthermore, in 1875, he abstained from voting for what became the constitution of the Third Republic. None the less, in 1879, he became the first undoubted Republican to preside over the Third Republic, whose constitution he undertook to respect.

Spanning some forty years, Grévy's career as a lawyer was twice as long as his two political careers (1848–51; 1868–87): hailing from modest landed peasant stock, he made a sizeable fortune through his law practice. A man of order and a parliamentarian, Grévy commanded respect not only for legal and constitutional expertise, but as a man of principle, for upholding the rule of law, and for the powerful sobriety of his arguments for a (one-Chamber) parliamentary republic – the sole regime that could end the strife brought about by those who opposed the revolution of 1789. Yet many followers of Gambetta (q.v.) – and they were influential long after the death of their champion in 1882 – portrayed Grévy as a man with an eye for the main chance: he – and his family or 'clan' – enjoyed the fruits of office while torpedoing the prospects of rising young Republicans – above all Gambetta – who were greater statesmen than he ever proved. Grévy ever preferred peace to glory. He opposed the declaration of war by Louis Napoleon (q.v.) in July 1870 and the continued prosecution of the war to the finish ('à l'outrance') by Gambetta, after the proclamation of the Republic in September. Later, angered by the bellicose talk of the war minister, General Boulanger (q.v.) in 1887, Grévy bestirred himself to assuage Bismarkian Germany by quiet diplomacy. Grévy considered Gambetta spoke 'un Français de cheval' and Boulanger a hothead. He likewise opposed the Commune and 'red agitators' in general – just as he did royalist and Bonapartist plots and machinations. The Republic should reassure: it must not frighten off the conservative and propertied classes including, above all, the peasantry.

Like Jules Favre and Jules Simon (q.v.) Grévy – who was not averse to concealing his true age – belonged to the generation of liberals and Republican parliamentarians born in the aftermath of the 1789 Revolution. Compared with Gambetta, or even Jules Ferry (q.v.), he was a member of the 'old school' – a 'man of 48' who abandoned active politics for most of the Second Empire. His education was classical; and he was a bibliophile, enamoured of Horace and Tacitus, Corneille and Racine (and, among contemporary authors, of Lamartine).

To establish the Republic as the 'definitive regime' for France was Grévy's chief concern. It motivated his support of Thiers (q.v.) between 1871 and 1873, when they were engaged in the delicate exercise – Thiers as the head of government and Grévy as president of the National Assembly – of establishing a regime that was Republican in name but a majority of whose parliamentarians were opposed to the Republic. In January 1879, on the resignation of the soldier-president, MacMahon (q.v.), Grévy was elected president by the two Houses of Parliament, gathered in 'Congress'. He left to his ministers the task of governing and the pattern of short-lived governments – set before he became president – continued. There was little cabinet solidarity and, save for the second Ferry administration (February 1883–April 1885), none of the twelve governments during Grévy's two mandates as president (January 1879–December 1887) lasted a full year. Defence, internal order and foreign relations were Grévy's chief preoccupations. Critics claim that Grévy set the tone for what would become standard presidential practice during subsequent parliamentary, and ministerial, crises. Grévy chose whom to appoint as prime minister, and then advised him on the wisdom, or otherwise, of some of his choices as ministers. Grévy deplored the difficulty of appointing a government assured of a stable majority; critics riposte that this was no reason to prefer accommodating, trimming, second-rate politicians to outstanding figures such as Gambetta. Grévy, runs this argument, did not appoint Gambetta, when the time was ripe (1879), but in late 1881; furthermore, through his parliamentary agent, his son-in-law Daniel Wilson (q.v.) Grévy allegedly sought to overthrow prime ministers whose policy he opposed – Gambetta who championed a departmental wide electoral system (which Grévy feared smacked of Louis Napoleon's plebiscitary democracy) and Ferry, set on colonial aggrandizement. Nemesis came in December 1887. Grévy had to resign when Wilson was implicated in the first major corruption scandal of the Third Republic (the sale of legion of honour decorations) and the octogenarian president had exhausted the list of politicians willing to accept an invitation to form a government.

Only de Gaulle and Mitterrand would subsequently preside over the Republic for as long as Grévy. The oblivion into which he has fallen is, however, more on a par with presidents of the Third and Fourth Republics.

Bibliography

Delabrousse, L. (1888), *Discours politiques et judiciaires, rapports et messages de Jules Grévy*, 2 vols, Paris: Maison Quantin.

Lavergne, B. (1966), *Mémoires: les deux présidences de Jules Grévy*, Paris: Fischbacher.

MP

GRIFFUELHES, Jean Victor (1874–1922)

After leaving school at the age of 14 Victor Griffuelhes was apprenticed as a cobbler. He moved to Paris and quickly became involved in trade union activities. After becoming secretary of the federation of trade unions for the Seine region, in 1901 he was elected national secretary of the leather workers' union, the Fédération Nationale des Cuirs et Peaux. The following year he was elected general secretary of the Confédération Générale du Travail (CGT), the only major trade union confederation of the time. He was to remain in office for a relatively short period, but one which was rich in incidents. He resigned in 1909, surrounded by scandal and intrigue.

Parallel to this, he was active in Socialist politics. Initially he allied himself with the followers of Auguste Blanqui (q.v.) and Edouard Vaillant (q.v.) but by the turn of the century he was increasingly drawn towards anarcho-syndicalism and the establishment of socialism through independent trade union action.

Under Griffuelhes' leadership, the CGT was to undergo a number of significant developments as regards its structures and objectives. It voted in 1902 to favour a unionism based on industrial sectors rather than one based on different trades and professions, but it also decided to retain a horizontal inter-professional structure based on the local *bourses du travail*. In 1906, the CGT agreed on the first major definition of French trade unionism, which came to be known as the *Charte d'Amiens*. The Guesdist Socialists led by Victor Renard, the secretary of the textile workers' union, had advocated a close association with the newly-founded Section Française de l'Internationale Ouvrière (SFIO), but Griffuelhes succeeded in obtaining the support of Auguste Keufer, the leader of the reformists and founder of the printers' union, to ensure that in theory at least trade unions should be independent of political parties.

In other spheres he differed radically from the reformists however. On the international front, he succeeded in withdrawing the CGT from the international secretariat of trade union organizations which tended to be dominated by the German trade unions which were a source of some inspiration for French reformists. On the domestic front, he committed the CGT to a number of important strikes, an initiative which failed not least because it coincided with a more aggressive stance on industrial relations assumed by successive governments. Indeed, after a series of violent strikes in 1908, Griffuelhes and other members of the executive of the CGT were imprisoned. Whilst in prison he was accused of mismanagement of the confederation's finances and so the following year he resigned. His resignation and the lack of opposition to it underlined the waning influence of the anarcho-syndicalists as a force in French trade unionism, even though their legacy is still to be found today at least in debates on ideology. From then until his death in 1922, Griffuelhes continued to play a significant role as an active elder statesman to the trade union movement, particularly as a trade union journalist.

Bibliography

There is no bibliography of Victor Griffuelhes in English. However he is the subject of a profile in the 12th volume of Jean Maitron (ed.) *Dictionnaire bibliographique du mouvement ouvrier français* (Paris: Les Editions Ouvrières, 1974). He wrote a number of works, such as *L'Action syndicaliste* (Paris: M. Rivière, 1908) and *Le Syndicalisme révolutionnaire* (Paris: La Publication Sociale, 1909), *Voyage révolutionnaire – impressions d'un propagandiste* (Paris: M. Rivière, 1910).

JB

GRIMAUD, Maurice (1913–)

Born in 1913 in the Ardèche, Maurice Grimaud first came to public prominence as prefect of police in Paris during the 'events' of May 1968. He was educated in Lyons, then at the Lycée Henri IV Secondary School in Paris, before obtaining an arts degree at the Ecole Normale Supérieure. After completing a post-graduate diploma at the Sorbonne, he entered military service in 1938 in Morocco, spent much of the Second World War in North Africa, and from 1943–4 worked in the Interior Ministry of the French provisional government in Algiers. He was to resume his connections with Morocco later when he spent three years up to 1954 as director of information in the resident-general's office. In 1955 he spent a brief period in François Mitterrand's private office. After seven years as a prefect and four years as head of the Sureté Nationale he was, to everyone's surprise, given his acknowledged Socialist sympathies, offered the post of prefect of police in Paris which he occupied from 1967–71. He re-entered political life in 1981 when he became director of Gaston Defferre's private staff (*cabinet*), following Defferre to the Planning Ministry in 1984. In 1986 he became a *délégué général* to the French ombudsman.

When Grimaud became prefect of police in January 1967, very much against his will, the signs were not good. He took over from the hardline Gaullist supporter Maurice Papon at a time when the reputation of the Paris police, never very high, had been rocked by incidents such as Charonne and the Ben Barka affair, and when de Gaulle was, as a consequence, anxious to ensure that the Ministry of the Interior exercised much closer control over the 'forces of order'. Eighteen months later, Maurice Grimaud had achieved the remarkable feat of emerging from the May events as one of the very few figures to have earned the respect of observers of all political shades of opinion, despite the well-documented examples of police violence in the first ten days of May.

The reasons for his success are not difficult to identify. His long friendship with Pierre Grappin, dean at Nanterre, meant that he understood at an early stage the growing discontent and agitation in the student body, and his frequent appearances in the thick of events in the streets increased his reputation as someone prepared to listen rather than simply repress. His intense dislike of police violence was well known, and was clearly demonstrated in his open letter to the Paris force. He also had a significant influence on political figures such as Louis Joxe, the acting prime minister during Pompidou's absence,

and on Christian Fouchet, the minister of the interior, invariably urging moderation on a government which often seemed prepared to resort to violence in the absence of any clear line of policy. There seems little doubt that the subtle blend of tolerance and firmness exercised by Grimaud, at a time when he occasionally seemed the only visible and active representative of the state, was a major factor in explaining the small numbers of fatal casualties incurred during the long succession of street battles. Grimaud's account of the May events, published in 1977, *En mai, fais ce qu'il te plaît* (Paris: Editions Stock), provides invaluable insights into the role of the government in May 1968, of which he is very critical, and of the relationship between the government and the police.

Bibliography

Brown, B.E. (1974), *Protest in Paris*, New Jersey: General Learning Press.

TH

GUÉRIN, Daniel (1904–88)

Writer, historian, revolutionary theorist and activist, anticolonialist, syndicalist activist, campaigner for gay rights, Daniel Guérin was active in many organizations and published in many fields. Those who write about him seldom do justice to this multiplicity of commitment or to what Guérin considered to be the importance of his attempt to reconcile anarchism and Marxism and, on a much broader level, the personal and the political. His second autobiography *Le feu du sang* (Paris: Grasset, 1977) was sub-titled *Autobiographie politique et charnelle*, and asserted the common well of the 'vital force' which motivated him in both his personal, emotional life and in his socio-political commitments. Thus, in the 1970s, when Guérin began to campaign for gay rights, it was through an organization called the Front Homosexuel d'Action Révolutionnaire. The identity of 'Daniel Guérin' – this 'son of the bourgeoisie' who 'sought to merge with the people in order ultimately to put himself at the service of the revolution' (*Autobiographie de Jeunesse*, Paris: Belfond, 1972, p. 9) was a central concern of his autobiographies, and he was to suffer often from simplistic pigeon-holing. It would not have surprised him to learn that, in different biographical and obituary articles, he was described by a writer in *Le Monde* as an anarchist; an anarchist-Communist declared his incomprehension of

Guérin's interest in the individualist Max Stirner; a Trotskyist lamented the fact that Guérin had not been quite Trotskyist enough; and a labour historian neglected any mention of his sexual proclivities and included *Le Feu du sang* in the 'sexology' section of the bibliography.

Guérin was born of a liberal, humanist, pro-Dreyfus family of the Left Bank, a very upper-class family with connections in banking, industry, commerce, transport and publishing.

In 1927 he finally escaped a quite restrictive family life by going to Syria and the Lebanon to work as a bookseller, and his long stay there, combined with a three-month visit to Indo-China, convinced him of the injustices of French colonialism. On his return to France in 1930 he contributed articles on the subject to H. Barbusse's *Monde*, and was later to be an active member of F. Jourdain's Comité d'Amnistie aux Indochinois.

At the same time, he became involved with the revolutionary syndicalists around Pierre Monatte, contributing articles to *La Révolution Prolétarienne* and *Le Cri du peuple*, and involving himself in the campaign for the reunification of the Confédération Générale du Travail and the Communist-controlled Confédération Générale du Travail Unifié. He joined the Belleville group of the Socialist Party (SFIO), but resigned again because of the anticommunism of certain municipal councillors. After visits to Germany in 1932 and 1933 Guérin wrote his studies of nazism and fascism, *La Peste brune* and *Fascisme et grand capital* (re-published together by Maspéro in Paris in 1969 as *Sur le fascisme*). In 1932 Guérin joined the Syndicat des Correcteurs, and was to remain a lifelong member. The following year, he was a co-founder of the Centre Laïque des Auberges de la Jeunesse.

In October 1935 Guérin re-joined the SFIO, and became a member of the recently-created Gauche Révolutionnaire (revolutionary left) tendency led by M. Pivert (q.v.). He was to hold several posts, and clashed not only with the Communists over their attempts to dominate trade union activities, but also with Marius Moutet, the SFIO minister for the colonies, and with M. Paz, secretary of the SFIO's colonies committee. In January 1938 the Gauche Révolutionnaire gained control of the SFIO's Seine Federation, and Guérin became one of the assistant secretaries. When the tendency was expelled from the SFIO (Royan Congress 1938), and the Parti Socialiste Ouvrier et Paysan was created, Guérin joined the new party, remaining firmly attached to the principles of revolutionary defeatism and proletarian internationalism. He had links with Trotsky, whilst disagreeing with him over the creation of a Fourth International.

Guérin had attended the International Congresses in Brussels (October 1938) and Paris (April 1939) of the Front Ouvrier International, and had been delegated by it to establish a secretariat in Oslo if war broke out. This he did, and he produced a monthly bulletin from October 1939 to April 1940, when he was arrested by the German army and taken to Germany. He managed to return to France in 1942 and was involved in an underground Trotskyist organization.

For just over two years, 1946–9 Guérin lived in the USA, and on his return produced the two-volume study *Où va le peuple américain?* (Paris: Julliard, 1950 and 1951), parts of which were later republished as more specific studies on the American labour movement, the position of black Americans and economic concentration.

Throughout the 1950s Guérin was heavily involved in anticolonial agitation. In 1952 he travelled to the Maghreb and established contact with syndicalist and nationalist militants there. From 1953 to 1955 he was a member of the Comité France-Maghreb led by F. Mauriac. In 1960 he was one of the first signatories of the 'Appeal of the 121' calling for the right not to fight in the Algerian War, and in 1963 he presented a report to President Ben Bella on Algerian self-management. After the coup of 1965, he helped found the committee which supported Ben Bella and opposed political repression in Algeria. He was also behind the creation of a committee to establish the truth about the disappearance of Moroccan leader Ben Barka in 1965.

Guérin's ideas regarding socialism evolved significantly from the 1950s. In 1955–7 he was active in the Nouvelle Gauche led by, among others, C. Bourdet; in 1957 this merged with the Mouvement de Libération du Peuple to become the Union de la Gauche Socialiste, then the Parti Socialiste Unifié. In May–June 1968 Guérin led open debates on self-management in the Sorbonne and in an occupied factory. The following year he joined G. Fontenis' Mouvement Communiste Libertaire, later to become the Organisation Communiste Libertaire, and he contributed to its newspaper, *Guerre de Classes*. In 1973 he joined the Organisation Révolutionnaire Anarchiste, and wrote for its paper, *Front Libertaire*. His evolution towards what he called libertarian communism – an attempted reconciliation of anarchism and Marxism (see *Vers un communisme libertaire*, Paris: Spartacus, 1984) – led him to become a member of the Union des Travailleurs Communistes Libertaires in 1980.

Bibliography

L'Anarchisme (Paris: Gallimard, 1965).

La Lutte de classes sous la Première République (1793–1797), 2 vols (Paris: Gallimard, 1968).

Essai sur la révolution sexuelle après Reich et Kinsey (Paris: Belfond, 1969).

Front populaire, révolution manquée (Paris, Maspéro, 1970).

Rosa Luxemburg et la spontanéité révolutionnaire (Paris: Flammarion, 1971).

Ci-gît le colonialisme (Paris/La Haye: De Gruyter/Mouton, 1973).

Les Assassins de Ben Barka (Paris: Guy Authier, 1975).

DGB

'GUESDE', Mathieu Bazile ('Jules') (1845–1922)

Jules Guesde's name is the one most closely associated with the introduction of marxism to France. Born in 1845, he was of the generation that witnessed the Paris Commune of 1871, which he supported in his newspaper articles. It was not until his return from the resulting exile however that he seriously embraced the philosophy he always described as 'collectivism'. Thereafter his life was wholly devoted to spreading the Marxist concept of class struggle. In 1882 he and his associates broke away from the new Socialist Party born of the Marseilles Congress of 1879, to create the Parti Ouvrier Français (POF). From then until the unification of French socialism in the SFIO in 1905, the POF (or the 'Guesdists' as they were generally known) formed a strongly-defined and coherent party, of which Guesde was the inspirational force and from which his own biography is inseparable. He was present throughout the conflicts that beset the early Socialist parties, and usually took an uncompromising stand. Several times elected to the National Assembly (in 1893–8, and continuously from 1906, as member for Roubaix in the Nord), he made history by accepting office as minister of state (1914–15) in the 'Union sacrée' government of René Viviani (q.v.) formed on the outbreak of war. By now elderly and in poor health, he survived to see the Russian Revolution, but at the time of his death in 1922, he was still in the SFIO and not in the Communist Party where many of his spiritual heirs found themselves.

Guesde's early years were very different from the life he was eventually to lead as a sort of roving apostle of socialism. Both his parents were devout Catholics, and his father ran a private school in Passy, which the young Jules attended. It was to avoid embarrassing the family establishment that Guesde later dropped his father's surname (Bazile), taking his mother's maiden name, under which history knows him. After a solid education from his father, leading to the *baccalauréat*, Guesde worked for a while as a civil servant, but read voraciously at night and, as a Republican under the Empire, eventually launched himself into the much less secure career of journalism, at first on provincial newspapers. Sentenced to five years in prison for his articles supporting the Commune, he fled in 1871 to Switzerland where he met other refugees and for a while became an anarchist, vigorously opposing the General Council of the International dominated by Karl Marx.

But extensive reading and, after his return to Paris in 1876, contact with the young intellectuals of the Latin Quarter, especially Karl Kirsch and Marx's son-in-law, Paul Lafargue, converted him to Marx's writings. The original series of his weekly paper *Égalité* (1877–8) has been described as 'the first Marxist paper in France'. Imprisoned for organizing an international congress, Guesde became well-known in the renascent workers' movement through his speech in his own defence, and through the manifesto he composed in prison, which proved influential at the Marseilles Congress of 1879. It was in order to provide a programme for the new Socialist Party that Guesde travelled to London with Lafargue in 1880, and met Marx and Engels in person. Together they drafted what became known as the 'Minimum programme' which combined a preamble by Marx, outlining long-term aims, with a set of short-term electoral demands. Guesde and his associates thus aimed to locate the Socialist Party's action firmly within a perspective of revolutionary change, and described themselves as 'collectivists'. Others, notably Paul Brousse (q.v.) who favoured 'possible reforms', called them 'Marxists', intending this as a term of abuse; the party split along these lines at Saint-Etienne in 1882.

Marx himself once famously remarked that he did not recognise his philosophy in that of the French 'Marxists', and it has often been pointed out that neither Guesde nor Lafargue knew German, nor had much background in economics. The Marxism they introduced to France was largely based on the *Communist Manifesto* of 1848, and on the text *Socialism Utopian and Scientific* (by Lafargue out of Engels). Few of Marx's writings were either available or widely read in France at the time. But if the Marxism professed by the Guesdists was somewhat simplified and often reduced to a series of formulas, not always applicable to France – 'dogmatic' and 'doctrinaire' were terms freely used of it – it was sympathetically received in certain parts of the French working class. And as a popularizer of the idea, Jules Guesde had no equal. His oratory held audiences spellbound at the hundreds of meetings he addressed up and down France in the 1880s and 1890s. With his flowing locks and beard, his intense blue eyes behind a pince-nez, and his grating voice, he was a figure instantly recognized and not easily forgotten. In the Assembly, he could be both eloquent and cutting. Throughout these years, he drove himself relentlessly, to the detriment of his health – speech-making, writing in any paper that would print him (for the Guesdists rarely had their own paper) and organizing the POF. The party, small at first, became the best-organized and most centralized of all the Socialist fractions, based on a devoted band of activists, and usually at odds with the other Socialist groups. By the 1890s, it had begun to recruit strongly in the industrial areas of northern France, which were to become its chief stronghold, and where Marxism corresponded to the popular militancy of the textile towns in particular. Nationally, it had about 16,000 members in 1898 – tiny numbers by German standards, but more than any of the other Socialist parties in France. Its share of the vote in 1898 was 3.6 per cent, and it had thirteen deputies in the Assembly.

Guesde's rhetoric in the 1880s was uncompromisingly millenarian: the revolution was inevitable. When in the 1890s the Guesdists made substantial progress in both municipal and parliamentary elections (with Guesde himself elected deputy for Lille in 1893), he conceded that the ballot box had its uses: we will fight for socialism, he said, 'by every means, *including* legal ones'. In this he was influenced by the German Socialist Party, the SPD, to which the Guesdists were particularly close within the framework of the Second International (1889–1914). But he never lapsed into electoralist reformism: revolutionary change was the end, whatever the means. And at times when other Socialist parties were inclined to rally to the Third Republic if it was under threat, as during the Boulanger and Dreyfus affairs, the Guesdists tended to stand aloof. They particularly condemned the participation of a Socialist minister (Millerand – q.v.) in a bourgeois government in 1899. Guesde once remarked that the best thing one could say about the Republic was that it revealed capitalism in all its nakedness.

Essentially he regarded the class struggle as the central fact of life, the revolutionary party as the spearhead of political action, and everything else – anticlericalism for instance – as a distraction (though he did apparently for a while encourage the simultaneous struggle of women for equality). The Guesdists saw the trade unions simply as the classic 'transmission belt' for the party, and successfully imposed their views on the Fédération Nationale des Syndicats in the years before the creation of the CGT (Confédération Générale du Travail) in 1895. But the new CGT, divided between reformists and revolutionary syndicalists, escaped their control: the Guesdists were scornful of syndicalist support for the general strike. They were no more sympathetic to the antimilitarist climate within the Socialist Party in the years leading up to the First World War – another distraction. Guesde's participation in the Union Sacrée did not represent an about-turn in this respect.

On antimilitarism, as on so many other things, Guesde was at odds with Jean Jaurès, especially after 1900 when Guesde's health was failing and the rising star of Jaurès tended to overshadow him. Guesde's apparent victory in stating the terms for the unification of the Socialist parties in 1905 preceded the real domination of Jaurès within the SFIO (though the Guesdists remained a party within the party). An element of personal rivalry accompanied the doctrinal differences between the two men, who are usually presented (with some over-simplification) as the twin poles of French socialism, with Jaurès increasingly gaining in attraction. It is probably true to say that the last twenty years of the nineteenth century were when Guesde, as the standard-bearer of Marxist ideas, really made his greatest mark on French socialism, a mark that would not quickly be obliterated.

Bibliography

Guesde's life is so closely associated with the POF that most general histories of French socialism do not separate them. A. Compère-Morel, *Jules Guesde, le socialisme fait homme* (Paris: Librairie A. Quillet, 1937), is a well-documented but uncritical biography; see also Claude Willard's monumental *Les Guesdistes* (Paris: Editions sociales, 1966); and the article on Guesde in Jean Maitron (ed.), *Dictionnaire biographique du mouvement ouvrier français* (Paris: Editions Ouvrières, 1974). In English, there is no single work, and references to Guesde reflect the writer's preoccupations. For a range of opinions see A. Noland, *The Founding of the French Socialist Party*, Cambridge, Mass.: Harvard University Press, 1956; T. Zeldin, *France 1848–1945*, vol. I (Oxford: Oxford University Press, 1972) and P. Hilden, *Working Women and Socialist Politics in France, 1880–1914* (Oxford: Oxford University Press, 1986).

SR

GUICHARD, Olivier-Marie Maurice, baron (1920–)

One of the most prominent Gaullists, Olivier Guichard began his political career with the Rassemblement du Peuple Français (RPF) in 1947. Born in Néac in the Gironde, he was the son of a naval officer who was also a baron. He read law at university in Paris and graduated from the Ecole Libre des Sciences Politiques. From 1962–7 he was mayor of Néac and in 1968 became deputy for the Loire-Atlantique. Currently a member of the Rassemblement pour la République (RPR) group in the National Assembly and president of the Loire Regional Council, he was General de Gaulle's *chef de cabinet* from 1951–8, press attaché to the atomic energy commissariat in 1955 and a member of the personal staff (*cabinet*) on de Gaulle's return to power in 1958. In 1959 he became a *conseiller technique*, saw service in the Sahara in 1960–2 and from 1963–7 worked closely with Georges Pompidou, the prime minister, as head of regional planning (DATAR). In 1968–9 he was minister of planning, in 1970–2 minister of education, in 1972–4 minister of development and in 1976–7 minister of justice under Valéry Giscard d'Estaing. Highly literate and articulate, his publications include *Aménager la Frànce* (1965), *L'Education nouvelle* (1970), *Un Chemin tranquille* (1975) and *Mon général* (Prix des Ambassadeurs) (1980). He is also the holder of the Médaille Militaire and the Croix de Guerre.

Olivier Guichard provides a classic example of a successful political career under three successive presidents in the Fifth Republic. Eminently a potential member of any number of cabinets (*ministrable*), he combines an impeccable background with high political skills and formidable administrative ability. Always close to de Gaulle, who held him in high regard, he was also able to form a close relationship with Pompidou in the years when the latter was establishing himself as party-leader and 'dauphin'. He served in Pompidou's cabinet when he became president. On Pompidou's untimely death, together with Debré and Sanguinetti, he supported, albeit as a 'chabaniste' with certain reservations, the candidature of Giscard on round two for president in 1974. A senior Gaullist, in 1976 he emerged triumphant as minister of justice and coordinator of the majority, appointed by Giscard to oversee, with Poniatowski and Lecanuet, the delicate negotiations over electoral strategy. In retrospect, he appears to have been in the right place at the right time, always close to the leader and his political instinct has served him well.

As a minister, he represented the school of Gaullist Jacobinism, with an emphasis on managerial efficiency and thus walked safely through the minefields of education, planning and decentralization. With characteristic humour and realism, he referred to the Education Ministry, with its 811,000 civil servants ('the largest administration in the world except the Red Army') as 'an impossible task', which he nevertheless tackled with energy, embarking on a far-reaching reorganization and 'management by objectives'. At planning (DATAR), he was in favour of retaining administrative supremacy rather than increased participation by the regions. In 1972 he presented the bill on regional reform as essentially an administrative and economic issue and was opposed to any suggestion of possible political autonomy for the regions. When asked by Giscard to prepare a report (the Guichard Report, 1975) on the problems of local government, his cautious estimate for the completion of the first stage was 1985. Olivier Guichard's political convictions and ability, combined with these mandarin skills, have ensured him a place at the top during most of the Fifth Republic.

Bibliography

Works by Olivier Guichard:
Aménager la France (Paris: Laffont-Gonthier, 1965).
L'Education nouvelle (Paris: Tribune Libre, Plon, 1970).
Un Chemin tranquille (Paris: Flammarion, 1975).
Mon général (Prix des Ambassadeurs) (Paris: Grasset, 1980).

Works on Gaullism:
Anderson, M. (1974), *Conservative Politics in France*, London: George Allen and Unwin.
Charlot, J. (1971), *The Gaullist Phenomenon*, London: Unwin.
Hartley, A. (1972), *Gaullism, the Rise and Fall of a Political Movement*, London: Routledge & Kegan Paul.
Hayward, J. (1973), *The One and Indivisible French Republic*, London: Weidenfeld & Nicolson.
Williams, P. and Harrison, M. (1973), *Politics and Society in de Gaulle's Republic*, London: Longmans.
DP

H

HABY, René-Jean (1919–   )

Born in Dombasle, René Haby attended the Ecole Normale in Nancy and began teaching in a primary school at 19. Continuing his studies at the University of Nancy, he later obtained a CAPES – the secondary teaching qualification. Thereafter he was appointed to a succession of secondary schools: Lons-le-Saunier (1947), Toul (1949), Nancy (1954). In 1954 he obtained the *agrégation*. He then became headmaster at the secondary schools of Saint-Avold (1954), Avignon (1958), Metz (1960) and Montgeron (1962). From 1962 to 1964 he worked at the Ministry of Education, where in 1963 he was made an *inspecteur général*. In 1964 he was put in charge of research as the principal private secretary to the head of the teaching section and remained there until 1965. He next lectured at the University of Nancy where he obtained his doctorate in 1965. From 1966 to 1968 he was principal private secretary to François Missoffe, minister of youth and sport, and then returned to the Ministry of Education to be in charge of the *information et orientation* section. (He also lectured at Paris IV in 1970.) In 1972 he became head (*recteur*) of the *académie* of Clermont-Ferrand, and from 1974 to 1978 he was minister of education. He was elected a deputy in 1978 and continued as a member of the Parti Républicain to represent Meurthe-et-Moselle.

He is a Chevalier de la Légion d'Honneur, Commandeur de l'Ordre National du Mérite and Officier des Palmes Académiques. He has published many articles on north-east France and education, as well as books such as *La Région des houillères lorraines* (1965), *Déformations rocheuses au-dessus des excavations souterraines* (1970) and *Combat pour les jeunes français* (1981).

Coming from a blue-collar background, Haby made up for his lack of connections by energy and ambition. His career reads like a railway timetable with its frequent brief stops on the way to Paris and fame. His advocacy of measured innovation during his period as headmaster finally earned him promotion to the prestigious secondary school at Montgeron. After only a few weeks there he was recruited to be principal private secretary to Jean Capelle at the Ministry of Education and they battled to establish the beginnings of a comprehensive system of secondary schooling in France with the creation of the CES (Collège d'enseignement secondaire). It was during his time under Missoffe that Haby really entered the world of politics, acting as unofficial adviser, especially to the Elysée, on reform in the secondary sector thereafter.

His appointment to Clermont-Ferrand brought him into Giscard's political fief and a short time later the new president made him minister of education. In 1975 he unveiled his controversial *loi Haby* which finally established, against much opposition, a uniform comprehensive school system. Other measures such as the introduction of mixed-ability classes in the secondary sector, with extra time allocated for both the bright and the less able pupils, were less successful. Despite the government's return after the 1978 elections, Haby had stirred up sufficient opposition – particularly among the teachers' unions – for Giscard to replace him in the new cabinet. First elected a deputy in 1981 to represent Meurthe-et-Moselle, he was re-elected in 1981 but in 1986 he was a substitute for André Rossinot (q.v.) whom he replaced when the Radical leader was made a minister.

Bibliography

There is a summary of Haby's years in office in *The Times Educational Supplement* (5 May 1978) and a profile (7 June 1974) as well as one in *Le Monde* (30 May 1974). Books on education in France which deal with the 1970s feature Haby. In English there is H.D. Lewis, *The French Education System* (London: Croom Helm, 1985), and in French Jacques Minot, *L'Education nationale* (Paris: Berger-Levrault, 1979).

HDL

HANOTAUX, Albert Auguste Gabriel (1853–1944)

More generally known as a distinguished historian than as a diplomat and politician, Gabriel Hanotaux helped shape French foreign and particularly colonial policy during the crucial period from 1894 until 1898.

Born in Beaurevoir (Aisne), he taught at the Higher Education Institute (Ecole des Hautes Etudes) in Paris before his distinction as an archivist and paleographer earned him a post in 1879 at the Ministry of Foreign Affairs. He rose rapidly through the diplomatic service in the next few years, and was elected to represent the Aisne constituency in 1885. When he failed to be re-elected in 1889, he returned to a diplomatic career, continuing at the Ministry of Foreign Affairs in a plenipotentiary post with responsibility for the French Protectorates.

This varied experience led eventually to office as foreign minister in Dupuy's cabinet (1894–5), and under Méline (q.v.) (1896–8). During the early part of this four-year period, Hanotaux played a significant part, constitutionally, by adopting a very independent line vis-à-vis President Casimir-Périer. The latter, elected after the assassination of Sadi Carnot (q.v.), was systematically ignored by Hanotaux and his other ministers, and after a few months resigned, demoralized by the powerlessness of his office.

A disciple of Jules Ferry (q.v.) in colonial matters, Hanotaux was sympathetic to the aims of the Parti Colonial (a pressure group in favour of colonial expansion), and his militant promotion of French claims in East and West Africa almost led to diplomatic rupture between England and France. He played a vital part in laying the foundations of French West Africa, and in the establishment of the boundaries of French possessions in Africa.

During his period as minister, Hanotaux had to tread a careful path on two important foreign policy fronts: during his second term, the Marchand mission to the Nile basin, of which Hanotaux was a main sponsor, brought to a head the clash of British and French colonial ambitions in Africa. During these years at the quai d'Orsay, Hanotaux managed to respect the letter of the Franco-Russian military agreement of 1892 without giving overmuch encouragement to Russian designs in the Balkans, and yet at the same time developing a policy of collaboration with Germany. After Hanotaux's fall, over the Fashoda crisis, French policy towards Germany was to change drastically under his successor, Delcassé (q.v.).

Hanotaux did not return to government, prefer-ring to devote most of his remaining years to historical writings, to lecturing, and to popularizing the colonial cause. He continued however to serve his country on special diplomatic missions, and was, from 1920–3, a delegate at the League of Nations. His many studies of Richelieu culminated in his six-volume *Histoire du Cardinal de Richelieu* (Paris: Firmin Didot, 1895). His *History of the French Nation*, 3 vols (Paris: Plon–Nourrit, 1921) is a classic of French history. They have been reprinted subsequently under many different imprints. His personal recollections, and also the access he had to private archives, make his works, particularly his four-volume *History of Contemporary France* (1903–9) – which was published in English by G.P. Putnam (New York) – indispensable tools for the historian of the period.

Bibliography

Heggoy, A.A. (1972), *The African Policies of Gabriel Hanotaux (1894–98)*, Athens, GA: University of Georgia Press.

Wright, G. (1981), *France in Modern Times*, 3rd edition, New York: W.W. Norton.

ACR

HENRIOT, Philippe (1889–1944)

Born the son of an army officer in Reims in 1889, Philippe Henriot studied classics and literature at the Sorbonne before embarking on a career as a private-school teacher. His political training-ground in the 1920s was General Castelnau's Fédération Nationale Catholique, a kind of Catholic counterpart to anticlerical Freemasonry, and he eventually won a parliamentary seat in 1932 as a deputy for Bordeaux. His oratorical skills won him a reputation in 1934, at the time of the Stavisky affair and the February riots, and thereafter he was one of the leading figures of the extreme-right in the Chamber of Deputies. Re-elected in 1936, he was a fervent opponent of war with Germany in the late 1930s and, having sided with Pétain in 1940, he became a vigorous propagandist for the Vichy regime's 'Révolution Nationale'. He is chiefly remembered for his polemical weekly broadcasts on Vichy Radio attacking the Allies and the Resistance movement, and in January 1944 he became minister of information in the government of Pierre Laval. In July 1944 he was killed by a Resistance commando unit in Paris.

Henriot was in many ways a classic exponent of the anti-Republican sentiments that were still rife in well-to-do Catholic and military milieux between the wars. Though he was initially affiliated in the Chamber of Deputies to Louis Marin's Fédération Républicaine, his true allegiance was to some of the extremist paramilitary formations that were flourishing outside. His name has been linked with Action Française, but more decisively he is known to have been involved in Taittinger's Jeunesses Patriotes. Along with others like Vallat, Ybarnégaray (q.v.) and Taittinger himself, Henriot thus acted as a bridge between the Catholic, nationalist right in the Chamber and those who were agitating on the streets for the establishment of a more authoritarian regime.

After the banning of the leagues by the Popular Front government in 1936, Henriot continued to collaborate with Taittinger, becoming one of the vice-presidents of the latter's Parti National Populaire, a movement without any significant following. This organization, along with Marin's Fédération Républicaine, formed the short-lived anti-Communist 'Front de la Liberté' with Jacques Doriot's Fascist Parti Populaire Français in 1937, and like Doriot, Henriot was calling openly for a *rapprochement* with Hitler's Germany by 1938. However, in his case this did not lead to outright defeatism, and he campaigned vigorously for a French victory once hostilities opened. Like so many sections of the traditional authoritarian right, he was unable to choose decisively between his patriotic and militaristic instincts on the one hand, and on the other his contempt for the Republic and his hatred of Bolshevism. Vichy rather than the occupied zone was his natural destination, as it was for most of the reactionary Catholic right, but his role there was none the less to make him one of the most hated symbols of collaboration.

Bibliography

A recent study of the Jeunesses Patriotes is R. Soucy, 'Centrist fascism: the Jeunesses Patriots' in *Journal of Contemporary History*, vol. 16 (2), April 1981, pp. 346–68. Henriot was the author of *Le 6 février* (Paris: Flammarion, 1934) and *Mort de la trêve* (Paris: Flammarion, 1935).

BJ

HERNU, Charles (1923–90)

Charles Hernu was born on 3 July 1923 in Quimper, the son of a civil servant, and was educated at the Collège des Minimes in Lyons. Hernu was a member of the Resistance army, the FFI, and was with the 1st Army in Germany. On demobilization he went into the Centre National du Commerce Exterieur and took up journalism first with the *Patriote de Lyon* and then with the *Démocrate de Lyon*.

In 1951 Hernu founded the Club des Jacobins which was Radical and supported Mendès France, and in 1956 he was elected as Radical deputy for the 6th constituency of the Seine. As a loyal Mendésiste he publicly called on his future leader, Mitterrand, to leave the Mollet government. Despite being the youngest deputy, he was made secretary of the powerful foreign affairs committee of the Assembly.

Losing his seat in 1958 he devoted himself to restructuring the non-Communist left, first by helping to found the PSU (as a member of its *bureau national* until 1963) and then as a member of the Convention des Institutions Républicains of which he was general secretary, then president. He was also secretary-general of the shadow cabinet which Mitterrand established for the FGDS (*contre-gouvernement* 1965–8). During the 1960s Hernu built up his reputation as a defence specialist, whilst remaining more an organizer and publicist than a personality of the first rank. He had transferred his allegiance from Mendès France to become a close 'fidèle' of Mitterrand by 1965.

In 1971 along with Mitterrand and the CIR, Hernu joined the Socialist Party at the Epinay Congress. He was then elected to the party's national bureau and became its specialist on defence, helping, through its national defence committee to develop Socialist defence policy. His book, *Soldat-Citoyen* (Paris: Club Socialiste du Livre, 1975) was, at a time when the Socialists and the left alliance were opposed to the French nuclear force, strongly in favour of nuclear defence and, along with CERES, he was one of the principal proponents on the left of deterrence.

Hernu developed contacts in military circles with the Socialist Convention pour l'Armée Nouvelle, and with his courses for the Institut des Hautes Etudes de la Défense Nationale. He also made contacts overseas in the German SPD and through the International Institute of Strategic Studies. This was important work at a time when the West, in general, and the French military, in particular, were somewhat uncertain as to what a left victory in France would mean.

Firmly on the social democratic wing of the party and a loyal supporter of Mitterrand, Hernu became mayor of Villeurbanne in the Lyons suburbs in 1977. The following year he was elected deputy for Villeurbanne (Rhône 6th constituency), was re-elected in 1981 and headed the Socialist list in the Rhône in 1986 when he was again returned. (He was re-elected in 1988.) When Mitterrand won the presidential election in 1981 Hernu was made minister of defence. At the ministry he was highly orthodox and hence widely popular, especially with the armed forces who approved the sharp increase in defence spending and reforms such as the rapid intervention unit designed to be used in Nato's front line against a conventional attack. The most controversial incident of his tenure was the French secret service sinking (in New Zealand) of the Greenpeace ship *Rainbow Warrior* which was protesting against French nuclear testing in the Pacific. The incident, though precipitating his resignation, made Hernu one of the most popular politicians and stimulated unrealistic presidential ambitions. Rather exotically Hernu combines the attributes of being a four times divorced Catholic Freemason.

Bibliography

Hernu's books include *Priorité à gauche* (Paris: Fayard, 1969) and *Soldat citoyen*. The Socialist Party's defence policy is discussed in J. Howorth and P. Chilton (eds), *Defence and Dissent in Contemporary France* (London: Croom Helm, 1984), especially Chapter 4 and J. Howorth, *France: The politics of peace* (London: Merlin, 1984).

BC

HERR, Lucien Charles (1864–1926)

Herr was one of the major Socialist intellectuals of his time and was responsible for the conversion of both Jean Jaurès and Léon Blum to socialism. He was an *agrégé de philosophie* (the elite corps of secondary school teachers), but became chief librarian of the renowned Ecole Normale Supérieure, of which he was a former student, in 1888, and occupied that post until 1926. His political influence owed more to his daily encounters and ideological debates with the bright young hopes of French socialism than to the pursuit of a personal political career.

In 1889, he joined Jean Allemane's Parti Ouvrier Socialiste Révolutionnaire, an antimilitarist and syndicalist Socialist group whose approach hinged on the concept of the general strike – i.e. a concept of Socialist transition based on the mobilization of trade unions and mass direct action. *Le Parti Ouvrier* (journal) published a number of articles by Herr, including some charging German Social Democrats with playing down the role of trade unions *vis-à-vis* the party, and with overemphasizing discipline in a way reminiscent of Prussian authoritarianism. Not an opponent of Marxism as such, Herr valued the contribution of French utopian Socialists, especially their idealism. The Russian refugee Lavrov shared with Herr an interest in Hegel, and converted him to the importance of intellectuals and rational education in the movement, as opposed to the reliance on instincts and emotions which characterized the age (e.g. Sorel and Bergson).

After converting Jaurès, a fellow philosophy teacher (*agrégé de philosophie*), to socialism, he became one of the first supporters of Captain Dreyfus in 1894. In spite of fierce attacks from Jules Guesde's Parti Ouvrier Français, on the grounds that Socialists should not associate with liberal bourgeois causes, Herr was instrumental in the subsequent demonstration 'for the defence of the Republic' in 1899, which paved the way for the Socialist Millerand's controversial acceptance of a ministry in Waldeck Rousseau's cabinet.

In the pre-First World War years, Herr somehow did not come up to his friends' expectations, i.e. he concentrated more on education and communication than on real theoretical and ideological work. One of the founders of a semi-independent Socialist study group, the Groupe de l'Unité Socialiste, he was one of the seventeen *agrégés* who sponsored Jaurès's non-sectarian Socialist daily *L'Humanité*, for which he wrote a regular column on foreign affairs.

Herr, who, as a native of Alsace, was fiercely anti-German, advocated Socialist support for Clémenceau's government in 1917. Yet, Léon Blum, whom Herr had met in 1893, and largely influenced, remained a lifelong friend and acknowledged his intellectual debt to Herr, who was his counsellor up to his last day. According to some testimonies, the speech Blum delivered in 1920 at the Tours Congress, where Communists and Socialists split, was written in Herr's flat. There is little doubt that, just as Jaurèsian humanistic idealism was reminiscent of Herr's conceptions, Blum's insistence on the freedom of trade unions to determine their own lines (as opposed to Communist fraction work), the importance of a mass party (as opposed to a vanguard), and his rejection of an underground leadership imposed by Moscow, owed much to Lucien Herr's views. Besides Jaurès and Blum, Herr also associated with a fellow Socialist intellectual, Charles Andler, as well as with Albert Thomas and Marcel Déat (q.v.).

199

Bibliography

Andler, C. (1932), *Vie de Lucien Herr*, Paris: Reider.

Goldberg, H. (1962), *The Life of Jean Jaurès*, Madison: University of Wisconsin Press.

Herr, L. (1932), *Choix d'écrits*, vol. I – Politique, Paris: Reider.

Lefranc, G. (1963), *Le Mouvement socialiste sous la 3eme république*, Paris: Payot.

JPR

HERRIOT, Edouard (1872–1957)

Better than any other politician Edouard Herriot came to symbolize the values and attitudes of French republicanism as it took shape in the late nineteenth century and would endure until the middle of the twentieth. His own career made him – like Daladier (q.v.) – a perfect example of the social mobility which the state education system allowed to the lower middle classes in the Third Republic. The son of an impoverished army officer who had risen from the ranks, he was able to study for the Ecole Normale Supérieure by virtue of a government grant. While a student he acquired the political beliefs that would mould his entire career: commitment to a parliamentary form of Republic, to the secular state, to a reformist rather than revolutionary model of social progress, to an internationalism based on peaceful coexistence but also on national defence.

Having obtained his higher teaching degree (*agrégation*) in 1893, Herriot taught at Nantes and then took over a class in advanced rhetoric at Lyons. He helped to found the Lyons branch of the League of the Rights of Man, joined the Radical Party and came to the attention of the mayor of Lyons, Augagneur, who included him on his list for the 1904 municipal elections. Thereafter he rapidly acquired prominence as a local notable while managing at the same time to complete a doctoral thesis. As assistant mayor he had charge of educational matters and then, when Augagneur was appointed governor-general of Madagascar in 1905, became mayor of Lyons. He was only 33. Seven years later he was elected to the Senate for the Rhône, having in the meantime become a prominent, but not front rank, figure in the Radical Party. He acquired a good reputation as a town hall administrator during the First World War and in December 1916 became minister of public works, transport and food in Briand's (q.v.) fifth government, a post that he held until March 1917. The countless difficulties that such a ministry had to deal with gave him his first experience of unpopularity.

Edouard Herriot's political career really took off in 1919 when he was elected, almost by chance and in his absence, president of a Radical Party that seemed moribund. He took on the task of recreating the party and of returning it to its left-wing origins (despite the desire of many of its parliamentarians to stay attached to the cross-party coalition known as the Union Sacrée). By 1923 he had succeeded in his aim; the Radical Party broke off its agreement with the governments of the right-wing *Bloc National* and signed an accord with the Socialists for the 1924 election. The election proved to be a triumph for the union of the left and for himself, since he was appointed prime minister. The government experience of the cartel, however, would bring him nothing but disappointment and bitterness. It soon became clear that his conception of left-wing values (parliamentarianism, secularism, international conciliation, social reform) was quite inadequate to satisfy the Socialists with whom he had sought to work. They defined the left in social terms and could accept neither the Radicals' liberalism nor their refusal to consider structural reform. Herriot also came up against the power of the business community, something of which he had hitherto been scarcely conscious. Because he was the ally of the Socialists, business refused him the confidence he had relied on to carry out his plans for economic recovery.

In April 1925 the Bank of France, which was a private institution run by the banking and industrial giants, brought about his downfall by compelling him to reveal the gravity of France's monetary position, as a result of which he was immediately overthrown by the Senate. When he returned to office in July 1926 the banks unleashed a financial panic which led the small investors to demand the immediate repayment of their Treasury bonds and hence to threaten the state's solvency. This 'plebiscite of the stockholders' led to the defeat of the government the very day it came before the Chamber of Deputies. In the face of such a serious crisis, Doumergue (q.v.), the president of the Republic turned to Poincaré (q.v.) the leader of the defeated right. Herriot's election triumph had been turned to ashes by what he himself would call the 'wall of money'. He drew from his defeat the lesson that it was impossible to govern against the interests of business but he also came to nurture a deep resentment against the Socialists whose impossible and constantly reiterated demands had played a large part in his government's downfall.

His disappointments, moreover, were not yet

over. The fact that no governing majority was possible in the 1924 Chamber without the support of the Radicals meant that he was forced to agree to join Poincaré's government, in which he became minister of education. His decision greatly angered the activists in the Radical Party, who were strong supporters of left unity. Faced with their growing hostility, Herriot abandoned the party presidency at the 1926 Congress, being replaced temporarily by Maurice Sarraut and then, in 1927 by Edouard Daladier (q.v.) who had the support of the party's left wing and also of Caillaux's group. At the 1928 Angers Congress, this coalition compelled Herriot and the other Radical members of Poincaré's government to resign, by passing a motion underlining the incompatability between the Radical Party's beliefs and government policy.

Herriot's political eclipse was, however, of short duration. By 1929 there was growing tension between Daladier and the Radical parliamentarians who disliked his authoritarianism. In 1931, to general acclaim, Herriot returned to the party presidency, covered in the glory of a brilliant victory in that year's municipal elections in Lyons when he managed to defeat both the Socialists and the right. And it was the same strategy that he proposed to the Radicals for the 1932 parliamentary elections. There would, of course be the usual 'republican discipline' agreements on round two of the election since without them there could be no left-wing majority in the Chamber; but there could be no question of reopening the experience of the cartel and the Radicals would define their own set of proposals for government, which they would invite all the other 'Republicans' to follow. The left, as in 1924, won the elections and Herriot formed a government of his choice. But, again as in 1924, Herriot was faced with the irreconcilable opposition between a left-wing parliamentary majority that included the Socialists and a policy of economic and financial deflation associated with the moderate minister of finances, Germain Martin, and backed by the right. Herriot decided that it was better to be defeated by the right (*tomber à gauche*): he organized his own overthrow by advocating the repayment of French war debts to the United States despite the Chamber's hostility to such a payment, given the Hoover moratorium on reparations.

Herriot was desperate to return to power and found it difficult to accept the succession of prime ministers who followed him, initially the Republican Socialist, Paul-Boncour and then his fellow Radicals, Daladier, Sarraut and Chautemps. Just when he thought his time had come, the Stavisky affair exploded in the face of the Radical Party, whose president thus became an impossible candidate for the premiership. To Herriot's fury it was his great rival Daladier who succeeded Chautemps. When he himself again returned to office after the 6 February 1934, it was in conditions very different from those he had imagined. As in 1926 – and for the same reasons – he agreed to become a minister of state in the government of national union formed by the former president of the Republic Doumergue whose behaviour at the time of the cartel had hardly been helpful to Herriot. He now embarked upon a calvary which would last for two years. Aware that no political majority was possible without the Radicals, Herriot – their president – agreed to give his support to governments of which he did not really approve in order to ensure the survival of the regime. As minister of state in the 'truce cabinets' of Doumergue, Flondin and Laval he had to endure the former's support for Tardieu who was violently hostile to the Radicals and to a foreign policy under the latter which rode roughshod over the League of Nations and flirted with Fascist Italy. Simultaneously, he became aware of an irresistible tide of opinion within his party in favour of the Popular Front, the alliance with those parties of the left who never stopped attacking the governments of which he was a member. In June 1935 he allowed the Radical Party's executive committee firstly to accept the offer to participate in the great meeting of the 14 July and subsequently to join the Popular Front. But the contradiction between his position as minister in Laval's government and president of a party that adhered to the Popular Front made his position untenable. In December 1935 he resigned the presidency of the Radical Party (where he was replaced, a month later, by Daladier) and in January of the new year he quit the Laval government, thereby provoking its fall.

He was reserved about, though not actually hostile to, the Popular Front and after the 1936 elections refused Léon Blum's (q.v.) offer of the Ministry of Foreign Affairs. The real problem was that this traditional Republican found it difficult to cope with the new terms of political debate in France. Hostile both to fascism and communism, ill at ease in the violent controversies of the 1930s, he sought refuge in honorary positions and steered clear of the risks of power. In so doing, he perhaps drew the lessons of his own successive failures and was realistic enough to appreciate that political values derived from the late nineteenth century no longer worked in the France of the 1930s. As president of the Chamber of Deputies from 1936 to 1940, he assumed the role of elder statesman, urging moderation on the governments (he dissuaded Blum from intervening in the Spanish Civil War), disapproving of the break up of the Popular Front and combating the spirit of Munich. He was critical of Daladier's passivity once war began and in 1940 became a strong supporter of Paul Reynaud, attempting to avoid an armistice and to arrange for the transfer of government to North Africa.

On 10 July 1940 he was hoodwinked by Laval, who pretended to offer concessions, into voluntary abstention in the vote granting full powers to Pétain. But the very next day, on reading the first constitutional acts, he joined with the president of the Senate, Jeanneney, in making a formal, juridical protest against the Vichy regime in the name of republicanism. His opposition was both undramatic and ineffective; but it became an outright break in July 1942 when the government dissolved the *bureaux* of the two Chambers. Herriot, who had been deprived of his functions as mayor of Lyons in 1940, was placed in guarded residence and then arrested. In August 1944 Laval brought him back to Paris, hoping that he might summon the National Assembly and thus institute a legal regime in opposition to de Gaulle's provisional government. The failure of the attempt owed less to Herriot's own hesitations than to the Germans' decision to deport him into Germany.

Liberated by the Russians, he returned to France in 1945 and to his roles as Mayor of Lyons, deputy for the Rhône and president of the Radical Party whose reconstruction was being undertaken by Henri Queuille. Herriot favoured a return to the Third Republic and combated both de Gaulle's provisional government and the emerging Fourth Republic. Yet as early as January 1947 he was back in his old position of president of the National Assembly and acquired once again his pre-war role of elder statesman of the regime. His hostility to communism and Gaullism made him one of the prophets of the Third Force and he played an important backstage role in the formation of governments. In 1951 he was elected life president of the Radical Party. Showered with honours and possessing considerable influence, his only problems were his age and his state of health. In 1954 he was compelled to give up the presidency of the National Assembly (which then created for him the unprecedented title of honorary president). A supporter of *Mendésisme* his last (1954) intervention in the National Assembly was to condemn the project for a European Defence Community. In 1956 he abandoned the presidency of the Radical Party which was, once again, being torn apart by a whole series of divisions. He died in 1957,

only a year before the collapse of the parliamentary Republic to which he had dedicated his life.

Bibliography

Berstein, S. (1985), *Edouard Herriot ou la république en personne*, Paris: Presses de la Fondation Nationale des Sciences Politiques.

Berstein, S. (1988), *Histoire du parti radical*, 2 vols, Paris: Presses de la Fondation Nationale, des Sciences Politiques.

Herriot, E. (1952), *In Those Days*, New York: Old and New World.

Soulie, M. (1962), *La Vie politique d'Edouard Herriot*, Paris: A. Colin.

SB

HERSANT, Robert Joseph Emile (1920–)

Robert Hersant is the best known media 'baron' in contemporary France. He is the owner of the leading French press group which publishes an impressive number of national and regional newspapers and magazines, including *Le Figaro* and *France-Soir*. Since 1987 he has also been the major shareholder in the commercial television channel, *La Cinq*. In addition, Hersant has been actively involved in party politics since the early 1950s, first as a supporter of the moderate left, but increasingly as a sympathizer of the right. He has occupied various elected posts, including those of mayor, departmental councillor, deputy in the National Assembly and member of the European Parliament (re-elected in 1989 on the RPR–UDF joint list). However, he has never held a ministerial position and it is in his capacity as a media entrepreneur of right-wing views that he has made his mark inside and, to a much lesser extent, outside France.

It was during the 1970s that Hersant rose to prominence as a key player in the changing landscape of the French media. In 1975 he took over the conservative daily, *Le Figaro*, and this was quickly followed in 1976 by *France-Soir*, the ailing mass market evening paper. In 1978 *L'Aurore* was added to the Hersant list of acquisitions and quickly incorporated into *Le Figaro*. By investing in new technology and breaking the hold of the Communist-dominated print union, the Hersant press empire spread its tentacles far and wide within France. His press group's dominant market position and the clear support of his newspapers for the political forces of the right made Hersant a natural target for attacks from the left. In particular, he was accused of infringing the 1944 legislation on concentration of press ownership. The electoral victories of the Socialists in 1981 led to the enactment of new legislation on the press three years later. However, the provisions of the so-called *loi anti-Hersant* of October 1984 were watered down by the Constitutional Council and in any case the act was repealed by the Chirac government at the end of 1986.

With the breakup of the state monopoly in broadcasting in the 1980s, Hersant spread his media interests to include television. After the victory of the right in the 1986 parliamentary elections he became chairman of the fifth channel, *La Cinq*, whose deputy chairman is the Italian media magnate Silvio Berlusconi. *La Cinq* is a lightly regulated, advertising-funded television channel and its programme schedules place an overwhelming emphasis on entertainment. None the less, in the increasingly competitive multi-channel television system of the late 1980s, *La Cinq* experienced severe problems in attracting viewers and advertisers and staggered from one financial crisis to another. Control of a satellite channel is the next goal for Hersant as France and Europe enter a new audiovisual age in which supranational competition will come from other well-known media entrepreneurs, including *inter alios* Rupert Murdoch and Robert Maxwell.

Bibliography

There is no biography in English on Hersant. On the press see P. Albert, *La Presse française* (Paris: La Documentation Française, 1983). On television see *Le Monde: dossiers et documents, la Télévision en 1987* (Paris, 1988).

RK

HERVÉ, Gustave Alexandre Victor (1871–1944)

Journalist and political extremist, Hervé was born at Brest in 1871. Though of poor origins, he became an *agrégé d'histoire*, his first post being at the Secondary School (*lycée*) of Rodez in 1897. Though his first political allegiance had been to Déroulède (q.v.), he had by now moved strongly to the left, and to a rejection of nationalism. Appointed to the *lycée* of Sens in 1899, he began contributing, under the pseudonym 'Un Sans-patrie', to the local Socialist paper *Le Travailleur Socialiste*, and to its supplement *Le Pioupiou de l'Yonne*. His violently antimilitarist articles led to his being taken to court in 1901, in what became known as 'l'affaire Hervé'. The graphic imagery in one of his articles gave rise to the first of the slogans universally associated with Hervé's name: 'Le drapeau dans le fumier' (the flag on the dung heap).

Hervé was acquitted, but was nevertheless removed from his post. He read for the Bar, to which he was called in 1905, the year which also saw the start of his major antimilitarist campaign within the Socialist group. At the congress called to found the SFIO, he declared that in the event of war the peasants of l'Yonne would not march. Later that year the distribution of an antimilitarist manifesto to recruits led to his being convicted to four years' imprisonment.

Freed under a general amnesty in 1906, he founded the newspaper *La Guerre Sociale*. 'Hervéisme' had by now become a major force among the French Socialists, and at the International Congress at Stuttgart in 1907 he tabled a motion inviting the working class of all countries to strike and rise in revolt on the outbreak of war.

Though French socialism was by now moving in his direction, by 1912 Hervé was, typically, changing course. Convinced by now that the German Socialists would not answer the call, he now saw the principal danger as Prussian imperialism. He gave up the idea of insurrection, and called instead for détente, including the return of Alsace-Lorraine to France, in exchange for Madagascar.

The outbreak of war witnessed an even greater shift in his ideas. Within days he had become violently patriotic, writing about 'La revanche' and invoking the name of Déroulède. By 1916 *La Guerre sociale* had been renamed *La Victoire*, and by 1918 he had been expelled from the Socialist Party.

After the war he moved progressively to the right, founding the Fascist-style Parti Socialiste National and producing continual press campaigns, in *La Victoire*, for an authoritarian Republic. These culminated in the famous *C'est Pétain qu'il nous faut* campaign of 1935–6. He also became converted to catholicism. On the international front, he called as early as 1930 for Franco-German reconciliation based on a fundamental revision of the Treaty of Versailles. He had always been favourable to Mussolini and Italian fascism, and in 1933 he welcomed Hitler as a defence against Bolshevism, stressing continually thereafter the need to come to terms with him: 'Il faut causer avec Hitler'. At the fall of France, *La Victoire* was the first collaborationist newspaper to reappear in Paris, on 17 June 1940. Unlike other such journals, however, it and its editor thereafter faded into obscurity.

Bibliography

Guy Bowman, introduction to Hervé's *My Country Right or Wrong* (London: Fifield, 1910); Catherine Slater, *Defeatists and their Enemies* (Oxford: Oxford University Press, 1981); F.F. Ridley, *Revolutionary Syndicalism in France* (Cambridge: Cambridge University Press, 1970); Hervé's own prefaces and books, and articles in *La Guerre sociale* (1906–15), and *La Victoire* (1916–40).

RMG

HERVÉ, Pierre (1913–)

Pierre Hervé was born in 1913 in the Finistère; he joined the Young Communists (the Jeunesse Communiste) in 1932, but was an unexceptional activist. The story which follows marks him out as an archetype of communism's resistance generation; it traces a deflationary path from moral enthusiasm to disenchantment with the Communist 'counter-society'.

Hervé served in the Army in 1939, was demobilized in 1940 and imprisoned in June 1941. In July 1941 he escaped, crossed into Vichy France and joined first, the Resistance group Libération, then the Mouvements Unis de la Résistance (MUR), and then the Mouvement de Libération Nationale (MLN). 'Officially' he was not a Communist, but simply a proponent of a line demanding a maximum of energetic activity. At the liberation, Hervé was spokesman for unity of action between the Resistance movements and the PCF. His was the most prominent political voice on behalf of a moral communism which identified the proletariat with suffering struggling humanity. The blending of Jesus and Prometheus strongly recommended Hervé to the Catholic existentialists at the review *Esprit*; it would prove a major strand in the surrogate communism of Merleau-Ponty and, belatedly, Sartre.

After the attempt to graft the Resistance on to the PCF had failed, Hervé the fellow-travelling mole was 'resurfaced'. He was PCF deputy for the Finistère in the 1945 Provisional and 1946 National Assemblies. He was an editorialist for *L'Humanité*. But things began to go wrong. Jhdanovism – the dictatorial politicization of culture wafting from Moscow – got on Hervé's nerves. He attacked Aragon as a culture dictator and fell out with Jean Kanapa (q.v.), Jhdanovism's leading enthusiast. In1948, out of favour, he was ordered to 'resign' from the Assembly; he was removed from *L'Humanité*. In 1949 the PCF launched a 'neutralist' journal, *Action*.

Its editors were Yves Farge, Hervé and the Abbé Boulier: Hervé was the only Communist, and the journal, as representative of the Mouvement pour la Paix, created an Indian summer for the Resistance. Ideologically, Hervé was connected with the Tillon side of the Marty–Tillon affair. Personally, he was isolated, while Marty was almost pathologically hostile.

Action was suddenly closed early in 1952, as part of the leftward shift preceding the Ridgway demonstrations. Hervé was, moreover, being tailed by Baranès, a party – and police – agent. To a man in Hervé's position, the beginnings of Soviet liberalization brought the light of hope: early in 1956 he published *La Révolution et les Fétiches* with a non-Communist editor. Hervé called on the PCF to facilitate a new Popular Front by repudiating Soviet-style dictatorship and cultural controls. The book became a *cause-célèbre* of the Parisian intelligentsia. That the PCF threw Hervé out was predictable – the sauce to the affair was the support they received from the leader of the Paris thought-police, a certain Jean-Paul Sartre. (Sartre lectured Hervé on his obligations under party discipline.) In the Café Flore, Hervé became a symbol of the metaphysical distance between 'the intellectual' and 'the activist', the one condemned to freedom, the other to obedience. Hervé joined the PSU, but his political career was finished.

Bibliography

See David Caute, *Communism and the French Intellectuals 1914–1960* (London: André Deutsch, 1964) or G. Lichtheim, *Marxism in Modern France* (New York: Columbia University Press, 1966). Hervé himself has written two major autobiographical accounts: *Lettre à Sartre et à quelques autres par la même occasion* and *Dieu et César sont-ils communistes?*, both Paris: La Table Ronde, 1956. Sartre's original strictures are in *Situations VI* (Paris: Gallimard, 1965).

MK

HERZ, Cornelius (1845–98)

Herz was an adventurer whose early years remain appropriately obscure. Born at Besançon to a Jewish family newly arrived from Germany, he was taken to the United States in 1848. He was said to speak in a strange jargon which mixed French, German and English, with the latter predominating. After various unsuccessful ventures on both sides of the Atlantic, he was (by 1879) installed in France, claiming to be a medical doctor, passing for a very wealthy man, and already decorated with the Legion of Honour. His wealth came ostensibly from the exploitation of patents for new inventions such as the telephone and electric light, but there seems to be no evidence that he had any real success in these enterprises. More certain is the fact that he prospered through connections with Republican politicians, notably Georges Clemenceau (q.v.). He became a central figure in the Panama affair, the biggest scandal of political corruption under the Third Republic. The company which was attempting to build a canal through the Panama Isthmus paid huge sums between 1885 and 1888 to bribe ministers and deputies for legislative favours – notably the right to raise money through a lottery. Herz was the leading intermediary between the Panama Company, its banker Baron Jacques Reinach (q.v.) and the politicians. Herz proceeded to blackmail Reinach and thus to divert huge sums into his own pocket. In 1892 Reinach's suicide brought the scandal into the open, at which point Herz fled to England where he lived until his death.

Herz's career had two major political consequences. His association with Clemenceau was a major factor in the latter's defeat in the parliamentary elections of 1893, a defeat which seemed to put an end to his political career: it was almost ten years before he was able to resume it. Although many other Radical politicians shared his fate as a result of their implication in the Panama affair, Clemenceau had been most closely involved with Herz who had financed his newspaper La Justice between 1881 and 1883. The second and broader political significance of the Panama affair arises from the fact that because its two central figures, Herz and Reinach, were Jewish, it gave a big push to the development of anti-Semitism. The theme of the exploitation of France by foreign-born Jewish bankers and financiers, linked to the Republican politicians who had so recently excluded the traditional ruling classes from power was given dramatic confirmation. The journalist Drumont (q.v.) wrote several best-selling anti-Semitic books and was able to publish a daily newspaper La Libre Parole in which anti-Semitic themes were prominent. The atmosphere was created in which the Dreyfus affair, after 1894, was able to install a long-lasting anti-Semitic strand into French political life.

Bibliography

Although Herz is mentioned in all general accounts of the period, there is very little detailed authenticated information about him in French, and none in English. The best sources remain: A. Dansette, *Les Affaires de Panama* (Paris: Perrin, 1934); and J. Bouvier, *Les Deux scandales de Panama* (Paris: Collection: Archives, 1964).

DRW

HERZOG, Philippe Albert Robert (1940–   )

Philippe Herzog, the son of an industrial chemist in the steel works at Pompy, has had a distinguished career. After graduating from the Ecole Polytechnique in 1959 he entered business (in cigarette manufacture) and then entered national military service (in Algeria). On demobilization he became an executive in the statistical and economic bureau, the INSEE, where he prepared for the teaching examination (*agrégation*) in economics which he passed in 1968. He now teaches economics at the University of Paris X-Nanterre.

He joined the Communist Party in 1965, became part of the PCF economic team and as such was at the centre of arguments about the joint left manifesto (common programme) of the 1970s. It was in fact Herzog who more or less wound up the renegotiation to update the programme for the 1978 legislative elections with a peremptory dismissal of Socialist propositions in the discussions of 22–3 September 1977.

Herzog was promoted to the Central Committee of the PCF in 1972 and to the Political Bureau in 1979 (along with other nominees of Georges Marchais – q.v.). His attempts to get himself elected to the Assembly were less successful and he seems content with his place as an expert. He is known to have been a hardline supporter of the leadership during the PCF's difficult years of dissidence in the 1980s and he led the party's list for the 1989 European elections in which the PCF polled a mere 7.7 per cent. Aside from André Lajoinie's poll in the 1988 presidential elections this was the party's worst result and it was reduced to sixth rank (after the centrists).

A genuinely able economist he has thus had two careers. He worked for a time in the prestigious Direction de la Prévision, the research division of the Finance Ministry where many of France's most distinguished economists have been employed. Moreover, like his party colleague Anicet le Pors (q.v.) whose work on industrial subsidies achieved considerable attention, he published a number of technical research papers from inside the ministry, mainly on economic forecasting. Since becoming a party propagandist, his writing has been at a more popular level, at the expense, some might feel, of intellectual rigour. His *Nouvelle economie à bras-le-corps* (2nd edition 1984) received considerable attention as a critique of the policies of the then Socialist government. Whilst it makes many points that would be widely respected even if not universally accepted, the reader is likely to be disconcerted by the somewhat over-generous praise for Georges Marchais as a fountainhead of ideas. In general, Herzog's considerable intellect would appear to have been put rather uncritically at the service of the party.

Bibliography

Herzog, P. (1972), *Politique economique et planification en régime capitaliste*, Paris: Editions Sociales, 1972.

Herzog, P. (1984), *L'Economie nouvelle à bras-le-corps*, Paris: Editions Sociales, 2nd edition, 1984.

PH

HOUPHOUËT-BOIGNY, Félix (1905–   )

Houphouët-Boigny was born in Yamoussokro in the central region of the Ivory Coast in 1905. The son of a Baoulé chief who was also a wealthy planter, he received his primary education at the Ecole Primaire Supérieure of Bingerville (1916–17) before going on to the Ecole Normale William Ponty and the school of medicine at Dakar where he graduated as a doctor in 1925. In 1944, when he was both a well-off planter and as a well-known doctor, he founded the agricultural unions the Syndicat Agricole Africain which was converted a year later into a political party, the Parti Démocratique de la Côte d'Ivoire (PDCI). Also in 1945 Houphouët-Boigny was elected as a deputy to the French Constituent Assembly where he carried through a bill to abolish both forced labour and the (*indigénat*) system which gave French administrations unlimited powers over Africans.

In October 1946 Houphouët-Boigny was founding member and president of the Rassemblement Démocratique Africain (RDA). Born out of discontent with the limited autonomy granted by the newly-adopted Constitution of the Fourth Republic, the RDA was a pan-African movement (with the PDCI as its Ivory Coast section) and was affiliated to the French Communist Party. Throughout the 1940s, the RDA organized or sponsored a series of demonstrations, boycotts and strikes in French West Africa which encountered increasingly severe repression from the colonial administration.

As the violence reached its climax in January 1950, the future of the RDA looked bleak and Houphouët-Boigny, although a member of the French National Assembly, only just escaped arrest. In a decisive tactical switch, however, Houphouët-Boigny and most of the other RDA leaders decided to end its association with the French Communist Party and to join forces with François Mitterrand's centre-left party, the UDSR. This belated move could not prevent losses for the RDA in the 1951 elections, but five years later the RDA recovered its electoral strength and won ten seats in the National Assembly. It was now a force to be reckoned with in French parliamentary politics and Houphouët-Boigny became a cabinet minister in the Socialist-led government of Guy Mollet (February 1956–June 1957). In this role he was closely involved in the preparation of the 1957 framework law on the overseas territories which divided the federations of French West Africa and French Equatorial Africa into autonomous territorial units. Houphouët-Boigny served as cabinet minister in all the remaining governments of the Fourth Republic until General de Gaulle became prime minister in June 1958. He was then, briefly, a member of the first government of the Fifth Republic, formed by Michel Debré in January 1959.

In April 1959 Houphouët-Boigny resigned his cabinet position in order to take up his post as the first elected prime minister of the Ivory Coast. De Gaulle's agreement to the independence of Mali within the French Community dashed Houphouët-Boigny's hopes for a Franco-African federation and, as a consequence he demanded and secured independence for the Ivory Coast. On 7 August 1960 the new state was born and on 27 November of the same year Houphouët-Boigny was elected president. Twenty-nine years later he is still in office. His parliamentary and ministerial experience in France have ensured him a continuing broad array of personal contacts with French politicians of his generation.

Bibliography

Fauré, Y.-A. and J.-F. Médard (eds) (1982), *Etat et bourgeoisie en Côte d'Ivoire*, Paris: Karthala.

Siriex, P.H. (1975), *Félix Houphouët-Boigny homme de la paix*, Paris: Séghers-NEA.

DCB

HUGO, Victor Marie (1802–85)

Poet, novelist, playwright and polemicist, Victor Hugo is the most imposing literary figure in nineteenth-century France. Though he attained widespread and enduring popularity through such novels as *Notre-Dame de Paris* (1831) and *Les Misérables* (1862), it is the virtuosity and innovative quality of his verse that are held to constitute the summit of his artistic achievement.

After an itinerant childhood in the train of the imperial armies (his father became a general under Napoleon), Hugo attended the secondary school Lycée Louis-le-Grand in Paris. His early literary productions were marked by an evolution from the classical to the romantic genres, culminating in his dramas *Cromwell* (1827) and *Hernani* (1830). Advocating a departure from the outmoded strictures of the classical convention, these literary 'charters' confirmed Hugo as the theorist and champion of the new Romantic movement.

From the First Republic to the Third, Hugo's life spans the whole turbulent period of nineteenth-century French politics. His literary development went hand in hand with an evolving political intuition. Having early inherited his mother's royalist sympathies, he moved towards a political liberalism which became increasingly reflected in his verse and prose. His literary achievement was acknowledged by his election to the Académie française in 1841 and by his nomination to the Chamber of Peers in 1845. With the Revolution of 1848 and the advent of the Second Republic, he was elected as a deputy first in the Constituent then in the Legislative Assembly. This new-found political role, inspired by a Republican commitment to the defence of freedom and the pursuit of social justice, was, however, to be short-lived. Having misread Louis-Napoleon's intentions when he supported his candidature for the presidency in 1848, Hugo greeted the *coup d'état* of December 1851 with token resistance and a self-imposed exile which was to last until 1870. His early writings in exile translate a mood of political wrath in which the full polemical power of his pen is deployed against Napoleon III and the Second Empire. *Napoléon le Petit* (1852) and *Les Châtiments* (1853) are mordant satirical indictments of the usurpation of power by a corrupt and autocratic ruler.

After the Prussian victory at Sedan and the proclamation of the Third Republic in 1870, Hugo returned in triumph to Paris. He was elected in 1871 to the National Assembly in Bordeaux, but almost at once fell out of sympathy with the right-wing majority and resigned his seat. His subsequent departure for Brussels coincided with the ill-fated episode of the Commune. Though he criticized the excesses of the latter, his offer of sanctuary to the defeated communards led to his expulsion from Belgium. He spent the last years of his life in Paris, where he was elected to the Senate and fêted as the bard and patriarch of the Republic. He died on 22 May 1885 and was given a national burial in the Pantheon. While his literary importance was never matched by his political achievements, he exerted a far-reaching influence on the taste and public opinion of his century, both as the leading light of the French Romantic school and as a celebrated exponent of Republican ideals.

Bibliography

Among the many studies which deal with Hugo's literary and political career, the following provide useful reading: M. Aref, *La Pensée sociale et humaine de Victor Hugo dans son oeuvre romanesque* (Geneva-Paris: Slatkine-Champion, 1979); J. Cornuz, *Hugo, l'homme des Misérables* (Lausanne-Paris: Favre, 1985); H. Juin, *Victor Hugo*, 3 vols (Paris: Flammarion, 1980); A. Maurois, *Olympio, ou la vie de Victor Hugo* (Paris: Hachette, 1954); English translation, *Victor Hugo* (London: Jonathan Cape, 1956); S. Petrey, *History in the Text: 'Quatrevingt-Treize' and the French Revolution*, Purdue University Monographs in Romance Languages, vol. 3 (Amsterdam: John Benjamins BV, 1980).

JS

I

ISORNI, Jacques Alfred Antoine Tibère (1911–)

Jacques Isorni is a lawyer by profession, and in 1931 was the first secretary of the Advocates Association of France as well as a barrister in the Paris Appeal Court. As a student he had been one of the co-founders of the journal *Rivarol* (the original, not the contemporary) of extreme left-wing Maurassian tendencies. He became famous for his defence of Marshal Pétain and of Robert Brasillach at the liberation. He thereafter campaigned indefatigably for the rehabilitation of Pétain as well as other extreme-right causes. (See Isorni's defence of Pétain, *Souffrances et mort du Maréchal*.) One of the few Vichy supporters who was eligible to stand for election, he headed the extreme right-wing lists (with Admiral Decoux) Union des Nationaux et des Independants Republicains in 1951. He was elected deputy for second district of the Seine and, because the Independent Republicans refused to accept him as a member, registered as a 'Peasant'. The Independent Republicans later relented and in 1956 he was re-elected as an Independent and a defendent of the French retention of Algeria.

Isorni was one of the few extreme right wingers to protest at de Gaulle's investiture in 1958 and he refused to vote for him in the Assembly. He remarked that the 'defender of Louis XVI cannot vote for Robespierre' and predicted that de Gaulle would decolonize Algeria ('politique d'abandon'). Isorni was not re-elected in 1958.

Isorni then defended French Algerian extremists in the courts. In February 1963 he was disbarred for three years by the Military Court for his behaviour during the trial of J.-M. Bastien-Thiry who had tried to assassinate de Gaulle. De Gaulle saw to it that Lt.-Col. Bastien-Thiry was executed. In 1966 Isorni was fined and made ineligible for election to the Assembly for ten years by the courts for certain defamatory passages about the president in his pamphlet *Jusqu'au bout de notre peine* (now unobtainable).

In the 1965 elections Isorni supported Lecanuet on the first ballot and Mitterrand on the second (arguing that Mitterrand had never said a word against Pétain – *Le Monde* 11 December 1965). Unlike many others on the extreme right (including Tixier-Vignancour) he was a severe critic of those who rallied to Pompidou in 1969 and supported Alain Poher (see *Le Monde* of 13 June 1969). He is the author of numerous books as well as several plays.

Bibliography

Isorni, J. (1951), *Souffrances et mort du maréchal*, Paris: Flammarion.

Isorni, J. (1957), *Le Silence est d'or*, Paris: Flammarion.

Isorni, J. (1959), *Ainsi passent les républiques*, Paris: Flammarion.

Isorni, J. (1986), *Memoirs 1948–58*, Paris: Laffont.

On Isorni's loss of civil rights in 1966 see *Le Monde* of 24 and 29 December 1966.

DSB

J

JAURÈS, Jean Léon (1859–1914)

Philosopher, teacher, journalist, orator, socialist leader and theoretician, Jean Jaurès was born in Castres (Tarn) on 3 September 1859. His family belonged to the urban bourgeoisie, predominantly woollen merchants and traders, but also military men (three of his uncles were army officers and two cousins were admirals). His own parents having fallen on hard times while working a smallholding of six hectares, Jaurès grew up in close proximity to the rude reality of rural France. A brilliant pupil at school, where his oratorical powers were already in evidence, he was channelled via the Collège Saint-Barbe towards the Ecole Normale Supérieure where, in 1878, he came first in the competitive entrance exam. Throughout the remainder of his life, the Ecole Normale Supérieure was to hold a special place in his affections. In 1881, he came third (behind Bergson) in the *agrégation de philosophie*, and began a teaching career at the Lycée d'Albi (1881–5) and the University of Toulouse (1883–5).

Alongside his teaching, Jaurès began to prepare his doctoral thesis and to participate in the political battles of the rural south-west. Both activities were informed by his radical break with catholicism which had taken place at the rue d'Ulm. An ardent supporter of Ferry (q.v.), with a quasi-religious belief in republicanism, Jaurès found himself, in large part as a result of his oratorical brilliance, included (in sixth place) on the Republican list for the 1885 elections. Emerging from the first round of the election in first place by voter preference, he was elected, shortly after his 25th birthday, as the youngest deputy in the 1885–9 Parliament. The following year, he married Louise Bois, the daughter of a wholesale cheese merchant from Albi.

His early years as a deputy constituted a turning-point during which he came to appreciate at first hand the superficiality and emptiness of Opportunist politics, the pitfalls and inadequacies of radicalism and the dangers of ideological inflexibility. Although he was shifting intellectually in the direction of 'socialism' (recognizing the structural existence of a social problem, the insolence of both money and

capital, the need for collective responsibility and, to some extent, control) he rejected the concept of class struggle currently being advocated by the few self-proclaimed socialists in the Chamber (whose dogmatism he found intolerable) and was still not exempt from an instinctive chauvinism stemming from blind conviction that France had a special universal mission to perform. In short, Jaurès felt desperately in need of a political home. The 'Boulangist' elections of 1889, with the return to *scrutin d'arrondissement*, saw Jaurès narrowly defeated in the Castres constituency by the forces of bribery and corruption which the aristocratic Reille and Solages families were able to muster against him. But in some ways, his return to the University of Toulouse saw the beginning of his real political education.

There, his insatiable thirst for ideas, and the progress of his doctoral thesis, finally brought him into contact with Socialist theory (Louis Blanc, Pierre-Joseph Proudhon, Ferdinand Lassalle and Karl Marx) but for the moment, his relationship with all these ideas was critical and reflective, stimulated by long discussions with Lucien Herr, rather than adulatory or partisan. His Socialist education came primarily as a result of his growing contact with the working class, especially the miners of Carmaux, whose cause he had already espoused in the 1885 Parliament. This early contact was complemented, after his election as a municipal councillor in Toulouse in 1890, by growing awareness of the real problems of the urban working class. He nevertheless remained, until 1892, convinced that the Republican party (as opposed to a specific *proletarian* party) was the political answer to the social problem. It was the Carmaux mining strike of 1892 which opened his eyes to the naked reality of class struggle and precipitated his crossing of the socialist Rubicon. Earlier that year, Jaurès completed his two doctoral dissertations, a subsidiary one, written in Latin, on *The Origins of German Socialism*, and his principal thesis, *De la Réalité du monde sensible*, in which he first attempted a philosophical synthesis of materialism and idealism.

The Carmaux strike shifted him abruptly from the ivory tower of theory to the crude arena of practice. When the workers of Carmaux elected one of their own, Jean-Baptiste Calvignac, as mayor, the feudal sensitivities of the marquis de Solages reached breaking-point. Refusing Calvignac the necessary time off work to carry out his civic duties, the mine-owners precipitated a crisis which led to the firing of the mayor and the outbreak of a bitter strike. No longer could Jaurès continue to believe that the *polit-ical* Republic alone sufficed to integrate all the sons and daughters of France. He threw himself into the strike with determination, stood for the parliamentary seat vacated by the haughty de Solages and was duly elected on a platform inspired by the Guesdist programme elaborated at their Marseilles Congress earlier that year. In the general election of 1893 he was re-elected with a substantially increased majority. From the cross-fire of class-struggle, the philosopher thus returned to the Chamber of Deputies as a *de facto* Socialist party leader.

The urgency and militancy of Jaurès' activities between 1893 and 1898 can in part be explained by his conviction that the advent of socialism was imminent. As a seminal theoretician and the supreme orator, he spoke with authority on a vast range of subjects, from education to agriculture, from military affairs to fiscal reform, from Greek philosophy to avant-garde literature. A prolific journalist, an indefatigable speaker at socialist and working-class meetings, Jaurès also maintained his links with the university and with the world of the arts and culture. Despite his 'conversion' to socialism, he never abandoned his faith that the 'intellectual' middle classes and those ranks of the petty bourgeoisie not organically tied to the interests of big capital would help reconcile his own two principal political objectives: the generalization of republicanism and the installation of socialism.

Although Jaurès was increasingly widely acknowledged within Socialist circles as a potential overall leader, he maintained absolute political and intellectual independence from any specific party or labour organization. During the bitterly-fought Carmaux strike of glassworkers in 1895, he braved the wrath of Socialist maximalists and syndicalist purists alike by advocating the creation of a workers' glassworks (*verrerie ouvrière*) at Albi. Against the Socialists who scorned the 'reformist naïveté' of cooperatives, and against the glassworkers who favoured a corporatist solution (*la verrerie aux verriers*), Jaurès pleaded in favour of his own nascent version of 'revolutionary reformism'. Likewise, at the international Congress of London in 1896, with the experiences of Carmaux fresh in his mind and the noise of anarchist bombs still ringing in his ears, he took a vigorous stance against those syndicalists who argued that 'po-litical action' was not an essential weapon in the struggle for socialism. On the contrary, for Jaurès, as the turn of the century approached and five years of unrelenting Socialist activism came to an end, the political dimensions of the task became ever clearer. By 1898, Jaurès was convinced that there was still a long and hard road to tread before any sign of the 'social republic' would begin to emerge. He was also mindful of the forces of reaction which still hankered after a return to pre-republican days.

The Dreyfus affair consolidated his belief that, before the walls of the Socialist temple could be constructed, the Republican foundation stones needed consolidating. The fate of Emile Zola, who, for having dared to write *J'Accuse*, was in February 1898 sentenced to prison without much more than a murmur from the streets of Paris, drove home for Jaurès the extent to which the popular masses underestimated the powers of the state and of the establishment. After his own defeat in the general election of 1898, he took full advantage of his political independence as editorialist on *La Petite République* to enter fully into the battle for Dreyfus (which the Socialist Party as a whole still officially dismissed as a mere power-struggle inside the ruling class). In a long series of editorials, which subsequently appeared as a book, *Les Preuves*, 'he dissected the case against Dreyfus until he had torn it to shreds' (Goldberg, p. 240). In so doing, for other Socialist leaders, he disturbed the previously clear demarcation line between class conflict and class collaboration. At the same time, Jaurès initiated a major push for Socialist unity, believing that any divisions in the Republican 'front' could prove fatal to the regime. But his desire to frog-march the various Socialist groups into organic unity, synchronizing as it did with his total involvement in what many Socialists persisted in seeing as an irrelevant campaign for the freedom of a bourgeois (and an army officer into the bargain) sparked off a major controversy pitting 'revolutionaries' against 'reformists'. When, in June 1899, in an effort to create a government of Republican unity, René Waldeck-Rousseau offered the rising Socialist lawyer Alexandre Millerand a ministerial portfolio, Jaurès energetically defended the course which rapidly became known as 'ministerialism'. Millerand's acceptance of office (and subsequent behaviour as a minister) split the Socialist forces down the middle, Jaurès, Briand and Viviani forming the Parti Socialiste Français while Guesde and Vaillant created the Parti Socialiste de France. The stakes were much more complex and far more subtle than the victory of 'reformism' over 'revolution'. At issue was an understanding of history, an interpretation of politics and a style of leadership. For Jaurès, socialism was the inevitable consequence of 1792, but, before its day could dawn, radicalism had to run its course. Politics was not some sort of gladiatorial stand-off where, at the end of the day, brute force prevailed, but rather a series of coalitions and compromises in which contending forces sought ultimately to promote their cause at the expense of their rivals. Leaders should not themselves be led by pre-ordained formulae, but should take each situation in the fullest possible context and assume the responsibility of a never-ending low of complex decisions.

For five years polemics held centre-stage. Jaurès, who was re-elected deputy in 1902, was determined to push his views to their logical conclusion. He therefore entered into a semi-formal parliamentary alliance with the radicals (the *bloc des gauches*) under the premiership of Emile Combes. Jaurès himself was elected vice-president of the Chamber of Deputies and, as such, devoted much of his time to pursuing the reformist programme of the radicals: separation of Church and state, republicanization of the army. But time and circumstances were, in one sense at least, against him. Although most of the radical programme was pushed through, the mood of the Socialist rank and file turned progressively against 'ministerialism'. The 'social' gains of the left bloc were embarrassingly thin, and although Jaurès' own integrity remained unblemished, for former firebrands of the Socialist movement like Millerand and Briand, the ministerialism and careerism became increasingly synonymous. Moreover, the German SPD, semi-official guardians of the Socialist temple, pronounced unequivocally, at their 1904 Dresden Conference, against any participation in 'bourgeois' governments short of final Socialist 'victory'. Finally, the shift in the international climate and the increasingly urgent need to devote attention to problems of war and peace helped nudge Jaurès ever closer to acquiescence in a 'revolutionary' basis for Socialist unity (the total rejection of 'ministerial participation') which he would not have accepted four years earlier. The final persuasion came when the Second International, despite an impassioned plea from Jaurès himself to allow each national section the latitude to seek its own way, voted massively, at its 1904 Amsterdam Congress, to condemn the Millerand experiment and its sequel and to demand that each national Socialist party move rapidly towards unity on 'revolutionary' bases. The French Socialist movements finally sealed their unity in 1905 with the creation of the Section Française de l'Internationale Ouvrière (SFIO).

The years between the Dreyfus affair and Socialist unity were, in Goldberg's words, 'years of anguish' for Jaurès. Isolated from the other major Socialist leaders, Vaillant and Guesde, increasingly suspect to most of the labour leaders, who detected in him the supreme example of the treacherous bourgeois politician, but at the same time mistrusted and kept at arm's length by his radical 'allies', Jaurès took intellectual solace in his friendship with Lucien Herr and in the monumental project of preparing the *Histoire socialiste de la révolution française*, which has subsequently become a classic, the first serious social, if not socialist, history of the Revolution. This breadth of intellectual vision, this thirst for new ideas continued unabated until his death in 1914. Subjects on which he wrote with freshness and lucidity as editor of the daily paper he created in 1904, *L'Humanité*, included aviation, the cinema, the engineering profession, literature and music. His previously Euro- (if not Franco-) centric horizons expanded rapidly, towards the Mahgreb, Africa, the Middle East, Asia and South America, whose cultural and political problems he studied with intensity. Increasingly fascinated by the richness of Islam, he gradually moved towards a consciousness of colonialism which, while never totally abandoning his early belief that France had something special to offer, nevertheless recognized the validity of movements of national liberation. His long speaking tour of Latin America in 1911 brought him into direct contact with a totally different concept of 'civilization'. The fruits of all this observation were to be harvested in his gradual intellectual dominance of the Second International.

After the creation of the SFIO, Jaurès emerged as the natural – though never entirely undisputed – leader of the united party, forging, with the old communard Edouard Vaillant, a political alliance which held fissiparous federations and sections together for almost ten years (the only period of left unity in the history of France). Although Jaurès took the leading role in formulating policy on almost every subject, two problems above all henceforth occupied his mind: internationalism against war and closer working unit between the CGT and the SFIO. Not only did he inject into Edouard Vaillant's twenty-year-old campaign for socialist recognition of syndicalist autonomy a remarkable degree of rhetorical passion and political subtlety, but he also began to develop a theory of the working class which historians have only recently begun to decipher.

On the international front, Jaurès worked ceaselessly, again alongside Edouard Vaillant, for Socialist mobilization against war. He avoided the twin pitfalls of a totally vacuous 'antipatriotism' (as advocated by Gustave Hervé) and an equally unrealistic

Guesdist determinism which held that, war being the logical consequence of capitalism, there was little point in wasting effort mobilizing against the former. The Vaillant–Jaurès motion, recognizing the reality of nation-states and the legitimacy of national defence, but calling on the international working classes to consider every means at their disposal, including an insurrectionary general strike, to prevent war, won large majorities at the party Congresses of Limoges (1906) and Nancy (1907) as well as more equivocal support at the International Congresses of Stuttgart (1907) and Copenhagen (1910). Jaurès' masterly study *L'Armée nouvelle*, first published in 1911, but still appearing in new editions in the 1980s, was the first (and remains by far the best) attempt to theorize a *Republican* organization, structure and credo for national defence. His impassioned orations in favour of peace, at Basel (1912), Pré-Saint-Gervais (1913) and Brussels (1914) made many feel that he alone was the last remaining barrier to the machinations of warmongers and militarists. Of his last speech, in Brussels two nights before his death, the novelist Martin du Gard has said, 'in such moments of paroxysm, a single cry or gesture from Jaurès would have sufficed to propel this fanaticized crowd head first into the storming of any Bastille to hand'. They were not to be given the chance. At 9.40 pm on 31 July 1914, a young right-wing fanatic, Raoul Villain, his head full of the 'Jaurès the German' stories he had read in the gutter press, fired two bullets into the Socialist leader as he dined with a group from *L'Humanité* at the Café du Croissant on the rue Montmartre. Minutes later, Jaurès was dead. His ashes were transferred to the Pantheon on 23 November 1924. He remains the undisputed founding father of French socialism.

Bibliography

Harvey Goldberg, *The Life of Jaurès* (Madison: University of Wisconsin Press, 1962); Madeleine Rebérioux, 'Jean Jaurès', in Jean Maitron (ed.), *Dictionnaire biographique du mouvement ouvrier français*, vol. 13 (Paris: Editions Ouvrières, 1975); Max Gallo, *Le Grand Jaurès* (Paris: Robert Laffont, 1984); Madeleine Rebérioux (ed.), *Jaurès et la classe ouvrière*. (Paris: Editions Ouvrières, 1981). See also the activities of the Société d'Etudes Jaurésiennes, who publish a quarterly *Bulletin*.

JH

JEANNENEY, Jean Marcel (1910–)

Jean Marcel Jeanneney was a university teacher, and an expert in economic theory, the author of *Forces et faiblesses de l'économie française* (Paris: Collin, 1956). He was appointed to the Pinay-Rueff committee established by the new de Gaulle government in autumn 1958 to revitalize the economy and plan the long-term economic future; the committee recommended devaluation, budgetary discipline, reduced state spending, and a 'heavy' franc worth a hundred old ones.

As minister for industry in the Debré government (1959–62), he fell out with Pinay, the finance minister, but began to gain influence with President de Gaulle. He became a fervent convert to the Fifth Republic regime and was always attracted by de Gaulle's non-conformist approach – to the Algerian problem, to international relations in general, to decentralization (1968–9), to 'participation' as a social doctrine. De Gaulle was attracted by Jeanneney's suggestion of an industrial development board through which industries in difficulties would receive state help.

He was 'exiled' with Debré (a personal friend) in 1962 and became ambassador to the newly independent Algeria, but both returned to government in 1966, Jeanneney to a new super-Ministry of Social Affairs; Jacques Chirac was his secretary for employment, and it was Jeanneney who first called him *'le bulldozer'*. Jeanneney, together with Debré and Pompidou had reservations about moves to foster profit-sharing, or a greater participation of people in decision-making in areas which affected them, but the events of May–June 1968 necessitated some concessions, and Jeanneney played a central role in the negotiations with labour organizations, leading to the Grenelle Agreements.

Jeanneney won Pierre Mendès France's Grenoble parliamentary seat from him in the June 1968 elections, and was made responsible in Couve de Murville's government for preparing the future referendum on Senate reform and regional reform, which, however, led to a 'No' vote. Returning to university teaching on de Gaulle's resignation, Jeanneney unsuccessfully opposed the devaluation of the franc, just as he had supported de Gaulle in his instinct not to devalue in autumn 1968. Jeanneney was one of the few people de Gaulle invited to his home between his resignation in April 1969 and his death eighteen months later.

In 1972, Jeanneney's increasing disillusionment with Gaullism without de Gaulle led him to resign from the Gaullist party, which he felt was no longer a vehicle for change, but an obstacle to innovation, and a mere buttress of President Pompidou's increased power. Jeanneney joined the Mouvement Réformateur, intent on adding his own brand of Gaullism to the Christian Democracy of the *Centre démocrate* and the Radical republicanism of the Radical Party, the two groups constituting the movement. This attempt to retain a separate Centrist identity in French politics soon collapsed in 1973–4, and Jeanneney returned once more to university teaching.

Bibliography

Jeanneney's political outlook is covered in his book *A mes amis gaullistes* (Paris: Presses-Pocket, 1973), which includes interviews and articles.

MS

JEANNENEY, Jules Emile (1864–1957)

Born in Besançon (Doubs) the son of an auctioneer, Jeanneney entered the legal profession, where he quickly acquired a reputation, particularly in the new realm of international law. Soon he was to combine this with a political career, and become mayor of the village of Rioz at the age of 32. In 1902 he was elected deputy for a Haute-Saône seat and in the Chamber he made his mark as a good constituency member. His efforts were amply repaid by an increased majority, and subsequent election, again for the department of the Haute-Saône, to the Senate in 1909. He remained a senator for the rest of the Third Republic.

It was in the Senate that Jeanneney was to emerge as a figure of national repute. Unlike many of his colleagues, he was not ambitious for office, accepting it twice in a long career and only when the country was deep in crisis, in 1917 and 1944. Instead his reputation was made through his work within the vital parliamentary commissions, particularly as president of the influential Finance Commission from 1928, where it fell to him to preside over the 'Poincaré devaluation', and other subsequent unsuccessful efforts to resist the onset of the Great Depression.

In 1932 Jeanneney was elected president of the Senate. His term of office covered a period when France suffered desperately from both internal and external conflicts. His authority and integrity were stretched to full. Nevertheless, his innate belief in constitutional republicanism bolstered him through the crisis of 6 February 1934, as it did during the election of a Popular Front government, and the traumatic passage of its social legislation through the Senate.

But of all the problems he had to face, the greatest was to be the voting of plenary powers to Marshal Pétain after the defeat of France in 1940. As presiding president over the joint session of the Chamber and Senate, Jeanneney sought to guide the Third Republic to a dignified demise. Yet, at the same time, he resolutely refused to give way to government pressure by insisting on reading the telegram from dissenting leaders of the Republic who had been tricked into leaving the country on the ship *Massilia*.

This same resolution was demonstrated in 1944 when leaders of the Vichy government attempted to persuade Jeanneney to recall the deputies and senators of the sixteenth legislature to a new assembly, thereby giving additional authority to the collapsing regime. His steadfast adherence to constitutionalism ensured that he would refuse to contemplate this, although his counterpart in the Chamber, Herriot, was more tempted. And it was this same steadfastness that was to lead to his recall to office on the 9 September 1944 when de Gaulle included him within a 'government of national unanimity' in an effort to display a continuity with France's Republican past.

Jeanneney was never a man to act purely as a figurehead. Though he staunchly defended Republican institutions (and *laïcité*) until the end of his life, he became increasingly disillusioned with the chaotic inefficiency of Fourth Republic parliamentarianism and often wrote in this vein to de Gaulle. His son was a Gaullist minister in the Fifth Republic and his grandson (Jean-Noël) is prominent in the world of letters and journalism.

Bibliography

Jeanneney's diaries, covering the period 1939–42, were edited by his grandson – J.-N. Jeanneney, *Journal politique* (Paris: A. Colin, 1972).

PT

JOBERT, Michel (1921–   )

Jobert has the distinction of having been a key minister in both a right-wing government under President Pompidou in 1973–4 (foreign minister) and a left-wing government under President Mitterrand from 1981–3 (minister of state – in France a prestigious senior minister – for foreign trade). Once seen as a potential leader of the Gaullists, now an independent critic and prominent gadfly, he is viewed primarily as a staunch defender of national independence and of an interventionalist state pursuing a Gaullist-style national interest.

Born in Morocco, he attended the Ecole Libre des Sciences Politiques and the Ecole Nationale d'Administration. In 1949 he joined the Cour des Comptes. He later was a member of several ministerial advisory staffs (*cabinets*), including that of Pierre Mendès France in 1954–6. He became director of the *cabinet* of the high commissioner of the Republic of French West Africa (1956–8), and dealt with issues of international cooperation until 1961.

In 1963, he began a close working relationship with then Prime Minister Georges Pompidou which lasted eleven years, first as director of his *cabinet*, then secretary-general of the presidential staff from 1969–73. He played a key advisory role in such issues as the events of May 1968, setting up the peace negotiations between US Secretary of State Henry Kissinger and Vietnamese leaders, and Britain's entry into the Common Market in 1972.

As foreign minister, he focused on European affairs – preparing, with Kissinger, the 1973 'Year of Europe'. He blamed the failure of this initiative – in the wake of the Arab-Israeli War of October 1973 and the subsequent oil crisis – on what he called 'superpower condominium', or the obsession of the United States and the Soviet Union with their bilateral relationships to the exclusion of third parties such as Europe.

Jobert's position at the US-inspired conference of oil-importing countries in February 1974 established his public image as pro-Arab and anti-American. Cultivating his style as a French 'Asterix' fighting the mighty American Goliath – Kissinger – he immediately gained public favour and demonstrated how style can be as important as content in foreign policy issues.

Pompidou's death in April 1974 put an abrupt end to Jobert's ascending career. In June 1974 he founded the left-Gaullist Mouvement des Démocrates, but his skills in political organization did not match those of his main rival for the Gaullist leadership, Jacques Chirac, and he was quickly marginalized.

In 1981, Mitterrand, looking to balance his Socialist–Communist coalition government on the right, appointed Jobert to the relatively minor Foreign Trade Ministry, but with the enhanced personal status of minister of state. His 'Asterix' image reappeared, this time fighting Japanese technology imports to defend French and European industry – as

symbolized in the 'Battle of Poitiers', when imported Japanese video recorders were diverted to the small, understaffed customs post in the city where Joan of Arc had once fought back the English.

Today he is largely out of the political mainstream, but remains active in international networks. He was, for instance, among the candidates for the position of secretary-general of the United Nations Educational, Scientific and Cultural Organization (UNESCO), based in Paris. But while Jobert's political future looks hazy, this is consistent with a certain style. Considered a 'conservative *mendésiste*', he may share Mendès's long-run political fate, remaining 'almost' a major figure, but unable to express his character or pursue his vision in foreign affairs in high office.

Bibliography

Jobert, M. (1974), *Mémoirs d'avenir*, Paris: Grasset.
Jobert, M. (1976), *L'Autre regard*, Paris: Grasset.
Jobert, M. (1984), *Par trente–six chemins*, Paris: Albin Michel.
Weed, M.K. (1988), *Michel Jobert et le diplomatie française*, Paris: Fernand Lanore.

MKW

JOFFRE, Joseph Jacques Césaire (1852–1931)

Between 1914 and 1916 Joffre must have been the most popular man in France, the embodiment of patriotism and the object of a personal cult: lay versions of the Lord's Prayer addressed to him ('Notre Joffre qui êtes au front') were widely circulated, his portrait was displayed in classrooms and in people's homes, baby girls were named after him (Joffrette) and puns on his name ('J'offre' meaning 'I offer') were used to evoke ideas of sacrifice and generosity. In epic popular representations, his fatherly figure appeared, surrounded by a halo, with such national heroes as Napoleon and Joan of Arc.

Up to 1914 Joffre's career has been that of an efficient professional soldier. Born in the Pyrenees, he came to Paris to study at the Ecole Polytechnique and was a second lieutenant at the time of the French defeat in 1870, when he was involved in the defence of Paris. He then worked in the Department of Fortifications and earned promotion to the rank of captain (1884).

The next phase of his life was spent in the colonies: there were some military exploits (expedition to Timbuktoo, 1894) but he was active chiefly as an administrator (in Indo-China, the Sudan and Madagascar he organized the military infrastructure and oversaw the building of roads, bridges, railways and hospitals). Having acquired a reputation for efficiency, he came back to higher and higher posts in the metropolitan French army, and found himself at its head on the eve of war.

If the weakness of his plan of attack was soon demonstrated by the German advance, few of his critics deny that Joffre was the main architect of the victory of the Marne (September 1914) which saved Paris and gave him considerable authority over the government and the army, as well as winning him the affection of the people. This prestige was to carry him through the next two years of inglorious war, marked by abortive offensives and enormous casualties. Delivering no visible results against the Germans he liked to say that he was 'nibbling away at them'. But at what cost!

By 1916 the war of attrition had begun to undermine his popularity: he had lost his allies in government and his critics were now more powerful. Public opinion needed a change but he still had to be treated with respect: he was dismissed in stages, keeping the rank of commander-in-chief without the power, then losing that title as well and being made 'Marshal of France' (December 1916). He later became a member of the Académie française, wrote his memoirs and at his death in 1931 was given a state funeral.

Today, although Joffre is remembered for the victory of the Marne, his reputation is in relative eclipse. However, leading the French army into trench warfare was a thankless task and his replacement, Nivelle, with his disastrous offensive at the Chemin aux Dames, was even less successful. Foch's enduring reputation, by contrast, owes much to the eventual unity of the Allied Forces which he came to command, and to the arrival of a million fresh American troops.

Bibliography

For Joffre's own account see *The Memoirs of Marshal Joffre* (London: Geoffrey Bles, 1932). Among many works on Joffre, see B.H. Liddel Hart, *Reputations* (London: J. Murray, 1928) which also deals with Falkenhayn and Haig, and J. d'Esme, *Le Père Joffre* (Paris: Editions France-Empire, 1962).

M-MH

JOLIOT-CURIE, Irène (1897–1956)

The elder daughter of Marie and Pierre Curie, Irène Curie was born in 1897 and educated privately at an 'alternative school' for academics' children, then at the Collège Sévigné, before studying science at the Sorbonne. During the First World War, she worked with her mother's X-ray unit at the front. After writing her doctoral thesis on polonium in 1926, she married fellow-scientist Frédéric Joliot and they linked their names. Over the next ten years, which also saw the birth of their two children, the Joliot-Curies worked together on the research which would bring them the Nobel Prize in 1935, for the discovery of artificial radioactivity. In 1936 Léon Blum created a government post for scientific research as one of his three junior ministries for women. Irène Joliot-Curie accepted his offer and became an under-secretary of state for several months before resigning to take up a post at the Sorbonne. After the war, during which her husband was active in the Resistance, both the Joliot-Curies were members of the French Atomic Energy Commission (CEA) and were closely associated with its early successes. Both were, however, dismissed from it in the early 1950s, for their Communist sympathies. Irène Joliot-Curie died of leukaemia in 1956, as a direct result of her lifelong work with radioactive materials.

Irène Joliot-Curie's brief ministerial appointment gives her a place in the political history of the Third Republic as one of Léon Blum's three women ministers at a time when French women did not have the vote. She was already famous as a scientist who, like her mother, had achieved great things in a male-dominated environment, and she could be regarded as a role model for the generation of young women entering higher education between the wars. During her tenure of the government post, she took part in discussions surrounding the reorganization of state funding for science in what would later become the CNRS (Conseil National de la Recherche Scientifique). While a left-wing sympathizer all her life, she was clearly much more at home in the laboratory than in politics and had accepted the post only to show her support for the right of women to exercise professions and hold office. She was not, however, in favour of granting the suffrage to all women immediately, sharing the fears of others on the left that it would lead to the return of reactionary governments of which 'women would be the first victims'.

It is as a scientist that Irène Joliot-Curie will best be remembered, but she brought to her political appointment the calm and unceremonious efficiency for which she was known in the laboratory. She and her family were part of the progressive scientific community of the period and she always championed the cause of women in science, several times making public applications to be admitted to the Académie des Sciences. Like her mother, she was refused admission.

Bibliography

There is some material on Irène Joliot-Curie in Eugènie Cotton, *Les Curie* (Paris: Séghers, 1963). In English there is a biography by Robin McKown, *She Lived for Science* (London: Macmillan, 1962) which contains more on science and private life than on politics, and apparently was written for young people.

SR

'JOLIOT-CURIE', Jean-Frédéric Joliot (1900–58)

Jean-Frédéric Joliot was the son of a communard and was a distinguished scientist (joint Nobel Prize for Chemistry in 1935). Following an orthodox career in chemistry, he became assistant to Marie Curie in 1925 and married her daughter in 1926. In 1932 he was a junior lecturer in the Paris Faculté des Sciences, then a lecturer in the Sorbonne. In 1937 he became a professor in the Collège de France and also head of the French atomic research institute. Joliot-Curie's political importance stems from this background because, not being a politician as such, he was one of the leaders of the scientific community and latterly devoted himself to Communist causes.

It seems to have been the quasi-insurrectional 6 February 1934, when the right-wing leagues tried to attack the Assembly, which drew Joliot-Curie into active politics as a member of the SFIO – Pierre Curie had much the same feeling. Although close to the PCF he was one of the intellectuals who signed the petition of 29 August 1939 expressing 'stupefaction at the volte-face which has reconciled leaders of the USSR to Nazi leaders at the very hour when the latter simultaneously threaten the invasion of Poland and the independence of all free peoples'. There is, as Robrieux points out, a degree of uncertainty about his wartime activities. He did organize the transfer of heavy water stocks from Norway to France and then to England, he was 'president' of the PCF's National Front Resistance, and he was active in the battle for Paris but he was also in Paris during the occupation

and was allowed a great deal of latitude by the authorities.

At the liberation he was made head of the CNRS and in 1946 became high commissioner of the Atomic Energy Authority. But at the same time he became an active party member and used his position in the world of science to draw in fellow-travellers and to extend the influence of front organizations. The most important of these was the Russian 'Peace Movement' which became active with the onset of the cold war. Although not at first an open party member he supported the August 1948 Wroclaw meeting of 'Intellectuals for Peace' (Paris), a committee which he headed, with Aragon and Fadeiev as vice-presidents; the organization had Picasso's dove as an emblem. In March 1950 the committee issued the Stockholm appeal 'for a ban on atomic weapons'. In April 1950 Joliot-Curie was evicted from the Atomic Energy Commission, but he and his wife already composed *le couple royal* of science for the PCF and in April 1951 he was awarded the Stalin Peace Prize. Joliot-Curie was a propagandist for the peaceful use of nuclear power but also a persuasive publicist of the danger of nuclear war (coming from the United States). When he got carried away by the prospect of nuclear disaster he was pulled back into line by Thorez (the PCF line being that the 'imperialists' would be destroyed, not all civilization).

It was the Khrushchev report which brought out one of Joliot-Curie's last major services to the PCF. His message to the French Communist 14th Congress in July 1956 (when he was promoted to the Central Committee) said that 'grave errors' had been committed in Russia but that these were not errors of Marxist–Leninist doctrine or of the system but of men. This is one of the first instances of the orthodox explanation of the 'Stalin phenomenon' which the party has used since that revelation. Joliot-Curie's position is summed up by two further statements: 'le Parti ne peut pas manquer de savoir mieux que chaque un d'entre nous' (hence no complaint about Lyssenko) and 'C'est si bon d'être au parti, on n'a plus besoin de penser' (R. Aron, *Mémoires*, Paris: Julliard, 1983, p. 289 for this last quotation). In 1958 he was still head of the Russian Peace Movement and outwardly showed no reservations about support for the PCF. Joliot-Curie was the last scientist of international stature to lead the PCF's scientists: the party replaced him with J.-P. Vigier.

Bibliography

There is no satisfactory political study of Joliot-Curie though there is a profile in P. Robrieux, *Histoire intérieur du parti communiste*, vol. IV (Paris: Fayard, 1984), pp. 334–8.

DSB

JOSPIN, Lionel Robert (1937–)

Lionel Jospin's political ascension has been a rapid one. He entered the PS in 1972, after a period spent oscillating between marginal political activity (PSU), and his career as a civil servant in the Foreign Affairs Ministry. He had refused to join either the old Socialist Party (SFIO) or Mitterrand's (q.v.) CIR. The date of joining was of great importance: the post-1971 party seemed sufficiently different from the old one to justify membership. Jospin is the earliest example of one of Mitterrand's protégés whose political experience has been gained almost exclusively within the post-1971 party. Mitterrand counted upon politicians such as Jospin to create a group of future party leaders whose loyalty to him was absolute.

Jospin's ascension owed everything to Mitterrand's early favour. In 1973 he was appointed as national secretary for political education, and then took control of Third World relations from 1975 to 1979. In 1979, Jospin moved sideways to international affairs, but became no. 2 in the party hierarchy. He became first secretary of the party in January 1981, having been proposed for the post by candidate Mitterrand. Jospin's nomination was accepted reluctantly by many, especially by Mitterrand's older political allies from the CIR (Mermaz (q.v.), Joxe (q.v.), Hernu (q.v.)).

Jospin led the party throughout the 1981–6 period. His position as first secretary was safeguarded by his own growing political stature and occasionally by Mitterrand calling other party lieutenants to order by backing Jospin (as before the 1983 Party Congress). As party leader and Mitterrand loyalist, Jospin facilitated the existence of normally uncomplicated relations. However, Jospin had considerable access to Mitterrand and made the party's viewpoint known on many contentious policies. He did not conceive of the party as a mere instrument of government policy; nor did he hesitate to criticize harshly certain government decisions: for example, Mitterrand's decision to withdraw Savary's church schools bill in 1984 was taken after discussion with Jospin and only then presented to Prime Minister Mauroy. In his capacity as PS leader, Jospin reacted strongly against Prime Minister Fabius's 1985 demand to lead the 1986 Socialist election campaign. He considered the PS to be an autonomous organization (not merely an arm of executive government): as its leader he should lead its campaign. After presidential arbitration in his favour, Jospin, Fabius and Mitterrand all played important roles in the campaign.

By a mixture of conviction, tactical manoeuvre and pragmatism, it was under Jospin's leadership that the PS began a process of ideological realignment away from theoretically intransigent socialism and towards a French version of social-democracy, which more accurately reflected its governmental practice. This process culminated in the 1985 PS Congress at Toulouse.

Jospin's leadership was openly criticized within the PS after the left's 1986 election defeat. The 1986 election inaugurated *cohabitation*, an unprecedented institutional development in the Fifth Republic in which a Socialist president, Mitterrand, coexisted with Jacques Chirac's conservative government. The new context was a difficult one for the PS: to ensure that *cohabitation* endured until the 1988 presidential election (thus preserving Mitterrand's best chances for re-election), Jospin was unwilling to criticize Chirac's government too harshly, since excessive criticism would allow Chirac to blame the PS for stabilizing *cohabitation* and possibly forcing a precipitate presidential election. Notwithstanding this, the PS stance led to charges of Jospin's leadership being ineffectual.

Jospin's tenure as first secretary since 1981 had tended to characterize him as a party *apparatchik* when the most prestigious political careers were conducted in government ministries. Gambling upon a Mitterrand victory, Jospin announced in February 1988 that, whatever the result of the 1988 presidential election, he would resign as first secretary of the party. After Mitterrand's re-election, he was rewarded for seven years loyal service as first secretary by being named as minister of state for education, research and sport, the top-ranking ministerial portfolio in Rocard's government. Jospin had a very difficult portfolio but also a position from which to campaign for the party's nomination when Mitterrand finally stepped down.

Bibliography

Cole, A. (1985), *Factionalism in the French Socialist Party, 1971–1981*, Oxford: Unpublished D. Phil thesis.

Pfister, T. (1977), *Les Socialistes*, Paris: Albin Michel.

Among the innumerable articles in the French press on Jospin, those in *Libération* (28 October 1983, 13 May 1988), *L'Express* (October 11–17 October,

1985) and *Le Monde* (14 May 1988) are particularly useful.

AC

JOUHAUX, Léon Henri (1879–1954)

Léon Jouhaux, the 'Pape du Syndicalisme', was at the very centre of trade union activities in France for half a century. He was a representative of the Matchworkers' Union, on the executive of the Confédération Générale du Travail (CGT), when in 1909 Victor Griffuelhes (q.v.) resigned as general secretary. After a brief interregnum of six months, Jouhaux became general secretary himself, a post he was to retain in one form or other until his resignation in 1947 when the 'reformists' broke away to form the Confédération Général du Travail – Force Ouvrière, better known by the latter part of its name Force Ouvrière (FO), of which he was president until his death. He was vice-president of the International Trade Union Federation from 1919 to 1945 and the World Federation of Trade Unions from 1945 to 1948. From 1945 onwards he was vice-president of the Administrative Council of the International Labour Office and then with the setting up of the International Confederation of Free Trade Unions – a by-product of the cold war – he became vice-president of this latter organization in 1949, remaining so until his death in 1954.

Jouhaux had been somewhat removed from the different ideological debates within the trade union movement in the early 1900s, thus making him an ideal compromise candidate as general secretary of the CGT. His sympathies lay initially with the anarcho-syndicalists, who advocated socialist revolution by means of the general strike and a policy of antimilitarism and independence from political parties and the state. Gradually however he began to distance himself from them and moved towards a more reformist view of social change, perhaps as a result of a certain respect for the improvements in wages and working conditions which had been achieved by British and German trade unions. He opposed a call for a general strike in September 1913 and again the following year at the outbreak of the First World War. Indeed, in a speech made on the day after Germany had declared war on France, he broke with the antimilitarism of the anarcho-syndicalists and committed the CGT to the French war effort, explaining that this was not because of 'hatred for the German people' but because of 'hatred for German imperialism'.

His wartime experiences alongside Albert Thomas, the minister for rearmament, and the gradual improvement in working conditions as a result of laws introducing collective bargaining and the eight-hour day were to reinforce his commitment to social reformism. However, opposition was growing within the CGT which was to experience the same pressures as the political left. In 1920 at the Tours Congress a majority of the Section Française de l'Internationale Ouvrière (SFIO) voted to join the Communist International which led to the founding of the French Communist Party, whilst a minority remained with the SFIO. In the trade union world Jouhaux succeeded the following year in ensuring that a majority stayed within the CGT, whilst a minority made up of Communists and anarcho-syndicalists left to found the Confédération Générale du Travail Unitaire (CGTU).

His major concern at this time was to compensate for these losses and after a considerable recruitment drive membership began to increase slowly. The presence of the more radical CGTU tended to reinforce the CGT's position as a reformist trade union confederation. During the 1930s the influence of the CGT and its general secretary was consolidated, if only briefly, for two reasons. After a number of years of intense opposition the CGTU changed its strategy and started to campaign for the reunification of the trade union movement. Jouhaux had feared Communist domination of the trade union structures but so great was the Communists' desire to rejoin the CGT that they agreed to new statutes which stated in article 10 that *le cumul des mandats* – holding office in a political party and in the trade union movement at the same time – was forbidden. In theory this would have led to a reduction in the influence of the French Communist Party within the trade union confederation. Secondly, although Jouhaux was undoubtedly caught unawares by the outbreak of strike activity which accompanied the election of the Popular Front government led by Léon Blum (q.v.), he became central to the negotiations which followed and which led to the laws introducing major social reforms, the forty-hour week, paid holidays, workplace representatives and an improvement in collective bargaining procedures. Jouhaux found himself, albeit briefly, at the head of a strong and influential trade union movement.

The international situation was to cast a shadow over the rest of the decade. The German-Soviet pact signed in August 1939 provided the Daladier (q.v.) government with an opportunity to dissolve the French Communist Party and the following month the executive of the CGT dismissed its Communist members. Later the existing trade unions were outlawed and at the age of 63 Jouhaux was arrested and sent to an internment camp where he was to stay for the second half of the war.

By the time Jouhaux returned, the CGT had already reconstituted itself on a unitary basis and he was to become one of the joint general secretaries, the other being Benoît Frachon (q.v.), who had gained control of the structures of the trade union confederation during the war. Jouhaux's supporters were no longer in the majority and at the national conference in 1946 it was decided that *le cumul des mandats* was to be reintroduced, which was to reinforce the position of the Communists within the trade union confederation. The relations between the two factions worsened and after a year in which there were further major disagreements within the CGT over strike tactics on the one hand and the position to be taken concerning the Marshall Plan on the other, Jouhaux decided to resign. A minority of CGT members followed him and the first national conference of the rival trade union confederation, Force Ouvrière (FO) took place the following year in 1948. At the age of 69 Jouhaux was elected president whilst the post of general secretary went to Robert Bothereau.

From then on, he tended to withdraw from national trade union activities in order to concentrate on his international responsibilities, for which he received the Nobel Peace Prize in 1951.

Bibliography

There is no biography of Léon Jouhaux in English. He has written a number of significant works, *Le Syndicalisme et la CGT* (Paris: Syrène, 1920), *Le Désarmement* (Paris: Alcan, 1927), *La CGT, ce qu'elle est, ce qu'elle veut* (Paris: Gallimard, 1937). The following biography in French exists: B. Georges, D. Tintant and M.-A. Renauld, *Léon Jouhaux dans le mouvement syndical français* (Paris: PUF, 1979).

JB

JOXE, Louis (1901–)

Louis Joxe, born at Bourg-la-Reine (Seine) in 1901, was one of the good and great of the Gaullist phase of the Fifth Republic, a senior public servant whose loyalty to General de Gaulle had been reflected in his secretary generalship both of the Comité de la Libération Nationale (1942–4) and of de Gaulle's provisional government (1944–6), and later in his role as resident minister in Algeria, steering the Evian Accords through the minefield of extreme right terrorism and army mutiny to the final extrication of France from the North African impasse.

The son of a *professeur agrégé* (and son-in-law of the famous historian, Daniel Halévy), Joxe was himself briefly an academic historian before entering the public service where he became *chef adjoint de cabinet* to Pierre Cot in the Paul-Boncour government in 1932. His career as a civil servant was spent in the diplomatic service. He was director-general at the Quai d'Orsay from 1946–52, during the long tenure of Georges Bidault and Robert Schuman, and subsequently ambassador to the Soviet Union from 1952 to 1955, and to West Germany (1955–6), whereafter he returned to Paris as secretary-general at the Foreign Ministry, ultimately to be awarded the distinction by de Gaulle of *Ambassadeur de France* in 1959.

Like so many of de Gaulle's men, an administrator and not a politician, Joxe served continuously in the Debré and Pompidou governments between 1959 and 1968, with high, minister of state status as successively minister for education (1960), Algerian affairs (1960–2), administrative reform (1962–7) and justice (1967–8). As became the custom with other Gaullist *caciques* drawn from similar backgrounds, he was, in 1967, 'parachuted' into a (Lyons) constituency for which he was re-elected in 1968 and 1973, until his retirement from the Assembly on elevation to the Constitutional Council in 1977.

As minister of justice (1967–8) he was briefly acting prime minister during Pompidou's absence abroad at the start of the student riots of May 1968 – an incongruously exposed position for one better known (as Dorothy Pickles has put it) for his reasonableness and conciliatory talents than for his forcefulness. Those diplomatic skills were most productively employed between November 1960 and November 1962, during which time he had responsibility for Algeria. This was the period of the generals' mutiny of April 1961 against the policy of self-determination and of the subsequent nine months of negotiation with the FLN from May 1961 to March 1962, in which Joxe led for the government. De Gaulle, in his memoirs, testified fulsomely to his skill, experience and character in ensuring that 'the emancipation of Algeria bore the stamp of France's generosity and dignity'. With his experience as a leading diplomat during the Fourth Republic and particularly his running of the Moscow embassy during the early Khrushchev years, Joxe was also an important agent in de Gaulle's policy of closer relations with the Eastern bloc.

This baron of Gaullism, a veritable *homme d'état*,

enjoys the distinction of having fathered a baron of Mitterrandism, Pierre Joxe, leader of the Socialist deputies in the 1980s and minister of the interior in the governments of Fabius (1984–6) and Rocard (1988–), and to whom it was shouted by one of his father's Gaullist parliamentary colleagues soon after he (Pierre) made his parliamentary debut in 1973, 'You are a traitor to your class!' Of Louis Joxe the same could not be said.

Bibliography

See Louis Joxe, *Victoire sur la nuit* (Paris: Flammarion, 1981).

BC

JOXE, Pierre (1934–   )

Despite a long and close association with François Mitterrand, Joxe has always insisted on proclaiming his Marxist faith. The son of a prominent Gaullist minister Louis Joxe (q.v.), he entered politics in the 1960s as a member of Mitterrand's CIR, of which he became general secretary in 1970. Joxe stood on the left wing of the Convention des Institutions Republicaines (CIR) and argued for closer cooperation between the non-Communist left and the PCF. That gradually became a reality after June 1971, when Mitterrand captured control of the PS. Within the post-1971 PS, Joxe's 'extremist' reputation (based on a ferocious anticlericalism and a repeatedly-avowed Marxism) probably explained why Mitterrand kept this undoubted loyalist on the margins of party affairs. From 1971–3 Joxe was national secretary for political education; from 1975–9 he acted as the party's agriculture spokesman, and became treasurer in 1979–81. In 1973 he was elected deputy in Saône-et-Loire (5th), a seat he held in 1978 and 1981; and in 1986 he was re-elected as head of the PS list in the same department. In 1988 he was returned for Saône-et-Loire (4th).

After a brief spell as Industry minister (May–June 1981) under Mauroy, Joxe served as president of the PS group in the National Assembly until July 1984. Under Joxe's leadership the PS group exercised considerable pressure on the Mauroy government: disputes occurred, for example, over nationalizations, tax reforms, the economy, education and the press. Joxe's reputation as a hardline Socialist was reinforced by his first spell as president of the PS group. In July 1984 Joxe became minister of the interior under Fabius. His passage at interior revealed a different Joxe: that of a competent, respected minister and it was heralded by many commentators as a frank success.

Joxe ended the state of perpetual rebellion that had existed among the police under Defferre, mainly by securing the passage of an expensive five-year (1986–1991) modernization plan for the police force; by raising the force's standard of living; by overhauling the organization of the Interior ministry; and by increasing the professional independence of the police, making them less directly dependent upon the interior minister, and more subject to independent rules and guidelines. Joxe's major contribution was probably to reconcile the left with the police. As interior minister, it was Joxe who – under Mitterrand's orders – introduced the proportional representation electoral system for the 1986 general election; as well as presiding over the final implementation of the decentralization programme initiated by his predecessor Defferre.

After the left's defeat in the 1986 general election, Joxe recovered his position as head of the PS group in the National Assembly. As spokesman for the PS deputies, he occasionally criticized the timidity of PS leader Jospin's opposition to Chirac's government, revealing the tensions that existed between the party organization and the PS deputies. After Mitterrand's re-election Joxe recovered the interior ministry portfolio under Rocard. In the final resort, Pierre Joxe remains an enigma: an unquestionable Mitterrand loyalist, and a proven minister, but also one of the more prominent representatives of a traditionally Marxist, and strongly anticlerical trend in French politics.

Bibliography

Cole, A. (1985), *Factionalism in the French Socialist Party, 1971–1981*, Oxford: D. Phil thesis.
Pfister, T. (1977), *Les socialistes*, Paris: Albin Michel.
Plenel, E. (1988), 'Police: peut mieux faire' in 'Bilan du septennat. L'alternance dans l'alternance', *Supplement aux Dossiers et Documents du Monde*, May.
Plenel, E. (1988), 'Intérieur: M. Pierre Joxe. Le retour "en administration" ', *Le Monde*, 14 May.
Roussillon, P.M. (1985), 'Pierre Joxe. Ministre dangereux', *Le Spectacle du Monde*, October.

AC

JUILLET, Pierre Armand (1921–   )

One of the barons of Gaullism but definitely a

worker in the corridors of power rather than a publicist, Juillet made a point of not seeking the limelight and of avoiding political journalists. Along with Marie-France Garaud (q.v.), Juillet is credited with running the Gaullist party in Pompidou's time and with the virtual creation of Jacques Chirac as a major political personality.

It is as a prince's counsellor that Juillet merits attention but it is an influence difficult to measure. Juillet's manoeuvrings are known but his precise political views are unclear: he was devoted to de Gaulle (and Pompidou) and to de Gaulle's ideas of France's *grandeur* but he had no truck with reformism (neither Chaban-Delmas' or Giscard's versions), nor the historic Gaullists – the other 'barons'.

Juillet was in the Maquis during the Resistance and was wounded – to the extent of leaving him with a slight limp – and entered the Ministry of the Interior in 1944 (with a law degree). The civil service was not to his liking and from 1947 to 1952 he was in the Rassemblement du Peuple Français becoming a power in the movement in the centre of France then in the south-west. He married one of de Gaulle's secretaries, Annick Mousnier, and has property in the Creuse – in Puy-Judeau where he was born and where he is at home. Juillet was closer to Pompidou than de Gaulle but he joined Malraux, as head of his private office, in 1958. When Pompidou became prime minister Juillet moved to the Matignon and then in 1969 he moved to the Elysée.

In 1971 Juillet, who believed Chaban-Delmas was 'leading France to socialism', left Pompidou's service and retired only after the disaster of the referendum on Europe. Chaban-Delmas was pushed out on 5 July 1972. He had, of course, been in close contact with Garaud in the interim.

Juillet and Garaud were also behind the rise of Chirac and Chirac's support for Giscard in the 1974 presidential elections: support which was instrumental in ending Chaban-Delmas' presidential hopes. This Juillet/Garaud 'tandem' mounted the operation which brought Chirac out of the prime minister's office and refashioned the Gaullist party into the Rassemblement pour la République in December 1976. When Chirac thanked Juillet for his help he replied that it was the first time a horse had thanked the jockey. Juillet and Garaud, who knew all the aspects of the Gaullist movement, were the law in the RPR at that time but their contemptuous treatment of Chirac contributed to their replacement (they also forced Jérôme Monod to resign as secretary general).

It was also the fiasco of the European elections of 1979 which finally undid their ascendancy over the Gaullist movement. This election saw the Gaullist party fall from first place among French parties (22 per cent in 1978) to fourth place (16 per cent). Chirac's anti-European declaration from the hospital of Cochin (Paris) had also been Juillet's work and Juillet's peremptory style also made an enemy of Mme Chirac who reportedly said 'either they (Juillet and Garaud) go or I go'. After the European elections they were obliged to quit.

Juillet retired to his property in the Creuse but helped write Giscard's 19 May farewell statement after the election defeat of 1981. Juillet refused to work for Giscard but helped Barre for a short period in the mid-1980s.

DSB

JUPPÉ, Alain Marie (1945–   )

Alain Juppé has been an economic adviser to Jacques Chirac since 1976 and a leading spokesman for the Rassemblement pour la République (RPR) since 1984. He has been responsible for the finances of the City of Paris since 1980, first as a civil servant and since 1983 as a councillor and assistant-mayor. He was budget minister and government spokesman between his election as deputy in March 1986 and François Mitterrand's second presidential victory in May 1988. Returned to a Paris seat in the June 1988 parliamentary elections, he succeeded Jacques Toubon as RPR secretary-general in the same month. His career has followed both a classic pattern (from the civil service to politics) and one particular pattern to a small number of Chirac's associates (from the Paris City Hall to high office in the government and the RPR).

Juppé was born into a comfortable farming family in Landes, in the Socialist south-west. A very able student at his local *lycée* in Mont-de-Marsan, at the prestigious Lycée Louis-le-Grand in Paris, at the Institut d'Etudes Politiques, at the Ecole Normale Supérieure (where he obtained the *agrégation* in classics), and finally at the Ecole Nationale d'Administration he graduated into the Inspection des Finances in 1972. His chief there, Jacques Friedmann, Chirac's oldest personal friend, arranged a post for Juppé as economic adviser and speechwriter in Chirac's *cabinet* in March 1976. After Chirac's resignation from the premiership in August, Juppé rapidly returned to his entourage as *délégué national aux études* for the RPR at its creation in December 1976, while retaining a post in the *cabinet* of cooperation minister Robert Galley. He helped prepare the RPR's economic platform for the 1978 parliamentary elections, but was himself an unsuccessful candidate in Landes. He suffered a second defeat there at the 1979 cantonal elections.

Juppé entered Chirac's *cabinet* in the Paris City Hall in 1978, was dissatisfied with his work there, tried to leave for a banking job with the Crédit National, but was turned down on political grounds. He then became assistant to the director of finance of the City of Paris in September 1979, and director himself a few months later. This meant running France's second largest public budget, which he did on the orthodox lines of his predecessors. At the same time he followed the 1980 US elections very closely, and as economic adviser to Chirac's 1981 campaign helped to convert him to the free-market economics that Gaullists had hitherto generally eschewed.

Juppé's first electoral victory, in the 18th *arrondissement* of Paris at the March 1983 municipal poll, was somewhat in Chirac's shadow but still against heavyweight Socialist opposition including Lionel Jospin. Although no longer director, he continued to run the City budget as Chirac's second assistant-mayor.

It was as secretary-general of the Club 89 (an RPR study group) that Juppé published *La Double rupture* (Paris: Economica, 1983), a generally thoughtful argument for breaking, not only with socialism, but also with the state interventionism that had preceded 1981. He also called for the rejuvenation of the RPR leadership in September 1984. At the November Congress that followed, he became *délégué national au redressement économique et social* – in effect the RPR's chief economic spokesman – while Toubon was elected secretary-general. Juppé also sat in the European Parliament from June 1984 until the 1986 parliamentary elections, when he was elected fifth on the RPR's Paris list.

Juppé's role in government was sometimes an uneasy one, being frequently overshadowed as budget minister by Edouard Balladur and as government spokesman by Chirac's press officer Denis Baudouin. And his management of Chirac's 1988 campaign failed to win the presidency for his patron. However, his good performance in the June 1988 parliamentary elections, when he won a seat in the 18th *arrondissement* of Paris against strong Socialist opposition, probably contributed to his appointment as RPR secretary-general ten days later. In this post he faced a particularly daunting task keeping the RPR together through the difficult period following Chirac's presidential defeat and the loss of the right-wing majority in the National Assembly. The price

of this, after discontent among leading RPR figures of his own generation broke out in the 'renovator' movement of spring 1989, was a relaxation on the Gaullists' traditional ban on organized tendencies within the party – though not before Juppé had threatened his colleagues with exclusion from the RPR if they ran their own list for the June 1989 elections. In the event Juppé was elected to the European Parliament as second on the joint UNR/RPR list.

Bibliography

There are profiles of Juppé in the *Financial Times* (26 June 1985), *Le Monde* (22 March 1986), in Alain Duhamel, *Les Prétendants* (Paris: Gallimard, 1983); Jacques Frémontier, *Les Cadets de la droite* (Paris: Seuil, 1984); and Thierry Desjardins, *Les Chiraquiens* (Paris: La Table Ronde, 1986).

AFK

JUQUIN, Pierre Louis Michel (1930–)

Pierre Juquin was born in Clermont-Ferrand, the son of a railway worker. He went to the Lycée Blaise-Pascal (secondary school) in his home town before moving to the Henri IV secondary school in Paris and then to the Ecole Normale Supérieure. Juquin joined the Communist Party at the age of 23 and took the prestigious teaching examination (*agrégation*) in German: he subsequently taught at the Lycée Lakanal. Juquin is probably best known as the leading 'renovator' – an opponent to the leadership of the party – in the mid-1980s, but he had a brilliant early career within the party apparatus. He became a substitute member of the Central Committee in 1964 (at 34), elected deputy for the Essonne three years later and became a Political Bureau member in 1979.

Juquin presented a youthful face and was talked of as a 'coming man'. His election victory in the Essonne in 1967 (where he saw off the Gaullist) was a good one for the party, but in 1968 he was reviled by the students of Nanterre and was defeated in the June elections that followed the May 'events'. Although he was re-elected in 1973 he did not immediately find a niche.

In the mid-1970s Juquin did symbolize the party's opening out and its attempts to come to terms with its own past which culminated in the 22nd Congress of 1976. In 1975 he published *Liberté* (Editions Sociales) which stated that 'socialism and liberty are synonymous' and then in 1976 there was his public handshake with the Soviet dissident Leonid Plyushch. This handshake was too much for the party hardliners and a 1978 election brochure with a photo of the event on the front was pulped.

In the run-up to the 1978 elections Juquin may (according to gossip) have expected a ministerial post were the left to win, but his ambition and a sharp tongue made him heartily disliked inside the party. Juquin seemed to have returned to the old orthodoxy when the union of the left broke up (Juquin published a book on the updating of the left's joint manifesto – *L'Actualisation à dossiers ouverts*, Paris: Editions Sociales, 1977) and in 1979 was promoted at the Congress – one of the Marchais loyalists. But Juquin was defeated in the 1981 elections by a Socialist and a period of breaking stones in the Place Colonel Fabien seemed the only vista; Juquin nevertheless became party spokesman (*porte-parole*) defending Communist participation in government.

As the party's vote sank and as differences with the Socialists became more pronounced, Juquin's disagreement with the party leadership became more evident. A partisan of continued participation in government, Juquin found himself in 1984 part of a wider movement of discontent (known as the 'renovators'). Juquin, through an exhausting number of engagements, made himself the 'intellectual' of the 'renovators' and expressed a clear criticism of the party's anti-Socialist line at the 1985 Party Congress and abstained in the vote. Since dissidence at such a Political Bureau level is unknown Juquin was listened to with attention: you could have cut the atmosphere with an ice-pick – it was frigid.

Like many others Juquin seemed to regard the Italian Communist Party with its open debates, competitive elections, suppler Marxism, and critical attitude to the USSR as a model for the French. Juquin's book *Autocritiques,* however, shows a complete disregard for novelty and contents itself with a vague allusion to a third way (between Communism and social democracy) where the rainbow is alleged to end. 'Aunt Sallies' of the Communist movement – the arms race, capitalist waste, famine, the CIA and Coca Cola – are set up and machine-gunned in rows. The book was influential because it expressed a, probably wide, discontent among Communist activists but it is not a *tour de force*.

Juquin remained on the Central Committee after the 1985 Congress and became a resident poltergeist. How long the leadership would tolerate this criticism was unclear and Juquin announced his intention to return to teaching. Juquin is yet another in a long line of victims of the 'intellectual delusion' that you can change the party from within. However, that Juquin who knew the apparatus from the inside, should have believed reform possible, is peculiar. Despite being a member of the Central Committee, Juquin was well on the way to exclusion in mid-1980s when there began to be talk about a 'renovator' candidate for the presidency in 1988, and he was excluded in October 1987.

Juquin's 1988 presidential campaign was supported by the PSU, Ligue Communiste Revolutionnaire as well as by intellectuals (Balibar, Labica, Molina) and from abroad the Grünen, the Italian Democrazie Proletaria and Gert Petersen of the Socialist Party of the Danish People. Juquin had two principal themes: votes for immigrants and unilateral French disarmament as well as a fanciful economic programme based on a reduction of the working week to create jobs. His 2.1 per cent of the votes did not presage an eminent future after 1988 and his support groups accused Juquin of authoritarianism almost as soon as the campaign was over. The 'renovators' polled a mere 0.4 per cent (74,383) in the 1989 European elections.

Bibliography

See in particular Pierre Juquin, *Autocritiques* (Paris: Grasset, 1985) aimed at the man in the public library, and *Fraternellement libre* (Paris: Grasset, 1987).

DSB

K

KANAPA, Jean (1924–78)

Born in Ezanville (Val-d'Oise), the son of a banker, Kanapa joined the Communist Party after the liberation (although he might have been involved in Resistance activities) was a student of Sartre's and qualified as a philosophy teacher before becoming a full-time party employee.

Kanapa soon made a name for himself as the author of venomous attacks on literary figures and for his aggressive Stalinism devoid of self-doubt. In *Existentialism is not a Humanism* (an allusion to Sartre's lecture) he attacked the 'petty ideological delinquency which actively plays the game of reaction . . . and anti-Communism' of his former professor. Kanapa relayed Zhdanov's view, that art and literature had to be subordinate to the party, in a French context and other writers were given similar treatment in *La Nouvelle Critique* (of which he was editor-in-chief) and *L'Humanité*. Kanapa was also on the powerful party committee on intellectuals and from this vantage accused French authors of creating a 'neutral literature', and demanded that they take the viewpoint of the 'labouring masses': 'literature of propaganda? Yes, but of propaganda for Man'. In addition to treating Sartre as an 'intellectual cop' (earning Sartre's rebuke 'Kanapa is a moron' – *con*), he accused Koestler of defending Fascists and so on.

At this time Kanapa assembled all the bigotries, clichés and resentments one medium-sized soul can accommodate and, at the 15th French Communist Party Congress in 1959 was nominated as a substitute member of the Central Committee. This promotion came after a speech – all italicized indignation and rage – in which Kanapa castigated the 'infantile liquidationism of the renegade Fougeyrollas' (this latter an unreadable Marxist) and demanded the execution or jailing ('liquidation') of Nagy and Lukacs (and the rest of the 1956 Hungarian government overthrown by the Russians). Kanapa was no routine droll.

Yet there seem to have been a proto-Kanapa and a deutero-Kanapa: sometime in the late 1950s or early 1960s Kanapa may have had a genuine change of heart. He was, however, able to organize his prin-ciples as required and take up the sensitive post of *L'Humanité*'s correspondent in Moscow until 1967. Alone in the hissing laboratory of his desires he may have had other plans but he stayed out of the top of the Stalinist French party (until he was 'adopted' by Waldeck Rochet who took over as party leader from Thorez in 1964) and he accompanied the French delegation to Prague in July 1968. The notes of this meeting with the reformist Czech government were handed over for use against Dubček. Kanapa's ascent was rapid and when Rochet was 'ill' in 1969 he went with Marchais (q.v.) as one of the French representatives to the World Conference of Communist Parties. According to François Hincker (*Le Parti Communiste au carrefour,* Paris: Gallimard, 1981) he was Marchais' inspiration and guide.

Kanapa became head of the French party's international department after the 20th Congress in December 1972 and was promoted to the Political Bureau in 1975. The new direction became evident when, in the first overseas visit, Marchais and Kanapa visited Olaf Palme in Sweden and the West German trade unions. After the 1973 elections Kanapa set out the agenda for the mid-1970s: a re-examination of the problems of liberty, property and the 'Socialist' countries. (This agenda led to Marchais' *Le Défi démocratique,* Paris: Grasset, 1973.) On the 'Socialist' countries Kanapa's line was a small marvel of defensive pleading: what they do in Eastern Europe is one thing but France is different. Kanapa was at the head of an international policy which led to a shift away from unconditional support for the USSR, noted that the 'workers aspired to socialism in liberty', and emphasized that 'international solidarity' meant reciprocal respect not a command relationship.

In 1978 Kanapa became an old man in a hurry. He was ill at a time when the party's position began to shift once again. It could be that the removal of Kanapa's impulse was important and his last actions lend some credence to this view. The visit with Marchais to the president of Mexico in April 1978 led to a series of proposals for a new world economic order; in September 1978 *France Nouvelle* published Kanapa's last lecture on what he called 'Eurocommunism'; and 1978 also saw F. Adler *et al.*, *L'URSS et nous* (Paris: Editions Sociales) and the party's second look at the Russian regime. Although these comments are made about Kanapa's commitment to a new libertarian vision the evidence of a genuine, rather than political, conversion is unclear. Some accounts portray Kanapa as disdainful, peremptory and condescending with a taste for the clumsy and the hispid, while others say he was tolerant to party workers and likeable.

Bibliography

Kanapa, J. (1947), *L'existentialisme n'est pas un humanisme*, Paris: Editions Sociales.

Fabien, J. (pseud.) (1984), *Kremlin – P.C.F., conversations secrètes*, Paris: Olivier Orban. (These contain Kanapa's notes on the meeting between Dubček and Waldeck Rochet.)

DSB

KASPAR, Jean (1941–   )

Jean Kaspar, who took over on 26 November 1988 from Edmond Maire as general secretary of the French Democratic Labour Confederation (CFDT) on the latter's retirement (six months earlier than originally envisaged) is not a well-known figure. He had been a CFDT full-time official since 1965 and one of Maire's closest supporters but a technocrat out of the public eye. He was born in the frontier town of Mulhouse (he is bilingual). After education as an electrical engineer, he became an electrician, in the potash mines in the Haut-Rhin and then, after an apprenticeship from 1955 to 1958, worked in the mines as a fully qualified skilled worker from 1958 to 1965.

Kaspar joined the Catholic Trade Union – CFTC in 1958. He was in charge of the youth committee and the Haut-Rhin Union from 1962 to 1963 and in 1965 became the general secretary of the tiny Potash Miners Federation. He joined the CFDT when it was formed in 1964. From 1966 to 1970 he was a member of the CFDT-confederal council (its 'parliament') whilst remaining general secretary of the CFDT Miners' Union from 1966 until 1976. In 1974 Jean Kaspar was elected to the CFDT National Bureau and remained in it until 1982 but was secretary of the Alsace CFDT from 1976 to 1982. In 1982 he was made a member of the executive committee of the CFDT and became responsible for wage bargaining.

Jean Kaspar is typical of the socially active union leaders of the CFDT and the younger generation. He was a member encouraged by Eugene Descamps of the Christian/Catholic wing of the CFTC (in a strongly religious region) and worked his way up the ranks of the newly-created CFDT. His outlook is similar to Maire's and he is a consensus minded reformist without being steeped in the Marxist outlook typical of the CGT or of his left-wing rival within the Federation, Pierre Héritier. He obtained the leadership against the left's candidate after a long bargaining session. He proved an able negotiator and a flexible tactician in a career which, whilst under Maire's shadow as 'dauphin', was one of steady success and constant promotion. He is warm and personable in face to face contacts and a capable committee organizer but he is less experienced as a public speaker and at mass media appearances. He is flanked by another of Maire's protégés (rumoured to have been a favourite to succeed at one point), Nicole Notat. Kaspar is faced with the problem of declining membership and confusion as to the federation's exact role. Kaspar, however, is neither a risk-taker nor a philosopher and is much more a pragmatist than an ideologue.

Bibliography

Lévy, C. (1987), *Les Trois guerres de succession*, Paris: Alain Moreau.

DSB

de KERILLIS, Henri Adrien Calloc'h (1889–1958)

Henri de Kerillis was born into a military family, and it was assumed that he would follow a military career. This he duly did during the First World War, serving first as a cavalry officer, and then as an aviator, flying over 250 missions. After the war he maintained his enthusiasm for flying, working for the Farman aeronautical factory, and becoming involved in such tasks as building the first Cuban aerodrome.

In a 1926 by-election he made the first of several unsuccessful forays into the political arena, when both he and his political mentor Paul Reynaud (q.v.) were beaten by the Communist candidates Duclos (q.v.) and Fournier. Subsequently de Kerillis managed to combine his career in aviation with inroads into politics when, in 1934, he published his first political critique entitled 'Paris-Moscou en avion'. More and more his taste for politics induced him to find a forum for his views, and he finally embarked on a full-time career in journalism, rapidly rising to the editorship of *L'Echo de Paris*.

From this base he formulated a policy of constitutional and economic reform and consolidated his reputation by his constant emphasis on the need for a strong and aggressive defence policy. He became convinced that the political prospects of French conservatives were gravely weakened by internal divisions and by the lack of an effective propaganda machine. To this end in 1926 he created the Centre de Propagande des Républicains Nationaux which sought to promote right-wing political opinions across the whole of France by means of posters, meetings, candidate training schools and so on. The centre had its own data bank and publishing house and played a large part in the election campaigns of 1928, 1932 and 1936.

Elected first to local office, he became a deputy in April 1936, and joined the Groupe des Indépendants Républicains. But in the machinations surrounding the creation of the Daladier cabinet in April 1938, he figured as a prominent member of the 'Reynaud group' in endorsing a more aggressive defensive policy than that favoured by the 'Flandin group' within the Alliance Démocratique. It was this fervent advocacy of an aggressive attitude towards Germany that was to prove de Kerillis' undoing, when on 4 October 1938 he was the only conservative deputy to vote against the Munich accords. In the debate he spoke out strongly against what he saw as the deceit practised by the French leadership in betraying not only Czechoslovakia, but France itself. In refusing his vote of confidence in the government, de Kerillis entered a self-imposed political isolation, that was only partially ameliorated as public opinion swung round to his viewpoint.

Undaunted, he continued to denounce the defeatist elements in the government. In 1940 he rejoined the air force and was one of the first to respond in London to de Gaulle's broadcast of 18 June. He soon went to the United States, however, and became one of the most violent critics of de Gaulle, publishing in 1945 *De Gaulle Dictateur* (Montreal: Beauchemin). He did not return to France at the liberation and spent the rest of his life farming in the United States.

Bibliography

Anderson, M. (1974), *Conservative Politics in France*, London: Allen and Unwin.

Coston, H. (1967), *Dictionnaire de la politique française*, Paris: La Librairie Française.

PT

KRASUCKI, Henri (1924–)

Henri Krasucki has been the general secretary of the Confédération Générale du Travail (CGT) since 1982 when he replaced Georges Séguy (q.v.).

The son of Polish Jewish immigrants who were active members of the French Communist Party (PCF), he joined the Resistance during the war and was arrested in 1943 and sent first to Auschwitz and then to Buchenwald. After the war he trained as a metal worker and joined the CGT. In 1950 he became a full-time trade union official and three years later a member of the executive of the Paris region of the CGT. In 1961 he became a member of the Bureau Confédéral, the executive of the confederation itself. At the same time as this, he was an active member of the French Communist Party and he rose rapidly up through its ranks; he became a fully-fledged member of its Central Committee in 1959 and of its Political Bureau eight years later.

During the 1960s and 1970s he was the editor of *La Vie Ouvrière*, the CGT's publication with the largest circulation. This was an ideal position to play an influential role in the internal politics of the confederation and indeed he was considered the automatic choice to replace Séguy. According to Robrieux, he was the major adviser on trade union affairs to the leader of the PCF, Georges Marchais, and given his reputation for Communist orthodoxy it was thought that he would align the CGT's position more closely with that of the French Communist Party. Ironically in the mid-1980s it has been suggested that he is himself on the defensive within the confederation because of his unwillingness to follow an increasingly insular and enfeebled PCF.

His term of office as general secretary of the CGT has coincided with a period in which the confederation has experienced a major reduction in its influence. Its membership has declined markedly, which has led to financial problems and a reduction in the number of its full-time officials. Its share of the votes in the elections to the enterprise committees has gone down to less than 30 per cent, indeed 26 per cent in 1986, which means that it is still the largest French trade union confederation but not in the dominant position it was ten years before. Moreover, with the notable exception of the demonstrations held in 1987 in opposition to the proposed changes in *Sécurité Sociale* provision, the CGT has largely lost its ability to mobilize large sections of the workforce.

After the 1981 legislative elections which led to a Socialist government with Communist participation, the CGT was caught between its desire to oppose some of the government's more socially regressive measures and its concern not to provide the parties of the right with political ammunition. This dilemma was somewhat resolved in 1984 when the Communist ministers resigned and the CGT tended to assume a more critical stance *vis-à-vis* the Socialist government, a policy it has continued subsequently and one with which its leader, Henri Krasucki, undoubtedly feels more comfortable.

Bibliography

There is no biography of Henri Krasucki in English. He is the subject of a short profile in the 4th volume of P. Robrieux, *Histoire intérieure du parti communiste français* (Paris: Fayard, 1984). He is the author of the following collections of views and articles, *Syndicats et luttes de classe* (1969), *Syndicats et socialisme* (1972), *Syndicats et unité* (1980), and *Un Syndicat moderne? Oui!* (1987), published by Editions Sociales (Paris).

JB

KRIVINE, Alain (1941–)

Alain Krivine was born in Paris on 10 July, of middle-class Russian Jewish origin. Active from childhood in Communist organizations, his assiduous fidelity to the PCF (the French Communist Party) earned him a visit to the USSR in 1957, which ironically was to trigger his disillusionment with Soviet-style socialism. Radicalized by the Algerian War and the rise of the neo-Fascist OAS (Secret Army Organization), he joined a group giving clandestine support to the Algerian independence movement and came under the influence of Trotskyism. While at the Lycée Condorcet, he had joined the Union of Communist Students (Union des Etudiants Communistes), but as a student of history at the Sorbonne, became a leader of the extreme-left Trotskyist opposition within that movement, gaining control of its 'Sorbonne Arts' Sector' (Secteur Lettres Sorbonne). Opposing the PCF's support for Mitterrand in 1965, the Arts Sector was dissolved in April 1966. But Krivine, expelled from the party, had already laid the foundations of an independent Trotskyist organization and in the same month the JCR, or Revolutionary Communist Youth (Jeunesse Communiste Révolutionnaire), held its first congress.

Its aim was to construct a revolutionary alternative to PCF 'reformism'. Faithful to the Fourth International, it attacked the state bureaucracies of capitalist and Communist regimes, brandishing Marx's view that the state, born of the class system, would disappear with it. It also protested against the Vietnam War: Krivine was a founder of the National Vietnam Committee (Comité Vietnam National), playing a key role in several major events, including the Berlin solidarity demonstration of February 1968, alongside the German student leader Rudi Dutschke. Krivine was later to see Berlin as having prepared the ground for the May 'events' through its street tactics and its display of the combined might of international youth.

During May the JCR distinguished itself by its size, discipline, and dedication. Krivine became a leader of the uprising and was arrested in June. The JCR was outlawed but resurfaced as the Communist League (Ligue Communiste). In 1969 it nominated Krivine, then doing his military service, as its presidential candidate, exploiting the event to demonstrate that only revolutionary change, not elections, would bring about worker control. He obtained 1.05 per cent of the vote. In June 1973 he was again arrested, and the League banned, after a violent street confrontation with an extreme-right organization. Released shortly afterwards, he fought the 1974 presidentials on behalf of a third Trotskyist manifestation, the Revolutionary Communist Front (Front Communiste Révolutionnaire), gaining only 0.36 per cent of the vote. In December the current name, the LCR, or Revolutionary Communist League (Ligue Communiste Révolutionnaire), was adopted. In the 1981 presidentials, he failed to obtain the necessary 500 signatures to enable him to stand in the elections. Today he is the spokesman of the LCR and a journalist on its newspaper *Rouge*.

Of all the leaders of May 1968 Krivine was the least known yet the most competent. An effective orator with years of disciplined militancy behind him, he probably came closer than any to giving this protean upsurge an ideological and tactical shape via the JCR and subsequently the Communist League, groups which clearly represented a substantial danger in the eyes of the State. But Krivine is also one of the rare veterans of 1968 to have remained true to his revolutionary past, transforming a radical student group into a small but effectively organized Trotskyist party which has demonstrably transcended its origins. Today the LCR claims some 2,500 members, of whom only 35 per cent are teachers or youths, while 60 per cent are employees in firms. Active on contemporary issues and hostile to the 1981–6 Socialist government and to cohabitation, the LCR gave qualified support to Pierre Juquin in the 1988 presidential elections. After Mitterrand's victory, Krivine supported the decision to dissolve the 'reactionary' 1986 Assembly. In June, he interpreted the ensuing election result as a rejection of the policy of 'openness towards the centre' and called for a Socialist–Communist government with a new set of policies.

Bibliography

Krivine himself has written *La Farce électorale* (Paris: Seuil, 1969); and *Questions sur la révolution* (Paris: Stock, 1973), conversations with R. Biard. The most detailed source on his life and political activity is H. Hamon and P. Rotman, *Génération: les années de rêve* (1987) and *Les Années de poudre* (1988), both Paris: Seuil. Other sources include J. Bertolino, *Les Trublions*, (Paris: Stock, 1969), pp. 103–21, and D. Bensaïd and H. Weber (former JCR organizers), *Mai 1968: Une répétition générale* (Paris: Maspero, 1968), which gives a detailed account of the creation and development of the JCR.

DL

L

LACORE, Marie Suzanne – 'Suzon' (1875–1975)

Suzanne Lacore spent almost all her career teaching in village schools in the Dordogne, but for a year was a junior minister in Léon Blum's Popular Front government of 1936–7. Born in the Corrèze in 1875, she trained at the Ecole Normale at Perpignan and taught in the region until 1930, when she retired as headmistress of the school at Ajat. A militant in the Socialist Party, the SFIO, from its foundation in the 1900s, she contributed to the party press under the pen-name 'Suzon', wrote several pamphlets and spoke at party conferences. But she was completely unknown to the general public when Léon Blum chose her as one of his three women ministers in 1936, giving her a post as under-secretary of state for the protection of children. During her year in office she set in motion a number of reforms, though the failure to appoint a successor prevented most from coming to fruition. She retired to her Dordogne village, where she lived to be a centenarian, being made an officer of the Légion d'Honneur on her hundredth birthday.

In 1936, much was made of the political inexperience of the 'little schoolteacher' suddenly projected into the limelight, and Suzanne Lacore later wrote that her first reaction was to refuse the job. But the press of both right and left were sympathetic to the idea of the ministry and it seems that beneath her demure appearance, Suzanne Lacore was an effective speaker and a practical reformer – as indeed might be expected of one who had been a friend of Jules Guesde (on whom she wrote a book) and had organized social services in her village. There was no precedent for the work of the childhood ministry, but there had been growing concern about juvenile delinquency and institutions for young offenders. Lacore made a point of trying to humanize the care of abandoned or delinquent children, appealing to the public for contributions, providing training for social workers and trying to organize diagnostic work among families at risk. She worked in close collaboration with her senior partner, the health minister, Henri Sellier, and it may be because of his departure from government in 1937 that the childhood ministry was not renewed. During its short history, it received much publicity, favourable on the whole, aided by Lacore's many provincial tours.

Suzanne Lacore undertook her work in the conviction that this was essentially a woman's task, on one occasion quoting Nietzsche: 'Woman has an insatiable desire to give'. She remained interested in children's problems, writing a book called *Enfance d'abord* in 1961. Her belief in women's rights was firmly subordinated both to the class struggle (working-class progress should take priority) and also to a fairly traditional view of women's role in the home. She also shared the fears of both the other women ministers that immediate enfranchisement of all French women might damage the left. In this she was a not untypical representative of women in the inter-war Socialist Party.

Bibliography

Suzanne Lacore wrote two articles about her ministerial experience in *Vétéran Socialiste* (no. 18, March 1960 and no. 19, May 1961), but there is very little information on her in any of the books on the Popular Front period, and none at all in English.

SR

LACOSTE, Robert (1898–1989)

Robert Lacoste, born in the Dordogne in 1898, was a controversial right-wing Socialist figure during the Fourth Republic, remembered for the tough policy he imposed as minister for Algerian affairs between 1956 and 1958 in the Mollet (q.v.), Bourgès-Maunoury (q.v.) and Félix Gaillard (q.v.) governments. The son of a railway inspector, Lacoste, after law faculty in Paris became a *fonctionnaire des finances* and CGT union organizer for the Fédération générale des fonctionnaires. He represented his native department in the National Assembly from 1945 to 1958, 1962 to 1968 and in the Senate from 1971 to 1980. He was elected mayor of his home town,

Azerat, in 1945 and served in early post-war governments between 1944 and 1950 as minister for industry.

But it is for the policy of 'pacification' (i.e. repression of the Arab insurgents) adopted by the Mollet government in Algeria after Mollet had faced an angry mob of white settlers, that Lacoste is recalled. Initially committed to a more liberal policy, the Socialist-led government (the first for ten years) adopted harsh anti-terrorist tactics, for which Lacoste became the bluff and blunt defender. He was minister at the time of the kidnapping of the nationalist leader Ben Bella, and he defended the summary justice meted out to the Arab lawyer Ali Boumendjel in March 1957, claiming that the 'apparatus of justice in Algeria was insufficient in means and personnel'. He favoured prompt execution of Muslim rebels as an example: 'You can think what you like about it; our action against terrorism has seriously decreased the number of victims'. With Mollet and Pineau, the secret collaborators with Eden and Selwyn Lloyd in the Suez affair, Lacoste also saw Nasser as the godfather of the guerrilla movement, the FLN, and believed that 'one French division in Cairo is worth four in Algeria'. The repressive policy against the FLN was vigorously attacked in the Socialist Party by such figures as Gaston Defferre, Alain Savary (who resigned from the Mollet government over the matter) and André Philip, who called at the 1956 Party Congress for Lacoste to be disciplined for not fighting the war in Algeria on *two* fronts, that is, against the *ultras* as well as the rebels. But the policy was irreversible in terms of public opinion and probably ensured the continued support for the government from the conservative parties. At the same time the issue badly split the Socialist Party as reflected in its reaction to the return to power of de Gaulle on the back of settler unrest in 1958 and the loss of some of the important opponents of the Mollet–Lacoste policy to the new PSA (later PSU). Defeated in the Gaullist landslide of 1958, Lacoste never lost his reputation for a policy which even de Gaulle swiftly discarded.

The new Socialist Party formed after Mollet's retirement in 1969, was not one in which Lacoste fitted at all easily. The alliance with the Communists was difficult for an old-style south-western SFIO politician, and in 1967 calls were made by elements in Mitterrand's CIR (though resisted by Mitterrand himself) to deny Lacoste the FGDS label in his Dordogne constituency because of his past record of anti-communism and support for *Algérie française*. Nevertheless, unlike his ex-ministerial colleague Max Lejeune who left the Socialists in 1973, Lacoste

remained a supporter of his party in the Senate until his 82nd year, despite the fact that in the Mitterrand Socialist Party fashioned in the 1970s he was little more than a beached curiosity. He died, aged ninety, in 1989.

BC

LAFARGUE, Paul (1842–1911)

Doctor, Marxist theoritician, polemicist and Socialist leader. Lafargue's grandmothers were both mulattos, his paternal grandfather a French Jew and his maternal grandfather of Caribo-Indian extraction. Born and raised in Cuba, he returned to Bordeaux with his relatively affluent parents in 1851. As a medical and pharmacy student in Paris in the 1860s, he participated in student agitation against the Empire and was eventually expelled from the Sorbonne University. Moving to London in 1866, he became a close associate of Karl Marx, whose daughter, Laura, he married in 1868. Despite his family's disapproval of his political activities, an allowance from his father ensured completion of his medical studies.

Coopted by Marx on to the General Council of the First International, where he served as corresponding secretary for Spain, Lafargue continued to work for the International after his return to France in 1870. Settling in Bordeaux, he played an obscure role in political circles, organizing opposition to the bourgeois republic. Already, he demonstrated his independence of mind and his penchant for political paradox by arguing, in contradiction to Marx, that a moderate Orleanist monarchy would be preferable to a bourgeois Republic. At the same time, he emerged as an ardent patriot, fulminating against the government's abandonment of Alsace and Lorraine. Fearing arrest (more because of his relationship with Marx than for his activities) he fled to Spain, eventually returning to London in 1872 where he lived, as he was effectively to do for the rest of his life, off the generosity of Engels. The deaths of his three children, all in infancy, contributed to his decision to abandon the practice of medicine.

Lafargue did not return to France until 1882, when he began to put his considerable energies as an organizer, journalist, translator, ideologue and polemicist to the service of Jules Guesde's nascent Parti Ouvrier, of which he became *de facto* second in command. His contribution to the creation of what was indisputably the biggest and best organized Socialist Party in France was significant. Never an orthodox 'Marxist', despite the best efforts of Engels to curb the worst excesses of his ideological and political idiosyncracies (in a voluminous correspondence which is still the most important source on Lafargue) this ebullient 'Jewish half-caste', as Marx once called him, revelled in paradox. After flirting openly with Boulangism, he was elected deputy for Lille in the wake of the Fourmies massacre of 1891 (when the troops opened fire on men, women and children who were celebrating May Day) but immediately threw his electors into confusion by declaring, in his maiden speech, that the best Socialist in the Chamber was the count, Albert de Mun. His most brilliant pamphlet, *Le Droit à la Paresse* (1880) can, at one level, be read as a profoundly anti-Marxist work.

Defeated in the parliamentary elections of 1893, Lafargue, while working tirelessly for the Parti Ouvrier Français and, after Socialist unification in 1905, for the Guesdist wing of the SFIO, became an increasingly eccentric character in the Socialist movement. Benefiting from a handsome inheritance on the death of Engels, he lived a life of semi-retirement, emerging regularly to enliven discussion at party congresses and meetings with his unpredictable but always penetrating insights. His death was as unconventional as his life. He and his wife Laura, unable to countenance the debilitating effects of old age, calmly injected themselves with potassium cyanide on 26 November 1911, shortly before his 70th birthday. At their funeral on 3 December 1911, Lenin referred to Paul as 'one of the most gifted and profound propagators of Marxism, whose ideas have been brilliantly confirmed' by the experience of the Russian revolution. Perhaps.

Bibliography

Bottigelli, E. (ed.), (1965–9), *Friedrich Engels, Paul and Laura Lafargue: Correspondance*, Paris: Editions Sociales, 3 vols.

Lafargue, P. (1883), *Le Droit à la paresse*, Paris: H. Oriol.

Lafargue, P. (1970), *Textes choisis*, introduction and notes by Jacques Girault, Paris: Editions Sociales.

Maitron, J. (ed.) (1969), *Dictionnaire biographique du mouvement ouvrier français,* Paris: Editions Ouvrières, vol. 6.

Oddly enough, Lafargue, whose life was in many ways the most interesting of all the socialist leaders, still awaits his biographer . . .

JH

LAGRANGE, François Léo (1900–40)

Although his family roots were in the Bordeaux region where he was born, Lagrange spent most of his childhood and youth in Paris. A gifted student and an ardent patriot, he interrupted his literary studies (he was preparing the entrance examination to the Ecole Normale Supérieure) and volunteered at the age of 17 in spring 1918. Demobilized in 1919, he went on to study law and politics, became a barrister in 1923, and began to play an active part in the Socialist Party. He was elected deputy for Avesnes (a northern industrial constituency) in 1932 and his parliamentary interests included army matters, civil and criminal legislation, the budget, and local issues such as strikes and unemployment. He also made important speeches on the Stavisky scandal and the disbandment of the right-wing leagues.

It is, however, mostly for his role in the Popular Front that Lagrange is now remembered: in 1936 he became the first head of the newly-created undersecretariat for leisure and sport. Mass leisure was a somewhat unfamiliar concept at the time: the new legislation reducing the working week to forty hours and introducing two weeks paid holiday had created a need for organization since it was feared by many that the extra leisure time would be wasted in bars or exploited by Fascist youth movements. Inspired by ideas of freedom and dignity, the efforts of Lagrange and his team were concentrated in three main areas. First, holidays and tourism: special train fares (still available today) were negotiated for those taking their annual paid holiday (*congés payés*) as were concessionary terms in hotels and resorts. To enable young people in particular to travel, great encouragement was given to youth hostels. Secondly, attempts were made to 'bring culture to the people' both by supporting popular culture and by shifting the emphasis away from Paris to provincial towns. Although today's *maisons des jeunes et de la culture* were not set up until the 1960s, less ambitious *clubs de loisirs* (many of them still active today and often known as *clubs Léo Lagrange*) were created throughout France at this time. Other projects such as film clubs and mobile libraries completed this ambitious infrastructure of popular culture but were not implemented until the post-war period, and then only partially. In the third area of action, sport and open air activities, a national inventory of existing facilities was drawn up; given the limited resources of his department new facilities had to be cheap (sports fields, campsites) and priority was given to deprived areas. Measures were also taken to improve physical education.

Lagrange's approach to leisure and sport was innovative in an elitist country where sport was practised by very few – if watched by many – and where culture was (and perhaps still is) very much a Parisian, middle-class preserve.

At the outbreak of war, Lagrange volunteered again at the age of 39 and was killed in action in June 1940.

Bibliography

For further information see E. Raude and G. Prouteau (eds), *Le message de Léo Lagrange* (Paris: Compagnie du Livre, 1950), which contains a contribution from Léon Blum, among others; among numerous works on the Popular Front: G. Lefranc, *Juin 36* (Paris: Julliard, 1970); J. Danos and M. Gibelin, *Juin 36* (Paris: La Découverte, 1986) contain pages on Lagrange.

M-MH

LAGUILLER, Arlette (1940–)

Arlette Laguiller has presented the unusual spectacle of a female, working-class candidate at the last three presidential elections, the only woman to stand in 1974 and one of three in 1981, and again the only woman in 1988. She was born in the suburbs of Paris in 1940, and after passing her certificate of secondary education left school at 16 to work as a clerical assistant in the Crédit Lyonnais bank, where she is still employed. She became a militant Socialist early in her career, first on a party level and subsequently as a trade unionist, appearing first before a national audience when she stood as the Trotskyist candidate in the 18th *arrondissement* of Paris at the 1973 general election, and spoke on television on behalf of her 171 fellow Lutte Ouvrière (Workers' struggle) candidates. Since then she has represented Lutte Ourvrière at all the major elections in France, parliamentary and European as well as presidential.

She can be defined above all by her active and single-minded commitment to socialism, well expressed in the title of her autobiography *Moi, une militante*. Her commitment began in the late 1950s when the French left's opposition to the Algerian War prompted her to join the leftist PSU. Her experience as a low-paid white-collar worker also led her to become an active trade unionist, and she was briefly a member of the CGT (France's largest, Communist-led union). She soon rejected what she saw as the bureaucratization of the French and the

Soviet Communist Parties and opted instead for the Trotskyist Voix Ouvrière (re-formed in 1968 as Lutte Ouvrière), moving at the same time to the more moderate and anti-Communist union Force Ouvrière. It was as an FO delegate that she helped to organize the 1974 strikes among the traditionally non-militant bank employees.

Arlette Laguiller has clearly never been in a position to win an election nor even significantly to split the left's vote. The repeated attempts to unify Lutte Ouvrière and France's other main Trotskyist grouping the LCR (Communist Revolutionary League), led by Alain Krivine, are unlikely to change this: the parties combined for the 1979 European elections and won 3.07 per cent of the vote. Her aim has been rather to use the first round of the elections to warn the traditional left – Communist and Socialist Parties – that they can not depend on the unqualified support of the working class, before helping to elect them as the lesser of two evils in the second. She considers the two major parties of the left to be reformist and bureaucratic, and mistrusts career politicians like François Mitterrand (q.v.). Her verdict on the Socialists' period in power from 1981 to 1986 was thus to be virtually indistinguishable from those of the right and denounced their failure to alter the distribution of wealth and power. Laguiller continues to work for the Crédit Lyonnais, though largely seconded to trade union duties, and to live in the same Paris suburb. Uncompromising in both her politics and her refusal to become a media 'personality', she uses the electoral system to attack its own inadequacy to produce radical social change.

Bibliography

Laguiller, A. (1974), *Moi, une militante*, Paris: Stock.

The following is a selection of French press articles: 'Interview d'Arlette Laguiller', *Paris Match* (17 April 1981); 'Entretien avec . . . Mlle Arlette Laguiller', *Le Monde* (19 April 1981); 'Mme Laguiller (LO): les hommes de gauche au pouvoir déconsidèrent les idées de gauche', *Le Monde* (8 June 1984).

DiH

LAJOINIE, André François (1929–)

The Communist Party's candidate for the 1988 presidential elections was born into a family of peasant smallholders in the tiny vilage of Chasteaux in the department of Corrèze. Lajoinie, who retains a regional accent also retained a strong interest in agricultural matters which facilitated his career in the party. Having joined the Young Communists at the age of 19, he became a member of the Corrèze Federation Political Bureau in 1954, a full-time party official for the Corrèze Federation in 1955 and was also departmental secretary of the departmental Union de la Jeunesse Républicaine de France (a front organization). As a Young Communist Lajoinie went to the World Youth Festival in Warsaw in 1955 and travelled widely in Eastern Europe. Very early on he became one of the PCF's stars and had his skull fractured in a demonstration in July 1958: he was in a coma for several hours and went to Czechoslovakia to recover and possibly for another operation.

Lajoinie was departmental secretary of the Syndicat d'Exploitants Agricoles, headed by the so-called 'Communist millionaire', Doumeng, but in the Corrèze Federation he was given responsibility for publicity and edited the weekly Le Travailleur de Corrèze (now defunct). He was an unsuccessful candidate for the 1963 cantonal elections. At this time his wife ran the Federation treasury (1961–3) and they both became party functionaries in Paris in 1964 and took up residence in Nanterre (Paulette Lajoinie is mayor in partibus of La Courneuve).

In 1964 Lajoinie attended the party college at Choisy-le-Roi and then (probably in July 1967) went for a year to the party college in Moscow, something leading Communists do not now do. On his return from Moscow he became director of the programme for agriculture activists at the party school and joined the Central Committee as a substitute member in 1972 taking charge of the agricultural department. As a party bureaucrat, Lajoinie wrote for La Terre, the Communist specialist weekly for small farmers and became its editor in 1977.

In 1978, when Pierre Villon died, Lajoinie 'inherited' a constituency in the agricultural department of the Allier. On entering the Assembly he quickly made a mark as specialist in agricultural questions and became a skilful parliamentarian. By 1979 he had become a vice-president of the Assembly Communist group and took over as group leader from Robert Ballanger in 1981 – this is a post which requires an exercise of all the political arts. Lajoinie was promoted substitute Political Bureau member with other Marchais loyalists on the party's 22nd Congress in 1976, entered the secretariat in 1982 and was spoken of as the third-ranking member of the party. Lajoinie is a Russophile, although more flexible on domestic politics. He is not a good speaker though,

and does not have Duclos' stamina (he is, however, a good TV interviewee).

In the outcome, Lajoinie's poll in the presidential elections was – at 6.3 per cent of the vote – a humiliation although the party recovered slightly at the subsequent legislative elections.

Bibliography

Although a journalist for the daily L'Echo du Centre, Lajoinie is one of the rare Communist leaders not to have produced a book although there is an interview, published as A coeur ouvert (Paris: Editions Sociales, 1987) for the 1988 electoral campaign.

DSB

LALONDE, Brice (1946–   )

Brice Lalonde was born in 1946 at Neuilly. A graduate in classical literature, he took part in the 'events' of May 1968 and was a leading figure in helping Friends of the Earth to get established in France in the early 1970s. He also edited the Green magazine Le Courrier de la Baleine, which gave him considerable freedom of action, as well as publicity, as a leading spokesman for the emerging Green movement in France. In 1972 he joined the Parti Socialiste Unifié (PSU), partly in protest against the motorway which at the time was proposed on the left bank of the River Seine in Paris, and partly because of his affinity for the self-management *autogestionnaire* ideology of the party. In 1973 he led a campaign in the Pacific against French nuclear tests and in 1974 supported René Dumont's (q.v.) campaign for the French presidency.

In November 1976 he was excluded from the PSU after standing as the Green candidate in a by-election in the 5th *arrondissement* in Paris, at which he gained 6.6 per cent of the vote. In 1978 he published, with Dominique Simonnet, *Quand vous voudrez,* which is essentially a Green movement manifesto and which sets out the ideological basis for his ecological ideas. He continued to be a leading figure in the French Green movement and was eventually selected as its candidate for the 1981 presidential elections, at which he gained 1.1 million votes (3.9 per cent of the total votes cast). His candidacy was far from obtaining the support of the whole Green movement however. Indeed he had always been viewed with suspicion by many grassroots activists, particularly outside Paris, who tended to regard him as something of a political careerist. Whether or not this was the case, it is certainly true that Lalonde has never felt at home within a structured organization, such as a political party, which does not give him considerable freedom of manoeuvre. It was attempts to unite the various disparate elements of the French Green movement into a single organization after the 1981 election that led Lalonde to part company with the movement. In an article in *La Baleine* in May 1983 he accused those who were trying to unify the movement of being 'Stalinists', and claimed that it was he who represented the *autogestionnaires* and 'authentic liberals' in France. He subsequently resigned from the Executive Council of Friends of the Earth and in the 1984 European elections presented himself as joint head, with the centrist politicians Olivier Stirn and François Doubin, of a list entitled Entente Radicale et Ecologiste Européene (ERE-Européenne), which was opposed by the official Green list. The latter obtained 3.36 per cent of the total vote, while Lalonde's list obtained 3.32 per cent. In the March 1986 parliamentary elections he stood as head of an independent Green list in Lyons against the list led by the former Socialist defence minister, Charles Hernu, in protest against the sinking of the Greenpeace ship *Rainbow Warrior* by French agents the previous year. He was however once again opposed by an official Green list and his list obtained just 1.4 per cent of the vote. Despite having been critical of the Socialists in government for many years, in May 1988 he accepted a post as secretary of state for the environment in Michel Rocard's government.

Bibliography

Lalonde, B. *et al.* (1978), *Pourquoi les écologistes font-ils de la politique?* Paris: Seuil.

Lalonde, B. and D. Simonnet (1978), *Quand vous voudrez,* Paris: J.-J. Pauvert.

See also a joint work (1981), *Ecologie. Le Pouvoir de vivre* (with an introduction by B. Lalonde), Montargis: Editions de la Surienne.

TC

LANG, Jack Mathieu Emile (1939–)

Jack Lang's career is one in which, emblematically perhaps, culture and politics are ultimately indivisible. Born in Mirecourt on 2 September, he read law at Nancy and Paris, where he qualified as a university lecturer in law, a profession he still pursues. As a student he campaigned for Algerian independence,

was excluded with Mendès France (q.v.) from the Radical Party in 1958, and helped form the Parti Socialiste Unifié. During the same period he developed his obvious talent as an actor and organizer and in 1963 launched the International Festival of University Theatre at Nancy. Within a few years, it had outgrown its student origins and acquired notoriety as an influential forum for radical theatre, anticipating the aesthetics and politics of May 1968. Lang became nationally known and was appointed director of the newly-created national theatre at Chaillot (Paris) in 1972. When his ambitious plans proved too revolutionary, he was sacked amid a storm of protest culminating in a theatrical and overtly political farewell ceremony in September 1974, attended by numerous arts luminaries and prominent Socialists including Mitterrand. Elected as a left-wing independent in the Paris municipal elections of 1977, Lang subsequently joined the Socialists, becoming a special adviser to Mitterrand. In 1979 he led the party's campaign for the European elections and was appointed its 'national delegate for cultural action'. He became minister of culture in May 1981.

Under the Socialists, culture was presented as a priority. With his budget doubled in November 1981 (by 1986 it had almost reached 1 per cent of public expenditure), Lang vigorously promoted culture as a key to the spiritual and economic regeneration of a France stricken by recession. Through a policy of 'cultural development' in the regions, hostility to the 'financial and intellectual imperialism' of the USA, support for new cultural forms – including rock, fashion, cartoons – Lang sought to give culture a renewed significance in the community. His plans were not always successful or universally acclaimed: the right accused him of a modish and demagogic disregard for the national heritage, left-wing intellectuals maintained a much publicized 'silence', and fellow ministers sometimes pursued policies which contradicted his own, particularly concerning the media. But he did succeed in making culture a live political issue and in the process became, according to at least one poll, the most popular minister in the government. Clearly his own style, theatrical background, and mastery of media imagery were contributory factors here, while also enabling him to act as socialism's fashionable front man in the run-up to the legislative elections of March 1986.

In March Lang left office after the Socialists' defeat but was elected to the National Assembly as member for Loir-et-Cher. In April 1987 he became the party's 'national delegate for culture and youth', a position which allowed him to maintain his following among the young and to legitimize his self-appointed position as minister of culture-in-exile, sniping at the policies of his successor François Léotard (q.v.). An omnipresent public figure and a devout, somewhat lyrical Mitterrandist, he was one of the president's campaign team for the 1988 elections and after 8 May was reappointed minister of culture – this time with the additional, and crucial, responsibility for the media and communication – in Michel Rocard's first and second governments. He was also re-elected to the National Assembly in June 1988, and in 1989 became Mayor of Blois.

Bibliography

Lang himself has written two books of note (in addition to occasional texts on international law): *L'Etat et le théâtre* (Paris: Librairie Générale de Droit et de Jurisprudence, 1968) (his doctoral thesis); and, together with Jean-Denis Bredin, *Eclats* (Paris: Simoën, 1978), a series of discussions concerning the Nancy Festival and Chaillot. His cultural policy is discussed in J. Renard (one of his collaborators at the Ministry of Culture), *L'Elan culturel: la France en mouvement* (Paris: PUF, 1987); D. Wachtel, *Cultural Policy and Socialist France* (New York: Greenwood Press, 1987); and J. Forbes, 'Cultural policy: The soul of man under socialism', in S. Mazey and M. Newman (eds), *Mitterrand's France* (London: Croom Helm, 1987), pp. 131–65.

DL

LANIEL, Joseph René (1889–1975)

Joseph Laniel came from a wealthy and long established Normandy family of textile manufacturers. Born in 1889, he was soon on his military service and became, at 19-and-a-half, the youngest officer in the French army. He served throughout the First World War, starting in the cavalry (working with General Grandmaison, the prophet of the offensive strategy) and later in the artillery. On demobilization, he joined the family business and at the same time engaged in gentlemanly public service as mayor of Notre-Dame de Courson and departmental councillor for Calvados. His father had been conservative deputy for Lisieux since 1896 (without ever holding a public meeting) but in 1932 he was outdistanced on the first round. To preserve the family seat, Laniel took advantage of the electoral law which enabled a candidate to enter the election on round two and was duly elected. In the Chamber of Deputies he sat with the parliamentary right –

Tardieu's Centre Républicain and then the Alliance Démocratique – and made little political impact. As a conservative, he naturally opposed the social and economic policies of the Popular Front. Yet he soon showed signs of the independence of judgement that would in the next ten years distance him from the majority of the French right. He opposed Laval's Ethiopian policy in 1935, he supported the idea of a national government under Léon Blum (q.v.) in 1938 and, above all, he believed in the need for the devaluation of the franc. This last issue brought him into contact with Paul Reynaud (q.v.) who became his political patron and brought him briefly into government in March 1940 as junior finance minister. In July 1940 Laniel voted with the majority to hand over power to Pétain (q.v.). But he almost immediately rejected both Vichy and collaboration and over the next four years would become a leading figure in the Resistance. He paid frequent visits to Reynaud in his various prisons, lived clandestinely in Paris and became Alliance Démocratique representative on the National Council of the Resistance.

This exemplary record – which contrasted favourably with that of most pre-war Conservatives – gave him a position in post-war politics that little in his earlier career had suggested. Continuously elected between 1945 and 1958, he was one of the founders of the Parti Républicain de la Liberté – later to become part of the Centre National des Indépendants – and became a useful addition to government coalitions in the period that followed the collapse of the Socialist, Communist and MRP alliance known as Tripartism. Junior finance minister in the Marie (q.v.) government of 1948, he was minister of posts and then minister of state under Pleven (q.v.) in 1951, keeping the latter post in the succeeding government of Faure (q.v.). The 1951 National Assembly, in which the right was strongly placed, had to face the enormously controversial issues of the European Defence Community and Indo-China. With the fall of René Mayer (q.v.) in 1953, a five-week ministerial crisis ensued at the end of which President Auriol (q.v.) turned to Laniel whose very anonymity made him acceptable to the Assembly. Voted in by 398 votes to 206, he formed a government of the centre right (Independents, MRP, Radicals, UDSR and Gaullists) that contained a clutch of Fourth Republic prime ministers (Bidault (q.v.), Pleven, Faure, Marie, Queuille (q.v.)) together with his old political mentor Reynaud and Mitterrand (q.v.). His government was (wrongly) seen as a temporary expedient and faced many familiar domestic problems – a shortage of Treasury funds, a huge wave of public sector strikes, peasant unrest due to falling prices, inflation. Yet Faure was able to pursue a vigorous expansion programme at finance, a process of modernization of the wine industry was started and Laniel refers proudly in his memoirs to the measures he took to improve France's housing stock. The government was no more able than any other to solve the problem of the European Defence Community – Laniel was roughly treated by Churchill at the 1953 Bermuda conference of the Western Allies, though Eisenhower was considerably more supportive – but its real importance was demonstrated over the rapidly worsening problems of the French Empire. Laniel underwrote the decisions of the Moroccan resident-general to deport the Sultan to Corsica and then to Madagascar – an action that led to the resignation of Mitterrand. In Indo-China he was not kept fully informed of the plans of his military commander, General Navarre; and his government was irrevocably linked with the military disaster of Dien-Bien-Phu in May 1954. Laniel failed in a last ditch attempt to get American military help to avoid the impending defeat of the French garrison. In fact negotiations with the Vietnamese were already close to a breakthrough and Laniel's defenders have claimed that he sacrificed his government to preserve their chances of success. His ministry fell on 12 June and was followed by that of Pierre Mendès France.

Fairly or unfairly, Laniel was one of the least suspected members of the political class of the Fourth Republic. Defeated in somewhat bizarre circumstances in his bid for the presidency of the Republic in 1953, he was savagely criticized and mocked by his opponents and his government seemed to survive by avoiding problems. The contrast between his leaden and tongue-tied slowness and the charismatic dynamism of his successor (and fellow Normandy deputy) Mendès France was too great. Re-elected in 1956, he took no part in the politics of the Fifth Republic though he was one of those who welcomed the return of de Gaulle on the grounds that he alone could keep Algeria French. He died in April 1975 and it is sadly revealing of his reputation that in its annual review of the year *Le Monde* did not see fit to include his name in its obituary column.

Bibliography

Daniel, J. (1971), *Jours de gloire et jours cruel*, Paris: Presses de la Cité.

Rioux, J.-P. (1987), *The Fourth Republic 1944–1958*, Cambridge: Cambridge University Press.

PM

LA ROCQUE, Comte de Severac François de (1885–1946)

Born in Lorient in 1885, the son of a general and descended from the Auvergne nobility, the Comte François de la Rocque de Severac entered the officer training school of Saint-Cyr at the age of 19. He served as a cavalry-officer in Algeria, and then in Morocco under Lyautey where he remained when the First World War broke out. Wounded in 1916, he returned to France and on his recovery was posted to the Somme as an infantry officer, where he was wounded and decorated several times. After the armistice he worked first for the Allied Command and then on the staff of Marshal Foch, a post which again took him to Morocco during the Rif War of 1920. He finally retired from the army in 1928 when Foch's staff was disbanded.

A year later he joined the Croix de Feu (Crosses of Fire), a war veterans' association for those decorated under fire, and became its president in 1931. Under his leadership the organization was transformed into a mass political movement of the far right with a paramilitary structure. When the Popular Front government of Léon Blum banned all such organizations in 1936, the Croix de Feu was converted into a political party, the Parti Social Français (PSF – French Social Party), which soon claimed over a million members. Though La Rocque rallied to Pétain after the armistice of 1940, he and most of his lieutenants were traditional anti-German and hostile to collaboration with the Nazis. If the official PSF position was pro-Vichy, anti-Gaullist and anti-Soviet, La Rocque was reluctant to involve his movement in Vichy's institutional structures and he later claimed Resistance credentials. He paid a heavy price for this ambiguity, being first arrested and deported by the Germans in 1943, and then re-arrested during the liberation purges of 1945. He was still in detention when he died on 28 April 1946.

La Rocque's name is now synonymous with the Croix de Feu/PSF movement which he led from 1931 until his arrest in 1943. When it was first formed in 1927 it was just one of the many ex-servicemen's associations that sought to keep alive the camaraderie of the trenches and to defend the economic interests of war veterans and their families. However, while some of these organizations were linked to the parties of the left, many of them were naturally drawn towards right-wing positions despite their claims to be apolitical. Applying military values to civilian life, they were often impatient with what they saw as the indecision and divisiveness of the democratic process, preferring the principles of order, authority, hierarchy and action. During the 1920s there was a growing bitterness in such circles towards the Republic, which was seen as having squandered the fruits of victory by failing to secure German reparation payments, by supporting disarmament and the League of Nations and by seeking *rapprochement* with Germany. The Croix de Feu first gave notice of its political preoccupations when, on 27 November 1931 La Rocque led a crowd of his supporters, backed by members of Action Française and Jeunesses Patriotes, into the Trocadero Hall in Paris and broke up a meeting of the International Disarmament Congress which was being addressed by former prime ministers Herriot (q.v.) and Painlevé (q.v.) and by foreign statesmen like Lord Robert Cecil and Salvador de Madariaga. As the meeting was being broadcast on the radio, the Croix de Feu suddenly achieved a national reputation.

By this time, however, the organization had become more than just an elite ex-servicemen's association reserved for those who had been decorated for combat duty. In 1929 membership rights had been extended to all those who had served more than six months at the front by the creation of the so-called 'Briscards' (old soldiers) section, and one year later a youth section was formed for the children of the membership. The most decisive change came, however, after La Rocque had taken over the leadership in 1931. In October 1933 the organization was opened to the entire population through the establishment of the ancillary movement known as the Volontaires Nationaux. Thanks to these successive moves, the membership passed from a mere 500 in 1928 to over 60,000 in early 1934.

For the left, however, the most disturbing feature of the Croix de Feu was the paramilitary structure La Rocque imposed once the Volontaires Nationaux had been set up. Through the establishment of armed and motorized mobile units (*disponibles* or *dispos*) La Rocque could call up at short notice commando-style groups, which often invaded left-wing municipalities, controlling traffic, occupying public buildings, rounding up Communists and provoking violence. Right-wing paramilitarism with its uniformed street-fighting units was not new, but La Rocque's movement appeared more professional, more disciplined and better-armed than older groups like Action Française and Jeunesses Patriotes, and above all more widely established in the provinces. The arms caches that were later found, the evidence of financial backing from powerful industrialists like Coty (q.v.), Mercier (q.v.) and de Wendel (q.v.), the systematic attempt to promote a climate of civil war, all of this made the Croix de Feu the centre of left-wing speculation about the dangers of a Fascist takeover in France.

Such fears were decisively aggravated by the events of January and February 1934, when the Stavisky (q.v.) scandal forced the Radical-led government of Chautemps to resign and the stage was set for the right-wing riots of 6 February. La Rocque had held his organization aloof from the demonstrations of January, but when the ineptitude of the new government under Daladier created a fresh crisis, La Rocque decided to support the demonstration called for 6 February. The riots and bloodshed which ensued brought down the Daladier government, which was replaced by a conservative coalition under Doumergue, and La Rocque did not hesitate to claim the victory as his own. His telegram to his section commanders on 7 February read: 'Government resigned. First objective attained. Suspend action until further notice. Maintain alert. Instructions follow.'

Though there was a considerable element of bluff in all this, the impression that the Croix de Feu were the main shock-troops of a Fascist conspiracy took root in left-wing circles, and won the movement increasing support on the extreme right. By the beginning of 1936 the organization had a membership of 450,000 and its activities caused increasing alarm. It called demonstrations in 'red' districts and bloody confrontations ensued in the Paris suburbs, in Lille and the Pas-de-Calais, and in Limoges. There was evidence that members were being trained in the use of arms by sympathetic elements in the police and armed forces, and when in October 1935 the Croix de Feu occupied parts of Paris and the main access roads, there were rumours of an imminent seizure of power. The formation and growth of the Popular Front against fascism on the left may be seen largely as a response to the threat of the Croix de Feu.

However, the violence of La Rocque's language and the spectacular displays of Croix de Feu strength had not convinced the other right-wing leagues that he was a reliable ally in their campaign against the Republic. For all his extravagant claims about his role on 6 February, the Action Française and Jeunesses Patriotes insisted that he had effectively saved the Republic that night by calling off the Croix de Feu column which was poised to invade the Chamber of Deputies. Their suspicions of him were confirmed when in December 1935, through the mediation of the Croix de Feu deputy, Jean Ybarnégaray (q.v.), La Rocque offered to wind up his paramilitary organization if all the other leagues were similarly disbanded. When the Popular Front government proceeded to introduce just such a measure in June 1936, La Rocque officially acquiesced, to the fury of the other leaders of the extra-parliamentary right. His movement was transformed into the Parti Social Français, and this drove a permanent wedge between him and other more radical opponents of the parliamentary regime. The gulf was further widened in 1937 when a former Croix de Feu leader, Pozzo di Borgo, alleged that La Rocque had been receiving secret government funds from prime-ministers Laval and Tardieu in 1931–2, a story that Tardieu confirmed.

In retrospect it is easy enough to discount the left's image of the Croix de Feu as a proto-Fascist movement. La Rocque's vague political programme, recorded in his 1934 book *Service Public*, envisaged a paternalistic conservative authoritarianism based on a strengthened executive, law and order, and a corporate economy 'reconciling' the interests of capital and labour. Its essential appeal was to bourgeois anti-Communism, which distinguished it from the more fundamentalist anti-Republicanism of groups like Action Française and Jeunesses Patriotes. At the same time, the Croix de Feu/PSF never developed that demagogic gloss of anti-capitalism which characterized foreign Fascist movements and which was the hallmark of the main extreme-right movement which developed in France after the banning of the leagues, Doriot's Parti Populaire Français.

However, if La Rocque's alleged ideological bankruptcy and political opportunism alienated some of his more combative supporters and antagonized his rivals on the right, the left still had every reason to be alarmed at the growing popularity of the new PSF, which had more than a million members by 1938 and which promised to become the dominant parliamentary force on the right at the elections due in 1940. Times had changed since 1934, when La Rocque and most of the conservative right had given the Republic a reprieve under Doumergue. With the Popular Front in power, right-wing bourgeois opinion after 1936 became increasingly disillusioned with parliamentary democracy and increasingly mesmerized by the threat of social revolution, and in such a climate the PSF looked more and more like the vehicle for an authoritarian backlash. Such speculation was inevitably heightened by the fact that, despite the official ban on paramilitary organizatons, the PSF retained its motorized units, its street-fighting tactics and its secret arms caches.

Some would argue that the conservative paternalistic regime imagined by La Rocque could never have come into being in a politically sophisticated democracy like France without the intervention of defeat and occupation. In many ways Pétain and the Vichy regime was the logical destination for the PSF (renamed Progrès Social Français in 1940), but curiously under the new order La Rocque briefly held only a very minor office and his movement never achieved real recognition. La Rocque's attitude under the occupation remains obscure. Some have identified him as an ardent *pétainiste*, constantly outmanoeuvred and embittered by the Marshal's entourage and eventually delivered to the Germans by the machinations of other collaborationist groups. Others have attempted to rehabilitate him by insisting that his traditional anti-German patriotism made Vichy's collaboration with the Nazis increasingly unacceptable to him. Accordingly his arrest by the Germans in 1943 is attributed to his sympathies for the Allies and his alleged organization of the 'spider's web' network which supplied military information to British Intelligence. This did not prevent La Rocque's imprisonment by the liberation authorities, and despite the pressure brought to bear by his friends on de Gaulle, he died in custody. However, in 1961 his widow was finally offered the posthumous medal honouring his status as a war deportee.

Bibliography

La Rocque's 1934 book *Service Public* has been translated into English as *The Fiery Cross* (London: Lovat Dickson, 1936). Otherwise there is nothing specifically on the Croix de Feu/PSF, or on La Rocque himself in English, surprisingly given the importance of his movement. In French there were several works published at the time: P. Chopine, *Six ans chez les Croix de Feu* (Paris: Gallimard, 1935); P. Creyssel, *La Rocque contre Tardieu* (Paris: Sorlot, 1938); F. Veuillot, *La Rocque et son parti* (Paris: Plon, 1938). More recent are: P. Rudeaux, *Les Croix de Feu et le PSF* (Paris: France-Empire, 1967) and Edith and Gilles La Rocque, *La Rocque tel qu'il était* (Paris: Fayard, 1962).

BJ

LA TOUR DU PIN, Chambly de la Charce, René-Charles-Humbert, Marquis de (1834–1924)

A soldier, landowner and Catholic social philosopher, La Tour du Pin was born at Avrancy in 1834. Having graduated from Saint-Cyr in 1854, he served as an officer in Algeria, and in the Italian War of 1859. In the Franco-Prussian War of 1870 he was taken prisoner at Metz, a fellow-prisoner being Albert de Mun. Their reading of German Social Catholic doctrines, and their later experience of the Commune, led them to realize the need for greater class understanding, and for social regeneration. The product of this was the *Oeuvre des Cercles Catholiques d'Ouvriers*, whose idealized conception of a feudal, corporate structure of society was based on the principles of social duty on the part of the upper classes; its creators believed in the possibility of peaceful co-operation between the classes. Not only in theory, but also in practice, it was basically paternalist.

From 1877 to 1880 La Tour du Pin was French military attaché in Vienna, where he was impressed by the Christian corporative doctrine which had been elaborated by Vogelsang and other theorists. In 1880 he retired from the army, with the rank of colonel, in order to take over the organization of the study section of the Oeuvre des Cercles. In the journal *L'Association catholique* he developed the theory of his particular brand of social catholicism; a series of his articles were later published in book form as *Vers un ordre social chrétien* (1907), which was to become a seminal book for the French Right.

Within the Oeuvre des Cercles La Tour du Pin stoood for theory, de Mun for practical politics. La Tour du Pin's far-reaching corporatist doctrine was developed as it were in abstract, while the movement itself was failing to obtain that support among the working-class which its idealistic view of society required and expected. Inevitably there were tensions. De Mun claimed that the Oeuvre was 'dying of theory', and that La Tour du Pin's philosophical speculations had made the movement lose sight of its true line of action. In 1890 de Mun withdrew official support from L'Association Catholique. Within two years there was an even more grave cause for division. With the *ralliement*, de Mun reluctantly obeyed the call to support the Republic; La Tour du Pin defiantly remained a royalist.

His royalism led him, in 1905, to join the Action Française, whose policies were to be strongly influenced by his theories (as Maurras – q.v. – himself was to proclaim). Despite a temporary withdrawal of his support at the time of the Action Française's flirtation with sydnicalism just before the First World War, he continued as a strong sympathizer with the movement until his death in Lausanne in 1924.

La Tour du Pin's effect on right-wing social doctrine in France in the twentieth century has been enormous. As late as 1941, he was being listed in an official Vichy publication as one of the greatest influences on contemporary opinion. His blend of paternalistic social concern and authoritarian political structures had considerable appeal for Catholic traditionalists, terrified by social change but seeking some outlet for their social consciences.

Bibliography

Dansette, A. (1961), *Religious History of Modern France*, London: Nelson.
Griffiths, R. (1966), *The Reactionary Revolution*, London: Constable.
McManners, J. (1972), *Church and State in France 1870–1914*, London: SPCK.
Weber, E. (1962), *L'Action Française*, Paris: Stock.

RMG

LAVAL, Pierre (1883–1945)

On 4 October 1945 Pierre Laval was brought before the High Court on charges of plotting against the state and of intelligence with the enemy. After the travesty of a trial, he was found guilty and executed eleven days later. As he himself claimed, his fate had been sealed before he opened his defence. In the politically charged atmosphere of post-war France, it was expedient to land all the sins of Vichy on one man. Since then, in the minds of many people, Laval has become the personification of all that was wrong with the Vichy regime. At worst, he is portrayed as the treacherous schemer, bent on the destruction of the Third Republic and determined on out-and-out collaboration with Germany. Even those who defend Vichy view Laval with suspicion. While they claim Pétain was playing a double game with the enemy, secretly working for the deliverance of his country, Laval was undermining this policy by desiring the outright victory of Germany. Only a dedicated minority persist in believing Laval had the best interests of France at heart, a realist in his attempts to reach a Franco-German settlement and a far-sighted statesman in his fear of Russia. Accordingly, the passion and the acrimony of these debates has made it difficult to unravel the controversy that surrounds Laval.

It is deeply ironic that Vichy should have come to be represented by a man who was, in many ways, the epitome of the Third Republic. Born in the Auvergne in 1883, the young Laval would have been unable, without the educational opportunities provided by the Republic, to have studied first science at Lyons then law at Paris in 1907. There he developed an interest in politics, entering parliament as the Socialist deputy for the working-class suburb of

Aubervilliers in northern Paris in 1914. This remained a political base until 1944, although in 1927 Laval switched his parliamentary constituency to become senator for the Seine. In the meantime he also built up an important power base in his native Puy-de-Dôme. This was founded on an influential radio and press empire he was able to procure through his lucrative law practice at Paris. In turn, the enormous personal wealth he amassed has been seen as the reason behind Laval's desertion of the left. But this is not altogether the case. As he himself claimed, his was a socialism of the heart, concerned not with doctrinal purity, but with the practical concerns of his constituents. Thus he was indifferent to the choice between Communists and Socialists when the two split in 1920, standing instead as an independent. Increasingly he moved centre stage in politics. It was appropriate that his name should have been a palindrone leading to the joke that whichever way one looked at it, backwards or forwards, it remained the same.

Yet this flexibility was the key to his success, enabling him to become a minister and prime minister in a succession of governments between 1925 and 1935. By then, however, Laval was clearly on the right. Two factors contributed to this shift. The growing radicalism of the French left (the emergence of the Popular Front alarmed him); the victory of the left-wing Popular Front government in 1936 embittered Laval, excluding him from power for the next four years. Secondly, and more importantly, his extensive dealings in foreign policy with the Italian and German dictatorships in the mid-1930s, convinced him that parliamentary democracy was out of date, incapable of matching fascism. Authoritarian government, free from domestic criticism, was crucial, argued Laval, if France was to ensure her security in an uncertain world. Consequently, he had no scruples about joining the right-wing government of Pétain at Vichy, first as deputy prime minister (12 July – 13 December 1940), then as prime minister (18 April 1942 – 17 August 1944), with the Marshal only as head of state.

What would provide a unity to this diverse career was a political style Laval made his own. This originated from his dealings with peasants in the Auvergne and workers in Aubervilliers. It was founded on the belief that the man in the middle, by remaining aloof of party and by developing extensive personal contacts on all sides of the political spectrum, could, by shrewd manoeuvre, sway the balance whichever way he chose. It was a technique that worked well in the ebb and flow of Third Republic politics where party ties remained loose and ministries frequently came and went. It also ensured Laval a place at Vichy. Following the armistice with Germany on 22 June 1940, it became clear to the group around Pétain that if they wanted to do away with the old Republic and inaugurate a new authoritarian regime better suited to deal with the exigencies of defeat, then they would require a seasoned negotiator to overcome the potential objections of Chamber and Senate. It was a task Laval would accomplish with considerable aplomb, steering through the law of 10 July 1940 suspending the 1875 Constitution and granting full powers to Pétain. Yet ultimately this style worked against Laval's ability to control events. His colleagues soon became tired of his constant bargaining, especially when it came to negotiations with the Germans. It was for this that Laval was excluded from government between December 1940 and April 1942. More seriously, Laval never understood that his techniques of conducting business were ill-suited to the ruthless world of international affairs. Arrogant bluff talk and personal charm worked well at a horse market in the Auvergne, but cut little ice in a world dominated by professional diplomats and dictators, where *raison d'état* constantly underlay policy decisions. It was always Laval's misfortune to overestimate his own powers of persuasion and underrate the intractability of international relations: it was France's misfortune too.

Due to the unsuitability of his methods, Laval's early interventions in foreign affairs in the 1930s met with little success. In 1931, his visits to Washington and Berlin did not ease the world depression or improve Franco-German relations. Later in 1935 he appeared to do nothing to restrain Italian aggression in Abyssinia, whereas that same year he failed to transform a mutual security pact with Stalin into something more solid, not even bothering to have it ratified by parliament at home. But, by then, he had little liking for parliamentary controls. Nor had he much time for domestic issues. His deflationary policy in 1935 did little to counteract the effects of the world depression in France. Indeed, as his critics point out, Laval's major contribution to the internal political life of the Third Republic was its destruction, when he secured the transfer of power to Pétain on 10 July 1940. To this his supporters reply such a move was essential as it would have been impossible to have maintained a garrulous assembly when the country was under occupation. In any case, they add, the deputies needed little persuading by Laval. In the extraordinary mood of self-recrimination of 1940, they were only too happy to relinquish their authority to the saviour-like figure of Pétain. There is some truth in these claims, but there can be no denying the zeal with which Laval undertook his work. After all, this was the Popular Front Parliament that had ousted him from power in 1936. 'This parliament made me sick,' he remarked. 'Now it is I who am going to make it sick.' But more important than revenge, Vichy offered Laval the possibility at long last of conducting a foreign policy free from democratic restraints.

Always supremely confident in his own abilities, Laval believed he alone held the key to that policy. He had little patience with those at Vichy who sought to promote French recovery through a National Revolution based on a restoration of spiritual values. Rather he would pin his faith on a Franco-German *rapprochement*. This was an old idea he had conceived during his early forays into foreign policy. At its heart lay a deep pessimism about France's position relative to Germany. 'We will always be neighbours of Germany,' he remarked in 1931. 'We face the alternative of reaching an agreement with her or of clashing every twenty years on the battlefield.' Should they clash, he believed it was obvious Germany would win due to her innate superiority in resources. Defeat in 1940 had merely confirmed that prognosis, and he had opposed France's entry into the war for this very reason. But now France had lost he did not give up hope. Because of her size and geographical position he did not believe Hitler wanted to vanquish France forever. He would have to include her in any new settlement of Europe. It was essential, therefore, to secure France's place within that settlement. This, he argued, would have numerous advantages. Not only would it remove the possibility of renewed Franco-German conflict, it would free France from her ties with Britain, whom Laval always viewed with suspicion. Furthermore, it would protect France from Russia. For Laval, it was Bolshevism, not nazism, that posed the greatest threat to European civilization.

Laval never lost faith in a settlement with Germany. In 1940, he considered France was strongly placed to negotiate a favourable position in Hitler's Europe. With her navy and colonies largely intact, Laval believed France could force Germany into making concessions to the harsh armistice agreement since Hitler would need to continue to count on French neutrality. Even in 1942, when America and Russia had entered the war, Laval pursued this policy. Yet to secure France's place in the new European order, he was forced to make more and more concessions to Hitler. At its most sordid, this policy led to the requisitioning of French labour for the Nazi war effort and the deportation of Jews. But Germany always remained unresponsive. Consistently overestimating his influence on Hitler, Laval never understood it was Germany's intention to keep France powerless lest she attempted a war of revenge.

It was for his collaboration with the enemy that Laval would be most upbraided both at his trial and after. But this is not a cross Laval should bear alone. Most Vichy ministers shared in his defeatism. After all, it was not Laval who concluded the armistice. Laval was not the sole collaborator, as some Vichy apologists would have us believe. It is quite clear that Pétain, rather than hoodwinking the Germans and working secretly for an Allied victory, was convinced of the need for collaboration. It was essential, he believed, to limit the demands of German occupation if he was to promote the new moral order of the National Revolution. Other Vichy ministers thought the same. It was significant, for instance, that collaboration continued during Laval's absence from power during 1941. Indeed, Laval was never quite the fully-blown collaborator he has been painted. It was part of the logic of his position that he could never completely accede to German demands, otherwise he would have nothing left to bargain with. Thus he would exert a restraining influence on those French Fascists at Paris who set their hearts on the nazification of France.

Because Laval was not always prepared to give in to Germany, his supporters have argued that he was actually part of the Resistance. This though is to misunderstand that he genuinely sought to collaborate. But even his collaborationism has been turned into his defence. Through his desire for Franco-German reconciliation he has been described as the forerunner of a united Europe. In this respect his vision has been compared to that of de Gaulle's; and, indeed, there are similarities between the two men. Both believed in a Franco-German entente as a prerequisite for European peace, although de Gaulle would never have entertained the humiliating terms Laval considered. The differences between the two are, however, substantial. While both men distrusted Britain, a loathing of perfidious Albion was never as strong in de Gaulle. Likewise, they varied in their attitude to America. Despite her intervention in the war, Laval always remained sympathetic to her, whereas de Gaulle, through his turbulent dealings with Roosevelt, felt nothing but suspicion. Yet it is in their approach to Russia they were most at odds. While de Gaulle believed Russia should be accommodated within Europe, Laval bitterly detested the Soviet Union. So great was his loathing that in 1942 he pronounced, 'I desire the victory of Germany.'

For Laval, communism always remained the real enemy of European peace.

After the war, Laval's supporters claimed he had been a realist in his fears of Russia. With the creation of the Eastern bloc, the evidence of Russian expansionism, they claimed, was all too plain to see. But, characteristically, Laval had done little to contain Soviet ambition in his lifetime. As we have already noted, in 1935 he was unable to build on a mutual security pact with Stalin. Yet what marks his career in foreign affairs was his inability to achieve anything more than fleeting success. Nowhere is this more apparent than in the field of Franco-German relations. While his desire for peace between the two was understandable, he failed to comprehend they could not cooperate on equal terms with nazism in the ascendant. He repeatedly misjudged Germany's intentions, not realizing that Hitler could never permit French recovery. But, confident as ever in his techniques of persuasion, he pressed on. This was his ultimate failing. As obdurate in his methods as he was convinced in the rightness of his decisions, Laval could never admit that he was wrong.

Bibliography

Kupferman, F. (1987), *Laval: 1883–1945*, Paris: Balland.

Paxton, R.O. (1972), *Vichy France: Old guard and new order, 1940–1944*, New York: Alfred A. Knopf. (Invaluable on Laval in Vichy.)

Thomson, D. (1951), *Two Frenchmen. Pierre Laval and Charles de Gaulle,* London: Cresset Press. (Useful interpretative essay on Laval.)

Warner, G. (1968), *Pierre Laval and the Eclipse of France,* London: Eyre and Spottiswoode. (The best introduction.)

NA

'LAVIGERIE', Charles Martial Allemand-Lavigerie (1825–92)

Lavigerie was born near Bayonne, where his father was a Customs inspector. He studied in the Parisian minor seminary of Saint Nicolas du Chardonnet, under the headmastership of Dupanloup (q.v.), and trained for the priesthood at the seminary of Saint Sulpice; he was ordained in 1849. A doctor of theology and Sorbonne professor of the subject, he spent two years in Rome as a kind of ecclesiastical diplomat (*Auditeur de la Rote*), before becoming bishop of Nancy in 1863 (and the youngest bishop in France).

In 1867 he became archbishop of Algiers, and cardinal in 1882 (Rome also conferring the title of archbishop of Carthage – i.e. Tunis – in 1884).

Lavigerie was probably best known at the time as the driving force behind Catholic missionary work in Africa. He fought the established government policy in Algeria of support for the Islamic faith (a policy which it was hoped would avoid alienating the Arabs), finally gaining freedom for Catholic proselytism. In 1868 he established the order of the White Fathers for missionary work, not only in Algeria but also in the Sahara and beyond, particularly in present-day Uganda. His missionary zeal was fired by a passionate desire to spread Christianity, but also by a profound hostility to Islam (which he saw as responsible for a morality of laziness and lubricity), and by a fierce French patriotism which made him a strong proponent of colonial expansion (especially in Tunisia). In the 1880s he campaigned strongly against the slave trade in Africa, partly because of a genuine revulsion (especially where female slavery was concerned), but also because the slave-traders were usually Muslim Arabs who stood in the way of French and Catholic penetration of the continent. In the public mind, he was firmly indentified with the French colonial cause in Africa.

Lavigerie is probably best known to history as the herald of Leo XIII's policy of calling on Catholics to accept the Republican regime (*ralliement*). Influenced by liberal Catholic circles in his youth, he evolved into a supporter of the reactionary Pius IX, and of the doctrine of papal infallibility at the First Vatican Council. His politics became equally reactionary, and in 1874 he even called on the royalist pretender, the comte de Chambord (q.v.) to stage a *coup d'état*. In 1880, however, he played a central role in trying to negotiate a compromise settlement between the religious orders and the Republican government that was trying to expel many of them, and on several occasions in the 1880s called on Catholics to accept – if not to approve of – the Republic. He may have been partly motivated by a desire not to alienate governments which could block his missionary activities. On 11 December 1890, at a dinner for the officers of the Mediterranean squadron, he proposed the famous 'Toast of Algiers', calling on Catholics to accept the Republic. In this he followed Leo XIII's encouragement, but also his own convictions. It was the act that effectively initiated the Catholic acceptance (*ralliement*) policy in France.

Lavigerie was aggressively authoritarian (particularly towards his clergy), and Euro-centric (to a degree that now seems deplorable) in his attitudes to Africans. He did, however, share with Leo XIII a perception that the Republic in France had come to stay, and that Catholics – despite their strong monarchist traditions – must learn to live with it. To Frenchmen of the time, he was the cardinal of Africa; today, he is the cardinal of the *ralliement*.

Bibliography

Baunard, Mgr. (1896), *Le Cardinal Lavigerie* (2 vols) Paris: C. Poussielgue. (The most comprehensive biography, though far too laudatory.)

Montclos X. de (1965), *Lavigerie, le Saint-Siège et l'église, 1846–1878*, Paris: Editions de Boccard. (Definitive on this aspect of his activities.)

Ward, J.E. (1965), 'The Algiers toast: Lavigerie's work or Leo XIII's?', in *Catholic Historical Review*, vol. LI, no. 2, July, pp. 173–91.

RG

LEBAS, Jean-Baptiste (1878–1944)

Jean Lebas was one of the outstanding leaders of the French Socialist Party (SFIO) in the inter-war years. The son of a textile worker who was also an early Socialist, Lebas grew up in the northern town of Roubaix and in 1906 was appointed deputy-secretary (later full secretary) of the Socialist Party's Federation in the Nord Department. In 1912 he became the mayor of Roubaix, a post which he held until 1940 and which enabled him to carry through an ambitious programme of social reforms in his home town.

His career in national politics began in 1919 when he was elected from the Nord department as a Socialist deputy in the Chamber of Deputies, in which he served from that year to 1928 and from 1932 to 1940. After the victory of the Popular Front in the general elections of 1936, he served as minister of labour in the first Blum government (June 1936– June 1937) and as minister for posts and telegraphs in the first Chautemps (q.v.) government (June 1937– January 1938) and in the second Blum government (March–April 1938). Throughout his career in Parliament, he showed a close interest in policies affecting labour, conditions of employment and social security.

Lebas was strongly influenced by the philosophy of Jules Guesde (q.v.), the early Socialist leader who had given the Nord Federation its formidable reputation for discipline and doctrinal rigour. He was a member of the minority at the Socialist Party's Tours Congress of 1920, when the majority of the dele-

gates supported the principle of affiliation to the Third International and prepared the way for the formation of the French Communist Party. He subsequently committed himself and his Federation to the task of rebuilding the Socialist Party and, until the period of the Popular Front, opposed the idea that Socialists should take part in coalition governments with other parties.

After the fall of France in 1940 he played a leading role in organizing resistance to German occupation in the Nord department. He established a Committee for Socialist Action and founded an underground newspaper, *L'Homme Libre* (The Free Man). Arrested by the Gestapo in May 1941, he was sentenced on 21 April 1942 to three years' hard labour at Sonnenburg, in Germany, where he died in March 1944 following a brief illness.

Bibliography

Maitron, J. (1975), *Dictionnaire biographique du mouvement ouvrier français*, vol. 13, 3rd part (1871–1914), Paris: Les Editions Ouvrières, pp. 228–30.

Piat, J. (1964), *Jean Lebas*, Paris: Editions du Parti Socialiste SFIO, Librairie des Municipalités.

BDG

LEBRUN, Albert François (1871–1950)

Irrevocably linked with the circumstances that led to the fall of France and the Republic in 1940, Albert Lebrun began his political career easily. Having graduated top of his year from the prestigious Ecole Polytechnique, he became a departmental councillor (*conseiller général*) for the Meurthe-et-Moselle at the age of 21 and was elected to the National Assembly for the same department in 1910 when he was 29. Only a year later he became minister of colonies, his first statement dealing with the Franco–German agreement drawn up after the Agadir crisis. In 1913 he was, for nine days, minister of war. Mobilization at the onset of the First World War interrupted his political career temporarily but in 1917 Clemenceau (q.v.) appointed him minister for the blockade and, subsequently, for the liberated regions. In 1920 he abandoned the Chamber of Deputies for the Senate, from which base he would achieve even greater prominence. He was elected its vice-president in 1926 and its president in 1931. It was this post that propelled him, by a massive majority, to the presidency of the Republic after the assassination of Doumer (q.v.) in 1932.

Sadly he did not fulfil the confidence placed in him, for he turned out to be a weak and ineffectual president at a time when France was embarking on a series of economic and political trials. He found himself at the head of a nation grappling with the problems caused by the Great Depression, the riots of 6 February 1934 and the German reoccupation of the Rhineland in March 1936. This was followed, only four months later, by the onset of the Spanish Civil War, where Lebrun was at the centre of an effort to persuade Blum (q.v.) not to back the Spanish government by sending arms to the Republican forces. Lebrun was hostile to the ideas and personalities of the Popular Front though he made no attempt to weaken Blum's domestic position.

Confronted by these problems, it was small wonder that Lebrun resolved not to stand for re-election in 1939. But the appointment of a new president would automatically enforce the government's resignation, and many politicians were anxious to avoid such an occurrence at this juncture. Lebrun was finally persuaded to stand on condition that he would do so unopposed, and the majority of party leaders agreed that he would be their official candidate. In fact his re-election was very far from being a ringing endorsement of his presidency.

The manipulation of this election failed to serve France well in the long run, for his tendency to vacillation was amply demonstrated in the final weeks before the defeat of France in June 1940. But in July, when the National Assembly accorded full powers to Marshal Pétain, Lebrun would not accept its mandate, refusing to sign a letter of resignation. This action eventually led to his arrest and deportation, but he was released soon afterwards on health grounds, spending the final years of his life mainly engaged in writing. He had become the symbol of the weakness of the political system of the Third Republic and the presidency created by de Gaulle was conceived as the anti-model to that exercised by Lebrun.

Bibliography

Albert Lebrun, *Témoignage* (Paris: Plon, 1945). On his role in the fall of France see R. Paxton, *Vichy France* (London: Barrie and Jenkins, 1972). A sympathetic portrait of Lebrun can be found in J. Zay, *Souvenirs et solitude* (Paris: Talus d'Approche, 1987).

PT

LECANUET, Jean Adrien François (1920–)

Jean Lecanuet presents three traits that are characteristic of a number of post-war politicians: he was a schoolmaster before entering politics (like Jean-Paul Sartre, Simone de Beauvoir and Raymond Aron, he achieved success in the *agrégation de philosophie*, the highly competitive examination leading to the top philosophy teaching posts in high schools and universities); secondly, he served his political apprenticeship in various *cabinets ministériels*, the ministerial private offices that play such an important part in French government machinery; and thirdly, he has established a firm local power base (as mayor of Rouen and, latterly, as president of the Seine-Maritime Departmental Council and the Haute-Normandie Regional Council). Although his early political career was not without its electoral setbacks, he has been a member of the Senate since 1959, except for periods of ministerial office (May 1974– March 1977).

A member of the Christian Democrat Mouvement Républicain Populaire, MRP, from the liberation, he was national president of the party during its death-throes (1963–5). He then attempted to bring together the various centre strands in French politics and on this ticket stood in the presidential election of 1965 against de Gaulle and Mitterrand. His relative youth and the 'Kennedy-image' he attempted to project in the first French election in which television was to play a major part probably contributed to his relative success, and – given that his 'natural' electorate coincided to a large extent with de Gaulle's – the 15.57 per cent he obtained in the first round probably contributed as much as Mitterrand's vote to forcing de Gaulle into a run-off with the left-wing candidate. With the demise of the MRP he founded in 1966 the Centre Démocrate as a centre opposition party hostile in particular to de Gaulle's European policy and to his presidential style of government. Given the increasing bi-polarization of French politics at the time, this – and the wider Mouvement Réformateur he founded with the Radical leader, Jean-Jacques Servan-Schreiber in 1972 – met with little success. In May 1976, by which time he had joined Giscard d'Estaing's presidential majority, his Centre Démocrate merged with the Centre Démocratie et Progrès (which Jacques Duhamel had founded) to form the new Centre des Démocrates Sociaux, CDS. The CDS is a constituent part of the Union pour la Démocratie Française, UDF, founded in 1978 by Giscard d'Estaing to counterbalance within the French right Jacques Chirac's Rassemblement pour la République. As president of the UDF, Lecanuet has attempted in the post-1981 period – with only limited success – to maintain some semblance of unity in a federal party rent by personal rivalries and ambitions and encompassing differing political sensibilities (the CDS has maintained a more pronounced pro-European stance and a greater concern for social justice than some of its partners).

Jean Lecanuet has always claimed to be a centre politician, although in many respects his options are those of the right. His political career has closely coincided with the fate of the centre in a regime strongly favouring bi-polarization. Protestations by some politicians (echoed by the media), especially since March 1986, about the continued existence of 'centrism' in contemporary France seem, to say the least, to be problematical. In any case, even if the centre does re-emerge as a powerful political force, it is likely to be too late for Lecanuet to achieve the sort of political success for which he once seemed destined, and indeed, in the wake of the defeat of the UDF candidate, Raymond Barre, in the first round of the presidential election of 1988, Lecanuet was forced to give way to Giscard d'Estaing as president of the UDF and has been left to devote his energies to his local and regional responsibilities. Although he was re-elected mayor of Rouen in 1989 this was despite advances in the department by the Socialist Party.

Bibliography

Lecanuet is the subject of a section of Alain Duhamel, *Les Prétendants* (Paris: Gallimard, 1983), but only as one of the Old Pretenders, and, before the publication of the same author's *Le Ve président* (Paris: Gallimard, 1987), Lecanuet's claims to becoming the fifth president of the Fifth Republic had disappeared. See also references to Lecanuet in R. Rémond, *Les Droites en France* (Paris: Aubier, 1982), R.E.M. Irving, *Christian Democracy in France* (London: George Allen & Unwin, 1973), and E.-F. Callot, *Le M.R.P., origine, structure, doctrine, programme et action politique* (Paris: M. Rivière, 1978).

HE

LECOIN, Louis (a.k.a. 'Léonic') (1888–1971)

Louis Lecoin is one of the best known names in the history of the French anarchist movement; between the wars he was, within the labour movement, an ardent defender of the principles of revolutionary syndicalism against both reformism and what he saw as the dangers of communism; and throughout his life – especially after the Second World War – he was an ardent pacifist.

Lecoin's father was an extremely poor agricultural labourer in Saint-Amand-Montrond (Cher). Louis gained his *certificat d'études*, moved to Paris in 1905 and worked first as a nurseryman, then as a building worker. Increasingly militant, Lecoin was forced like so many other revolutionaries to earn his living as a proof-reader, and he was to hold positions of responsibility within the Syndicat des Correcteurs. In 1936 he married Marie Morand, a PTT (post office) worker, with whom he had been living, in the 10th *arrondissement*, since 1922; their daughter Josette was born in 1924. Lecoin died in Pavillons-sous-Bois (Seine).

It was at the age of 17 that Lecoin first became involved with the syndicalist movement, taking part in a gardeners' strike and in the riotous May Day demonstrations of 1906, during which he was arrested. Lecoin was at first an admirer of Jaurès, but was discouraged by the Socialists' electoralism. In 1910, during his military service, he was court-martialled for refusing to help break a railway workers' strike, and this refusal was given prominent coverage in the press. In March 1912 Lecoin joined the Foyer Populaire de Belleville, a group of the Fédération Communiste Anarchiste, created the previous year. In October 1912 he became the federation's secretary, and in November he was sentenced to five years' imprisonment for producing a leaflet encouraging insubordination and desertion. Lecoin was released in 1916, only to be imprisoned once more, again because of his antimilitarist activities, in 1917. Whilst in prison he helped produce a clandestine number of *Le Libertaire*, the federation's newspaper. Using the pseudonym Léonic, he continued to contribute to the paper from his prison-cell, after it reappeared in 1919.

After his release in 1920 Lecoin was to be a member of the Union Anarchiste, the successor of the pre-war federation, but the activities he engaged in were increasingly the result of his personal initiative. His work for the Comité pour le Droit d'Asile, his organization of the Comité Sacco-Vanzetti and later of the Comité pour l'Espagne Libre and its successor Solidarité Internationale Antifasciste, were all criticized by some anarchists on the grounds that they were not revolutionary campaigns, but humanitarian ones. It is nevertheless true that the success of such campaigns, although (or because) they involved famous 'personalities' from political, trade union and intellectual circles, gave the anarchist movement a

245

much higher profile than it would otherwise have had.

At the outbreak of war, Lecoin was imprisoned for having distributed the famous appeal 'Paix Immédiate'. After his release from gaol in 1941, he wrote and published his first autobiography, *De prison en prison*, and in 1948 began to publish the monthly review *Défense de l'Homme*. This period represented a low-point in Lecoin's relations with the anarchists, who equated his passivity during the war with collaborationism; they criticized the humanism of the new review and attacked his absolute pacifism with regard to the national liberation movements in Indo-China and North Africa. Similarly, and through the mouthpiece of André Breton, Lecoin was attacked for his prominent role in supporting 'citizen of the world' Gary Davis in 1949. In 1956, after the sudden death of his wife, Lecoin began to campaign for the right to conscientious objection. To this end, in 1958, he launched a new weekly paper, *Liberté*, which counted among its contributors Albert Camus (q.v.). In 1962, at the age of 74, Lecoin went on hunger strike for twenty-two days, and the following year conscientious objection was finally legalized. In 1964 a committee was formed around Mme Albert Camus in order to propose Lecoin for the Nobel Peace Prize, but he withdrew his own name in favour of Martin Luther King. At Lecoin's burial at Père Lachaise in 1971, the 500 mourners included members of the Union Pacifiste de France, French and Spanish anarchists, syndicalists from the Confédération Française Démocratique du Travail and Force Ouvrière, and individuals such as Simone Signoret, Yves Montand, Bernard Clavel and Eugène Descamps (q.v.).

Bibliography

As well as his contributions to the periodicals already cited, Lecoin wrote (and published) two autobiographies: *De prison en prison* (Paris: Fresnes-Antony, 1946), and *Le Cours d'une vie* (Paris: Fédération Anarchiste, 1965).

The best biographical source, and one which includes a good bibliography, is Sylvain Garel's booklet, *Louis Lecoin et le mouvement anarchiste* (Paris: Fresnes-Antony – Editions du Groupe Fresnes-Antony de la Fédération Anarchiste, 1982), no. 19 in the Volonté Anarchiste series.

DGB

LÉGER, Alexis Léger Saint- (a.k.a. Saint-Jean Perse) (1887–1975)

Alexis Léger, poet and diplomat, was born into a settler family on 31 May 1887 on an island near Guadeloupe in the Antilles. In 1889 the family returned to France, settling near Pau. Léger attended the local *lycée* and Bordeaux University. He entered the French diplomatic service in 1913 and served for five years at the French legation in Peking. His literary interests brought him friendship with a small group of writer diplomats – Paul Claudel, Paul Morand and Jean Giraudoux.

As a Far East expert he attended the Washington Conference (1921) where he was noticed by foreign minister Aristide Briand. Briand appointed him head of his private office (*chef de cabinet*) and he played a considerable role in the negotiation of the Locarno treaties (1925), the Briand-Kellogg Pact outlawing war (1928), and he was the author of the French proposal for a federal European union (1930). In March 1933 he succeeded Philip Berthelot as secretary-general, the highest post in the Foreign Ministry. In May 1940 on the eve of France's fall, Prime Minister and Foreign Minister Paul Reynaud (q.v.), influenced by intrigues, dismissed him. Refusing the sop of a post as ambassador to Washington he went first to London and then to the United States. Many observers credit Léger with a behind-the-scenes influence on Washington against de Gaulle, and with stiffening American hostility to the Gaullists. He did not want to work with General de Gaulle. Although he did not officially retire until 1950, his diplomatic career ended in 1940 and thereafter he gave himself to poetry, under the pseudonym Saint-Jean Perse. He won the Nobel Prize for literature in 1960. In 1957 he returned to France for the first time since 1940.

Léger has been called the permanent master of French foreign policy in the 1930s. However, assessing his influence is far from easy since the archives reveal little of his personality and ideas and he left no memoirs. He refused to give evidence to the parliamentary commission of enquiry created in 1945 to investigate the period 1933 to 1945. Seemingly he wanted to efface his diplomatic career and be known only as a poet. Unlike his predecessor Philip Berthelot, an indefatigable worker, Léger spent much of his day receiving visitors, especially a small circle of sympathetic journalists. Contemporary judgements on him vary considerably. A senior colleague at the Quai d'Orsay, Jean Chauvel, recalled that Léger was not always well-informed even on his speciality of Far Eastern affairs and preferred to talk about the Chinese character. Nor was he easy to meet. More generously, the journalist Pertinax (André Géraud) considered the secretary-general a man 'of absolute intellectual and moral integrity' who never sought to 'impose his own ideas'. Pertinax summed up Léger's key ideas as: 'primacy of the entente and collaboration with Great Britain, the necessity to maintain the Polish and Czechoslovak alliances, to keep Russia away from Germany, to transform the League of Nations . . . into a military and economic league supporting the Western powers'.

The main criticism to be made of Léger's diplomacy is that he was too content simply to follow the ideas of his patron Briand. By the late 1930s, as the international dangers mounted Briand's policy needed rethinking and re-adapting. Contrary to the widely-held belief at the time, Léger was not the grey eminence of French policy because he lacked both the will and personality to impose himself.

Bibliography

Knodel, A.J. (ed. and trans.) (1979), *Saint-John Perse Letters*, Princeton, NJ: Princeton University Press.

Cameron, E.R. (1977), 'Alexis Saint-Léger Léger', in Gordon A. Craig and Felix Gilbert (eds), *The Diplomats 1919–1939*, vol. 2, New York: Atheneum.

APA

LÉOTARD, François Gérard Marie (1942–)

François Léotard has been general secretary of the Republican Party (PR) since 1982, vice-president of the Union for French Democracy (UDF) since 1983 and in 1986 minister of culture and communication (after July 1986 his portfolio was changed to minister of culture) in the conservative government of Jacques Chirac. He has been mayor of Fréjus since 1977, and since 1978 a deputy and departmental councillor for the Var department. François Léotard is the son of a member of the *Cour des comptes*. He was educated at the prestigious Lycées Charlemagne and Henri IV from where he entered first the Paris Institut d'Etudes Politiques, and then in 1971, after working in the Foreign Ministry, the Ecole Nationale d'Administration. He spent 1973–5 in the Ministry of the Environment and Equipment, in the course of which he was, for a brief period, sub-prefect in the department of the Dordogne. Between 1975 and 1977 he was attached to the personal staff (ministerial *cabinet*) of the influential supporter of Giscard, Michel Poniatowski (q.v.), minister of the interior.

His career provides an almost 'ideal type' example of the recruitment patterns for the governing elite of the Fifth Republic. His social background, educational training, administrative expertise and contacts helped to give him an entrée in the world of politics. It was during the period in the Dordogne that he began to develop his political career and his post in Poniatowski's *cabinet* brought him closer to the world of national politics; Poniatowski made Léotard head of Agir (the association for potential Giscardien parliamentary candidates). His victory at the Fréjus municipal elections meant that he inherited his father's former position as mayor, and consolidated his local power base. His successful parliamentary campaign in 1978 as a Republican Party candidate was initially won against the incumbent Gaullist deputy. Giscard, who was anxious to gain parliamentary allies against his powerful Gaullist competitor on the right, Jacques Chirac, gave him his support in the Assembly. His career 'took off' after 1981. He was one of the few young Republican Party deputies to survive the débâcle that followed Giscard's defeat in the presidential elections and was astute enough not to criticize the fallen leader. Thus he was well placed to succeed Jacques Blanc as head of the Republican Party in 1982 when Giscard decided that a new image was needed.

Léotard set about creating a party machine and identity that could rival the Gaullist RPR juggernaut and strengthen the position of the Republican Party within the Union for French Democracy (of which it was a constituent part). At the same time he established himself as an effective and energetic spokesperson for the parliamentary opposition to the Socialist government. In 1984 he proved himself a tough negotiator in the formation of a joint UDF–RPR list for the European elections. His youthful energy, engaging personality and keen sense of image made him by 1985 one of the most popular figures in the 'new generation' of political leaders. By 1986 he was the second most popular politician in the right and an influential figure within the UDF. As a minister with a high public profile he has fought hard battles to steer through the difficult and contentious legislation of deregulating the French television network. While carefully projecting himself as a 'man of the centre' he is nevertheless closely associated with the liberal anti-interventionist free-marketism of his close radical enthusiast allies, Alain Madelin and Gerard Longuet. His popularity with the activists in the Republican Party, his ability to appeal to the electorate and his increasing ministerial experience, all combine to place him in a powerful position within the UDF, as a potential candidate for the presidency or the premiership. In 1989 he was both re-elected as mayor of Fréjus and elected to the European Parliament third on the joint RPR/UDF list. After a clash with former president Giscard d'Estaing, Léotard failed to be elected as leader of the UDF parliamentary group in succession to J.-C. Gaudin in September 1989. Léotard got fewer votes (35) than his own Parti Républicain (55) and another member (Millon) was elected in what was a considerable setback to Léotard's ambitions.

Bibliography

There is very little in English on Léotard although he was the subject of a short profile in *Le Monde* (21 January 1986), in A. Duhamel, *Les Prétendants* (Paris: Gallimard, 1983) and in J. Frémontier, *Les Cadets de la droite* (Paris: Seuil, 1984). See also F. Léotard, *Pendant la crise le spectacle continue* (Paris: Belfond, 1989).

ER

LE PEN, Jean-Marie (1928–   )

Born in Brittany in 1928 Le Pen is the son and grandson of sailors and a war orphan. He was educated by the Jesuits. At 16 he joined a *maquis* and became violently opposed to the Communists for their monopolization of the Resistance movement. Between 1947 and 1953, he was registered, on and off, as a law student in Paris. He became president of the students union (Corpo de Droit), as a belligerent anti-Marxist. Known as a *baroudeur* or fighter, he was repeatedly in trouble with the police for violence (e.g. in a Pigalle night club in 1948). Without having completed his studies, he joined the Foreign Legion in 1953 and went to Indo-China as a parachutist. He arrived there after the fall of Dien-Bien-Phu and became a political journalist on the staff of the army paper.

Back at the law faculty in 1954, he became a student leader again. He happened to meet Pierre Poujade, improvised an impassioned speech in support of Poujade's *Union de Défense des Commerçants et Artisans* at a rally in Rennes, and stood as its parliamentary candidate in a working-class Paris district. In January 1956 he became one of fifty-two *Poujadiste* deputies and the youngest French MP. He gained a reputation as a violent, but effective speaker.

In order to protest against the lengthened period of national service, he took six months' leave from Parliament to rejoin his former regiment. He was sent to Suez first and then to Algeria from September 1956 to May 1957. Lieutenant Le Pen was accused of having tortured a young Algerian arrested by the parachutists on 8 March 1957, and released on 31 March. Although a police report was drawn up at the complainant's request, there was no prosecution. On his return to Parliament, Le Pen embraced the course of French Algeria with characteristic violence. He lost an eye in a fight during an electoral meeting in which he was supporting a Muslim friend. By late 1957, he had left the *Poujadiste* group and sat as an independent. Re-elected in November 1958, he joined the conservative parliamentary group of Indépendants et Paysans. His anti-Gaullism and his militancy lost him his seat in November 1962.

Out of Parliament, Le Pen experienced financial difficulties. These were allegedly reduced by his marriage to Pierrette Lalanne, the former wife of a theatrical impresario and friend of his. Having launched a firm which re-issued historical recordings, Le Pen was sued for comments alleged to have eulogized national-socialism which appeared on the sleeve of a record entitled 'Nazi songs of the Third Reich'. He remained politically active, becoming secretary-general of the support committee for Tixier-Vignancourt's campaign in the presidential campaign of 1965. However, it was only in 1972 that he decided to 'go it alone' by creating his own party, the Front National (FN). One of its early recruits, Hubert Saint-Julien Lambert, a writer and former member of several extreme-right organizations, was the descendant of a very wealthy industrial dynasty. He made a will leaving his fortune, valued at about 30 million francs and derived from the cement industry, to Le Pen and his wife. So did his mother, Madame Lambert, a close friend of Pierrette Le Pen. In the event, both Lamberts died in quick succession, the son at 42 in the summer of 1976. His relatives challenged the will, but settled out of court in September 1977. Part of the estate was a mansion at Saint-Cloud, to which Le Pen moved with his wife and his three daughters after an attempt on their lives which wrecked their Paris flat in late 1976. Those who planted the bombs were never found and there were no victims.

Relieved from financial worries, Le Pen devoted all his energy to politics. The early days of the FN were hardly promising. In the presidential election of 1974 only 0.74 per cent of the votes cast went to Le Pen. In the legislative elections of March 1978 the national vote of the FN was 0.33 per cent and Le Pen's himself managed only 3.19 per cent in his Paris constituency. It was only in 1981 that the Parti des Forces Nouvelles which had, since 1974, competed with the FN for the votes of the extreme right, disintegrated into a mere fragment (*groupuscule*). In that same year Le Pen gained full control of his own party. In the parliamentary elections of June 1981 he won 4.38 per cent of votes cast in his constituency – a big personal achievement since the extreme right as a whole could boast only 0.35 per cent (Le Pen had been unable to acquire enough signatures to qualify as a candidate for the 1981 Presidential election.) In mid-1982, the FN claimed 15,000 members. Its political role was still marginal, but its message was clear – nationalist, moralist, anti-Communist and focused on the emotive issue of law and order.

In 1983, the FN began to achieve a measure of success in local elections and in the European elections of 1984 it broke through with 10.95 per cent of the poll. These were the years in which Le Pen became a media personality, particularly after his successful performance on the TV network *Antenne 2* in February 1984. He had gained 11.26 per cent of the vote in the Paris municipal elections of March 1983 and in a by-election in Brittany (in the constituency where his native town is located) he polled 12.02 per cent. His credibility was no longer in doubt.

In the legislative elections of 1986, Le Pen was returned as MP for Paris – he was back in Parliament after twenty-four years. Yet his party's results (9.80 per cent of the votes cast) were not up to the level of the European elections or to his own expectations of 15 per cent, though well in excess of opinion poll predictions. Throughout the mid-1980s, the personality of Le Pen became more and more charismatic through media exposure. Simultaneously the electoral message of his party was increasingly identified with the repatriation of immigrants and with tougher policing. By April 1987 Le Pen was a candidate to the presidency of the Republic and was taken seriously in this capacity. This might have been the crest of the wave as 1987 turned out to be a difficult year for Le Pen. His divorce from Pierrette resulted in acrimonious exchanges and the picture of his ex-wife wearing only an apron (in retaliation for his suggestion that she should become a domestic cleaner if she needed cash) did not enhance the image of a politician who advocated Catholic traditionalism. The interview he gave in mid-September 1987, in which he described the Holocaust as a 'point of detail', proved extremely damaging even among sympathizers.

Once again, Le Pen effected a remarkable recovery. He projected a new, rejuvenated image during the pre-electoral campaign and proved all the opinion polls wrong by achieving a poll of 14.4 per cent in the first round of the presidential election in 1988. Despite his personal achievement, his party was the biggest loser of the legislative elections only weeks later. It ended with only one MP, as the main victim of the shift away from proportional representation to 'first past the post'.

Whether by accident or by design, just a year after his Holocaust blunder, Le Pen did it again. A crude pun about gas ovens entailed the estrangement of Madame Yann Piat, depriving the Front of any parliamentary representation. Even more damagingly, it prompted the first ever repudiation by the RPR of any local or national alliance in future elections.

After the death of Stirbois in a car accident on 5 November 1988 and his replacement as general secretary by Carl Lang, the moderate section appeared to be on the ascendant. Le Pen's public hope for 15–20 per cent in the elections for the European Assembly in June 1989 were disappointed when the party polled only 11.73 per cent. Although it was a respectable result (third in France) 11 per cent was well below expectations and gave the FN only ten members which caused difficulties in composing a group in Strasbourg. However, the proverbial cat has several lives and the Front National several avatars.

Bibliography

Marcilly, J. (1984), *Le Pen sans bandeau*, Paris: Graucher.
Plenel, E. and A. Rollat (1984), *L'Effet Le Pen*, Paris: Le Monde.

MV

LE PORS, Anicet (1931–)

Following the general election of June 1981 President Mitterrand appointed four members of the French Communist Party (PCF) to his government. Among these was Anicet Le Pors, who was made junior minister, under the prime minister, for the civil service and adminstrative reform. Le Pors had concluded his education at the national meteorological training school, and then joined the meteorological service. However, 'exchanging' he is alleged to have said 'one inexact science for another' he subsequently gained a doctorate in economics. He joined the Communist Party in 1955.

Le Pors brought to his ministerial post active experience of political life. He had been a senator for the department of the Hauts-de-Seine since 1977, and a member of the Central Committee of the PCF since 1979. He also, however, had long experience of the civil service, having spent the decade from 1965 to 1975 in a senior post as head of the industry branch of the forecasting division of the Ministry of Finance. He had, in the context of the preparation of the Sixth and Seventh Plans, been particularly concerned with investment options and the effects of state transfers to industry. From 1975 to 1977 he was the head of the Interministerial Commission on Immigration.

His appointment as minister for the civil service may be taken as evidence of attention by President Mitterrand to the continuities of French political tradition and the sensitivities of the PCF. The post had a special importance for the party, for PCF leader Maurice Thorez (q.v.) held these responsibilities from 1945 to 1947 during the period of *tripartisme*. That period had seen major reforms introduced by a combination of the efforts of the Gaullist Michel Debré (q.v.) and Thorez which laid the basis for the post-war structures of the French civil service. Le Pors undertook, during his period of office, an overhaul of these structures which, whilst involving the rewriting of the legislation, he nevertheless saw as a continuation of the French principles of administration exemplified in the reforms of Debré and Thorez. The most notable points of his own reforms were the opening up, in the name of improved democratization, of a new method of recruitment to the elite civil service training school (the Ecole Nationale d'Administration), the formal strengthening of trade union consultation within the civil service, and the introduction of national conditions of service for local government officials. Despite having been active since 1955 in the civil service union attached to the Confédération Générale du Travail, he proved to be a tough negotiator in wage bargaining when the government began to restrain public expenditure in 1983. He left office with the other Communist ministers in July 1984, and in 1985 was appointed to the Conseil d'Etat. Although mentioned as a possible presidential candidate for the PCF, Le Pors did not have a strong position in the Communist Party and did not play a prominent part in the 1986-7 internal party squabbles.

Bibliography

On the activity of the Ministry for the Civil Service under Le Pors see: Ministère de la Fonction Publique et des Réformes Administratives, *La Fonction publique en 1981-1982-1983-1984* (Paris: Documentation Française, 1982-5).

Le Pors has published a number of books, notably: *Les Béquilles du capital* (Paris: Seuil, 1977), and *L'Etat efficace* (Paris: Robert Laffont, 1985).

AS

LE TROQUER, André Lucien Alexandre (1884-1963)

André Le Troquer was Socialist president of the French National Assembly in May–June 1958, a time when de Gaulle's return to power, which he opposed, marked the beginning of the end of the Fourth Republic. As such, he would have become provisional head of state if the President of the Republic, René Coty, had been unable or unwilling to continue in office.

During military service in the First World War, Troquer lost an arm, and thereby qualified as a 'grand mutilé de guerre'. At the key SFIO (Socialist Party) Conference held at Tours in 1920, he was prominent in the group calling itself 'the rebuilders' (*les Reconstructeurs*) opposed to the nascent French Communist Party; he was elected to Parliament for the Seine department in the Popular Front election of 1936.

He was the chief defence lawyer of Léon Blum at his trial by the Vichy regime at Riom, near Clermont-Ferrand, in 1942, and in the same year joined the executive committee of the reconstituted SFIO. Later, he was a member of the organization set up by de Gaulle in Algiers which became the provisional government after the liberation of Paris. When de Gaulle celebrated the latter event on 26 August 1944 by walking down the Champs Elysées to the acclamation of the crowd, Le Troquer was one of those at his side.

Thereafter, he was a rather minor Socialist politician, though with two brief ministerial spells (at defence in Blum's 1946 government and at the interior in Bidault's 1946 government) until he became president of the Chamber of Deputies. He was first elected to this post in January 1954 as an 'anti-European' candidate against Pierre Pflimlin, of the European-minded Mouvement Républicain Populaire (MRP). Beaten by another MRP candidate in 1955, he turned the tables a year later, and was president of the Chamber of Deputies when the return to power of de Gaulle became a growing possibility during May 1958. Together with the president of the Senate, he met de Gaulle during the night of 28–29 May; de Gaulle said that if the rest of the National Assembly was as hostile to him as Le Troquer, he could do nothing other than leave Le Troquer to explain himself to the parachutists – underlining that a military takeover was not ruled out.

At this time, de Gaulle's entourage considered Le Troquer to be public enemy number one to the Gaullist cause. On 29 May, President Coty said openly that he would resign if the National Assembly were to prevent de Gaulle's return by refusing to invest him as prime minister a few days later. In the confused situation of May–June 1958, one hypothesis is reasonably clear – if Coty had resigned, Le Troquer as interim president of the Republic would have called on an anti-Gaullist to form a left-wing government, and an invasion by army rebels from Algeria and a military dictatorship might well have been the result.

In 1959 Le Troquer was implicated in the 'affaire des ballets roses', involving strip-tease parties in his 'grace and favour' residence outside Paris. He was given a suspended prison sentence, and retired from active politics.

MS

Leygues's most famous moment came in 1920 when Millerand, then prime minister, was elected President of the Republic after Deschanel (q.v.) (who had gone mad) had resigned. Millerand was determined that he should continue to direct the country's foreign policy (and much else) and he chose Leygues as prime minster. The centre-left of the Chamber of Deputies had always esteemed Leygues, but more generally, it seemed that Leygues had become prime minister in order to carry out the wishes of the president who was fearful of having walked into a trap whereby his ceremonial duties would become his only duties. Leygues simply took over Millerand's existing government. But he did not have the authority to impose his will on his cabinet colleagues. He was not particularly interested in foreign policy and it was evident that in that domain he was simply there to execute his master's orders. But public opinion was anxious to understand why reparations were still not coming from Germany, and, unable to answer that question, Leygues suffered a vote of no-confidence and resigned in January 1921. He continued to serve in subsequent ministries.

DJ

LEYGUES, Jean-Claude Georges (1857–1933)

Born in Villeneuve-sur-Lot, Leygues is famous for having been minister for the marine in eleven different governments. Coming from a relatively prosperous background, he was invariably recognized as able, hard-working and a conscientious politician. He early became a supporter of Clemenceau, but he showed, from time to time, a certain independence. When, in October 1918, the question arose of how the French would negotiate an armistice, whilst Clemenceau thought that it would be wise to consider seriously any German proposals and Poincaré said that it was unthinkable that any negotiation should take place as long as German troops occupied the slightest morsel of French or Belgian territory, it was Leygues who said that Clemenceau wished to 'couper les jarrets' of the French army. When Poincaré repeated this remark Clemenceau immediately threatened his resignation. In 1919 Leygues again opposed Clemenceau when he wished to abandon any French intervention against Soviet Russia in the Black Sea. However he remained a supporter of Clemenceau in 1919 and would have wished him to be elected President of the Republic.

LOCKROY, Edouard Etienne Antoine Simon (1840–1913)

Born in Paris, the son of author and dramatist Joseph-Philippe Simon Lockroy (1803–91), Edouard studied painting, and at the age of 22 took part in Garibaldi's Sicilian campaign (1860). He accompanied the historian and man of letters Ernest Renan as photographer and illustrator on his travels in the Middle East (1860–1), before turning to journalism where his mordant wit and ironic style made him a valued contributor to *Le Figaro*, and, later, with Henri Rochefort, to the Radical opposition paper, *Le Rappel*.

He commanded a battalion during the siege of Paris, and was elected as Radical deputy to the National Assembly in February 1871, where he allied himself with the extreme left. Though he attempted, in March 1871, to mediate between the Commune and Versailles and resigned his seat as deputy in April, Lockroy was arrested in May by the government in Versailles, but freed a month later. His journalistic activity continued unabated, and in May 1872 he took over the fortunes of the popular political paper, *Peuple Souverain*. In July 1871 he had been elected to the Municipal Council of Paris, and two years later became deputy for the Bouches-du-Rhône (April 1873); re-elected in 1876, he was one of the group of twenty-five deputies who published a manifesto in August denouncing clericalism as the enemy to be resisted, and spearheading opposition to the newly-formed Senate. In the forefront of Republican agitation for reform, he proposed legislation to repeal the Chapelier law which still restricted freedom of association. A member of the '363' who opposed the Broglie-Fourtou ministry after the sacking of Jules Simon, he was among the 221 re-elected in October 1877. With Clemenceau and Louis Blanc, he represented the extreme left on the Committee of Eighteen who, in November, sought to combat a MacMahon not yet ready either to give in or give up (*se soumettre ou se démettre*).

Lockroy was a deputy, almost without interruption, for some thirty years. He was vice-president of the Chamber in 1894, and retained that post in 1895. His ministerial experience included office under Freycinet (q.v.) as minister of commerce and industry (January 1886), and under Goblet (q.v.) afterwards, and, in 1889, he was active in preparing the Universal Exhibition. Responsible for *Instruction Publique et Beaux Arts* under Floquet (q.v.) (1888–9), he was also in Léon Bourgeois's (q.v.) cabinet of 1895, and he retained this post at the Ministry for the Navy until 1899, carrying through a series of important naval reforms.

He had married the widow of Charles Hugo in 1877, and, a prolific author, he published several works, including a book on Moltke (*Moltke ses mémoirs et la guerre future*, Paris: E. Dentu, 1892) and a book of political memoirs. Somewhat of an eccentric and bohemian, Lockroy, though a man of many gifts and who served with some distinction in several cabinets, never quite reached the front rank of the politicians of his time.

Bibliography

Lockroy, E. (1913), *Au hasard de la vie: notes et souvenirs*, Paris: Grasset.

ACR

LONGUET, Jean Frédéric Laurent (1876–1938)

Jean Longuet was born on 10 May 1876 in London, where his father, the communard Charles Longuet, was in exile. His mother was Jenny, the eldest of Karl Marx's daughters. After the amnesty of the commu-

nards, the family moved to Caen, where Jean pursued his secondary schooling before going to university in Paris, graduating in law. Although he was called to the Bar in Paris, it was perhaps inevitable, given the background in which he grew up, that Jean Longuet instead devoted his life to socialism. His father, his uncle and aunt, Paul and Laura Lafargue, and his aunt Eleanor Marx-Aveling were all early influences. As a student he joined a collectivist group. Like Lafargue a Guesdist, Longuet then became active in the Paris Parti Ouvrier Français and participated in its 1896, 1897 and 1898 Congresses. During the Dreyfus affair, however, he moved away from the Guesdist position and closer to that of Jean Jaurès.

Longuet, an advocate of unity, took part in the general Socialist Congresses of 1899 and 1900 and worked with Renaudel to try to unite the various Socialist factions. He remained close to Jaurès whilst opposing Alexandre Millerand in the ministerial participation debate. In 1904 he moved from *La Petite République* to Jaurès' new paper *L'Humanité*, where he was responsible for international affairs. This was an area to which Longuet, with his international contacts and especially knowledge of the English language and labour movement, was particularly suited. He used the example of Socialist Parties abroad to support his own arguments in favour of party discipline and class solidarity, which eventually won through and enabled the Guesdists to unite with the independents in 1905. Longuet was elected on to the adminstrative committee of the newly-unified party, a post he retained until his death. Between 1905 and 1914, Longuet was a leading figure in the Aisne Federation, where he stood three times as parliamentary candidate, without success. He was finally elected in May 1914 in a Seine constituency, which he represented until 1919 and then again from 1932 to 1936.

Longuet accepted the idea of national defence and, as a deputy, voted for the war budget in 1914 (for the sake of party discipline, he later said). However, he felt that Socialist internationalism should be upheld even during the war, and participated in a labour movement conference of the allied countries, held in London in February 1915. He soon became one of the leading figures in the minority Socialist movement which criticized the leadership's position during the war, and represented this faction at the second Allied Conference in Paris in March 1917. He was closely involved with the organ of the minority, *Le Populaire*. The minority took over the leadership of the SFIO at the party's 1917 Congress, and it was in the name of the party that Longuet opposed the Peace Treaty in 1919.

There were disappointments in store, however. Longuet was defeated in the 1919 elections (a personal as well as a party defeat). A year later, his pleas for Socialist unity failed when the party split over membership of the Third International. Longuet favoured instead the creation of an international organization open to all revolutionary Socialist groupings. He remained within the SFIO and for a while collaborated with Léon Blum on *Le Populaire*, then the party paper.

In 1925, he was elected mayor of Chatenay-Malabry and departmental councillor for Sceaux, the constituency which had sent him to Parliament in 1914. He was re-elected deputy for the same constituency in 1932 but lost his seat in 1936. He died after a holiday accident in Savoie in 1938.

Bibliography

Agulhon, M. (ed.) (1989), *Jean Longuet la conscience et l'action* (Paris: OURS with *Revue Politique et Parlementaire*).

Jean Maitron, *Dictionnaire biographique du mouvement ouvrier française* (3rd part: 1871–1914) (Paris: Editions Ouvrières, 1973–7), vol. XIII (1975), pp. 308–10 has a profile of Longuet. There is a biographical dossier in the Archives de l'Assemblée Nationale. Jean Longuet's own works include *Le mouvement socialiste international (Encyclopédie socialiste, syndicale et coopérative de l'Internationale ouvrière*, vol. 5) (Paris: F. Alcan, 1918).

SM

LOUBET, Émile (1838–1929)

Born in Marsanne in the Drôme, Loubet is usually seen as a very typical politician of the Third Republic. A lawyer practising in Montélimar, he gained the reputation of being an opponent of the Second Empire and then, after 1870, he easily ascended into the political hierarchy becoming mayor, departmental councillor (*conseiller général*), deputy, senator and eventually, in 1892, prime minister. In the latter office he played the role which he was frequently to play, that of endeavouring to diffuse situations that were potentially dangerous. One was that which arose from a strike among the miners of Carmaux in the Tarn. It was Clemenceau who suggested that an arbitration committee should be formed, with four representatives on each side (those who were chosen by the strikers were Clemenceau, Millerand, Pelletan and the mayor of Carmaux, Cal-

vignac, whose dismissal from working in the mines had been the cause of the strike). Loubet was chosen to be the chairman of this arbitration committee and although his decision (announced on 26 October 1892) was not immediately accepted by the miners, it contained the elements of amnesty and the strike was eventually called off on 3 November.

The other question was that of winding up the scandal of the Panama affair. Loubet opposed the prosecution of the director of the company as he oppposed the appointment of a committee of inquiry. The mysterious death of Baron Jacques de Reinach (a German Jew, Italian baron and naturalized Frenchman) who had directed the affairs of the Panama company and organized many of its political contacts made it impossible for an inquiry to be avoided. Loubet fell from power, became president of the Senate and when, in 1899 Félix Faure died suddenly, he seemed the obvious candidate to become president. The centre-right parties would have preferred Méline, but since excitement was rife over the Dreyfus affair, that prudent politician withdrew his name. Loubet's role in the end of the Panama scandal was not forgotten and he was booed and insulted when he arrived in Paris after being elected (there were various plots and demonstrations by the right wing over the following days, all of them being totally ineffective).

Loubet was also insulted over the Dreyfus affair, he and his wife being physically attacked at the Longchamp races. He was in favour of reopening the case, but it was only after much hesitation that he agreed to give an official pardon to Dreyfus. He accepted the expulsion of the congregations, and used his influence to reduce violence. But it was his official visit to the king of Italy in Rome in July 1904 which led to the Vatican breaking off diplomatic relations with France. He showed more interest in foreign affairs than many other presidents and he was a warm supporter of Delcassé (q.v.). His visit to England in July 1903 was part of the process which led to the *entente cordiale*.

Loubet is usually presented as the presidential figure who was entirely devoted to ceremony. In fact he was an intelligent and respectable politician whose influence was far from negligible.

DJ

LOUCHEUR, Louis Albert Joseph (1872–1931)

Born in Roubaix (Nord), the son of a modest

architect, Loucheur graduated from the Ecole Poly-technique in 1890 and served an engineering apprenticeship with the Compagnie des Chemins de Fer du Nord. In 1899, he and a friend founded a highly successful company specializing in the application of the new technique of reinforced concrete to factory construction and public works projects.

Mobilized in 1914, Loucheur placed his expertise at the disposal of France's fledgling munitions effort, building and adapting factories for arms production. In 1916 Loucheur proved his indispensability to Albert Thomas (q.v.), Socialist minister of armaments, by galvanizing production of crucial heavy artillery, whose inadequacy had been revealed by the battle of Verdun. Appointed under-secretary at the Armaments Ministry in December 1916 by Briand, he succeeded Thomas as minister in September 1917. He remained in place when Armaments was converted into the Ministry for Industrial Reconstitution (November 1918–January 1920).

Brought by the accident of war to government, Loucheur was one of a new breed of managerial and technocratic politicians from an industrial background, and he pursued the remainder of a prominent career in French and European politics. The war marked him profoundly in several ways. It qualified his faith in private enterprise by a critical perception of the low degree of professional and economic self-organization of French industry; it gave him insights into the claims of organized labour for social reform; above all, it made him suspicious of unbridled economic competition and national rivalries.

As minister for industrial reconstitution, Loucheur favoured a rapid withdrawal of the state from direct intervention in the economy, but only on condition that French industrialists rationalized their organization in order to modernize and meet international competition. First elected deputy in the 1919 general election – for the Nord, where he was re-elected until his death – Loucheur became minister for the liberated regions in Briand's 1921 government. He was a notable advocate of the more restrained approach to German reparations which resulted in the government's downfall.

A voice of moderation during the French occupation of the Ruhr in 1923–4, Loucheur remained closely linked to Briand when the latter, as foreign minister, became the 'apostle' of Franco-German *rapprochement* and European federation. In 1927, Loucheur was elected president of the French section of an influential pressure group, the pan-European Union. But he was especially prominent as the advocate of European economic integration. In 1921, at Wiesbaden, Loucheur had discussed with Rathenau, German foreign minister, a consortium to organize reparations in kind while minimizing disruption to Franco-German economic relations and in the mid-1920s he proposed European economic cooperation by means of a customs union and regulated international cartels, and in 1926 endorsed the International Steel Agreement as a first step along this path.

Loucheur's final bout of minsterial activity came as minister for labour, hygiene and social provision (1928–30). He advocated state arbitration in industrial disputes and holidays and social welfare for workers. In 1928, he introduced the first major legislation to tackle the housing crisis through state funding for public housing schemes.

Bibliography

Loucheur's papers are in the Hoover Institution on War, Revolution and Peace, Stanford University, California.

Carls, S.D. (1982), *Louis Loucheur. A French Technocrat in Government, 1916–1920*, PhD thesis, University of Minnesota.

Chevrier, J.-M. (1972), *Le Rôle de Louis Loucheur dans l'économie de guerre 1914–1918*, Paris: Maîtrise.

Godfrey, J. (1987), *Capitalism at War. Industrial Policy and Bureaucracy in France, 1914–1918*, Leamington Spa: Berg.

Kuisel, R. (1981), *Capitalism and the State in Modern France. Renovation and Economic Management in the Twentieth Century*, Cambridge: Cambridge University Press.

Loucheur, L. (1962), *Carnets secrets 1908–1932*, Brussels: Brépols (ed. J. de Launay).

Loucheur, L. (1926), *Le Problème de la coopération économique internationale*, Paris: Editions de la Revue Mondiale.

Loucheur, L. (1922), *La Reconstruction de l'Europe et le problème des réparations*, Paris: Imprimerie Commerciale.

Pegg, C. (1983), *Evolution of the European Idea 1914–1932*, Chapel Hill: University of North Carolina Press.

Trachtenberg, M. (1980), *Reparation in World Politics: France and European economic diplomacy*, New York: Columbia University Press.

JohnH

LOUSTUNAU-LACAU, Georges
(1894–1955)

A graduate of Saint-Cyr, the French military academy, Loustunau (sometimes spelt Loustaunau)-Lacau was a hero of the First World War who also saw active service in France's colonial Rif War in Morocco (1925–6). In 1934 he became one of Pétain's staff officers at the War Ministry and, although pensioned off in 1938 on the orders of the Ministry of Defence because of his close association with extreme right-wing conspiracies, he remained unofficially in Pétain's service until 1941. In that year he was disowned by the Vichy government and then arrested for making contact with de Gaulle in London. He later joined the Resistance, was captured and survived deportation to become an important witness at Pétain's trial. He died, whilst still a member of Parliament, in 1955.

By 1934 Major Loustunau-Lacau was in command of the 24th *chasseurs* batallion at Villefranche-sur-Mer where the future Marshal Pétain had been posted soon after graduating, also from Saint-Cyr, some fifty years earlier. It was no doubt because of this association that when Pétain was war minister in 1934 he appointed the major to his staff where one of his duties involved writing the marshal's articles, especially for the *Revue des Deux Mondes*, and some of his speeches. On Pétain's resignation in November 1934 Loustunau-Lacau remained at the War Ministry until 1935 when he joined the marshal's staff again. Put in charge of political affairs he was disappointed that Pétain did not use his influence with politicians and with the military to further the interests of the nation. By 1936 in a France rife with rumours of Communist, Jewish and Freemason plots to overthrow the State, Loustunau-Lacau formed a secret right-wing movement within the army called *Corvignolles*. The object was to stamp out what the major viewed as Communist orchestrated subversion to spread antimilitarism among the troops. By early 1937 *Corvignolles* had some 10,000 members among the military and its leader had reached an agreement with the more violently antiparliamentarian secret organization known as the La Cagoule ('hood') to pool information on Communists. Loustunau-Lacau also became involved with another clandestine organization called the *Spirale* which by 1938 had a similar understanding with Doriot's Fascist Parti Populaire Français. Retired from active service in February 1938 by Daladier, the defence minister, the major was nevertheless employed by Pétain in the autumn of 1939 as his contact with Pierre Laval, the future leader of the Vichy government. At that time

Pétain was ambassador to Spain where Loustunau-Lacau visited him frequently.

Between 1940 and 1941, but without seeking Pétain's approval, the major tried to establish a dialogue between Vichy and de Gaulle's Free French forces. He also tried to set up a Gaullist Resistance group in the unoccupied zone. Both offers were rejected by London and, tired of the endless conspiratorial activities of Loustunau-Lacau Vichy arrested the 'schemer'. After escaping and joining the *Alliance* Resistance network he was captured by the Gestapo and deported to Mauthausen concentration camp from which he returned to testify largely in Pétain's favour at the Marshal's trial for high treason in 1945.

A caricature of the extreme right-wing mavericks who dabbled in ultra-patriotic conspiracies in the late 1930s, Loustunau-Lacau ended his days as MP for the Basses-Pyrénées, elected in 1951 on an extreme right-wing Unité des Indépendants Républicains ticket. The end of his political career confirmed his maverick reputation in that he canvassed his support for the most liberal of the Fourth Republic's prime ministers, Mendès France.

Bibliography

Very little exists in English or French on Loustunau-Lacau. He is mentioned in R. Griffiths, *Marshal Pétain* (London: Constable, 1970) and H.R. Lottman, *Pétain, Hero or Traitor?* (London: Viking 1985). For further information see his own memoirs: G. Loustunau-Lacau, *Chiens maudits, souvenirs d'un rescapé des bagnes hitlériens* (Paris: Réseau Alliance, 1946) and *Mémoires d'un français rebelle* (Paris: Robert Laffont, 1948).

GTH

LYAUTEY, Marshal Louis Hubert Gonsalve
(1854–1934)

Soldier and colonial administrator, Marshal Lyautey was born at Nancy in 1854. As a young cavalry officer, this Catholic legitimist came strongly under the influence of Albert de Mun (q.v.). His article 'Du rôle social de l'officier', published in the *Revue des Deux Mondes* in 1891, extended to the military sphere de Mun's views on social reform, based on the principles of social duty on the part of the upper classes.

Lyautey served under General Galliéni in Indo-China (1894–7) and in Madagascar (1897–1902), and in this period successfully began to develop his later techniques and attitudes. Another article, 'Du rôle colonial de l'armée', preached a new, paternalistic view of France's colonial mission.

After his return to France in 1902, he was sent to restore order on the Algerian-Moroccan border. After a further period in France he was sent, in April 1912, to the new French protectorate of Morocco as resident-general. Morocco was in anarchy. The sultan's central power was almost non-existent. After the initial subjugation of the area around Fez, Lyautey slowly but surely penetrated the rest of the territory, using as in Madagascar the spreading stain – 'tache d'huile' – method. Small areas were won over, in turn, by a mixture of military and political means, which ensured lasting relationships rather than resentment and subjugation. The aim was not French conquest, but indirect rule through the Moroccan elites.

On declaration of war in 1914, he was ordered to evacuate the interior and send most of his troops to the Western Front. He sent the troops, but with inspired insubordination maintained and even extended the pacified territory. In this, however, he came to place inordinate powers in certain friendly tribes. The subsequent career of El Glaoui, so prominent in the final crisis of the protectorate in the 1950s, owed much to this time. In 1917 Lyautey was appointed war minister, but resigned after three months, returning to Morocco. He had found himself incapable of coping with the restraints of democratic government, in a wartime situation.

After the war he further consolidated the Moroccan protectorate, making of it one of the wonders of the French Empire. In 1921 he was created Marshal of France. But all was not to end happily. In 1925 the Rif rebellion spilled over from the Spanish zone of Morocco. Lyautey, initially starved of reinforcements, contained the attack. But those in France who had always criticized Lyautey's methods, and wanted swift and crushing military victories, now had their way. Marshal Pétain (q.v.) was given sole military command and set about joint operations with the Spanish, which were to crush the rebellion. Lyautey resigned. He retired to his property in Lorraine, full of bitterness. He was to die there in July 1934.

Lyautey was a man of many contradictions; a royalist legitimist who gave an empire to the Republic ('légitimiste qui a donné un empire à la République';); a Catholic soldier who was a Dreyfusard (and a close friend of Joseph Reinach) and yet a supporter of the leagues in February 1934; a man of culture who hated militarists. He was to remain, for many, the example of what French colonial policy might have been; a moral, unselfish, yet paternalistic mission. Yet in his policies there lay the seeds of the eventual dissolution of that empire.

Bibliography

A. Maurois, *Lyautey* (London: John Lane, 1931); J.G.P.M. Benoist-Méchin, *Lyautey l'Africain* (Lausanne: Clairefontaine, 1966); *L'Illustration* (special Lyautey number), 11 August 1934; unpublished Lyautey-Terrier correspondence in Bibliothèque de l'Institut.

RMG

M

de MACMAHON, Marie-Edmonde Patrice Maurice, comte de, duc de Magenta (1808–1893)

Marshal de MacMahon was the second president of the Third Republic from 24 May 1873 to 30 January 1879. His period of office was the last time the royalist right controlled the French government, the last time that a monarchist restoration was a serious possibility in France, and the last time that a peacetime French government attempted to use its powers to reverse the advance of democracy and republicanism. The failure of all these enterprises, of which MacMahon was the figurehead rather than the directing force, demonstrated that there was no alternative to a parliamentary Republic in France.

MacMahon was born into a military family descended from Irish Jacobite exiles. At first destined for the Church, he was educated at a minor seminary, the Saint-Cyr military college and the Staff School. He took part in the 1830 Algiers campaign, and decided, after hesitation, not to resign following the 1830 revolution. His career thereafter was one of the most brilliant in the French army in the gilded years before 1870. His courage and aristocratic origins brought speedy promotion and the nickname 'the Young Lion'. In the Crimea he led the final assault on Sebastopol, taking the vital Malakoff redoubt with the famous (and perhaps apocryphal) words 'J'y suis; j'y reste'. Further renown and a Marshal's baton came in the Italian war, in the battles of Turbigo, Magenta (which won him his dukedom) and Solférino. He was governor-general of Algeria, and known as a critic of the Second Empire. Like many of the brilliant 'African' generals, he was found wanting against the Prussians in 1870, when his army was surrounded and defeated at the catastrophe of Sedan, which brought the fall of the Second Empire. A serious wound in the early stages of the battle saved MacMahon from some of the opprobrium. His marshal's rank, earlier military glory, political discretion and pliability of character led Thiers to appoint him to command the Army of Versailles against the Paris Commune in 1871, and his success made him potentially a political figure of importance in the eyes of conservatives seeking a safe guardian of order, or even – given his royalist background – a French General Monck. Consequently, his name was soon mentioned in political circles as a replacement for Thiers.

When Thiers resigned in May 1873 a reluctant MacMahon was drafted into office by the royalist majority in the National Assembly, with the duc de Broglie, leader of the Orleanist right-centre party, as head of the government. The royalists hoped that he would hold the fort until the Bourbon pretender, the comte de Chambord, was ready to ascend the throne as Henri V. But Chambord's Legitimist intransigence (symbolized by his determination to replace the tricolour with the Bourbons' white flag) made a restoration impossible by parliamentary means, as moderate royalists were unwilling to give him a free hand. MacMahon, to the disappointment of the extreme Legitimists, would not contemplate conspiracy to force the Assembly's hand: he refused even to see Chambord when he came secretly to Versailles in November 1873. Without MacMahon's support, there was not the slightest chance of a restoration by extra-parliamentary means. 'I thought I was dealing with a Constable of France,' said the disappointed Chambord, 'but I found only a Captain of Gendarmes.'

The right as a whole, unable to effect a restoration and alarmed at the by-election successes of the Radical Republicans, saw no alternative to keeping MacMahon in office to gain time (in the hope that Chambord might change his mind or possibly die) and in the knowledge that he would act as a barrier to the left by repressing radical agitation and pursuing policies to restore 'moral order' to the country. In November 1873 he was voted a term of office of seven years. However, the divisions among the royalists (which brought the downfall of the de Broglie government in May 1874, replaced by a weak government under General de Cissey) left MacMahon in a political predicament for which nothing in his experience had prepared him. Conservative but legalistic, he was trying to keep the Republicans at bay without defined powers or a clear source of legitimacy, without a clear majority in parliament or the country, and without the use of force.

An alarming rise in Bonapartist support showed that the prolongation of provisional government was dangerous for both royalists and Republicans. In 1874 MacMahon made a speech calling for 'regular institutions' – i.e. a constitution – to ensure 'calm, security and appeasement', and the National Assembly voted constitutional laws in February 1875. These provided for a President and a Senate, both elected indirectly, to check the feared excesses of universal suffrage. A Republican electoral victory in 1876 obliged MacMahon to accept governments under the moderate Republicans Dufaure and Simon, both former ministers of Thiers. However, this peaceful if cool *cohabitation* was ended on 16 May 1877, when MacMahon, apparently on his own initiative, practically dismissed Simon for his halfhearted opposition to radicalism – the famous *coup d'état* of the 16 May. MacMahon recalled the Duc de Broglie to form a government, and when the Chamber voted no confidence he dissolved it. For years conservatives had nursed the illusion that a determined government, using press control, patronage, the prestige of power and, if necessary, martial law, could influence or coerce the mass of the electorate into rejecting the 'agitators' of the left. This illusion was exposed in October 1877, when a general election again gave the Republicans a majority despite official pressure. MacMahon at first turned to a soldier, General de Rochebouët, to form a non-parliamentary ministry of officials, but the Chamber would not recognize it. Warned by Gambetta that his choice was 'se soumettre ou se démettre' (submit or resign), MacMahon, who had never wanted a *coup d'état*, recalled Dufaure to form a government and announced that he had no intention of 'erecting the exercise of the right of dissolution into a system of government'. He then withdrew to the dignified figurehead position for which he was admirably suited; 'J'y reste, mais je n'y suis plus', quipped Republicans. Opening the Paris Exhibition in 1878 he appealed for 'the spirit of concord, absolute respect for the law, ardent and disinterested love of the fatherland'. However, in January 1879, after the Republicans had finally obtained a majority in the Senate as well as the Chamber of Deputies, they forced his resignation. He died on 5 October 1893, reviled by Republicans as a would-be destroyer of the Republic, and by diehard monarchists as a feeble bungler who had thrown away the last chance of a restoration.

MacMahon was an honourable soldier of limited intelligence and narrow political vision. Both his virtues and his weaknesses helped to restrain the extreme royalists from taking illegal action to overthrow the Republic. But his abortive attempt to halt the advance of the Radicals in 1877, though remaining within the constitution, increased partisan bitterness and weakened for good the authority of the presidency. No future incumbent would dare to dissolve a Chamber before the end of its term, and the few attempts to strengthen the executive against Parliament during the Third Republic were successfully resisted.

Bibliography

Outside the standard textbooks there is nothing on MacMahon in English. A solid traditional biography is Jacques Silvestre de Sacy, *Le Maréchal de MacMahon duc de Magenta 1808–1893* (Paris: Les Editions Inter-Nationales, 1960) and on his period as president see Fresnette Pisani-Ferry, *Le Coup d'état manqué du 16 mai 1877* (Paris: Robert Laffont, 1965).

RT

MAGINOT, André (1877–1932)

Although associated nowadays only with the line that bore his name, Maginot was in fact a charismatic political figure who enjoyed both popularity and respect, particularly from the First World War until his death. Physically and intellectually, he was out of the ordinary: extremely tall and with a record that made him a national hero (his imposing crutches can still be seen at the Musée des Invalides), he was also a brilliant student (top of his year at the Ecole Libre des Sciences Politiques) and was only 23 when he entered the Council of State (*Conseil d'Etat*). As a politician his main interests were matters of war and peace (defence, war prevention and the fate of soldiers and veterans).

Originally a man of the left, Maginot joined governments of various political complexions (Republican or 'union nationale' coalitions) at the request of such diverse figures as Ribot, Briand, Poincaré, Tardieu and Laval, who sought to add his personal appeal as well as his reputation for efficiency to their cabinets. His achievements in the areas for which he was responsible to a large extent justify this reputation; given the usual constraints of Third Republic politics, the short-lived governments and fragile coalitions, Maginot had a degree of success where many failed. He first proved to be a good administrator during a pre-war appointment in Algeria. As a minister for the colonies in the mid-1920s, however, his plan for the development of the Empire's local resources and human potential was very much diluted in its application. It was in the field of defence that Maginot distinguished himself. Already respected before 1914 for his views on the war effort and the extension of military service, he spoke after 1915 with the first-hand experience of a much decorated, wounded war hero. Determined that such a war should never be allowed to happen again, he denounced the weaknesses of the Treaty of Versailles, its lack of commitment to reconstruction, to the protection of borders and to guarantees. A hardliner on the issue of reparations, he was minister of war at the time of the occupation of the Ruhr (1924); he was later strongly opposed to withdrawal from the Rhineland, and spoke at the League of Nations on the fragility of peace and the need for world arms limitation. Failing this, he wanted a non-aggressive France to enjoy total security behind impregnable defences. Thus the French soldier would not have to endure the horrors of improvised trench warfare. If the Maginot Line failed, as we know, to save France, this was for a variety of reasons (budget cuts, incomplete execution of the project, mismanagement) many of which were not the fault of Maginot, who died in 1932 and was therefore unable to see his plan through to the end. His name, however, with its associations of courage, resilience and non-aggression, remained attached to the project, which appealed so much to the generation of war veterans for which he had spoken.

Indeed, his role as spokesman for the war veterans is arguably his most distinctive achievement, since he gave some unity to this bitter and fragmented grassroots movement and helped promote many of its claims. As the minister for war pensions in 1920, he had to break new ground: existing legislation regarding compensation dated back to the nineteenth century when wars were on a much smaller scale and there were relatively few injured veterans to be cared for. At a time of great financial constraint he obtained what were regarded as humane and even generous terms. On a symbolic level, he also gave the war veterans and victims a central place in French life by the creation of the ceremonial of the Unknown Soldier, still observed today at the Arc de Triomphe.

Bibliography

Maginot's war diaries, *Carnets de patrouille*, were published posthumously (Aurillac: Imprimerie Moderne, 1964). A biography by P. Belperron was translated as *Maginot of the Line* (London: Williams & Norgate,

1940). For his work on behalf of war veterans see A. Prost, *Les Anciens combattants et la société française* (Paris: Presses de la Fondation Nationale des Sciences Politiques, 1977).

M-MH

MAIRE, Edmond Louis (1931–)

Edmond Maire was general secretary of the trade union confederation Confédération Française Démocratique du Travail (CFDT) between 1971 (when he took over from Eugène Descamps – q.v.) and December 1988 when he retired to make way for Jean Kaspar (q.v.).

He was a technician with the chemical company Pechiney when he decided to join the Confédération Française des Travailleurs Chrétiens (CFTC), the forerunner of the CFDT, a somewhat late arrival to the world of trade unionism at the age of 23. In 1958 he became a full-time official and in 1964, the year of the 'deconfessionalization' of the CFTC, when the reference to Christianity was modified in its statutes and it changed its name to the CFDT, he was elected general secretary of the Chemical Workers Union, Fédération des Industries Chimie – CFDT. In 1970 he became a member of the executive body of the confederation, the *Commission Executive*.

He has presided over a CFDT whose membership continued to grow until about the late 1970s before declining quite rapidly in the 1980s. The CFDT remains particularly strong in certain traditionally Catholic regions, parts of the east and west of France, and still obtains approximately 20 per cent of the votes at the election for enterprise committees, which makes it the second most important trade union confederation after the CGT.

In political terms the CFDT has traditionally emphasized the independence *vis-à-vis* political parties but there is no doubt that the revival of the Socialist Party in the 1970s owed much to the support provided by the CFDT and by Edmond Maire in particular. However, towards the end of the 1970s Marie encouraged the CFDT to change its strategy again and, with its new policy of 'resyndicalization', the CFDT turned its back on party politics and re-emphasized its commitment to industrial trade unionism.

In the 1970s there was a real, if conflictual, unity of action between the CFDT and the CGT, which in fact was to outlive the union of the left, if only briefly, and on a number of occasions Maire and

Séguy (q.v.), the leader of the CGT, were to be seen defending similar positions. By the 1980s relations had soured and Maire was rarely to be seen in the company of the subsequent leader of the CGT, Henri Krasucki (q.v.). The CFDT has always criticized the excessive subordination of the CGT to the political wishes of the French Communist Party.

When the Socialist government was elected in 1981, the CFDT played a significant supporting role in spite of its proclaimed autonomy, particularly in the preparation of the Auroux laws which were intended to increase the influence of employees and trade unions in the workplace. When the Socialist government started to introduce certain austerity measures in 1982 and 1983, the CFDT was left in an uncomfortable position, caught between its desire to oppose these measures and its concern not to provide the parties of the right with political ammunition.

Whereas in the 1970s the CFDT had a recognizable, if hazy, ideological commitment to a concept based on workers' control, on the socialization of the means of production and exchange and on decentralized planning (*socialisme autogestionnaire*), this objective was to be gradually dropped and Maire has been engaged in a difficult exercise, searching for a new identity which would provide a realistic definition of trade unionism in the 1980s and ensure the identity of the CFDT *vis-à-vis* the other trade union confederations.

Bibliography

There is no biography of Edmond Maire in English nor in French, but he is the subject of a major profile in H. Hamon and P. Rotman, *La Deuxième gauche* (Paris: Ramsay, 1982). He has published a series of speeches and interviews entitled *Pour un socialisme démocratique* (Paris: Epi, 1971), *Reconstruire l'espoir* (Paris: Seuil, 1980) and *Nouvelles frontières pour le syndicalisme* (Paris: Syros, 1987). He has written *La CFDT aujourd'hui* (Paris: Seuil, 1975) with J. Julliard and *Demain L'Autogestion*, (Paris: Séghers, 1976) with C. Pérignon.

JB

MALRAUX, Georges André (1901–76)

An autodidact, Malraux was involved in adventures in the Far East in his early twenties and by his mid-thirties had acquired a reputation as a left-wing militant and a highly successful novelist. He fought in the Spanish Civil War from August 1936 to February 1937 and from 1944 in the Resistance. At the liberation he became a member of de Gaulle's cabinet, one of the General's closest associates and a founder member, in April 1947, of his anti-Communist and anti-Fourth Republic Rassemblement du Peuple Français. In the 1950s he began publishing a series of highly controversial studies on the plastic arts and on the General's return to power in 1958 rejoined his cabinet. From 1959 until de Gaulle's resignation in 1969 he was his minister of state for culture. From 1969 until his death Malraux wrote prolifically, publishing notably semi-autobiographical essays and further art studies.

Tired of post-war French society, Malraux embarked in 1923–25 upon his Indo-China adventures. The first of these involved the theft of sculptures from Khmer temples in Cambodia and ended with Malraux's trial and ten months' detention in the then French protectorate. The second adventure began in 1925 in Saigon where for six months he co-directed a newspaper attacking the local French colonial administration. Although inspired by his Cambodian experience the newspaper was not, as is so often claimed, a revolutionary organ. However, Malraux's mythical participation in the 1925 Chinese blockade of Hong Kong has lent credence to such an interpretation and the myth, never debunked by Malraux, was reinforced by the documentary style of his two novels inspired by the Chinese revolution, *Les Conquérants* (1928), and *La Condition humaine* which won the Goncourt prize in 1933. His reputation as a left-wing militant was further bolstered by *L'Espoir* (1937), the novel based on his experiences in the Civil War in Spain where for some months he commanded a Republican air squadron.

In the Second World War he fought in the tank corps, was captured and escaped in November 1940. He joined the Resistance in spring 1944 and eventually commanded the Alsace-Lorraine brigade. Disliked by the Communists in the Resistance of whom, like de Gaulle, he was very suspicious, he was instrumental at the First National Conference of the Mouvement de Libération Nationale in January 1945, in defeating their bid for total control of the Resistance movement. Malraux's political career as an unconditional Gaullist had thus begun and he joined the General's cabinet in 1945. His life-story immediately appeared as a bi-partite one comprising a left-wing pre-Gaullist phase followed by a nationalistic Gaullist period, although in fact Malraux's commitment to any left-wing ideology has been exaggerated. In April 1947 he was put in charge of propaganda for the Rassemblement du Peuple

Français and his virulently anti-Communist rhetoric would become the trademark of the movement.

As de Gaulle's minister of state for culture from 1959, Malraux was responsible for re-establishing the primacy of France's artistic and cultural achievements internationally although he is probably best remembered for initiating the cleaning of public buildings in Paris and for creating the politically adventurous *maisons de la culture*. Symbolic of the esteem in which France holds her intellectuals, Malraux's career as a Gaullist owes as much to the General's attachment to this prestigious if controversial figure as to Malraux's fascination with de Gaulle as a world leader.

Bibliography

The best overview of Malraux's life and works is, J. Lacouture, *André Malraux* (New York: Pantheon, 1975). The extended and updated edition of this study exists only in French, *Malraux, une vie dans le siècle 1901–1976* (Paris: Seuil, 1976).

For a more succinct overview see W.G. Langlois, 'The humanism of André Malraux: A commitment for modern man', *Studies in Language and Culture*, vol. XII (Minneapolis: University of Minnesota Press, 1986), pp. 223–40; and for a detailed study of Malraux as a Gaullist see J. Mossuz, *Malraux et le gaullisme* (Paris: A. Colin, 1970).

GTH

'MANDEL', Georges Louis Rothschild (1885–1944)

Mandel adopted his mother's maiden name when he embarked, aged 17, on a career in journalism and politics. Although he moved in Clemenceau's circle from the first, it was only after 1910 that he became one of his main assistants. During the second Clemenceau ministry, from November 1917 until his resignation in 1920, he was his right-hand man. As *chef de cabinet* (principal private secretary) Mandel controlled domestic politics during two dramatic years in which his ruthless tactics and arrogant manner made many enemies. This background, and a political stance modelled on that of Clemenceau's final years, handicapped his own political prospects. Although elected deputy for the Gironde in the Bloc National landslide of 1919, he was defeated in 1924, re-elected by narrow margins in 1928 and 1932, only achieving a secure local base in 1936. He was not a successful speaker in the Chamber, and joined

no political party, being one of the independent 'moderates', or conservatives. Not until 1934 did he achieve ministerial office as minister of posts and telecommunications; he pushed through important developments in airmail, telephones and radio, at the cost of confrontation with the trade unions. Excluded from office by the Popular Front, he returned as minister for the colonies in the Daladier cabinet of April 1938, moving to the key post of the Interior Ministry on 18 May 1940 in the last chaotic days of the collapsing Third Republic. He was the leader of the section of the cabinet opposing an armistice, and was excluded from Pétain's cabinet on 17 June 1940. With a few other deputies who still hoped that France would continue the war he embarked on the ship *Massilia* for Morocco. He arrived to find the armistice concluded, and was arrested on vague and spurious charges. If he had been able to get to England he would almost certainly have headed the Resistance, in place of de Gaulle. But he was never to be released; after four years of imprisonment in France, and at Buchenwald concentration camp, he was murdered by members of the collaborationist French militia on 7 July 1944.

Mandel's career must be deemed a failure. Although as minister of posts and for the colonies he had solid achievements to his credit, he failed to occupy an important post except for his days as minister of the interior in a helpless government on the run before the advancing German armies. Throughout the inter-war period he had argued in vain for stronger French policies towards Germany. He opposed appeasement, although he did not resign at the time of the Munich agreement. His proposals for constitutional change designed to permit stronger and more stable government – he advocated a British-type first past the post electoral system – were equally unachievable. His lack of success was partly due to his political isolation – he was never close to Tardieu (q.v.), another assistant of Clemenceau's whose position on many questions mirrored his own. Other reasons for his failure are his arrogance, although this diminished as he grew older; the somewhat mysterious image he cultivated, and the enmities dating from 1917–19. (The Radical Party's vendetta against Clemenceau weighed in the balance against Mandel until 1936 at least.) But this failure was rooted in the political stance he inherited from Clemenceau in the changed conditions of the post-1919 years. Much of the right was reluctant to accept him because of his anticlericalism – and for some his Jewish race also counted – while the left hated him for his record under Clemenceau.

Bibliography

The authoritative work is John M. Sherwood, *Georges Mandel and the Third Republic* (Stanford, Cal.: Stanford University Press, 1970).

In French, useful as personal reminiscences by men who knew him well are, F.Varenne, *Mon Patron, Georges Mandel* (Paris: Défence de la France, 1947) and G. Wormser, *Georges Mandel, L'homme politique* (Paris: Plon, 1967). Also in French, an account which centres on the local side of his political career, B. Favreau, *Georges Mandel, un Clémenciste en Gironde* (Paris: Pedone, 1969).

DRW

MARCELLIN, Raymond (1914–)

Raymond Marcellin acquired considerable notoriety in the period following the events of May 1968 as a tough and illiberal minister of the interior. His actions in banning organizations and suppressing dissent aroused much protest and contributed to the decline of the electoral popularity of Gaullism; yet he himself had no doubt that France faced an international conspiracy of subversion and his policy reassured those on the right who saw repression rather than reform as the only solution to 1968.

Marcellin's background differed from that of most Gaullists and he has never been a member of a Gaullist party. Born in Sezanne in Britanny, he trained as a lawyer and, like many others, combined support for the values of Pétainism – he taught at Vichy's Université Jeune-France – with Resistance activity. He entered politics as deputy for Morbihan, a traditionally conservative area in 1946 and since then has known no other career than politics (he is unmarried). He has been mayor of Vannes since 1965 and is president of the departmental council of the Morbihan and of the regional council of Britanny. Several times a junior minister in the Fourth Republic, he was also a leading member of the right-wing (but non-Gaullist) Centre National des Indépendants et Paysans. Like most conservatives he supported the return of de Gaulle in 1958; unlike many of them, he took the president's side in the great political drama of 1962 that followed the successful censure motion on the Pompidou (q.v.) government. He was rewarded for his support by being invited to join the new Pompidou administration that followed the Gaullist triumph in the 1962 elections. Between 1962 and 1968 he held the portfolios of public health, industry and planning.

It was the May events, however, that propelled him to the centre of governmental activity. On 31 May de Gaulle appointed him minister of the interior with the comment: 'It is not a pleasant job but Marcellin will do it. He has courage.' His nomination was unexpected but he soon showed his vigour in rousing the police from their disarray and organizing the 1968 elections. He also showed his loyalty to the status quo and in particular to Pompidou by refusing to participate in the campaign of criticism that Giscard d'Estaing (q.v.) had launched against them (though a member of Giscard's party, the Independent Republicans, he was always much closer to Pompidou than to his own party leader). Thus it was no surprise that Pompidou kept him at the Interior Ministry after he became president. Marcellin had an uncomplicated view of his task. With no desire, as he said in a significant aside, to end up like Kerensky, he set about dismantling the organizations which he saw as threatening the survival of the state – extremist groups of the left (Gauche Proletarienne, Ligue Communiste) and right (Ordre Nouveau). He greatly increased the police budget, announcing that if it needed 50,000 police to keep Paris orderly then 50,000 police there would be. He pushed through the 'anti-wreckers' bill of 1971 which made mere attendance at a meeting where violence occurred illegal and attempted to tighten the regulations governing the registration of associations. His actions – and his deliberately heavy style – attracted growing criticism, particularly as the panic of 1968 receded. The discovery that the police had bugged the editorial offices of France's celebrated satirical weekly the *Canard Enchâiné*, contributed to the malaise that accompanied the last stage of Pompidou's presidency and weakened Marcellin. He had always been unpopular with ministerial colleagues who resented his authoritarianism and meddling; and in February 1974 when the dying Pompidou, in an attempt to assure his succession, finally replaced him at the interior with Chirac (q.v.), Marcellin went to the Ministry of Agriculture.

The election of Giscard d'Estaing meant an immediate end to the ministerial career of someone who represented the down side of the Gaullist state (and with whom the new president got on badly). Marcellin retreated in 1974 to the Senate and thereafter devoted himself to the consolidation of his position as political boss of his city and his department.

Bibliography

Marcellin, R. (1969), *L'Ordre public et les groupes révolutionnaires*, Paris: Plon.

Marcellin, R. (1978), *L'Importune vérité*, Paris: Plon, 1978.

DSB/PM

MARCHAIS, Georges René Louis (1920–)

Born in La Hoguette (Calvados) in 1920, Georges Marchais came from a working class, mining background. His early career was as a skilled mechanic (fitter) in the aeronauticals industry with the Société National de Construction Aéronautique du Centre. In this profession, Marchais worked briefly in wartime Germany at the Messerschmitt factory, Neu-Ülm. Following the Second World War, he became involved in trade union activity in the Paris region and, in 1947, joined the French Communist Party (PCF). In 1956, Marchais became secretary of the Seine-South federation of the PCF, where he enjoyed the patronage of PCF leader Maurice Thorez and his wife, Jeanette Vermeersch. Marchais' rise through the party was rapid: he joined the Central Committee and Political Bureau in 1959 and two years later was made responsible for party organization, a key role. In 1970, Marchais became joint general secretary alongside the ailing Waldeck-Rochet and, in 1972, sole leader of the PCF. Whilst leader, Marchais served as a deputy for Val-de-Marne (1973–), a European deputy (1979–) and a member of the Regional Council of Ile-de-France (1976–81). In 1981, Marchais contested unsuccessfully the election for the presidency of France.

A controversial aspect of Marchais' career was his wartime record. Critics, especially former members of the PCF such as Charles Tillon and Auguste Lecoeur, insist that Marchais volunteered to work for Germany before the introduction of compulsory labour regulations in 1943. Marchais denies this accusation and claims to have been forced to work in Germany, before escaping. Intermittently, this issue has resurfaced – especially in the 1970s when Marchais was appointed as leader and then when the PCF seemed on the verge of taking office – and remains a grey area in Marchais' biography. Certainly, there have been doubts among the French Resistance generation in the PCF about the wisdom of choosing Marchais as leader, on account of his apparent non-participation in the Resistance.

In the post-war decade, Marchais worked hard as a trade union (CGT) official and PCF activist before conquering the higher echelons of the party. Throughout the 1960s he earned a reputation for efficiency, plain speaking and pro-Soviet sentiments. In particular, Marchais gained a certain notoriety for his uncompromisingly critical response to the May 1968 social unrest. In *L'Humanité*, the PCF daily press, Marchais attacked the student leader Daniel Cohn-Bendit as a 'German anarchist' and criticized 'false revolutionaries' and left-wing splinter groups. In effect, Marchais minimized and played down the significance of the May events. In the same year, the Soviet Union invaded Czechoslovakia and Marchais led the 'normalization' of this process by which the PCF leadership, despite initial hesitations, accepted the legitimacy of the Soviet intervention in Czechoslovakia. On both these issues (May 1968 and Czechoslovakia), Marchais clashed with leading PCF intellectual Roger Garaudy, and one of Marchais' first tasks as general secretary was to help expel Garaudy from the party.

In the late 1960s and early 1970s, Marchais began effectively to lead the PCF, given Waldeck-Rochet's deteriorating health. Marchais won the seal of approval from all the relevant 'king-makers' – the Thorez family, Waldeck Rochet and the Soviet Union's leadership. In addition, he was popular within the PCF rank and file. At the 20th Conference of the PCF (1972), Marchais became party leader and brought a new dynamism to the movement. With the media and in debate, Marchais earned a well-deserved reputation for sharpness. In the opinion polls, Marchais' image was assessed positively. As leader, he aspired to modernize the party, promote wider debate and formulate a common programme with the Socialist Party.

In 1972, Marchais signed the historic common programme for left-wing government with François Mitterrand (Socialist Party) and Robert Fabre (left-wing Radicals), which realized left-wing gains in the 1973 general election. With left-wing unity strengthened, Marchais committed the PCF to supporting Mitterrand as the left's common presidential candidate in 1974. The course of left-wing unity involved the PCF tying its flag to the slogan 'socialism in French colours', a concept which had figured in Marchais' 1973 book *Le Défi démocratique* and signified the 'opening out' of the PCF. Under Marchais' robust leadership, the PCF adopted a proclaimed liberal democratic face and, alongside the Italian and Spanish Communist Parties especially, posed as 'Eurocommunists'. For Marchais, this entailed snubbing the Soviet Union's international leadership, rejecting the idea of following Communist 'models', opting for a specifically French way to socialism, i.e., full democratic rights, a multi-party system, religious tolerance, free elections, etc., and even abandoning basic Marxist–Leninist doctrine to some extent.

The new direction of the PCF paid mixed dividends. On the one hand, the party enjoyed a better public image and aroused less animosity; on the other, the PCF failed to increase its electorate. Instead, the Socialist Party benefited mostly from the renewed credibility of the left in France. The Soviet leadership had warned Marchais of this possibility. After 1976–7, the PCF moved away from union of the left with Marchais guiding the PCF back towards the Soviet Union on major issues such as the Soviet role in Afghanistan and events in Poland. In 1978, left-wing disunity deprived the left of an anticipated general election victory whilst in 1981 Marchais' presidential campaign was as much against Mitterrand as against the French right.

With the succession of policy and tactical changes during Marchais' leadership, much intra-party criticism was released. For example, intellectuals and activists complained about changes being imposed from above, via Marchais and his supporters, rather than being given full democratic discussion within the party. Some prominent PCF members (notably Louis Althusser and Etienne Balibar) opposed Marchais' Eurocommunist dilution of Marxist–Leninist theory, whilst others (such as Jean Elleinstein and Henri Fizsbin) criticized the subsequent retreat from Eurocommunism. Opposition to Marchais increased as the PCF declined electorally between 1981–6, commencing with Marchais' presidential bid. In a series of elections (presidential, parliamentary, local, European, etc.), the PCF plummeted to less than 10 per cent of the electorate (March 1986), a reduction of 50 per cent or more compared to previous decades.

Inevitably, Marchais' leadership emerged as a bone of contention among party members and was much discussed in popular and academic writing. The decline of the PCF could be attributed to various factors including the rise of the Socialist Party, rejuvenation of the electorate, changing socio-economic class structures and inadaptability of the PCF to rapid societal change. However, for some critics, Marchais' authoritarian style of leadership was a contributory factor to decline. Without doubt, Marchais' public image declined appreciably after 1978. In 1974 31 per cent of French public opinion wanted to see Marchais 'play an important role in the future'. By 1985 this percentage was down to 10 per cent. In 1976 62 per cent (against 16 per cent) of the French opinion viewed Marchais as a 'good' leader for the PCF. In 1985 only 31 per cent (against 51 per cent) shared this viewpoint. Significantly, in 1987

the PCF – with Marchais' approval – chose another candidate (André Lajoinie – q.v.) to represent the party in the 1988 presidential election. By 1987, however, the PCF's opinion poll ratings had fallen and it polled only 6.3 per cent in the presidential election in 1988, though it recovered somewhat at the legislative elections. Moreover, an increasingly organized group of dissident 'renovators' contested the party leadership and Marchais' role.

Marchais' career is notable for several landmarks but the most significant is his accession to the leadership of the PCF. Marchais took over the reins of the largest party on the French left and formerly France's biggest post-war political force. Quickly, Marchais exerted his authority and control over the apparatus. His trade union and organizational background was an invaluable asset. Not unfairly, Jacques Fauvet portrays Marchais as an *apparatchik*.

Under Marchais' direction, the PCF claimed a vocation to govern – the party would 'assume its responsibilities' and accept office in the event of left-wing victory. Paradoxically, the PCF entered the government (four ministers between 1981–4) at a time of electoral decline. After 1982, however, the PCF found difficulty coming to terms with the Socialist Party's policy reformulations and left the government in 1984 following bad PCF electoral results in the European election. Outside the cabinet, the PCF was more able to criticize the Socialist Party's U-turns.

For Marchais, the PCF had erred in some of its political strategy over recent years. For example, too much emphasis had been placed upon leadership negotiations without sufficiently involving rank and file members. Support for Mitterrand's presidential candidature in 1974 and overestimation of the class perspective of the Socialist Party were apparent failings. However, whilst accepting mistakes had been made, Marchais was unwilling to accept any personal blame for the PCF's electoral decline. Unsurprisingly, therefore, internal dissension dogged the party and the optimism of Marchais' 'early' leadership gave way in the 1980s to a phase of 'historic decline'. A common observation was that the party had lost its identity, its sense of direction – strategic U-turns, ambivalence in relations *vis-à-vis* the Socialist Party and doubts over the practice of genuine internal party democracy (i.e., the concept of 'democratic centralism') – leaving members and electors unsure of the essence of the PCF in the 1980s. In the 1988 presidential election Marchais played an important role in André Lajoinie's electoral campaign but the PCF vote slumped to 6.7 per cent.

Marchais' career is dominated by his attachment

to the PCF over four decades and, in particular, his leadership of the party. His leadership may be divided into two phases: first, a relatively successful Eurocommunist period with Marchais' abilities helping to soften the PCF's public image; second, a more unhappy decade of electoral decline, deteriorating public appeal and political crisis. Over both phases, Marchais' authoritative and authoritarian style of leadership prevailed. Despite the 'reformist' nature of the initial period, the PCF proved unable to keep pace with the rapid social changes operative within France and arguably, therefore, Marchais' leadership will be remembered more for the decline of the PCF than the union of the left.

Bibliography

Among Marchais' own writings are *L'Espoir au présent* (Paris: Editions Sociales, 1980), which complements Marchais' campaign for the 1981 presidential election and *Le Défi démocratique* (Paris: Grasset, 1973), which represents Marchais' appeal for 'socialism in French colours'. Also in the Eurocommunist vein are *Parlons franchement* (Paris: Grasset, 1977) and *Communistes et chrétiens, communistes ou chrétiens* (co-author) (Paris: Desclée, 1976). Other major publications include *La Politique du parti communiste français* (Paris: Editions Sociales, 1974), and *Les Communistes et les paysans* (co-author) (Paris: Editions Sociales, 1972), on the PCF's agricultural policy.

Most writings on Marchais are critical and sometimes emotive. Michel Dansel, *Georges Marchais* (Paris: Regine Deforges, 1977) is superficial and dated. Auguste Lecoeur, *Le PCF: continuité dans le changement* (Paris: Laffont, 1977) is written by an ex-PCF stalwart critical of Marchais' wartime record. Pierre Viansson-Ponté, *Lettre ouverte aux hommes politiques* (Paris: Albin Michel, 1976) picks up the same theme but is less persecutionist. Two books are useful for dealing with the early Marchais' leadership: André Laurens and Thierry Pfister, *Les Nouveaux communistes* (Paris: Editions Stock, 1973) and Jacques Fauvet, *Histoire du parti communiste français 1920–76* (Paris: Fayard, 1977). Sofres, *Opinion publique 1986* (Paris: Gallimard, 1986), examines Marchais' image and leadership via opinion polls.

Howard Machin (ed.), *National Communism in Western Europe: A third way for socialism?* (London: Methuen, 1983), is very readable, and especially relevant is Vincent Wright's chapter on the PCF. A view of PCF rank and file is given in Jane Jensen and George Ross, *The View from Inside* (Berkeley, Cal.: University of California Press, 1984). R.W. Johnson, *The Long March of the French Left* (London:

Macmillan, 1981), deals with the common programme phase and its aftermath. Also relevant are the contributions by John Gaffney and François Hincker in Stuart Williams (ed.), *Socialism in France* (London: Pinter Publishers, 1983).

PH

MARIE, André Désiré Paul (1897–1979)

André Marie, whose name is remembered with that of Barangé (q.v.) for his promoting of legislation in 1951 on the financing of the private sector in education in 1951, was a Norman, born in Honfleur. A Radical at a time when the secular ethos in radicalism was becoming less of an absolute, André Marie became a deputy in 1928, was deported to Buchenwald during the war and was, in the Fourth Republic, to be the professional politician par excellence, a man of little passion, even less colour, but supremely available as a last resort to fill cabinet vacancies. At a time when (after the demise of the Communist, Socialist, Centrist governments' *tripartisme*), ephemeral centre left 'Third Force' cabinets struggled to preserve the Republic against the centrifugal forces of Gaullist RPF and the Communist Party, André Marie served in several ministries (he was minister of education for a total of four years) and headed one, for five brief weeks, in July–August 1948. His government was dominated by Paul Reynaud (q.v.) and was chiefly significant as the return to respectability of the men and the political forces thought to have been disqualified by the events of 1940–4.

Marie's was one of those ministries which fell, without a vote in the Assembly, abandoned by one of its constituent parties (the SFIO). It was thus that constitutional arrangements intended to prevent irresponsible overturning of governments were shown not to work, the cabinets themselves, as in this instance, often breaking up even before the constitutional safeguards came into play. A further contribution of André Marie to constitutional practice was the so-called 'Marie constitution'. By the use of an 'unofficial' '*question of confidence*' and by letting it be known that the very existence of his cabinet depended on the support of the Council of the Republic, Marie tacitly encouraged the Second Chamber in its attempt to regain the prerogatives of the Third Republican Senate.

At a difficult moment in the history of decolonization, André Marie struggled manfully with the Indo-China problems; the Bao-Dai solution of June

1948 which he had inherited, and which provided for an independent Vietnam but with associate member status in the French Union (*Union française*) could not be 'sold' to army or to settlers, and was soon shown to be unworkable. It was however as education minister under René Pleven (q.v.) in 1951 that Marie found himself in the church school (*école libre*) controversy, an embarrassment set up by Gaullists, who thereby drew attention to the ideological divide between Socialists (SFIO) and Christian Democrats (MRP) on this contentious issue. The Marie Law (September 1951) provided for the extension to the private sector of the grants (*bourses*) given to secondary school pupils. It was a reversion to a practice advocated by Vichy, but repudiated at the liberation.

André Marie was one of seven politicians approached in May 1953 to break the deadlock after the fall of the Mayer cabinet. He was opposed to Mendès France and to the abandonment of French Algeria and together with Queuille (q.v.) formed a dissident Radical Party in 1956. He disappeared from political view in the Fifth Republic.

Bibliography

Arné, S. (1962), *Le Président du conseil des ministres de la IVe république*, Paris: Librairie Générale de Droit et de Jurisprudence.

MacRae, D. (1967), *Parliament, Parties and Society in France (1946–58)*, London: Macmillan.

de Tarr, F. (1961), *The French Radical Party from Herriot to Mendès France*, Oxford: Oxford University Press.

ACR

MARIN, Louis (1871–1960)

Conservative republicanism, catholicism and intransigent, Germanophobic nationalism were the hallmarks of Louis Marin's ideological standpoint. Born in 1871, the son of a notary, he spent his childhood and adolescence in Lorraine, where he was educated at Catholic schools, including the Collège de la Malagrange, near Nancy, at which Maurice Barrès had been a pupil. Marin took a law degree in Paris, but later turned his interest to ethnology. Elected a deputy for Nancy in 1905, he held the seat with substantial majorities until 1940. After the liberation he was re-elected in Nancy and served until his retirement in 1951. His extreme nationalism disbarred him from the major governmental portfolios, but he served as a junior minister in six governments during the inter-war years. He was respected in the Assembly for his tireless activity in preparing bills and reports, or serving on commissions, though the sanctimonious verbosity of many of his speeches won less admiration.

Marin joined the Republican Federation at its inception in 1903 and was elected one of its Secretaries in 1906. As president of the Federation from 1924 onwards, he so dominated it that it was often referred to as the Marin party. His autocratic leadership aroused antagonisms and caused desertions which depleted the parliamentary group in the 1930s. Yet he also attracted fierce loyalty among the Federation's deputies and grassroots members. Under his presidency, the Federation continued to recruit particularly among the upper bourgeoisie and aristocracy, though its membership extended to the middle and lower bourgeoisie. There were always financiers and industrialists to provide material support. Marin himself was a close friend of the steel magnates, François de Wendel (q.v.) and Edouard de Warren, who became deputies for the Federation.

Marin was a sincere, if critical supporter of the parliamentary system, but his obsessive nationalism and social conservatism (tempered, it is true, by a willingness to support limited welfare and labour reforms) pushed the Federation increasingly to the right, so that in the 1930s it attracted a number of well-known, extreme right-wingers, such as Pierre Taittinger, Jean Ybarnégaray, Xavier Vallat and Philippe Henriot. Many of the Federation's adherents were also members of the right-wing leagues, Les Jeunesses Patriotes or the Croix de Feu. Marin himself showed an equivocal sympathy towards the extraparliamentary leagues of the new right, for so long as he perceived them as subordinate adjuncts, rather than rivals. As with many conservatives, Marin's increasing fear of Soviet influence, and of the possibility of social revolution in France came to outweigh his Germanophobia by the mid-1930s, producing inconsistencies and ambiguities in his views on foreign policy. Nevertheless, in May 1940, he was among those of Reynaud's ministers who opposed the defeatist faction around Pétain. While many former members of the Federation were to be closely associated with the Vichy regime, Marin distinguished himself in the Resistance movement, but when he returned to Parliament following the liberation, the Federation was tarnished by its past associations. After 1946, the organization was no more than a shell. Marin could not prevent the haemorrhage of parliamentary and other members to newer, more vigorous groupings.

Bibliography

In the absence of a serious biography in English or French, see William D. Irvine, *French Conservatism in Crisis. The Republican Confederation of France in the 1930s* (Baton Rouge and London: Louisiana State University Press, 1979) which gives a wider coverage of Marin's career than its title suggests. Most of the material in French is hagiography.

CF

MARQUET, Adrien Théodore Ernest (1884–1955)

The career of Adrien Marquet was intimately linked to the city of Bordeaux (Gironde) where he was born in 1884. In 1924 he was elected as a Socialist for the Gironde and in the following year became mayor of Bordeaux. He was among those Socialists who opposed their party's policy of non-participation in Radical governments. At a party congress in 1933 Marquet, Déat (q.v.) and Montagnon made sensational speeches advocating a whole reconsideration of Socialist ideology. Later that year they broke with the SFIO and founded their own party, popularly known as the 'neo-Socialists'. After the Stavisky riots in February 1934 Marquet became labour minister in the national union government of Gaston Doumergue. In 1939 he was one of the deputies most opposed to war. When the government fled to Bordeaux in June 1940 he provided practical help to the advocates of an armistice, especially his friend Pierre Laval (q.v.). Laval entered Pétain's cabinet on 23 June 1940 and was joined by Marquet, who became interior minister. But on 6 September all Third Republic politicians, except Laval, were sacked by Pétain, and Marquet's moment of glory ended. Brought to trial in 1947, he was sentenced to ten years of 'indignité nationale'. Although he was able to use his continuing popularity in Bordeaux to mount a serious challenge to its new mayor Chaban-Delmas (q.v.), he never regained local power.

Marquet's career was typical of many revisionist Socialists who moved towards fascism and collaboration. They originally quarrelled with the party because they believed that its refusal to accept office and failure to elaborate antidepression strategy were paving the way for fascism. But ironically they ended up proposing remedies against fascism that were indistinguishable from the disease they wanted to cure. Searching for a middle way between doctrinaire socialism and unregulated capitalism, they found it in

'planism': the idea of a national economic recovery plan implemented by a strong state. At the 1933 Congress Marquet, Déat and Montagnon summarized their ideas under the slogan 'order, authority, nation'.

Marquet's greatest influence came in the last days of the battle of France. He turned Bordeaux's town hall into the centre of the peace party, and made things as difficult as possible for those who wanted to continue the war: the British ambassador was originally allocated a chateau 50 kilometres from the city while Laval was put up in the town hall. Marquet's reward for these services was his place in Pétain's government. But, like many politicians who hoped to forge a new career out of defeat, he quickly found himself marginalized. In July 1940 he had approached the Germans in Paris, telling them that Pétain was too old and Laval too tarnished by participation in the fallen regime to carry out a real national revolution. But this race to get the ear of the Germans was won by Laval. And Marquet soon discovered that the Germans had no intention of sweeping away the Vichy conservatives.

When Laval returned to power in April 1942, Marquet refused a place in his government. He displayed similar caution towards Déat's RNP. It was probably this prudence which ensured Marquet's fairly lenient treatment at the liberation. Like many collaborators, he had aspired to a larger role than he had been allowed to play.

Bibliography

Marquet's speech to the 1933 Socialist Congress is published in A. Marquet, B. Montagnon and M. Déat, *Néo-Socialisme? Ordre, autorité, nation* (Paris: Grasset, 1933). R. Dufourg, *Adrien Marquet devant la haute cour* (Paris: Grasset, 1947), summarizes Marquet's defence at his trial.

JTJ

MARTY, André Pierre (1886–1956)

The name Marty recalls heroic moments in the inheritance of revolutionary France: the Commune, the Black Sea Mutiny of 1919, the International brigades. Auguste Marty, father of André, was an escaped communard, and was honoured by a death sentence *in absentia*. He was later pardoned and André was born on 6 November 1886 in his father's Languedoc, at Perpignan.

In 1908, Marty joined the navy as an engineer,

winning officer rank in 1917. In 1919 his ship was with the Black Sea fleet, supporting the Whites. In April Marty, in conjunction with the local Bolsheviks, prepared a mutiny. He was betrayed, and sentenced to twenty years' hard labour. The intensity of support in the fleet made execution dangerous; popular support explains Marty's release in 1923. That year, Marty entered the PCF; his membership was dated from the day of his arrest, in recognition of the living symbol of the insurrectionary spirit.

As the years passed, Marty added to his legend. Elected deputy in 1924, he sat without a tie. In 1927, imprisoned for his part in the PCF's antimilitary campaign, he wrote a vitriolic 'Open letter to Marshal Foch'. War against the military so entered his soul that Marty made inflammatory speeches even after the Popular Front was formed.

In the meantime, Marty, released in 1928 (re-elected in 1928 and released in 1929, member of the Political Bureau in 1931) became, in 1932, a Comintern executive, and in 1935 the Comintern's French section secretary. In 1936 the Comintern sent him to Spain: there he entered world literature, 'immortalized' as 'Massart' in *For Whom the Bell Tolls*. Hemingway's novel makes Marty-Massart the exterminator of the non-Communist left. But the real Marty had been recalled from Spain in April 1937, before the Communist massacres began. Marty's language was full of murder, but he did not organize the death of revolutionaries.

In 1939, the day after the Soviet–German pact, the Comintern summoned Marty to Moscow. In 1943 he was allowed to broadcast to France and, after the dissolution of the Comintern, he was sent to Algiers: there he openly expressed his contempt for Thorez. 'The mutineer of the Black Sea' was never cabinet material: Thorez sought to channel his aggressiveness by appointing him a party secretary, but Marty's tongue made him many enemies. However, he remained the Marat of communism, the man the French bourgeoisie feared and hated most.

On 26 May 1952, just before the demonstrations against General Ridgeway, the new Nato commander, the Political Bureau accused Marty of forming an oppositional centre with Tillon. On 4 September the Central Committee convicted them of 'fractionalism', dropped Marty from the secretariat and forced his self-criticism – *autocritique*. But the fall had only begun: his party guards and car went. A new *autocritique* came, but on 6 November the party doctor who injected the diabetic with insulin left; on 8 November Raymonde Marty obeyed party orders and left. (Marty, a hunted man, took refuge with his brother Jean.) In January 1953 the PCF discovered that Marty had been a police spy, a Titoist and finally an admiralty informer during 1919. Marty was expelled.

Crushed morally and physically, Marty still fought frenetically. In *L'Affaire Marty* (1955) he denounced a plot to eliminate true revolutionaries; but his obsessive aim was readmission. He failed. He died in November 1956, but the same month he sent his congratulations to the Polish Communists as true revolutionaries.

In destroying Marty, the PCF destroyed its own heroic past. Nothing could be more Stalinist. Warts and all, Marty should have been their Saint André; instead, as the French say, he was *martyrisé*.

Bibliography

Yves Le Braz, *Les Réjétés du P.C.F. L'Affaire Marty-Tillon* (Paris: La Table Ronde, 1974), is virtually a biography. See also Philippe Robrieux, *Histoire intérieure du parti communiste*, vols 1 and 2 (Paris: Fayard 1980–81) or Irwin Wall, *French Communism in the Era of Stalin: The quest for unity and integration 1945–1962* (Westport, Conn.: Greenwood Press, 1983). Marty himself wrote about *L'Affaire Marty* (Paris: Deux-Rives, 1955) as well as *La Révolte de la Mer noire* (Paris: Bureau d'Editions, 1927). For a strongly pro-PCF view see Max Adereth, *French Communist Party: A critical history, 1920–1984* (Manchester: Manchester University Press, 1984).

MK

MASSU, Jacques Emile Charles-Marie (1908–)

General Massu was an experienced professional soldier, an active combatant through the Second World War, largely with colonial forces, with General Leclerc's division in Africa and with paratroops in Indo-China after 1945. His posting to Algeria plunged him into politics, a turn of events that he seemed not to have wished and did not sustain. General Massu was above all a decisive officer, determined to carry out orders and to maintain public order. His great wartime operational experience made him an appropriate commander of the 10th Parachute Division in Algeria, a division which included the elite Foreign Legion parachute regiments. He went with the French paratroops to Egypt in the Suez campaign of 1956.

General Massu became a popular figure among soldiers and the white population of Algeria. This reputation rested on the decisive operation known as the 'Battle of Algiers'. This police and military campaign commenced in January 1957 and broke the organization of the Muslim insurgents in the capital by direct, often brutal pressure, based on excellent intelligence and carried out by the paratroop units. Massu always defended the methods of his men on the grounds that they were the only means of carrying out the duties assigned to him. There is no doubt that they were successful in so far as the terror campaign based on the casbah in Algiers was broken.

The fear that the government in Paris would betray the cause of French Algeria drew Massu towards support for de Gaulle. Before a vast crowd in the Forum in Algiers on 13 May 1958, Massu addressed his appeal to de Gaulle. His forthright military approach carried the day and he became president of the committee of public safety. Massu rather than General Salan, his superior officer, was the hero of May 1958. He was rewarded with the position of prefect of Algiers in June 1958, and promoted *général de division*, commandant of the 10th military region. However, in common with other officers he began to doubt de Gaulle's loyalty to the preservation of a French Algeria. This doubt was made public in an interview that Massu gave to a former legionnaire, Klaus Kempski, a journalist on the *Suddeutsche Zeitung*, in January 1960; he suggested that there were limits to the loyalty of the army in Algeria. Perhaps the political outcome of May 1958 had been a mistake. Massu was recalled to Paris.

General Massu did not forsake his duty as a French officer. He served France in Europe, was loyal to de Gaulle in the crisis of May 1968, and never (unlike many other officers) became politically involved in the tragic developments in Algeria after his departure in 1960. He was not a revolutionary, but devoted to his army and the need for order.

Bibliography

Droz, B. and E. Lever (1982), *Histoire de la guerre d'Algérie*, Paris: Seuil. (A full, authoritative account.)

Horne, A. (1977), *A Savage War of Peace*, New York: Viking. (The best account in English, not accurately up to date with the latest work.)

Massu, J.E.C.M. (1971), *La Vraie bataille d'Alger*, Paris: Plon.

Massu, J.E.C.M. (1972), *Le Torrent et la digue*, Paris: Plon.

Montagnon, P. (1984), *La guerre d'Algérie*, Paris: Pygmalion. This is a sharp account by a former officer, a participant in the events.

PS

'MAULNIER, Thierry', Jacques André Talagrand (1909–88)

Thierry Maulnier, a pen-name for Jacques Talagrand, was born in 1909 at Alès (Gard). A brilliant school career enabled him to study in Paris like his father before him at the prestigious Ecole Normale Supérieure, where he entered in the same year-group as Robert Brasillach (1928). Indeed, with his fellow students Brasillach and Maurice Bardèche, Maulnier very soon began to move in circles associated with the *Action Française*. In 1930 he was invited to contribute to the Maurrasian periodical *La Revue Universelle*, and from 1931 onwards he wrote regularly for the daily newspaper *Action Française* as a literary critic: here, in Maurras' orbit, he served his apprenticeship as a writer, critic and journalist.

However, like many other intellectuals of his generation, Maulnier felt increasingly frustrated by the sterility of the Third Republic, and dissatisfied by the political inaction of Maurras' movement. Thus, in the company of other 'non-conformist' intellectuals, as the 1930s went on Maulnier became associated with some of the most important groups and newspapers of the so-called 'jeune droite' ('young right'). In collaboration with young men like Jean-Pierre Maxence, Maulnier contributed regularly to small reviews such as the *Revue Française, Réaction* and *Revue du XX-ème Siècle*. These reviews, by no means united in a doctrinal sense, were all to one degree or another antidemocratic, anticapitalist, and in favour of the renewal of French political and spiritual thinking. As early as 1933, only months after Hitler had come to power in Germany, in a preface to a work on the Third Reich, Maulnier showed how his doctrinal thinking was evolving: he confessed that as a member of the 'young right', he 'felt closer and more readily understood by a German national-socialist than by a French pacifist'. By 1936, Maulnier and his co-editor friend Jean de Fabrègues had set up the review *Combat*, a small but none the less influential venture on the political and intellectual right which, although it was essentially a doctrinal publication, tried to take account of the increasingly critical international situation.

After the election of the Popular Front in 1936, in 1937 Maulnier and Maxence founded *L'Insurgé*, a polemical weekly newspaper in violent opposition to Blum's government. This short-lived publication illustrates Maulnier's continued desire to attempt to wed nationalism, derived but divorced from Maurras, and socialism, freed from Marxist internationalism. His work in *Combat* and *L'Insurgé* inevitably led to accusations from his opponents that Maulnier was espousing fascism. Yet whether or not he was a true Fascist, he did not follow Robert Brasillach in his pro-Nazi sentiments and he did not express the blatant anti-Semitism of those around the *Je Suis Partout* newspaper.

Despite his disenchantment with Maurras's movement, Maulnier continued to write for *L'Action Française*. Once this newspaper had settled in Lyons during the occupation, he resumed his collaboration with it. During this phase, he firmly believed that the appalling tragedy of defeat provided the ideal opportunity for the renewal of France: to this extent, he supported the 'National Revolution', all the while insisting that France should remain free from foreign – including Nazi-German – ideological influences. From mid-1942, as Vichy France became ever more indissolubly embroiled with the Nazis, Maulnier grew further away both from the collaborators and from Maurras: he indicated his change of position with what would be the beginning of his long association with the newspaper *Le Figaro*.

After the liberation Maulnier continued his writing activity. Although in disrepute and on the defensive because of their collaboration, intellectuals on the right had by no means disappeared from the scene. They had however been deprived of many of their publishing outlets and periodicals. In 1948, with François Mauriac, Maulnier was instrumental in setting up the influential review *La Table Ronde*. In a cultural climate dominated by the polarizing effect of the cold war, Maulnier adopted a fiercely anti-Communist position, as demonstrated by the collection of articles published in 1951 entitled *La Face de méduse du communisme*. This work, and his play *La Maison de la nuit* (1953), established Maulnier as a sort of 'anti-Sartre' during the early 1950s.

In September 1958, like so many of his friends on the intellectual right, Maulnier gave his public support to de Gaulle; by 1959 Maulnier's public standing was enhanced by his being accorded the 'Grand Prix de littérature' for his literary output, and in February 1964 he was further rewarded by his election to the Académie Française (French Academy).

Apart from his activities as a playwright and essayist, Maulnier is remembered today as an untiring polemical journalist on the political right. He remained until the very end a vehement opponent of communism, reaffirming in 1983, in a preface to a work on André Gide's flirtation with the Soviet Union, that Western humanism and communism are totally incompatible.

Bibliography

Works by Maulnier
La crise est dans l'homme, Paris: Rieder, 1932.
Preface to *Le 111 Reich* by Van den Bruck, Paris: Rieder, 1933.
Mythes socialistes, Paris: Gallimard, 1936.
Au-delà du nationalisme, Paris: Gallimard, 1938.
La France, la guerre et la paix, Lyons: Lardanchet, 1942.
Violence et conscience, Paris: Gallimard, 1945.
La Face de méduse du communisme, Paris: Gallimard, 1951.
Preface to *André Gide et l'URSS* by R. Maurer, Berne: Editions Tillier, 1983.
Other works
Loubet del Bayle, J.-L. (1969), *Les Non-conformistes des années 30*, Paris: Seuil.
Sérant, P. (1978), *Les Dissidents de l'action française*, Paris: Copernic (esp. pp. 211–44).

MC

MAURIAC, François Charles (1885–1970)

Although best known as a Catholic novelist, Mauriac was also an influential political commentator and polemicist. He was one of the few French Catholics to condemn Franco's 'Christian' crusade in Spain. During the Second World War he was a Resistance writer, but at the liberation he acquired the nickname 'Saint Francis of the Assizes' because of his pleas for clemency for writers condemned to death for collaboration crimes. It was, however, in the 1950s that Mauriac came to the forefront of French political controversy. As president of France-Maghreb, an association working for the reconciliation of French Catholics and Moroccan Muslims, he castigated successive French governments for the repression in Morocco and called for negotiations and ultimate independence for that country and for Tunisia. He relentlessly inveighed against what he saw as the humiliating spectacle of Fourth Republic ministerial instability; the only party political figure he thought capable of restoring national self-respect was the Radical, Pierre Mendès France (q.v.), whose cause he championed in his weekly column in *L'Express*. In de Gaulle, Mauriac was to find his undisputed hero: a leader imbued with authority but within the democratic framework of Fifth Republic institutions, who could restore France's pride and place in the world. It would not be an exaggeration to say that his political writings of the years 1958–70, often repetitive, verge on idolatry.

One should not attempt to discover a high degree of consistency in Mauriac's political journalism or link him closely to any of the established French political traditions. Jealously guarding his political independence, his weekly articles – the *bloc-notes* – often reflected his impulsive reaction to events, a reaction, moreover, usually of a moral rather than of a political nature. Neither can one ignore his obvious delight in engaging in the dubiously Christian, but perhaps typically French, activity of verbal warfare, in which he excelled. In his best period, the 1950s, his *bloc-notes*, a genre he made very much his own, became an institution in French political life. By temperament and upbringing a social conservative, his early association with Marc Sangnier's Christian Democrat Sillon was, however, to leave its mark on him throughout his life. A believer in strong political authority and scornful of Third and Fourth Republic parliamentarianism, he remained a democrat. Though he was a nationalist, he always spurned Charles Maurras and the extreme right.

Bibliography

None of Mauriac's political writings, the five volumes of collected *Bloc-notes* (Paris: Flammarion, 1958–71), his *De Gaulle* (Paris: Grasset, 1964), his *Mémoires politiques* (Paris: Grasset, 1967), has been translated into English. He has been the subject of innumerable biographical and critical studies, but his political development has been most closely studied by Malcolm Scott, *Mauriac, the Politics of a Novelist* (Edinburgh: Scottish University Press, 1980). The most detailed biography published to date is that, in French, of Jean Lacouture, *François Mauriac* (Paris: Seuil, 1980); in English, Robert Speight, *François Mauriac – a Study of the Writer and the Man* (London: Chatto & Windus, 1976), is a useful and readable general study.

HE

MAURIN, General Louis Félix (1869–1956)

Born just before the disintegration of the Second Empire, Louis Maurin pursued a military career that spanned the great dramas between soldiers and statesmen under the Third Republic, from the Boulanger crisis of the 1880s to the challenge of Hitler fifty years later. Maurin had a conventional training, through the officer academies, before spe-

cializing as an artilleryman. Promoted steadily, he gained renown as one of the rising gunnery specialists in the French army in the approach to the First World War. Involved in the 75-mm field gun programme, the famous *Soixante-quinze*, that re-equipped the French artillery with up-to-date firepower by the eve of the conflict, Maurin was secretary to the artillery committee of the general staff in 1914. With the onset of trench warfare and the tactics of attrition by 1915, the gunnery arm assumed an unexpected pre-eminence in the French army, whilst the intensive bombardments made demands of unimagined voraciousness for munitions and artillery. Maurin's career progressed in step with the elevation of the artillery as the new god of war. In 1917, promoted general of division, he consolidated his reputation as a military technocrat by successfully reorganizing the French army's artillery general reserve, a new concept in the massed concentration of firepower for breakthrough or counterattack. After the return of peace Maurin became inspector-general of the artillery in 1921, was appointed to the Conseil Supérieur de la Guerre (the army council) in 1926 and was, the following year, made the French army's first inspector-general of mechanization. In 1934, reaching the age of 65 (the retirement limit for his rank), Maurin was removed from the army's active list and placed on the reserve. This, however, opened the way for the final and political phase of his career, during which he served as war minister in the governments of Pierre-Etienne Flandin (November 1934 to May 1935) and Albert Sarraut (January to June 1936).

Maurin's service record approximates to be a model for a 'Republican general' of the *Troisième*. He was politically favoured by his bourgeois background and technical specialization. For the artillery, along with the infantry, was considered to be more sympathetic to the regime, more reliably Republican, than the allegedly aristocratic and reactionary cavalry officers. In this sense, Maurin is to be located in the school of Joffre and Gamelin; with both of whom he enjoyed friendships and professional connections, not in the conservative cavalrymen's tradition of Foch and Weygand. Contemporaries thought highly of Maurin, a British report in 1935 praising him for having 'brought French artillery to a high standard of technical efficiency and rapidly developed the mechanization of the French army'. Popular with the army itself (which was not universally true of generals who turned politician), Maurin was reckoned a sophisticated artilleryman and a competent 'technocratic' minister.

Politically, Maurin embraced the strategic

orthodoxies of the French establishment of the 1930s. It was in 1935, to the Chamber of Deputies, that he uttered his enduring contribution to anthologies of military quotation with his apologia for the defensive French doctrine between the wars: 'Who can suppose that, after spending millions on fortifying our frontiers, we would ever be so foolish as to leave the safety of the Maginot Line to launch ourselves into who knows what adventure'. In March 1936, when Germany remilitarized the Rhineland, Maurin preached caution. He associated with Gamelin, then commander-in-chief designate and chief of general staff, in advising his colleagues in Sarraut's government that they had to undertake general mobilization and be ready to wage a war if they genuinely wished to respond militarily to Hitler's coup. Maurin, however, was no defeatist. Rather, he understood the cumbersome character of the French mobilization procedure and drew the conclusion from 1914–18 that twentieth-century wars between industrialized European states could not be other than long attritional affairs of the whole nation.

Indeed, Maurin's record as war minister in 1935–6 is creditable. He guided the first serious French military responses to Hitlerism. For, when Germany tore up the military restrictions of Versailles in March 1935, re-establishing compulsory military service and refounding the *Luftwaffe*, Maurin obtained the retaliatory extension of conscription from one to two years. Likewise it was Maurin, later in 1935, who secured 800 million francs of special defence credits for new tank and munitions contracts. It was the beginning of the real rearmament of France.

Bibliography

There is no study of Maurin. The general himself, however, wrote a book of military reflections, *L'Armée moderne* (Paris: Flammarion, 1938).

MSA

MAUROY, Pierre (1928–)

Born in 1928 in the north of France, Mauroy is one of the few French political leaders of genuinely modest origins. He started his career as a secondary school teacher in 1952, before becoming general secretary of the secondary school technical branch of the main teacher's union, FEN from 1955 to 1959. But party political rather than trade union activity was Mauroy's main attraction. From 1950 to 1958

he held the position of general secretary of the Socialist Party's (SFIO) Young Socialists; unlike many contemporaries (such as Michel Rocard) Mauroy remained within the SFIO after 1958. In 1963, he entered the SFIO's *Comité Directeur* and in 1966, he became deputy general secretary of the Socialist Party. That made him appear to be party leader G. Mollet's main protégé, but the image was always somewhat misguided. Mauroy had a strong regional base in North France, and became first secretary of the SFIO *Nord* Federation in 1961 – a position he owed to the support of A. Laurent, the powerful mayor of Lille. Moreover, from 1966 to 1971, Mauroy formed and led CEDEP, a political club operating within the SFIO, but independent of Mollet. The final breach between Mollet and Mauroy came in 1969, when the SFIO leader backed A. Savary rather than Mauroy to lead the new Socialist Party (PS).

Mauroy exacted revenge over Mollet in 1971. In genuine alliance with G. Defferre and conspiratorial collusion with the left-wing CERES group, Mauroy helped Mitterrand take over the leadership of the Socialist Party (PS) in June 1971 at the Epinay Congress and defeated Mollet's candidate, Savary. Mauroy thereby enabled Mitterrand's accession as head of the PS, while providing an indispensable element of continuity with the older SFIO. From 1971 to 1979, Mauroy was national coordination secretary of the new PS, as well as first secretary of the PS *Nord* Federation and reputed to be the 'strong-man' of the organization. In 1973 he was elected mayor of Lille (and regularly re-elected thereafter) to replace Laurent. In October 1974 it was on Mauroy's initiative that the *Assises* of socialism were held, at which Rocard (q.v.) and a minority of the PSU joined the PS, along with some CFDT and associative group activists. For Mauroy, that signalled the new party's determination to include all democratic Socialists within its ranks, but was interpreted by Mitterrand as a possible threat to his leadership.

After the left's defeat in the 1978 general election, serious divergences appeared between Mitterrand and Mauroy, which led to Mauroy's defeat at the PS Congress of 1979 and his eviction from the party leadership (along with Rocard). Mauroy's 'crossing of the desert' lasted until November 1980, when he was appointed as director of candidate Mitterrand's presidential election campaign. Once elected president, Mitterrand appointed Mauroy to be the first Socialist prime minister of the Fifth Republic. The choice of Mauroy as prime minister helped to unite the PS behind the new president. It was also of symbolic value: Mauroy's modest origins would help stress that the left's accession to power had modified the composition of the Fifth Republic's political personnel. Mauroy headed three governments. The first (21 May to 22 June 1981) was formed primarily to prepare for the imminent general election of June 1981, and was composed exclusively at Socialists and their non-Communist sympathizers. The second Mauroy government lasted from June 1981 to March 1983. It included four Communist ministers and carried through the major reforms of the Mitterrand presidency.

The third Mauroy government was formed in March 1983, after the left's defeat in the 1983 municipal elections. It was considerably reduced in size, although it continued to include two Communist ministers of cabinet rank. Mauroy resigned as prime minister in July 1984 (to be replaced by L. Fabius) after he had been disavowed by President Mitterrand over reform of secondary school education.

Before 1981 Mauroy's main significance was as a powerful symbol of the continuity of the French Socialist Party, from SFIO to PS; as a representative *par excellence* of the influence of solid local roots in building political careers in France, and as the personality best embodying the reconciliation of different Socialist traditions (especially those of Christian and lay socialism). Mauroy's crucial early support for Mitterrand facilitated the rallying to the latter's leadership of the most traditional ex-SFIO elements within the new PS, for it was among the large traditionalist federations, along with Socialist local authorities and the solid core of Socialist deputies and senators, that Mauroy counted his supporters within the party.

Mauroy could occasionally impose his choices on Mitterrand against the latter's will. In October 1974 the *Assises* of socialism were held on Mauroy's insistence, despite Mitterrand's lack of enthusiasm. At the June 1977 PS Congress Mauroy publicly criticized Mitterrand's monarchical control of the PS. After the 1978 election defeat, Mauroy demanded a change in party strategy (towards more Socialist 'autonomy'), and a more collegial government of the party. That act of *lèse-majesté* forced Mauroy to confront Mitterrand at the 1979 PS Congress, at which support for his motion trailed a poor third behind those of Mitterrand and Rocard. His party standing suffered from the presidentialization of internal PS politics, which led party members to group themselves around plausible presidential candidates (Mitterrand and Rocard), rather than Mauroy or the left-wing CERES faction. The same effect continues to limit his party audience. However, Mauroy was valued by

Mitterrand after 1979 as a personality who genuinely sought to keep the party united and who represented the organizational continuity of French socialism. After heading Mitterrand's presidential campaign, he was an obvious choice for prime minister.

Mauroy's career illustrates that in the technocratically-inclined Fifth Republic, solid local roots could still (as in the Fourth) act as a substitute to an elitist education at a Parisian *grand école* as a means of succeeding in politics. The elective offices having been held by Mauroy are legion: county councillor in Nord from 1967 to 1973; town councillor from 1971 to 1973, replacing A. Laurent as mayor of Lille in 1973 (and regularly re-elected); deputy for Lille South and South-West (Nord) in 1973, 1978, 1981 and again in 1988, and returned in 1986 as head of the PS list in Nord; European MP from 1979 to 1984; regional deputy since 1986. He was re-elected as deputy for Lille (1), the first constituency of Lille, in June 1988. A number of indirectly-elected offices have added to this elective burden (for example, as president of the Nord Pas-de-Calais region from 1974 to 1981). But the public will remember Mauroy as prime minister.

Mauroy was one of the more original prime ministers of the Fifth Republic. He was the only Socialist prime minister of the first ever united left-wing government alliance (apart arguably from the post-war *tripartite* one). He initially surrounded himself with political advisers who were as likely to have entered politics through the teaching profession, as through one of the elitist *grandes écoles*. Moreover in 1981 two-thirds of his prime minister's office was composed of PS activists, many from his Nord Federation. This break undoubtedly reflected an initial distrust of the permanent civil service. Despite important changes, especially after March 1983 (fewer political advisers, more technocrats on secondment from the full-time civil service), Mauroy's office remained far more politically self-conscious than most of its predecessors.

Mauroy's tenure as prime minister can be divided into three periods, which only partially corresponded with changes of government. From May 1981 until March 1982, Mauroy's government benefited from a 'state of grace' from an electorate anxious to enable a peaceful alternation of power. This period was marked by a spate of important social and political reforms (nationalization, decentralization, redistributive fiscal policies) and an economic strategy aimed at fighting unemployment by reflating the economy. Mauroy was initially closely identified with these policies. For government adversaries, Socialist generosity was bought at the expense of unpardonable economic profligacy, marked by growing balance of trade and budget deficits and an initial devaluation of the franc in October 1981.

As prime minister, Mauroy was acutely aware of pending economic 'catastrophe' should the government not alter its economic policies. It was Mauroy who persuaded Mitterrand to devalue in June 1982 and to adopt a series of deflationary economic measures, notably a wages and prices freeze. The resulting government unpopularity widened the psychological breach between Prime Minister Mauroy and President Mitterrand. None the less, Mauroy remained in firm overall control of the government until the left's resounding defeat in the March 1983 municipal elections.

Mauroy's third government lasted from March 1983 to July 1984. His renomination as prime minister by Mitterrand surprised many political commentators, but it was probably the only means of retaining the Communists in the government. However, Mauroy's effective control over the government was drastically reduced by Mitterrand's appointment of two 'super-ministers' (Delors – q.v. – and Bérégovoy – q.v.) who had prime responsibility for applying the new series of economic austerity measures that accompanied the third devaluation of the franc in March 1983. Control over economic policy, by far the main government preoccupation, now virtually escaped him, while in other areas presidential interventionism increased at Mauroy's expense (in industrial and employment policy for example). Mauroy's position was the unenviable one, often reserved for prime ministers in the Fifth Republic: that of assuming responsibility for unpopular decisions taken elsewhere and of diverting popular discontent away from the president. By June 1984 Mauroy's popularity ratings had sunk to an all-time low, and the left-wing parties had been separately humiliated in the 1984 European election. To add insult to injury, Mitterrand announced in July 1984 that he intended to shelve Savary's contentious education bill, the passage of which Mauroy had made a point of honour. Mauroy resigned shortly afterwards.

As prime minister from 1981 to 1984, Mauroy embodied the changing fortunes of French Socialism during that crucial period. Although inevitably somewhat misleading, a comparison with Blum's (q.v.) Popular Front government of 1936–7 is useful. Both leaders were initially lauded by their supporters for presiding over important social reforms, only to be criticized later for decreeing a 'pause' (a phrase avoided by Mauroy). Both were condemned by political opponents for preferring false social generosity

to rigorous financial management – and later by erstwhile supporters for reversing these priorities. Perhaps more profoundly, the nature of the initial reformism had changed surprisingly little. However, the comparison must not be pushed too far.

Unlike Blum, Mauroy headed a government with a durable parliamentary majority, which was primarily responsible to the presidency for its existence. After three years of increasingly unpopular stewardship, Mauroy resigned, worn out by the exercise of power. That indicated presidential supremacy (with the prime minister holding office on the president's terms). It also pointed to the difficult relationship that exists between president and prime minister in the Fifth Republic, even when they are from the same political camp.

Moreover, Mauroy headed a government which included Communist ministers (for the first time since 1947). He embodied the strategy of the union of the left in government, and continued to advocate a version of this strategy while no longer prime minister. After his resignation as prime minister, there followed a second crossing of the desert from July 1984 until 1986. Despite occasional friction with PS leader Jospin, Mauroy eventually succeeded in joining forces with Mitterrand's supporters at the party's Congress of Lille in April 1987 to create a new mainstream force (the Jospin–Mauroy *courant*) within the PS. This consolidation of his party position concealed a recognition by Mauroy that he would never achieve the party's presidential nomination. His manoeuvring finally paid off in May 1988, after Mitterrand's re-election as president, when Mauroy succeeded Jospin as first secretary of the Socialist Party. The event was of considerable importance: President Mitterrand had made clear his preference for his second prime minister Laurent Fabius, the modernizer, over his first, Pierre Mauroy, the traditionalist social-democrat. Mauroy's accession marked the most serious rebellion ever against Mitterrand by his own lieutenants within the PS: even most of Mitterrand's closest supporters preferred Mauroy to Fabius. Many observers concluded that this act of defiance towards the founding father marked the beginning of a new era within the PS: that of *l'après-Mitterrand*. Under a leader of Mauroy's stature there were likely to be limits to which the party, albeit the 'presidential' party, would allow itself to be treated as a mere tool of Mitterrand's will. By preferring Mauroy to Fabius, the Socialist Party regained a degree of autonomy from the president, emphasized its public refusal to be transformed into an 'American Democratic Party', and reaffirmed its Socialist identity, as it had become personified by Mauroy.

Bibliography

Bauby, P. (1984), *Le Cabinet du premier ministre depuis l'alternance au pouvoir de 1981*, Institut d'Etudes Politiques de Paris: DEA thesis.

Bizot, J.F. (1976), *Au Parti des socialistes*, Paris: Grasset.

Cole, A.M. (1985), *Factionalism in the French Parti Socialiste, 1971–1981*, University of Oxford: D. Phil thesis.

Pfister, T. (1977), *Les Socialistes*, Paris: Albin Michel. (Bizot and Pfister are both interesting on Mauroy's early career.)

Pfister, T. (1985), *La Vie quotidienne à Matignon au temps de l'union de la gauche*, Paris: Hachette. (An excellent study of the 1981–4 governments.)

AC

MAURRAS, Charles Marie Photius (1868–1952)

Few writers in twentieth-century France have caused as much passionate and controversial debate as Charles Maurras. Indeed some would argue that it is impossible to remain objective when assessing the achievement of this leader of the intellectual right. Some commentators have seen him as an incomparable and genuinely original thinker, while others would consider him the most dangerous sophist and political charlatan the century has ever known. In brief, with his distillation and mixture of positivist thought, right-wing traditionalism, anti-republicanism and monarchism, Maurras, inseparably linked with the Action Française movement, stands as a major figurehead among the forces of counter-revolution in France between the turn of the century and the end of the Second World War.

He was born on 20 April 1868 in Martigues into a Provençal family which counted magistrates, officers, doctors and sailors among its ancestors. His father, a local tax-collector, died in 1876 when the young Maurras was only 9. Although he had been exposed to a variety of political influences, the greatest was that of his mother, a devout Catholic, and whose own mother had harboured a visceral horror of the 1789 Revolution. The family moved to Aix-en-Provence where Maurras attended the Catholic College; here he received an intensive Catholic education. When he was 14, he was suddenly afflicted by an almost total deafness which caused him to abandon his hopes of becoming a naval officer. A little later he lost his religious faith, and he steeped himself in studies of philosophy. He was a successful student and, after gaining the *baccalauréat* he moved to Paris in December 1885 to pursue his studies and begin his writing career.

Paris made a very profound impression on the young provincial. He began to move in Catholic and conservative circles, and contributed articles of mainly literary criticism to a wide range of periodicals. According to his autobiography *Au signe de Flore* (1931), he was deeply disturbed by the number of foreign names on the Paris boulevards: from this time on a blend of aestheticism, xenophobia and nationalism developed in Maurras, a blend which evolved rapidly during these lively formative years and which would not substantially change. Historical circumstances too bore an influence: these were the troubled years of the early Third Republic, marked by events such as the publication of Drumont's *La France juive*, the Panama scandal and the Boulanger affair. He struck up a friendship with Jean Moréas, the anti-symbolist poet, met and was patronized by Maurice Barrès (q.v.) and Anatole France, among the major literary figures of the day; they gave Maurras much encouragement.

In Paris he had become deeply nostalgic for his native Provence: he joined with the Félibres, a Parisian group of followers of the Provençal poet Mistral. This had a political significance in so far as Maurras himself made demands which went beyond regional folklore or aesthetics: he called for provincial decentralization, restoration of the former provinces and recognition of the Provençal language. Maurras saw Provence and, in an ideal world, the French nation, as the real inheritors of the Graeco-Roman tradition. These Mediterranean cultures, infused with warmth, light and goodness, stood in opposition to the cold, misty or barbarian cultures of the north and east. Judaism and (particularly Protestant) Christianity and their traditions had, believed Maurras, corrupted Europe ever since their spread through western Europe.

A further element in Maurras' intellectual development is his anti-Germanism. This is in part attributable to the ever-present atmosphere of revenge for France's defeat in the Franco-Prussian War of 1870–1; yet through his reading of Fichte's work he became increasingly aware of German nationalism. The experience of reporting the Olympic Games in Athens in 1896 was a further spur to his realization that the nation should be considered as paramount – 'politique d'abord!' (politics first!) – this would become Maurras' rallying cry, based on the premise that it is the state, or national interest, which dictates the order and meaning of human existence; everything else can only be accessory. Subsequently Maurras was to fuse nationalism and monarchies together into his own 'doctrine' and that of the *Action Française* – it came to be known as 'integral nationalism'.

The major turning point for Maurras was the Dreyfus affair. In its early stages the affair was seen as little more than a controversial legal matter, despite the extraordinary circumstances surrounding it. Through the persistence of the Dreyfus family, and the support of such as Emile Zola (q.v.) ('J'accuse!' appeared in *L'Aurore* on 13 January 1898), the affair became an issue in which the 'national interest' was a major factor. When, in September 1898, Colonel Henry committed suicide after his arrest for forging documents, many took this as an admission of guilt. The complicity in the affair of the army would be openly exposed and beyond doubt; Maurras, however, in the first of a series of articles in the *Gazette de France* entitled 'Le premier sang' ('The first blood'), came unequivocally to Henry's defence. Using heavily emotive language he characterized Henry's suicide as a martyrdom for France: Henry had only acted in the interests of France. Looking back thirty years later Maurras saw this 'action' as the beginning of his career as a polemical journalist: he wrote that it was 'the best action and, in any case, the most useful action of all those for which I have reason to rejoice' (*Au signe de Flore*, p. 82).

This period also represents Maurras's most intensive phase of activity as regards the development of his 'doctrine'. In the 1899 essay 'Les Monod peints par eux-mêmes' (collected in *Au signe de Flore*, 1931) he outlined the famous Maurrassian doctrine of the 'quatre états confédérés ('four confederated states') to which he adhered throughout his life. In it he identified the Jews, Protestants, Freemasons and aliens (his word is 'métèques') as the sworn enemies of France; through their manipulation of liberal democracy they intended to subjugate the nation to further their own interests. Maurras' blatant anti-Semitism, in part derived from his earlier cultural musings and spurred on by the Dreyfus affair, would develop into a frenzy later in the 1930s. In 1900 there followed the wide-ranging *Enquête sur la monarchie* in which Maurras substantiated his neo-royalist 'doctrine', and in 1905 appeared the influential essay *L'Avenir de l'intelligence*, in which he berated the subservience of intelligence and opinion to plutocracy: his alternative 'elitist' system would be genuinely liberating.

In a successful attempt to rally the right-wing anti-Dreyfus intelligentsia, the Ligue de la Patrie Française came into being in late 1898; elements from this and another group formed in the wake of a manifesto called 'Action française', fused in the summer of 1899 into the movement which Maurras then came to dominate. The major difference between Maurras and the other founding figures (Maurice Pujo (q.v.) and Henri Vaugeois (q.v.) was that Maurras was the only monarchist in the group. Although many of the founders of Action Française came from liberal and Republican backgrounds, they were eventually persuaded by Maurras in works such as *Enquête sur la monarchie* (1900) that French nationalism would never be complete – or 'integral' – until it had been totally dissociated from the ideas and heritage of the French Revolution. Since the execution of Louis XVI the only ideology to serve the interests of the 'real France', by countering the political legacy of the Revolution – liberal and parliamentary democracy – was monarchism; thus integral nationalism should be essentially monarchist. Yet Maurras' movement, Action Française, was certainly not exclusively monarchist in terms of its adherents' own backgrounds or beliefs. Part of its strength was precisely that it gathered together personalities from so many different, sometimes nonconformist, political or intellectual *milieux*. This was because, as René Rémond puts it, nationalism led them to monarchism, not the inverse. What initially united such as Jacques Bainville, Léon Daudet (q.v.), Louis Dimier and Pierre Lasserre in the first years of the Action Française was not necessarily their monarchism, it was rather their common opposition to the Third Republic and its social works. Yet this diversity would, in the long run, also ensure that there were many personality clashes. Because of Maurras' own doctrinaire intransigence, there were numerous 'dissidents' from the Action Française, including figures such as Georges Bernanos, Louis Dimier and Robert Brasillach.

During the 1900s Maurras' ceaseless polemical writings lent Action Française increasing momentum: by March 1908 the movement had its own daily newspaper. Financially supported by Léon Daudet, it appeared uninterrupted until August 1944 in a total circulation which never exceeded, on average, 100,000 copies (see Eugen Weber). After the consolidation of the Radical Republic in 1905, Action Française and its street gangs, Les Camelots du Roi, demonstrated frequently and violently until 1914. In fact the years 1900 to 1914 were the best years for Maurras and his followers, and the outbreak of the First World War seemed for many to justify adopting a strong nationalist position, since the war was seen as a struggle between European imperialisms. The war effort forced Maurras into supporting a domestic political truce in the shape of the *Union Sacrée* (Sacred Union), yet this did not prevent him from relentlessly pursuing those whom he considered as traitors. After the war Maurras' reputation was at its zenith. Action Française benefited from the election of the so-called 'sky-blue' Chamber – 'Chambre bleu horizon': Léon Daudet was elected as an Action Française deputy. Yet thanks to Clemenceau (q.v.) the Republic had emerged fortified from the war and any hopes of a royalist restoration seemed ever more remote. In the 1924 elections Action Française candidates were thoroughly defeated and Daudet lost his seat.

One major setback was the condemnation of Maurras' movement by the Vatican in 1926. During the 1900s the extreme anti-republican conservatism of Action Française had appealed to a great many Catholics, and in turn they had given him much support for his attacks on the 'anticlerical' Republic. Yet Maurras' relationship with the Catholic Church was ambiguous. If he had endeared himself to traditional antimodernist Catholics in his attacks on Marc Sangnier's (q.v.) liberal-democratic Sillon movement (see *Le Dilemme de Marc Sangnier,* 1906), he himself was considered with much suspicion by the Vatican hierarchy, not so much for his professed agnosticism, but because the doctrine of 'politique d'abord!' subordinated the spiritual authority of the Church to a political creed. After a series of warning signs, Pope Pius XI's condemnation finally came in December 1926: Catholics were not permitted to belong to a movement which placed party interests above religion. If they disobeyed they would be denied the Church's sacraments. Maurras's forthright reply only compounded the crisis and, in addition to the ground lost to the conservative Poincaré (q.v.), Action Française entered its long phase of decline. Within a few months the movement's newspaper also lost half its readers.

However, the extreme right tends to flourish in times of crisis. In the wave of antiparliamentary protest after the 1932 elections, culminating in the riots of 6 February 1934, Maurras and his followers were again a force to be reckoned with. But Maurras missed the opportunity presented by this attack on the National Assembly and, once again, triggered the dissatisfaction of many young intellectuals who had hopes of a Maurras-led 'coup de force'. For fascist sympathizers such as Lucien Rebatet, Maurras' movement was now 'Inaction française'. None the less, between the election of the Popular Front under Léon Blum (q.v.) in 1936 and the outbreak of the Second World War, Maurras continued his relentless daily attacks on what he saw as the two principal enemies of France: Hitler and the democratic Third Republic.

On the one hand Maurras never tired of warning his readership about the menace of Hitler: he predicted that one of the aims of Nazi expansionism was to crush France and recommended that in order to avoid war, treaty obligations in eastern Europe should be broken. French blood should not be split, he believed, for Czechs, Jews or any other 'foreign Nation'. This attitude explains his pro-Munich stance when Britain and France capitulated to Nazi demands on Czechoslovakia.

On the other hand, Maurras and his satellites throughout the right-wing press waged a war of words and calumny against the personalities of the Popular Front both before and after its election in June 1936. It was a concerted attack against what many on the extreme right saw as the 'Jewish Republic' led by Léon Blum who, tired of the endless stress fighting and after being physically attacked by members of the Ligue d'Action Française, banned the leagues.

If the political influence of Action Française went on declining (in December 1937 the pretender to the French throne disavowed the movement's claim to represent the royalist cause), Maurras himself continued to enjoy great national and international prestige. Between October 1936 and July 1937 he served his sentence for 'incitements to murder' (particularly against the person of Blum); this provided him with an aura of martyrdom which the right-wing press exploited lavishly. He was nominated for the Nobel Peace Prize whilst in prison and, on 9 June 1938, he was finally elected to the Académie française (French Academy). With the outbreak of war and the ignominious routing of the French by the German blitzkrieg, Maurras and his newspaper were forced to flee the capital. For him the defeat was an atonement for the fact that France had suffered '70 years of democracy'; and it is no surprise that he expressed 'joy and hope' in the 10–12 July 1940 issue of *L'Action Française* on learning that Marshal Pétain had been granted full powers.

Maurras gave Pétain much support. Although at first the Vichy regime appeared to put into practice all the principles of the counter-revolution as advocated by Maurras over the last forty years, with Pétain as a sort of surrogate king figure, from mid-1942 Vichy became ever more enmeshed in the Nazi machine. Although Maurras criticized many of his former pupils active in the pro-Nazi collaboration, he continued to publish *L'Action Française* in Lyons throughout the occupation. In it he berated all those working against France, including Jews, Freemasons, Communists, Gaullists, Christian-Democrats, the Allies and the Resistance, to the point of encouraging the betrayal of potential Nazi victims to the authorities. Arrested on 8 September 1944 and charged with 'intelligence with the enemy', he was condemned to life imprisonment in January 1945, aged 76, uttering the legendary cry 'this is the revenge of Dreyfus!'. In March 1953 he was transferred to a clinic near Tours and died there on 16 November.

Thus Republican France lost one of its own most persistent opponents. As regards any assessment of his political achievement, his sheer persistence and energy ensured that he had always been at the front of the public stage: in his journalism alone, with at least one daily and often substantial text in the *L'Action Française*, he produced well over 13,000 articles. It is arguably of secondary importance that Maurras' doctrine was in character reactionary and in practice sterile, and thus condemned to failure. Yet for some, even if they were aware of the impossibility of a royalist restoration, once monarchism was subtracted from Maurrassianism, it represented a body of ideas as coherent as Marxism. Most important is that despite his constant claims that all he did was in the best interest of 'the real' France, Maurras did more in the inter-war period to sap the morale and strength of the French nation than any other single individual.

His influence was undoubtedly greatest in intellectual circles. Successive generations of young writers in France and elsewhere, many of them highly talented, came under the spell of Maurras and some served their apprenticeship in his sphere of influence. Even before he died, after the war a further generation of 'Maurrassians' emerged, setting up and editing numerous periodicals (*Aspects de la France, Ecrits de Paris, La Nation Française* (Pierre Boutang), *L'Esprit Public* (Jacques Laurent), *La Parisienne, Défense de l'Occident* (Maurice Bardèche) and *Rivarol*. And, although Jean-Marie Le Pen's (q.v.) National Front accepts Republican parliamentary democracy, much of the rhetoric used in debates about immigration and the search for French 'identity' ('La France aux Français! – 'France for the French') may be traced to Maurras and his ideas. For as long as the extreme right survives in France, its followers will always owe a debt to Maurras.

Bibliography

Works by Maurras (dates given are of first editions)
Kiel et Tanger, Paris: Bibliothèque des oeuvres politiques, 1910.
Au signe de Flore, Paris: Les Oeuvres représentatives, 1931 (autobiography).

Dictionnaire politique et critique, 5 vols, Paris: Cité des livres, 1932–5.
Mes idées politiques, Paris: Fayard, 1937 (the best introduction).
La seule France, Paris: Lardanchet, 1941.
Works relating to Maurras
Birnbaum, P. (1988), *Un Mythe politique: la 'République juive'*, Paris: Fayard.
Capitan Peter, C. (1972), *Charles Maurras et l'idéologie de l'Action française. Etude sociologique d'une pensée de droite*, Paris: Seuil.
Chebel d'Appollonia, A. (1988), *L'Extrême-droite en France de Maurras à Le Pen*, Brussels: Complexe (concise, accessible and up-to-date).
Curtis, M. (1959), *Three Against the Third Republic, Sorel, Barrès and Maurras*, Westport, Conn.: Greenwood Press, 1959 (good general study in English, placing Maurras in context).
Girardet, R. (1957), 'L'Héritage de l'Action française', *Revue française des sciences politiques*, vol. VIII, no. 4, October–December, pp. 765–92 (excellent, remains useful).
Weber, E. (1962), *Action française: Royalism and reaction in twentieth century France*, Stanford, Cal.: Stanford University Press (remains the best history of the movement).

MC

MAYER, Daniel (1909–)

A journalist by profession, Daniel Mayor was general secretary of the French Socialist Party (SFIO) in the immediate post-war period and served as a minister in a number of governments in the late 1940s.

He was born in Paris and attended primary school in the 20th *arrondissement* of the city. He joined the Socialist Party at the end of 1927 and was active in the Young Socialists' organization in the early 1930s. In July 1933 he was appointed to the staff of his party's main newspaper, *Le Populaire*, and reported for it on social affairs throughout the years of the Popular Front.

During the war he played a prominent part in the Resistance movement. At first he was general secretary of the underground party in the southern, unoccupied portion of France and then, in 1943, after a mission to London, he became secretary-general of the clandestine Socialist Party for the whole of France. He also represented his party on the National Council of the Resistance. He continued as general secretary after the liberation of the country and tried to make his party more effective and better organized than it had been before the war. However, disappointing election results and frustration with the heavy responsibilities which the Socialists had to bear in post-war politics caused a reaction against his leadership and his annual report to the party's National Congress in August 1946 was rejected. He then resigned as secretary-general and Guy Mollet was appointed in his place.

Daniel Mayer was now on the threshold of a distinguished parliamentary career. He was a Socialist deputy representing the Seine department in the National Assembly throughout the Fourth Republic and was a minister in the Blum administration of December 1946 to January 1947 and in six successive governments from May 1947 to October 1949, in which his chief responsibility was the labour portfolio. In the early 1950s he opposed the idea of a European Defence Community and in 1956 he criticized the Mollet government's Algerian policy and its part in the Suez intervention. During the political crisis of 1958, he was one of several Socialists who opposed General de Gaulle and in September 1958 he joined with Edouard Depreux and others in forming the Autonomous Socialist Party (PSA), which was absorbed into the Unified Socialist Party (PSU) in 1960. He later joined the new Socialist Party, founded in 1971.

He has devoted a great deal of his time to work for human rights in recent years, serving as president of the League for the Rights of Man from 1958 to 1975. In 1977 he became president of the International Federation for the Rights of Man. In 1983 President Mitterrand appointed him president of the Constitutional Council.

Bibliography

Juin, C. (1982), *Liberté . . . Justice . . . Le combat de Daniel Mayer*, Paris: Anthropos.
Mayer, D. (1969), *Pour une histoire de la gauche*, Paris: Plon.

BDG

MAYER, René Joël Simon (1895–1972)

Born in Paris in 1895, René Mayer had a short but influential political career under the Fourth Republic. After joining the French liberation committee in Algiers in 1943, he served in de Gaulle's provisional government in 1944. Returning to ministerial office in 1947, he held a series of important posts (finance, justice, defence), before himself win-

ning the premiership of 1953. As deputy for Constantine in Algeria from 1946 to 1955, he was leading member of the North African lobby and of the aggressively conservative 'neo-radical' grouping which controlled the Radical Party machine in the early and mid-1950s. He was also an advocate of the cause of European integration and before the war played a big role in the creation of the French national railway system (SNCF).

Mayer came late to politics, having built a successful career as a business administrator in the inter-war years. The son of a businessman, educated at the Lycée Carnot school in Paris, Mayer took degrees in law and literature and gained a diploma from the Ecole Libre des Sciences Politiques in Paris before serving as an artillery officer in the First World War. After joining the Conseil d'Etat in 1919, Mayer gained useful experience of the governmental process, serving with three ministers as head of their private office in the mid-1920s. He also taught a course on administrative law at Sciences Po from 1927 to 1933. From 1925 his expertise in this field earned him a growing number of posts in business administration, primarily in the public sector (with the autonomous port of Strasbourg and the Rhine Navigation Company, followed by posts in a broader range of utilities including railways, electricity, water, and Air France). His Jewish origins, however, led to his removal from all these posts in 1941.

His short premiership, from January to May 1953, was noteworthy primarily because his investiture was the first occasion on which the bulk of the Gaullist parliamentary group voted in support of a candidate prime minister, thus helping precipitate de Gaulle's dissolution of the Gaullist movement later in the year. In February 1955 his biting attack on Mendès France's liberal proposals for France's North African protectorates was the signal for the end of the latter's premiership. In the subsequent struggle for control of the Radical Party, Mayer found himself summarily expelled from the party in December 1955 along with Martinaud-Deplat and Lafay. However, he had already been nominated as president of the high authority of the European Coal and Steel Community, replacing Jean Monnet there in June 1955. When he left this in September 1957, he returned to business adminstration, joining a number of international companies.

Bibliography

R. Mayer, *Etudes, témoignages, documents* (Paris: PUF, 1983), a collection edited by his widow, Denise Mayer, provides a full account of Mayer's career in

French. In English useful details on his role in the Radical Party under the Fourth Republic can be found in F. de Tarr, *The French Radical Party from Herriot to Mendès-France* (Oxford: Oxford University Press, 1961) and F. O'Neill, *The French Radical Party and European Integration* (Aldershot: Gower, 1981).

JL

MÉDECIN, Jacques François Xavier Paul (1928–)

Jacques Médecin exemplifies two continuous features of political life in modern France – the existence of city bosses whose power resides in the assiduous use of clientelism and the persistence of a hard right that, even before the emergence of Le Pen (q.v.) was only loosely attached to mainstream political organizations. Médecin's position at Nice owes everything to his father, Jean, who was mayor of the city and its parliamentary representative from the Third Republic to the Fifth. Jean Médecin created a powerful political machine – known locally as the 'Camorra' – which linked town hall to powerful business interests (notably in tourism) and also, via a series of ward organizations, to the ordinary citizens. He had the good fortune to be deprived of his town hall by the Vichy government in 1943 an act which enabled him to shake off his earlier associations with Fascist leaders like Doriot (qv.) and Darnand (qv.). Yet his sympathies remained with the far right. His support of de Gaulle in 1958 had been based on the belief that de Gaulle would keep Algeria French. As French policy moved towards independence, Médecin was a resolute defender of the cause of French Algeria; Nice received many of the returning settlers (*rapatriés*) and its mayor voted the censure motion on the Pompidou government in autumn 1962.

When Jean Médecin died in 1965, his son Jacques, who had hitherto pursued a career in journalism, inherited the town hall, the parliamentary seat, the system and the political beliefs of his father. At that stage a strong anti-Gaullist (he once ejected from a municipal reception one of the judges who had condemned de Gaulle's would-be assassin to death) he was linked to the extreme right Alliance Républicaine pour les Libértés et le Progrès of Tixier-Vigancour (qv.), before moving to the centre. First elected to Parliament in 1967 on a local label (the Rassemblement Républicain) he later joined the centrist Progrès et Démocratie Moderne and campaigned for Poher (q.v.) against Pompidou (q.v.) in 1969 using the slogan 'Why sack the master and keep the servant?' In 1973 he was a member of the opposition centrist grouping, the Mouvement Réformateur, led by Lecanuet (q.v.) and Servan-Schreiber (q.v.). In the great simplifying duel of left and right in 1974, he naturally supported Giscard d'Estaing (q.v.) and became a member of the new president's Parti Républicain. In 1976 he was appointed junior minister of tourism and leisure in the government of Raymond Barre (q.v.) but was dropped after the 1978 elections. Joint head of a wholly unsuccessful dissident right list in the 1979 European elections, he became increasingly attracted to the muscular neo-Gaullism of Chirac (q.v.) and it was as a member of the RPR that he was elected for the last time, to the National Assembly in 1986. He did not stand in 1988.

Médecin is the kind of politician whom it is polite to call colourful. He claims to be descended from the Italian Medicis, he defends the twinning of Nice with Cape Town and he has been assiduous promoter of his city (e.g. the Nice International Book Fair). He has also been accused of links with the underworld, notably the neo-Fascist bank robber Spaggiari, and has been the subject of a strong attack from the author Graham Greene. Too controversial to be a significant national figure, his easy victory in the 1989 municipal election in Nice showed his continuing local appeal. But by the end of 1989 he was in serious legal difficulties over allegations of malpractice.

Bibliography

Franca, M. and J. Crozier, *Nice, la baie des requins* (Paris: A. Moreau, 1982) is a hostile book.

PM

MÉHAIGNERIE, Pierre (1939–)

Pierre Méhaignerie has been deputy for Ille-et-Vilaine since 1973, president of the centrist Centre des Démocrates Sociaux (CDS) since 1982 and minister of equipment, land-use planning, environment, housing and transport since March 1986. He was born into a Breton family with long political ties; his father was a deputy for the Christian Democrat Mouvement Républicaine Populaire and his grandfather a departmental councillor. He was born in Baluze, educated in Paris and Rennes and after graduating top from the Ecole Nationale Supérieur des Sciences Agronomiques trained as an *ingenieur des eaux et forêts* (waterways and forestry engineer). He worked as an engineer firstly in Tunisia (1965–7) and then in Bordeaux before being seconded in 1969 to work in the personal staff (*cabinet*) of Jacques Duhamel, firstly at the Ministry of Agriculture (1969–71) and then at Cultural Affairs (1971–3). As well as holding national office, Mehaignerie has been a departmental councillor since 1973, mayor of Vitré (Ille-et-Vilaine) since 1976, and president of the Ille-et-Vilaine departmental council since 1982. In 1976, at the age of 37 he became junior minister for agriculture in the Barre government, holding full ministerial responsibility for agriculture from 1977 until the defeat of Giscard d'Estaing (q.v.) and the conservative government in 1981.

From his well-embedded local roots, Méhaignerie has become a powerful spokesman for the centre right and has established himself as an extremely competent and assiduous minister. As for many young civil servants with political leanings his years in a ministerial *cabinet* helped to familiarize him with the corridors of power and provided a useful jumping-off point for a political career. Once elected in 1973 he became attached to the reformist and centrist group in the National Assembly where he soon established himself as a skilled negotiator. He has held the seat for Ille-et-Vilaine since 1973, being re-elected at the first ballot in 1981, in the face of a national swing to the left, with the biggest majority in France. As president of the CDS he has done much to strengthen their position within the Union for French Democracy (UDF), of which they are a constituent part, and he has naturally emerged as the spokesman for the seven CDS ministers in the government. His ministerial career has been equally impressive. As minister of agriculture, the youngest member of the Barre government of 1976, he soon established a reputation for himself both in Paris and Brussels. His knowledge of local politics gave him an empathy for the problems of farming and the main French agricultural lobby, the FNSEA, appreciated his honesty and robustness as a minister. Unusually, he held the post for sixty-four months, one of the longest ministerial tenures of the Fifth Republic. The portfolio of the giant Ministry of Equipment and Environment was given partly as a recognition of his ministerial skills of management and negotiation.

Politically Méhaignerie can be placed, along with his close associates Jacques Barrot and Bernard Stasi, on the progressive and reformist wing of the CDS. He sees the party as a corrector to some of the excesses of economic liberalism of the Chirac administration and has argued, discreetly, since 1986, for a more humane approach to social and employment policy. Like most of his CDS colleagues he supported Raymond Barre as the potential UDF presidential candidate. However, a pragmatist by nature, he has not ruled out alternative alliances for his party.

Bibliography

Pierre Méhaignerie is the subject of a short profile in A. Duhamel, *Les Prétendants* (Paris: Gallimard, 1983).

ER

MÉLINE, Jules Félix (1838–1925)

Méline was a politician of the Third Republic, associated especially with protectionism and the defence of agriculture. As prime minister between 1896 and 1898, Méline headed one of the longest-lasting governments of the Third Republic, based on an alliance of conservative forces. His brand of socially conservative republicanism, associated with the defence of established economic interests, came to be known in the early twentieth century as 'progressism'.

An advocate by profession, Méline represented the Vosges department, as deputy or senator, from 1872 to 1925. He was a promotor of the tariff law of 1881, France's first major departure from free-trade principles, and was minister of agriculture in 1883–5. As chairman of the Chamber's committee on tariffs, he was largely responsible for the protectionist system known as the 'Méline tariffs' enacted in 1892. These tariffs covered both industry and agriculture, but Méline was identified especially with the latter. He saw the peasant base of French society as a source of stability and moral virtue, and this 'agrarian' theme was a feature of his speeches. He adopted the slogan 'Neither revolution nor reaction', which corresponded to the attitudes of many peasant supporters of the Republic.

Méline claimed throughout his career to be faithful to the Republican heritage of Gambetta and Ferry (q.v.), in which social reform had little place. But in the 1890s the rise of socialism created new priorities, and politics became more polarized: moderate Republicans and Catholics sought to abandon the old religious conflicts for the sake of social defence. The income-tax proposals of the Radical government of Léon Bourgeois (1895–6) led to its overthrow, and Méline took office as head of a government which relied on the votes of Catholic deputies who had accepted the Republic (*Ralliés*). On social questions, the government took a strong anti-Socialist line, while promoting such alternative reforms as the law of 1898 on compensation for industrial accidents. Its other feature, supported by

Méline as representative of a frontier department, was reinforcement of the alliance with Russia; Tsar Alexander III's state visit to Paris was a notable event of 1896.

Méline's government came under mounting pressure from the campaign to reopen the Dreyfus case, which he resisted, declaring at one point that 'There is no Dreyfus affair'. His government was responsible for the prosecution of Zola, which initiated the affair's decisive stages. One of its effects was to make Méline's compromise between conservative Republicans and moderate Catholics unworkable. The 1898 election saw a shift to the left, and the new Chamber passed a resolution calling for an 'exclusively Republican majority', on which Méline resigned.

He was an unsuccessful candidate for president of the Republic in 1899, and devoted the rest of his career to the defence of agriculture; he returned to office briefly as minister of agriculture during the First World War.

Bibliography

There is no modern biography of Méline. G. Lachapelle, *Le Ministère Méline* (Paris: Editions de l'Art J.L.L. D'Artey, 1928) is a first-hand account by a collaborator and admirer; P. Barral, *Les Agrariens français de Méline à Pisani* (Paris: FNSP, 1968) deals with a central area of his policies.

RDA

MENDÈS FRANCE, Pierre Isaac Isidore (1907–82)

One of the most praised – and also insulted – French leaders of his time, Pierre Mendès France occupies a unique place in French contemporary history. In a political career that spanned three Republics, he led France for only 'seven months and seventeen days, June 1954–February 1955' (the title of one of his books). During this short but very active period as premier, he dramatically extricated France from Indo-China; granted autonomy to Tunisia; brought the long European Defence Community debate to an end and helped negotiate a basis for German rearmament; and by his dynamic approach to political life inspired a generation of his young compatriots. An early admirer of de Gaulle, in whose provisional government he served in 1944–5 (after having flown numerous combat missions with the Free French air force in 1943), he bitterly opposed de Gaulle's return

to power in 1958 and adamantly refused to accept the institutions of the Fifth Republic.

After a precocious beginning in politics in the Third Republic, and his brief but spectacular premiership in the Fourth, he was largely on the sidelines during the Fifth. But in 1981, in a tribute due more to his widespread intellectual influence than to specific political collaboration or support, he received a warm accolade from President François Mitterrand, newly-elected to the office whose prerogatives Mendès France had so firmly opposed: 'If I am here, it is really thanks to you.' A non-practising Jew, he was often villified during his life, and not only for political reasons (in an interview in 1957, François Mauriac declared: 'Nobody admits it, but what really broke him was racial feeling'). At the time of his death in 1982, however, he was the subject of an almost unanimous outpouring of eulogies.

The future premier was born in Paris in 1907, the only son of a manufacturer of women's clothing whose family, of Portuguese-Jewish origin, had been in France since the seventeenth century. Mendès France's father served as a non-commissioned officer and as a lieutenant in the First World War; his grandfather was a corporal in the Franco-Prussian War of 1870. Brilliant and industrious, the young Mendès France began life with a series of records. At age 15 the youngest graduate of his secondary school, he was at 19 the youngest lawyer in France. He won a law doctorate two years later, and was also a graduate of Sciences Po. Politically active very early, he was secretary-general of a left-wing student movement which engaged in street fighting with right-wing students. In a more moderate step, when only 16 and after hearing a speech by Edouard Herriot, he decided to join the Radical Party, an allegiance he was to maintain for over thirty-five years. When he was first elected deputy, in 1932, he was only 25 and was the youngest member of parliament. The following year he married Lily Cicurel, whose family owned a large department store in Cairo (they were to have two sons; she died in 1967). In 1935 he was elected mayor of Louviers, the town in Normandy where he had established a law practice and which was to be his political fief until 1958. In 1938 Léon Blum named him under-secretary of state for the treasury in his short-lived second government; at age 31 Mendès France was the youngest member of a government in the history of the Third Republic.

Mendès France's life was to reach new peaks – as well as a disheartening low point – during the Second World War. At the outbreak of war in September 1939, he immediately volunteered for training as an aerial observer and navigator with the air force, despite his relatively senior age and his status as a deputy. After service in Syria, he was in France on leave when the Germans invaded France in May 1940. In an effort to join his unit which had been transferred to Morocco, he sailed with other parliamentarians on the *Massilia* from Bordeaux to Casablanca. Grotesquely charged with desertion, he was arrested and brought back to France where, in a mockery of justice, he was sentenced to six years in prison. After a dramatic escape and several months in hiding he managed to reach England where, after meeting with General de Gaulle on the day of his arrival, he served with the Free French air force in a bomber squadron from May 1942 until November 1943. He then agreed to accept de Gaulle's call to join him in Algiers as commissioner (i.e. minister) of finance in what was to become in May 1944 the provisional government of France. In this capacity he led the French delegation to the Bretton Woods Conference on international monetary problems in June 1944; in July he returned to the United States to help negotiate the creation of the World Bank; and in September, after the liberation of Paris, he was named by de Gaulle as minister of the national economy. It was in this post that Mendès France established a reputation as a man of principle in advancing unpopular ideas that was to mark him for the rest of his political career. Strongly advocating drastic anti-inflationary measures and currency reform, he was opposed by Minister of Finance René Pleven, who wanted to proceed by using more traditional, cautious measures. Forced to choose, de Gaulle opted for Pleven's approach. Unable to get his way, and refusing to compromise, Mendès France resigned from the government in May 1945.

Vowing not to accept political office unless he had the power to do what he believed to be right, Mendès France spent the next nine years on the political sidelines. Offered the post of minister of finance by the Socialist premier, Félix Gouin who succeeded de Gaulle in January 1946, Mendès France declined after being refused the power to carry out a drastic programme of deflation. During the years that followed, regularly re-elected as deputy and as mayor of Louviers, he accepted various assignments of an economic and financial nature, serving as head of the French delegation to the Savannah Monetary Conference in 1946; as French representative to the International Monetary Fund in 1947–50; as permanent representative to the UN Ecoomic and Social Council; and as chairman of the National Assembly's finance committee. Occasionally giving courses in France's most prestigious institutions of higher education (among his students at the Ecole

Nationale d'Administration was Valéry Giscard d'Estaing), his reputation was spreading among France's future decision-makers. He was, above all, becoming the Cassandra of French politics, bluntly calling for economic rigour and for the balancing of commitments and resources, notably in regard to the long war in Indo-China that was bleeding France's army and economy. In June 1953, during one of the long governmental crises that marked the Fourth Republic, he was unexpectedly offered – and hesitantly accepted – a chance to try to form a government. After relentlessly outlining his diagnosis for France's ills, he failed to be elected premier by only thirteen votes.

A year later, after the French army suffered a disastrous defeat at Dien-Bien-Phu, Mendès France's moment came. Pledging a satisfactory settlement of the war in Indo-China in a month or the resignation of his government, a 'coherent programme' for economic recovery, and a decision on the European Defence Community ('France can no longer prolong an equivocal situation which harms the Western Alliance'), Mendès France was voted in as premier on 18 June 1954 by a comfortable margin. By stating that he would accept office only if he obtained a majority independent of the votes of Communist deputies, he won added support from the right but earned the undying enmity – and opposition – of the Communist party (a party, he said, which 'insults the army'). Mendès France began his period in office with his most spectacular victory. Serving as his own foreign minister (for which John Foster Dulles later called him 'superman'), working against and almost around the clock, he brought the negotiations at Geneva to a successful close. France's Indo-China war was over, and Mendès France the most popular man in France. Maintaining his momentum, he flew to Tunisia a few days later and – having disarmed his critics by having Marshal Juin accompany him – was able to defuse an explosive situation by granting internal autonomy, a step which led to Tunisian independence.

Henceforth, every decisive step that Mendès France took was to further weaken his power base and infuriate new categories of his varied opponents. Unable to negotiate a compromise which could get a majority in the National Assembly, he let the bitter debate on the European Defence Community culminate in a vote in the National Assembly on 30 August. This resulted in the demise of a project which had long divided France's political parties and French public opinion, a demise for which some of his opponents, notably in the Christian Democrat MRP, never forgave him. Defending the need to maintain Western solidarity, Mendès France subsequently lost left-wing support by negotiating and then steering through the National Assembly the London and Paris agreements which, with a British commitment to maintain troops in Germany, provided for the rearmament of Germany and its entrance into Nato. Mendès France aroused still more ire by denouncing the excessive production and consumption of alcohol and by imposing measures that enraged France's powerful alcohol interests as well as her then 3 million private distillers. In weekly radio broadcasts (modelled after President Roosevelt's fireside chats), he explained his projects and actions directly to the public, but pressures were clearly building up against him in parliament.

These pressures finally came to a head on the subject of Algeria, where hostilities broke out in November 1954. Mendès France was forceful in announcing his government's determination to crush the rebellion ('One does not compromise when it is a question of maintaining the nation's internal peace and the integrity of the Republic . . . Algeria is France, and not a foreign country we are protecting,' he declared in the National Assembly on 12 November). But he also was to argue for the need for reforms. Many of his enemies, moreover, were ready to use any occasion to bring him down. After a vituperative and often violent debate in the National Assembly during the night of 4–5 February 1955, a debate in which the accumulated resentment against Mendès France took precedence over the debate's formal subject, his government's Algerian policy, Mendès France's varied opponents joined forces to vote him out of office.

Unable to continue his efforts to renovate France as premier, Mendès France devoted much of his time during the next two years to trying to renovate the Radical Party and to make it an instrument of change. This was a task of mammoth proportions (in the dramatic roll-call in which he had been voted out of office, seventeen Radicals voted against him and four abstained), and one which proved impossible to attain. After gaining control of the party in May 1955, Mendès France finally submitted his resignation as leader in June 1957. In September 1959 he was formally declared to be no longer a member; by this time France's oldest party was only a shadow of its former self, and the Fourth Republic relegated to history. In his last major electoral campaign effort during this period, Mendès France led the Republicain Front alliance which won the legislative elections of January 1956, but only to see Socialist Guy Mollet, as leader of the largest parliamentary group, chosen as premier. After four

months as minister of state without portfolio, a position of no power and little influence, and in increasingly strong disaccord with Mollet's Algerian policy, Mendès France resigned from the government in May 1956. Returning to his familiar role as Cassandra, he was to remain adamantly in opposition for the next twenty-five years.

Isolated during the end of the Fourth Republic, Mendès France opposed the advent of the Fifth. Although sharing some of de Gaulle's political attitudes and personal characteristics (the personalization of power, use of media to reach the public over the head of parliament, force of character and personal rectitude) Mendès France was never to forgive de Gaulle for the way he came to power in 1958. Born in the wake of military disobedience in Algiers, the Fifth Republic was in his view conceived in original sin. And, unlike most of France's political leaders – including François Mitterrand – who opposed to de Gaulle's return to power, Mendès France was to remain stubbornly opposed to the constitution of the Fifth Republic, notably including the provision added in 1962 for the election of the president by direct universal suffrage.

Mendès France's last long period in opposition was to take disparate forms. Unsuccessful in attempts to win election in Normandy in the legislative elections of 1958 and 1962, he was returned to parliament in 1967 in Grenoble, only to be narrowly defeated – by lack of Communist votes on the second ballot – in the elections held after the student riots of May 1968. During the tumultuous events of May he had attracted new controversy by appearing at a student rally and by being briefly billed – by François Mitterrand – as the prospective prime minister of a transitory government. In his electoral campaigns during these years Mendès France campaigned primarily as Mendès France and as a prominent leader of the French left, but also as a member of the Parti Socialiste Unifié (PSU). After having joined a left-wing splinter group in 1959, the Parti Socialiste Autonome, he moved with it when it joined in the formation of the PSU the following year, but he never played an active leadership role. In the presidential elections of 1969, he unexpectedly agreed to join the nominal Socialist candidate Gaston Defferre as his prospective prime minister, a 'ticket' which received an abysmal 5.01 per cent of the votes cast (with the PSU candidate, Michel Rocard receiving 3.6 per cent).

During the years that followed, Mendès France's activities on the French political scene were primarily those of an observer and commentator. In 1971 he married a second time, to Marie-Claire de

Fleurieu, *née* Servan-Schreiber. Ill-health prevented him from contesting Grenoble in the 1973 legislative elections. Later in 1973 he was received in Israel by President Sadat at the time of the latter's dramatic peace mission to Jerusalem. During the final decade of his life, Mendès France characteristically devoted much of his time to the challenging if not hopeless task of seeking an agreement between Israel and the Palestinians.

In the year before his death in October 1982, Mendès France supported François Mitterrand in the presidential elections of May 1981. The man who since 1965 had supplanted Mendès France as the leader of the French left gave him a warm accolade after his victory, but – a final irony – subsequent contacts between Mendès France and the new government (then following a policy of reflation alien to the economic rigour that Mendès France had spent his life advocating) were minimal. Stubborn and uncompromising, a better statesman than politician, Mendès France remained intransigent in defending his principles until the end. Liked or disliked, he was, after de Gaulle, the most memorable French political figure of his time.

Bibliography

Two biographies of Mendès France in English were published in the mid-1950s: Donald McCormick, *Mr. France* (London: Jarrolds, 1955) and Alexander Werth, *The Strange History of Pierre Mendès-France and the Great Conflict over French North Africa* (London: Barrie & Jenkins, 1957). Also in English, Francis de Tarr, *The French Radical Party from Herriot to Mendès-France* (Oxford: Oxford University Press, 1961; Westport, Conn.: Greenwood Press, 1980). In French, see especially Jean Lacouture's complete and detailed biography, *Pierre Mendès France* (Paris: Seuil, 1981). A prolific writer of books and articles, Mendès France's *Oeuvres complètes* are being published by Gallimard (Paris) in six large volumes, of which three have thus far been published: *S'engager 1922–1943* (1984), *Une politique de l'économie* (1985), and *Gouverner, c'est choisir 1954–1955* (1986). For Mendès France's economic ideas, see also (in translation) *Economics and Action*, co-authored with Gabriel Ardant (London: Heinemann, 1955).

FdeT

de MENTHON, François count (1900–   )

The de Menthon are an aristocratic family from Savoy, but one devoted to reformist Catholic politics. Count Henri-Bernard de Menthon, François' father, was deputy for Haute-Saône from 1919–28 and as such headed the liberal wing on the MRP. Although a Christian Democrat activist and city councillor in Nancy before the war, his main career was as a university economics teacher first in Nancy and then, in 1941, in Lyons.

François de Menthon joined de Gaulle's movement and became CNR commissioner for justice (1943–4) and was made justice minister in the government of September 1944. He had the misfortune to preside over the settling of accounts (*épuration*) at the liberation (about which the state could do little) and departed to work in the Nuremburg Tribunals soon after (Teitgen – q.v. – took over the Ministry of Justice). When he returned he was briefly education minister but he represented Haute-Savoie in the Assembly continuously from 1945–58 and was minister of the national economy in the Bidault government of June 1946.

De Menthon was also a member of the Fourth Republic's first constitutional committee but he resigned with *éclat* on 3 April 1946 because an MRP draft was rejected and the committee had adopted a Socialist–Communist position – he was replaced by Pierre Cot (q.v.) As president of the assembly committee he had displayed a resolute hostility to de Gaulle.

Apart from the brief stints at the variety of ministries, de Menthon led the interventionist, Keynesian, wing of the MRP arguing the need for government regulation of the economy and for an active state role. He was a supporter of planning as well as of the small and medium-sized industries and, somewhat daringly, urged the case for a radical restructuring of French agriculture. He voted for the MRP to leave the Pinay government in protest against its restrictive economic policy.

De Menthon was a European federalist, a defender of the European Defence Community (a proposed merger of the French and German armies) and the European Political Community: against both Munich and Maurras. He also became increasingly critical of the Fourth Republic's policy in Algeria and criticized the renewal of special powers for the Algerian Commissioner Lacoste in 1957.

De Menthon was opposed to de Gaulle's return to power and headed a demonstration against him in 1958. De Menthon was the only MRP dissenter against the investiture of de Gaulle as prime minister on the grounds that it was the illegitimate result of a military coup.

Defeated in the 1958 Assembly elections, he

returned to the University of Nancy and in 1962 headed its European research centre.

DSB

MERCIER, Ernest (1878–1955)

Born in Constantine, Algeria in 1878, Ernest Mercier studied at the Ecole Polytechnique and went on to specialize in the field of electrical energy. In 1914 he joined the board of the company Le Triphasé and became managing director of Energie Électrique de la Seine. He was called up shortly afterwards, but finished the war as a technical advisor to the Armaments Ministry. In 1919 he founded the Union d'électricité in order to participate in the electrification of the Paris region, and with the aid of the Rothschilds Bank he amalgamated the Paris electricity companies and linked them up with the major firms Alsthom and Compagnie Générale d'Electricité. By the mid-1920s Mercier was the dominant figure in electrical power with parallel interests in electrical equipment, mechanical engineering and oil, a veritable industrial tycoon. After the Second World War he was to become both a director of the Suez Canal Company and honorary president of the International Chamber of Commerce. Mercier's well-known anti-Nazism did not save him from the general post-liberation backlash against the business community at large. The law of April 1946 nationalizing the electric power and gas industries deprived him of his last major managerial positions. He returned to research and spent the last years of his life studying means of improving electric turbines. He died of cancer on 10 July 1955.

Mercier's remarkable success as an entrepreneur is not, however, the chief source of his historical interest. In 1925 he founded an economic study group, Redressement Français (French Resurgence), under the patronage of Marshal Foch, and the organization soon took on a political dimension. Mercier was a capitalist innovator with a vigorous commitment to industrial rationalization, high productivity and state planning, and he applied the same logic to his project for political reform. He saw politicians as too incompetent to handle the complex economic affairs of state in the new technological age, and the task should instead, he argued, be assigned to technicians. Such a regime would have to be based on authoritarian principles, and hence Redressement Français also called for the reassertion of the 'traditional values' of order, hard work and patriotic duty.

Given the relationship between sections of big business and the Fascist movements in Italy and Germany, the French left could not fail to be alarmed by such views. Mercier was known to be one of the financial backers of La Rocque's right-wing paramilitary Croix de Feu in the early 1930s, and he had openly identified himself with the agitation of the extremist leagues against the Republic during the Stavisky affair of January 1934. When the left talked of the threat of fascism in France, Mercier's name was inevitably cited alongside those of François Coty (q.v.) and François de Wendel (q.v.) to illustrate the support of large-scale capitalist interests for authoritarian political solutions.

In fact Mercier had little sympathy for genuine fascism and he was well known for his anti-Germanism. However, while his image as the capitalist *éminence grise* of French fascism is false, there is no doubt that the ideas he helped to advance in business circles played their part in undermining the Third Republic and in paving the way for its successor. Indeed, Vichy's institutions and ideology are an echo of the curious contradiction in Mercier's own thinking – the attempt to combine modern technocratic economic ideas with an outdated paternalistic vision of politics.

Bibliography

The main biography of Mercier is in English: Richard F. Kuisel, *Ernest Mercier: French technocrat* (Berkeley, Cal.: University of California Press, 1967). The most specific references to him in French are to be found in historical works concentrating on the leagues and the extreme right and in E. Beau de Loménie, *Les responsabilités des dynasties bourgeoises*, vol. IV: Du cartel à Hitler (Paris: Denoël, 1954).

BJ

MERMAZ, Louis (1931–)

Louis Mermaz began his professional career as a teacher of contemporary history at the Lycée d'Etat du Mans, the Lycée Lakanal at Sceaux and finally at the University of Clermont-Ferrand where he was appointed as a teacher (*assistant*) in 1963. Since then, history, with a social/literary bias, has provided an individual flavour to the style and content of his politics. Of his four published works, three are literary/social/historical: *Madame de Maintenon* (Lausanne: Rencontre, 1965), *Madame Sabatier* (Lausanne: Rencontre, 1967), *La Dynastie des Hohenzollern* (Lausanne: Rencontre, 1969), and the one work of political discourse *L'Autre volonté* (1984) opens with quotations from classical authors.

The major stimulus to political action came in 1955 when he met François Mitterrand, then the leader of a small centre group, L'UDSR (L'Union Démocratique et Socialiste de la Résistance). Since then he has been the intimate friend and faithful disciple of the future president and an untiring exponent of Mitterrandist social democracy.

An energetic campaigner, he was elected to most of the posts of local, departmental and regional responsibility and, at national level, held high office within the party. He was first elected deputy for the FGDS (Fédération de la Gauche Démocratique et Socialiste) in the Isère department in March 1965. Rejected by the electorate in 1968, he was re-elected in 1973, 1978, 1981 and 1986. He was elected mayor of Vienne in 1971 (a post which he still occupies), departmental councillor for Vienne-Sud (1973–9) and Vienne-Nord (1979 to the present), and president of the *Conseil Général* (Departmental Council) from 1976 to 1985.

At national party level, he was general secretary of the early Socialist grouping, the Convention des Institutions Républicaines, and was at Mitterrand's side when Mitterrand's CIR entered the Parti Socialiste at the Epinay Congress in 1971. Mermaz was first a member, then later in 1979, President of the Comité Directeur of the new party, a stalwart champion of Mitterrand's cause for a united left in France. When Mitterrand became President of the Republic in May 1981, Louis Mermaz was appointed transport minister (*ministre de l'equipement et des transports*) in the first brief Socialist government of 1981 and, after the June 1981 elections, president of the National Assembly. This post, officially the third highest in the French State, is the apogee of his career to date, but provides something of a mystery. Was Louis Mermaz after so many years of self-effacing service to Mitterrand, disappointed at not being appointed prime minister? Mitterrand had earlier declared that Mermaz had the 'stuff' of a prime minister and he was a firm favourite with the political pundits. However, nothing that this Socialist grandee (*vieux baron du socialisme*) has done or said since, suggests disappointment or detracts from his image as Mitterrand's faithful lieutenant.

Following the re-election of Mitterrand to the presidency in 1988, Louis Mermaz was appointed leader of the Socialist group in the National Assembly. Though little known in England, he is often a regular guest in televised debates in France, is still an energetic campaigner, and has been the subject of a number of press articles.

Bibliography

Conan, E. (1985), 'Louis Mermaz: en campagne avec ses gros sabots', Libération, 8 March.
Duhamel, A. (1984), 'Le Vicaire général de Mitterrand' (following publication of *L'Autre volonté*), *L'Express,* 4 May.
Mermaz, L. (1984), *L'Autre volonté*, Paris: Laffont.
Villeneuve, B. and F.-H. De Virieu (1984), *Le Nouveau pouvoir*, Paris: J.-C. Lattès (pp. 321 *et seq.*).

John B

MERRHEIM, Alphonse Adolphe (1871–1925)

Alphonse Merrheim, leader of the metalworkers' union and one of the most important trade union activists of his time, was born in La Madeleine (Nord) on 7 May 1871, into a working-class family. He left school at the age of 10 to work in a soap factory and two years later began an apprenticeship as a coppersmith. For health reasons he had to leave this job, and became a weaver at the age of 18. Attracted first to the socialism of Jules Guesde and then, briefly, to that of Jean Allemane, Merrheim soon turned instead to trade union organization. After resuming his trade as a coppersmith, he worked to set up a trade union, of which he was secretary from 1893 to 1904. In 1904, he became secretary of the Copperworkers' Federation, a post which took him to Paris. He then set about trying to merge the various metalworkers' organizations, a goal which was achieved in 1909 with the formation of the Metalworkers' Federation. He was involved in the organization of miners' strike movements, but after 1908 questioned the utility of such strikes, and became convinced that trade union organization depended on a solid knowledge of capitalism. With the help of economic experts he published many articles on capitalist concentration and, in the pre-war years, on the build up of the arms industry.

Merrheim developed close ties with the revolutionary syndicalist leadership of the CGT, whose position he defended at the 1906 CGT Congress of Amiens, against both the socialists led by Victor Renard and the 'antipatriots' such as Georges Yvetot. He found himself in a similar position in 1908, when he successfully steered the congress, in the absence of the confederal committee, between reformism and insurrectionism. From 1909 onwards, he was associated with the CGT leadership's attempts to build organization and make policies more realistic. Merrheim's brand of revolutionary syndicalism was above all pragmatic. For this he was expelled from his own union in January 1914 in a bitter ideological dispute, but he never actually left his post.

In August 1914, Merrheim supported the CGT leadership's stance, but was among the first to criticize its participation in government, and withdrew his federation's support for the confederal committee in December 1914. He spoke at various meetings against the war and urged closer ties with German antiwar Socialists such as Karl Liebknecht. He represented the CGT minority at the February 1915 London Conference of Socialists of the Allied countries, and attended Lenin's extreme antiwar Zimmerwald Conference in September 1915. After 1916 and particularly after the Russian Revolution of October 1917, however, Merrheim drew closer to the majority and supported the Wilson initiative. Although a pacifist, he acknowledged the necessity of national defence and for this reason condemned the Brest-Litovsk Treaty. At the CGT congress in September 1919, he defended Léon Jouhaux, and in 1921 he intervened on the side of the majority. His support of the majority brought him into conflict with his own federation in 1920, although he remained its secretary. Illness forced him out of trade union activity after 1923, and he died during the night of 22–3 October 1925.

Bibliography

The major biography in English is Nicholas Papayanis, *Alphonse Merrheim. The Emergence of Reformism in Revolutionary Syndicalism 1871–1925* (Dordrecht: Martinus Nijhoff, 1985), in which particular attention is paid to Merrheim's reformist influence within the syndicalist movement. There is a biographical entry on Merrheim in Jean Maitron, *Dictionnaire biographique du mouvement ouvrier français*, 3rd part (1871–1914) (Paris: Editions Ouvrières 1973–77), vol. XV (1977), pp. 70–3.

SM

MESSMER, Pierre-Auguste Joseph (1916–)

Pierre-August Messmer, born on 20 March 1916 at Vincennes, the son of an industrialist from Alsace, followed a classic middle-class schooling at the Lycées Charlemagne and Louis-le-Grand before engaging in law studies in Paris. Having completed his doctorate, he trained for a career in the colonial service at the prestigious Ecole Nationale de la France d'Outre-mer, entering the colonial service just before the war in 1938. Called up on the outbreak of war, he joined the Free French forces in 1940 alongside de Gaulle in London and participated with distinction in the Foreign Legion in the campaigns in Africa, Italy, France and Germany, as well as Indo-China. After a brief period in central government service in 1946 as secretary general of the interministerial committee on Indo-China, he filled several important posts during the 1950s in the French colonial service in Africa: governor of Mauritania, then of the Ivory Coast, and high commissioner to the Cameroons, to French Equatorial Africa and French West Africa. In the meantime in 1956 he had headed the private office (*directeur de cabinet*) of Gaston Defferre (q.v.), the Socialist minister for the French overseas territories, at the time of the preparation of the framework law on the independence of the French colonies.

In 1960, at the height of the Algerian War crisis, he was personally chosen by de Gaulle, without reference to Prime Minister Debré, to be defence minister (*ministre des armées*), a post he retained for the rest of de Gaulle's presidency under successive prime ministers. He was joint founder in 1969 of the Association Presence et Action du Gaullisme. Nominated President Pompidou as minister of state in 1971, he succeeded J. Chaban-Delmas as prime minister in 1972, remaining in Matignon until President Giscard succeeded the interim President Poher in May 1974. Subsequently he has been an important parliamentarian (elected deputy for Lorraine in 1968, a seat he retained until his surprise defeat in 1988), an influential local politician (becoming mayor of Sarrebourg in 1971, and president of the Regional Council of Lorrain 1978–86) and an important figure in national politics as a loyal supporter of the neo-Gaullist Rassemblement pour la République (RPR) from its foundation.

Messmer is a classic example of the Fifth Republic phenomenon of a career civil servant building a political career after having been called into government. 'Politics is not my calling and I am proud of it' ('La politique n'est pas mon métier, et j'en suis fier'), he once said. Described by some as dour or colourless, he may be seen as a model public servant, loyally following the leadership of others in the national interest. As the longest serving defence minister in French Republican history, he faithfully carried out President de Gaulle's defence policy, accepting the General's deep knowledge of military matters and his own executive role. He helped establish an independent French deterrent (he was present alongside de Gaulle at the first French nuclear test in Mururoa), military independence from Nato being a key element in de Gaulle's determination to maintain national independence and French influence in world politics.

He accepted the post of prime minister less out of personal ambition than from fidelity to a certain idea of Gaullism and a desire to further its continuation in power. Similarly he was prepared to let his name go forward as the single candidate on the right for the 1974 presidential election in order to effect a compromise when a plethora of candidates presaged electoral suicide, but immediately withdrew when Chaban and Giscard maintained their candidacies. As Pompidou's prime minister he showed absolute loyalty and deference to the President of the Republic, and total discretion at the time of Pompidou's terminal ilness. His period in Matignon has been seen as a further step on the road of presidentialization of power in France and of parliamentary impotence. His government was installed for three months before parliament came into session and he did not ask the Assembly for a vote of confidence on his programme, the confidence of the Elysée seemingly offering sufficient legitimacy to his government.

His periods in office were characterized by a deep-rooted conservatism. He was brought into the Chaban-Delmas government in 1971 as minister of state to satisfy the Gaullist deputies who thought Chaban was going too far in the direction of a new liberal society and risked closing the great book of Gaullism. His nomination as prime minister re-assured the Gaullist rank-and-file, but it was difficult to find a new political direction, other than swinging between immobilism and repression (whether in the field of industrial relations with the Lip factory occupation, in broadcasting, or with the dissolution of the extreme-left movement Ligue Communiste and for good measure the extreme-right Ordre Nouveau). His term of office coincided with a downturn in the economy. Inflation and unemployment started to rise and in January 1974, three years after the dollar went off the gold standard, all that Messmer's government was prepared to do was to institute the floating franc, a devaluation in disguise.

Messmer is the most prominent example of the continuity of the Gaullist tradition into the RPR party. Despite his connections with the Socialist Defferre his Gaullist credentials are immaculate: the FFL, the liberation campaigns, de Gaulle's right-hand man in the key field of defence, one of only four former ministers to be invited to see de Gaulle in his retirement in 1969. His creation of Presence et Action du Gaullisme, bringing together those most closely concerned to keep alive a certain idea of Gaullism, and an analysis in book form of de Gaulle's military writings. However he was not a traditional right-winger (as his early espousal of decolonization showed), but a great pragmatist, for he saw Gaullism as intelligent pragmatism rather than as a set dogma. In the interests of winning the 1973 legislative elections he had readily incorporated the centre into the ruling coalition (Lecanuet − q.v. − and Servan-Schreiber − q.v. − had of course been strong opponents of de Gaulle in 1965). He has had no ideological or other qualms about supporting the party which has emerged out of the Gaullist movement or its new leader Jacques Chirac (q.v.). He had after all appointed Chirac (a protégé of Pompidou) to key posts in his own government. He is the last of the historic Gaullists to remain close to Chirac, who found him indispensable in various ways: he was official spokesman for the Chirac presidential campaign in 1981, and then president of the RPR parliamentary group in the Assembly from 1986 to 1988 when the power-sharing prime minister needed discipline in the ranks of his small majority. As an elder statesman of the RPR, he has found a public role which has allowed a more colourful personality to emerge than was evident in his days in high office.

GH

MICHEL, Clémence Louise (1830 or 1836–1905)

Louise Michel's political career began in earnest when she was 40 years of age. Her commitment to revolution came as a gradual break with the values of her upbringing and her youth when she was a keen supporter of Napoleon III. Illegitimate, born in Vroncourt-La Côte, Haute-Marne, she was well educated by the de Mahis family for whom her mother was a servant. She was devoutly religious in her youth and wrote poetry. In fact her admiration for Victor Hugo, then in exile, encouraged her to correspond with him. When it came to finding a job in order to support herself and her mother to whom she was devoted, this interest in writing and education decided her career. It was as a schoolteacher in Paris that Louise Michel began frequenting Republican opposition groups. She joined the First Internationale and fought in the ranks of the communards in their final struggles against the Versailles troops. Many of her close friends were executed. She herself refused to escape and was sentenced to deportation to New Caledonia in 1873. During her captivity she had time to become familiar with the theories of socialism and anarchism and with the local conditions. She studied local plant life and gave classes to fellow deportees. It was not long before she was taking sides in the local power struggle; she supported the indigenous New Caledonians – the Kanaks – in their struggle against the French settlers. Amnestied in 1880 she returned to France via Australia and was given a heroine's welcome back to France by the left. Louise Michel then became the spokesperson for anarchism and spent the next thirty-five years leading demonstrations of workers, lecturing and raising funds in Europe. Despised and feared by the ruling classes for her abilities as a rabble rouser, her standing rose as she was constantly followed by the police, convicted and imprisoned on several occasions and even threatened by assassins.

Although she wrote prolifically for the cause of anarchism, her writing was not limited to political tracts but included poetry, plays, literature for children, and personal memoirs. However, few of her works had extensive distribution or achieved notable success. Often she was in too much of a hurry as all her outpourings were dedicated to raising funds for her many causes with little attention to success as a theorist or writer. Her only regular source of income was from Rochefort (q.v.), a fellow communard and deportee who gave her an allowance from his paper, *L'Instrinsigeant*. Known as the red Virgin (*la vierge rouge*) and kind Louise (*la bonne Louise*), it was the extraordinary generosity and devotion to the idea of total revolution that gave Louise Michel her reputation more than any of her writings. She gave away everything she could to people in dire straits, often going without food and minimum comforts herself. Her frugal life style was as much part of her commitment as were her public appearances as a passionate and powerful orator. Like many other idealists, she was uninterested in the practical details of party organization or in internal squabbles of the Socialist and anarchist movement in France at the end of the nineteenth century. On the question of feminism, she supported the demand for equal pay for equal work but was as dismissive of suffragettes as she was of parliamentary Socialists. Like Guesde, she dismissed the Dreyfus affair as a bourgeois scandal. Despite their increasing differences, anarchists, socialists and syndicalists united for a huge demonstration at her funeral, each group claiming her as their own.

Bibliography

La Commune: histoire et souvenirs, Paris: Stock, 1970.
Mémoires, 'La Mémoire du peuple', Maspéro, 1977.
Légendes et chants de gestes canaques, Paris: 1980.
A Travers la vie et la mort, edited by D. Armogathe and Marion Vilynie, Paris: Maspéro, 1982.
Le Livre du jour d l'An, Paris: Opale, 1983.

As Edith Thomas indicates, Louise Michel does not admit to the full extent of her religious fervour and Bonapartism of her youth in her memoirs. Her biography is the most comprehensive, *Louise Michel*, translated by Penelope Williams (Montreal: Black Rose Books, 1980). See also Paule Lejeune, *Louise Michel l'indomptable* (Paris: Editions des Femmes, 1978).

MCr

MICHELET, Edmond (1899–1970)

A First World War hero, Edmond Michelet joined the ultra-conservative royalist movement Action Française but soon identified more closely with left-wing Christian thinking and what would become the Christian democratic tradition. By 1922 he was chairman of the Catholic Youth Movement in the Béarn region and ten years later founded the Equipes Sociales, a movement of militant young Christians with progressive social ideals. A very early member of the Resistance he took command first of the *Combat* movement in the Limousin region and later of the nation-wide Mouvements Unis de la Résistance. In February 1943 he was captured by the Gestapo and eventually deported to Dachau concentration camp. On his return from Dachau he was introduced to General de Gaulle, a meeting which marked the beginning of his career as a politician. Elected on the MRP list to Parliament for the Corrèze department (1945–51) he was de Gaulle's army minister of defence from 1945 to 1946. From its formation in 1947 to 1953 he played a major role in the General's nationalistic movement, the Rassemblement du Peuple Français (RPF) but, failing in 1951 to win a parliamentary seat on an RPF ticket in the Corrèze became senator for the Seine department (1952–9). After de Gaulle's return to power Michelet was appointed minister for ex-servicemen before becoming minister of justice from 1959 until he resigned in 1961. In 1962 he was appointed to the Constitutional Council where he remained until 1967 when, having been elected to Parliament for the department of Finistère, he became minister of state for the civil service until 1968. After André Malraux's resignation, Michelet was appointed minister of culture in Chaban-Delmas' government from June 1969, a post he retained until his death in 1970.

Although an unconditional Gaullist, Michelet commanded wide respect on account of his outstanding Resistance record and his left-wing stance. One of his most difficult posts was the key Justice Ministry in the Debré government during the Algerian War. Eventually in 1961 he resigned, no longer able to reconcile his ideals with the unpleasant realities of France's involvement in what amounted to a colonial war. By no means a politician's politician he was at once a man of action, a devout Christian with a social conscience, and a patriot with a strong sense of history and the type of earthy mysticism derived from Péguy, on which the Gaullist movement, never strong on ideology, thrived. Michelet had such an unshakeable faith in the notion of the 'people' that André Malraux once called him France's chaplain, *L'Aumônier de la France*.

Bibliography

Very little exists on Michelet in English or in French. The best source of information is his own memoirs: *Le Gaullisme, passionnante aventure* (Paris: Fayard, 1962); *Rue de la Liberté, Dachau 1943–1945* (Paris: Seuil, 1970); *La Querelle de la fidélité: peut-on être gaulliste aujourd'hui?* (Paris: Fayard, 1971). See also the volume edited by his son: C. Michelet, *Mon père Edmond Michelet, d'après ses notes intimes* (Paris: Presses de la Cité, 1971); and also J. Charlot, *Le Gaullisme d'opposition* (Paris: Fayard, 1988) and J. Charbonnel, *Edmond Michelet* (Paris: Beauchesne, 1988).

GTH

MILLERAND, Etienne-Alexandre (1859–1943)

Born in Paris on 10 February 1859, the future president of the Republic Alexandre Millerand trained for the bar and quickly earned a reputation for his defence of cases involving breaches of the social order. Continuing to represent a clientele drawn from this constituency for some two decades, his career broadened into legal journalism and politics. Elected to the chamber of deputies as a Socialist for the department of the Seine in 1885, he soon became the leader of the Socialist left, editing until 1896 their daily newspaper *La Petite République*. His

first serious encounter with controversy came when he was appointed minister of commerce in Waldeck-Rousseau's cabinet of 'republican defence' in 1899, which led many Socialists to brand him a traitor for participating in a 'bourgeois' government. Though not a member of Combes' 1902 ministry, he was expelled from the party in 1904 with the 'Millerand case', as it became known being a subject of fervent debate at the 6th Congress of the Socialist International. He re-entered government in 1909, this time as minister for public works in Artistide Briand's cabinet, again provoking controversy over his willingness to crush the railway strike in 1910 with troops. Appointed minister of war in Raymond Poincaré's cabinet of 1912, he returned to the same post at the outbreak of the war until October 1915.

In 1920, following the defeat of Clemenceau's bid for the presidency, Millerand was called upon to form his own cabinet in which he combined the premiership with the foreign affairs portfolio. When the incumbent president of the Republic was forced to resign on grounds of ill-health, Millerand, now leader of the Bloc National (a right-centre coalition), was elected his successor. He again provoked controversy in departing from the traditional presidential neutrality in the elections of 1924 by openly favouring conservatives. In the face of violent attacks from the left majority he was unable to appoint a new government and was forced to resign.

From here on Millerand played only a secondary role in politics, being elected on his second attempt to the Senate in 1927 – where he remained until 1940. He died at Versailles on 7 April 1943.

Alexandre Millerand remains a controversial figure to this day. At first the right saw in him a revolutionary, a self-proclaimed 'collectivist', a defender of unpopular worker and Socialist causes; then the left rejected him as a renegade and traitor to the Socialist cause. From being the first Socialist, with the exception of Louis Blanc (q.v.), ever to sit in a European government, he had become by 1920 the leader of a centre-right coalition. For some, Millerand is viewed as having provoked the dispute which once more split the Socialist Party and set back its unification in 1899. Others have suggested that it was not so much Millerand who moved to the right at the beginning of the present century as French socialism which, from the reformist years of the 1890s, reverted to its revolutionary stance of the beginning of the Third Republic. What can be said about Millerand is that in his early years he exemplified the problems faced by a Socialist attempting to reconcile party principles with the demands of ministerial life. Thus his Socialist years typify the early efforts of socialism itself to adapt to modern industrial society.

The controversy of Millerand's Socialist years has to a certain extent overshadowed the good work he carried out while minister in various governments, much of which was characterized by a firm belief in state involvement in the economy. As minister of commerce from 1899 to 1902, he devoted his attentions to upgrading the mercantile marine, promoting trade, developing technical education and the postal system and improving labour conditions. During his term as minister of public works in Briand's first cabinet in 1909, his principal achievement was to reorganize the state railways even though he is better remembered for his adoption of strong measures to crush the railway strike of October 1910.

While minister of war from 1912 to 1913, he was able to reorganize the higher command and to give definite status to aeronautics as a military force. His recall to the same post during the early war years brought him less success, as the government was criticized for its slowness in providing the necessary heavy artillery for France's war effort. He resigned with other members of Viviani's cabinet in October 1915. Following the war, as premier and foreign minister in 1920 he was preoccupied with ensuring that the Versailles Treaty was correctly applied, but he is also remembered for frustrating the attempts to organize revolutionary strikes and for providing military supplies to Poland during the Polish–Soviet war.

In standing for the post of president of the Republic in 1920, Millerand made clear his belief in the need for constitutional revision which would give more power to the head of state. It is not surprising therefore that he should come into conflict after the elections of May 1924 with the new majority in the Chamber of Deputies composed of Radicals and Socialists and known as the *Cartel des Gauches*. Millerand had made little secret of his antipathy towards this group who now refused to form or support any government unless he resigned, which he finally agreed to do. Thus Millerand's life in high political office ended in the controversy which had marked its beginning. Overall Millerand emerges as a strong, independently-minded politician unwilling to toe the line of party loyalty at a time when the localized nature of parliamentary politics in the Third Republic made such independence possible.

In 1918 Millerand was elected to the Academie des Sciences Morales et Politiques having published *Le Socialisme Réformiste* (1903) and *Pour la défense nationale* (1913).

Bibliography

Millerand and the 'Millerand case' are often dealt with in general histories of French and European Socialism. There is also R. Persil, *A. Millerand* (Paris: Société d'Editions Françaises et Internationales, 1949) and the very useful Leslie Derfler, *Alexandre Millerand: The socialist years* (The Hague: Mouton, 1977) which as its title suggests only deals with Millerand's life until his expulsion from the Socialist Party in 1904, but which makes use of much new material in the form of private papers and police archives.

JFVK

MITTERRAND, François Maurice (1916–)

The first man in French history to be twice elected by universal suffrage as president of the Republic (1981–8, 1988–), Mitterrand's main contributions have been as a national policy-maker and as an international statesman. None the less, his earlier career as a minister and party leader during the Fourth Republic, as an opposition leader since 1958 and as the first secretary of the Socialist Party (PS) since 1971, and his achievements as a writer and as a builder of national monuments are also noteworthy.

Like many of his generation, Mitterrand entered politics through the Resistance, where he was transformed from a practising Catholic student into a centre-left political activist. Little in his pre-war youth presaged such a change. Born on 26 October 1916, at Jarnac in the Charente, one of eight children, he grew up in a prosperous and Catholic family. It was the profitable vinegar factory of his maternal grandfather, rather than his father's career as station-master at Angoulême which provided the wealth. Like his brothers, he was educated by diocesan priests at the Collège Saint Paul, at Angoulême. An able, but not brilliant, student, he failed his oral exam for the *baccalauréat* at the first attempt. His higher education, in law and political science, also took place in a Catholic, right-wing atmosphere – as a student at Sciences Po (the then private Ecole Libre des Sciences Politiques) and as a resident at the Marist student house at 104, rue de Vaugirard. He had just completed his degree, and begun his military service when the war started. In his pre-war years, his major activism was not political, but religious, as a member of the Society of St Vincent of Paul.

He changed dramatically during the war. As a sergeant in 1940, he faced his first battle, near

Verdun, and his courage merited the award of a Croix de Guerre. He was wounded, and taken prisoner by the Germans. Soon he was playing a lively role in prison camp activities, and not least in escape attempts. His third attempt, in December 1940, was successful, but the problems of prisoners of war had become one of his major preoccupations. After a brief visit to his family in the occupied zone, he moved to Vichy, where pre-war friends found him a job with the government service concerned with prisoners of war. This job, and the later award of Marshal Pétain's personal decoration, the *Francisque*, were subsequently to be cited by his enemies as evidence of his right-wing, probably Pétainist political sympathies. Whilst he had right-wing friends, there is no proof of pro-Pétain views. Indeed, he started working for the Resistance, making false papers, as soon as he got his government job. Furthermore, he soon gave up his job, and assumed a new identity, as 'Morland', leader of the RNPG (a prisoner of war Resistance organization). He was, in fact, in London, on Resistance work when the award of the *Francisque* was announced.

In the Byzantine world of Resistance politics, Mitterrand proved a shrewd operator and an effective leader, although this won him few friends among the Gaullists or the Communists, since his own RNPG had centre-left political views. His first meeting with de Gaulle, in Algiers, to discuss the merger of the three prisoner of war Resistance organizations, was icily distant, as Mitterrand rejected the Gaullists' pretensions to assume the leadership of the merged body. In fact, it was Mitterrand himself who became the national leader when the merger took place. There was little surprise when he was appointed general secretary of the Ministry for Prisoners of War when the provisional government was set up. Hence, when Paris was liberated in August 1944, he became – albeit for only a few weeks – the acting minister. He thus emerged from the war, aged only 27, with a Croix de Guerre, a *Francisque*, the prestigious *Rosette de la Resistance*, and a brief ministerial experience.

He did not stay on at the Ministry when the minister arrived, but helped to found, and became first president of, the National Movement of Prisoners of War and the Deported. This pressure group leadership led to another glacial meeting with de Gaulle, after a demonstration in Paris for improved benefits. It also facilitated his entry to Parliament. In 1946 he successfully campaigned for election as deputy in the Nièvre, as a candidate of the centre, ex-Resistance UDSR.

Château Chinon and the Nièvre were to remain his political base until 1981. Although he arrived in 1946 as a carpet-bagger, and only retained a hotel room as his local residence, he set down strong political roots. He won election to the General Council of the Nièvre, and later became its chairman, and he was also elected as a municipal councillor, before taking over as mayor of Château Chinon. Until 1981, when as president he gave up all other elected offices, he was regularly re-elected as deputy – except in 1958 when his opposition to de Gaulle cost dearly. Even then, however, his exile from national politics was short, for in 1959 he was elected as senator for the Nièvre.

During the Fourth Republic, Mitterrand quickly emerged as a major political actor – a party leader and a minister. His own talents as a debater and an organizer were soon revealed, but the key pivotal position of his own small party also helped his career. In January 1947, still aged only 30, he was appointed to his first full ministry (war veterans), and over the next eleven years held many ministerial posts, including the ministries of the interior, in 1954, and of justice, in 1956. He took over the leadership of the UDSR in 1953 by a carefully calculated coup. He made some firm friends, but also many enemies. The communists attacked him as a right-winger, whilst the extreme right and Gaullists accused him of being a fellow-traveller. One real attempt was made to destroy his reputation, if not his career, in the 'defence leakages scandal' of 1954, when he was accused, by right-wingers, of passing defence secrets to the Communists. He emerged unscathed from this first (but not last) scandal. None the less, accusations of unprincipled, Machiavellian opportunism still abounded, based on the evolution of his policy stances and his willingness to serve in a variety of coalitions. There was, however, some evidence of firm views and clear principles. He was fully consistent in his support for European integration. In 1953, he resigned over Laniel's policies in the North African colonies. In 1958, he was one of the few political leaders who resisted de Gaulle's return to power. He marched in the Communist-led demonstration in Paris, and argued strongly that it was unacceptable to appoint de Gaulle as prime minister under pressure from the army in Algeria. De Gaulle's investiture, however, marked the start of a twenty-three year exile from office for Mitterrand.

In October 1959, shortly after his return to parliament as a senator, Mitterrand again achieved national notoriety as the central figure in the 'rue de l'Observatoire' scandal (also called 'the Mitterrand affair'). He made a complaint as the victim of an assassination attempt from which he had only escaped by leaping over a fence into the Luxembourg Gardens. His right-wing enemies, however, produced evidence that he knew in advance about the attack, and had connived with his attackers. He was accused of contempt of court, and the Senate, after a strained debate, lifted his parliamentary immunity to prosecution. The case was never brought to court, and Mitterrand continued to claim that he was the victim of a right-wing plot to discredit him. Statements in 1965 and 1975 by Pesquet, his main accuser in 1959, seemed to confirm this. Whatever the case, Mitterrand's disgrace was shallow and short-lived.

In 1962 he was again campaigning against de Gaulle, against the referendum proposal that the president be elected by universal suffrage. The success of the General's referendum did not prevent Mitterrand's return to the Assembly in the elections which followed. Here, he became an effective, but not unchallenged, leader of the opposition on the left. First, he made his mark as a writer, by publishing, in 1964, *Le Coup d'etat permanent*, a well-argued critique of the 'presidential deviation' inherent in the Fifth Republic. Secondly, he organized a national network of political clubs, the Convention des Institutions Républicaines (CIR), aimed at drawing into politics those outside traditional parties, and especially those repulsed by the ideological discourse and ultra-pragmatic practices of the Socialist Party. Finally, he actively sought to bring together a coalition to defeat de Gaulle. In 1964, he supported Defferre's attempt to federate all non-Gaullist and non-Communist forces in support of his candidature for the 1965 presidential election. When Defferre (q.v.) failed, Mitterrand presented himself as a candidate, but with a different strategy. His proposal was for a federation solely of the parties of the centre-left, but also for a negotiated second ballot alliance between this federation and the Communist Party. In this way, he became the presidential candidate of the entire 'union of the left', and leader of the Fédération de la Gauche Démocrate et Socialiste (FGDS), which comprised the Socialist and Radical parties and the Convention.

At the election, in December 1965, Mitterrand was beaten, but his 45 per cent second ballot score was sufficient to ensure that the FGDS stayed together and that he remained its leader. After the 1967 Assembly elections, when the FGDS and Communists again fought together, and gained seats, but not a majority, Mitterrand initiated talks on the questions he thought essential for a victory of the left. These were the transformation of the FGDS from a loose grouping of declining parties into a united and dynamic single party, the setting up of a 'shadow cabinet' – a recognized team of opposition spokesmen – and the drafting by the FGDS and Communists of an agreed and clear governmental programme. However, he faced such suspicions from his partners that none of these goals was achieved when the 'Events of May 1968' exploded, and his whole strategy, leadership and political career were called into question.

If Mitterrand was as surprised by this outburst as were all other political leaders, he did not hesitate to join the attack on de Gaulle and his government. Indeed, when de Gaulle appeared incapable of any action, it was Mitterrand who promised (at a press conference on 28 May) that he was ready and willing to take over if de Gaulle withdrew. When de Gaulle did not resign, but instead dissolved the Assembly, this speech was attacked as rashly irresponsible, if not downright treasonable. The FGDS and Communists faced the elections in hopeless disarray, and Mitterrand was treated as more of a liability than an asset. By the end of this year of electoral disaster, the FGDS had collapsed, the union of the left seemed shattered, and Mitterrand was again in the political wilderness. In 1969, when de Gaulle resigned, he was not even considered by his erstwhile partners as a presidential candidate. In disgrace, he turned his attention to building up his club network.

It was as leader of the CIR that he returned to prominence in 1971, when he negotiated a merger between his clubs and the Socialist Party. At the special merger conference at Epinay, it was Mitterrand, the newcomer to the PS, who was elected as its leader (first secretary), a post he was to hold until 1981. His programme was to revive, rejuvenate and popularize the PS, but also to renew the alliance with the Communist Party to provide a credible alternative to the Gaullists. This latter strategy bore fruit in 1972, when the PCF, the PS and the left Radicals agreed a common programme of government. The PS began to grow in membership, and the 1973 elections saw appreciable gains in votes and seats. Under his leadership the Socialist Party was at last rebuilding. In 1974, when Pompidou died, he was the obvious choice as the presidential candidate of the left. He was backed not only by the PS and PCF, but also by Rocard and many PSU members (who later joined the PS).

Although Mitterrand lost the election, he did so by such a narrow margin that his leadership of the left seemed unchallengeable. Furthermore, after Giscard's initial popularity faded, a victory for the left in the 1978 Assembly elections became increasingly probable. After the large gains in the 1977 municipal elections, however, the PCF demanded an 'updating' of the common programme. For Mitterrand, 'updating' meant broadening its electoral appeal, not the radicalization which the PCF was demanding. Negotiations broke down, and the two parties entered the election campaign in disarray. Once again, the divided left was defeated, albeit narrowly.

To many within the PS, Mitterrand's leadership and his insistence on attempting to renew the union of the left alliance (if and when the PCF turned back from its Muscovite tack) seemed out of date. At the party conference at Metz in 1979, Rocard, with support from Mauroy, proposed an alternative party platform to that of the leader. The highly ideological debate masked a real power struggle for the leadership of the party and its candidature for the 1981 presidential election. Mitterrand won, but only by compromising with the left-wing CERES faction.

From such a poor start, he went on to fight an impressive campaign, aided by the entire PS, including his rivals, and advised by Seguela, the advertising expert. With a simple theme, *la force tranquille*, a 'radical but reasonable' series of '110 proposals for France', impressive television and poster presentation, Mitterrand fought his most professional campaign to date. He was helped by the poor score of Marchais, the fratricidal attacks of Chirac and the unpopularity of Giscard, but he won with a comfortable majority on 10 May and took office ten days later. As president, his first acts were to appoint a new government, led by Mauroy, and to dissolve the Assembly. The June elections produced the best ever result for the PS: 38 per cent of the vote and an overall majority in the Assembly. Under his leadership the left had, for the first time, the prospect of at least five years in power. Whilst his victories had reduced the Communist share of the vote, he still invited the PCF to provide four ministers after the June elections. It was the first time since 1947 that a major Western government included Communists.

As president, Mitterrand was primarily, but not exclusively, concerned with foreign affairs and defence. In defence policy, he maintained a high level of spending, the nuclear research programme, and the independence from military integration within Nato. He even opted for the construction of an additional nuclear submarine. In addition to this Gaullist traditionalism, his policies had a clearly European bent. He relaunched ideas of European defence cooperation, revived the West European Union, extended the French nuclear umbrella to cover West Germany, created a Rapid Deployment Force, initiated joint manoeuvres with German forces, and even

began joint procurement consultations with European allies. He offered Britain immediate support during the Falklands crisis, and argued strongly for the arms embargo by the whole EEC.

In other aspects of foreign policy, his aim of greater European cooperation was also clear. He maintained French membership of the European Monetary System, despite strong temptations to leave in the 1982 and 1983 devaluation crises. He accepted the steel production quotas in 1981, and the milk quotas in 1983. He pushed for ratification of the Single European Act, and for the 1992 deadline for the completion of a single market. He also played a key role in negotiating the budget contribution compromise with Britain, and signed the treaty for the Channel Tunnel. The Eureka Programme of research cooperation among all European firms was also a Mitterrand proposal, albeit in response to the American Strategic Defense Initiative.

Mitterrand maintained good relations with the Reagan administration, despite the unpromising start of appointing Communist ministers and giving support to the Sandinista regime in Nicaragua. His critical attitude towards Soviet policies in pre-Gorbachev days, his support for the deployment of Cruise and Pershing missiles in Western Europe, and his decisions to intervene militarily in Chad and the Lebanon were especially appreciated in Washington.

Despite his keen interest in international questions and his rising prestige as an international statesman, he was often drawn into domestic policy-making. Whilst some of his top domestic priorities (notably the nationalization and decentralization programmes) were largely left to the ministers and prime minister, others were subject to presidential interference. Cultural policy was one such area in which Mitterrand not only fixed the objectives, but also decided such precise questions as the composition of the broadcasting control authority, the choice of Pei as the architect for the Louvre, and the choice of the consortia to run the 5th and 6th television channels. The 'presidential projects' for great new public buildings, included not only the Louvre extension, but also the Bastille opera, the arch at La Défense, the Arab cultural centre, the science museum at La Villette, and, in 1988, the 'mega-library'. Aesthetic appreciations may vary, but the Mitterrand presidency will certainly be remembered for its buildings.

It was over economic and education policies, where Mitterrand's interventions were more sporadic, that the Socialists became unpopular. After the raising of expectations during the presidential election campaign and the mild reflationary measures of 1981, the cuts of 1982 and the 'rigour' package adopted – after presidential arbitration – in 1983 were unpopular and seen as a sign of incompetence. More significantly, they exacerbated, rather than solved, the growing problem of unemployment, despite Mitterrand's specific electoral pledges. Furthermore, the cuts in, and limitation of, social security benefits for the unemployed meant that the Mitterrand presidency witnessed the appearance of the 'new poor' who were to depend on private charities for help. Governmental unpopularity reached its depth, however, over the attempt to integrate private schools into the state education system by the 'Savary bill' of 1984. Millions took to the streets to demonstrate their protest, and the PS vote plummeted in the European Assembly elections in June. The polls showed that Mitterrand had become the most unpopular president since polling began.

In July 1984, he made a dramatic attempt to reverse the situation. He withdrew the Savary bill, accepted the resignation of the government and appointed a new government led by the youthful, moderate Fabius, and including no Communist ministers. The president and his new team adopted a very different image – one of modernization and managerial competence – to regain popularity before the 1986 Assembly elections. By early 1985, however, despite a slight improvement in the polls, prospects were still bleak, especially as the PCF was increasingly hostile. In these circumstances, Mitterrand respected his campaign promise to change the electoral system for the Assembly elections, and introduced a form of proportional representation. Despite the Greenpeace scandal, the signs of success in economic policies helped the PS and its leader to win back some support.

After the March 1986 elections, however, for the first time in the Fifth Republic, the President faced a hostile majority in the Assembly. He immediately appointed the leader of the new majority, Chirac, as prime minister, and began the novel experience of 'cohabitation'. Behind a courteous façade of peaceful coexistence, with clear policy responsibilities, Mitterrand waged a war for prestige and power against Chirac. He claimed two constitutional roles, as 'arbiter and guarantor of the Constitution' and as the representative of France abroad. In the first, he avoided any association with Chirac's domestic policies, but made rare, but noteworthy condemnations of divisive, unpopular, or clearly partisan measures. He also demonstrated his old prowess in avoiding any blame in the scandals revealed by the Chirac government about its PS predecessor. In the second, he kept a high public profile as a respected international statesman. He continued to rise in the opinion polls, so that by late 1987, the widely disliked president of 1984 had become the favourite candidate to win the 1988 presidential election.

His 1988 campaign was a model of professionalism, from the striking *Génération Mitterrand* posters, to the theme of *La France Unie*. He attacked his rivals as divisive and partisan but promised few specific changes, except an 'opening' to new coalition partners if re-elected. Once elected, and by a margin of votes greater than in 1981, he appointed his old rival, Rocard, as prime minister to lead a government including centrist politicians. After a brief search for new allies, he dissolved the Assembly. The single-member constituency, two-ballot electoral system reintroduced by Chirac, did not, however, produce the expected majority for the PS. Mitterrand's second term thus began with yet another institutional innovation – a minority government. Its opening months, facing major industrial disputes, but surviving by concessions to the PCF and the centrists demonstrated once more his political professionalism.

By late 1988, however, his personal popularity was once again declining. The amiable image of the good, if distant 'Tonton' was being replaced by the more autocratic, if not monarchical style of 'Dieu'. But the television puppet show, and the right-wing attacks of Catherine Nay (*Les sept Mitterrand*) and *Le Point* were not solely responsible. The public prominence of the Mitterrand family (one brother sometimes serves as a presidential envoy, one son is a deputy, the other a top adviser at the Elysée Palace), the appointments of close friends to state posts, absence of any Socialist ideology in governmental policies, and the increasingly regal style of his 'court' have been attacked by a leading PS journalist, Thierry Pfister (*Lettre ouverte à la génération Mitterrand qui marche à côté de ses pompes*).

Despite a long and impressive political career, and the publication of a dozen quite successful books which are largely about his own experiences and ideas, Mitterrand remains a surprising enigma. Evaluations of Mitterrand vary widely: for some he is a hero of the left, who rebuilt the PS and took the left to unequalled triumphs, for others a moderate social democrat, for others still an unprincipled 'Florentine', a professional politician pursuing no particular end except staying in power – historians will argue over his achievements and methods for years to come. For a man as fascinated by history as Mitterrand, there must be considerable satisfaction in having already marked French history in so many ways, and in still keeping so many people watching for his next move.

Bibliography

Daniel, J. (1988), *Les Réligions d'un president*, Paris: Grasset.

Duhamel, A. (1982), *La République de M. Mitterrand*, Paris: Grasset.

Estier, C. (1981), *Mitterrand President*, Paris: Stock.

MacShane, D. (1982), *François Mitterrand: A political odyssey*, London: Quartet.

Mitterrand, F. (1964), *Le Coup d'état permanent*, Paris: Plon.

Nay, C. (1984), *Le Noir et le rouge*, Paris: Fayard.

Nay, C. (1988), *Les Sept Mitterrand*, Paris: Fayard.

Pfister, T. (1988), *Lettre ouverte à la génération Mitterrand qui marche à côté de ses pompes*, Paris: Albin Michel.

HM

MOCH, Jules-Salvator (1893–1985)

A graduate of the prestigious Ecole Polytechnique and an engineer, Jules Moch's political career began as an SFIO deputy for the Drôme constituency (1928–36), and almost to the end of his life he remained a Socialist. A strong advocate of planning in the 1930s, he was secretary-general in the prime minister's office in Blum's Popular Front government. He briefly served as an under-secretary of state in the second Blum cabinet in 1938. A Resistant, he joined de Gaulle in 1942 and was a member of the Consultative Assembly in Algiers in 1944.

After the war, he was to make his name as a no-nonsense politician, strongly anti-Communist and with firm convictions on constitutional and other matters. A member of both Constituent Assemblies, he served in eight ministries, first of all at public works and transport under Gouin, Blum and Ramadier (1945–7) but most controversially as interior minister in the troubled years after 1947. His appointment of eight 'super-prefects' or IGAME (*inspecteurs généraux de l'administration en mission extraordinaire*) to administer the regions was an innovation which owed something to Vichy and to Liberation precedents. But it was his firm treatment of industrial unrest in the strike-torn years of 1947–8 which attracted most attention. His stand in the winter of 1947–8 was a factor in persuading the moderate Force Ouvrière trade union to split away from the CGT in April 1948. He did not hesitate to use the security forces to reoccupy coking plants within days of the start of the pit-strikes of October 1948, and, never afraid to be controversial, he claimed that Cominform money had helped to foment the unrest. A minister again under Queuille (q.v.), Moch was nominated as his successor in October 1949 but was unable to form a government. However he served as deputy premier and minister of the interior under Georges Bidault (q.v.) in October 1949.

A general strike against his candidature in 1948 had failed; however the so-called *affaire des généraux* involving leaked documents (1950) nearly caused him to appear before the High Court. A wine scandal dating back to 1946 was also brought up to embarrass the embattled Jules Moch and other Socialists like Félix Gouin (q.v.) and Christian Pineau. A man with friends as well as enemies, Moch benefited from the 1951 electoral system of joint lists (*apparentements*) that gained for his Hérault constituency three seats for 39,000 votes, while the 69,000 Communist votes gained not a single seat.

During the second legislature of the Fourth Republic, Moch, who had been Pleven's minister of national defence (1950–1), played a vital part in the parliamentary back-peddling over the ratification of the EDC agreements. Notoriously hostile to the European Defence Community, it was Moch who was chosen to be *rapporteur* on one of the two main committees set up to examine the question in 1953.

Ever a clear-sighted politician, Jules Moch, as minister of the interior in Pflimlin's cabinet – chosen for his firmness ten years before – realized how powerless were ministers, himself included, during the last weeks of the Fourth Republic. In his memoirs, De Gaulle comments scathingly on Moch's use of tanks to try to prop up the régime. With the fall of the Republic that he had served so conscientiously, Moch never again held ministerial office. He continued until 1962 to sit as a Socialist deputy in the National Assembly, but left the party in 1974 over its alliance with the Communists.

Bibliography

Moch, J. (1952), *Confrontations, doctrines, déviations, expériences, espérances*, Paris: Gallimard.

Moch, J. (1976), *Une si longue vie*, Paris: Robert Laffont.

Moch, J. (1977), *Le Communisme, jamais!* Paris: Plon.

Quilliot, R. (1982), *La SFIO et l'exercice du pouvoir, 1944–58*, Paris: Fayard.

ACR

MOLLET, Guy Alcide (1905–75)

Secretary-general of the French Socialist Party (SFIO) from 1946 to 1969 and premier of France from 1956 to 1957, Guy Mollet played a prominent part in the politics of the Fourth and early Fifth Republics.

The second of three children, he was born in the Norman town of Flers, where his father was a commercial employee (later a textile worker) and his mother a dressmaker. She later obtained the post of concierge at the local savings bank, whose basement flat became the family's home. His father served in the First World War but was badly gassed in 1917 and, although he returned to work for a time, became an invalid until his death in 1931.

Mollet, who won a state scholarship and passed his *baccalauréat* at the age of 17, was drawn to the Socialist Party during his student days in Normandy, joining the Young Socialists in 1921 and the party proper in 1923. At this stage he belonged to the party's Calvados Federation, whose leading intellectual was Ludovic Zoretti, a teacher in the science faculty at the University of Caen, and it was he who introduced Mollet to the writings of Marx and Engels and strengthened his pacifism.

After brief teaching appointments in Le Havre and Lisieux, in November 1925 Mollet became a tutor in a school in Arras, in the Pas-de-Calais department, and here carried further an earlier interest in teachers' trade unions. He helped to establish the General Federation of the Teaching Profession which belonged to the General Confederation of Labour (CGT). In 1930 he married Odette Fraigneau and they had two daughters, one being born in 1931 and the other in 1932. It was after his move to the north that Mollet came to know one of the founder members of his party, Alexandre-Marie Desrousseaux, familiarly known as Bracke, who encouraged his interest in Marxism. By at least 1934 Mollet belonged within the SFIO to a group known as Bataille Socialiste (Socialist Struggle) but in that year he joined Révolution Constructive (Constructive Revolution), a team of radical intellectuals who were in sympathy with the ideas of Henri de Man, the Belgian Socialist, regarding the desirability of systematic economic planning. Subsequently, Mollet rejoined Bataille Socialiste but in 1938 and 1939 he was associated with another small group known as Redressement (Rectification), which had attracted some of the former members of Révolution Constructive, and which took the line that a European war could be avoided by a new economic and political settlement between the great powers.

Mollet was mobilized at the outbreak of war. He was wounded and taken prisoner by the Germans in May 1940 but was released in January 1941. In the resistance movement, he worked with the Civilian and Military Organization in underground activities in the Pas-de-Calais and became secretary of the committee of liberation for that department. In the municipal elections of May 1945 he was elected to the Arras Municipal Board and became mayor of this city, a post which he was to occupy until his death.

From this relatively narrow base he rose within the space of eighteen months to the top position in his party. He was elected in the general elections of 21 October 1945 to the first Constituent Assembly, where he served as a member and, from January 1946, as president of its constitutional committee. In the elections of 2 June 1946 he was returned to the second Constituent Assembly and was appointed to the constitutional committee of this body as well. He attracted attention not only at this level but also at party meetings, such as the 37th National Congress of August 1945 and the extraordinary congress of March 1946, where he showed that he was willing to challenge the party's leaders, who were being blamed by critics for committing the party to onerous responsibilities in government, for various supposed errors of strategy and for disappointing election results. With the 38th National Congress of August 1946 in view, Mollet and a group of such critics drew up a lengthy motion calling for a doctrinal and strategic reorientation of the party. This statement aroused considerable interest and weakened the position of the central leaders in the weeks preceding the congress, which rejected the annual report of the incumbent general secretary, Daniel Mayer, and thus precipitated his resignation. After the congress, on 4 September, the party's executive chose Mollet to take his place.

He was elected to the first National Assembly of the Fourth Republic in the elections of 10 November 1946 and served as a minister of state in Léon Blum's government of December 1946 to January 1947, but his power within the party was still relatively limited, as was shown when he failed to persuade its National Council to vote in favour of the resignation of the Ramadier government, in which the Socialists were well represented, following the departure of the Communist ministers in May 1947. However, in later years, as the Socialists came to accept their place in the broad centre grouping, the 'third force', which held at bay the Communists on one side and the Gaullists on the other, Mollet made a firm alliance with Augustin Laurent of the powerful Nord Federation and won widespread support among the party's rank-and-file members, who respected his tolerant didacticism, his sound judgement and his loyalty to the party. Although he was a member of two successive governments in 1950–1, under René Pleven as a minister of state and under Henri Queuille as vice-premier, his main concern in the 1946–51 and 1951–5 legislatures was to ensure that the party organization and the parliamentary group worked together towards agreed objectives and he encountered particular difficulty in restraining a number of deputies who objected to the policy of supporting the European Defence Community. Mollet was a firm believer in European unity, and in 1954 became president of the Consultative Assembly of the Council of Europe.

After the general elections of 2 January 1956, Mollet was appointed premier and formed a coalition government consisting mainly of Socialists and Radicals. His aims were to bring peace to Algeria, where a civil war had been in progress since November 1954, and to carry out reforms in France, including measures for three weeks of paid holidays and for an old-age pensions fund. The appointment of General Georges Catroux as resident minister in Algeria was meant to signify the government's liberal intentions but when Mollet arrived in Algiers on 6 February he found himself in the midst of a mob of Europeans demonstrating against the apparent change of policy. In an attempt to avoid further divisions, he accepted Catroux's resignation and appointed Robert Lacoste, a Socialist, to take his place. Mollet subsequently proposed that a cease-fire should be followed by free elections to choose representatives with whom the government would negotiate a new legal status for Algeria within the French state. That the French government had sufficient control of its agents to carry out such a policy was placed in doubt when it chose to condone, after the event, the diversion of a Moroccan aircraft to Algiers in October 1956 so that Ben Bella and other National Liberation Front (FLN) leaders on board could be arrested. Some within the Socialist Party severely criticized the government for having agreed to the Suez operation by Anglo-French forces but it was an attempt to increase its financial resources which eventually led to the ministry's downfall. On 21 May 1957 the National Assembly defeated a proposal for new taxes by 250 votes to 213 (with seventy abstentions) and Mollet submitted his resignation.

In 1958 Mollet was at the centre of the events which led to the creation of the Fifth Republic. On 14 May, the day after the Algiers insurrection, he became vice-premier in the cabinet which had just been formed by Pierre Pflimlin, but he wrote to and later met with General Charles de Gaulle in an effort to ascertain his views and his intentions. Convinced that de Gaulle represented the only means of avoiding a military dictatorship, Mollet voted for the General's investiture as premier and accepted a post as minister of state in his cabinet. He was a member of the small inter-ministerial council which prepared the draft text of the new constitution and he recommended that it should be approved in the constitutional referendum of 28 September. Once the constitution had been ratified, steps were taken to elect a new National Assembly and the President of the Republic. Although Mollet won his seat in the assembly poll, the Socialists' numbers in the house were disappointingly small and he was soon indicating that the party was unlikely to be associated with the next administration. On 27 December he submitted a letter of resignation to de Gaulle, citing his objections to the government's economic and financial policy, but was asked to remain in office until 8 January 1959. The Socialists finally moved into opposition when, under de Gaulle's presidency, Michel Debré formed the first ministry of the Fifth Republic.

When the Algerian settlement was finally agreed in 1962, Mollet faced the difficult problem of showing his party a way forward against the entrenched position of the Gaullists, who shared with the president the credit for having brought about peace. Once the referendum of 28 October 1962 had resulted in approval of de Gaulle's proposal to have the president elected by universal suffrage, it was evident that future campaigns for presidential elections would transform the party system. A Socialist nominee could have offered the SFIO its first real chance in decades to broaden its audience but Mollet gave only qualified support to the candidature of his colleague, Gaston Defferre, and, after the latter's venture had collapsed in June 1965, the party found itself bound up with the Communists in backing François Mitterrand for the presidency. Mitterrand lost to de Gaulle, but only on the second ballot, and he emerged from the campaign as an arbiter of alliances on the left of the party spectrum. His supporting front, the Federation of the Democratic and Socialist Left (FGDS), acquired much more cohesion than had at first seemed possible. The SFIO fought the elections of 1967 as part of this alliance but resumed its independent existence after the events of May 1968 and the elections of the following June had thrown the opposition parties into disarray. However, there was still pressure to produce a greater measure of unity on the left and in December 1968 an SFIO congress agreed to form a new party. Despite the confusion caused by the unexpected presidential elections of 1969 – as a result of de Gaulle's resignation – a congress held in July 1969 did finally establish a new organization. It was at this stage that Mollet retired from the office of general secretary to devote himself to work in his research centre, the Office Universitaire de Recherche Socialiste (OURS).

Bibliography

Cahier et Revue de l'Ours published two issues in commemoration of the tenth anniversary of the death of Guy Mollet: no. 164 (October 1985), 'Textes et discours (1946–1973)'; and no. 169 (May–June 1986), 'Actes du colloque d'Arras, samedi, 5 octobre 1985'.

See also Bernard Ménager *et al.*, *Guy Mollet: un camarade en république* (Lille: Presses Universitaires de Lille, 1987); Guy Mollet, *Quinze ans après . . . 1958–1973* (Paris: Albin Michel, 1973); Guy Mollet *13 mai 1958 – 13 mai 1962* (Paris: Plon, 1962); and Harvey G. Simmons, *French Socialists in Search of a Role 1956–1967* (Ithaca and London: Cornell University Press, 1970). *Le Monde* published an obituary article by André Laurens and Thierry Pfister (4 October 1975) and related letter by Georges Lefranc (15 October 1975).

By far the best account of Mollet's early life is that by Denis Lefebvre, 'Du pacifisme à la résistance', in B. Ménager *et al.*, pp. 197–217. Most of Guy Mollet's archives are deposited at the OURS in Paris where there is also a substantial collection of material relating to Mollet and to the SFIO.

BDG

MONIS, Ernest Antoine Emmanuel (1846–1929)

Ernest Monis has some claim to be the most obscure of all the prime ministers of twentieth-century France. Born in the Charente, he studied law at Poitiers and Paris, entered the bar at Cognac (Charente) and immediately set himself up in opposition to the local Bonapartist magnate, Cuneo d'Ornano. He later moved his law practice to Bordeaux and it was as deputy for the Gironde that he entered the Chamber of Deputies in 1885. He lost his seat to a Boulangist in 1889 but was almost immediately elected senator in a by-election and would stay in the upper house until 1920. He was an active parliamentarian but his appointment as minister of justice in the Waldeck Rousseau (q.v.) government of Republican defence

in 1899 was a surprise. In 1911 he was, equally unexpectedly, chosen as prime minister, largely as a low-profile alternative to highly ambitious political grandees like Berteaux and Caillaux (q.v.). His period as prime minister was cut short by an aviation accident – attending an air show with his war minister Berteaux, he was seriously injured by a falling plane. (Berteaux, a millionaire stockbroker who wanted to be president of the Republic, was decapitated.) He was briefly navy minister in the Doumergue (q.v.) government of 1913–14.

Despite his lack of political weight, Monis was savagely attacked by the extreme right for his supposed willingness to pervert the course of justice for political (or commercial) ends. His old enemy, Cuneo d'Ornano pursued him over a complicated story of alcohol fraud; more seriously, he succumbed to the pressure of his powerful colleague Caillaux in 1911 to postpone the appeal against conviction of a crooked financier, Rochette. The affair led to a parliamentary commission of inquiry chaired by Jaurès (q.v.) and indirectly to the murder of the editor of *Le Figaro* (which published details of the case) by the wife of Caillaux. The Jaurès commission strongly criticized Monis (and Caillaux) for abuse of influence. Monis resigned from the Doumergue government and took no further part in government. The savage portrait of him painted by Barrès in *Dans la cloaque* is virtually his only memorial; however unjustly, he is an example of that connection between politics and corruption that would be so damaging to the parliamentary Republic in the 1930s.

Bibliography

Jeanneney, J.-N. (1981), *L'Argent caché: milieux d'affaires et pouvoirs politiques dans la France du XX siècle*, Paris: Fayard.

PM

MONNERVILLE, Gaston (1897–)

Born into an indigenous family in Cayenne (French Guyana) and a lawyer by training, Monnerville represented Cayenne as a Radical deputy in the 1930s and held junior ministerial office in 1937 and 1938. His political career flourished as a member of the Council of the Republic (1946–8), and in the Senate of the Fifth Republic. In both bodies, he was a distinguished and sometimes controversial president. He achieved notoriety late in life, being a leader of the opposition in 1962 to de Gaulle's proposed referendum on the election of the President of the Republic by universal suffrage. When, several years later, the referendum of 1969 on regionalization and on the reform of the Senate was mooted, it only served to confirm Monnerville's anti-Gaullism. In 1974, he was chosen to be a member of the Constitutional Council, nominated by Alain Poher (q.v.) who had replaced him in October 1968 as president of the Second Chamber.

A notable member of the Resistance after 1940, Monnerville had been elected to the Constituent Assemblies at the end of the war, once again for Cayenne. Before the outbreak of war, he had briefly served as under-secretary of state for the colonies (1937–8) and in 1946 he was to play an important part in the negotiating of full departmental status for Guadeloupe and Martinique, for the island of La Réunion and for his native Guyana. Elected senator in 1946 and representing, from 1948, the Lot department, he became president of the Council of the Republic in 1947, and served in that capacity throughout the lifetime of that body. Had he not been considered by some to be an 'overseas' candidate, he might have been a more serious contender to succeed Vincent Auriol (q.v.) as President of the Republic in 1953. A combative president of a body sometimes unsure of its role under the 1946 constitution, he regularly complained that the Assembly ignored the senators' amendments to legislation, and he worked successfully to restore to the Council of the Republic some of the power of which it had seemingly been deprived in 1946.

His relationship with de Gaulle was to undergo an interesting change; it had been the Socialist group in the Upper House which, with Monnerville playing a leading role, had swayed the SFIO to vote the investiture of the General in 1958. Yet in a much publicized speech in September 1963 he described de Gaulle's France as 'no longer a Republic', though later withdrawing remarks in which he had likened Frenchmen of his day to prisoners in a concentration camp. Monnerville would have become interim president of the Republic if de Gaulle had resigned in 1968. This fact may have played some part in the General's determination to stay on, since he had never forgiven Monnerville for denouncing the 1962 referendum as unconstitutional. In October 1968, Poher took over as president of the Upper House; in that same year, Monnerville published a monumental political biography of Georges Clemenceau.

Bibliography

Monnerville, G. (1975), *Témoignage: de la France Equinoxiale au Palais de Luxembourg*, Paris: Plon.

Monnerville, G. (1980), *Vingt-deux ans de présidence*, Paris: Plon.

Williams, P.M. (1970), *French Politicians and Elections, 1951–69*, Cambridge: Cambridge University Press.

Wright, G. (1948), *The Reshaping of French Democracy*, London: Methuen.

ACR

MONNET, Jean-Marie Omer Gabriel (1888–1979)

Jean Monnet, the father of French post-war economic planning, and of the community approach to European unification, was thus the source of the two main policy innovations of the Fourth Republic. Yet he never held elected office, never fitted into normal civil service routines, was not an economist, nor even directly fathered the Common Market. Difficult to pigeon-hole and controversial, he has been revered by many as the strategist and conscience of European integration, suspect to others as an *éminence grise*, and abominated by hard-core Gaullists as an alleged agent of America. Certainly, with de Gaulle, he has been one of the two archetypal figures of post-war French statecraft – at the opposite, internationalist end of the spectrum.

Jean Monnet was born in Cognac on 9 November 1888, the eldest of four. His father was head of a wholesale brandy firm, a cooperative set up by smallholders to compete with the major merchants. At 16 the son was apprenticed in the City to learn English. At 18 he became a salesman for the firm, travelling in Canada, the United States, England, Sweden, Russia and Egypt.

He might have continued but for 1914. Declared unfit for the army, in September he persuaded a lawyer friend of the family to introduce him to the French prime minister, René Viviani (q.v.). He argued that the French and British should coordinate purchases of scarce overseas supplies to underpin the war effort. Such far-reaching commitments were unheard-of between states at the time and Monnet was only 26. Yet he played a prominent part, in London, in the slow, reluctant creation, from 1916 to 1918, of eight Allied Executives, first coordinating supply of commodities such as wheat, then in 1918, and hardest of all, pooling transport. When peace came, the French put him up as deputy secretary-general of the new League of Nations. He plunged into rehabilitation programmes, especially in Austria and the Saar, but soon realized that Allied cooperation stopped at victory. His experiences at the League seem to have vaccinated him (like others) against both punitive policies of the Versailles Treaty type and inter-governmental institutions where each state can veto action.

After this long public interlude, in 1923 he reverted to business, originally to set the ailing family firm back on its feet. Then he became the Paris partner in an American investment bank, Blair & Co. His international activity included the refloating of the Rumanian and Polish currencies, the liquidation of the Transamerica and Kreuger financial empires after the great crash, and the building of railways in China in 1936. His banking produced many contacts of later importance. For instance, René Pleven (q.v.) was his secretary, John Foster Dulles his lawyer, in refloating the Polish zloty (1927).

In 1938, when already 50, Monnet was drawn back into public service by impending war. The premier, Edouard Daladier (q.v.) used him in the highly delicate operation of placing big warplane orders in a still neutral United States. In October 1939 he became head of the Anglo-French coordinating committee in London. When France fell, he promoted a plan for an Anglo-French Union. Churchill (persuaded by Chamberlain) and even de Gaulle (q.v.) endorsed it, but the disintegrating French government of Paul Reynaud (q.v.) did not. The idea seems to have been to prevent Hitler treating England and France separately and to stimulate resistance in the French empire.

Monnet then went to the British Supply Council in Washington on a passport signed by Churchill. In 1941, he seems to have established himself, as an influential adviser to Beaverbrook and Roosevelt; and as such to have overcome much of the political, administrative and industrial opposition in non-belligerent America to huge war production goals. Within weeks of Pearl Harbour, President Roosevelt was able to announce the victory programme and make America the 'arsenal of democracy' (the phrase itself may be Monnet's). When the Allies landed in North Africa, Roosevelt sent Monnet to Algiers as political adviser to General Giraud. Monnet soon gauged Giraud's political incompetence and helped negotiate de Gaulle's take-over of power in the French committee of national liberation.

After the liberation, in late 1945, Monnet proposed to de Gaulle an investment plan to lay the economic bases of revival. Though the Ministry of Economics, inspired by Pierre Mendès France (q.v.), had a planning department, on 3 January 1946 Monnet was put in charge of the new, independent Commissariat-Général du Plan attached to the Prime Minister.

In effect, the Monnet Plan was devised as a prospectus for raising scarce US dollars. It succeeded in this before and after Marshall Aid. Exceptionally, France was allowed to earmark Marshall counterpart funds for the plan's investment goals. These were a major resource from 1948 to 1950.

The Commissariat had no formal powers of decision. Its influence was based on ability to give a lead. Strains with the Ministry of Finance, controlling funds led to a formal compromise in October 1948 by which the Finance Ministry approved investment payments but normally on Commissariat proposals. The parallel with the European Communities later is interesting.

Monnet took pride in having a full-time staff of less than one hundred including secretaries and chauffeurs. The strategy instead was to produce a 'democratic' kind of corporative plan in which a wide range of industrialists, trade unionists – a novelty at the time – and civil servants from important ministries (especially finance) would all take part. Eighteen sectoral Commissions were set up involving, indirectly, hundreds of people, and chairmen were hand-picked usually by Monnet or his close subordinates. Industrialists were chosen for their reforming outlook, not from spokesmen of the sectoral associations. Monnet and the Commissariat staff, including people like Félix Gaillard (q.v.) and Robert Marjolin, coordinated the sectoral plans.

Investment priorities were concentrated on six 'basic activities': coal, electricity, transport, steel, cement and agricultural equipment. Two key decisions were taken early, with Communist help. The first was to sacrifice (dire) housing needs to production. The second was to raise the working week above the forty hours won by the Popular Front in 1936. Virtually Soviet quantitative targets were set, and despite delays and cutbacks in funding by governments struggling with inflation, were met sufficiently by 1952 to convey a badly needed sense of success. The plan also threw off important technical by-products like national accounting, initially conceived as an instrument to measure, and act against, the 'inflationary gap'.

The general thrust of the plan was to reverse prewar decline through 'modernization', constant adjustment ('the plan is a continuous creation'), and an expansionist outlook. With thirty years of world-wide boom ahead, this turned out to be just the right prescription. But the reconstruction period and Monnet's influence were exceptional, the first plan had no economic doctrine and it was never fully grafted on to the bureaucracy. Its later decline may have been built into the very nature of its initial success.

Success consisted less perhaps in achieving specific targets or rates of growth (which were not exceptional) than in injecting the beginnings of an expansive mentality in industry and the bureaucracy. The plan also laid material foundations to reduce the French inferiority complex towards Germany. Targets, especially for coal and steel, seen as the sinews of power, betrayed a desire to establish a more equal manufacturing balance with Germany and the Ruhr. But by 1949 France's initial post-war policies of 're-gionalizing' Germany, absorbing the industrial Saar, and placing administrative ceilings on German production, were all bankrupt. America was strongly backing West Germany's revival as the key to the West European economy and to the cold war balance with the Soviet Union. French governments could only delay the process and seemed unable to devise alternatives.

It was this which finally drew Monnet, now 61-years-old, into international politics. In March–April 1950, he prepared a plan to pool the coal and steel of France, Germany and any countries willing to join them in a common market under a European High Authority, enjoying federal powers, with right of appeal to a European Court. Monnet had exposed some such ideas to colleagues during the war. He sent the plan to the prime minister, Georges Bidault (q.v.), who had other priorities, and then to the foreign minister, Robert Schuman (q.v.). Schuman was under pressure from the United States and Britain to present an alternative to existing ceilings on German output at their next tripartite foreign ministers' meeting in London on 11 May. But he had promised Parliament he would not lift controls on the Ruhr. Monnet's plan resolved the dilemma. Schuman pushed the plan through cabinet on the morning of 9 May and announced it the same afternoon.

Part of the force of the Schuman Plan lay in its stress on the coal and steel pool as a first step to federation. This harnessed the diffuse desire in continental Europe for unity to the structure designed to meet the concrete problems of France's fear of Germany. It offered a common goal to the founder states. Added drama came from the knowledge that Britain would not accept the federal approach. To go ahead with Germany alone was a bold choice five years after the end of the war. Yet Monnet's sharp line that Britain would 'accept facts' once the new community existed, but not before, prevailed both then and later.

Monnet, not the diplomats, with whom Schuman's relations were rather strained, negotiated with the Germans and French and chaired the conference to negotiate what became the Treaty of Paris, signed on 18 April 1951 setting up the European Coal and Steel Community (ECSC). He and his team behaved as if the community already existed and they were chairing a joint exploration of its necessary features. Later European achievements owed much to the committed 'European' personal networks created in these negotiations and the first years of the ECSC High Authority in Luxembourg, when Monnet was its president (1952 to 1955).

The Korean War broke out only six weeks after the Schuman Plan was launched. This gave a new twist to American policy for Germany: insistence on rearmament. To head off the political dangers of a revived national German army, Monnet and others in autumn 1950 prepared for the premier, René Pleven, what later became the European Defence Community (EDC) project. In the end, the EDC was too much for the French Parliament to swallow and ratification was shelved on 30 August 1954. Monnet, despite reservations about the project, was deeply involved in the politics of promoting the EDC.

However, though many thought the rejection of the EDC marked the end of European integration, Monnet and Paul-Henri Spaak, the Belgian foreign minister, seem to have agreed only two days later that the initiative must be regained through further plans in the economic area. The winter of 1954–5 was dominated by the now inevitable talks to bring Germany directly into Nato. But in February and April, Monnet presented proposals to Spaak for a new start of which the centre-piece was a European Atomic Energy Community. Spaak shared these with the Dutch foreign minister, Jan Beyen, who argued the greater importance of a general Common Market (a longstanding Dutch idea). The Messina conference of the six Community countries, on 1–3 June 1955, agreed to examine both proposals. Slowly, the talks led to the Rome treaties, signed on 25 March 1957, which set up the Common Market (EEC) and Euratom and so extended the European Community more or less to its present functional frontiers.

Leaving the High Authority on 10 June 1955, Monnet set up the Action Committee for the United States of Europe on 14 October 1955 to ensure parliamentary and public support for the post-Messina treaties. The committee was composed of all the major political parties and trade unions in the six countries, as organizations not individuals, except the Communists, Gaullists and, at first, Italian (Nenni) Socialists. The German Social Democrats, who had voted against the Schuman Plan and EDC, now committed themselves to European integration; so did the French Socialists who had split down the middle over the EDC. The action committee recreated the presumption that integration schemes could be ratified in the parliaments of the Community's member states; and actually widened the original base of support of the Schuman Plan days.

Yet at first Monnet's energies were poured only into Euratom. In 1955, most French thought a Common Market ruinous and, like other observers, Monnet long felt it could not be ratified. He also seems to have thought it would either mean free trade without political commitment or demand a degree of economic union beyond immediate reach. He vigorously promoted a Euratom for electric power but renouncing nuclear weapons; and, after Suez, in 1956, persuaded the six governments to commission a Wise Men's report which proposed a huge nuclear power programme to reduce European dependence on Middle East oil. All this failed in the end, despite strong US support for (a) a Euratom operating its own controls outside the UN control agency (IAEA) and (b) for a massive Euratom–US cooperative programme. One reason was the 'bomb', the French right's price for Euratom, later confirmed by de Gaulle; a second was costs, which fell below expectations for conventional energy in the 1960s and rose above them for capital invested in nuclear power; a third was that the French ensured in the treaty that all quinquennial research programmes except the first would be subject to a national veto. Nevertheless, Euratom provided vital time in 1955–6 for French opinion, wedded to protection, to come round to the Common Market.

De Gaulle's arrival in power five months after the establishment of the new European Communities on 1 January 1958 cut off Monnet's influence at the root in France. This was not immediately apparent, since de Gaulle accepted the Common Market and promoted his brand of political cooperation between the six, which Monnet, interestingly for a supposed functionalist, at first supported.

Foreign relations of the new communities also absorbed much energy. Monnet prompted the Americans in June 1959 to join the OEEC to coordinate western economic policies with those of Europe. They responded by setting up a new body, the OECD. Monnet's immediate objective in this – to

outflank the UK-sponsored Free Trade Area and force Britain to try to enter the Common Market – was reached in mid-1961. Prospects of British entry then led to the idea of the 'partnership of equals' between the USA and 'a uniting Europe' which President Kennedy celebrated in a famous speech on 4 July 1962. Monnet's longer-term aim was nothing less than to outgrow the cold war and establish stable relations with the USSR. But hopes now outran reality. De Gaulle's veto on British entry of 13 January 1963 put an abrupt end to all the best-laid schemes of Western 'interdependence'. Thereafter, though Monnet remained active and astonishingly mobile for a man of his age, with easy access to nearly all Western leaders, his prime influence was at an end. He closed the action committee in 1975 when 86. His *Mémoires* were published in 1976. He died in March 1979.

Monnet's career is of exceptional interest on several counts. First and foremost, he launched the Community approach which underpins European integration.

Second, from the Allied Wheat Executive of 1916 to as late (some claim) as the European Council of 1974, he has been France's, perhaps Europe's most fertile begetter of administrative and political schemes. His failure rate has been fairly high, but that seems to have been the price of a unique record of innovation.

Third, Monnet was both a visionary and a pragmatist. His strategy was essentially to promote his long-term goals through plans to deal with immediate problems. The Schuman Plan is the purest case, using the impasse in Franco-German relations to give a concrete base to schemes for European unity. His influence with successive elites in different countries was the product, not the cause, of his capacity to fuse tactics and strategy, practice and ideas.

Fourth, Monnet's internationalist outlook stood outside, and to some extent against, state traditions. Characteristically: 'we are uniting men not states'. Far more deliberately than other post-war 'Europeans', he sought to implant in the international arena rules of law familiar within states but not between them. This was not inherently limited to Europe nor the West; and explains attitudes few contemporaries, especially French ones, ever fully grasped, such as his refusal to be a European nationalist, but also his determination that a uniting Europe should achieve 'equal' relations with the United States. He was the arch-proponent of Europe as the 'ferment of change' for international relations.

However, Monnet's main achievements, the Monnet plan and the community method, succeeded in the special circumstances of post-war reconstruction and cold war. Support in America and Adenauer's Germany for a supranational Europe did not fail so long as France gave the lead. But this flagged in France, at first briefly in 1954 over the EDC, and later for a longer period under the Fifth Republic. The European policy rested on an alliance of France, Germany and the United States and could not work without all three.

Bibliography

Literature on the Monnet Plan and European integration is enormous. But there is no critical biography of Jean Monnet. The only sizeable source in English is his *Memoirs* (ghosted under close direction by François Fontaine and translated by Richard Mayne) (London: Collins, 1978), which he saw as a political testament to his 'method' rather than as autobiography. French sources (all from the Monnet camp, or near it) include *Les Etats-Unis d'Europe ont commencé*: useful brief extracts from Monnet speeches (Paris: Robert Laffont, 1955); texts from the Fondation Jean Monnet pour l'Europe in Lausanne (e.g. *Ainsi va la vie* by Etienne Hirsch and *Plus loin avec Jean Monnet* by François Fontaine); Pascal Fontaine, *Jean Monnet: l'inspirateur* (Paris: Gaucher, 1988); and good portraits in Jacques van Helmont, *Options Européennes* (Brussels: Commission des Communautés Européenes, 1986); and Robert Marjolin, *Le Travail d'une vie* (Paris: Robert Laffont, 1986).

FD

de MONZIE, Pierre Armand Anatole (1876–1947)

Anatole de Monzie was one of the most glittering members of the parliamentary class of the later Third Republic. A brilliant orator and conversationalist, he was also extremely erudite and brought to politics great personal ability as well as driving ambition. He had the kind of intelligence which can be described as ruthless and he prided himself on his realism. Yet these very qualities meant that he never attained the first rank positions for which he yearned; and his actions both before and after the defeat of 1940 showed both the moral, and practical limitations of a political style which seemed to be too clever by half. By the time of his death in 1947, he was a virtual outcast, reviled as a symbol of the frivolity and decadence of the political order that had collapsed in 1940.

De Monzie was born in 1876, the son of a tax officer who eventually settled in the department of the Lot. Educated at the *lycée* in Agen (Lot et Garonne), he was prevented by a childhood accident from entering his favoured profession of the navy and turned instead to the law. He acquired great fame (and wealth) as a barrister but showed very early that he wanted to combine law with politics. At the age of 26 he was head of the private office of Chaumié, minister of education in the Combes (q.v.) government and two years later, in 1904, he became a departmental councillor for the Lot. He was elected a Lot deputy in a 1909 by-election. Describing himself as an Independent Socialist, he always clung to his independence and it was in a government headed by a conservative Republican, Louis Barthou (q.v.) that he first acquired ministerial office, as under-secretary of state for the merchant navy (a new department). He would hold this post again in the war time governments of Ribot (q.v.) and Painlevé (q.v.).

His career took off in the 1920s. Defeated in the 1919 elections, he was almost immediately returned to Parliament as a senator for the Lot. He built up an enormously strong local position in the Lot, acquiring a landed estate and becoming president of the Departmental Council and mayor of Cahors (where he was energetic promotor of municipal enterprise and arts). He consolidated his position as a man of the democratic left by acting as Caillaux's (q.v.) defender in the latter's 1920 trial in the High Court of the Senate. Well placed to acquire office when the left won power in 1924, he held the Ministries of Finance (twice), Education and Justice in the cascade of governments that succeeded each other in 1925–6. Bored with the Senate, he returned to the Chamber of Deputies in a 1929 by-election and then became a long serving minister of education in the Radical-led governments of 1932–4. As minister, he invited Einstein, after his departure from Nazi Germany, to a special chair at the Collège de France and initiated the publication of a vast French encyclopaedia. (He is also credited with the famous remark that as minister of education he knew at any moment what was being taught in every class-room in France.) In August 1938 Daladier (q.v.) made him minister of public works, a position he held until June 1940 and which involved him in building up French supplies (notably of oil) for the impending war.

De Monzie's restless intelligence and ambition could not be satisfied with the essentially technical posts he was given. He was fascinated by foreign affairs and dreamed of becoming another Tallyrand. Believing that there were only two principles in foreign affairs – the politics of presence and the need not to allow interstate relations to be affected by internal political values – he was instrumental in the process whereby France established diplomatic relations with the Vatican (1920) and with the Soviet Union (1924). But in the changed circumstances of the 1930s, hard-headed realism could easily slide into full-hearted appeasement and so it did with de Monzie. Like many 'realists' he was passionately devoted to the chimera of an alliance with Mussolini's Italy and believed that peace with Germany could be brought by handing over colonies. Inexplicably – but violently – hostile to the Czech president, Beneš he was a strong supporter of Munich and in September 1939 he clung to the hope that a deal could be struck over Poland via Mussolini's good offices. (His Ministry became the meeting place for the anti-war party.) It was not until June 1940 that Reynaud (q.v.) felt able to sack him.

De Monzie unsurprisingly voted for Pétain (q.v.) in July 1940 and thereafter continued to play what became an increasingly futile independent game. He held no official post under Vichy (he would have liked the Rome Embassy) and criticized various elements of government policy, notably in *La Saison des Juges*. But he also settled scores with the pre-war resisters in *Ci-Devant* and was among those who in 1943–4 urged the summoning of the National Assembly. It was the sort of realism that no longer made sense. The liberation found him quite unprepared for the hostility he faced and which led, in September 1944, to a prosecution for having threatened the external security of the state and the loss of his right to exercise his profession of barrister. Deeply angered and depressed, he died in 1947.

Bibliography

de Monzie, A. (1942), *Ci-Devant*, Paris: Flammarion.
de Monzie, A. (1943), *La Saison des juges*, Paris: Flammarion.
Duroselle, J.-B. (1979), *La Décadence*, Paris: Imprimerie Nationale.
Jeanneney, J. (1972), *Journal politique*, Paris: A. Colin.
Planté, L. (1955), *Un Grand seigneur de la politique: Anatole de Monzie*, Paris: Clavreuil.

PM

MOULIN, Jean (1899–1943)

After studying law at the University of Montpellier Jean Moulin joined the civil service and by 1930 was the youngest sub-prefect in France. In 1936, as principal private secretary to Pierre Cot, aviation minister in the Popular Front government, he played a major role in circumventing the official French non-intervention policy in the Spanish Civil War. Moulin was in particular responsible for organizing the smuggling of air-crew and Soviet aircraft from France to the Republican forces in Spain. He rejoined the prefectoral corps in 1937. It is however, as Max, the most famous hero and martyr of the French Resistance movement that Jean Moulin is best remembered.

In 1937 he became the youngest prefect in France taking up his post in Chartres in the Eure-et-Loir department. It was there in June 1940 that he was arrested by the Germans soon after they had captured the town and was tortured for refusing to sign a document falsely accusing Senegalese troops of atrocities in his department. To avoid signing Moulin eventually tried to commit suicide and, given the scandal created at a time when the occupying forces were trying to win over French public opinion, was released. From 22 June until November 1940 when the Vichy government relieved him of his duties, accusing him of being a Freemason, Moulin defended the population of Eure-et-Loir against the exactions and brutality of the Germans. On his dismissal he made contact with the embryonic Resistance movement and in September 1941 joined General de Gaulle in London where he was appointed coordinator of Resistance groups in the unoccupied zone. Dropped by parachute near Salon-de-Provence in late December 1942 with the necessary funds and transmitting equipment he immediately set about persuading the leaders of the three major Resistance groups in the unoccupied zone – Combat, Franc-Tireur and Libération – to acknowledge de Gaulle's authority and to merge their movements into a single fighting force. By March 1943 this had been achieved and the Mouvements Unis de la Résistance came into existence. Moulin was the official intermediary between de Gaulle and the internal French Resistance, setting up a communications and information network in preparation for a unified Resistance movement throughout France.

Given the rivalry and general atmosphere of mutual suspicion between the different factions within the Resistance, the degree of unity which Moulin managed to achieve is a tribute to his organizational ability and to his dedication. Largely as a result of his efforts the Resistance gained recognition on the international scene and became the major political force to be reckoned with in France at the liberation.

In May 1943 he became the first chairman of the national committee of the Resistance which grouped together eight Resistance movements in the two zones. No doubt as a result of a betrayal, he was captured by the SS at Caluire on 26 June 1943. At the Gestapo headquarters in Lyons he was quickly identified as Max, the legendary leader of the Resistance, was interrogated and tortured but remained silent. Although the German authorities maintained that he died during his deportation to Germany it is almost certain that he was tortured to death in Lyons in July 1943 at the hand of the Gestapo officer Klaus Barbie. In 1964 his remains were ceremoniously transferred from the Père-Lachaise cemetery in Paris to the Panthéon.

Bibliography

Virtually all the reliable sources of information on Moulin are in French:

Bédarida, F. and J.-P. Azéma (1983), *Jean Moulin et le Conseil National de la Résistance: études et témoignages,* Paris: CNRS.

Calef, H. (1980), *Jean Moulin: une vie, 20 juin 1899 – 21 juin 1943,* Paris: Plon.

Frénay, H. (1969), *L'Enigme Jean Moulin,* Paris: Presses de la Cité; 2nd edition 1982.

Michel, H. (1964), *Jean Moulin l'unificateur,* Paris: Hachette.

Moulin, J. (Max) (1983), *Premier Combat,* Paris: Editions de Minuit (his own account of his experiences in Chartres, June 1940).

GTH

MOUNIER, Emmanuel (1905–50)

Mounier came from a modest background in Grenoble where he became a student of Jacques Chevalier, a Catholic philosopher who was later to be responsible for the Vichy government's attempts to Christianize French education. Moving to Paris and to the Ecole Normale Supérieure, he came under the influence of Jacques Maritain who published his first book, a collaborative work on Charles Péguy (q.v.). It was in Maritain's circle, which met at Meudon, that he developed the idea of a new review with one of his co-authors on the Péguy book, Georges Izard. Mounier and Izard believed that the bases of bourgeois capitalist society were crumbling and that the evidence for this was all around – the World War, the Bolshevik Revolution, the Wall Street Crash, the scandals of the Third Republic. If this was the established order, for Mounier it was the *désordre etabli*. Since the corrupting influence of materialism penetrated all areas of life, it was therefore urgent to create a Renaissance (*refaire la Renaissance* and bring about the break between Christian order and the established disorder (*la rupture entre l'ordre chrétien et le désordre établi*). The role of Mounier's review *L'Esprit*, was to provide a new set of moral and political values based on the primacy of the spiritual. Aimed primarily at Catholics *L'Esprit* sought to win them away from their traditional allegiance to the right.

The Popular Front government earned grudging support from Mounier who was impressed by its popular support though he denounced its demagogy. During the Spanish Civil War Mounier was a strong supporter of the Republic and worked tirelessly to produce evidence of right-wing atrocities against Catholics to match the stories appearing in the Catholic press of Republican excesses.

The economic and social policies advocated by Mounier at this time were decentralization, the establishment of cooperatives with workers involved in decision-taking, and a communal life (*la vie communautaire*) which would provide the opportunity for the full development (*l'épanouissement*) of the personality. Mounier's personalism was opposed to the pervading individualism based on the power of money. In common with much Catholic thinking, Mounier did not see wealth as a sign of divine grace but as a corrupting influence.

The collapse of France in 1940, the chaotic exodus towards the south and the installation of Pétain's administration, led Mounier to think that in the breathing space left before the barbarians took over completely some work was possible and indeed necessary. Above all he was determined to prevent Maurras' Action Française from holding a monopoly position in the establishment of the new ideology. He urged that the mobilization of youth, an enormous issue given the exodus from Northern France and the absence of national service and of normal employment policies, should not be into a single youth movement as in totalitarian countries. In general, Mounier sought to establish a forum from which new ideas could develop. To this end he brought *L'Esprit* out again from his base in Lyons, when the Vichy censor decided that such opposition could not be tolerated. Shortly afterwards Mounier was arrested and imprisoned.

In the euphoria of the liberation, *L'Esprit* reappeared on a permanent basis with its influence greatly enhanced. Mounier was by now closer to Marxism (particularly of the 1844 variety) and his influence was bearing fruit as new generations of Catholics came through the Jeunesse Agricole Chrétienne, the Jeunesse Ouvrière Chrétienne and the Jeunesse Etudiante Chrétienne. *L'Esprit* was in the forefront of those defending the worker priest movement against Vatican hostility and was loud in its denunciation of anti-communism. This was not through any special affection for the Communist Party; rather it was the recognition that attacks on communism hit the millions of French poor and deprived those who had only the party and its union, the CGT to defend them.

Mounier's greatest successes were to come after his premature death at the age of 44. The transformation of the Catholic trade union, the CFTC into the more open and more progressive CFDT reflected his earlier influence on the JOC. A less dramatic change took place in agricultural politics in the 1960s when the young progressive farmers of the JAC and the Centre National des Jeunes Agriculteurs took over the farmers' union the FNSEA. Henri Nallet, minister of agriculture in the 1988 Rocard (q.v.) government is a product of that evolution. But it was at the centre of the Catholic Church, at the Vatican Council (Vatican II) called by Pope John XXIII that Mounier's influence was most powerful. Pope John had previously been Apostolic Nuncio in Paris and had used his office to defend *L'Esprit* on more than one occasion when it was threatened by Pius XII with being placed on the Index. The council of experts which prepared the agenda for the Council was dominated by theologians who had been close to Mounier. Several of the issues put before Vatican II had been discussed in the 1930s in a small group comprising Mounier, Gabriel Marcel and Teilhard de Chardin and two Dominicans who would appear as experts at Vatican II, Chenu and Congar.

Mounier's influence came not from an elaborate ideology, which he abhorred, but from a 'stance' or a 'style', a commitment to involvement in the world, to bringing moral principles rather than political calculation to bear on decisions, to devoting oneself to the service of others and to being always ready to listen to others. His death at the age of 44 was through exhaustion. His legacy can be seen in the fact that neither the bishops nor the laity in France can be automatically labelled right-wing. In the last bastion of Catholicism – Latin America – priests guided by the theology of liberation consciously use his arguments and the Solidarity movement in Poland also felt his influence.

Bibliography

Emmanuel Mounier's complete works are published as follows (Ouvrages [de] Emmanuel Mounier): *1931–1939*, vol. 1 (Paris: Seuil, 1961); *Traité de caractère*, vol. II (Paris: Seuil, 1961); *1944–50*, vol. III (Paris: Seuil, 1962); *Recueils posthumes; correspondence*, vol. IV (Paris: Seuil, 1963).

Mounier's short text, *Le Personalisme*, is published as number 395 of the *Que sais-je?* series (Paris: Presses Universitaires de France, 1959). There is useful biographical material in J.-M. Domenach, *Emmanuel Mounier* (Paris: Seuil, 1972) and in English see E. Mounier, *Existentialist Philosophies* (London: Rockliff, 1948).

BD

MOUTET, Marius (1876–1968)

Marius Moutet was born in Nîmes in the Gard in April 1876. A student first at Lycée Henri IV (Paris) and then Ampère (Lyons), he took his degree in law. His political baptism came with the Dreyfus affair: a socialist from 1896, he and Herriot founded the Lyons section of the Ligue des Droits de l'Homme in 1898. Eventually, he became its vice-president.

Moutet's home base stretched along the Rhône from Lyons southward. A municipal councillor representing the 'proletarian fortress' of the Croix-Rousse in Lyons from 1902 to 1925, he founded there the Unified Socialist Party of 1905. In 1925 he moved to Valence. A deputy for the Rhône between 1914 and 1928, he shifted appropriately to the Drôme, which he represented between 1929 and 1942.

The main thrust of Moutet's career, however, stemmed from the universalist significance of the Dreyfus affair. It had two aspects: his presence at the Bar and his involvement with the policy of 'overseas France'. At the Bar, Moutet's most famous client was Caillaux. For Moutet, the Caillaux trial, in 1920, replayed 'the affair' – the rights of man against *raison d'état*. Moutet himself had been an 'ardent patriot' in the war: he went to Russia in May 1917 to help persuade Kerensky to launch the June offensive. Moutet's judicial training and interests spilled over into his approach to colonial and extra-European affairs.

Moutet's colonial involvement began in 1919: as a member of parliamentary commissions, he sought to invest the name of 'overseas France' with a minimum of juridical plausibility. Thus he promoted a law admitting Algerian Muslims to French citizenship. He also predicted that Indo-China must become autonomous if it was to be retained as a colony. Moutet founded the Institut Franco-Chinois; mixing his 'universal' and 'parochial' roles, he received Chinese students in Lyons; his friendship with Sun Yat Sen would still earn him greetings as late as 1945 from Chiang Kai Shek.

That this man, who saw France, human rights and the law as inextricably connected should have been minister for colonies from 1936 to 1938 and 1945 to 1947 speaks loudly about the non-revolutionary policies of those governments and the nature of the colonial regime Moutet tried to transform. His principal reform, in 1936, dealt with Indo-China: he proposed to establish full political and trade union rights for the natives. His admiring biographer says the policy was 'unfortunately not always faithfully and loyally observed'. Nevertheless free elections were held in 1937 and a Trotskyist party with Pivertiste tendencies (see Pivert) won a major electoral victory in Vietnam. But they were interned by Moutet's successor in 1940.

In 1945, Moutet tried again. In Indo-China his policy ran into the Vietminh. He was more successful with Black French Africa. The educated elites welcomed political openings such as representation in the National Assembly. At a conference in Valence, Senghor – the future president of Senegal – paid tribute to Moutet's spirit of justice.

Moutet's ministerial career ended in 1947. Afterwards he accumulated prestigious honorific positions. A senator, he was president of the French representatives at Strasbourg; in 1958 he was president of the Sahara commission and vice-president of the foreign affairs and armed forces committee. He died in 1968.

Bibliography

There is no biography that could be recommended. The dictionary of French deputies and the Paris 'Who's Who' in the Bibliotheque National are at least safe. His role in the Caillaux trial is discussed in J.C. Allain, *Joseph Caillaux*, 2 vols (Paris: Imprimerie Nationale, 1981). His role as minister of colonies is discussed by Daniel Guérin, *Front populaire, révolution manqué* (Paris: Julliard, 1963), and Jean Rabaut, *Tout est possible* (Paris: Denoël, 1974). On French socialism and the colonial question, see André Philip, *Le Socialisme trahi* (Paris: Plon, 1957). On French Indo-China in these years, see W. Duiker, *The Rise of Nationalism in Vietnam* (New York: Cornell University Press, 1976).

MK

MULLER, Emile (1915–88)

Emile Muller was mayor of Mulhouse (Haut-Rhin) for twenty five years and a founder of the centrist (anti-Communist) Social Democrat movement which was to become part of the Union for French Democracy. He was born and brought up in Mulhouse in Alsace where he was a typesetter and later the owner of a printing business. He joined the Young Socialists of the SFIO and was a member of the provisional City Council of Mulhouse in 1945, becoming an assistant to the mayor.

In the elections of 1947 the Gaullists won the municipal elections but standing on a 'third force', on a Socialist and Christian Democrat (MRP) list. Muller was elected in the 1953 elections, became mayor in 1956 and was regularly returned until he retired in 1977. As a mayor, Muller was better known for the extensive building programme and the creation of new facilities than more adventurous forms of policy. He was also a member of the Council of Europe, Western European Union and a strong Mendès supporter in 1954. He was always a strong anti-Communist, a supporter of the right in the SFIO, and refused to stand down for Communists in the 1970 department (cantonal) elections. The same month, March 1970, he left the Socialist Party, disillusioned with its alliance policy and founded the Parti de la Démocratie Socialiste. He was one of the founders of the Réformateur Party in November 1971 but his anti-Communist stance held up his entry into its governing body – Bureau National. He was thus elected to the Assembly as a Réformateur Social Democrat in 1973, then as a UDF Social Democrat in 1978 but was defeated in 1981 by a Socialist.

The Parti Social Démocrate became (in December 1973) a part of the Mouvement Social Démocrate de France (MSDF) of which he became vice-president. Muller stood for the MSDF in the 1974 presidential elections but polled only 176,279 votes (0.69 per cent of votes). On the second ballot the MSDF supported Giscard.

DSB

de MUN, comte Adrien Albert-Marie (1841–1914)

After an early career in the army, de Mun entered Parliament in 1876, with the dual purpose of defending Catholic interests and improving working-class conditions. Apart from two short breaks, he was to be a deputy for the Morbihan and then Finistère for the rest of his life – and was widely respected for his oratorical skill and personal courage. He had considered founding a specifically Catholic party in the 1880s; but Leo XIII dissuaded him, fearing that it might further envenom Church-state relations and embarrass the Vatican's dealings with France. Although sympathetic to the royalists, de Mun had discounted all serious hope of a restoration as early as 1873; and, despite private misgivings about what he saw as Leo's appeasement policies, he obediently accepted the papal *ralliement* to the Republic in 1892. As he later wrote, 'I have had an ardent Catholic faith and a social doctrine. I no longer have a political faith; I have sought only expedients.' The anticlerical legislation of 1900–6 found him in the forefront of the government's critics – and increasingly disposed to intransigent attitudes. He wholeheartedly supported Pius X's disastrous decision to reject the property and legal framework left to the Church by the disestablishment law of 9 December 1905, and erroneously imagined that popular indignation at government policy would give the Catholic party, Action Libérale Populaire, massive electoral support. This was a major miscalculation, on a par with his advice to the royalist pretender in the 1880s to stake his chances on General Boulanger, or his sorry part in the anti-Dreyfusard campaign of the late 1890s.

De Mun will chiefly be remembered for the foundation of the Oeuvre des Cercles Catholiques Ouvriers (1871) and the Association Catholique de la Jeunesse Française (1886), which rose to a membership of 140,000 by the time of his death. His career exemplifies the fact that many of the sharpest spurs to the social conscience of the Church were men who were politically and theologically conservative. In the 1880s he was advocating not only accident and sickness insurance, but also unemployment insurance and a long overdue income-tax, while the early years of the twentieth century found him defending the right of state employees to strike. Towards the end of his life, French military security became increasingly one of his preoccupations; and President Poincaré, who valued his support on military issues, invited him to accompany the government to Bordeaux in the early months of the war.

Bibliography

The most recent studies on de Mun are Benjamin F. Martin, *Count Albert de Mun: Paladin of the Third Republic* (Chapel Hill: University of North Carolina Press, 1978) and Philippe Levillain, *Albert de Mun: catholicism français et catholicisme romain du syllabus au ralliement* (Rome: Ecole Française de Rome, 1983).

ML

N

NAPOLEON III (Louis-Napoleon Bonaparte) (1803–73)

Louis-Napoleon Bonaparte was the third of three sons (two survived to adulthood) of Louis Bonaparte, brother of the Emperor Napoleon and king of Holland from 1805 to 1810, and Hortense de Beauharnais, daughter of Josephine de Beauharnais who had been the emperor's first wife. The marriage however was already falling apart when Louis-Napoleon was born (some historians have cast doubts on Louis Bonaparte's paternity, as he did himself when it suited him) and the young prince was looked after by his mother and grandmother. On the latter's death in 1814, he was brought up by his mother alone, in exile on the Swiss–German border and later in Italy, where, as a young man, he became embroiled in anti-papal and anti-Austrian adventures.

On the death of his older brother on 1831, Louis-Napoleon became recognized leader of the young generation of Bonapartes. His political thought was developing on the Napoleonic model: power emanating from the will of the people (hence his dislike of the Orleanist regime of Louis-Philippe), and reconciliation of aristrocracy and common people: equality and national independence assured by a centralized system; the fostering of freedom, including that of oppressed nations, except when crisis or war necessitated a firm hand to ensure order; the grasping of political opportunities instead of merely waiting to see what would happen, as Louis-Napoleon's uncles were doing.

However, one such opportunity misfired. Accompanied by a group of adventurers and malcontents who had assembled in Southern Germany, Louis-Napoleon tried to rally the Strasbourg garrison to the Bonapartist cause prior to a march on Paris, but was arrested. King Louis-Philippe accepted his mother's plea that he should not be brought to trial, which would have shown the latent strength of Bonapartist opinion, on condition that he left Europe; seven fellow-plotters faced trial, but were acquitted. Returning to Switzerland as his mother's death from cancer approached, he soon launched himself again into political intrigue and went to London, which he already knew from short visits, in order to pursue, by plotting and writing (*Des idées napoléoniennes,* 1839) his campaign against the July Monarchy. Another attempted *coup d'état* failed, however, when he was arrested after landing at Boulogne-sur-Mer in 1840 with a small group intent on taking over the town's garrison. He was tried, with sixteen others, sentenced to life imprisonment, and spent the next six years in the fortress prison of Ham, in a rather damp part of the department of the Somme. The rigours of prison life however were mitigated by his being allowed to employ a laundress by whom he had two sons; he also continued to write, adding social and economic dimensions to his basic political message. Escaping from prison in 1846, he returned to England, though his wish to visit his dying father in Italy was frustrated by the Austrian authorities.

The Revolution of February 1848 overthrew the July Monarchy and installed a Republican government, which however refused to have Louis-Napoleon on its territory when he arrived in Paris to announce his adherence to the new regime. Between March and September 1848, when he finally returned to France, Louis-Napoleon's support grew steadily, and what had started as a position of weakness, isolated from both the victorious Republicans and the royalists of the former regime, allowed him to appear as the candidate of national reconciliation and unity by the time of the December elections for the presidency. He won easily, attracting nearly three-quarters of the seven-and-a-half million votes cast. This success meant above all that the peasants voted overwhelmingly for Louis-Napoleon, and that Republican suspicion of him had dwindled, but more fundamentally, that France, again plunged into chaotic times by the 'unexpected' Revolution of February 1848, had opted once more for a providential saviour.

The new president, helped by the plebiscitary nature of his election, was soon able to appoint his own supporters to key positions, and succeeded in his first test in foreign policy by using French troops to restore the Pope to his temporal powers while insisting these should be applied in a spirit of justice and liberalism. But internal political affairs were still in turmoil, with strong Republican and royalist elements not reconciled to the regime, and contemplating taking power by force. The Constitution did not allow the re-election of Louis-Napoleon as president after his term expired in spring 1852, and he failed in an attempt to have this provision changed. The way out of the impasse was the *coup d'état* of 2 December 1851 which was well prepared and executed by Louis-Napoleon and his followers; opponents were arrested, printing presses seized, sporadic barricades dismantled, and the people were invited to approve the new state of affairs in a plebiscite characterized by repression of opposition. The regime, though still a Republic, was backed by the 'party of order', and quickly assumed a monarchical colour; a new constitution in January 1852 greatly increased the personal power of the president, now officially called 'Prince'. The plebiscite empowered him to exercise national sovereignty for ten years, and re-election was not explicitly ruled out; all state servants and parliamentarians were required to give an oath of allegiance; the president was the head of the executive, the government being simply the apex of the administrative pyramid, and not accountable to the Lower House (*Corps législatif*). Louis-Napoleon soon imposed severe limitations on press freedom, took control of higher education, made concessions to the Catholic Church (especially on education), and organized a system of official candidates at elections, which effectively nullified universal suffrage – though independent-minded candidates were sometimes elected in surprisingly large numbers. Louis-Napoleon's popularity with the masses was still great, however, and a plebiscite in November 1852 overwhelmingly ratified a decree naming him emperor, with the name of Napoleon III. Conscious of the need for an heir, he married Eugénie de Montijo in January 1853. A son was born in 1856.

The new emperor capitalized on his immense prestige; opposition was minimal and disorganized, though assassination attempts were not infrequent. Napoleon III doubled the number of state officials, and used the institution of prefects in each department to get official candidates elected, impose government policy, and gather intelligence; like ministers and members of the Council of State (Conseil d'Etat), they were from the bourgeois class. In economic matters, Napoleon III was a liberal, though he realized that the State had a general duty to regulate and stimulate economic activity; in any case post-1852 stability, following social and political turmoil, favoured economic growth. Napoleon's

favourite schemes were to complete the railway network begun during the July Monarchy and to foster urban renewal, especially in Paris, where the new railway stations, gateways to the rest of France, needed to be linked by a new inner network of boulevards. This transformation of Paris is closely associated with the name of Haussmann, who in 1853 was transferred from the south-west to be prefect of the Seine until 1870; in fact, Napoleon had already begun the process when he was still president.

Having consolidated his power, the emperor was able to put into effect his ideas on foreign policy. His aim was no less ambitious than that of his uncle – to recast the European system on the basis of nation-states sustained by plebiscites and universal suffrage, by negating the consequences of the 1815 treaties. The very establishment of a new French empire was already a challenge to the guarantors of the 1815 system – Russia, Austria and Prussia. He needed, however, to avoid the two major defects in his uncle's policy, firstly by not incurring the implacable hostility of Great Britain (which meant that his designs on Belgium came to naught) and secondly by going to war only to the limited extent necessary to bring about negotiated settlements. French involvement in the Crimean War (1854–6) as well as mutual state visits by the emperor and Queen Victoria, reinforced the British connection. Although Napoleon failed to bring Austria into the war against Russia (he wanted an independent Polish nation to result from a widening of the war) the 1856 Congress of Paris marked the success of French political and military assertiveness, just as the Vienna Congress in 1815 had signalled its failure.

This assertiveness showed itself in the late 1850s over the Italian question: the emperor wanted to establish a confederation of three or four Italian states free from Austrian control. This was a logical step in his policy of dismantling the 1815 treaties, and would serve also to diffuse growing Republican opposition in France, and to absorb Nice and French-speaking Savoie as compensation for French help to the kingdom of Piedmont. Napoleon proceeded in his favoured way – personal intrigues with European sovereigns, a two-month war in Northern Italy in 1859, and a negotiated settlement with Austrian Emperor, though the union of most of Italy in 1860 went beyond Napoleon's plans for that nation. The early 1860s were characterized by relative political calm in Europe, and by extra-European adventures by Napoleon to which French opinion was largely hostile: an expedition to protect Christians in Lebanon and Syria, which aroused British suspicions, especially since French capital was behind the building of the Suez Canal; an expedition, this time in conjunction with Britain, to Peking; the first trade settlements in Indo-China, beginning an era of colonization lasting until 1954; an expedition to suppress a revolt in Algeria; and most significant (and least successful) of all, an attempt to establish Maximilian of Austria as emperor of Mexico.

In domestic politics, the second half of the decade of the 1860s saw growing economic stagnation, and increased political opposition to the regime, often articulated by a legislature (*corps législatif*) which had managed to win a small increase in its powers. The emperor had prematurely aged, suffering from a stone in the bladder; the prince imperial, heir to the empire, was still young (born 1856). During the months after the 1869 elections, Napoleon was obliged to accept political change and a 'liberal empire'; the *corps législatif* gained even more independence, and the government at last became accountable to it. The emperor's health however was further deteriorating; but just when, in June 1870, he and Eugénie had decided to abdicate when their son reached the age of 18 in 1874, a crisis broke which precipitated their departure.

Napoleon objected to the suggestion that a member of the Prussian royal family should be the new king of Spain, but he was outmanoeuvred by Bismarck. He went to war with Prussia without allies, with defective strategic planning, and with a weaker army, despite the military reforms occasioned by the 1866 Prussian defeat of Austria. Napoleon made a half-hearted attempt to command the armies in the field, then handed over to Marshal Bazaine, who capitulated in Metz in October 1870. Already in September 1870, however, Napoleon had been caught in Sedan by the advancing Prussians; and he passed through Belgium to begin a short captivity in the castle of Wilhelmshöhe, near Kassel, where he had spent some time as a child. In Paris on 4 September (hence the name of a street near the Opéra), a Republic was declared, which concluded an armistice and a peace treaty with the victorious Prussians, and suppressed the insurrectionary Paris Commune.

In March 1871 Napoleon left Wilhelmshöhe to join Eugénie and their son in exile in Chislehurst, Kent. When Queen Victoria saw him briefly in Windsor soon afterwards (the first time since 1857), she found him 'very fat and grey'. The ex-emperor's health deteriorated rapidly in the second half of 1872, and he died in January 1873 after two operations on his bladder; his grave is in Farnborough, Hampshire. French opinion was split between royalists and Republicans, and it is hardly likely that a 'return from Elba' hoped for by a handful of associates for spring 1873 would have succeeded. His only son died in Zululand in 1879.

Bibliography

The life of Napoleon III and the history of the Second Empire are the subject of numerous works, but the following biographies are recommended:

Girard, L. (1986), *Napoléon III*, Paris: Fayard.

Roux, G. (1969), *Napoléon III*, Paris: Flammarion.

Smith, W.H.C. (1982), *Napoléon III*, Paris: Hachette.

Thompson, J.M. (1980), *Louis Napoleon and the Second Empire*, Oxford: Blackwell.

MS

NAQUET, Alfred-Joseph (1834–1916)

Principally associated with the parliamentary law of 1884, re-establishing divorce, Alfred Naquet, a Jew, born in Carpentras in the Vaucluse was by training and profession a pharmacist. Awarded his doctorate in medicine in 1859, he occupied a number of teaching posts, and published widely on medical matters, spending some years in a post at Palermo.

In 1867, shortly after his return to Paris, he was imprisoned for his involvement in secret societies. The publication of his book *Religion, propriété, famille* (Brussels: H. Kistemaeckers, 1877) earned him a further period of imprisonment. Naquet took refuge in Spain during the last months of Empire, returning in the aftermath of the 4 September and serving on the defence committee with the government delegation at Tours and at Bordeaux. Elected to represent Vaucluse in 1871, he joined the ranks of the extreme-left and, in 1876, tried briefly to form a breakaway movement whose aim was to revise the constitution and to rewrite Gambetta's Radical Belleville programme.

His campaigns for state control of railways and mines, for the separation of Church and state, and for freedom of speech and of association had already earned him the suspicion of moderate Republican opinion, and he was an eloquent opponent of Mac-Mahon's *moral order* ministries. One of Gambetta's '363' Republicans at the time of the Broglie-Fourtou ministry of June 1877, Naquet lost his seat in the October elections. He was re-elected however in 1878, and his parliamentary career continued until 1898, the years 1882–90 being spent as senator for the Vaucluse.

As early as 1876, Naquet had put his name to a bill demanding the abrogation of all legislation restrictive of press freedom. When, two years later, he submitted a watered-down series of proposals, he gave the required momentum to a process which was to result in the epoch-making law of 29 July 1881 establishing press freedom. The campaign to re-establish divorce, another essential plank in the secularization platform of the Republic, bore fruit in 1883. Having become a senator for the Vaucluse, he was able to pilot his legislation through the Upper House in 1884.

In later years, Naquet was, perhaps strangely for a Jew, involved in Boulangism. In June 1888, with Socialist deputies of Boulangist sympathies, he helped relaunch the journal *La Presse*, which became the main organ of the 'democratic' wing of the Boulangist movement. Some years later, he was implicated in the Panama scandal and fled to London; he had also become involved in anarchist activities, and he left public life after his acquittal in 1898. His published works, including *La République radicale* (Paris: Germer-Baillière, 1873), *Le Divorce* (Paris: Dentu, 1877) and *Collectivism, Socialism and the Liberal School* fairly reflect the pattern of Naquet's career and the range of his interests.

Bibliography

Naquet, A. (1895) *Collectivism, Socialism and the Liberal School,* trans. W. Heaford, London: S. Sonnescheim.
Naquet, A. (1939) *Autobiographie*, Paris: E. Pillias.

ACR

NIZAN, Paul Yves (1905–40)

Paul Nizan was born in 1905, son of a father who rose from skilled worker (1,800 francs a year in 1888) to railway manager-engineer (7,200 francs in 1914). In 1916 he entered the Lycée Henri IV in Paris, main gate to the Ecoles Normales (academies), from which the administrative–academic elite was formed. Nizan's teachers sensed an exceptional talent destined for the Panthéon. One day, Nizan and his pal, 'wonderchild' no. 2 (Sartre) climbed Montmartre. Nizan ogled Paris as if she was a victim to devour, and exclaimed 'Hey, hey Rastignac'. Sartre echoed 'Hey, hey'. Nizan and Sartre entered the Ecole Normale Supérieure at rue d'Ulm in 1924. Nizan was a dandy, Sartre a blob. As a bourgeois aspiring to aristocracy and a male bluestocking, Nizan confused

insolence with dignity: a woman who offered herself was told 'Madam, we would be soiled'.

In 1926, Nizan absconded to Aden (in Arabia). He was to serve as a secretary, but potentially partner, to the Anglo-French tycoon Antoin Besse. In 1927 he returned to the Ecole Normale Supérieure in the rue d'Ulm, disillusioned. In December 1927 he married Henriette Alphon; the witnesses were Sartre (q.v.) and Aron (q.v.). In racialist discourse he soiled his pure Breton roots, henceforth implanted in the daughter of a 'banker' (Jew). In religious terms, this civil marriage was no marriage, in Sartrean eyes marriage is bad faith, and for a 'Rastignac', a man who lives in obsessive fidelity is finished.

Just before marrying, Nizan joined the PCF. His rage had grown against a 'civilization' which tempted him to prattle of Wagner, while doing the real job of exploiting the other class, the other sex, and other peoples. Nizan entered an anti-French PCF; it incited revolts against French imperialism in 'overseas France' and even in Alsace.

During 1929 Nizan joined the first existentialist–Marxist journal in France, the short-lived *Revue Marxiste*. The rage overflowed into two *succès de scandale* – *Aden, Arabie* (1931) and *The Watchdogs* (1932), a denunciation of the idealist philosophers of the rue d'Ulm. If the 'class against class' PCF (see Thorez) distrusted intellectuals, Nizan hated them.

Maybe Nizan's rage derived from the purity of his 'Heideggerian' struggle with death. If Marxism could merely offer authentic life, Nizan's despair in the face of death would not be quelled. When he visited the Soviet Union during 1934 he asked young Soviets if they feared death; forgetting that the five-year plans had collectivized death, they answered yes.

1934 saw the introduction of the Popular Front, Stalin's great transformation of 'Leninism'. Nizan's antibourgeois rage was henceforth unacceptable; the PCF wanted Nizan the celebrity. His activities took three main directions. He was a leading figure in assembling a front of 'antifascist' intellectuals, with special responsibility for Catholics. In 1935 he 'admitted' to Mounier that he had been wrong. Ideologically, he told the Catholics, we are incompatible, but otherwise we have many points of contact. The second line was journalism: as foreign correspondent for *L'Humanité* (1935–7) and *Ce Soir* (1937–9) he identified passionately with the struggle against Hitler. Thirdly he wrote novels. The post-1934 novels, *The Trojan Horse* (1935) and *The Conspiracy* (1938) retained a metaphysical rage haunted by fears of treachery. *The Conspiracy* was an intellectual's fantasy: what would Dostoevsky do had he joined the

PCF? Nizan's fears make sense: his activities were mutually supportive in political terms (the angry novelist was ideal bait for Catholic vanities), but ideologically 'the Party' had pushed Nizan to the brink of self-betrayal. As with all fantasy fears, Nizan knew the answer – in Russia, he wrote, the Grand Inquisitor is now in power.

The Soviet–German pact of August 1939 buffeted the entire PCF. For Nizan, the blow was doubly cruel. His letter of resignation, published in the Catholic journal *L'Oeuvre,* was provoked by the Soviet invasion of Poland. Nizan claimed that the PCF should learn cynicism from Stalin and disown the pact. He might as well have said that the Third International should be dissolved. The real point was touched when he described the invasion as 'too Dostoevskian'. Nizan discovered that twelve years of communism had led only to moral suicide.

Nizan was mobilized in September 1939. In March 1940 he obtained a posting as interpreter with the British Expeditionary Force. In May 1940 he was at the centre of the Panzer attack; along with almost all the officers in the sector he was killed.

In March 1940 the PCF launched the story of Nizan as a police spy. In 1947 Sartre challenged them – there was no evidence. Nizan was however 'forgotten'. In 1960 Sartre, now 'Panthéonized', sensed a new leftism, and prefaced *Aden, Arabie.* Sartre envied Nizan the misfortune of dying pure; more sincerely he speculated that Nizan would have rejoined the PCF in the Resistance. Some Communists accepted Sartre's version. This 'Hegelian atheist' variant on Catholic stories of deathbed repentance gave Nizan a limited readership. It is the last 'conspiracy' which Nizan occasioned.

Bibliography

Thanks to Sartre's preface, *Aden, Arabie* was translated in 1968 (New York: Monthly Review Press). A quite contrary view of Nizan will be found in Henri Lefèbvre, *La Somme et le reste,* vol. I (Paris: La Nef, 1951).

David Caute, *Communism and the French Intellectuals, 1914–1960* (London: André Deutsche, 1964), is useful. Despite his reverence for Henriette Nizan, Pascal Ory, *Paul Nizan, destin d'un revolté* (Paris: Ramsay, 1980) is most incisive. W. Redfern, *Paul Nizan: Committed literature in a conspiratorial world* (Princeton, NJ: Princeton University Press, 1972), is acceptable, but literary rather than political.

MK

NOËL, Léon (1888–1987)

Noël was born in Paris, in 1888, the son of a member of the Conseil d'Etat. He followed his father into this most select branch of French public administration but after the First World War moved increasingly into government circles. He worked in the private office of Maurice Colrat under-secretary of state of the interior in 1921, was a member of the High Commission for the Rhineland, was head of the private office of both Laval (q.v.) and Tardieu (q.v.) and briefly became director of the national police force, the Sûreté-générale. In the 1930s his career moved into diplomacy. He was minister plenipotentiary between 1932–5 (working as head of the French legation in Czechoslovakia) and in 1935 was secretary-general of government during the preparation of the Stresa Pact. The same year he was sent to the highly sensitive Warsaw embassy, where he remained for five years. His relations with Colonel Beck, Poland's leader, were bad and he became so alarmed at what he saw as the ludicrously pro-German policy of Warsaw that he suggested after Munich that the Franco-Polish alliance should cease to be automatic. A year later he was involved in the last desperate efforts to stop the Nazi–Soviet Pact, extracting from Poland, when it was too late, limited agreements to military collaboration with the Soviet Union. His role as ambassador has been highly rated by historians and he acquired the beginnings of his subsequent, more public reputation when in 1940, as a member of the team sent to negotiate the armistice, he refused to sign the agreed terms.

After the war he joined the boards of various industrial companies but also took on a much more high-profile political role. Enormously impressed with de Gaulle, he became a leading member of the Rassemblement pour la France, was appointed to its *conseil de direction* and was elected to the national Assembly (for the department of the Yonne) in 1951. His real importance to Gaullism came, however, in the early years of the Fifth Republic. A member of the consultative constitutional committee, he was appointed by de Gaulle to head the new Constitutional Council. The Council was an innovation in French constitutional practice, since its very existence was a challenge to the hitherto dominant doctrine of unfettered parliamentary sovereignty and thus to traditional republicanism. Noël proved to be the agent de Gaulle needed in his bid to reshape French constitutional practice. It is a measure of his commitment to the strict constitutional Gaullism that he criticized the excessively conciliatory attitude of Prime Minister Debré (q.v.) towards parliament. In his memoirs, which reveal an energetic and even aggressive temperament, he is extremely hostile to those like Auriol (q.v.), the former president of the Republic and Monnerville (q.v.) president of the Senate, who sought to combat the new order by using the Constitutional Council. Noël saw no incompatibility between his official function as guardian of the constitution and his unofficial role as adviser to de Gaulle and his refusal to declare unconstitutional the use of Article 11 for the 1962 amendment on the direct election of the president which caused great controversy. Noël himself had no doubt that the procedure was illegal, and told de Gaulle so; but convinced his fellow members of the Council that they had no power to quash a law passed by referendum. When Noël left the Constitutional Council in 1967, he could fairly say, in the words of a chapter of his memoirs, that he had contributed to the strengthening of the regime: but it is not surprising that for some years after the reputation of the Council as an independent watchdog of constitutional propriety remained low. He supported the 1974 constitutional amendment that enabled parliamentarians to have access to the Constitutional Council.

Bibliography

Duroselle, J.-B. (1979), *La Décadence*, Paris: Imprimerie Nationale.
Noël, L. (1956), *Notre dernere chance*, Paris: Gedalge.
Noël, L. (1976), *De Gaulle et les débuts de la Ve République*, Paris: Plon.
See also his obituary in *Le Monde* (9–10 August 1987).

PM

NOIR, Michel (1944–)

Michel Noir was elected RPR deputy for Lyons in 1978, 1981, 1986 and 1988, and was foreign trade minister in the second Chirac government (March 1986 to May 1988). He has also been a Lyons councillor since 1977, regional councillor for Rhône-Alpes since March 1986, and RPR national secretary for industrial questions since November 1984. In 1989 he was elected mayor of Lyons at the second attempt, a victory which put him in the forefront of the new generation of leaders on the moderate right.

His career has not been that of an orthodox member of the Fifth Republic elite. Born into a working-class family in Lyons (his father fought in a Gaullist Resistance network), he studied at the Lycée Ampère and the Institut d'Etudes Politiques in his home city. He took part in de Gaulle's 1965 campaign, his initial asset for the Gaullists (against the Lyonnais extreme right) being his great size. On graduating in 1966, he worked full-time for the party as *chargé de mission* then federal secretary in the Rhône department, campaigning in Lyons for the 1967 elections and organizing, with guidance from Charles Pasqua, a Lyons equivalent to the big Gaullist demonstration in Paris on 30 May 1968. He then moved into the private sector, first as a product executive for an aluminium subsidiary of the Pechiney group and then, from 1972 to 1978, as an independent management and marketing consultant.

Noir's political activities continued, if less intensely. In 1972 he helped Alain Peyrefitte to found the Gaullists' Ecole des Cadres, and two years later he campaigned vigorously for Chaban-Delmas, reacting with dismay to Chirac's sabotage of the former prime minister. Pasqua then reconciled him to Chirac, whom Noir encouraged to stand as secretary-general in December 1974 (Noir emerged from the same Central Committee meeting as *délégué national à la communication*). He was elected to the Lyons Council on a united right-wing list in 1977, and the following year won his parliamentary seat against the far-right incumbent Jacques Soustelle.

In the 1981 parliament he made a mark as one of the four 'musketeers' (with Philippe Séguin, François d'Aubert and Charles Millon), all young deputies who staged a filibuster against the Socialist government's nationalization bill. They formed the nucleus of the Cercle, a study group of a dozen or so young RPR and UDF deputies. Like most Cercle members, Noir is a moderate: several of his electoral battles have been fought with the far right, and he detests the Front National (FN). He also writes. *Réussir une campagne électorale: suivre l'exemple américain?* (Paris: Editions de l'Organisation, 1977) is a study of Carter's 1976 campaign, with practical guidance on applying American techniques in France. *1988, le Grand rendez-vous* (Paris: J.C. Lattès, 1984) is a reasoned if unexciting statement of policy objectives for a right wing restored to power.

Noir's record as foreign trade minister was undistinguished: his ministerial overlord, Edouard Balladur (q.v.) left him little independent power, and trade figures were generally disappointing. A year after his appointment few poll respondents knew who he was and most of those who did had a negative opinion of him. He increased his national notoriety in May 1987 when he made an outspoken attack on Le Pen's Front National (FN) and argued that the right should be ready to lose the presidential elections rather than make any tactical or ideological concessions to it. This earned him a reprimand from Chirac, but his attacks on the FN continued into the campaign and beyond.

Noir's political base remains in Lyons. For some time, though, both the local UDF establishment and Raymond Barre represented obstacles to his ambitions there. At the 1983 municipal elections, he came in a poor second against the colourless incumbent UDF mayor, Francisque Collomb. In March 1986 he did better: his RPR list and Barre's list won almost the same number of votes, and three parliamentary seats each. Noir retained his parliamentary seat in the June 1988 elections following Mitterrand's re-election as president. And his triumphant election as mayor in 1989 against an aged and intransigent Collomb placed France's second city in the hands of a leading Gaullist who owes almost nothing to Jacques Chirac.

Noir was quick to seize the implications of this, and became a leading member of the Mouvement des Rénovateurs within the RPR, with Philippe Seguin, François Fillon and others. The *rénovateurs*, drawn from both the RPR and the UDF, called for a renewal of the right under the colours of youth, non-sectarianism, moderation and social conscience, particularly in the run-up to the June 1989 European elections. Threatened with exclusion from the RPR if they ran their own Euro-list, the *rénovateurs* backed down, but they had sufficient impact for the RPR to permit the existence of organized tendencies within its ranks for the first time in the Gaullist movement's history.

Bibliography

There are profiles of Noir in *Le Monde* (22 March 1986), Alain Duhamel, *Les Prétendants* (Paris: Gallimard, 1983), and Thierry Desjardins, *Les Chiraquiens* (Paris: La Table Ronde, 1986), as well as many references in Jacques Frémontier, *Les Cadets de la Droite* (Paris: Seuil, 1984). See also Michel Noir, *La Chasse au mammouth* (Paris: Robert Laffont, 1989).

AFK

O

ORLÉANS, Prince Henri, duc d' (1838–94)

Orléans, grandson of Louis-Philippe, was a pious Catholic although his mother was a German Protestant princess and he was educated in England from the age of 10, where he spent most of his life (he owned Sheen House near Richmond). He became Pretender in 1883 and was endowed with a lively political interest which he cultivated by travelling widely and by trying to unite the squabbling royalist factions. He was outstandingly rich, partly as a result of his own endowments and partly through his royalist bequests and legacies, and he was overwhelmingly ambitious. He tried to broaden the appeal of the royal family by using his wealth to create a royalist press and royalist organizations.

It was Orléans who conceded the right of succession to Chambord (q.v.) in 1873 although the occasion was missed to restore the throne by the Legitimist insistance on having the royal flag. Since Chambord was childless, Orléans would have succeeded within a few years.

In the elections of 1885 Orléans was able to present a more-or-less united conservative thrust which capitalized on discontent. On the first round monarchists came close to defeating the Republicans (who were disunited). However the second round saw a Republican rally, unification and a narrow victory. The Republicans countered the menace of this conservative, and flexible, pragmatic, monarchism by exiling the pretender (who settled permanently in England).

In exile he continued to try to develop an appealing monarchist platform based on social stability, liberty of education, and to propose plebiscites to undermine parliamentary sovereignty. He was, however, opposed to conspiracy or violence and expected to return to power when the Republic proved unviable and collapsed. He did break with this principle to support General Boulanger (q.v.), who was financially aided by the duchesse d'Uzes (q.v.). The failure of the Boulangist movement was a catastrophe for monarchism. The royalists lost support and split with one group objecting to anti-parliamentary movements (consistent with Orleanist parliamentary tradition) and the others retreating into rancorous opposition. When the Republicans dropped their attacks on the Church and Pope Leo XII urged Catholics to accept the Republic (the *ralliement*) the monarchists lost mass support.

The series of hammer blows to the monarchist cause would have required real political skill to redress but the Count of Paris died on 8 September 1894 with the movement in disarray. His son, the duc d'Orléans, was 'a playboy of mediocre ability' who was not interested in politics and who allowed Action Française to make the running on the extreme right.

Bibliography

See T. Zeldin, *France 1848–1945*, vol. I: Kings and Aristocrats (Oxford: Oxford University Press, 1973), pp. 393–427.

DSB

ORLÉANS, Prince Henri, Robert, comte de Paris (1908–)

The current pretender to the French throne was born in Nouvion-en-Thierarche (Aisne) on 5 July 1908 and married Princess Isabelle of Orléans and Bregance on 8 April 1931. They had eleven children. The death of the Duke of Orléans, who was childless, on 28 March 1926, meant that the succession passed to the lateral branch and the Count was then obliged to leave France and finish his studies at the University of Louvain in Belgium.

At the time the Action Française, under the impulse of Charles Maurras (q.v.), was the principal force on the extreme right and there were great hopes of a royalist restoration. However, in 1934 the Count created *Le Courrier Royal* journal and preferred his own advisers to those of Action Française. The comte de Paris' closest adviser was Count Pierre de la Roque who thought that his brother (q.v.) might support the royal cause (which he did not). Action Française, which had been criticized by the

Pope in 1928, grew steadily more antagonistic to the Count of Paris. In 1937 the Duke of Guise repudiated Action Française and the break became definitive in November of that year.

The Count was unable to win the French army and the Vichy regime was not willing to give the Pretender any hopes (even though he backed Pétain). After the Allied landings in Algeria the Pretender's supporters hoped that he would be proclaimed head of the provisional government but these hopes were shattered in the course of complicated machinations (and when Admiral Darlan was assassinated). De Gaulle, of course, profited from Anglo-American support and his own skill enabled him to dominate the provisional government.

When the 1886 law, which enforced exile on the royal family, was repealed in 1950 the pretender returned to France and began a long campaign for support among politicians of the Fourth Republic. In the turmoil of the collapse of the Republic the pretender seems to have entertained hopes of a restoration and even that de Gaulle would make France a constitutional monarchy. (On what basis the pretender thought that de Gaulle would is unclear.) As is well known de Gaulle turned on the partisans of French Algeria and dashed the hopes of remaining monarchists.

Unlike his father, the comte de Paris had expected to be able to revive the royalist cause and he is cultured and politically well-read man. He still issues statements to the people of France at New Year, but has no serious expectation of a restoration.

Royalists still hold rallies in the summer in one of the villages in the Midi-Cointat (the so-called Vendée provençale-Baux-de Provence or Saint-Martin-de-Crau) and *Aspects de la France* (founded in 1947) is published weekly.

Bibliography

See T. Zeldin, *France 1848–1945*, vol. I (Oxford: Oxford University Press, 1973).

DSB

d'ORNANO, Michel, comte (1924–)

An industrialist from an aristocratic family dating back to Philippe d'Ornano under Napoleon (1784–1863), Michel d'Ornano is important politically because of his devotion to Giscard d'Estaing and his position as a local potentate in the Lower Normandy

(Calvados). In 1962 d'Ornano was elected mayor of Deauville and he became president of the Lower Normandy business group in 1967. In 1967 he was also elected as an Independent Republican deputy for Lower Normandy and became one of the main partisans of the overthrow of the Gaullist domination of the right declaring, notably, 'Nous voulous que demain la majorité soit différente! Nous ne le cachons pas'. He was regularly re-elected thereafter as an Independent Republican and served on the party's national committee, where he remains.

When Giscard won the 1974 presidential elections d'Ornano was made minister for industry and was one of the president's closest confidants. In 1977 reforms of local government restored the post of mayor to Paris and Giscard asked d'Ornano to stand. With exemplary loyalty d'Ornano stood for mayor on a centrist (Giscardian) ticket but despite favourable opinion polls at the onset the City Hall was won by Chirac (q.v.) for the Gaullists. In a bitter struggle Chirac won 26 per cent of the vote, against d'Ornano's 22 per cent: under the rules of right-wing coalition politics then prevailing, d'Ornano stood down in eleven of eighteen sectors and Chirac swept to victory on the second ballot (winning 54 of 109 seats to d'Ornano's 15). D'Ornano was rewarded for this battle with demotion to the Ministry of Culture where he remained until the 1978 election when he was nominated minister of the environment.

After Giscard's defeat in 1981, d'Ornano devoted his energies to the Calvados and to preparing hopefully for Giscard's eventual return to the national scene. He was elected general councillor for the Calvados and his collaborator in his 1974–81 private office (René Garrec) was elected president of the region in 1986.

D'Ornano's position in the Calvados region remains unchallenged but he has never been able to exert much authority in the Union Pour la Démocratie Française, the coalition of non-Gaullist parties of the centre right that was founded by Giscard in 1978 and which (in 1989) showed signs of disintegrating, thanks to the rival ambitions of a new generation of leaders.

Bibliography

Lecomte, B. and C. Sauvage (1978), *Les Giscardiens*, Paris: Albin Michel.
d'Ornano, M. (1977), *Une Certaine idée de Paris*, Paris: J.T. Lattès.

DSB

P

PAINLEVÉ, Paul (1863–1933)

Paul Painlevé is perhaps the most outstanding member of that school of professors which, in the title of Thibaudet's famous book (*The Republic of Teachers*), provided part of the governing personnel of the Third Republic. A classic example of the poor boy made good, he was a brilliant mathematician; a leading figure in wartime and post-war governments, he entered politics via the great symbolic struggle of republicanism, the Dreyfus affair.

Born in Paris, Painlevé came from a Breton family and quickly revealed the intellectual brilliance that would take him to the Lycée Louis Le Grand and the elite training school for teachers, the Ecole Normale Supérieure. After a period studying in Germany, he taught in Lille Faculty of Science before returning to Paris to teach at various times at the Collège de France, the Sorbonne, the Ecole Polytechnique and the Ecole Normale Supérieure. He was fascinated in particular by mathematics and physics and in 1900 was elected to the Academy of Sciences. His appearance and manner made him look like an absent-minded professor but he was in fact a man of strong convictions and organizing energy. Appalled by the injustice done to Dreyfus, he was one of the first members of the Ligue des Droits de l'Homme and testified at the retrial of Dreyfus in Rennes (1899). In 1910 he entered the Chamber of Deputies as a Republican Socialist, replacing Viviani (q.v.) in the 5th *arrondissement* of Paris, and quickly made his mark as a specialist on military questions. He was president of the Chamber Navy Commission but also took a very keen interest in aviation, on which he wrote a book. (He also flew with Wilbur Wright and the great French aviator, Henri Farman.)

It was as minister of education and inventions that he first entered government in the Briand (q.v.) ministry of October 1915 to December 1917. He took the War Ministry in the Ribot (q.v.) government of March 1917 and held on to the post in his own brief ministry of September to November of that year. It was a terribly difficult time to hold such responsibility and Painlevé's record was hardly successful. Despite his misgivings he gave the go-ahead

for the catastrophic Nivelle offensive in spring and had to deal with the mutinies that followed. He was always proud of the fact that he responded to the disaster by appointing Foch (q.v.) and Pétain (q.v.) to the top positions in the French army. War weariness, the disintegration of the all-party pact known as the *Union Sacrée*, the desire among some prominent politicians for a negotiated peace, and a growing climate of defeatism posed problems Painlevé lacked the political authority to solve. In the face of disasters outside – the Russian Revolution, the Italian defeat at Capovetto – and tension within, notably the alleged treason of the Interior Minister Malvy, his government came under great pressure and was eventually overthrown (the only ministry to be defeated in the course of the war). He was replaced by Clemenceau (q.v.) about whose determination there could be no doubt.

Painlevé survived the electoral triumph of the right in 1919 to become one of the most prominent members of the French democratic left. Without in any sense abandoning his scientific and pedagogic interests (he drew up a report for the Chinese government on the reform of its higher education system), he was one of the leaders of the opposition to the right-wing governments of the Bloc National. He was the driving force behind the Ligue de la République a highly successful supraparty grouping of the forces of the left that campaigned vigorously in the 1924 elections and attracted many bright young men into politics. With the victory of the Socialist–Radical coalition (*Cartel des gauches*) in 1924, Painlevé became president of the Chamber and seemed well placed to replace Millerand (q.v.) as president of the Republic after the latter's forced resignation. In fact he was easily defeated by the Senate president Doumergue (q.v.), a result that showed the limitations of the left's victory. In April 1925 Painlevé replaced the exhausted Herriot (q.v.) as prime minister. He showed his instinctive republicanism by giving the Finance Ministry to the 'victim' of the wartime right, Caillaux (q.v.) and his commitment to international reconciliation by making Briand (q.v.) foreign minister. But if his government was able to articulate the spirit of Locarno, to reduce national tensions by dropping Herriot's anti-clerical legislation and to bring the troubles in Morocco to a successful conclusion, it was quite unable to resolve the worsening financial situation. Caillaux failed to be a miracle worker and, after a short period when Painlevé himself took the finance portfolio, his government fell.

The last years of his career were spent at the Ministries of War (November 1925 to October 1929) and Aviation (December 1930 to January 1931 and June 1932 to January 1933). In the former position he played a central role in the decisions to create what became known as the Maginot Line and to reduce the length of military service. His republicanism led him to view Pétain as the right sort of military leader for a France that could no longer afford the reactionary luxury of an offensive strategy. When he died in 1933, his illusions unshattered, the Republic showed its respect for this greatest of its professors, by transferring his ashes to the Panthéon.

Bibliography

Though Painlevé's papers are available at the Archives Nationales no modern biography exists. An affectionate portrait exists in G. Bonnet, *Vingt ans de vie politique* (Paris: Fayard, 1969); and see also J. Hughes, *To the Maginot Line* (Cambridge, Mass.: Harvard University Press, 1971); D.R. Watson, *George Clemenceau: A political biography* (London: Eyre Methuen, 1974).

PM

PALEWSKI, Gaston (1901–84)

One of the most committed Gaullists, Gaston Palewski was principal private secretary to Paul Reynaud, having earlier worked in Morocco with marked loyalty from 1924 to 1925, when he first met de Gaulle in 1934. Immediately convinced of the then colonel's political potential he was among the first to contact de Gaulle's Free French movement in London in 1940. Initially in charge of establishing contacts within occupied France he was subsequently entrusted with the difficult mission of organizing the Free French forces in East Africa. Recalled early in 1942, he became de Gaulle's principal private secretary first in London, until May 1943, then in Algiers where the General headed the Comité Français de Libération Nationale (May 1943 to August 1944) and finally in Paris until de Gaulle founded the nationalistic and

anti-Communist Rassemblement du Peuple Français in April 1947.

Palewski played an important role, still as de Gaulle's efficient *éminence grise*, in the creation and organization of the RPF. In 1951 he was elected to parliament on a RPF ticket as member for the Seine department and, although he sought to preserve the Gaullist line in the Assembly after the movement's poor showing in the municipal elections of 1953, he became a member of Edgar Faure's government for eight months. This brief flirtation outside the unconditional Gaullist camp possibly explains his subsequent four-year period of, albeit comfortable, exile as ambassador to Italy from 1957 to 1962 (he lost his seat in parliament in 1956). He hoped for but did not receive, the foreign secretaryship in 1958 when de Gaulle returned. He eventually returned to France in 1962 to become minister of state for scientific, atomic and space research in Pompidou's first and second governments until February 1965 when he was appointed president of the Constitutional Council, a post he held until 1974. His vast range of contacts in France and abroad, and his skills as negotiator and conciliator made him one of the most valuable of the so-called 'barons' who surrounded de Gaulle from 1940 onwards.

Bibliography

Little or no information on Palewski is available in English, and there is not much more in French although the following can be consulted: G. Palewski, *Hier et aujourd'hui 1974* (Paris: Plon, 1975) and G. Pilleul (ed.), *'L'Entourage' et de Gaulle* (a collection of reminiscences including one by Palewski) (Paris: Plon, 1979).

GTH

PARODI, Alexandre (1901–79)

Parodi was born in Paris, where his father was an education inspector. Parodi had a masters degree in literature and in law and became a *conseiller d'état* in 1926. Although there was no French equivalent to Beveridge in the founding of the welfare state, Alexandre Parodi did play a roughly similar role behind the scenes along with Pierre Laroque. Parodi had worked on social legislation through the 1930s at the Ministry of Labour (and had recruited Pierre Laroque); in 1934 he had worked in the CGT's *bureau d'études* where he had been influenced by de Man's 'planisme' – social engineering – and had favoured the unification of the dispersed social funds under the troika of union management and government control. Parodi also wanted to increase benefits.

Parodi, who was thus immersed in the details of social legislation, was well placed to head a special Vichy commission in 1943 to study social benefits although at the same time he was organizing the Gaullist Resistance. Pierre Laroque had been in London since 1942 with de Gaulle's government-in-exile and Parodi took over as head of de Gaulle's General Delegation in March 1944. This last body was intended to prevent a drift of power to the divided, but Communist-dominated, National Resistance Council. In the event this manoeuvre proved impossible.

On 10 September 1944 Parodi became minister of labour in de Gaulle's government and held that post until he was replaced by the Communist Croizat on 21 November 1945. Despite subsequent myths – which attribute a determining role to the PCF – it was Parodi and his right hand Laroque who designed the legislation for the French National Security Fund (Caisse Nationale de la Sécurité Sociale) and put it into place during this short period. Laroque headed a special commission in June 1945 and Parodi steered policy by using his position as head of the Conseil Supérieur des Assurances Sociales. Many competing sectional and local interests had to be reconciled (not completely successfully) at a time when the Consultative Assembly was beginning to assert its authority as 'tripartite' agreement between the Christian Democrats (MRP), Socialists (SFIO) and Communists was breaking down. In July 1945 Parodi had to make one of his rare speeches in the Assembly to argue for a simplification of the social security system, to point out that there was no law obliging all firms to provide disability protection, and to reassure the defenders of 'free institutions' (private charities). Parodi none the less pushed through a national system which, however, partially exempted agriculture and created a separate family allowance organization.

The break up of 'tripartism' led to squabbles about the participant management arrangement of the social security fund and the reform process lost its impetus. The Family Allocation Law of August 1946 was the only initial proposal by Parodi and Laroque which was fully implemented. This law made family support a universal payment: it included pre-natal payments for seven months, an additional payment on a third child, a rising scale and instituted payment to the person in charge of children (not the head of family).

Parodi was a civil servant and technocrat rather than a politician as such but in the reformist climate

of the liberation he was able to implement Fabian-style reforms without an independent political position or any of the traditional political backing. On leaving politics he followed a distinguished diplomatic career being ambassador to the United Nations (1946–9), secretary-general of foreign affairs, (1949–55), ambassador to Nato, ambassador to Morocco, and finally vice-president of the Conseil d'Etat in 1960.

Bibliography

See Dominique Ceccaldi, *Histoire des prestations sociales en France* (Paris: Association Nationale des Allocutions Familiales, 1951) and D.E. Ashford, *The Emergence of the Welfare States* (Oxford: Blackwell, 1986). There is a tribute to Parodi in *Espoir*, no. 29, p. 59 by G. Palewski.

DSB

PASQUA, Charles Victor (1927–   )

Charles Pasqua was one of very few members of the second Chirac government to have been an active Gaullist since the Resistance. His importance in French politics has been fourfold: as a superlative mass organizer, as an internal party broker on behalf of Chirac, as an orator and parliamentarian (deputy from 1969 to 1973, senator from 1977 to 1986, and again in 1988, and leader of the Senate Gaullist group after 1982) and, from March 1986 to May 1988, as a controversial minister of the interior.

Pasqua was born in Alpes-Maritimes, the son of a Corsican policeman. His first career was with the Ricard drinks firm, which he joined in 1952 after the *baccalauréat*, two years' law studies, and various short-term jobs; by 1962 he was the group's sales manager. At the same time, his adolescent Resistance activities led him first to the Union Gaulliste and then to the Rassemblement du Peuple Français, the Alpes-Maritimes section of which he set up almost single-handed in 1947. In 1958 he reactivated his RPF contacts on the south coast in readiness for a Gaullist *coup d'état*, and four years later was a co-founder of the Service d'Action Civique, a more or less shady group ostensibly committed to the personal protection of leading Gaullists (it was implicated in a multiple murder case and dissolved in 1981). Two networks – the SAC and Ricard – proved particularly useful when Pasqua organized the massive Gaullist demonstration that turned the tide of May 1968 in favour of the right. As national secretary for 'animation' from 1974, he ensured the material organization for the relaunch of the Gaullist movement as the Rassemblement pour la République (RPR) in 1976 and for every election campaign since then.

Pasqua's organizational influence within the Gaullist movement allowed him to stage-manage Chirac's spectacular leadership take-over of December 1974, and to keep enough of a hold on it to allow its transformation into the RPR two years later after Chirac's resignation from the premiership.

Pasqua became deputy for Hauts-de-Seine in June 1968, *conseiller général* in 1970, and president of the General Council (*Conseil Général*) in 1973, thus pioneering the Gaullists' implantation in the 'Red belt' of Communist-dominated Paris suburbs in highly aggressive campaigns that suited his political style. This implantation did not 'take' immediately, however: Pasqua lost his parliamentary seat back to the Communists in 1973 and his place on the General Council in 1976, returning to the legislative branch the following year in the indirectly-elected post of senator. From this position he remained the RPR's chief in Hauts-de-Seine, and the younger men promoted by him are of a similar populist, authoritarian, right-wing stamp. As president of the RPR group in the Senate from 1982, he won national notoriety with his vocal opposition to Socialist bills on New Caledonia and the press and with obstructionist tactics that killed the education bill and referendum project linked to it in the summer of 1984.

As interior minister from 1986 to 1988, Pasqua showed indifference to victims of police violence (particularly during the student demonstrations of December 1986, which he hoped would benefit the right as much as those of May 1968), expelled illegal – and some legal – immigrants *en masse*, instigated lawsuits against hostile reporters and led an antipornography crusade. He also – after the wave of Paris bombings in September 1986 – produced impressive results in the shape of falling crime figures and arrests of several key domestic and foreign terrorists. These helped him to recover from very low popularity ratings early in 1987 and so to stay in the government.

In the final week of Chirac's second presidential campaign Pasqua was instrumental in organizing the return of all French hostages held in Lebanon, of a score of gendarmes held by New Caledonian independence fighters, and of a pregnant *Rainbow Warrior* bomber from her captivity in the Pacific. These spectacular but somewhat dubious coups failed to achieve their goal of a last-minute surge of support for Chirac, and Pasqua returned to his Senate seat

within days of Mitterrand's re-election and the government's resignation. The right then lost the ensuing parliamentary elections despite a constituency redistribution that Pasqua had designed to benefit the RPR. In the period of factional struggle within the RPR that followed, Pasqua confirmed his role as the party's chief right-wing populist, having argued during the presidential campaign that there was no fundamental difference between the RPR's ideas and those of the Front National.

Bibliography

Alain Duhamel's thumb-nail sketch *Les Prétendants* (Paris: Gallimard, 1983) is useful but has been largely superseded by more recent profiles in Thierry Desjardins, *Les Chiraquiens* (Paris: La Table Ronde, 1986) (sympathetic) and *Le Monde* of 6 December 1986 (hostile). Full-length biographies are Pierre Pellissier, *Charles Pasqua* (Paris: Lattès, 1986) and A. Rollat and P. Boggio, *Ce terrible Monsieur Pasqua* (Paris: O. Urban, 1988). There is nothing on Pasqua in English. His own book, *L'Ardeur nouvelle* (Paris: Albin Michel, 1985), is partisan, often simplistic, and thus a good reflection of its author.

AFK

PATENÔTRE, Raymond (1900–51)

Raymond Patenôtre was born in Atlantic City, New Jersey, whilst his father, Jules Patenôtre, was French ambassador to the United States. From an early age he was fascinated by what became the three principal interests of his public career: politics, the operation of international finance, and journalism. In 1925 he made his political debut, being elected to the Council of the Seine-et-Oise department. Three years later he entered the Chamber of Deputies by winning Rambouillet in the April 1928 elections, crushing his opponent by a ten to one margin on the first ballot in a conservative landslide inspired by the resurgence of the economy after Raymond Poincaré's 1926 revaluation of the franc. At the Palais Bourbon, Patenôtre joined the moderate Indépendants de Gauche parliamentary group. Soon he was appointed to the Chamber's agricultural commission. In the May 1932 elections he was again returned at Rambouillet on the first ballot and again sat with the Left Independents. His abilities as a debater and an economist had drawn him to the attention of the Radical-Socialist leader Edouard Herriot. When the latter formed a government on 3 June 1932, he brought

Patenôtre into the prime minister's office with junior ministerial rank, as under-secretary of state for the national economy. Patenôtre performed so capably that he retained his post under five successive centre-left (*Cartel des Gauches*) prime ministers (Herriot, 3 June to 18 December 1932; Joseph Paul-Boncour, 18 December 1932 to 31 January 1933; Edouard Daladier, 31 January to 26 October 1933; Camille Chautemps, 26 October 1933 to 30 January 1934; and Daladier again, 30 January to 9 February 1934). In the middle 1930s Patenôtre returned to the back benches. There he concentrated on acquiring a newspaper empire and publishing several bold treatises on the economic crisis. On the former count he purchased the Parisian *Petit Journal*, controlled an important provincial press including *Le Petit Niçois*, *Le Petit Var* and *Lyon Républicain*, helped launch the weekly *Marianne* and bought interests in several American papers. Meanwhile Patenôtre brought out three contributions to the contemporary economic debate: *La Crise et le Drame Monétaire* (Paris: Editions de la Nouvelle Revue Française, 1932), *Voulons-nous sortir de la crise?* (Paris: Plon, 1934), and *Vers le bien-être par la réforme de la monnaie et du crédit* (Paris: Hachette, 1936). In 1936 he held off the tide of Popular Frontism, being returned a third time for Rambouillet, although only after a tough fight on the second ballot. For this legislature, the sixteenth and last of the Third Republic, Patenôtre switched allegiance to a different centrist group, the Union Socialiste et Républicaine, which nominated him to one of the Chamber's most influential watchdogs, the commission for foreign affairs. The ending of Popular Front governments in April 1938 brought Patenôtre a return to office that year. This time he secured cabinet rank, as minister for the national economy in Daladier's government. He retained this post for a year and a half, playing an important part in reorganizing French industry for the accelerated rearmament drive that was one of the administration's overriding concerns. On 15 September 1939 he left office when Daladier restructured his government to meet the demands of war, placing powers of economic mobilization with a new ministry of armaments headed by the businessman and transport expert, Raoul Dautry.

Patenôtre is a good example of the exceptions to Alfred Sauvy's rule about the ignorance of economics prevailing among the French political class between the wars. As the ephemeral prosperity that France enjoyed in the Poincaré boom years of 1926–9 disappeared into the deepening world depression of the early 1930s, Patenôtre made a name by his radical prescriptions for monetary and economic re-organization. He was, with the former finance minister Paul Reynaud and the young Popular Front under-secretary Pierre Mendès France, one of a select band of parliamentarians who possessed sufficient technical understanding and political courage to escape the stranglehold into which contemporary orthodoxies of a gold-standard based currency and balanced budgets had confined French economic thought. Where Reynaud's observations of the 1931 and 1933 adjustments of sterling and the US dollar led him, from 1934, to preach French devaluation, and Mendès had made a special study of Poincaré's reform of the franc, Patenôtre offered genuine economic innovation. Throughout the 1930s he argued relentlessly that nothing short of a new global financial regime would cure the international economic chaos of the age. Convinced that the protracted crisis on such a world-wide scale imperilled the permanency of democratic civilization itself, he contended that imaginative and internationally coordinated economic reform was essential. Without it he feared that another depression would be inevitable in the future, bringing the collapse of an already weakened Western economic order.

Knowledgeable about American banking, business and Taylorized scientific management, Patenôtre used his papers, his parliamentary platform and his books to urge devaluation of the franc to a level that would stick, state control over credit and open markets. But his major contribution to the economic debate came via his proposals for long-term international measures to bring world-wide production and consumption into balance and, chief of all, his advocacy of a new global monetary order. This was to be introduced through an international financial conference, which he pressed the French government to host, leading to the revaluation of the world's gold stocks and the rebasing of all national currencies on a dual gold and silver standard. Too revolutionary for the inter-war era, Patenôtre's conception of political economy was on the grand scale. Its time came not in the France of the 1930s but at Bretton Woods in 1944.

Bibliography

The best guide to Patenôtre's thought is the trio of books that he wrote, *La Crise et le drame monétaire* (Paris: Gallimard, 1932), *Voulons-nous sortir de la crise?* (Paris: Plon, 1934), *Vers le bien-être par la réforme de la monnaie et du crédit* (Paris: Hachette, 1936).

MSA

PAUL-BONCOUR, Joseph Alexandre Alfred (1873–1972)

Born 4 August 1873 at Saint-Aignan (Loire-et-Cher), Paul-Boncour became a major figure of the parliamentary left in the inter-war period and an international statesman. He originally planned a naval career but, after graduating as a doctor of arts, became a lawyer. After making a name for himself by defending trade unionists and strikers in court, he entered political life by joining the staff of Prime Minister Waldeck-Rousseau in 1898. During this period Paul-Boncour supported Alexandre Millerand's participation in government. He headed René Viviani's Labour Ministry staff between 1906 and 1909. In 1909, he stood for parliament in his own right as an Independent Socialist. Re-elected in 1910, he kept his seat until 1914 and was appointed minister of labour for a brief spell in 1911. Mobilized in the reserves, Paul-Boncour was a major by the end of the war and received military honours.

During the war he joined the Socialist Party, the SFIO, and was elected to parliament in 1919 on the Socialist list. He joined the permanent administrative committee of the SFIO after the split in 1920 and headed a committee on military affairs. After 1924, when he was returned to parliament as deputy for the mining town of Carmaux, his main sphere of interest was defence and foreign affairs. From 1924 to 1926, he was attached to the French delegation to the United Nations and succeeded Aristide Briand as head of the French mission in 1927. In 1931, the year when Paul-Boncour was elected senator for his native department, he left the Socialist Party because of its opposition to a defence bill and formed a group of Independent Socialists, but he maintained links with Léon Blum. He was minister for war in the Edouard Herriot cabinet in 1932, foreign affairs minister in the government which he headed from December 1932 until January 1933, and subsequently remained at the Foreign Affairs Ministry until February 1934 in the governments of Edouard Daladier, Albert Sarraut and Camille Chautemps. In the 1936–7 Blum cabinets Paul-Boncour was a minister of state.

In July 1940 Paul-Boncour was one of the eighty deputies who refused to vote the transfer of power to Marshal Pétain. He retired from public life during the war to write his memoirs, but returned after the liberation. He was delegated to the Consultative Assembly in 1944. In 1944 he rejoined the Socialist Party. He was senator (councillor of the Republic) from 1946 to 1948.

He was the author of several political works in-cluding *Un Débat nouveau sur la République et la dé-centralisation* (Toulouse: Société Provinciale d'Edi-tion, 1904) and *Entre deux guerres, souvenirs sur la IIIe République*, 3 vols (Paris: Plon, 1945–6). The latter, written during the Second World War, gives an ac-count of Paul-Boncour's parliamentary career.

Bibliography

In English, there is a biographical entry on Paul-Boncour in Patrick H. Hutton, *Historical Dictionary of the Third French Republic, 1870–1940* (Westport, Conn.: Greenwood Press, 1986), p. 756. A very short account of Paul-Boncour's political life appears in Henry Coston (ed.), *Dictionnaire de la politique française* (Paris: La Librairie Française, 1967), p. 829. A fuller biography will appear in Jean Maitron and Claude Pennetier, *Dictionnaire bi-ographique du mouvement ouvrier français* (4th part: 1914–39), which is currently published up to the letter H (Paris: Editions Ouvrières, 1983). A dossier on Paul-Boncour exists in the Archives de l'As-semblée Nationale.

SM

PAUWELS, Louis François (1920–   )

Pauwels was brought up in a working-class Paris environment by his printer mother, and Socialist stepfather, who revered Victor Hugo. He was later to dedicate a book to the latter's 'boundless spirit' and 'impassioned heart', but his upbringing left him with a taste for political controversy and mysticism rather than the politics of the left.

After a brief interlude as a teacher during the Second World War, Pauwels turned to journalism, novels and film adaptations. This mercurial career brought him many honours. In 1977 his *L'Appren-tissage de la Sérénité* won the Prix Chateaubriand, and in 1986 he was made a member of the Académie des Beaux-Arts. However, his political views, which were closely entwined with his artistic ones, also led to considerable controversy.

In the early years he worked for *Carrefour*, edited *Combat* from 1949 to 1955, and *Arts* from 1952 to 1955. In 1961 he was director and founder of *Planète*, which after 1968 became *Le Nouveau Planète*. During this period he was known for attacks on communism, the bourgeoisie, and avant-garde forms of literature. He was attracted by Gurdjieff's school of esoteric mysticism, and more generally by the occult. His views involved a revolt against intellectualism, and a search for traditions. These views helped lead him to flirt with nazism during the late 1950s and 1960s.

However he was also interested in science, and this helped lead him to the work of GRECE (Groupement de Recherche et d'Etudes pour la Civilisation Européenne), which emerged in the late 1960s. This sought to create a more intellectual right in France. GRECE sought to popularize the work of writers such as Jensen and Eysenck on hereditary intelligence. It also featured the new writings of American socio-biologists, as well as a rather older social Darwinism. It sought to develop cultural racism, in particular the need to defend European values. A key tactic of this 'nouvelle droite' derived from the adaptation of the ideas of the Italian Marxist theorist Gramsci: it sought to establish a right-wing intellectual hegemony. By the late 1970s Pauwels was in a key position to develop such themes. In 1977 he was appointed director of 'services culturels' for the leading daily newspaper, *Le Figaro*, and the following year he became editor in chief of *Le Figaro Magazine*. He subsequently used this weekly colour supplement as a major forum for the dissemination of his ideas. By late 1979 there was considerable discussion in France of this 'nouvelle droite'.

On the economic front, Pauwels's views owed more to the Anglo-Saxon new right. In the 1980s he described himself as a defender of the capitalist system because it was most likely to lead to individual freedom. He rejected socialism, communism, fascism and all forms of totalitarianism. He argued that during his lifetime capitalism had overcome crises, whereas the totalitarian ideologies had all failed. This was a remarkable change from his views of the 1950s. Pauwels's intellectual development therefore offers an interesting insight into the metamorphosis of a section of the French right in the post-Second World War era.

Bibliography

Pauwels, L.F. and J. Bergier (1960), *Le Matin des magiciens*, Paris: Gallimard.

Pauwels, L.F. (1978), *Comment devient-on ce que l'on est?*, Paris: Stock.

Pauwels, L.F. (1984), *La Liberté guide mes pas*, Paris: Albin Michel.

RE

PÉGUY, Charles Pierre (a.k.a Pierre Baudoin) (1873–1914)

Political writer, philosopher and poet, Péguy was born in Orléans the son of a cabinet-maker: he remained proud of his descent from generations of French peasants. He grew up as a Catholic in the city of Joan of Arc, and was acutely conscious as a child of the Prussian enemy who had so recently defeated France. By 16, however, he had become a rebel and an atheist; progressing brilliantly via scholarships to Paris *lycées*, he entered the Ecole Normale Supérieure in 1894, and in 1895 announced his conversion to socialism. He became a leader of the young Dreyfusards, both intellectually and in the street, and upbraided the parliamentary Socialists for their slowness to commit themselves to defend Dreyfus. His own near-anarchist socialist ideal can be seen in his prose poem *Marcel premier dialogue de la cité harmonieuse* (1898; reissued by Gallimard, Paris, 1973). He soon broke with the Socialist Party to found, in 1900, the *Cahiers de la Quinzaine*, which remained for a decade, under his fiercely independent direction, a small and struggling Latin Quarter fortnightly. He published in the *Cahiers* the work of many young and little-known authors, notably Romain Rolland, and all his own polemical and literary writings. The early years of the century were spent castigating the moral and political failings of Socialists and Radicals. In 1904, he broke with Jaurès (q.v.). By 1905, the German emperor's sabre-rattling at Tangier had brought about in Péguy a patriotic awakening to the German threat, expressed in *Notre patrie*. He was soon to abandon all hope for European socialism. He launched a campaign against scientism and the domination of the neo-positivist 'Intellectual Party' and, by 1908, had confessed to friends that he was a Catholic again.

It was only in 1910 that Péguy emerged as a major literary figure, largely thanks to the publicity given by Maurice Barrès to his would-be Christian work, the *Mystère de la charité de Jeanne d'Arc* (Paris: Plon, 1910). Seizing on Péguy's apparent renunciation of his left-wing past, Barrès sought to portray him as a renegade Socialist and Dreyfusard, and the nationalist extreme right followed suit. Feeling misconstrued, Péguy quickly reacted with his major prose work, *Notre jeunesse*, a vindication and re-affirmation of his early Dreyfusism and republicanism. In *Notre jeunesse*, he elaborated his celebrated distinction between *mystique* and *politique*: all movements begin with la *mystique*, a spirit of disinterested idealism, and finish up in the corrupt world of political expediency. From now on Péguy produced, in a creative torrent, a series of Christian poems, culminating in *Eve* (1913), as well as two philosophical works, the *Note sur M. Bergson* and the *Note conjointe sur M. Descartes*, in which he appeared as the outstanding disciple of the intuitive philosophy of Bergson. The Christian Péguy now adhered, in terms of day-to-day politics, to the right-wing republicanism of Poincaré and the French government. By 1913 he was so convinced that France was in a war situation that he virulently denounced Jaurès' ceaseless peace efforts in *L'Argent, suite*, calling for 'Jaurès in a tumbril and a drum-roll to cover that great voice'. In 1914, he left for the front, in his own words, as a 'soldier of the Republic leaving to fight for general disarmament and the war to end wars'. He was killed at the head of his platoon in the first skirmishes of the battle of the Marne. For decades after his death, Péguy was for most Frenchmen essentially the Catholic poet who had written: 'Happy are they who have died/But only if it was in a just war.' He remained identified with nationalism and the far right, and it was not until the 1960s that scholarly work in France and abroad revived interest in and understanding of his early socialism and Dreyfusism.

Despite his apparently violent turnabouts from atheist to fervent Catholic and from revolutionary Socialist to right-wing patriot, there certainly lay beneath the turbulent surface of his life a continuity of commitment to a series of moral absolutes: salvation for the whole of mankind, absolute justice, absolute truth and absolute freedom for the individual. His only reason for rejecting catholicism as a schoolboy was that the doctrine of eternal damnation conflicted with his desire that the whole of mankind should be saved. He then simply transferred his desire for universal salvation to the temporal sphere and expressed it in the form of socialism: all men were now to be saved from the damnation of poverty and war. Through Péguy's early socialism, through his Dreyfusism and his republicanism (the two latter were for him identical) ran the same moral absolutes: absolute justice for Dreyfus and in society at large; absolute truth, to be established in respect of Dreyfus, and then to be disseminated through his journal, the *Cahiers de la quinzaine* as the means to the social revolution; and absolute freedom for the individual. These absolutes also underlay his break with the Socialist Party and his remorseless critique of the parliamentary politics of both Socialists and Radicals: he was morally outraged at their compromises and manoeuvrings, the half-truths and untruths of their discourse, the authoritarianism inherent in their party organization. When their moral decline had reduced the Socialists to impotence, Péguy transferred his hopes of universal salvation to Christianity again. But as a Christian he still believed that the absolutes of his republicanism and even of his socialism coincided with the tenets of his rediscovered Christian faith: his Christianity stood for freedom, not authority, and he never ceased to believe that to talk to men of eternal salvation was meaningless until their poverty had been alleviated.

By 1913 Péguy's moral absolutes had to take a back seat in face of urgent military realities. Péguy now claimed to speak in the name of a Jacobin war republicanism, which must not flinch from the execution of the 'internal enemy', Jaurès, and must ensure adequate military defence through the law on three-year military service. But he remained an anti-authoritarian at heart and his republicanism aimed only the better to defend Republican freedom against German imperialism, and to remove for good the threat of war.

Péguy is a major figure in twentieth-century French literature and a prophetic thinker who anticipated libertarian trends in world catholicism, as well as much of the later libertarian critique of parliamentary democracy, socialism and communism.

Bibliography

The Pléiade *Oeuvres en prose complètes*, ed. Robert Burac, vols 1 and 2 (Paris: Gallimard, 1987), for the first time give a complete chronological presentation of the prose works. There are no recent studies in English but see Daniel Halévy, *Péguy and les cahiers de la quinzaine*, trans. R. Bethell (London: Dennis Dobson, 1946). The French version was edited and updated with many footnotes as *Péguy* (Paris: Le Livre de Poche, 1979). See also W.B. Gallie, 'Péguy the moralist', *French Studies*, vol. II, no. 1, 1948, pp. 68–82; C.F.N. Mackay, 'Péguy's harmonious city', *The Times Literary Supplement* (22 December 1945) and E. Cahm, *Péguy et le nationalisme français* (Paris: Amitié Charles Péguy, 1972).

EC

PELLETAN, Camille Charles (1846–1915)

Camille Pelletan was a leading figure among Radical politicians during the first half of the Third Republic. Contemporaries regarded him as the embodiment of left-wing radicalism. He inherited his republicanism from his father, Eugène, who had been an opposition journalist and deputy during the Second Empire. Eugène Pelletan had also served as a member of the Third Republic's provisional government in the winter of 1870–1. Camille came of age then in the intersecting social, intellectual and political worlds which formed the amorphous left of the 1860s and 1870s. After studies in law and history, he began a lifelong career as a journalist, joining the Radical journal *Le Rappel* in 1870. Pelletan's first assignment was the Franco-Prussian War. He then covered the tortuous deliberations of the National Assembly at Versailles.

Journalism led naturally to electoral politics. After an unsuccessful campaign in 1879, he entered the Chamber of Deputies in 1881, elected in two districts, the Paris 10th *arrondissement* and the rural villages surrounding Aix-en-Provence. Pelletan chose to represent the southern rural district and he remained its deputy for thirty-one years without interruption. He sat on the extreme-left of the Chamber, joining Georges Clemenceau and the other deputies who took the label Radical-Socialist. He also collaborated closely with Clemenceau on the editorial board of his new journal, *La Justice*. From 1880 to 1893 Pelletan served as its editor-in-chief. During the 1880s and 1890s Pelletan followed an intransigent Radical position: opposing colonialism, demanding constitutional revision, denouncing clerical influence, calling for tax reform, proposing the nationalization of the railroads, sympathizing with the plight of strikers, and supporting labour legislation. His long-time service on the budget committee of the Chamber made him a parliamentary power and gave his denunciations of the banks and 'la féodalité financière' greater force.

From the time of Dreyfus' first conviction until the suicide of Colonel Henry, Pelletan remained convinced of Dreyfus' guilt. Even after he had been won to the Dreyfusard camp, he was reluctant to support the Waldeck-Rousseau government of Republican defence. He was outraged that the general who had brutally repressed the Commune should be the minister of war in this government. In 1901 Pelletan was instrumental in the creation of a formal Radical-Republican and Radical Socialist Party. Each year party militants selected him as a member of the executive committee and in 1906 he was elected party president. Following the 1902 legislative election, during which the Radical Party became the largest party in France, Pelletan served as the controversial minister of the navy in the government of Emile Combes. As minister he supported the demands of naval arsenal workers for unionization, defended ordinary sailors against their officers, and proposed a new strategic policy based on smaller ships, submarines and torpedoes. During the 1902–6

legislature he had a key role in the creation and functioning of the *bloc des gauches*, the electoral and parliamentary alliance of Radicals with Socialists. Pelletan always remained a strong advocate of this alliance as one consistent with the traditions of French radicalism and as one necessary for the implementation of an interventionist social reform programme which he championed in the Chamber and at party congresses.

During the Clemenceau ministry of 1906–9 Pelletan differed sharply with the premier from whom he had become increasingly distant since the mid-1890s. He attempted to organize Radical opposition to Clemenceau's anti-syndicalist stance and to revive the *bloc des gauches*. In both these efforts he failed and became a steadily more marginal voice in the Radical Party. In 1912 he exchanged his position as deputy, which was no longer as secure as it had once been, for that of senator from the Bouches-du-Rhône. The following year he was defeated in his bid for the presidency of the Radical Party. At the time of his death in 1915, while still applauded by Radical militants, he no longer spoke for the majority of Radical Party members, deputies or voters.

Bibliography

Revillon, Tony, *Camille Pelletan 1846–1915. Quarante-cinq ans de lutte pour la République* (Paris: M. Rivière, 1930). This is the only biography of Pelletan, written by an admiring political protégé.

JFS

PELLETIER, Madeleine née Anne (1874–1939)

Unlike many women who played a leading role in the radical movements at the end of the nineteenth century in France, Madeleine Pelletier did not come from a well-off family. She was in fact born and reared in squalor. Nevertheless, she gained access by her own efforts to two male preserves: the medical profession and the Socialist Party (SFIO). Her medical work in working-class districts confirmed her sense of injustice, and taunts from male colleagues about her unconventional appearance strengthened her commitment to feminism. Indeed her appointment as the first woman house doctor in a mental institution in France came only after a year-long struggle against sexual discrimination on the grounds that the requirement to have completed military service excluded women.

Little is known of Madeleine Pelletier's medical career; she did spend some years in research and published her studies. She achieved more notoriety for her political stances and manner of dress. Having become a writer in medical journals on scientific work, she turned her attention to political activity and wrote for feminist and socialist journals. She published numerous articles and brochures, and between 1908 and 1914 issued her own review, *La Suffragiste*. During the same period she entered the Socialist Party (SFIO); in 1906 she became the first woman to speak at a national assembly of the newly unified party; by 1910 she had become an executive committee member. Until the war, Madeleine Pelletier was frequently a speaker at national and international congresses. In this capacity she waged a campaign to get the SFIO to present a bill in the Assembly on women's suffrage. It was put on the agenda at the Limoges Congress in 1906 but got no further. She had to contend with the commonly held belief that votes for women would give the right an advantage. Madeleine Pelletier believed strongly that women's suffrage was as important a demand as the right to work. The Socialist deputies were divided over the issue at this time and failed to carry out their promises of legislative action.

Madeleine Pelletier sought support from the many Socialist groups in existence as long as they advanced her cause. Becoming more and more disillusioned with electoral politics, she associated more with the anarchist groups of the extreme-left. She was also an active member of the most radical feminist group of the time, Solidarity of Women (*La Solidarité de femmes*), became its president and led a protest group of suffragettes to the Chamber of Deputies in December 1906. However she represented an extreme position compared to most feminists. She was unconventional and her ideas on the family as a unit of oppression did not blend in with those of other women in the movement. She was far ahead in her development of feminist ideology. Economic independence for women was the cornerstone of her belief. However French workers were divided over the question of women working. Madeleine Pelletier found herself on the fringe of the Socialist and feminist movements. Unwilling to abandon feminism in socialism or socialism in feminism she left party politics. In the later part of her life she wrote fiction. As a practical means of implementing her beliefs she turned to individual direct action – practising abortions – for which she was incarcerated in the same Paris mental hospital where she had begun her medical career. She died six months later.

Madeleine Pelletier was the most outstanding woman to associate herself with the Socialist movement in France in the early years of the century. Her life is the tragic story of the attempt, against all odds, to advance both feminism and socialism. Her radicalism challenged not only the assumptions of the establishment but also those of reformist socialism, to such an extent that she would have been quietly forgotten were it not for recent interest in historical links between feminism and socialism that was engendered by the feminist movement of the 1960s.

Bibliography

In the series *Mémoire des Femmes* an anthology of works has been reprinted including Madeleine Pelletier, *L'Education féministe des filles et autres textes*, preface by Claude Maignien (Paris: Editions Syros, 1978).

Two articles in English by Marilyn J. Boxer contain comprehensive bibliographical references on Pelletier and on background topics of feminism and socialism of the period: 'When radical and socialist feminism were joined: The extraordinary failure of Madeleine Pelletier' in Jane Slaughter and Robert Kern (eds) *European Women on the Left: Socialism, feminism, and the problems faced by political women, 1880 to the Present* (Westport, Conn. and London: Greenwood Press, 1981), pp. 50–73; 'Socialism faces feminism: The failure of synthesis in France 1879–1914' in Marilyn J. Boxer and Jean H. Quataert (eds) *Socialist Women: European socialist feminism in the nineteenth and twentieth centuries* (New York: Elsevier, 1978), pp. 75–110.

MCr

PELLOUTIER, Fernand Léonce Emile (1867–1901)

A major figure of the late nineteenth-century French labour movement (although true recognition of his role only came after his death), Fernand Pelloutier was a champion of trade union autonomy, which he furthered through his work with the Bourses du Travail (local trade union centres). He was born in Paris on 1 October 1867, but the family moved to Nantes and then Saint-Nazaire. In Saint-Nazaire the two Pelloutier brothers attended a Catholic seminary, but after two attempts to run away and the discovery of anticlerical literature in his possession, Fernand was expelled in 1882 and enrolled instead at a secular school, where he proved to be a brilliant but erratic pupil. He failed his *baccalauréat* in 1885.

He then entered journalism and from 1885 to 1892 worked for the radical paper *La Démocratie de l'Ouest*, where he collaborated with Aristide Briand. In 1889, Pelloutier worked in support of Briand's unsuccessful electoral bid as Radical-Republican candidate.

By 1892, when Pelloutier took over as editor of *La Démocratie de l'Ouest*, his political allegiance had shifted towards socialism. He joined Jules Guesde's Parti Ouvrier Français, and at the same time became interested in the 'economic' wing of the labour movement, helping to set up the Saint-Nazaire Bourse du Travail. Soon, however, his support for the idea of the general strike brought him into conflict with the Guesdists, and he left the party. After his move, with his family, to Paris in 1893, Pelloutier developed his ideas on the general strike and made contact with anarchist circles. He became assistant secretary in 1894, and then general secretary in 1895, of the National Federation of Bourses du Travail (founded in February 1892). In the same year, he joined the secret society, the Chevalerie du Travail.

It is as the driving force behind the Bourses du Travail that Pelloutier left a lasting influence on the French labour movement. Pelloutier's ideas were set out in a famous article published in the anarchist paper *Les Temps Nouveaux* (20 October 1895), in which he urged anarchists to join labour organizations as the best means of preparing the revolution. From 1895 to 1901 Pelloutier guided the activities of the Bourses du Travail, which he saw as a means of helping workers to educate and organize themselves. A libertarian and an ardent defender of labour autonomy, Pelloutier combated not only Guesdist attempts to recruit trade unions to socialism, but also what he regarded as the centralizing tendencies of the newly-formed Confédération Générale du Travail. During this period he also continued his journalistic activities; his major project was the launch in February 1897 of *L'Ouvrier des Deux Mondes*, but he was forced to halt publication in July 1899. For Pelloutier, journalism corresponded to a vision of working-class emancipation which depended on education, and which provided a basis for the activities of the Bourses du Travail.

Pelloutier's journalistic work and his post as head of the Fédération des Bourses brought him little income, and friends found him in a state of such poverty and ill-health in 1899 that Alexandre Millerand was asked to find him a temporary job as researcher at the Labour Office. From the beginning of 1901, Pelloutier was laid low by the tuberculosis which had sapped his health (forcing long periods of convalescence) and disfigured him since adolescence. He died on 31 March 1901 — a slow and agonizing death.

Bibliography

One of Pelloutier's major works, published posthumously, *Histoire des Bourses du Travail: origine, institutions, avenir* (London: Gordon and Breach, 1971) (first published Paris: Schleicher, 1902; 1946 edition, reprinted) contains a biographical preface by Victor Dave. Jacques Julliard, *Fernand Pelloutier et les origines du syndicalisme d'action directe* (Paris: Seuil, 1971), combines a biography of Pelloutier with a collection of his writings, and gives a useful bibliography. A short account of Pelloutier's life is in Jean Maitron, *Dictionnaire biographique du mouvement ouvrier*, 3rd part: 1871–1914 (Paris Editions Ouvrières 1973–7), vol. XIV (1976), pp. 231–3. The Musée Social in Paris holds Pelloutier's personal papers.

SM

PÉRI, Gabriel (1902–41)

Péri was born in Toulon on 9 February 1902. His father worked as a technical services director in the docks at Marseilles; Gabriel attended the *lycée* there and completed his studies in 1918. His formative years were heavily influenced by the war; indeed, his whole life and career were to be dominated by his interpretation and responses to the First World War. In his autobiography, written in captivity in 1941, Péri describes the path he began to follow:

> I became aware in a world still at war. War was the major fact of life one met everywhere, it sprang up at every stage of one's thinking. I was looking for an explanation of the War, considered not just as a source of suffering, but as a complete upheaval, the meaning, the interpretation of which I wanted to discover.

'The struggle for socialism', he wrote, 'was to be my life.'

In 1919 he joined the French Socialist Party (the SFIO — Section française de l'Internationale ouvrière) and, after the Congress held at Tours in 1920, Péri joined the newly-formed Communist Party as a Young Communist militant. Having already been imprisoned for his activities, in 1922, Péri, aged 20, became secretary-general of the Young Communists. He continued his work as a journalist, writing for Henri Barbusse's *Clarté*, and for *Avant-garde*, the organ of the Young Communists. His meteoric rise within the echelons of the PCF (the French Communist Party) was further marked in 1929 by his election to the Central Committee, and by his appointment as the chief foreign affairs correspondent of *L'Humanité*, the party's major daily newspaper. This post enabled Péri to travel widely, and he covered many of the important international conferences of the inter-war period, visiting the Balkans, Spain, England, Indo-China, North Africa and Czechoslovakia.

In 1932 his political activism was rewarded when he was elected as deputy for the Seine-et-Oise district, a seat which had been won for the Communists for the first time by André Marty in 1924. In 1938, at the time of the Munich accords, Péri wrote a series of powerful articles in *L'Humanité* denouncing the peace agreement as an illusion which would soon 'give way to the appalling reality of war'. With the outbreak of war in September 1939 and the banning of the French Communist Party, Péri went underground. He continued to write articles for the Communist *Cahiers* which were published clandestinely; indeed Péri was among the few well-known Communists to adopt a clear anti-German stance before the beginning of Hitler's campaign to invade the Soviet Union in June 1941.

On 18 May 1941, however, Péri was arrested by the German occupying forces in France. Despite being tortured by the Gestapo, Péri refused to denounce his commitment to the Communist cause and, on 15 December 1941 at the Mont-Valérien fortress, he was shot by firing-squad.

Péri remains a hero in the Communists' pantheon. The many French streets named after him honour the memory of an activist who, for some, was martyred in the struggle against Fascism.

Bibliography

Péri, G. (1947), *Un grand français, Gabriel Péri*, Paris: Editions Sociales.

MC

PÉTAIN, Henri Philippe Benoni Omer Joseph (1856–1951)

Marshal of France and head of state, Philippe Pétain was born at Cauchy-la-Tour (Pas-de-Calais) on 24 April 1856. Of peasant stock, he received a Catholic education, and entered the military school of Saint-Cyr in 1876, leaving in 1878 as a *sous-lieutenant*. From then until the age of 58, Pétain's career was hardly exceptional. It took him twelve years to reach the rank of captain, ten more to become a major, and ten more to become a colonel, the rank he still held in 1914 at the outbreak of war. His promotion had been slow even by peacetime standards. This was in part, however, due to the unpopularity of the theories he had put forward during a number of stints as war college lecturer at the Ecole Normale de Tir and the Ecole de Guerre. In contrast with the accepted strategy based on the offensive, Pétain took full account of the new conditions of war: heavy artillery, machine guns and barbed wire. His own strategy was based on the simple dictum firepower kills ('le feu tue'), and stressed the fact that the new conditions created an advantage for the defensive. One must not exaggerate his prescience, however; at this stage he could not foresee the completely static nature of the warfare to come, and still saw the offensive as remaining the way to win a battle (albeit an offensive tempered with caution). These views were anathema to those who saw war as a heroic business: the official line ignored Pétain's views, which were to be justified only by war itself.

In 1914 Pétain was two years from retirement. The next thirty years were, however, to be the most active and the most public of his life.

At the outbreak of war, he was in command of the 4th Infantry Brigade. During the advance into Belgium, and the subsequent retreat, Pétain was swiftly promoted to general (as one early replacement for the many removed for incompetence). In September, having taken over the 6th Infantry Division, he took part in the advance after the Marne. Once this attack was checked, his division started digging in as part of the extensive trench system which from now on was to stretch from Switzerland to the sea.

The experience of the ill-fated Artois and Champagne offensives of 1915 confirmed Pétain's view of the futility of such attacks, and the unreality of the vision of the 'percée', or breakthrough. Ironically, his own comparative success in these offensives (based on meticulous preparation) brought him the respect both of the high command and of the politicians, and his advancement was swift. By June 1915 he was in command of the 2nd Army.

It was the defence of Verdun, in 1916, which was to make him a household name. Called in suddenly, three days after the initial German onslaught in February when all appeared on the verge of collapse, he organized a stubborn defence which over a number of months was crowned with success, based partly on defensive lines in depth and partly on the brilliant organization of reinforcements via the 'Voie Sacrée', but above all on the maintenance of morale. Verdun was to make of Pétain one of the first public heroes of the war. For the rest of his life he was to remain the 'Saviour of Verdun', reputed, as well, for his personal commitment to the welfare of the troops under his charge.

This reputation was to serve him well in his next important test. In May 1917, after the disastrous Nivelle offensive, Pétain was made commander-in-chief. The immediate result of the offensive had been the widespread mutinies which by June affected fifty-four divisions (i.e. over half the French army). The prospect was one of French collapse, and a German victory. By the end of June, however, by a judicious mixture of stern discipline and positive morale-raising initiatives, Pétain had solved the problem. This almost miraculous result was to form the other part of Pétain's subsequent heroic reputation.

That reputation was to be dented, among leading generals and politicians, in 1918 – though the public was to be unaware of it. The German breakthrough in March led to doubts about his nerve. Pétain gave orders for the French to withdraw and cover Paris, thus losing contact with the British and opening the front. Haig, deciding that what was needed was a 'French commander-in-chief who would fight', agreed with the politicians that General Foch should be made supreme commander, with Pétain and Haig serving under him. Whether Pétain had merely been his usual cautious, pessimistic self or, as Haig suggests, 'was in a funk and had lost his nerve', has always been a matter for debate.

Be that as it may, after the armistice Pétain was, on 8 December 1918, made a Marshal of France. To the general public he was with Foch the symbol of their victory. Foch's political intrigues in the aftermath of the war, interfering in, and publicly criticizing the Versailles negotiations, and actively encouraging Rhineland separatism, led to his almost immediate disappearance from the public scene. Pétain remained unscathed, to become the dominant figure in military affairs. In 1920 he was appointed vice-president of the Conseil Supérieur de la Guerre (the nominal president being the war minister). The vice-president commanded the French armies in time of war, and in peace the General Staff were under his authority. Pétain was also appointed inspector-general of the army, with the stipulation that the chief of general staff should submit for his approval anything to do with the structure or mobilization of the army, before sending it to the minister. In the

years 1920–31 Pétain thus ran army policy, having even greater power than the minister himself.

During this period Pétain took part personally in one more military campaign, when he was sent in 1925–6 at the height of the Rif rebellion in Morocco to take over command of the French troops from Marshal Lyautey. In close liaison with the Spanish, Pétain delivered a crushing victory over Abd-el-Krim, the Rifi leader.

From 1931, when at the age of 75 he retired from these military posts, until 1934 Pétain spent three years in comparative limbo despite several attempts to return to the centre of operations. Suddenly, in 1934, all this was changed. In the aftermath of the February 1934 riots Gaston Doumergue was brought in as premier, to restore confidence. Into his government he brought Pétain as minister for war, to provide added reassurance. Pétain held this post until the fall of the government in November.

As minister he reversed the roles with regard to the Conseil Supérieur de la Guerre. Where, when he had been vice-president of that body, he had seemed almost more powerful than the minister, he now, as minister exerted a great deal of power over his successor, Weygand, and over the chief of general staff, Gamelin. This period was short but its result was to restore Pétain to military power. Though he refused in November 1934 to serve in Flandin's government, the new minister for war was his old friend General Maurin who set up a Haut-Comité Militaire with very wide powers, on which Pétain was to sit by personal right (the only person not there by virtue of his function). Maurin also made Pétain in his own right a permanent member of the Conseil Supérieur de la Guerre, with a *voix délibérative*. From now until the war Pétain was to be once more one of the most powerful voices in French military policy.

Throughout the inter-war period Pétain insisted on a policy based on what he took to be the lessons of the First World War. It was based on defence, and on the use of strong fortified positions; out of it grew the Maginot Line. He was completely unaware of the revolutionary part to be played in modern warfare by tanks and aeroplanes, which were to restore a war of movement. By a strange paradox he now became the equivalent of those died-in-the-wool generals against whom he had reacted before the war. His dogged determination and his enormous influence did much to produce France's unpreparedness for modern warfare in 1940.

Pétain's influence between the wars was not purely military. For the public he had become the symbol of victory, a charismatic figure. His name was indissolubly connected with the defence of Verdun, the ultimate symbol of French valour; Pétain was seen, too, as the general who had had closest to his heart the welfare of his men. For the old soldiers' associations, Pétain stood for their sacrifice. There was more than this, however. The aura of a Marshal of France made him seem more than a military man, and someone on whom the country could count in all circumstances. He became a figure of political reassurance – particularly as he was seen as a 'Republican Marshal', unconcerned with *coups d'état* of the right. His own views, as publicly expressed in this period, were however fairly typical of military men of this type – against politics, but by that very attitude political, in a traditional and reactionary mould.

In the mounting pre-war crisis there were a number of calls for Pétain to take power. Hervé in *La Victoire* ('C'est Pétain qu'il nous faut'), Suarèz and Bailby in *Le Jour*, the old soldiers in *La Voix du combattant*, Daudet in *L'Action Française*, d'Ormesson in *Le Figaro*, Taittinger in *L'Ami du peuple*, Lémery in *L'Indépendant*, all called at one time or other for Pétain's leadership in face of the external threat and of parliamentary chaos at home. Though most of these calls were from the right, it is typical of Pétain's universal appeal that he should also have been seen by left-wingers such as Pierre Cot as the 'Republican Marshal', a man of perfect loyalty and of absolute political independence, who should take full powers to stem the threat from the Fascist leagues (*ligues*). When, at the age of 83, Pétain was in 1939 appointed France's first ambassador to Franco's Spain, the left was furious, not with Pétain, but with the government for sending 'Le plus noble, le plus humain de nos chefs militaires'.

It would be wrong to see Pétain as having encouraged any of these campaigns. He gave them no public approval, nor did he show any inclination to go along with the various more solid attempts to involve him in practical politics. In 1939, for example, a number of leading politicians tried to get him to stand for the presidency of the Republic, but he refused. This atmosphere of adulation, however, could hardly leave him unaffected. He was convinced, after the Doumergue experience, that parliamentary government was leading France to disaster. He was convinced, too, that when that occurred he would be needed. One of his greatest characteristics in this period was unconscious vanity; by now he believed himself to be the great figure he was reputed to be.

For the first eight months of the Second World War, Pétain remained at his post in Madrid. On 18 May 1940 he was called to Paris after the initial disastrous week of the German invasion to become deputy premier in Reynaud's cabinet. His presence caused immediate public relief. Amid the worsening situation, however, Pétain's attitude was one of pessimism and phlegmatic acceptance of defeat. In the cabinet he became the rallying-point of those desiring an armistice. At Bordeaux on 16 June Reynaud resigned and Pétain took over as premier. Negotiations started, and on 22 June the armistice was signed, whereby half of France came under military occupation with the rest remaining under French control as a neutral state. The armistice was welcomed with relief by a large majority of the French nation. On 1 July the government moved to Vichy, and on 10 July, thanks in large part to the skilful activities of Pierre Laval, the National Assembly of the Third Republic voted itself out of existence, and a new regime was set up with Pétain as *chef de l'état* and *chef du gouvernement* (premier), with Laval as deputy premier.

Pétain had full powers; and in the first period of Vichy he was firmly in charge. His accession was greeted with joy and with reassurance by a large section of the French population. He himself appears to have seen his role in almost mystical terms; his statement 'I offer my self to France' ('J'ai fait à la France le don de ma personne') carries overtones of religious sacrifice, as well as hints of unconscious self-satisfaction. To many he 'incarnated' France; he himself seems to have subscribed to this view. What must not be discounted, however, is the sincerity of his belief that he was the man for the situation.

Despite the urgency of negotiations with Germany, one of Pétain's major concerns from the start was with the internal regeneration of France. The defeat was seen as a punishment for France's shortcomings, which must now be expiated. The 'National Revolution' was introduced, a series of reforming policies based on the traditional teachings of the right, such as the importance of the family, the land, duty, order and patriotism. The motto 'Travail, Famille, Patrie' replaced the Republican 'Liberté, Egalité, Fraternité'. Alongside the moral exhortations, the new government introduced anti-Semitic legislation, way ahead of any German demands.

In foreign policy there was a determined effort to establish a policy of collaboration with Germany, for which Pétain was (despite later myths) as enthusiastic as Laval or anyone else. Pétain's meeting with Hitler at Montoire in October 1940 was a major moment in these negotiations. His dismissal of Laval in December was not, as has sometimes been suggested, based on disagreement on this policy; indeed Vichy's attempts at collaboration remained just as strong in the succeeding months. Germany's attitude, however, became increasingly resistant to such ideas.

By early 1941 the pattern of Pétain's Vichy experiences was already established. The armistice agreement, based originally on a belief in Germany's imminent victory, had become an ongoing battle, with the French striving for collaboration, and Germany's demands becoming more insistent. Pétain was to be continually pushed further down a slope caused by his original decision. Darlan, Laval's successor, attempted a 'grand design' in 1941, in which France collaborated more closely with the German war effort. The sole result was the loss of Syria to the British and even more strained relations with Germany. In April 1942 Pétain was forced to readmit Laval, this time as head of government, with Pétain now merely fulfilling the role of figurehead.

The Allied landings in North Africa in November 1942 were the watershed of Vichy's fortunes. Many believed that now was the moment for Pétain to fly to North Africa to link with the Allies; but he firmly rejected the idea, determined to remain in France and continue to share his people's fate. This had been his last chance to reverse the downward slope; now not only was it clear that Germany's victory was less certain, but also much of the French army, and a considerable section of the French public (as well as most of France's overseas territory) had gone over to what had previously been seen as a dissident minority. Not only this, but the aftermath of the North African situation was the German invasion of France's unoccupied zone. Pétain's dignified condemnation of the German action was, as always, followed by his acceptance of it. He remained in office as the nominal head of what was now a purely puppet government. France was entirely occupied; one of her trump cards, the fleet, had been scuttled; the other, the empire, had been lost. Laval held most of the little power that was going, and effectively became the government. The regime was now widely discredited, and during 1943 became more so when under German pressure it set up the *Milice*, a paramilitary force to combat the Resistance. Meanwhile the Germans began to institute a more comprehensive policy for the deportation of Jews.

Despite the growing effects of his great age, and his comparative powerlessness, Pétain began in late 1943 to try to work towards the removal of Laval, in order to set up a new government which would disband many of Vichy's structures and prepare for an orderly hand-over of power. In November he attempted to broadcast to the nation, but the Germans forbade it. The Marshal thereupon declared himself unable to exercise his functions. For three weeks there was stalemate, but faced by threats of force Pétain eventually had to give in and resume his office. A further step downwards; the Germans now insisted on his cabinet containing some of the most extreme of the Paris collaborators.

From now on Pétain was a mere onlooker as France disintegrated into civil war, and as Vichy's policies became even more extreme. From May 1944 onwards he was moved from place to place by the Germans, who feared his disappearance. On 17 August, in face of the Allied advance, the Germans ordered the French government to Belfort; Laval and Pétain both refused, but were removed there by force. From there, in early September, they were taken to the castle of Sigmaringen in Southern Germany, where they remained until April 1945 when, with Germany collapsing, Pétain was taken to the Swiss frontier. He declined, however, to remain in that neutral country and voluntarily returned to France to face trial. At the trial, in July–August 1945, he was condemned to death. Given his great age, the sentence was commuted to life imprisonment. From then until his death on 23 July 1951, at the age of 95, he was kept in prison on the Ile d'Yeu, declining into senility.

Pétain was neither a villain nor a saint. He was a man of limited experience and capabilities, except in military matters, who came to believe that he was the saviour of his nation. He thus found himself having to deal with matters completely outside his competence. Though he usually acted in good faith, and for what he believed to be the good of France, his vanity led him down paths which were disastrous both to France and to himself.

Bibliography

Griffiths, R. (1970), *Marshal Pétain*, London: Constable.

Paxton, R. (1972), *Vichy France*, London: Barrie and Jenkins.

Ryan, S. (1969), *Pétain the Soldier*, London: Yoseloff.

Tournoux, J. (1964), *Pétain et de Gaulle*, Paris: Plon.

RMG

PEYREFITTE, Alain Antoine (1925–)

Alain Peyrefitte has been a deputy, diplomat and former conservative minister, departmental councillor for Bray-sur-Seine since 1964 and mayor of Provins since 1965 and an intellectual and author, member of the prestigious Académie Française since

1977 and member of the editorial board of *Le Figaro* since 1983. The son of teachers, he was educated in Montpellier and Paris, at the Faculté de Droit and the Ecole Normale Supérieure. After graduating from the National School of Administration in 1947 he pursued a career as a diplomat throughout the Fourth Republic. He was elected as a Gaullist deputy for Provins (Seine-et-Marne) successively in 1962, 1967, 1968, 1973, 1978, 1982 (after a by-election) and in 1986. Peyrefitte had an impressive ministerial career, briefly holding a junior ministerial post of education in 1962, followed by ministerial posts for repatriation (1962), information (1962–6), scientific research (1966–7), education (1976–8), administrative reform (1973–4), culture (1974) and justice (1977–81). He has also been a prolific and much acclaimed writer, publishing most notably on contemporary French political life (*Le Mal français*, Paris: Plon, 1976) on China (*Chine immuable et changeante*, Paris: Fayard, 1984) and on conservative thought (*Réponses à la violence*, Paris: Presses-Pocket, 1988; *Quand la rose se fânera*, Paris: Plon, 1983).

Although close to de Gaulle, Peyrefitte was not among the ranks of 'historic' Gaullists who had come out of the Resistance. Rather, he can best be identified with a second generation of 'institutional' Gaullists who emerged with the Fifth Republic. During the early 1960s he shared the concern of many young Gaullist deputies about the future of the party after de Gaulle. Whilst stressing the importance of the institutions of the Fifth Republic, this group also realized the need for an effective party organization and tactics. It was therefore quite natural for de Gaulle's successor Pompidou to choose Peyrefitte to revitalize the Gaullist party organization. He held the post of secretary-general of the Gaullists between 1972 and 1973, where he did much to build up the party for the 1973 legislative elections. During the struggle for the leadership of the right in 1974 Peyrefitte supported the unsuccessful Gaullist candidate Jacques Chaban-Delmas. However, he soon transferred his support to the new Independent Republican president, Giscard d'Estaing, becoming one of the most pro-Giscardian Gaullists. Although in policy terms Peyrefitte was a traditionalist and a conservative, who rejected many of the more liberal social policies of Giscardian administration, he was above all else a 'legitimist' who believed in the stability of the regime and hence he was able to work closely with Giscard and helped to ensure Gaullist parliamentary support. Since 1986 he has retired to the 'backbenches' of the Gaullists, where he has continued to be an active parliamentarian.

As a politician Peyrefitte is cautious and calculating, and as a minister vigorous and assertive. He came to public attention as minister of education during the student revolt of 1968, although his most important contributions to the Gaullist regime were steering through many complex pieces of legislation which aimed to strengthen the State. As minister of information under de Gaulle he was responsible for increasing governmental influence over news output. As minister of justice he was the author of the highly controversial law 'securité et liberté' which increased and strengthened penal policies against offenders. This made him the target of criticism not only from the left but from many moderates within the governmental majority.

Peyrefitte's crusade against the left has also been voiced in his essays and articles for *Le Figaro* where he continually asserts the need for traditional values, the importance of freedom of choice in all sectors and the key role of the state in enforcing order and reducing dissent. In 1986 he narrowly survived an assassination attempt by Action Directe.

Bibliography

Peyrefitte was the subject of a short profile in A. Duhamel, *Les Prétendants* (Paris: Gallimard, 1983); for details of his role in the Gaullist party see Jean Charlot, *The Gaullist Phenomenon* (London: George Allen & Unwin, 1971).

ER

PFLIMLIN, Pierre Eugène Jean (1907–   )

Pflimlin will probably be best remembered as the Mouvement Républicain Populaire (Christian Democrat) leader whose nomination as president of the Council (prime minister) on 13 May 1958 was to precipitate the demise of the Fourth Republic. By the spring of 1958 the successive governments in Paris, reduced to impotence by internal divisions and the absence of a stable parliamentary majority, had completely lost control of the situation in Algeria, orders from Paris were being openly flouted and the army, in collusion with the European settlers, was increasingly taking matters into its own hands. After a ministerial crisis lasting thirty-eight days, Pflimlin was nominated president of the Council. The army and the European settlers, believing he favoured independence for Algeria (he had advocated negotiations with the Algerian National Liberation Front), staged an insurrection in Algiers. The army took control of Corsica and the only alternative to civil war in metropolitan France seemed to lie in de Gaulle. On 1 June the National Assembly approved his nomination as president of the Council and, accepting his condition that a new constitution be drafted and submitted for popular approval by referendum, effectively signed the death warrant of the Fourth Republic.

Pflimlin had previously held several important ministerial appointments between 1947 and 1954 under the Fourth Republic, and was to be a minister under de Gaulle in 1958 and again briefly in 1962. He was one of the five MRP ministers who resigned in May 1962 after de Gaulle's 'anti-European' press conference, in which the latter stated: 'The only possible Europe is one of independent nation-states.' In the same year Pflimlin also came out against the direct election of the president of the Republic. Parallel with his national political career, Pflimlin has been active in local politics (as mayor of Strasbourg) and in promoting the regional development of his native Alsace. In recent years much of his energy has been directed towards European Community affairs, as vice-president and (from 1984 to 1986) president of the European Parliament.

In the early years of the Fifth Republic Pflimlin supported de Gaulle, partly for tactical reasons (opposition would have been suicidal for his party) and partly because he believed that de Gaulle's Algerian policy offered the only hope of a solution to the problem and that decolonization was inevitable. Subsequently, as one of the more conservative members of his party, he expressed general if not unconditional support for de Gaulle's economic and social policies. However, he shared the reservations of some of his colleagues in the MRP in respect of de Gaulle's personality and style of government and of the increasingly presidential nature of the regime; he also opposed de Gaulle's anti-Nato stance and his blocking of the process of European integration. The limited part played by Pflimlin in the French national scene since the mid-1960s is perhaps symptomatic of the difficulty the Christian Democrats have encountered in establishing a place in Fifth Republic politics, whether inside or outside the majority during the Gaullist era and subsequently in the left/right polarization. As one of the 'elder statesmen' of the European Parliament, he has pursued the ideals of his former MRP colleague, and one of the 'fathers of Europe', Robert Schuman (q.v.), namely: realistic progress towards European unity, increased powers for the European Parliament, rejection of 'Euro-pessimism', while at the same time ill-concealing his sense of frustration at the immobilism of the EEC Council of Ministers.

Bibliography

For Pflimlin's role in the MRP, see R.E.M. Irving, *Christian Democracy in France* (London: George Allen & Unwin, 1973) and, in French, E.-F. Callot, *Le MRP, origine, structure, doctrine, programme et action politique* (Paris: M. Rivière, 1978). There is, of course, an abundant literature on the events of May 1958, and A. Horne, *A Savage War of Peace* (London: Macmillan, 1977) and, in French, B. Droz and E. Lever, *Histoire de la guerre d'Algérie (1954–1962)* (Paris: Seuil, 1982) may profitably be consulted; J.-L. English and D. Riot, *Entretiens avec Pierre Pflimlin* (Strasburg: Nuée Bleue, 1990) is a quasi-autobiography.

HE

PHILIP, André (1902–70)

André Philip, a Protestant, was born in 1902 in the Gard. By 1924 he had written a doctoral thesis on guild socialism (based on research in London) and formulated a lifelong philosophy, in which he placed Christ just beyond the horizon of socialism. In 1926 he entered the SFIO as well as the Faculty of Law at Lyons. In the early 1930s he defended Protestant conscientious objectors; in 1934, together with Karl Barth and Dietrich Bonhöffer, he adumbrated a radical Christian front against fascism.

But Philip was no pacifist: entering the Chamber of Deputies in 1936, he would urge Blum to take a vigorous anti-Munich stand. In 1940, after voting against the Vichy enabling laws he organized 'Libération Sud', a resistance movement in Lyons. In 1942 he escaped to London. Thence followed his special relationship with de Gaulle, the uneasy friendship of an autocrat and a democrat united by their cause and by a lofty moralism. He undertook a mission to Roosevelt on de Gaulle's behalf (1942), but criticized his concept of executive power. In 1945, while president of the Constitutional Commission, he helped launch the attack which prompted de Gaulle to leave government in January 1946. Philip was to follow shortly: he had been the Consultative Assembly's budgetary expert (1944–5), minister of economy and finance under Gouin (1946) and Blum (1946–7) and finally of the economy under Ramadier (1947).

With the breakup of the post-Resistance coalition, Philip returned to his 'vocation' of eminent dissidence: it would be incarnated in three directions: education, European Unity and the 'Third

World'. In 1944–5 he had presided over a commission on education; more lastingly, he was president of the Federation of Youth Centres from 1944 to 1968. Here he sought to inculcate his socialism, concerned less with distributive justice than with the ethic of dignity in work and leisure. Member of the parliamentary committee on European unity in 1949, he lost his place when beaten in the 1951 elections; he remained president of the Socialist Movement for the United States of Europe (1950–64). His opposition to colonial ventures (Suez, Algeria) evolved into a leading role among European sympathizers with the Third World concept. Philip proved the opposite of a party man – he left the SFIO (1957) and then the PSU. His vision found some consummation in a guarded welcome for May 1968.

The portrait of Philip speaks volumes: a professor and a loner.'I have always felt entirely in this world and yet not of this world.' His career illuminates the significance of the Resistance both as a cultural–ideological achievement and a political failure: the only years he occupied office were those which witnessed a front which, at its widest, stretched from de Gaulle to Thorez. The Resistance introduced Philip's Barthian socialism into the mainstream of French political culture, but the logic of everyday politics soon drove Philip back into 'dissidence'. In a sense, he was a morally absolute version of his friend Léon Blum.

Bibliography

A selection of his writings with biographical prefaces by Paul Ricoeur and L. Philip (his son) can be found in *André Philip par lui-même. Les Voies de la liberté* (Paris: Aubier Montaigne, 1970). See also Philip's *Les Socialistes* (Paris: Seuil, 1967). For the years 1944–7, consult B.D. Graham, *The French Socialists and Tripartisme, 1944–1947* (London: Weidenfeld & Nicolson, 1965).

MK

PINAY, Antoine (1891–)

Born in Saint-Symphorien (Rhône) the son of a hatmaker, Antoine Pinay enjoyed a long and distinguished career spanning three Republics and became the popular symbol of prudent non-Gaullist conservatism. He was mayor of Saint-Chamond (Loire) for nearly fifty years and member and president of the Council (Conseil Général) of the Loire from 1948 to 1979. First elected to the Chamber of

Deputies in 1936, he became a senator in 1938. After the war he was elected to the second Constituent Assembly in 1946, despite problems over his wartime record, and sat in the National Assembly from 1946 to 1958. Having first held office as junior minister for economic affairs in the Queuille government of 1948, he was minister of public works in four administrations between 1950 and 1952. With the unexpected help of twenty-seven members of the Gaullist RPR, he acquired enough votes in the National Assembly to become prime minister in 1952; the election of this one-time member of Pétain's National Council, who had retained mayoral office during the occupation seemed to mark the return to respectability for the non- if not actually anti-Gaullist right, known as the 'Moderates'. He was a leading member of the moderate Centre National des Indépendants et Paysans (CNIP) and in 1953 became president of a political formation which was a valuable focus of moderate conservative opinion at a time of dangerous polarization in French politics.

As *président du conseil*, Pinay took for himself the difficult finance portfolio and owed his popularity, like some latter day Poincaré (q.v.) to his declared desire to defend the franc and halt inflation. He hoped by sound economic management and reduced taxation to win over the small saver and the business world in general. Referring to himself as the consumer's friend (*M. Consommateur*), he won early popularity by cancelling electricity price increases. He preferred to cut expenditure rather than raise new taxes; he introduced a sliding scale for wages indexed to prices. More controversially he declared an amnesty on tax evasion and his taxation pledges seemed to many a dangerous reversion to Third Republic habits. The famous Pinay loan (*emprunt Pinay*) of March 1952, with its tax and death duties exemptions and its linkage to the price of gold, ensured his long-term reputation as a financial master. There were costs to the Pinay strategy – reduced investment, unproductive hoarding, slightly higher unemployment – but he did restore confidence in the currency and inflation did fall.

After his defeat in December 1952 Pinay never again formed a government though he made three attempts (in 1953, 1955 and 1957) to do so. He was, however, foreign minister in Edgar Faure's (q.v.) government in 1955–6. At a significant moment in French decolonization, he came to support Faure's independence policy for Morocco and his conservatism did not make him a French Algeria (*Algérie Française*) diehard, as it did for many of his political allies. He coined the memorable phrase 'independence within interdependence' to characterize the new relationship between France and her overseas possessions.

Pinay was among the first parliamentarians to approach de Gaulle in 1958 and his enduring economic reputation made him a natural choice as minister of finance and economic affairs in the government formed by de Gaulle in June. His name and reputation were crucial in ensuring the success of the June loan and he participated in the elaboration of the Jacques Rueff (q.v.) Stabilization Plan. He was a member of the 1959 Debré (q.v.) government, but resigned within a year. Very much the Fourth Republic politician he criticized the Gaullist style of government and the notion of a reserved presidential domain (*domaine réservé*); he frequently argued for the right of ministers to speak on matters for which they were collectively responsible. He was frequently mentioned as a possible anti-de Gaulle presidential candidate and in 1969 Pompidou (q.v.) sounded him out as a possible finance minister. But he declined all offers to re-enter national politics, though he did accept the newly created post of ombudsman (*médiateur*) for a short period in 1973–4.

His remaining political energies were reserved for the more congenial atmosphere of the town hall of Saint-Chamond where he could enjoy to the full his reputation as the eldest of elder statesmen.

Bibliography

Anderson, M. (1974), *Conservative Politics in France*, London: Allen & Unwin.

Campbell, P. (1953), 'Discipline and loyalty in the French Parliament during the Pinay Government' in *Political Studies*, vol. I, September, pp. 247–57.

Guillaume, S. (1984), *Antoine Pinay ou la confiance en politique*, Paris: Presses de la Fondation Nationale des Sciences Politiques.

Rimbaud, C. (1990), *Pinay*, Paris, Perrin.

ACR

PINEAU, Christian (1904–)

Socialist politician and trade union activist, Christian Pineau, the son-in-law of the playwright Jean Giraudoux, was French foreign minister at the time of the Suez crisis in 1956, and during the negotiations leading to the Treaty of Rome in 1957.

Active in the Confédération Générale du Travail (CGT) in the 1930s, Pineau soon became a prominent member of the internal Resistance after 1940, and was sent as an emissary to London to see de Gaulle, whom he regarded as but one representative among many of republican legitimacy; his aim was to get de Gaulle to commit himself firmly to a future democratic France. Later, he spent two years in prison in Lyons, and was deported to Buchenwald concentration camp.

As a deputy in the Constituent Assembly in 1945–6 and a prominent member of its finance committee, he was the instigator of the nationalization of banks and credit institutions, though the final measure of this was not as great as he had wanted. He held a wide variety of ministerial posts, including that of minister of finance – the only Socialist to hold that post during the Fourth Republic. During the long-running debate (1950–4) on the supranational European Defence Community, Pineau, despite having been a deportee, urged his fellow countrymen not to base policy towards Germany on experiences of the inter-war period.

Pineau tried unsuccessfully to form a government in February 1955, but his experience of European and colonial matters earned him the portfolio of foreign minister in the Socialist-led government of Guy Mollet in 1956–7. The independence of Morocco was recognized, and Pineau tried to increase diplomatic influence with the Soviet Union and in the Third World.

The worsening situation in Algeria, however, led Pineau and Mollet to plan secretly, with Anthony Eden, Selwyn Lloyd, and the Israeli government, the invasion of Egypt in 1956 to overthrow Nasser, who was helping the Algerian nationalist struggle. As with Eden, it was clear that Pineau was influenced by analogies with Hitlerian aggression in the 1930s. He later said he had been 'haunted by the memory of March 1936', when Germany reoccupied the Rhineland.

1956–7 was the period of the 'relaunch' of Europe, and Pineau, having made sweeping changes in the Quai d'Orsay (the French Foreign Ministry), was instrumental in tailoring the EEC Treaty (1957) to French needs in the matter of the absorption of agricultural surpluses and the association of overseas territories and colonies.

After the fall of the Mollet government in December 1957, Pineau was retained as foreign minister by succeeding governments until May 1958. Pineau was in favour of the return to power of de Gaulle as a solution to the Algerian problem, though he opposed the new Fifth Republic Constitution in September 1958. He lost his parliamentary seat soon after, and though remaining a member of the organizing committee of the SFIO (the Socialist Party) until 1966, he gradually retired from active politics.

Bibliography

Pineau's own account of the Suez operation is covered in *1956 – Suez* (Paris: Robert Laffont, 1976). His wartime experiences are dealt with in *La Simple vérité 1940–45* (Paris: Robert Laffont, 1960).

MS

PISANI, Edgard Edouard Marie-Victor (1918–)

Born into an Algerian settler (*pied noir*) family, this brilliant and adaptable civil servant-turned-politician is in many ways an archetype of the Fifth Republic 'technocracy'. Schooling in Tunis and at the prestigious Lycée Louis-le-Grand in Paris led to a degree and a doctorate in literature at the Sorbonne; but during the Occupation Pisani was already drawn to the movement where he would spend much of his career, Gaullism. While many of his contemporaries went to ENA at the liberation, Pisani plunged into a career in the prefectoral corps; during the Fourth Republic he was in charge of Haute-Loire and Haute-Marne, as well as heading the office (*cabinet*) of the Paris prefect of police and being *directeur de cabinet* to the ministers of the interior and of defence. In 1954 he moved into electoral politics with election as senator for Haute-Marne (till 1961), sitting with the *gauche démocratique* group which he saw, typically, as quite compatible with his Gaullist feelings. The General's return in 1958 meant a trouble-shooting task for Pisani, who was called in as agriculture minister while farmers rioted against shrinking incomes and rising costs. In 1966 he moved to the Infrastructure Ministry, resigning in April 1967 to become UDR deputy for Angers but leaving this office in 1968 in protest at the government's handling of the 'events'. He had meanwhile become a real notable in local government, being both a mayor and *conseiller général* in Maine-et-Loire from 1964–75. His break with party Gaullism meant a brief exile from national politics until 1974 when he re-emerged as senator for Haute-Marne, but now as a member of the Socialist Party or more accurately of its Rocardian wing. Mitterrand (q.v.) made him one of the European Commissioners in 1981; but he was soon fire-fighting again, first as special delegate (1984), then as minister for New Caledonia (1985).

Despite apparent paradoxes (technocrat or notable? Socialist or Gaullist?), Pisani's career has a consistency typical of the governmental mandarin (*grand commis*). Having a strong sense of the state and of

French interests abroad, such men are compulsive modernizers and political realists rather than ideologues. They will work for governments that get things done. Pisani's reforms typify his problem-solving pragmatism. The 1962 Agriculture Act tried to humanize the inevitable decline of the farm population by offering money inducements to farmers to vacate plots, encouraging rational redistribution of available land and cooperative practices in the name of efficiency. Similarly in New Caledonia Pisani was ready to gerrymander local government boundaries in a sophisticated way so as to offer the indigenous Kanak population (now outnumbered by later immigrants) a significant share of power in the hope of persuading them to retain strong but flexible links with France. His ingenious solution to the colony's troubles was promptly undone by the right on its return to office in 1986. In party politics Pisani played no major role, though his sharp wit and common sense undoubtedly helped the credibility of the Rocardians.

Bibliography

Pisani's own work includes *L'Utopie foncière* (Paris: Gallimard, 1977) and *Socialiste de raison* (Paris: Flammarion, 1978). For the context of his work in agriculture see G. Wright, *Rural revolution in France* (Stanford, Cal.: Stanford University Press, 1964) and on New Caledonia see J.-M. Colombani, *L'Utopie calédonienne* (Paris: Denoël, 1985).

DH

PIVERT, Marceau (1895–1958)

Pivert's significance rests on his botched attempt to transform the Popular Front into a Socialist revolution. Born in 1895, mobilized in 1914, he was a victim of water pollution in 1917, and never fully recovered. He joined the Socialist Party (SFIO) in 1920. Like many future Communists, he came to socialism through war, but Pivert's was not that absolute faith which leads to communism. A teacher, Pivert was strongly impregnated with the Masonic anticlericalism of his profession: in 1927 he wrote a report advocating standardized national education – the document was exemplary of 'petty bourgeois' radicalism.

By 1934, Pivert had veered left and was a leader of the Bataille Socialiste group, headed by Zyromski (q.v.). Their stronghold was the Paris region (Seine-et-Marne). They sought to reunify Socialists and

Communists as the key to the Socialist revolution. With fascism looming, this 'united front' unity (see Thorez q.v.) was identified as the only means of defeating fascism. The insistence on counter-attack led Pivert to organize a militia (TPPS) in response to the 'Fascist' riot of 6 February 1934.

The Communist strategy of the Popular Front forced Pivert and Zyromski to split. Zyromski held unity paramount. Pivert retained this goal (even as late as 1937) but could not approve alliance with 'bourgeois parties', especially if this legitimized national defence. Pivert became the focal point for Socialists who privileged Socialist revolution: these 'Pivertistes', the Gauche Révolutionnaire, were thereby closely connected with the Trotskyists, then seeking entry into the SFIO. More gentle than Trotsky, Pivert saw the revolutionaries as a ginger group, not a vanguard: they should persuade the proletariat's established organizations to advance from the defensive to the offensive, that is, Socialist, stage of the Popular Front.

The unforeseen sit-in strikes of May 1936 seemed a fulfilment of 'Pivertisme': Pivert's article 'Tout est Possible' defined a widespread mood (27 May). The mood got nowhere: Pivert was an enthusiastic amateur, and the Gauche Révolutionnaire lacked proletarian members. Once the strikes were defused, 'Pivertisme' was on the road to disintegration.

In June Pivert accepted a post in charge of cinema and radio. Ideologically, he was cracked by the approach of war. His original interpretation of the slogan 'If you want Peace make Revolution' excluded aid to the Spanish Popular Front. By the time he changed his mind, his allies, the POUM were being exterminated by the Communists. In January 1937 he left the government, saying 'no' to 'social peace' and national defence. When the Popular Front ebbed, the incompatibility of the Gauche Révolutionnaire with the SFIO became palpable: eventually, but unwillingly, in June 1938 Pivert formed the Workers' and Peasants' Socialist Party – PSOP. After Munich, many 'Psopists' slid from 'revolutionary defeatism' to straightforward pacifist defeatism. Pivert was in America in September 1939, and so missed the final collapse of the PSOP.

In June–August 1940 Pivert wrote twice to de Gaulle, offering to serve France in his own way. De Gaulle answered only the first letter. Pivert got to Mexico and returned to France in 1946. He rejoined the SFIO. By 1955 he decided that the Communists were as bad as the Catholics. 'Marceau' was universally liked; he was honourable and charming, but hardly a serious revolutionary.

Bibliography

No biography exists, but his role in the Popular Front is usefully discussed in Nathanael Green, *Crisis and Decline: The French Socialist Party in the Popular Front* (Ithaca, NY: Cornell University Press, 1969). Two former 'Pivertistes' may also be consulted: Jean Rabaut, *Tout est possible* (Paris: Denoël, 1974), and Daniel Guérin, *Front Populaire, révolution manqué* (Paris: Julliard, 1963), but Guérin often confuses what Pivert should have done with what Pivert did.

MK

PLEVEN, René (1901–)

Born in 1901, René Pleven was educated at the *lycées* of Rennes and Laval and then at Paris University where he obtained a doctorate in law and a diploma from the Ecole Libre des Sciences Politiques. His national political career began in 1940 when he joined the Free French movement, working in Africa and in London and becoming de Gaulle's right-hand man. After the war, as Deputy for the Côtes-du-Nord (1945–73) and president of the Fourth Republic party, the Democratic and Socialist Resistance Union (Union Démocratique et Socialiste de la Résistance – UDSR) between 1945 and 1953, Pleven played a key role in several 'Third Force' coalition governments of the Fourth Republic. Re-elected deputy for the Côtes-du-Nord in 1958 he joined the centrist Progressive Democratic Party National Assembly group (Progrès et Démocratie Moderne). From 1958 until 1969 Pleven was a French delegate to the European Assembly and chairman of the Assembly's Liberal group. In 1969, he was among four non-Gaullists brought into the government by President Pompidou and was justice minister in the administrations of Jacques Chaban-Delmas (June 1969 to July 1972) and Pierre Messmer (July 1972 to March 1973).

Under Pleven's conservative leadership the centrist UDSR played a pivotal role in the parliamentary politics of the Fourth Republic. As its president, Pleven refused to join the RPF, something for which de Gaulle never forgave him. Pleven then participated in several 'Third Force' governments. He was finance minister (1944–6), defence minister (October 1949 and March 1952 to June 1954) and minister for foreign affairs in the Pflimlin government between 14–31 May 1958. He was also prime minister twice during the Fourth Republic; From July 1950 to February 1951 and again from

from July 1950 to February 1951 and again from August 1951 to January 1952 when he presided over the ratification of the Schuman Plan in December 1951.

Pleven was an archetypal *grand notable* – a national politician with an extensive local and regional power base. As departmental councillor for Dinan-Est and president of the Departmental Council of the Côtes-du-Nord (1948–76), he led the regional campaign for the economic development of Brittany. He was both co-founder and president (1951–72) of the regional economic pressure group, the committee for the study and defence of Breton interests (Comité d'Etudes et de Liaisons Breton – CELIB), which successfully campaigned for higher public investment in the region. Between 1964 and 1973 he was president of the official consultative planning body, the Commission pour le Développement Economique Régional (Commission for Regional Economic Development – CODER) in Brittany. Finally, from its establishment in 1974 until he retired in 1976, Pleven was president of the Brittany Regional Council. His book *L'Avenir de la Bretagne* (Paris: Calmann-Lévy, 1961), reflects his interest in regional development.

Bibliography

Nothing has been written in English specifically on René Pleven. His national political career is dealt with in P.M. Williams, *Crisis and Compromise* (London: Longman, 1964) and P.M. Williams and M. Harrison, *Politics and Society in de Gaulle's Republic* (London: Unwin, 1971). His involvement in regional affairs is covered in detail in M. Phlipponneau, *Débout Bretagne* (St Brieuc: Presses Universitaires de Bretagne, 1970) and details of his time with de Gaulle can be found in Jean Lacouture, *De Gaulle*, vol. II (Paris: Seuil, 1985).

Sonia M

PLISSONNIER, Gaston Désiré (1913–)

Plissonnier was born to a family of artisan furniture-makers in the Saône-et-Loire (Bantanges) and retained the regional – Burgundian – accent throughout his Parisian career. At the age of about 20, Plissonnier joined the Young Communists and moved up the hierarchy of the Union de la Jeunesse Agricole de la France and from there went into the Communist Party school in 1938. During the war Plissonnier was in the Resistance in Toulouse and at the liberation moved into Waldeck Rochet's agricultural department. In 1949 he was sent to rebuild the Loir-et-Cher Federation; in 1950, at the 12th Congress, he became a substitute member of the Central Committee; in 1964 he was a substitute member of the Political Bureau. From 1956 Plissonnier's work in the party was initially with agricultural questions, then as controller of the cadres; but he is probably best known as 'Moscow's man' in the PCF. Plissonnier, who lives in Hauts-de-Seine, is the real power in Nanterre despite the Communist mayor, Yves Saudmont.

Even though Plissonnier was, until 1982, in control off the party functionaries department, he seems to have been the servant of the leadership and to have refrained from exercising the department's power on his own behalf. In this Plissonnier was the very model of 'organization man': a vapid personality with a formidable lack of imagination but an unparalleled knowledge of the apparatus. Nevertheless as a loyal second in command, Plissonnier could have been important at various junctures including Waldeck Rochet's mysterious illness after 1969 and the rise of Marchais. Yet the key aspect to Plissonnier's position was his close link with the CPSU: Plissonnier has consistently been dedicated to Soviet interests. Plissonnier stated to the CPSU's 27th Congress that 'In attaching a great importance to the people's self-government, your party has revealed the democratic nature of socialism and in that way contributed to the creation of the New Man who has access to the knowledge and the socio-political activity which develops the personality (applause)' (*Ici Moscou*, May 1986, no. 1). This is the voice of the authentic Russophile and Plissonnier was probably as responsible as anybody for toning down the only criticism the PCF ever made of Russian foreign policy (condemnation of the invasion of Czechoslovakia in 1968).

In the 1960s and 1970s Plissonnier was the principal contact for those in the CPSU in charge of Western CPs (Ponomarev and Zagladin) and represented the PCF at foreign Communist Congresses. In the mid-1970s, when the PCF had its differences with the Russians, it was Plissonnier who went to Moscow (to the 25th CPSU Congress in 1976, for example). Plissonnier was also probably the leading architect of the party's return to the Russian fold at the end of the 1970s (marked by the 23rd Congress in 1979) and conducted a quasi-*tutelle* over the foreign affairs department which Gremetz ostensibly ran; he is credited with the phrase 'a globally positive balance' used by the PCF to describe the Eastern bloc after 1979.

Bibliography

Plissonnier's insultingly unrevealing autobiography *Une Vie pour lutter* (interview with D. Bleitrach) was published by Messidor in Paris in 1985.

DSB

POHER, Alain Emile Louis Marie (1909–)

Born in Ablon-sur-Seine near Paris, Alain Poher followed his father into engineering after taking a degree in law. His political career as a militant Christian Democrat, began in 1945 when he became mayor of Ablon, a post he retained for nearly forty years. He represented the Seine-et-Oise constituency in the Council of the Republic and Senate for all but four years of the Fourth Republic, and continued his career in the Senate (Upper House) after 1958. In 1968, when he represented the Val-de-Marne as a member of the Centrist group in the Senate, he was elected president to replace Gaston Monnerville (q.v.), and held that office continuously under de Gaulle, Pompidou, Giscard-d'Estaing and Mitterrand.

He held minor government posts in 1946 and 1948, as secretary of state for financial affairs, and between 1955 and 1957 was president of the European Common Market Commission. A member of the European Parliament since 1958, he had been, since 1966, president of the European Assembly, yet he was still a comparative unknown in French politics. He was projected into national prominence when, partly as a sop to Gaullists, he was unexpectedly chosen to replace Monnerville, *persona non grata* at the Elysée Palace after his six-year campaign of opposition to Gaullism. On the death of de Gaulle in 1970, and by virtue of a constitutional provision – which a clause in the rejected referendum proposals of 1969 would have altered! – Alain Poher, as incumbent president of the Senate, became interim president of the Republic. Between April 28 and June 19 his moderation and reasonableness ensured his popularity, and this encouraged him to challenge the Gaullist heir presumptive, Georges Pompidou (q.v.), in the June presidential elections. Poher was helped by his new prestige as champion of the Senate in the recent referendum campaign, and Jean Lecanuet's (q.v.) Democratic Centre group, with the Radicals, seemed prepared to support him.

Those who yearned for a return to the political style of the Fourth Republic also supported him. A victorious Poher might have dissolved the Gaullist-dominated Assembly, thereby bringing perhaps an Assembly with no clear-cut majority. Encouraged moreover by his good showing in the first ballot in which he came second to Pompidou, he maintained his candidature in the second ballot, but hardly threatened Pompidou who polled 58 per cent of the second-round votes.

Five years later, on the death of Pompidou, Poher was again interim president of the Republic, between 2 April and 27 May 1974. Having no further presidential ambitions, he contented himself henceforth with the presidency of the Senate, taking over also in that same year the presidency of the Association of Mayors of France. In October 1989, after twenty-one years as president of the Senate he was elected for a further and surely final term.

Bibliography

Linotte, D. (1985), *Les Constitutions françaises*, Paris: MA Editions.
Pado, D. (1969), *Les 50 jours d'Alain Poher. L'intérim. La campagne présidentielle*, Paris: Denoël.

ACR

POINCARÉ, Raymond (1860–1934)

Born at Bar-le-Duc (Meuse) in Lorraine on 20 August 1860, Raymond Poincaré occupied most of the major offices of state, including president of France, in a political career which established him as one of the foremost statesmen of the Third Republic. The only son of an engineer he was educated at the secondary schools (*lycées*) of Bar-le-Duc and Louis-le-Grand in Paris from where he went on to graduate from the Sorbonne with an arts and a law degree. He was called to the Paris Bar in 1882.

Poincaré's political career began with his election in 1887 as deputy for his native Meuse department. He sat on the left centre of the Chamber with the Progressists. Quickly establishing a name for himself in legal and financial matters he was made minister of education and culture (April–November 1893) at the age of 33. The following year he became minister of finance (May 1894 to January 1895) in Charles Dupuy's cabinet, then minister of education again (January–October 1895) under Alexandre Ribot. Apart from a brief period as minister of finance in 1906 he refused any further ministerial responsibility until 1912, preferring to devote his attention to his new legal firm. He did not however give up parliamentary life being elected vice-president of the

Chamber of Deputies in 1895 and a member of the Senate for the Meuse in 1903.

Following the Agadir crisis Poincaré became both premier and foreign minister in January 1912 and the following year (17 January 1913) was elected President of the Republic. During his seven-year stewardship France entered and emerged triumphant from the First World War. At the expiry of his mandate he was re-elected to the Senate and became chairman of the commission on the reparations due from Germany. On 15 January 1922 he again became premier and foreign minister but following a left-wing victory in the general elections of May 1924 he resigned (1 June). He was recalled as premier and finance minister to solve the financial crisis on 23 July 1926 and remained in office until he fell dangerously ill and was forced to resign on 26 July 1929. This was the end of his political career, leading him to devote his remaining years to completing his memoirs. He died in Paris on October 1934.

Poincaré has gone down in folk memory as epitomizing the values and way of life of middle-class Third Republic France, as the patriotic Lorrainer willing to stand up to Germany, the leader who was able to unite France before the First World War and to save the franc after it. If those middle-class values were hard-work, thrift, honesty, modesty and a deep respect for order he certainly typified them. He grew up in a solidly middle-class environment in which success, and even fame, were not unknown; his first cousin was the famous mathematician Henri Poincaré. At school he worked hard and demonstrated intellectual powers which won him several prizes and ensured him of brilliant results in his *baccalauréat*. A mere 20 when he graduated with degrees in law and arts which he had read concurrently, he went on to do his pupillage and begin his career as a barrister while preparing a law doctorate. He doubtless found satisfaction in the detail, rigour and order of French legal texts and codes. His passion for work throughout his life surprised even his hard-working contemporaries. He was said to rise at five o'clock in the morning and begin his day by reading a page of the four or five languages he knew. From his youth he had literary aspirations and began as a student to write articles for a number of newspapers and literary journals and would continue to do so until his death; as in everything he did he would achieve the supreme distinction in this field with his election to the Académie française in 1909.

Much has been exaggerated about Poincaré's Lorraine origins being synonymous with *revanche*, the desire to retrieve from Germany, if necessary by conflict, the French provinces of Alsace and Lorraine lost in 1871 after the Franco-Prussian War. The defeat of 1870 certainly had a profound effect on this 10-year-old boy uprooted from his home, forced to move from hotel to hotel for three months, only to return to live under German occupation for four years. Throughout his life he would harbour a profound mistrust of Germany and display an ardent patriotism and a strong sense of national pride. But his experience of the chaos and destruction of war would make him wish to guard against further defeat and further war, which would inevitably be fought on Lorraine soil, by ensuring that France always be prepared diplomatically and militarily.

It is not surprising that he should represent a Lorraine department throughout his parliamentary career. From the outset his legal brain and fastidiousness applied to financial matters quickly earned him ministerial office at a characteristically young age and gained him the reputation for financial rigour and stringency. In a broader sense he gained a reputation for moral rectitude, moderation and intellectual honesty. He kept his distance from the politico-financial scandals such as Panama which affected parliamentary circles in the 1880s and 1890s and emerged with a reputation so white as to be dubbed 'the White Ermine'. Though opposed to the Radicals he was no reactionary. He followed a centre-left path and during the Dreyfus affair spoke out in favour of the alleged traitor's innocence. But though a champion of secularism and a supporter of Waldeck-Rousseau's 1899 government he soon found that his moderate views clashed with its severe anticlerical policy and his intellectual honesty forced him to refuse to vote the 1901 Law on Associations. His ability to see both sides of an argument and to weigh its pros and cons often led him to agonize for long periods when making political decisions, preferring as often as not to stay as close as possible to the status quo. Some described this rather exaggeratedly as a phobia of responsibility and it was rumoured that when his colleagues saw him rushing from the courthouse to the Chamber of Deputies they were said to remark 'He's hurrying to abstain'. But once he had finally decided on a course of action he was not easily swayed from it. Thus after 1906 when Poincaré withdrew from ministerial life to concentrate on his legal career his clean political record, intelligence, capacity for hard-work, personal integrity and tolerance annoyed some who would have loved to have found a flaw in this image, which explains his political rival Georges Clemenceau's bitter pun: 'Il devrait être moins carré' (He shouldn't be so square).

It was this reputation which inevitably led to his recall to cabinet office at a time of crisis. That crisis was the Agadir incident of 1911 in which France and Germany had almost come to blows over Morocco. The confusion in which different diplomatic negotiations between the two countries had been taking place to resolve the conflict led to the resignation of the Radical premier Joseph Caillaux (q.v.). As *rapporteur* of the Senate commission of inquiry into the matter Poincaré was well qualified to settle the problem and was entrusted by the President of the Republic with the formation of a new government on 12 January 1912.

Wounded French national pride looked to Poincaré's unquestionable patriotism for assistance, ensuring the new government of considerable popular acclaim. By combining the premiership with foreign affairs, Poincaré demonstrated the importance he would give to diplomacy which during the next year would be given a stronger and more rigorous style. Convinced that Germany only had respect for strength he set about strengthening France's diplomatic links with Russia and Britain. In the case of the former it was a case of repairing cracks in the alliance which had been allowed to develop under successive Radical ministries who viewed France's autocratic ally with suspicion. But Poincaré refused to go to the opposite extreme to shore up the alliance, and give *carte blanche* to Russia to pursue her Balkan interests because this could lead France into a war in southeast Europe in which she had no interests. Instead Poincaré pursued a middle-of-the-road policy which reaffirmed the alliance while making Russia aware that France would not support an adventurous policy in the Balkans. It was to this effect that he visited St Petersburg in August 1912. In the case of Britain he attempted to have the entente converted into an alliance and though unsuccessful he was able to put Franco-British relations on a more solid footing in November 1912 through the agreement with the British foreign secretary whereby the two governments should consult at moments of international crisis and if necessary invoke the plans drawn up by their naval and military authorities.

By the end of 1912 France's diplomatic security within the triple entente with Russia and Great Britain had been tightened up. In his dealings with the opposite grouping, the triple alliance of Germany, Austria-Hungary and Italy, Poincaré was firm and distant, believing strongly that a balance of power and a rigid separation of the two alliance groupings was the best safeguard for peace.

With presidential elections timed for January 1913 and his popularity at a peak Poincaré was encouraged to stand. He did so against the left's candidate strongly backed by Clemenceau and was elected president on 17 January 1913 after a close-run finish. Once again he had achieved the highest distinction. But he was intent that his new office should not be merely decorative. By a judicious interpretation of the constitution, which gave the president considerable powers in foreign affairs and in the choice of new governments, he ensured that the main tenets of his foreign policy went unchanged up to the war. Maintaining that France must be prepared militarily for any eventuality, he firmly supported an extension of the length of compulsory military service from two to three years, which would bring the number of French troops with the colours into line with Germany's. Although the general election of May 1914 gave the left a majority in the Chamber and encouraged the belief that the Three Years Law might be repealed, Poincaré did all he could to see that this did not happen.

In his dealings with Germany, contrary to popular belief he did not act aggressively towards her but was able to work with her on colonial matters and even accepted to dine at the German embassy in Paris in January 1914, the first time a French president had done so since 1870.

Poincaré was on a three-week state cruise to Russia and Scandinavia accompanied by his premier and foreign minister and the director of the French Foreign Office when he learnt of the Austro-Hungarian ultimatum to Serbia in July 1914 which began the slide towards the First World War. At a time when radio cabling was in its infancy there was little that he could do to stop the tragic course of events in train. Two weeks had passed in which the effective political and diplomatic masters of France had been isolated from the European scene, to return to French soil only five days before Germany declared war on France on 3 August 1914. Because he gave support to Russia and was willing to stand up to Germany before the war Poincaré has been cast as a warmonger. This misrepresentation is largely the result of post-war propaganda from Germany and Russia and Poincaré's political opponents who were intent on blocking his return to power in the 1920s. In reality he sincerely desired peace but once war was declared he was able to unite Frenchmen against the invader following his famous message to the French Parliament appealing for a national coalition (*Union Sacrée*) on 4 August 1914.

Throughout the war Poincaré carried out his duties energetically, but with greater discretion. A further test of his patriotism and ability to put country before politics came in November 1917 when he entrusted his bitter rival Georges Clemenceau (q.v.) with the premiership. Their rivalry surfaced again at the peace negotiations when Clemenceau disregarded his advice. Though his selfless and tireless action in favour of national unity contributed substantially to French victory it is Clemenceau who is remembered as the Father of Victory (*Père-La-Victoire*). Poincaré's presidential term ended on 18 February 1920.

Though this ended the first period of Poincaré's political career the second was just as eventful. Re-elected to the Senate in 1920 and chairman of the reparations commission, he also made clear in the press the need to make Germany pay and respect the Versailles Treaty against the more conciliatory line of the British and Americans. This firm stance ensured his recall to the premiership and foreign ministry in January 1922 in place of the more moderate Aristide Briand (q.v.). Poincaré was unable to reach an agreement with the British on reparations, rejecting Andrew Bonar Law's compromise at the Paris conference in January 1923. Following the reparations commission's declaration (which did not include the British), that Germany was not fulfilling her obligations, in agreement with Belgium and Italy Poincaré ordered French troops to occupy the Ruhr. This controversial measure was greeted with 'passive resistance' in the area at the German government's request. But Poincaré would not back down and retaliated by taking complete control of railways and mines in the Ruhr which brought the 'resistance' to an end on 26 September 1923. Unwilling to abuse his dominant position, he returned to negotiations with the British and Americans and eventually accepted a suggestion that the problem of reparations be placed in the hands of a group of experts which led to the adoption of the reparation commission's Dawes Plan which suggested the resumption of German payments on a heavy scale. His action over the Ruhr has, in the light of subsequent appeasement of Germany, begun to be regarded with greater respect.

Poincaré's reputation for having solved France's financial crisis is more firmly established and earned him the title *Poincaré-le-franc*. That crisis began in the first quarter of 1924 and was solved in the first instance by Poincaré's success in convincing Parliament that new taxes should be voted. However opposition to these measures by the Radicals and the Socialists united in a broad left alliance or *Cartel des Gauches* forced him to reshuffle his cabinet. The *cartel* was victorious in the general elections of May 1924 and on 1 June Poincaré was forced to resign. With his departure French finances deteriorated further so that by July 1926 the exchange rate of the franc fell to forty-eight to the US dollar (as against five in 1914). On 23 July Poincaré was recalled as premier in a coalition government of national union in which he reserved the finance portfolio for himself and foreign affairs for Briand. With public opinion on his side he brought in a number of new taxes, refused to contract any foreign loans and with the financial stringency characteristic of him was able to stabilize the franc at twenty-four to the dollar by the end of 1926 and keep it buoyant until the general election of 1928 in what has become recognized as one of the most successful financial operations of its kind.

He was duly rewarded at the elections in April but in November 1928 saw the withdrawal of the Radical ministers from his government. He resigned but immediately formed a new government which increasingly relied for its support on the centre and right. His task was now to convince Parliament to accept the Washington and London agreements on Inter-Allied debts but at 69 the strain proved too much and reluctantly he was forced to resign office on 26 July 1929.

Even through ill-health he remained industrious to the last, writing for newspapers and continuing his memoirs, ten volumes of which appeared between 1926 and 1933. Their title *Au service de la France* was fitting for a man whose life service to his country was recognized by a state funeral. However, despite the fact that from 1912 to 1929 Poincaré virtually headed the country, that on a number of occasions his role was fundamental for France's well-being, he has never been close to the hearts of Frenchmen in a way that Gambetta (q.v.), Jaurès, Clemenceau or de Gaulle have. Ironically the best of the middle-class values he so well represented have faded in Frenchmen's minds bringing to the fore traits of austerity and narrow-mindedness. It is much to the pity that a brilliant intellect, a man of honour, a major statesman, and a great Frenchman is not better served in the memory of his countrymen.

Bibliography

Huddleston, S. (1924), *Poincaré: A biographical portrait*, London: T. Fisher Unwin.

Keiger, J.F.V. (1983), *France and the Origins of the First World War*, London: Macmillan.

Miquel, P. (1961), *Poincaré*, Paris: Fayard.

Wright, G. (1942), *Raymond Poincaré and the French Presidency*, Stanford, Cal.: Stanford University Press.

JFVK

POINSO-CHAPUIS, Germaine (1901–81)

Germaine Poinso-Chapuis will be remembered above all for being the first woman to hold a full ministerial post in France. Her lifelong involvement with Catholic, conservative politics made her one of the defenders of the interests of the family throughout her political career, but particularly during the Fourth Republic when she held her ministerial post.

Born in Marseilles, Germaine Poinso-Chapuis became a lawyer and was involved in the Parti Démocrate Populaire (a small Catholic, conservative party) before the war. During the war she participated in the Mouvement de Libération Nationale (pro-de Gaulle) network of the Resistance and was one of the founder members of the MRP (Mouvement Républicain Populaire – the new Christian Democratic Party) at the liberation.

Her political career took off at this point: she was a municipal councillor in Marseilles; deputy on an MRP ticket for Bouches-du-Rhône at both constituent assemblies and then, from 1946 to 1956 in the National Assembly.

In Robert Schuman's government (November 1947 to July 1948), she was minister of health and of population at a time when both of these were among issues at the top of the political agenda. Her name is associated with the 1948 'Poinso-Chapuis decree' which proposed government support for parents of children at private (i.e. Catholic) schools. This law provoked a crisis in the governing coalition, notably with the SFIO (Socialist) partners.

Other areas where Poinso-Chapuis intervened in the Assembly included the fight against alcoholism, and legislation concerning reintegration of the disabled into society.

Active before the war in the Ligue Française pour le Droit des Femmes (League for Women's Rights) Poinso-Chapuis was considered to be a feminist of a very traditional and 'bourgeois' kind: she fought for women to play a full role in public life, but she shared her party's views on motherhood and the family and believed in the role of woman as guardian of traditional values and virtues within the home.

CD

POMPIDOU, Georges Jean René (1911–74)

Georges Pompidou was the second prime minister of the Fifth Republic, from April 1962 to July 1968. After his dismissal by de Gaulle in July 1968 he was described as being 'in the reserve of the Republic', and when de Gaulle's second term of office as president came to an end with his resignation in April 1969, Pompidou, as the natural successor to the regime shaped by de Gaulle, won the ensuing presidential election. His own term of office as the second president of the Fifth Republic came to a premature end with his death in April 1974.

Pompidou came from Auvergne peasant stock; though his great grandfather had been illiterate, his father benefited from the institution of compulsory education in the last decades of the nineteenth century to the extent that he became a primary school teacher and then a secondary school teacher. After schools in Albi and Toulouse, Pompidou went to a secondary school in Paris to prepare for the prestigious Ecole Normale Supérieure (for intending secondary school teachers); he taught in Marseilles and Paris after his marriage and completion of military service.

After meritorious war service in 1939–40, Pompidou returned to his teaching post in Paris, where he stayed for the rest of the war. He had, in keeping with millions of French people, respect for the person and basic patriotic stance of Marshal Pétain, while having the reservations about the Vichy regime of which Pétain was the figurehead. And while his anti-Nazi sentiments during this period are not in doubt, he was never an active member of the Resistance. This wait-and-see approach later left him open to attacks both from the Communist Party, whose members and supporters had made up a large proportion of Resistance personnel inside France, and from those Gaullists who had joined de Gaulle and the Fighting French in London and later in Algiers.

His first glimpse of de Gaulle was when the latter strode triumphantly down the Champs Elysées after the liberation of Paris. Pompidou used his pre-war contacts to obtain a job on de Gaulle's staff. During this time he became closer to de Gaulle, but was still more of an unquestioning admirer rather than an intimate associate at the time of de Gaulle's resignation in January 1946. Devoid of political ambition, he was the person in whom de Gaulle confided, and this continued even after he gave up the post of head of de Gaulle's personal staff – *chef de cabinet* – and got a job in Rothschild's Bank.

Pompidou played no active part in the plots which preceded de Gaulle's return to power at the end of May 1958, but he was the obvious choice to become once more his head of personal staff for the second half of 1958. This was a post where, as the institutions of the new Fifth Republic were being set up,

Pompidou's tactful and self-effacing diplomacy was at a premium. Pompidou, not wanting to be a member of Debré's new government in 1959, returned to his job at Rothschild's, but was also appointed by de Gaulle as one of nine members of the new Constitutional Council. In 1961 he smoothed the way for another round of negotiations with the Algerian provisional government, but once more refused to join the government. By this time, however, he was virtually certain that he would take over from Debré as prime minister when the Algerian problem was solved by independence.

Pompidou's appointment as prime minister in April 1962 was a sign not only that de Gaulle intended to carry on directing the main thrusts of policy but also that he continued to have little respect for party politicians. Pompidou had never been elected to political office, and his appointment was taken as a calculated affront by many parliamentarians.

In October 1962 Pompidou's government was defeated on a vote of censure – the only time that this has happened in the Fifth Republic. He submitted his resignation to de Gaulle, as he was constitutionally obliged to do, but was asked to continue in office. In fact, it was really de Gaulle who was the object of the National Assembly's disapproval and he won popular approval not only of the new method of electing the president, when 62 per cent voted Yes in the 28 October referendum, but also of his way of running the Fifth Republic, when Gaullist candidates were returned as a majority in the November 1962 parliamentary elections. This new majority in the National Assembly meant that Pompidou's government could pursue, without risk of being thrown out of office, the task of implementing policies decided on by de Gaulle. Already, however, differences of perspective between the two men were becoming apparent, as Pompidou favoured a less *dirigiste* approach to economic planning and the industrial modernization of France. Pompidou and de Gaulle also had different perspectives on the 1965 presidential election, and on the future of the Gaullist Party. To de Gaulle, it acted as a rally (*rassemblement*), uniting as many French people as possible under the banner of national interest; to Pompidou, it had to become an effective electoral machine able to get a post-de Gaulle candidate elected president. To this end, Pompidou promoted a new generation of Gaullists such as Jacques Chirac, within his team and the party.

Pompidou's replacement by Couve de Murville as prime minister in June 1968 was provoked by a more dramatic manifestation of the differences between de Gaulle and Pompidou – their reaction to the crisis of May–June 1968. Whereas de Gaulle was wavering and uncertain, Pompidou was perspicacious and calmly resolute. He showed tactical flexibility in reopening the Sorbonne to assuage students and in agreeing to improvements in workers' wages and conditions; and he persuaded de Gaulle to change his plan for a referendum into one whereby Parliament was dissolved and new elections held, resulting in a Gaullist landslide.

In 1967, Pompidou became deputy for one of the seats in his native department of Cantal, an office he held until he became president of the Republic. His removal from the centre of the political stage gave him time to write *Le Noeud Gordien*, outlining his political views. Already however he was taking large doses of cortisone for a blood disorder, as yet unspecified. Politically, he had the delicate task after mid-1968 of not being so prominent as to embarrass Couve's government, but of not appearing to retire from politics in circumstances where he remained the natural successor to de Gaulle. This period was made more dramatic when the underworld murder of Stephan Markovic was exploited for political ends. In the 'Markovic affair', false accusations of involvement with the Parisian underworld were made against Pompidou and his wife; worse still, de Gaulle and Couve appeared not to be totally on his side. There was also the strong suspicion that elements of the secret services were implicated, possibly manipulated by the Eastern bloc, which would have preferred the more anti-American Couve to succeed de Gaulle. De Gaulle's apparent lack of total belief in Pompidou's innocence broke any links of devotion the latter may still have had, and he felt free to announce early in 1969 that he would be a candidate for the presidency. De Gaulle's resignation in April 1969 after the failure of his referendum precipitated presidential elections, and Pompidou was elected on 15 June in the second round against Alain Poher, president of the Senate and interim president of the Republic.

Pompidou's victory signified that the presidency as developed by de Gaulle had become institutionalized, in the sense that the office of President continued to be the keystone of the institutional structure of the Fifth Republic. Victory for any of Pompidou's opponents would have meant a return to the letter of the 1958 Constituion in which the President does not initiate policies, but mediates to prevent any internal political discord from paralysing the state.

Within a month of taking office, Pompidou announced in a press conference that he wanted to make France 'a proper industrial country', but the most pressing need was to halt the drain on currency reserves, which had been steadily worsening since mid-1968. This he did by devaluing the franc as a prelude to a whole package of economic measures. Pompidou's approach was change within continuity – 'continuité et ouverture' – continuation of the institutional structure of the Fifth Republic, including the Gaullian embellishments, but flexibility in areas such as devaluation and the enlargement of the EEC, which meant that some Centrist deputies felt able to join the parliamentary majority of Gaullists and Giscardians supporting the government of Pompidou's prime minister, Jacques Chaban-Delmas (q.v.). It was Chaban who announced to Parliament in September 1969 that his government wanted to bring about a 'New Society' which would cure the triple ills of 'a tentacular and inefficient state, archaic and conservative social structures, and a fragile economy'. However, Chaban had omitted to submit his speech to the Elysée beforehand (he explained in his book *L'Ardeur* (1975) that he had been 'carried away by enthusiasm for his job') thus jeopardizing the Gaullian logic of the Fifth Republic whereby it is the president who determines policy and the prime minister who carries it out. It became rapidly evident that post-de Gaulle Gaullism was an uneasy mixture of 'barons' of the first generation, of younger, more forward-looking elements, and of provincial conservative *notables* (local bigwigs). It was with the latter that Pompidou felt most in sympathy; they represented, in his view, the real France – hard-headed, non-intellectual, and above all heirs of the traditional catholicism to which Pompidou himself returned in the late 1960s, and which served as a solace for the cares of the presidential office.

Despite a less solid basis of Gaullist support, Pompidou pressed ahead with policy initiatives which led commentators to speak of 'Pompidolism'. At the summit conference of The Hague in December 1969, the way was opened to negotiations for EEC enry by four applicant countries – the United Kingdom, Ireland, Denmark and Norway. But Pompidou insisted that two other aspects should proceed in parallel – completion of the complex common agricultural policy by adequate financing arrangements, and extension of cooperation in the areas of monetary policy and tax harmonization. On the Middle East, Pompidou continued de Gaulle's arms embargo on Israel, imposed in 1967; however, it was clear that pro-Israeli elements within France helped the Israelis to make off in December 1969 with five torpedo boats built for them in Cherbourg, but impounded since 1967. On a visit to the United States in February 1970 Pompidou and his wife felt the

backlash of his Middle East policy when a pro-Israel demonstration in Chicago came dangerously close to getting out of hand.

Domestic policy initiatives dating from the first year of Pompidou's presidency were the setting up of an Institute of Industrial Development to encourage foreign investment in French industry; the commissioning of nuclear power stations using the more efficient US-developed enriched uranium technology, while making sure US firms themselves could not dominate the industry; and the decision to create a major centre for contemporary art in Paris – opened in 1977 as the Centre Georges Pompidou.

The death of de Gaulle in 1970 allowed 'Pompidolism' to flourish. Pompidou's approach to the presidential function was markedly different from de Gaulle's. Far from restricting his policy initiatives to a 'reserved area' of foreign and defence matters, Pompidou took charge, if not on a day-to-day basis, at least on a week-to-week basis, of economic and social matters as well. Pompidou's influence on policy was further extended by a greater use than before of Elysée-based meetings, restricted to the ministers involved. These inter-ministerial councils were not under the prime minister's aegis and they declined in importance as compared with the pre-1969 situation.

A major example of Pompidou's involvement in policy-making was the preparation and adoption of the Sixth Economic Plan in 1971. It was this which concretized Pompidou's wish to promote the modernization of France through industrialization, by encouraging economic growth, industrial concentration, and exports. Nuclear power, telecommunications, and computerization received massive investment. By the early 1970s, industrial productivity in France was increasing at the rate of 7 per cent per annum, and investment by industrial firms had reached 20 per cent; in terms of growth, France had outstripped the United States and Western Europe, and was not far behind Japan.

In European policy, preparation for enlargement of the EEC was facilitated by Pompidou's meeting, for the first time, with the British Prime Minister Edward Heath in May 1971. The two men struck a bond of sympathy, but progress through 1971 was bedevilled by international monetary issues as the post-war Bretton Woods system disintegrated. In spring 1972, Pompidou decided to go ahead with an initiative which he had been thinking about for more than a year – a referendum asking the French people whether they approved of the enlargement of the EEC. The referendum of April 1972 gave a 67 per cent Yes vote, but was in all other respects a failure – the abstention rate was almost 40 per cent. In what seemed like an attempt to reimpose his authority, Pompidou dismissed Jacques Chaban-Delmas; in fact the distance between the two men had been growing in many areas, and Pompidou's instinctive conservatism had been offended by Chaban's rather immoderate style of politics and desire to assert the powers of political initiative which the Constitution gives to the prime minister. In *L'Ardeur*, Chaban reports that Pompidou said to him, 'one knows where one is with a Communist or a Socialist. One can take the necessary precautions. But what *you* are, no one knows.' With Chaban's successor, Pierre Messmer, there was no doubt – he was intensely loyal, and as a former colonial governor and army minister had a firm sense of discipline.

Pompidou's health was steadily deteriorating, and his blood disorder was diagnosed in 1972 as Waldenström's disease. Obviously he could have taken the advice of doctors, and those close associates who dared raise the matter, to prepare the ground for his successor and then resign; whether he was 'courageous' and 'stoic' to carry on to the end, as some observers described him, especially in retrospect, appeared to depend very much on one's place in the political spectrum. Despite his illness, Pompidou master-minded the campaign for the March 1973 parliamentary elections, warning the electorate (including on the day before the second round of the elections, in true Gaullian tradition) of the dire consequences of a left-wing victory. The loss of some seats after the Gaullist landslide of 1968 was inevitable, but a majority coalition of right-wing parties was re-elected. The president interpreted the election as a victory for 'the real France'.

The 1973 election however heralded a time of uncertainty for France which the ailing president appeared unable to deal with adequately. In the economic sphere, growth and optimism gave way to fears about inflation, which was gaining pace as the money supply increased and credit expanded. Freed from the constraints of government office after March 1973, Michel Debré, as spokesman for the Gaullist 'fundamentalists', bitterly attacked what he regarded as a soft economic policy. Such attacks, however, were but one example of the way in which the majority in Parliament supporting Pompidou and his government was becoming less cohesive. Giscard's group of Independent Republicans more and more asserted their independence, not least as the backing for a future attempt on the presidency by their leader. In October 1973, Alexandre Sanguinetti, openly hostile to Pompidou, became general

secretary of the Gaullist party, the largest component of the majority. In November, doubts about whether support in the National Assembly and Senate was sufficiently solid had led to the postponement of an attempt by Pompidou, which in any case had taken many people by surprise, to get Parliament to change the Constitution and reduce the presidential term of office to five years. On the international front, the Arab-Israeli war of 1973 showed up the basic weakness, not to say irrelevance, of French Middle East policy – Pompidou admitted it was 'misunderstood'. France also refused to cooperate in attempts to set up an organization of oil-consuming industrial countries.

Pompidou, in the final phase of his leukaemia, was not spared political attack even in the last three months of his life. He was accused by Gaullists of being isolated from his government, and though he still thought Messmer the right man as prime minister, the latter was also under attack from his own side. The government was paying in unpopularity for its handling of the workers' protracted sit-in at the Lip factory in Besançon, and for bugging the offices of the satirical weekly *Canard enchaîné*. Pompidou, true to his policy of not stepping down, went to the Soviet Union to meet Brezhnev in mid-March 1974. He was still performing political duties in the days, even the very morning, before his death, which occurred on 2 April 1974. His son Alain is a member of the European Parliament, elected on the joint UDT/RPR list of 1989.

Bibliography

Pompidou's two works of political memoirs are *Le Noeud gordien* (Paris: Plon, 1974) and *Pour rétablir une vérité* (Paris: Flammarion, 1982). His interviews and speeches (*Entretiens et discours*, 2 vols) were published, with an introduction by Edouard Balladur (Paris: Plon, 1975). Pompidou's period of office as prime minister is covered in Philippe Alexandre's aptly named book *Le Duel Pompidou–de Gaulle* (Paris: Grasset, 1970). Academic treatment is given in S. Rials, *Les Idées politiques de Georges Pompidou* (Paris: PUF, 1977) and F. Decaumont, *La Présidence de Georges Pompidou* (Paris: Economica, 1979). A more recent biography is E. Roussel, *Georges Pompidou* (Paris: J.-C. Lattès, 1984); paperback edition (Brussels: Marabout, 1985). His relations with de Gaulle are covered in J. Lacouture, *de Gaulle*, vol. III (Paris: Seuil, 1986).

MS

PONIATOWSKI, Michel Casmir, prince de (1922–)

Michel Poniatowski has been a conservative politician, member of the European Parliament, minister of health (1973) and the interior (1974–7) and eminent historian and political commentator. A direct descendant of the last king of Poland, he was educated in Paris at the Faculté de Droit and the Ecole Nationale d'Administration (1947–8). After entering the Ministry of Finance as a civil servant he alternated between postings abroad and working as a ministerial adviser in the *cabinets* of Faure, Pflimlin and Buron. In 1959 he became a close adviser to the young deputy, Giscard d'Estaing, following him in 1962 to the Ministry of Finance as a special assistant. He continued to work closely with Giscard during the 1960s and at the same time built up his own career as a civil servant and as a politician, with his election to the National Assembly as Independent Republican deputy for the Val d'Oise in 1967 (–1978) and to the mayorship of d'Isle Adam in 1971. After holding ministerial office, he continued to be a prominent presidential adviser from 1977 to 1981. Having lost his Assembly seat in 1978 he was elected to the European Parliament in 1979 and re-elected in 1984. Poniatowski has also been a prolific and significant writer on nineteenth-century French history (among other works *Talleyrand aux Etats Unis* (1967), *Talleyrand et Le Directoire* (1976), *Louis Philippe et Louis XVIII* (1980) and on contemporary French politics *Les choix de l'espoir* (1970), *Cartes sur la table* (1972), *L'Europe ou la morte* . . (1984)).

Poniatowski's influence was far reaching in the political world of the 1960s and 1970s as the adviser, confidant, chief lieutenant and political henchman of Giscard d'Estaing. Sharing Giscard's dream of creating a great centrist party in France, he played a key role in developing the strategy and structure of the non-Gaullist right and in establishing a firm party organization behind Giscard. He was instrumental in setting up both the National Federation of Independent Republicans (FNRI) in 1966 and from May 1965 the political 'clubs' (Perspectives et Réalites) which were 'think tanks' for the elaboration of a Giscardien social and economic doctrine and a training ground for potential Giscardien deputies. While secretary-general of the FNRI from 1967 to 1973, he did much to develop both a parliamentary and a local support base for Giscard and he was the key organizer in the 1974 presidential campaign.

As minister of the interior in the new administration he continued to hold a privileged position with Giscard, often circumventing the Gaullist prime minister, Chirac, over policy decisions. His ministerial career was however short-lived. Although an experienced and shrewd politician, Poniatowski was frequently outspoken and his often illiberal policies in the Ministry of the Interior did not fit into the image and style of a 'humane and advanced society' which Giscard was trying to project as president. This eventually led to his removal from office in 1977 some months after the establishment of the Barre government. However, between 1977 and 1981 he continued to work closely with Giscard as a 'roving ambassador' for special missions overseas and to have the personal protection of his patron.

By the 1980s his influence both in national and Republican Party politics had diminished as a younger generation of politicians took over; although he continued to hold an important honorary office in the Republican Party. His immense energies and enthusiasm became largely devoted to writing and to the European Parliament, of which he was an active member from 1979 to 1989, chairing the important committees of economic development and cooperation (1979–84) and energy research and technology (1984–).

Bibliography

Poniatowski was the subject of short profiles in B. Lecomte and C. Sauvage, *Les Giscardiens* (Paris: Albin Michel, 1978), and A. Duhamel, *Les Prétendants* (Paris: Gallimard, 1983); for details of Poniatowski's role in the FNRI see Jean-Claude Colliard, *Les Républicains indépendants: Valéry Giscard d'Estaing* (Paris: PUF, 1971).

ER

POUGET, Jean-Joseph Emile (1860–1931)

Emile Pouget was a major figure of late nineteenth-century French anarchism, notably through his creation of the famous (or notorious) *Père Peinard* newspaper. Later he became one of the main proponents of what came to be known as revolutionary syndicalism: he was the first editor of *La Voix du Peuple* (organ of the Confédération Générale du Travail), secretary of the federations within the CGT 1902–8, and a signatory of the legendary Amiens Charter in 1906.

Pouget – whose real name was Jean Joseph, not Emile – was born of a bourgeois family in Pont-de-Salars (Aveyron), but he was forced by the death of his stepfather to abandon secondary education in

1875. He moved to Paris and took work in a shop, and it was then that he began to attend the meetings of different political groups. In 1879 he helped create the Syndicat des Employés du Textile. By this time he was already an anarchist, and violently antimilitarist: in 1881 he was one of the delegates representing the French anarchists at the international conference in London. In 1883 he and Louise Michel led a demonstration of unemployed workers in the Boulevard Saint-Germain which turned into a bread riot. Pouget was arrested and, when the police found 600 copies of an antimilitarist pamphlet at his home, he was sentenced to three years' imprisonment.

It was in 1889 that Pouget launched the small-format weekly *Père Peinard*. The symbolic shoemaker 'Père Peinard' was typical of the sociology of the anarchist movement at that time, and this remarkable paper was clearly aimed at the working class, pulling no punches and employing the *argot* familiar to the workers of the suburbs. In *Père Peinard* Pouget attacked the government, politicians and the military, and advocated the general strike, and as a consequence did several terms in prison. Like most other anarchist newspapers, *Père Peinard* was eventually closed down altogether in 1894 in the wave of repression provoked by the anarchists' terrorist phase of 1892–4. Pouget himself was one of the accused in the 'trial of the thirty' [see under S. Faure], but he fled to Algiers and then to England. In London he produced a further eight numbers of *Père Peinard* (1894–5), and after an amnesty he returned to France to produce another weekly, *La Sociale* (1895–6), and further series of *Père Peinard*. During this period he also contributed to S. Faure's pro-Dreyfus *Journal du Peuple*.

This was a period in which the nascent French labour movement was increasing in strength, and in which anarchist-communists were turning more and more to the organized working class. Pouget was one of the first to encourage fellow revolutionaries to join or create unions, at the same time as he attacked party political influence over the new organizations. The Confédération Général du Travail was created in 1895, and in 1897 Pouget began to attend its congresses, delegated by various workers' organizations. In 1900, when the CGT decided it needed its own organ, Pouget was a member of the committee which studied the question, and he was given the job of editing the new paper: *La Voix du Peuple*. Two years later, he was elected secretary of the federations section (i.e. the section based on the national trade or industrial federations). Pouget worked very well together with V. Griffuelhes, gen-

eral secretary of the CGT 1901–9, and was very influential within the organization. In 1906 he was one of the signatories of the motion which was passed by an overwhelming majority at the Amiens Congress, and which came to be seen as the definitive statement of revolutionary syndicalism. The 'Amiens Charter' emphasized working-class solidarity and autonomy, the independence of the trade unions from the political parties, and the 'dual task' of the CGT: the strategic struggle for social revolution, coupled with the daily struggle for the improvement of wages and conditions.

In 1909 Pouget put a great deal of effort into launching a weekly which was intended to be the organ of the revolutionary syndicalist tendency: *La Révolution*. The paper was not a success, however, and only survived a year. Shortly afterwards, he retired with his second wife to Lozère (Seine-et-Oise), and played no further role in the movement, beyond contributing some articles to Hervé's *La Guerre sociale*, and some in a patriotic vein to *L'Humanité* during the First World War.

Bibliography

Books and pamphlets by Pouget:

L'Action Directe (Paris: Editions de *La Guerre Sociale*, Bibliothèque Syndicaliste, no. 4, 1910).

Les Bases du Syndicalisme (Paris: Editions de *La Guerre Sociale*, Bibliothèque Syndicaliste, no. 1; translated as *The Basis of Trade Unionism* (London: T.H. Keel, 1908 – A Voice of Labour pamphlet).

La Confédération Générale du Travail (Paris: M. Rivière, Bibliothèque du Mouvement Socialiste, 1908).

Le Parti du Travail (Paris: Bibliothèque Syndicaliste, no. 3, 1905).

Le Syndicat (Paris: Bibliothèque Syndicaliste, no. 2, n.d.).

With E. Pataud, *Comment nous ferons la révolution* (Paris: J. Tallandier, 1909); with E. Pataud, *Syndicalism and the Co-operative Commonwealth* (Oxford: New International Publishing Co., 1913). With F. de Pressensé, *Les Lois scélérates de 1893–1894* (Paris: Editions de La Revue Blanche, 1899), [Extracts from *La Revue Blanche*, 1–15 July 1898 and 15 January 1899.]

DGB

POUJADE, Pierre-Marie (1920–)

Poujade's father was an architect who died while

young. His mother, whom he adored, subsequently struggled to bring up her family in the small town of Saint-Céré (Lot). Poujade showed little aptitude for school, but proved an able sportsman, and fervent organizer of his fellow youth. A psycho-historian would find ample material here to help explain the career of the man who was to become known as 'Poujadolf' to his enemies, and 'Pierrot le petit gars' to his many friends.

In the late 1930s Poujade was attracted by the ideas of French Fascists, such as Doriot (q.v.). He had been brought up in a strongly monarchist family, who despised the Republic. He had relatives in Spain, who fled from the ravages of the Republican forces in 1936. Perhaps most importantly, Poujade was an activist rather than a thinker. He was attracted by Fascism's promise of national regeneration, and the social reconciliation he believed impossible within Republican structures. It was therefore not surprising that he was attracted to the Vichy regime after the fall of France. However, by late 1942 Poujade had become disillusioned with the increasing subservience to the Germans. He crossed the Pyrenees into Spain, was arrested, but liberated in 1943. He finished the war training for the air force in Britain.

Returning to his beloved Saint-Céré, he became a travelling book salesman. By the early 1950s he was a small wholesaler, covering the department of Lot and beyond. Poujade had become part of the large number of small businesses, especially shops, which still characterized French life. In the era of shortages immediately after the war, many had done well. By the early 1950s they were threatened by the rise of larger units. This was compounded by a complicated tax system, often administered by officials from large towns such as Paris. For the tax inspector, and many others, small businesses were the epitome of fraud and evasion. For the artisan and shopkeeper on the margin of survival, 'le fisc' was an enemy engaged in a battle to the death. Pressure groups in France tended to be weak, and the two main business groups paid little attention to those on the economic edge. Moreover, the Fourth Republic was remote from everyday provincial life. Deputies and senators retained strong local links, but the administration tended to be highly technocratic.

Against this background, in 1953 Poujade began to organize demonstrations. It began as a revolt against tax *contrôles*, local shopkeepers gathering to prevent the inspector conducting audits. By 1954 Poujade had formed the UDCA (Union de Défense des Commerçants et Artisans), which held its first national rally in Algiers. Specific economic interests welded the movement together, but it quickly took on a wider set of concerns. It was defined more by what it opposed than what it was for. It was against foreign influences in France, the Republic, faceless bureaucrats, Paris, and urbanization. It defended a vague, idealized vision of French life in which the small town, and entrepreneur, were the very essence of *Liberté, Egalité,* and *Fraternité.*

These broader themes grew stronger in 1955 when Poujade established a political party, the UFF (Union et Fraternité Française). By this time the movement had two national journals, plus many local ones, and it issued a large amount of printed propaganda. Vast rallies were held throughout France, in which the star demagogue was 'le petit papetier'. A new *Etats Généraux* was demanded to decide on a replacement for the loathed republic. American and Jewish influence was discerned everywhere. Remarkably, in the January 1956 parliamentary elections the UFF won 11.6 per cent of the vote, and fifty-two seats. Poujade had rallied a significant rural and small town following, and added to this a group of *mécontents* from across the political spectrum, especially from the largely dormant proto-fascists.

However, it was a highly unstable coalition, both in the Chamber and electorally. Some Poujadists deputies like the young Le Pen, were primarily interested in broader issues such as *Algérie française,* or in parliamentary dealing. Others longed to return to their businesses, or the politics of the parish pump. In the provinces many shopkeepers had opposed the movement into electoral politics. Politics could be bad for trade; they also correctly saw that it would divert attention from specific economic issues. The UFF had little formal organization, and relied heavily on immediate issues, and the weakness of other parties. Thus it was in difficulties even before de Gaulle's return in 1958, and the creation of a new Gaullist party put the final nail in its coffin as a serious electoral force.

Poujadists were active in the Algerian events which led to de Gaulle's return to power, and were subsequently involved in various plots against the General. Poujade dabbled in conspiratorial politics, but never ultimately committed himself to a coup. Although he operated in a strongly *Algérie française* milieu, he admired de Gaulle in many ways, and realized that the remnants of the UDCA remained primarily interested in business issues. There was no small town maquis waiting to rise at the news of de Gaulle's assassination.

A change was also taking place in Poujade's outlook. He had been in contact with Gaullists in the

1950s, and by the mid-1960s was looking for an accommodation with the Fifth Republic rather than confrontation. During Pompidou's presidency he became a frequent adviser on issues affecting small business. However, new shopkeeper *enragés* were emerging, and Giscard d'Estaing had no desire to flatter the ego of the leader of the dwindling UDCA. Poujade countered by launching an 'apolitical' UDI (Union de Défense Interprofessionnelle) list in the 1979 European elections, but it gained only 1.4 per cent of the vote. A new campaign was launched to encourage the efficient use of agricultural produce. Poujade spoke to a handful in the towns where twenty-five years before he had addressed thousands. He duly received his meetings with government representatives, but this was clearly part of the manoeuvring for the 1981 presidential elections. Poujade was not deceived, and he endorsed Mitterrand's candidacy. The scourge of the Fourth Republic ended his political career by supporting one of its doyens.

Bibliography

Borne, D. (1977), *Petits bourgeois en révolte? Le mouvement poujade*, Paris, Flammarion.

Eatwell, R. (1982), 'Poujadism and neo-Poujadism: From revolt to reconciliation', in P. Cerny (ed.), *Social Movements and Protest in France*, London: Pinter Publishers.

Hoffmann, S. (1956), *Le Mouvement poujade*, Paris: A. Colin.

Poujade, P. et al. (1977), *A l'heure de la colère*, Paris: Albin Michel.

RE

de PRESSENSÉ, Francis Dehaut de (1853–1914)

The son of a distinguished Protestant theologian, Francis de Pressensé first embarked on a diplomatic career in 1879, becoming a secretary at the French embassy in Constantinople, then in Washington in 1880; he soon resigned, first to take up the post of *chef de cabinet* of the minister for public instruction in 1887, then to devote himself entirely to journalism. Having become the main foreign affairs analyst of *Le Temps*, where he remained for nineteen years, he was drawn into domestic politics by the Dreyfus affair. Himself an ardent Dreyfusist, he joined the newly-founded League of the Rights of Man of which he was elected president in 1903. Won over to social-

ism, he became Jaurès' (q.v.) friend and one of his closest and most trusted collaborators.

Elected deputy for Lyons in 1902, Pressensé channelled his energies in three major directions. Firstly, in the Chamber of Deputies he was a noted orator, taking up causes like that of the Armenians (he was a delegate to the Pro-Armenia Congress held in Brussels in 1902); he also drafted the bill on the separation of Church and state in 1905. Secondly, he remained a well-known journalist, having switched his loyalty to suit his personal evolution, from *Le Temps* to *L'Aurore*, whose columns he incidentally used to castigate the Radicals for their conservatism; meanwhile, he played a crucial role in the foundation of Jaurès' paper *L'Humanité* in 1904, making a financial contribution of 30,000 francs, and henceforward sharing the writing on foreign policy with Lucien Herr (q.v.). Finally, he helped Jaurès in the management of internal party affairs. He was one of the three deputies who represented the Jaurès fraction (Parti Socialiste Français) in the left-wing parliamentary group 'Délégation des gauches'. He took part in the Amsterdam Congress of 1904 and supported Jaurès' successful endeavours to maintain Socialist unity. And he was Jaurès' constant adviser on the main orientations of party policies.

Returned to Parliament in 1906, he was beaten in 1910 when the centre and right-wing parties formed a majority in the Chamber of Deputies. Afflicted with poor health, he died in January 1914, much grieved by Jaurès, who paid tribute to him at a memorial meeting at the Salle des Sociétés Savantes in Paris two days after his death: 'What he accumulated in the solitude of his study, what he gleaned from the wisdom of the past, he did not absorb for his own sake. Nor did his wide knowledge lead him, in the manner of our reactionary dilettantes, to scorn for the masses and isolation from them.'

A prominent member of the 'haute société protestante', Pressensé provides an interesting example of a French intellectual whose espousal of socialism arose from a combination of cool-headed speculation and the emotional shock of the Dreyfus affair. His devotion to socialism was further nurtured by his mutually rewarding relationship with Jaurès. His experience, in that sense, is not unlike that of Léon Blum. It is not surprising to hear the nationalist Barrès exclaim: 'In the Chamber (of Deputies), I constantly experience this painful feeling of witnessing talent, education, culture emanating from the extreme left – Jaurès, Pressensé, Sembat – but this culture merely helps them to express in an interesting manner an erroneous doctrine.'

Francis de Pressensé is the author of a number of

books on wide ranging issues, including *L'Irlande et l'Angleterre depuis l'acte d'union jusqu'à nos jours*, *Le Cardinal Manning*, *Les lois scélérates de 1893–1894*, *L'idée de la patrie*, and *Un héros*. *Le lieutenant-colonel Picquart*.

Bibliography

There is no sustained study of Pressensé in English, and the relatively few references to him in the French literature are mostly found in biographies of Jaurès. The following books can usefully be consulted: Charles Andler, *Vie de Lucien Herr* (giving a somewhat negative opinion of Pressensé, often a rival of Herr) (Paris: Editions Rieder, 1932); Max Gallo, *Le Grand Jaurès* (Paris: Robert Laffont, 1984); Harvey Goldberg, *The Life of Jean Jaurès* (Madison, Wisc.: University of Wisconsin Press, 1968); Jacques Kayser, *Les Grandes batailles du radicalisme* (on Pressensé's articles in *L'Aurore*) (Paris: M. Rivière, 1961).

AM

PUCHEU, Pierre Firmin (1900–43)

Pierre Pucheu was born in Algeria of relatively humble parents. After graduating brilliantly from the Ecole Normale Supérieure (a prestigious Paris college) he entered industry. He worked for Pont à Mousson, a steel marketing syndicate (not the Comité des Forges); and Japy Frères. After the defeat in 1940 he became president of the government-sponsored committee which regulated the engineering industry; he was minister of industrial production (from February until July 1941) and then minister of the interior until May 1942. In this latter office Pucheu displayed little sympathy for his former associates in the Doriot's Parti Populaire Français; he banned the PPF in the southern zone and prevented recruitment for Doriot's Légion Français de Volontiers Français. He also effectively signed his own death warrant by handing over Communists in French prisons for reprisal shootings by the Germans.

Because of his links with big business it is often suggested that Pucheu formed part of an enclave of ministers and officials who sought to protect industrial interests at Vichy. More specifically some talked of a 'synarchic' group, a semi-Masonic conspiracy said to be manipulated by the Worms bank. Certainly it is true that Pucheu had close links with certain other ministers and officials – Barnaud, the Leroy Ladurie brothers and Lehideux. They were united by similar professional backgrounds, by regular meetings in Paris, and, to a more limited extent, by their views. But it would be crude to describe any of these men as simple representatives of big business. Pucheu illustrates the ideological distance which could exist underneath the apparent professional links between businessmen and Vichy ministers. Even when he had worked in industry Pucheu displayed an interest in politics which went well beyond the ordinary concerns of running a business. He had been involved in Ernest Mercier's *Redressement Français* campaign and later in the Parti Populaire Français which Doriot (q.v.) had founded – until he broke with it because of his disapproval of Munich. Indeed his political beliefs marked him out sharply from his colleagues. Where most industrialists saw the Popular Front as a problem Pucheu saw it as an opportunity to install a more humane and better organized economy – he was later to talk of 'les beaux jours de 1936'.

Pucheu saw Vichy as another chance to impose his ideas. These ideas were far from being an expression of business opinion. Most businessmen had less time than ever for grand schemes of reform during the uncertain and difficult conditions of the war. The clash between Pucheu and his peers was illustrated by his attempts to impose the 'rationalization' scheme drawn up by his friend Robert Loustau upon the coal industry in 1941. By 1943 Pucheu had become disillusioned with Vichy. At considerable risk to himself he travelled across France to join the Free French in Algeria. He was repaid by a firing squad.

Bibliography

Pucheu, P. (1948), *Ma vie*, Paris: Amiot Dummont.

RCV

PUJO, Maurice (1872–1955)

Maurice Pujo was born at Lorrez-le-Bocage (Seine-et-Marne) in 1872, and studied first at the *lycée* (secondary school) in Orléans and then at the Sorbonne, where he revealed precocious talents for literature and literary criticism. His early political tendencies, like those of his friend Henri Vaugeois, were towards anarchism, but the Dreyfus affair drove both of them firmly towards the nationalist right. In an 1898 article, Pujo coined the phrase 'action française' which was to become the title of the review and movement founded by him and Vaugeois, and by 1903 the decisive influence of Charles Maurras had converted the group to the royalist programme which was the hallmark of Action Française. When in 1908 the review became a daily newspaper, Pujo was put in charge of the Camelots du Roi, a volunteer organization formed to sell the paper, but which under his leadership was soon to become a combative youth movement, Action Française's main political presence on the streets. After the First World War, in which he served as a private soldier, Pujo continued to devote his skills as an organizer and propagandist to the royalist cause. A supporter of Pétain in 1940, he none the less remained hostile to Nazi Germany, and was arrested by the occupation authorities in Lyons in June 1944. Freed when the Germans retreated, he was re-arrested when Lyons was liberated and imprisoned for his Vichyite sympathies. After his release in 1947 he resumed his involvement in royalist journalism. He died in 1955.

As leader of the Camelots du Roi, Pujo played an important part in establishing Action Française's ideological influence in right-wing circles before and during the First World War, and in maintaining its hold on student milieux in the Paris Latin Quarter during the 1920s. He will also be remembered, along with Léon Daudet (q.v.) for a violent and scurrilous brand of journalism which spasmodically boosted the notoriety and the sales of the *L'Action Française* newspaper between the wars. The vicious personal campaigns against Aristide Briand and Franco-German *rapprochement* in the 1920s against politicians implicated in the financial scandals of the early 1930s, and against Léon Blum and the Popular Front, have won Pujo and his associates an unenviable place in the annals of the French press.

Pujo embodied that curious mixture of elitism and demagogy which characterized the Action Française, a man of refined literary tastes who at the same time revelled in the political street-brawl and in abusive polemics. However, the movement reached the zenith of its political influence between the wars during the Stavisky scandal and the riots of 6 February 1934, and thereafter it was increasingly marginalized by the growth of new organizations on the extreme right. Pujo himself was accused by certain *Camelots* of having deserted them on 6 February, when the Republic was allegedly on the brink of collapse, and a group of them were later to break away to form the secret right-wing terrorist Cagoule. Many of the intellectuals who had been schooled in the doctrines of Action Française came to see its royalism as an irrelevant anachronism, and moved towards more modern political movements like Doriot's Parti Populaire Français. Pujo and his mentor Maurras were increasingly isolated figures in the closing years of the Third Republic, and during the occupation their uncompromising allegiance to their specific political principles won them enemies on every side.

Bibliography

Pujo figures in several works on the Action Française, notably in E. Weber, *Action Française: Royalism and reaction in twentieth century France* (Stanford Cal.: Stanford University Press, 1963); E. Tannenbaum, *Action Française: Die-hard reactionaries in twentieth century France* (New York: Wiley, 1962); E. Nolte, *Three Faces of Fascism* (New York: Holt, Rienhart and Winston, 1965).

BJ

Q

QUEUILLE, Henri (1884–1970)

One of the most durable political figures of the Third and Fourth Republics, Henri Queuille was minister of agriculture eleven times during the Third Republic, acting president of the provisional government of the French Republic at Algiers during de Gaulle's absences in 1944, and premier three times during the Fourth Republic.

Queuille was born in 1884 at Neuvic d'Ussel in the department of Corrèze, a mountainous area in central France that always was to be close to his heart as well as his political base. After the death of his father, a pharmacist, in 1895, Queuille's mother brought her children to the nearby town of Tulle, where Queuille completed his secondary school studies before going to Paris on a scholarship to study medicine. He received his medical degree in 1908, but due to his mother's death the same year and his resultant family responsibilities he renounced competing for a coveted Paris internship and returned to Neuvic to practise medicine. Four years later, in 1912, 'the good Dr Queuille' started his long political career with his election as mayor of Neuvic, a post which – except for the wartime years after his dismissal in 1941 by the Vichy government – he was to hold until 1965. A member of the then dominant Radical Party, Queuille was elected deputy in 1914. At the outbreak of the First World War shortly afterwards, he volunteered for military service, serving as a doctor on the front lines; his decorations included the Croix de Guerre. Reelected deputy in 1919, Queuille was henceforth secure in his political fief: deputy without a break until 1935 when he was elected senator, he was again deputy from 1946 to 1958, i.e. during the entire life of the Fourth Republic.

But more remarkable was Queuille's almost unparalleled ministerial record. From 1920 to 1940, he served in nineteen governments, usually as minister of agriculture, but also as minister of public health, of posts, of public works, and of food (in 1940). After joining de Gaulle in London in April 1943, he subsequently became a member of de Gaulle's provisional government serving as interim president when de Gaulle was absent from Algiers. During the Fourth Republic he was a minister – or premier – without a break from July 1948 to June 1954. His first government made post-war history by lasting from September 1948 to November 1949 (a record surpassed only by Guy Mollet's government in 1956–7). His second government lasted for only two days in July 1950, and his third for four months, March–July 1951.

Queuille was on occasion criticized for temporizing and for being the 'father of immobilism', but he also has been credited with saving the Fourth Republic. Governing during difficult times, he often showed impressive firmness and courage (e.g. in contending with a violent miners' strike in 1948), and his political astuteness helped keep the Fourth Republic afloat despite attacks by the Gaullist RPF and the Communist Party. Modest and unpretentious, with no flair or apparent desire for personal publicity, he played a more significant and forceful leadership role in governing France than he usually has been credited with by French opinion.

Bibliography

Queuille is the subject of the first half of the chapter on '*radicaux de gestion*' in Francis de Tarr, *The French Radical Party from Herriot to Mendès-France* (Oxford: Oxford University Press, 1961; Westport, Conn.: Greenwood Press, 1980). In French, see *Henri Queuille et la Corrèze. (Actes du Colloque de Tulle)* (Limoges: Editions Souny, 1986); and, especially, *Henri Queuille et la République. (Actes du Colloque de Paris)* (Limoges: Université de Limoges, 1987).

FdeT

QUILÈS, Paul (1942–)

Quilès, an able politician but a somewhat grey figure, is typical of the new generation of Socialists promoted after the Metz Congress: efficient, technocratic and devoted to Mitterrand. The son of an army officer he went to secondary school in Casablanca and in Paris at the prestigious Lycée Louis-le-Grand. He went on to the Ecole Polytechnique and was an executive with Shell Oil from 1964–78.

Quilès started work in the Socialist Party as its energy specialist in 1974 and quickly made a reputation in this field. In 1978 one of the rare Socialist victories was Quilès' winning of the Paris 13th *arrondissement* from the Gaullist Alexandre Sanguinetti: the victory, although a pleasing one for the left, was not entirely against the run of the election. After the 1979 Metz Congress Quilès was voted on to the executive of the PS and helped prepare an alliance with CERES (which gave Mitterrand control of the party against Rocard and Mauroy). As national secretary for organization in the PS, Quilès devoted himself to preparing Mitterrand's supporters for the nomination battle for the 1981 presidential elections; this was successful and Mitterrand made him campaign director in 1981.

Quilès was not rewarded with an immediate government post but was given the unofficial title of no. 3 in the Socialist Party. He played a prominent, if unfortunate role, in the post-victory October 1981 Congress in Valence. Referring to the replacements of top jobs in the civil service Quilès said that if heads were to roll it would be necessary to say which heads and quickly. This, popular with the activists at that time, earned him the nickname of 'Robespaul'. Quilès was then eclipsed for two years in a party where there was little room for him to exercise influence and in 1983 he ran as Socialist mayoral candidate for Paris. This was a disaster and he preserved his own seat on the council only as a result of the introduction of proportional representation.

In July 1984. when Fabius became prime minister, Quilès was made minister for urban affairs, housing and transport. This government, unlike Mauroy's, was not a radical reforming one and was concerned more to prepare for the 1986 elections. Quilès had no room to make much of a mark. The same holds true for Quilès' unexpected promotion to minister of defence in September 1985 when Hernu resigned because of the Greenpeace affair. Hernu's had been a high spending ministry and Quilès had to damp down expectations – always difficult to do – and, for example, postponed the decision on the mobile land-based missile system until 1990. However he had no time other than to issue a few declaratory statements and try to reassure the public after the turmoil of the 'Affair'. In the 1988 Rocard government Quilès was made minister for post and telecommunications.

Bibliography

On the Socialist Party and defence see J. Howorth and P. Chilton (eds), *Defence and Dissent in Contemporary France* (London: Croom Helm, 1984) and also see Paul Quilès, *La Politique n'est pas ce que vous croyez* (Paris: Robert Laffont, 1985).

BC

R

RACAMOND, Julien (1885–1966)

As one of the first French Communists, Racamond played an important, though largely secondary, role in the Communist trade union movement in the 1920s and 1930s. He was born in Dijon into a family of agricultural labourers and worked on the land (from 1897 to 1903) before taking up the trade of baker and progressing up the ladder of the bakery workers' union from 1905–14. By the eve of the First World War he had become a full-time trade unionist and deputy secretary of the union's Paris region. In 1914 Racamond was called up for service in the army and won the Croix de Guerre but by 1919 he was back in the bakery workers' union, this time as secretary of the Paris region.

Racamond participated in the extreme, quasi-revolutionary, strikes of the post-war period, was elected to the executive of the revolutionary union committees (*comités syndicalistes révolutionnaires*) in 1921 as a scourge of 'reformism'. Racamond was thus typical of the cadres recruited from the unions into the early Bolshevik parties and as such, *noblesse de robe*. When the CGT split (and the CGTU founded) in 1921–2 Racamond was, with Gaston Monmousseau, a member of the Vie Ouvrière group in the Communist unions and, at the St Etienne Congress of 25 June 1922, called for adherence to the International of Communist unions (Profintern). At the Bourges Congress of the CGTU (17 November 1923) Racamond supported Sémard's resolution which 'unreservedly approved' adhesion to Profintern (also subordinating unions to the party) and he was put on the new executive along with Monmousseau. Racamond was to remain a national secretary until the reunification of the French unions in 1936.

The rest of Racamond's career is characterized by a promiscuous servility: following every twist in Comintern line, he remained a party member until his death. In Moscow in July 1924 he was given the privilege of addressing the 3rd Profintern Congress. From 1926 to 1936 he was on the French Communist Central Committee and was a Political Bureau member from June 1926 to July 1928. In 1928

Racamond addressed with 6th Comintern Congress and was in Moscow dealing with French party matters in 1933. Racamond weathered the rise of Stalin, which many of the early Bolsheviks did not. In 1936, when CGTU merged into the CGT, Racamond was made an assistant secretary of the CGT and was active in promoting the new Popular Front. In the late 1930s Racamond marched in lockstep with Russian policy, and, after the signature of the Nazi–Soviet pact embraced revolutionary 'defeatism'. As a result of opposing the war effort he was arrested in October 1939 and interned for a short while before being liberated under surveillance: he was interned again but then freed in June 1942 after signing a statement condemning attacks on German forces – he seems, like Cachin (q.v.) at the same time, not to have realized that the Comintern line would change. Racamond may have been in Resistance work but when the CGT resumed public activity he emerged, along with Frachon (q.v.) and Reynaud, on the confederal bureau (with the assistance of fellow-travellers they had the upper hand). Racamond was on the CGT secretariat from the liberation until his retirement in 1953.

Racamond was a good public speaker but not an organizer or tactician of genius: however politics is not a meritocracy and Racamond stayed at the top of the greasy pole for a long time. He was important in the Bolshevization of the CGTU (by Treint – q.v.) in 1925 as well as in the political thimble-rigging of the CGT in the 1930s and 1940s.

Bibliography

See E. Mortimer, *The Rise of the French Communist Party* (London: Faber, 1984). There is a sketch of Racamond in P. Robrieux, *Histoire intérieur du parti communiste* (Paris: Fayard, 1984).

DSB

RACINE, Pierre (1909–   )

As *directeur des stages* (director of practical training)

from 1945 to 1957 and then as director from 1969 to 1975 Pierre Racine had a major influence on the nature and consistency of the development of the Ecole Nationale d'Administration (ENA), the elite civil service college which has trained many of France's top civil servants and also some of the leading post-war politicians. Racine was brought up in southern France and then studied commerce for a year at the Catholic University of Lille. This experience convinced him of the formative value of a period spent outside a familiar environment. Study at Aix-en-Provence, combined with work in the family business preceded the standard route into the higher civil service through the Paris Ecole Libre des Sciences Politiques and the competitive entry to the Conseil d'Etat, which he joined in 1935 along with his friend Michel Debré (q.v.). He married an American fellow student.

In 1945 after five years as a prisoner of war Racine was appointed by Debré to the tiny staff of the newly-created ENA. Here he developed the system that places students for their first year in different government offices outside Paris, especially prefectures. Most importantly he created a coherent theory of the aims of such training, stressing the importance of the move away from familiar backgrounds, of close contact with senior officials in developing a sense of civil service behaviour and style, of attention to actual problems from a broad viewpoint and of 'a sense of the state' and the exigencies of state service.

Racine returned to the Conseil d'Etat in 1957 and when Debré became prime minister in 1959 was appointed as head of his personal staff (*directeur de cabinet*). Between 1963 and 1983 Racine was, in addition to his other duties, head of the inter-ministerial mission for the development of Languedoc-Roussillon. This government body was set up outside the normal structures in the hope that it would galvanize all concerned into concerted and rapid action. The futuristic resorts, such as La Grande Motte, along the formerly mosquito-ridden marshy Languedoc coastline are the visible, if not entirely uncontroversial, results.

Racine returned to the ENA as its director in 1969. He oversaw a period of reform, induced largely by the upheavals of May 1968, restructuring both entry and curriculum without abandoning his rather austere principles of the worth of state service and the importance of a broad, vocational but perhaps technocratic training. He encouraged larger intakes with a higher proportion of women. He returned to a very senior post in the Conseil d'Etat in 1975, retiring in 1979.

Bibliography

For a description of the ENA which closely reflects Racine's approach see: *L'Ecole Nationale d'Administration* (Paris: Documentation Française, 1975).

AS

RAMADIER, Paul (1888–1961)

Paul Ramadier was one of the most prominent members of that generation of French Socialists who saw socialism as an extension of, rather than an alternative to, liberal republicanism. A major figure in the last twenty years of the parliamentary Republic, his political career came to an abrupt end with the arrival in 1958 of a new constitutional order. The product of a bourgeois and Catholic family, Ramadier grew up in Rodez (Aveyron), was educated at the local *lycée* and studied law at Toulouse and Paris. While at Toulouse he discovered the labour movement and in Paris he was briefly attracted to the doctrine of revolutionary syndicalism, perhaps remembering the antimilitarism of a Rodez school teacher, Gustave Hervé (q.v.). But he quickly rejected what he saw as the unreality and catastrophism of syndicalism and the rigid orthodoxy of (Guesdist) Marxism in favour of a practical, reformist socialism that acknowledged both the liberties won by the Third Republic and such key Republican themes as secularism (*laïcité*). He was an admirer of the leader of reformist socialism Albert Thomas (q.v.) (in whose ministerial office he worked during the First World War and whom he would follow into the International Labour Office). He viewed Bolshevism as dangerous fanaticism and thus gave strong support to Blum (q.v.) at the time of the Socialist Party split in 1920. A lifelong supporter of the cooperative movement, he was also a prominent Freemason. It would be wrong to see Ramadier as a closet centrist – he disliked the Radical Party's complacency and insisted on the need for structural reform of capitalist society – but he did believe in electoral and governmental alliances between the parties of the democratic left.

Ramadier became Socialist mayor of the mining town of Decazeville in 1919 and in 1928 was elected to the National Assembly for Villefranche-de-Rouergue (Aveyron). His commitment to practical reformism led him in 1933 to join the dissident 'neos', whose split with the Socialist Party over its refusal to contemplate a governmental alliance with the Radicals brought about the formation of the Parti Socialiste de France. Yet his equally deep commitment to Republican democracy led to his rapid estrangement from the authoritarianism of other neos like Déat (q.v.) and Marquet (q.v.). Highly susceptible to the theme of Republican defence which emerged after the riots of the 6 February 1934, he supported the Popular Front once the entry of the Radicals had enabled him to overcome his innate distrust of the Communists. Despite his 1933 decision to leave the SFIO, he was re-elected in 1936 as the Popular Front candidate. He served in the governments of Blum, Chautemps (q.v.) and Daladier (q.v.) first as under-secretary of state for mines and energy and then as minister of labour. In the former post he was active in developing new sources of energy and in promoting the electrification of rural communes and in the latter he was a strong supporter of compulsory arbitration in labour disputes. He resigned from the Daladier government over the authoritarian use of decree laws to reform the forty-hour week. His commitment to Republican due process of law would be abundantly demonstrated in July 1940 when he was one of the eighty parliamentarians who voted against handing over power to Marshal Pétain (q.v.) at Vichy; his opposition to the constitutional plans of the Vichy *Etat Français* was absolute. Removed from his town hall by Vichy, he refused to renounce his Freemasonry, protected a number of Socialist and Jewish friends, and was in close contact with local Resistance organizations. Thus he had a good occupation. Yet his continuing dislike of what he saw as Bolshevik fanaticism meant that he rejected the armed struggle of the Maquis; this estrangement from a rapidly growing Communist movement would ultimately prove fatal to his electoral position.

Ramadier's reputation at the liberation was high. Having rejoined the Socialist Party, he served in the politically difficult Ministry of Food in de Gaulle's provisional government, was parliamentary *rapporteur* of the electricity nationalization bill (in which he again clashed with the Communists) and was minister of justice in Blum's short-lived 1946 government. In January 1947 President Auriol (q.v.) nominated him as the first prime minister of the Fourth Republic and he was accepted by the National Assembly by 549 votes to nil, with 66 abstentions. It was an extraordinarily difficult time in which to take office. Appalling social and economic conditions made worse by bad weather meant a reduction in the bread ration to a level lower than during the occupation and earned Ramadier the enduring nickname of Ramadan. The situation in Indo-China was rapidly deteriorating into one of all out war between the French and the Vietnamese,

there was a bloody uprising in Madagascar and the Algerian statute which Ramadier passed quickly became a dead letter. A series of strikes and demonstrations took place in protest against high prices and the government's wage policy. Above all, 1947 was the year when domestic and international political tensions collided and exploded. The government had to face not only the emergence of a mass antisystem party of the right (de Gaulle's Rassemblement Pour la France) but also the changing political stance of the Communists. The caricature of Resistance unity known as tripartism finally disintegrated in May 1947 when Ramadier sacked the Communist ministers for their refusal to abide by collective government responsibility, that pillar of parliamentary government. Ramadier was not at this stage a cold war warrior and hoped for diplomatic collaboration with the Soviet Union. His action in dismissing the Communists was not, as has been often claimed, imposed by Washington. Yet by the end of the summer, French acceptance of Marshall Aid, the establishment of the Cominform, the ever worsening situation in Central Europe and the violent repression of the equally violent Communist strikes meant that France was firmly in the Atlantic camp. Ramadier's government fell in November, largely because of the hostility of the Socialist Party secretary Guy Mollet (q.v.) but he was back in office in September 1948 as minister of defence in the Queuille (q.v.) ministry. During this period he was involved in the discussions leading to the creation of Nato – and also in the measures to protect the army establishment from scandals in Indo-China.

Ramadier was defeated in the 1951 parliamentary elections but returned to the National Assembly in 1956 and was, somewhat surprisingly, appointed minister of finance in Mollet's government. Galloping inflation, a hugh budgetary deficit (made worse by the Algerian War which he supported) and a weak franc made his tenure of office controversial; though he himself strongly defended the government's social measures – a third week's holiday with pay and old age pensions – which fitted in perfectly with his reformism. He participated in the discussions on the formation of the EEC and acquired much odium for his decision to introduce a road tax (the *vignette*) on car drivers. In 1958 he supported the return to power of de Gaulle whom he saw as the only person capable of solving the Algerian crisis and as an authentic Republican. He immediately became, however, one of the principal victims of the Fifth Republic. The intense hostility of the Decazeville Communists (memories of 1947–8 were still red) and his identification with a discredited system meant that he lost in rapid succession his parliamentary seat (November 1958) and his position as mayor (March 1959). The latter defeat was particularly humiliating since he was the only Socialist on his list not to be re-elected. He died in 1961, only a year before the referendum on the presidency that would finally destroy the parliamentary Republic to which his political career had been devoted.

Bibliography

Ramadier, P. (1961), *Les Socialistes et l'exercice du pouvoir*, Paris: Robert Laffont.
Auriol, V. (1970), *Mon septennat*, Paris: A. Colin.
Rioux, J.P. (1987), *The Fourth Republic 1944–1958*, Cambridge: Cambridge University Press.

PM

RANC, Arthur Joseph (1831–1908)

A prominent Republican journalist and pamphleteer for half a century, a noted opposition spokesman under the Second Empire and briefly a communard, Arthur Ranc was trained in law and studied at the School of Archivists (Ecole des Chartes). At the age of 22 he was implicated in the 1853 *opéra comique* plot to assassinate Napoleon III, prosecuted for belonging to a secret society, and condemned to a term of one year in prison. In 1856 he was deported to Lambessa, the penal establishment in Algeria, for his part in a plot against the empress, whence he fled to Switzerland, returning to France after the amnesty of 1859.

A continual thorn in the side of the imperial regime, and a frequent contributor to opposition newspapers, he was imprisoned again in 1867 for articles written in the radical daily *Le Nain jaune*. Ranc played an important part in the events of 1870–1. He participated in the storming of the Palais Bourbon (4 September), was mayor of the 9th *arrondissement* of Paris and served as Gambetta's (q.v.) head of police in the Government Delegation at Tours. A deputy in February 1871, he allied himself with the extreme left. His brief flirt with the Commune when he was elected to the City Council in March 1871 was motivated, he claimed, by the desire to keep Gambetta informed, but it was to jeopardize seriously his subsequent career.

As a close collaborator of Gambetta, he was to be a chief target of the 1873 Broglie (q.v.) ministry. His prosecution was voted overwhelmingly by the Assembly and, condemned to death in October, he fled to Brussels. From there, he continued to render yeoman service as informant and contributor to Gambetta's daily newspaper, the *République Française* until his return to France with the 1879 amnesty. Like other polemical journalists of his time, Ranc had occasion to defend his honour in a sword duel – an occupational hazard at the time! – notably against the editor of the Bonapartist newspaper *Le Pays*.

His journalistic career continued, and in 1880 he shared with Paul Bert the political editorship of *La Petite République*, an offshoot of Gambetta's *République Française*. His political career also was far from over for he was deputy for the Seine (1881–5), became a senator (1891–1908), all the while continuing to be a leading contributor to the radical press.

A notable defender of the Republican cause during the Boulangist episode, he was associated with Clemenceau (q.v.) in founding in May 1888 the Société des Droits de l'Homme et du Citoyen in defence of the Republic and against Caesarean dictatorship. An unrepentant anticlerical and Freemason, his brushes with Archbishop Lavigerie (q.v.) of Tunis in 1890 over the coming round (*ralliement*) of the Church to the Republic were much publicized. Among his last campaigns was the Dreyfus affair. A combative journalist to the end, Ranc spent the last two years of his life as political editor of *L'Aurore*. His *Correspondance* – particularly that with Gambetta during Ranc's exile – is a valuable source of information on the Radical *milieu* and on the world of polemical journalism in the formative decades of the Third Republic.

Bibliography

Depasse, H. (1883), *Ranc* (Coll. Célébrités contemporaines), Paris: A. Quantin.
Ranc, A. (1913), *Souvenirs et correspondances 1831–1908*, Paris: E. Cornély.

ACR

'RAVACHOL' (pseud), Koenigstein, François Claudius (1859–92)

Born in Saint-Chamand in the Loire, Ravachol was baptized François Claudius Koenigstein: Ravachol was his mother's name. His father, a worker in a rolling-mill, abandoned his wife and four children to return to his native Holland. To support the family, Ravachol worked on local farms from the age of 8, beginning a three-year apprenticeship as a dyer at the age of 11. At 18, he read Eugène Sue's *Le Juif errant*, and lost his faith. He began to attend public meetings, became a collectivist, then an anarchist. He and his brother were both sacked, and this combined with the birth of an illegitimate child to his elder sister meant great hardship for the family. Ravachol turned to petty crime in an attempt to support his family and his companion.

The incidents for which he became famous began in May 1891, when, in Terrenoire (Loire), he disinterred the body of the comtesse de la Rochetaillée in a vain attempt to steal jewels with which she had supposedly been buried. In June, in Chambles, he strangled a 92-year-old man and stole about 15,000 francs. Ravachol was arrested, but he escaped to Paris and lived in Saint-Denis.

Ravachol then decided to avenge the treatment by the police and by the court of two anarchists arrested during a demonstration on May Day 1891. In March 1892 he planted bombs in the homes of the judge and the public prosecutor who had been involved in the court case, injuring no one but causing a great deal of damage. He was arrested, tried and condemned to forced labour for life for the explosions. The restaurant where he had been betrayed by a waiter blew up the day before the trial started in April. All those who knew him and gave evidence testified to his good character: he was kind and gentle, and had been good to his family. He justified his acts as being in revenge for the unjust treatment of his comrades.

In June he was tried for the desecration of the tomb and for the murder, and was accused of several other crimes, for which he denied responsibility. His justification was that he killed first in order to survive and secondly in order to help the anarchist cause, 'because we work for the happiness of the people'. He greeted the pronouncement of the death penalty with the cry: 'Vive l'anarchie!' He was guillotined on 11 July 1892 at Montbrison.

The anarchists originally disapproved of Ravachol's apparently selfish motives and even suspected him of being an *agent provocateur*. After his behaviour at the trials – accepting all responsibility and shielding his co-defendants – and the exposure of his political motives, their attitude changed, criticism turned to praise, and vengeance was called for. His physical strength, his generosity towards the poor and his mercilessness towards the bourgeoisie combined to turn him into a hero of the anarchist cause, even a Christ-figure. The verb *ravacholiser* was coined (meaning to dispose of one's enemies), a novel about his exploits was serialized in a local anarchist newspaper, and three songs were written, the most famous being 'La Ravachole', sung to the tune of 'La Carmagnole' and 'Ça ira'.

Belief in the imminence of the Revolution was widespread within the French anarchist movement, and 'propaganda by the deed' had been sanctioned by the First International at its London Congress in 1881. There was also much admiration for the Russian nihilists. Thus it had been a tactic of the French movement to encourage acts of violence with the aim of increasing popular awareness of the nature of social and economic oppression. Despite a decade of such propaganda there were only a few minor incidents in the 1880s, but a spate of them in the years 1892–4. Although those responsible for such actions – Ravachol, Henry, Vaillant, Caserio – were far from typical, the image of the anarchist terrorist became the stereotype of nineteenth-century anarchism, and thanks to the efforts of both the bourgeois state and anarchism's political enemies on the left, the figure of a Ravachol is still very much the typical anarchist.

Bibliography

Maitron, J. (1964), *Ravachol et les anarchistes*, Paris: Julliard.

Maitron, J. (1975), *Le Mouvement anarchiste en France*, vol. 1, Paris: Maspéro.

Maitron, J. (ed.) (1975), *Dictionnaire biographique du mouvement ouvrier français*, vol. 15, Paris: Les Editions Ouvrières.

DGB

RECLUS, Jean-Jacques Elisée (1830–1905)

Elisée Reclus, the anarchist-geographer, was born in 1830 in Saint-Foy-la-Grande (Gironde). His mother ran a small school and his father was a Calvinist minister. Reclus, however, came to denounce religion and reject ceremonies associated with it. His three 'marriages' (the first two partners died in childbirth) and those of his two daughters were celebrated by a simple gathering.

Expression of Republican sentiments forced him and his elder brother Elie to leave France after the December 1851 coup. The first of many travels took him to England, Southern United States and New Grenada (Columbia) and were to provide him with material for numerous articles on geography and politics after his return to France in 1856. In the 1860s he became involved in various organizations – the International Working Men's Association, Paris section, founded in 1864, and Bakunin's International Brotherhood. From 1868 onwards relations with Bakunin became strained over Reclus' belief in the possibility of social and political change through alliances with the bourgeoisie. However, Reclus was entrusted with the editing of Bakunin's papers after his death in 1876.

By this time, the experience of the Paris Commune and the brutal repression of the communards had led Reclus to reject totally any revolutionary activity within the existing political order. He had been imprisoned in 1871–2, but adamantly refused to be pardoned because he was a well-known geographer. The idea for his enormous *Nouvelle géographie universelle* (19 volumes, 1872–95) came to him in prison and was then begun during his exile in Switzerland. Curiously, he wrote very little on the Commune except for a few pages, for example, in his last major work *L'Homme et la terre* (1905–8). Yet he realized that it was not just the elected representatives of the Commune who had failed, but also the people who had not shown themselves capable of carrying through a revolution. They had adopted the existing institutions even to the extent of escorting money from the Banque de France to the National Assembly at Versailles!

Anarchism, as a distinctive political theory opposing activity within the context of the bourgeois political system, was not clearly defined until the late 1870s. Reclus used the term in 1851 to refer to the harmonious operation of stateless societies based upon principles of justice, equality and brotherly love, but would not apply the label to himself until 1876. Anarchists sought to destroy the state which was the bourgeoisie's means of maintaining its economic system without, however, first taking possession of it. For Reclus, the ultimate social revolution would be achieved through the interrelated processes of evolution and revolution; equality could not be brought about at a single stroke since consciousness had first to be changed, as Reclus stated in his main political work *L'Evolution, la révolution et l'idéal anarchique*. Science, especially the Darwinian theory of evolution, provided the rationale and justification for the eventual creation of the universal social Republic.

As an anarchist and a geographer, Reclus was for long consigned to the recesses of history. Although one of the major anarchist theoreticians, he could not match the flamboyance of Bakunin who was involved in several abortive revolts. Kropotkin described him as 'a real puritan in his lifestyle, and intellectually, a sort of eighteenth-century French philosopher'. In true French tradition, he was unable to obtain a teaching post in France because he did not hold formal qualifications, and so, accepted

in 1894 an invitation from the Université Libre in Brussels.

Bibliography

M. Fleming, *The Anarchist Way to Socialism. Elisée Reclus and nineteenth-century European anarchism* (London: Croom Helm, 1979); for his geographical work, see P. Girot and E. Kofman (eds) *International Geopolitical Analysis: Selections from Hérodote* (London: Croom Helm, 1987) and for a recent biography, H. Sarrazin, *Elisée Reclus ou la passion du monde* (Paris: La Découverte, 1985).

EK

REINACH, Joseph Herman (1856–1921)

Joseph Reinach was the eldest of three brothers who were exceptionally brilliant students and thus immediately enhanced the intellectual reputation of the French Jewish community. A lawyer turned journalist, he joined the staff of Gambetta's newspaper *La République Française* in 1876, and when Gambetta put together his 'great cabinet' in 1881, it was Reinach who headed his 'cabinet office', and who drafted most of the bills. When the cabinet fell in 1882, Reinach, who reverted to journalism, remained a member of Gambetta's Opportunist Party and unsuccessfully stood for election in 1885. In 1886 he bought *La République Française* (with fellow Opportunists) and became its chief editor. A vigorous opponent of Boulangism, he was elected deputy of the Basses-Alpes in 1889, and re-elected in 1893. He was an active parliamentarian, a member of several standing committees of the Chamber of Deputies (and a rapporteur of the budget committee), the author of a number of proposals for legal and tax reform, and a talented and polemical orator.

Reinach unwittingly found himself in the eye of the political cyclone that devastated the French Parliament in the early 1890s, when the Panama scandal, in which his uncle and father-in-law Baron de Reinach was deeply implicated, was uncovered. That episode provides at least a partial explanation why such an eminent politician as Joseph Reinach never reached the upper rungs of the Third Republican ladder.

Dreyfus's 'admirable brother' (Reinach's phrase) Mathieu excepted, Reinach was the first Jew to intervene in favour of Dreyfus. As early as 1894 he personally but unsuccessfully appealed to his friend the President of the Republic to ensure that the military trial would not proceed in camera. From August 1896 onwards, Reinach tirelessly mobilized his political and personal contacts to campaign for a second trial; he wrote and held public meetings, all at considerable risk and personal cost to himself. He lost his seat in 1898, having been one of the very few candidates who dared mention Dreyfus in the electoral campaign; he was sacked from the French territorial army, and was prosecuted for libel. In 1899, within a few days of the infamous verdict of the Rennes court martial, he suggested that Dreyfus apply for a presidential pardon. Unlike Clemenceau, Reinach placed humanity above ideology, and understood that the hapless Dreyfus was mentally and physically too exhausted to take on more punishment for the sake of justice.

Reinach himself had exhausted his reserves of political energy. He spent his phenomenal mental energy continuing to write books, which he had done ever since he was 20. The work of lasting fame is his monumental *Histoire de l'Affaire Dreyfus*, in seven volumes, still one of the cornerstones of the historiography of the affair.

Reinach's career provides one of the most interesting examples of the life and opinions of a member of the French Jewish upper bourgeoisie. As an Opportunist, i.e. a moderate who advocated for France 'religious peace through tolerance and social peace through solidarity', he made enemies at both ends of the political spectrum. His campaign to curb the excessive freedoms granted to the press by the 1881 legislation was motivated by his revulsion against virulent articles aimed not only at Jews, but also at Catholic associations. He should also be remembered when accusations of cowardice are levelled at the Jewish community for distancing itself from Dreyfus. That which brought him opprobrium at the time, now stands as one of the best testimonials to his courage and perspicacity in the judgement of history.

Bibliography

Mentioned in virtually all books dealing with the Dreyfus affair, Joseph Reinach gets interesting notices in Jean-Denis Bredin, *L'Affaire* (Paris: Julliard, 1983); Douglas Johnson, *France and the Dreyfus Affair* (London: Blandford, 1966); and above all in Michael R. Marrus, *The Politics of Assimilation. A study of the French Jewish Community at the time of the Dreyfus Affair* (Oxford: Oxford University Press, 1971).

AM

REYNAUD, Paul (1878–1966)

Born in the Alps of a prosperous business family, Paul Reynaud was educated in Paris. He became a barrister, married the daughter of a leading Paris lawyer and entered parliament for the Basses-Alpes in 1919. Defeated in 1924, he was re-elected for Paris in 1928 and emerged as rising star of the right, his first appointment being as finance minister in the 1930 Tardieu (q.v.) government. He was then successively minister of colonies (1931) and of justice (1932) in two more right-wing governments. After the left's victory in 1932, he remained out of office until entering Daladier's (q.v.) government in 1938, first as minister of justice and then (from November 1938) as finance minister.

On 21 March 1940 he succeeded Daladier as premier. After France's military defeat he opposed the policy of seeking an armistice, and, feeling he had lost the support of his government, he resigned on 16 June to be succeeded by Marshal Pétain (q.v.). In September 1940 he was arrested by the Vichy government and (in November 1942) handed over to the Germans. After 1945 he resumed his political career in the Fourth Republic, becoming finance minister (for one month) in 1948, and vice-premier in the Laniel (q.v.) government of 1953–4. Although initially supporting de Gaulle's return to power in 1958, and chairing the consultative constitutional committee set up to examine the new constitution, Reynaud broke with de Gaulle in 1962, objecting to the introduction of universal suffrage for the presidential election. He was subsequently opposed, and defeated, by a Gaullist candidate at the 1962 parliamentary elections. This ended his political activity.

Although Reynaud's career stretches over three Republics, his life, like that of his younger British contemporary, Anthony Eden, is tragically overshadowed by the events of one year: in Reynaud's case, 1940 and the fall of France. When he became premier in 1940, many believed that France had found a new Clemenceau (q.v.). There were good reasons for this: in the 1930s Reynaud had been one of the rare conservatives to oppose appeasement: he supported sanctions against Mussolini's Abyssinian invasion, and came close to resigning from Daladier's government over Munich. He backed the idea of a Franco-Soviet treaty to resist Hitler, and, as a domestic corollary of this, favoured a national unity government including the left – at a time when most conservatives feared communism more than nazism. Since 1934 Reynaud was also the leading political advocate of de Gaulle's ideas on military reorganization. By the outbreak of war, Reynaud had therefore become alienated from many of his former political allies. This was one clue to his problems in 1940: to win a parliamentary majority he was forced to include in his government ministers who were hardly enthusiastic supporters of the war. Even so the government obtained a majority of only one vote.

Up to the German invasion of 10 May, Reynaud, as war premier, attempted to reinvigorate France's war effort, hoping, as it were, to play Churchill to Daladier's Chamberlain. On 28 March he signed an agreement with Britain forbidding either country to sign a separate peace: this was a source of much future recrimination. In reality, however, although his rhetoric was more pugnacious than Daladier's, Reynaud's war strategy was identical: to avoid a frontal attack on Germany while increasing the economic pressure on her. This was the purpose of the Norwegian expedition – to cut off German iron ore supplies – and of plans to bomb the Caucasus oilfields – to cut off German oil supplies. Although this second policy was rejected owing to well-founded British fears about alienating Russia, Reynaud, despite later protestations, was favourable to it.

But Reynaud, who bore no responsibility for French military planning before March 1940, cannot be blamed for France's collapse after the German invasion. He had indeed been about to replace the commander-in-chief, Gamelin, in whom he had no confidence. The controversy over 1940 concerns not so much Reynaud's handling of the war as his responsibility for the armistice: why did he resign on 16 June knowing that he would be succeeded by Pétain (whose lack of enthusiasm for the war was well known) rather than remain in government and continue resistance from abroad? However sincerely Reynaud wanted to keep France in the war, his actions frequently undermined that objective. First, in various cabinet reshuffles after 10 May, he appointed several notorious defeatists – for example, Paul Baudouin and Yves Bouthillier – to important posts. Such people actively sabotaged his policy of continued resistance. Some observers attributed these appointments to Reynaud's defeatist mistress, the Comtesse de Portes, and even if her influence has been exaggerated, she and other defeatists in Reynaud's entourage undoubtedly sapped his determination. Secondly, if Reynaud genuinely wished to fight on, why did he resign without first forcing a cabinet vote on whether to sue for an armistice? Later calculations showed a probable 14:9 majority *against* armistice negotiations, but the demoralized Reynaud seems not to have realized this. Later he claimed that numbers were not the central issue and

that he would not have been able to carry on if such leading figures as Pétain had resigned. Thirdly, however ardently Reynaud later claimed to have opposed an armistice, he displayed surprising indulgence to Pétain's government in its early days, even briefly accepting an ambassadorial posting to Washington, and disapproving of de Gaulle's first broadcasts from London.

In defence of Reynaud's intentions – if not his perspicacity – when he resigned he does seem to have believed that Pétain's government would find the armistice terms unacceptable thus making way for a Reynaud led government of resistance. Although this may have been self-delusion – a means of rationalizing weakness – other politicians harboured the same hope.

Ultimately, it seems that, although opposed to the signing of an armistice, Reynaud was only half-convinced this solution could be avoided, a position that put him, so to speak, mid-way between Pétain and de Gaulle. His behaviour during the last days of the Battle of France was thus characterized by extreme indecision. He was torn between his own active temperament and the defeatism of many of his advisers, between the firmness of de Gaulle (whom he had appointed secretary of state for war on 5 June) and the pessimism of his military counsellor Paul de Villelume, between ordering preparations to move the army to Algeria and telling the British that all was lost. Beneath his bombast Reynaud was weaker than many had suspected. And he lacked confidence in Britain's ability to resist after France's defeat: having failed to assume the mantle of Clemenceau in May, he passed over the chance to anticipate de Gaulle in June.

Reynaud's failure in 1940 should not entirely obscure the rest of his career. He was one of the ablest politicians of his generation, although always a maverick. His background itself was unusual. The Alpine village where he was born had a tradition of emigration to Mexico. Reynaud's father was an example of this: having made a fortune in Mexico, he returned to France in 1875, the year in which the Third Republic was founded. Reynaud's father was a typical product of the conservative provincial bourgeoisie on which that Republic was built, and Reynaud himself remained faithful to this political tradition throughout his life. His first book was a eulogy of the moderate Republican Waldeck-Rousseau (q.v.). Being born into a family with extensive contacts outside France – his father continued to spend much time in Mexico – Reynaud was more open to the outside world than many of his Third Republic contemporaries. He was an inveterate traveller and spoke good English: a long trip to America in 1932 was to make him more sympathetic to Roosevelt's policies than any other French conservative.

In the inter-war years Reynaud was a member of the centre-right Alliance Démocratique. But conservative politicians in this period relied less on the support of a party than on networks of local influence. Reynaud's career did not fit this pattern; both as a deputy for Paris between the wars and then as deputy for the Nord after 1945, Reynaud was essentially a carpet-bagger. Like the conservative politician Henri de Kerillis (q.v.), to whom he was close, Reynaud believed that France needed an organized conservative party firmly anchored to the right of centre: France should adopt a two-party system on the Anglo-Saxon model.

But in the 1930s Reynaud adopted a number of unpopular policies which precluded his playing any central role even if such a political realignment had occurred. It was Reynaud's advocacy, between 1934 and 1936, of devaluation, as a remedy to the depression, which turned him into a political pariah. Although devaluation was a minimum prerequisite of French economic recovery, the opposition to it was hysterical: Reynaud's family even received death threats. Although accused of propounding immorality, inflation and monetary collapse, Reynaud claimed, with reason, to be offering a rational conservatism, saving a bourgeoisie wedded to the sanctity of the franc from the consequences of its blindness.

Unfortunately Reynaud was not an effective advocate of the causes he defended. Although a brilliant parliamentary debater, he repelled supporters by his ambition and self-importance. He disliked the backslapping camaraderie of the French parliament. His arrogance disguised a certain lack of self-confidence; possibly this derived from the diminutive stature of which he was very self-conscious (Mickey Mouse was one of his nicknames). Lacking effective party support, or a wide following in parliament, he was unable to compensate for this, like Poincaré (q.v.) or Pinay (q.v.), by popularity in the country at large. Thus much of the time Reynaud was confined to the role of political Cassandra.

After 1936 he partially rehabilitated himself on the right by attacking the economic policy of the Popular Front, and his appointment as finance minister in 1938 was rightly seen as a victory for *laissez-faire* economics. The centre-piece of Reynaud's policy was the ending of the forty-hour week to allow an increase in industrial production, especially armaments, and to win the confidence of investors, thereby encouraging a return of expatriated capital. This policy was brilliantly successful: the government found no difficulty in raising funds for rearmament, gold reserves increased, and industrial production went up. This achievement, however, occurred at the cost of antagonizing labour: on the eve of the war France was more divided than ever.

As wartime finance minister the liberal Reynaud was not afraid to resort to *dirigiste* controls on consumption in order to avoid inflation. Keynes' *How to Pay For The War* (1940) pays tribute to the financial management of the French war economy which, he claimed, went further than he would have dared hope of the British chancellor; Reynaud in fact wanted to go further. Jean Monnet (q.v.), negotiating the purchase of American planes for the Allies between 1938 and 1940, felt that Reynaud was too cautious as finance minister in his stewardship of France's finances. But the tension between Reynaud and Monnet really derived from a lack of clarity about respective delimitations of responsibility. Most would agree that Reynaud was a successful finance minister.

Even if Reynaud's reputation never totally recovered after 1940, during the Fourth Republic he remained quite an influential conservative politician (he was president of the powerful parliamentary Finance Commission for eleven years). He became an ardent supporter of European unity, was liberal on decolonization, and from 1953 argued for constitutional reform to strengthen the executive. It was the two latter causes which led him to support de Gaulle's return to power. But, besides his growing opposition to de Gaulle's European and anti-Atlanticist policies, he could not accept what seemed to him the Bonapartism of de Gaulle's directly elected presidency.

Reynaud's relationship to Gaullism is emblematic of his whole political temperament. He had been a patron of de Gaulle in the 1930s: some of de Gaulle's closest political collaborators – Gaston Palewski (q.v.), Michel Debré (q.v.) – had first worked for Reynaud; Reynaud in his very person was therefore a bridge between traditional conservatism and Gaullism. And inasmuch as in his advocacy of a conservative party, of devaluation, of increased production, of decolonization, of constitutional reform, Reynaud had consistently stood in the camp of the modernizing right, there was much in Gaullism that might have appealed to him. But in the end Reynaud, like Pierre Mendès France (q.v.), remained faithful to the model of parliamentary republicanism with which he had grown up. The irony of his career is that he should have been so bad at playing by the rules of that system.

Bibliography

There is no biography of Reynaud in French or English. E. Demey, *Paul Reynaud, mon père* (Paris: Plon, 1980), by Reynaud's daughter by his second marriage, contains some useful information on his wartime imprisonment and post-war career. Reynaud wrote various tendentious versions of memoirs: *La France a sauvé L'Europe*, 2 vols (Paris: Flammarion, 1947); *Au coeur de la mêlée* (Paris: Flammarion, 1951); *Mémoires*, 2 vols (Paris: Flammarion, 1960, 1963). The second of these is translated as *In The Thick of the Fight* (London: Cassels; New York: Simon & Schuster, 1955).

JTJ

RIBOT, Alexandre Félix Joseph (1842–1923)

After a short career in the magistrature as an assistant public prosecutor (*substitut*) on the *tribunal de la Seine*, Ribot became a *conseiller d'état* (1875), an office which he resigned in 1877. He was elected as a centre-left Republican deputy for his native Saint Omer (Pas-de-Calais) in 1878, a position he was to hold, almost without a break, until 1909. In that year he became a senator, retaining this office until his death. In 1903 Ribot became a member of the Académie des sciences morales and, in 1906, was admitted to the Académie française. He produced a number of written works, notably a biography of Lord Erskine and his *Lettres à un ami: souvenirs de ma vie politique* were published in 1924.

Now a somewhat neglected figure, Ribot, from 1878 onwards, was to play an important role in the political life of the Third Republic. As deputy for Saint Omer from 1878–85 and again from 1887–1909, he distinguished himself as a genuinely gifted orator, whose eloquence perhaps contributed to the fall of Gambetta's ministry of 1881–2, or that of Ferry early in 1885.

Ribot had to wait until March 1890 and the fourth Freycinet government before capturing an important ministerial appointment, that of foreign minister. During the brief Loubet government which followed, Ribot retained the post and his major achievement during this period was, without doubt, the contribution he made to the setting-up of the Franco-Russian Alliance of 1892. In December of that year, Ribot himself headed a fragile administration which collapsed less than four months later, largely as a result of pressures exerted by the Panama canal scandal.

Ribot found himself at the head of a government again in 1895 and, during that year, aided by his foreign minister, Hanotaux, he made his mark on French colonial expansion by establishing a French protectorate in Madagascar, albeit after a rather costly campaign.

Ribot was *président du Conseil* on three further occasions, including a brief ministry at a critical stage of the First World War. Among Ribot's other important achievements were the part he played in helping Briand to draft the 1905 law on the separation of the church and the state and, as finance minister from 1914–17, the credit measures he brought in to help France's war effort: most notably, the *Bons de la défense nationale*.

There is no doubt that Ribot was a formidable, if not spectacular parliamentarian, who never seriously challenged the pre-eminence of some of his close contemporaries, such as Poincaré and Clemenceau, possibly even protecting the latter on occasions. Until he withdrew from active involvement in political life, late in 1917, Ribot laboured to impose his moderate Republican views on a regime under constant threat, in the early part of his career, first from the right and then from the left. Boulangist fever, stoked up by nationalists intent on forcing constitutional reform and rampant anticlericalism were both equally unacceptable to him. His belief in the ultimate efficacy of parliament and his insistence on conciliation, compromise and consensus, point to the possible influence of Anglo-Saxon models. An early admiration for Tocqueville and a visit to the United States in 1886, during a brief lull in his career as deputy, were clearly important factors here.

Bibliography

A.S. Kanya-Forstner's 'French African policy and the Anglo-French Agreement of 5 August 1890' (*Journal of Contemporary History*, vol. 12, no. 4, 1969, pp. 628–50) includes some discussion of Ribot's contribution to French colonial expansion, while the fullest account available in English of Ribot's career is Martin E. Schmidt's *Alexandre Ribot: Odyssey of a liberal in the Third Republic* (The Hague: Martinus Nijhoff, 1974).

TAleVH

RIGOUT, Marcel (1928–)

Before becoming one of the four Communist ministers in 1981, Marcel Rigout was not well known, nor were his opinions accorded much attention. But Rigout is a long-serving Communist who joined the Young Communists when he was 15, was promoted into the secretariat of the Communist Union of Republican Youth in 1953 and was involved in demonstrations against the Algerian War in the late 1950s. He is a man of the Limousin area and his promotion within the PCF was very much a reflection of the importance of the Haute-Vienne Federation although he was also one of the beneficiaries of the clean out of Georges Guingoin's Resistance generation. In 1961 he was promoted substitute Central Committee member and in 1967 became deputy for Haute-Vienne. Though he was to be defeated in 1968, he won the seat in 1973 and in subsequent elections up to and including 1986. Rigout made some mark in the Assembly (where he shared the agriculture portfolio with André Lajoinie), but was more active in party politics, concentrating on the Haute-Vienne where he was councillor after 1970. He managed the regional Communist daily *L'Echo du Centre* (Limoges) and worked in the Departmental and Regional Councils.

Rigout was minister for professional training in the second Mauroy government (1981–3) and then minister for employment in the third Mauroy government (March 1983 to July 1984). As a cabinet minister for three years Rigout did not make much of an impact, neither gaining the popularity of Fiterman (q.v.) nor committing the blunders of Jack Ralite but there were tributes to his ministerial competence. The Haute-Vienne is one of the most solid of French Communist Federations (Communists regularly polled over 30 per cent of the first ballot) and is dependent for its success on alliances with the Socialists; this fact probably explains Rigout's enthusiasm for participation in government and his willingness to take on the Employment Ministry in 1983 when the Socialists turned to an 'austerity' policy and abandoned attempts to reduce unemployment to 1 million.

In June 1984, after the European election setback for the PCF, Rigout made a widely reported speech which criticized both the disarray of the Party leadership and anti-Socialist views of hardliners. Rigout advocated staying on in government but the Party decided to pull out and (along with Pierre Juquin – (q.v.) and Felix Damette) he then emerged as a 'renovator', arguing for a more flexible strategy. This dissidence was formally expressed when the Haute-Vienne (along with Corse-du-Sud and Hautes-Alpes) amended the leadership motion to the 15th Congress in February 1985: Haute-Vienne called for a change in relations with Eastern Europe and the reform of democratic centralism and was implicitly critical of the leadership. Although Rigout managed his own Federation he emerged neither as a pamphleteer of the 'renovators', a job taken on by Juquin, nor as the organizer, a job taken on by nobody. The leadership isolated the Haute-Vienne, and Rigout, but the Federation was too important to be dissolved (like Finistère) or just ignored.

Rigout's Federation survived the 1986 elections, a small island of entropy in a collapsing Communist system, but with a vote reduced to 20.9 per cent. In his biography Rigout states that he is a 'lathe worker' but he has been a Communist functionary since 1953 and his future is bound up with a party over which he has little influence; a lack of influence tacitly recognized by a retreat into silence when the attempts to change the party line failed in 1986, and then by his resignation from the Central Committee in January 1987.

Bibliography

See Denis Jeambar, *Le P.C. dans la maison* (Paris: Calmann-Lévy, 1984) (chapter II is on Rigout in government) and Marcel Rigout, *L'Autre Chance* (Paris: Messidor, 1982). This last is prefaced by Pierre Mauroy and explains the philosophy of Rigout's Employment Ministry.

DSB

ROCARD, Michel Louis Léon (1930–)

Michel Rocard was educated at the Institut des Etudes Politiques in Paris and then at the prestigious Ecole Normale d'Administration, the breeding ground for so many members of the elite ranks of the upper civil service as well as for politicians of the main parties of the right and the left. After ENA, Rocard joined the Inspection des Finances, becoming, by 1965, the secretary-general of La Commission des Comptes et des Budgets Économiques de la Nation. His political career was pursued in tandem with his professional career, and, until the mid-1960s, he used the pseudonym Georges Servet in his political life.

Rocard's involvement in politics began in the mid-1950s when he was a student. He was National Secretary of the Association of Socialist Students (1955–6) which was allied to the Socialist Party (SFIO), but, like many of his generation, he split with the party over the Mollet government's Algerian policy. The SFIO's official support for de

Gaulle in 1958 saw many more defectors from the party. Rocard, on leaving the SFIO in that year, became a member of the new Autonomous Socialist Party (PSA) which, along with the Union des Gauches Socialistes, formed the Unified Socialist Party (PSU) in 1960. In the 1960s, Rocard was associated briefly with the Club Jean Moulin. He was National Secretary of the PSU between 1967 and 1973, the period in which he attained national prominence (within leftist circles he had already attained a certain name for himself at the 1966 Grenoble colloquium of what came to be seen as the 'new left').

Although he was not actively involved in the street fighting of 1968 (he was adamantly opposed to violence), Rocard became, in the aftermath of the student rebellion, the public and political, organizationally-expressed voice of that movement. His intelligence and moderate appearance, and the fact that he headed a significantly organized political force (unlike many of the student leaders), gave him a certain status. In 1967, at the age of 36, he was the youngest leader of an organized political party, and his image contrasted strongly with that of other, older, national leaders. This impression of youthfulness has remained with him throughout his political career.

Two electoral battles in 1969 took Rocard to even greater national prominence. In June 1969 he stood as the PSU candidate in the presidential elections, gaining 800,000 votes. In October of the same year, in a by-election in Les Yvelines, he stood against a Gaullist baron, Maurice Couve de Murville, and won. Although he stood as the PSU's candidate, he remained politically and personally associated with Les Yvelines after his departure from the PSU. He lost his parliamentary seat in the 1973 elections, but regained another Yvelines constituency as a PS candidate in 1978 (and held it in 1981, 1986 and 1988). In 1977 he became mayor of Conflans-St-Honorine.

By the time François Mitterrand took the leadership of the PS in 1971, it had become clear to many people including Rocard that the small think-tank, faction-riven PSU which, unlike the PS, had no strong social base, would not effect a rally of opinion around a new, modern socialism as it had hoped to do after its formation in 1960. For Rocard, it became a question of how and when to join the PS with the maximum advantage to himself and his PSU support. He worked for Mitterrand in the 1974 presidential elections, and joined the PS after the 'Assises du socialisme' of November 1974, which saw the reconciliation of the near-totality of the non-Communist left, divided since the late 1950s.

In the PS, Rocard's 'courant' represented the 'autogestionnaires' (a claim disputed by the left-wing CERES group led by J.-P. Chevènement), much of the left-wing Catholic tradition, many CFDT activists, and those from the PSU (about 40 per cent) who had followed Rocard into the PS.

Rocard's career since 1974 has been part of the history of the PS. He soon became the only serious rival to Mitterrand and, as such, he provoked a great deal of hostility among Mitterrand's supporters and other rival leaders (which often matched the hostility shown towards him by the French Communist Party). His strategy was always to gain the party's presidential candidacy and so become president of the Republic. His political fortunes, therefore, were tied, after 1974, to those of Mitterrand himself.

His politics followed two main and interrelated lines. Firstly, he represented the evolution of the new left, 'autogestionnaire' socialism towards a 'realist' social-democracy. Secondly, a personality politics grew up around him as the personification of his 'courant'. By the late 1970s and into the 1980s, he became, according to opinion polls, consistently the most popular politician in France, this a popularity which increased hostility towards him within the party, but which, nevertheless, the party could not ignore.

Rocard's public distancing from mainstream Socialist strategy and from Mitterrand's unquestioned leadership dates from the PCF/PS/MRG talks on the updating of the Common Programme of Government of 1972, in September 1977. Public knowledge of his disapproval of the PS's dependence upon the union of the left and of what he considered to be the Common Programme's unrealistic economic policy enhanced his status as the spokesperson for an alternative strategy. The left's failure to win the 1978 legislative elections enhanced his public standing further, especially after his post-election television broadcast, where he urged the left to accept its responsibility for the defeat, and used a form of address which subsequently developed into the 'parler vrai' style associated with his political image.

At the party's Metz Congress of 1979, his supporters ('courant') were voted out of the party's ruling majority. From this point he also had to contend with a younger generation of Mitterrandists (represented in particular by Laurent Fabius and Lionel Jospin) who had been promoted in part to counter the Rocard threat to Mitterrand. However, his extra-party support, the 'vital forces' ('forces vives'), as the Rocardians called them, remained strong, as did the support and sympathy he enjoyed not only from the CFDT but also from industry and the financial world.

In the name of party unity, Rocard was forced in 1980 to assert that he would not stand against Mitterrand in the presidential elections of 1981. Mitterrand gained the party's nomination and the presidency.

In the first Mauroy government, Rocard was minister of the plan (June 1981 to March 1983), and in March 1983 he became minister of agriculture. Both were relatively lowly ministerial posts, given his status in the Socialist movement and in the country at large. He resigned in April 1985 over his opposition to the Socialists' decision to introduce proportional representation for the 1986 legislative elections. This distancing from government allowed him to concentrate upon his presidential ambitions, and in June 1985 he let it be understood that he would be a presidential candidate in 1988. He also kept his distance from the mainstream of party life to the point where his activity during the 1986 legislative election campaign was considered minimal.

In the post-March 1986 period, which saw the return of the right to government, his continuing popularity meant that he remained the only serious Socialist contender for the presidency apart from Mitterrand. This situation was recognized at the party's Lille Congress in April 1987 where it became clear that, if Mitterrand did not run, Rocard would be the party's presidential candidate.

Rocard's influence on French Socialism has been significant, though often unacknowledged within his own party: the party's developing economic 'realism', its abandonment of its Marxist rhetoric, its distancing from the Communists, its orientation towards the political centre, all of these ideas, previously voiced by Rocard, were adopted by the party during and after its first period of office between 1981 and 1986.

It would be a mistake, however, to assume, as many observers have, that Michel Rocard represents only the pragmatic social-democracy of contemporary French Socialism (or a contemporary manifestation of Mendèsism). The early lyricism of self-managing ('autogestionnaire') Rocardianism evolved into an equally utopian treatment of the National Plan as both the means of attaining and a metaphor of an ideal society. The straight speaking ('parler vrai') style, moreover, projected not only a practical realism but also a morally-charged approach to politics. Both of these idealistic aspects of Rocardianism became an integral part of his personal philosophy and combined with the philosophy of economic soundness and realism to create a very specific public persona for Rocard. The moral aspect of his public image was developed throughout 1987 in the run-up to the 1988 presidential elections, where he represented himself as the guardian not only of a new social-democracy but also of the European humanist tradition.

Like most major political figures of the Fifth Republic, Rocard has responded to the logic imposed upon political activity by the Fifth Republic's institutions: the need to deploy a personal philosophy and highly personalized style, and to create a strong public image, and these within the context of a concerted attempt to mobilize a political party in order to gain the presidency of the Republic. One of the problems with this form of politics, however, is that, because the presidential factor is the organizing principle of political action, Rocard's political fortunes since 1969 have been tied almost exclusively to the presidential elections of 1969, 1974, 1981 and 1988, and, therefore, to the political fortunes of François Mitterrand.

In 1988, Mitterrand declared his candidacy for the presidency once again. Rocard again withdrew and kept a relatively low profile throughout the campaign. On 8 May 1988, Mitterrand regained the presidency with 54 per cent of the vote. Mitterrand's campaign placed great emphasis on an *ouverture* towards the centre. Two days after his victory, Mitterrand asked Rocard to form a government, thus conferring upon Rocard, at 58, a status which reflected his national popularity, confirmed his political legitimacy within modern French socialism, and which would enhance his national prominence still further and project his presidential aspirations towards the next presidential election.

Bibliography

Rocard, M. (1969), *Le PSU et l'avenir socialiste de la France*, Paris: Seuil.

Rocard, M. (1971), *Les Militants au PSU*, Paris: Editions Epi.

Rocard, M. (1973), *Le Marché commun contre l'Europe* (with B. Jaumont and D. Lenègre), Paris: Seuil.

Rocard, M. (1973), *Un député pour quoi faire?*, Paris: Syros.

Rocard, M. and J. Gallus (1975), *L'Inflation au coeur*, Paris: Gallimard.

Rocard, M. (1979), *Parler vrai*, Paris: Seuil.

Rocard, M. *et al.* (1979), *Qu'est-ce que la social-démocratie?*, Paris: Seuil.

Rocard, M. (1986), *A l'épreuve des faits: textes politiques, 1979–1985*, Paris: Seuil.

Rocard, M. (1987), *Le cœur à l'ouvrage*, Paris: Jacob.
See also:

Bensaïd, D. (1980), *L'Anti-Rocard ou les haillons de l'utopie*, Paris: La Brèche.

Evin, K. (1979), *Michel Rocard ou l'art du possible*, Paris: Simoen.

Hamon, H. and P. Rotman (1980), *L'Effet Rocard*, Paris: Stock.

Heurebise, G. (1983), *Michel Rocard vu par trois quotidiens nationaux: Le Figaro, L'Humanité, Le Monde*, Mémoire, Paris: Université de Paris X.

Pélissier, P. (1981), *L'Idéologie rocardienne: repérage et articulations des concepts fondamentaux*, Mémoire, Paris: Institut d'Etudes Politiques.

Rocard, M. (1987), *Au four et au moulin*, Paris: Albin Michel.

Schneider, R. (1987) *Michel Rocard*, Paris: Stock.

JG

de ROCHEBOUËT, Gaëtan de Grimaudet (1813–99)

General de Rochebouët was surely the most obscure and unsuccessful of the many heads of government of the Third Republic. A *polytechnicien*, he had an unremarkable military career which began under the July Monarchy and continued during the Second Republic, when he was noted for his conservative views. He took part in Louis-Napoleon's *coup d'état* of 2 December 1851, and was decorated for his services a few days afterwards. He was promoted to general of division in 1867, but held no prominent post during the War of 1870 or against the Commune. In January 1874 he was appointed by the Broglie government to the command of the 18th Army Corps at Bordeaux, no doubt because of his known monarchist sympathies.

He was to play his first – and unexpected – political role in 1877. On 16 May of that year, the president, Marshal de MacMahon, had dismissed the Republican government – the famous 'coup' of *seize mai* – installed a royalist ministry and dissolved the Chamber of Deputies. The ensuing elections in October, however, gave a sizeable majority to the Republicans. MacMahon, at a loss, summoned Rochebouët from Bordeaux to head a non-parliamentary caretaker government of officials, and he obediently took office on 23 November. This was a remarkably inept appointment given Rochebouët's past, for it was inevitably taken as evidence that MacMahon and his supporters intended to try a military coup. As this was not the case, one can only speculate that the president had preferred, in a crisis, to turn to a military man he knew well, and also, perhaps, that more suitable men had declined. The Chamber of Deputies immediately voted no confidence and refused to recognize the government. Rochebouët and his colleagues made minor military preparations to maintain order – for example sending telegrams in schoolboy code to military units putting them on the alert – which only made matters worse when the news leaked out. Rochebouët might have been willing to risk stronger measures, but MacMahon was far too prudent, and perhaps too honest, to attempt a *coup d'état*. With the Chamber refusing to vote funds, the government resigned on 12 December, after a semi-existence of less than three weeks. Rochebouët returned to his command at Bordeaux, and was placed on the reserve list in March 1878.

This farcical episode amply demonstrates how unable and indeed unwilling the French army was in the 1870s to play any political role in the absence of a clear lead from the divided parties of the right. Soldiers were called upon to be figureheads in the hope that they would symbolize patriotism and strength, but were far too unsure of their support within the army and outside it to heed promptings from the extreme right to overturn the new constitution and pursue the chimera of a monarchist restoration.

Bibliography

There is nothing written on Rochebouët in English, and little in French. The outlines are given in A. Robert, E. Bourloton and G. Cougny, *Dictionnaire des parlementaires français*, vol. 5 (Paris: Bourloton 1889–91) and there is some detail in Fresnette Pisani-Ferry, *Le Coup d'état manqué du 16 mai 1877* (Paris: Robert Laffont, 1965).

RT

ROCHEFORT, Marquis de Rochefort – Luçay, Victor ('Henri') (1830–1913)

Rochefort was one of the most startling, brutal and scurrilous pamphleteers of the Third Republic: his fanatical mien and his quiff of hair became familiar features in the caricatures of the late nineteenth century. His career was one of successive enthusiasms which he embraced one after the other with the shamelessness of Mr Toad: starting as a communard he ended as a nationalist extremist. Rochefort's talent for running different hares was allied to an undoubted talent for phrase-making and coining epithets which stuck.

Rochefort's entry on to the political scene came with glass-shattering effect when the Second Empire liberalized its press laws in 1868. The first issue of Rochefort's periodical *La Lanterne* started with the famous sentence 'France has, according to the Imperial Almanach, 36 million subjects, not counting the subjects of discontent'. A publication which was expected to have a restricted audience sold 120,000 copies and showed the limits of Bonapartist liberalism: Rochefort suffered spells in prison for the violation of press laws.

Rochefort fled to Belgium but was elected to the legislature in 1869. He used his parliamentary immunity to return to France and make speeches in which he declared that the empire of Louis-Napoleon was dismembering France and criticized the nullity of parliamentary debates. On the fall of the empire Rochefort became a member of Gambetta's government of national defence and then supported the communards, against the brutal reprisals of the Versailles government. As a result of this Rochefort was exiled, first to the Ile-de-Ré and then to New Caledonia. He returned to France after the amnesty of 1880.

In the late 1880s Rochefort was one of the most prominent activists in the Boulangist movement (he was on its governing committee) and put his formidable polemical talents at the service of General Boulanger (q.v.). It was Rochefort who called for Parisians to write in the name of the general at the by-election of May 1887 – 38,000 did so. Rochefort took a quasi-insurrectionary view, one which Boulanger himself eschewed, and he fled to London when he was condemned for libel (*contumace*).

After his return to France in 1895 he put his temperamental rebelliousness at the service of various causes. He was briefly involved with the Jaurès (q.v.) wing of the Socialists and was the conduit for Madame Demburg's gift of 100,000 francs to establish a workers cooperative glassworks in Jaurès' constituency. He was in his element with the discovery of various scandals. It was Rochefort who described the Republicans as 'Opportunists': not because they were 'opportunist' but because they said they would bring reforms when the time was opportune, i.e., riposted Rochefort, 'never'. He likened Charles Dupuy (q.v.) to 'a cow gazing at a passing train'.

The Dreyfus affair saw him turn on his recent allies and associate in a spectacular manner with his erstwhile enemies on the right, the monarchists and the clericals. The Dreyfus affair made clearer Rochefort's extreme nationalism and anti-Semitism, characteristics which had always been present in his writing. He used his journal *L'Intransigeant* for violent anti-Dreyfusard propaganda. He called Dreyfus the 'Judas of Devil's Island' and he claimed that a document in Dreyfus' hand had been annotated by the Kaiser himself. Similar nonsense led to a trial for libel against Joseph Reinach which was a curtain raiser to the trial of Emile Zola (q.v.). He also turned on Jaurès in a famous tirade in which *L'Intransigeant* accused him of being the 'mouthpiece of traitors'.

Rochefort's role in the Dreyfus affair was minor, and he was soon eclipsed by a new generation of extremist pamphleteers. It was his last campaign. Rochefort was a formidable adversary and a publicist of genius but a fanatical hater.

Bibliography

de Rochefort, H. (1868–9), *La Lanterne* (1st series) Paris-Brussels.

de Rochefort, H. (1874–6), *La Lanterne* (2nd series) Brussels-Geneva.

de Rochefort, H. (1880), *Napoleon dernier*, Paris: Librarie Anti-clerical.

Williams, R.L. (1976), *Le Prince des polémistes: Henri Rochefort*, Paris: Editions de Trevise.

Williams, R.L. (1966), *Henri Rochefort: Prince of the Gutter Press*, New York: Schreiber.

DSB

ROCHET, 'Waldeck' Emile Eugène (1905–83)

His baptismal register spoke of him pessimistically as Emile Eugène, but he left that behind with the other maladies of infancy, and his friends knew him under the front-name of Waldeck. His father, an artisan in the small village of Saint-Croix (Saône-et-Loire), gave him the name for which he is known in hommage to Waldeck-Rousseau: this name was not pronounced over the font.

At school Rochet seems to have been a promising pupil but at 17 he went to work in market gardening. Nothing of Waldeck's early career marked him out as the potential John XXIIIrd of French communism, in fact the reverse: he was typical of the young Communists who were promoted by the Comintern in the 1920s. In 1923 Waldeck Rochet moved into the Communist Party, having been an admirer of revolutionary syndicalism and of the Russian revolution; he joined when the party was in a deeply sectarian phase and in 1926 he was reprimanded by the military for political work and, in 1932, was given an eight-day prison sentence for picket-line violence. From 1930 to 1932 Waldeck Rochet attended the Comintern's Lenin School in Moscow (he was a PCF delegate to the 7th Comintern Congress in 1935). On return from Russia he became secretary-general of the Lyons region Communists and his ascent as part of the 'Thorez' group was steady: in 1936 he was elected deputy for Colombes (in the Paris red belt) and he also became an alternative member of the Central Committee in that year; in 1937 he became a full member and he started editing *La Terre*, the party journal for peasant farmers.

When, after the Hitler–Stalin pact in 1939, the French Communist Party was outlawed, Waldeck Rochet was one of the twenty-six party deputies condemned to five years in prison and interned in Algeria. Allied occupation of Algeria freed Waldeck Rochet and in November 1943 he was sent to London as the Communist representative to de Gaulle's French national liberation committee (of the united Resistance). In August 1944, at the liberation, Rochet returned to Paris, became head of the peasant farmers section of the party and resumed work on *La Terre*. Rochet was elected to the subsequent Assemblies for the Saône-et-Loire constituency from 1945 to 1958: for the Fifth Republic he was moved back to the Paris region and was elected for the Seine-Saint-Denis constituency until 1973. In 1945 he was made an alternative member of the Political Bureau and in 1959, at the 15th Congress, he joined the secretariat.

As head of the agricultural section Waldeck Rochet was not in the front line of the cold war although he did have to reaffirm the Party's commitment to ownership of land. The Lyssenko affair, which demanded that the Communists, in the name of 'proletarian science', defend the 'inheritance of acquired characteristics', did produce a famously fatuous article from Rochet (*L'Humanité*, 10 December 1948). In the 1950s Waldeck stuck close to Thorez although there were improbable rumours that he was conspiring against the leadership and it is quite likely that he was promoted as crown prince by Khrushchev. However, Rochet never went too far out from Thorez' ambit and carefully 'defended' Thorez in the 'Servin–Casanova affair'.

It is probable that Waldeck Rochet was moved by the Khrushchev secret report 'revealing' Stalin's crimes – he was one of the French delegation sent to enquire about it in Moscow. In public Waldeck's response was similar to Thorez' – that the French party had no responsibility – but he was probably pushing for 'change without risk' in private; according to *Le Monde* (4 April 1956) he clashed with Vermeersch (q.v.) about the line to take. Both Robrieux (in *La Secte*, Paris: Stock, 1985) and François Hincker (*Le Parti Communiste au carrefour*, Paris: Gallimard, 1981, pp. 52–80) agree that Waldeck Rochet was a genuine reformer although one who was waiting for the right moment.

Waldeck's time came when in 1961 he was made deputy secretary-general and then in May 1964 at the party's 17th Congress secretary-general. He inherited a policy of left unity (alliance with the Socialists) around a common manifesto from Thorez and his subsequent actions make sense in that light. Waldeck Rochet understood that the party's commitment to democracy would not be taken seriously unless they criticized repression in Russia (Aragon was licensed to criticize the trials of Russian dissidents Siniavsky and Daniel) and the Central Committee meeting at Argenteuil in March 1966 buried the party's crude constraint of the arts. Waldeck is supposed to have said that Argenteuil ended 'thirty years of sclerosis under Stalin', but it must be noted that the party – through Waldeck – still claimed sovereignty over the social sciences.

Although the Communist Party had been looking for an alliance with the Socialists since at least 1956, when they voted credits for the war in Algeria with this consideration uppermost, it largely fell to Waldeck Rochet to take the first practical measures. Rochet had to persuade the non-Communist left that an alliance was feasible and that Socialists would not be crushed by the dominating and much larger PCF. Waldeck set about wooing the Socialists (SFIO) and in this he was aided by his outgoing personality and his wide political contacts (often Resistance). The main step came in the party's promotion of Mitterrand as a united left candidate against de Gaulle in 1965 which led to a creditable first ballot vote and an unexpected run-off against General de Gaulle.

As the main, or perhaps only, substantial organization on the left the party gained activists and probably prestige from the 1965 campaign. It has, nevertheless, been criticized as a strategic error. Yet the party had very limited alternatives and the error, if error there was, was not perceived until much later. As a result of the 1965 campaign a joint manifesto was agreed with the Socialists in 1968 although the confusion of May 1968 and the Russian invasion of Czechoslovakia put an end to it. Thus Waldeck did briefly achieve the party's main aim and probably perceived the need to change the party as well. But

Waldeck was not a 'liquidationist' and for all his talk of democracy, liberty and the 'peaceful road to socialism' party functioning remained rigidly totalitarian. Many ex-Communists look back to Waldeck Rochet's leadership as the period when opportunities were available and being taken. Party loyalists look back to the time as one of the creation of a Frankenstein's monster of a unified non-Communist left. Waldeck was instructed to encourage intellectuals to justify the new line as early as 1961 – and gained a good many friendships in doing so – but it was left to the unfortunate Marchais to discover that the PCF had gambled all its resources and found that they still didn't cover the bet.

Yet the peaceful (if not exclusively parliamentary) road to power was impeccably orthodox. The same would be said of Waldeck Rochet's book (*L'Avenir du PCF*, Paris: Grasset, 1969) which was an elaboration of the 'Champigny manifesto' of December 1968. In this Waldeck Rochet outlined the party's policies for an 'advanced democracy' – the intermediate stage between capitalism and socialism which would permit a peaceful transition whilst safeguarding liberties, democracy and private property. This translated the theory of state monopoly capitalism, developed by Russian ideologists, to French conditions.

During the 1960s Waldeck Rochet made frequent visits to Moscow and often met Russian leaders. In March 1966 he gave a speech to the 23rd CPSU Congress and in November 1967 spoke of the French delegation at the fiftieth anniversary of the Russian Revolution. A rift with Moscow did open up with the Russian invasion of Czechoslovakia: Waldeck immediately expressed 'surprise and reprobation' but within a week the party was backtracking and later disowned Roger Garaudy's criticisms of Russian behaviour. The tension between the party's domestic strategy (of alliance with the Socialists) and its unconditional loyalty to Moscow became acute and was resolved, eventually, in the traditional manner – the party supported 'normalization' in Czechoslovakia. One account of the attempt Waldeck Rochet made to mediate between Moscow and Prague is given in Kanapa's notes (*Kremlin PCF* by J. Fabien, Paris: Oliver Orban, 1984) but neither Waldeck nor the French party came out of these at all well. Moreover, they show a timid and hesitant Waldeck repeating the Soviet view and putting reservations in most guarded terms, saying: 'extreme measures should be avoided if possible'.

In February 1969, whilst in Moscow, Waldeck Rochet suffered a severe health breakdown, the start of a long debilitating illness. The accounts of this are confusing and contradictory (particularly from the party) but leaving aside the more lurid speculations, Waldeck Rochet was re-elected secretary-general at the PCF 19th Congress in February 1970, became president of honour in 1972 (when Marchais became secretary-general) but was dropped from the Central Committee in 1976. It is likely that Waldeck was struck by a degenerative brain disease (he underwent surgery in Moscow and in Paris) but his exact state of health, and lucidity, are unknown after 1969.

Bibliography

There is a profile of Waldeck Rochet in P. Robrieux, *Histoire intérieur du parti communiste*, vol. 2 (Paris: Fayard, 1983), pp. 620–3 and some of his speeches (in translation) can be found in P. Lange and M. Vanicelli (eds), *The Communist Parties of France and Spain* (London: Unwin, 1981). These last, although important in a French communist context, are devoid of personality.

DSB

ROSSINOT, André (1945–)

Born the son of a rural primary school teacher in Briey (Lorraine), André Rossinot went to the Lycée Henri-Poincaré in Nancy before going on to Nancy medical school. At university Rossinot was active in the student union (to the detriment of his work), joined the European Federalist movement, and got involved in local citizens' associations, something which led him, bit by bit, into full-time politics.

Rossinot became a local councillor on the Nancy City Council, then led by the centrist Marcel Martin, and began, in 1969, to work in the university hospital as an ENT consultant. Jean-Jacques Servan-Schreiber (q.v.) had just won the Nancy by-election and was undertaking the Kennedyesque process of renovating the old Radical Party. In 1974 Rossinot, who had followed Servan-Schreiber's movement 'with interest', joined the Radical Party and started a club in Meurthe-et-Moselle. In 1974 a new mayor also took over (Claude Coulais) and Rossinot became second adjoint responsible for social affairs and head of the public housing department. In 1978 Rossinot was elected to Parliament for the third constituency against the former mayor (Pierre Weber) and in 1981 he was elected on the first round.

At the same time as Rossinot was building a local following he was rebuilding the national Radical Party, left at a loose end after the departure of

Servan-Schrieber. In 1979, aided by Didier Bariani, he became secretary-general of the Radicals and in 1983 president. Rossinot used the small party's position of balance to support Raymond Barre inside the UDF and started discussions with the Left Radicals (MRG) with a view to merging. In 1983 Claude Coulais decided not to stand again as mayor of Nancy and, under suspicion of having engineered the mayor's resignation, Rossinet took the head of a list composed of all the parties of the right then in opposition to the Socialists in the Assembly.

Rossinot became mayor and began to implement a consensus-style politics to cope with the city's slow decline. He also began to extend his influence in the region and the city. He continued with the fêtes, inaugurating and 'electoralist' events in the old tradition. The city, which had declined from 130,000 to 95,000 inhabitants, had severe social difficulties and a new dynamic was needed to rebuild the economy based once on coal – a declining industry.

Originally a supporter of Raymond Barre (q.v.) he changed sides in 1986 and supported Chirac (q.v.). In the 1986 Chirac government, Rossinot became minister for relations with Parliament and devoted himself to achieving a consensus around the government's programme. Rossinot's sympathy with the Gaullist Prime Minister Chirac's 'cohabitation' government and his *rapprochement* with the RPR undermined his position with Barre's supporters in the UDF. In 1988 Rossinot changed position and supported the UDF's candidate Raymond Barre for the presidential elections.

After 1959 a four-year limitation of tenure of the presidency of the Radicals was introduced (to avoid another Herriot) and in 1988 he tried to amend this to remain leader. This manoeuvre failed and Yves Galland became president. Rossinot is a gladhanding politician of the old school, an active, hail-fellow-well-met canvasser who personally embodies the old radicalism and who is a local politician from Nancy above all. He is a Freemason.

DSB

ROUDY, Yvette (1929–)

Yvette Roudy, whose place in history is guaranteed by her role as the first minister for women's rights in France, was born at Pessac in the Gironde, daughter of Joseph Saldou, a municipal employee and Jeanne Dicharry. Her working life began as a secretary in a fish-canning factory at the age of 16. After her marriage to Pierre Roudy, she spent several years in Glasgow where he was a teacher and she learned English well enough to translate several works including the influential *The Feminine Mystique* by Betty Friedan.

Roudy's political involvement began in the early 1960s, inspired by Colette Audry and Marie-Thérèse Eyquem with whom she participated in the Mouvement Démocratique Féminin (women's democratic movement), a women's political club of the non-Communist left. She was involved first in Mitterrand's Convention des Institutions Républicaines and then in the FGDS (Fédération de la Gauche Démocrate et Socialiste), an electoral coalition of the non-Communist left in the 1960s, which supported François Mitterrand after 1965. She has been a close supporter and colleague of François Mitterrand ever since. Her first attempt at winning a seat in the National Assembly met with resounding defeat and awoke her awareness of the masculine orientation – 'machisme' – of the left and her battle against the 'misogyny, inherited from Proudhon, that permeates the left'.

Roudy was elected to the European Parliament in 1979 and in 1981 entered Pierre Mauroy's cabinet as France's first minister for women's rights. Roudy was one of four ministers who kept her ministry throughout the Socialist legislature of 1981–6.

As minister, Yvette Roudy was responsible for a number of actions and reforms on behalf of women. Among the best known actions are the reimbursement of abortion by social security; the *loi Roudy* on equality at the workplace; programmes for training girls in science and technology; the commissions revizing images of women in school books; opening refuges for battered women; the status at last accorded to wives of agricultural workers; information centres set up all over France for women; financial support given to countless women's projects.

After the Socialist defeat of 16 March 1986, Yvette Roudy remained a Socialist deputy, but was no longer on the top Socialist Party committees. The Ministry for Women's Rights was abolished by Jacques Chirac's right-wing government and replaced by a delegation concerned with the condition of women; it has not subsequently been restored. Paradoxically, Roudy is much in demand abroad, and is still considered to be the voice of women's rights in France.

Bibliography

See Sîan Reynolds, 'Whatever happened to the Ministry of Women's Rights?' in *Modern and Contemporary France*, no. 33, March 1988; Yvette Roudy,

A Cause d'elles (Paris: Albin Michel, 1985); and *Les Femmes en France dans une société d'inégalités*, report to the Ministry of Women's Rights (Paris: Documentation Française, 1982).

CD

ROUVIER, Pierre Maurice (1842–1911)

A prominent politician in the Third Republic and a noted financial expert, Rouvier symbolized the close connection of the Republic with business interests. Entering politics in 1871, Rouvier became a follower of Gambetta (q.v.), and was minister of commerce in the one government which he formed, in 1881–2. Rouvier soon established a reputation in the economic field, and held the finance portfolio under several governments. This appeal to 'technical' experts – both as ministers and as chairmen of parliamentary committees – was a feature of Third Republic politics, and was one of the factors which counteracted the frequent changes of government. Also characteristic was the respect accorded, both by business interests and by the small property-owners who were such a large element in the electorate, to exponents of financial orthodoxy. Like Poincaré (q.v.) or Pinay (q.v.) in the twentieth century, Rouvier was a reassuring figure who stood for a balanced budget, low taxes, a sound currency and high returns on government stock.

Rouvier's wider political ambitions met with difficulties. As prime minister in 1887, he had to cope with the early stages of the Boulangist agitation, and his government fell because of the 'Wilson affair' – a scandal over the sale of decorations which involved the president of the Republic. In 1892 he was one of the deputies accused of corruption in the Panama scandal. He was forced to resign as a minister, but the case against him was eventually dismissed. He returned to office as minister of finance in the left-wing Combes (q.v.) government (1902–5). He then succeeded Combes as prime minister, and his government put through the final stages of the law separating Church and state.

Thus in political matters, Rouvier was fully committed to the cause of 'Republican defence', and his government also enacted the reduction of military service to two years, seen as a rebuff to the army after the Dreyfus affair. But it then had to confront the first Morocco crisis (1905–6), arising from the German challenge to French economic and political penetration of Morocco. The danger of war and the pressure of public opinion led Rouvier to dismiss Delcassé (q.v.) as foreign minister, and to take over this portfolio himself. The Algeciras conference which followed was a triumph for French diplomacy, though Rouvier had by then left office.

Rouvier's conciliatory policies towards Germany foreshadowed those of Caillaux. Both men had banking interests, and approached politics from the financial and business angle; but whereas Caillaux was a champion of income tax, Rouvier was faithful to older Republican traditions in resisting this radical measure.

RDA

ROYER, Jean-François (1921–)

Jean Royer is important on two counts: as a representative of old-style local notability whose influence resides in a network of local contacts and as the author of the 1973 'Royer Law' which promoted the rights of small shopkeepers. Royer was also an unsuccessful presidential candidate in 1974.

Royer is very much a figure of Tours and the Indre-et-Loire department. He was the son of school teachers, started a career in 1945 as a primary school teacher and taught in Tours for four years from 1954–8. His political career started in the Gaullist RPF of which he was departmental head from 1947 to 1951. When the RPF was dissolved by de Gaulle Royer did not rejoin a political party but usually the main formations of the right (Gaullist and UDF) did not put candidates up against him in the parliamentary elections of the Fifth Republic. In 1958 Royer was elected deputy, the following year he became mayor of Tours; and he was constantly re-elected to those positions through the 1960s, 1970s and 1980s. Royer made the Tours City Hall very much his own and it was as mayor that he made his mark with policies subsequently developed at a national level: the protection of small business and the crusade against 'pornography' (going so far as to use local powers to ban films). Royer also achieved impressive construction projects, normal for mayors at that time and, very unusually, the fusion of Tours with two neighbouring communes. Royer was a popular mayor regularly re-elected with 57–70 per cent of the vote (in 1977, his worst year, he polled 57.4 per cent and in 1983 64 per cent).

Royer's appointment as minister of commerce and small business by Pompidou in the reshuffle of 1972 came as surprise but was probably explained by the resurfacing of discontent among small shopkeepers. Poujade (q.v.) had fomented a similar discontent to destabilize the Fourth Republic and Gerard Nicoud was using a similar grievance in the early 1970s through the small shopkeepers association. Royer's principal act as minister was to barnstorm around the country reassuring the small business community and then to pilot a bill (*loi Royer*) which gave small shopkeepers a virtual majority on the local planning committees which decided on the allocation of land for supermarkets. The same law also allowed disaffected children to leave school at 14 if they went into a job-training scheme; this reflected Royer's educational background. Royer used threats of resignation to push his bill through the Assembly in 1973 against stiff opposition. Royer was transferred to the Ministry of Posts a few months before Pompidou's death but on this, his last ministerial position, he had no time to make an impact.

Royer resigned from the Messmer government in April 1974 and stood as a presidential candidate. This campaign was marked chiefly by an anti-permissive theme (the inheritance of an old lay tradition) and earned him the reputation of 'père-le-pudeur'. In an unpleasant incident an election meeting was invaded and one girl stripped to the waist: Royer emerged from the confrontation with wide publicity but with no dignity. The campaign was not a success: Royer polled a mere 808,825 votes (3.22 per cent) though the 33.8 per cent he obtained in Indre-et-Loire showed his local popularity. Royer remained an influential back-bencher in the 1970s and 1980s but devoted his time to the city of Tours.

Bibliography

Jouet, M. and J.-M. Marin (1975), *Jean Royer: Un réformisme autoritaire*, Paris: Notre Temps.

DSB

RUEFF, Jacques Léon (1896–1978)

Jacques Rueff was the foremost French advocate of economic liberalism of his generation and the first economist to be elected a member of the Academie française. Rueff was a distinguished product of the French elite educational system, a former student of the Ecole Polytechnique, schooled in the disciplines of economics and law, who successfully pursued several careers throughout his life.

Rueff's progress through the French establishment speaks volumes for his ability as well as for the variety of doors that can be opened to those who attain the exalted administrative rank of Inspecteur des Finances. In the 1920s he was drawn into Poincaré's cabinet before seeing service at the League of Nations. Four years as financial attaché at the French embassy in London preceded five years' service in the Trésor, ultimately as director. From the Finance Ministry, Rueff moved to the Banque de France as vice-governor for two years from 1939–41.

After the war Rueff became immersed in reparations issues among the Allied powers and then for ten years served as a judge at the European Court of Justice, first for the European Coal and Steel Community and later for all three European Communities.

Rueff's place in history is assured by two aspects of his life – his major achievements as an economic adviser to the French government and his seminal influence as a writer and advocate of liberal economics.

As a public servant Rueff played a crucial part in ensuring the successful transition of the French economy away from its traditionally protected character to a more open economy able to survive and grow within the newly-formed EEC. As a leading member of the committee of experts advising the government, he co-authored the Rueff-Pinay Plan of 1958. This called for higher taxes, higher public sector charges, high public investment and a 17½ per cent devaluation of the French franc, with the creation of the new Fifth Republic franc – the 'franc lourd'. Most of the plan was implemented and within eighteen months economic order and prosperity had been restored. In 1960 Rueff produced a further report which analysed the main rigidities in the economy which remained as obstacles to France's evidently rapid growth within the European Community environment.

Rueff could not resist entering economic debate at an academic as well as a practical level, and was no respecter of political sensitivities. For twenty years he taught at the Ecole Libre des Sciences Politiques in Paris, expounding the merits of market forces and criticizing France's protectionist and *dirigiste* policies. After the Second World War, Rueff was a keen advocate of full convertibility of the franc, and membership of the EEC.

Rueff's economic ideas received world-wide attention when in 1973 he published 'La réforme du système monétaire international'. This advocated a return to the gold standard as the basis of international monetary transactions. Rueff argued that as governments began to borrow abroad to finance consumption rather than investment, thus much stricter international monetary discipline was called for. The existing international monetary order was being undermined by excess dollars circulating as a reserve currency, and was conceived too much in the interests of the United States. Rueff's ideas did not find much favour outside France and even within France were rejected by liberals such as Raymond Barre (q.v.).

Bibliography

Rueff, J. (1949), *Epîtres aux dirigistes*, Paris: Gallimard.
Rueff, J. (1979), *La Réforme du système monétaire*, Paris: Plon.
Rueff, J. (1979), *Théorie monétaire*, 2 vols, Paris: Plon.
See also *The Times* obituary (25 April 1978).

ABP

S

SABIANI, Simon Pierre (1887–1956)

Hero of the First World War, founder of the Communist Party in Marseilles, premier adjoint and mayor of the city in all but name for four years, regional leader of the 'Fascist' Parti Populaire Français, leading collaborationist during the German occupation – Simon Sabiani's varied claims to fame reflect his unique personality and career. But his evolution from left to right and his type of patriotism, leading him into seemingly paradoxical acts of collaboration with the enemy, were not unique and therein, probably, resides his chief historical interest.

Born in a Corsican village in 1887, Sabiani emigrated to Marseilles in 1906 and led an unsettled life until the First World War, in which three of his brothers were killed and he himself lost an eye. In 1918 he entered Marseilles politics as an extensively decorated veteran and revolutionary socialist, and in 1920 joined the newly-created French Communist Party. He took poorly to Bolshevization, however, and left the party in 1923, continuing to hold local office as a left-wing apostate throughout the 1920s. Tactical alliances with the right won him election to the Chamber of Deputies in 1928 and 1932 and kept him in local office as deputy-mayor of Marseilles during a turbulent and scandal-ridden period in the city's history. After losing the mayoralty in 1935 and his deputy's seat in Marseilles in 1936 to the Socialist/Communist/Radical Popular Front it was no surprise that he joined Jacques Doriot's Parti Populaire Français (PPF) later in the year and devoted the rest of his career and life to an obsessive anti-communism which ultimately led him to give vocal support to the German occupiers during the war: he saw Stalin as a greater danger than Hitler. In 1942 his son was killed fighting alongside the Germans on the Russian front. He joined the exodus of French collaborators to Germany in 1944, and lived on in exile in South America and Spain, where he died in 1956.

During his years in office and even during the occupation Sabiani rendered many individual services to friends and clients, and to this day former friends recall his generosity. His foes recall his politics. Sabiani's language after 1936, like that of his 'chef' Doriot, often earned him the label 'Fascist', and although he was equivocal about the term, the PPF in which he so enthusiastically participated, it is arguably the closest approximation in French history to a mass Fascist party. Although he seems to have had little regular contact with the Germans, restricting his collaborationism to propaganda and ideological utterances, the PPF in his area degenerated into a rabble of blackmailers, bounty-hunters and German agents over whom he had little control but with whom his name is now indissolubly associated.

Bibliography

J.-A. Vaucoret, *Un Homme politique contesté: Simon Sabiani* (Aix-en-Provence: Université de Provence, 1979, unpublished doctoral thesis) and Paul Jankowski, *Communism and Collaboration: Simon Sabiani and politics in Marseille, 1919–1944* (London: Yale University Press, 1989).

PFJ

SALAN, Raoul Albin Louis (1899–1984)

A certain mystery, suggested by his nickname 'the Mandarin', always surrounded this man, elusive and perhaps rather uncertain of himself. General Salan was the most decorated officer in France, a professional soldier of great experience. He fought through the First World War, was injured in the Levant in 1921 and went to Indo-China in 1924. He became an expert in intelligence operations and subversion against the Italians in North Africa. This work took him to Dakar in 1942 and Algiers in 1943. By 1945 he was the youngest general with command in the French army. The Far East held particular attraction for Salan. He was involved in peace negotiations in 1945, and was on Marshal de Lattre de Tassigny's staff in the Indo-China war. He succeeded to the position of commander-in-chief in 1952 until the

French withdrawal in 1954. This serious, moderately left-wing Republican officer nevertheless became a leader of the insurrection in Algeria in May 1958, and in 1961–2 was plotting to overthrow the government of President de Gaulle.

Raoul Salan was appointed commander-in-chief in Algeria on 1 December 1956. He was initially unpopular among the 'colonists'. An attempt by the protagonists of French Algeria to assassinate him on 16 January 1957, killed one of his aides (the 'Bazooka Affair'). Within a year Salan had shown his ability with successful military operations. He was determined not to see the cause of French Algeria betrayed by the government in Paris. Salan was given full civil and military authority by the last two governments of the Fourth Republic. On 14 May 1958, he demanded the resignation of premier Pflimlin (q.v.). Despite his diffidence in public, Salan masterminded support for de Gaulle in Algeria. The return of de Gaulle brought Salan's appointment as delegate-general and commander-in-chief in Algeria. The harmony did not last; on 19 December 1958 Salan left Algeria for a less demanding post, president of the Old Soldiers' Association.

He retired to Spain in October 1960, where he began active work for French Algeria. Although he missed the planning, he arrived in Algiers for the April 'putsch' in 1961. After the failure of the operation he returned to Madrid where he was inolved in preparing the Organization of the Secret Army (OAS). This organization coordinated opposition to the negotiations for Algerian independence, and plotted de Gaulle's assassination. Salan's National Council for Resistance had some support in France; deputies debated the 'Salan amendment', to mobilize Algerian civilians. Divisions within the OAS and violence necessitated Salan's presence in Algeria. Disguised as a school inspector, he travelled there but was arrested on 20 April 1962. He vainly appealed for a stop to the violence. His trial ended with a life sentence which was amnestied on 14 July 1968.

Bibliography

B. Droz and E. Lever, *Histoire de la guerre d'Algérie* (Paris: Seuil, 1982) is a full, authoritative account; A. Horne, *A Savage War of Peace* (London: Macmillan, 1977) is the best account in English, not accurately up to date with the latest work; P. Montagnon, *La guerre d'Algérie* (Paris: Pygmalion, 1984) is a sharp account by a former officer, a participant in the events; and see also R. Salan, *Mémoires* (Paris: Presses de la Cité, 1972–4).

PS

SALENGRO, Roger Henri Charles (1890–1936)

Roger Salengro was born in Lille in 1890, and his political training-ground was the powerful *Nord* department federation of the Socialist Party where the influence of Jules Guesde (q.v.) was still strong. Salengro's career followed the classic path for a Third Republic politician, through the various echelons of local elected office to a seat in the Chamber of Deputies. By 1925 he was mayor of Lille, and three years later he was elected deputy for his home town. He retained the seat at the parliamentary elections of 1932, and again in 1936 when the Popular Front victory brought the Socialists into government for the first time. For a party that had never held power before, local administrative experience became a major qualification for ministerial office, and the mayor of Lille suddenly found himself raised to the key Ministry of the Interior. Salengro's new responsibility for public order was immediately put to the test by the mass sit-in strikes which had broken out in celebration of the Popular Front's election victory. Alongside Léon Blum, he was to play a crucial role in setting up the tripartite talks between government, unions and employers which were eventually to end the strikes and which produced the famous social reforms of the so-called 'Matignon agreements'.

Salengro is, however, remembered less for his achievements as a minister than for the circumstances of his death. The response of the extreme right to the Popular Front victory was a press campaign of hate and vilification laced with violent anti-Semitism, but the case of Salengro proves that all politicians of the left were legitimate targets, irrespective of their racial origins. In October 1936 the royalist *Action Française* and the weekly periodical *Gringoire* accused Salengro of having deserted to the enemy when serving as a dispatch rider in 1915, and of having been condemned to death in his absence by a court martial. Other conservative newspapers took up the charge, and some sections of the parliamentary right did not hesitate to exploit the affair against the government.

There appears to have been no substance in these allegations. Salengro had crossed enemy lines to recover the body of a friend, and had been captured. The charge brought before the court martial was one of indiscipline, not desertion. He was cleared of all suspicion by a commission of war veterans under General Gamelin, and was further exonerated in the 14 November debate in the Chamber of Deputies by 427 votes to 63. Significantly, two-thirds of the opposition deputies refused to associate themselves with the press campaign. However, Salengro, already depressed by the recent death of his wife, was not consoled by this rehabilitation of his honour, and he took his own life in his home in Lille on 18 November. His death is testimony to the violent polarization of French political conflict in the 1930s.

Bibliography

The main sources for the affair leading to his suicide are General Gamelin, *Servir*, 3 vols, vol 2: 1930–9 (Paris: Plon, 1947); L. Bodin and J. Touchard, *Front Populaire 1936* (Paris: A. Colin, 1961); J. Zay, *Souvenirs et solitude* (Paris: Julliard, 1945).

BJ

SANGNIER, François–Marie Marc (1873–1950)

A devout Catholic and staunch Republican, Marc Sangnier was an important precursor of Christian democracy in France. Born in Paris in 1873, he abandoned a career in the army to found the Sillon (the Furrow) in 1898 – a militant Catholic social movement devoted to the reconciliation of Church and Republic and the exposure of social injustice. This proved too radical for the Church and was disbanded by Pius X in 1910. Afterwards Sangnier attempted to keep its ideals alive through a political party, Jeune République (1912), and a youth organization, the Auberges de la Jeunesse (1930). But neither of these two bodies was to leave the same impression on the political and religious life of France as the Sillon.

Why the Sillon was to have such an impact was largely due to the boldness of Sangnier's message. His belief that Catholics should accept the Republic and work within its framework to transform society along Christian ideals was a brave one at a time when the institutional Church appeared an implacable opponent of democracy. Bold too were Sangnier's ideas on social questions. As well as seeking the reconciliation of Catholics and Republicans, he advocated the cooperation of workers and employers. Yet Sangnier never possessed a clear notion how to attain these goals, and the Sillon remained without a specific plan of action. Its dynamism was always more dependent on Sangnier's forceful personality than on his abilities as a theorist.

With his striking good looks and powerful oratory, Sangnier commanded a near total devotion among the adherents of the Sillon. Numbering no more than 5,000, these were largely drawn from the ranks of students and adolescents. Many were organized into a Young Guard, akin to modern Crusaders with their own uniforms and ritualistic ceremonies, charged with protecting the Sillon's meetings from disruption by right-wing extremists. But increasingly Sangnier experienced difficulties from his own supporters. His high-handed methods and unwillingness to tolerate rivals, alienated many who had first been captivated by his personal charm.

In turn, Sangnier's domineering personality has been blamed for his inability to convert the Sillon into a political party. Yet far more destructive was the opposition of the Church hierarchy. Following the separation of Church and state in 1905, few members of the French episcopate were willing to consider reconciliation with the Republic. Thus they were deeply suspicious of the Sillon, and tolerated it only as a social movement. When Sangnier considered transforming it into a political party, they became alarmed. So too did the Pope, Pius X, who would condemn the movement in 1910, fearful it was slipping out of clerical control into the political arena.

At the moment of its demise, the Sillon had accomplished little in practical terms. None the less, Sangnier had made a lasting contribution to Christian democracy in France. In unfavourable circumstances he had kept alive the idea that it was both possible and desirable to be a Christian and a democrat. This was an ideal he would never relinquish, not even during the darkest hours of the Vichy regime (1940–4) when most of the institutional Church rallied to the authoritarian government of Marshal Pétain. It was a fitting tribute, therefore, that in the more liberal atmosphere of post-war France the newly-formed Christian Democratic Party, Mouvement Républicain Populaire, would make Sangnier its honorary president.

Bibliography

J. Caron, *Le Sillon et la démocratie chrétienne, 1894–1910* (Paris: Plon, 1967) is a detailed study which is as much a biography of Sangnier's early life as a history of the Sillon; A. Dansette, *A Religious History of Modern France* (Freiburg: Herder, 1961) contains a useful chapter on Sangnier and the Sillon which helps to compensate for the absence of a biography in English; R.E.M. Irving, *Christian Democracy in France* (London: George Allen & Unwin, 1973) – the first chapter provides a succinct evaluation of Sangnier's contribution to Christian Democracy.

NA

SANGUINETTI, Alexandre (1913–81)

An Algerian settler (*pied noir*), born in Cairo, one of the most flamboyant Gaullists, Alexandre Sanguinetti was on the extreme right of the Gaullist movement and a hate-figure for the left. He was a Camelot du roi (Action Française) as a student but had an outstanding war record in the infantry, as a war prisoner then escapee, and officer with the French units in North Africa, Italy and Corsica. During the course of his wartime service he lost a leg.

Sanguinetti was not, at the outset, a Gaullist. In 1946 he entered the private office of the MRP minister, François de Menthon, but thereafter moved rapidly rightward and he became a colonial die-hard and a supporter of French Algeria as well as a Gaullist. He also became secretary-general of the Comité National des Anciens Combattants, the powerful veteran's association, which was linked to Algerian interests but which he persuaded to support de Gaulle. He was, with Roger Frey, one of the clandestine organizers of de Gaulle's return to power. Ironically he headed the Ministry of the Interior's attack on the French Algerian right-wing terrorist organization, the OAS.

Sanguinetti was elected deputy for Paris in 1962 and became a *rapporteur* for the defence estimates, but he became a minister for ex-servicemen later that year. In 1967 he was one of the four ministers defeated in the election. He then moved to Toulouse where he was elected in 1968. He used his seat in the Assembly to attack the students and to criticize Edgar Faure's education reforms which he refused to vote for. He also made his unhappiness about de Gaulle's attitude to Israel clear by leading a demonstration in November 1968.

Sanguinetti developed a dislike for Pompidou and his election as head of the Gaullist movement in October 1973 was a severe embarrassment to the president. He used his position as head of the UDR to conduct a war against Pompidou's supporters in support of Chaban-Delmas (q.v.). Sanguinetti was defeated by Alain Savary (q.v.) in the 1973 elections and when he moved back to Paris he was defeated in 1978 by Paul Quilès (q.v.). Sanguinetti led the inquest into the defeat of the Gaullists in the 1974 presidential elections and, as secretary-general was very hostile to Giscard d'Estaing. It was probably as a result of this intense dislike that he facilitated Chirac's takeover in 1974 and the transformation of the party into the RPR. He retained, throughout his political career, extensive business interests in a variety of companies.

Bibliography

Sanguinetti rates a mention in J. Charlot, *The Gaullist Phenomenon* (London: Unwin, 1970) and is mentioned in most histories of the Gaullist movement. Estier's book about the FGDS describes the 1967 election in which he defeated Sanguinetti but the portrait is radically hostile. See Claude Estier, *Journal d'un fédéré* (Paris: Fayard, 1970). For his views on military policy and strategy, see A. Sanguinetti, *Histoire du soldat* (Paris: Ramsay, 1979).

DSB

SARRAUT, Albert (1872–1962)

The son of Omer Sarraut, mayor of Carcassonne and a leading figure in Midi radicalism, Albert Sarraut entered politics young. First elected deputy for the Aude in 1902, he was continually re-elected until 1924 and then, after a two-year gap, entered the Senate where he would remain, still representing the Aude, until the end of the Third Republic.

His career rested on three major strengths – the powerful south-west Radical daily the *Dépêche de Toulouse* which was run by his brother Maurice; the Radical Federation of the Aude which he and his brother controlled; and the compact group of Radical parliamentarians from the south-west who owed their electoral position to the *Dépêche* and whose leader he was, initially in the Chamber and then in the Senate. In these circumstances, it is not surprising that Sarraut embarked early on a brilliant ministerial career that began in 1906 as junior minister of the interior in the governments of Sarrien (q.v.) and Clemenceau (q.v.) and was interrupted only by his two spells as governor-general of Indo-China between 1911 and 1914 and 1916 and 1919. He became a specialist on colonial questions and used his experience to publish *Grandeur et servitude coloniales* in 1931.

Sarraut was essentially a man of government, unquestionably 'Republican' in his principles but politically very moderate and thus quite happy to serve as minister of colonies in the right-wing governments of the Bloc National between 1920 and 1924. His position became more difficult in 1923 when the Radical Party broke with the government and in 1924 his decision to vote for the Poincaré (q.v.) decree laws led to his expulsion from the party and his decision not to stand for re-election in 1924. Yet his withdrawal was of short duration. Herriot (q.v.) was anxious not to offend the Sarrauts and appointed

Albert ambassador to Turkey. In 1926 he returned to France to become minister of the interior in the Poincaré government of national union. He stayed in his post until 1928, devoting much of his energy to the struggle against the French Communists whose anticolonialist and antimilitarist policies he detested. (In a speech at Constantine in 1928 he coined the famous phrase 'Communism is the real enemy' (Le Communisme, voilà l'ennemi).)

Henceforth Sarraut, who had been readmitted to the Radical Party in 1925, was a member of all the ministerial combinations in which the Radicals participated. In 1933 he became for the first time prime minister of a government which the left thought was too moderate and which succumbed to economic difficulties after only a month. He was again at the Interior Ministry in the post-6 February government of Doumergues (q.v.) but resigned in October, holding himself responsible for the assassination in Marseilles of the King of Yugoslavia and Louis Barthou (q.v.) the minister of foreign affairs. Barely a year later, however, he was once again, in January 1936, prime minster in succession to Laval (q.v.). His task was a limited one: to ensure the peaceful running of the elections at a time when the opposition between the right and the Popular Front meant that political passions ran high. It was thus without any real authority that he had in March to respond to Hitler's reoccupation of the Rhineland. His robust declaration ('We will not leave Strasbourg exposed to enemy cannons') and his own determination would be nullified by the High Command's refusal to engage in a 'gamble' and by the British rejection of any military riposte.

Sarraut was too conservative to be a member of Blum's (q.v.) first government but he was a minister of state in the Chautemps (q.v.) ministries of 1937–8 and in Blum's brief second government; and he was yet again interior minister under Daladier (q.v.) from April 1938 to March 1940. He voted full powers to Pétain (q.v.) in July 1940 but had very little to do with the Vichy regime, whose behaviour offended his Republican values. After the war, Sarraut sat in the Assembly of the French Union and became its president in 1951.

Bibliography

Bernstein, S. (1980–2), *Histoire du parti radical*, 2 vols, Paris: Presses de la Fondation Nationale des Sciences Politiques.

Lerner, H. (1978), *La Dépêche, journal de la démocratie: contribution à l'histoire du radicalisme en France sous la troisième république*, Le Mirail: Publications de l'Université de Toulouse (series A, vol. 35).

SB

SARRAUT, Maurice (1869–1943)

Unlike his younger brother Albert (q.v.), Maurice Sarraut avoided ministerial office and the political limelight; yet through his dominant role in the regional press of the south-west he became one of the most powerful figures in the later years of the Third Republic. Having joined the daily newspaper *Dépêche de Toulouse* in 1889 at the age of 20, three years later he was head of its Paris agency and his position became even stronger when he married the sister of its director, Arthur Huc. Sarraut played a major part in the expansion of the *Dépêche*, which had been founded in 1870 and which became enormously influential in the politics of south-western France. His father had been mayor of Carcassonne (Aude) and Maurice combined his press work with the organization of political radicalism in his home department. He was both founder (in 1903) and boss of the Aude Radical Federation and acquired such an ascendancy that in 1913, without even having posed his candidature (let alone running a campaign) he was elected senator for the Aude. Apart from war service, he spent the next nineteen years as a senator and, for all his avoidance of publicity, proved to be an assiduous participant in parliamentary affairs. Yet the *Dépêche* remained his real passion and the source of his power. In 1920 he became joint director of the newspaper and henceforth he exercised a near total, if hidden, control over the destinies of the Radical Party in the south-west, a region where it had had no serious rival. Maurice was perfectly content to let Albert enjoy the fruits of office which their privileged position gave them – he himself was content with the role of political conscience and mentor.

The Radical Party viewed Sarraut as an elder statesman (though he was only in his fifties) and it was as such that he became its president in 1926, after the row over Radical participation in the Poincaré (q.v.) government between Herriot (q.v.) and Caillaux (q.v.) and the party left. He made it clear that he accepted the presidency only to avoid a party split and that he would serve for only one year. In 1927 he handed over to Daladier (q.v.). He demonstrated his view of his priorities of radicalism – which he defined as centrism – by resigning his senate seat in 1932, when Huc died, to take over the direction of the *Dépêche*, a position he kept for the rest of his life. After 1936, however, his influence started to wane. His republicanism was of the traditional sort that refused to acknowledge the existence of enemies on the left. He was thus out of sympathy with the rise of a violent anti-Marxism among the younger Radicals of the south-west who came to advocate an alliance with the parliamentary right. In the tense politics of the late 1930s Sarraut seemed to the younger generation to be an out-of-date symbol of an out-of-date value system; it was as such that he was assassinated, in circumstances that remain mysterious, by the Vichy *milice* in December 1943.

Bibliography

Bernstein, S. (1980–2), *Histoire du parti Radical*, 2 vols, Paris: Presses de la Fondation Nationale des Sciences Politiques.

Lerner, H. (1978), *La Dépêche, journal de la démocratie: contribution à l'histoire du radicalisme en France sous la troisième république*, 2 vols, Le Mirail: Publications de l'Université de Toulouse (series A, vol. 35).

SB

SARRIEN, Jean-Marie Ferdinand (1840–1915)

Jean Sarrien was a second rank, but important, figure in the first forty years of the Third Republic. He built up an impregnable political position in his native Saône-et-Loire, was frequently a minister in the mid-1880s and became the influential leader of a parliamentary group, the *Gauche Radicale*, in the period of left-wing ascendancy in the early 1900s. Briefly prime minister in 1906, he is usually remembered for being the first man to dare to bring Clemenceau (q.v.) into government; students of the period contrast his lethargy with the aggressive dynamism of his minister of the interior who would succeed him as prime minister in October 1906. Yet his government contained as well as Clemenceau, six other future prime ministers of the Third Republic and Sarrien's lack of leadership qualities does not mean he was uninfluential.

He was born in Bourbon-Lancy in 1840, the son of a tanner, who was mayor of the commune. Having studied law in Paris and fought in the Franco-Prussian War, he returned home and became mayor on the death of his father. He had the correct Republican credentials; dismissed by the right from his town hall in 1873 and reintegrated in 1876, he was elected to the Chamber of Deputies the same year,

defeating a Bonapartist. Between April 1885 and April 1888 he held the Ministries of Posts, Justice and the Interior – and he was again at the Interior in the first wholly Radical government of Léon Bourgeois (q.v.) in 1895. At the height of the Dreyfus affair, his solid republicanism led him to take the justice portfolio in a Brisson (q.v.) ministry. It was the same quality that the new president, Fallières (q.v.), sought when he invited Sarrien to head a government of all the Republican talents to preside over the 1906 election. After the conflicts caused by the aggressive anticlericalism of the Combes (q.v.) government and by the separation of Church and state, a government that contained Poincaré (q.v.), Barthou (q.v.) and Leygues (q.v.) as well as Clemenceau (and did not contain any hardline *combists*) was a guarantee of moderation. In fact the election campaign was marked less by conflicts of the past than by the future – a miners' strike following a catastrophic pit disaster in Northern France and the threat of mass syndicalist violence on the 1 May.

It was Clemenceau, rather than Sarrien, who dealt with these problems and managed to stave off the sort of social conflict that might have helped the right. The election was a success for the Radicals (and the Socialists) and appeared to presage the arrival of the Radical Republic and in particular its programme of social reform. In an atmosphere of heightened political expectations, Clemenceau, the historic chief of radicalism, went round the country making inspirational speeches. There was no further place for Sarrien, who resigned in October. Shortly afterwards, in 1908, he entered the Senate where he stayed until his death in 1915.

Bibliography

Duroselle, J.-B. (1988), *Clemenceau*, Paris: Fayard.
Watson, D.R. (1974), *Georges Clemenceau, a Political Biography*, London: Eyre Methuen.

PM

SARTRE, Jean-Paul (1905–80)

Jean-Paul Sartre was born in Paris in 1905. After a lonely childhood, he attended schools in La Rochelle and Paris, before studying philosophy and becoming a philosophy teacher. In 1945, he gave up teaching for a full-time career as a writer.

His claim to have had no interest in politics in the early part of his career is belied by the strong note of hostility to the middle class in his first novel, *La*

Nausée (Nausea), in 1938, as well as in the uncompleted tetralogy *Les Chemins de la liberté* (*Paths of Freedom*, 1945–9). He became more overtly political in 1946 with his plea *Qu'est-ce que la littérature?* (*What is literature?*) for the writer to take sides on the issues of his day, automatically assuming that this would be on the left. His early existentialism, which he defined as 'the attempt to draw all possible conclusions from a consistently atheist position', gave way after 1952 to a greater sympathy with Marxism. The change is most obvious in the contrast between *L'Etre et le néant* (*Being and Nothingness*, 1943) and *La Critique de la raison dialectique* (*Critique of Dialectical Reason*, 1960). The second presents existentialism as a partial ideology which will be absorbed into the general truth of Marxism. His study of Flaubert, *L'Idiot de la famille* (*The Family Idiot*, 1971) tries to combine Marxism and existentialism. It is less readable than the 1946 essay on Baudelaire.

Sartre's plays are more obviously political than his novels. *Les Séquestrés d'Altona* (*The Damned of Altona*, 1959) uses the allegory of German history to attack French policy in Algeria, and the 1965 adaptation of Euripides's *The Trojan Woman* does the same for American involvement in Vietnam. He was very sympathetic to the student rebels in 1968 and to all wars of colonialist liberation, arguing that violence in this cause was fully justifiable. His concern for the relationship between literature and politics was shown in his brief autobiographical fragment, *Les Mots* (*Words*, 1963), which also has the advantage, especially in the early pages, of being very funny.

Sartre had an enormous following, especially among the young, who admired his total commitment to revolutionary values and activity. Whether he actually achieved anything politically is an open question, especially in the light of his fierce opposition to de Gaulle, the man who did in fact solve the Algerian problem. Ironically, his best plays – *Les Mains sales* (London: Methuen, 1963), *Crime Passionnel* (London: Methuen, 1961) – are a denunciation of Communist opportunism, and much of his work remained banned for a long time in the Soviet Union. His review *Les Temps Modernes* (1946–) nevertheless had a deep influence on the development of left-wing thought in France, and his lifetime association with Simone de Beauvoir enabled many of his ideas to be developed in more assimilable form in the women's movement.

Bibliography

Hayman, R. (1986), *Writing Against*, London: Weidenfeld & Nicolson.

PTh

SAUNIER-SEITÉ, Alice Louise (1925–)

Born 26 April 1925 at Saint-Jean-le-Centenier (Ardèche), Alice Saunier has been married twice, first to Elie-Jacques Picard in 1947 (the marriage produced two sons) and then to Jérome Seïté (deceased). She was educated at the Lycée de Tournon then at the Faculté des Lettres et des Sciences in Paris and the Ecole Nationale des Langues Orientales Vivantes. From 1958 to 1963 she was employed specializing in geography at the Centre National de la Recherche Scientifique (CNRS) then, after obtaining her *doctorat*, from 1963 to 1965 as lecturer in geography in the University of Rennes; then lecturer and later professor and dean at the Collège Littéraire Universitaire at Brest. Whilst at Rennes she was a member of the national committee of the CNRS. From 1970 to 1973 she was professor then director of the Institut Universitaire de Technologie at Sceaux. She was *recteur* of the *académie* of Rheims 1973–6; secretary of state for the universities 1976–7; minister for universities 1978–81; from 1981 onwards she worked at the Conservatoire des Arts et Métiers, Paris. She has been a member of a variety of organizations principally with a geographical orientation such as the Société des Explorateurs Français or the Institut Géographique and has received a multiplicity of honours from organizations at home such as the CNRS or the Société de Géographie de Paris; and abroad, for example, Camaroon, Ivory Coast, Egypt, Greece, Indonesia and Sweden. She has contributed to geographical publications and written *En première ligne* (1982), *Remettre l'état à sa place* (1984), *Une Europe à la carte* (1985).

Alice Saunier-Seïté is a unidimensional politician and that dimension is education. Her career was a textbook one of the able administrator who quickly moved ever upward through the ranks of higher education. Her time in the French cabinet was solely (if one excludes her very brief assumption of the role of secretary of state for 'la condition féminine' in 1981) concerned with higher education and she always saw her role as being exclusively in that area.

She has the distinction of being France's first female dean of faculty, *recteur* (of an education region) and also secretary of state (later minister) for the universities. She might have continued in the world of educational administration had she not met President Giscard d'Estaing by chance in October 1975. Thus she did not take up her next appointment as *recteur* in Corsica but entered Giscard's cabinet under the then prime minister, Jacques Chirac as secretary of state for universities being classed as belonging to the 'presidential majority', the euphemism for non-party members chosen personally by Giscard. She was promoted to minister in the January 1978 cabinet re-shuffle though by now Raymond Barre was prime minister. Her tenure only ended with the fall of Giscard from office in 1981.

Alice Saunier-Seïté's period in charge is best remembered for the firm hand of government vigorously shaking the universities by the scruff. Like René Haby, another *recteur* turned minister, Alice Saunier-Seïté knew the educational world from the inside and came to office with a clear idea of the direction she wished to move, and if the universities did not share her vision (they often did not) she was prepared to rely upon decree and forget consensus. Since all the important degrees and diplomas in France are validated by the state, the Ministry is in a strong position to make its feelings known. Mme Saunier-Seïté began her period in charge of the universities with a flying start by taking over her predecessor's plans for degree reform (in an attempt to make them more relevant) but if this made the universities uncomfortable, her withdrawal of validation for hundreds of courses had vice-chancellors up in arms. She was also intimately involved in moving the University of Paris VIII from Vincennes to Saint-Denis despite the vigorous protests of academia. In addition she introduced proposals to strengthen the position of senior staff on university councils (composed of representatives of all those working on a university site, plus some from the outside world) – seen by some as an attempt to return to the *mandarinat* of pre-1968 – and to tighten conditions of service for junior lecturers. Relations between the universities and the Ministry were frequently strained between 1976 and 1981. This probably had as much to do with Mme Saunier-Seïté's style as with the content of the reforms. Nevertheless her outspokenness (she was eminently quotable for newspapers), her vigour (and perhaps her good looks) went down well with the French public, particularly as the universities have not often enjoyed a good reputation with the French (in contrast to the selective system of *grandes écoles*). Demonstrations, for example, in protest against Ministry reforms by students and lecturers only reinforced the position of Mme Saunier-Seïté who often declared herself wary of laxity and left-wing influence in the university sector.

Bibliography

Articles on Alice Saunier-Seïté can be found in *Le Monde* (14 January 1976) and the *Times Higher Educational Supplement* (26 June 1981).

HDL

SAVARY, Alain François (1918–88)

Alain Savary's political career covered nearly half a century. Born in 1918, he became a wartime resistant and after the war held a number of important positions in the Fourth Republic. From 1951 to 1958, Savary represented Saint-Pierre-et-Miquelon in the National Assembly for the Socialist Party (SFIO), but he was frequently ill at ease with that organization. His consistent *Mendésiste* anticolonialism partly explained this. In February 1956, Savary became secretary of state for African and Moroccan affairs in the Republican Front government formed by the Socialist leader Guy Mollet. Despite the SFIO's anticolonialist rhetoric during the 1956 election campaign, Mollet's government adopted a tough attitude towards the Algerian nationalists fighting for their country's independence from France. By October 1956 Savary had resigned from Mollet's government on a question of anticolonialist principle (protesting against the hijacking by the French army of the Algerian nationalist leader, Ben Bella, an action which Mollet subsequently claimed as his own). In September 1958 Savary finally broke with the SFIO, since, unlike his former party, he refused to back either de Gaulle or his proposed constitution. He then helped form the Autonomous Socialist Party (PSA).

Never more than a marginal splinter group, Savary's PSA joined with other minor groups in 1960 to form the Unified Socialist party (PSU). Savary endured the faction-ridden PSU until 1963, when he quit the party and formed his own organization (Socialism and Democracy, which transformed itself into the UCRG in 1965). The UCRG refused to support François Mitterrand, the candidate backed by most left-wing organizations, in the 1965 presidential election, mainly because he distrusted Mitterrand as an opportunist. Although Savary's UCRG participated in Mitterrand's Federation of the Left (FGDS) from 1966 to 1968, it brought together those political clubs which remained suspicious of Mitterrand's intentions. After having failed to gain the Socialist nomination for the May 1969 presidential election, Savary succeeded in becoming first secretary of the new Socialist Party (PS) formed in July 1969, thanks to his alliance with Guy Mollet (the old SFIO leader from 1946 to 1969). Although most observers suspected that he remained subordinated to Mollet's control, it was under Savary's leadership from 1969 to 1971 that the Socialist Party's electoral fortunes and organizational strength began to revive. Savary was overturned as PS leader by Mitterrand in June

1971. Despite initially opposing Mitterrand, he rallied to the latter's leadership in 1973. However, Savary once again sided with the opposition to Mitterrand (led by Pierre Mauroy and Michel Rocard) at the 1979 PS Congress. From 1973 to 1981 Savary represented Toulouse North in the National Assembly, and was president of the Midi-Pyrénées Regional Council from 1974 to 1981.

In the final stage of his career, Savary served as education minister in the three Mauroy governments (May 1981 to July 1984). His educational reforms covered a broad spectrum of interests (universities, secondary schools, decentralization in education). His name is most commonly associated with the 1984 education bill. Under pressure from anticlerical PS deputies and teachers unions, this bill attempted to impose stricter public sector control over private (mainly religious) schools, especially in terms of funding and staffing. Although his bill would neither have abolished private schools, nor the right to a religious education (as some Socialists would have liked), it unleashed a massively unfavourable public reaction, and was promptly denounced by the right-wing opposition as an affront to liberty. Savary resigned as education minister on 14 July 1984, after President Mitterrand had announced his decision to shelve the proposed educational reforms without consulting his minister. That was indeed a cruel paradox: Savary had consistently advocated a moderate, consensual approach towards reforming the pivate schools, but – thanks to amendments passed by zealous PS backbenchers – he became associated by the public as the representative of a sectarian and uncompromising left. His political career never recovered and he died in February 1988.

For supporters, Savary's political career illustrated both moral commitment (over decolonization, or education) and a principled reformist stance; whereas for his critics he acted too impulsively, resigned too easily and lacked sufficient public stature ever fully to succeed in politics.

Bibliography

Cole, A.M. (1985), *Factionalism in the French Socialist Party*, Oxford: D. Phil thesis.

Lhomeau, J.-Y. (1988), 'Une Conscience de la gauche', *Le Monde*, 18 February.

Pfister, T. (1977), *Les Socialistes*, Paris: Albin Michel.

Savary, A. (1985), *En toute liberté*, Paris: Hachette.

AC

SAY, Léon Jean-Baptiste (1826–96)

Say was born in a well-known and distinguished family: his father had been a *conseiller d'état* and his grandfather was the political economist and free-trade publicist, Jean-Baptiste Say. An opponent of the Second Empire and critic of Baron Hausmann's management of Paris finances, Say was elected for the first time to the National Assembly in 1871 where he voted for the Treaty of Peace with Germany. The same year Thiers appointed him prefect of the Seine where he played a major role in remodelling the administration of Paris after the *Commune*. At the end of 1872 he entered the government of Adolphe Thiers as finance minister and was instrumental in successfully arranging the payment of the massive war indemnity to Germany. At the fall of Thiers in May 1873 he retired with him but resumed the finance portfolio in the Buffet administration, a post he held in various other cabinets between 1876 and 1882. Ambassador in London (1882) with the special mission of renewing the commercial treaty between the two countries, he left this post after a few weeks having been elected to the presidency of the Senate. Member of the Academie française, Professor of Political Economy at the Ecole Libre des Sciences Politiques, he was a regular contributor to the *Journal des Débats* (which he directed) and wrote extensively on economic matters. He also maintained a lifelong association with the Rothschilds, being a member of the board of directors of the Compagnie du Chemin de Fer du Nord as well as chairman of the French company of the Channel Tunnel.

The career of Léon Say is closely associated with the beginnings of the Third Republic and as such his activities from 1871 to 1890 encompass the life of parliamentary government in France during this period. As the member of the centre-left in the National Assembly he was a firm defender of the conservative Republic advocated by Thiers which he saw as the surest guarantee of order and peace after the crushing defeat of 1870 and the Commune. He therefore strenuously opposed all attempts by the de Broglie administrations to re-establish the monarchy. By birth and education he was a thorough liberal and a free trader (which made him a trusted friend of Britain and British statesmen like Gladstone) and he vigorously upheld throughout his life his free-trade beliefs against strong protectionists like Thiers. At the same time his prestige in international circles assured the financial stability of France in the first years of the Republic. As such he was regarded in the Assembly as the most influential adviser in regard to all financial matters. In his later term as finance minister he voiced his disapproval of the constant state of indebtedness of the Third Republic. Even if he recognized the need for government intervention to support public works his politics became increasingly anti-Socialist, seeing socialism as great a danger as protectionism and he looked with growing apprehension to the tide of new taxes and state expenditure which he denounced in a multitude of books, articles and lectures.

Bibliography

Michel, G. (1899), *Léon Say, sa vie, ses oeuvres*, Paris: Calmann-Lévy.

Valynseelee, J. (1971), *Les Say et leurs alliances*, Paris: private printing.

BS

SCHEURER-KESTNER, Auguste (1833–1899)

Scheurer-Kestner was born in Mulhouse, the son of a Protestant textile print manufacturer who was a disciple of Fourier. Much influenced by his father, Scheurer-Kestner studied chemistry in Paris and later on ran a chemicals factory, trying to introduce into it a system of workers' participation. He pursued his family's liberal tradition and was a declared opponent of the Second Empire, as a result of which he was arrested and jailed for a few months in 1862. From the beginning of the Franco-Prussian war he endeavoured to organize the defence of Alsace. Elected delegate from the Haut-Rhin department to the National Assembly in February 1871, he was one of 107 deputies who voted against the Frankfurt peace treaty and, leaving his native Alsace, he threw in his lot with France after the loss of Alsace-Lorraine to the German Empire.

Sympathetic to the cause of the Commune, he was denounced in a police report of June 1871 as one of those who had 'financed the uprising'. Returned to Parliament by the Seine department in July 1871, he soon joined Gambetta and others to found the Union Républicaine, later to become the Opportunist Party. A friend and close associate of Gambetta's, he partly financed and directed his newspaper *La République Française* from 1879 to 1884. His unblemished record as a committed Republican and the high degree of respect he widely enjoyed earned him in 1875 a seat as one of the eight 'left wing' out of the seventy-five life senators installed according to the provisions of the new constitution.

Very predictably Scheurer-Kestner vigorously opposed the reactionary 'government of the 16 May' 1877, and again about a decade later he denounced the dangers of Boulangism. His diligence as a high-ranking parliamentarian (he was elected vice-president of the Senate) and as a scientist (with a good list of publications to his name) and a businessman, also found a focus in his tireless endeavours to help the oppressed. Two examples of his devotion to just causes are the organization of a welfare committee for the persecuted Jews of Russia in the 1880s and his much more widely publicized campaign for the rehabilitation of Dreyfus.

Features which stand out in examining Scheurer-Kestner's role in the Dreyfus affair are his extreme conscientiousness in ascertaining facts and in keeping within the strict limits of legality, and his unshakeable devotion to Dreyfusism in the face of the most vicious aspersions on his own reputation. Approached first by Mathieu Dreyfus and later on by the Jewish publicist Bernard Lazare, Scheurer-Kestner undertook his own personal enquiry as to the circumstances of the court martial. Having become convinced by Dreyfus's innocence, he then conducted a private and a public campaign to obtain a revision of the trial. In vain he paid a visit to the president of the Republic Félix Faure who, embarrassed, dismissed him rather than discuss the case. A visit to another personal friend, Minister for War Billot, yielded no better results; and the less than discreet Billot allowed leaks to occur which generated a nasty press campaign denouncing Scheurer-Kestner's 'anti-patriotic manoeuvres'. By then, discretion was no longer relevant, and at the end of 1897 Scheurer-Kestner wrote a letter to *Le Temps*, in which he publicized proofs of Dreyfus's innocence. The judges' response was to acquit the prime suspect Esterhazy who was at the time standing trial, and the response of the politicians was to deprive Scheurer-Kestner of the vice-presidency of the Senate. The weight of Scheurer-Kestner's opinion, however, greatly strengthened the Dreyfusard camp, and influenced the Waldeck-Rousseau government in deciding to ask the Supreme Court of Appeal to quash the verdict. Scheurer-Kestner died on 19 September 1899, the very day when the then president of the Republic Emile Loubet signed the decree granting Dreyfus a pardon.

Scheurer-Kestner's involvement in the Dreyfus affair did not stop with his death. The Senate voted (by 181 to 29 votes) in July 1906 to erect a statue to its late vice-president in the Palais du Luxembourg, and that statue was later wilfully damaged by unrepentant anti-Dreyfusards.

Bibliography

As a major actor in the drama of the Dreyfus affair, Scheurer-Kestner is mentioned in all accounts of that drama, as well as in most histories of the Third Republic. Interesting comments can be found in Jean-Denis Bredin, *L'Affaire* (Paris: Julliard, 1983); Cécile Delhorbe, *L'Affaire Dreyfus et les écrivains français* (Paris: Victor Attinger, 1932); Douglas Johnson, *France and the Dreyfus Affair* (London: Blandford, 1966); Jean-Marie Mayeur and Madeleine Rebérioux, *The Third Republic from its Origins to the Great War, 1871–1914* (Cambridge: Cambridge University Press, 1984).

AM

SCHUMAN, Robert Jean–Baptiste Nicolas (1886–1963)

In the course of a long career in politics Robert Schuman held the highest offices of state in France but it is for the decisive impetus that he gave to the process of European integration that he is best remembered. Schuman's early life could scarcely have been more suited to instilling a 'European' outlook. Born in Luxembourg he grew up in Metz, then under German rule, and went on to study law at Bonn (alongside Konrad Adenauer), Munich and Berlin. On the return of Alsace Lorraine to France in 1918 Schuman entered French political life with the support of the influential de Wendel family and was elected deputy for the Moselle in 1919. In Parliament Schuman aligned himself with the Christian Democrat Parti Républicain Populaire and specialized in financial affairs. It was not until 1940, however, that a long-standing friendship with Paul Reynaud saw him appointed under-secretary of state for refugees in Reynaud's war cabinet. Schuman then briefly supported Pétain but quickly resigned from the Vichy government and went on to cultivate discreet links with the Resistance.

Having joined the newly constituted Mouvement Républicain Populaire and having been appointed to its National Bureau, he was re-elected for the Moselle in 1945. With the MRP constituting a key element in post-war coalition governments, Schuman rose rapidly to prominence, being appointed minister of finance by Bidault in 1946 and by Ramadier in 1947. Schuman pursued orthodox financial policies in combating inflation and the weakness of the franc but the divisions among these short-lived coalition governments afforded him little

opportunity to impose strict fiscal rectitude. Schuman's growing political stature and the constitution of the centre right 'Third Force' coalition excluding Communists on the left and Gaullists on the right resulted in his election to the premiership following the fall of Ramadier's government and from November 1947 to July 1948 his government battled against a continuing financial crisis and mounting industrial unrest. Schuman was on the right wing of the MRP, which was itself shifting to the right following the collapse of 'tripartism', which had linked Communists, Socialists and the MRP in post-war coalition governments. He took a hard line in the face of Communist militancy and the CGT-led general strike collapsed. It was in fact finally to be French fears over the re-emergence of a powerful Germany which led to the fall of his government.

Translated to a wider European context these two issues – the containment of communism and the place of Germany in Europe – were to dominate Schuman's career from then on since, from July 1948 to January 1953, in ten successive governments Schuman held the foreign affairs portfolio – a remarkable example of stability in the quicksand of Fourth Republic politics. French attempts to restrict German economic and military potential were clearly doomed as the United States and United Kingdom called for Germany to add its weight to the defence of Western Europe. The only alternative was to integrate West Germany into the framework of Western Europe so as to make renewed aggression against its neighbours impossible and also consolidate Western Europe against the Soviet threat. The federalist movement, which aimed at political integration, had failed and Schuman looked to economic integration. In May 1950 Jean Monnet (q.v.) of the French Planning Commission presented Schuman with a plan to merge the French and German coal and steel industries under a 'supranational' executive with the power to impose binding decisions on member governments. Schuman immediately adopted the plan which was to bear his name and tenaciously defended it against pressure from the United Kingdom and in bitter parliamentary debates. The eventual creation of the European Coal and Steel Community laid the foundations of the EEC. Schuman himself continued to pursue the goal of European integration and it was his close association with the yet more bitterly contested – and ultimately defeated – 'Pleven plan' for a European Defence Community which led to his departure from the Quai d'Orsay in 1953.

Schuman's political life, like that of his party, the MRP, was subject to the peculiar constraints of

Fourth Republic parliamentary politics. The need to compromise with coalition partners made it difficult for any party or politicians to pursue distinctive policies. The MRP in particular was often restricted to a negative role, exercising a restraining influence on partners of the left or right. However the MRP was distinguished by the fervour of its Europeanism springing from links with other Christian Democratic parties in Europe, a catholic universalism and a belief in a common European heritage characterized by an adherence to Western democratic and Christian values, which it saw as under threat from the extension of Soviet hegemony in Europe. For a brief period, following the exclusion of the PCF from government and before the resurgent nationalism of the classical right and the Gaullist movement asserted itself, there was a fragile consensus among parties of government in favour of European integration. Schuman seized the opportunity and exploited it to the full with a personal commitment born of his devout catholicism and personal experience of the transient nature of national frontiers.

Bibliography

C. Ledre, *Robert Schuman* (Paris: Spes, 1954), covers the essential part of Schuman's career as does the more recent R. Hostiou, *Robert Schuman et l'Europe* (Paris: CUJAS, 1969).

RobertT

SCHUMANN, Maurice (1911–   )

A politician, author and journalist, Schumann's loyalty to de Gaulle dates from June 1940 when he joined de Gaulle in London, where throughout the war he was to be de Gaulle's spokesman in the BBC broadcasts to occupied France (a selection of these broadcast messages was published in 1964 under the title *La Voix du couvre-feu*) (Voice of the curfew). Previously, in the 1930s, his first job had been as foreign affairs correspondent with the Havas Press Agency from where he was able to follow at close hand the rise of nazism in Germany and fascism in Italy (and to establish friendly relations with Anthony Eden); this early experience was to be crucial for his future political career as a foreign affairs specialist. At the same time, a Jewish convert to catholicism, he was an active member of the minuscule Christian Democrat Party Jeune République and, using a variety of pseudonyms (in order not to jeopardize his career with Havas), contributed art-

icles to the reviews of the progressive Dominican Order as well as to Francisque Gay's Christian Democrat *L'Aube*. He was an outspoken critic of the Munich agreement. Elected deputy for the Nord department in 1945, he has represented that area ever since (except, under the Fifth Republic, during his periods of ministerial office), until 1973 in the National Assembly and subsequently in the Senate. He was also in 1945 one of the founder members of the Christian Democrat Mouvement Républicain Populaire, MRP, its national president from 1945 to 1949, and subsequently its honorary president. He was a junior foreign affairs minister from 1951 to 1954 (the period of the European Defence Community negotiations). Appointed to ministerial office at the beginning of the Fifth Republic, he resigned – with his four MRP colleagues and only after heated debate within the party leadership – in protest at de Gaulle's 'anti-European' press conference of May 1962. It was not until 1967 that he received another ministerial appointment. From 1969 to 1973, during Pompidou's presidency, and at the time of the final negotiations for British entry to the EEC, he was foreign minister. He has also been for long periods chairman of the parliamentary foreign affairs committee. He was a leading member of Jacques Chirac's support committee in the 1988 presidential campaign.

In parallel with his political career, Maurice Schumann has pursued a successful literary career, publishing, in addition to works of more topical interest, a novel, a historical work, memoirs of the war period and several works reflecting his metaphysical and philosophical preoccupations. In 1974 he was elected to the Académie française, an election which seems more justified in terms of his literary talent than that of most other political members, past and present, of that august body.

Fidelity, loyalty, are two words often used in respect of Maurice Schumann, and it was he who, in 1945, coined the expression 'the party of fidelity' (to de Gaulle) to designate the MRP. Its loyalty was, however, to be short-lived, and Schumann can perhaps best be described in terms of a dual loyalty: to the historic figure of de Gaulle, whom he refuses to see either as a representative of the traditional French right or of Bonapartism, and to the Christian Democrat ideals of the 1930s, the political expression of a Christian humanism forged in the company of thinkers and writers such as Maritain, Mauriac, Daniel-Rops. Although Schumann himself admits to no contradiction between the two, this dual loyalty has not been without its problems. In office, under the Fourth Republic, Schumann and the MRP can hardly be said to have pursued relentlessly its generous aims of social justice, and, in the early years of the Fifth Republic (before its demise in 1965), the party was divided between those (including Schumann) who supported de Gaulle and Gaullist institutions and those in opposition. Schumann and de Gaulle differed over Europe, and it is perhaps significant that, in spite of his personal loyalty, Schumann did not enter into formal links with the Gaullist parliamentary group until 1967 and did not join the Gaullist party until 1974, after de Gaulle's resignation and death.

Although Schumann's effectiveness in ministerial office has been criticized, there can be no denying his gifts as a public speaker, his sincerity, energy, enthusiasm and affability, qualities which, in particular in foreign affairs during the Gaullist era, usefully served to soften the abrasiveness of some of the General's pronouncements. Although, as far as Europe is concerned, he has not maintained the maximalist or federalist stance he adopted at the early MRP congresses, he remains in the MRP tradition as a firm advocate of European Political Union, in which, however, for Schumann agreement on common policies should precede the creation of new institutions. For Schumann, the corner-stone of France's European policy, and indeed, perhaps, of French foreign policy in general, must remain the irreversibility of Franco-German reconciliation, embodied in the 1963 Treaty of Alliance between de Gaulle and Adenauer. In his preoccupation with the 'German problem' – the danger of German reunification and neutralization, the relationship between the Federal Republic and the United States – Schumann should perhaps be seen as typical of his generation, a generation that reached political maturity in the 1930s.

In the last resort, history may well judge Maurice Schumann (and his fellow ex-MRP Gaullists) on the extent to which they have been, and are able, to influence Gaullism from within.

Bibliography

None of Schumann's works has been translated into English. A sympathetic view of the man is to be found in Pierre Viansson-Ponté, *Les Gaullistes, rituel et annuaire* (Paris: Seuil, 1963). For Schumann and the MRP see: R.E.M. Irving, *Christian Democracy in Modern France* (London: George Allen & Unwin, 1962) and E.-F. Callot, *Le MRP, origine, structure, doctrine, programme et action politique* (Paris: M. Rivière, 1978). For Schumann and Gaullism, see J. Touchard, *Le Gaullisme (1940–1969)* (Paris: Seuil, 1978) and J. Charlot, *The Gaullist Phenomenon* (London: George Allen & Unwin, 1971).

HE

SÉGUIN, Philippe Daniel Alain (1943–)

Philippe Séguin is regarded as one of the rising stars of the Gaullist movement but is distinctly social democrat in orientation – a 'left-wing Gaullist'. Born in Tunis in 1943 the son of a school teacher, he trained as a teacher at the Ecole Normale in the Var but eventually chose an administrative career. He graduated from the Ecole Nationale d'Administration in 1970 and joined the Cour des Comptes. In 1973 he joined what was to be the nursery of so many *Chiraquien* ministers – President Pompidou's private staff. During the Giscard presidency he became in 1977 head of the office for R. Poncelet, minister responsible for relations with Parliament, and then, the same year a *chargé de mission* on the staff of the Prime Minister Raymond Barre. At the same time with the support of RPR leader Jacques Chirac, he was 'parachuted' into the constituency of Epinal, Vosges – a seat he won in 1978.

Up until the period of opposition, which began in 1981, one could have considered Séguin just another of the clever ENA graduates who made their way in politics through membership of ministerial staffs. However in opposition his real political qualities shone through. He was a highly effective parliamentarian, playing a leading role in the legislative battles over nationalization and decentralization. He was elected mayor of Epinal in 1983 and he became one of the regional notables which are such a feature of French political life. He was the first Gaullist to denounce any idea of an electoral deal with the National Front. He was the first to call for a moderate and responsible approach to the future coexistence of a centre-right majority with President Mitterrand, and to oppose blind systematic opposition to the Socialists. He was the first to remind Gaullists, during all their talk of 'liberalism', of their tradition of state intervention in economic affairs to promote industrial modernization and the national interest.

After the election victory of 1986, Séguin was given the very senior Ministry of Social Affairs and Employment, and was considered one of the most successful ministers in the Chirac government. In the parliamentary election of 1988, though President Mitterrand had 'won' the Epinal constituency and though the National Front called on their electors to oppose Séguin, he was narrowly re-elected. He emerged as the leader of the 'reformist' wing of the RPR and by 1988 was widely regarded as a future prime minister or president.

Bibliography

Séguin, P. (1983), *Réussir l'alternance: contre l'esprit de revanche* (Paris: Robert Laffont).
Séguin, P. (1989), *Force de convaincre* (Paris: Payot).
See also J. Fromentier, *Les Cadets de la droite* (Paris: Seuil, 1983).

JF

SÉGUY, Georges (1927–)

Séguy succeeded Benoît Frachon (q.v.) in 1967, general secretary of the Confédération Générale du Travail (CGT), the largest trade union confederation in France, a post he was to retain until 1982 when he was succeeded by Henri Krasucki (q.v.).

Séguy joined the Resistance in 1942 and two years later at the age of 16 he was arrested and sent to the Mauthausen concentration camp. After the war he worked as an electrician on the French railways (SNCF) and quickly became involved in trade union activities. By 1949 he was a member of the executive of the CGT Railwayworkers Union and he became its general secretary in 1961. In 1965 he was elected to the Bureau Confédéral, the executive body of the confederation itself and within two years he had become the general secretary. Parallel to this, he was an active member of the French Communist Party. In 1956 he was elected to its Central Committee and in 1964 he became a fully-fledged member of its Political Bureau. In fact the more prominent part of his life was to be spent in the trade union movement.

A year after he became general secretary, France was to experience an unprecedented level of strike activity, in the events of 16 May 1968, which caught the CGT somewhat unawares. Séguy headed the CGT delegation which participated in the negotiations between the trade unions, the employers and the government that led to an initial agreement on a number of issues, notably wage increases and the reinforcement of trade union rights. Although it was rejected by the workers in Renault factory in Boulogne-Billancourt, it provided the basis for further negotiations in each individual industry.

The failure of the events of 16 May to provide any long-term political alternative persuaded Séguy to campaign for the Union of the Left which was established in June 1972 when the French Communist

Party (PCF), the Socialist Party (PS) and the rump Mouvement des Radicaux de Gauche (MRG) signed the common programme of government. However when the Union of the Left broke up in September 1977, the ostensibly autonomous CGT openly blamed the Socialist Party and supported the French Communist Party; Séguy took part in an election rally on behalf of the PCF. This overt and blatant alignment of the CGT with the positions of the PCF was heavily criticized within the confederation.

The 1970s was to see a high level of agreement between the CGT and the Confédération Française Démocratique du Travail (CFDT). They often held similar views in terms of industrial demands and engaged in industrial conflict together, to an extent which had not occurred before or since.

At the 40th Conference held in Grenoble 1978, Séguy advocated a certain 'ouverture' which implied greater unity of action with the CFDT and a democratization of the internal workings of the CGT itself. However, this strategy was announced at a time when the PCF was becoming more sectarian. The spirit of the 40th Conference was to be disavowed and the CGT also entered a period of isolation within the trade union world. In the wake of these major changes, Séguy retired at the next conference in 1982, when he took over responsibility for the Institut d'Histoire Sociale, a small organization charged primarily with preserving the archives of the Confédération Générale du Travail.

Bibliography

There is no biography of Georges Séguy in English. He has written two autobiographical works, *Le Mai de la CGT* (Paris: Julliard, 1972) and *Lutter* (Paris: Stock, 1975). There is a short profile of him in the fourth volume of P. Robrieux, *Histoire intérieure du parti communiste* (Paris: Fayard, 1984).

JB

SELLIER, Henri Charles (1883–1943)

Born in Bourges, the son of a munitions worker, Henri Sellier became a scholarship boy and studied law in Paris before working first in a bank, then as a civil servant. At the same time he was both an active trade union official and a cooperative administrator. He was first elected to the Council of the Seine department (that is Greater Paris) in 1910, played a leading role in its pioneering activity in providing cheap housing (*habitations bon marché*), and became the Council's *rapporteur* and later chairman. In 1919, he was elected mayor of Suresnes on the western outskirts of Paris, which became experimental terrain for his ideal of a garden suburb run on Socialist principles. Originally a follower of Edouard Vaillant, he had joined the Socialist Party, the SFIO, on its foundation in 1905, and apart from a brief spell in the Young Communist Party after the 1920 split, he remained in the SFIO all his life. During the 1930s, he was in national politics for a while as senator from 1935, and as minister of health in Léon Blum's Popular Front government of 1936–7. He was one of the comparatively few Socialists who did not vote full powers to Marshal Pétain in July 1940. Dismissed as mayor of Suresnes by the Vichy regime in 1941, he died in 1943.

It is extraordinarily difficult to resume the varied career of Henri Sellier in a few lines. To describe it as devoted to municipal or welfare socialism is perhaps reductive, since Sellier was no stranger to theoretical debate and was always keen on international contacts. But he was one of the pioneers in France of what has been described as 'modernist social realism': a belief that socialism had to do with the better organization of everyday life – health, welfare, education, leisure – and with the rational ordering of urban services to that end. All this at a time when many Paris suburbs – *la zone* – were the scene of notorious poverty and chaos.

In all his indefatigable activity – whether shrewdly buying up land during the First World War for cheap housing, planning the garden city at Suresnes with its world-famous open-air school, or outlining a national programme of public health during the Popular Front, Sellier believed in applying modern technology and social science to concrete problems like infant mortality and the particular scourge of the inter-war period, tuberculosis. Not all of his thoroughgoing intervention was universally approved at the time or in retrospect: as health minister, he made many enemies with his attempt to clamp down on prostitution, and the garden city concept never became widely accepted in France; but the pioneering work of 'le Barbu', the enthusiastic and outspoken champion of public health, is now, after inexplicable historical neglect, beginning to be recognized, and Suresnes and the other *cités-jardins* round Paris are in a sense his monument.

Bibliography

There is nothing on Sellier in English and until recently Louis Boulonnois' contemporary account, *La Municipalité en service social. L'Oeuvre municipale*

d'Henri Sellier à Suresnes (Paris: Berger-Levrault, 1938) was the only full-length book in French. The recent collection of essays, edited by Katherine Burlen, *La Banlieue oasis, Henri Sellier et les cités-jardins 1900–1940* (Paris: Presses Universitaires de Vincennes, 1987), makes handsome amends, and contains a full bibliography of Sellier's own writings.

SR

SELLIER, Louis (1885–1978)

Although one of the founding members of the French Communist Party and briefly party secretary-general, Sellier is yet another of the many enthusiasts for the Russian revolution who fell victim to the internal battles in the Kremlin during the 1920s. Sellier was born in the small commune of Dorms in the Nièvre into a modest family (his father was a grocer). He joined the SFIO in 1909, and was elected councillor for the 18th *arrondissement* of Paris in 1914. However, in 1914 Sellier was mobilized and only returned to active politics in 1919 when he went along with the SFIO majority in favour of the Third International and at Tours supported the split to form the French Communist Party.

Sellier, and his ally Cachin (q.v.), belonged to the soft centre in the Communist Party, which was manipulated by Zinoviev, and Sellier's ascension began as the position of the party's first secretary-general – Frossard – weakened. Thus in March 1922 Sellier was promoted to the executive committee of the International (as the sectarian 'United Front' line was inaugurated) and in May 1922 participated in the Moscow committee meeting which condemned Frossard and the French leadership. Sellier was promoted to the directing committee of the French party at the 2nd Congress (in Paris) in October 1922 and was featured prominently in *L'Humanité* (praising the Russian regime). In December 1922, when Frossard was convoked to Moscow, Sellier and Treint (q.v.) became co-secretaries of the party and in January 1923 when Frossard resigned Sellier became interim secretary-general.

Although promoted to full secretary-general (flanked by Jean Cremet of the Young Communists and Georges Marrane ex-SFIO) at the party's 3rd (Lyons) Congress in January 1924, the 'colourless' Sellier was always dominated by the powerful tandem of 'Captain' Treint and (the 'backstairs Catherine the Great') Suzanne Girault who virtually ran the French party during these years. Thus the 'centrist' Sellier presided over the 'clear-out' of the party and the elimination of those suspected of potential 'Trotskyism': work accomplished with exemplary brutality by the fell 'Captain'. However, as the power balance in the Kremlin shifted and as Stalin promoted new cadres Sellier received condign punishment. In June 1924 the 5th Comintern Congress promoted Pierre Sémard (q.v.) to Sellier's post and on 12 August 1924 the French party Central Committee formally made Semard secretary-general. At the party's 4th Congress (Clichy) in January 1924 Sellier was again on the Political Bureau, but too closely associated with Treint who had been criticized by Moscow for the 'brutality' of the struggle against dissidents in the party: those who had supported Zinoviev were eliminated although at the Lille Congress of 1926 Sellier was put back on the Political Bureau.

As the party plunged into its ultra-sectarian 'class against class' phase – and as Stalin's appointees took the reins – Sellier, who had had no difficulties with the 'United Front' sectarianism, raised objections (along with Cachin – q.v. and Doriot – q.v.). Sellier wanted an alliance with the SFIO and led the so-called 'rightist opposition' to 'left sectarianism', that is to the violent demonstrations and the disastrous election results. On 15 November 1929 *L'Humanité* published a letter from Sellier and five other Paris councillors protesting against the party policy. A diatribe of mounting venom was then mounted by *L'Humanité* and 'the six' were excluded at the Saint-Denis Congress in 1929 (or had resigned already – it is not quite clear). Sellier and the others then founded the Parti Ouvrier et Paysan which, after various transmutations, became the radical left-wing Parti d'Unité Proletarienne (PUP). As a 'pupist' Sellier was elected – along with ten others – to the Assembly for the Paris 13th *arrondissement* defeating his old friend Cachin in 1932 and he was re-elected in 1936. In 1937 he rejoined the SFIO and three years later voted full powers for Pétain. He remained a city councillor through to 1944 (and was vice-president of the Council in 1943) and retired from active politics (a brief interlude excepted) at the liberation.

Bibliography

See Edward Mortimer, *The Rise of the French Communist Party 1920–1947* (London: Faber, 1984); M. Drachkovich, *Bibliographical Dictionary of Comintern* (Stanford, Cal.: Stanford University Press, 1973).

DSB

SÉMARD, Pierre (1887–1942)

Sémard, a railway worker, began his political career in the Confédération Général du Travail (CGT) railway workers' trades union in 1910, joined the Socialist Party (SFIO), rose to the executive committee of his union in 1916 and moved to the French Communist Party (PCF) after the Tours Congress in 1920. He became general secretary of his union in 1921 and continued in that post with the Confédération Général du Travail Unitaire when it broke from the CGT in 1922. In 1923 he was arrested during the protests against Poincaré's occupation of the Ruhr and then went to Moscow with a delegation from the PCF to hear Lenin's demand that they 'Bolshevize' the party. During this visit he made contacts with the Soviet leadership. He emerged as Moscow's choice for the party leadership during the damaging dispute between Albert Treint (q.v.) and Souvarine, which mirrored the Stalin, Trotsky, Zinoviev struggles. Thus it was that he became secretary-general of the party in 1924, a member of the Praesidium of the International and a trusted lieutenant of the Soviet leadership. In 1925 he managed to hold the party together during the turbulent national congress, but he had a difficult position between the older 'rightist' leaders, the 'leftists' and the younger, more radical generation. In the April 1929 Congress Sémard found that most of his 'old Bolshevik' colleagues had been eliminated from the Central Committee and his control over the Secretariat and Politbureau was badly weakened. He was arrested by the police at the secret Central Committee meeting in May 1929 as it was planning the general strike and demonstration of 1 August. Whilst Sémard was in gaol the younger leaders of the PCF, Thorez, Frachon, Barbé and Célor emerged and took power. Thus in 1930, Sémard was 'retired' to the directorship of *L'Humanité* and became secretary of the Paris regional committee.

Arrested by Daladier on the 19 October 1939, he was later handed over to the Germans by the French police. He was shot as a hostage on the 7 March 1942 at Evreux. In a letter to Duclos, smuggled out of prison just before his execution, he confirmed his unwavering belief in the future of the working class, in Marxism and in the French Communist Party. He was important to the Communist movement in France because he was one of the 'Bolshevik old guard' who took a central position in the 1920s and held together the factions of an increasingly weak and disorganized party, until his demotion in 1930. He represented the traditional French 'ouvriériste' tradition of Marxist socialism, which despite his re-education in Moscow, he never entirely lost. He was a simple man, whose emotional socialism appealed to his audience and whose career linked the PCF back to 1917 and the pre-First World War workers movement.

JCS

SEMBAT, Marcel Etienne (1862–1922)

Marcel Sembat, born on 19 October 1862 in Bonnières (Seine), came to socialism from a relatively comfortable family background. After obtaining his degree and doctorate from the Paris law faculty, he was called to the Bar but, after studying the works of French and English thinkers, he became involved instead in Socialist activity and journalism. Still in his early twenties, he made contact with activists involved with *La Revue Socialiste* before moving on to *La Petite République*, which he soon transformed into a Socialist paper. Sembat saw journalism as an important part of the struggle for socialism.

It was as an Independent Socialist that Sembat won his first election victory in 1893 (in Paris), but within the parliamentary Socialist group he moved closer to Edouard Vaillant and joined the Comité Central Révolutionnaire in 1895. His oratorical skills and intellectual powers quickly won him a leading place in the Socialist group. He was re-elected in 1898 on a Socialist platform (transformation of society and, in the shorter term, abolition of the Senate and of the presidency, nationalization of mines and monopolies, income tax, female emancipation). Again successful in 1902, this time as a Parti Socialiste de France candidate, was even more explicitly revolutionary-collectivist. He continued to be re-elected in 1906, 1910 and 1914 (at the first round, although with decreased majorities each time). An assiduous parliamentarian, he sat on various committees including those on income tax and the press laws. He took an active part in major debates on domestic and foreign policy.

Sembat remained close to Vaillant's position during the Dreyfus affair and the debate on ministerial participation, and after the parliamentary group split in two he was, with Vaillant, the leading spokesman for the Unité Socialiste Révolutionnaire group. He was, however, able to stay on reasonably good terms with other Socialist factions. He chaired several sessions at the first General Socialist Congress in 1899 and was present at the following congresses. In 1904–5, Sembat's support of the Combes government during the Russo-Japanese conflict won him

some criticism within his own party but brought him closer to other Socialist groups. At the Socialist Unity Congress in 1905, Sembat was thus seen as a bridging figure. He contributed regularly to *L'Humanité* from 1906 onwards. He moved closer to Jaurès and became one of the latter's most trusted supporters in the parliamentary group.

The approach of war placed Sembat in an awkward position. After the passage in 1913 of the three-year military service law, which he had vigorously combated in parliament, Sembat published a curiously-titled book (*Faites un roi, sinon, faites la paix*, Paris: E. Figuière et cie, 1913) which puzzled his Socialist colleagues but was acclaimed by the far right. In the book, Sembat tried to show that war and the Republic were incompatible. But when war broke out Sembat supported national defence and from August 1914 to December 1916 was minister for public works under Viviani and then Briand. The ideological problems caused by such a stance weakened somewhat Sembat's position within the party and it was with some hesitation that he stood on the Socialist list for the Seine in 1919 (although he was elected with an impressive score).

Sembat spoke out roundly against membership of the Third International, claiming that French socialism was closer to the English than to the Russian movement. After the split he stayed with the SFIO and was elected on to its decision-making bodies. However, ill-health forced him to retire from political life to convalesce in the mountains of Haute-Savoie, where he died suddenly in 1922. He was succeeded by only a few hours by his wife, the artist Georgette Agutte, who committed suicide.

Bibliography

In French, there are profiles of Sembat in: Victor Méric, 'Marcel Sembat', in *Coulisses et tréteaux. A travers la jungle politique et littéraire* (2nd series) (Paris: Librarie Valois, 1931), pp. 107–43; Jean Maitron, *Dictionnaire biographique du mouvement ouvrier français* (3rd part: 1871–1914) (Paris: Editions Ouvrières, 1973–7), vol. XV (1977), pp. 152–4. Sembat's own work *La Victoire en déroute* (Paris: Editions du Progrès, 1925), is an important account of socialism in the 1914–20 period.

SM

SENGHOR, Léopold Sédar (1906–)

Léopold Senghor was born in 1906 to a prosperous

Serer family in French West Africa. He was educated at a Catholic mission school near his birthplace in the predominantly Muslim area of Joal and at a seminary. He obtained his *baccalauréat* at a state secondary school in Dakar and was then awarded a scholarship to study literature in France. He prepared his examination to the Ecole Normale Supérieure at the prestigious Lycée Louis Le Grand in Paris where one of his best friends was the future president of the Fifth Republic, Georges Pompidou (q.v.). Graduating with a degree in African languages in 1931, Senghor became the first African to pass the highly competitive *agrégation* to enable him to teach in a *lycée*. He acquired French nationality and taught at secondary schools in Tours, and then in Paris. When the war broke out he joined the French army, and was captured by the Germans. After two years in a prisoner of war camp he returned to teaching but in 1945 decided to give up a purely academic career in order to enter politics. At the same time he emerged as a major poet with the publication in 1945 of his first volume *Chants d'Ombre* (Seuil).

Senghor was first elected a deputy to the Constituent Assembly in 1945 with the backing of the Socialist Party (SFIO) and of the senior Senegalese politician Lamine Guèye; he would remain a member of successive legislatures until 1958. Together with Alioune Diop he founded in 1947 the magazine *Présence Africaine* which became the advocate of the philosophy of 'negritude' (the term had been coined in the 1930s by the Martinique born Aimé Cesaire – q.v.). 'Negritude' sought to challenge French cultural assimilation and to emphasize the uniqueness of the values of Negro civilization.

Senghor broke with Lamine Guèye in 1948, established his own party, the Bloc Démocratique Sénégalais (BDS) which won sweeping electoral victories in Senegal. Senghor made successful appeals to the rural electorate, something which had been at the heart of his disagreement with Lamine Guèye. In a period when Houphouët-Boigny's (q.v.) Communist affiliated Rassemblement Démocratique Africain (RDA) faced increasing repression from the French colonial administration, Senghor's BDS was its chief rival and seemed likely to emerge as the leading force in French West Africa. But by 1955, when Senghor became a minister in Edgar Faure's (q.v.) government, the RDA had broken with the Communist Party and joined Mitterrand's (q.v.) centre grouping, the UDSR. In the 1956 elections, the RDA's new position enabled it to outdistance the BDS throughout West Africa, with the sole exception of Senegal. That same year Senghor fought in vain in the National Assembly to defeat the out-

line law for overseas France which he saw as a factor in the 'Balkanization' of the Dakar-based French West Africa Federation; the Federation was subsequently divided into autonomous territories. Despite this setback, Senghor continued, as pressure for independence increased, to fight for the creation of a political federation in West Africa. He was, however, unsuccessful and in 1960, after the breakup of a short-lived Federation with the French Sudan (now called Mali) Senghor became the first president of Senegal. In December 1981, after twenty-one years as head of state he took the unusual step of voluntarily retiring. He now lives in France and has been, since 1984, a member of the French Academy.

Bibliography

J.L. Huymans, *Léopold Sédar Senghor: An intellectual biography* (Edinburgh: Edinburgh University Press, 1971). On 'negritude' see 'Negritude and African socialism', in K. Kirkwood, *African Affairs: Number two*, St Anthony's Papers no. 15 (London: Chatto & Windus, 1963) pp. 9–22; L. Senghor's poetry is collected in *Poems* (Paris: Seuil, 1964); his lectures and essays are published in the four volumes of *Libertés*. These are: *Négritude et humanisme* (1964); *Nation et voie Africaine du socialisme* (1964); *Négritude et civilisation de l'universel* (1977); *Socialisme et planification* (1985) (Paris: Seuil). For L. Senghor's informative address to the French Academy, see *Le Monde* (30 March 1984).

DCB

'SERGE', Victor (Victor Kibalchich) (1890–1947)

Victor Serge was born in Brussels in 1890. His father, Léo Kibalchich, was a revolutionary tsarist officer on the run, his mother a Polish noblewoman. He died, stateless, in Mexico in 1947. Yet he is rightly included in this dictionary as his life embodies the fate and metamorphoses of the last heroic generation of French anarchism.

In 1908 Serge came to Paris as a pilgrim. He had already adopted the exalted existence of Kropotkinite communism. His Paris was Montmartre, where the visitors were Russian revolutionaries, not American tourists. Here, working-class individualism shaded into *La Vie bohème*, criminality and anarchism by deed. Serge befriended the famous criminal gang known as the *bande à Bonnot* whose acts of defiance were expiated by the guillotine. Their prophets had been Nietzsche and Elisée Reclus, not Marx. Serge was netted by the police as their accomplice in 1912, and released in 1917.

In 1917 began years of revolutionary wanderings under the pseudonym of Victor Serge. He left Paris for Barcelona in time to catch its Bakuninist uprising of June–July 1917 – its setback demonstrated to him the impossibility of a pure anarchist revolution and he returned to France intending to go to Russia. He had begun to identify the Soviets with the organization a revolution must have. He was placed in a concentration camp until the armistice. He reached Russia in January 1919.

Serge served in the siege of Leningrad and was affected to the Comintern under Zinoviev. But the inner anarchist never died. After the Kronstadt uprising, Serge became increasingly critical. A widespread, mistaken convention calls him a Trotskyist. Serge was really an 'anarchist-leaning' ally of the opposition. Like the Kronstadt rebels, he hoped to liberate the Soviets from Bolshevik control, a 'petty-bourgeois' deviation, according to Trotsky.

Serge was arrested in 1928. But he was released within a month, thanks to his French connections. The depth of his implantation in the French political community also proved the key to his subsequent destiny. Between 1928 and 1933, he published, in Paris, several works on the Russian Revolution. When he was re-imprisoned in 1933, a Paris-centred committee was formed on his behalf. Headed by the left Socialists Maurice and Magdaleine Paz, they recruited Romain Rolland and André Malraux. Serge was the one victim of Stalinism in Russia for whom a major left-wing campaign developed. His release in 1936 was Stalin's tribute to the 'Frenchness' of Serge and his significance for the Parisian intelligentsia.

When Serge returned west, he retraced the path from Brussels (April 1936) to Paris (June 1936). He was like a visitor from another planet. His prophecies of the impending destruction of European socialism only served to isolate him. Trotsky invited Serge to join the Fourth International, but he declined – he sensed a lack of revolutionary will in the Western proletariat. Once the Spanish Civil War began, he saw his role as saving as many as he could from the NKVD (Russian secret police). Working in close contact with the Pivertistes, he animated a defence committee which rescued several Socialists and especially the Spanish Partido Obrero de Unificación Marxista leaders in 1937–9.

In June 1940 Serge headed for Marseilles. As a French author of renown, he obtained a visa and managed to reach Mexico in 1941. Serge still dreamed of the eventual rebirth of European socialism, but he wished to see the defeat of nazism and the containment of Stalinism, in that order. He is buried as a posthumous Spanish national in the French cemetery in Mexico City.

Bibliography

His autobiography, *Memoirs of a Revolutionary 1901–1941* (Oxford: Oxford University Press, 1963), is prefaced with a biographical account by Peter Sedgwick. The 1957 French *Mémoires d'un révolutionnaire 1901–1941* (Paris: Club des Editeurs) has a portrait of Serge in Mexico by Julian Gorkin. His contacts with the French left in the 1930s are best covered by Jean Rabaut, *Tout est possible* (Paris: Denoël, 1974).

MK

SERVAN-SCHREIBER, Jean-Jacques (1924–)

For the best part of twenty-five years, Jean-Jacques Servan-Schreiber acted as an imaginative irritant in French politics. Though he was a member of parliament for only eight years and a minister for less than a fortnight, he was able, through his magazines, his books and his talent for publicity, to gain an audience for ideas that challenged prevailing orthodoxies of both right and left.

Servan-Schreiber came from a family of journalists. His father and uncle were co-owners of the financial daily *Les Echos* and his brothers, sisters and cousins have all been involved in the press. Educated during the occupation at the elite Ecole Polytechnique, he joined the Gaullists in Algeria via Spain and acquired considerable contempt for what he saw as the complacent Pétainism of most members of the French bourgeoisie. At the end of the war, he spent a period running a hotel in Brazil and then returned to France to become a foreign policy analyst for the influential daily, *Le Monde* (he opposed the organization of the Atlantic Alliance). In 1953 he founded the weekly magazine *L'Express*, which became the basis of his subsequent influence and the instrument for his ruthless dynamism. Enormously impressed by the ideas and unideological modernism of Mendès France (q.v.) he vigorously supported Mendès' attempts to break through the archaic party system of the French left. For a period he turned *L'Express* into a daily. The failure of Mendésism did not discourage Servan-Schreiber who wrote an account of his national service period in Algeria and then plunged into the anti-Gaullist politics of the Fifth Republic.

Impressed with American styles of political campaigning (though his most famous book warned against American domination of the European economy), he used *L'Express* to build up the candidature of Gaston Defferre (q.v.) ('Monsieur X') for the 1965 presidential election.

The campaign foundered on the entrenched hostilities of the parties of the centre and democratic left. Servan-Schreiber turned to writing and his book *The American Challenge* attracted great attention, both in France and elsewhere, for its urgent pleas for greater European cooperation against a menacing United States and for awareness of the emerging computer revolution. His political prospects were further strengthened by the discredit into which the non-Communist left fell as a result of 1968. In 1969 Maurice Faure (q.v.) invited him to take over the management of the Radical Party, whose very decay made it a potential instrument for his brand of dynamic reformism, as it had once been for Mendès France. Servan-Schreiber wrote a new manifesto for the party, rejuvenated its personnel and got himself elected deputy for a constituency in Meurthe-et-Moselle.

A constant critic of Gaullist themes of state and nation, he saw the future lying in regions and in Europe and continued to see himself as a man of the left. But he came up against the new dynamism of the orthodox left, symbolized by the common programme of the left agreed by the Communist and Socialist Parties; he also showed poor political judgement in a hopeless attempt to defeat Chaban-Delmas (q.v.) in a by-election in the latter's Bordeaux constituency. In 1973 he joined with the Christian Democrat leader Lecanuet (q.v.) in an autonomous electoral cartel called the Mouvement Réformateur. His action, however, had split the Radical Party (most of whose deputies relied on Socialist/Communist votes) and only four Radicals were elected under his banner in the 1973 elections. The following year, almost inevitably, he came out for Giscard d'Estaing (q.v.) who rewarded him by imposing him on Chirac (q.v.) as minister of reform. A characteristically impetuous criticism of France's nuclear weapon policy led to his almost immediate dismissal, to the great joy of the Gaullists who hated him. He was president of the Radical Party from 1971 to 1975 and again in 1977 and was influential in the creation of the Giscardian cartel, the Union Pour la Démocratie Française for the 1978 elections. He just held on to his own seat in 1978; but the election result was quashed by the Constitutional Council and he was soundly beaten in the subsequent by-election by a Socialist.

His political career seems over and in the 1970s he sold *L'Express* to Sir James Goldsmith. The Socialist government of Mauroy (q.v.), however, recognized his part in alerting France to the realities of the new world by appointing him president of a world committee for micro-computers.

Bibliography

Rioux, J.P. (1985), *Mendès et le mendésisme*, Paris: Fayard.

Servan-Schreiber, J.-J. (1968), *The American Challenge*, London: Hamish Hamilton.

Vajou, J.C. (1971), *J-JSS par J-JSS*, Paris: La Table Ronde.

PM

'SÉVERINE' Rémy, Caroline (1855–1929)

The only daughter of a postal worker, Séverine became the first professional woman journalist in France. After a disastrous marriage, which had been arranged by her parents, Séverine was ill-prepared for a career. Indeed she had no choice but to return to her parents' home where she had been given a strict upbringing with little formal schooling. Her great chance came when the communard and Socialist journalist, Jules Vallès, on his return from exile in 1880, employed her as his secretary and taught her all he knew about his trade and politics. Through her second marriage to a wealthy doctor she was able to help finance *Le Cri du Peuple*, a newspaper that had been begun under the Commune.

After the death of Vallès, Séverine attempted to continue the editorship of this Socialist paper, but was unable to prevent rifts and arguments among the activists involved, including Jules Guesde. Throughout the 1880s, like many Socialists, Séverine was highly critical of the conservative Republic and admired the Boulangist spirit, though she did not go as far as supporting Boulanger (q.v.). She opposed the Marxist tendency of Jules Guesde who left the *Cri du Peuple*.

Séverine herself gave up running the paper and took to professional journalism. From then on she wrote for a number of newspapers, not always on the left, including *Le Gil Blas* (fashionable), *Le Gaulois* (royalist), *Le Figaro*, *Paris-Soir*, *La Libre Parole* (anti-Semitic), *La Fronde* (feminist) to name but a few. At the same time she was a keen observer of politics, often an active participant, but not always a member of an organization or party. She preferred to have a free hand in politics just as she preferred being a freelance journalist. As a sympathizer, events forced her to participate and take sides, supporting strikes, anarchists and the Dreyfus family in their demand for justice. In fact Séverine lost a lot of work because of her position during the Dreyfus affair; she wrote a daily account of the retrial in Rennes for the feminist paper *La Fronde*, whereas it was a forbidden topic in others. It was her enthusiasm for the Russian Revolution which led her to become a member of the Communist Party for a very brief period, but in fact she was one of the first to be expelled. Her pacifist convictions led her to another public sphere: speaking at meetings during the war years and after, condemning the waste of human lives. She defended Hélène Brion, also a pacifist, at her trial.

Séverine's position on feminism altered somewhat during her career. At first she refused to have anything to do with any feminist organization and turned down the invitation to attend the Feminist Congress in 1892. She did take a stand on the right to abortion, having had the experience of two unwanted pregnancies. She was also vociferous on the question of the right to work and equal pay. Gradually, she recognized the weakness of the position of an individual in the struggle for emancipation, but she detested the parliamentary system so much that it was only in 1914 that she recognized the need for a suffrage movement. War interrupted the efforts of herself and Marguerite Durand to develop a suffrage campaign. She continued her work as a pacifist and libertarian Socialist defending the oppressed through her writings until her death.

Bibliography

Evelyne Le Garrec (ed.), *Séverine (du Cri du peuple à la Fronde)* (Paris: Editions Tierce, 1982) is an anthology of articles written by Séverine in the period from the 1880s to the end of the Dreyfus affair, preceded by a short biography. See also Bernard Lecache, *Séverine* (Paris: Gallimard, 1931) and Evelyne Le Garrec, *Séverine une rebelle (1855–1929)* (Paris: Seuil, 1982).

MCr

SIMON, Jules François Suisse, 'Simon' (1814–96)

Born in Lorient (Morbihan), Jules Simon (Suisse), was a student at the prestigious Ecole Normale Supérieure in Paris and a pupil of Victor Cousin. He taught philosophy at the Sorbonne in 1839, and it was at this time that Cousin suggested he change his name from Suisse to Simon. His political career began when he was elected deputy to the Constituent Assembly of 1848. When he refused to take an oath of fidelity to Napoleon III, he was suspended from holding office in a public institution. Philosophical and historical writings occupied Simon during the next few years. He narrowly failed to be re-elected in 1857, but was more successful in 1863. His social convictions found expression in a number of books including *L'Ouvrière* (1863), *Le Travail* (1866), and *L'Ouvrier de 8 ans* (1867).

Jules Simon was, with Jules Grévy and Jules Favre, a leading member of the Republican left during the last years of Empire, writing an eloquent plea for liberal representative institutions in *La Politique Radicale* in 1868. It was Simon who, as a member of the government of national defence, had the delicate task in February 1871 of negotiating with Gambetta's delegation at Bordeaux over elections and the negotiation of peace. In 1877, after the abrupt termination of his ministry, he was to turn for a time to journalism; he had been editor of the daily *Le Siècle* (1875–7) and was to direct the fortunes of the Legitimist daily *Le Gaulois* in 1881, turning it into an organ of moderate republicanism. While at the Education Ministry under Thiers (q.v.), Simon had advocated compulsory primary education, but he was a leading opponent of the Ferry education bill of 1879; his successful opposition in the Senate to the notorious Article 7 meant that the bill was eventually passed in a much diluted form. Hostile to Boulangism, against which he wrote *Souviens-toi du 2 décembre* (1889), he pursued an active career as politician and man of letters into his final years.

Elected a senator for life in 1875, when that body was overwhelmingly conservative, Simon was often distrusted, particularly when, on taking office in December 1876, he claimed to be 'profoundly Republican and profoundly conservative'. An orator to rival Gambetta, he seemed to some a clever and persuasive parliamentary tactician, to others, mealy-mouthed, even duplicitous. The ambiguity of his position was to be his downfall. Chosen, albeit reluctantly, by MacMahon to lead a cabinet after the clear Republican gains of 1876, he was soon in a cleft stick. His failure to condemn firmly ultramontane agitation in France pleased neither MacMahon, to whom it was too timid, nor the left to whom it was proof that, even under Simon, it was clericalism which was the real enemy, and shortly afterwards he received from MacMahon the celebrated letter which was tantamount to dismissal. Nothing in Simon's subsequent career was to be as significant as this episode which was, with MacMahon's eventual submission, and premature retirement in 1879, to so gravely weaken the authority of all subsequent presidents of the Third Republic.

Bibliography

Daudet, E. (1883), *Jules Simon* (Célébrités Contemporaines), Paris: A. Quantin.

Seche, L. (1898), *Figures bretonnes: Jules Simon*, Paris: E. Lehavalier.

Seche, L. (1887), *Jules Simon: sa vie et son oeuvre*, Paris: A. Dupret.

ACR

SOISSON, Jean-Pierre Henri Robert (1934–)

A former Giscardien minister and councillor at the Court of Accounts, Soisson has been a deputy for Auxerre in the Yonne since 1968, mayor of Auxerre since 1971, departmental councillor for Auxerre 1970–6, and from 1982 onwards, and vice-president of Burgundy Regional Council since 1983. The son of an industrialist, Soisson was born and educated in Auxerre, and then at the Faculté de Droit and the Institut d'Etudes Politiques in Paris. After studying at the National School of Administration (1959–61) he entered the Court of Accounts, from which he was briefly seconded to Algeria before spending several years working as a ministerial adviser in the *cabinets* of Morin, Bourgès and Faure (q.v.). After standing unsuccessfully in the 1967 legislative elections, Soisson went on to win a seat as an Independent Republican in 1968. He rose through the ranks of the party first holding the post of deputy general secretary under Poniatowski, then the vice-presidency before becoming general secretary of the revamped Republican Party in 1977. He helped to organize Giscard's presidential campaign in 1974 and was rewarded with a junior ministerial post for universities (1974–6) followed by professional training (1976) and youth and sports (1976–7). His ministerial career culminated with the full portfolio of youth, sport and leisure which he held between 1976–7.

Soisson's career is typical of that of many of the governing elite in Fifth Republic France. His position as a member of a prestigious *grands corps*, his experience of policy-making circles, contacts gained in his years working in ministerial *cabinets* and a well entrenched foothold in local politics, all combined to place him in a strong position for a career in national politics.

From the early 1960s he had much admiration for Giscard d'Estaing and once elected became very active within the small parliamentary group of Independent Republican deputies. He soon became established as one of the leaders of the new generation of image conscious and professional Giscardiens. A close political ally of Giscard's he shared his desire to renovate the Fédération Nationale des Républicains Indépendants and to extend the party beyond its deputies and their local fiefdoms. The need for change was more than apparent after the poor results for the party in the 1977 municipal elections. Giscard relieved Soisson of his governmental duties and put him in charge of constructing the new Parti Républicain (PR). Although his office as general secretary was short-lived, Soisson did much to revitalize the party by changing its personnel, establishing a new image and by laying down principles which were to shape the PR in the following years. In 1978 he was one of the team which assisted Giscard in the setting up of the Union pour la Démocratie Française (UDF), a new presidential alliance of all non-Gaullist centre and right-wing groupings.

After 1982 Soisson became a close supporter of Raymond Barre in his presidential aspirations and was one of the key movers in organizing parliamentary support for Barre within the UDF. As a deputy he had been much concerned with the problems of agriculture and the impact of technological change on agricultural communities. In 1988, after Mitterrand's re-election he became minister of labour in Rocard's second government and as such, the most prominent example of the new policy of opening out ('ouverture') towards the centre which the Socialist leadership had initiated.

Bibliography

For general biographical details see J.-P. Soisson, *La Victoire sur l'hiver* (Paris: Fayard, 1978) and *Mémoires d'ouverture* (Paris: Belfond, 1989); and for a discussion of Soisson's role within the Republican Party see D. Seguin, *Les Nouveaux Giscardiens* (Paris: Calmann-Lévy, 1979).

ER

SOREL, Georges (1847–1922)

Sorel was a political autodidact. Coming from no tradition (except the blameless life of a servant of the bourgeois state), he was able to see what the problems were in other traditions of political theorizing and to blend those insights into a political position so remarkably original that it can only be called Sorelian. Sorel's revolutionary syndicalism is one of only three possible revolutionary positions (the other two were monarchical dictatorship and fascism) which could be held in France with any hope of success after the pretended revolutionary doctrines of republicanism and socialism had been seen through as shams. In the *Reflections on Violence* (1908), Sorel contrasted Marxistically the claims of republicanism and socialism with Republican and Socialist practice. The Republic was easy to see through: 1848, and especially the brutal suppression of the Paris Commune in 1871, showed how literally the Republic was bourgeois. The French working class was expected to be Republican in a Republic which would never be theirs. The alternative was socialism, and by 1900 France had a Socialist Party with impeccable Marxist credentials, but Sorel saw that it was already revisionist. M. Jaurès practised a Socialist version of the politics of clientage, making deals with parliamentary groups on behalf of his working-class electoral following by telling other parliamentarians that it was only by dealing through *him* that the workers could be prevented from taking up the weapons of the cruder forms of class struggle. For Sorel, the recently invented 'iron law of oligarchy' necessarily meant the *embourgeoisement* of leaders of the working class (and of working-class leaders).

True to Marx's own reading of French politics, Sorel saw that the apparent victories of all French oppositionism and insurrectionism since 1789 had strengthened the French state, that glittering prize which Jaurès and his Socialist parliamentary colleagues had their eyes on just as much as Robespierre, Napoleon or Napoleon III. The guilty secret of democratic socialism was now out: Socialists wanted to capture the State's legal force through the ballot-box rather than to destroy the class enemy. The working class would be turned into just another special interest within the parliamentary game, anodynely competing with other, bourgeois, interest groups.

Sorel contrasted the 'force' of the state, the sneaking violence of lawyers, with heroic 'violence'. He was impressed with Gustave Le Bon's *The Crowd: A study of the popular mind* (1895), which argued that the elite had more to fear from a dark undercurrent of popular and barbarous violence than from universal suffrage. Sorel turned Le Bon on his head by arguing that only violence could revitalize decadent, *fin-de-siècle* society (he was an admirer of Bergson's).

Sorel saw as clearly as anyone how recent the state's claim to monopolize violence was. The institutionalization of violence in the state, which men had come to confuse with civilization, meant that a cowardly bourgeoisie failed to confront a proletariat now tamed by the show of political rights. Both the great historical classes had lost their taste for action. Sorel looked for groups likely to begin the class *war* again and thought he had found them in those trade unions (*syndicats*) which could be energized by the 'myth' of the general strike as Napoleonic battlefield and take on the class enemy, or its state agents, direct. Sorel greeted the Russian Revolution in its Soviet phase with considerable enthusiasm, believing it to be a genuine workers' movement with those bourgeois intellectuals who always seem to muscle in on the workers' act for once conspicuously absent. Mussolini claimed ideological descent from Sorel but is unlikely ever to have read a line of him.

Bibliography

Stanley, J.L. (1981), *The Sociology of Virtue: The political and social thought of Georges Sorel*, Berkeley, Cal.: University of California Press.
Sorel, G. (1925), *Reflections on Violence* (trans. T.E. Hulme), London: Unwin.

JSM

SOUSTELLE, Jacques Emile Yves (1912–)

The political career of Jacques Soustelle is inextricably intertwined with that of Charles de Gaulle. For twenty years Soustelle was one of de Gaulle's most loyal servants, but in the final decade of the president's life they became arch-enemies. The turning point came with the Algerian War, launched by Muslim guerrillas against French rule in 1954. Soustelle broke with de Gaulle in 1960 and fled France the following year to escape arrest under emergency powers introduced by the president to deal with the Algerian crisis. He remained in exile until 1968, and in a steady stream of pamphlets, articles and books bitterly criticized de Gaulle, whom he accused of setting up a personal dictatorship.

Soustelle was born into a working-class Protestant family in 1912. He studied at the prestigious Ecole Normale Supérieure in Paris from 1929 to 1932, and then began an academic career as an ethnologist, doing field work in South America. A prominent anti-Fascist in the 1930s, Soustelle quickly rallied to the London headquarters of General de Gaulle's Free

French forces after the fall of France. Having headed de Gaulle's wartime intelligence services, he was appointed minister of information and then colonial minister in 1945.

Soustelle followed de Gaulle into opposition in 1946. The following year, he became secretary-general of the newly-formed Rassemblement du Peuple Français (RPF), a movement designed to further de Gaulle's political ambitions while enabling the general himself to remain aloof from parliamentary politics. After winning a seat in the National Assembly in 1951, Soustelle served as leader of the RPF's parliamentary group until its dissolution by de Gaulle two years later amid a decline in its electoral support.

Early in 1955, under the premiership of Pierre Mendès France, Soustelle was appointed governor-general of Algeria, where the insurrection which was eventually to lead to independence in 1962 had just begun. He remained in Algeria until 1956, combining social and economic reforms with increasingly vigorous military repression. Two years later he played a leading role in the orchestration of de Gaulle's return to power after rebellious army officers joined with right-wing settlers in Algeria with the aim of forcing a more resolute stand by the authorities in Paris. In de Gaulle's distribution of ministerial portfolios, Soustelle was kept away from the formulation of Algerian policy, which turned increasingly against the hardliners. Early in 1960 Soustelle resigned from the government in protest. Fearing that his support for the die-hards would lead to his arrest, he fled abroad in 1961 following the collapse of an army *putsch* in Algeria. A warrant for his arrest on charges of plotting against the state was issued the following year. Not until an amnesty was called in 1968 was Soustelle able to return to France, where he resumed his academic career and won a seat in Parliament from 1973 to 1978 with the help of old political friends in Lyons. He was elected to the Académie française in 1983.

Bibliography

Jacques Soustelle, *Vingt-huit ans de gaullisme* (Paris: La Table Ronde, 1968) presents a polemical but wide-ranging overview of Soustelle's relations with de Gaulle. English-language accounts of the Algerian War which contain illuminating references to Soustelle include Alistair Horne, *A Savage War of Peace: Algeria 1954–1962* (London: Macmillan, 1977) and John Talbott, *The War Without a Name: France in Algeria 1954–1962* (London: Faber and Faber, 1981).

AGH

'SOUVARINE', Boris; pseudonym of Liefschitz, Boris (1885–1984)

Boris Souvarine was one of the founders of the PCF (French Communist Party), to which he came via left-wing journalism rather than the wider workers' movement; he was one of the thirty-two members of its first organizing committee, and the last survivor. Stern, ascetic and impulsive, he was a seeker after the unvarnished truth, and a non-conformist *par excellence*.

Born in Kiev, Boris Liefschitz went to France at the age of 3 and later took the name of the revolutionary intellectual in Zola's *Germinal*. An activist in the SFIO from about 1910, he wrote for a pacifist Socialist weekly, *Le Populaire*, but nevertheless served in the army from 1913 to 1916. He became acquainted with Trotsky in Paris, and engaged in written polemics with Lenin; he showed his independence of spirit when he surmised in an article written just after the October Revolution of 1917 that the only people to benefit from the dictatorship of the proletariat would be the Bolshevik leaders.

By 1919 however he had espoused the Bolshevik cause and, being convinced of the necessity of a party dictatorship, pressed for the SFIO to join Lenin's new Third International. He edited the daily *L'Humanité* and founded *Bulletin Communiste*, the journal of the French committee for the Third International, and until 1924 one of the theoretical journals of the PCF. Unable to attend the key SFIO Conference at Tours in 1920 because he was temporarily in prison for 'plotting against the state' (i.e. striking), he drafted the victorious resolution which led to the founding of the PCF. 'The most important thing concerning the Conference took place in the Santé prison', he later said in *L'Express* (6 December 1980).

While in Moscow during most of 1921, he was made a member of the Secretariat and Praesidium of the Communist International. However, after Lenin's death, he backed Trotsky against Stalin, and was expelled from both the PCF, as the party became 'Bolshevized', and the Comintern. He broke with Trotsky in the early 1930s, but he remained even more firmly anti-Stalinist, objecting particularly to Stalin's anti-Semitism.

He devoted the rest of his life to attacking Stalinism, and to urging the view that the Revolution had been betrayed, and that in retrospect it amounted to no more than a military takeover. He continued *Bulletin Communiste* after 1924 as an opposition Communist journal, attacking the Bolshevization of the PCF. Souvarine remained an inveterate journalist and founder of journals and discussion circles up to his death in December 1984; he inspired the journal *Socialisme ou Barbarie*, founded in 1947 and dominated by Cornelius Castoriadis.

Bibliography

Souvarine's *magnum opus* was a long biography of Stalin, published in Paris in 1935 and reissued in 1977, and also in English as *Stalin: A critical survey of Bolshevism* (London: Secker & Warburg, 1939): it hinted at everything which was made public later, in the 1950s. See also his *A contre-courant: écrits 1925–1939* (Paris: Denoël, 1985).

MS

STAVISKY, Alexandre Sacha 'Serge' (1886–1934)

A Russian emigré of Jewish extraction, born in Slobovda in 1886, Alexandre Stavisky, along with his beautiful wife, cut something of a dash in fashionable French society in the 1920s. Though it later transpired that the police were also aware of his existence, the public at large knew nothing of him until the 'affair' which bears his name broke in the press at the end of December 1933. An associate of Stavisky revealed to a judicial enquiry the fraudulent character of the Bayonne municipal pawnshop, which Stavisky had established with the aid of the local Radical Party deputy, Joseph Garat. When Stavisky disappeared from Paris on 25 December, the right-wing press began to investigate his past activities and to implicate a series of Radical Party politicians and public officials in an alleged cover-up of the swindler's fraudulent operations over a number of years. However, it was the manner of Stavisky's death on 9 January which turned the scandal into a major political 'affair'. Tracked by the police to a house in Chamonix, Stavisky was supposedly found dying by his own hand. The right-wing press (and indeed the Communist *L'Humanité*) unanimously rejected this official version in favour of the thesis that Stavisky had been silenced to prevent disclosure of his previous connections.

The Stavisky affair was in the classic mould of the politico-financial scandal which the extreme right under the Third Republic traditionally seized on to discredit the 'corrupt' parliamentary regime. A succession of similar episodes in the early 1930s (*Hanau, Oustric, Aéropostale*) had sunk without trace, but the Stavisky case broke against a background of mount-ing economic insecurity and political instability. The right's contention that Stavisky's financial support for the Radical Party and his involvement in Masonic circles had been used to buy official acquiescence in his shady dealings enjoyed some credibility. Some eighty dossiers on his fraudulent activities were apparently circulating in various departments of the police and judiciary, and on nineteen occasions charges against him had been mysteriously dropped. The Radical deputies Garat and Bonnaure were both indicted, and the Radical minister Dalimier was forced to resign. Most damaging of all, the Radical prime minister Chautemps' own brother-in-law, public prosecutor Georges Pressard, was accused of involvement, and this fuelled press speculation about an even wider political conspiracy. Chautemps' refusal to allow a parliamentary commission of enquiry raised the temperature still further, and increasingly lost him the support of the SFIO (Socialists) who were unwilling to see themselves compromised alongside the government and the whole Radical Party. The eventual resignation of the Chautemps cabinet paved the way for the formation of a new government under Edouard Daladier, whose handling of an already delicate situation sparked off the right-wing riots of 6 February 1934.

The obscure personality of Alexandre Stavisky was thus the catalyst for a series of events that were to be decisive in the closing years of the Third Republic. The affair further weakened the credibility of the parliamentary regime and set in motion a process that polarized French society sharply between left and right.

Bibliography

The key primary source for the Stavisky affair is the published proceedings and findings of the parliamentary Commission d'Enquête set up to investigate the scandal. See also 'Scandales politiques et démocratie' by René Rémond in *Etudes* 1972, p. 849.

The Stavisky affair is also the subject of a film directed by Alain Resnais, 'Stavisky' starring Jean-Paul Belmondo.

BJ

STEEG, Théodore Jules Joseph (1868–1950)

Active in politics for over fifty years in the twentieth century and a leading figure in the government of France (and the colonies) between 1911 and 1931, Steeg always resembled one of the great nineteenth-century Republicans. His father was a Protestant minister of Prussian origin who became a Gironde deputy in 1881 (before he acquired French nationality). He himself was a professor of philosophy in Paris before turning to the law and politics. This combination of Republicanism, Protestantism and education was similar to that of Buisson (q.v.) with whom he collaborated in the Dreyfus affair and politics of the late 1890s. He entered the Chamber of Deputies as a Radical Socialist in a 1904 by-election in Paris, and became a Seine senator in 1914. He was minister of education in two governments before the First World War and for three years during it. As such, he was responsible for organizing the education of war orphans – the *pupilles de la nation.*

The kind of Radical who believed in good government at least as much as in ideology, he was willing to accept the Interior Ministry in the government of Millerand (q.v.) that following the conservative victory in the elections of 1919. (He was a passenger on the train off which the president of the Republic Deschanel – q.v. – fell in August 1920.) Having succeeded Deschanel as president, Millerand sent Steeg, with whom he got on well, to be governor-general of Algeria. Steeg managed to calm the settlers' agitation over a law enabling the enfranchisement of some Algerians and in his four-year period as governor presided over considerable economic development. In the crisis of the presidency that followed the left's victory in 1924, he refused Millerand's offer of the premiership and returned to his Radical family by accepting the Justice Ministry under Painlevé (q.v.) in April 1925. In October of that year Painlevé sent him to be resident-general in Morocco, following the resignation of Lyautey (q.v.) and he played a large part in the ending of the Rif rebellion led by Abd el Krim.

He was prime minister only once, for a brief six-week period in December 1930–January 1931. It was a time of darkening economic (and political) prospects. His predecessor, Tardieu (q.v.) had fallen victim to the long standing hostility of the Senate but the majority in the Chamber was essentially centre-right and Steeg was quite unable to reconcile the opposing groups. A number of his ministers, including René Coty (q.v.) resigned when it became clear that the Socialists would vote for the government. The Chamber of Deputies voted to amnesty the Communist deputies, Marty (q.v.) and Duclos (q.v.). Disagreements between ministers over how to deal with the growing crisis of agricultural prices led to the government's defeat. It was significant of Steeg's priorities that he tried to argue that such economic disagreements were less important than the right's

opposition to secular education. Steeg returned to office in the brief Chautemps (q.v.) and Blum (q.v.) ministries of 1938, as if to demonstrate his concern for Republican defence. Choosing to abstain in the 10 July 1940 vote at Vichy that gave power to Pétain (q.v.) his Republican integrity led him in December 1944 to be appointed acting president of the Radical Party. It was totally unsurprising that this pure product of Third Republican politics should have advocated the maintenance of the constitution of 1875.

Bibliography

Bonnefous, G. (1962), *Histoire politique de la IIIème république* (vol. 5), Paris: Presses Universitaires de France.

Bonnet, G. (1969), *Vingt ans de vie politique*, Paris: Fayard.

PM

STIRBOIS, Jean-Pierre (1945–88)

Until his death in a car accident in November 1988, Jean-Pierre Stirbois, the secretary-general of the Front National, was among the strongest of the contenders to succeed Jean-Marie Le Pen as future party leader. Born in Paris in 1945, Stirbois, the son of a boilermaker, took a diploma in marketing from the Ecole des Cadres et du Commerce before pursuing a career in printing. His political activism dates from the mid-1960s, when he played a leading role in the youth wing of the movement in support of Jean-Louis Tixier-Vignancour's presidential campaign. After spells in a number of far-right activist groups, such as the Mouvement Jeune Révolution (MJR), the Mouvement Solidariste Français (MSF) and the Groupe Action Jeunesse (GAJ), Stirbois joined the Front National in 1977. He quickly became a prominent figure in the party and succeeded Alain Renault as secretary-general in 1981.

An effective party organizer and important aide to Jean-Marie Le Pen, Stirbois was known for his hard-right views, most notably on immigration. His political and ideological roots lay firmly in a tradition of French right-extremism for which the Indo-China War, *Algérie française* and opposition to de Gaulle still stand as powerful reference points. Stirbois came to political prominence in September 1983, when he led the Front National to its first electoral performance of note in the municipal by-election of Dreux in the Eure-et-Loir department. Polling almost 17 per cent of the first round vote, the

Front National was able to negotiate a controversial local alliance with the RPR and UDF, which secured victory for the right and the post of deputy mayor for Stirbois. While putting the Front National on the political map, the municipal by-election of Dreux first signalled the importance which the immigration issue was to develop in the French political debate of the 1980s and presaged a string of electoral successes for Le Pen's party. It represented, too, an important step in the latter's long-term strategy of seeking acceptance by the mainstream French right.

As the architect of the Dreux alliance, Stirbois' stock within the Front National rose. His political achievement, however, soon advanced beyond the municipal level. In the European elections of June 1984 Stirbois took one of ten seats won by the Front National in the European Assembly of Strasbourg. In the French legislative elections of March 1986, he was one of thirty-five members of the Front National elected for the first time to the National Assembly, where he represented the Hauts-de-Seine constituency and was vice-president of the party's parliamentary group until losing his seat in the election of June 1988. He was also at the time of his death a councillor for the Ile-de-France region, a seat which he won in the regional elections of March 1986.

Between 1983 and 1988, Stirbois played a leading role in transforming the Front National from an electoral irrelevance into a major national political force. An important voice in party policy-making, he articulated an uncompromising political philosophy which placed him clearly on the right wing of an already ultra-right party. In late 1989 his widow won Dreux for the Front National in a by-election.

Bibliography

Though there is no study devoted to Jean-Pierre Stirbois, aspects of his political career are discussed in a number of recent publications. See J. Lorien, K. Criton, S. Dumont, *Le Système Le Pen* (Antwerp: EPO, 1985); A. Rollat, *Les Hommes de l'extrême droite: Le Pen, Marie, Ortiz et les autres* (Paris: Calmann-Lévy, 1985); J. Chatain, *Les Affaires de M. Le Pen* (Paris: Messidor, 1987). Brief obituary profiles of Stirbois were published in *Le Monde* and *Le Figaro* of 7 November 1988.

JS

T

TABOUIS, Geneviève Rapatel (née Le Quesne) (1892–1985)

Born in 1892, Geneviève Le Quesne was the daughter of an artist and the niece of the diplomats Paul and Jules Cambon (q.v.). Educated at the Faculty of Arts of the Sorbonne and at the Ecole du Louvre, she married industrialist Robert Tabouis, and it was only at the age of 32, after bringing up two children, that she embarked upon her career as a journalist. She began as the League of Nations correspondent at Geneva for a French provincial newspaper, and soon became an authoritative voice on diplomatic and foreign affairs. From 1932 she wrote regular articles for the Paris daily *L'Oeuvre*. Her accurate predictions, of Hitler's expansionist policies in particular, earned her the nickname of Cassandra. In 1940, she left France for New York, where she edited a paper called *Pour la Victoire*. Back in France after the war, she wrote for a number of newspapers, French and foreign, and became known to a new and wide audience through her broadcasts for RTL (Radio Luxembourg). She carried on working in radio until well into her eighties and died in 1985 at the age of 93.

Her family connections no doubt gave her the confidence to deal with the world of diplomacy. Women journalists were beginning to make names for themselves in the 1920s, but rarely wrote on foreign affairs, and Geneviève Tabouis was often the only woman present at press briefings. She later revealed that her first editor insisted she sign her work with her initial, so that his readers would not know she was a woman. Her articles quickly became known for being remarkably well informed and for their pungent, astute and prophetic summaries of world affairs. Her forthright attacks on the Nazi regime earned her the publicly expressed hate and fear of its leaders. (Hitler is supposed to have said: 'Frau Tabouis is under my table when I telephone and in my inkwell when I write'.) By the outbreak of war, she was described as the 'French journalist best known outside France'. Her flamboyant style sometimes brought accusations of sensationalism, but her colleagues respected her professionalism and her undeflectable pursuit of information.

Her heyday was the inter-war period, when the written press was highly influential, and when statesmen could still hope to achieve their ends through diplomacy. But she adapted to the new world of radio, and her famous expressions, 'Attendez-vous à savoir' and 'J'ai appris', became familiar to her listeners, as did her distinctive voice. She never overcame her distrust of Germany and was opposed to integrationist policy within the EEC, approving de Gaulle's policy of *rapprochement* with the Soviet Union. Although a critical observer, she once said that she had a great deal of respect for world statesmen, since she had seen at close quarters how difficult international negotiations could be. Geneviève Tabouis wrote a number of books, including several on ancient history, but it was her book on the approach of war, *Blackmail or War*, that caused most sensation when published as a Penguin Special in 1938.

Bibliography

Geneviève Tabouis published two books of memoirs, *They Called Me Cassandra* (New York: Scribner's, 1942) and *Vingt ans de 'suspense' diplomatique* (Paris: Albin Michel, 1958). Some of her other books have been translated, but there is little on her in English.

SR

TAITTINGER, Pierre-Charles (1887–1967)

Born in Paris in 1887 into the prestigious champagne house of his name, Pierre Taittinger established himself with a flourishing business career in his family firm by the eve of the First World War. In Rheims, the location of the company's viticultural business, and in Paris where it owned hotels and property, Taittinger essayed his first steps in local government and city politics. Following commissioned service in the 1914–18 war he won a seat in the Chamber in 1919 as a deputy for the Charente-Maritime, a Biscay constituency reputed for its royalist political ancestry and conservatism. Taittinger's success was part of the triumph at the polls of the list of the right-centre nationalists

(Bloc National) and he affiliated to the parliamentary group of the Republican Federation, then France's chief conservative party, led by Louis Marin (q.v.). In the 1924 elections, defying the national swing to the left which brought victory for the Radical-Socialist *Cartel des Gauches*, Taittinger switched constituency and gained a seat in the 1st *arrondissement* of Paris, the fashionable and prosperous financial quarter of the Bourse, the Bank of France and the Finance Ministry. Retaining the seat down to the Second World War, he not only turned it into a personal parliamentary fief but used it as a springboard into the capital's administration, being elected to the Paris Municipal Council in 1937. In 1924, meanwhile, alarmed at the inability of the traditional right to retain office, Taittinger joined other disgruntled Republican Federation politicians, particularly Charles Marquis des Isnards, and Jean Ybarnégaray, to found the Mouvement des Jeunesses Patriotes. A populist right-wing anti-Communist grouping that harboured ambitions to amend the constitution and strengthen the executive at the expense of the powers of Parliament, the Jeunesses Patriotes was heavily subventioned from Taittinger's own business profits. It sought to rejuvenate French politics by allying the camaraderie of war veterans to the dynamism of students and teenage youth. On 6 February 1934 the movement took a leading role in the violent anti-parliamentary demonstrations, on the Place de la Concorde opposite the Chamber of Deputies, which provoked the resignation of the Radical government of Edouard Daladier. The outcome was the installation of a conservative 'National Union' administration, under former President of the Republic Gaston Doumergue, and, in response, the creation of the Popular Front, a new union of the left. Taittinger partially withdrew from the national stage, reducing his role with the Jeunesses, and resuming a more conventional political career. In particular he devoted himself to defence questions, becoming an activist on the influential army commission of the Chamber of Deputies. He used this platform for vociferous advocacy of watchfulness towards Germany, speedy French rearmament, alliance with England and abandonment of the Popular Front's attempted *rapprochement* with Soviet Russia.

By 1939 he was a leading light in the Anglo-French parliamentary association, working intensively alongside francophile British MPs, notably Major-General E.L. Spears, to cement the revived Anglo-French alliance. In March 1940 Taittinger's inspections with the Chamber army commission led him to warn vainly about the inadequacies of the French arms industry, and the vulnerability of the Ardennes front just two months before the fall of France (in which one of his sons was killed in action serving with the French mechanized cavalry). President of the Paris Municipal Council in 1943, Taittinger's finest hour came in August 1944 when, through negotiations with General Dieter Von Choltitz, the capital's German governor, he persuaded the German military garrison to let the Allied armies liberate Paris in defiance of Hitler's Wagnerian orders to raze it to the ground.

Taittinger typified the French *haute bourgeoisie* which had experienced the carnage of the Western front at first hand. His political outlook and career choice was conditioned by this formative military experience. For Taittinger and his fellow veterans and war wounded (*mutilés de guerre*) like Sergeant André Maginot and Colonel Jean Fabry, both war ministers in the 1920s and 1930s, the hegemonic ambitions and untrustworthiness of the Germans were self evident. German–French rivalry was thus regarded as an immutable fact of life. The hardline nationalism of those like Taittinger earned the first post First World War Parliament its soubriquet of the 'Sky Blue Chamber', (*Chambre Bleu Horizon*) after the scores of blue army great-coated veterans who first took their seats in 1919. *Si vis pacem, para bellum* never epitomized a political outlook better than it did that of Taittinger. His anti-communism at home was as characteristic of the inter-war conservative style he embodied as was his phobia of Bolshevik Russia abroad.

Of especial interest is Taittinger's straddling of two political traditions: on the one hand his retention of his membership of Parliament and adherence to the Republican Federation, a respectable and mainstream conservatism; on the other hand, his parallel career as founder and financier of a demagogic and populist movement in the Boulangist mould, dedicated to a reordering of executive and parliamentary powers. The paradox, however, may not be as great as it appears. For Taittinger was an Anglophile, a student and admirer of British societal stability and political procedure, which he wished France might emulate. His public life, it may be concluded, was dedicated not to the Republic's overthrow or emasculation but to the restoration of its respectability and regeneration of its energies. He would live into the 1960s, seeing the constitution of the Fifth Republic and the *rapprochement* with Adenauer, by which de Gaulle realized the vision at home and reconciled the old adversary abroad.

Bibliography

Pierre Taittinger, *Notre dernière chance* (Paris: Flammarion, 1937); Pierre Taittinger, *Et Paris ne fut pas détruit* (Paris: L'Elan, 1948); Robert J. Soucy, 'Centrist fascism: the jeunesses patriotes', in *Journal of Contemporary History*, vol. 16 (1981), pp. 349–68; M.S. Alexander, 'Prophet without honour? The French high command and Pierre Taittinger's report on the Ardennes defences, March 1940', in *War and Society*, vol. 4, no. I (May 1986), pp. 53–77.

MSA

TARDIEU, André Pierre Gabriel Amédée (1876–1945)

The career of André Tardieu could be a paradigm for the short-comings of the right in the second half of the Third Republic. A journalist, with a brilliant war record, deputy from 1914 to 1924 and again 1926–36, prime minister on three occasions between 1929 and 1932, he ended in an impasse largely of his own making. The three great projects of his life – the Treaty of Versailles, the National Retooling Plan, and constitutional reform of the state – represented a diplomatic, economic and political vision, which, if fulfilled, might have broken the stalemate gripping France between the wars. Some aspects of Tardieu's ideas make an interesting analogy to Gaullism, in others he seems closer to fascism; what is certain is that he failed to communicate the urgency of his views to followers inside or outside Parliament.

Tardieu was born in 1876, the elder child of an upper-middle-class Parisian family which, even in the Second Empire, had been conspicuous for combining Republican sympathies with traditional catholicism. As a young man he scored a remarkable series of successes, winning first place in three national entry-competitions – Ecole Normale Supérieure (this only for the challenge: he left within weeks), the Foreign Office, and the Ministry of the Interior. By the time he entered Parliament in the 1914 general election, winning the Versailles constituency on the first ballot, he had already made a mark in public life, first as personal aide to René Waldeck-Rousseau and later as a journalist specializing in foreign affairs. His outspoken defence of the Three Years' Law, a measure to increase the duration of national service, marked him as a right-winger. When war broke out, he displayed a characteristic mix of principle and impulsiveness: although over-age, he insisted on active duties, serving first on Foch's general staff and then at the front, where he was wounded and decorated; later, he used his seat on the Chamber's Army Commission to press for more aggressive policies.

Within days of America declaring war in 1917, Tardieu was named 'High Commissioner to the Unit-ed States', and went out to manage France's military supplies there. Seven months later, Clemenceau took over the premiership and Tardieu gained a powerful patron: from June 1918, as US landings in France accelerated, his responsibilities also covered American needs in France, as well as French buying in America; and his title was accordingly widened to 'Commissioner-General for Franco-American War Questions'. The job continued in a different guise after the armistice, for Tardieu was Clemenceau's closest confident during the Paris Peace Conference, and his good relations with President Wilson's negotiating team were crucial to achieving a compromise between American and French objectives. He became a full minister when the new liberated regions portfolio fell vacant in November 1919; in the general election a week later, he was comfortably re-elected at the head of a centre-right list which won all the seats in the Seine-et-Oise.

During the 1919–24 Legislature, however, Tardieu condemned himself to back-bench politics, for he figured prominently in a small ginger group of Clemenceau supporters invoking the letter of the Treaty of Versailles, and demanding a firm line against Germany. These Clemenceau supporters ('Clemencistes') were in an ambiguous position; their foreign policy put them to the right of the already reactionary coalition (the *Bloc National*), but they resented the way that religious traditionalists had vetoed Clemenceau becoming President of the Republic. To publicize his views, Tardieu launched a new daily newspaper, the *Echo National*, and produced a full-length account of the peace negotiations (*La Paix*, Paris: Payot, 1921, published in the United States as *The Truth about the Treaty*, Indianapolis: Bobbs Merrill, 1921). In 1924, he became a victim of the pseudo-proportional representation system then in use: 76,000 votes were insufficient to hold his seat, while other lists in the same constituency were successful with as few as 24,000.

This experience led Tardieu to decline to stand in various multi-member by-elections, but in February 1926 he had the chance of fighting a one-man campaign. He captured the Belfort constituency from the Radicals in the first round, and was to hold it similarly in the general elections of 1928 and 1932.

The event marks an important turning point in several respects. First, for Tardieu's career: within a few months, he became a minister again, and was to remain in government virtually uninterrupted until June 1932; during this period he managed most of the great offices of state – the interior, war, and foreign affairs; and in the last two-and-a-half years, he was either prime minister (on three occasions: November 1929 to February 1930; March–December 1930; and

February–June 1932) or at the very centre of power in the cabinet. Indeed, it would be no exaggeration to describe 1929–32 as the Tardieu era. Second, his main tactical concern was no longer division among the conservatives, but instead the Radical Party, and whether it could be persuaded to rally to the right permanently. Third, and arguably most important, Tardieu can be seen already to have begun considering structural reforms of the state, long before it became a commonplace response to the 6 February 1934 riots – moreover, his point of departure was economic, not political.

As minister of public works between 1926 and 1928, Tardieu managed to go ahead with many important construction projects, despite the prevalent mood of budgetary austerity. This brought him into contact with the younger generation of technocrats who founded the Redressement Français movement, men such as Ernest Mercier, Raoul Dautry and Auguste Detoeuf; in general terms, his association with businessmen makes a striking contrast to Poincaré, who was closer to the banking interest. Tardieu played a central role in persuading his prime minister to accept a lower-value 'stabilization' of the franc, as requested by traders and export manufacturers, rather than the outright 'revaluation' which the banks preferred. So when he inherited leadership of Poincaré's majority in 1929, Tardieu seemed to be offering a really new departure, not just a change of generation: the Radicals put up maximum resistance before he completed his cabinet, provoking the fourth longest crisis which the Republic had known.

Tardieu's insensitivity to religious politics – another facet of his relative modernity – only served to highlight tensions with the Radicals. In his first cabinet, four major *congrégations* were represented for the first time since 1906 – yet he dared celebrate the fiftieth anniversary of the Ferry educational laws and indeed to extend free state education to the first year of secondary school. The Radicals would not respond to either flattery or threats: in 1929 they refused to join his government, despite being offered twice as many seats as they had held under Poincaré; by 1930, Tardieu was frustrated by their opposition to his social reform programme which, he alleged, they simply envied. Later disillusionments led him to declare a savage, fatal vendetta against radicalism – but the crucial breakdown in relations occurred during his premiership.

The third element in Tardieu's new persona is at once the least clear-cut and potentially the most important: at its minimum, it was no more than a tendency to consult economic interest-groups when drafting government policy; at its maximum,

Tardieu came close to espousing a fully-fledged authoritarian corporatism. Between 1926 and 1932, he made repeated use of the new consultative National Economic Council (Conseil National Economique – CNE); he quickly became dissatisfied with *laissez-faire* liberalism as a method of mobilizing private initiatives; finally, there are suggestions that he really wanted to devolve on to organized business certain administrative and financial functions of the state.

In November 1929, Tardieu announced a controversial 'Plan for National Retooling', which allocated 5 billion francs' extraordinary expenditure to rebuilding the economic infrastructure. This plan was less radical than it seemed – there was no deficit financing, and much of the work had already been scheduled against reparations repayments; moreover, due to heavy parliamentary opposition, it was never completed. Yet, despite his own supporters' doubts about the plan, Tardieu accepted the CNE's recommendations to expand it by involving professional groups such as private water authorities, cooperatives, and Chambers of Commerce or Agriculture. Indeed, the plan's top management committee, composed entirely of CNE members plus civil servants, was to be kept distant from parliamentary control.

Tardieu repeatedly urged businessmen, farmers, and sometimes even workers to form associations and to work together more openly: he emphasized the potential benefits for industrial relations, and seemed to ignore big business' dogmatic rejection of collective contracts; he also implied that professional bodies might take over other tasks, such as technical training, family insurance, selecting key economic growth areas, and defending these against illegitimate foreign competition. By and large his ideas remained vague, and apparently little was done to win employers over to them; but, as a further point, it should be noted that in 1932 Tardieu did draft a bill to give big business virtually exclusive control over the level of cartelization and price fixing in the national economy.

Defeated in the 1932 elections by an electoral pact between the Radicals and Socialists, Tardieu organized a new parliamentary group, Centre Républicain, whose objective was to block all short-term deals with the ensuing Radical governments. His outlook was increasingly conservative: in foreign policy, he denounced revisionism wherever he saw it – suspension of war debts, the Four-Power Pact, alliance with the Soviets; in economics, he advised stricter protectionism, and disowned the campaign of his old ally, Paul Reynaud, to devalue the franc. During 1933, Tardieu began to expose the failings of the Third Republican parliamentary system, and in January 1934 he published a full-length book on the subject, *L'Heure de la* décision (Paris: Flammarion, 1934). In contrast with earlier preoccupations, his solutions were now political and institutional: allowing the government to dissolve the Chamber without recourse to the Senate; removing deputies' right to propose new expenditure; votes for women; and a restricted form of referendum (on the substance of an issue, before government and Parliament decided a formal text). The 6 February riots posed a direct challenge to the competence and legitimacy of Parliament, so Tardieu seemed a natural choice as an expert minister without portfolio in Doumergue's new National Union cabinet. But even before any proposals to reform the state had been produced, he became embroiled with his Radical coalition partners in a series of mutual accusations arising from the Stavisky case, and was nearly forced out of office. Later in 1934, these Radicals rejected his programme for constitutional reform, and Doumergue allowed the government to collapse – so it is possible that Tardieu had deliberately been pre-empting the issue. However that may be, this marked the end of his active political career: Tardieu refused to participate in all subsequent cabinets, ceased attending Parliament, and announced that he would not be seeking re-election. Henceforth, he hoped to achieve by journalism what he had failed to do in the Chamber: in 1936, he began his (unfinished) magnum opus, *La Révolution à refaire* (Paris: Flammarion, 1937), repeating earlier strictures against deputies' irresponsibility and the weakness of the executive; the first volume was widely read, but produced no practical results. From the mid-1930s onwards, Tardieu suffered from an unspecified chronic illness: in 1939 he was totally incapacitated by a stroke, and he died in 1945.

Bibliography

André Tardieu, *France in Danger* (London: D. Archer, 1935), a translation of *L'Heure de la décision* (Paris: Flammarion, 1934) is the neatest summary of Tardieu's constitutional ideas. Many of Tardieu's political papers are available to researchers; above all, in the *Archives Nationales* (series 324 AP, requiring permission from the Société des Amis d'André Tardieu) but also at the Quai d'Orsay and in the Service Historique de l'Armée de Terre (Vincennes). See also Rudolph Binion, *Defeated Leaders: The political fate of Caillaux, Jouvenel and Tardieu* (New York: Columbia University Press, 1960). Slightly sensational but well researched for its time, this book is more reticent about Tardieu's own political prejudices than he would probably have wished himself.

Monique Clague, 'Vision and myopia in the new politics of André Tardieu', in *French Historical Studies*, vol. VIII, no. 1 (spring 1973), pp. 105–29, is a detailed rebuttal of any Keynesian gloss on Tardieu's plan, but it does not adequately consider in what other respects he was unconventional.

AR

TEITGEN, Pierre-Henri (1908–)

Henri Teitgen, Pierre-Henri's father, was an early follower of Mounier's (q.v.). He was a lawyer, president of the Bar in Nancy, briefly a deputy for the Gironde (1945–53), and was editor of the daily *Ouest-Eclair*. The daily *Ouest-Eclair* was the largest selling provincial newspaper and did more to spread the ideas of the Sillon than other specialist publications. Pierre and his brother Paul were both steeped in Christian Democratic politics and both made their marks on the liberal left of the movement.

Pierre-Henri was also a lawyer. He had the good fortune to escape from the train taking him to a concentration camp in 1944, after which he joined the Resistance. He was an important Resistance figure and sat on the committee to vet post-war appointments. He was de Gaulle's information minister (issuing licences for newspapers at the liberation) and then minister of justice during the settling of scores ('épuration'), against the excesses of which he spoke out. When de Gaulle resigned he became deputy prime minister and held that post in successive MRP–SFID Radical governments until 1950.

Teitgen's refusal to countenance independence for Indo-China and his hardline against the Vietminh insurgents when he was Laniel's deputy prime minister camouflaged his otherwise essentially progressive positions. On Algeria he prepared MRP congress reports urging reform rather than repression. His brother, Paul Teitgen, resigned as chief of police in Algeria because of torture. He was minister for the colonies in the Faure government of 1955 and supported the Defferre law preparing the African colonies for independence.

Teitgen was a pro-European and in 1950 he proposed a European Army for a United Europe (in the Council of Europe) and in 1953 saw the European Defence Community as a step towards European integration. (He did not, however, support the Western European Union and made a venomous speech against the Western European Union in the Assembly debate.) In 1957 he supported the creation of a European market, to reinforce Europe's influence, such as part of a strategy of strengthening Europe by small steps.

In 1958 Teitgen represented the MRP on the constitutional committee and, like other drafters, believed that the Fifth Republic placed the premier in control of policy and responsible to Parliament. However, by March 1960 he was telling the MRP Congress (somewhat exaggeratedly) that the French people were 'no longer living in a regime which can strictly speaking be called democratic'. Teitgen had early doubts about de Gaulle's European policy, was opposed to direct election of the president (in the 1962 referendum) and condemned the French nuclear strike force. Teitgen also maintained a sceptical attitude to Pompidou with whom he had been in conflictual contact in 1945 but although he remained on the MRP's leadership he returned to academic life as a professor of law in Rennes and then in Paris.

Bibliography

On the Christian Democrat movement see R.E.M. Irving, *Christian Democracy in France* (London: Unwin, 1973) and the memoirs of Pierre-Henri Teitgen, *Faites entrez le témoin suivant* (Paris: Ouest-France, 1988).

DSB

TESSIER, Gaston (1887–1960)

The son of a Parisian carpenter, Gaston Tessier was educated at a Catholic primary school and a commercial college before beginning his career as an office worker. In 1905 he joined the Catholic Syndicat des Employés du Commerce et de l'Industrie which had been created in 1887, becoming its assistant general secretary in 1908 and its general secretary in 1914. In his formative years he was influenced by the writings of Albert de Mun, La Tour du Pin and Canon Garigues and by the example of Léon Harmel and Marc Sangnier. However, opposed to Sangnier's Sillon (which sought to rally democrats from the Catholic world) Tessier devoted his life to an organization whose doctrine was specifically Catholic in nature and was, throughout his life, to adhere to a Christian Democratic and Catholic social outlook.

Soon after the outbreak of the First World War he was demobilized and occupied a number of positions in the Catholic trade union movement. When the Confédération Française des Travailleurs Chrétiens (CFTC) was formed from the various strands of that movement in 1919, Tessier became its first general secretary. As the CFTC's membership expanded and diversified in the inter-war period Tessier played an important role in taking the Confederation beyond the paternalist influences prevalent in French catholicism and in affirming its organizational if not doctrinal independence from Church authorities. While rejecting economic liberalism, the CFTC of this period was opposed to the dominant class-struggle tradition of French syndicalism and was clearly reformist, seeking social harmony through a form of corporatism. In 1922, as a member of the Conseil Supérieur du Travail, Tessier drafted the first plan for social insurance in France and, unlike the CGT, favoured the development of collective bargaining. However, he backed the CFTC's participation in the 1936 strike movement.

In 1940 Tessier opposed the armistice and was among the first Frenchmen to rally to de Gaulle and to the Resistance. Following the banning of the CFTC he joined with representatives of the CGT in signing the 'Manifeste des 12', which reaffirmed the principles of independent trade unionism. As a result of the CFTC's stance Tessier became a member of the Conseil National de la Résistance. At the liberation he was responsible for the Ministry of Supplies for several months and became a member of the Provisional Parliamentary Assembly. Although he had been co-director of the Christian Democratic daily *L'Aube*, which he had helped to launch in 1932, and had played a role in creating the Mouvement Républicain Populaire (MRP), Tessier was not eager to embark on a political career and turned down the invitation to stand as a MRP candidate.

In 1948 Tessier relinquished the position of CFTC general secretary, assuming instead the presidency of the movement. The post-war history of the CFTC was marked by the progress of the minority which was eventually to bring about the *déconfessionalisation* of the movement in 1964. In 1946 Tessier accepted a revision of the CFTC's statutes which henceforth no longer defined the organization's doctrine by reference to papal encyclicals, but spoke in a more general vein of 'la morale sociale chrétienne'. However, he interpreted the latter to mean the social doctrine of the Church. The CFTC's 1953 Congress moved further towards an affirmation of the non-confessional nature of the movement. Tessier, who opposed any such dilution of the CFTC's original principles, was marginalized in the preparations for the Congress and, now aged 65, did not seek re-election to the presidency. From this time until his death in 1960 he devoted his energies to the Confédération Internationale des Syndicats Chrétiens to whose presidency he had been elected in 1948.

Gaston Tessier also occupied a considerable number of other positions of national and international importance. He took part in the activities of the ILO and in the 1940s and 1950s was a frequent member of French delegations to the UN General Assembly. He devoted particular attention to the questions of world peace and disarmament. He was a member of the board of Crédit Lyonnais and of a number of social insurance and mutualist bodies. He was the recipient of many honours including the Légion d'Honneur and the Croix de Guerre 1939–45.

Bibliography

By G. Tessier, *Les Catholiques et la paix* (Paris: Editions Spes, 1927). See also:

Adam, G. (1964), *La CFTC 1940–1958. Histoire politique et idéologique*, Paris: A. Colin.

Bouladoux, M. (1961), 'Un Homme au service d'une cause: Gaston Tessier et la CFTC', in *CFTC La Revue du Militant 'Formation'*, no. 32, February, pp. 1–12.

Lefranc, G. (1967), *Le Mouvement syndical sous la troisième république*, Paris: Payot.

LAB

THIERS, Louis-Adolphe (1797–1877)

Thiers was 'Head of the Executive Power' and then the first President of the Third Republic from 17 February 1871 to 24 May 1873. He was responsible for the peace negotiations with Germany following the defeat of 1870–1, in which France lost the territories of Alsace and Lorraine. He crushed the insurrection of the Paris Commune in May 1871, restored the French army and civil administration, raised the money to pay off the German war indemnity and end the military occupation of French soil, and did more than any other individual to convince an uncertain nation that a Republic was the only safe regime for France.

The witty, voluble and immensely energetic only son of a modest Marseilles family, he had been educated at the *lycée* at Marseilles and the law faculty at Aix-en-Provence. By 1870, he had already had a long and distinguished career as journalist and politician under the Restoration (when he was a leading liberal propagandist), the July Monarchy (when he held frequent ministerial office, including twice the premiership), and the Second Republic and Empire (when he was a leading spokesman and latterly elder statesman of conservative liberalism, and an influential critic of the personal government of Napoleon III). He was also a renowned historian, the author of monumental works on the French Revolution, the consulate and the Empire.

In July 1870 he tried to avert the war with Germany, and when disaster came in August and September he refused to take office under the dying Empire or the new-born Republic, being unwilling to shoulder responsibility for the French defeat that he believed inevitable. From September to October 1870, he undertook a diplomatic mission to London, St Petersburg, Vienna and Turin to seek the support of the neutral powers in peace negotiations, but obtained no more than assistance to meet Bismarck for talks in November. Following these, he urged the French government to accept German terms which, though harsh, would inevitably grow worse, he believed, if the war dragged on. His advice was rejected. On 8 February 1871, after an armistice was finally signed, elections were held for a National Assembly to negotiate peace. Royalists won a large majority, and Thiers was elected in twenty-six departments, an unequalled feat: he was seen as the enemy of the discredited Empire, the prescient opponent of war, the advocate of peace, and the only man with the prestige to confront Bismarck at the negotiating table. Consequently, he was the inevitable choice as head of the new government, with the title of 'Head of the Executive Power', to which that of President of the Republic was added in August. On 19 February 1871, Thiers proposed the 'Pact of Bordeaux', a truce between the parties under which no decision would be taken concerning the future regime of France until 'the existence and safety of the country' were secure.

Immediately, Thiers had to face a challenge from Paris. The city's huge citizen militia, the National Guard, angry at the defeat of France and suspicious that the National Assembly was planning restoration of the monarchy, set up a military–political Republican Federation outside government control. Thiers' rash attempt on 18 March to disarm the National Guard by seizing their artillery provoked a popular uprising which forced the government to flee to Versailles. A revolutionary Paris Commune was elected on 26 March. After abortive negotiations, fighting began on 1 April and developed into full-scale civil war, with Paris besieged by the French army. Thiers prosecuted the war with energy. He was determined not only to defeat the Parisian insurgents, but also to prevent the spread of unrest to the provinces (which he did both by intimidation and by promising Republican leaders privately that he would not lend himself to a monarchist restoration), to prevent power from falling into the hands of the royalists in the National Assembly, and to stave off intervention by the Germans. Finally, in a week of street fighting (21–8 May) – *la Semaine Sanglante* – marred by appalling bloodshed and massive physical damage to the capital, the insurrection was crushed, leaving bitter and enduring resentments. Thiers, who had done little to prevent mass executions by the army, has always been blamed for the carnage: 'We do not consent to any execution once a man is taken prisoner,' he wrote. 'During the fighting we can do nothing and it would be useless to get ourselves mixed up in it.'

His second pressing task was to repair the damage done by the German war. He had long been convinced that the defeat was inevitable in the short term, and that a limitation of the damage and a return to normal was the best that the government could achieve. He bargained personally with Bismarck in February 1871, and through intermediaries in May, when the Treaty of Frankfurt was signed, but was resigned to the loss of Alsace-Lorraine and a large indemnity (5,000 million francs). His policy was to raise the money quickly (by the largest international loans ever floated), pay the indemnity and secure the rapid end of German occupation. That the sum was raised without difficulty showed the confidence that Thiers inspired in financial circles in spite of the recent civil war.

He also laboured to restore the army, though without agreeing to fundamental reforms in its organization. He clung to the belief that only a long-service standing army was suitable for France, both for military and political reasons, and almost alone blocked the Assembly's plan to institute short-term (three years) military service on the Prussian pattern, insisting on five years' service. He also blocked reforms in other important areas: resisting income tax (which was not introduced until the First World War), insisting on the retention of central powers over local government (which remained until the 1980s), and working doggedly to reintroduce import tariffs (he was a diehard protectionist). On all these questions, his habitual conservatism was strengthened by a desire to return the country to normal as quickly as possible and with the minimum of upheaval. He used the threat of resignation to force the Assembly's acquiescence. In foreign affairs, his aim was to secure a period of tranquillity for France until German troops were withdrawn and her own political and military situation had improved. His long-term aspiration, foreshadowed by his diplomatic mission in 1870, was *rapprochement* with Russia as a counterbalance to Germany.

Hanging over every other question was the unsolved problem of France's future regime. The National Assembly claimed constituent powers, and its majority was royalist. Thiers, however, had long doubted whether a monarchy could provide France with durable stability, and at least since 1850 he had been willing to contemplate a Republic, which he had called 'the government that divides us least'. These views were confirmed after 1871, when it became increasingly plain that the royalist parties were divided over the kind of regime a restored French king should institute: the Bourbon comte de Chambord – the would-be Henri V – envisaged divine-right paternalism, symbolized by his insistance on replacing the *tricolore* with the Bourbon white flag – demands acceptable to only the most extreme Legitimists. Thiers quipped that Chambord would be the French Washington – the founder of the Republic. Consequently, Thiers took the step on 13 November 1872 of calling formally in his message to the Assembly for a Republican constitution: 'The Republic exists, it is the legal government of the country: to want anything else would be a new revolution, and the most fearsome of all.' He wanted a 'conservative Republic': a parliamentary regime of the sort he had advocated throughout his career, a barrier to dangerous social and financial demagogy, governed by men like himself and his colleagues of the left-centre – experienced men of affairs of the professional and landed classes, often former royalists. This would require an agreement between reasonable moderate men, as Thiers saw them, both Republican and Orleanist, to exclude the dangerous extremists of the Legitimist right and the Radical left and set up an ideologically bland compromise Republican regime with a constitution comprising a strong president and a nominated or indirectly elected Senate to balance the democratic tendencies of the lower Chamber.

However, the Radicals, led by Gambetta, refused to stand by while Thiers manoeuvred them into the political wilderness by negotiating with the Orleanists. In April 1873, a Radical, Barodet, stood as a parliamentary candidate in Paris against Thiers' protégé and foreign minister, Rémusat, and convincingly beat him. This showed dramatically the growing strength of the Radicals (although Paris was far from typical of France, with its left-wing traditions and bitter memories of the Commune). It panicked many moderate royalists, on whom Thiers was relying to give him a majority for his conservative Republic, into demanding repression of left-wing agitation and another attempt to restore the monarchy. They now believed that Thiers' advocacy of republicanism was merely paving the way for dangerous radicalism. Nevertheless, Thiers persisted in presenting his draft constitution to the Assembly: France would be a Republic, but with safeguards against democratic excess. The right was no longer willing to consider this, and on 24 May 1873 the combined royalist groups, with a handful of Thiers' former centrist followers tipping the balance, voted no confidence in the government by sixteen votes. Thiers at once resigned, and was replaced by Marshal de MacMahon as president and the Duc de Broglie as head of the government. Thiers' strategy of building a centrist majority had failed, and French politics had split down the middle into right and left.

Thiers sided unambiguously with the left. He bitterly resented what he considered the short-sighted opposition of the royalists, and had realized that Gambetta and the Radical leaders were on the whole sensible men with whom he could work. For their part, they were glad to have as symbolic leader a man who could reassure the electorate and foreign opinion that the Republican party could be trusted. The continuing failure of the royalists to persuade the comte de Chambord to accept reasonable terms for his restoration (which led indirectly to the fall of de Broglie in 1874) and repeated Republican successes in by-elections showed that time was on the side of the latter. In February 1875 the Assembly, at last convinced that prolonged uncertainty was politically dangerous, voted constitutional laws embodying the main features of Thiers' 1873 draft, and agreed that the regime should be entitled 'Republic'. The Assembly then dissolved, and the Chamber of Deputies elected in 1876 gave the Republicans a majority. Thiers' predictions were thus borne out. However, MacMahon's dismissal of the moderate Republican Simon ministry in the so-called 'coup' of seize mai (16 May 1877), and his recall of de Broglie, marked a return to the royalist policy of 'combat' against the left that had caused Thiers' fall in 1873. This time, however, the left, not the right, had a majority in the Chamber, and after a vote of no confidence in June 1877 (when Thiers was one of the 363 voting against the government) MacMahon used his presidential powers to dissolve it. In the ensuing election campaign, Thiers, at the age of 80, abandoned his philosophical studies to return to the political limelight as the Grand Old Man of the combined Republican party. In the event of victory, it was planned that he would assume the presidency with Gambetta as head of the government. But he died suddenly on 3 September 1877, a month before the elections. His funeral in Paris became a silent mass demonstration of support for the Republic: it seemed that the repression of the Paris Commune had been forgiven. His posthumous electoral manifesto became the Republicans' watchword, and doubtless contributed to their success in retaining their majority in the Chamber. As MacMahon was unwilling to contemplate further resistance, let alone a coup d'état, this was a decisive victory for the Republic.

Thiers' importance in the early years of the Third Republic was enormous. By crushing the Paris Commune he ended for good the danger of armed revolt against the regime, and also staved off monarchist reaction and German intervention. While in office he liquidated the effects of the 1870–1 defeat, rapidly restoring French independence and confidence, though at a heavy price in territory and money. Eager to return the country to normality and to repair the machinery of the state with a minimum of delay and upheaval, he re-established the military, financial and administrative machinery along familiar lines, stubbornly blocking far-reaching reforms. Thus he helped to set the Third Republic on the traditional course that it was to follow for generations. The confidence he inspired among middle-class and peasant voters (commemorated in the inevitable 'Rue Thiers' in innumerable provincial towns) meant that his espousal of a 'conservative Republic' as the only safe and sensible regime was of decisive importance. He aimed to arrange an ideologically neutral compromise between converted royalists like himself and conservative Republicans, embodied in a liberal constitution with checks and balances to restrain democracy. This satisfied neither right nor left and brought about his fall. In the Republican camp during the struggle against MacMahon and de Broglie, he helped consolidate the Republican victory in 1877.

Bibliography

The most recent biography of Thiers in English is J.P.T. Bury and R.P. Tombs, *Thiers 1797–1877: A political life* (London: Unwin, 1986). A shorter summary is R. Albrecht-Carrié, *Adolphe Thiers or the Triumph of the Bourgeoisie* (Boston, Mass.: G.K. Hall, 1977). For the general political background of these years, see J.-M. Mayeur and M. Rebérioux, *The Third Republic from its Origins to the Great War* (Cambridge: Cambridge University Press, 1984).

RT/JPTB

THOMAS, Albert Aristide (1878–1932)

Albert Thomas, born on 16 June 1878 at Champigny-sur-Marne (Seine), was an influential figure in the French labour movement and gained international repute as the first head of the International Labour Office (ILO). Growing up in his father's bread shop in a poor district, he became aware of poverty and inequality at an early age, and as a student professed his Socialist beliefs. An outstanding student, he graduated in history from the Ecole Nationale Supérieure in 1902 and went on to gain his doctorate in 1910. Although he taught for a period at the Sévigné secondary school and gave private lessons, his teaching career was soon abandoned in favour of political activity. An article on the trade union movement in Germany, where he spent a year after graduation, made Thomas known in Socialist circles, and in 1904 he started to cover social questions for *L'Humanité* and *La Petite République*. In 1905 he started his own paper, *La Revue Syndicaliste*.

Thomas's first contacts were with the independent Socialists, and he joined the Parti Socialiste Français in 1902. An advocate of Socialist unity, Thomas was elected on to the administrative committee of the newly unified Socialist Party in 1905. He was elected councillor in his home town in 1904, and was mayor from 1912 to 1925. He also represented the constituency in the Senate from 1910. After his election as deputy for the Tarn constituency, he became a leading figure of the parliamentary Socialist group.

An ardent supporter of trade union organization, Thomas was active in the cooperative movement, and was elected on to the administrative council of the Bourse des Coopératives Socialistes in 1909. He saw trade unions and cooperatives as a vital part of the Socialist movement, because of their working-class nature. Because of the importance he attached to the economic side of the labour movement, Thomas refused to see legislative reform as the only means of Socialist action, but he rejected the idea of the revolution as a goal and saw himself as a reformist.

The war gave Albert Thomas the chance to promote his ideas of social reform. After taking responsibility for the coordination of railways and arms production, in May 1915 he became under-secretary of state for artillery and military equipment, and in December 1916 arms minister. He also acted as intermediary between the French government and the first Russian revolutionary governments, and travelled to Russia in August 1917. By collaborating with the government, he hoped to improve conditions for workers, as was shown by his act of July 1916 restricting night-work for women, and the setting-up of arbitration committees in the arms industry. His actions brought him into disfavour within the post-war Socialist Party, and the Seine Federation refused to place him on their list for the 1919 elections. He was, instead, the only Socialist elected on the Tarn Federation list.

It was at the ILO in Geneva that Albert Thomas's influence was felt. Here, as head of the ILO, he promoted his view that the labour movement had a role to play in post-war reconstruction. For him, labour legislation depended on the harmonization of conditions in the various countries. Ill health restricted his activities, however, and he resigned as deputy in October 1921 and as mayor of Champigny in 1925. He died in Paris on 7 May 1932.

Bibliography

The standard biography of Albert Thomas remains B.W. Schaper, *Albert Thomas: trente ans de réformisme social (1894–1932)* (Paris: Presses Universitaires de France, 1963) (translated from the original Dutch). Jean Maitron, *Dictionnaire biographique du mouvement ouvrier français* (part 3: 1871–1914) (Paris: Editions Ouvrières, 1973–7), vol. XV (1977), pp. 223–7, contains a profile of Thomas. Several ILO publications pay tribute to Albert Thomas's international work; see, for instance, Edward Joseph Phelan (ILO Director), *Albert Thomas et la création du bureau international du travail* (Paris: Grasset, 1936). A collection of Thomas's speeches and writings relating to his work with the ILO was published in French in 1947: *Politique sociale internationale* (Geneva: Bureau International du Travail) and in English as *International Social Policy* (Geneva: ILO, 1948). On Thomas's contribution to the French Socialist movement, see Georges Lefranc, *Le Mouvement socialiste sous la troisième république*, vol. II (1920–40) (Paris: Payot, 1977) pp. 442–4. Albert Thomas was himself author of many articles, pamphlets and books, notably *Le Syndicalisme allemand, résumé historique (1848–1903)* (Paris: G. Bellais, 1903). The Archives Nationales holds an Albert Thomas archive.

SM

THOREZ, Maurice (1900–64)

Maurice Thorez was born in 1900 in the mining town of Noyelles-Godault in the Pas-de-Calais. He died in 1964: this happened on a Soviet ship taking him from France for a Russian holiday. At the age of twelve-and-a-half he was employed as a 'stone picker' in the mines, but as a result of the 1914 war, was evacuated and resumed his studies. Mobilized in 1918, re-employed as a clerk in the mines at Dourges in 1919, he joined the CFT and the Socialist Party (SFIO) almost simultaneously in March 1919. A supporter of entry into the Third International on the basis of the '21 conditions', he was one of the founding generation of the PCF when that party emerged from the split at the Congress of Tours in 1921. He was a leading activist in the mining districts of the North; in 1923 he became secretary for the Federation of the Pas-de-Calais.

In 1924 he was promoted from the regional to the national level as a member of the PCF Central Committee. Boriz Souvarine, among others, noted him as a genuine proletarian, and Thorez' sympathies in that year were Trotskyite. But by 1925 he had 'bitten the bullet' and visited the Soviet Union as part of a delegation honoured by meetings with the anti-Trotsky 'troika' – Zinoviev, Kamenev and Stalin (in order of official importance). On his return came another promotion: in July 1925 he joined the Political Bureau and became a Central Committee secretary. This series of rapid promotions was connected to the 'Bolshevization' or 'Russification' of the PCF. The operation called for injecting proletarian blood into a party which still smelled of Bohemian anarcho-syndicalism (Souvarine, Rosmer, Monatte). Thorez' blood was proletarian red. His entry into the Political Bureau was part of a response to Stalin's victory over Zinoviev.

As a leading PCF cadre, Thorez was pitched into the campaign of military disobedience against the suppression of the Rif uprising in Morocco. In 1927 he was arrested for 'anarchist propaganda'. In fact Thorez was not very good as a street-level revolutionary: a police raid on the Central Committee in 1929 netted Thorez because he hid in the wrong place, where 'les flics' could see his shoes – he alone was caught. His imprisonment lasted nine months, but in April 1930 he was released after paying off his fine: this he did on his own initiative and against all the customs of the PCF. Thorez was on the threshold of rapid ascent. He had built up an asset highly appreciated by Stalin – namely a 'biography with spots on it', and was to add yet another huge spot after meeting a French girl in Moscow in May 1930. Eventually, he and Julie Vermeersch, known publicly as Jeannette, were husband and second wife. Thorez had married Aurore Memboeuf in 1922: in the PCF, deserting a wife was more than a venial sin. Thorez was then perfectly poised to fill his role as

'sub-Stalin' in a world movement permeated by the cult of Socialist personality.

In 1929 Thorez was recruited by Henri Barbé (q.v.) and Pierre Célor (q.v.). On Comintern initiative, they formed a dictatorial caucus within the PCF's leadership. Their brief was to implement the ultra-left 'class against class' line. Thanks to his imprisonment, Thorez was morally on the margin of the group, even if in July 1930 he was appointed first secretary. He could therefore profit from the manifest failure of the Barbé-Célor leadership. (By 1931 the PCF was little more than an isolated sect, thriving only among the unemployed.) In 1931, the Comintern decided to eliminate Barbé-Célor as a 'group' of saboteurs. Thorez became a 'non-tenured' leader. He relaxed the 'class against class' line, but executed its essential strategy: this line designated Socialists as 'social Fascists' and characterized the existing regime in France as effectively Fascist. In this he faced the barely concealed opposition of Jacques Doriot, PCF mayor of the Paris suburb of Saint-Denis. Doriot agitated for a 'united front', that is Communist-Socialist alliance, and defined fascism as the anti-parliamentary right.

A crisis came with the Croix de Feu-led riots of 6 February 1934, when the PCF activists joined the right (nationalists) against the police. But on the 12 February Communist and Socialist demonstrators spontaneously joined forces. Thorez disappeared for a month.

Faced with the bankruptcy of 'class against class', the Comintern hesitated to sanction measures against Doriot's open insubordination. Thorez and Doriot were both summoned to Moscow. Thorez went. Doriot did not. Thorez returned undisputed leader (April–May 1934).

From 1931, Thorez had a political 'minder'. Eügen Fried, a Czechoslovak Jew, known as Clément (to the party), was appointed by the Comintern to supervise the PCF. He did not merely back Thorez, he entered a 'Freudian' symbiosis with him – Aurore became Fried's mistress. The biography of Thorez in these years thus poses a double kink. Officially Thorez was leader. Unofficially, the Comintern exercised control through several channels. Thorez' institutional dependence (for example a section of cadres set up in 1932 excluded Thorez) was overlaid by the introjected psychological relationship with Fried.

Thorez' first initiative certainly was a Comintern directive: in June 1934 the PCF approved a United Front (by this time Doriot had left, en route for real fascism). The United Front that had first emerged after the revolutionary upsurge of 1917–19 had patently failed. But this time it was a response, not just to a failed offensive, but to Hitler's victory. The Comintern approved a startling innovation: Communists should form alliances with bourgeois European parties to contain the Nazi menace. The details were left to local leaderships. Here Thorez, or Thorez–Fried, probably introduced a new political idea, termed Popular Front. By October 1934 Thorez had decided that the alliance must include the Radicals. His most dazzling stroke came in 1936 with the 'outstretched hand' (*La Main tendue*) offered to all anti-Fascist Catholics. This abandonment of post-1848 Socialist anticlericalism complemented the PCF's about turn on militarism. After the Franco-Soviet pact of 1935 was signed, Stalin pronounced his support for French armed force: the next day posters declared 'Stalin is right'. Between 1934 and 1936 Thorez had presided over the transformation of French communism from a culture of dictatorial anarchism to one clothed in the rhetoric of populist patriotism.

Consistent with the strategic function of the Popular Front as support for the Franco-Soviet pact, Thorez used his authority to inhibit any attempt to transform the Popular Front into a Socialist revolution. The most notorious occasion came in June 1936. Thorez countered Pivert's left Socialist battle cry 'Tout est possible' (All is possible), with a stern 'Tout n'est pas possible' (Not all is possible) and explained 'We must know when to end a strike'. Thorez did not, could not, never did repudiate proletarian dictatorship. He reaffirmed it at Arles in 1937, but reserved it until after the defeat of fascism. Naturally in this vein, Thorez' principal quarrel with Blum concerned the latter's failure to help significantly the Republican government in the Spanish Civil War.

The Popular Front era witnessed the launching of the cult of Thorez. Was it a substitute for revolutionary action? This major step in Stalinizing the PCF involved Thorez as little more than an inert idol. A ghosted autobiography *Fils du peuple*, published in 1937, gave the signal. But the decision to publish had been taken in the Comintern, probably in 1935, and corresponded to similar semi-divinity granted to other national leaders, such as Togliatti, Thälmann and Gallacher. In 1936 he received a French equivalent of Stalin's title 'general secretary'. Increasingly, Thorez was presented as the incarnation of the French people: in a system where Stalin was Son of Man, Thorez could aspire to be Son of France. Thorez' status, however, conferred no increased autonomy either for him or the PCF. This was abruptly demonstrated in August 1939, when he was

not even informed about the Soviet–German pact. Indeed, his obedience to Moscow was most perfect between 1939 and 1944.

After the pact, the PCF still reaffirmed the patriotism it had discovered in 1935. Accordingly Thorez obeyed his conscription orders on 3 September. Only around 20 September would Raymond Guyot bring new orders: the war was an 'imperialist struggle' particularly on the Anglo-French side. The PCF swung around 179° to denounce the imperialist war and demand negotiations with Hitler. Thorez, however, counted for nothing in all this, even at the formal level, since he was at the front. His destiny was determined by two decisions beyond his control. In mid-September (before the PCF received its official orders) Fried communicated an order to desert. Possibly Thorez hesitated: he did not desert until 4 October, but his decision was facilitated since the PCF was banned on 26 September.

Thorez escaped to Brussels; *in absentia* he was condemned by a French military tribunal for desertion and stripped of French citizenship. He became a pawn in Stalin's game: as a satrap in exile, at court in Moscow, he was denied all contact with his party base. His isolation would last until November 1944. At some time in 1940 he left Brussels and arrived in Moscow. No one can say exactly how, but a sealed train through Germany is distinctly possible. But certainly he was not in France: consequently the anti-Vichy (but not anti-German) manifesto of 10 July 1940, signed Thorez–Duclos, was not his work – as official chief his name was lent to others' doings. This position of a legal and political 'unperson' contrasted by 1943 with that of the detested rival André Marty (q.v.).

Thorez' fortunes changed after de Gaulle's Moscow visit in November 1944. On 28 October Thorez was amnestied and the 'popular militias' dissolved: on 26 November de Gaulle landed in Moscow, and on 27 November Thorez was in Paris. De Gaulle wanted a 'PCF respectueux'. Stalin distrusted national communism. Thorez was their man: both held 'dossiers' which could destroy him politically (de Gaulle held the evidence that the PCF had fabricated Thorez' supposed presence in occupied France). Thorez' first major speech (30 November) announced that the popular militias must be disbanded – there could be only one French state, one army. (An explicit deal is, however, unlikely.)

Thorez returned, as he had left, a political servant, but the lines of command had changed since 1939. In feudal terms he was a man with a liege lord – Stalin – but owing a secondary fealty to another – de Gaulle. But the terms of his allegiance to Stalin were greatly altered. In 1939 the chain of command was mediated by the Comintern. But not only had the Comintern been dissolved, Fried, Thorez' 'minder', was shot down in Brussels in 1943. The killers are unknown, but probably worked for Stalin. Thorez was now directly responsible to Stalin, which does not mean that his moves were ordered by Stalin.

Between 1944 and 1947 Thorez and the PCF were allowed considerable latitude. Thorez was one of three Communist ministers in the November 1945 coalition headed by de Gaulle. He proved very good at being a minister. As minister of state, he produced an effective reform regulating conditions in the civil service. He worked hard to ensure that the workers gave of their best. His efforts earned him recognition from de Gaulle: Thorez, he wrote, served France well. After de Gaulle left at the beginning of 1946, Thorez remained: in May 1947 he was still a minister, despite the difficulties posed by the Indo-China war against the Vietminh. To *The Times* he declared in November 1946 that France was following her own road to socialism.

The crisis of May 1947 was certainly not provoked by the PCF. They were caught between American pressure and a strike at Renault emanating from pro-Trotskyist elements. Unable to support the government's wage freeze, the PCF was ousted from government, but Thorez spoke of the expulsion as a technical problem. To the Party Congress of June 1947 at Strasbourg he declared that the PCF was a party of government, even if it was not 'in government'. In September 1947 the newly-created Cominform invited the French and Italian Communist Parties to send delegates to its inaugural meeting. They were the only two parties invited who were not in power. Thorez either smelled trouble or received a warning. He did not go to the Cominform, but sent Duclos and Fajon. The storm broke over Duclos: the PCF was savaged for its 'opportunistic subservience to the bourgeoisie' and for missing the revolutionary bus in 1944. Being absent, Thorez avoided personal degradation and indeed could strengthen the cult of 'Maurice' both privately and publicly.

The post-Cominform line could only build up pressure. The PCF sought to combine its Popular Front, Resistance claims to be the most patriotic of French parties with a sub-revolutionary street-level combativity. The latter role sat most uneasily on Thorez; he hinted that he had been forced to resign from government by the PCF: this may have been a manoeuvre, but he was conspicuous by his reticence towards the great strikes which nearly paralysed France in late 1947 and in 1948. After the strikes,

Jeanette Vermeersch, Thorez' more combative half, and from April 1950 member of the Political Bureau, began to hit out at the PCF's trade union leadership, Benoît Frachon especially.

A marked feature of Thorez' cult character after 1944 was the development of a viceregal style which he maintained even after the end of his ministerial career. Before 1939 he lived modestly, was available: 'one of the lads'. After the war the party bought a *château* for his use and he lived there in semi-reclusion with 'Jeannette'. This lifestyle soon produced the elevation of Jeannette Vermeersch as an autonomous component of PCF politics. The cult became that of the couple 'Maurice' and 'Jeannette'. At Strasbourg 'Jeannette' was admitted into the Central Committee. 'Jeannette' was not a demure wilting rose, and many of Thorez' subordinates had enough French chauvinism to remember that in France monarchy could not be held by or through women. A most unstable condition built up within the PCF: the spark which began the explosions was the stroke which paralysed Thorez in October 1950.

Thorez' stroke was a cruel political blow. It illuminated his dependence on Stalin, since in November 1950 he was flown to the Soviet Union to be cured by Stalin's doctors. He was to stay there until after Stalin died, returning in April 1953. That he should remain the unchallenged party leader marks the discipline (or subservience?) of his lieutenants. Thorez himself experienced the sojourn as half cure, half detention. His primary channel of communication with the PCF was Vermeersch – the leadership became akin to a family business. Vermeersch brought the instructions which initiated the Marty–Tillon affair. But other channels still operated: François Billoux (q.v.) brought the signal for the ultra-leftist anti-Ridgway demonstration. Their simultaneity represented a typical Stalinist manoeuvre – Thorez swung left and covered his flank by eliminating Marty, symbol of Revolution, and Tillon, symbol of Resistance.

Stalin's death came as a climacteric moment. As Thorez loved Stalin, he wept, but now the feared monster was gone Thorez could return to France. The PCF proclaimed it as a Second Coming – Aragon's poem *He Returns* was published by *L'Humanité* as an editorial. Thorez brought the ghost of Stalin to France: his last years were dominated by struggle against de-Stalinization. The immediate objective to preserve Stalin as a French cult led, inevitably, to intervening in Soviet politics – through loyalty to his dead master, Thorez paradoxically accelerated the de-Stalinization of world communism. The 'polycentrism' – decentralization – deliberately promoted by Togliatti was unwittingly helped by Thorez.

Thorez' struggle began in 1953: on holiday in the Soviet Union, he received a sketch of the 'crimes' of Stalin and Beria. With Duclos' connivance, he withheld the document from his subordinates. In February 1956 he was in Moscow and received a copy of Krushchev's secret speech within hours of its delivery. The PCF, however, knew nothing until excerpts were published in the 'bourgeois' press. Thorez joined a world Communist counteroffensive led by Mao. Thorez indeed went further: he backed Molotov and Kaganovitch against Krushchev. That he survived their defeat indicates the independence the PCF now possessed.

As a 'post-Stalin', Thorez sought to preserve the theoretical bases of the leftism of Stalin's last years: in 1955 he reaffirmed the thesis of absolute working-class impoverishment. This precluded analysis of the French economy's great leap forward which had just begun. In line with this theoretical conservatism, Thorez saw de Gaulle's 1958 coup as a return to fascism. Against these positions, the renovators, headed but hardly led by Casanova and Servin, analysed the Fifth Republic as the state of a new capitalism, one unforeseen by Lenin. They hoped to persuade Thorez, unaware of the bitter hostility both 'Maurice' and 'Jeannette' held for 'Krushchevism'. Thorez purged them from their leading positions during 1960–1.

Krushchev forced Thorez to repudiate the formula 'Le parti de Maurice Thorez', but Thorez ensured the survival of the cult. His sixtieth birthday was marked as a festival in which Stalin received muted worship. But unlike Stalin, Thorez knew he was mortal. In 1959 he began to groom Waldeck Rochet as his immediate successor, and possibly envisaged the young Georges Marchais as eventual leader. The selection of Waldeck Rochet, called the 'French Krushchev' (for peasant origins but hardly ebullience), suggests that Thorez knew his successor could not be a 'Maurice II', but hoped to limit the damage. Indeed, where liberalization and defiance of Krushchev coincided, Thorez gave discreet support (see Gaurady entry).

Death came on 11 July 1964. He was buried by the PCF with great pomp; he also received homages from the entire political world, including de Gaulle – Thorez' life suggests they mourned the wasted statesman, not the 'Révolutionnaire malgré lui' (unwilling revolutionary).

Thorez' biography illuminates a hierarchy of problems: (a) In what sense was the PCF a revolutionary party? (b) What were its relations with the Soviet Union and international communism? (c) Did the PCF represent a repudiation of French culture and society, or a different way of being French? This last question leads to the celebrated position of Annie Kriegel (another ex-Communist) that 'Le Parti de Maurice Thorez' became a 'counter society': in its political ghetto it duplicated or recreated the socio-cultural world of official France.

The second question is easiest to answer. The speed of Thorez' ascent was a function of the 'Bolshevization' of the PCF. During the years of Stalin's absolute power, Thorez ruled as a satrap of Stalin: the cult of Thorez was not due to any personal charm. In that respect, Thorez suffered patently, not only if compared to a Mao or Ho Chi Min, but even with the Italian communist leader Togliatti. The difference between Togliatti and Thorez is neatly symbolized by Togliatti's successful evasion of Stalin's demand, in 1952, that he become the Cominform's coordinator stationed in Prague. Thorez, while Stalin lived, presided over a 'Stalinist Revolutionary Party', one for whom revolutionary success was envisaged as a function of Kremlin control – Thorez' paradigm of revolution was the one which occurred in Czechoslovakia in 1948, but definitely not Yugoslavia in 1945. The PCF was consequently organized in a state of 'revolutionary expectancy', where the signal was to come from outside. We know that in fact the signal never came.

The above analysis is the key to the third question. Thorez presided over the practical transformation of the PCF from a revolutionary movement to a society trapped inside the real France of his time. As a very ordinary Frenchman, Thorez easily symbolized the PCF's assimilation to traditional French culture; the cult of Thorez, his principal legacy, was a cult of the Frenchness of the PCF.

Bibliography

There is no biography in English. French readers can consult Philippe Robreiux, *Maurice Thorez. Vie secrète et vie publique* (Paris: Fayard, 1975), as well as *Histoire intérieure du parti communiste*, vols 1 and 2 (Paris: Fayard, 1980–1). The seminal works of Annie Kriegel on French communism are largely untranslated. An exception is *The French Communists. Profile of a people* (Chicago: University of Chicago Press, 1972). Ronald Tiersky, *French Communism 1920–1972* (New York: Columbia University Press, 1974) is strongly influenced by Kriegel. Max Adereth, *French Communist Party: A critical history, 1920–1984* (Manchester: Manchester University Press, 1984) is sympathetic to the PCF. The most comprehensive English interpretation is Irwin Wall, *French Communism in the Era of Stalin: The quest for unity and integration 1945–1962* (Westport, Conn.: Greenwood Press, 1983).

MK

TILLON, Charles Joseph (1897–)

Primarily, Tillon's name is the other half of the Marty–Tillon affair. Both biographies are pages of Communist heroism destroyed by the PCF. Tillon was younger, less illustrious, but a cooler leader. Tillon was born on 3 July 1897, in a family of Breton workers; his uncle, a CGT loyalist, persuaded Charles to join the navy in 1916. In 1919, his ship was anchored off Greece en route for the Black Sea (in support of the Whites). Tillon led a failed mutiny, and got five years' hard labour. He hung on to life, was released, and in 1922 joined both the PCF and the Communist CGTU (Unions).

By 1924 Tillon was CGTU secretary for Brittany, and in 1925 a municipal councillor in Douarnenez, Brittany. After his only Moscow trip in 1931 he was promoted to the national level, both in the CGTU and in the Party – Central Committee in 1931, Political Bureau in 1931. In 1936 he was deputy for the Paris suburb of Aubervilliers. He volunteered for Spain, but his role involved back-up rather than political operations.

When the PCF was outlawed in September 1939, (its security network failed), Tillon escaped and became responsible for underground survival. Benoît Frachon sent him to Bordeaux in March 1940. While in Paris the PCF sought legalization from the Germans in June 1940, Tillon remained 'underground', issued an anti-Nazi manifesto and organized a skeletal Resistance. Since collaborationism failed, September saw a leadership group of Duclos, Frachon and Tillon. Tillon's moment came when Germany invaded Soviet Russia. As head of the FTP (Partisans) Tillon imposed the maximum of armed struggle; he opposed integration with other Resistance organizations. He envisaged a leading role for the Partisans, both in and after the liberation.

After the 'Gaullist' liberation, Tillon received ministerial posts as 'consolation prizes': first, the Air Ministry (1945), then Armaments (1946), then Reconstruction (1947). In May 1947 he rejoiced when his ministerial career ended. In 1948, Tillon directed the Communist-controlled 'Movement for Peace', whose principal brief was to oppose German rearmament. Unfortunately, the line changed in 1951:

Stalin proposed a neutral, armed Germany. Tillon failed to respond with proper alacrity. He had to perform a self-criticism – 'autocritique' – of his chauvinist tendencies.

Tillon later recognized 'L'affair Marty–Tillon' as a 'Moscow Trial in Paris'. The directives came proximately from Jeanette Vermeersch, but ultimately from Beria. On 26 May 1952, Tillon was named *in camera*; the direct confrontation came on 4 September. The accusers (Duclos, Mauvais) fantasized about a Marty–Tillon conspiracy. They reinterpreted Tillon's contempt for the non-revolution of 1944 from an attitude of disapproval to political opposition. Tillon was removed from his posts, confessed to fractionalism, but denied embezzling Partisan funds. He took refuge in upland Provence. Unlike Marty, he was not expelled; in 1956 the embezzlement charge was dropped.

Tillon kept silent on the 'Marty–Tillon' affair, but, aware of its parallels to the Prague trials of 1952, he found the 1968 Czech invasion hard to digest. For Tillon, the ascent of Marchais transformed the PCF from a Party of Resistance to a Party of Collaboration: Marchais, he pointed out, had worked for Messerschmidt in Germany from 1942. Naturally, Tillon was expelled. Much PCF dirty linen was exposed subsequently by Tillon.

Bibliography

Biographies of Tillon can be derived from Yves Le Braz, *Les Réjétés du P.C.F. L'Affair Marty-Tillon* (Paris: La Table Ronde, 1974), or from Raymond Jean, *L'Interrogation,* which is a preface to Tillon's *Un Procès de Moscou à Paris* (Paris: Seuil, 1971). See also Philippe Robrieux, *Histoire intérieure du parti communiste,* vols 1 and 2 (Paris: Fayard, 1980–1), and Pierre Daix, *J'ai cru au matin* (Paris: Robert Laffont, 1976). In English, the most extensive is Irwin Wall, *French Communism in the Era of Stalin: The quest for unity and integration 1945–1962* (Westport, Conn.: Greenwood Press, 1983). For a strongly pro-PCF stance see Max Adereth, *French Communist Party: A critical history, 1920–1984* (Manchester: Manchester University Press, 1984).

MK

TIRARD, Paul-Emmanuel (1837–93)

Born in Geneva, Tirard combined a successful career in business with strong Republican convictions. After the fall of Napoleon III, he became mayor of the 2nd *arrondissement* of Paris and was elected as a left-winger to the National Assembly (he was elected to the Paris Commune but refused to acknowledge its authority). In the National Assembly he voted the straight Republican ticket and was one of the 363 deputies to oppose the installation of the de Broglie government after the crisis of the 16 May. Re-elected in 1877, his expertise in financial and commercial matters led to his being appointed minister of commerce in most of the Opportunist-led governments between 1879 and 1885. He was the first prime minister to be appointed by President Carnot (q.v.) in 1887. A staunch opponent of Boulangism, he was again prime minister in February 1889, shortly after Boulanger's sensational victory in a Seine by-election. The tough methods of his interior minister Constans (q.v.) saw off the immediate crisis and Tirard made much of the diversion offered to public opinion by the opening of the Universal Exhibition in May 1889. He also withdrew the exile imposed on the Orleanist duc d'Aumale and slowed down the secularization of hospices and schools, both measures being designed to woo conservatives away from anti-republicanism. Tirard's government fell in March 1890 but he was back in office in 1892–3 as minister of finance under Ribot (q.v.).

Bibliography

Rudelle, O. (1982), *La Republique absolue*, Publications de la Sorbonne.

PM

'TIXIER-VIGNANCOUR', pseud. Jean-Louis (Tixier) (1907–89)

Born in October 1907 in a family of the Paris bourgeoisie, Jean-Louis Tixier was a pupil of the prestigious Lycée Louis-le-Grand and read law at the University of Paris, from which he received a doctorate. His brilliant mind and personality earned him a position as a barrister (*avocat*) at the Paris Appeals Court as early as 1927, and he became a member and secretary of the Barristers' Standing Conference in 1931. His reputation eventually earned him a place in the Professional Council of the Paris Bar (Conseil de l'Ordre des avocats au barreau de Paris) from 1963 to 1967.

His notoriety is, however, linked far more directly to his political than to his professional activities. Elected deputy for the Basses-Pyrénées in 1936, he had joined extreme right-wing groups in the inter-war period, when 'extreme right-wing' inevitably indicated strong sympathies with, if not total commitment to the Fascist ideology. Indeed, he held a particularly sensitive position during the Vichy years, as deputy general-secretary for information, in other words in charge of the government's propaganda (he has always displayed remarkable talents not just as an orator but also as a pamphleteer). Unsurprisingly, he was arrested and gaoled in 1944, and sentenced to the loss of his civic rights (a standard punishment for Vichy collaborators), including that of exercising his profession and of holding elected office for a number of years.

This temporary eclipse from professional and public life gave him plenty of leisure to revive his interests in extreme right-wing groups. An active member of the Pétainist Union of Independent Intellectuals, he was one of the leading organizers of the European Social Movement linked with the neo-Fascist Malmö Conference, and was involved in the publication of its periodical *Défense de l'Occident*.

He also involved himself with the leadership of the Fascist movement 'Jeune Nation' founded in 1949 by Pierre Sidos, which developed dubious connections with some Indo-China veterans and mercenary soldiers, one of whom, Roger Holeindre, would become Tixier-Vignancour's electoral agent for the 1965 capaign. Assaults and beatings of Communist newspaper sellers were a common form of entertainment for 'Jeune Nation' activists. Feeling some distaste for the violence and coarseness of the movement, Tixier-Vignancour resigned in 1953. Almost immediately he launched and was president of a new nationalist movement, 'Rassemblement National', which at once gained the support of the influential review *Rivarol* and spawned local committees in various French regions. Like the others, this movement was opposed to the projected European Defence Community, purported to fight against the disintegration of the French Union, and claimed to be at the vanguard of the antiparliamentarian campaign in order to build a strong national state, defend the Empire and promote the 'Europe of Fatherlands'. But the Paris leadership of 'Rassemblement National' was itself racked by dissensions, and the movement unsuccessfully coped with competition from the raucous populism of the Poujadists (q.v.).

Whereas the latter obtained fifty-two seats, six deputies were elected on the 'Rassemblement National' and its sister movement 'Réforme de l'Etat' platform, including Tixier-Vignancour who regained his old seat of Basses-Pyrénées.

Tixier-Vignancour was not returned to the Assembly on the Fifth Republic elections and he therefore set his sights on a higher plane. In 1963 Jean-Marie Le Pen founded an 'Action Committee for a National Candidature' (to the presidency of the Republic) designed to support Tixier-Vignancour's own candidature with the specific aim of 'routing de Gaulle'. As early as 1964, that committee launched an election campaign with a mass meeting at the Palais de la Mutualité in Paris (with members of the Fascist 'Occident' movement as ushers and bouncers). This was followed by an amazingly modern and mediatic twenty-nine-day tour of French beaches from Dunkirk to Menton organized by Le Pen, in the course of which more than 600,000 copies of *TV Demain* (the Tixier-Vignancour paper) were distributed, and an indefatigable Tixier-Vignancour introduced himself as the 'candidate of youth and fatherland' and expatiated on the necessity to oust de Gaulle as a sacred patriotic duty.

In spite of this brash, American-type campaign, Tixier-Vignancour obtained a mere 5.27 per cent of votes cast in the first ballot of the December 1965 presidential election (instead of the 15 per cent he expected), and advised his electors to cast their votes for François Mitterrand in the second ballot having, meanwhile, broken up with Le Pen. He went on to found and become life president of yet another nationalist movement, the innocuously named 'Republican alliance for Liberty and Progress'.

In 1968 Tixier-Vignancour, appalled by what he perceived as the inexorable rise of Bolshevism in France, resigned himself to support the Gaullist regime, then the Giscard presidency 'so that European youth can effectively fight Marxism and its spiritual heir terrorism'. Attempts to make it up with Le Pen have all foundered.

Beside his direct political involvement, Tixier-Vignancour is famous for having defended in court such notorious figures as the collaborationist literary critic Maurice Bardèche, the leader of the 1961 anti-Gaullist *putsch* General Salan, and the would-be murderer of General de Gaulle, Bastien-Thiry.

His prolific writings include such telling titles as *Défense de Bastien-Thiry* (Paris: Presses du Mai, 1963), *Des Républiques, des justices et des hommes* (Paris: A. Michel, 1976) and *La France Trahie* (Paris: Amiot-Dumont, 1956).

Bibliography

It must be surmised that Tixier-Vignancour's colourful life will eventually tempt the talents of a biographer but see J.-C. Tixier-Vignancour, *Le Contre-* *mal français* (Paris: Albin Michel, 1977). He seems to have attracted relatively little notice from English language writers but useful data in French can be obtained from such sources as Joseph Algari, *La tentation néo-fasciste en France, 1944–1965* (Paris: Fayar, 1984); Serge Dumont, *Les Brigades noires* (Bruxelles: Editions EPO, 1983) and François Duprat, *Les Mouvements d'extrême-droite en France depuis 1944* (Paris: Editions Alabatros, 1972), as well as Tixier-Vignancour's own works (ops. cit.). See also the obituary in *Le Monde*, 1–2 October, 1989.

AM

TOUBON, Jacques (1941–)

Jacques Toubon's political fortunes have been closely linked since 1970 to those of his political patron Jacques Chirac. Secretary-general of the Rassemblement pour la République (RPR) from November 1984 to June 1988, he has been a Paris deputy since June 1981 and mayor of the 13th *arrondissement* since March 1983.

From relatively modest beginnings (his father was a croupier who rose to manage a casino) Toubon has followed a typical Fifth Republic *cursus honorum*. After the Lycée Jean Perrin, the Institut d'Etudes Politiques and the Law Faculty in Lyons, he studied at the Ecole Nationale d'Administration and became *directeur de cabinet* to the prefect of Pyrénées-Atlantiques. This posting gave him his first experience of electoral politics (organizing the return of two Gaullist deputies to Parliament in 1967) as well as contacts that brought jobs in two ministerial private offices (*cabinets*) in 1968–9 and a position as secretary-general of the Pompidou Foundation in 1970. It was this last appointment that led to his crucial meeting with Chirac.

Toubon's subsequent career divides into three phases. First, he worked continuously in Chirac's various ministerial *cabinets* from 1971 to 1976. Secondly, after Chirac's resignation from the premiership in 1976, Toubon became one of his chief electoral advisers. He helped to plan the re-launch of the Gaullist party as the RPR in December 1976, and to run the campaigns that re-elected Chirac as deputy for Corrèze (November 1976) and elected him mayor of Paris (March 1977). Appointed RPR delegate for elections in April 1977, he has played a key organizational role in every RPR campaign since then. Thirdly, his own election as a Paris deputy in 1981 led to a rapid rise to the top of the RPR. A hard-hitting parliamentary opponent of the

Socialist government, he won a notable success in the March 1983 municipal elections by defeating Paul Quilès, Chirac's Socialist rival for the Paris Town Hall, in the 13th *arrondissement*. His appointment as RPR secretary-general exemplified the injection of young *chiraquiens* into the party leadership, a policy Toubon was expected to apply at section level across France. He also led negotiations on common candidacies with the Union pour la Démocratie Française (UDF) for the March 1986 parliamentary elections, and participated both in constituency redistribution when the new government returned to the 1958 electoral law immediately afterwards, and again in candidate selection for the next National Assembly elections. Finally, during the period of 'cohabitation' between March 1986 and May 1988, he voiced partisan criticisms of President Mitterrand that Chirac, as prime minister, could not utter.

Despite his rhetoric, Toubon is not simply a politician of the authoritarian right: he is opposed to the death penalty, and has written a surprisingly moderate book on the law-and-order issue (*Pour en finir avec la peur*, Paris: Robert Laffont, 1984). Rather more accurately, he has been portrayed as a Chirac clone, displaying the same energy and verbal excess in pursuing personal and partisan ambition. Like his patron, he also underwent a political eclipse following Chirac's second presidential defeat in May 1988, hesitating publicly in his choice of constituency before the June parliamentary elections before being narrowly returned in the 13th *arrondissement*. Criticism of the performance of the RPR machinery during the two campaigns inevitably reflected on him, and he was succeeded as RPR secretary-general by Alain Juppé in June 1988. Toubon remains a Chirac loyalist, and refused to throw in his lot with other RPR figures of his generation who emerged as the 'renovators' in spring 1989.

Bibliography

There is nothing in English on Toubon. Profiles can be found in *Le Monde* (20 November 1984); Alain Duhamel, *Les Prétendants* (Paris: Gallimard, 1983); Jacques Frémontier, *Les Cadets de la droite* (Paris: Seuil, 1984) and (the fullest but most overly sympathetic) Thierry Desjardins, *Les Chiraquiens* (Paris: La Table Ronde, 1985). Pierre Saurat's *Jacques Toubon, Premier ministre de Jacques Chirac* (Paris: Cinq Diamants, 1985) is a wordy hagiography.

AFK

TREINT, Albert Edmund (1889–1971)

Albert Treint is remembered mainly for the cynical *vantardise* that the Communist alliance policy would 'pluck the Socialist chicken' (*plumer la volaille socialiste*) but he did play an important part in the early Bolshevization of the PCF. He was promoted to be PCF co-secretary by the Comintern (with Louis Sellier – q.v.) from January 1923 to January 1924 – when Sellier became full secretary-general. In other respects Treint bore the hallmarks of the Third Republic Socialist activist. A Parisian, a schoolteacher from a modest background, he joined the SFIO in 1910, was badly wounded in the First World War (was awarded the Croix de Guerre), was a reserve 'captain', and became a left-winger in the leadership of the teachers' union in 1919.

Treint was an enthusiast for Lenin's 1917 October coup and was a lobbyist for the pro-Russian left at the 1920 Tours Congress of the SFIO. After the Tours split Treint became a full-time party activist, had support from the International (in February 1922 he was at a Comintern meeting in Moscow) and became the impresario of 'Bolshevization' in the French party, starting by evicting Frossard (q.v.) and Cachin (q.v.) from the leadership. (Frossard noted that Treint's faction 'treated the party like a conquered country'.) Like other West European Communist Parties at the time, French communism was a shambles: Treint was among the 'leftists' who resigned because the 1921 Marseilles Congress did not elect Souvarine. Yet Treint benefited from the clean-out of the French party and from Zinoviev's promotion of reliable cadres. As a hardened union activist (and of undoubted courage), Treint was arrested for attending the Essen Congress in January 1923 which called on French troops to fraternize with German workers (he was, as a result, in prison from January to May 1923).

In 1923–4 Treint carried out Comintern policy to eliminate Trotsky's supporters, 'intellectuals', and others who were less than totally devoted to the party's cause. It was Treint who reorganized the party to make the Secretariat the power house and to establish control through regional delegates; Treint ensured that, at the 1924 elections, 90 per cent of candidates were workers or peasants as the Comintern instructed. Thus Treint was, with Suzanne Girault (q.v.), the real power in the party because he controlled the Paris region despite Pierre Semard's promotion to secretary: in August 1924 it was Treint who administered the violent word-whipping to Zinoviev's opponents Rosmer and Monatte. After their ejection Treint rejoined the Political Bureau and remained there until the defeat of Zenoviev and may have been responsible for organizing street-fighting, for violent clashes at demonstrations during 1924 and for a network of narks – his own informers.

Treint objected to Stalin's orders during 1926 but this rebelliousness was not a result of prescience. Treint had anticipated Stalin's ultra-sectarian line when he had declared about the 1924 *Cartel des Gauches*: 'fascism is already here'. There are colour-able political reasons for Treint's outspokenness. As Zinoviev's nominee, Treint had the run of the French party in 1923 and 1924 but the political balance in Moscow tilted away from Zinoviev and towards Stalin once Trotsky had been disposed of: in 1926 Sauvage (Girault's creature) was replaced by Thorez as organization secretary. Treint criticized Stalin, especially his mismanagement of the International (the suicidal policy imposed on the Chinese party, for example) but he fell victim to the change of leadership in Moscow. He was criticized by the International in March 1926, evicted from the Political Bureau in June, excluded from the Central Committee in November 1927 and then expelled from the party in January 1928.

On expulsion from the Communist Party Treint's career followed an unusual path but not in the top echelons. After meeting Trotsky at Prinkipo he joined the Trotskyists he had previously excruciated and then, in 1934, joined the SFIO. In 1936 he took up teaching again (he had been excluded by the government in 1921) only to become active as a trade union extreme left-winger (in the 'Class Struggle' group) in 1937. When the Second World War ended Treint had become a commanding officer in the 1st Free French Army. Treint, a habitual convert, nevertheless seems to have faded from political life after the Second World War.

Bibliography

See Edward Mortimer's *The Rise of the French Communist Party 1920–1947* (London: Faber and Faber, 1984); and there is a profile of Treint in J. Humbert-Droz (Moscow's nominee in the French party) who deals with this period in *L'Oeul de Moscou à Paris* (Paris: Juillard, 1973), where he notes that Treint had 'all the faults of a junior master and a subaltern'.

DSB

U

D'UZÈS, Marie Anne Clémentine, duchesse de Rocheouart et Mortemart (1847–1933)

Woman of letters, sculptress and sportswoman; committed monarchist, moderate suffragist and feminist, Anne de Mortemart was born in 1847 into one of the most noble of French families: the granddaughter of 'la Veuve Cliquot', her ancestry may be traced to the counts of Limoges of the early Middle Ages. She is best known for her early association with Boulangism, for clandestinely financing the campaign of General Georges Boulanger, in support of whose abortive attempt to undermine the Republic she provided the sum of 3 million francs. Her fame further derives from her considerable and various contributions to the origins of the French feminist movement.

Anne de Mortemart's entry into politics was facilitated initially by her marriage to Emmanuel de Crussol, duc d'Uzès, who, on her persuasion, stood as a parliamentary candidate and was elected to the National Assembly in 1870 as a monarchist politician. He retained his seat until his death in 1878, whereupon the duchesse became one of the most independently wealthy women in France (her income from investments alone amounting to an annual total of several million francs) – a critical factor in her subsequent conversion to feminism.

D'Uzès was one of the exceptionally few nobles to support the feminist groups. She was one of the most notable converts of the British-born feminist activist Jeanne Schmal, whose society Avant-courrière she joined and financed. This organization had been formed in 1893 with the specific objective of obtaining an earnings law comparable to the Married Woman's Property Act of 1882 in Britain, an end which was attained in 1907 when the law according married women in France control of their own wages was finally passed. D'Uzès' commitment to feminism then became more overtly political. Urged by Schmal, she became, in 1909, co-founder and vice-president of the French Union for Woman's Suffrage (Union Française pour le Suffrage Feminin), in an effort to extend the appeal of the movement to less radical, more right-wing feminists. She advocated suffragism for many years, contributing regularly to *La Française*, the first feminist newspaper to achieve a general circulation.

Despite her commitment to the above-mentioned movements, D'Uzès remained to the last above all an individualist: as an eminent sculptress who presided over the Union of Women Painters and Sculptors; as an energetic sportswoman who continued to ride to the hunt even in her eighties; and as president of the Feminine Automobile Club, for which – perhaps most remarkably of all – she led a caravan to Rome at the age of 85.

Bibliography

Dansette, A. (1946), *Le Boulangisme*, Paris: Fayard.
Hause, S.C. with A.R. Kenney (1985), *Women's Suffrage and Social Politics in the French Third Republic* Princeton, NJ: Princeton University Press.
Puget, J. (1972), *La Duchesse d'Uzès*, Paris: Peladan.
Seager, F. (1969), *The Boulanger Affair*, Ithaca, NY: Cornell University Press.
d'Uzès, A. (1939), *Souvenirs*, Paris: Plon.

MMac

V

VAILLANT, Marie-Edouard (1840–1915)

Engineer, doctor, Socialist leader and parliamentarian, Edouard Vaillant was born into a wealthy bourgeois family in Vierzon (Cher) on 29 January 1840. After degrees at the Ecole Centrale and the Sorbonne, culminating in a doctorate in engineering, he moved to Germany in 1865 and studied both philosophy and medicine at Heidelberg, Tubingen and Jena. Here he came into contact with the young Hegelians and was a personal friend of Ludwig Feuerbach. He retained certain links with revolutionary movements in Paris and corresponded with Proudhon. Returning to the capital at the outset of the Franco-Prussian War, he emerged as one of the leading thinkers of the nascent communard revolution. He was appointed minister for education under the Commune and was responsible for introducing free, secular and professional schooling for both sexes.

After escaping from Paris on 28 May 1871, he settled in London where Marx and Engels sought his support against Bakunin by nominating him for the General Council of the First International. He broke with Marx in 1872 for largely tactical reasons (he felt Marx was wrong in assuming the revolutionary tide had broken in Europe) and threw in his lot with the French exiles in London, the majority of whom were Blanquists. During this period, Vaillant completed his medical studies and became a member of the Royal College of Surgeons. After the 1880 amnesty, he returned to France, settling in Vierzon where he devoted himself to organizing the Socialist Party in the central departments. Although formally a member of the Blanquist Comité Révolutionnaire Central, he increasingly distanced himself from the knee-jerk insurrectionism of Eudes and Granger, seeking to instil some elements of Marxist historical and structural analysis into the Socialist Republican movement. In this, he sought allies in Jules Guesde (q.v.) Paul Brousse (q.v.), Jean Allemane (q.v.) and the other aspiring Socialist leaders. His quest for Socialist unity was to become a lifelong passion.

In 1889, the 'old-guard' Blanquists, seduced by Boulangism, broke away from Vaillant and espoused an ambiguous form of national socialism. Vaillant galvanized his followers into a national party, the Parti Socialiste Révolutionnaire which, in the general elections of 1898, became the second largest Socialist Party in France. During the Dreyfus (1898) and Millerand (1899) affairs, Vaillant's conception of a tactical approach which eschewed the twin 'dangers' of open support for bourgeois governments (Jaurès) and crude revolutionary rhetoric (Guesde) paved the way for the political compromise which was to inform the infant united party (Section Française de l'Internationale Ouvrière) after 1905. Vaillant's leadership of the SFIO Fédération de la Seine, the largest federation in the party, was along with his growing closeness to Jaurès, a vital factor in the preservation of unity between 1905 and 1914.

Vaillant was an active municipal councillor (1884–93) and deputy (1893–1915) for the Père Lachaise district of Paris and succeeded in implementing many practical reforms which helped transform the lives of his constituents. An ardent champion of syndicalist autonomy, Vaillant, more than any other Socialist leader, ensured that the infant Confédération Générale du Travail was able to avoid the sectarianism of Socialist politics and devote itself to organizing the direct labour action of the working class. He has been called by one historian 'the founding father of the CGT'. Vaillant was also a dedicated and lifelong internationalist who devoted the last fifteen years of his life to the cause of peace. He was the most active member of the SFIO on the International Socialist Bureau and was instrumental in forcing the Second International to examine and re-examine potential measures to be adopted against war. Shattered by the death of Jaurès in 1914, Vaillant espoused the cause of Union Sacrée, but died a year later, in December 1915. He is buried in Vierzon and must be regarded (with Jaurès and Guesde) as one of the three founding fathers of French socialism.

Bibliography

Howorth, J. (1982), *Edouard Vaillant et la création de l'unité socialiste en France*, Paris: Editions Syros.

Pennetier, C. (1982), *Le Socialisme dans le Cher*, Paris: Delayance La Charité.

JH

VALLAT, Xavier Joseph (1891–1972)

Xavier Vallat was born in Villedieu (Vaucluse) in 1891, received a Catholic education, and was teaching in a Catholic college when called to military service in 1913. He began the war as a corporal and finished as a lieutenant in the Alpine Division, three times decorated and three times wounded, blind in his right eye and his left leg amputated. He was to become a distinctive figure on the right in the Chamber of Deputies, where he first won a seat in 1919, being re-elected in 1928, 1932 and 1936. Outside the Chamber he practised as a barrister and, more significantly, was involved with a succession of extremist right-wing leagues – Action Française, Valois' Faisceau (1925–6), the Croix de Feu (1928–36). After the fall of France he was nominated by Pétain as secretary to the Ministry of War Veterans (1940) and then as commissioner for Jewish affairs in 1941. He was also the founder of the Légion Française des Combattants which sought to bring all war veterans associations into a single movement in service of the Vichy regime. The post-liberation purge of collaborators saw him condemned to ten years' imprisonment and to national disgrace for life. A former close friend of Charles Maurras (q.v.), he remained true to his royalist principles to the end, and was director of the royalist newspaper *Aspects de la France* from 1962 to 1966. He died in 1972.

Vallat was an authentic son of the right-wing Catholic nationalist tradition which confirmed its implacable hostility to the Republic at the time of the Dreyfus affair. His extra-parliamentary connections were eclectic, including several right-wing leagues, Castelnau's Fédération Nationale Catholique and, after 1936, Taittinger's Parti National Populaire (ex-Jeunesses Patriotes). The positions he came to occupy under the Vichy regime were particularly appropriate to his reputation. His physical disabilities made him a symbolic figure for the right-wing war veterans' associations, whose mystique of order, national unity and military virtues was a powerful source of hostility to parliamentary democracy between the wars. Similarly the responsibility he was given in 1941 for 'Jewish affairs' reflected the brutal anti-Semitism he had expressed throughout his political career. He is particularly notorious for his speech in the Chamber of Deputies in 1936 greeting the investiture of Léon Blum as prime minister, when despite warnings from the president of the Chamber, he registered his disgust that 'this ancient Gallo-Roman country' was to be governed by 'a Jew'.

Defending himself at his trial after the liberation, Vallat insisted that Vichy's anti-Jewish legislation had the effect of averting Hitler's 'final solution' in the non-occupied zone. Subsequent research has discredited this notion of Vichy as a 'shield' against the worst excesses of nazism. However, there is evidence that Vallat's anti-Semitism was cultural rather than racial, that his attempts to preserve a degree of French sovereignty in this domain did antagonize the occupying power, and that Vichy's worst crimes against Jews followed his replacement as commissioner for Jewish affairs in March 1942. Vallat's role as the initiator of French anti-Semitic laws under the occupation has none the less made him one of the most notorious symbols of collaboration.

Bibliography

Vallat's role at Vichy is discussed in most of the major studies of the regime, of which the most accessible in English is probably R.O. Paxton, *Vichy France: Old guard and new order 1940–44* (London: Barrie and Jenkins, 1973). For his earlier career there are no biographical works, but of interest may be A. Prost, *Les Anciens combattants et la société française 1914–39*, 3 vols (Paris: FNSP, 1977), and a study of the Jeunesses Patriotes: R. Soucy, 'Centrist Fascism: The Jeunesses Patriotes' in *Journal of Contemporary History*, vol. 16, no. 2, spring 1962, pp. 273–307.

BJ

VALLÈS, Jules (1832–85)

A democratic Socialist and member of the Paris Commune of 1871, Vallès was most important in his own time as a political journalist, though his reputation today rests more on his fiction and *reportage*.

He was born at Le-Puy-en-Velay (Haute-Loire), the son of a schoolteacher, and the family moved in 1845 to Nantes. His childhood and adolescence were unhappy and disturbed. He was first involved in revolutionary activity in Nantes and Paris during the Second Republic, and his father placed him for a while in a lunatic asylum in Nantes in 1852 apparently to escape the consequences of his opposition to the *coup d'état* of Napoleon III. He soon returned to Paris, where he frequented 'bohemian' and anti-governmental circles. He was implicated in an abortive plot against the emperor in 1853. After various temporary jobs, he was able to earn his living as a journalist. In June 1867, he founded a literary weekly *La Rue*, which was suppressed after six months because of its left-wing and oppositional stance. Vallès spent three months in prison in 1868–9 for writing further articles against the regime. He attempted to start other papers, and he stood as a revolutionary Socialist candidate in Paris in the legislative elections of 1869. The same year he became a Freemason.

He was prominent in the events leading up to the creation of the Commune. He participated in the insurrectionary movements of 14 August and 31 October 1870 and he helped to constitute the important Comité Central Républicain des Arrondissements in September. He was one of the authors and signatories of the proclamation of 6 January 1871 calling for the establishment of a Commune, the *Affiche Rouge*, and the following month he founded *Le Cri du Peuple*, which was to become almost the 'official voice' of Paris's revolutionary government. He was elected to the Commune for the 15th *arrondissement* on 26 March. He attended and spoke at its meetings regularly and was in the minority opposing dictatorial measures, notably the suppression of the liberty of the press, arbitrary arrests and the setting-up of a committee of public safety. He was a member of the Commune's education committee, which put forward advanced proposals for comprehensive education for both sexes, and he wrote the Declaration to the French People of 19 April. He fought on the barricades in Belleville in the last days of the Commune in May 1871 and was reported dead. He managed to escape, however, and went via Belgium to England. He was condemned to death in his absence in 1872.

He spent most of his exile in London, from where he sought to resume his journalistic career. After initial difficulties, he was able to do this, and he also played a role in maintaining contacts and morale among those banned as a result of their communard activities – the *proscrits*. It was during his exile, too, that he wrote his masterpiece, the autobiographical trilogy *Jacques Vingtras*. *L'Enfant* first appeared in serial form in 1876, while *Le Bachelier* and *L'Insurgé* were published in 1881 and 1882. In 1880 he had returned to France following the general amnesty for the communards. In 1883, *Le Cri du Peuple* was revived and became France's most successful Socialist paper of the day. It was doctrinally eclectic, publish-

ing contributions from Blanquists, Guesdists and Independents as well as by Vallès himself and his anarchist companion Séverine. Vallès became seriously ill with diabetes in 1884 and died in February the following year. His funeral in Paris attracted large crowds.

Vallès' brand of socialism was instinctive and romantic. He was primarily a rebel, against family, school and university and then against the authoritarian Second Empire. He refused to accept the constraints of sects, parties or set doctrines. Positively, he was a passionate advocate of liberty for the individual and justice for the socially deprived.

Bibliography

There are two modern editions of Vallès' writings: *Oeuvres Complètes,* edited by Lucien Scheler (Paris: Editeurs Français Réunis, 1951–); and *Oeuvres,* edited by Roger Bellet (Paris: Gallimard, 1975–). See also Gaston Gille, *Jules Vallès (1832–1885). Ses révoltes, sa maîtrise, son prestige* (Paris: Flammarion and Jouve, 1941; reprinted Geneva: Slatkine, 1981); Marie-Claire Bancquart, *Jules Vallès* (Paris: Editions Pierre Seghers, 1971); and Roger Bellet, *Jules Vallès journaliste du second empire, de la commune de Paris et de la IIIe République (1857–1885)* (Paris: Editeurs Français Réunis, 1977).

SW

'VALOIS', pseudonym Alfred Georges Gressent (1878–1945)

Valois was born Alfred Georges Gressent in 1878, adopting his literary pseudonym in 1906. His father was a butcher who died young, and Valois was brought up in relative poverty by strict grandparents. These factors may have been important in his subsequent deep-rooted hatred of money-dominated bourgeois society and his emphasis on discipline. Before 1914 he was influenced by two main theorists, Sorrel and Maurras. After a youthful flirtation with anarchism and syndicalism, he joined the Action Française. Valois sought to reconcile the working class with order and authority, believing these concepts were embodied in Catholicism and monarchism. Valois was a social Darwinist, who turned Rousseau upside down: he believed that in the state of nature man was an ignoble savage until he was forced to be creative by strong leaders. He was a key figure in the Cercle Proudhon, which he saw as offering a common platform for nationalists and leftist anti-democrats. After 1912 these ideas were disseminated in particular through the Nouvelle Librairie Nationale, which later became the Librairie Valois.

After serving with distinction in the First World War, Valois became disillusioned with the Action Française. Maurras had never liked him, and Valois had become increasingly critical of his leader's lack of dynamism. He believed that the war had shown the great mobilizing power of nationalism, and he sought to amalgamate this with a social programme based on corporatism. These factors eventually led to a break with the elitist Action Française.

In November 1925 he went on to found the Faisceau. He had been impressed by Mussolini, but Valois saw the Faisceau in terms of a French tradition – a fusion of Barrès's nationalism and Sorel's attack on the bourgeois state. Valois's fascism did not seek to defend an idealized past. His programme sought a strong government, directing a corporatist economic system which involved real cooperation of workers and management. The ultimate goal was not only social stability, but technical and economic progress. Aspects of this programme, which Valois had partly developed before 1925, attracted some business support. However, business saw the movement mainly in terms of controlling labour. Moreover, the break with the Action Française led to bitter attacks on Valois from his former colleagues, who were nothing if not masters at the art of vilification. In 1926 the Faisceau was estimated to have over 50,000 members. Great ceremonies were held, with uniformed activists, but the movement was already cracking up. It was plagued by internal divisions, weakened by Action Française pressure on key supporters, and finally doomed by the formation of a government of 'national union', and the stabilization of the franc.

In 1928 the Faisceau was dissolved, and Valois began a political journey which led him back to an interest in small economic units, such as cooperatives. In the 1930s he was strongly critical of the main trade union federation's plans which he said did not involve the working class enough. Although interested by some aspects of the 1930s planning debates, he ultimately believed it would place too much power in the hands of technocrats. During the war he was arrested, and died in Bergen-Belsen in 1945.

Bibliography

Douglas, A. (1984), 'Violence and fascism: The case of the Faisceau', *Journal of Contemporary History*, vol. 19, no. 4, pp. 689–712.

Guchet, Y. (1975), *Georges Valois*, Paris: Editions Albatros.

Sternhell, Z. (1976), 'Anatomie d'un mouvement fasciste en France: le Faisceau de Georges Valois', *Revue Française de Science Politique*, vol. 26 no. 1, pp. 5–40.

Sternhell, Z. (1986), *Neither Left nor Right*, Berkeley, Cal.: University of California Press, French edn, Paris: Seuil, 1983.

RE

VAUGEOIS, Henri (1864–1916)

Vaugeois was one of the founders of the right-wing Action Française and a leading figure in the movement in its early 'radical' phase. He was born at Laigle (Orne) in Normandy into an academic and Republican family. His father was dean of the Law Faculty at the University of Caen, and one of his forebears had been a member of the Revolutionary Convention. Vaugeois himself became a philosophy professor, teaching at the college of Coulommiers (Seine-et-Marne), and his first political inclinations were to the left and radical-socialism. He was a committee member of Paul Desjardins' Union pour l'Action Morale until it became Dreyfusard.

In the atmosphere of the 'affair', he then sought a new vehicle for his neo-Jacobin nationalism. With Maurice Pujo, he constituted an ephemeral Comité d'Action Française in April 1898, and he was a prime mover in the creation of the Ligue de la Patrie Française in January 1899. This association of intellectuals quickly established itself as one of the main anti-Dreyfusard leagues. Vaugeois and others, however, were unhappy with its conservative and legalistic stance. He and Charles Maurras broke away in mid-1899 and revived the Comité d'Action Française. They held their first public meeting in Paris in June that year and launched a bi-monthly *Bulletin* (later *Revue*) *de l'Action Française* in July.

The new movement and its organ were explicitly counter-revolutionary, advocating political violence and direct action against the Republican régime. Vaugeois opposed any involvement in elections and stressed the centrality of anti-Semitism in his programme for national revival. He was converted in 1901 to Maurras' brand of political monarchism but remained hostile to the style and personnel of traditional royalism. He was keen at this time to forge links between the Action Française and the 'corporatist' Syndicats Jaunes movement.

In 1905, the Comité became the Ligue d'Action Française with Vaugeois as president, and in 1908 he was founding co-editor with Léon Daudet of the daily *L'Action Française*. He played an active role in the administration of both the league and the newspaper, fund-raising, making speeches, visiting local branches and writing regular columns until his premature death in April 1916.

Bibliography

There is no study of Vaugeois. Henri Vaugeois, *Notre Pays* (Paris: Nouvelle Librairie Nationale, 1916) is a collection of articles, preceded by short memorial notices by Maurras and Daudet. His political views receive most extensive discussion in Jacques Paugam, *L'Age d'or du maurrassisme* (Paris: Denoël, 1971).

SW

VEIL, Simone Annie (neé Jacob) (1927–   )

Simone Veil has been emerging from opinion polls as France's most popular politician since 1974, though since 1979 she has been working in a European rather than a national context. She was minister of health from 1974 to 1979 under the presidency of Giscard d'Estaing, President of the European Parliament from 1979 to 1982, and continues to sit as a European MP and as leader of the European Parliament's liberal-democratic grouping.

The distinguishing feature of Simone Veil's career is that despite having been consistently allied with the centre-right, she is a figure of some sympathy to the left. She was born Simone Jacob in Nice in 1927, one of four children of a middle-class French Jewish family, and, shortly after the completion of her *baccalauréat*, was arrested as a Jew by the occupying Nazis and deported with her mother and sister to the concentration camp at Auschwitz. Her mother died there of typhus, and her father and brother, deported elsewhere, were never traced. Simone and her sister survived and returned to France in 1945. She studied law and political science at the Institute for Political Studies in Paris, and married a fellow student, Antoine Veil, in 1946. Over the next ten years Simone Veil had three children and completed her studies, so that in 1956 she qualified as a magistrate and the following year accepted an appointment in the Ministry of Justice. Working in the department concerned with prison administration during the Algerian War, she fought for the reclassification of captured Algerian nationalists as *political* prisoners. She became technical adviser to the minister of justice in 1969, secretary-general of the High Council

of Magistrates in 1970, and in 1972 joined the administrative board of the French broadcasting authority (the ORTF).

Simone Veil's career as a major public figure began in 1974 with her appointmemt as minister of health in the first cabinet of President Giscard d'Estaing, newly elected after a campaign that emphasized liberal social policies. She thus became the first woman to hold full ministerial office under the Fifth Republic, and it is for her work on questions essentially affecting women that her ministry will be remembered. Since the repressive anti-contraception laws of 1920 abortion had been a criminal offence in France and women who could not afford to pay for private treatment had been forced into dangerous 'backstreet' abortions at the rate, on the figures quoted by Veil, of some 300,000 a year. The new minister's first major task was to steer through Parliament a bill legalizing abortion under certain carefully defined circumstances. Despite vitriolic attacks from the right, and enforced dependence on the votes of the left opposition rather than those of her own severely divided majority party, the 'Veil law' as it came to be known was passed in December 1974 after a lengthy televised Assembly debate. During the rest of her period as minister of health Simone Veil also helped to promote greater availability of contraception and some improvements in maternity services, as well as sponsoring preventive medecine with, for example, a large scale anti-smoking campaign. Her ministry was extended to include social security in 1977, and in this capacity she was also responsible for managing a steep and unpopular rise in social security contributions.

Though she had never joined a political party or stood for election to public office, the polls indicated that the minister of health was a popular figure in the country. At the same time, her relations with Giscard's second prime minister, Raymond Barre, were distinctly less cordial than they had been with his predecessor Jacques Chirac, and there were some disagreements with the president himself over, for example, the government's response to the worsening recession. Partly for these reasons she was invited to head Giscard's centre-right slate for the first elections to the European Parliament, and, having accepted, campaigned on the theme of a more integrated Europe, whilst the other half of the French governmental majority, the Gaullists, emphasized the defence of France's interests in Europe. Elected in June, she resigned as minister of health, then stood for president of the new Parliament and won on the second ballot, supported by a voting coalition of centrist Liberals, Christian Democrats and British Conservatives. In her inaugural address she drew attention to the fact that with her election two 'minorities' achieved significant representation in the Parliament of Europe, for she was both a woman and a Jew. Her term of office as president ended in January 1982. At the second European parliamentary elections in June 1984 she headed a combined slate of UDF (Giscard's Union for French Democracy Union) and the Gaullist RPR, and she has been president of the liberal-democratic group throughout this Parliament. Veil is a wholehearted European and centrist in her political sympathies, and at the 1989 elections she abandoned the major right coalition to head, instead, the centre list. She was elected to become one of seven French Euro-MPs of the centre.

It has been strongly suggested that had Giscard won the presidential election of 1981, Simone Veil might have become prime minister. There has also been much press speculation on the possibility of her being a future candidate for the presidency. Though she has denied any intention to stand for this office, certain features of her career and public image justify the speculation. Public perception of her seems to focus on the qualities of integrity and reasoned calm; the radicalism associated with her pro-abortion stance is offset by the reassuring image of a devoted mother and grandmother. The fact that she has never become completely identified with one political party is clearly an advantage, for the ideal of a president who would be above party conflicts is written into the constitution of the Fifth Republic. It remains to be seen how heavily these political advantages could weigh against what the polls also suggest is a widespread national disinclination to elect a female head of state.

Bibliography

There have been numerous articles in the French press over the last few years. One of the more useful is 'Politoscopie de Simone Veil', *Le Point*, 23 January 1984.

In the English press articles and interviews can be found in: *The Times* (3 March 1975), *The Guardian* (6 August 1975), *The Observer* (10 September 1978), *The Economist* (30 December 1978).

There is a published biography of Simone Veil by Michel Sarazin, *Une femme, Simone Veil* (Paris: Robert Laffont, 1987).

DiH

VERMEERSCH, Julie 'Jeannette' (1910–)

Jeannette Vermeersch, companion of Maurice Thorez, was a leading member of the French Communist Party until the death of Thorez and one of the dominant forces in the Union des Femmes Françaises (Union of Frenchwomen – the Communist Party women's para-political organization).

Born in Lille, one of nine children of a docker's family, Julie Vermeersch (known as Jeannette) began work as a weaver at the age of 12. She joined the Jeunesses Communistes (Young Communists) a few years later and in 1929 paid her first visit to the Soviet Union.

During the 1930s, she held posts in the Communist trade union organization (CGTU) and the national executive of the Jeunesses Communistes (very unusual for a young woman at the time). She was a founder-member of the Union des Jeunes Filles de France (Communist youth movement for young women and girls) with Danièle Casanova and Marie-Claude Vaillant-Couturier. Vermeersch spent some of the war years in the USSR with Maurice Thorez, and on her return, became increasingly prominent in the UFF (Union des Femmes Françaises) and the Communist-dominated Fédération Démocratique Internationale des Femmes (International Democratic Women's Federation). She gained a place in the party's central committee in 1947. She was a PCF deputy from 1945–58, and a senator from 1959 to 1968.

Vermeersch dominated the UFF with three other women (also wives or companions of PCF leaders) who were collectively known as 'the four musketeers'. In the 1950s, with Thorez ill but still general secretary of the PCF, Vermeersch was considered to be the unofficial 'no. 2' of the PCF, an influence she maintained until the death of Thorez in 1964. After his death, she remained in the Central Committee until 1968, when she resigned over the PCF's criticism of the Soviet invasion of Czechoslovakia.

She was outspoken in the National Assembly on issues concerning working-class women but is better remembered for her unquestioning loyalty to the Soviet Union, her Stalinism and her relationship with Thorez. As far as women were concerned, she is better remembered for her hostility to the introduction of contraception, calling it the vice of bourgeois women, than for her statements about women's rights at work (and the married woman's right to work – subject of much discussion in the 1950s), or on state provision of childcare facilities.

Today, Vermeersch lives quietly in a Paris suburb.

Bibliography

Robrieux, P. (1975), *Maurice Thorez, vie secrète et vie publique*, Paris: Fayard.

Rousseau, R. (1983), *Les Femmes Rouges*, Paris: Albin Michel.

CD

VIVIANI, René Jean Raphaël Adrien (1863–1925)

René Viviani was an independent Socialist deputy, who became the first minister of labour (1906–10), and prime minister (1914–15). Born and educated in Algeria, he studied law first in Algiers then Paris and followed his father into the legal profession. At the Paris Bar he made his reputation defending the rights of trade unions. Drawn to the politics of the left, he joined the staff of Millerand's newspaper *La Petite République* and was elected deputy for the 5th *arrondissement* of Paris in 1893. A skilled orator (he had taken elocution lessons at the Comédie Française) he soon made his mark in the Chamber alongside Millerand (q.v.) and Jaurès (q.v.). A noted anticlerical, he also consistently championed the cause of women's rights throughout his career. (His commitment was doubtless reinforced by a long liaison with Marguerite Durand, founder of the first feminist daily newspaper *La Fronde*.) He strongly defended Millerand over 'ministerialism' and broke altogether with the new SFIO in 1905.

Having lost his seat in 1902, he was returned to Parliament in 1906 with largely Radical votes and was appointed minister of labour by Clemenceau. In nearly four years in office he implemented social reforms already passed and helped enact the law of 1910 on workers' pensions. He resigned from the Briand government in opposition to its policy of mobilizing striking railway workers. Following the elections of 1914 he became prime minister (and his own foreign minister) after assuring President Poincaré (q.v.) that he would uphold the three-year law on military service, which earlier he had opposed. Partly because of his inexperience in foreign affairs and partly on account of illness he relinquished the direction of French foreign policy during the July crisis to the president of the Republic. Similarly, after the outbreak of war until the overthrow of his cabinet in October 1915 he was overshadowed by commander-in-chief Joffre and minister of defence Millerand. Increasingly the victim of a brain disorder, he never regained major office but made a decisive speech in May 1919 which helped persuade the Chamber of Deputies to pass a bill on women's suffrage. Recurrence of his mental illness ended his legal career in 1923 and he died in a mental hospital in 1925.

Bibliography

Gallup, S.V. (1965), *The Political Career of René Viviani*, Oxford: B. Litt. thesis.

Keiger, J.F.V. (1983), *France and the Origins of the First World War*, London: Macmillan.

Hause, S. and A. Kenney (1984), *Women's Suffrage and Social Politics in the French Third Republic*, Princeton, NJ: Princeton University Press.

JFM

W

WADDINGTON, William Henry (1826–94)

Waddington was of English descent and had two careers, those of a scholar and a politician. Son of a rich English manufacturer who had settled in Normandy, he was educated in Paris before going to Rugby and Trinity College, Cambridge. At Cambridge he distinguished himself by being bracketed equal as chancellor's medallist and rowing in the victorious crew against Oxford, both in 1848. Having chosen French nationality, he spent the next sixteen years pursuing his interests in classical archaeology. He travelled in Greece and Asia Minor and became eminent as a numismatist and epigrapher, some of whose published work is still highly regarded.

By 1865, when he was elected to the Académie des Inscriptions et Belles Lettres, his second career was beginning. Political activity under the Second Empire was reviving and Waddington, a man of moderate liberal leanings, aspired to enter Parliament. Unsuccessful in 1865 and 1869, he was returned in February 1871 to the first National Assembly of the Third Republic. Thence forward he represented the Aisne department, first as a deputy and then as a senator for twenty-three years. A supporter of Thiers in the National Assembly, he was rewarded in May 1873 with the post of minister of education. But Thiers fell five days later and it was nearly three years before Waddington resumed charge of education in the Dufaure and Simon cabinets of 1876–7. After the *seize mai* crisis he became minister for foreign affairs, a post he held for two years combining it with the premiership from February to December 1879. He then gave way to de Freycinet (q.v.), who was preferred by the influential Opportunist leader Gambetta. This was the end of his ministerial experience, but in 1883 he accepted the London embassy where he represented France until 1893.

Waddington is remarkable as being the only premier of the Third Republic who was half English, a Cambridge rowing blue and with an American second wife. His ancestry and upbringing made him politically vulnerable to Anglophobes but a useful ambassador at a time when Anglo-French relations were bedevilled by overseas rivalries. Ancestry apart, he exemplified a type of politician who, a generation earlier, might have won prominence under the July Monarchy but now loyally served the Third Republic. He was a well-to-do 'notable' with a provincial power-base, erudite and level-headed, a Protestant like his successor, de Freycinet, but less wily. Two sensible measures, a partial amnesty for communards and the return of Parliament to Paris from Versailles, were voted during his premiership and he created the useful Ministry of Posts and Telegraphs. In foreign affairs his freedom of action was necessarily circumscribed by France's weakness after the Franco-Prussian War, but he helped to secure France's representation at the Berlin Congress (1878), going there himself, and he strongly favoured French occupation of Tunis as compensation for Britain's taking Cyprus in that same year.

JPTB

WAECHTER, Antoine (1949–   )

Born in Mulhouse (Haut-Rhin), Antoine Waechter is an ecologist of long standing who came to public notice as the youthful ecology candidate in the 1988 presidential elections with a forceful campaign. He polled a creditable 1,149,642 votes (3.78 per cent) which was virtually the same as Brice Lalonde (q.v.) in 1981 (3.7 per cent). However, Waechter represents a new autonomous strategy for the ecology movement which split shortly before the presidential nominating convention with the more left-wing groups (Lalonde, for example) leaving. The new outlook, 'neither left nor right', in Waechter's words, was also more pragmatic about political power.

Waechter, in 1963, was in the Student Christian movement but had joined the ecology movement by 1965. He has a doctorate in animal ecology and since 1978 has worked for the Ministry of Agriculture. He has participated in many local elections in the Haut-Rhin and in 1986 was elected to the Regional Council and in 1989 to the Mulhouse City Council. The ecology movement's shift to Alsace is a reflection of the power of regional personality and was reflected in the 1988 vote (9.37 in Bas-Rhin and 9.24 per cent in Haut-Rhin) – although Waechter retained the same vote as Lalonde it fell in Paris itself (it was still only 200 behind the Communists and this result was effaced in 1989 when the ecologists polled well).

Waechter's presidential campaign called for a halt to the building of nuclear power stations but also proposed the further democratization of society through such measures as the popular initiative for referendums. Waechter also took up the more familiar environmental issues as well as giving pre-eminence to the ecologist view that the mainstream parties with their obsession with 'growth' were outmoded.

The 1989 European elections were another boost for Waechter who led the ecologist list to 10.39 per cent in fourth position (a whisker behind the National Front) and nine European Seats.

Bibliography

Guillaume Saintenay, 'Les verts: limites et intérprétations d'un succès électoral', *Revve Politique et Parlementaire*, no. 940, March–April 1989, pp. 25–33; Sara Parkin, *Green Parties* (London: Heretic Books, 1989).

DSB

WALDECK-ROUSSEAU, Pierre-Marie René Ernest (1846–1904)

Waldeck-Rousseau embarked on a parliamentary career as a deputy for Ille-et-Vilaine in 1879. Only two years later, at the early age of 35, he was given the Ministry of the Interior in Gambetta's short-lived '*grand ministère*' of 1881–2. But he subsequently moved in a conservative direction, as his legal practice took him into the world of big business and high finance. His skill and reputation as a barrister brought him eminent clients from a variety of milieux, including such diverse figures as Coquelin, Zola and Leo XIII. Yet this fish-eyed man of cold aspect did not make friends easily, and had little of his wealthy wife's taste for social occasions, preferring the opera and theatre which was increasingly reflected in the cases he undertook. He might well

have devoted himself entirely to his practice, had he not been persuaded to stand for a vacant Senate seat in the Loire in 1894. Untainted by the parliamentary scandals of the period – while enhancing his professional reputation in the attendant litigation – he inspired a respect that went far beyond the ranks of his fellow Opportunists. After an unsuccessful bid for the presidency of the Republic in 1895 – in which he came a modest third – the Dreyfus crisis of 1899 brought him the premiership, after Poincaré had declined the offer.

His ministry (22 June 1899 – 7 June 1902) was to be the longest in the history of either the Third or Fourth Republics; and it was also remarkable for its initial political breadth, ranging from the first Socialist to sit in a Third Republican cabinet (Alexandre Millerand) to General Gallifet, the so-called 'butcher of the Commune'. Waldeck-Rousseau saw public confidence as the main issue. Confidence in the law had been shaken by procedural irregularities in the handling of the Dreyfus case, and faith in the stability of public order had been undermined by the subversive activities of the Nationalists. He accordingly arraigned the leaders of subversion before the Senate in its High Court capacity, where they were sentenced to varying terms of exile and imprisonment. But the widely-held belief that he artificially strengthened the case against them by manufacturing a dossier of dubious evidence is not borne out (in the present writer's view) by the documents on which the charge is based. When, to the government's embarrassment, Dreyfus was again found guilty by court martial, Waldeck-Rousseau arranged to have him pardoned. But he was initially disinclined to see the question of confidence in the army as a major issue, since the main lesson of Déroulède's abortive coup was the reluctance of the army to respond to nationalist and royalist invitations to help overthrow the regime. With notable exceptions, Gallifet's shake-up of its senior echelons was mainly on grounds of efficiency rather than political security. But his successor as war minister, General L.J.N. André, inaugurated a systematic watch on the private lives and opinions of officers who were candidates for promotion. Waldeck-Rousseau was aware in general terms of what was going on, and indeed had been at pains to impress on ministers and prefects that civil servants, teachers and other public employees should be chosen with an eye to their Republican sentiments. What he appears not to have known was that André was making use of a network of Masonic informers – a fact that was eventually to lead to André's disgrace and resignation under the next ministry.

On the remaining issue of public confidence – the state's ability to control the Church – Waldeck-Rousseau considered the Church a declining force and regarded the Concordat as an adequate means of controlling the secular clergy, provided that the state fully exercised its legitimate rights. The regular clergy were a different matter. Many of the orders had no formal legal status in France, and lay outside any normal machinery of governmental control over ecclesiastics. The government consequently brought about the associations law of 1 July 1901, which among other things effectively obliged the religious orders to apply for the authorization of their continued residence in France. It is not clear which orders Waldeck-Rousseau would himself have authorized and which expelled, since the implementation of the law largely fell to his successor, Emile Combes; moreover the examining parliamentary committee had sharpened the provisions of the premier's original bill. He had in any case already had the Assumptionists dissolved. Their chief crime in his eyes was the venom they had put into politics during the Dreyfus affair, and the fact that the venom reached half a million readers through the multiple channels of the Assumptionist press. The Jesuits were also a likely target for his disfavour in that their schools had a high entry rate into the military academies and were popularly if simplistically associated with the alleged clerico–military conspiracy to subvert the regime. As for the rest of the orders, Waldeck-Rousseau was subsequently to express alarm at his successor's wholesale rejection of the vast majority of requests for authorization.

His resignation in June 1902 was largely the result of ill-health – cancer was to carry him off two years later – but it was also hastened by the size of the large anticlerical majority elected to the Chamber in the previous month. The achievement of a balanced solution to the clerical question would not be easy; and, perhaps with the presidential election of 1906 in mind, he preferred to retire on his laurels rather than risk his reputation in the ungrateful role of urging moderation on a belligerent Parliament. It has been suggested that his choice of successor was intended to enhance the memory of his own ministry and improve his standing for the presidential election.

Bibliography

The indispensable study of his career is Pierre Sorlin's *Waldeck-Rousseau* (Paris: A. Colin, 1966).

ML

WEISS, Louise (1893–1983)

A lifelong campaigner, journalist and woman of action, Louise Weiss ended her long career as doyenne of the European Parliament of 1979. Born in Arras in 1893 into a dynasty of public servants, she fought for independence against a reluctant family. Her education, at the Lycée Molière and the Collège Sévigné in Paris, also included a spell as a 'Mädchen in uniform' in Germany and an Oxford diploma. She succeeded in the *agrégation* on the eve of the First World War, and spent the war nursing, and organizing hospitals. Soon after the war, she co-founded a weekly paper, *Europe Nouvelle*, which she directed until 1934: devoted to the cause of international understanding, it became closely identified with the views of Aristide Briand (q.v.). In 1921 she organized the safe evacuation of over a hundred French governesses caught up in the Russian Revolution. In 1934, feeling pacifism to be no longer an adequate response to the dictators, she left *Europe Nouvelle* and flung herself energetically into a campaign for women's suffrage. Her group, Femme Nouvelle, organized direct action on similar lines to the British suffragettes. When in 1936, a franchise bill yet again failed in the Senate, Louise Weiss turned once more to international affairs as war threatened. (She was particularly close to the leaders of the Czech government whom she had long known.) As secretary-general of the committee for refugees, she was instrumental in 1938 in finding refuge for the Jewish passengers of the steamer *Saint-Louis*, who were in danger of becoming stateless. During the Second World War, she edited a Resistance newspaper. In the post-war period, she remained a prolific journalist and writer, bringing out memoirs, travel books and novels, and winning several literary prizes. Louise Weiss unsuccessfully campaigned to become the first woman member of the French Academy in 1974, but five years later was elected, on the list led by Jacques Chirac, to the European Assembly. She died in 1983.

Louise Weiss probably became best known to the public during her Femme Nouvelle campaign in the 1930s and her Academy candidature in the 1970s, but hers was a life lived in close proximity with the political and diplomatic world. Highly intelligent, resourceful and afraid of no one, she bitterly resented her exclusion from formal politics on account of her sex. During the 1920s and 1930s she was on familiar terms with many political leaders, and for want of power fell back on influence. But hers was a temperament suited to action and oratory rather than discreet pressure. Her undisguised impatience with others and her unconventional way of going about things sometimes made enemies, and certainly made her life difficult and isolated at times. She was briefly married; by her own account, the chief virtue of the marriage was to provide her with a more secure social status. Much honoured in her old age, she nevertheless strikes one forcibly as being someone who was, as Simone de Beauvoir would put it, 'flouée': cheated of the life she might have led. Her memoirs are a lively and detailed, if far from objective, account of her times.

Bibliography

Ample details of Louise Weiss's life will be found in her *Mémoires d'une européenne*, 6 vols (Paris: Albin Michel, 1980), a definitive edition replacing earlier versions, but there is nothing available on her in English.

SR

de WENDEL, François Augustin Marie (1874–1949)

Steel industrialist, newspaper owner, chairman of the renowned iron and steel pressure group the Comité des Forges, regent of the Bank of France, deputy, then senator and member of the Republican Federation, François de Wendel figured more than prominently among his generation of Third Republican politicians. He was a man who, perhaps more than any other of his time, combined in one person the many attributes of the 'grande bourgeoisie': enormously wealthy and wielding influence in the worlds of business, politics and finance, he appeared, at least to his detractors and to the makers of myths, to incarnate the powers of the infamous 'deux cent familles' – the 200 capitalist families who, for certain sections of the left, were the true rulers of France behind its democratic, Republican façade.

In reality, the powers of de Wendel and others of his circle have been greatly exaggerated, as is shown by the work of historian Jean-Noël Jeanneney. But this is not to deny that de Wendel was a man of enormous influence. Already a leading steel baron (*maître des forges*) in the first decade of this century, with an industrial empire based on iron ore and steel which spanned the border of France and annexed Alsace-Lorraine, de Wendel became a regent of the Bank of France in 1912 and was elected deputy for Briey-Sud in April 1914. Between 1914 and 1918, he held a series of positions in the War Ministry,

with special responsibility for munitions, and by the end of the war had begun to discover the extent and potential of his powers. It was also from this early period that the powerful myths surrounding de Wendel, his family and the other steel barons of Lorraine began to emerge.

If de Wendel's early years in Parliament and at the Bank of France were ones of new opportunities and apprenticeship in power, then the years between the wars which followed revealed the multiple constraints on that power. As a regime dominated by middle classes, the political class and electorate of the Third Republic shared a deep mistrust of the industrial and financial bourgeoisie. And certain sections of the political community were actively hostile to the likes of de Wendel and the barons of steel. In the 'Briey affair', the *maîtres des forges* of Lorraine were accused of prolonging the First World War by preventing the French military from bombing their steel plants and ore mines in annexed and invaded Lorraine. This particular myth – which, as the historical record reveals, was quite unfounded – was perpetuated by the left-wing press for several decades, and was linked in the popular mind to other instances of boss power – *pouvoir patronal*. But if it was true that the de Wendels were able to dominate Lorraine through paternalism, company towns and the sheer weight of their industry in the regional economy, national political affairs were quite another matter.

The conviction that what was good for steel and Lorraine was also good for France could not easily be imposed on government policy, despite de Wendel's elevated position among the political elite. Contrary to popular belief at the time, his influence over the Treaty of Versailles was virtually non-existent; nor was he able to force the government's hand over occupation of the Ruhr when the Germans began to renege on their reparations commitment to deliver coke to French steel plants. His ownership of the Parisian *Journal des Débats* and holdings in other papers failed to provide a clear and controllable voice for his views on domestic and foreign policy; nor did his controversial funding of leagues such as the Jeunesses Patriotes prevent the decline of his individual influence in the uncertain and increasingly chaotic environment of the early and mid-1930s. It was really only through his position at the Bank of France that, in league with colleagues such as Rothschild, he was able directly to influence government policy. But even then, such direct influence was limited to the crisis years of 1924 to 1927 when the precarious monetary situation rendered Herriot, Caillaux and Briand dependent on the Bank's goodwill and financial expertise.

By the 1930s, even these limited powers were fully on the wane. In his own world of steel, he had never been able to dominate the Comité des Forges due to his preoccupations in other spheres and to the growing role of full-time bureaucrats such as Robert Pinot in employers' organizations. By the mid-1920s, the impact of recession was beginning to weaken his industrial base in Lorraine. And within his own party, his name, wealth and notoriety began to limit his capacity for striking alliances, gaining allegiance and playing a leading role. He admired Mussolini but implacably opposed both Hitler and Vichy, and this kept him politically isolated from the late-1930s on. Despite his honourable behaviour in these difficult years, it was to be a political wilderness from which he never returned: the liberation saw a resurrection of attacks on de Wendel based in small part on fact, but largely on innuendo, and as a man of advanced years he was denied a role in the early post-war political order. He died in January 1949.

Bibliography

Berstein, S. (1978), 'L'argent et le pouvoir: à propos de François de Wendel', *Revue d'Histoire Moderne et Contemporaine*, vol. 25, July–September, pp. 487–99.

Jeanneney, J.-N. (1976), *François de Wendel en République: l'argent et le pouvoir 1914–1940*, Paris: Seuil.

MR

WEYGAND, Maxime (1867–1965)

General Weygand was a professional soldier, recalled from retirement to serve as commander-in-chief of the French forces facing the German invasion in 1940. After the defeat of France and the armistice, General Weygand played an important political role in the years 1940–42 until he was arrested by the Gestapo and imprisoned until the end of the Second World War.

Maxime Weygand was born in Brussels but moved to France, training as a cavalry officer at Saint-Cyr and serving in the Hussars in 1914. He worked closely with Marshal Foch in a staff job until 1923, being the permanent representative of France at the Versailles Conference. His military career took him to Warsaw and Syria. He was appointed chief of staff in 1930 and retired in 1935. The impending tragedy of 1940 when the French forces and their British allies failed to defend France against the Ger-

man invasion led to Weygand's recall. He became supreme army commander on 19 May 1940. The overrunning of the defences and the serious weaknesses which had been left in the French military preparations by Weygand's predecessor, General Gamelin, left Weygand a supporter of an armistice with Hitler.

General Weygand served in the government of the French Vichy regime, as minister of national defence under Marshal Pétain. However, he was mistrusted by Pierre Laval, Germany's firmest support in Pétain's cabinet, and on 9 September General Weygand was appointed delegate-general in French North Africa. He was indeed not a strong sympathizer of Franco-German collaboration, but determined to prevent as far as he was able a German invasion of North Africa and any extension of their occupation of French lands. He opposed the Vichy government's plan to allow the Germans to use facilities at Dakar and Bizerta in May 1941, an opposition which earned Weygand the displeasure of Admiral Darlan (q.v.). On 18 November 1941, persistent pressure from pro-German interests led to the dismissal of Weygand and an enforced retirement in Vichy France. The contacts which he had developed with the United States, particularly with Robert Murphy, the special representative of the American government in North Africa, also offended key interests in the Pétain cabinet. He had arranged for supplies to be sent to North Africa as early as February 1941 and was active in maintaining the links between Vichy France and the United States in the period before the entry of the Americans into the war.

Weygand's retirement was not peaceful; he was arrested in November 1942 and spent the rest of the war years in Germany. He was placed on trial as a member of the Vichy cabinet, having been incarcerated by the French in 1945, but he was released on the grounds that there was no basis for the accusations. General Weygand was already 78 years old at the end of the war and he lived a further twenty years in quiet retirement.

Bibliography

Churchill, W.S. (1949), *The Second World War* (vol. 2), London: Cassell. (The classic account with much detail and grasp of the realities facing Weygand.)

Horne, A. (1969), *To Lose a War: France 1940*, London: Macmillan. (A usefully prepared history of the key events.)

Werth, A. (1956), *France 1940–1944*, London: Hals.

(A sympathetic narrative of the military and political history of France during the war.)

Weygand, M. (1948), *The Role of General Weygand*, London: Eyre and Spottiswoode.

Weygand, M. (1955), *Recalled to Service: The memoirs of General Maxime Weygand*, London: Cassell.

PS

Y

YBARNÉGARAY, Michel Albert Jean Joseph (1883–1956)

Born at Uhart-Cize in the Basque country in 1883, Jean Ybarnégaray, a lawyer by training, was deputy for the department of his birth (Basses-Pyrénées) from 1914 to 1942. He first rose to public prominence during the parliamentary debates on the Stavisky affair in January 1934, when his local knowledge of Stavisky's fraudulent operations in Bayonne enabled him to spearhead the right's campaign to discredit the Chautemps government. He emerged in 1935 as the spokesman in the Chamber of Deputies for La Rocque's right-wing league, the Croix de Feu (Crosses of Fire), a role he continued to play when the organization was transformed into the Parti Social Français (PSF – French Social Party) in 1936. He was among those who voted plenary powers to Marshal Pétain in the parliamentary debate of July 1940 following the fall of France, and he briefly held office in the early months of the Vichy regime, first as minister for war veterans and then as minister for youth. Evidence of individual acts of resistance saved him from the initial sentence of national dishonour imposed by the courts after the liberation. He unsuccessfully sought re-election to Parliament in the post-war years, notably in 1956 on the list of another ex-PSF member, Tixier-Vignancour. He died in the same year.

Ybarnégaray was one of several conservative deputies who were affiliated to one or other of the various extreme-right extra-parliamentary organizations which flourished in the 1930s. After playing a leading role in Pierre Taittinger's Jeunesses Patriotes (Patriotic Youth), he was by 1934 involved with La Rocque's Croix de Feu, whose paramilitary structure and spectacular growth between 1934 and 1936 led the left to regard it as France's most dangerous proto-Fascist movement. As its parliamentary mouthpiece, Ybarnégaray thus earned a certain notoriety.

However, there had been a progressive estrangement between the Croix de Feu and the other leagues ever since the riots of 6 February 1934, when La Rocque had allegedly squandered the opportunity to invade the Chamber of Deputies. The rift was made irreparable when, in December 1935, Ybarnégaray offered to disarm the Croix de Feu and proposed the disbanding of all paramilitary organizations. This drew on him the opprobrium of all the other leagues, who accused him of capitulating to the growing Popular Front movement.

This incident heralded a new phase in the development of the Croix de Feu which, following the ban imposed on the leagues by the Popular Front government in 1936, was transformed into a political party (Parti Social Français). Ybarnégaray was influential in this change of strategy, which saw the movement shed its earlier image in favour of a more traditional conservative authoritarianism. By 1937, with over 1 million members, the PSF had become by far the largest organized force on the French right, and as it never had the opportunity to fight a legislative election campaign and increase its parliamentary representation, Jean Ybarnégaray remained its principal voice in the Chamber of Deputies in the closing years of the Third Republic.

Bibliography

Jean Ybarnégaray was himself the author of a book on the events of 6 February 1934, *Le Grand soir des honnêtes gens* (Paris: Editions des Ambassadeurs, 1934). See also M. Anderson, *Conservative Politics in France* (London: Allen and Unwin, 1974).

BJ

Z

ZAY, Jean Elie Paul (1904–44)

Jean Zay was minister of education and the fine arts under five successive prime ministers continuously from June 1936 until September 1939. A man of ability, vision and energy, he brought forward a wide range of major reforms to the education systems; many of them were not fully achieved on the outbreak of war. However, his reforming zeal and political common sense set an important agenda for change in a notoriously recalcitrant area. Zay was born and educated in Orléans. He took a law degree, and practised as a lawyer and a journalist. In 1932 and again in 1936 he was elected member of Parliament for one of the Orléans constituencies. Between 1932 and 1935 he was active as a backbench member of the Radical Party. In January 1936 he became a junior minister in the prime minister's department, and in June, at the age of 31, joined Léon Blum's (q.v.) Popular Front government. In September 1939 he refused the exemption from mobilization to which, as minister, he was entitled. He served with an active unit until June 1940, when he joined other members of Parliament including Pierre Mendès France (q.v.) leaving for North Africa on the steamship *Massilia* in the hope of continuing the war. Returning to France he was convicted on trumped up charges of desertion. Strongly anti-Fascist and opposed to the Munich settlement, he became a symbol of those aspects of pre-war France which the Vichy regime strongly attacked. In June 1944 three members of the French special police, the *milice*, removed him from prison in Riom alleging orders to transfer him elsewhere. During the journey they killed him.

As minister of education Zay was the founder of the main umbrella organization for government sponsored research, the Centre National de la Recherche Scientifique. He reorganized the national theatres and founded the Paris Museum of Modern Art. The school leaving age was raised to fourteen. He made physical education compulsory in schools. In his concern to open up educational access he brought both the primary schools and the elementary classes of the *lycées* (the selective academic secondary schools) under a single director of primary education. In 1937 experimental 'orientation classes' designed to provide a common first year of secondary education for all pupils were introduced in forty-five centres. This experiment, like his plans to nationalize the Ecole Libre des Sciences Politiques and provide a new system for the recruitment and training of top civil servants, was abandoned at the outbreak of war but was influential in shaping postwar developments.

Bibliography

The only biography of Zay is Marcel Ruby, *La Vie et l'oeuvre de Jean Zay* (Paris: l'Auteur, 1969). Zay's prison diary was posthumously published as: Jean Zay, *Souvenirs et solitude* (new edition with an introduction by A. Prost, Paris: Talus d'Approche, 1987). John E. Talbott, *The Politics of Educational Reform in France 1918–1940* (Princeton, NJ: Princeton University Press, 1969).

AS

ZOLA, Emile (1840–1902)

Zola was the author of some twenty-five novels, and of the letter to the President of the French Republic published in *L'Aurore* on 13 January 1898 under the title (coined by Clemenceau) 'J'accuse'.

Born in Paris in 1840 of an Italian father who died only five years later, Zola first encountered the world of publishing when he worked for Hachette & Cie in his early 20s. His own first major work was the novel *Thérèse Raquin*, published in 1867. Four years later he published the first volume of *Les Rougon-Macquart*, by which time he had become one of France's best known novelists; from that series at least two novels: *L'Assommoir* and *Germinal*, have become classics of world fame. This prolific writer was also a noted literary critic and the political correspondent of several newspapers (including a Russian one, *Vestnik Evropy*).

Zola developed the literary doctrine of naturalism,

a doctrine of the experimental novel derived from the scientific doctrine of the French biologist Claude Bernard (author of *Introduction à la méthode expérimentale*). The aim of the novelist – who must base his work on a meticulous documentation – is to expose evil in its most repulsive aspects, in order to generate in the reader a longing for that which is good. Thus in *Les Rougon-Macquart* it is less the personal history of the characters than the social deprivation around them which form the interest of the writing. From the mid-1880s onwards Zola, whose doctrine was under severe attack from the anti-naturalists who found his works immoral and abhorrent, became increasingly pessimistic about the evils that assailed France, and held the Church and clericalism as major culprits, responsible for growing intolerance and anti-Semitism in the country.

It comes as no surprise, therefore, that Zola quickly became a militant Dreyfusard. Two of his articles for *Le Figaro* deal with the scourge of anti-Semitism (1896) and the inevitability of victory for the forces of truth and honesty (1897) respectively. But the catalyst of Zola's passionate indictment of the French establishment, the letter 'J'accuse', was the acquittal of Esterhazy which, coming after the wrong conviction and deportation of Dreyfus, seemed a deliberate flouting of the most elementary principles of justice.

'J'accuse', written in an explosion of anger, is indeed explosive. In it, Zola accuses by name highly placed members of the General Staff and of the War Ministry of lies and deliberate malversations, and reviles traditional bourgeois values, religious and military narrow-mindedness, and the distorted sense of hierarchy that produced Dreyfus's conviction and Esterhazy's acquittal. Zola knew and intended that the explicitness of the accusations and the violence of the tone should expose him to charges of libel, as the purpose of his intervention was to give the affair maximum publicity. Publicity it got: 300,000 copies of *L'Aurore* sold that day, and the ensuing trial held in February 1898 was also well publicized, although the prosecution tried to minimize the issue, much to Zola's indignation and frustration. Zola was sentenced to one year in gaol and received a heavy fine. A second trial was called because of a technical error; but Zola fled to England where he stayed for almost a year.

Almost personally ruined as a result of his initiatives, Zola nevertheless achieved his aim: he converted the Dreyfus affair from a lonely campaign by a few tenacious believers in Dreyfus's innocence into a nationwide joust between the defenders of traditional values and those who consisdered a miscarriage of justice as the germ of a potential plague in the body politic.

Zola's last novel, *Vérité*, is a transposition of the Dreyfus affair. It was published posthumously, as Zola died at home in September 1902 in suspicious circumstances, asphyxiated by coal-gas as a result of a blocked chimney-pot. When his ashes were transferred to the Panthéon in 1908, Dreyfus, who attended the function, was slightly wounded by a journalist who fired two shots at him. The journalist was tried and acquitted.

Zola is the archetypical example of the 'intellectual' who takes on a role of moral leadership in the midst of a political crisis. Both the Dreyfusard and the anti-Dreyfusard camps managed to gather a constellation of 'intellectuals' as spokesmen for their 'truth', but as the one who invested most into this role, Zola stands as the herald of the French social conscience in those troubled days.

Bibliography

Apart from Zola's own day-to-day commentaries of the Dreyfus affair under the title *La Vérité en marche*, and his novel *Vérité*, his position is analysed in biographies of the writer, and in accounts of the Dreyfus affair. One of the pioneer works on the role played by writers was Cécile Delhorbe, *L'Affaire Dreyfus et les écrivains français* (Paris: Victor Attinger, 1932), and interesting light is also shed by Henri Mitterand, *Zola journaliste. De l'affaire Manet à l'affaire Dreyfus* (Paris: A. Colin (Kiosque), 1962) and Henri Guillemin, *Zola, légende ou vérité?* (Paris: Juillard, 1960). See also the two following articles: Eric Cahm, 'Pour et contre Emile Zola, les étudiants de Paris en janvier 1898', *Bulletin de la Société d'Etudes Jaurésiennes*, October–December, 1970 and Madeleine Rebérioux, 'Zola, Jaurès et France: trois intellectuels devant l'affaire', *Cahiers Naturalistes,* no. 54, 1980. Of biographies of Zola in English, two useful ones are Elliott M. Grant, *Emile Zola* (Boston, Mass.: Twayne Publishers, 1966), and Bettina L. Knapp, *Emile Zola* (New York: F. Unger, 1980).

AM

ZYROMSKI, Jean (1890–1975)

Jean Zyromski was one of the leading figures in the French Socialist Party (SFIO) in the 1920s and 1930s, serving as a member of its central executive between 1924 and 1940 and playing a prominent part in the affairs of its large Seine Federation, which encompassed the Paris area. Born at Nevers, he studied law at Toulouse and wrote a thesis on the legal protection of labour. Drawn to socialism as a young lawyer, he joined the SFIO in 1912. During the First World War he served in the Balkans and afterwards settled in Paris, where he worked in the Prefecture of the Department of the Seine and eventually became an inspector of its welfare division. During the Second World War he was active in the Resistance movement but the coming of peace saw a change in his allegiance: in 1945 he joined the Communist Party and sat with its parliamentary group during the two years, 1946–48, that he was a member of the Council of the Republic representing the Department of Lot-et-Garonne.

In the inter-war period his main interest was in the possibility of reuniting the Socialist and Communist Parties. He played a leading role in the negotiations which led to unity of action between Communists and Socialists from 1934 onwards but he was soon attaching more importance to international than domestic issues: he supported the signing of the mutual defence pact between France and the Soviet Union in May 1935, opposed the Blum government's policy of non-intervention in the Spanish Civil War, and, in 1938–39, stood out against the pacifist wing of his party on the grounds that it was necessary to contain Germany and Italy within a system of defensive alliances and to prepare France for the possibility of war.

Intellectually, Zyromski was influenced not only by the Marxist ideas of Jules Guesde (as interpreted by A.M. Desrousseaux – q.v.) but also by the theories of Hubert Lagardelle regarding revolutionary syndicalism and by those of Otto Bauer, the Austrian Socialist, on the ultimate fusion of communism and socialism. However, his almost continual involvement in issues of party tactics gave him little scope for developing his philosophy systematically and he invested most of his energies as a journalist and writer in the service of the journal *Bataille Socialiste* (Socialist struggle) and of the group of the same name which played an important part in the internal politics of the Socialist Party between 1927 and 1940. Affectionately known as 'Zyrom', he was for many of his colleagues the very model of an activist, an inspiring orator, a courteous and fair opponent, and a disciplined soldier of his party.

Bibliography

Baker, D.N. (1971), 'The politics of socialist protest in France: The left wing of the Socialist Party, 1921–39', *The Journal of Modern History*, vol. XLIII, no. 1, March, pp. 13–16.
Greene, N. (1969), *Crisis and Decline: The French Socialist Party in the popular front era*, Ithaca, NY: Cornell University Press, pp. 48–55.
Lefranc, G. (1963), *Le Mouvement socialiste sous la troisième République (1875–1940)*, Paris: Payot, pp. 353–5.
Zyromski, J. (1936), *Sur le chemin de l'unité,* Paris: Editions Nouveau Prométhée.

BDG

APPENDICES

FRENCH PRESIDENTS

Third Republic

Adolophe Thiers (1871–73)
Marshal de MacMahon (1873–9)
'Jules' Grévy (1879–87)
M.F. Sadi Carnot (1887–94)
Jean Casimir-Périer (1895–9)
Emile Loubet (1899–1906)
Armand Fallières (1906–13)
Raymond Poincaré (1913–20)
Paul Deschanel (1920)
Alexandre Millerand (1920–4)
Gaston Doumergue (1924–31)
Paul Doumer (1931–2)
Albert Lebrun (1932–40)

Vichy

The office of president was abolished in 1940, Marshal Pétain became head of state.

Fourth Republic

Vincent Auriol (1947–53)
René Coty (1953–9)

Fifth Republic

General Charles de Gaulle (1959–69)
Georges Pompidou (1969–74)
Valéry Giscard d'Estaing (1974–81)
François Mitterrand (1981–   )

PRIME MINISTERS (*PRÉSIDENTS DU CONSEIL*)

Third Republic

Adolphe Thiers, Head of the Executive (1871)
Then President of the Republic (1871–73)

J. Dufaure (19 February 1871)
A. de Broglie (25 May 1873)
A. de Broglie (26 November 1873)
E. de Cissey (22 May 1874)
L. Buffet (10 March 1875)
J. Dufaure (23 February 1876)
J. Dufaure (9 March 1876)
J. Simon (12 December 1876)
A. de Broglie (17 May 1877)
G. de Rochebouët (23 November 1877)
J. Dufaure (13 December 1877)
W. Waddington (4 February 1879)
C. de Freycinet (28 December 1879)
J. Ferry (23 September 1880)
L. Gambetta (14 November 1881)
C. de Freycinet (30 January 1882)
C. Duclerc (7 August 1882)
A. Fallières (29 January 1883)
J. Ferry (21 February 1883)
H. Brisson (6 April 1885)
C. de Freycinet (7 January 1886)
R. Goblet (11 December 1886)
M. Rouvier (30 May 1887)
P. Tirard (12 December 1887)
C. Floquet (3 April 1888)
P. Tirard (22 February 1889)
C. de Freycinet (17 March 1890)
E. Loubet (27 February 1892)
A. Ribot (6 December 1892)
A. Ribot (11 January 1893)
C. Dupuy (4 April 1893)
J. Casimir-Périer (3 December 1893)
C. Dupuy (30 May 1894)
C. Dupuy (1 July 1894)
A. Ribot (26 January 1895)
L. Bourgeois (1 November 1895)
J. Méline (29 April 1896)
H. Brisson (28 June 1898)
C. Dupuy (1 November 1898)
C. Dupuy (18 February 1899)

R. Waldeck-Rousseau (22 June 1899)
E. Combes (7 June 1902)
M. Rouvier (24 January 1905)
M. Rouvier (18 February 1906)
J. Sarrien (14 March 1906)
G. Clemenceau (25 October 1906)
A. Briand (24 July 1909)
A. Briand (3 November 1910)
E. Monis (2 March 1911)
J. Caillaux (27 June 1911)
R. Poincaré (14 January 1912)
A. Briand (21 January 1913)
A. Briand (18 February 1913)
J.L. Barthou (22 March 1913)
G. Doumergue (9 December 1913)
A. Ribot (10 June 1914)
R. Viviani (13 June 1914)
R. Viviani (27 August 1914)
A. Briand (29 October 1915)
A. Briand (12 December 1916)
A. Ribot (20 March 1917)
P. Painlevé (12 September 1917)
G. Clemenceau (16 November 1917)
A. Millerand (20 January 1920)
A. Millerand (18 February 1920)
G. Leygues (24 September 1920)
A. Briand (16 January 1921)
R. Poincaré (15 January 1922)
R. Poincaré (29 March 1924)
F. François-Marsal (9 June 1924)
E. Herriot (14 June 1924)
P. Painlevé (17 April 1925)
P. Painlevé (29 October 1925)
A. Briand (28 November 1925)
A. Briand (9 March 1926)
A. Briand (23 June 1926)
E. Herriot (19 July 1926)
R. Poincaré (23 July 1926)
R. Poincaré (11 November 1928)
A. Briand (29 July 1929)
A. Tardieu (3 November 1929)
C. Chautemps (21 February 1930)
A. Tardieu (2 March 1930)
T. Steeg (13 December 1930)
P. Laval (27 January 1931)

P. Laval (13 June 1931)
P. Laval (14 January 1932)
A. Tardieu (20 February 1932)
E. Herriot (3 June 1932)
J. Paul-Boncour (18 December 1932)
E. Daladier (31 January 1933)
A. Sarraut (26 October 1933)
C. Chautemps (26 November 1933)
E. Daladier (30 January 1934)
G. Doumergue (9 February 1934)
P.-E. Flandin (8 November 1934)
F. Bouisson (1 June 1935)
P. Laval (7 June 1935)
A. Sarraut (24 January 1936)
L. Blum (4 June 1936)
C. Chautemps (22 June 1937)
C. Chautemps (18 January 1938)
L. Blum (13 March 1938)
E. Daladier (10 April 1939)
E. Daladier (11 May 1939)
E. Daladier (13 September 1939)
P. Reynaud (21 March 1940)
P. Pétain (16 June 1940)

Vichy

Marshal P. Pétain–P. Laval (12 July 1940)
Marshal P. Pétain–P.-E. Flandin (13 December 1940)
Marshal P. Pétain-Admiral F. Darlan (10 February 1941)
P. Laval (18 April 1942)
  (Pétain and Laval leave for Germany, 7 September 1944)

French Provisional Government

C. de Gaulle (29 August 1944)
C. de Gaulle (9 September 1944)
C. de Gaulle (21 November 1945)
F. Gouin (26 January 1946)
G. Bidault (23 June 1946)

L. Blum (16 December 1946)

Fourth Republic

P. Ramadier (28 January 1947)
R. Schuman (22 November 1947)
A. Marie (24 July 1948)
R. Schuman (31 August 1948)
H. Queuille (11 September 1948)
G. Bidault (27 October 1949)
H. Queuille (30 June 1950)
R. Pleven (13 July 1950)
H. Queuille (9 March 1951)
R. Pleven (8 August 1951)
E. Faure (17 January 1952)
A. Pinay (6 March 1952)
R. Mayer (7 January 1953)
J. Laniel (26 June 1953)
P. Mendès France (18 June 1954)
E. Faure (25 February 1955)
G. Mollet (5 February 1956)
M. Bourgès-Maunoury (12 June 1957)
F. Gaillard (5 November 1957)
P. Pflimlin (13 May 1958)
C. de Gaulle (1 June 1958)

Fifth Republic

M. Debré (8 January 1959)
G. Pompidou (14 April 1962)
G. Pompidou (8 January 1966)
G. Pompidou (7 April 1967)
M. Couve de Murville (10 July 1968)
J. Chaban-Delmas (20 June 1969)
P. Messmer (5 July 1972)
J. Chirac (27 May 1974)
R. Barre (25 August 1976)
P. Mauroy (21 May 1981)
L. Fabius (17 July 1984)
J. Chirac (20 March 1986)
M. Rocard (9 May 1988)

POST-WAR UNION LEADERSHIP

CFTC   Secretary-General
  Gaston Tessier (1919–48)
  Maurice Bouladoux (1948–53)
  Georges Levard (1953–64)
  Jacques Tessier (1964–71)
  Jean Bornard (1971–81)
  Guy Drilleaud (1981–   )

CFDT   Secretary-General
  Eugène Descamps (1964–71)
  Edmond Maire (1971–89)
  Jean Kaspar (1989–   )

CGT   Secretary-General
  Benoît Frachon (1945–67)
  Georges Séguy (1967–82)

  Henri Krasucki (1982–   )

CGT – Force Ouvrière   Secretary-General
  Léon Jouhaux (1948–54)
  Robert Bothereau (1954–63)
  André Bergeron (1963–1989)
  Marc Blondel (1989–   )

French Employers' Federation –
CNPF   President
  Georges Villiers (1946–66)
  Paul Huvelin (1966–72)
  François Ceyrac (1972–82)
  Yvon Gattaz (1982–86)
  François Perigot (1987–   )

FIFTH REPUBLIC PARTY LEADERSHIP

Communist Party (PCF) General Secretary
Maurice Thorez (1932–64)
Waldeck Rochet (1964–72)
Georges Marchais (1972–   )

Socialist Party (SFIO) General Secretary
Guy Mollet (1946–69)

Socialist Party (PS) First Secretary
Alain Savary (1969–71)
François Mitterrand (1971–81)
Lionel Jospin (1981–8)
Pierre Mauroy (1988–   )

Gaullists (UNR) Secretary General
Roger Frey (1958–9)
Albin Chalandon (1959)
Jacques Richard (1959–61)
Roger Dusseaulx (1961–2)
Louis Terrenoire (1962)

(UNR–UDT) Secretary General
Jacques Baumel (1962–7)

(UDVe) Secretary General
Robert Poujade (1968)

(UDR) Secretary General
Robert Poujade (1968–71)
René Tomasini (1971–2)
Alain Peyrefitte (1972–3)
Alexandre Sanguinetti (1973–4)
Jacques Chirac (1974–5)
André Bord (1975–6)
Yves Guéna (1976–   )

(RPR) President
Jacques Chirac (1976–   )
    Secretary General
Jérôme Monod (1976–8)
Alain Devaquet (1978–9)
Bernard Pons (1979–84)
Jacques Toubon (1984–8)
Alain Juppé (1988–   )

Christian Democrats (MRP) President
André Colin (1954–63)

Jean Lecanuet (1963–5)
(CD) President
Jean Lecanuet (1966–1976)
(CDP) President
Jacques Duhamel (1969–74)
(CDS) President
Jean Lecanuet (1976–82)
Pierre Méhaignerie (1982–   )

Radical Party (Valoisien) President
Félix Gaillard (1958–61)
Maurice Faure (1961–5)
René Billères (1965–9)
Maurice Faure (1969–71)
Jean–Jaques Servan Schreiber (1971–5)
Gabriel Peronnet (1975–7)
Jean-Jacques Servan-Schreiber (1977–9)
Didier Bariani (1979–83)
André Rossinot (1983–9)
Yves Galland (1989–   )

MRG (Left Radicals) President
Robert Fabre (1972–8)
Michel Crépeau (1978–81)
Roger-Gerard Schwarzenberg (1981–3)
Jean-Michel Baylet (1983–5)
François Doubin (1985–   )

Giscardians (RI) Secretary General
Michel Poniatowski (1966–74)
Michel d'Ornano (1974)
Roger Chinaud (1975–7)
(PR)
Jean-Pierre Soisson (1977–8)
Jacques Blanc (1979–82)
François Léotard (1982–   )

Independents (CNIP) Secretary General
Roger Duchet (1949–61)
Camille Laurens (1961–79)
Maurice Ligot (1980–1)
F.-X. Parent (1981–4)
M. Junot (1984–6)
Y. Briant (1987–   )

INDEX

Note: Bold names denote subjects of biographies listed on pages ix–xiii and shown in bold type in the dictionary. Bold numbers denote the main references to those subjects. Bold numbers over 443 refer to entries in the appendices. Political parties, organisations etc., as listed by their acronyms on pages xv–xvii, are entered under those acronyms: other groups mentioned in the book are entered under their textual titles.